Business Planning for Mergers and Acquisitions

Business Planning for Mergers and Acquisitions

Corporate, Securities, Tax, Antitrust, International, and Related Aspects

FOURTH EDITION

Samuel C. Thompson, Jr.

Professor of Law, Arthur Weiss Distinguished Faculty Scholar,
and Director, Center for the Study of Mergers and Acquisitions
The Pennsylvania State University Dickinson School of Law

Carolina Academic Press
Durham, North Carolina

ISBN 978-1-61163-169-2
LCCN 2014954900

Carolina Academic Press
700 Kent Street
Durham, NC 27701
Telephone (919) 489-7486
Fax (919) 493-5668
www.cap-press.com

Printed in the United States of America

This book is dedicated to the professors
at the University of Pennsylvania School of Law
who introduced me to the topics covered here:

Professor Robert H. Mundheim,
Corporations

Dean Bernard Wolfman,
Corporate Tax

Visiting Professor David S. Ruder,
Securities Regulation

Professor Louis B. Schwartz,
Antitrust

Professor Martin J. Aronstein,
Legal Accounting and Creditor Rights

Summary of Contents

Contents

Part III
Regulation of Mergers and Acquisitions in the European Union

Table of Principal Cases

Preface to the Fourth Edition

About the Book

The book provides a transactional approach to many of the issues that arise in mergers and acquisitions, including corporate, securities, antitrust, Federal income taxation, accounting, and valuation. The principal purpose of this book is to help train law students in the art of doing merger and acquisition deals. The statutes, rules, regulations, and documentary appendices referred to in this book are contained in a companion volume: Thompson, *M&A Statutes, Rules, and Documents for Business Planning for Mergers and Acquisitions* (Carolina Academic Press, 2015) (available without charge at www.cap-press.com/files/thompson_bpma4e_supp).

As set forth more completely in Section 1.1, Scope of the Book, the book is divided into four parts:

Part I, The Building Blocks,
Part II, Consensual Transactions,
Part III, Hostile Transactions, and
Part IV, Special Topics.

Part I, The Building Blocks, looks at issues likely to be faced in both consensual and hostile transactions, including shareholder voting and dissenting rules, directors' fiduciary duties, basic securities considerations, tax aspects, accounting treatment, valuation, antitrust, pre-merger notification, due diligence, and preliminary deal documents.

Part II, Consensual Transactions, looks at the following types of M&A transactions:

(1) acquisitions of the stock of closely-held corporations;
(2) acquisitions of the assets of closely-held corporations;
(3) acquisitions of publicly-held corporations by merger;
(4) leveraged buy-outs;
(5) going private transactions; and
(6) the drafting of various types of acquisition agreements.

Part III, Hostile Transactions, addresses the following Federal and state law aspects of these transactions:

(1) proxy contests;
(2) the impact of the Williams Act provisions of the Securities Exchange Act of 1934 on open market purchases;
(3) the impact of the Williams Act on tender offers;
(4) state regulation of tender offers; and
(5) state regulation of defensive tactics employed by a target's management.

Part IV, Special Topics, examines or provides an introduction to the following advanced M&A topics:

(1) spin-offs (*i.e.*, transactions in which a parent corporation distributes the stock of a subsidiary to the parent's shareholders);
(2) shareholder activism;
(3) international acquisitions, including inbound acquisitions (*i.e.*, acquisitions by foreign acquirors of U.S. targets) and outbound acquisitions (*i.e.*, acquisitions by U.S. acquirors of foreign targets);
(4) brief introductions to (a) M&A in three regulated industries (*i.e.*, the banking, telecom and public utility industries), (b) bankruptcy M&A, and (c) joint ventures, which are an alternative to M&A; and
(5) ethical issues in M&A.

All of the topics covered in this book are also addressed in my five volume treatise *Mergers, Acquisitions, and Tender Offers* (PLI 2010, updated periodically) (*MATO*).

Changes from the Third Edition

This edition follows the structure of the third edition with the following major changes and additions:

(1) the materials dealing with freeze-out mergers and going private transactions, which previously were addressed in Chapter 24, have been integrated into the coverage of LBOs in Chapter 14;
(2) in view of the increasing importance of shareholder activism, Chapter 25 now focuses on that topic; and
(3) Chapter 27 now provides brief introductions to the following topics, which were covered in greater detail in the third edition: banking M&A (former Chapter 27); telcom M&A (former Chapter 28); public utility M&A (former Chapter 29), bankruptcy M&A (former Chapter 30) and joint ventures (former Chapter 31).

My *MATO* treatise contains chapters dealing with each of the special topics covered in Chapter 27.

How to Use the Book

I generally cover the entire book in two three-semester-hour courses. Most of the material in the first three parts (Building Blocks, Consensual Transactions and Hostile Transactions) could be covered in a four-semester-hour course. Part IV, Special Topics, could be covered in a two-semester-hour course or seminar. It would be difficult to cover all of the materials in this book in one course. I also occasionally teach a broad range of topics in the book in an M&A drafting course.

The book can be used flexibly in a variety of courses. For example, the book could be used in a two-semester-hour course focusing on friendly transactions by covering the Building Block chapters in Part I (with the exception of the chapters on valuation, antitrust, and pre-merger notification) and the Consensual Transactions chapters in Part II. A three-semester-hour course could cover these materials, plus the materials on Hostile Acquisitions in Part III.

Use of Terms: Acquirer, Acquiror, Acquiring Corporation, AC, Target, Target Corporation, and TC

The terms "Acquirer," "Acquiror," "Acquiring Corporation," and "AC" all refer to the acquiring corporation in a merger or acquisition transaction. The terms "Target," "Target Corporation," and "TC" all refer to the target corporation in a merger or acquisition transaction.

The Genesis of the Book

This book had its genesis in several of the courses I had as a student at the University of Pennsylvania School of Law 44 years ago. Those courses excited my interest in mergers and acquisitions. All editions of this book are, therefore, appropriately dedicated to my Penn Law professors who introduced me to this subject: Professors Robert H. Mundheim, Bernard Wolfman, David S. Ruder, Louis B. Schwartz, and Martin J. Aronstein.

I was first exposed to mergers and acquisitions by Professor Mundheim in my second year Corporations course. That course, undoubtedly one of the best Corporations courses ever offered, opened my eyes to the fascinating world of corporate and securities law. In that course, I first read many of the cases examined in this book (such as *Farris v. Glen Alden, see* Chapter 2).

The "icing on the cake" was provided by Visiting Professor David Ruder in his Securities Regulations course and Rule 10b-5 seminar. I distinctly remember studying SEC Rule 133, which has now been replaced by Rule 145 (*see* Chapter 13) in Professor Ruder's Securities Regulations course. His Rule 10b-5 seminar, which was by far the best seminar I have experienced, explored in depth topics addressed at several points in this book (*see* Chapters 4, 13, and 20). In that seminar, the title of my paper was: *It is Time to Render a Death Blow to the Ill-Reasoned Birnbaum.* Notwithstanding my position, *Birnbaum* still lives and is set out in Chapter 11.

Dean Wolfman's Corporate Tax course introduced me to taxable acquisitions and tax-free reorganizations (*see* Chapter 5). Indeed, after I finished Professor Mundheim's Corporations course, I was certain that I wanted to be a corporate and securities lawyer, but Dean Wolfman sent me off in the direction of the tax law, which I have pursued for most of my career. Indeed two of my other casebooks published by Carolina Academic Press deal with tax law, with a particular focus on tax aspects of M&A: *Corporate Tax Through the Lens of M&A*, and *U.S. International Tax Planning and Policy, Including Cross-Border M&A*.

Professor Louis Schwartz introduced me to antitrust law and to Section 7 of the Clayton Act (*see* Chapter 8). Even though the law under Section 7 has changed significantly in the past 44 years, the foundation Professor Schwartz provided has helped me to better appreciate the evolving landscape of Section 7.

Finally, the ideas explored in several chapters can be traced to Professor Aronstein, who introduced me to M&A accounting (*see* Chapter 6) in his Legal Accounting course and to fraudulent conveyance law in his Creditor Rights course. Fraudulent conveyance law has become important in LBOs (*see* Chapter 14), which were not nearly as visible when I first studied Creditor Rights.

In this book, I return to my roots in Professor Mundheim's Corporation's course, and also explore other merger and acquisition topics that piqued my interest at Penn, such as tax, antitrust, and accounting.

I am forever indebted to Penn Law and the great education I received there. Indeed, Penn set me on a path I could not have dreamed of before it. It is my privilege again to publicly thank Professors Mundheim, Wolfman, Ruder, and Aronstein, and all my other great professors at Penn Law.

Thanks

First, thanks to the input from the students in my Mergers and Acquisitions courses who have used prior editions of this book at Penn State Law, the UCLA School of Law, the University of Virginia School of Law, the University of Miami School of Law, and the University of Pretoria School of Law, Pretoria, South Africa.

Second, thanks to my Penn State Law research assistants for their helpful comments and suggestions on this edition: Mulhim Almulhim, Hasan Celebioglu, Gene M. Chung, Alexandra Cumings, Matt Harostock, James Peavler, Rebecca Salko, Keana Williams, and Ouqing Wu.

Third, thanks to my Fellows at the Penn State Center for the Study of Mergers and Acquisitions: Taimoor Choudhry and Joshua Bam.

Fourth, thanks to my former student Dao Fu, who is now an associate at Davis Polk in New York City, for his helpful comments on the China M&A section of Chapter 26.

Finally, I thank my wife, Becky, and our son, Samuel C. Thompson, III, (Tommy), for their love, support, and understanding.

Samuel C. Thompson, Jr.
Professor of Law and Director of the
Center for the Study of Mergers and Acquisitions
Penn State Law School
February 15, 2015

Business Planning for Mergers and Acquisitions

Chapter 1

Introduction

§ 1.1 Scope of Book

This book considers numerous topics arising in merger and acquisition (M&A) transactions, including corporate, securities, antitrust, pre-merger notification, federal income taxation, accounting, and valuation. The book integrates the consideration of these topics by focusing on various types of M&A transactions. Most of the statutes and rules referred to in this book are contained in the companion text, Thompson, *M&A Statutes, Rules, and Documents for Business Planning for Mergers and Acquisitions*, [hereinafter *M&A Statutes, Rules, and Documents*], available without charge at http://www.cap-press.com/files/thompson_bpma4e_supp. Also, this companion has several Documentary Appendices, such as merger agreements and SEC disclosure documents for various types of transactions examined in this book.

Throughout the book, problems are used to illustrate the many varied and interrelated principles, and most of the chapters begin with a problem designed to present a real life setting for an examination of the topics covered in that chapter. The approach taken here is intended to help the law student gain both a practical and theoretical understanding of many of the legal problems a business lawyer will likely encounter in practice when working on M&A deals. These deals present some of the most challenging and intellectually rewarding work for business lawyers, and virtually every business lawyer at one point or another will represent either a buyer or seller in a merger or acquisition.

This book is divided into four parts. Part I, which consists of Chapters 1 through 10, discusses basic legal concepts that impact mergers and acquisitions, such as the rules governing directors' actions; the shareholders' right to vote and to dissent and seek appraisal; federal securities law; federal income tax; accounting; antitrust; and valuation.

Part II, which consists of Chapters 11 through 15, focuses on consensual transactions, including stock and asset acquisitions of closely-held corporations and mergers of publicly-held corporations.

Part III, which consists of Chapters 16 through Chapter 23, focuses on hostile transactions, including proxy contests, open market purchases, tender offers, and defensive tactics.

Part IV, which consists of Chapter 24 through Chapter 28, examines special types of M&A transactions and issues, including: spin-offs; shareholder activism; international M&A; regulatory issues in M&A, including issues involving the Affordable Care Act (*i.e.*, Obamacare); and ethical issues in M&A. This section also provides an introduction to bankruptcy M&A and joint ventures.

The M&A topics covered in this book, as well as some topics that are not covered here, such as state taxation of M&A transactions, are addressed in greater detail in my treatise on M&A: *Mergers Acquisitions and Tender Offers* (MATO), *infra* Section 1.10, which is published by PLI. Several excerpts from MATO are included in this book with the permission of PLI.

Chapter 1 provides an introduction to the topics covered herein. Chapter 2 considers the rules regarding the shareholders' right to vote and to dissent and seek appraisal in various types of M&A transactions. The focus is on the law of Delaware, California, Pennsylvania, and the ABA's Model Business Corporation Act (MBCA), which has been adopted at least in part by many states. The last section in Chapter 3 compares the voting and dissenting rules in Pennsylvania to those in Delaware, California, and the MBCA. Chapter 3 considers the legal standards governing the actions of a corporation's directors in various types of mergers and acquisitions. The emphasis here is on the law of Delaware, which has the most highly developed law governing directors. The last section of this chapter discusses the different approach to these issues taken in Pennsylvania.

Chapter 4 presents an introduction to the impact of the federal securities laws generally and in mergers and acquisitions. This chapter introduces the registration process under the Securities Act of 1933 (the 33 Act) and examines the private offering exemption under Regulation D and the resale exemption under Rule 144. The chapter also introduces the Securities Exchange Act of 1934 (the 34 Act) and Rule 10b-5 thereunder. The purpose of Chapter 4 is to lay the foundation for the exploration of more advanced federal securities issues in subsequent chapters, such as the proxy rules (*see* Chapters 13 and 16) and the tender offer rules (*see* Chapters 17–21).

Chapter 5 provides an introduction to the federal income tax aspects of mergers and acquisitions. This chapter looks at both taxable and tax-free acquisitions and illustrates the operation of both concepts.

Chapter 6 considers the accounting rules for mergers and acquisitions. This chapter looks at the rules of the Financial Standards Accounting Board (FASB) and the SEC's financial reporting guidelines, Regulation S-X.

Chapter 7 provides a guide to the use of modern valuation techniques, such as the net present value concept and the Capital Asset Pricing Model (CAPM), in mergers and acquisitions. These concepts are illustrated by referring to an actual valuation study for an M&A transaction.

The antitrust aspects of mergers and acquisitions are considered in Chapter 8. This chapter first gives a broad introduction to the antitrust laws and to Section 7 of the Clayton Act, the principal antitrust statute governing mergers and acquisitions. The chapter next introduces the microeconomic principles that provide the theoretical underpinning for antitrust merger policy. The chapter then examines the 2010 Horizontal Merger Guidelines promulgated by the Department of Justice (DOJ) and the Federal Trade Commission (FTC). These Guidelines set forth the enforcement standards generally followed by the DOJ and FTC in deciding whether to challenge a horizontal acquisition under Section 7. The chapter also briefly looks at antitrust enforcement of vertical and conglomerate M&A transactions. In addition, this chapter examines some of the leading cases interpreting Section 7.

The Hart-Scott-Rodino pre-merger notification rules are examined in Chapter 9. Under these rules, prior to completing a merger or acquisition, certain acquiring and target corporations must provide the federal antitrust authorities (*i.e.*, the DOJ and FTC) with certain information regarding the transaction to permit the authorities to determine whether to challenge the transaction on antitrust grounds. The examination of basic concepts is completed in Chapter 10, which considers confidentiality agreements, due diligence, exclusivity agreements, and letters of intent. These agreements and concepts will apply prior to the structuring of a consensual transaction (*see* Chapters 11–14) and the drafting of the acquisition agreement (*see* Chapter 15).

Part II, consensual transactions, starts with Chapter 11, which considers issues arising in a stock acquisition of a closely-held corporation. This chapter illustrates the application in such transactions of many concepts covered in previous chapters, including federal income tax, accounting, Hart-Scott-Rodino, and Regulation D under the 33 Act. This chapter also considers the law governing partial stock acquisitions.

Chapter 12 examines issues arising in an acquisition of assets of a closely-held corporation, such as the developing law on successor liability. This chapter also illustrates the application of previously covered concepts, such as the federal income tax provisions, the accounting rules, and the federal securities laws, in such transactions.

Chapter 13 explores issues arising in the acquisition of a publicly-held target corporation in a consensual (negotiated) merger. In particular, this chapter builds on many of the federal securities law concepts studied in Chapter 4 and also examines the proxy rules under the 34 Act.

Chapter 14 deals with freezeout mergers and acquisitions by private equity firms in leveraged buyouts (LBOs) and management buyouts (MBOs). Private equity firms, such as KKR, raise funds from a small number of wealthy individuals and institutions such as pension funds. The equity capital raised is then used, together with a substantial amount of cash raised through the issuance of debt (*i.e.*, leverage), to acquire publicly-held firms, that is, to take the publicly-held firms private. In addition to examining the structure of a typical freezeout merger and leveraged acquisition, the chapter also examines (1) the corporate governance rules for such transactions; (2) the SEC's going private rules under Rule 13e-3, which are applicable to certain freezeout mergers and MBOs; (3) the application of the law of fraudulent conveyances to LBOs; and (4) the impact of the federal margin rules on the structuring of LBOs. LBOs may also be used in the acquisition of a closely-held target.

Chapter 15 presents an introduction to the principles governing the drafting of the three most common types of acquisition agreements: the merger agreement, the stock acquisition agreement, and the asset acquisition agreement. To bring this topic alive, in discussing the various drafting principles, this chapter refers to acquisition agreements set out in *M&A Statutes, Rules, and Documents*.

The book then turns in Part III to an examination of hostile transactions involving publicly-held corporations. Chapter 16 considers proxy contests. Chapter 17 provides an introduction to the Williams Act, which added Sections 13(d) and (e) and Sections 14(d), (e) and (f) to the 34 Act. Section 13(d) regulates open market purchases of the stock of publicly-held corporations, for example, the purchase of stock that is traded on an exchange. Sections 14(d) and (e) regulate third-party tender offers for the stock of publicly-held corporations. These are transactions in which an acquiring firm makes an offer directly to the shareholders of a publicly-held target corporation. Section 13(e) regulates (1) tender offers by an issuer for its own shares, and (2) going private transactions, which involve the acquisition of all of the stock of a publicly-held firm by a controlling shareholder.

Chapter 18 examines the regulation under Section 13(d) of open market purchases. Chapter 19 considers the definition of "tender offer." Here it will be seen that the rules under Sections 14(d) and (e) can be avoided if an acquisition does not constitute a "tender offer." Chapter 20 considers third-party tender offers under Sections 14(d) and (e). This chapter also addresses the use of a tender offer followed by a merger in a consensual transaction. Chapter 21 examines the rules governing issuer tender offers. Chapter 22 looks at the law governing state regulation of tender offers, and Chapter 23 considers the defensive actions that may be taken by a target's board of directors. This chapter builds on many of the concepts addressed in Chapter 3, which discusses the legal standards governing a corporation's directors in mergers and acquisitions.

Part IV addresses several special topics. Chapter 24 considers spin-offs, that is, a transaction in which a parent corporation distributes to its shareholders the stock of a controlled subsidiary. Spin-offs are becoming more prevalent, and they may be used in connection with a merger or acquisition, such as in the spin-off by AT&T of AT&T Broadband, which was immediately followed by the acquisition of Broadband by Comcast. Chapter 25 looks at issues involved with shareholder activism, with particular emphasis on activist hedge funds. Chapter 25 also introduces a related concept: merger arbitrage.

Chapter 26 looks at some of the international aspects of mergers and acquisitions focusing on both acquisitions by foreign firms of U.S. firms (inbound acquisitions) and acquisitions by U.S. firms of foreign firms (outbound acquisitions). This chapter considers some of the corporate, securities, tax, and antitrust issues arising in such transactions under both U.S. law and the law and directives of the European Union. Chapter 26 has two case studies illustrating outbound acquisitions under the laws of: (1) South Africa, as illustrated in Walmart's acquisition of a controlling interest in South Africa's Massmart, a publicly held South African firm; and (2) China, as illustrated in Coca-Cola's proposed, but blocked, acquisition of China's Huiyuan Juice Group, a publicly held company.

Chapter 27 examines some of the unique regulatory issues that arise in acquisitions in the following industries: (1) banking, (2) telecom, (3) public utility, and (4) health care. The chapter also briefly introduces (1) acquisitions of bankrupt companies, and (2) joint ventures, which can be an alternative to a merger. Finally, Chapter 28 presents a problem and related cases highlighting some of the ethical issues that can arise in mergers and acquisitions.

§ 1.2 Scope of Chapter

This chapter introduces some of the underlying concepts and theories of mergers and acquisitions. Section 1.3 discusses consensual transactions in which a willing target corporation is acquired by an acquiror in an arm's length transaction. Section 1.4 introduces tender offers and open market purchases. Section 1.5 gives a historical and economic perspective on the merger and acquisition process. Section 1.6 presents an assessment of various theories explaining mergers and acquisitions, and Section 1.7 takes a look at the use of event studies for determining the wealth effects of mergers, and actually conducts an event study of the acquisition in 2004 by J.P. Morgan Chase of Bank One. Section 1.8 provides an introduction to the state of the dynamic M&A marketplace. Section 1.9 sets out an introduction to the Sarbanes–Oxley Act, and Section 1.10 provides references to the vast literature on mergers and acquisitions.

§ 1.3 Introduction to Consensual Transactions

This section is a modification of an excerpt from Chapter 1 of Thompson, *Mergers, Acquisitions and Tender Offers*, *infra* Section 1.10.

A. The Starting Point: Valuation and Due Diligence

The starting point for any consensual M&A transaction is the determination by the acquirer of the amount it would be willing to pay for the target and the determination by the target's directors or shareholders of the amount they would be willing to accept from the acquirer. This requires that the target be properly valued, and Chapter 7 discusses the principles underlying modern valuation techniques. Before a target can be properly valued, the acquirer must have access to confidential information on the target so that the acquirer can complete its due diligence, and Chapter 10 provides a guide to drafting a confidentiality agreement and the conduct of due diligence. If the acquirer will be paying cash, the target will generally not conduct extensive due diligence regarding the acquirer. However, if the acquirer will be issuing stock the target's shareholders will be making an investment in the acquirer, and the target will generally conduct extensive due diligence on the acquirer, which will require access to confidential information pursuant to a confidentiality agreement. In some cases, the parties may come to a basic agreement before they have completed the due diligence process, and they may enter into a letter of intent or similar document, also discussed in Chapter 10.

B. Structuring the Transaction: Tax and Corporate Law Considerations

1. In General

Once the parties have come to an agreement on price and the other basic terms, the transaction will have to be structured. This will principally present corporate and tax law issues addressed in Chapter 2 (transaction structures and shareholder voting and dissenting rules), Chapter 3 (directors' fiduciary duties), and Chapter 5. There is a potential "chicken and egg" problem in creating the structure, because as explained in Chapter 5, in a taxable acquisition an acquirer should generally pay less in a stock acquisition of a stand-alone (*i.e.*, non-subsidiary) target than in an asset acquisition. Thus, if an acquirer has valued the target on the assumption that the acquirer will have a cost basis for the target's assets, but the transaction is structured as a stock acquisition without a cost basis for those assets, the acquirer may be overpaying.

In general the structure of the transaction will not be sensitive to the financial accounting treatment of the transaction, because as discussed in Chapter 6, without respect to the form of the acquisition, the transaction will be accounted for as if the acquirer purchased the target's assets. This purchase accounting rule will create goodwill on the acquirer's balance sheet when the purchase price exceeds the book value of the target's assets.

The following sections discuss the most common structures used in consensual, *i.e.*, non-hostile, deals: the stock purchase, the asset purchase, the direct merger, the reverse subsidiary merger, the forward subsidiary merger, the compulsory share exchange, and the short form merger. The diagrams employ the following short-hand definitions of the various parties to the transactions:

1. Acquiring Corporation = AC
2. Wholly-owned Subsidiary of AC = AC-S
3. Target Corporation = TC
4. Shareholders of AC = AC-SHs
5. Shareholders of TC = TC-SHs

2. Stock Purchase Structure

In the case of an acquisition of a stand-alone closely held corporation, the principal acquisition structure is a stock purchase pursuant to a stock purchase agreement such as

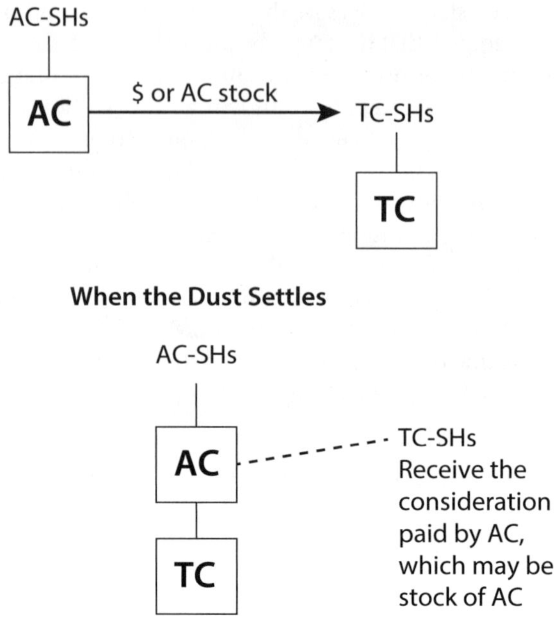

Diagram 1-A: Stock Purchase Structure

Documentary Appendix U, Annotated Sample Stock Purchase Agreement. The consideration paid by the acquirer is usually cash or its stock, but there are essentially no limitations on the consideration that can be paid. This is true with all of the acquisitions. The following discussions assume that the consideration is either cash or stock.

This structure, which can also be utilized in the acquisition of a subsidiary, is illustrated in Diagram 1-A, above.

3. Asset Purchase Structure

In some cases the acquisition of a closely held corporation or a subsidiary will be structured as an asset acquisition pursuant to an asset acquisition agreement such as Documentary Appendix V, Annotated Sample Asset Acquisition Agreement. Pursuant to the agreement, and after any required shareholder vote, the acquirer acquires specified assets of the target and assumes specified liabilities of the target. Thus, whereas in a merger all of a target's assets pass over to the acquirer, in an asset acquisition, only the specified assets and generally only the specified liabilities pass over. As discussed in Chapter 12, in certain asset acquisitions non-specified liabilities may pass-over.

Usually the target is liquidated after the sale, and the shareholders receive the consideration, unless pursuant to the applicable state law they dissent and have their shares appraised. If a shareholder exercises "dissenter's rights," a court will appraise the value of the shares, which the shareholder will receive in lieu of the basic consideration specified in the agreement. This structure is illustrated in Diagram 1-B.

4. Direct Merger Structure

In the direct merger structure, pursuant to the applicable state law (*see* Chapter 2), the acquirer and target enter into a merger agreement. Pursuant to that agreement, and after

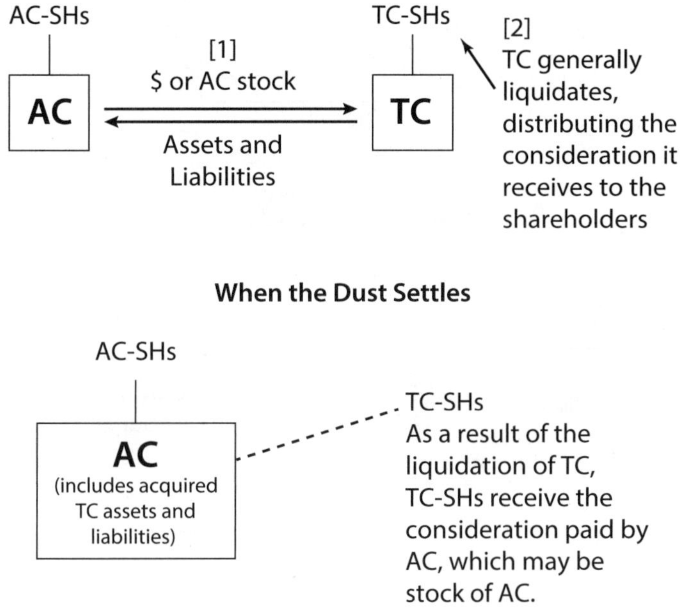

Diagram 1-B: Asset Purchase Structure

the required shareholder vote, the target merges into the acquirer. By operation of law, all of the targets assets and liabilities pass over to the acquirer, and the target's shareholders receive the consideration specified in the merger agreement, unless they dissent and seek appraisal of their shares. This type of transaction can be used in the acquisition of a closely held or publicly held target. For an illustration of a merger of a publicly held target into a publicly held acquirer see Documentary Appendix D, JP Morgan Chase–Bank One Direct Stock Merger Agreement. This structure is illustrated in Diagram 1-C on the next page.

5. Reverse Subsidiary Merger Structure

In the case of a consensual acquisition of a stand-alone publicly held corporation, the principal acquisition structure is a reverse subsidiary merger. This type of transaction is sometimes referred to as a reverse triangular merger, because three corporations are involved.

In this transaction, the acquirer forms a subsidiary (AC-Sub), and pursuant to the applicable state corporate law, the acquirer, AC-Sub, and the target enter into a merger agreement. When, after the requisite shareholder vote, the merger becomes effective, (1) AC-Sub merges into the target; (2) the target's shareholders receive the merger consideration, unless they dissent and have their shares appraised; and (3) the acquirer ends up owning all of the target's stock. Thus, the target becomes a wholly-owned subsidiary of the acquirer.

For reasons discussed in Chapter 2, structuring deals, and Chapter 5, Federal income tax, the reverse subsidiary merger is generally employed in a taxable acquisition where the consideration is cash, as with Documentary Appendix F, Toys (R Us) Reverse Subsidiary Cash Merger Agreement. The reverse subsidiary merger is also generally employed when the consideration is stock as in Documentary Appendix A, Time-Warner Reverse Subsidiary

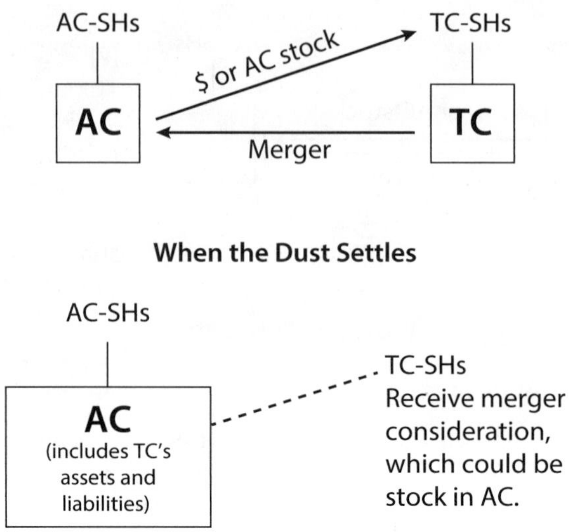

Diagram 1-C: Direct Merger Structure

Stock Merger. Where stock is used the transaction may qualify as a tax-free reorganization. *See* Chapter 5. This structure can be employed in the acquisition of closely held and publicly held targets, and Diagram 1-D illustrates the transaction.

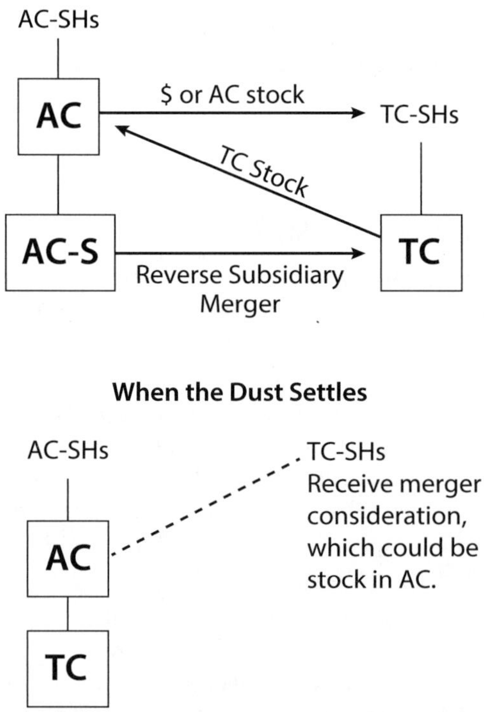

Diagram 1-D: Reverse Subsidiary Merger Structure

6. Forward Subsidiary Merger Structure

In some subsidiary or triangular mergers, the target merges into the subsidiary of the acquiring corporation (AC-Sub), with AC-Sub holding all of target's assets and liabilities and the target's shareholders receiving the merger consideration, subject to exercising their dissenters' rights to appraisal. This type of transaction is called a forward subsidiary or triangular merger. As indicated in Chapter 5, the tax consequences of engaging in a forward subsidiary merger can be dramatically different from the tax consequences of engaging in a reverse subsidiary merger. This type of transaction can be utilized in acquisitions of both closely held and publicly held targets. Diagram 1-E illustrates the transaction.

7. Compulsory Share Exchange Structure

As discussed in Chapter 2, the Model Business Corporation Act and some state laws permit the acquisition of a target's shares in a compulsory share exchange. In this transaction, pursuant to operation of law and after the required shareholder vote, the target's shareholders are required to transfer their shares directly to the acquirer in exchange for the consideration required to be paid in the transaction. In certain cases the target's shareholders can exercise dissenters' rights. Although Delaware law does not have a compulsory share exchange provision, the end result of a reverse subsidiary merger, which is permitted in all states, is generally the same as the end result with a compulsory share

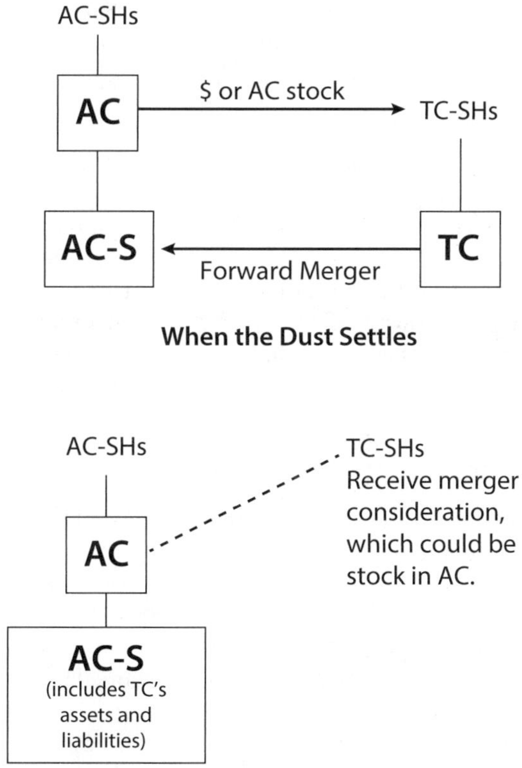

Diagram 1-E: Forward Subsidiary Merger Structure

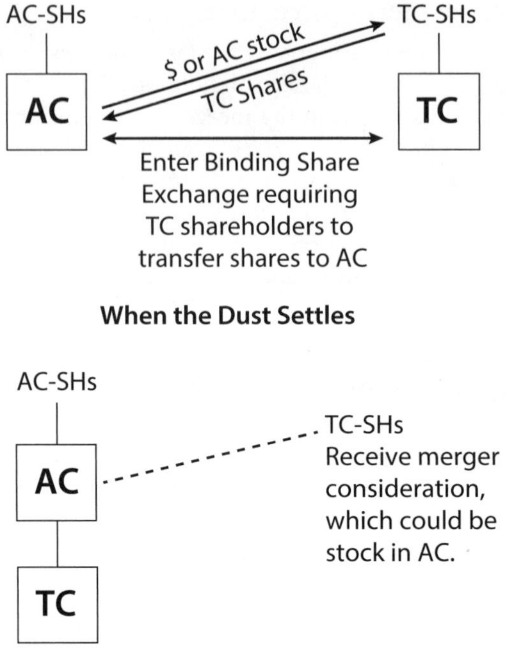

Diagram 1-F: Compulsory Share Exchange Structure

exchange, that is, the acquirer ends up owning all of the shares of the target. Diagram 1-F illustrates an acquisition of a publicly held target in a compulsory share exchange.

8. Short Form Merger Structure

Where a parent corporation owns 90% or more of the stock of a subsidiary, under the laws of most if not all states, the parent can acquire the assets and liabilities of the subsidiary without a vote of the subsidiary's shareholders. This type of transaction is called an upstream short form merger, and is explored in Chapter 2. Also, the parent can merge downstream into the sub, and some states permit a short form merger to be used in a merger of sister subs. Also, in some states the ownership level for a short form merger is less than 90%. A short form merger may be utilized (1) to acquire a long-held sub, and (2) as the follow-up step after a tender offer. Diagram 1-G illustrates an upstream short form merger.

C. Drafting the Acquisition Agreement

As discussed in Chapter 15, the provisions of the acquisition agreement generally will follow the same basic structure without regard to the type of agreement. The agreement will start with the parties and the "whereas" clauses or "recitals, which set out the basic framework of the deal. The agreement will then address the heart of the transaction, specifying (1) the assets or stock to be acquired or the form of merger, (2) the consideration to be paid, and (3) the mechanics for closing the transaction. The agreement next contains representations and warranties, which are statements of fact. The target or its shareholders generally will make extensive representations and warranties, as will the acquirer if the consideration is stock. However, if the consideration is cash, the acquirer's representations and warranties usually are quite limited. The agreement then generally sets out covenants

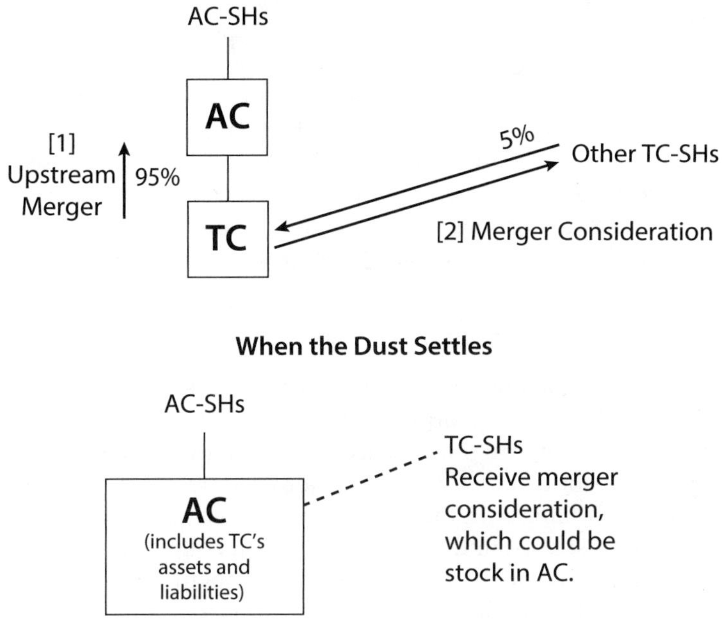

Diagram 1-G: Short Form Merger Structure

which deal with matters the parties "will do" (*i.e.*, affirmative covenants) and "will not do" (*i.e.*, negative covenants) between the signing and the closing. The covenants generally are followed by the conditions to closing, which are followed by the provisions governing the termination of the agreement and miscellaneous provisions. If the transaction involves the acquisition of a closely held corporation, the selling shareholders generally will provide the acquirer with indemnification against certain losses, including losses resulting from materially inaccurate representations and warranties, which generally will survive the closing. On the other hand, in acquisitions of publicly held targets, the representations and warranties generally do not survive the closing and there is no indemnification.

D. Federal Securities Laws

The Federal securities laws treatment of the transaction is generally not sensitive to the structure of the transaction. As explained in Chapters 4 and 13, without respect to the structure of the transaction, if the acquirer does not issue securities in the transaction, the acquirer will not have to register the transaction under the Securities Act of 1933 (the 33 Act). On the other hand, without respect to the structure of the transaction, if the acquirer issues securities, such as its stock, in the transaction, (1) in the case of an acquisition of a publicly held target, the acquirer will have to register such stock on Form S-4, and (2) in the case of an acquisition of a closely held target, the acquirer will have to register the stock or establish an exemption from registration, such as an exemption under Regulation D. If the stock is issued pursuant to an exemption from registration, the target's shareholders will have limits on their ability to resell the securities; such resales are generally made pursuant to Rule 144.

In the acquisition of a publicly held target, the target's shareholders will always have the right to vote on the transaction under the applicable corporate law (*see* Chapter 2), and the acquirer's shareholders may have the right to vote if, *inter alia*, the acquirer issues more than 20% of its stock in the transaction (*see* Chapter 2). As discussed in Chapter 13, in the acquisition of a public target (1) a proxy statement under Section 14(a) of the Securities Exchange Act of 1934 (the 34 Act) will have to be prepared for the target's shareholders and for the acquirer's shareholders if they have the right to vote, and (2) a registration statement will have to be prepared by the acquirer if it issues securities in the transaction. The registration statement and the proxy statement or statements can all be included in one disclosure document on Form S-4. If the consideration is cash, only a proxy statement for the target's shareholders is required.

E. Antitrust, Pre-Merger Notification

As discussed in Chapter 8, the antitrust laws are designed to prevent, *inter alia*, mergers that will substantially lessen competition or lead to a monopoly of a market. In order to give the antitrust authorities the time needed to analyze the antitrust implications of a merger or acquisition, for certain large transactions, the parties are required to make a pre-merger notification filing with the applicable antitrust authorities, such as the FTC and DOJ in the U.S. (discussed in Chapter 9), the Competition Commission in the E.U. (discussed in Chapter 26), or the antitrust (*i.e.*, "competition") authorities in other countries where the parties conduct business.

Antitrust and regulatory issues generally will be addressed in the representations, covenants, and conditions provisions of the acquisition agreement (*see* Chapter 15). The representations and warranties section will identify the antitrust and regulatory approvals required; the covenants section will address how the parties will deal with the antitrust and regulatory issues between signing and closing; and the conditions section will make receipt of the antitrust and regulatory approvals conditions to closing.

§ 1.4 Introduction to Tender Offers and Related Transactions

This section is a modification of an excerpt from Chapter 1 of Samuel C. Thompson, Jr., *Mergers, Acquisitions and Tender Offers* (PLI, 2010, updated periodically).

A. The Basic Tender Offer Structure

In a third party tender offer an acquirer pursuant to an "offer to purchase," makes an offer directly to the shareholders of a publicly held target to purchase their shares for cash, stock, or any other type of consideration. This type of transaction is illustrated in Diagram 1-H.

As discussed in Chapters 17, tender offers for, and open market purchases of, the securities of publicly held targets are subject to regulation under the Williams Act provisions of the 34 Act, that is, principally Sections 13(d) and (e) and Section 14(d) and (e) and the regulations thereunder. Also, many states have laws, sometimes referred to as "Baby Williams Acts," regulating these transactions.

Section 13(d) sets out an early warning system to alert the target and the market whenever an acquirer or other person acquires more than 5% of the target's securities. *See* Chapter 18. Under Section 13(d), the acquirer is required to make a public filing regarding its ownership interests in the target within ten days of crossing the 5% threshold.

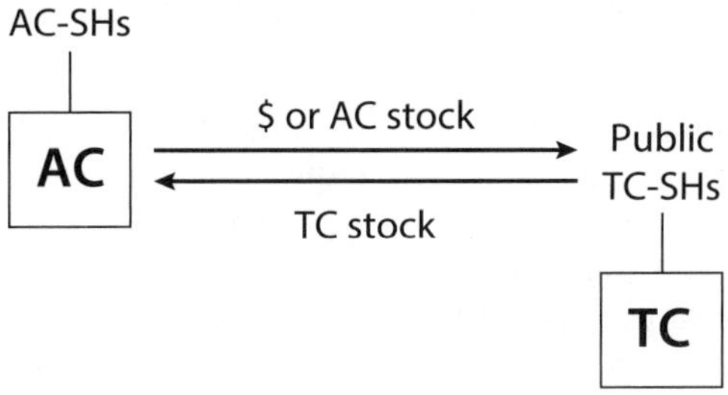

When the Dust Settles

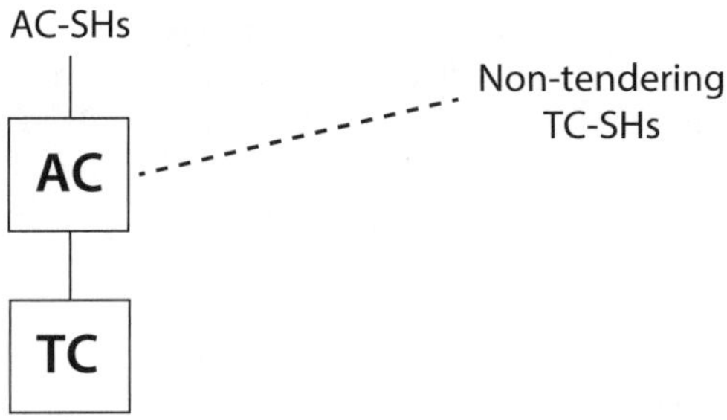

Diagram 1-H: Tender Offer Structure

Further, as discussed in Chapter 3, the flip-in provisions of a firm's poison pill will prevent an acquirer from acquiring more than a specified percentage of the target's shares. In addition, the premerger notification rules will prevent an acquirer from acquiring more than a specified amount of a target's shares prior to filing with the antitrust authorities and having the transaction cleared. Depending on the size of the target, the premerger filing may be required before the acquirer crosses the 5% threshold in Section 13(d).

The acquirer can offer either cash or securities, such as its stock, in a tender offer. Where the acquirer offers securities the transaction is referred to as an exchange offer, and the transaction is subject to regulation under the 33 Act as well as the 34 Act. Cash tender offers are not subject to regulation under the 33 Act; only the 34 Act applies.

B. Hostile and Consensual (Noncontested) Tender Offers

Tender offers can be either hostile or consensual. Consensual tender offers are generally set out in a merger agreement that provides for a first step tender offer, which is to be followed by a second step long form or short form merger. These transactions are discussed in Chapter 20 and can be made pursuant to the type of merger agreement set out in Documentary Appendix P, Cox Communications Combined Tender Offer and Going Private Merger Agreement. As discussed in Chapter 20, consensual tender offer-mergers can allow the acquirer to get a controlling interest in the target in a shorter period of time than with a one step merger.

Both consensual and hostile tender offers are basically subject to the same rules set out in Sections 14(d) and (e) of the 34 Act and the regulations thereunder, including the following: (1) the tender offer must remain open for 20 business days, (2) there must be unlimited withdrawal rights, and (3) all shareholders must receive the highest price offered during the tender offer.

Tender offers are made pursuant to an "offer to purchase" like Documentary Appendix M, Oracle Tender Offer for Peoplesoft. The acquirer generally publishes a summary advertisement in the financial press such as Documentary Appendix, N, Oracle-PeopleSoft Summary Advertisement. The tender offer can commence upon the filing of a Schedule T-O. *See* Documentary Appendix M. No pre-clearance of the tender offer is required, although if the SEC discovers material inaccuracies, the acquirer may be required to extend the tender offer. Within ten business days of the commencement of a tender offer the target's board must file Schedule 14D-9 and take a position on the tender offer or state that it cannot take a position. *See* Documentary Appendix O, PeopleSoft 14D-9 Statement.

Hostile tender offers will face defensive tactics employed by the target's directors, and these tactics are discussed in both Chapters 3 (fiduciary duties) and 23 (defensive actions). Also, the acquirer will have to give careful attention to any Baby Williams Act that may be applicable. *See* Chapter 22. The acquirer may have to conduct a proxy contest (*see* Chapter 16) to remove the target's board and dismantle the defensive measures, such as a poison pill.

C. Second-Step Mergers

Most tender offers are followed by a second step merger to eliminate the remaining public shareholders of the target. The acquirer generally does not want to own less than 100% of the stock of the target because the presence of minority shareholders can lead to litigation brought by shareholders regarding transactions between the parent and the sub. Section 251(h) of the Delaware Corporate law, which was enacted in 2013, in many instances, makes it easier to effectuate second step mergers. Second step freezeout mergers as well as freezeout mergers that are not preceded by a tender offer may be subject to the SEC's going private rules under Section 13e-3 (*see* Chapter 14). These rules require the acquiring parent or controlling group to explain why the transaction is fair to the minority shareholders. Also, such transactions may be subject to scrutiny under the entire fairness standard of review in Delaware and other states (*see* Chapter 3 and 14).

§ 1.5 A Historical and Economic Perspective on Mergers and Acquisitions

Senate Judiciary Committee Hearings on Mergers and Corporate Consolidation

June 16, 1998, *Testimony of Dr. Janet Yellen, Chair, Council of Economic Advisers*

Mr. Chairman and members of the Committee, it is a pleasure to be here this morning to talk about some of the economic issues raised by the current merger wave. My testimony contains four sections. The first puts the current merger wave into historical perspective. The main message from that section is that merger activity has certainly increased substantially in the past few years, but it is not clear that the level of merger activity is "unprecedented." The second section examines the question of what the current increase in merger activity means for the economy. Here the main message is that mergers affect economic performance primarily through their impact on competitive conditions in specific markets rather than on broader macroeconomic conditions. The third section looks at the causes and consequences of mergers. Here there is no simple conclusion. Many, if not most mergers are motivated by the desire to achieve greater operating efficiencies and lower costs. But it is impossible to rule out anticompetitive motives or simple managerial hubris as explanations for mergers. * * *

Mergers: A Historical Perspective. [In 1998 the] United States [was] in the midst of its fifth major merger wave in a hundred years. The previous four merger waves provide background and perspective for assessing today's merger activity.

> —*The Great Merger Wave of the 1890s.* The first great merger wave at the turn of the last century was the culmination of the trust movement, when numerous small and mid-sized firms were consolidated into single dominant firms in a number of industries. Examples include Standard Oil and U.S. Steel. One estimate is that this merger wave encompassed at least 15 percent of all plants and employees in manufacturing at the turn of the century. An estimated 75 percent of merger-related firm disappearances occurred as a result of mergers involving at least five firms, and about a quarter involved 10 or more firms at a time. The sharp decline in merger activity during 1903 and 1904 was probably related to the onset of a severe recession and the legal precedent for prohibiting market-dominating mergers under the antitrust laws that was established by the Northern Securities Case.
>
> —*The Roaring Twenties.* The merger movement of the 1920s saw the consolidation of many electric and gas utilities as well as manufacturing and minerals mergers. Some of the most prominent manufacturing mergers (such as the one that produced Bethlehem Steel) created relatively large number-two firms in industries previously dominated by one giant.
>
> —*The "Go-Go" Sixties.* The 1960s conglomerate wave represented a deflection of the "urge to merge" away from horizontal (same-industry) mergers, perhaps due to stronger antitrust enforcement. The constant-dollar value of mergers in manufacturing and minerals surpassed the prior peak attained in 1899 (though it remained much smaller as a share of the economy). The 1960s boom was also fueled by a strong stock market and financial innovation (such as convertible preferred stocks and debentures). This merger wave ended with a decline in stock prices that was especially severe for companies that had aggressively pursued conglomerate mergers.
>
> —*The Deal Decade of the 1980s.* Unlike other merger booms, this one began in a depressed stock market. With stock prices low relative to the cost of building new capacity, it appeared cheaper to expand by takeover. The 1980s boom was marked by an explosion of hostile takeovers and financial innovation (such as junk bonds and leveraged buyouts). The 1980s wave was unique in the prevalence of cash purchases (as opposed to acquisition through stock). Efforts to dismantle conglomerate firms put together in the previous wave and redeploy their assets more efficiently may have been an important driving force. Finally, the antitrust environment was more permissive and companies were more willing to attempt horizontal mergers.

Qualitatively, the current merger wave appears to be a reversion to pre-1980s form in some ways: It is taking place in a strong stock market, and stock rather than cash is the preferred medium. But many mergers are neither purely horizontal (in general large horizontal mergers would raise antitrust issues) nor purely conglomerate. Rather they represent market extension mergers (companies in the same industry that serve different and currently non-competing markets) or mergers seeking "synergy," in which companies in related markets expect to take advantage of "economies of scope."

By almost any quantitative measure, the current merger boom is substantial. * * * The total value of all deals announced in 1992—a year of especially low activity—was only $150 billion. The value of all deals announced in 1997 ($957 billion) was equivalent to about 12 percent of GDP, and activity so far in 1998 suggests another record year by this measure. * * * The last time merger activity was this large a share of GDP was during the Great Merger Wave at the turn of the last century.

One reason current merger activity is so large relative to the size of the economy is the run up in stock prices in the past few years. When merger activity is expressed relative to the market value of U.S. companies, its level remains lower than it was in the 1980s. * * *

§ 1.6 An Assessment of Various Theories of Mergers and Acquisitions

There are numerous studies of the economic effects of mergers, acquisitions and takeovers. One of the most comprehensive guides to this extensive literature is an article by Professor Roberta Romano of the Yale Law School entitled: *A Guide to Takeovers: Theory, Evidence, and Regulation,* 9 Yale Journal on Reg. 119 (1992).

As indicated by the following excerpt from this article, target shareholders benefit in all forms of acquisitions:

> One important, and undisputed, datum about acquisitive transactions should be noted from the outset: acquisitions generate substantial gains to target company shareholders. All studies find that target firms experience statistically significant positive stock price responses to the announcement of takeover attempts or merger agreements. On average, there is a 20% increase over the pre-announcement market price for mergers and a 30% increase for tender offers in the period around the takeover announcement. Abnormal returns in going-private transactions (leveraged buyouts) are of similar magnitude, ranging across studies between 20% and 37%. Without question, the announcement of a bid is good news for target shareholders. *Id.* at 122.

Also, as indicated from the following excerpt, the evidence on the benefit to the shareholders of acquirors is less certain:

> The data are more ambiguous, however, concerning acquiring firms' returns. Depending on the sample and time period, acquirers experience positive, negative, or zero abnormal returns on a bids announcement and completion. From the acquirer's perspective, there are two classes of explanations or motivations for a takeover: value-maximizing and non-value-maximizing ones. Value-maximizing explanations view takeovers as undertaken in order to increase the equity share price of the acquiring firm. Non-value-maximizing explanations consider takeovers in diametrically opposite terms, as transactions that maximize managers' utility rather than shareholder wealth. These two explanations therefore predict a different stock price reaction, positive and negative, respectively. *Id.* at 123.

Professor Romano sets out several possible explanations of why the returns to the acquirors are ambiguous:

> There are, however, theoretically plausible reasons for not finding positive abnormal returns to bidders even when acquisitions are value-maximizing transactions. First, acquiring firms are typically much larger than target firms, making it more difficult to measure abnormal returns. Second, a bid may reveal

> information about the bidding firm unrelated to the particular acquisition, confounding the stock price effect. Third, if the takeover market is competitive, then bidders will earn only normal returns, as abnormal profits are competed away. Finally, for acquiring firms that have an active mergers and acquisitions program, the gain from a specific acquisition may have been anticipated in the bidder's stock price at the time the mergers and acquisitions program was announced. *Id.* at 123–124.

Most of the studies relied on by Professor Romano are "event studies," and these studies are explored in the next section.

In his book, *The Synergy Trap: How Companies Lose in the Acquisition Game*, Professor Mark L. Sirower, a professor of business strategy and competitive analysis at the NYU Business School, has emphasized the significant challenges facing acquirors in mergers and acquisitions:

> Few, if any, corporate resource decisions can change the value of a company as quickly or dramatically as a major acquisition. Yet the change is usually for the worse. Shareholders of acquiring firms routinely lose money right on announcement of acquisitions. Sirower, *Imagined Synergy: A Prescription for a No-Win Deal*, a chapter from *The Synergy Trap*, excerpted in Mergers and Acquisitions 23 (January/February 1998).

He goes on to say that in many acquisitions, the acquiror is making a gift to the target's shareholders:

> When executives play the acquisition game, they pay, in addition to the current market price, an up-front premium for an uncertain stream of payoffs sometime in the future. Since shareholders do not have to pay a premium to buy the shares of the target on their own, these payoffs, the synergies, must represent something that shareholders cannot get on their own. They must mean improvements in performance greater than those already expected by the markets. If these synergies are not achieved, the acquisition premium is merely a gift from the shareholders of the acquirer to the shareholders of the target company. *Id.*

§ 1.7 Introduction to Event Studies: Determining the Wealth Effects of Mergers

This section provides an illustration of the event study methodology for determining the market reaction for both the target and bidder firms upon the announcement of a merger or acquisition.[1] Event studies are based on the efficient capital markets hypothesis, which holds that markets react quickly and accurately to new information. Thus, this hypothesis predicts, for example, that upon the announcement of a merger of two publicly-held firms, the market will quickly and accurately assess the prospects of the transaction

1. This section is based on and a modification of a paper entitled, *The Wealth Effects of Mergers and Acquisitions: Analysis of Recent M&A Sample from 2004*, written in April 2004 for my Investment Banking course by Katherine Splan, at the time a third year student at the UCLA Law School (with permission). Her paper and the above section follow the methodology set out in Weston, Mitchell, and Mulherin, *Takeovers, Restructuring, and Corporate Governance* 218–226 (Fourth Edition, 2003) [hereinafter *Weston*].

for both firms and such assessment will be reflected in the share price of the firms. The purpose of this section is to give the student an introduction to an important methodology for critically thinking about the wealth effects of mergers. An event study analysis of a merger can easily be done with an Excel spread sheet, which was used in the following illustration.

This section conducts an event study of the market's reaction to the announcement of the acquisition by J.P. Morgan Chase of Bank One in January 2004. Both companies were large publicly-held financial institutions. The merger agreement and SEC disclosure document for this transaction are Documentary Appendices D and E of *M&A Statutes, Rules, and Documents*, *supra* Section 1.1. The Delaware Supreme Court's decision in a shareholders' suit brought over this merger is set out in Chapter 3, and the U.S. district court's decisions in a federal proxy securities case, involving this merger is set out in Chapter 13.

This study has three basic purposes: (1) determine the return for the target's shareholders, the Bank One shareholders; (2) determine the return for the bidder's shareholders, the J.P. Morgan Chase shareholders; and (3) determine the combined return for the target's and bidder's shareholders. As Professor Weston points out: "The most important query concerning the wealth effects of mergers and acquisitions is whether the transactions create wealth. In other words are mergers positive net present value (NPV) projects?"[2] The NPV concept is explored in Chapter 7. As indicated above in most acquisitions the target's shareholders benefit and the acquiror's shareholders have slight gains or losses. The combined returns are more ambiguous. The following illustration proceeds with background information and then computes the target's returns, the bidder's returns, and finally the combined return.

Basic Data. Table 1 sets out information regarding the outstanding shares of J.P. Morgan Chase and Bank One:

Table 1 Target and Bidder Information

Announcement Date	Target Firm	Shares Outstanding	Industry Classification	Bidder Firm	Shares Outstanding
January 14, 2004	Bank One Corp	1,120,000,000	Banking Institutions	J.P. Morgan Chase & Co.	2,060,000,000

Table 2 provides basic information on the characteristics of the transaction:

Table 2 Merger Characteristics

Announcement Date	Target Firm	Bidder Firm	Type of Transaction	Merger Consideration
January 14, 2004	Bank One Corp	J.P. Morgan Chase & Co.	Merger	Stock of J.P. Morgan Chase

2. *Id.* at *Weston* at 222.

Computing Three Day Window Returns. The next step in this analysis is to compute the actual stock returns of the target and bidder firms for the 3-day window around the announcement of the merger. This is the return over the (–2 day, +1 day) period, where day 0 is the announcement date, day –2 is two days before the announcement date, and day +1 is the day after the announcement date. The 3-day window is employed here because even when the merger is announced on a particular day, which is the normal situation, there is still difficulty in determining exactly when the news of the merger first became available to the public and the market. Indeed, in many cases there is speculative trading in stocks of potential merger partners on the basis of inside information or rumors. For that reason, sometimes the stock price for a day that is long before the announcement date, such as 30 days before, may be used in the analysis.

The price formula for the 3-day return is $(P_{+1} - P_{-2}) \div P_{-2}$, that is, the return over this window period is the price of the security the day after the announcement date (P_{+1}), minus the price two days before the announcement date (P_{-2}), divided by the price two days before (P_{-2}). For example, if the price the day after the announcement date (P_{+1}) is \$110 and the price two days before the announcement (P_{-2}) is \$100, then the 3-day window return is 10%, computed as follows: [P_{+1} (\$110) – P_{-2} (\$100)] ÷ P_{-2} (\$100) = \$10 ÷ \$100 = 10%.

To control for factors other than the announcement of the merger that is being studied, an estimate of the movement in the stock market over the same 3-day window is needed. As a proxy for the market, the S&P 500, an index of 500 stocks, is often used, which is the case here. Alternatively, an index of the stocks in the particular industry could be used. The market return is subtracted from the return of the target or bidder firm to estimate the "net-of-market abnormal return" related to the given transaction (*i.e.*, the target's or bidder's return that cannot be explained by movements in the market).

Target Returns. Table 3 reports the estimation of the returns for the target, Bank One, the returns on the S&P 500, and the net of market return for Bank One.

Table 3 Estimated Target, Bank One, Returns

		Estimating Target Return			Estimating Market (S&P 500)			
Announcement Date	Target Firm	P_{-2}	P_{+1}	Return (%) $\frac{(P_{+1}-P_{-2})}{P_{-2}}$	P_{-2}	P_{+1}	Return (%) $\frac{(P_{+1}-P_{-2})}{P_{-2}}$	Net of Market Return (%)
January 14, 2004	Bank One Corp	44.18	50.01	13.20	1127.23	1132.05	0.43	12.77

Key: P_{-2} is the stock price two days before the announcement of the merger
P_{+1} is the stock price one day after the announcement of the merger

Bank One's stock return for the 3 days window period is equal to (50.01–44.18) ÷ 44.18 = 13.20%. The S&P 500 returned only 0.43% over the same window. Therefore, the net-of-market or abnormal return for Bank One was 12.77% (*i.e.*, 13.20 – 0.43%). This type of return is consistent with the studies discussed by Professor Romano above.

Bidder Returns. Table 4 reports the estimates of the returns to the bidder firm, J.P. Morgan-Chase, the returns on the S&P 500, and the net of market return for J.P. Morgan-Chase.

Table 4 Estimated Bidder, J.P. Morgan Chase, Returns

		Estimating Bidder Return			Estimating Market Return (S&P 500)			
Announcement Date	Bidder Firm	P_{-2}	P_{+1}	Return (%) $\frac{(P_{+1} - P_{-2})}{P_{-2}}$	P_{-2}	P_{+1}	Return (%) $\frac{(P_{+1} - P_{-2})}{P_{-2}}$	Net of Market Return (%)
January 14, 2004	J.P. Morgan Chase & Co.	38.48	38.61	0.34	1127.23	1132.05	0.43	–0.09

Key: P_{-2} is the stock price two days before the announcement of the merger
P_{+1} is the stock price one day after the announcement of the merger

The analysis of the returns for the bidder follows the same procedure that was used in analyzing the returns of Bank One. First, the 3-day return for the bidder is estimated and then subtracted from the market return over the same window period to provide the net-of-market return. J.P. Morgan-Chase had a stock return for the 3 day window period equal to (38.61–38.48)/38.48 = 0.34%. However, the S&P 500 returned 0.43% over the same window. Therefore, the net-of-market return for J.P. Morgan-Chase was –0.09%, indicating that there was a slight negative reaction by the J.P. Morgan-Chase shareholders. This type of return is consistent with the studies discussed by Professor Romano above.

The Combined Return. The combined return is the weighted average of the returns of the two parties in the merger where the weights are the equity value (*i.e.*, total market capitalization) of the particular target and bidder. The formula is:

$$\frac{[(\text{Target Value at } P_{-2} \times \text{Target Return} + \text{Bidder Value at } P_{-2} \times \text{Bidder Return})]}{(\text{Target Value at } P_{-2} + \text{Bidder Value at } P_{-2})}$$

The logic behind this formula is easily discernable. The numerator is computed by multiplying each firm's pre-announcement value (*i.e.*, the outstanding shares times the price per share) by the firm's net of market return and then adding these two amounts to get the estimated wealth gain or loss from the merger transaction. Since the target firm Bank One has a wealth gain of approximately $6.3 billion, and the bidder firm J.P. Morgan Chase has a wealth loss of roughly $71 million, the combined wealth creation is roughly $6.25 billion. This equates to a 4.85% return on the pre-announcement combined firm value of $129 billion, the denominator in the formula. Thus, although this merger produced a slight wealth loss for the shareholders of J.P. Morgan Chase, on an aggregate basis the merger produced a significant gain. Transactions in which the shareholders of both the target and acquiror experience wealth gains are unambiguously economically beneficial.

§ 1.8 The Current M&A Scene

This section presents a macro-picture of the M&A marketplace, principally over the period from 2004 through 2013. It is important for the M&A attorney or adviser to have a basic understanding of the macro-trends in M&A activity. This section employs two of the graphs and two of the tables employed in the review of the Current M&A scene in Chapter 1 of Thompson, *Mergers, Acquisitions and Tender Offers*, *infra* Section 1.10. That review is updated annually in July of each year.

Graph 1. Trends in U.S. Mergers and Acquisition Activity 2004–2013

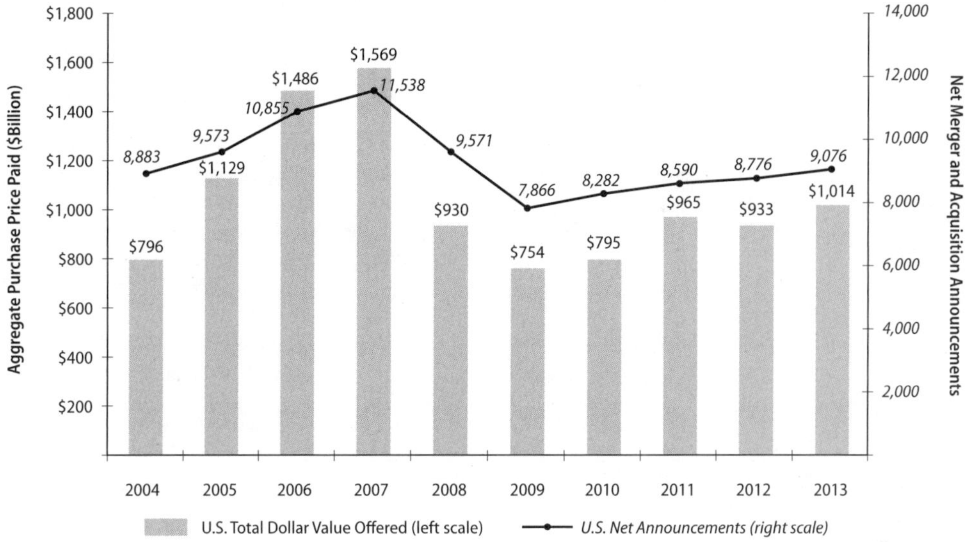

Source: Thomson Reuters Data, as of May 2014

The financial press has periodic articles on M&A trends, and several private firms provide analyses of this marketplace. An excellent source of information on U.S. M&A is the annual *Mergerstat Review*, which is published by FactSet Mergerstat, LLC. Most of the information in the graphs comes from *Mergerstat Review 2014*. Two other excellent sources of M&A data are Thomson Reuters and Deal Logic.

In 2012 and 2013, the M&A market in the U.S. continued to recover from the financial crisis of 2007 and 2008. Graph 1, *Trends in U.S. Mergers and Acquisition Activity 2004–2013*, above, shows both the dollar value of deals and the number of deals for each of these years, and Table 1, *Percent Change in U.S. Deals Volume and Percent Change in US Number of Deals 2009–2013*, shows the year-to-year percentage changes in U.S. deal value and number of deals for this period. Table 1 also shows the number of deals above $100 million and above $1 billion for this period.

Table 1. Percent Change in U.S. Deals Volume and Percent Change in U.S. Number of Deals 2009–2013

Year	2009	2010	2011	2012	2013
Percent Change in U.S. Deals Volume	–18.96%	5.44%	21.37%	–3.32%	8.76%
Percent Change in No. of Deals	–17.81%	5.36%	3.64%	2.17%	3.42%
U.S. $100 Million + Deals	535	912	932	1,013	1,016
U.S. $1 Billion + Deals	90	161	147	187	177

Source: Thomson Reuters Data, as of May 2014

Table 2. Breakdown of U.S. M&A Activity by Type of Transaction: Number of Deals and Deal Value 2009–2013

Year	Public		Foreign		Divestitures		Private	
	No. of Deals	Deal Value ($ Billions)	No. of Deals	Deal Value ($ Billions)	No. of Deals	Deal Value ($ Billions)	No. of Deals	Deal Value ($ Billions)
2009	292	289.4	591	33.4	2440	195.0	3473	38.6
2010	364	259.7	970	60.7	3066	287.5	4716	83.0
2011	325	355.7	1059	100.0	2919	319.9	5216	94.2
2012	343	205.4	979	65.5	2958	378.2	5330	130.5
2013	314	284.4	939	59.4	2789	470.7	4735	80.0

Source: Composition of Net Merger and Acquisition Announcements, Mergerstat Review 2014, FactSet Mergerstat, LLC pg. 9, 12.

Table 2, *Breakdown of U.S. M&A Activity by Type of Transaction: Number of Deals and Deal Value 2009–2013*, provides a breakdown on the type of M&A deals for the years 2009 through 2013. The deals are divided into the following categories:

1. Public Sellers,
2. Divestitures,
3. Privately Owned Sellers, and
4. Foreign Sellers.

Table 2 shows that for 2013 there were only 314 acquisitions of publicly-held U.S. targets, whereas there were (1) 4,735 acquisitions of privately-held U.S. targets; (2) 2,789 U.S. divestiture transactions, which involve the sale of a subsidiary or division of a U.S. parent corporation; and (3) 939 acquisitions of foreign targets.

Of the 343 public company acquisitions in 2012, 100 were tender offers, but 90 of these were uncontested, consensual deals; only 10 were hostile. The success rate of these hostile deals was 60%, whereas the success rate of uncontested tender offers was 94%. (*Mergerstat Review 2013* at 39–40)

The low number of hostile tender offers and their low success rate is attributable in part to the effectiveness of the poison pill defensive tactic, which is explored in Chapters 3. Chapter 20, which deals with third party-tender offers, explains how a tender offer can be combined with a merger in one agreement.

The consideration paid in most deals is cash; for example, in 2012, 71% of deals were for cash, 13% for stock, 16% for mixed cash and stock, and 1% other. The predominance of cash is probably attributable in substantial part to (1) the increasing activity of private equity firms in the M&A marketplace, (2) the fact that many potential acquirors have significant cash on their balance sheets, and (3) the low cost of debt financing.

From a U.S. regional perspective, historically the bulk of both buy-side (*i.e.*, acquirors) and sell-side (*i.e.*, targets) has been located in either the mid-eastern states or the far western states.

Graph 2. Recent U.S. M&A Volume Related to S&P 500 Index* 2004–2013

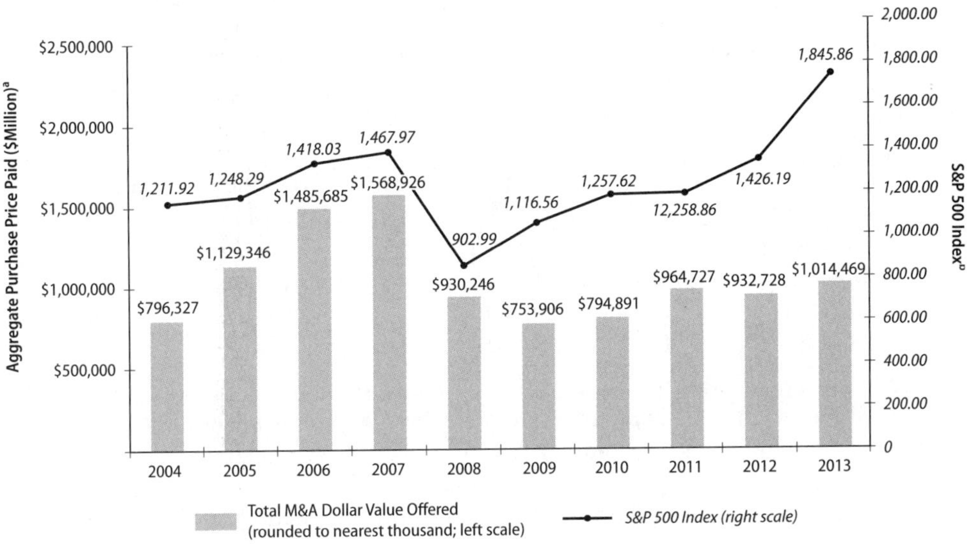

Sources: (a) Thomson Reuters Data, as of May 2014
(b) Yahoo finance Historical Prices S&P 500 2001–2013
*S&P Composite Index on 500 Stocks

Graph 2, *U.S. M&A Volume Related to S&P 500 Index 2004–2013*, shows the aggregate value of U.S. M&A over this period as compared with movements in the S&P 500.

Graph 2 shows that movements in the value of M&A activity have generally been in lock-step with movements in the S&P 500. As the S&P 500 increased, the amount of deal value increased, and as the S&P 500 decreased, deal value decreased. This may be an indication that when the market is doing well, managers may be more inclined to do M&A deals and to pay more in such deals.

§ 1.9 Introduction to the Sarbanes-Oxley Act and the Dodd-Frank Act

The Sarbanes-Oxley Act of 2002, which was enacted in response to the Enron and other corporate accounting scandals, dramatically changes the law governing publicly held corporations. This section introduces the Act. Chapter 3, directors' duties, examines the provisions of the Act that are most likely to have an impact on corporate governance: (1) the rules governing public company audit committees, (2) the rules on audit committee financial experts, (3) the rules governing codes of ethics, and (4) the related rules of the NYSE and NASDAQ Stock Market requiring public companies to have a majority of independent directors. Chapter 4 reviews the following provisions of the Act: (1) the rules regarding management assessment of internal controls, (2) the rules requiring officer certification of financial reports, and (3) the rules dealing with enhanced disclosure of beneficial interest under Section 16 of the 34 Act. The rules dealing with the professional responsibility for attorneys are addressed in Chapter 32, which focuses on ethical issues in M&A.

Some of the provisions of Sarbanes-Oxley amended the Securities Exchange Act of 1934 (34 Act) and other provisions imposed obligations on the SEC without amending the 34 Act. The Senate Report explained the purpose of the Act:

> The purpose of the [the Act] is to address the systemic and structural weaknesses affecting our capital markets which were revealed by repeated failures of audit effectiveness and corporate financial and broker-dealer responsibility in recent months and years. The [Act] creates a strong independent board to oversee the conduct of the auditors of public companies, and it strengthens auditor independence from corporate management by limiting the scope of non-audit services that auditors can offer their public company audit clients. * * * The [Act] also requires steps to enhance the direct responsibility of senior corporate management for financial reporting and for the quality of financial disclosures made by public companies. * * *

The Dodd-Frank Wall Street Reform and Consumer Protection Act of 2010 added several sections to the 34 Act relating to corporate governance, including the following: (1) provisions giving the shareholders a "say on pay" and "say on golden parachutes" (*see* Chapters 4 and 13); (2) a provision authorizing the SEC to adopt rules relating to proxy access (that is, permitting certain shareholders to include their own director nominees on the company's proxy card at the company's expense) (*see* Chapter 16); and (3) a provision authorizing the closing of the ten-day window in section 13(d), the early warning system (*see* Chapter 18).

§ 1.10 References

The literature dealing with mergers and acquisitions is quite extensive. The purpose of this section is to set out some of the most important references. References are also provided at the end of each chapter.

The topics addressed in each of the chapters of this book, as well as other topics, are addressed in treatise form in Samuel C. Thompson, Jr., *Mergers, Acquisitions and Tender Offers* (PLI, 2010, updated periodically) [hereinafter Thompson, *Mergers, Acquisitions and Tender Offers*]. The excerpts in this book from Thompson, *Mergers, Acquisitions and Tender Offers* are reprinted with permission. In reviewing any of the references in this section and throughout the book, the reader should consult the latest version of the referenced document.

One of the leading books dealing with negotiated acquisitions is Kling and Nugent, *Negotiated Acquisitions of Companies, Subsidiaries and Divisions*, (2005) [hereinafter Kling and Nugent, *Negotiated Acquisitions*]. Another important, but somewhat dated, book addressing negotiated acquisitions is Freund, *Anatomy of a Merger* (1975) [hereinafter Freund, *Anatomy of a Merger*]. Detailed information dealing with tender offers, takeovers and freezeouts is contained in Lipton and Steinberger, *Takeovers & Freezeouts* (2000) [hereinafter Lipton and Steinberger, *Takeovers & Freezeouts*]; Brown, Ferrara, Bird, Kubek and Regner, *Takeovers: A Strategic Guide to Mergers and Acquisitions*(2nd Edition, 2004) [hereinafter Brown *et al*, *Takeovers: A Strategic Guide*]; and Fleischer and Sussman, *Takeover Defense* (6th Edition, 2004) [hereinafter Fleischer and Sussman, *Takeover Defense*]. For a treatment of going private transactions *see* Borden, *Going Private* (1994) [hereinafter Borden, *Going Private*]. For a discussion of both negotiated acquisitions and takeovers, *see* Lorne, *Acquisitions and Mergers: Negotiated and Contested Transactions* (2006) [hereinafter

Lorne, *Negotiated and Contested Transactions*]. For a student's hornbook treatment of M&A *see* Bainbridge, *Mergers and Acquisitions* (2003).

The Negotiated Acquisitions Committee of the American Bar Association has published several excellent books on various aspects of mergers and acquisitions: ABA, *Model Stock Purchase Agreement with Commentary* (1995) [hereinafter *ABA Model Stock Purchase Agreement*]; ABA, *Model Asset Purchase Agreement with Commentary* (2001) [hereinafter *ABA Model Asset Purchase Agreement*]; ABA, *Manual on Acquisition Review* (1995) [hereinafter *ABA Acquisition Review*]; ABA, *The M&A Process* (2005) [hereinafter *ABA M&A Process*]; and ABA, *Model Merger Agreement for the Acquisition of a Public Company* (2011) [hereinafter ABA, *Model Public Company Merger Agreement*].

For a general treatment of Delaware corporate law *see* Balotti and Finkelstein, *Delaware Law of Corporations & Business Organizations* (1999) [hereinafter Balotti and Finkelstein, *Delaware Corporate Law*] and Ward, Welch and Turezyn, *Folk on the Delaware General Corporate Law: Fundamentals,* (4th Edition 2006) [hereinafter *Folk on Delaware Corporate Law*]. For a general treatment of corporate law, *see* American Bar Association, *Model Business Corporation Act* (Revised through 2005)[hereinafter *Model Business Corporation Act*]. For a treatment of the fiduciary duties of directors and the related business judgment rule, *see* Block, Barton, and Radin, *The Business Judgment Rule: Fiduciary Duties of Corporate Directors* (5th Edition 1998) [hereinafter Block et al, *Business Judgment Rule*]. *See also* ALI's *Principles of Corporate Governance: Analysis and Recommendations* (1994) [hereinafter the ALI *Corporate Governance Project*) and Thompson, *The Merger and Acquisition Provisions of the ALI Corporate Governance Project As Applied to the Three Steps in the Time-Warner Acquisition,* 1996 Columbia Business Law Review 145 (1996) [hereinafter Thompson, *The M&A Provisions of the ALI Corporate Governance Project*].

Two of the leading authorities on federal securities law related to mergers and acquisitions are Loss and Seligman, *Securities Regulation,* (3rd Edition, 1995) [hereinafter Loss and Seligman, *Securities Regulation*] and Hazen, *The Law of Securities Regulation* (5th Edition 2005) [hereinafter Hazen, *Securities Regulation*].

Two of the leading authorities on taxation of mergers and acquisitions are Ginsburg and Levin, *Mergers, Acquisitions and Buyouts* (Jan. 2006) [hereinafter Ginsburg and Levin, *Mergers and Acquisitions*] and Bittker and Eustice, *Federal Income Taxation of Corporations and Shareholders* (7th Edition, 2000) [hereinafter Bittker and Eustice, *Corporate Tax*]. For a casebook treatment of taxation of mergers and acquisitions, *see* Thompson, *Corporate Taxation Through the Lens of Mergers and Acquisitions* [hereinafter Thompson, *Corporate Taxation Through the Lens of M&A*]. *See also* Thompson, *U.S. International Tax Planning and Policy, Including Cross-Border M&A* (2006) [hereinafter Thompson, *U.S. International Tax Planning and Policy*].

For an exploration of the antitrust aspects of mergers and acquisitions *see* Areeda and Turner, *Antitrust Law,* Chapters 9, 10, and 11 (2004) [hereinafter Areeda and Turner, *Antitrust*]; Hovenkamp, *Federal Antitrust Policy,* Chapters 12 and 13 (3rd Edition 2005) [hereinafter Hovenkamp, *Antitrust Policy*]; Sullivan and Grimes, *The Law of Antitrust* (2000) [hereinafter Sullivan and Grimes, *Antitrust*]; and American Bar Association, *Mergers and Acquisitions, Understanding the Antitrust Laws* (2nd Edition 2004) [hereinafter *ABA Mergers and Acquisitions*]. For a comprehensive look at antitrust pre-merger notification *see* Axinn, Fogg, Stoll, & Prager, *Acquisitions Under the Hart-Scott-Rodino Antitrust Improvements Act* (Revised Edition, 2005) [hereinafter Axinn et al., *Hart-Scott-Rodino*] and ABA, Section of Antitrust Law, *The Merger Review Process* (3rd Edition 2006) [hereinafter *ABA The Merger Review Process*].

For an excellent review of banking acquisitions *see* Herlihy et al, *Financial Institutions Mergers and Acquisitions* (2005) [hereinafter Herlihy et al, *Financial Institutions M&A*].

The literature dealing with the finance and economics of mergers and acquisitions is also quite extensive. One of the best surveys of this literature is Romano, *A Guide to Takeover Theory, Evidence and Regulation,* 9 Yale Journal on Reg. 119 (1992). An excerpt from this article is set out in this chapter. *See also* the excellent collection of materials in *Part II, Motives for Acquisitions,* of Gilson and Black, *The Law and Finance of Corporate Acquisitions,* 253–638 (1995).

General information on M&A is available from many publications, including the *Wall Street Journal,* the *New York Times, The Economist, Corporate Control Alert, Mergers and Acquisitions,* and *The Deal.*

Chapter 2

Voting and Dissenting in Mergers, Asset Acquisitions, and Compulsory Share Exchanges

§2.1 Scope

This chapter examines the rules governing the shareholders' right to vote and to dissent and seek appraisal in mergers, compulsory share exchanges, and asset acquisitions. Section 2.2 presents an introductory problem, and Section 2.3 provides a brief introduction to (1) the role of the corporation's organizational documents, that is the certificate of incorporation and the by-laws, in determining the voting rights of directors and shareholders in M&A transactions, and (2) the default shareholder voting and proxy rules in Delaware. Section 2.4 explains that voting and dissenting rights are not available for a target's shareholders in a stock acquisition or tender offer, and consequently, these transactions are not covered in this chapter. Section 2.5 considers the requirements of various stock exchanges for the approval of an acquiror's shareholders in certain transactions. Although this chapter focuses principally on mergers and other acquisitions of corporations, Section 2.6 briefly discusses mergers between corporations and other business entities, such as limited liability companies (LLCs).

Section 2.7 discusses the legal effect of a merger, and Section 2.8 addresses the documents to be filed to effectuate a merger or share exchange. Section 2.9 addresses the long form merger provisions and the compulsory share exchange provisions of the ABA's Model Business Corporation Act (MBCA), and Section 2.10 addresses the Delaware long form merger provisions. These long form provisions govern mergers between firms that are unrelated or substantially unrelated; on the other hand short form mergers involve the merger of a subsidiary into its parent corporation. Delaware does not have a compulsory share exchange provision.

Section 2.11 considers the provisions of the MBCA governing the sale of substantially all of a target's assets, and Section 2.12 addresses the Delaware provision governing this type of transaction. Section 2.13 considers the *de facto* merger doctrine, and Section 2.14 discusses triangular (*i.e.*, subsidiary) acquisitions. These are transactions in which an acquiring corporation (acquiring parent) sets up a wholly-owned subsidiary and either the target merges into the sub in a "forward subsidiary (triangular) merger," or the sub merges into the target in a "reverse subsidiary (triangular) merger." In both the forward and reverse triangular mergers the target's shareholders end up with the merger consideration, which can be stock of the acquiring parent, and the acquiring parent ends up controlling the target. Most acquisitions of publicly-held companies are structured as reverse subsidiary mergers. Section 2.15 addresses the question of when class voting is required in a merger, and Section 2.16 considers (1) short form mergers under the MBCA and Delaware law, and (2) second-step freezeout mergers taking place after certain first-step tender offers under Section 251(h) of the Delaware corporate law, which was adopted in 2013.

Section 2.17 addresses the California approach to long form mergers, sales of assets, short form mergers, and dissenters' rights. Section 2.18 compares the approach to these issues in Pennsylvania[1] with the approach taken in Delaware, California, and the MBCA. The treatment of mergers and acquisitions in the MBCA and under the law in Delaware, California, and Pennsylvania broadly reflect the different approaches of the various states to these transactions. Finally, Section 2.19 refers to the treatment of these issues in the ALI's *Principles of Corporate Governance, supra* Section 1.10.

M&A Statutes, Rules, and Documents, supra Section 1.1, contains the statutory provisions discussed in this chapter. The materials in this chapter are covered in greater detail in Chapter 4 of Thompson, *Mergers, Acquisitions and Tender Offers, supra* Section 1.10.

§ 2.2 Introductory Problem on Shareholders' Right to Vote and Dissent

The boards of J.P. Morgan Chase & Co. (J.P. Morgan), and The Goldman Sachs Group, Inc. (Goldman Sachs), both NYSE-traded Delaware corporations, have entered into a merger agreement pursuant to which a newly-formed wholly-owned subsidiary (Sub) of J.P. Morgan will merge into Goldman Sachs. In the merger, the Goldman Sachs shareholders will receive voting common stock of J.P. Morgan, and J.P. Morgan's shares in Sub will be converted into Goldman Sachs shares. Thus, when the dust settles, the Goldman Sachs common shareholders will own J.P. Morgan stock, and J.P. Morgan will own all of the common stock of Goldman Sachs. J.P. Morgan has sufficient authorized and unissued shares to effectuate the transaction.

What are the voting and dissenting rights of the shareholders of J.P. Morgan and Goldman Sachs in this transaction? What if J.P. Morgan and Goldman Sachs were incorporated in states that had adopted the MBCA? What if J.P. Morgan and Goldman Sachs were incorporated in California?

§ 2.3 Introduction to the Impact of a Corporation's Articles of Incorporation and By-Laws on Shareholder and Director Voting and the Number and Classification of Directors

A. Introduction

This chapter focuses on the rights of the shareholders to vote and to dissent in a variety of M&A transactions. In determining the voting rights of directors and shareholders it is necessary to review the corporation's organizational documents to determine if these documents modify the voting rules set out in the provisions of the applicable state corporate law.

1. I thank Taimoor Choudhry, a 2014 graduate of Penn State Law and my former research assistant, for his very helpful assistance in preparing the materials dealing with Pennsylvania law.

As discussed in the *Ford Holdings* case in Section 2.10.I, state corporation laws are "enabling statutes;" thus, except for a few mandatory rules, such as a minimum voting requirement for mergers, the parties can structure the corporation in accordance with their desires. Also, corporate statutes set out certain "default" rules that apply in the event the parties have not specifically set forth an alternative rule, such as a super-majority rule for mergers.

Corporations are formed by filing with the appropriate state authority, usually the Secretary of State, an organizational document generally referred to as a "certificate of incorporation" [*see e.g.*, Delaware General Corporate Law (DGCL) §§ 101 and 102] or the "articles of incorporation" [*see e.g.*, Model Business Corporation Act (MBCA) § 2.02]. These documents are sometimes referred to as the corporation's charter.

Section 102(a) of the DGCL requires that the certificate contain the following basic information:

(1) the name of the corporation,

(2) the address of the corporation, including an address of a registered office and agent in Delaware,

(3) the nature of the business or purpose of the corporation, which could be and usually is a purpose of "engag[ing] in any lawful act or activity * * *,"

(4) if the corporation is "authorized"[2] to issue only one class of stock (*i.e.*, voting common stock), the number of shares of stock the corporation is authorized to issue and the par value, if any, of such shares,

(5) if the corporation is "authorized" to issue more than one class of stock, the total number of shares of all classes and the number of shares in each class (for example, common and preferred shares) and the par value, if any, and the "designations and the powers, preferences and rights, and the qualifications, limitations or restrictions * * *" of such shares [the directors can be granted the authority to determine the attributes of, for example, preferred stock, which is referred to as "blank check preferred"], and

(6) the name and mailing address of the incorporator or incorporators.

See also MBCA § 2.02(a).

While Section 102(a) sets forth barebones charter provisions, Section 102(b) sets out certain provisions that may (but are not required to be) set forth in the certificate, including:

(1) provisions limiting the powers of the shareholders or directors, provided such provision is not contrary to the laws of Delaware,

(2) a provision granting the shareholders preemptive rights (*i.e.*, the right to purchase on a pro rata basis any newly issued shares),

(3) "provisions requiring for any corporate action, the vote of a larger portion of the stock or of any class or series thereof, or of any other securities having voting power, or a larger number of the directors, than is required by this chapter," and

(4) a provision limiting the liability of directors for violations of the duty of care (this provision is examined in detail in Chapter 3).

---

2. The number of "authorized" shares represents the shares that the corporation has the legal authority to issue. The "outstanding" shares are the shares that have actually been issued by the corporation.

See also MBCA § 2.02(b).

The provision above relating to enhanced voting rights is sometimes used by a corporation to require a higher shareholder or director vote for a particular corporate action, such as a merger, than is required by the DGCL.. For example, as discussed below, under Section 251 of the DGCL, a merger generally must be approved by a majority of the outstanding shares of a corporation. However, a corporation's certificate of incorporation could require a larger, but not a lower, percentage shareholder vote to approve a merger.

Corporations will also generally adopt by-laws. Section 109(b) of the DGCL provides that the by-laws "may contain any provision, not inconsistent with law or with the certificate of incorporation, relating to the business of the corporation, the conduct of its affairs, and its rights or powers or the rights or powers of its stockholders, directors, officers or employees." After the corporation has received consideration for its stock, the power to "adopt, amend, or repeal" a bylaw is held by the shareholders entitled to vote, unless the certificate grants such power to the directors. *See* DGCL § 109(a). By-Laws generally deal with issues such as the procedures for calling and running the meetings of the corporation's directors and shareholders.

In the absence of a provision in the certificate of incorporation or the by-laws, the particular issue is governed by the applicable corporate law. For example, Section 141 of the DGCL sets out rules regarding the directors, including (1) the requirement that the business and affairs of the corporation be managed under the direction of the board, unless otherwise provided in the charter (this provision is examined in detail in Chapter 3), (2) the quorum and required vote for action, unless otherwise provided in the charter, and (3) the number of directors and any classes of directors (for example, if there are three classes, each class would stand for reelection every three years). Section 141(d) of the DGCL sets out the following rule pursuant to which a corporation may have a classified board:

> (d) The directors of any corporation ... may, by the certificate of incorporation ... or by a bylaw adopted by a vote of the stockholders, be divided into 1, 2 or 3 classes; the term of office of those of the first class to expire at the first annual meeting held after such classification becomes effective; of the second class 1 year thereafter; of the third class 2 years thereafter; and at each annual election held after such classification becomes effective, directors shall be chosen for a full term, as the case may be, to succeed those whose terms expire.

Under Section 152 of the DGCL, unless provided otherwise in the certificate [*see* DGCL § 152(d)], the directors of the corporation have the power to issue shares for "consideration consisting of cash, any tangible or intangible property or any benefit to the corporation, or any combination thereof." *See also* MBCA §§ 6.21(a) and (b). Once shares are issued they are "outstanding," and the number of outstanding shares is limited by the number of authorized shares.

Subsequent sections of this chapter assume that there are no provisions in the corporation's organizational documents regarding shareholder or director voting.

B. Certificate of Incorporation and By-Laws of the Goldman Sachs Group, Inc.

Documentary Appendices W and X of *M&A Statutes, Rules, and Documents, supra* Section 1.1, contain, respectively, annotated copies of the certificate of incorporation and the by-laws of The Goldman Sachs Group, Inc., a publicly-held Delaware corporation. Both the certificate and the by-laws contain several provisions not commonly found in the certificates and by-laws of closely-held firms. Several of the provisions of both documents can have an impact on M&A transactions that Goldman might enter into. These provisions will be referred to in subsequent chapters.

C. The Default Shareholder Voting and Proxy Process in Delaware

This section introduces the basic rules in the Delaware General Corporation Law (DGCL) concerning the shareholder voting and proxy process. This discussion does not discuss the nuances in these rules, such as the voting mechanics when a class vote is required.

Stockholder Action by Voting at a Meeting or by Consent. Stockholders may take action at an annual or special meeting of stockholders, and they may also take action by consent without a meeting of stockholders. Section 228 of the DGCL, which is titled "Consent of shockholders ... in lieu of meeting" provides:

> Unless otherwise provided in the certificate of incorporation, any action required by [the DGCL] to be taken at any annual or special meeting of stockholders of a corporation, or any action which may be taken at any annual or special meeting of such stockholders, may be taken without a meeting, without prior notice and without a vote, if a consent or consents in writing, setting forth the action so taken, shall be signed by the holders of outstanding stock having not less than the minimum number of votes that would be necessary to authorize or take such action at a meeting at which all shares entitled to vote thereon were present and voted....

Thus, for example, as discussed more fully later in this chapter, a merger governed by Section 251 of the DGCL must be approved by a "majority of the outstanding stock of the corporation" at an "annual or special meeting" of stockholders. Pursuant to Section 228, in lieu of approval at such an annual or special meeting, a merger could be approved by the filing of consents by a "majority of the outstanding stock of the corporation."

Calling of a Stockholders' Meeting. Section 211(a)(1) of the DGCL, provides that "[m]eetings of stockholders may be held at such place, either within or without this State as may be designated by or in the manner provided in the certificate of incorporation or bylaws, or if not so designated, as determined by the board of directors." Where the board is authorized to determine the place of the stockholders' meeting, the board may specify that the meeting be held "by means of remote communication."

Calling of Special Meeting. Section 211(d) provides that "[s]pecial meetings of the stockholders may be called by the board of directors or by such person [*e.g.*, Chairperson] or persons as may be authorized by the certificate of incorporation or by the bylaws." Thus, stockholders cannot call a special meeting unless they are granted such a right in the certificate or bylaws.

Fixing of Record Date for Determining Stockholders Entitled to Vote. Section 213(a), which deals with the fixing of the date for determination of stockholders of record," provides in part:

> In order that the corporation may determine the stockholders entitled to notice of any meeting of stockholders..., the board of directors may fix a record date, which record date shall not precede the date upon which the resolution fixing the

> record date is adopted by the board of directors, and which record date shall not be more than 60 nor less than 10 days before the date of such meeting.

Thus, the record date must be between the 10th and 60th days before the date of the meeting.

Notice of Stockholders' Meeting. Section 222(a) sets out the following requirements regarding notice of stockholders' meetings:

> Whenever stockholders are required or permitted to take any action at a meeting, a written notice of the meeting shall be given which shall state [1] the place, if any, date and hour of the meeting, [2] the means of remote communications, if any, by which stockholders and proxy holders may be deemed to be present in person and vote at such meeting, [3] the record date for determining the stockholders entitled to vote at the meeting, if such date is different from the record date for determining stockholders entitled to notice of the meeting, and, [4] in the case of a special meeting, the purpose or purposes for which the meeting is called.

Pursuant to Section 229 a waiver of notice is "deemed equivalent to notice."

Time for Giving Notice of Stockholders' Meeting. Pursuant to Section 222(b), unless otherwise provided in the DGCL, the "written notice of any meeting [must] be given not less than 10 nor more than 60 days before the date of the meeting to each stockholder entitled to vote at such meeting as of the record date for determining the stockholders entitled to notice of the meeting."

The shortest period between the record date and a stockholder meeting is 10 days. This is because (1) under Section 213(a), the record date must be at least 10 days before the meeting, and (2) under Section 222(b) the notice must be given at least 10 days before the meeting. Consequently, if, for example the record date is December 1 and notice is given on December 1, a shareholders' meeting could be held on December 11.

The List of Stockholders. Pursuant to Section 219, "at least 10 days before every meeting of stockholders," the "officer in charge of the stock ledger," must prepare "complete list of the stockholders entitled to vote at the meeting."

Right to Vote by Proxy. Section 212(b) of the DGCL provides that "[e]ach stockholder entitled [1] to vote at a meeting of stockholders or [2] to express consent or dissent to corporate action in writing without a meeting[,] may authorize another person or persons to act for such stockholder by proxy, but no such proxy shall be voted or acted upon after 3 years from its date, unless the proxy provides for a longer period." Section 212(c) sets out non-exclusive ways in which a stockholder can authorize a person to act for such stockholder as proxy.

If a purchaser acquires stock after the record date, the purchaser should get from the seller a proxy that will allow the purchaser to vote the shares.

Quorum and Votes Needed to Approve an Action. Section 216 provides that the quorum for a stockholders' meeting and the required votes needed for approval of an action shall be determined by the certificate of incorporation or bylaws, but the quorum cannot be less than 1/3rd of the shares entitled to vote at the meeting. This section also sets out the following default rules regarding the quorum and the number of votes needed for approval of an action:

> (1) A majority of the shares entitled to vote, present in person or represented by proxy, shall constitute a quorum at a meeting of stockholders;

> (2) In all matters other than the election of directors, the affirmative vote of the majority of shares present in person or represented by proxy at the meeting and entitled to vote on the subject matter shall be the act of the stockholders; [and]
>
> (3) Directors shall be elected by a plurality of the votes of the shares present in person or represented by proxy at the meeting and entitled to vote on the election of directors....

The One Vote Per Share Default Rule. In setting out the default voting rule, Section 212(a) of the DGCL provides that "[u]nless otherwise provided in the certificate of incorporation and subject to [the rules under Section 213 for fixing the date for determining the Stockholders of record], each stockholder shall be entitled to 1 vote for each share of capital stock held by such stockholder."

Annual Election of Directors. Section 211(b) provides that as a general rule, "an annual meeting of stockholders shall be held for the election of directors on a date and at a time designated by or in the manner provided in the bylaws." Under certain circumstances, the election of directors may be made by consent.

Section 211(c) prevents the indefinite deferral of an annual meeting by providing:

> If there be a failure to hold the annual meeting or to take action by written consent to elect directors in lieu of an annual meeting for a period of 30 days after the date designated for the annual meeting, or if no date has been designated, for a period of 13 months after the ... last annual meeting or the last action by written consent to elect directors in lieu of an annual meeting, the Court of Chancery may summarily order a meeting to be held upon the application of any stockholder or director.

Filling Director Vacancies. Pursuant to Section 223(a), unless the certificate of incorporation or bylaws provide otherwise, director "[v]acancies ... may be filled by a majority of the directors then in office, although less than a quorum, or by a sole remaining director...."

Cumulative Voting. Pursuant to Section 214, the certificate of incorporation may provide for cumulative voting for directors.

§ 2.4 Voting and Dissenting Rights in Stock Acquisitions

This chapter examines transactions that require action by the directors and shareholders, including corporate mergers, compulsory share exchanges, and sales of all or substantially all of a corporation's assets. This chapter does not address stock acquisitions of closely-held corporations and tender offers, which are stock acquisitions of publicly held corporations. These stock transactions do not involve collective action by the shareholders of the target corporation. Thus, in a stock acquisition or tender offer each shareholder of the target must decide whether or not to sell her shares; on the other hand, in a merger, compulsory share exchange, or sale of all or substantially all of a target's assets followed by a dissolution of the target, all of the target's shareholders are forced to give up their equity interests in the corporation.

Although the target's shareholders do not have the right to vote or dissent in stock acquisitions and tender offers, as discussed below, state corporate law or stock exchange rules may give the acquiror's shareholders the right to vote if the acquiror issues a significant amount of its stock in the acquisition. Stock acquisitions of closely held corporations are examined in Chapter 11, and tender offers are addressed in Chapters 17 through 22.

§ 2.5 Stock Exchange Requirement of Approval by Acquiror's Shareholders

A. Introduction

The rules of the New York Stock Exchange, the American Stock Exchange, and the NASDAQ Stock Market may require that the shareholders of corporations listed on such organizations be given a vote on certain transactions even though a shareholder vote is not required under the applicable state business corporation statute. For that reason, the applicable rules of the NYSE, which are essentially the same as the rules of the other exchanges, are set out here before studying the state law corporate rules regarding voting.

B. New York Stock Exchange

Section 312.03 Shareholder Approval of NYSE Listed Company Manual

Shareholder approval is a prerequisite to listing in the following situations …

(c) Shareholder approval is required prior to the issuance of common stock, or of securities convertible into or exercisable for common stock, in any transaction or series of related transactions if:

(1) the common stock has, or will have upon issuance, voting power equal to or in excess of 20 percent of the voting power outstanding before the issuance of such stock or of securities convertible into or exercisable for common stock; or

(2) the number of shares of common stock to be issued is, or will be upon issuance, equal to or in excess of 20 percent of the number of shares of common stock outstanding before the issuance of the common stock or of securities convertible into or exercisable for common stock.

However, shareholder approval will not be required for any such issuance involving: any public offering for cash * * *.

§ 2.6 Mergers Between Corporations and Other Entities Such As Limited Liability Companies

Before beginning the examination of mergers involving corporations, it is appropriate to introduce a relatively new type of transaction: cross-specie mergers between corporations and other types of business entities. Although these transactions are not examined in detail in this book, it is important for the M&A practitioner to have a basic familiarity with these transactions.

The MBCA, Delaware law, California law, and the law of many other jurisdictions permit mergers between a corporation and an "other entity," such as a limited liability company. For example, Section 11.01 of the MBCA defines an "other entity" as "any association or legal entity, other than a domestic or foreign corporation, organized to conduct business, including, without limitation, limited partnerships, general partnerships, limited liability partnerships, limited liability companies, joint ventures, joint stock companies, and business trusts," and Section 11.02 of the MBCA provides that "[o]ne or more domestic corporations may merge with a domestic or foreign corporation or other entity pursuant to a plan of merger."

In any merger between a corporation and an "other entity" the applicable corporate law sets out the procedures governing the approval of the merger by the directors and shareholders of the corporation, and the law governing the "other entity" sets out the procedures for approval of the merger by the owners of the other entity. For example, Section 18-209(b) of the Delaware Limited Liability Company Act requires a majority vote of the members of an LLC to approve a merger.

Significant federal income tax issues can arise in mergers, particularly mergers involving "other entities."

The balance of the discussion in this chapter focuses on mergers and other acquisitions involving corporations.

§ 2.7 Legal Effect of a Merger and Share Exchange

A. Comment on Rule Governing Legal Effect of Merger or Share Exchange under MBCA § 11.07

Committee on Corporate Laws, Changes in the Model Business Corporation Act—Fundamental Changes

54 Bus. Law. 685, 744–746 (1999)

Official Comment. Under section 11.07(a), in the case of a merger the survivor and the parties that merge into the survivor become one. The survivor automatically becomes the owner of all real and personal property and becomes subject to all the liabilities, actual or contingent, of each party that is merged into it. A merger is not a conveyance, transfer, or assignment. It does not give rise to claims of reverter or impairment of title based on a prohibited conveyance or transfer. It does not give rise to a claim that a contract with a party to the merger is no longer in effect on the ground of nonassignability, unless the contract specifically provides that it does not survive a merger. [In a merger it is necessary for the acquirer's attorney to determine whether contracts the target has entered into, particularly material contracts, will terminate as a result of the merger.] All pending proceedings involving either the survivor or a party whose separate existence ceased as a result of the merger are continued. * * *

In contrast to a merger, a share exchange does not in and of itself affect the separate existence of the parties, vest in the acquiring corporation the assets of the corporation whose stock is to be acquired, or render the acquiring corporation liable for the liabilities of the corporation whose stock the acquiring corporation acquires.

Under section 11.07(a)(8), on the effective date of a merger the former shareholders of a corporation that is merged into the survivor are entitled only to the rights provided in the plan of merger (which would include any rights they have as holders of the consideration they acquire) or to any rights they may have under chapter 13 [relating to appraisal rights]. Similarly, under section 11.07(b), on the effective date of a share exchange the former shareholders of a corporation whose shares are acquired are entitled only to the rights provided in the plan of share exchange (which would include any rights they have as holders of the consideration they acquire) or to any rights they may have under chapter 13. * * *

B. The Delaware Law

1. The Law

Read Delaware Gen. Corp. Law Section 259(a), which sets out the rights and liabilities of the surviving corporation in a merger, and Section 261, which provides the rules regarding the impact of a merger on pending legal actions.

2. Illustration

Read Section 1.3(b) of the Time/Warner Merger Agreement, Documentary Appendix A, of *M&A Statutes, Rules, and Documents, supra* Section 1.1, which sets out the effect of the merger on the surviving corporation. Even without Section 1.3(b), the merger would still have this effect under Section 259(a) of the Delaware Gen. Corp. Law.

§ 2.8 Illustration of Documents to Be Filed with State to Effectuate Merger or Share Exchange

A. Comment on Rules Governing Articles of Merger or Share Exchange under MBCA § 11.06

Committee on Corporate Laws, Changes in the Model Business Corporation Act—Fundamental Changes

54 Bus. Law. 685, 743 (1999)

Official Comment. The filing of articles of merger or share exchange makes the transaction a matter of public record. The requirements of filing are set forth in sections 1.20 and 1.25. The effective date of the articles is the effective date of their filing, unless otherwise specified. Under section 1.23, a document may specify a delayed effective time and date, and if it does so the document becomes effective at the time and date specified, except that a delayed effective date may not be later than the ninetieth day after the date the document is filed.

B. The Delaware Law

Read Section 251(c) of the Delaware Gen. Corp. Law, which sets out requirements for filing with the Secretary of State either the merger agreement or a certificate of merger.

§ 2.9 The MBCA Long Form Merger and Share Exchange Provisions

A. Comment on Rule Regarding Issuance of Shares under MBCA § 6.21(f)

Committee on Corporate Laws, Changes in the Model Business Corporation Act — Fundamental Changes
54 Bus. Law. 685, 712–715 (1999)

Section 6.21(f) provides that an issuance of shares or other securities convertible into or rights exercisable for shares, in a transaction or a series of integrated transactions, for consideration other than cash or cash equivalents, requires shareholder approval if either the voting power of the shares to be issued, or the voting power of the shares into which those shares and other securities are convertible and for which any rights to be issued are exercisable, will comprise more than 20 percent of the voting power outstanding immediately before the issuance. Section 6.21(f) is generally patterned on New York Stock Exchange Listed Company Manual Rule 312.03, American Stock Exchange Company Guide Rule 712(b), and NASDAQ Stock Market Rule 4310(c)(25)(H)(i). * * *

Section 6.21(f) does not apply to an issuance for cash or cash equivalents, whether or not in connection with a public offering. * * *

B. Comment on Rules Regarding Definitions Relating to Mergers and Share Exchanges under MBCA § 11.01

Committee on Corporate Laws, Changes in the Model Business Corporation Act — Fundamental Changes
54 Bus. Law. 685, 730 (1999)

*Official Comment. **In General.*** The provisions of section 11.01 fall into two broad categories. The definitions in sections 11.01(a)–(c) [defining "merger," "party to a merger," and "share exchange"] are intended principally to simplify the language of the remaining sections in chapter 11, through the adoption of short defined terms. * * * The definition of "voting power" in section 1.40 also has important substantive implications, because whether shareholder approval is required for a transaction under chapter 11 depends in part on the proportion of voting power that is carried by shares that would be issued and issuable as a result of the transaction. * * *

C. Comment on Rules Relating to Adoption of Plan of Merger under MBCA § 11.02

Committee on Corporate Laws, Changes in the Model Business Corporation Act — Fundamental Changes
54 Bus. Law. 685, 732–734 (1999)

*Official Comment. **In General.*** Section 11.02 authorizes mergers between one or more domestic corporations, or between one or more domestic corporations and one or more foreign corporations or domestic or foreign other entities. Upon the effective date of the merger the survivor becomes vested with all the assets of the corporations or other entities that merge into the survivor and becomes subject to their liabilities, as provided in section 11.07.

Applicability. A merger of a domestic corporation with a foreign corporation or a domestic or foreign other entity is authorized by chapter 11 only if the merger is permitted by the laws under which the foreign corporation or the domestic or foreign other entity is organized, and in effecting the merger the foreign corporation or the domestic or foreign other entity complies with such laws and with its articles of incorporation or organizational documents. Whether and on what terms a foreign corporation or a domestic or foreign other entity is authorized to merge with a domestic corporation is a matter that is governed by the laws under which that corporation or other entity is organized or by which it is governed, not by chapter 11. * * *

Terms and Conditions of Merger. Chapter 11 imposes virtually no restrictions or limitations on the terms or conditions of a merger, except for those set forth in section 11.02(e) concerning provisions in a plan of merger for amendment of the plan after it has been approved by shareholders. Owners of shares or interests in a party to the merger that merges into the survivor may receive shares or other securities of the survivor, shares or other securities of a party other than the survivor, interests, obligations, and rights to acquire shares or other securities, cash, or other property. The capitalization of the survivor may be restructured in the merger, and its articles or organizational documents may be amended by the articles of merger, in any way deemed appropriate. * * *

Adoption and Approval; Abandonment. A merger must be adopted and approved as set forth in sections 11.04 and 11.05. * * *

D. Comment on Rules Relating to Adoption of Plan of Share Exchange under MBCA § 11.03

Committee on Corporate Laws, Changes in the Model Business Corporation Act — Fundamental Changes

54 Bus. Law. 685, 735–737 (1999)

Official Comment. ***In General.*** It is often desirable to structure a corporate combination so that the separate existence of one or more parties to the combination does not cease although another corporation or other entity obtains ownership of the shares or interests of those parties. This objective is often particularly important in the formation of insurance and bank holding companies, but is not limited to those contexts. In the absence of the procedure authorized in section 11.03, this kind of result often can be accomplished only by a reverse triangular merger, which involves the formation by a corporation, A, of a new subsidiary, followed by a merger of that subsidiary into another party to the merger, B, effected through the exchange of A's securities for securities of B. Section 11.03 authorizes a more straightforward procedure to accomplish the same result. * * *

Terms and Conditions of Share Exchange. Chapter 11 imposes virtually no restrictions or limitations on the terms or conditions of a share exchange. * * *

E. Comment on Rules Relating to Action on Plan of Merger or Share Exchange under MBCA § 11.04

Committee on Corporate Laws, Changes in the Model Business Corporation Act—Fundamental Changes

54 Bus. Law. 685, 739–741 (1999)

*Official Comment. **In General.*** Under section 11.04, a plan of merger or share exchange must be adopted by the board. Thereafter, the board must submit the plan to the shareholders for their approval, unless the conditions stated in section 11.04(g) or section 11.05 are satisfied. A plan of share exchange must always be approved by the shareholders of the class or series that is being acquired in a share exchange. Similarly, a plan of merger must always be approved by the shareholders of a corporation that is merged into another party in a merger, unless the corporation is a subsidiary and the merger falls within section 11.05 [dealing with short form mergers]. However, under section 11.04(g) approval of a plan of merger or share exchange by the shareholders of a surviving corporation in a merger or of an acquiring corporation in a share exchange is not required if the conditions stated in that section, including the fundamental rule of section 6.21(f), are satisfied.

Section 11.04(f) provides that a class or series has a right to vote on a plan of merger as a separate voting group if, pursuant to the merger, the class or series would be converted into shares or other securities, interests, obligations, rights to acquire shares or other securities, cash, or other property, or if the class or series would have the right to vote as a separate group on a provision in the plan that, if contained in an amendment to the articles of incorporation, would require approval by that class or series, voting as a separate voting group, under section 10.04. * * *

Submission to the Shareholders. Section 11.04(b) requires the board of directors, after having adopted the plan of merger or share exchange, to submit the plan of merger or share exchange to the shareholders for approval, except as provided in subsection (g) and section 11.05. [Section 11.05 deals with short form mergers. *See* § 2.16.] When submitting the plan of merger or share exchange the board of directors must make a recommendation to the shareholders that the plan be approved, unless the board of directors makes a determination that because of conflicts of interest or other special circumstances it should make no recommendation. * * *

Quorum and Voting. Section 11.04(e) provides that approval of a plan of merger or share exchange requires approval of the shareholders at a meeting at which a quorum consisting of a majority of the votes entitled to be cast on the plan exists and, if any class or series of shares are entitled to vote as a separate group on the plan, the approval of each such separate group at a meeting at which a quorum consisting of at least a majority of the votes entitled to be cast on the plan by that class or series exists. If a quorum is present, then under sections 7.25 and 7.26 the plan will be approved if more votes are cast in favor of the plan than against it by the voting group or separate voting groups entitled to vote on the plan. * * *

In lieu of approval at a shareholders' meeting, approval can be given by the consent of all the shareholders entitled to vote on the merger or share exchange, under the procedures set forth in section 7.04. * * *

F. Comment on Rules Relating to Definitions Regarding the Right to Dissent under MBCA § 13.01

Committee on Corporate Laws, Proposed Changes in the Model Business Corporation Act—Appraisal Rights

54 Bus. Law. 209 (1998)

*Official Comment. **Overview.*** Chapter 13 deals with the tension between the desire of the corporate leadership to be able to enter new fields, acquire new enterprises, and rearrange investor rights, and the desire of investors to adhere to the rights and the risks on the basis of which they invested. Contemporary corporation statutes in the United States attempt to resolve this tension through a combination of two devices. On the one hand, through their approval of an amendment to the articles of incorporation, a merger, share exchange or disposition of assets, the majority may change the nature and shape of the enterprise and the rights of all its shareholders. On the other hand, shareholders who object to these changes may withdraw the fair value of their investment in cash through their exercise of appraisal rights. * * * [Thus, appraisal may be viewed as the price corporations must pay for the ability to engage in fundamental changes, like mergers, with less than unanimous approval of the shareholders.]

Chapter 13 proceeds from the premise that judicial appraisal should be provided by statute only when two conditions co-exist. First, the proposed corporate action as approved by the majority will result in a fundamental change in the shares to be affected by the action. Second, uncertainty concerning the fair value of the affected shares may cause reasonable persons to differ about the fairness of the terms of the corporate action. Uncertainty is greatly reduced, however, in the case of publicly-traded shares. This explains both the market exception described below and the limits provided to the exception.

Appraisal rights in connection with mergers and share exchanges under chapter 11 and dispositions of assets requiring shareholder approval under chapter 12 [*see* the discussion of asset acquisitions below] are provided when these two conditions co-exist. Each of these actions will result in a fundamental change in the shares that a disapproving shareholder may feel was not adequately compensated by the terms approved by the majority. Except for shareholders of a subsidiary corporation that is merged under section 11.05 (the "short-form" merger) [*see* Section 2.16], only those shareholders who are entitled to vote on a transaction are entitled to appraisal rights. The linkage between voting and appraisal rights is justified because the right to a shareholder vote is a good proxy for assessing the seriousness of the change contemplated by the corporate action. This is especially true where the action triggers group-voting provisions.

Notwithstanding this linkage, amended chapter 13 eliminates appraisal for voting shareholders in several instances where it would have been available under the 1984 Act. Shareholders who are entitled to vote on a corporate action, whether because such shareholders have general voting rights or because group voting provisions are triggered, are not entitled to appraisal if the change will not alter the terms of the class or series of securities that they hold. Thus, statutory appraisal rights are not available for shares of any class of the surviving corporation in a merger or any class of shares that is not included in a share exchange. * * *

Chapter 13 also is unique in its approach to appraisal rights for publicly-traded shares. Approximately half of the general corporation statutes in the United States provide exceptions to appraisal for publicly-traded shares, on the theory that it is not productive to expose the corporation to the time, expense and cash drain imposed by appraisal demands when shareholders who are dissatisfied with the consideration offered in an appraisal-triggering transaction could sell their shares and obtain cash from the market. This exception to appraisal is generally known as the "market-out" and is referred to here as the "market exception." * * *

For the market exception to apply under chapter 13, there must first be a liquid market. Second, unique to chapter 13, the market exception does not apply in specified circumstances where the appraisal-triggering action is deemed to be a conflict-of-interest transaction.

Definitions. Section 13.01 contains specialized definitions applicable only to chapter 13. * * * *Fair Value.* Subsection (i) of the definition of "fair value" in section 13.01(4) makes clear that fair value is to be determined immediately before the effectuation of the corporate action, rather than, as is the case under most state statutes that address the issue, the date of the shareholders' vote. This comports with the purpose of this chapter to preserve the shareholder's prior rights as a shareholder until the effective date of the corporate action, rather than leaving the shareholder in an ambiguous state with neither rights as a shareholder nor perfected appraisal rights. The corporation and, as relevant, its shares are valued as they exist immediately before the effectuation of the corporate action requiring appraisal. Accordingly, section 13.01(4) permits consideration of changes in the market price of the corporation's shares in anticipation of the transaction, to the extent such changes are relevant. Similarly, in a two-step transaction culminating in a merger, the corporation is valued immediately before the second step merger, taking into account any interim changes in value. *Cf. Cede & Co. v. Technicolor, Inc.*, [Section 2.10.F.4].

The definition of "fair value" in section 13.01(4) makes several changes from the prior version. * * *

The new formulation in paragraph (ii), which is patterned on section 7.22 of the Principles of Corporate Governance promulgated by the American Law Institute, directs courts to keep the methodology chosen in appraisal proceedings consistent with evolving economic concepts and adopts that part of section 7.22 which provides that fair value should be determined using "customary valuation concepts and techniques generally employed * * * for similar businesses in the context of the transaction requiring appraisal." Subsection (ii) adopts the accepted view that different transactions and different contexts may warrant different valuation methodologies. * * *

Modern valuation methods will normally result in a range of values, not a particular single value. When a transaction falls within that range, "fair value" has been established. Absent unusual circumstances, it is expected that the consideration in an arm's-length transaction will fall within the range of "fair value" for purposes of section 13.01(4). Section 7.22 of the ALI Principles of Corporate Governance also provides that in situations that do not involve certain types of specified conflicts of interest, "the aggregate price accepted by the board of directors of the subject corporation should be presumed to represent the fair value of the corporation, or of the assets sold in the case of an asset sale, unless the plaintiff can prove otherwise by clear and convincing evidence." That presumption has not been included in the definition of "fair value" in section 13.01(4). * * * Nonetheless, under section 13.01(4), a court determining fair value should give great deference to the aggregate consideration accepted or approved by a disinterested board of directors for an appraisal-triggering transaction.

Subsection (iii) of the definition of "fair value" establishes that valuation discounts for lack of marketability or minority status are inappropriate in most appraisal actions, both because most transactions that trigger appraisal rights affect the corporation as a whole and because such discounts give the majority the opportunity to take advantage of minority shareholders who have been forced against their will to accept the appraisal-triggering transaction. * * *

G. Comment on Rules Relating to the Right of Appraisal under MBCA § 13.02

Committee on Corporate Laws, Proposed Changes in the Model Business Corporation Act—Appraisal Rights

54 Bus. Law. 209 (1998)

Official Comment. ***Transactions Requiring Appraisal Rights.*** Section 13.02(a) establishes the scope of appraisal rights by identifying those transactions which afford this right. * * * [S]tatutory appraisal is made available only for corporate actions that will result in a fundamental change in the shares to be affected by the action and then only when uncertainty concerning the fair value of the affected shares may cause reasonable differences about the fairness of the terms of the corporate action. The transactions that satisfy both of these criteria are:

(1) A merger pursuant to section 11.04 or a short-form merger [*see* Section 2.16] pursuant to section 11.05. Holders of any class or series that is to be exchanged or converted in connection with a merger under section 11.04 are entitled both to a vote under section 11.04(f) and to appraisal under section 13.02(a)(1). Although shareholders of a subsidiary that is a party to a merger under section 11.05 [*see* the discussion of short form mergers below] are not entitled to a vote, they are entitled to appraisal under 13.02(a)(1) because their interests will be extinguished by the merger. Section 13.02(a)(1)(i) denies appraisal rights to any class or series of shares in the surviving corporation if such class or series remains outstanding.

(2) A share exchange under section 11.03 if the corporation is a party whose shares are being acquired in the exchange. Consistent with the treatment in section 13.02(a)(1) of mergers requiring shareholder approval, subsection (2) provides appraisal only for those shares that will be exchanged.

(3) A disposition of assets requiring shareholder approval under section 12.02 [*see* the discussion below of asset acquisitions]. * * *

(5) Any other merger, share exchange, disposition of assets or amendment to the articles to the extent the articles, by-laws, or a resolution of the board of directors grants appraisal rights to a particular class or series of stock. A corporation may voluntarily wish to grant to the holders of one or more of its classes or series of shares appraisal rights in connection with these important transactions whenever the Act does not provide statutory appraisal rights. * * *

Market Exception to Appraisal Rights. * * *

For purposes of this chapter, the market exception is provided for a class or series if two criteria are met: the market in which the class or series is traded must be "liquid" and the value of the shares established by the appraisal-triggering event must be "reliable." Liquidity is defined in section 13.02(b)(1) and requires the class or series of stock to satisfy either of two requirements: the class or series is either listed on the New York Stock Exchange or the American Stock Exchange or is designated as a national market system security on an interdealer quotation system by the National Association of Securities Dealers, Inc.; or * * *.

Because section 13.02(b)(3) excludes from the market exception those transactions that require shareholders to accept anything other than cash or securities that also meet the liquidity tests of section 13.02(b)(1), shareholders are assured of receiving either appraisal rights, cash from the transaction, or shares or other proprietary interests in the survivor entity that are liquid. * * *

Appraisal Rights in Conflict Transaction. The premise of the market exception is that the market must be liquid and the valuation assigned to the relevant shares must be "reliable." Section 13.02(b)(1) is designed to assure liquidity. For purposes of these provisions, section 13.02(b)(4) is designed to assure reliability by recognizing that the market price of, or consideration for, shares of a corporation that proposes to engage in a section 13.02(a) transaction may be subject to influences where a corporation's management, controlling shareholders or directors have conflicting interests that could, if not dealt with appropriately, adversely affect the consideration that otherwise could have been expected. Section 13.02(b)(4) addresses two groups of conflict transactions: those in clause (i), which involve controlling shareholders [20%]; and those in clause (ii), which involve senior executives and directors [in management buyouts, *see* Chapter 14]. * * *

Elimination of Appraisal Rights for Preferred Shares. Section 13.02(c) permits the corporation to eliminate or limit appraisal rights for the holders of one or more series or classes of preferred shares. * * *

Exclusivity of Appraisal Rights. With two exceptions, section 13.02(d) provides that appraisal is the exclusive remedy for a corporate action that has been completed. The theory underlying this section is that when a majority of shareholders has approved a corporate change, the corporation should be permitted to proceed even if a minority considers the change unwise or disadvantageous. * * * Thus, an exclusivity principle is generally justified. Nevertheless, there may be exceptional circumstances where the process by which the corporate action was approved was so flawed that it is appropriate to provide more general relief on behalf of all affected shareholders. Thus, section 13.02(d)(1) does not preclude challenges to serious procedural defects in approving the action, such as a failure to obtain the votes required by statute or by the corporation's own articles, bylaws, or board resolution authorizing the transaction. Similarly, subsection (2) creates an exception for cases where fraud or material misrepresentation have affected the shareholder vote to such an extent as to have caused the corporate action to be approved mistakenly. * * *

H. Comment on Rules Regarding Notice of Appraisal Rights under MBCA § 13.20

Committee on Corporate Laws, Proposed Changes in the Model Business Corporation Act — Appraisal Rights

54 Bus. Law. 209 (1998)

Official Comment. Before a vote is taken on a corporate action, the corporation is required by section 13.20(a) to notify record shareholders that a transaction is proposed and that the corporation has concluded either that appraisal rights are or are not available; alternatively, if the corporation is unsure about the availability of appraisal rights, it may state that appraisal rights may be available. * * *

I. Comment on Rules Relating to Notice of Intent to Demand Payment under MBCA § 13.21

Committee on Corporate Laws, Proposed Changes in the Model Business Corporation Act—Appraisal Rights

54 Bus. Law. 209 (1998)

Official Comment. Section 13.21 applies to all transactions requiring appraisal, except short-form mergers under section 11.05. In the latter case, shareholders of the subsidiary do not vote on the transaction but are nevertheless entitled to appraisal.

Section 13.21(a) requires the shareholder to give notice of an intent to demand payment before the vote on the corporate action is taken. This notice enables the corporation to determine how much of a cash payment may be required. * * *

J. Comment on Rules Regarding Payment under MBCA § 13.24

Committee on Corporate Laws, Proposed Changes in the Model Business Corporation Act—Appraisal Rights

54 Bus. Law. 209 (1998)

Official Comment. * * * Section 13.24 changes the relative balance between the corporation and shareholders demanding appraisal by requiring the corporation to pay in cash within 30 days after the required form is due the corporation's estimate of the fair value of the stock plus interest. Section 13.24(b)(2) requires that estimate to at least equal the corporation's estimate of fair value given pursuant to section 13.22(b)(2)(iii). * * *

K. Comment on Rules Regarding Procedure if Shareholder Is Dissatisfied with Payment or Offer under MBCA § 13.26

Committee on Corporate Laws, Proposed Changes in the Model Business Corporation Act—Appraisal Rights

54 Bus. Law. 209 (1998)

Official Comment. A shareholder who is not content with the corporation's remittance under section 13.24, or offer of remittance under section 13.25, and wishes to pursue appraisal rights further must state in writing the amount the shareholder is willing to accept. A shareholder whose demand is deemed arbitrary, unreasonable or not in good faith, however, runs the risk of being assessed litigation expenses under section 13.31. These provisions are designed to encourage settlement without a judicial proceeding. * * *

L. Comment on Rules Regarding Court Action under MBCA § 13.30

Committee on Corporate Laws, Proposed Changes in the Model Business Corporation Act—Appraisal Rights

54 Bus. Law. 209 (1998)

Official Comment. Section 13.30 retains the concept of judicial appraisal as the ultimate means of determining fair value. The proceeding is to be commenced by the corporation within 60 days after a timely demand for payment under section 13.26 was received. If the proceeding is not commenced within this period, the corporation must pay the additional amounts demanded by the shareholders under section 13.26. * * *

M. Comment on Rules Regarding Court Costs and Counsel Fees under MBCA § 13.31

Committee on Corporate Laws, Proposed Changes in the Model Business Corporation Act—Appraisal Rights

54 Bus. Law. 209 (1998)

Official Comment. Section 13.31(a) provides a general rule that the costs of the appraisal proceeding should be assessed against the corporation. Nevertheless, the court is authorized to assess these costs, in whole or in part, against all or some of the shareholders demanding appraisal if it concludes they acted arbitrarily, vexatiously, or not in good faith regarding the rights provided by this chapter. Similarly, under section 13.31(b), the court may assess fees and expenses of counsel and experts against the corporation or against all or some of the shareholders demanding appraisal for the reasons stated in this subsection. * * *

N. Problems on Direct Mergers and Share Exchanges under the MBCA: Acquiror Directly Acquires Target

1. Merger Consideration: 30% of Acquiror's Stock

Closely-Held Target Corporation (CHTC) is going to merge into Closely-Held Acquiring Corporation (CHAC) with the CHTC shareholders receiving common stock of CHAC amounting to 30% of the outstanding common stock of CHAC after the merger. CHAC and CHTC each have one class of voting common stock outstanding. Both corporations are incorporated in states with the MBCA. CHAC has a sufficient number of authorized and unissued shares to complete the transaction.

a. What action is required by the boards of CHAC and CHTC?
b. Do the shareholders of CHAC and CHTC have the right to vote?
c. Do the shareholders of CHAC and CHTC have the right to dissent?
d. Would the answers to Question b or c change if CHAC and CHTC were publicly-held?

2. Merger Consideration: 15% of Acquiror's Stock

The facts are the same as in Section 2.9.N.1, except the CHTC shareholders will receive stock of CHAC amounting to 15% of the outstanding stock of CHAC after the merger.

a. What action is required by the boards of CHTC and CHAC?
b. Do the shareholders of CHTC and CHAC have the right to vote?
c. Do the shareholders of CHTC and CHAC have the right to dissent?
d. Would the answers to Question b or c change if CHAC and CHTC were publicly-held?

3. Merger Consideration: Cash

The facts are the same as in Section 2.9.N.1, except the CHTC shareholders will receive cash.

a. What action is required by the boards of CHTC and CHAC?

b. Do the shareholders of CHTC and CHAC have the right to vote?
c. Do the shareholders of CHTC and CHAC have the right to dissent?
d. Would the answers to Question b or c change if CHAC and CHTC were publicly-held?

4. Share Exchange

Closely-Held Target Corporation (CHTC) is going to be acquired by Closely-Held Acquiring Corporation (CHAC) in a compulsory share exchange under MBCA § 11.03. CHAC and CHTC each have one class of voting common stock outstanding. Both corporations are incorporated in states with the MBCA. The shareholders of CHTC will receive stock of CHAC amounting to 30% of CHAC's outstanding stock after the acquisition. CHAC has sufficient authorized and unissued shares to effectuate the transaction.

a. What action is required by the boards of CHTC and CHAC?
b. Do the shareholders of CHTC and CHAC have the right to vote?
c. Do the shareholders of CHTC and CHAC have the right to dissent?
d. Would the answers to Question b or c change if CHAC and CHTC were publicly-held?
e. Would the answer to Questions a to c change if CHAC issued in the exchange stock amounting to 15% of its outstanding stock after the acquisition?
f. What is the end result of the share exchange?
g. What result in Questions a to c, if either CHAC or CHTC is not subject to the MBCA?

O. Observation on Absence of a Vote by Acquiror's Shareholders Where Cash Is the Consideration

Note that in all of the situations discussed above, the acquiror's shareholders do not get a vote when cash is the consideration. This is the case even where a minnow is swallowing a whale, that is, a small acquiror is acquiring a large target for cash. As will be seen from the subsequent discussions in this chapter, the same "no vote" rule applies under Delaware, California, and Pennsylvania law. And the "no vote" rule applies where the acquiror issues its debt instruments. Is this a wise policy? The laws of some countries require a vote by the acquiror's shareholders where the acquiror makes a major acquisition even when the consideration is cash.

§ 2.10 Delaware Long Form Merger Provisions

A. Mergers of Domestic Delaware Corporations

Read Section 251 of the Delaware General Corporation Law, which sets out the basic requirements for a merger. Section 251(a) authorizes mergers and refers to the merging corporations as "constituent corporations" without defining the term. Section 251(b) sets out the action the board of directors of each corporation is required to take. Section 251(c) addresses the required shareholder approvals and the filing requirements; Section 251(f) eliminates a vote by the shareholders of the acquiror in certain circumstances. Section 146 allows a corporation to "agree to submit a matter to a vote of its shareholders whether or not the board of directors determines at any time subsequent to approving such matter that such matter is no longer advisable and recommends that the stockholders reject or vote against the matter." In the context of mergers, this is referred to as a "force the vote" provision. The origin of this provision is discussed after the *Van Gorkom* case in Chapter 3. Section 251(d) deals with amendments to and termination of the merger agreement. Section 251(e) addresses amendments to the certificate of incorporation of the surviving corporation, and Section 251(g) provides for the formation of certain holding companies by merger without a shareholder vote.

Section 251(h), which was added to the DGCL in 2013, permits certain second-step mergers after a tender offer to be effectuated without a shareholder vote. Section 251(h) is explored in greater detail in connection with the look at short form mergers, *infra*.

B. Mergers of Delaware and Non-Delaware Corporations

Section 252 of the Delaware General Corporation Law sets out the rules for mergers between Delaware and non-Delaware corporations.

C. Illustrative Merger Agreement under Delaware Law

Read the Introduction and Articles I and II of the Time/Warner Merger Agreement, Documentary Appendix A of *M&A Statutes, Rules and Documents, supra* Section 1.1. Scan the balance of the Merger Agreement.

D. No Compulsory Share Exchange

Delaware does not have a compulsory share exchange provision like § 11.03 of the MBCA.

E. Dissenters' Rights under Delaware Law

1. The Statute

See § 262 of Delaware General Corporation Law.

2. Example

For a discussion of dissenters' rights under Delaware law, *see* Section [20] of the Time/Warner Joint Proxy Statement, Documentary Appendix B of *M&A Statutes, Rules, and Documents, supra* Section 1.1.

3. The Market-Out Exception to Appraisal Rights in a Cash/Stock Election Merger—*Wesco*

Krieger v. Wesco Financial Corp.,
Delaware Court of Chancery, 2011, 30 A.3d 54

[In *Wesco*, Vice Chancellor Laster of the Delaware Court of Chancery addressed the "market-out" exception in Section 262 of the Delaware General Corporation Law. The transaction was a long-form merger under Section 251 in which the shareholders of the publicly held target could elect either publicly traded stock of the acquirer or cash, with the default election being cash. The court reasoned:]

Notwithstanding the general availability of appraisal rights for mergers effected pursuant to the sections enumerated in Section 262(b) [including this long form merger under Section 251], Section 262(b)(1) creates the "market-out" exception. Under this exception,

> no appraisal rights under this section shall be available for the shares of any class or series of stock, which stock ... at the record date fixed to determine the stockholders entitled to receive notice of the meeting of stockholders to act upon the agreement of merger or consolidation, [was] either (i) listed on a national securities exchange or (ii) held of record by more than 2,000 holders....

8 Del. C. § 262(b)(1). Wesco's common stock was listed on a national securities exchange before the merger, so at this point in the analysis, Wesco's stockholders would not be entitled to appraisal rights.

But the appraisal statute continues. In what is known affectionately as the "exception to the exception," Section 262(b)(2) restores appraisal rights to a class or series of stock otherwise covered by the market-out exception if the holders are required to accept certain types of consideration:

> (b)(2) Notwithstanding paragraph (1) of this subsection, appraisal rights under this section shall be available for the shares of any class or series of stock of a constituent corporation if the holders thereof are required by the terms of an agreement of merger or consolidation ... to accept for such stock anything except:
>
> a. Shares of stock of the corporation surviving or resulting from such merger or consolidation ...
>
> b. Shares of stock of any other corporation ... which shares of stock ... at the effective date of the merger or consolidation will be either listed on a national securities exchange or held of record by more than 2,000 holders;
>
> c. Cash in lieu of fractional shares ... ; or
>
> d. Any combination of the shares of stock ... and cash in lieu of fractional shares ... described in the foregoing subparagraphs a., b. and c. of this paragraph.

8 Del. C. § 262(b)(2), ... As noted, Wesco stockholders could elect to receive (i) cash, (ii) shares of Berkshire Class B common stock listed on a national securities exchange, or (iii) a mix of cash and shares. Wesco stockholders who opted for Berkshire Class B shares would receive cash in lieu of fractional shares.

Under the terms of the merger agreement, holders of the class of Wesco common stock were not "required" to accept any type of consideration that would restore appraisal rights under the "exception to the exception." Berkshire had sufficient authorized shares of Berkshire Class B common stock and agreed to make sufficient shares available such that all holders of Wesco common stock could receive shares of Berkshire Class B common stock listed on a national securities exchange. The merger agreement did not contemplate proration or impose any cap on the number of shares available for individual stockholders or the class as a whole. No other eventuality has been identified that could have resulted in holders of Wesco common stock being "required" to accept appraisal-triggering consideration.... The "exception to the exception" therefore did not apply, and appraisal rights were not available for shares of Wesco common stock in the Wesco-Berkshire merger.

F. Determination of Fair Value in a Delaware Appraisal Proceeding

1. The Traditional Delaware Block Method

Francis I. DuPont & Co. v. Universal Studios

Delaware Court of Chancery, 1973 312 A.2d 344

DUFY, JUSTICE:

This is the decision upon exceptions to an Appraiser's final report determining the value of minority shares in a corporation absorbed in a short form merger [*see* Section 2.16]. * * *

On March 25, 1966 Universal Pictures Co. (Universal) was merged into Universal City Studios, Inc. (defendant) under 8 Del.C. § 253 effected by MCA, Inc., the common parent. MCA owned 92% of Universal and 100% of defendant. The minority stockholders of Universal were offered $75 per share which plaintiffs rejected and then perfected their appraisal rights.

On March 29, 1973 the Appraiser filed a final report, in which he found the value of the Universal stock to be $91.47 per share. Both parties filed exceptions and this is the decision thereon after briefing and oral argument. [The plaintiffs based their valuation on earnings, market, and assets, with different weights assigned to each. The defendant based its valuation on earnings, dividends, and assets, with different weights. And, the appraiser based his valuation on earnings and assets, with different weights assigned to each. After considering the parties' positions on the value factors, the court turned to the proper weights.] * * *

I conclude that the value of a share of Universal stock on the date of merger should be determined to be as follows [under the "Delaware block" or weighted average method]:

Value Factor	Value	Weight	Result
Earnings	$92.89	87.5%	$81.28
Assets	91.72	12.5%	11.47
		Value Per Share	$92.75

2. The Modern Approach

Excerpt from Weinberger v. UOP, Inc.

Delaware Supreme Court, 1983 457 A. 2d. 701

(*Weinberger* is also set out in Section 2.10.G.1 and Section 3.14.B)

[In *Weinberger*, a parent corporation Signal, acquired its partially owned subsidiary, UOP, in a freezeout merger. The minority shareholders brought an action alleging unfair treatment. The court held that the parent's action did not satisfy the entire fairness test which involved an analysis of whether the transaction satisfied the test of fair dealing and fair price. The facts of *Weinberger* and the fair dealing analysis are set out in Section 3.14.B. The portion of the opinion dealing with the determination of fair price in general and in an appraisal proceeding under Section 262 of the Delaware General Corporation Law is set out below. The portion of the opinion dealing with the exclusivity of an appraisal proceeding is set out in Section 2.10.G.1].

Turning to the matter of price, plaintiff also challenges its fairness. His evidence was that on the date the merger was approved the stock was worth at least $26 per share. In support, he offered the testimony of a chartered investment analyst who used two basic approaches to valuation: a comparative analysis of the premium paid over market in ten other tender offer-merger combinations, [*i.e.*, a comparable transactions approach, *see* Chapter 7], and a discounted cash flow analysis [*see* Chapter 7].

In this breach of fiduciary duty case, the Chancellor perceived that the approach to valuation was the same as that in an appraisal proceeding. Consistent with precedent, he rejected plaintiff's method of proof and accepted defendants' evidence of value as being in accord with practice under prior case law. This means that the so-called "Delaware block" or weighted average method was employed wherein the elements of value, *i.e.*, assets, market price, earnings, etc., were assigned a particular weight and the resulting amounts added to determine the value per share. This procedure has been in use for decades. However, to the extent it excludes other generally accepted techniques used in the financial community and the courts, it is now clearly outmoded. It is time we recognize this in appraisal and other stock valuation proceedings and bring our law current on the subject.

While the Chancellor rejected plaintiff's discounted cash flow method of valuing UOP's stock, as not corresponding with "either logic or the existing law," it is significant that this was essentially the focus, *i.e.*, earnings potential of UOP, of Messrs. Arledge and Chitiea [Signal employees] in their evaluation of the merger. Accordingly, the standard "Delaware block" or weighted average method of valuation, formerly employed in appraisal and other stock valuation cases, shall no longer exclusively control such proceedings. We believe that a more liberal approach must include proof of value by any techniques or methods which are generally considered acceptable in the financial community and otherwise admissible in court, subject only to our interpretation of 8 *Del.C.* § 262(h). This will obviate the very structured and mechanistic procedure that has heretofore governed such matters. * * *

It is significant that section 262 now mandates the determination of "fair" value based upon "all relevant factors." Only the speculative elements of value that may arise from the "accomplishment or expectation" of the merger are excluded. We take this to be a very narrow exception to the appraisal process, designed to eliminate use of *pro forma* data and projections of a speculative variety relating to the completion of a merger. But elements of future value, including the nature of the enterprise, which are known or susceptible of proof as of the date of the merger and not the product of speculation, may be considered. * * *

3. Modern Valuation Techniques

Chapter 7 explores the use of modern valuation techniques in mergers and acquisitions.

4. Determining Value of Target in Second-Step Freezeout Merger

Cede & Co., and Cinerama, Inc. v. Technicolor, Inc.

Delaware Supreme Court, 1996 WL 601475

Holland, Justice:

This appeal is from a final judgment of the Court of Chancery in an appraisal action. The proceeding arises from a cash-out merger of the minority shareholders of Technicolor Incorporated ("Technicolor"), a Delaware corporation. With the approval from a majority of Technicolor's shareholders, MacAndrews & Forbes Group Incorporated ("MAF") merged its wholly-owned subsidiary, Macanfor Corporation ("Macanfor"), into Technicolor. The only defendant-appellee in this appraisal action is Technicolor, the surviving corporation of the merger. The plaintiffs-appellants are Cinerama, Incorporated, the beneficial owner of 201,200 shares of Technicolor common stock, and Cede & Company, the record owner of those shares. (collectively "Cinerama.") * * *

[**Issue**] Cinerama argues that the Court of Chancery should have valued Technicolor as it existed on the date of the merger and, in particular, with due regard for the strategies that had been conceived and implemented following the merger agreement by MAF's controlling shareholder, Ronald O. Perelman ("Perelman Plan"). [MAF acquired Technicolor pursuant to an agreed to two-step tender offer followed by merger. After the tender offer, which gave MAF control of Technicolor, but before the merger, MAF instituted the Perelman Plan at Technicolor.] Technicolor argues that the Court of Chancery properly considered Technicolor without regard to the Perelman Plan and only as it existed on or before [the tender offer], with the then extant strategies that had been conceived and implemented by Technicolor's Chairman, Morton Kamerman ("Kamerman Plan"). * * *

The Court of Chancery recognized that the parties' disagreement about valuing Technicolor based upon either the Perelman Plan or the Kamerman Plan presented a question of law with regard to the proper interpretation of the appraisal statute. *See* 8 Del. C. § 262(h). * * *

In a two-step merger, to the extent that value has been added following a change in majority control before cash-out, it is still value attributable to the going concern, *i.e.*, the extant "nature of the enterprise," on the date of the merger. The dissenting shareholder's proportionate interest is determined only after the company has been valued as an operating entity on the date of the merger. Consequently, value added to the going concern by the "majority acquiror," during the transient period of a two-step merger, accrues to the benefit of all shareholders and must be included in the appraisal process on the date of the merger. * * *

The judgment of the Court of Chancery in the appraisal action is reversed. This matter is remanded for further proceedings in accordance with this opinion.

Note

As pointed out in a footnote in the case, Cinerama's expert valued the Technicolor shares at $62.75 per share, and Technicolor's expert valued the shares at $13.14 per share. The valuation methodologies used by these experts are explored at various points in Chapter 7.

5. Minority Discounts

Minority shares, particularly in a public company, may trade at what is referred to as a minority discount, reflecting the lack of control of a company. In *Cavalier Oil Corp. v. Harnett*, 564 A.2d 1137 (Del. 1989), the Delaware Supreme Court affirmed the Vice Chancellor's rejection of a minority discount in an appraisal proceeding. The Supreme Court agreed with Vice Chancellor's statement that the "objective of a Section 262 appraisal is 'to value the corporation itself, as distinguished from a specific fraction of its shares as they may exist in the hands of a particular shareholder.'"

G. Exclusivity

1. Basic Exclusivity Rule in Delaware

Excerpt from Weinberger v. UOP, Inc.

Delaware Supreme Court, 1983 457 A.2d 701

(*Weinberger* is also set out in Section 2.10.F.2 and Section 3.14.B)

While a plaintiff's monetary remedy ordinarily should be confined to the more liberalized appraisal proceeding herein established, we do not intend any limitation on the historic powers of the Chancellor to grant such other relief as the facts of a particular case may dictate. The appraisal remedy we approve may not be adequate in certain cases, particularly where fraud, misrepresentation, self-dealing, deliberate waste of corporate assets, or gross and palpable overreaching are involved. Under such circumstances, the Chancellor's powers are complete to fashion any form of equitable and monetary relief as may be appropriate, including rescissory damages. [Rescissory damages are the court's determination of the monetary equivalent of the position the plaintiff would have been in if the transaction had been rescinded.] * * *

2. Evidence of Fraud

Cede & Co. v. Technicolor, Inc.

Delaware Supreme Court, 1988 542 A.2d 1182

HORSEY, Justice:

We accepted this interlocutory appeal from the Court of Chancery to address a question of first impression in this Court: the standing and right of a minority shareholder who has dissented from a cash-out merger and commenced an appraisal proceeding under 8 *Del.C.* § 262 to assert and pursue a later-discovered individual claim of fraud in the merger through an action for rescissory damages against the participants for breach of fiduciary duty to the shareholder. This issue arises from a cash-out merger of the minority shareholders of Technicolor Incorporated (Technicolor), a Delaware corporation, accomplished by MacAndrews & Forbes Group Incorporated (MAF) through the merger of its wholly-owned subsidiary, Macanfor Corporation (Macanfor), into Technicolor, following approval by a majority of Technicolor's shareholders.

The appeal encompasses two suits, a first-filed statutory appraisal proceeding (the "appraisal action") and a later-filed shareholders' individual suit for damages for alleged fraud, conspiracy, self-dealing and waste of corporate assets (the "fraud action"). The plaintiffs are Cinerama, Incorporated, a beneficial owner of * * * approximately 4.5% of the total issued and outstanding common stock, and Cede & Company, the record owner. * * * Cinerama seeks to proceed to trial on both its appraisal remedy and its equitable claim against the several defendants, individual and corporate, for breach of fiduciary duty occurring in the merger.

The sole defendant in the appraisal action is Technicolor, the surviving corporation of the merger. The several individual and corporate defendants in the fraud action include Technicolor, all but two of the members of Technicolor's Board of Directors at the time of the merger, and the chief architects of the merger, MAF, Macanfor, and Ronald O. Perelman, controlling shareholder and Chairman of MAF.

Cinerama instituted its appraisal action pursuant to 8 *Del.C.* § 262 after voting against the merger. Approximately two years later, in the course of appraisal discovery, Cinerama came upon evidence of wrongdoing by Technicolor management associated with the merger. Cinerama then filed in the Court of Chancery its fraud action, charging the above-described defendants with conspiracy, fraud, breach of fiduciary duty, and other wrongdoing in the merger.

Defendants moved to dismiss the fraud action, asserting that Cinerama lacked standing to institute a fraud action after electing appraisal relief under section 262.

We affirm the Chancellor's ruling declining to dismiss Cinerama's fraud action, but we reverse the court's ruling declining to consolidate Cinerama's appraisal and fraud actions, requiring Cinerama to make a binding election of remedies before trial. Under the facts as alleged, Cinerama should not be put to an election of such disparate remedies; rather, the actions should be consolidated for trial. If Cinerama prevails, the court will determine the appropriate remedies warranted by its findings. * * *

[I]n a section 262 appraisal action the only litigable issue is the determination of the value of the appraisal petitioners' shares on the date of the merger, the only party defendant is the surviving corporation and the only relief available is a judgment against the surviving corporation for the fair value of the dissenters' shares. In contrast, a fraud action asserting fair dealing and fair price claims affords an expansive remedy and is brought against the alleged wrongdoers to provide whatever relief the facts of a particular case may require. In evaluating claims involving violations of entire fairness, the trial court may include in its relief any damages sustained by the shareholders. In a fraud claim, the approach to determining relief *may* be the same as that employed in determining fair value under 8 *Del.C.* § 262. However, an appraisal action may not provide a complete remedy for unfair dealing or fraud because a damage award in a fraud action may include "rescissory damages [*i.e.*, damages as if the contract were rescinded] if the [trier of fact] considers them susceptible of proof and a remedy appropriate to all issues of fairness before him." *Weinberger.* * * *

Applying these principles to the record before us, we find the Chancellor was clearly correct in refusing to dismiss Cinerama's fraud action. * * *

Cinerama's motion to consolidate, for purposes of trial as well as discovery, its fraud and appraisal actions should have been granted. No rule of law required the Court to put Cinerama to an election of remedies before judgment. * * *

Questions

Why would Cinerama want rescissory damages instead of an appraisal? Which shareholders could recover rescissory damages? Which shareholders recover in an appraisal proceeding?

H. Duty of Disclosure in Transaction with Appraisal Rights—*Skeen*

Skeen v. Jo-Ann Stores, Inc.
Delaware Supreme Court, 2000
750 A.2d 1170

Opinion: Berger, Justice:

In this appeal, we consider the adequacy of corporate disclosures to minority stockholders who were "cashed out" in a merger approved by the majority stockholder. The minority stockholders complain that they were not given enough financial information to decide whether to accept the merger consideration or seek appraisal. * * * We hold that there is no different standard for appraisal decisions. Directors must disclose all material facts within their control that a reasonable stockholder would consider important in deciding how to respond to the pending transaction. The Court of Chancery applied the proper standard and correctly concluded that the minority stockholders' disclosure claims were legally insufficient. Accordingly, we affirm. * * *

Omitted facts are not material simply because they might be helpful. To be actionable, there must be a substantial likelihood that the undisclosed information would significantly alter the total mix of information already provided. [This materiality standard is also explored in Chapter 3, dealing with director's duties and Chapter 4, dealing with the Federal securities laws.] The complaint alleges no facts suggesting that the undisclosed information is inconsistent with, or otherwise significantly differs from, the disclosed information. Appellants merely allege that the added information would be helpful in valuing the company. * * *

Note

Chapter 3 explores other disclosure issues.

I. Right of Preferred Stock to Appraisal—*Ford*

In the Matter of the Appraisal of Ford Holdings, Inc. Preferred Stock

Delaware Court of Chancery, 1997 698 A.2d 973

ALLEN, Chancellor.

This is an appraisal proceeding under Section 262 of the Delaware General Corporation Law. It arises from a merger in which Ford Holdings, Inc. ("Holdings"), a subsidiary of Ford Motor Company, merged with Ford Holdings Capital Corporation, its own wholly owned subsidiary. The effect of the merger was to cash-out various types and series of Holdings' preferred stock. In each instance, the holders of preferred were paid the liquidation value of their security, plus a "merger premium" if the certificate creating the preferred called for it, plus any accumulated and unpaid dividends. Holdings asserts that under the various documents creating these securities that is exactly what the holders of the preferred stock are entitled to in the event of a merger. Plaintiffs in this appraisal action are certain holders of preferred stocks of Holdings. They seek a judicial appraisal of the "fair value" of their shares at the time of the merger, which they contend is higher than the amount Holdings calculated as due to them. * * *

I conclude that properly expressed terms of a Certificate of Designation of preferred stock may establish the consideration to which holders of the stock will be entitled in the event of a merger and, when the documents creating the security do so, that the amount so fixed or determined constitutes the "fair value" of the stock for the purposes of dissenters' rights under Section 262 of the Delaware General Corporation Law. With respect to some series of Holdings, preferred stock, I conclude that the documents creating the security do so limit merger consideration; for others, in my judgment, they do not. * * *

Delaware's General Corporation Law, like most general laws of incorporation in the twentieth century U.S., is an enabling statute. * * * [U]nlike the corporation law of the nineteenth century, modern corporation law contains few mandatory terms; it is largely enabling in character. It is not, however, bereft of mandatory terms. Under Delaware law, for example, a corporation is required to have * * * shareholder concurrence in the authorization of a merger; and is required to have shareholder approval in order to dissolve. Generally, these mandatory provisions may not be varied by terms of the certificate of incorporation or otherwise.

Among these mandatory provisions of Delaware law is Section 262, the appraisal remedy. * * * It is this provision upon which petitioners rely. * * *

Defendant asserts that the Designations of the Cumulative Preferred and the Auction Preferred limit the appraisal rights of holders of these shares. Specifically, defendant contends that the Designations define the consideration to which the holders are entitled in the event of a merger. According to defendant, while shareholders may be statutorily entitled to an appraisal of fair value, the instrument creating their security fixes that value. * * *

All of the characteristics of the preferred are open for negotiation; that is the nature of the security. There is no utility in defining as forbidden any term thought advantageous to informed parties, unless that term violates substantive law. Particularly, there is no utility in forbidding the parties creating a preferred stock (the issuer, its advisors and counsel, and the underwriter and its counsel) from establishing a security that has a stated value (or a value established by a stated formula) in the event of stated contingencies. * * *

I cannot conclude that a provision that establishes the cash value of a preferred stock in the event of a cash-out merger would violate the public policy reflected in Section 262, given the essentially contractual nature of preferred stock. Thus, the relevant question in this case is whether the instruments establishing the rights and preferences of these various series of preferred stocks do contractually limit the right of a holder to seek judicial appraisal in the event of a cash-out merger. * * * [The court found that certain series of the preferred were so limited.]

J. Problems on Direct Mergers under Delaware Law: Acquiror Directly Acquires Target

1. Merger Consideration: 30% of Acquiror's Stock

Same questions as in Section 2.9.N.1, except CHAC and CHTC are incorporated in Delaware.

2. Merger Consideration: 15% of Acquiror's Stock

Same questions as in Section 2.9.N.2, except CHAC and CHTC are incorporated in Delaware.

3. Merger Consideration: Cash

Same questions as in Section 2.9.N.3, except CHAC and CHTC are incorporated in Delaware.

§ 2.11 The MBCA Sale of "Substantially All" of Assets Provision

A. Introduction

As noted above, in a merger of a target into an acquiror, all of the target's assets and liabilities pass over to the acquiror by operation of law. If the acquiror does not want to acquire all of the target's assets and liabilities, the transaction may be structured as an asset acquisition in which the acquiror acquires specified assets and liabilities from the target. This type of transaction is effectuated by a contract of sale between the acquiror and the target, specifying the assets to be acquired and the liabilities to be assumed. The contract may be labeled: Asset Acquisition Agreement. A Sample Asset Acquisition Agreement is set out in Documentary Appendix V of *M&A Statutes, Rules and Documents, supra* Section 1.1. In many cases, after the acquisition, the target is liquidated, distributing the proceeds of the sale plus any other assets to its shareholders in exchange for their stock. This and succeeding sections deal with the sale of assets transaction.

B. Comment on Rules Regarding Disposal of Assets Not Requiring Shareholder Approval under MBCA § 12.01

Committee on Corporate Laws, Changes in the Model Business Corporation Act—Fundamental Changes

54 Bus. Law. 685, 747–748 (1999)

Section 12.01 provides that no approval of the shareholders is required for dispositions of assets of the types described therein, unless the articles of incorporation otherwise provide. Dispositions other than those described in section 12.01 require shareholder approval if they fall within section 12.02.

Under subsection (1), shareholder approval is not required for a disposition of the corporation's assets in the usual and regular course of business, regardless of the size of the transaction. * * *

Subsection (3) provides that no approval of shareholders is required to transfer any or all of the corporation's assets to a wholly owned subsidiary or other entity. This provision may not be used as a device to avoid a vote of shareholders by a multi-step transaction.

Subsection (4) provides that no approval of the shareholders is required to distribute assets pro rata to the holders of one or more classes of the corporation's shares. A traditional spin-off—that is, a pro rata distribution of the shares of a subsidiary to the holders of one or more classes of shares—falls within this subsection. * * * [Spin-offs are discussed in Chapter 24.]

C. Comment on Rules Regarding Shareholder Approval of Certain Dispositions under MBCA § 12.02

Committee on Corporate Laws, Changes in the Model Business Corporation Act—Fundamental Changes

54 Bus. Law. 685, 749–753 (1999)

In General. Section 12.02(a) requires shareholder approval for a sale, lease, exchange or other disposition by a corporation that would leave the corporation without a significant continuing business activity. The test employed in section 12.02(a) for whether a disposition of assets requires shareholder approval differs verbally from the test employed in past versions of the Model Act, which centered on whether a sale involves "all or substantially all" of a corporation's assets. The "all or substantially all" test has also been used in most corporate statutes. In practice, however, courts interpreting these statutes have commonly employed a test comparable to that embodied in 12.02(a). For example, in *Gimbel v. Signal Cos.[Section 2.12.C.1]*, the court stated that "While it is true that [the all or substantially all] test does not lend itself to a strict mathematical standard to be applied in every case, the qualitative factor can be defined to some degree. * * * If the sale is of assets quantitatively vital to the operation of the corporation and is out of the ordinary [course] and substantially affects the existence and purpose of the corporation then it is beyond the power of the Board of Directors." * * *

Whether a disposition leaves a corporation with a significant continuing business activity, within the meaning of section 12.02(a), depends primarily on whether the corporation will have a remaining business activity that is significant when compared to the corporation's business prior to the disposition. [Under] * * * a safe harbor, embodied in the second sentence of section 12.02(a), * * * a significant business activity exists if the continuing business activity represented at least 25 percent of the total assets and 25 percent of either income from continuing operations before income taxes or revenues from continuing operations, in each case of the company and its subsidiaries on a consolidated basis for the most recent full fiscal year. * * *

In determining whether a disposition would leave a corporation without a significant continuing business activity, the term "the corporation" includes subsidiaries that are or should be consolidated with the parent under generally accepted accounting principles. * * *

Submission to Shareholders. Section 12.02(b) requires the board of directors, after having adopted a resolution authorizing a disposition that requires shareholder approval, to submit the disposition to the shareholders for approval. When submitting the disposition to the shareholders, the board of directors must make a recommendation to the shareholders that the disposition be approved, unless the board makes a determination that because of conflicts of interests or other special circumstances it should make no recommendation. * * * [*See* Section 2.9.E, Submission to the Shareholders]

Section 12.02(c) permits the board of directors to condition its submission of a proposed disposition to the shareholders. * * * [*See* Section 2.9.E]

Quorum and Voting. Section 12.02(e) provides that approval of a [transaction under Section 12.02] requires approval of the shareholders at a meeting at which at least a majority of the votes entitled to be cast on the plan is present, including, if any class or series of shares are entitled to vote as a separate group on the plan, the approval of each such separate group at a meeting at which a similar quorum of the voting group exists. If a quorum is present, then under sections 7.25 and 7.26 the plan will be approved if more votes are cast in favor of the plan than against it by the voting group or separate voting groups entitled to vote on the plan. This represents a change from the Act's previous voting rule, which required approval by a majority of outstanding shares.

In lieu of approval at a shareholders' meeting, approval can be given by the consent of all the shareholders entitled to vote on the merger or share exchange, under the procedures set forth in section 7.04. * * *

D. Comment on Rules Relating to Dissolution by Board of Directors and Shareholders and Articles of Dissolution under MBCA §§ 14.02 to 14.03

Committee on Corporate Laws, Changes in the Model Business Corporation Act—Fundamental Changes

54 Bus. Law. 685, 749–753 (1999)

[A sale of all or substantially all of a corporation's assets will generally be followed by a dissolution of the corporation.] Section 14.02(b) requires the board of directors, after approving a proposal to dissolve, to submit the proposal to the shareholders for their approval. When submitting the proposal the board of directors must make a recommendation to the shareholders that the plan be approved, unless the board of directors makes a determination that because of conflicts of interest or other special circumstances it should make no recommendation. * * *

Section 14.02(c) permits the board of directors to condition its submission of a proposal for dissolution on any basis. * * *

Section 14.02(d) provides that if the proposal is required to be approved by the shareholders, and if the approval is to be given at a meeting, the corporation must notify each shareholder, whether or not entitled to vote, of the meeting of shareholders at which the proposal is to be submitted. * * *

Section 14.02(e) provides that approval of a proposal for dissolution requires approval of the shareholders at a meeting at which a quorum consisting of a majority of the votes entitled to be cast on the proposal exists. If a quorum is present, then under sections 7.25 and 7.26 the proposal will be approved if more votes are cast in favor of the proposal than against it by the voting group or separate voting groups entitled to vote on the proposal. * * *

E. Dissenters' Rights on a Disposition of Assets Where Shareholder Approval Is Required under the MBCA

Committee on Corporate Laws, Changes in the Model Business Corporation Act—Fundamental Changes

54 Bus. Law. 685, 753 (1999)

Appraisal Rights. Shareholders of a domestic corporation that engages in a disposition that requires shareholder approval under section 12.02 may have appraisal rights. *See* chapter 13. [*See* Section 2.9.G. There it will be seen that a disposition of assets requiring shareholder approval under Section 12.02 gives rise to appraisal rights. However, the commentary explains: "As provided in section 12.02(g), a disposition of assets by a corporation in the course of dissolution under chapter 14 is governed by that chapter, not chapter 12, and thus does not implicate appraisal rights." Thus, there are no appraisal rights in a sale of all or substantially all of a target's assets if the target is liquidated and dissolved as part of the transaction.]

F. Problems on Sales of Assets under the MBCA

1. Acquisition Consideration: 30% of Acquiror's Stock

Closely-Held Target Corporation (CHTC) is going to sell all of its assets and transfer certain of its liabilities to Closely-Held Acquiring Corporation (CHAC) in exchange for stock of CHAC amounting to 30% of the outstanding stock of CHAC after the acquisition. Immediately after the transfer, CHTC will be dissolved and liquidated, with CHTC transferring to its shareholders the CHAC stock in exchange for the CHTC stock, which will be cancelled. Both corporations are incorporated in states with the MBCA. CHAC has a sufficient number of authorized and unissued shares to complete the transaction.

a. What action is required by the boards of CHAC and CHTC?

b. Do the shareholders of CHAC and CHTC have the right to vote on the transaction?

c. Do the shareholders of CHAC and CHTC have the right to dissent?

d. Would the answers to Questions b and c change if CHAC or CHTC were publicly-held?

2. Acquisition Consideration: 15% of Acquiror's Stock

The facts are as set forth in Section 2.11.F.1 above, except CHAC issues in the acquisition its stock amounting to 15% of its outstanding stock after the acquisition. Same questions as in a through d under Section 2.11.F.1.

3. Acquisition Consideration: Cash

The facts are as set forth in Section 2.11.F.1 above, except CHAC pays cash in the acquisition. Same questions as in a through d under Section 2.11.F.1.

§ 2.12 The Delaware Sale of "Substantially All" Assets Provision

A. Sale of Assets Provision

See § 271 of Delaware General Corporation Law, which sets out the board and shareholder voting requirements for a sale of all or substantially all of the corporation's assets.

B. No Dissenters' Rights

See § 262 of Delaware General Corporation Law, which does not provide for dissenters rights in sale of asset transactions. However, pursuant to Section 262(c), a corporation "may provide in its certificate of incorporation that appraisal rights under this section shall be available for the shares of any class * * * of its stock as a result of * * * the sale of all or substantially all of the assets of the corporation."

C. Determination of Meaning of "Substantially All" the Assets

1. Quantitative and Qualitative Approach

Gimbel v. The Signal Companies, Inc.
Delaware Court of Chancery, 1974 316 A.2d 599

QUILLEN, Chancellor:

This action was commenced on December 24, 1973 by plaintiff, a stockholder of the Signal Companies, Inc. (Signal). The complaint seeks, among other things, injunctive relief to prevent the consummation of the pending sale by Signal to Burmah Oil Incorporated (Burmah) of all of the outstanding capital stock of Signal Oil and Gas Company (Signal Oil), a wholly-owned subsidiary of Signal. The effective sale price exceeds 480 million dollars. The sale was approved at a special meeting of the Board of Directors of Signal held on December 21, 1973. * * *

In Count 3, the plaintiff alleges a class action on behalf of all Signal stockholders who, according to the complaint, were entitled to vote upon the proposed sale. * * *

I turn first to the question of 8 Del.C. § 271(a) which requires majority stockholder approval for the sale of "all or substantially all" of the assets of a Delaware corporation. A sale of less than all or substantially all assets is not covered by negative implication from the statute.

It is important to note in the first instance that the statute does not speak of a requirement of shareholder approval simply because an independent, important branch of a corporate business is being sold. * * * The statute requires shareholder approval upon the sale of "all or substantially all" of the corporation's assets. That is the sole test to be applied. While it is true that test does not lend itself to a strict mathematical standard to be applied in every case, the qualitative factor can be defined to some degree notwithstanding the limited Delaware authority. But the definition must begin with and ultimately necessarily relate to our statutory language. * * *

If the sale is of assets quantitatively vital to the operation of the corporation and is out of the ordinary and substantially affects the existence and purpose of the corporation, then it is beyond the power of the Board of Directors. With these guidelines, I turn to Signal and the transaction in this case. * * *

Based on the company's figures, Signal Oil represents only about 26% of the total assets of Signal. While Signal Oil represents 41% of Signal's total net worth, it produces only about 15% of Signal's revenues and earnings. * * *

While it is true, based on the experience of the Signal-Burmah transaction and the record in this lawsuit, that Signal Oil is more valuable than shown by the company's books, even if, as plaintiff suggests in his brief, the $761,000,000 value attached to Signal Oil's properties by the plaintiff's expert Paul V. Keyser, Jr., were substituted as the asset figure, the oil and gas properties would still constitute less than half the value of Signal's total assets. Thus, from a straight quantitative approach, I agree with Signal's position that the sale to Burmah does not constitute a sale of "all or substantially all" of Signal's assets.

In addition, if the character of the transaction is examined, the plaintiff's position is also weak. While it is true that Signal's original purpose was oil and gas and while oil and gas is still listed first in the certificate of incorporation, the simple fact is that Signal is now a conglomerate engaged in the aircraft and aerospace business, the manufacture and sale of trucks and related equipment, and other businesses besides oil and gas. * * * I conclude that measured quantatively and qualitatively, the sale of the stock of Signal Oil by Signal to Burmah does not constitute a sale of "all or substantially all" of Signal's assets. * * *

2. Qualitative Approach

Katz v. Bregman

Delaware Court of Chancery, 1981 431 A.2d 1274

Marvel, Chancellor:

The complaint herein seeks the entry of an order preliminarily enjoining the proposed sale of the Canadian assets of Plant Industries, Inc. to Vulcan Industrial Packaging, Ltd., the plaintiff Hyman Katz allegedly being the owner of approximately 170,000 shares of common stock of the defendant Plant Industries, Inc. * * *

The complaint alleges that during the last six months of 1980, the board of directors of Plant Industries, Inc., under the guidance of the individual defendant Robert B. Bregman, the present chief executive officer of such corporation, embarked on a course of action which resulted in the disposal of several unprofitable subsidiaries of the corporate defendant located in the United States. * * * As a result of these sales Plant Industries, Inc. by the end of 1980 had disposed of a significant part of its unprofitable assets.

According to the complaint, Mr. Bregman thereupon proceeded on a course of action designed to dispose of a subsidiary of the corporate defendant known as Plant National (Quebec) Ltd., a business which constitutes Plant Industries, Inc.'s entire business operation in Canada and has allegedly constituted Plant's only income producing facility during the past four years. The professed principal purpose of such proposed sale is to raise needed cash and thus improve Plant's balance sheets. * * *

In seeking injunctive relief, as prayed for, plaintiff relies on two principles, one that is found in 8 Del.C. § 271 to the effect that a decision of a Delaware corporation to sell * * * all or substantially all of its property and assets * * * requires not only the approval of such corporation's board of directors but also a resolution adopted by a majority of the outstanding stockholders of the corporation entitled to vote thereon at a meeting duly called upon at least twenty days' notice. * * *

Turning to the possible application of 8 Del.C. § 271 to the proposed sale of substantial corporate assets of National to Vulcan, it is stated in *Gimbel v. Signal Companies, Inc.*, [Section 2.12.C.1] as follows: "If the sale is of assets quantitatively vital to the operation of the corporation and is out of the ordinary and substantially affects the existence and purpose of the corporation then it is beyond the power of the Board of Directors."

According to Plant's 1980 10K form [the annual report filed with the SEC, *see* Chapter 4], it appears that at the end of 1980, Plant's Canadian operations represented 51% of Plant's remaining assets. Defendants also concede that National represents 44.9% of Plant's sales' revenues and 52.4% of its pre-tax net operating income. * * * [D]efendants concede that " * * * National accounted for 34.9% of Plant's pre-tax income in 1976, 36.9% in 1977, 42% in 1978, 51% in 1979 and 52.4% in 1980." * * *

In the case at bar, I am first of all satisfied that historically the principal business of Plant Industries, Inc. has not been to buy and sell industrial facilities but rather to manufacture steel drums for use in bulk shipping as well as for the storage of petroleum products, chemicals, food, paint, adhesives and cleaning agents, a business which has been profitably performed by National of Quebec. Furthermore, the proposal, after the sale of National, to embark on the manufacture of plastic drums represents a radical departure from Plant's historically successful line of business, namely steel drums. I therefore conclude that the proposed sale of Plant's Canadian operations, which constitute over 51% of Plant's total assets and in which are generated approximately 45% of Plant's 1980 net sales, would, if consummated, constitute a sale of substantially all of Plant's assets. By way of contrast, the proposed sale of Signal Oil in *Gimbel v. Signal Companies, Inc.*, *supra*, represented only about 26% of the total assets of Signal Companies, Inc. And while Signal Oil represented 41% of Signal Companies, Inc. total net worth, it generated only about 15% of Signal Companies, Inc. revenue and earnings.

I conclude * * * that an injunction should issue preventing the consummation of such sale at least until it has been approved by a majority of the outstanding stockholders of Plant Industries, Inc. * * *

Questions

What percentage of plaintiff's assets, revenues, and income were proposed to be disposed of in *Katz*, and how do these percentages compare with those in *Gimbel*? Are the above percentage differences sufficient enough to justify the different results? Are there any other significant differences between *Katz* and *Gimbel*? *See* the *CERBCO* case in Chapter 11.

3. Sale of Assets of Subsidiary

Hollinger Inc. v. Hollinger International, Inc.

Delaware Court of Chancery, 2004, 858 A.2d 342

STRINE, Vice Chancellor

* * * Hollinger Inc. (or "Inc.") seeks a preliminary injunction preventing Hollinger International, Inc. (or "International") from selling the *Telegraph* Group Ltd. (England) to Press Holdings International, an entity controlled by Frederick and David Barclay (hereinafter, the "Barclays"). The *Telegraph* Group is an indirect, wholly owned subsidiary of International and publishes the *Telegraph* newspaper and the *Spectator* magazine. The *Telegraph* newspaper is a leading one in the United Kingdom, both in terms of its circulation and its journalistic reputation.

The key question addressed in this decision is whether Inc. and the other International stockholders must be provided with the opportunity to vote on the sale of the *Telegraph* Group because that sale involves "substantially all" the assets of International within the meaning of 8 Del. C. § 271. The sale of the *Telegraph* followed a lengthy auction process whereby International and all of Hollinger's operating assets were widely shopped to potential bidders. As a practical matter, Inc.'s vote would be the only one that matters because although it now owns only 18% of International's total equity, it, through high-vote Class B shares, controls 68% of the voting power.

Inc. argues that a preliminary injunction should issue because it is clear that the sale of the *Telegraph* satisfies the quantitative and qualitative test used to determine whether an asset sale involves substantially all of a corporation's assets. The *Telegraph* Group is one of the most profitable parts of International and is its most prestigious asset. After its sale, International will be transformed from a respected international publishing company controlling one of the world's major newspapers to a primarily American publishing company whose most valuable remaining asset, the *Chicago Sun-Times*, is the second leading newspaper in the Second City. * * *

In response to these arguments, International makes several points.

Initially, it contends that the sale of the *Telegraph* Group does not trigger § 271. However prestigious the *Telegraph* Group, International says its sale does not involve, either quantitatively or qualitatively, the sale of substantially all International's assets. Whether or not the *Chicago Sun-Times* is as prestigious as the *Daily Telegraph,* it remains a profitable newspaper in a major city. Along with a group of profitable Chicago-area community newspapers, the *Chicago Sun-Times* has made the "Chicago Group" International's most profitable operating segment in the last two years and its contribution to International's profits has been comparable to that of the *Telegraph* Group for many years. Moreover, International retains a number of smaller newspapers in Canada and the prestigious *Jerusalem Post.* After the sale of the *Telegraph* Group, International therefore will quantitatively retain a sizable percentage of its existing assets and will qualitatively remain in the same business line. Although the *Telegraph* sale is admittedly a major transaction, International stresses that § 271 does not apply to every major transaction; it only applies to transactions that strike at the heart of a corporation's existence, which this transaction does not. * * *

As an alternative argument, International contends that § 271 is inapplicable for another reason. International argues that none of *its* assets are being sold at all, because the *Telegraph* Group is held through a chain of wholly owned subsidiaries and it is only the last link in that chain which is actually being sold to the Barclays. * * *

In this opinion, I conclude that Inc.'s motion for a preliminary injunction motion should be denied as neither its § 271 nor its equitable claims have a reasonable probability of success. [Only the § 271 claim is examined here.]

As to the § 271 claim, I choose not to decide whether International's technical statutory defense has merit. It is common for public companies to hold all of their operating assets through indirect, wholly owned subsidiaries. International wants me to hold that a parent company board may unilaterally direct and control a process by which its indirect, wholly owned subsidiary sells assets that would, if held directly by the parent, possibly comprise substantially all of the parent's assets and by which the sale proceeds under a contract that the parent corporation itself negotiates, signs, and fully guarantees. In that circumstance, International says that § 271 would have no application unless the selling subsidiary has no corporate dignity under the strict test for veil piercing. A ruling of that kind would, as a practical matter, render § 271 an illusory check on unilateral board power at most public companies. And while that ruling would involve a rational reading of § 271, it would not represent the only possible interpretation of that statute. Because this motion can be resolved on substantive economic grounds and because the policy implications of ruling on International's technical defense are important, prudence counsels in favor of deferring a necessarily hasty decision on the interesting question presented.

Instead, I address the economic merits of Inc.'s § 271 claim and treat the *Telegraph* Group as if it were directly owned by International. An application of the governing test, which was originally articulated in *Gimbel v. Signal Cos.* [Section 2.12.C.1] to the facts demonstrates that the *Telegraph* Group does not come close to comprising "substantially all" of International's assets. Although the *Telegraph* Group is a very important asset of International's and is likely its most valuable asset, International possesses several other important assets. Prominent among these is its so-called Chicago Group, a valuable collection of publications that, by any objective standard approaches the *Telegraph* Group in economic importance to International. * * *

Put simply, after the *Telegraph* Group is sold, International will retain considerable assets that are capable of generating substantial free cash flow. Section 271 does not require a vote when a major asset or trophy is sold; it requires a vote only when the assets to be sold, when considered quantitatively and qualitatively, amount to "substantially all" of the corporation's assets.

Inc.'s inability to meet this economically focused test has led it to place great weight on the greater journalistic reputation of the *Telegraph* newspaper when compared to the *Sun-Times* and the social importance of that newspaper in British life. The problem with this argument is that § 271 is designed as a protection for rational owners of capital and its proper interpretation requires this court to focus on the economic importance of assets and not their aesthetic worth. The economic value of the *Telegraph's* prestige was reflected in the sales process for the *Telegraph* Group and in the cash flows projected for that Group. * * *

Inc.'s demand for a vote places great weight on the qualitative element of *Gimbel.* In its papers, Inc. stresses the journalistic superiority of the Telegraph over the Sun-Times and the social cachet the Telegraph has. If you own the Telegraph, Inc. notes, "you can have dinner with the Queen." * * *

[I]nvestors in public companies do not invest their money because they derive social status from owning shares in a corporation whose controlling manager can have dinner with the Queen. Whatever the social importance of the Telegraph in Great Britain, the economic value of that importance to International as an entity is what matters for the *Gimbel* test, not how cool it would be to be the Telegraph's publisher. * * *

It may be that there exists somewhere an International stockholder * * * who values the opportunities that Conrad Black had to dine with the Queen and other eminent members of British society because he was the Telegraph's publisher. But the qualitative element of the *Gimbel* test addresses the rational economic expectations of reasonable investors. * * *

Note

In considering the issue in *Hollinger*, note that Section 271(c) of the DGCL, which was adopted after *Hollinger*, provides as follows:

> (c) For purposes of this section only, the property and assets of the corporation include the property and assets of any subsidiary of the corporation. As used in this subsection, "subsidiary" means any entity wholly-owned and controlled, directly or indirectly, by the corporation and includes, without limitation, corporations, partnerships, limited partnerships, limited liability partnerships, limited liability companies, and/or statutory trusts. Notwithstanding subsection (a) of this section, except to the extent the certificate of incorporation otherwise provides, no resolution by stockholders or members shall be required for a sale, lease or exchange of property and assets of the corporation to a subsidiary.

4. Impact of Splitoffs and Spinoffs on the "Substantially All" Issue

The Bank of New York Mellon Trust Com., N.A. v. Liberty Media Corp.

Delaware Supreme Court, 2011, 29 A.3d 225.

HOLLAND, Justice:

[Before reading this case, a brief introduction will be helpful. In a splitoff, a parent corporation distributes the stock of a subsidiary to some of the shareholders of the parent in exchange for their stock in the parent. Thus, the parent's shareholders who participate in the splitoff have their interest in the parent decreased but have an interest in the stock of the splitoff sub. On the other hand, the parent's shareholders who do not participate in the splitoff have their interest in the parent increased. A splitoff is different from a spinoff, which is a transaction in which a parent corporation distributes stock of a subsidiary to the shareholders of the parent on a prorate basis. Both splitoffs and spinoffs can be effectuated on a tax-free basis. These transactions are discussed further in Chapter 24.]

The plaintiffs-appellees, Liberty Media Corporation ("LMC") and its wholly owned subsidiary Liberty Media LLC ("Liberty Sub," together with LMC, "Liberty") brought this action for declaratory and injunctive relief against the defendant-appellant, the Bank of New York Mellon Trust Company, N.A., in its capacity as trustee (the "Trustee"). Liberty proposes to split off, into a new publicly traded company ("SplitCo") the businesses, assets, and liabilities attributed to Liberty's Capital Group and Starz Group (the "Capital Splitoff"). * * * After Liberty announced the proposed splitoff of the businesses and assets attributable to its Capital and Starz tracking stock groups, Liberty received a letter from counsel for an anonymous bondholder.

In that letter, counsel for the bondholder stated that Liberty has pursued a "disaggregation strategy" designed to remove "substantially all" of Liberty's assets from the corporate structure against which the bondholders have claims, and shift those assets into the hands of Liberty's stockholders. Therefore, the bondholder contended that the transaction might violate the Successor Obligor Provision in the Indenture and threatened to declare an event of default. [If a default occurred, the bonds would become due and payable.] In response to that threat, Liberty commenced this action against the Trustee under the Indenture [*i.e.*, one of the provisions governing the rights of the bondholders], seeking injunctive relief and a declaratory judgment that the proposed Capital Splitoff will not constitute a disposition of "substantially all" of Liberty's assets in violation of the Indenture. [Thus, the Indenture contained a "substantially all" concept that is similar to the substantially all provision in Section 271 of the DGCL.]

The Capital Splitoff will be Liberty's fourth major distribution of assets since March 2004. The Trustee argues that when aggregated with the previous three transactions, the Capital Splitoff would violate a successor obligor provision in an indenture dated July 7, 1999 (as amended and supplemented, the "Indenture") pursuant to which Liberty agreed not to transfer substantially all of its assets unless the successor entity assumed Liberty's obligations under the Indenture ("Successor Obligor Provision"). It is undisputed that, if considered in isolation, and without reference to any prior asset distribution, the Capital Splitoff would not constitute a transfer of substantially all of Liberty's assets or violate the Successor Obligor Provision. [In other words, in the Splitoff, Liberty transferred less than substantially all of its assets.]

The Court of Chancery concluded, after a trial, that the four transactions should not be aggregated, and entered judgment for Liberty. The Court of Chancery concluded that the proposed splitoff is not "sufficiently connected" to the prior transactions to warrant aggregation for purposes of the Successor Obligor Provision. * * *

We conclude that the judgment of the Court of Chancery must be affirmed....

The Indenture. While it was a subsidiary of AT&T, Liberty entered into the Indenture with the Trustee. From July 7, 1999 through September 17, 2003, Liberty issued multiple series of publicly traded debt under the Indenture, the proceeds of which totaled approximately $13.7 billion. Liberty has since retired or repurchased much of that debt. As of September 30, 2010, debt securities with a total balance of approximately $4.213 billion remained outstanding....

The Terms of the Indenture. The Indenture includes a successor obligor provision. This provision prohibits Liberty from selling, transferring, or otherwise disposing of "substantially all" of its assets unless the entity to which the assets are transferred assumes Liberty's obligations under the Indenture (thereby releasing Liberty from its obligations). Section 801 of the Indenture provides, in pertinent part:

> [Liberty] shall not consolidate with or merge into, or sell, assign, transfer, lease, convey or other[wise] dispose of all or substantially all of its assets and the properties and the assets and properties of its Subsidiaries (taken as a whole) to, any entity or entities * * * unless:
>
> (1) the successor entity [*i.e.*, SplitCo] ... shall expressly assume, by an indenture * * * executed by [Splitco] and delivered to the Trustee, the due and punctual payment of the principal of, any premium and interest on and any Additional Amounts with respect to all the Securities and the performance of every obligation in this Indenture and the Outstanding Securities * * *;
>
> The Indenture does not define the phrase "substantially all." * * *

The Court of Chancery acknowledged that, as a theoretical matter, a series of transactions can be aggregated for purposes of a "substantially all" analysis. * * *

[*Analysis*] The Court of Chancery began its analysis with the Second Circuit's 1982 decision in *Sharon Steel Corp. v. Chase Manhattan Bank, N.A.*, [691 F.2d 1039, 1051–52 (2d Cir. 1982)] which the court characterized as "the leading decision on aggregating transactions for purposes of a 'substantially all' analysis" in the context of a successor obligor provision. In *Sharon Steel*, the Second Circuit addressed a transaction in which a corporation, subject to a successor obligor provision in a bond indenture, had transferred corporate assets to multiple purchasers pursuant to a plan of liquidation. The court held that "boilerplate successor obligor clauses do not permit assignment of the public debt to another party in the course of a liquidation unless 'all or substantially all' of the assets of the company at the time the plan of liquidation is determined upon are transferred to a single purchaser." [*Sharon* is set out in Chapter 12, which deals with asset acquisitions. Note that in *Sharon*, the transferor wanted the transaction to be treated as a transfer of "substantially all" of the assets so that the transferee could assume the transferor's debt. On the other hand, here Liberty wants the transaction not to be treated as a transfer of "substantially all" of the assets so that the maturity of the debt will not be accelerated.] * * *

In *Sharon Steel*, the Second Circuit found that aggregation was appropriate because the individual sale transactions at issue were part of a "plan of piecemeal liquidation" and an "overall scheme to liquidate." Conversely, where asset transactions are not piecemeal components of an otherwise integrated, pre-established plan to liquidate or dispose of nearly all assets, and where each such transaction stands on its own merits without reference to another, courts have declined to aggregate for purposes of a "substantially all" analysis. * * *

The Court of Chancery carefully considered and applied *Sharon Steel* to the facts before it, and concluded that the Capital Splitoff "is not sufficiently connected to the LMI and Discovery spinoffs or the [Entertainment] splitoff to warrant aggregating the four transactions." * * *

The Trustee concedes that the Capital Splitoff, viewed in isolation, does not constitute a disposition of substantially all of Liberty's assets. On the facts of this case, the Court of Chancery properly held that aggregation is not appropriate. Accordingly, Liberty was entitled to a declaration that the Capital Splitoff does not violate the Successor Obligor Provision in the Indenture.

Note on Step Transaction Analysis

The excerpt above does not contain the discussion of the "step-transaction" alternative analysis that the Chancery Court applied for determining if the "substantial all" test was satisfied. Although the Chancery Court had found that even under the step-transaction analysis the substantially all test had not been met, the Supreme Court found that the step-transaction analysis was unnecessary because the *Sharon Steel* test was the controlling law. The Supreme Court described as follows the three branches of the step-transaction doctrine (which apparently is based on Federal Income Tax principles):

> The step-transaction doctrine applies if the component transactions meet one of three tests. First, under the "end result test," the doctrine will be invoked "if it appears that a series of separate transactions were prearranged parts of what was a single transaction, cast from the outset to achieve the ultimate result." Second, under the "interdependence test," separate transactions will be treated as one if "the steps are so interdependent that the legal relations created by one transaction would have been fruitless without a completion of the series." The third and "most restrictive alternative is the binding-commitment test under

which a series of transactions are combined only if, at the time the first step is entered into, there was a binding commitment to undertake the later steps."

D. Dissolution after Sale of Assets

See § 275 Delaware General Corporation Law, which sets out the board and shareholder voting requirements for a dissolution of a corporation, including a dissolution after the sale of all or substantially all the assets of a corporation.

E. Problems on Sales of Assets under Delaware Law

1. Acquisition Consideration: 30% of Acquiror's Stock

Same questions as in Section 2.11.F.1, except CHAC and CHTC are incorporated in Delaware.

2. Acquisition Consideration: 15% of Acquiror's Stock

Same questions as in Section 2.11.F.2, except CHAC and CHTC are incorporated in Delaware.

3. Acquisition Consideration: Cash

Same questions as in Section 2.11.F.3, except CHAC and CHTC are incorporated in Delaware.

§ 2.13 The De Facto Merger Doctrine

A. Absence of Dissenters' Rights in a Sale of Assets under § 271 of Delaware General Corporation Law

Hariton v. Arco Electronics, Inc.

Delaware Supreme Court, 1963 188 A.2d 123

SOUTHERLAND, Chief Justice.

This case involves a sale of assets under § 271 of the corporation law, 8 Del.C. It presents [the following question]:

A sale of assets is effected under § 271 in consideration of shares of stock of the purchasing corporation. The agreement of sale embodies also a plan to dissolve the selling corporation and distribute the shares so received to the stockholders of the seller, so as to accomplish the same result as would be accomplished by a merger of the seller into the purchaser. Is the sale legal?

[**Facts**] The defendant Arco [a Delaware corporation] and Loral Electronics Corporation, a New York corporation, are both engaged, in somewhat different forms, in the electronic equipment business. In the summer of 1961 they negotiated for an amalgamation of the companies. As of October 27, 1961, they entered into a "Reorganization Agreement and Plan." The provisions of this Plan pertinent here are in substance as follows: (1) Arco agrees to sell all its assets to Loral in consideration (*inter alia*) of the issuance to it of 283,000 shares of Loral; (2) Arco agrees to call a stockholders meeting for the purpose of approving the Plan and the voluntary dissolution; and (3) Arco agrees to distribute to its stockholders all the Loral shares received by it as a part of the complete liquidation of Arco. At the Arco meeting all the stockholders voting (about 80%) approved the Plan. It was thereafter consummated.

Plaintiff, a stockholder who did not vote at the meeting, sued to enjoin the consummation of the Plan on the grounds * * * that it was illegal. * * *

[**Issue**] Plaintiff [argues that the] the several steps taken here accomplish the same result as a merger of Arco into Loral. In a "true" sale of assets, the stockholder of the seller retains the right to elect whether the selling company shall continue as a holding company. Moreover, the stockholder of the selling company is forced to accept an investment in a new enterprise without the right of appraisal granted under the merger statute. Section 271 cannot therefore be legally combined with a dissolution proceeding under § 275 and a consequent distribution of the purchaser's stock. Such a proceeding is a misuse of the power granted under § 271, and a *de facto* merger results. * * *

Plaintiff's contention that this sale has achieved the same result as a merger is plainly correct. * * * Accepting it as correct, we noted that this result is made possible by the overlapping scope of the merger statute and § 271. * * *

We now hold that the reorganization here accomplished through § 271 and a mandatory plan of dissolution and distribution is legal. This is so because the sale-of-assets statute and the merger statute are independent of each other. They are, so to speak, of equal dignity, and the framers of a reorganization plan may resort to either type of corporate mechanics to achieve the desired end. This is not an anomalous result in our corporation law. As the Vice Chancellor pointed out, the elimination of accrued dividends, though forbidden under a charter amendment * * * may be accomplished by a merger. * * *

In *Langfelder v. Universal Laboratories*, D.C., 68 F.Supp. 209, Judge Leahy commented upon "the general theory of the Delaware Corporation Law that action taken pursuant to the authority of the various sections of that law constitute acts of independent legal significance and their validity is not dependent on other sections of the Act." 68 F.Supp. 211, footnote. * * *

We are in accord with the Vice Chancellor's ruling, and the judgment below is affirmed.

Question

How would the transaction in *Hariton v. Arco* be treated under the MBCA?

B. Avoiding Dissenters' Rights by Having Real Target Act As Acquiror

1. Illustration of the Problem

Closely-Held Acquiring Corporation (CHAC) is planning to acquire all of the assets and assume all of the liabilities of Closely-Held Target Corporation (CHTC) in exchange for stock of CHAC amounting to 15% of the stock of CHAC after the acquisition. Both CHAC and CHTC are incorporated in a state that provides for dissenters rights for the target's shareholders in both mergers and sales of substantially all of the assets followed by a liquidation of the target. Otherwise, the state corporate law is the same as the MBCA. Several shareholders of CHTC have indicated they will dissent, pursuant to their right under the applicable corporate law. On the other hand, all of the shareholders of CHAC are enthusiastic about the transaction.

To avoid dissenters' rights, the transaction is restructured to have CHTC acquire all of the assets and assume all of the liabilities of CHAC in exchange for stock of CHTC amounting to 85% of the stock of CHTC after the acquisition. CHTC has a sufficient number of authorized and unissued shares to complete the transaction. As part of the transaction, CHAC will be liquidated, with CHAC distributing the CHTC stock to its shareholders in exchange for their CHAC stock, which will be cancelled. After the dust settles, the former shareholders of CHAC will own 85% of the stock of CHTC and the former shareholders of CHTC will own 15% of the stock of CHTC. The name of CHTC will be changed to CHAC. None of the CHAC shareholders will exercise the right to dissent.

2. The Original Pennsylvania Approach

Farris v. Glen Alden Corp.

Supreme Court of Pennsylvania, 1958 143 A.2d 25

Cohen, Justice.

We are required to determine on this appeal whether, as a result of a "Reorganization Agreement" executed by the officers of Glen Alden Corporation [a Pennsylvania corporation] and List Industries Corporation [a Delaware Corporation], and approved by the shareholders of the former company, the rights and remedies of a dissenting shareholder accrue to the plaintiff.

[**Facts**]* * * October 1957, List, * * * purchased through a wholly owned subsidiary 38.5% of Glen Alden's outstanding stock. This acquisition enabled List to place three of its directors on the Glen Alden board.

On March 20, 1958, the two corporations entered into a "reorganization agreement," subject to stockholder approval, which contemplated the following actions: (1) Glen Alden is to acquire [essentially] all of the assets of List * * * (2) In consideration of the transfer, Glen Alden is to issue 3,621,703 shares of stock to List. List in turn is to distribute the stock to its shareholders * * *. In order to accomplish the necessary distribution, Glen Alden is to increase the authorized number of its shares of capital stock from 2,500,000 shares to 7,500,000 shares without according pre-emptive rights to the present shareholders upon the issuance of any such shares. (3) Further, Glen Alden is to assume all of List's liabilities * * *. (4) Glen Alden is to change its corporate name from Glen Alden Corporation to List Alden Corporation. (5) The present directors of both corporations are to become directors of List Alden. (6) List is to be dissolved and List Alden is to then carry on the operations of both former corporations. * * *

[Upon completion of the transaction, the former List shareholders will own 76.5% of the List Alden outstanding shares and the former Glen Alden shareholders will own 23.5% of such shares.]

[**Plaintiff's Position**] On the day of the shareholders' meeting, plaintiff, a shareholder of Glen Alden, filed a complaint in equity against the corporation and its officers seeking to enjoin them temporarily until final hearing, and perpetually thereafter, from executing and carrying out the agreement.

The gravamen of the complaint was that the notice of the annual shareholders' meeting did not conform to the requirements of the Business Corporation Law, 15 P.S. § 2852–1 *et seq.*, in three respects: (1) It did not give notice to the shareholders that the true intent and purpose of the meeting was to effect a merger or consolidation of Glen Alden and List; (2) It failed to give notice to the shareholders of their right to dissent to the plan of merger or consolidation and claim fair value for their shares, and (3) It did not contain copies of the text of certain sections of the Business Corporation Law as required.

By reason of these omissions, plaintiff contended that the approval of the reorganization agreement by the shareholders at the annual meeting was invalid and unless the carrying out of the plan were enjoined, he would suffer irreparable loss by being deprived of substantial property rights. * * *

[**Lower Court**] The court below concluded that the reorganization agreement entered into between the two corporations was a plan for a *de facto* merger, and that therefore the failure of the notice of the annual meeting to conform to the pertinent requirements of the merger provisions of the Business Corporation Law rendered the notice defective and all proceedings in furtherance of the agreement void. Wherefore, the court entered a final decree denying defendants' motion for judgment on the pleadings, entering judgment upon plaintiff's complaint and granting the injunctive relief therein sought. This appeal followed. * * *

[**Analysis**] [I]t is no longer helpful to consider an individual transaction in the abstract and solely by reference to the various elements therein determine whether it is a "merger" or a "sale." Instead, to determine properly the nature of a corporate transaction, we must refer not only to all the provisions of the agreement, but also to the consequences of the transaction and to the purposes of the provisions of the corporation law said to be applicable. We shall apply this principle to the instant case.

Section 908, subd. A of the Pennsylvania Business Corporation Law provides: "If any shareholder of a domestic corporation which becomes a party to a plan of merger or consolidation shall object to such plan of merger or consolidation * * * such shareholder shall be entitled to * * * [the fair value of his shares upon surrender of the share certificate or certificates representing his shares]."

This provision had its origin in the early decision of this court in *Lauman v. Lebanon Valley R. R. Co.*, 1858, 30 Pa. 42. There a shareholder who objected to the consolidation of his company with another was held to have a right in the absence of statute to treat the consolidation as a dissolution of his company and to receive the value of his shares upon their surrender.

The rationale of the *Lauman* case, and of the present section of the Business Corporation Law based thereon, is that when a corporation combines with another so as to lose its essential nature and alter the original fundamental relationships of the shareholders among themselves and to the corporation, a shareholder who does not wish to continue his membership therein may treat his membership in the original corporation as terminated and have the value of his shares paid to him. * * *

Does the combination outlined in the present "reorganization" agreement so fundamentally change the corporate character of Glen Alden and the interest of the plaintiff as a shareholder therein, that to refuse him the rights and remedies of a dissenting shareholder would in reality force him to give up his stock in one corporation and against his will accept shares in another? If so, the combination is a merger within the meaning of section 908, subd. A of the corporation law.

If the reorganization agreement were consummated plaintiff would find that the "List Alden" resulting from the amalgamation would be quite a different corporation than the "Glen Alden" in which he is now a shareholder. Instead of continuing primarily as a coal mining company, Glen Alden would be transformed, after amendment of its articles of incorporation, into a diversified holding company whose interests would range from motion picture theaters to textile companies, Plaintiff would find himself a member of a company with assets of $169,000,000 and a long-term debt of $38,000,000 in lieu of a company one-half that size and with but one-seventh the long-term debt.

While the administration of the operations and properties of Glen Alden as well as List would be in the hands of management common to both companies, since all executives of List would be retained in List Alden, the control of Glen Alden would pass to the directors of List; for List would hold eleven of the seventeen directorships on the new board of directors.

As an aftermath of the transaction plaintiff's proportionate interest in Glen Alden would have been reduced to only two-fifths of what it presently is because of the issuance of an additional 3,621,703 shares to List which would not be subject to pre-emptive rights. In fact, ownership of Glen Alden would pass to the stockholders of List who would hold 76.5% of the outstanding shares as compared with but 23.5% retained by the present Glen Alden shareholders.

Perhaps the most important consequence to the plaintiff, if he were denied the right to have his shares redeemed at their fair value, would be the serious financial loss suffered upon consummation of the agreement. While the present book value of his stock is $38 a share after combination it would be worth only $21 a share. In contrast, the shareholders of List who presently hold stock with a total book value of $33,000,000 or $7.50 a share, would receive stock with a book value of $76,000,000 or $21 a share. [Chapter 7 will demonstrate that companies generally cannot be valued on the basis of book value.]

Under these circumstances it may well be said that if the proposed combination is allowed to take place without right of dissent, plaintiff would have his stock in Glen Alden taken away from him and the stock of a new company thrust upon him in its place. He would be projected against his will into a new enterprise under terms not of his own choosing. It was to protect dissident shareholders against just such a result that this court one hundred years ago in the *Lauman* case, and the legislature thereafter in section 908 granted the right of dissent. And it is to accord that protection to the plaintiff that we conclude that the combination proposed in the case at hand is a merger within the intendment of section 908. * * *

Note

The *de facto* merger doctrine has been legislatively overruled in Pennsylvania. *See* Act of November 10, 1959 (P.L. 1406, No. 502). Delaware does not follow the *Glen Alden* approach, but strictly rejects the *de facto* merger doctrine. New Jersey, on the other hand, generally follows the doctrine. *See e.g., Applestein v. United Board and Carton Corp.*, 159 A.2d 146, aff'd 161 A.2d 474 (Superior Court, N. J., 1960).

§ 2.14 Triangular (or Subsidiary) Acquisitions

A. Introduction

The parties to an acquisition may desire to use a merger transaction in order to force the target's shareholders to either sell or dissent. Also, a merger eliminates the need for the specific transfer of a target's assets in a sale of assets transaction. The acquiring corporation may not want to directly own the target's assets and be subject to the target's liabilities. Rather, the acquiring corporation may want the target to be a subsidiary, thereby insulating the acquiring corporation's assets from the target's liabilities.

The twin goals of (1) acquiring the target by merger, and (2) holding the target as a subsidiary, can be accomplished by a "subsidiary" merger. In the transaction, which is also known as a "triangular" merger, either the target merges into a subsidiary of the acquiring corporation (a forward triangular merger), or the subsidiary merges into the target (a reverse triangular merger). In both cases the target's shareholders receive the merger consideration which can be anything, including cash or stock of the acquiring corporation. The acquiring corporation ends up owning all of the stock of either the target in the case of a reverse subsidiary merger or the surviving subsidiary in the case of a forward subsidiary merger. For an illustration of a reverse subsidiary merger, *see* the Preamble and Article I, §§ 1 to 1.3 and 2.1(a) to (c) of the Time/Warner Merger Agreement, Documentary Appendix A of *M&A Statutes, Rules and Documents, supra* Section 1.1.

B. Triangular Mergers in Delaware

Excerpt from Balotti and Finkelstein, The Delaware Law of Corporations and Business Organizations

Sections 9.5 and 9.7 (1988)

Forward Triangular Merger. The forward triangular merger permits A to acquire T without A being a constituent corporation. A forms a new Delaware subsidiary (S) into which T is merged. The stockholders of A do not have the right to vote on the merger, [*See* § 251(c)] nor are they entitled to appraisal rights since A is not a constituent corporation. [*See* § 263] As the sole stockholder of S, A votes all of the stock of S in favor of the merger. The stockholders of T, of course, will have the same rights as in a two party merger.

The result of the forward triangular merger is that T becomes part of S, a wholly-owned subsidiary of A, since the merger agreement would normally provide for the outstanding shares of stock of S (all of which are owned by A) to remain outstanding and be unaffected by the merger. The shares of stock of T outstanding immediately prior to the effective time of the merger are converted into securities of A, cash or other consideration. [*See* § 251(c)] Such a merger would not have been possible prior to 1967, when stock of the surviving corporation(s) was the only form of permissible consideration in a merger under Section 251.

Reverse Triangular Merger. In a reverse triangular merger, the merger proceeds in the same manner as a forward triangular merger except S is merged into T, with T surviving. The outstanding shares of stock of S (all of which are owned by A) are converted into shares of stock of T. The shares of stock of T outstanding immediately before the effective time of the merger are converted into securities of A, cash or other consideration. [*See* § 251(b)(5)] The advantage of this type of merger is that T will become a wholly-owned subsidiary of A without any [change] in its corporate existence. Thus the rights and obligations of T, the acquired corporation, are not transferred, assumed or affected. For example, obtaining consents for the transfer of governmental or other licenses may not be necessary, absent a provision to the contrary in the licenses or agreement, since the licenses will continue to be held by the same continuing corporation.

C. Do the Shareholders of the Acquiring Parent Have the Right to Vote?

Equity Group Holdings v. DMG, Inc.

United States District Court, Florida, 1983 576 F.Supp. 1197

Aronovitz, District Judge.

[**Facts**]* * * The undisputed facts as stipulated by the parties can be summarized as follows: Defendant, DMG, Inc. (DMG), a Florida corporation, is a holding company which has no assets or operations. It is the listed (New York Stock Exchange) parent corporation of a wholly-owned subsidiary, Defendant Diversified Mortgage Investors, Inc. (DMI), a Florida corporation. * * *

Defendant Carlsberg Corporation (Carlsberg), a Delaware corporation, is the parent corporation of Defendant Carlsberg Resources Corporation (Carlsberg Resources), which in turn is wholly owned by Carlsberg. * * *

Plaintiff Equity Group Holdings ("Equity" or "Equity Group" and related parties) owned approximately * * * 27.1% of [DMG's] shares. * * *

DMG, DMI and Carlsberg entered into an Agreement and Plan of Merger (the "Merger Agreement"). Pursuant to the Merger Agreement, Carlsberg will merge into DMI; outstanding shares of Carlsberg will then be converted into DMG common. To accomplish this plan, approximately 12.5 million new shares of Common will be issued to shareholders of Carlsberg. Thereafter, some 64% of DMG Common Stock will be owned by Carlsberg shareholders. * * *

The New York Stock Exchange, wherein DMG is listed, requires that to validate the issuance of the authorized twelve and one-half million shares of DMG common stock that are to be issued to Carlsberg, a majority of DMG shareholders who are represented in person or by proxy at a meeting of shareholders must so vote. *See* NYSE Company Manual, A-283–284 (January 25, 1978). [*See* Section 2.5.A] This election is necessary in order to maintain DMG's listing on the Exchange. Consequently, a shareholders' meeting of DMG has been currently scheduled for December 22, 1983, to vote on a corporate resolution approving the issuance by DMG of the 12.5 million shares of DMG common stock to shareholders of Carlsberg. DMG has also announced that officers and directors of Carlsberg will stand for election to the DMG Board of Directors at the shareholders' meeting scheduled for December 22, 1983, and that Carlsberg will seek to fill by election four of the seven directorial seats on the DMG Board. * * *

[**Discussion of Issues**] On the basis of the foregoing record and stipulated facts, the issues presented to the court, in the procedural posture of a motion for preliminary injunction, can be summarized as follows:

> Plaintiff contends that the * * * the merger of DMI and Carlsberg which results in issuance of 12.5 million shares of DMG common to Carlsberg, * * * constitute[s] a *de facto* merger of three corporations: the present DMG, its subsidiary, DMI and Carlsberg; that the real merger is not only that between DMI and Carlsberg, but between DMG, the parent company, and Carlsberg; that, because Carlsberg is approximately three times the size of DMG, it is really Carlsberg which is surviving and DMG which is ceasing to exist after the merger; and that, if in fact these transactions together do constitute a *de facto* merger of DMG into Carlsberg, then Florida Corporation Law Section 607.221 requires a full majority of *all outstanding* shares to approve the transaction, rather than a *quorum of shares voted*

> *either at the December 22, 1983 meeting or by proxy*, which is all that is required under the rules of the New York Stock Exchange. *See* NYSE Company Manual A-283, 284 (January 25, 1978).

Plaintiff concedes that the transactions do not fall within the strict statutory wording of Florida Statute Section 607.221, and that therefore this court would have to declare the transactions a *de facto* merger in order to find that the statute applies. * * *

Defendants' central contention is that the Florida Merger Statute is inapplicable to the instant transaction because it does not require that the shareholders of a parent corporation be given the opportunity to vote upon the issuance of already authorized shares; that the merger between DMI and Carlsberg does not constitute a merger of DMG, the parent; and that all of the relevant shareholders—those of DMI and Carlsberg, which are the merging corporations—have been given or will be given the opportunity to vote upon the proposed transaction. * * *

The parties seem to agree that the DMI-Carlsberg Merger * * * is a forward triangular merger: a wholly-owned subsidiary is acquiring the assets, liabilities, and stock of the target, a third-party corporation, after which the parent company and its original subsidiary will survive and the target will become part of the subsidiary. * * *

The court finds that under these facts and circumstances, on the basis of the record before it, Florida law does not necessarily stop or prevent the minnow from swallowing the whale where the business judgment of both the minnow and the whale is that the event will be mutually beneficial to both parties. Without evidence of a breach of fiduciary duty by the Officers/Directors of DMG or DMI or fundamental unfairness, or without allegations or proof of fraud, misrepresentation, *mala fides* or economic harm resulting from such merger, there is not presented to this court a basis to invoke its equity jurisdiction. * * *

The reason that the minnow may swallow the whale here is simply that nothing appears to prevent this from occurring. Each gets the opportunity to vote on the transaction. Florida law does not define the dilution of voting rights through the issuance of authorized stock as a matter which requires a full shareholder vote and the Florida legislature has specifically abolished preemptive rights. *See* Florida Corporation Act Section 607.077(1). DMG could go forward with the issuance of every one of its authorized but unissued shares, without asking the shareholders for approval. This is not to say that if this were done for fraudulent reasons or illegitimate business purposes, the shareholders would not have numerous causes of action on which to sue, both under state law and under the Federal Securities Laws. * * *

D. Problems on Triangular Mergers under the MBCA and Delaware Law

1. Merger Consideration: 30% of Acquiring Parent's Stock

Closely-Held Acquiring Corporation (CHAC) forms Acquiring Corporation Subsidiary (ACS) for the purpose of acquiring Closely-Held Target Corporation (CHTC) in a triangular merger. The transaction will be structured as either a forward subsidiary merger or as a reverse subsidiary merger. In a forward subsidiary merger, CHTC merges into ACS, with the CHTC shareholders receiving stock of CHAC amounting to 30% of CHAC's outstanding stock after the merger. In a reverse subsidiary merger, ACS merges into CHTC, with the shareholders of CHTC receiving 30% of CHAC's outstanding stock in exchange for their CHTC stock and CHAC having the stock it holds of ACS converted into stock of CHTC; when the dust settles, CHTC is a wholly owned subsidiary of CHAC. CHAC, ACS and

CHTC are each incorporated in Delaware and in the alternative in a state with the MBCA. CHAC has a sufficient number of authorized and unissued shares to complete the transaction.

a. What action is required by the boards of CHAC, ACS and CHTC?

b. Do the shareholders of CHAC and CHTC have the right to vote?

c. Do the shareholders of CHAC and CHTC have the right to dissent?

d. Would the answers to Questions b and c change if CHAC and CHTC were publicly-held?

2. Merger Consideration: 15% of Acquiror's Stock

The facts and questions are the same as in Section 2.14.D.1 above, except CHAC issues in the merger its stock amounting to 15% of its outstanding stock after the acquisition.

3. Merger Consideration: Cash

The facts and questions are the same as in Section 2.14.D.1 above, except CHAC pays cash in the merger.

E. Does a Reverse Subsidiary Merger Result in an Assignment of the Target's Contractual Rights?

Meso Scale Diagnostics, LLC v. Roche Diagnostics Gmbh

Delaware Court of Chancery, 2013 Del. Ch. LEXIS 51

PARSONS, Vice Chancellor.

[In this transaction a target, BioVeris, was acquired by the defendant, Roche, in a reverse subsidiary merger, and the plaintiff, Meso, who had certain contract rights with the target, asserted that the reverse triangular merger was an assignment by operation of law that required Meso's consent.]

I grant summary judgment [for Roche, the defendant] on the basis that the reverse triangular merger was not an assignment by operation of law or otherwise, such that it would have required the [Meso's] consent....

Specifically, Roche asserts that BioVeris remained intact as the surviving entity of the merger, and, therefore, BioVeris did not assign anything. Meso, on the other hand, contends that mergers generally, including reverse triangular mergers, can result in assignments by operation of law.... .

To interpret an anti-assignment provision, a court "look[s] to the language of the agreement, read as a whole, in an effort to discern the parties' collective intent." Roche contends that the language "by operation of law or otherwise" makes clear that the parties did not intend [that the anti-assignment provisions of] Section 5.08 to cover reverse triangular mergers. I find Roche's interpretation of Section 5.08 to be reasonable. Generally, mergers do not result in an assignment by operation of law of assets that began as property of the surviving entity and continued to be such after the merger.

Upon the completion of a merger, Section 259 of the DGCL provides:

> When any merger or consolidation shall have become effective under this chapter, for all purposes of the laws of this State the separate existence of all the constituent corporations, or of all such constituent corporations except the one into which the other or others of such constituent corporations have been merged, as the

> case may be, shall cease and the constituent corporations shall become a new corporation, or be merged into 1 of such corporations ... the rights, privileges, powers and franchises of each of said corporations, and all property, real, personal and mixed, and all debts due to any of said constituent corporations on whatever account ... shall be vested in the corporation surviving or resulting from such merger or consolidation; and all property, rights, privileges, powers and franchises, and all and every other interest shall be thereafter as effectually the property of the surviving or resulting corporation as they were of the several and respective constituent corporations.

In *Koppers Coal & Transport Co. v. United States*, [122 107 F.2d 706 (3d Cir. 1939)], the United States Court of Appeals for the Third Circuit concluded that "the underlying property of the constituent corporations is transferred to the resultant corporation upon the carrying out of the consolidation or merger as provided by Section 259." Other courts in Delaware have held that Section 259(a) results in the transfer of the non-surviving corporation's rights and obligations to the surviving corporation by operation of law.... The language in Section 259, "except the one into which the other or others of such constituent corporations have been merged," ... suggests that the surviving corporation would not have effected any assignment. In sum, Section 259(a) supports Roche's position that a reverse triangular merger generally is not an assignment by operation of law or otherwise, and that, therefore, Section 5.08 was not intended to cover reverse triangular mergers.

I also note that Roche's interpretation is consistent with the reasonable expectations of the parties. Pursuant to the widely accepted "objective theory" of contract interpretation—a framework adopted and followed in Delaware—this Court must interpret a contract in a manner that satisfies the "reasonable expectations of the parties at the time they entered into the contract." The vast majority of commentary discussing reverse triangular mergers indicates that a reverse triangular merger does not constitute an assignment by operation of law as to the nonsurviving entity. For example, this Court has recognized that "it is possible that the only practical effect of the [reverse triangular] merger is the conversion of the property interest of the shareholders of the target corporation." Similarly, in *Lewis v. Ward*, [2003 Del. Ch. LEXIS 111 (Del. Ch. Oct. 29, 2003)], then-Vice Chancellor Strine observed:

> In a triangular merger, the acquiror's stockholders generally do not have the right to vote on the merger, nor are they entitled to appraisal. If a reverse triangular structure is used, the rights and obligations of the target are not transferred, assumed or affected. Because of these and other advantages to using a triangular structure, it is the preferred method of acquisition for a wide range of transactions.

Leading commentators also have noted that a reverse triangular merger does not constitute an assignment by operation of law. Based on the commentary on this subject, I consider it unlikely that the parties would have expected a clause covering assignments by operation of law to have applied to reverse triangular mergers.

Meso disagrees and has advanced three theories in support of its interpretation of Section 5.08, i.e., that the anti-assignment clause was intended to cover reverse triangular mergers. Those theories are: (1) the acquisition of BioVeris was nothing more than the assignment of BioVeris's intellectual property rights to Roche; (2) Delaware case law regarding forward triangular mergers compels the conclusion that a provision covering assignment "by operation of law" extends to all mergers; and (3) this Court should embrace a California federal court's holding that a reverse triangular merger results in an assignment by operation of law.

[After rejecting Meso's first two arguments the court said:] As a final argument, Meso suggests that this Court should embrace the United States District Court for the Northern District of California's holding in *SQL Solutions, Inc. v. Oracle Corp.* [1991 U.S. Dist. LEXIS 21097 (N.D. Cal. Dec. 18, 1991)] that a reverse triangular merger results in an assignment by operation of law. There the court stated, "an assignment or transfer of rights does occur through a change in the legal form of ownership of a business." The court in *SQL Solutions* applied California law and cited a line of California cases for the proposition that whether "an assignment results merely from a change in the legal form of ownership of a business ... depends upon whether it affects the interests of the parties protected by the nonassignability of the contract."

I decline to adopt the approach outlined in *SQL Solutions*, however, because doing so would conflict with Delaware's jurisprudence surrounding stock acquisitions, among other things. Under Delaware law, stock purchase transactions, by themselves, do not result in an assignment by operation of law. For example, in the *Baxter Pharmaceutical Products* case [1999 Del. Ch. LEXIS 47 (Del. Ch. Mar. 11, 1999)], this Court stated, "Delaware corporations may lawfully acquire the securities of other corporations, and a purchase or change of ownership of such securities (again, without more) is not regarded as assigning or delegating the contractual rights or duties of the corporation whose securities are purchased." Similarly, in Branmar Theatre Co. v. Branmar, Inc., [1999 Del. Ch. LEXIS 47 (Del. Ch. Mar. 11, 1999)], the Court held that "in the absence of fraud ... transfer of stock of a corporate lessee is ordinarily not a violation of a clause prohibiting assignment...."

Delaware courts have refused to hold that a mere change in the legal ownership of a business results in an assignment by operation of law. *SQL Solutions*, on the other hand, noted, "California courts have consistently recognized that an assignment or transfer of rights does occur through a change in the legal form of ownership of a business." The *SQL Solutions* case, however, provides no further explanation for its apparent holding that any change in ownership, including a reverse triangular merger, is an assignment by operation of law. Both stock acquisitions and reverse triangular mergers involve changes in legal ownership, and the law should reflect parallel results. In order to avoid upsetting Delaware's well-settled law regarding stock acquisitions, I refuse to adopt the approach espoused in *SQL Solutions*.

In sum, Meso could have negotiated for a 'change of control provision." They did not. Instead, they negotiated for a term that prohibits "assignments by operation of law or otherwise." Roche has provided a reasonable interpretation of Section 5.08 that is consistent with the general understanding that a reverse triangular merger is not an assignment by operation of law. On the other hand, I find Meso's arguments as to why language that prohibits "assignments by operation of law or otherwise" should be construed to encompass reverse triangular mergers unpersuasive and its related construction of Section 5.08 to be unreasonable.

For the foregoing reasons, I conclude that Section 5.08 was not intended to cover the BioVeris Merger and that Roche is entitled to summary judgment in its favor as to [this] Count.

§ 2.15 Is Class Voting Required?

A. The Delaware Approach

Warner Communications, Inc. v. Chris-Craft Industries, Inc.

Delaware Court of Chancery, 1989 583 A.2d 962

ALLEN, Chancellor.

Pending is a motion for judgment on the pleadings. Plaintiffs seek a determination that the related holders of Warner Communications, Inc.'s Series B Variable Rate Cumulative Convertible Preferred stock (Series B Preferred) are not entitled to a class vote upon a proposed merger among Warner, its controlling shareholder Time Incorporated (now renamed Time Warner Inc.) and TW Sub Inc., a wholly owned subsidiary of Time Warner.

Plaintiffs in this declaratory judgment action are the parties proposing the merger—Warner, Time and TW Sub, all of which are Delaware corporations. Defendants are two corporations, Chris-Craft Industries, Inc. and its controlled subsidiary, BHC, Inc., which together with its wholly owned subsidiary, is the holder of the Series B Preferred stock. For purposes of this opinion, plaintiffs generally will be referred to as Warner; Time Warner, for purposes of clarity, will be referred to as Time and the holders of the Series B Preferred will be referred to as BHC.

[**Facts**] The merger in question is the proposed "back end" of a transaction, the first stage of which was a public tender offer for 51% of Warner's common stock for cash that closed on July 24, 1989. In that merger, the Series B Preferred stock would be cancelled and BHC as the holder of it would receive a new senior security, Time Series BB Convertible Preferred. For purposes of this motion (but for those purposes only), plaintiffs have stipulated that that substitution would adversely affect defendants.

[**Parties Positions**] * * *

[D]efendants argue that Section 3.3(i) of the certificate of designation gives BHC the right to a class vote. It contends that Section 3.3(i) protects against any corporate action that alters or changes "any rights or preferences" of the preferred stock so as to adversely affect the preferred shareholders. The proposed merger, it says, will alter the rights of the Series B Preferred (and on this motion presumptively in an adverse way) by substituting a new security, Time BB Preferred, for the Series B Preferred. Thus, it concludes, Section 3.3(i) requires that BHC be afforded the opportunity to vote on that merger separately. * * *

Warner answers that it is Section 3.4(iii) of the certificate of designation that is the dispositive provision relating to mergers. That section requires supermajority approval of a merger by the holders of Series B Preferred if in the merger they receive equity securities that are not the highest ranked equity securities of the surviving, resulting or acquiring corporation. Warner points out that under the merger the holders of Series B Preferred stock will receive Time Series BB Preferred stock which will be the senior equity security of Time. Thus, plaintiffs contend that Section 3.4(iii) is the pertinent provision and it grants no right to vote on the back-end merger to the Series B Preferred shareholders. * * *

[**Discussion**] In evaluating these contending positions, it should first be noted that the existence and extent of special stock rights are determined by reference to the issuer's certificate of incorporation; such rights are essentially contractual in nature. In determining them, a court should apply the same techniques of contract interpretation generally applied to contractual disputes. * * *

[T]he core issue here may be said to be whether the predicate words of Section 3.3(i), "alter or change," are to be read to include "convert pursuant to a merger." I conclude that Section 3.3(i) does not create a right to a class vote on a merger that will convert the Series B Preferred stock into other securities, other property or cash. * * *

The language of Section 3.3(i) is closely similar to the language of Section 242(b)(2) of the corporation law statute governing amendments to a certificate of incorporation. That section creates a right to a class vote under certain circumstances. It provides in pertinent part:

> The holders of the outstanding shares of a class shall be entitled to vote as a class upon a proposed amendment * * * if the amendment would * * * *alter or change the powers, preferences or special rights of the shares of such class so as to affect them adversely.*

The parallel language of Section 3.3(i), as quoted above, provides in pertinent part:

> * * * the affirmative vote of at least two-thirds of the * * * outstanding shares of Series B Stock * * * shall be necessary *to alter or change any rights, preferences or limitations of the Preferred Stock so as to affect* the holders of all such stock *adversely.*

The parallel is plain. It is therefore significant, when called upon to determine whether Section 3.3(i) creates a right to a class vote on a merger, to note that the language of Section 242(b)(2) does not itself create a right to a class vote on a merger. The voting requirements for a merger are generally set forth in Section 251(c) of our corporation law statute. Under Section 251, unless a charter provision creates a right to a class vote, a merger is authorized by the company's shareholders when "a majority of the outstanding stock of the corporation entitled to vote thereon shall be voted for the adoption of the agreement [of merger]." 8 Del.C. § 251(c). Unlike Section 242(b), Section 251 contains no class vote requirement.

Our bedrock doctrine of independent legal significance (*e.g., Hariton* [Section 2.13.A]) compels the conclusion that satisfaction of the requirements of Section 251 is all that is required legally to effectuate a merger. It follows, therefore, from rudimentary principles of corporation law, that the language of 242(b)(2), which so closely parallels the language of 3.3(i), does not entitle the holders of a class of preferred stock to a class vote in a merger, even if (as we assume here) the interests of the class will be adversely affected by the merger. Indeed, this is so apparent that Chris-Craft does not argue that it has such rights under Section 242. * * *

Note

In *Elliot Associates, L.P. v. Avatex Corporation*, 715 A.2d 843 (Del. 1998), the Delaware Supreme Court distinguished *Warner* and found that a class vote by preferred shareholders was required in a merger. The court's decision applies when the certificate of incorporation of the merging corporation expressly provides for such right where the holder's rights are "materially and adversely" affected by any "amendment, alteration or repeal, whether by merger, consolidation or otherwise * * * of the certificate of incorporation." In distinguishing *Warner*, the court reasoned:

> We note again that nowhere in the [Warner] Series B certificate of designations was found the phrase "by merger, consolidation or otherwise," which is the key phrase in the present case. Nevertheless, the heart of the *Warner* rationale, which we must address here, is that it was not the amendment, alteration or repeal of the Warner certificate that adversely affected the Warner Series B stock. The

> Chancellor held that it was only the conversion of the Warner Series B Preferred to Time Series BB Preferred that caused the adverse effect, and, moreover, that the conversion was permissible under 8 Del.C. Sec 251, which (unlike 8 Del.C. Sec 242) does not require a class vote on a merger. Further, the Chancellor held that no contractual protection of the Warner Series B stock provided for a class vote on a merger.

The court gave the following guidance on drafting class vote provisions:

> The path for future drafters to follow in articulating class vote provisions is clear. When a certificate (like the Warner certificate or the Series A provisions here) grants only the right to vote on an amendment, alteration or repeal, the preferred have no class vote in a merger. When a certificate (like the First Series Preferred certificate here) adds the terms "whether by merger, consolidation or otherwise" and a merger results in an amendment, alteration or repeal that causes an adverse effect on the preferred, there would be a class vote.

B. The MBCA Approach

1. For Mergers and Share Exchanges

a. **The Statute.** ***See* MBCA Sections 11.04(f), 10.04, and 1.40(26).**

b. **Comment on Class Voting Requirement for Mergers and Share Exchanges under the MBCA**

Committee on Corporate Laws, Changes in the Model Business Corporation Act — Fundamental Changes

54 Bus. Law. 685, 739–740 (1999)

Section 11.04(f) provides that a class or series has a right to vote on a plan of merger as a separate voting group if, pursuant to the merger, the class or series would be converted into shares or other securities, interests, obligations, rights to acquire shares or other securities, cash, or other property, or if the class or series would have the right to vote as a separate group on a provision in the plan that, if contained in an amendment to the articles of incorporation, would require approval by that class or series, voting as a separate voting group, under section 10.04. * * *

[The comments to the MBCA provide: "Section 1.40(26) defines 'voting group' for purposes of the Act as a matter of convenient reference. A 'voting group' consists of all shares of one or more classes or series that under the articles of incorporation or the revised Model Act are entitled to vote and be counted together collectively on a matter."]

2. For Sales of Substantially All the Assets

See MBCA § 12.02, Section 2.11.C.

C. Problem on Class Voting

Target Corporation (TC) has 100 shares of voting common stock outstanding, 50 shares of Class A voting preferred stock, and 50 shares Class B non-voting preferred stock. Acquiring Corporation (AC) has proposed to acquire TC in a merger transaction in which TC's common stock and Class A preferred stock would be converted into cash and TC's Class B preferred stock would be converted into Class B preferred of AC with the same terms and conditions. The articles of incorporation of TC do not address class voting.

The certificates of designation for the preferred have no provisions bearing on the proposed transaction.

All of the stockholders of TC are prepared to vote, and if they are permitted to vote they would vote as follows:

	For	Against	Total
Common	60	40	100
Class A Preferred	20	30	50
Class B Preferred	0	50	50
TOTAL	80	120	200

1. Delaware Law. What are the voting requirements for the merger under the Delaware law, and are those requirements satisfied?

2. MBCA. What are the voting requirements under the MBCA, and are those voting requirements satisfied?

§ 2.16 Short Form Mergers and Second-Step Mergers Pursuant to DGCL Section 251(h)

A. The MBCA: Comment on Rules Regarding Merger Between Parent and Subsidiary or Between Subsidiaries under MBCA §§ 11.05 and 13.02

Committee on Corporate Laws, Changes in the Model Business Corporation Act—Fundamental Changes

54 Bus. Law. 685, 749–753 (1999)

Under section 11.05, if a parent owns 90 percent of the voting power of each class and series of the outstanding shares of a subsidiary that have voting power, the subsidiary may be merged into the parent or another such subsidiary, or the parent may be merged into the subsidiary, without the approval of the subsidiary's shareholders or board of directors, subject to certain informational and notice requirements. Approval by the subsidiary's shareholders is not required partly because if a parent already owns 90 percent or more of the voting power of each class and series of a subsidiary's shares, approval of a merger by the subsidiary's shareholders would be a foregone conclusion, and partly to facilitate the simplification of corporate structure where only a very small fraction of stock is held by outside shareholders. Approval by the subsidiary's board of directors is not required because if the parent owns 90 percent or more of the voting power of each class and series of the subsidiary's outstanding shares, the subsidiary's directors cannot be expected to be independent of the parent, so that the approval by the subsidiary's board of directors would also be a foregone conclusion. In other respects, mergers between parents and 90 percent-owned subsidiaries are governed by the provisions of chapter 11.

B. Short Form Mergers in Delaware

1. The Delaware Short Form Merger Statute

See § 253 (short form merger) and § 262(b)(3) (appraisal rights in a short form merger) under Delaware General Corporate Law.

2. Exclusivity of Appraisal in a Short Form Merger in Delaware

Glassman v. Unocal Exploration Corporation

Delaware Supreme Court, 2001
2001 Del. LEXIS 317

BERGER, Justice:

In this appeal, we consider the fiduciary duties owed by a parent corporation to the subsidiary's minority stockholders in the context of a "short-form" merger. Specifically, we take this opportunity to reconcile a fiduciary's seemingly absolute duty to establish the entire fairness [the entire fairness doctrine is explored in Chapter 3, dealing with directors' duties] of any self-dealing transaction with the less demanding requirements of the short-form merger statute. The statute authorizes the elimination of minority stockholders by a summary process that does not involve the "fair dealing" component of entire fairness. Indeed, the statute does not contemplate any "dealing" at all. Thus, a parent corporation cannot satisfy the entire fairness standard if it follows the terms of the short-form merger statute without more.

Unocal Corporation addressed this dilemma by establishing a special negotiating committee and engaging in a process that it believed would pass muster under traditional entire fairness review. We find that such steps were unnecessary. By enacting a statute that authorizes the elimination of the minority without notice, vote, or other traditional indicia of procedural fairness, the General Assembly effectively circumscribed the parent corporation's obligations to the minority in a short-form merger. The parent corporation does not have to establish entire fairness, and, absent fraud or illegality, the only recourse for a minority stockholder who is dissatisfied with the merger consideration is appraisal.

Factual and Procedural Background. * * * At the time of the merger at issue Unocal [Corporation] owned approximately 96% of the stock of Unocal Exploration Corporation ("UXC"). * * *

In December 1991 the boards of Unocal and UXC appointed special committees to consider a possible merger. The UXC committee consisted of three directors who, although also directors of Unocal, were not officers or employees of the parent company. The UXC committee retained financial and legal advisors and met four times before agreeing to a merger exchange ratio of .54 shares of Unocal stock for each share of UXC. Unocal and UXC announced the merger on February 24, 1992, and it was effected, pursuant to Section 253 [the Delaware short form merger provision] on May 2, 1992. The Notice of Merger and Prospectus stated the terms of the merger and advised the former UXC stockholders of their appraisal rights.

Plaintiffs filed this class action, on behalf of UXC's minority stockholders, on the day the merger was announced. They asserted, among other claims, that Unocal and its directors breached their fiduciary duties of entire fairness and full disclosure. The Court of Chancery conducted a two day trial and held that: (i) the Prospectus did not contain any material misstatements or omissions; (ii) the entire fairness standard does not control in a short-form merger; and (iii) plaintiffs' exclusive remedy in this case was appraisal. The decision of the Court of Chancery is affirmed.

Discussion. The short-form merger statute, as enacted in 1937, authorized a parent corporation to merge with its wholly-owned subsidiary by filing and recording a certificate evidencing the parent's ownership and its merger resolution. In 1957, the statute was expanded to include parent/subsidiary mergers where the parent company owns at least 90% of the stock of the subsidiary. The 1957 amendment also made it possible, for the first time and only in a short-form merger, to pay the minority cash for their shares, thereby eliminating their ownership interest in the company. * * * [The court here reviews the history of the applicability of the entire fairness doctrine to parent-sub mergers in Delaware. As illustrated in *Kahn v. Lynch* in Chapter 3, the doctrine applies to non-short form parent-sub mergers.] * * *

[W]e must decide whether a minority stockholder may challenge a short-form merger by seeking equitable relief through an entire fairness claim. Under settled principles, a parent corporation and its directors undertaking a short-form merger are self-dealing fiduciaries who should be required to establish entire fairness, including fair dealing and fair price. The problem is that § 253 authorizes a summary procedure that is inconsistent with any reasonable notion of fair dealing. In a short-form merger, there is no agreement of merger negotiated by two companies; there is only a unilateral act-a decision by the parent company that its 90% owned subsidiary shall no longer exist as a separate entity. The minority stockholders receive no advance notice of the merger; their directors do not consider or approve it; and there is no vote. Those who object are given the right to obtain fair value for their shares through appraisal.

The equitable claim plainly conflicts with the statute. If a corporate fiduciary follows the truncated process authorized by § 253, it will not be able to establish the fair dealing prong of entire fairness. If, instead, the corporate fiduciary sets up negotiating committees, hires independent financial and legal experts, etc., then it will have lost the very benefit provided by the statute—a simple, fast and inexpensive process for accomplishing a merger. We resolve this conflict by giving effect the intent of the General Assembly. In order to serve its purpose, § 253 must be construed to obviate the requirement to establish entire fairness.

Thus, we again return to *Stauffer,* and hold that, absent fraud or illegality, appraisal is the exclusive remedy available to a minority stockholder who objects to a short-form merger. In doing so, we also reaffirm *Weinberger's* statements about the scope of appraisal. The determination of fair value must be based on *all* relevant factors, including damages and elements of future value, where appropriate. So, for example, if the merger was timed to take advantage of a depressed market, or a low point in the company's cyclical earnings, or to precede an anticipated positive development, the appraised value may be adjusted to account for those factors. * * *

3. Delaware Supreme Court's Adoption of the Quasi-Appraisal Remedy—*Berger*

Berger v. Pubco Corporation

Supreme Court of Delaware, 2009
976 A.2d 132

Jacobs, Justice:

The issue on this appeal is what remedy is appropriate in a "short form" merger under 8 *Del. C.* § 253, where the corporation's minority stockholders are involuntarily cashed out without being furnished the factual information material to an informed shareholder decision whether or not to seek appraisal. The Court of Chancery held that because the notice of merger did not disclose those material facts, the minority shareholders were entitled to a "quasi-appraisal" remedy, wherein those shareholders who elect appraisal must "opt in" to the proceeding and escrow a portion of the merger proceeds they received. We conclude that although the Court of Chancery correctly found that the majority stockholder had violated its disclosure duty, the court erred as a matter of law in prescribing this specific form of remedy.

Under *Glassman v. Unocal Exploration Corporation*,[3] the exclusive remedy for minority shareholders who challenge a short form merger is a statutory appraisal, provided that there is no fraud or illegality, and that all facts are disclosed that would enable the shareholders to decide whether to accept the merger price or seek appraisal. But where, as here, the material facts are not disclosed, the controlling stockholder forfeits the benefit of that limited review and exclusive remedy, and the minority shareholders become entitled to participate in a "quasi-appraisal" class action to recover the difference between "fair value" and the merger price without having to "opt in" to that proceeding or to escrow any merger proceeds that they received. Because the trial court declined to order that remedy, we must reverse. * * *

In cases where the corporation does not comply with the disclosure requirement mandated by *Glassman*, the quasi-appraisal remedy that operates in the fairest and most balanced way and that best effectuates the legislative intent underlying Section 253, is the one that does not require the minority shareholders seeking a recovery of fair value to escrow a portion of the merger proceeds they received. We hold, for these reasons, that the quasi-appraisal remedy ordered by the Court of Chancery was legally erroneous in the circumstances presented here.

To summarize: where there is a breach of the duty of disclosure in a short form merger, the *Gilliland* approach [*i.e.*, shareholder opt-in and escrow requirements] does not appropriately balance the equities. If only a technical and non-prejudicial violation of 8 *Del. C.* § 253 had occurred, the result might be different. In some circumstances, for example, where stockholders receive an incomplete copy of the appraisal statute with their notice of merger, the *Gilliland* remedy might arguably be supportable. But the majority stockholder's duty of disclosure provides important protection for minority stockholders being cashed out in a short form merger. This protection the quasi—appraisal remedy for a violation of that fiduciary disclosure obligation—should not be restricted by opt in or escrow requirements.

C. Section 251(h), Facilitating Two Step Transactions, a 2013 Amendment to Delaware Law

In response to a recommendation by the Delaware Corporate Bar, the Delaware legislature has added new Section 251(h) to the Delaware corporate law effective August 1, 2013.[4] As explained in the following synopsis by the Bar, the purpose of this section is to facilitate second-step mergers that take place after a tender offer:

> Section 6 amends § 251(h) to permit a merger agreement to include a provision eliminating the requirement of a stockholder vote to approve certain mergers if a statutorily defined minimum number of shares is tendered in a tender or exchange offer consummated by an arms'-length third-party acquiror. The subsection does not change the fiduciary duties of directors in connection with such mergers or the level of judicial scrutiny that will apply to the decision to enter into such a merger agreement, each of which will be determined based on the common law of fiduciary duty, including the duty of loyalty.

---

3. 777 A.2d 242 (Del. 2001) ("Glassman").

4. Delaware Corporate Council, An Act to Amend Title 8 of the Delaware Code Relating to the General Corporation Law (May 2013).

The original 2013 version of Section 251(h) was amended in 2014, and the amended provision reads in substantial part as follows:

> (h) Notwithstanding the requirements of subsection (c) of this section, unless expressly required by its certificate of incorporation, no vote of stockholders of a constituent corporation whose shares are [publicly traded] immediately prior to the execution of the agreement of merger by such constituent corporation shall be necessary to authorize a merger if:
>
> (1) The agreement of merger expressly:
>
> a. Permits or requires such merger to be effected under this subsection; and
>
> b. Provides that such merger shall be effected as soon as practicable following the consummation of the offer referred to in paragraph (h)(2) of this section if such merger is effected under this subsection;
>
> (2) A corporation consummates a tender or exchange offer for any and all of the outstanding stock of such constituent corporation on the terms provided in such agreement of merger that, absent this subsection, would be entitled to vote on the adoption or rejection of the agreement of merger; provided, however, that such offer may exclude stock of such constituent corporation that is owned at the commencement of such offer by:
>
> a. Such constituent corporation;
>
> b. The corporation making such offer;
>
> c. Any person that owns, directly or indirectly, all of the outstanding stock of the corporation making such offer; or
>
> d. Any direct or indirect wholly-owned subsidiary of any of the foregoing;
>
> (3) Following the consummation of the offer referred to in paragraph (h)(2) of this section, the stock irrevocably accepted for purchase or exchange pursuant to such offer and received by the depository prior to expiration of such offer, plus the stock otherwise owned by the consummating corporation equals at least such percentage of the stock, and of each class or series thereof, of such constituent corporation that, absent this subsection, would be required to adopt the agreement of merger by this chapter and by the certificate of incorporation of such constituent corporation;
>
> (4) The corporation consummating the offer referred to in paragraph (h)(2) of this section merges with or into such constituent corporation pursuant to such agreement; and
>
> (5) Each outstanding share of each class or series of stock of the constituent corporation that is the subject of and not irrevocably accepted for purchase or exchange in the offer referred to in paragraph (h)(2) of this section is to be converted in such merger into, or into the right to receive, the same amount and kind of cash, property, rights or securities to be paid for shares of such class or series of stock of such constituent corporation irrevocably accepted for purchase or exchange in such offer. * * *

By eliminating the vote on the second step merger, this provision has the effect of, in essence, expanding the short form merger concept, which is discussed *supra*, to second step mergers where after the tender offer, the acquirer owns "at least such percentage of the stock ... of such constituent corporation that [otherwise] would be required to adopt the agreement of merger by this chapter [generally more than 50% of the outstanding shares]...."

§ 2.17 The California Approach to Long Form Mergers, Sales of Assets, Short Form Mergers and Dissenters' Rights

A. Introduction

This section examines the approach California takes to voting and dissenting in mergers and sales of substantially all the assets. The provisions of the California Corporations Code cited in this section are in *M&A Statutes, Rules, and Documents*, *supra* Section 1.1.

B. The Definition of "Reorganization"

1. The Provision

See § 181 of California General Corporation Law.

2. Explanation

Marshall L. Small, Corporate Combinations under the New California General Corporation Law

23 UCLA L. Rev. 1190; 1194–1195 (1976)

Chapter 12 of the new law applies to all reorganizations. [*See* the definition of "reorganization" in Section 181 of the California Corporations Code.] Mergers are additionally regulated by chapter 11. Sale-of-assets and exchange reorganizations are dealt with only in chapter 12. Certain sales of assets for cash or for a form of consideration which was thought not to subject the recipient to the risk of-long-term investment in the acquiring corporation (herein referred to as "cash equivalent") are not treated as "reorganizations" at all and are dealt with separately in chapter 10. Dissenters' appraisal rights are dealt with in chapter 13. * * *

C. Board of Directors' Authorization

1. The Provision

See § 1200 of California General Corporation Law.

2. Explanation

Marshall L. Small, Corporate Combinations under the New California General Corporation Law

23 UCLA L. Rev. 1190; 1195–1196 (1976)

Board of Directors' Authorization. * * * In effect section 1200 requires approval of the board of each corporation which is a party to the reorganization [including the acquiring parent in a triangular merger]. The only board approval not needed is that of the [acquired corporation] in an exchange reorganization because individual shareholders must decide whether or not to sell their stock in such a reorganization. * * *

D. Shareholder Authorization

1. The Provision

See § 1201 of California General Corporation Law.

2. Explanation

Marshall L. Small, Corporate Combinations under the New California General Corporation Law

23 UCLA L. Rev. 1190; 1196–1202 (1976)

Shareholders' Authorization. Subsection 1201(a) provides that the principal terms of a reorganization must be approved by the outstanding shares[5] of each class of each corporation where the board of directors is required by section 1200 to approve the reorganization, unless one of two exceptions discussed below applies [*See* § 1201(a) and (b)]. A majority vote, or a higher proportion if mandated by the articles or a shareholder's agreement, is required by the shares of each class, regardless of any limitations on the voting power of a class. For purposes of determining what constitutes a class of shares, two classes of common shares differing only as to voting rights are to be considered a single class of stock. [*See* § 1201(a)].

The first exception to the requirement of shareholder approval is fairly simple. Preferred shares in the surviving or acquiring corporation or its parent [do not vote if the] "rights, preferences, privileges and restrictions granted to or imposed upon" such shares remain unchanged by the reorganization [*See* § 1201(a)]. * * *

The second exception to the requirement of shareholder consent is more complex. Neither preferred nor common shareholder approval is needed if the corporation, or its shareholders immediately before the reorganization, or both, will own immediately after the reorganization equity securities of the surviving or acquiring corporation or its parent possessing more than five-sixths of the voting power of the surviving or acquiring corporation or its parent [*See* § 1201(b)]. This exception, however, does not apply under two circumstances:

> (1) Shareholder approval is needed despite retention of five-sixths of the voting power for the surviving or acquiring corporation or its parent if any amendment which would otherwise require shareholder approval is made to the articles of the surviving corporation in connection with a merger reorganization [*See* § 1201(c)]. * * *
>
> (2) Under section 1201(d) of the new law the outstanding shares of a class in a disappearing corporation must give their consent to a merger reorganization even though the five-sixths rule applies if the holders of such class receive shares of the surviving corporation that have different rights than those surrendered. * * *

3. Illustration of Shareholder Voting in a Triangular Merger

Kirschner Bros. Oil, Inc. v. Natomas Co.

California Court of Appeals, 1986 299 Cal.Rptr. 899

Scott, Associate Justice.

Plaintiffs, all holders of [preferred stock of] Natomas Company (Natomas) [a California corporation and the target] filed similar actions against Natomas, one of its directors, and

5. "Approved by or approval of the outstanding shares" means approved by the affirmative vote of a majority of the outstanding shares entitled to vote. [*See* § 152]

Diamond Shamrock Corporation [the acquiror]. Plaintiffs sought to enjoin a proposed merger * * * According to [the terms of the merger], each share of Natomas preferred was exchanged for a share of the preferred stock of another corporation, New Diamond. * * *

[**Facts**][T]he boards of Diamond Shamrock and Natomas approved a plan and agreement of reorganization between the two companies. * * *

According to the plan, a new holding company, New Diamond, was to be formed, which in turn would form two wholly owned subsidiaries, D. Sub, Inc., and N Sub, Inc. In two reverse triangular "phantom" mergers, D Sub, Inc., would merge into Diamond Shamrock, and N Sub, Inc., into Natomas; New Diamond would issue New Diamond common shares to common shareholders of Natomas and Diamond Shamrock in exchange for their shares. New Diamond would thus become the sole shareholder of Natomas' common shares. * * *

The agreement was to be submitted to Natomas common and preferred shareholders, voting as separate classes. Upon the approval of each class, the Natomas common shares would be converted into New Diamond common shares and the Natomas preferred into New Diamond preferred, convertible into New Diamond common. Failure to obtain the approval of the Natomas preferred shareholders would not prevent consummation of the merger, however, and it is that feature of the reorganization plan which is at the heart of this litigation. If a majority of Natomas common shareholders approved the agreement but its preferred shareholders did not, the reorganization would still take place. The Natomas common shares would be converted into New Diamond common, but the Natomas preferred would remain outstanding and continue to be convertible into Natomas common. * * *

[**Issue**]* * * [Plaintiffs allege] that consummation of the merger without an affirmative vote of a majority of the preferred shareholders would violate Corporations Code section 1201 and the certificate of determination specifying the rights of Natomas preferred shareholders. * * *

[**Discussion**] The Corporations Code recognizes several methods of reorganization whereby two or more corporations are combined into a single business enterprise. (§ 181) * * * Section 1201 spells out when a vote by the shareholders of any corporation involved in a reorganization is required. Subdivision (a) of section 1201 provides in pertinent part: "The principal terms of a reorganization shall be approved by the outstanding shares * * * of each class of each corporation the approval of whose board is required under Section 1200 * * * except that (unless otherwise provided in the articles) *no approval of any class of outstanding preferred shares of the surviving or acquiring corporation or parent party shall be required if the rights, preferences, privileges and restrictions granted to or imposed upon such class of shares remain unchanged* * * *." (Emphasis added)

Plaintiffs contend that despite the appearance of the transaction at issue, in reality Natomas was acquired by Diamond Shamrock. Therefore, plaintiffs reason, Natomas was not a "surviving corporation" under either reorganization alternative and the preferred shareholders' approval was required by section 1201, subdivision (a), for either to become effective.

Ignoring for the moment the fact that a majority of the preferred shareholders *did* approve the reorganization, we consider the argument unpersuasive. The reorganization at issue here was structured as a "reverse triangular 'phantom' merger," well-recognized as a method of reorganization which preserves the existing corporate entity of the target corporation. Notwithstanding the fact that the parent holding company, New Diamond, would wholly own Natomas, it is still undisputed that N Sub, Inc., corporation merged into Natomas, leaving the latter intact as a legal entity. Similarly, D Sub, Inc., merged into Diamond Shamrock, which also remained a legal entity. The Corporations Code defines a "surviving corporation" simply as "a corporation into which one or more other corporations are merged." (§ 190) * * * [Consequently, the court held for the defendant.]

Note

Each of the reverse subsidiary mergers presumably qualified as a tax-free reorganization under Section 368(a)(2)(E) of the Internal Revenue Code. *See* Chapter 5. This type of holding company structure with two reverse subsidiary merger was utilized by Oracle in its acquisition of Siebel, Documentary Appendix H of *M&A Statutes, Rules, and Documents, supra* Section 1.1.

4. Is Class Voting Required by a Delaware Corporation under California's "Quasi California Corporation" Provision?

VantagePoint Venture Partners 1996 v. Examen, Inc.

Delaware Supreme Court, 2005, 871 A.2d 1108

HOLLAND, Justice:

[Examen, a Delaware corporation with its principal business activities in California, entered into a merger pursuant to which it was to be acquired by a subsidiary of Reed Elsevier Inc. The issue was whether VantagePoint Venture Partners, Inc. ("VantagePoint"), a Delaware Limited Partnership and an Examen Series A Preferred shareholder was entitled to a class vote on the merger under California law because Examen was a "quasi California corporation" under Section 2115 of the California Corporations Code.[6] Thus, the question is: which merger law governs, the Delaware law, which does not have a class vote, or the California law which does?]

California Section 2115.VantagePoint contends that section 2115 of the California Corporations Code is a limited exception to the internal affairs doctrine. Section 2115 is characterized as an outreach statute because it requires certain foreign corporations to conform to a broad range of internal affairs provisions. Section 2115 defines the foreign corporations for which the California statute has an outreach effect as those foreign corporations, half of whose voting securities are held of record by persons with California addresses, that also conduct half of their business in California as measured by a formula weighing assets, sales and payroll factors.

VantagePoint argues that section 2115 "mandates application of certain enumerated provisions of California's corporation law to the internal affairs of 'foreign' corporations if certain narrow factual prerequisites [set forth in section 2115] are met." * * *

State Law of Incorporation Governs Internal Affairs.* * * Applying Delaware's well-established choice-of-law rule—the internal affairs doctrine—the Court of Chancery rec-

---

6. Section 2115 of the California Corporations Code purportedly applies to corporations that have contacts with the State of California, but are incorporated in other states. *See* Cal. Corp. Code §§ 171 (defining "foreign corporation"); and Cal. Corp. Code §§ 2115(a), (b). Section 2115 of the California Corporations Code provides that, irrespective of the state of incorporation, foreign corporations' articles of incorporation are deemed amended to comply with California law and are subject to the laws of California if certain criteria are met. *See* Cal. Corp. Code § 2115 (emphasis added). To qualify under the statute: (1) the average of the property factor, the payroll factor and the sales factor as defined in the California Revenue and Taxation Code must be more than 50 percent during its last full income year; and (2) more than one-half of its outstanding voting securities must be held by persons having addresses in California. *Id.* If a corporation qualifies under this provision, California corporate laws apply "to the exclusion of the law" of the jurisdiction where [the company] is incorporated. *Id.*

ognized that Delaware courts must apply the law of the state of incorporation to issues involving corporate internal affairs, and that disputes concerning a shareholder's right to vote fall squarely within the purview of the internal affairs doctrine.

Examen is a Delaware corporation. The legal issue in this case—whether a preferred shareholder of a Delaware corporation had the right, under the corporation's Certificate of Designations, to a Series A Preferred Stock class vote on a merger—clearly involves the relationship among a corporation and its shareholders. As the United States Supreme Court held in *CTS*, "no principle of corporation law and practice is more firmly established than a *State's authority* to regulate domestic corporations, including the authority to *define the voting rights of shareholders*."

In *CTS*, the Supreme Court held that the Commerce Clause "prohibits States from regulating subjects that 'are in their nature national, or admit only of one uniform system, or plan of regulation,'" and acknowledged that the internal affairs of a corporation are subjects that require one uniform system of regulation. In *CTS*, the Supreme Court concluded that "so long as each State regulates voting rights *only in the corporations it has created*, each corporation will be subject to the law of only one State." Accordingly, we hold Delaware's well-established choice of law rules and the federal constitution mandated that Examen's internal affairs, and in particular, VantagePoint's voting rights, be adjudicated exclusively in accordance with the law of its state of incorporation, in this case, the law of Delaware.

E. Merger Reorganizations

1. The Provision

See § 1101 of California General Corporation Law.

2. Explanation

Marshall L. Small, Corporate Combinations under the New California General Corporation Law

23 UCLA L. Rev. 1190; 1202–1203 (1976)

In addition to the reorganization provisions of chapter 12, merger reorganizations and short-form mergers are regulated by the provisions of chapter 11. Section 1100 states the general proposition that any two or more corporations may be merged into one under chapter 11. Although "corporation" is defined to include only domestic corporations, [*see* § 162] section 1108 makes clear that mergers are authorized between domestic and foreign corporations and that the surviving corporation may be either domestic or foreign. * * *

As explained above, a merger reorganization must be approved by the board of each constituent corporation. [*See* § 1200(a)] Section 1101 requires that the merger agreement also be approved by each board.

A merger agreement is required by section 1101 of the new law to include: the terms and conditions of the merger; any amendments to the articles of the surviving corporation to be effected by the merger; the name and place of incorporation of the constituent corporations, and which shall be the surviving corporation; the manner of converting the shares of each constituent corporation into shares or other securities of the surviving corporation; and, under section 1101(d), if the shares are not to be converted solely into securities of the surviving corporation,

> the cash, property, rights or securities of any corporation which the holders of such shares are to receive in exchange for such shares, which cash, property,

> rights or securities of any corporation may be in addition to or in lieu of shares or other securities of the surviving corporation * * *.

The reorganization provisions clearly contemplate that shareholders of a constituent corporation may, in a triangular merger, receive *equity* securities of a parent corporation. [*See* § 1200(d)] These provisions should not be construed to limit the type and source of securities to be issued in a merger to equity securities of a constituent corporation or parent, or to securities of a corporation which is technically in "control" of one of the constituent corporations within the meaning of section 160(b). Section 1101(d) certainly suggests a broader range of alternatives. * * *

F. Sale of Assets Transactions

1. The Provisions

See § 1001 and § 181(c) of California General Corporation Law.

2. Explanation

Marshall L. Small, Corporate Combinations under the New California General Corporation Law
23 UCLA L. Rev. 1190; 1209–1214 (1976)

Unlike statutory mergers under chapter 11, all of which (except for short-form mergers) constitute reorganizations under chapter 12, sale-of-assets transactions are divided into two distinct categories, depending upon the types of consideration issued in the transaction. Chapters 12 (reorganizations) and 13 (dissenters' rights) govern "sale-of-assets reorganizations." [*See* § 181(c)] Such a sale will occur if the acquiring corporation issues any of its equity securities, any equity securities of a corporation which controls the acquiring corporation, any debt securities of the acquiring corporation which are not "adequately secured" and which have a maturity date more than five years after completion of the reorganization, or a combination of equity securities and such debt securities, in exchange for all or substantially all of the property and assets of the selling corporation. If none of these securities is issued as a part of the consideration for transfer of all or substantially all of the assets, then chapters 12 and 13 are inapplicable; instead, the provisions of chapter 10 (sale of assets) apply to the transaction. Chapter 10 governs only sales of assets which are not "sale-of-assets reorganizations"; it is expressly made inapplicable to such reorganizations. [*See* § 1001(a)] * * *

Section 1001 sets forth the general rule that a corporation may sell or otherwise dispose of all of its assets if its board of directors approves the principal terms of the transaction. The principal terms of the transaction must also be approved by the holders of a majority of the outstanding shares entitled to vote unless the transaction is in the usual course of business. * * *

The distinctions drawn in the new law between sales of assets which are reorganizations and those which are for cash or cash equivalents may produce some rather incongruous results, as noted above. * * *

G. Exchange Reorganizations

1. The Provisions

See § 181(b) of the California General Corporation Law.

2. Explanation

Marshall L. Small, Corporate Combinations under the New California General Corporation Law

23 UCLA L. Rev. 1190; 1215–1217 (1976)

As in the case of sale-of-assets reorganizations, no separate chapter in the new law sets forth the procedural provisions governing exchange reorganizations subject to chapter 12. The basic requirements are set forth solely in chapter 12.

An "exchange reorganization" is defined as:

> The acquisition by one corporation in exchange in whole or in part for its equity securities (or the equity securities of a corporation which is in control of the acquiring corporation) of shares of another corporation if, immediately after the acquisition the acquiring corporation has control of such other corporation * * *. [*See* § 181(b)]

Section 160(b) provides that control in section 181 means the ownership directly or indirectly of shares possessing more than 50 percent of the voting power. * * *

H. Share Exchange Tender Offer

See § 183.5 and § 1201.5 of California General Corporation Law.

I. Interested Party Proposal or Tender Offer

See § 1203 of California General Corporation Law.

J. Short Form Mergers

California has a 90% ownership requirement for short form mergers, the same as under Delaware law and the MBCA. *See* § 1110(a) of the California General Corporation Law.

K. Dissenters' Rights

1. The Provision

See § 1300 and § 1312 of California General Corporation Law.

2. Explanation

Marshall L. Small, Corporate Combinations under the New California General Corporation Law

23 UCLA L. Rev. 1190; 1209 (1976)

If the approval of outstanding shares of a corporation is required for a * * * reorganization under section 1201(a), (b) or (e), each shareholder of that corporation may require it to pay, in cash, the fair market value of all "dissenting shares." [*See* § 1300(a)] A similar right is accorded to each shareholder of a disappearing corporation in a short-form merger [*See* § 1300(a)]. Certain shares, including shares listed on a national securities exchange certified by the Commissioner of Corporations to be exempt securities, or listed on the list of over-the-counter margin stocks issued by the Board of Governors of the Federal

Reserve System, are not "dissenting shares" subject to the appraisal procedures [*See* § 1300(b)(1)].

3. Exclusivity of Dissenters' Rights in California. *See* § 1312.

Steinberg v. Amplica, Inc.

Supreme Court of California, 1986 729 P.2d 683

Mosk, Justice.

The Corporations Code provides that the holder of shares in certain types of corporations may require the corporation to purchase his shares for fair market value if the corporation merges with another, and the shareholder dissents from the merger. (Corp. Code, § 1300, § 1301) The corporation must offer the dissenting shareholder a price which it determines to be fair market value for his shares (§ 1301, subd. (a)). In the event of a failure to agree on a price, he may file an action in the superior court to determine such value, and the court may either decide the issue or refer the matter to an appraiser to do so (§ 1304, § 1305).

Section 1312(a) provides in relevant part, "No shareholder of a corporation who has a right under this chapter to demand payment of cash for the shares held by the shareholder shall have any right at law or in equity to attack the validity of the reorganization or short-form merger, or to have the reorganization or short-form merger set aside or rescinded * * *." We are concerned in this case with whether under section 1312(a) appraisal is the exclusive remedy for a shareholder who alleges that his shares were undervalued because of fraud and breach of fiduciary duty by the majority stockholders and others in connection with the merger, and whether an action for compensatory and exemplary damages will lie for such purported misconduct. * * *

If a minority shareholder were confined to appraisal when he claimed that the undervaluation of his shares resulted from the breach of fiduciary duty by corporate insiders, the wrongdoers would go unpunished, for only the corporation would be liable for the fair market value of the shares. Exemplary damages would not be available, and there would be no deterrent to individual misconduct, since the corporation would be liable for the fair value of the shares no matter what the cause of their undervaluation. * * *

The resolution of the problem in this case requires balancing the need to deter misconduct by corporate insiders against the risk that desirable corporate changes will be hampered by minority stockholders who seek to "exercise leverage for [their] own aggrandizement." * * * We conclude that at least in a case such as this, where the plaintiff was aware of all the facts leading to his cause of action for alleged misconduct in connection with the term of the merger prior to the time the merger was consummated but deliberately opted to sue for damages instead of seeking appraisal, section 1312(a) acts as a bar. * * *

L. Problems

1. Long Form Direct Merger

Work the problems in Section 2.9.N on the assumption that both Closely-Held Target Corporation and Closely-Held Acquiring Corporation are incorporated in California.

2. Sale of Assets

Work the problems on sales of assets in Section 2.11.F on the assumption that both Closely-Held Target Corporation and Closely-Held Acquiring Corporation are incorporated in California.

3. Problems on Triangular Mergers

Work the problems on triangular mergers in Section 2.14.D on the assumption that both Closely-Held Target Corporation and Closely-Held Acquiring Corporation are incorporated in California.

4. Class Voting

Work the problems on Class Voting in Section 2.15.C on the assumption that both Acquiring Corporation and Target Corporation are incorporated in California.

§ 2.18 Comparing the Pennsylvania Approach to Long Form Mergers, Sales of Assets, Short Form Mergers and Dissenters' Rights with the Approaches of Delaware, the MBCA, and California[7]

A. Introduction

This section discusses the basic rules set out in the Pennsylvania Business Corporation Law (Pa. BCL) relating to shareholder voting and dissenting in (1) long form direct and reverse subsidiary mergers, (2) share exchanges, (3) sales of all or substantially all of at target's assets, and (4) short form mergers. The section also compares these Pennsylvania rules with the rules governing these transactions under the corporate laws of Delaware, California, and the MBCA.

In each of the transactions, it is assumed that (1) all corporations are Pennsylvania corporations; (2) the bylaws of the corporation do not set out a higher voting rule than the Pa. BCL; (3) in any triangular merger, AC Parent is the ultimate acquirer and AC Sub is the wholly-owned sub of AC Parent. The discussion does not address the impact of the stock exchange voting requirements. It must be emphasized that this discussion focuses on the basic principles of Pennsylvania law applicable in each of these transactions and not on many of the nuances under that law.

Before examining the ins and outs of the voting and dissenting rules in Pennsylvania, it is important to note that Section 1721(a) of the Pa. BCL, the Pennsylvania analogue to Section 141(a) of the Delaware corporate law, provides that the "all [corporate] powers ... shall be exercised by or under the authority of, and the business and affairs of every business corporation shall be managed under the direction of, a board of directors."

B. Long Form Direct Mergers

1. The Provisions

See §§ 1921 to 1929 of Pa. BCL.

---

7. As indicated previously, I thank Taimoor Choudhry, a 2014 graduate of Penn State Law and my former research assistant, for his very helpful assistance in preparing the materials dealing with Pennsylvania law.

2. Board of Directors' Authorization, Explanation and Comparison

Like the three other jurisdictions, Section 1922 of the Pa. BCL requires that the board of directors of each of the merging corporations pass a corporate resolution adopting the plan of merger. *See* Pa. BCL § 1922.

3. Shareholder Authorization, Explanation and Comparison

Target Shareholders Vote. Like the three other jurisdictions, under Section 1924 of the Pa. BCL, the shareholders of the target corporation always have the right to vote in a long form merger.

The Voting Rule. Pennsylvania follows the MBCA rule in providing in Section 1924(a) that the merger must be approved by the "affirmative vote of a majority of the votes cast by all shareholders of the business corporation entitled to vote." In addressing the quorum requirement, Section 1756 provides that "unless otherwise provided in a bylaw adopted by the shareholders: (1) The presence of shareholders entitled to cast at least a majority of the votes that all shareholders are entitled to cast on a particular matter to be acted upon at the meeting shall constitute a quorum for the purposes of consideration and action on the matter." Thus, in the absence of a bylaw providing for a higher quorum, the quorum for a merger vote is effectively 51% of the outstanding shares. Consequently, as with the MBCA, assuming that only 51% of the shares are voted on a merger, the merger will be approved with an affirmative vote of just 26% of the outstanding shares. Section 251 of the Delaware law and Section 1201(a) of the California law require that the merger be approved by a majority of the outstanding shares.

Class Vote Rule. Section 1924(a) provides that "if any class or series of shares is entitled to vote thereon as a class," then the merger will be approved upon the "affirmative vote of a majority of the votes cast in each class vote." Presumably, if the governing instrument of the shares does not require a class vote, there is no class vote. This is the same as the Delaware rule (*see* § 251(c)) and contrary to the mandatory class voting rules in California (*see* § 1201(a)) and the MBCA (*see* § 11.04(f)). The following language in Section 1924(a) granting a class vote on certain amendments to the articles of incorporation would seem to be inapplicable where the target goes out of existence in the merger:

> The holders of any class or series of shares of a domestic corporation that is a party to a merger or consolidation that effects any change in the articles of the corporation shall be entitled to vote as a class on the plan if they would have been entitled to a class vote under the provisions of section 1914 (relating to adoption of amendments) had the change been accomplished under Subchapter B (relating to amendment of articles).

Acquiror Shareholder Vote. Under Section 1924(b) of the Pa. BCL, the shareholders of the acquiror have the right to vote unless all of the following three conditions are satisfied:

> (1) the acquiror's articles are not changed;
>
> (2) each share of the acquiror "outstanding immediately prior to the effective date of the merger * * * is to continue as ... an identical share of the [acquirer] after the effective date of the merger;" and
>
> (3) "the plan provides that [after the merger] the [acquiror's] shareholders * * * are to hold in the aggregate shares of the [acquirer that are] entitled to cast at least a majority of the votes entitled to be cast generally for the election of directors."

Conditions (1) and (2) are also present in the laws in Delaware, California and the MBCA. However, condition (3) is much more liberal than the laws of these other jurisdictions. With regard to condition (3), each of Delaware (*see* § 251(f)), California (*see* § 1201(b)), and the MBCA (*see* § 6.21(f)) eliminate the need for a vote of the shareholders of the acquiror only when the acquiror's shareholders hold 80% or more of the acquiror's outstanding shares after the acquisition, that is, the acquiror issues in the merger no more than 20% of its pre-merger outstanding shares. On the other hand, under condition (3), Pennsylvania eliminates the need for a vote of the acquiror's shareholders when those shareholders hold 51% or more of the acquiror's outstanding shares after the acquisition. Thus, for example, if in a merger, the acquiror's shareholders end up with 60% of the acquiror's outstanding stock after the transaction, the acquiror's shareholders have no vote in Pennsylvania, whereas they would have a vote in the other jurisdictions.

4. Shareholder Dissenter's Rights

a. The Provision

See § 1930 of Pa. BCL.

b. Explanation and Comparison

In long form mergers, Section 1930(a) of the Pa. BCL grants dissenter's rights to "any shareholder, of a domestic business corporation that is to be a party to a merger ... [who] objects to the plan of merger ... and complies with the provisions of Subchapter D of Chapter 15 (relating to dissenters' rights)." While this provision would seem to give all the shareholders of both the target and the acquiror the right to dissent, whether or not the shareholders had the right to vote, Section 1930(b), takes dissenters' rights away from the acquiror's shareholders unless they have the right to vote on the transaction. (*See* § 1930(b) and its reference to § 1924(b)(1)(i), which denies the vote to the acquiror's shareholders unless more than 50% of the acquior's stock is issued in the transaction.) This rule is similar to the rules regarding dissenting rights of acquiror shareholders in Delaware, California, and the MBCA.

Dissenters' rights in Pennsylvania are subject to a market out exception under Section 1571(b)(1), which is similar to the market out exception in the MBCA. Delaware and California have more limited market-out exceptions.

C. Triangular Mergers

1. The Provisions

See §§ 1922(d) & 1924 of Pa. BCL.

2. Board of Directors' Authorization, Explanation and Comparison

As in Delaware and the MBCA, the board of directors of both the target and AC Sub must adopt a plan of merger. The board of AC Parent is not required to adopt a plan of merger because the parent is not (1) a "party to the merger" under Pennsylvania law (*see* § 1924(a)), (2) a "constituent corporation" under Delaware law (see § 251(a), or (3) a "party to the merger" under the MBCA (*see* § 11.01). However, as a practical matter, all three companies are included as parties to the merger agreement. Under California's approach, the board of the parent corporation in a triangular merger must adopt a plan of merger if the parent corporation is issuing securities. (*See* 1200)

3. Shareholder Authorization, Explanation and Comparison

In a triangular merger, shareholders of the target corporation will have the same voting rights as in a two party merger. (*See* discussion of the *Voting Rule* and the *Class Vote Rule* under the section above dealing with direct long-form mergers.) Shareholders of AC Sub may also have a right to vote. However, given that AC Parent is the sole shareholder of AC Sub, AC Parent would always vote in favor of the transaction.

As in Delaware, shareholders of AC Parent do not have voting rights under the Pa. BCL because AC Parent is not a "party to the merger." Thus, in a triangular merger, AC Parent can issue any amount of its shares without triggering a shareholder vote. Of course, AC Parent would have to have sufficient authorized and unissued shares; otherwise a shareholder vote would be required to authorize the shares that are issued in the merger.

This is in contrast to both the MBCA and California. Under Section 6.21(f) of the MBCA and Section 1201(b) of California law, shareholders of AC Parent have a right to vote if AC Parent issues more than 20 percent of its voting stock in the merger.

4. Shareholder Dissenter's Rights

a. The Provision

See § 1930 of Pa. BCL.

b. Explanation and Comparison

Shareholders will have the same dissenting rights as in a long form merger. Thus, the acquiror's shareholders will not have dissenter's rights unless they have the right to vote on the transaction, and even if they have the right to vote, if the market-out exception applies there would be no dissenter's rights.

5. Illustration of the Pa. Approach to Triangular Mergers

Terry v. Penn Central Corporation

United States Court of Appeals, Third Circuit, 1981 668 F.2d 188

ADAMS, Circuit Judge.

The Penn Central Corporation (Penn Central), an appellee in this case, has sought to acquire Colt Industries Inc. (Colt), also an appellee, by merging Colt with PCC Holdings, Inc. (Holdings), a wholly-owned subsidiary of Penn Central. Howard L. Terry and W. H. Hunt, the appellants, are shareholders of Penn Central who objected to the transaction. * * *

[**Parties Positions**] Terry and Hunt contend that under Pennsylvania law they are entitled to dissent and appraisal rights if a merger is approved by the Penn Central shareholders. As the district court concluded, this assertion is unsupported by Pennsylvania statute or case law. * * * Briefly, appellants' argument is that the proposed merger between Holdings and Colt constitutes a *de facto* merger between Colt and Penn Central, and that the Penn Central shareholders are therefore entitled to the protections for dissenting shareholders that Pennsylvania corporate law provides for shareholders of parties to a merger. Although this reasoning, with its emphasis on the substance of the transaction rather than its formal trappings, may be attractive as a matter of policy, it contravenes the language employed by the Pennsylvania legislature in setting out the rights of shareholders.

Section 908 of the Pennsylvania Business Corporation Law (PBCL), 15 P.S. § 1908, provides that shareholders of corporations that are parties to a plan of merger are entitled to dissent and appraisal rights, but adds that for an acquisition other than such a merger, the only rights are those provided for in Section 311 of the PBCL. Section 311, in turn, provides for dissent and appraisal rights only when an acquisition has been accomplished by "the issuance of voting shares of such corporation to be outstanding immediately after the acquisition sufficient to elect a majority of the directors of the corporation." In this case the shares of Penn Central stock to be issued in the Colt transaction do not exceed the number of shares already existing, and thus the transaction is not covered by Section 311. Any statutory dissent and appraisal rights for Penn Central shareholders are therefore contingent upon Penn Central's status as a party to the merger within the meaning of Section 908. And as the district court points out, the PBCL describes the parties to a merger as those entities that are *actually* combined into a single corporation. * * *

Appellants argue that Penn Central is nevertheless brought into the amalgamation by the *de facto* merger doctrine as set out in Pennsylvania law in *Farris v. Glen Alden Corp.*, [Section 2.13.2].

[**Discussion**] *Farris* was the penultimate step in a *pas de deux* involving the Pennsylvania courts and the Pennsylvania legislature regarding the proper treatment for transactions that reached the same practical result as a merger but avoided the legal form of merger and the concomitant legal obligations. In the 1950s the Pennsylvania courts advanced the doctrine that a transaction having the effect of an amalgamation would be treated as a *de facto merger*. The legislature responded with efforts to constrict the *de facto* merger doctrine. *Farris*, addressing those efforts, held that the doctrine still covered a reorganization agreement that had the effect of merging a large corporation into a smaller corporation. In a 1959 response to *Farris*, the legislature made explicit its objection to earlier cases that found certain transactions to be *de facto* mergers. The legislature enacted a law, modifying *inter alia* Sections 311 and 908, entitled in part: "An Act * * * changing the law as to * * * the acquisition or transfer of corporate assets, the rights of dissenting shareholders,* * * abolishing the doctrine of *de facto* mergers or consolidation." * * *

Following this explicit statement, the *de facto* merger doctrine has rarely been invoked by the Pennsylvania courts. * * * This court, sitting in diversity in *Knapp v. North American Rockwell Corp.*, [Section 12.9.A] made reference to the *de facto* merger doctrine to hold that a transaction structured as a sale of assets could nevertheless be deemed a merger for purposes of requiring the merging corporation to assume the acquired corporation's liability for damages to a worker who was injured by a faulty piece of equipment manufactured by the acquired company. * * *

[This does not persuade] us that a Pennsylvania court would apply the *de facto* merger doctrine to the situation before us. Although * * * dissent and appraisal rights might be available if fraud or fundamental unfairness were shown, we are not faced with such a situation. * * * [T]he denial of appraisal rights to dissenters cannot constitute fundamental unfairness, or the *de facto* merger doctrine would apply in every instance in which dissenters' rights were sought and the 1959 amendments by the legislature would be rendered nugatory.

Knapp was not concerned with the rights of shareholders as the Pennsylvania legislature was in 1959. * * * We therefore hold that appellants do not possess such rights if a transaction such as the one involved here is consummated. * * *

D. Share Exchanges

1. The Provision

See § 1931 of Pa. BCL.

2. Board of Directors' Authorization, Explanation and Comparison

In contrast to the MBCA, only the board of directors of the exchanging corporation is required to adopt a plan of share exchange under the Pa. BCL. Neither Delaware nor California have a share exchange provision.

3. Shareholder Authorization, Explanation and Comparison

In contrast to the MBCA, only shareholders of the exchanging corporation (*i.e.*, the target) are required to vote on a share exchange. This means that the acquiror can issue any amount of its stock in the share exchange without triggering a shareholder vote. Of course, the acquiror would have to have sufficient authorized but unissued shares. In contrast, under Section 6.21(f), the MBCA provides voting rights to the acquiror's shareholders whenever the acquiror issues voting stock in the transaction that amounts to more than 20% of its pre-merger outstanding voting stock.

The *Voting Rule* and the *Class Vote Rule* applicable to long-form mergers are also applicable to the target's shareholders in a share exchange. Thus, Pennsylvania does not have the mandatory class vote requirement that is applicable under the share exchange provision of the MBCA (*see* § 11.04(f)).

4. Shareholder Dissenter's Rights

a. The Provision

See § 1931(d) of Pa. BCL.

b. Explanation and Comparison

Subject to the market-out exception in Section 1571(b)(1), Section 1931(d) grants dissenters rights to "[a]ny holder of shares that are to be canceled, exchanged or converted pursuant to a plan of exchange who objects to the plan and complies with the [rules regarding dissenter's rights]." The MBCA has a similar provision. (*See* § 13.02(a)(2)).

E. Sale of Assets Transactions

1. The Provision

See § 1932 of Pa. BCL

2. Board of Directors' Authorization, Explanation and Comparison

All or Substantially All Requirement. Section 1932 of the Pa. BCL governs the sale of "all or substantially all" of the assets of a "transferring corporation" (*i.e.*, the target). The "all or substantially all" concept is also in Delaware (*see* § 271)) and in California (*see* § 1001). However, it is not in the MBCA (*see* § 12.02), which has the similar concept of a transfer that "will leave the corporation without a significant continuing business activity."

Dissolution. Section 1932(b)(3) provides that "the plan may provide for the distribution to the shareholders of some or all of the consideration to be received by the corporation ..."

In Delaware, California and the MBCA, the dissolution is made pursuant to the dissolution provisions.

Board Approval. As in Delaware and the MBCA, only the board of directors of the target is required to adopt the "plan of asset transfer" for the disposition of "all or substantially all" of the target's assets. In this regard, Section 1932(b)(4) explicitly states that the "procedures of this subchapter shall not be applicable to the person acquiring the property or assets of the transferring corporation." This is in contrast to California, in which the boards of both the acquiror and the target must adopt the asset transfer if the consideration paid by the acquiror consists of its equity securities or certain debt securities (*see* §§ 181(c) and 1200)). However, if the underlying consideration is cash, then only the board of the transferring corporation needs to adopt the plan. Even though the board of the acquiror is not required by the asset transfer provisions of the Pa. BCL to adopt the plan of asset transfer, in fulfilling its fiduciary duties regarding the management of the corporation under Section 1721 of the Pa. BCL, the board of the acquiror would normally approve the asset acquisition.

3. Shareholder Authorization, Explanation and Comparison

As with Delaware, California, and the MBCA, the approval of the target's shareholders is required, and pursuant to Section 1932(b)(4), these shareholders have the same voting rights as in a two party merger. (*See* discussion of the *Voting Rule* and the *Class Vote Rule* under the section above dealing with direct long-form mergers.)

As in Delaware, shareholders of the acquiror are not entitled to vote on an asset acquisition. This is the case even if the acquiror issues more than 50% of its stock in the acquisition. This is in contrast to California (*see* § 1201(b)) and the MBCA (*see* § 6.21(f)) under which shareholders of the acquiror will have voting rights if the acquiror issues 20 percent or more of its voting stock pursuant to an asset transfer.

4. Shareholder Dissenter's Rights

a. The Provision

See § 1932(c) of Pa. BCL.

b. Explanation and Comparison

The Target's Shareholders. Section 1932(c)(1) provides that "[i]f a shareholder of a [target] that adopts a plan of asset transfer objects to the plan and complies with Subchapter D of Chapter 15 [relating to dissenter's rights], the shareholder shall be entitled to the rights and remedies of dissenting shareholders therein provided, if any." This provision seems to give all of the shareholders of the target the right to dissent, whether or not they have a right to vote, subject, of course, to the market-out exception.

This rule is the opposite of the rules in Delaware (*see* § 271), California (*see* § 1300(a)), and the MBCA (*see* § 12.02(g)), which deny dissenter's rights to the target's shareholders in these transactions.

The Acquiror's Shareholders. Pursuant to Section 1571(b)(3), the acquiror's shareholders do not have the right to dissent in an asset acquisition. This provision states:

> (3) The shareholders of a corporation that acquires by purchase, lease, exchange or other disposition all or substantially all of the shares, property or assets of another corporation by the issuance of shares, obligations or otherwise, with or without assuming the liabilities of the other corporation and with or without

> the intervention of another corporation or other person, shall not be entitled to the rights and remedies of dissenting shareholders provided in this subchapter regardless of the fact, if it be the case, that the acquisition was accomplished by the issuance of voting shares of the corporation to be outstanding immediately after the acquisition sufficient to elect a majority or more of the directors of the corporation.

This is the same as the rule in Delaware, California, and the MBCA.

5. The *De Facto* Merger Doctrine in PA.

a. See *Farris v. Glen Alden*, Section 2.13.B.2.

b. Repeal of the *De Facto* Merger Doctrine in PA.

Section 1904 of the Pa. BCL, which overrides the de facto merger doctrine in Pennsylvania, provides:

> § 1904. De facto transaction doctrine abolished
>
> The doctrine of de facto mergers, consolidations and other fundamental transactions is abolished and the rules laid down by *Bloch v. Baldwin Locomotive Works*, 75 Pa. D. & C. 24 (C.P. Del. Cty. 1950), and *Marks v. The Autocar Co.*, 153 F.Supp. 768 (E.D. Pa. 1954), and similar cases are overruled. A transaction that in form satisfies the requirements of this subpart may be challenged by reason of its substance only to the extent permitted by section 1105 (relating to restriction on equitable relief).

F. Short Form Mergers

1. The Provision

See § 1924(b)(1)(ii) of Pa. BCL.

2. Board of Directors' Authorization, Explanation and Comparison

Under all four bodies of law, only the board of the parent corporation is required to adopt a plan of merger. However, whereas under Delaware, California, and the MBCA, the parent must own at least 90% of the sub's outstanding stock, under Pennsylvania law, the parent must own at least 80% of the sub's outstanding stock.

3. No Shareholder Authorization

4. Shareholder Dissenter's Rights

a. The Provision

See § 1930 of Pa. BCL.

b. Explanation and Comparison

Under all four bodies of law, the target shareholders have an absolute right to dissent, which is not subject to the market-out exception.

§ 2.19 The ALI's Rules Relating to Director Action and Shareholder Voting and Dissenting in Arm's Length Mergers and Acquisitions

The ALI *Corporate Governance Project, supra* Section 1.10, contains proposals on shareholder voting and dissenting. *See generally* Thompson, *The M&A Provisions of the ALI Corporate Governance Project, supra* Section 1.10. The rules in general follow the MBCA.

References

ALI, *Corporate Governance Project, supra* Section 1.10, at Sections 6.01, 7.21–7.24.

Balotti and Finkelstein, *Delaware Corporate Law, supra* Section 1.10.

Easterbrook and Fischel, *The Economic Structure of Corporate Law* 145–161 (1991).

Folk on Delaware Corporate Law, supra Section 1.10.

Kling and Nugent, *Negotiated Acquisitions, supra* Section 1.10, at Chapter 4.

Thompson, *Mergers, Acquisitions and Tender Offers, supra* Section 1.10, Chapter 4.

Chapter 3

Directors' Fiduciary Duties in M&A Generally and in Using Poison Pills: Delaware with a Quick Look at Pennsylvania, the Model Act, and the ALI's Proposals

§ 3.1 Scope

This chapter provides an introduction to the legal standards governing the conduct of a corporation's board of directors in a merger and acquisition transaction. The focus is principally on the acquisition of publicly held target corporations. This chapter principally contains Delaware cases because (1) most publicly held corporations are incorporated in Delaware, and (2) Delaware law is the most highly developed law in this area. The chapter also presents several Pennsylvania cases, which, for the most part, take a different approach from the Delaware cases. In addition, the chapter presents a summary of the approaches taken to these issues by the Model Business Corporation Act (MBCA) and the American Law Institute. The topics addressed here are put to work in later chapters, principally Chapter 13, acquisitions of publicly-held firms in negotiated mergers, Chapter 14, management buyouts, and Chapter 23, defensive tactics. The materials in this chapter are covered in greater detail in Chapter 5 of Thompson, *Mergers, Acquisitions and Tender Offers*, *supra* Section 1.10.

Section 3.2 presents an introductory problem, and Section 3.3 introduces the duty of loyalty and duty of care. Section 3.4 presents an early duty of loyalty case, and Section 3.5 explores the parties who are owed the duty of loyalty. Section 3.6 sets out an early duty of care case and an early business judgment rule case. Section 3.7 introduces the entire fairness doctrine, and Section 3.8 sets out the *Schell* case, which demonstrates that a legal action may be enjoined because the action is not equitable. Section 3.9 introduces the duty of candor, which is also a fiduciary duty. Many cases dealing with fiduciary duties are addressed pursuant to motions to dismiss or motions for summary judgment, and Section 3.10, introduces the Delaware rules dealing with these motions. Section 3.11 discusses the differences between direct and derivative actions by shareholders; the distinction between these two types of actions can be important in litigation involving mergers and acquisitions. Section 3.12 discusses provisions of charters and bylaws dealing with the forum in which shareholder litigation is to take place. Section 3.13 discusses the concept of independence, an essential element in qualifying for the business judgment standard of review.

Section 3.14 sets out the "big-six" Delaware cases dealing with fiduciary duties: *Weinberger*, *Van Gorkom*, *Unocal*, *Moran*, *Revlon* and *Blasius*. An understanding of these six cases is the starting point for addressing fiduciary duty issues in M&A transactions. Section 3.15 examines the application of the business judgment rule in arm's length negotiated mergers and acquisitions. Thus, this section builds on *Van Gorkom*, probably the leading business judgment rule case in the country.

Section 3.16 elaborates on the application of the entire fairness doctrine to acquisitions by controlling shareholders, such as mergers in which a parent corporation acquires all of the stock or assets of a partially-owned subsidiary. Thus, this section builds on *Weinberger* by presenting, *inter alia*, the *MFW* case which was decided by the Delaware Supreme Court in March 2014. Section 3.17 addresses the following question: Does the entire fairness doctrine apply in a tender offer by a controlling shareholder for the stock of a sub held by minority shareholders where the tender offer is followed by a second step merger?

Section 3.18 elaborates on the enhanced business judgment rule standard of review that applies to takeover defenses under the Delaware Supreme Court's decision in *Unocal*. This section also provides an introduction to poison pills and discusses developments after the Delaware Supreme Court's decision in *Moran*, which involved the application of the enhanced business judgment rule on the adoption of a poison pill. Section 3.19 introduces the "quasi" duty to auction under the Delaware Supreme Court's decision in *Revlon*. This section also considers the Delaware Supreme Court's decisions in *Time*, involving Time's "Just Say No" defense against Paramount, and in *QVC*, involving Paramount's defensive strategy against QVC. The applicability of the *Revlon* doctrine in connection with negotiated mergers where cash is the consideration is also examined in Chapter 13, which deals with negotiated acquisitions of public companies.

Section 3.20 elaborates on fiduciary duty issues arising with the use of deal protection devices, such as "no solicitation," "lock-up" and "break-up fee" provisions of acquisition agreements. Section 3.21 elaborates on the compelling justification test adopted by the Delaware Chancery Court in *Blasius* and further developed by the Delaware Supreme Court in *Liquid Audio*. This test applies to attempts to interfere with the voting rights of shareholders.

Section 3.22 explores several issues that can arise when a controlling shareholder of a partially-controlled, publicly held target (1) disposes of the target, (2) receives a premium for itself over the amounts paid to the public shareholders, (3) sells itself rather than the sub, (4) causes the target to sell shares to a third party, and (5) acquires at a bargain the target's publicly held shares. Section 3.23 addresses the manner in which Pennsylvania law addresses many of these issues.[1] Section 3.24 briefly introduces the manner in which these issues are dealt with in the MBCA and Section 3.25 introduces the business judgment rule and the standard governing defensive actions adopted in the ALI's *Principles of Corporate Governance*.

§ 3.2 Introductory Problems on Directors' Duties

(1) The boards of directors of J.P. Morgan Chase & Co. (J.P. Morgan) and The Goldman Sachs Group, Inc. (Goldman Sachs), both publicly-held Delaware corporations, are negotiating a merger transaction in which a newly formed subsidiary of J.P. Morgan will merge into Goldman Sachs in a reverse subsidiary merger. *See* Chapter 2. In the merger

1. I thank Taimoor Choudhry, a 2014 graduate of Penn State Law and my former research assistant, for his very helpful assistance in preparing the materials dealing with Pennsylvania law.

the Goldman Sachs shareholders will receive stock of J.P. Morgan, and J.P. Morgan will end up owning all of the stock of Goldman Sachs. The directors of J.P. Morgan and of Goldman Sachs have no interest in the transaction other than their normal interests as directors, shareholders, and employees, if applicable. What standard governs the actions of J.P. Morgan's board? Goldman Sachs's board? Under what circumstance can the Goldman Sachs directors be held personally liable for structuring a transaction that gives the Goldman Sachs shareholders less than their shares are worth? Under what circumstances can the J.P. Morgan directors be personally liable if J.P. Morgan overpays for the Goldman Sachs shares? In negotiating the terms of the merger to what extent do the directors of J.P. Morgan and Goldman Sachs have an obligation to the holders of preferred stock or debt?

(2) Before the merger discussed in Question 1 is completed, Citigroup, Inc., a publicly-held Delaware corporation, makes an unsolicited tender offer for J.P. Morgan. J.P. Morgan and Goldman Sachs respond by restructuring their merger as a friendly tender offer by J.P. Morgan for the stock of Goldman Sachs to be followed with a second-step freezeout merger of the Goldman Sachs shareholders that do not have their shares acquired in the tender offer. If this tender offer is allowed to proceed, Citigroup will not complete its tender offer for J.P. Morgan. Many of the J.P. Morgan shareholders very much want the opportunity to tender their shares to Citigroup. What standard governs the actions of the boards of Citigroup, J.P. Morgan, and Goldman Sachs? Are any of the directors exposed to possible personal liability?

J.P. Morgan also has a standard flip-in and flip-over poison pill. What standard applied to J.P. Morgan's board upon adoption of the poison pill? What standard applies to the decision of J.P. Morgan's board not to redeem the pill in the face of Citigroup's tender offer?

(3) J.P. Morgan has completed its tender offer for Goldman Sachs and J.P. Morgan now owns 50% of the outstanding Goldman Sachs shares. Citigroup has terminated its tender offer. What standard governs transactions between J.P. Morgan and its partially owned subsidiary, Goldman Sachs? If, pursuant to an arrangement worked out with the Goldman Sachs directors before the tender offer, J.P. Morgan completes the freezeout merger shortly after the tender offer, what standard applies to the J.P. Morgan and Goldman Sachs directors in the freezeout merger? If, on the other hand, J.P. Morgan waits and completes the merger after holding the Goldman Sachs stock for several years, what standard applies to the J.P. Morgan and Goldman Sachs directors?

§ 3.3 Introduction to Director's Duty of Loyalty and Duty of Care

ALI, Principles of Corporate Governance: Analysis and Recommendations

Vol. I, P. 137 (1994)

The relationship between duty of care and duty of fair dealing. The legal obligations of directors and officers have traditionally been divided into the categories of duty of care and duty of loyalty; the latter is referred to in Part V of these *Principles* as the duty of fair dealing. *The Corporate Director's Guidebook* properly distinguishes between the two as follows:

Duty of Loyalty. By assuming his office, the corporate director commits allegiance to the enterprise and acknowledges that the best interests of the corporation and its shareholders must prevail over any individual interest of his own. The basic principle to be observed is that the director should not use his corporate position to make a personal profit or gain other personal advantage * * *.

Duty of Care. In addition to owing a duty of loyalty to the corporation, the corporate director also assumes a duty to act carefully in fulfilling the important tasks of monitoring and directing the activities of corporate management. * * *

§ 3.4 Illustrative Duty of Loyalty Case—*Loft*

Guth v. Loft, Inc.

Delaware Supreme Court, (1939) 5 A.2d 503

[The issue was whether the defendant, Guth, had appropriated for himself an opportunity to acquire the right to manufacture Pepsi-Cola that belonged to the corporation, Loft.] Corporate officers and directors are not permitted to use their position of trust and confidence to further their private interests. While technically not trustees, they stand in a fiduciary relation to the corporation and its stockholders. A public policy, existing through the years, and derived from a profound knowledge of human characteristics and motives, has established a rule that demands of a corporate officer or director, peremptorily and inexorably, the most scrupulous observance of his duty, not only affirmatively to protect the interests of the corporation committed to his charge, but also to refrain from doing anything that would work injury to the corporation, or to deprive it of profit or advantage which his skill and ability might properly bring to it, or to enable it to make in the reasonable and lawful exercise of its powers. The rule that requires an undivided and unselfish loyalty to the corporation demands that there shall be no conflict between duty and self-interest.

Upon a consideration of all the facts and circumstances as disclosed we are convinced that the opportunity to acquire the Pepsi-Cola trademark and formula, goodwill and business belonged to the complainant, and that Guth, as its President, had no right to appropriate the opportunity to himself. * * *

Note

Guth v. Loft, Inc. is one of the leading duty of loyalty cases in Delaware. State precisely the holding of the case. *See e.g.*, Kenneth B. Davis, Jr., *Corporate Opportunity and Comparative Advantage*, 84 Iowa L. Rev. 211 (1999).

§ 3.5 To Whom Is the Duty of Loyalty Owed?—*Marriott*

HB Korenvaes Investments, L.P. v. Marriott Corporation

Delaware Court of Chancery, (1993) CCH Fed Sec Law Rep ¶ 97, 728

Opinion of Allen, Chancellor.

Plaintiff's claim that the proposed distribution of a special dividend to the common stockholders of Marriott Corporation consisting of securities representing a large part of the net worth of that company would, if accomplished, constitute a breach of duty owed to them as holders of Marriott's preferred stock. The transaction is to be voted upon by holders of common stock of the company at a forthcoming shareholders' meeting. * * * This spin-off will be effectuated through the transfer of the spin-off assets to International (presently a wholly-owned Marriott subsidiary) followed by a dividend to the holders of Marriott's common stock of all of the stock of International. It is alleged that in this spin-off most of Marriott's assets that generate a positive cash flow will be transferred to International. * * *

[A]mong other things, plaintiffs complain that the planned transaction constitutes a breach of the terms of the certificate of designation that defines the relative rights of the Series A Preferred Stock. Most notably, the proposed transaction will have the effect, it is said, of allowing the Marriott common stockholders to receive cash dividends while the preferred stock receives none, in contravention of a basic right of the preferred. The proposed transaction is also said to constitute a breach of a fiduciary duty of loyalty and care and of the contractual obligations of good faith and fair dealing. * * *

In what follows I set forth my opinion that, with respect to the proposed special dividend, the rights of plaintiffs are contractual in nature and not equitable. That is, I conclude that with respect to this transaction, the directors of Marriott Corporation owe no duty of loyalty to holders of the preferred stock. * * *

Rights of preferred stock are primarily but not exclusively contractual in nature. The special rights, limitations, etc., of preferred stock are created by the corporate charter or a certificate of designation which acts as an amendment to a certificate of incorporation. Thus, to a very large extent, to ask what are the rights of the preferred stock is to ask what are the rights and obligations created contractually by the certificate of designation. * * *

[G]iven the terms of the certificate of designation I conclude that the proposed transaction does not implicate or engage the directors' duty of loyalty but must be evaluated under the contractual law governing the special rights and preferences of the preferred. * * *

§ 3.6 Illustrative Duty of Care and Business Judgment Rule Cases—*Lutz* and *Puma*

A. Duty of Care—*Lutz*

Lutz v. Boas

Delaware Court of Chancery, (1961) 171 A.2d 381

Seitz, Chancellor.

[An action was brought against both inside directors and non-affiliated directors of certain mutual funds for failure to properly supervise.]

The non-affiliated directors had the same responsibility as that of the ordinary directors of a Delaware corporation. * * *

Based upon my view of the evidence I make certain findings of fact: these non-affiliated directors gave almost automatic approval to the Management Agreement; they did not examine the registration statements carefully; they did not discuss securities at their meetings or discuss any of the other facts which would have been pertinent to a reasonable discharge of their duties; most of the time at the directors' meeting was spent in determining dividends * * *; the directors did not know who selected securities for purchase or sale; they did not inform themselves about the rate of turnover and how the brokerage business was being distributed. * * *

What is the extent of the liability of these grossly negligent directors? * * *

I conclude that because of this negligence these directors must be held jointly and severally liable with [the other defendants] for the payments made to Associates after June 12, 1954. * * *

Note

Lutz v. Boas is one of the leading duty of care cases in Delaware. State precisely the holding of the case.

B. Business Judgment Rule, Requirement of Disinterestedness—*Puma*

Puma v. Marriott

Delaware Court of Chancery, (1971) 283 A.2d 693

SHORT, Vice Chancellor.

This is a stockholder's derivative action which challenges the fairness of a transaction entered into by Marriott Corporation (Marriott), a Delaware corporation, whereby Marriott, in exchange for 313,000 shares of its common stock, acquired all of the stock of six corporations principally owned by members of the Marriott family. [The transaction was approved unanimously by Marriott's outside directors.] * * *

Plaintiff contends that since the case involves insiders dealing with their corporation the test of validity of the transaction is fairness. That our courts have frequently so held is without question. Thus in *Sterling v. Mayflower Hotel Corp.* the Supreme Court said: "Since they stand on both sides of the transaction, they bear the burden of establishing its entire fairness." * * * [*See also, Levien v. Sinclair Oil Corp.*, Section 3.7] * * * In each of the cited cases, however, it either affirmatively appeared that the insider or insiders dominated the board of directors or the court found such to be the fact. Except to point out that the Marriott Group owned some 46% of the Marriott stock plaintiff here has utterly failed to make any showing of domination of the outside directors. * * *

I conclude that since the transaction complained of was accomplished as a result of the exercise of independent business judgment of the outside, independent directors whose sole interest was the furtherance of the corporate enterprise, the court is precluded from substituting its uninformed opinion for that of the experienced, independent board members of Marriott. * * *

Question

In reviewing subsequent cases in this chapter, consider whether *Puma* is still good law in Delaware.

§ 3.7 Transactions Between Parent and Sub Corporations, Business Judgment Rule or Entire Fairness—*Sinclair*

Sinclair Oil Corporation v. Levien

Delaware Superior Court, 1971 280 A.2d 717

This is an appeal by the defendant, Sinclair Oil Corporation (hereafter Sinclair), from an order of the Court of Chancery in a derivative action requiring Sinclair to account for damages sustained by its subsidiary, Sinclair Venezuelan Oil Company (hereafter Sinven), organized by Sinclair for the purpose of operating in Venezuela, as a result of dividends paid by Sinven, the denial to Sinven of industrial development, and a breach of contract between Sinclair's wholly-owned subsidiary, Sinclair International Oil Company, and Sinven.

The Chancellor held that because of Sinclair's fiduciary duty and its control over Sinven, its relationship with Sinven must meet the test of intrinsic [entire] fairness. * * * Under this standard the burden is on Sinclair to prove, subject to careful judicial scrutiny, that its transactions with Sinven were objectively fair. *Guth v. Loft, Inc.*, [Section 3.4]

Sinclair argues that the transactions between it and Sinven should be tested, not by the test of intrinsic fairness with the accompanying shift of the burden of proof, but by the business judgment rule under which a court will not interfere with the judgment of a board of directors unless there is a showing of gross and palpable overreaching. A board of directors enjoys a presumption of sound business judgment, and its decisions will not be disturbed if they can be attributed to any rational business purpose. A court under such circumstances will not substitute its own notions of what is or is not sound business judgment.

We think, however, that Sinclair's argument in this respect is misconceived. When the situation involves a parent and a subsidiary, with the parent controlling the transaction and fixing the terms, the test of intrinsic fairness, with its resulting shifting of the burden of proof, is applied. *Sterling v. Mayflower Hotel Corp.* The basic situation for the application of the rule is the one in which the parent has received a benefit to the exclusion and at the expense of the subsidiary. * * *

A parent does indeed owe a fiduciary duty to its subsidiary when there are parent–subsidiary dealings. However, this alone will not evoke the intrinsic fairness standard. This standard will be applied only when the fiduciary duty is accompanied by self-dealing—the situation when a parent is on both sides of a transaction with its subsidiary. Self-dealing occurs when the parent, by virtue of its domination of the subsidiary, causes the subsidiary to act in such a way that the parent receives something from the subsidiary to the exclusion of, and detriment to, the minority stockholders of the subsidiary.

We turn now to the facts. The plaintiff argues that, from 1960 through 1966, Sinclair caused Sinven to pay out such excessive dividends that the industrial development of Sinven was effectively prevented, and it became in reality a corporation in dissolution. * * *

[I]t must be determined whether the dividend payments by Sinven were, in essence, self-dealing by Sinclair. The dividends resulted in great sums of money being transferred from Sinven to Sinclair. However, a proportionate share of this money was received by the minority shareholders of Sinven. Sinclair received nothing from Sinven to the exclusion of its minority stockholders. As such, these dividends were not self-dealing. We hold therefore that the Chancellor erred in applying the intrinsic fairness test as to these dividend payments. The business judgment standard should have been applied.

We conclude that the facts demonstrate that the dividend payments complied with the business judgment standard and with 8 Del.C. § 170. * * *

[The court, however, applied the intrinsic fairness [i.e., the entire fairness] test to claims of denial of industrial development and breach of contract.]

Questions

The Court here says that under the business judgment rule, "[A] board of directors enjoys a presumption of sound business judgment, and its decisions will not be disturbed if they can be attributed to any rational business purpose." What test should be applied in determining whether a business purpose is "rational"? Is this "rational" standard sound?

§ 3.8 The Difference Between What Is Legal and What Is Equitable—*Schnell*

Schnell v. Chris-Craft Industries, Inc.

Delaware Supreme Court, 1971 285 A.2d 437

HERRMANN, Justice (for the majority of the Court):

This is an appeal from the denial by the Court of Chancery of the petition of dissident stockholders for injunctive relief to prevent management from advancing the date of the annual stockholders' meeting from January 11, 1972, as previously set by the by-laws, to December 8, 1971.

It will be seen that the Chancery Court considered all of the reasons stated by management as business reasons for changing the date of the meeting; but that those reasons were rejected by the Court below in making the following findings:

> "I am satisfied, however, in a situation in which present management has disingenuously resisted the production of a list of its stockholders to plaintiffs or their confederates and has otherwise turned a deaf ear to plaintiffs' demands about a change in management designed to lift defendant from its present business doldrums, management has seized on a relatively new section of the Delaware Corporation Law for the purpose of cutting down on the amount of time which would otherwise have been available to plaintiffs and others for the waging of a proxy battle. * * *"

In our view, those conclusions amount to a finding that management has attempted to utilize the corporate machinery and the Delaware Law for the purpose of perpetuating itself in office; and, to that end, for the purpose of obstructing the legitimate efforts of dissident stockholders in the exercise of their rights to undertake a proxy contest against management. These are inequitable purposes, contrary to established principles of corporate democracy. The advancement by directors of the by-law date of a stockholders' meeting, for such purposes, may not be permitted to stand. * * *

Management contends that it has complied strictly with the provisions of the new Delaware Corporation Law in changing the by-law date. The answer to that contention, of course, is that inequitable action does not become permissible simply because it is legally possible. * * *

Accordingly, the judgment below must be reversed and the cause remanded, with instruction to nullify the December 8 date as a meeting date for stockholders; to reinstate January 11, 1972 as the sole date of the next annual meeting of the stockholders of the corporation; and to take such other proceedings and action as may be consistent herewith regarding the stock record closing date and any other related matters.

§ 3.9 Duty of Candor and the Materiality Standard in Delaware

A. General Principles—*Arnold, Gantler, Malone,* and *Skeen*

The Delaware Supreme Court in *Arnold v. Society for Savings Bancorp, Inc.*[2] discussed as follows the disclosure duty applicable to directors and controlling shareholders:

2. Arnold v. Soc'y for Sav. Bancorp, Inc., 650 A.2d 1270 (Del. 1994).

> The genesis of Delaware law regarding disclosure obligations can be traced to the seminal case of *Lynch v. Vickers Energy Corp.*, Del.Supr., 383 A.2d 278 (1978), where, in the context of a self-tender, this Court held that a majority stockholder "owed a fiduciary duty ... which required 'complete candor' in disclosing fully 'all the facts and circumstances surrounding the' tender offer." 383 A.2d at 279 (quoting *Lynch v. Vickers Energy Corp.*, Del.Ch., 351 A.2d 570, 573 (1976)); *accord Shell Petroleum, Inc. v. Smith, Del.Supr.*, 606 A.2d 112, 114–115 (1992) (majority stockholder bears burden of showing full disclosure of all facts within its knowledge that are material to stockholder action). A number of subsequent decisions have recognized the existence of fiduciary disclosure obligations....
>
> In *Stroud* [*v. Grace*, Del.Supr. 606 A.2d 75 (1992)] the Court explicated that the disclosure obligation "represents nothing more than the well-recognized proposition that directors of Delaware corporations are under a fiduciary duty to disclose fully and fairly all material information within the board's control when it seeks shareholder action." The obligation attaches to proxy statements and any other disclosures in contemplation of stockholder action.[3]

The *Arnold* court also set out the standard for determining whether the disclosure obligation has been satisfied:

> The essential inquiry is whether the alleged omission or misrepresentation is material. *e.g.*, *Stroud*, 606 A.2d at 84.
>
>> Materiality is defined as follows: An omitted fact is material if there is a substantial likelihood that a reasonable shareholder would consider it important in deciding how to vote.
>
> *TSC Indus. v. Northway, Inc.*, [defining materiality under the Federal securities laws, *see* Chapter 4].... [M]ateriality is to be assessed from the viewpoint of the "reasonable" stockholder, not from a director's subjective perspective.[4]

In its 2009 decision in *Gantler*[5] the Delaware Supreme Court describes the "fiduciary duty to disclose" as follows:

> It is well-settled law that "directors of Delaware corporations [have] a fiduciary duty to disclose fully and fairly all material information within the board's control when it seeks shareholder action." That duty "attaches to proxy statements and any other disclosures in contemplation of stockholder action." The essential inquiry here is whether the alleged omission or misrepresentation is material. The burden of establishing materiality rests with the plaintiff, who must demonstrate "a substantial likelihood that the disclosure of the omitted fact would have been viewed by the reasonable investor as having significantly altered the 'total mix' of information made available."[6]

In its 1998 decision in *Malone v. Brincat*, the Delaware Supreme Court said the following concerning the origin of the disclosure duty: "The duty of directors to observe proper disclosure requirements derives from the combination of the fiduciary duties of care, loyalty and good faith."[7]

---

3. *Id.* at 1276–1277.
4. *Id.* at 1277.
5. Gantler v. Stephens, No. 132, 2008, 2009 Del. LEXIS 33 (Del. Jan. 27, 2009).
6. *Id.* at *34–*35.
7. Malone v. Brincat, 722 A.2d 5, 11 (1998).

Without respect to whether the disclosure duty is a free standing fiduciary duty or merely part of the duties of care, loyalty and good faith, in virtually all merger cases there will be a claim that the directors or controlling shareholder failed to satisfy the disclosure duties. Thus, in executing any merger or acquisition transaction, the directors and controlling shareholders should be careful to ensure that they fully comply with the disclosure duty. Review the discussion of the disclosure requirement in appraisal transactions as addressed in *Skeen*, Section 2.10.H, and in going private transactions as addressed in *Pure Resources*, Section 3.9.B.

B. Disclosure of Investment Banker's Valuation Opinions—*Pure Resources*

In Re Pure Resources, Inc., Shareholders Litigation

Delaware Court of Chancery, 2002 Del. Ch. Lexis 112

STRINE, Vice Chancellor.

[In this case, Unocal, the controlling shareholder of Pure Resources, made a tender offer for the minority stock of Pure with a plan to follow the tender offer with a second-step short form merger. Set out below is then Vice Chancellor Strine's discussion of the rule that he thinks should apply relating to the disclosure of an investment banker's valuation of the stock of a company.]

The Plaintiffs' Disclosure Claims. As their other basis for attack, the plaintiffs argue that neither of the key disclosure documents provided to the Pure stockholders—the S-4 Unocal issued in support of its Offer and the 14D-9 Pure filed in reaction to the Offer—made materially complete and accurate disclosure. The general legal standards that govern the plaintiffs' disclosure claims are settled. * * *

The plaintiffs advance a plethora of disclosure claims, only the most important of which can be addressed in the time frame available to me. I therefore address them in order of importance, as I see them.

First and foremost, the plaintiffs argue that the 14D-9 is deficient because it does not disclose *any* substantive portions of the work of First Boston and Petrie Parkman [investment banking firms] on behalf of the Special Committee, even though the bankers' negative views of the Offer are cited as a basis for the board's own recommendation not to tender. Having left it to the Pure minority to say no for themselves, the Pure board (the plaintiffs say) owed the minority the duty to provide them with material information about the value of Pure's shares, including, in particular, the estimates and underlying analyses of value developed by the Special Committee's bankers. This duty is heightened, the plaintiffs say, because the Pure minority is subject to an immediate short-form merger if the Offer proceeds as Unocal hopes, and will have to make the decision whether to seek appraisal in those circumstances.

In response, the Pure director-defendants argue that the 14D-9 contains a great deal of financial information, including the actual opinions of [Pure's investment bankers,] First Boston and Petrie Parkman. * * *

[T]he director-defendants cite Delaware case law that indicates that a summary of the results of the actual valuation analyses conducted by an investment banker ordinarily need not be disclosed.

This is a continuation of an ongoing debate in Delaware corporate law, and one I confess to believing has often been answered in an intellectually unsatisfying manner. Fearing stepping on the SEC's toes and worried about encouraging prolix disclosures, the

Delaware courts have been reluctant to require informative, succinct disclosure of investment banker analyses in circumstances in which the bankers' views about value have been cited as justifying the recommendation of the board. But this reluctance has been accompanied by more than occasional acknowledgement of the utility of such information, acknowledgement that is understandable given the substantial encouragement Delaware case law has given to the deployment of investment bankers by boards of directors addressing mergers and tender offers.

These conflicting impulses were manifested recently in two Supreme Court opinions. In one, *Skeen v. Jo-Ann Stores, Inc.*, [Section 2.10.H], the Court was inclined towards the view that a summary of the bankers' analyses and conclusions was not material to a stockholders' decision whether to seek appraisal. In the other, *McMullin v. Beran,* [Section 3.22.B], the Court implied that information about the analytical work of the board's banker could well be material in analogous circumstances.

In my view, it is time that this ambivalence be resolved in favor of a firm statement that stockholders are entitled to a fair summary of the substantive work performed by the investment bankers upon whose advice the recommendations of their board as to how to vote on a merger or tender rely. I agree that our law should not encourage needless prolixity, but that concern cannot reasonably apply to investment bankers' analyses, which usually address the most important issue to stockholders—the sufficiency of the consideration being offered to them for their shares in a merger or tender offer. Moreover, courts must be candid in acknowledging that the disclosure of the banker's "fairness opinion" alone and without more, provides stockholders with nothing other than a conclusion, qualified by a gauze of protective language designed to insulate the banker from liability.

The real informative value of the banker's work is not in its bottom-line conclusion, but in the valuation analysis that buttresses that result. This proposition is illustrated by the work of the judiciary itself, which closely examines the underlying analyses performed by the investment bankers when determining whether a transaction price is fair or a board reasonably relied on the banker's advice. Like a court would in making an after-the-fact fairness determination, a Pure minority stockholder engaging in the before-the-fact decision whether to tender would find it material to know the basic valuation exercises that First Boston and Petrie Parkman undertook, the key assumptions that they used in performing them, and the range of values that were thereby generated. After all, these were the very advisors who played the leading role in shaping the Special Committee's finding of inadequacy. * * *

Although there are other reasons why I find this type of information material, one final policy reason will suffice for now. When controlling stockholders make tender offers, they have large informational advantages that can only be imperfectly overcome by the special committee process, which almost invariably involves directors who are not involved in the day-to-day management of the subsidiary. The retention of financial advisors by special committees is designed to offset some of this asymmetry, and it would seem to be in full keeping with that goal for the minority stockholders to be given a summary of the core analyses of these advisors in circumstances in which the stockholders must protect themselves in the voting or tender process. That this can be done without great burden is demonstrated by the many transactions in which meaningful summary disclosure of bankers' opinions are made, either by choice or by SEC rule.[8]

---

8. In certain going private transactions, the SEC requires that the entire investment banker board presentation books be made public as an exhibit. This requirement has hardly had a deal-stopping effect.

For all these reasons, I conclude that the plaintiffs have shown a reasonable probability of success on their claim that the 14D-9 [the disclosure document issued by Pure] omits material information regarding the First Boston and Petrie Parkman analyses. * * *

§ 3.10 Delaware Motions to Dismiss and for Summary Judgment

A. Introduction

The merger and acquisition area produces a significant amount of litigation. This litigation can involve many parties including: the acquiror, the target, the acquiror's directors and shareholders, and the target's directors and shareholders. Often the litigation revolves around claims that the directors of the target corporation have violated their duty of loyalty or duty of care.

In many of the cases, the defendant will (1) move to dismiss the action at the pleading stage, or (2) move for summary judgment after discovery and before trial. This section introduces the rules of the Delaware Court of Chancery governing motions to dismiss and for summary judgment. The next section addresses the difference between direct and derivative actions in Delaware and discusses motions by a corporation to defeat the control by shareholders of a derivative action.

B. Delaware Court of Chancery, Rule 12(b)(6), Motion to Dismiss

1. Rule 12(b)(6)

Rule 12. Defenses and objections—When and how presented—By pleading or motion—

Motion for judgment on pleadings. * * *

(b) How presented.—Every defense, in law or fact, to a claim for relief in any pleading, whether a claim, counterclaim, cross-claim or third-party claim, shall be asserted in the responsive pleading thereto if one is required, except that the following defenses may at the option of the pleader be made by motion: * * * (6) failure to state a claim upon which relief can be granted * * *. If, on a motion asserting the defense numbered (6) to dismiss for failure of the pleading to state a claim upon which relief can be granted, matters outside the pleading are presented to and not excluded by the Court, the motion shall be treated as one for summary judgment and disposed of as provided in Rule 56, and all parties shall be given reasonable opportunity to present all material made pertinent to such a motion by Rule 56.

2. Discussion of Rule 12(b)(6)—*Malpiede*

Malpiede v. Townson

Delaware Supreme Court, 2001 780 A.2d 1075

We review de novo the dismissal by the Court of Chancery of a complaint under Rule 12(b)(6). The complaint ordinarily defines the universe of facts from which the trial court may draw in ruling on a motion to dismiss. Because a motion to dismiss under Chancery Rule 12(b)(6) must be decided without the benefit of a factual record, the Court of Chancery may not resolve material factual disputes; instead, the court is required to assume as true the well-pleaded allegations in the complaint. The trial court may dismiss a complaint under Rule 12(b)(6) only where the court determines with "reasonable certainty" that the plaintiff could prevail on no set of facts that may be inferred from the well-pleaded allegations in the complaint. This standard is based on the "notice pleading" requirement established in Ct. Ch. R. 8(e) and is "less stringent than the standard applied when evaluating whether a pre-suit demand has been excused in a stockholder derivative suit filed pursuant to Chancery Rule 23.1." [Rule 23.1 is discussed below.]

Of course, the trial court is not required to accept every strained interpretation of the allegations proposed by the plaintiff, but the plaintiff is entitled to all reasonable inferences that logically flow from the face of the complaint. Moreover, a claim may be dismissed if allegations in the complaint or in the exhibits incorporated into the complaint effectively negate the claim as a matter of law. * * *

C. Delaware Court of Chancery Rule 56, Motions for Summary Judgment

1. Rule 56

Rule 56. Summary judgment

(a) For claimant.—A party seeking to recover upon a claim, counter claim, cross-claim or declaratory judgment may, at any time after the expiration of 20 days from the commencement of the action or after service of a motion for summary judgment by the adverse party move with or without supporting affidavits for a summary judgment in the party's favor upon all or any part thereof.

(b) For defending party.—A party against whom a claim, counterclaim, cross-claim or declaratory judgment is asserted may, at any time, move with or without supporting affidavits for a summary judgment in the party's favor as to all or any part thereof.

(c) Motion and proceedings thereon.—* * *The judgment sought shall be rendered forthwith if the pleadings, depositions, answers to interrogatories and admissions on file, together with the affidavits, if any, show that there is no genuine issue as to any material fact and that the moving party is entitled to a judgment as a matter of law. A summary judgment, interlocutory in character, may be rendered on the issues of liability alone although there is a genuine issue as to the amount of damages, or some other matter. * * *

2. Discussion of Rule 56 and Its Relationship to Rule 12(b)(6)—*Zapata, Lyondell,* and *Malpiede*

Zapata Corp. v. Maldonado

Delaware Supreme Court, 1981, 430 A.2d 779

[T]he moving party should be prepared to meet the normal burden under Rule 56 that there is no genuine issue as to any material fact and that the moving party is entitled to dismiss as a matter of law.

Lyondell Chemical Company v. Ryan

Delaware Supreme Court, 2009, 970 A.2d 235

Summary judgment [under Rule 56] may be granted if there are no material issues of fact in dispute and the moving party is entitled to judgment as a matter of law. The facts, and all reasonable inferences, must be considered in the light most favorable to the nonmoving party.

Malpiede v. Townson

Delaware Supreme Court, 2001 780 A.2d 1075

[O]n a Rule 12(b)(6) motion to dismiss, if matters outside the pleading are presented to and not excluded by the Court the motion shall be treated as one for summary judgment and disposed of as provided in Rule 56. * * * .

Under Rule 56 in this context, there may be an opportunity for either side to submit affidavits or engage in discovery to explore the "matter outside the pleadings [that had been] ... presented to and not excluded by the Court."

Simply because a matter outside the pleading has been presented under Rule 12(b)(6) and thereby must be "treated as one for summary judgment" with "all parties ... given a reasonable opportunity to present all material made pertinent to such a motion by Rule 56," it does not follow that the "floodgates of discovery" have to be opened. The Rule 56 opportunity to present affidavits or engage in discovery is not absolute. * * *

§ 3.11 Introduction to Direct and Derivative Actions in Delaware

A. Significance for Mergers and Acquisitions

An action brought by shareholders against directors can be either derivative, brought for the benefit of the corporation, or direct, brought for the benefit of the shareholders directly. One of the principal differences between direct and derivative actions is that in a derivative action the shareholder-plaintiff may have to give the corporation the opportunity to pursue or not pursue the litigation. On the other hand, in a direct action, the shareholder-plaintiff is in complete control of his side of the case. Thus, shareholders would generally prefer to have litigation classified as direct.

B. Delaware Court of Chancery Rule 23.1

Rule 23.1. Derivative actions by shareholders.

(a) In a derivative action brought by one or more shareholders * * * to enforce a right of a corporation * * *, the corporation * * * having failed to enforce a right which may properly be asserted by it, the complaint shall allege that the plaintiff was a shareholder * * * at the time of the transaction of which the plaintiff complains or that the plaintiff's share * * * thereafter devolved on the plaintiff by operation of law. The complaint shall also allege with particularity the efforts, if any, made by the plaintiff to obtain the action the plaintiff desires from the directors * * * and the reasons for the plaintiff's failure to obtain the action or for not making the effort.

C. Delaware Supreme Court's View on Derivative and Direct Actions-Two Prong Test—*DLJ*

Tooley v. Donaldson, Lufkin, & Jenrette, Inc.

Delaware Supreme Court, (2004) 845 A.2d 1031

VEASEY, Chief Justice.

* * **The Proper Analysis to Distinguish Between Direct and Derivative Actions.*The analysis must be based solely on the following questions: Who suffered the alleged harm—the corporation or the suing stockholder individually—and who would receive the benefit of the recovery or other remedy? This simple analysis is well imbedded in our jurisprudence. * * *

Determining whether an action is derivative or direct is sometimes difficult and has many legal consequences, some of which may have an expensive impact on the parties to the action. For example, if an action is derivative, the plaintiffs are then required to comply with the requirements of Court of Chancery Rule 23.1, that the stockholder: (a) retain ownership of the shares throughout the litigation; (b) make pre-suit demand on the board [*i.e.*, demand that the board undertake the action on behalf of the corporation]; and (c) obtain court approval of any settlement. Further, the recovery, if any, flows only to the corporation. The decision whether a suit is direct or derivative may be outcome-determinative. Therefore, it is necessary that a standard to distinguish such actions be clear, simple and consistently articulated and applied by our courts. * * *

The proper analysis has been and should remain that stated in *Grimes*, *Kramer* and *Parnes*. That is, a court should look to the nature of the wrong and to whom the relief should go. The stockholder's claimed direct injury must be independent of any alleged injury to the corporation. The stockholder must demonstrate that the duty breached was owed to the stockholder and that he or she can prevail without showing an injury to the corporation. * * *

D. The Relationship between Derivative Actions, Demand Futility and the Business Judgment Rule in Delaware—*Aronson*

Aronson v. Lewis

Delaware Supreme Court, (1984) 473 A.2d 805

MOORE, Justice.

In the wake of *Zapata Corp. v. Maldonado*, Del.Supr., 430 A.2d 779 (1981), this Court left a crucial issue unanswered: when is a stockholder's demand upon a board of directors, to redress an alleged wrong to the corporation, excused as futile prior to the filing of a derivative suit [pursuant to Rule 23.1]? * * *

[**The Business Judgment Rule**] In our view the entire question of demand futility is inextricably bound to issues of business judgment and the standards of that doctrine's applicability. The business judgment rule is an acknowledgment of the managerial prerogatives of Delaware directors under Section 141(a). It is a presumption that in making a business decision the directors of a corporation acted on an informed basis, in good faith and in the honest belief that the action taken was in the best interests of the company. Absent an abuse of discretion, that judgment will be respected by the courts. The burden is on the party challenging the decision to establish facts rebutting the presumption. *See Puma v. Marriott*, [Section 3.6.B]. * * *

The function of the business judgment rule is of paramount significance in the context of a derivative action. It comes into play in several ways—in addressing a demand, in the determination of demand futility, in efforts by independent disinterested directors to dismiss the action as inimical to the corporation's best interests, and generally, as a defense to the merits of the suit. However, in each of these circumstances there are certain common principles governing the application and operation of the rule.

First, its protections can only be claimed by disinterested directors whose conduct otherwise meets the tests of business judgment. From the standpoint of interest, this means that directors can neither appear on both sides of a transaction nor expect to derive any personal financial benefit from it in the sense of self-dealing, as opposed to a benefit which devolves upon the corporation or all stockholders generally. Thus, if such director interest is present, and the transaction is not approved by a majority consisting of the disinterested directors, then the business judgment rule has no application whatever in determining demand futility. *See* § 144(a)(1).

Second, to invoke the rule's protection directors have a duty to inform themselves, prior to making a business decision, of all material information reasonably available to them. Having become so informed, they must then act with requisite care in the discharge of their duties. While the Delaware cases use a variety of terms to describe the applicable standard of care, our analysis satisfies us that under the business judgment rule director liability is predicated upon concepts of gross negligence. * * *

[I]t should be noted that the business judgment rule operates only in the context of director action. Technically speaking, it has no role where directors have either abdicated their functions, or absent a conscious decision, failed to act. But it also follows that under applicable principles, a conscious decision to refrain from acting may nonetheless be a valid exercise of business judgment and enjoy the protections of the rule. * * *

Our view is that in determining demand futility the Court of Chancery in the proper exercise of its discretion must decide whether, under the particularized facts alleged, a reasonable doubt is created that: (1) the directors are disinterested and independent [or] (2) the challenged transaction was otherwise the product of a valid exercise of business judgment. Hence, the Court of Chancery must make two inquiries, one into the independence and disinterestedness of the directors and the other into the substantive nature of the challenged transaction and the board's approval thereof. As to the latter inquiry the court does not assume that the transaction is a wrong to the corporation requiring corrective steps by the board. Rather, the alleged wrong is substantively reviewed against the factual background alleged in the complaint. As to the former inquiry, directorial independence and disinterestedness, the court reviews the factual allegations to decide whether they raise a reasonable doubt, as a threshold matter, that the protections of the business judgment rule are available to the board. * * *

In sum, we conclude that the plaintiff has failed to allege facts with particularity indicating that the [company's] directors were tainted by interest, lacked independence, or took action contrary to [the company's] best interests in order to create a reasonable doubt as to the applicability of the business judgment rule. Only in the presence of such a reasonable doubt may a demand be deemed futile. * * *

E. Demand Futility in the Context of the Absence of a Business Decision—*Stone, Caremark,* and *Rales*

Stone v. Ritter

Delaware Supreme Court 2006, 911 A.2d 362

HOLLAND, Justice: * * *

This is an appeal from a final judgment of the Court of Chancery dismissing a derivative complaint against fifteen present and former directors of AmSouth Bancorporation ("AmSouth"), a Delaware corporation. The [shareholder] plaintiffs * * * filed their derivative complaint without making a pre-suit demand on AmSouth's board of directors (the "Board").

Unlike a challenge to a business decision made by the board, which possibly is protected by the business judgment rule, the [Court of Chancery characterized the allegations in the derivative complaint as a "classic *Caremark* claim," a claim that derives its name from *In re Caremark Int'l Deriv. Litig* [698 A.2d 959 (Del. Ch. 1996)].

[In *Caremark*, the Court of Chancery recognized that: "[g]enerally where a claim of directorial liability for corporate loss is predicated upon ignorance of liability creating activities within the corporation ... only a sustained or systematic failure of the board to exercise oversight—such as an utter failure to attempt to assure a reasonable information and reporting system exists—will establish the lack of good faith that is a necessary condition to liability."] * * *

The Court of Chancery held that the plaintiffs had failed to adequately plead that such a demand would have been futile. The Court, therefore, dismissed the derivative complaint under Court of Chancery Rule 23.1. * * *

In this appeal, the plaintiffs concede that "[t]he standards for determining demand futility in the absence of a business decision" [which would be governed by *Aronson*] are set forth in *Rales v. Blasband.*[9] To excuse demand under *Rales*, "a court must determine whether or not the particularized factual allegations of a derivative stockholder complaint create a reasonable doubt that, as of the time the complaint is filed, the board of directors could have properly exercised its independent and disinterested business judgment in responding to a demand." The plaintiffs attempt to satisfy the *Rales* test in this proceeding by asserting that the incumbent defendant directors "face a substantial likelihood of liability" that renders them "personally interested in the outcome of the decision on whether to pursue the claims asserted in the complaint," and are therefore not disinterested or independent. * * * [The court found that because, *inter alia*, of the Section 102(b)(7) exculpatory provision in the corporation's charter, which as discussed subsequently prevents liability for breaches of the duty of care, the directors did not face any personal liability.]

F. Note on Derivative and Direct Actions

Tooley, Section 3.11.C, provides the basic test for determining if an action is direct or derivative: "Who suffered the harm" and "Who would receive the benefit of the recovery?" If the action is direct under this test, the company has no role in the litigation. However, if the action is derivative, the *Aronson*, Section 3.11.D, test of (1) lack of independence, or (2) "reasonable doubt as to the applicability of the business judgment rule" applies for determining if the demand on the board is excused. If demand is not excused, the board's

9. Rales v. Blasband, 634 A.2d 927 (Del. 1993).

action with regard to the matter will generally be protected by the business judgment rule. If demand is excused, the plaintiff can proceed with the action; however, as indicated in the discussion of *Oracle* in the *Stewart* case, Section 3.13.A, the board can appoint a special litigation committee, which can seek to dismiss the action.

To illustrate, assume that a controlling shareholder purchases property from a corporation at a bargain price. An action against the shareholder is derivative, because under *Tooley*, the corporation suffered the harm and is entitled to the recovery. On the other hand, assume that a controlling shareholder through a merger transaction acquires all of the stock of a corporation at a bargain price. An action my the non-controlling shareholders against the controlling shareholder is direct, because under *Tooley*, the non-controlling shareholders suffered the harm and are entitled to the recovery.

One peculiarity with the *Tooley*, formulation is: Can there be a situation where the person who suffered the harm is different from the person who would receive the benefit of the recovery? If the answer is no, why have the two-part test? And if the answer is yes, is such a situation direct or derivative?

§ 3.12 Forum Selection and Fee Shifting Bylaws[10]

Boards and controlling shareholders may want to ensure that any shareholder direct or derivative action be litigated in Delaware. For example, Article IX of the certificate of incorporation of LinkedIn, a Delaware corporation that went public in May 2011, contains the following choice of forum provision:

> Unless the Corporation consents in writing to the selection of an alternative forum, the Court of Chancery of the State of Delaware shall be the sole and exclusive forum for (i) any derivative action or proceeding brought on behalf of the Corporation; (ii) any action asserting a claim of breach of a fiduciary duty owed by any director, officer or other employee of the Corporation to the Corporation or the Corporation's stockholders; (iii) any action asserting a claim against the Corporation arising pursuant to any provision of the General Corporation Law, the Restated Certificate or the Bylaws of the Corporation; or (iv) any action asserting a claim against the Corporation governed by the internal affairs doctrine. Any person or entity purchasing or otherwise acquiring any interest in shares of capital stock of the Corporation shall be deemed to have notice of and to have consented to the provisions of this Article IX.

In a January 2011 decision in *Galaviz v. Berg*,[11] the U.S. District Court in San Francisco addressed the validity of a bylaw adopted by the board of Oracle requiring that any derivative action be brought in the Delaware Chancery Court. The court set out the issue as follows: "May corporate directors control the venue for shareholder derivative actions brought against them by adopting a bylaw purporting to require that such cases be filed in a particular forum?"[12] In finding that the bylaw in this circumstance was not valid and, therefore, denying Oracle's motion to dismiss the federal action, the court reasoned:

> Under federal procedural law that controls such venue issues, parties may enter into contracts—including those where elements of adhesion exist—that

10. This section is adapted from Thompson, *Mergers, Acquisitions and Tender Offers*, *supra* Section 1.10, at Section 5.2.8.

11. Galaviz v. Berg, 2011 U.S. Dist. LEXIS 1626 (N.D. Cal. Jan. 3, 2011).

12. *Id.* at *1.

> contain legally enforceable forum selection clauses. Even when bringing a claim under a contract offered on a "take it or leave it" basis, however, a plaintiff can be said to have consented to the forum selection clause when he or she elected to enter into that contract.
>
> A bylaw unilaterally adopted by directors, however, stands on a different footing. Particularly where, as here, the bylaw was adopted by the very individuals who are named as defendants, and after the alleged wrongdoing took place, there is no element of mutual consent to the forum choice at all, at least with respect to shareholders who purchased their shares prior to the time the bylaw was adopted.[13]

In addressing the shareholders' claim that "only a charter amendment, approved by a majority of the shareholders, could properly limit venue in derivative actions against the corporation,"[14] the court responded:

> Certainly were a majority of shareholders to approve such a charter amendment, the arguments for treating the venue provision like those in commercial contracts would be much stronger, even in the case of a plaintiff shareholder who had personally voted against the amendment.[15]

Obviously, this is not the last word on this issue. Note, however, that in the case of LinkedIn, the choice of forum provision was in the charter of the corporation at the time the corporation went public.

In 2013, Chancellor Strine of the Delaware Chancery Court found in *Chevron*[16] that a board-adopted forum selection bylaw was statutorily valid under Delaware law, and in 2014, Chancellor Bouchard of the Delaware Chancery Court found in *Providence*[17] that a board adopted forum selection bylaw was valid even though the bylaw (1) required that litigation of the Delaware corporation be brought in North Carolina, and (2) was adopted on the day of announcement of a merger.

Also in 2014, the Delaware Supreme Court held in *ATP*[18] that a fee shifting bylaw that required that the losing party pay the prevailing party's legal expenses was valid in the context of a non-stock company. It remains to be seen if the same rule will be adopted for stock corporations. If so extended, such a rule would likely cause a significant decrease in litigation relating to M&A transactions.

---

13. *Id.* at *1–*2.
14. *Id.* at *13.
15. *Id.*
16. *Boilermakers Local 154 Retirement Fund v. Chevron Corp.*, 73 A.3d 934 (Del. Ch. 2013).
17. *City of Providence v. First Citizens Bancshares, Inc.*, 2014 BL 250170 (Del. Ch. 2014).
18. *ATP Tour, Inc. v. Deutscher Tennis Bund*, 91 A.3d 554 (Del. 2014).

§ 3.13 Meaning of Independence under Delaware Law and the NYSE and NASDAQ Rules: Impact of Sarbanes–Oxley

A. Independence under Delaware Law for Purposes of the Business Judgment Rule—*Stewart*

Beam v. Stewart

Delaware Supreme Court, (2004) 845 A.2d 1040

Veasey, Chief Justice.

[The court considered if a majority of directors of Martha Stewart Living Omnimedia, Inc. (MSO) were independent of Martha for purposes of determining if demand on the board for a derivative action against Martha would be excused. The plaintiff argued that "Stewart breached her fiduciary duties of loyalty and care by illegally selling ImClone stock in December of 2001 and by mishandling the media attention that followed, thereby jeopardizing the financial future of MSO." Three of the six directors were not independent and the case focused on the independence of the other three directors. In finding that the plaintiff failed to establish that these directors were not independent the court reasoned:]

Demand Futility and Director Independence. * * * The issue in this case is the quantum of doubt about a director's independence that is "reasonable" in order to excuse a presuit demand.

The key principle upon which this area of our jurisprudence is based is that the directors are entitled to a *presumption* that they were faithful to their fiduciary duties. In the context of presuit demand, the burden is upon the plaintiff in a derivative action to overcome that presumption. The Court must determine whether a plaintiff has alleged particularized facts creating a reasonable doubt of a director's independence to rebut the presumption at the pleading stage. If the Court determines that the pleaded facts create a reasonable doubt that a majority of the board could have acted independently in responding to the demand, the presumption is rebutted for pleading purposes and demand will be excused as futile.

A director will be considered unable to act objectively with respect to a presuit demand if he or she is interested in the outcome of the litigation or is otherwise not independent. A director's interest may be shown by demonstrating a potential personal benefit or detriment to the director as a result of the decision. "In such circumstances, a director cannot be expected to exercise his or her independent business judgment without being influenced by the * * * personal consequences resulting from the decision." The primary basis upon which a director's independence must be measured is whether the director's decision is based on the corporate merits of the subject before the board, rather than extraneous considerations or influences. This broad statement of the law requires an analysis of whether the director is disinterested [that is, has no personal interest] in the underlying transaction and, even if disinterested, whether the director is otherwise independent. More precisely in the context of the present case, the independence inquiry requires us to determine whether there is a reasonable doubt that any one of these three directors is capable of objectively making a business decision to assert or not assert a corporate claim against Stewart. * * *

Personal Friendship. A variety of motivations, including friendship, may influence the demand futility inquiry. But, to render a director unable to consider demand, a relationship must be of a bias-producing nature. Allegations of mere personal friendship or a mere outside business relationship, standing alone, are insufficient to raise a reasonable doubt about a director's independence. * * *

The facts alleged by [plaintiff] regarding the relationships between Stewart and these other members of MSO's board of directors largely boil down to a "structural bias" argument, which presupposes that the professional and social relationships that naturally develop among members of a board impede independent decision making. * * *

In the present case, the plaintiff attempted to plead affinity beyond mere friendship between Stewart and the other directors, but her attempt is not sufficient to demonstrate demand futility. Even if the alleged friendships may have preceded the directors' membership on MSO's board and did not necessarily arise out of that membership, these relationships are of the same nature as those giving rise to the structural bias argument. * * *

A Word About the* Oracle *Case. In his opinion, the Chancellor referred several times to the Delaware Court of Chancery decision in *In re Oracle Corp. Derivative Litigation* [824 A.2d 917 (Del. Ch. 2003)]. Indeed, the plaintiff relies on the *Oracle* case in this appeal. *Oracle* involved the issue of the independence of the Special Litigation Committee (SLC) appointed by the Oracle board to determine whether or not the corporation should cause the dismissal of a corporate claim by stockholder-plaintiffs against directors. The Court of Chancery undertook a searching inquiry of the relationships between the members of the SLC and Stanford University in the context of the financial support of Stanford by the corporation and its management. The Vice Chancellor concluded, after considering the SLC Report and the discovery record, that those relationships were too close for purposes of the SLC analysis of independence.

An SLC is a unique creature that was introduced into Delaware law by *Zapata v. Maldonado* in 1981. The SLC procedure is a method sometimes employed where presuit demand has already been excused and the SLC is vested with the full power of the board to conduct an extensive investigation into the merits of the corporate claim with a view toward determining whether—in the SLC's business judgment—the corporate claim should be pursued. Unlike the demand-excusal context, where the board is presumed to be independent, the SLC has the burden of establishing its own independence by a yardstick that must be "like Caesar's wife"—"above reproach." Moreover, unlike the pre-suit demand context, the SLC analysis contemplates not only a shift in the burden of persuasion but also the availability of discovery into various issues, including independence. * * *

Moreover, because the members of an SLC are vested with enormous power to seek dismissal of a derivative suit brought against their director-colleagues in a setting where presuit demand is already excused, the Court of Chancery must exercise careful oversight of the bona fides of the SLC and its process. * * *

B. Impact of Sarbanes–Oxley Act on Independence Issue

This section examines the following provisions of the Sarbanes–Oxley Act of 2002, which is introduced in Section 1.9: (1) the rules governing public company audit committees, (2) the rules on audit committee financial experts, and (3) the rules governing codes of ethics. The next section examines the related rules of the NYSE and NASDAQ Stock Market requiring public companies to have a majority of independent directors. These provisions can have a significant impact on issues discussed in this chapter. Chapter 4, securities regulation, reviews other provisions of the Sarbanes–Oxley Act. This is just a brief introduction to these complex rules.

Public Company Audit Committees. SEC Release 34–47654 (April 9, 2003) describes the final audit committee rules as follows:

> As directed by the Sarbanes–Oxley Act of 2002, [*see* Section 10A(m)(1) of the 34 Act] we are adopting a new rule to direct the national securities exchanges and national securities associations to prohibit the listing of any security of an issuer that is not in compliance with the audit committee requirements mandated by the Sarbanes–Oxley Act of 2002. These requirements relate to: the independence of audit committee members; the audit committee's responsibility to select and oversee the issuer's independent accountant; procedures for handling complaints regarding the issuer's accounting practices; the authority of the audit committee to engage advisors; and funding for the independent auditor and any outside advisors engaged by the audit committee. The rule implements the requirements of Section 10A(m)(1) of the Securities Exchange Act of 1934, as added by Section 301 of the Sarbanes–Oxley Act of 2002. * * *

Code of Ethics for Senior Financial Officers. SEC Release 34–47235 (January 23, 2003) gives the following explanation of the code of ethics rules:

> We are adopting rules and amendments requiring companies, other than registered investment companies, to include two new types of disclosures in their annual reports filed pursuant to the Securities Exchange Act of 1934. * * * [T]he rules require a company to disclose whether it has adopted a code of ethics that applies to the company's principal executive officer, principal financial officer, principal accounting officer or controller, or persons performing similar functions. A company disclosing that it has not adopted such a code must disclose this fact and explain why it has not done so. A company also will be required to promptly disclose amendments to, and waivers from, the code of ethics relating to any of those officers. These rules implement the requirements in Sections 406 * * * of the Sarbanes–Oxley Act of 2002. * * *

Disclosure of Audit Committee Financial Expert. SEC Release No. 34–47235 (January 23, 2003) summarizes the new financial expert requirements:

> We are adopting rules and amendments requiring companies * * * to include two new types of disclosures in their annual reports filed pursuant to the Securities Exchange Act of 1934. First, the rules require a company to disclose whether it has at least one "audit committee financial expert" serving on its audit committee, and if so, the name of the expert and whether the expert is independent of management. A company that does not have an audit committee financial expert must disclose this fact and explain why it has no such expert. * * *

C. Required Director Independence under NYSE and NASDAQ Rules

NASD and NYSE Rulemaking Relating to Corporate Governance

SEC Release No. 34–48745 (November 4, 2003)

Introduction. * * * In January 2003, pursuant to the Sarbanes–Oxley Act of 2002 ("Sarbanes–Oxley Act"), the Commission proposed Rule 10A-3 under the Exchange Act, which directs each national securities exchange and national securities association to prohibit the listing of any security of an issuer that is not in compliance with the audit committee requirements specified in Rule 10A-3. * * *

Independence of Majority of Board Members. NYSE Section 303A(1) of the NYSE Manual would require the board of directors of each listed company to consist of a majority of independent directors. Pursuant to NYSE Section 303A(2) of the NYSE Manual, no director would qualify as "independent" unless the board affirmatively determines that the director has no material relationship with the company (either directly or as a partner, shareholder or officer of an organization that has a relationship with the company). The company would be required to disclose the basis for such determination in its annual proxy statement or, if the company does not file an annual proxy statement, in the company's annual report on Form 10-K filed with the Commission. In complying with this requirement, a board would be permitted to adopt and disclose standards to assist it in making determinations of independence, disclose those standards, and then make the general statement that the independent directors meet those standards.

Definition of Independent Director. In addition, the NYSE proposes to tighten its current definition of independent director as follows. First, a director who is an employee, or whose immediate family member is an executive officer, of the company would not be independent until three years after the end of such employment relationship ("NYSE Employee Provision"). * * *

Separate Meetings for Board Members. NYSE proposes to require the non-management directors of each NYSE-listed company to meet at regularly scheduled executive sessions without management. * * *

Nominating/Corporate Governance Committee. NYSE proposes to require each listed company to have a nominating/corporate governance committee composed entirely of independent directors. * * *

Compensation Committee. NYSE proposes to require each listed company to have a compensation committee composed entirely of independent directors. * * *

Audit Committee. Composition. NYSE Sections 303A(6) and 303A(7) would require each NYSE-listed company to have a minimum three-person audit committee composed entirely of directors that meet the independence standards of both NYSE Section 303A(2) and Rule 10A-3. * * *

Audit Committee Charter and Responsibilities. NYSE Section 303A(7)(c) would require the audit committee of each listed company to have a written audit committee charter that addresses: (i) the committee's purpose; (ii) an annual performance evaluation of the audit committee; and (iii) the duties and responsibilities of the audit committee ("NYSE Audit Committee Charter Provision"). * * *

Internal Audit Function. NYSE Section 303A(7)(d) would require each listed company to have an internal audit function.

Corporate Governance Guidelines. NYSE Section 303A(9) would require each listed company to adopt and disclose corporate governance guidelines. * * *

Code of Business Conduct and Ethics. NYSE Section 303A(10) would require each listed company to adopt and disclose a code of business conduct and ethics for directors, officers and employees, and to promptly disclose any waivers of the code for directors or executive officers. The commentary to this section sets forth the most important topics that should be addressed, including conflicts of interest; corporate opportunities; confidentiality of information; fair dealing; protection and proper use of company assets; compliance with laws, rules and regulations (including insider trading laws); and encouraging the reporting of any illegal or unethical behavior. * * *

Discussion. After careful review, the Commission finds that the NYSE [and NASDAQ] Corporate Governance Proposals, as amended, [are] consistent with the Exchange Act. * * *

D. Impact of Dodd–Frank on Independence Issues, Including Approval of Golden Parachutes

The 2010 Financial Reform Act, the Dodd–Frank Wall Street Reform and Consumer Protection Act, contains several provisions addressing corporate governance, some of which bear on director independence and shareholder oversight of director compensation. Although a careful examination of these provisions is beyond the scope of this chapter, the M&A attorney should generally be aware of these provisions. The most significant of these provisions have been summarized by the applicable House and Senate staffs as follows:

> **BRIEF SUMMARY OF THE DODD–FRANK WALL STREET REFORM AND CONSUMER PROTECTION ACT**
>
> EXECUTIVE COMPENSATION AND CORPORATE GOVERNANCE
>
> *Gives Shareholders a Say on Pay and Creating Greater Accountability Vote on Executive Pay and Golden Parachutes*: Gives shareholders a say on pay with the right to a non-binding vote on executive pay and golden parachutes. [Golden parachutes are payments made to executives as a result of a company being taken over in a change of control transaction. The Dodd–Frank provisions on golden parachutes are examined further in Chapter 13.] This gives shareholders a powerful opportunity to hold accountable executives of the companies they own, and a chance to disapprove where they see the kind of misguided incentive schemes that threatened individual companies and in turn the broader economy. [*See* section 951.]
>
> *Nominating Directors*: Gives the SEC authority to grant shareholders proxy access to nominate directors. These requirements can help shift management's focus from short-term profits to long-term growth and stability. [*See* section 971.]
>
> *Independent Compensation Committees*: Standards for listing on an exchange will require that compensation committees include only independent directors and have authority to hire compensation consultants in order to strengthen their independence from the executives they are rewarding or punishing. [*See* section 952.]
>
> *No Compensation for Lies*: Requires that public companies set policies to take back executive compensation if it was based on inaccurate financial statements that don't comply with accounting standards. [*See* section 954.]
>
> *SEC Review*: Directs the SEC to clarify disclosures relating to compensation, including requiring companies to provide charts that compare their executive compensation with stock performance.

§ 3.14 The "Big Six" Foundational Delaware Fiduciary Duty Cases Dealing with Mergers and Acquisitions

A. Introduction

This section presents the following six foundational Delaware fiduciary duty cases dealing with various aspects of mergers and acquisitions: *Weinberger*, decided in 1983,

Van Gorkom, decided in 1985, *Unocal*, decided in 1985, *Moran*, decided in 1985, *Revlon*, decided in 1986, and *Blasius*, decided in 1988. *Blasius* was decided by the well-respected Chancellor Allen, who is now a professor of law at the NYU School of Law, and all of the other cases were decided by the Delaware Supreme Court. Most of the subsequently decided Delaware cases addressing fiduciary duties in mergers and acquisitions build on one or more of these six cases. Thus, an understanding of the "Big Six" is an essential element of the M&A lawyer's tool kit.

After presenting the "Big Six," the chapter turns to some of the most significant Delaware cases that have elaborated on the themes developed in the "Big Six."

B. The Entire Fairness Doctrine for Parent-Subsidiary Mergers: Fair Dealing and Fair Price—*Weinberger*, Decided in 1983

Weinberger v. UOP, Inc.

Delaware Supreme Court, 1983 457 A.2.d 701

Moore, Justice:

[T]he class action plaintiff below, a former shareholder of UOP, Inc., * * * challenged the elimination of UOP's minority shareholders by a cash-out merger between UOP and its majority owner, The Signal Companies, Inc. * * * The present Chancellor held that the terms of the merger were fair to the plaintiff and the other minority shareholders of UOP. Accordingly, he entered judgment in favor of the defendants. * * *

[**Basic Facts**] [Signal, the acquirer, was a publicly held corporation and UOP, the target, was a Delaware corporation. Signal owned 50.5% of UOP's shares, and the balance of its shares was publicly traded.] * * * .

The trial court found that at the instigation of certain Signal management personnel, including William W. Walkup, its board chairman, and Forrest N. Shumway, its president, a feasibility study was made [in 1977] concerning the possible acquisition [by Signal] of the balance of UOP's outstanding shares. This study was performed by two Signal officers, Charles S. Arledge, vice president (director of planning), and Andrew J. Chitiea, senior vice president (chief financial officer). Messrs. Walkup, Shumway, Arledge and Chitiea were all directors of UOP in addition to their membership on the Signal board.

Arledge and Chitiea concluded that it would be a good investment for Signal to acquire the remaining 49.5% of UOP shares [which were trading at around $14.50 per share] at any price up to $24 each. * * * It was ultimately agreed that a meeting of Signal's executive committee would be called to propose that Signal acquire the remaining outstanding stock of UOP through a cash-out merger in the range of $20 to $21 per share.

The executive committee meeting was set for February 28, 1978. As a courtesy, UOP's president, Crawford, was invited to attend, although he was not a member of Signal's executive committee. On his arrival, and prior to the meeting, Crawford was asked to meet privately with Walkup and Shumway. He was then told of Signal's plan to acquire full ownership of UOP and was asked for his reaction to the proposed price range of $20 to $21 per share. * * *

Crawford voiced no objection to the $20 to $21 price range, nor did he suggest that Signal should consider paying more than $21 per share for the minority interests. * * *

Two days later, on March 2, 1978, Signal issued a second press release stating that its management would recommend a price in the range of $20 to $21 per share for UOP's

49.5% minority interest. This announcement referred to Signal's earlier statement that "negotiations" were being conducted for the acquisition of the minority shares.

Between Tuesday, February 28, 1978 and Monday, March 6, 1978, a total of four business days, Crawford spoke by telephone with all of UOP's non-Signal, *i.e.*, outside directors. Also during that period, Crawford retained Lehman Brothers to render a fairness opinion as to the price offered the minority for its stock. * * * James W. Glanville, a long-time director of UOP and a partner in Lehman Brothers, had acted as a financial advisor to UOP for many years. * * *

Glanville's immediate personal reaction was that a price of $20 to $21 would certainly be fair, since it represented almost a 50% premium over UOP's market price. Glanville sought a $250,000 fee for Lehman Brothers' services, but Crawford thought this too much. After further discussions Glanville finally agreed that Lehman Brothers would render its fairness opinion for $150,000. * * *

Glanville assembled a three-man Lehman Brothers team to do the work on the fairness opinion. These persons examined relevant documents and information concerning UOP. * * * [O]n Friday, March 3, 1978, two members of the Lehman Brothers team flew to UOP's headquarters in Des Plaines, Illinois, to perform a "due diligence" visit, during the course of which they interviewed Crawford as well as UOP's general counsel, its chief financial officer, and other key executives and personnel.

As a result, the Lehman Brothers team concluded that "the price of either $20 or $21 would be a fair price for the remaining shares of UOP". They telephoned this impression to Glanville, who was spending the weekend in Vermont.

On Monday morning, March 6, 1978, Glanville and the senior member of the Lehman Brothers team flew to Des Plaines to attend the scheduled UOP directors meeting. Glanville looked over the assembled information during the flight. The two had with them the draft of a "fairness opinion letter" in which the price had been left blank. Either during or immediately prior to the directors' meeting, the two-page "fairness opinion letter" was typed in final form and the price of $21 per share was inserted.

On March 6, 1978, both the Signal and UOP boards were convened to consider the proposed merger. * * *

While Signal's men on UOP's board participated in various aspects of the meeting, they abstained from voting. However, the minutes show that each of them "if voting would have voted yes".

On March 7, 1978, UOP sent a letter to its shareholders advising them of the action taken by UOP's board with respect to Signal's offer. * * *

Despite the swift board action of the two companies, the merger was not submitted to UOP's shareholders until their annual meeting on May 26, 1978. * * * [At that meeting the merger was approved by] 51.9% of the total minority. * * * When Signal's stock was added to the minority shares voting in favor, a total of 76.2% of UOP's outstanding shares approved the merger while only 2.2% opposed it.

By its terms the merger became effective on May 26, 1978, and each share of UOP's stock held by the minority was automatically converted into a right to receive $21 cash. * * *

[**The Intrinsic (Entire) Fairness Standard of Review Applies**] A primary issue mandating reversal is the preparation by two UOP directors, Arledge and Chitiea, of their feasibility study for the exclusive use and benefit of Signal. This document was of obvious significance to both Signal and UOP. Using UOP data, it described the advantages to Signal of ousting the minority at a price range of $21–$24 per share. * * *

Having written those words, solely for the use of Signal, it is clear from the record that neither Arledge nor Chitiea shared this report with their fellow directors of UOP. We are satisfied that no one else did either. This conduct hardly meets the fiduciary standards applicable to such a transaction. * * *

Certainly this was a matter of material significance to UOP and its shareholders. Since the study was prepared by two UOP directors, using UOP information for the exclusive benefit of Signal, and nothing whatever was done to disclose it to the outside UOP directors or the minority shareholders, a question of breach of fiduciary duty arises. This problem occurs because there were common Signal-UOP directors participating, at least to some extent, in the UOP board's decision-making processes without full disclosure of the conflicts they faced.[19] * * *

Given the absence of any attempt to structure this transaction on an arm's length basis, Signal cannot escape the effects of the conflicts it faced, particularly when its designees on UOP's board did not totally abstain from participation in the matter. There is no "safe harbor" for such divided loyalties in Delaware. When directors of a Delaware corporation are on both sides of a transaction, they are required to demonstrate their utmost good faith and the most scrupulous inherent fairness [*i.e.*, entire fairness] of the bargain. The requirement of fairness is unflinching in its demand that where one stands on both sides of a transaction, he has the burden of establishing its entire fairness, sufficient to pass the test of careful scrutiny by the courts. *Sterling v. Mayflower Hotel Corp.*

[**Determining if the Transaction Was Entirely Fair—Fair Dealing and Fair Price**] The concept of fairness has two basic aspects: fair dealing and fair price. The former embraces questions of when the transaction was timed, how it was initiated, structured, negotiated, disclosed to the directors, and how the approvals of the directors and the stockholders were obtained. The latter aspect of fairness relates to the economic and financial considerations of the proposed merger, including all relevant factors: assets, market value, earnings, future prospects, and any other elements that affect the intrinsic or inherent value of a company's stock. However, the test for fairness is not a bifurcated one as between fair dealing and price. All aspects of the issue must be examined as a whole since the question is one of entire fairness. However, in a non-fraudulent transaction we recognize that price may be the preponderant consideration outweighing other features of the merger. Here, we address the two basic aspects of fairness separately because we find reversible error as to both.

[**Fair Dealing**] Part of fair dealing is the obvious duty of candor required by *Lynch I*, *supra*. Moreover, one possessing superior knowledge may not mislead any stockholder by use of corporate information to which the latter is not privy. * * *

The Arledge–Chitiea report is but one aspect of the element of fair dealing. How did this merger evolve? It is clear that it was entirely initiated by Signal. The serious time constraints under which the principals acted were all set by Signal. * * *

As we have noted, the matter of disclosure to the UOP directors was wholly flawed by the conflicts of interest raised by the Arledge–Chitiea report. All of those conflicts were resolved by Signal in its own favor without divulging any aspect of them to UOP.

---

19. Although perfection is not possible, or expected, the result here could have been entirely different if UOP had appointed an independent negotiating committee of its outside directors to deal with Signal at arm's length. *See, e.g., Harriman v. E.I. duPont de Nemours & Co.*, 411 F.Supp. 133 (D.Del.1975).

This cannot but undermine a conclusion that this merger meets any reasonable test of fairness. The outside UOP directors lacked one material piece of information generated by two of their colleagues, but shared only with Signal. True, the UOP board had the Lehman Brothers' fairness opinion, but that firm has been blamed by the plaintiff for the hurried task it performed, when more properly the responsibility for this lies with Signal. There was no disclosure of the circumstances surrounding the rather cursory preparation of the Lehman Brothers' fairness opinion. Instead, the impression was given UOP's minority that a careful study had been made, when in fact speed was the hallmark, and Mr. Glanville, Lehman's partner in charge of the matter, and also a UOP director, having spent the weekend in Vermont, brought a draft of the "fairness opinion letter" to the UOP directors' meeting on March 6, 1978 with the price left blank. We can only conclude from the record that the rush imposed on Lehman Brothers by Signal's timetable contributed to the difficulties under which this investment banking firm attempted to perform its responsibilities. Yet, none of this was disclosed to UOP's minority.

Finally, the minority stockholders were denied the critical information that Signal considered a price of $24 to be a good investment. * * * Under the circumstances, an approval by a majority of the minority was meaningless.

Given these particulars and the Delaware law on the subject, the record does not establish that this transaction satisfies any reasonable concept of fair dealing, and the Chancellor's findings in that regard must be reversed.

[**Fair Price**] Turning to the matter of price, plaintiff also challenges its fairness. His evidence was that on the date the merger was approved the stock was worth at least $26 per share. In support, he offered the testimony of a chartered investment analyst who used two basic approaches to valuation: a comparative analysis of the premium paid over market in ten other tender offer-merger combinations, and a discounted cash flow analysis. [As discussed in Section 2.10.F.2, the court accepted these approaches to valuation.]

The judgment of the Court of Chancery, finding both the circumstances of the merger and the price paid the minority shareholders to be fair, is reversed. The matter is remanded for further proceedings consistent herewith. Upon remand the plaintiff's post-trial motion to enlarge the class should be granted. * * *

REVERSED AND REMANDED.

C. The Business Judgment Rule and the Gross Negligence Standard—*Van Gorkom*, Decided in 1985

1. The Decision

Smith v. Van Gorkom

Delaware Supreme Court, (1985) 488 A.2d 858

Horsey, Justice (for the majority).

This appeal from the Court of Chancery involves a class action brought by shareholders of the defendant Trans Union Corporation ("Trans Union" or "the Company"), originally seeking rescission of a cash-out merger of Trans Union into the defendant New T Company ("New T"), a wholly-owned subsidiary of the defendant, Marmon Group, Inc. ("Marmon"). Alternate relief in the form of damages is sought against the defendant members of the Board of Directors of Trans Union, New T, and Jay A. Pritzker and Robert A. Pritzker, owners of Marmon.

Following trial, the former Chancellor granted judgment for the defendant directors. * * * Judgment was based on two findings: (1) that the Board of Directors had acted in an informed manner so as to be entitled to protection of the business judgment rule in approving the cash-out merger; and (2) that the shareholder vote approving the merger should not be set aside because the stockholders had been "fairly informed" by the Board of Directors before voting thereon. The plaintiffs appeal. [Only the first issue is discussed here.]

Speaking for the majority of the Court, we conclude that both rulings of the Court of Chancery are clearly erroneous. Therefore, we reverse and direct that judgment be entered in favor of the plaintiffs and against the defendant directors for the fair value of the plaintiffs' stockholdings in Trans Union, in accordance with *Weinberger v. UOP, Inc.*, [Section 3.14.B].

We hold: (1) that the Board's decision, reached September 20, 1980, to approve the proposed cash-out merger was not the product of an informed business judgment; (2) that the Board's subsequent efforts to amend the Merger Agreement and take other curative action were ineffectual, both legally and factually; and (3) that the Board did not deal with complete candor with the stockholders by failing to disclose all material facts, which they knew or should have known, before securing the stockholder' approval of the merger. * * *

[**Basic Facts**] Trans Union was a publicly-traded [Delaware corporation.] [The] Company had difficulty in generating sufficient taxable income to offset increasingly large investment tax credits (ITCs). * * *

On August 27, 1980, Van Gorkom [Trans Union's Chairman and Chief Executive Officer] met with Senior Management of Trans Union. * * *

Various alternatives were suggested and discussed preliminarily, including the sale of Trans Union to a company with a large amount of taxable income.

Donald Romans, Chief Financial Officer of Trans Union, stated that his department had done a "very brief bit of work on the possibility of a leveraged buy-out." * * *

On September 5, at another Senior Management meeting, which Van Gorkom attended, Romans again brought up the idea of a leveraged buy-out as a "possible strategic alternative" to the Company's acquisition program. * * * [Romans indicated that his] "figures indicated that $50 [per share] would be very easy to do but $60 would be very difficult to do under those figures." * * *

At this meeting, Van Gorkom stated that he would be willing to take $55 per share for his own 75,000 shares. He vetoed the suggestion of a leveraged buy-out by Management, however, as involving a potential conflict of interest for Management. * * * It is noteworthy * * * that he was then approaching 65 years of age and mandatory retirement.

Van Gorkom decided to meet with Jay A. Pritzker, a well-known corporate takeover specialist and a social acquaintance. However, rather than approaching Pritzker simply to determine his interest in acquiring Trans Union, Van Gorkom assembled a proposed per share price for sale of the Company and a financing structure by which to accomplish the sale. Van Gorkom did so without consulting either his Board or any members of Senior Management except one: Carl Peterson, Trans Union's Controller. Telling Peterson that he wanted no other person on his staff to know what he was doing, but without telling him why, Van Gorkom directed Peterson to calculate the feasibility of a leveraged buy-out at an assumed price per share of $55. * * * [T]he record is devoid of any competent evidence that $55 represented the per share intrinsic value of the Company. * * *

Van Gorkom reviewed with Pritzker his calculations based upon his proposed price of $55 per share. Although Pritzker mentioned $50 as a more attractive figure, no other price was mentioned. However, Van Gorkom stated that to be sure that $55 was the best price obtainable, Trans Union should be free to accept any better offer. Pritzker demurred, stating that his organization would serve as a "stalking horse" for an "auction contest" only if Trans Union would permit Pritzker to buy 1,750,000 shares of Trans Union stock at market price which Pritzker could then sell to any higher bidder. After further discussion on this point, Pritzker told Van Gorkom that he would give him a more definite reaction soon.

On Monday, September 15, Pritzker advised Van Gorkom that he was interested in the $55 cash-out merger proposal and requested more information on Trans Union. * * *

On Thursday, September 18, Van Gorkom met again with Pritzker. At that time, Van Gorkom knew that Pritzker intended to make a cash-out merger offer at Van Gorkom's proposed $55 per share. Pritzker instructed his attorney, a merger and acquisition specialist, to begin drafting merger documents. There was no further discussion of the $55 price. However, the number of shares of Trans Union's treasury stock to be offered to Pritzker was negotiated down to one million shares; the price was set at $38.75 cents above the per share price at the close of the market on September 19. At this point, Pritzker insisted that the Trans Union Board act on his merger proposal within the next three days, stating to Van Gorkom: "We have to have a decision by no later than Sunday [evening, September 21] before the opening of the English stock exchange on Monday morning." Pritzker's lawyer was then instructed to draft the merger documents, to be reviewed by Van Gorkom's lawyer. * * *

On Friday, September 19, Van Gorkom called a special meeting of the Trans Union Board for noon the following day. He also called a meeting of the Company's Senior Management to convene at 11:00 a.m., prior to the meeting of the Board. * * * Van Gorkom did not invite Trans Union's investment banker, Salomon Brothers or its Chicago-based partner, to attend. * * *

Van Gorkom disclosed the offer and described its terms, but he furnished no copies of the proposed Merger Agreement. Romans announced that his department had done a second study which showed that, for a leveraged buy-out, the price range for Trans Union stock was between $55 and $65 per share. * * * .

Senior Management's reaction to the Pritzker proposal was completely negative. * * *

Ten directors served on the Trans Union Board, five inside * * * and five outside * * *. All directors were present at the meeting, except O'Boyle who was ill. Of the outside directors, four were corporate chief executive officers and one was the former Dean of the University of Chicago Business School. None was an investment banker or trained financial analyst. All members of the Board were well informed about the Company and its operations as a going concern. * * *

Van Gorkom began the Special Meeting of the Board with a twenty-minute oral presentation. * * * Van Gorkom did not disclose to the Board, however, the methodology by which he alone had arrived at the $55 figure, or the fact that he first proposed the $55 price in his negotiations with Pritzker.

Van Gorkom outlined the terms of the Pritzker offer as follows: Pritzker would pay $55 in cash for all outstanding shares of Trans Union stock upon completion of which Trans Union would be merged into New T Company, a subsidiary wholly-owned by Pritzker and formed to implement the merger; for a period of 90 days, Trans Union could receive, but could not actively solicit, competing offers; the offer had to be acted on by the next evening, Sunday, September 21; Trans Union could only furnish to competing bidders published information, and not proprietary information; the offer was subject to Pritzker obtaining the necessary financing by October 10, 1980; if the financing contingency were met or waived by Pritzker, Trans Union was required to sell to Pritzker one million newly-issued shares of Trans Union at $38 per share.

Van Gorkom took the position that putting Trans Union "up for auction" through a 90-day market test would validate a decision by the Board that $55 was a fair price. * * *

Attorney Brennan advised the members of the Board that they might be sued if they failed to accept the offer and that a fairness opinion was not required as a matter of law.

Romans attended the meeting as chief financial officer of the Company. He told the Board that he had not been involved in the negotiations with Pritzker and knew nothing about the merger proposal until the morning of the meeting; that his studies did not indicate either a fair price for the stock or a valuation of the Company; that he did not see his role as directly addressing the fairness issue; and that he and his people "were trying to search for ways to justify a price in connection with such a [leveraged buy-out] transaction, rather than to say what the shares are worth." Romans testified: I told the Board that the study ran the numbers at 50 and 60, and then the subsequent study at 55 and 65, and that was not the same thing as saying that I have a valuation of the company at X dollars. But it was a * * * first step towards reaching that conclusion. Romans told the Board that, in his opinion, $55 was "in the range of a fair price," but "at the beginning of the range."

The Board meeting of September 20 lasted about two hours. Based solely upon Van Gorkom's oral presentation, Chelberg's supporting representations, Romans' oral statement, Brennan's legal advice, and their knowledge of the market history of the Company's stock, the directors approved the proposed Merger Agreement. * * * [I]t is undisputed that the Board did not reserve the right to actively solicit alternate offers.

The Merger Agreement was executed by Van Gorkom during the evening of September 20 at a formal social event that he hosted for the opening of the Chicago Lyric Opera. Neither he nor any other director read the agreement prior to its signing and delivery to Pritzker. * * *

On Monday, September 22, the Company issued a press release announcing that Trans Union had entered into a "definitive" Merger Agreement with an affiliate of the Marmon Group, Inc., a Pritzker holding company. Within 10 days of the public announcement, dissent among Senior Management over the merger had become widespread. Faced with threatened resignations of key officers, Van Gorkom met with Pritzker who agreed to several modifications of the Agreement. Pritzker was willing to do so provided that Van Gorkom could persuade the dissidents to remain on the Company payroll for at least six months after consummation of the merger.

Van Gorkom reconvened the Board on October 8 and secured the directors' approval of the proposed amendments sight unseen. The Board also authorized the employment of Salomon Brothers, its investment banker, to solicit other offers for Trans Union during the proposed "market test" period.

The next day, October 9, Trans Union issued a press release announcing: (1) that Pritzker had obtained "the financing commitments necessary to consummate" the merger with Trans Union; (2) that Pritzker had acquired one million shares of Trans Union common stock at $38 per share; (3) that Trans Union was now permitted to actively seek other offers and had retained Salomon Brothers for that purpose; and (4) that if a more favorable offer were not received before February 1, 1981, Trans Union's shareholders would thereafter meet to vote on the Pritzker proposal.

It was not until the following day, October 10, that the actual amendments to the Merger Agreement were prepared by Pritzker and delivered to Van Gorkom for execution. As will be seen, the amendments were considerably at variance with Van Gorkom's representations of the amendments to the Board on October 8; and the amendments placed serious constraints on Trans Union's ability to negotiate a better deal and withdraw from the Pritzker agreement. Nevertheless, Van Gorkom proceeded to execute what became the October 10 amendments to the Merger Agreement without conferring further with the Board members and apparently without comprehending the actual implications of the amendments. * * *

Salomon Brothers' efforts over a three-month period from October 21 to January 21 produced only one serious suitor for Trans Union, General Electric Credit Corporation ("GE Credit"), a subsidiary of the General Electric Company. However, GE Credit was unwilling to make an offer for Trans Union unless Trans Union first rescinded its Merger Agreement with Pritzker. When Pritzker refused, GE Credit terminated further discussions with Trans Union in early January.

In the meantime, in early December, the investment firm of Kohlberg, Kravis, Roberts & Co. ("KKR"), the only other concern to make a firm offer for Trans Union, withdrew its offer. * * *

On December 19, this litigation was commenced. * * * On January 21, Management's Proxy Statement for the February 10 shareholder meeting was mailed to Trans Union's stockholders. On January 26, Trans Union's Board met and, after a lengthy meeting, voted to proceed with the Pritzker merger. The Board also approved for mailing, "on or about January 27," a Supplement to its Proxy Statement. The Supplement purportedly set forth all information relevant to the Pritzker Merger Agreement, which had not been divulged in the first Proxy Statement. * * *

On February 10, the stockholders of Trans Union approved the Pritzker merger proposal. Of the outstanding shares, 69.9% were voted in favor of the merger; 7.25% were voted against the merger; and 22.85% were not voted.

[**Business Judgment Rule**] We turn to the issue of the application of the business judgment rule to the September 20 meeting of the Board.

The Court of Chancery concluded from the evidence that the Board of Directors' approval of the Pritzker merger proposal fell within the protection of the business judgment rule. * * *

The Court of Chancery made but one finding; *i.e.*, that the Board's conduct over the entire period from September 20 through January 26, 1981 was not reckless or improvident, but informed. * * *

[W]e conclude that the Court's ultimate finding that the Board's conduct was not "reckless or imprudent" is contrary to the record and not the product of a logical and deductive reasoning process. * * *

Under Delaware law, the business judgment rule is the offspring of the fundamental principle, codified in 8 Del.C. § 141(a), that the business and affairs of a Delaware corporation are managed by or under its board of directors. * * * In carrying out their managerial roles, directors are charged with an unyielding fiduciary duty to the corporation and its shareholders. *Loft, Inc. v. Guth*, [Section 3.4]. The business judgment rule exists to protect and promote the full and free exercise of the managerial power granted to Delaware directors. The rule itself "is a presumption that in making a business decision, the directors of a corporation acted [1] on an informed basis, [2] in good faith and [3] in the honest belief that the action taken was in the best interests of the company." Thus, the party attacking a board decision as uninformed must rebut the presumption that its business judgment was an informed one.

The determination of whether a business judgment is an informed one turns on whether the directors have informed themselves "prior to making a business decision, of all material information reasonably available to them."

Under the business judgment rule there is no protection for directors who have made "an unintelligent or unadvised judgment." A director's duty to inform himself in preparation for a decision derives from the fiduciary capacity in which he serves the corporation and its stockholders. *Lutz v. Boas*, [Section 3.6.A]. Since a director is vested with the responsibility for the management of the affairs of the corporation, he must execute that duty with the recognition that he acts on behalf of others. Such obligation does not tolerate faithlessness or self-dealing. But fulfillment of the fiduciary function requires more than the mere absence of bad faith or fraud. Representation of the financial interests of others imposes on a director an affirmative duty to protect those interests and to proceed with a critical eye in assessing information of the type and under the circumstances present here. *See Lutz v. Boas, supra*; *Guth v. Loft, supra.*

Thus, a director's duty to exercise an informed business judgment is in the nature of a duty of care, as distinguished from a duty of loyalty. Here, there were no allegations of fraud, bad faith, or self-dealing, or proof thereof. Hence, it is presumed that the directors reached their business judgment in good faith and considerations of motive are irrelevant to the issue before us.

The standard of care applicable to a director's duty of care has also been recently restated by this Court. In *Aronson*, [Section 3.11.D], we stated:

> While the Delaware cases use a variety of terms to describe the applicable standard of care, our analysis satisfies us that under the business judgment rule director liability is predicated upon concepts of gross negligence. (footnote omitted)

We again confirm that view. We think the concept of gross negligence is also the proper standard for determining whether a business judgment reached by a board of directors was an informed one.

In the specific context of a proposed merger of domestic corporations, a director has a duty under 8 Del.C. § 251(b), along with his fellow directors, to act in an informed and deliberate manner in determining whether to approve an agreement of merger before submitting the proposal to the stockholders. * * *

It is against those standards that the conduct of the directors of Trans Union must be tested, as a matter of law and as a matter of fact, regarding their exercise of an informed business judgment in voting to approve the Pritzker merger proposal. * * *

[T]he question of whether the directors reached an informed business judgment in agreeing to sell the Company, pursuant to the terms of the September 20 Agreement presents, in reality, two questions: (A) whether the directors reached an informed business judgment on September 20, 1980; and (B) if they did not, whether the directors' actions taken subsequent to September 20 were adequate to cure any infirmity in their action taken on September 20. We first consider the directors' September 20 action in terms of their reaching an informed business judgment.

On the record before us, we must conclude that the Board of Directors did not reach an informed business judgment on September 20, 1980 in voting to "sell" the Company for $55 per share pursuant to the Pritzker cash-out merger proposal. Our reasons, in summary, are as follows:

The directors (1) did not adequately inform themselves as to Van Gorkom's role in forcing the "sale" of the Company and in establishing the per share purchase price; (2) were uninformed as to the intrinsic value of the Company; and (3) given these circumstances, at a minimum, were grossly negligent in approving the "sale" of the Company upon two hours' consideration, without prior notice, and without the exigency of a crisis or emergency. * * *

We now examine the Board's post-September 20 conduct for the purpose of determining first, whether it was informed and not grossly negligent; and second, if informed, whether it was sufficient to legally rectify and cure the Board's derelictions of September 20. [The Court found the subsequent actions did not cure the gross negligence in approving the sale on September 20.]

[**The Stockholder Vote**] The defendants ultimately rely on the stockholder vote of February 10 for exoneration. The defendants contend that the stockholders' "overwhelming" vote approving the Pritzker Merger Agreement had the legal effect of curing any failure of the Board to reach an informed business judgment in its approval of the merger. * * *

The settled rule in Delaware is that "where a majority of fully informed stockholders ratify action of even interested directors, an attack on the ratified transaction normally must fail." The question of whether shareholders have been fully informed such that their vote can be said to ratify director action, "turns on the fairness and completeness of the proxy materials submitted by the management to the * * * shareholders." In *Lynch v. Vickers Energy Corp.*, [383 A.2d 278 (1978)], this Court held that corporate directors owe to their stockholders a fiduciary duty to disclose all facts germane to the transaction at issue in an atmosphere of complete candor. We defined "germane" in the tender offer context as all "information such as a reasonable stockholder would consider important in deciding whether to sell or retain stock."

Applying this standard to the record before us, we find that Trans Union's stockholders were not fully informed of all facts material to their vote on the Pritzker Merger and that the Trial Court's ruling to the contrary is clearly erroneous. * * *

[**Summary**] To summarize: we hold that the directors of Trans Union breached their fiduciary duty to their stockholders (1) by their failure to inform themselves of all information reasonably available to them and relevant to their decision to recommend the Pritzker merger; and (2) by their failure to disclose all material information such as a reasonable stockholder would consider important in deciding whether to approve the Pritzker offer.

We hold, therefore, that the Trial Court committed reversible error in applying the business judgment rule in favor of the director defendants in this case.

On remand, the Court of Chancery shall conduct an evidentiary hearing to determine the fair value of the shares represented by the plaintiffs' class, based on the intrinsic value of Trans Union on September 20, 1980. Such valuation shall be made in accordance with *Weinberger v. UOP, Inc.,*[Section 3.14.B]. Thereafter, an award of damages may be entered to the extent that the fair value of Trans Union exceeds $55 per share. * * *

Questions and Note

What are the elements of the Delaware business judgment rule? In *Van Gorkom* the Court found no evidence of fraud or lack of good faith. What then is the basis of the

Court's finding that the directors did not receive the benefit of the business judgment rule? What was the basis of the Court's finding that the shareholder vote did not cure any breach by the directors? On the basis of *Van Gorkom*, what advice would you give to a target's board of directors that is considering an acquisition proposal? Does *Van Gorkom* eliminate the use of a single bidder strategy with a post-signing "market check" through the active solicitation of a topping bid?

Why did Pritzker negotiate to acquire one million newly-issued shares of Trans Union at $38 per share? What was the value of this transaction to Pritzker assuming a topping acquisition had been made at a price of $60 per share? What percentage of the aggregate purchase price for Trans Union was represented by the bargain element received by Pritzker on the purchase of the one million shares? The acquisition by Pritzker of these shares was a deal protection device. Would this type of deal protection device pass scrutiny under the Delaware law, discussed *infra*, governing such devices?

As a result of *Van Gorkom*, in virtually all acquisitions of a publicly held company by another publicly held company, both the target's board and the acquiror's board will obtain a fairness opinion from an investment banker. Fairness opinions are examined in Chapter 7, which deals with valuation.

2. Pritzker's Reaction to *Van Gorkom*

Symposium: Theory Informs Business Practice: Roundtable Discussion: Corporate Governance, Chicago-Kent College of Law April 6, 2001

77 Chi.-Kent L. Rev. 235, 236–243 (2001)

[In connection with a symposium interview sponsored by the Chicago-Kent College of Law, Robert Pritzker, one of the head people at the acquiror in *Van Gorkom*, expressed the following views on the case and explains why his family paid most of the damages imposed on the directors.]

William Carney: [E]xactly how did the $55 number come about, that wound up as the purchase price in this case?

Robert Pritzker: It was a number that was selected by Jerry Van Gorkom. And as I understand it—and I wasn't there when they made the decision what price they wanted—it was on the advice of their internal people. Mr. Romans[, Chief Financial Officer of Trans Union,] and some others had wanted to have a management buyout. * * *

William Carney: One week seems like an awfully short time in which to negotiate and to sell a company, and the supreme court was critical of that timetable. Who initiated that timetable?

Robert Pritzker: Van Gorkom, but I think he had a good reason. I don't agree with the supreme court on that point, either. His general logic was this: he was generating tax credits faster than he could use them, by a lot. So, he could buy a company that had use for tax credits, he could sell it to a company that had use for tax credits, or merge. His feeling was that he wouldn't get more than $55 per share in any event, and he didn't want his company kicked around and auctioned. * * *

William Carney: I think $ 37 or $ 38 was the range that the court referred to.

Robert Pritzker: Yes, one or the other. It had been selling below that, so the premium was pretty great. And, of course, the proof in the pudding that he was right was later, as you know. It was put out to bid in an auction and Salomon Brothers had a $5 million commission riding on it. And in four months they couldn't top the bid. So, apparently

$55 was the right price to charge us. Now, from our point of view it didn't look like such a slam dunk. We had a huge loan against it, and for the first couple of years I thought we may have made a mistake. But ultimately it's worked out fine.

William Carney: The court was critical of the lockup arrangement that your family had. I believe it turned out to be a million shares of stock at $ 38. The supreme court seemed to suggest that that might have been a deal killer. Was that your view of why they didn't come up with any other offers?

Robert Pritzker: I don't quite see why it would be a deal killer. * * * I think history has proved that it was a good price.

William Carney: The other question that has, I think, fascinated many people is the settlement of this case, which, I believe, was for $23 million, and there was, I think, $10 million worth of directors' and officers' liability insurance, and your family contributed $13 million. * * * Could you tell us what motivated you to make that kind of a contribution?

Robert Pritzker: Well, we didn't think the directors had done anything wrong. They were a very knowledgeable group; as I recall, four of them were CEOs of conglomerates that had been put together by buying companies. They surely knew what they were doing. There was an academic, Allen Wallis, who had been, I think, head of one of the [Chicago] business school. * * *

He was quite knowledgeable about this. And there was another director who was in the hospital during this entire transaction. In fact, I'm not sure I've ever met him, but he knew nothing about it. Now, let's start with him. For him to pay $1.3 million which he didn't have would have bankrupted him. It just didn't seem quite appropriate. One of the directors had passed away and his widow was the one who was supposed to come up with the $1.3 million. It just didn't seem fair. As a matter of fact, I think it was $13-and-a-half million, as I recall now. So we felt that we were the beneficiaries of the whole event. The directors didn't do anything wrong, why should they bear the responsibility? They had nothing to gain and everything to lose. Our feeling was that morally we owed it to them. So, our deal was we would pay 90 percent of that $1.35 million for each one, and they would pay 10 percent to charity. We felt they ought to have something, but not so gross a number. And, incidentally, Van Gorkom paid three or four of their charity contributions. He was about as high class as you could be. He asked for nothing, he didn't want any final settlement or bonus. * * *

Richard Painter: It seems to me the court focused in most of its opinion on the procedural due care that went into the transaction on the part of the Trans Union directors, rather than the fairness of the price. Were there aspects of the procedure in the negotiations that in retrospect perhaps could have been handled in a way that would have provided more legal cover? The short time between when the board was notified and when the contract had to be signed was an issue the court was concerned about; it was only a matter of forty-eight hours. Indeed, I think the contract was signed at the Lyric Opera Ball.

Robert Pritzker: * * * A week is too short. Van Gorkom had some ghosts in his closet that bothered him. Personally, I'd have given more time, but not for the reason that the supreme court said. I thought he wasn't fair to his management, who felt that they had created a lot of this wealth, to just pull the rug out from under them with two hours' notice. And they rebelled. * * *

A week's notice was not our idea. It was their idea completely. Can you imagine how frustrated I was trying to evaluate something where you have one week, and you're only privy to three people? * * *

3. The Legislative Reaction to *Van Gorkom*

a. Section 102(b)(7) of the Delaware General Corporate Law

Excerpt from Veasey, Finkelstein and Bigler, Delaware Supports Directors with a Three Legged Stool of Limited Liability, Indemnification and Insurance

42 Bus. Lawyer 399, 399–404 (1987)

* * * No doubt every director of a public company is painfully aware of the celebrated damage case of *Smith v. Van Gorkom*, where directors were found personally liable in damages for gross negligence in hastily approving a merger transaction.

The corporate governance system depends on the self-governing mechanism of outside directors to provide independent, objective oversight of management and reasoned business decisions. Yet, the very courts that have emphasized the necessity of strong outside director involvement have imposed the pain of personal liability for gross negligence. In view of the substantial judgments rendered against directors by the courts in recent years and the ever-increasing amount of information that must be considered by directors in their deliberations, directors are demanding increased protection from personal liability. Simultaneously, many D & O insurers have withdrawn from the market completely or have dramatically altered their policies to decrease the availability and scope of coverage and/or increase the premiums and the amounts deductible under existing policies. The result has been the ultimate irony in corporate governance—outside directors refusing to serve. Obviously, if competent directors are not willing to serve because of an unreasonable risk of exposure of their personal assets, the laudable policy of having independent directors as decision makers is seriously undermined. * * *

Consistent with the other provisions of section 102(b), new paragraph (7) is an enabling provision only. [Read carefully Section 102(b)(7)] To grant the protection authorized by the new legislation, a corporation is required to amend its certificate of incorporation to add the liability-limiting provision (or to include such a provision in its original certificate of incorporation). * * *

The new amendment authorizes either a partial limitation (such as a dollar "cap," either per director or for the board collectively) or the total elimination of the directors' liability for duty of care violations. The proposed legislation thus provides flexibility, allowing the authorized certificate provision to be tailored to include such conditions or restrictions as might be appropriate in particular circumstances. * * *

Section 102(b)(7) is not, and was not intended to be, a panacea for directors. It only allows a certificate of incorporation to limit liability of directors in certain circumstances. Indeed, as mentioned above, it specifically excludes certain classes of behavior. Moreover, while some commentators have suggested that the new Delaware legislation exempts directors from liability for recklessness actions—somewhere in between ordinary negligence and intentional wrongdoing—whether the new statute would protect a director against reckless acts is not altogether clear. To the extent recklessness involves conscious disregard of a known risk, it could be argued that such an approach is one not taken in good faith and thus would not be a liability subject to limitation under the new statute. On the other hand, to the extent recklessness only involves sustained inattention to duty, it could be labeled "grossly negligent" and thus any resulting liability would be subject to limitation. * * *

Section 102(b)(7) authorizes limitation or elimination of monetary liability only for directors' actions as directors. It does not limit the liability of a director for actions taken in a capacity other than a director, such as that of an officer or a majority stockholder. Nor does it apply to officers, employees, or agents.

While section 102(b)(7) may not be a panacea, it provides a layer of protection for directors by allowing stockholders to dramatically reduce the types of situations in which a director's personal wealth is put "on the line." * * *

Notes

Event studies (*see* Chapter 1) of the impact on the stock price of Delaware corporations resulting from (1) the announcement of the *Van Gorkom* decision, and (2) the adoption of Section 102(b)(7), found (1) no impact from the announcement of *Van Gorkom*, and (2) a significant decrease in value resulting from the adoption of Section 102(b)(7). *See* Michael Bradley and Cindy A. Schipani, *The Relevance of the Duty of Care Standard in Corporate Governance*, 75 Iowa L. Rev. 1 (1989).

In *Arnold v. Society for Savings Bancorp, Inc.*, 650 A.2d 1270 (Del. 1994), the court held that Section 102(b)(7) applies to a disclosure claim in a merger.

b. Section 102(b)(7) Affirmative Defense—*Emerald*

In *Emerald Partners v. Berlin*, 726 A.2d 1215 (Del. 1999), the Delaware Supreme Court said:

> [T]he shield from liability provided by a certificate of incorporation provision adopted pursuant to 8 Del. C. § 102(b)(7) is in the nature of an affirmative defense. Defendants seeking exculpation under such a provision will normally bear the burden of establishing each of its elements. * * * [T]he burden of demonstrating good faith, however slight it might be in given circumstances, is upon the party seeking the protection of the statute.

4. Indemnification and Insurance for Directors

In addition to exculpation under Section 102(b)(7), Section 145(a) of the DGCL permits Delaware corporations to provide indemnification for directors' actions as long as such actions are taken in good faith, and Section 145(g) of the DGCL authorizes the corporation to purchase insurance on behalf of directors. *See e.g.*, Monteleone and Conca, *Directors and Officers Indemnification and Liability Insurance: An Overview of Legal and Practical Issues*, 51 Bus. Law. 573 (1996).

D. The Enhanced Business Judgment Test—*Unocal*, Decided in 1985

Unocal Corporation v. Mesa Petroleum Co.

Delaware Supreme Court, 1985 493 A.2d 946

Moore, Justice.

We confront an issue of first impression in Delaware—the validity of a corporation's self-tender for its own shares which excludes from participation a stockholder making a hostile tender offer for the company's stock.

The Court of Chancery granted a preliminary injunction to the plaintiffs, Mesa Petroleum Co., Mesa Asset Co., Mesa Partners II, and Mesa Eastern, Inc. (collectively

"Mesa"),[20] enjoining an exchange offer of the defendant, Unocal Corporation (Unocal) for its own stock. The trial court concluded that a selective exchange offer, excluding Mesa, was legally impermissible. We cannot agree with such a blanket rule. The factual findings of the Vice Chancellor, fully supported by the record, establish that Unocal's board, consisting of a majority of independent directors, acted in good faith, and after reasonable investigation found that Mesa's tender offer was both inadequate and coercive. Under the circumstances the board had both the power and duty to oppose a bid it perceived to be harmful to the corporate enterprise. On this record we are satisfied that the device Unocal adopted is reasonable in relation to the threat posed, and that the board acted in the proper exercise of sound business judgment. We will not substitute our views for those of the board if the latter's decision can be "attributed to any rational business purpose." *Sinclair Oil Corp. v. Levien*, [Section 3.7] Accordingly, we reverse the decision of the Court of Chancery and order the preliminary injunction vacated.

[**Basic Facts**] The factual background of this matter bears a significant relationship to its ultimate outcome.

On April 8, 1985, Mesa, the owner of approximately 13% of Unocal's stock, commenced a two-tier "front loaded" cash tender offer for 64 million shares, or approximately 37%, of Unocal's outstanding stock at a price of $54 per share. The "back-end" was designed to eliminate the remaining publicly held shares by an exchange of securities purportedly worth $54 per share. However, pursuant to an order entered by the United States District Court for the Central District of California on April 26, 1985, Mesa issued a supplemental proxy statement to Unocal's stockholders disclosing that the securities offered in the second-step merger would be highly subordinated, and that Unocal's capitalization would differ significantly from its present structure. Unocal has rather aptly termed such securities "junk bonds".

Unocal's board consists of eight independent outside directors and six insiders. It met on April 13, 1985, to consider the Mesa tender offer. Thirteen directors were present, and the meeting lasted nine and one-half hours. The directors were given no agenda or written materials prior to the session. However, detailed presentations were made by legal counsel regarding the board's obligations under both Delaware corporate law and the federal securities laws. The board then received a presentation from Peter Sachs on behalf of Goldman Sachs & Co. (Goldman Sachs) and Dillon, Read & Co. (Dillon Read) discussing the bases for their opinions that the Mesa proposal was wholly inadequate. Mr. Sachs opined that the minimum cash value that could be expected from a sale or orderly liquidation for 100% of Unocal's stock was in excess of $60 per share. In making his presentation, Mr. Sachs showed slides outlining the valuation techniques used by the financial advisors, and others, depicting recent business combinations in the oil and gas industry. * * *

Mr. Sachs also presented various defensive strategies available to the board if it concluded that Mesa's two-step tender offer was inadequate and should be opposed. One of the devices outlined was a self-tender by Unocal for its own stock with a reasonable price range of $70 to $75 per share. The cost of such a proposal would cause the company to incur $6.1–6.5 billion of additional debt, and a presentation was made informing the board of Unocal's ability to handle it. The directors were told that the primary effect of this obligation would be to reduce exploratory drilling, but that the company would nonetheless remain a viable entity.

---

20. T. Boone Pickens, Jr., is President and Chairman of the Board of Mesa Petroleum and President of Mesa Asset and controls the related Mesa entities.

The eight outside directors, comprising a clear majority of the thirteen members present, then met separately with Unocal's financial advisors and attorneys. Thereafter, they unanimously agreed to advise the board that it should reject Mesa's tender offer as inadequate, and that Unocal should pursue a self-tender to provide the stockholders with a fairly priced alternative to the Mesa proposal. The board then reconvened and unanimously adopted a resolution rejecting as grossly inadequate Mesa's tender offer. Despite the nine and one-half hour length of the meeting, no formal decision was made on the proposed defensive self-tender.

On April 15, the board met again with four of the directors present by telephone and one member still absent. This session lasted two hours. Unocal's Vice President of Finance and its Assistant General Counsel made a detailed presentation of the proposed terms of the exchange offer. A price range between $70 and $80 per share was considered, and ultimately the directors agreed upon $72. The board was also advised about the debt securities that would be issued, and the necessity of placing restrictive covenants upon certain corporate activities until the obligations were paid. The board's decisions were made in reliance on the advice of its investment bankers, including the terms and conditions upon which the securities were to be issued. Based upon this advice, and the board's own deliberations, the directors unanimously approved the exchange offer. Their resolution provided that if Mesa acquired 64 million shares of Unocal stock through its own offer (the Mesa Purchase Condition), Unocal would buy the remaining 49% outstanding for an exchange of debt securities having an aggregate par value of $72 per share. The board resolution also stated that the offer would be subject to other conditions that had been described to the board at the meeting, or which were deemed necessary by Unocal's officers, including the exclusion of Mesa from the proposal (the Mesa exclusion). Any such conditions were required to be in accordance with the "purport and intent" of the offer.

Unocal's exchange offer was commenced on April 17, 1985, and Mesa promptly challenged it by filing this suit in the Court of Chancery. On April 22, the Unocal board met again and was advised by Goldman Sachs and Dillon Read to waive the Mesa Purchase Condition as to 50 million shares. This recommendation was in response to a perceived concern of the shareholders that, if shares were tendered to Unocal, no shares would be purchased by either offeror. The directors were also advised that they should tender their own Unocal stock into the exchange offer as a mark of their confidence in it.

Another focus of the board was the Mesa exclusion. Legal counsel advised that under Delaware law Mesa could only be excluded for what the directors reasonably believed to be a valid corporate purpose. The directors' discussion centered on the objective of adequately compensating shareholders at the "back-end" of Mesa's proposal, which the latter would finance with "junk bonds." To include Mesa would defeat that goal, because under the proration aspect of the exchange offer (49%) every Mesa share accepted by Unocal would displace one held by another stockholder. Further, if Mesa were permitted to tender to Unocal, the latter would in effect be financing Mesa's own inadequate proposal. * * *

On April 29, 1985, the Vice Chancellor temporarily restrained Unocal from proceeding with the exchange offer unless it included Mesa. * * *

[**Issues**] The issues we address involve these fundamental questions: Did the Unocal board have the power and duty to oppose a takeover threat it reasonably perceived to be harmful to the corporate enterprise, and if so, is its action here entitled to the protection of the business judgment rule?

Mesa contends that the discriminatory exchange offer violates the fiduciary duties Unocal owes it. Mesa argues that because of the Mesa exclusion the business judgment rule is inapplicable, because the directors by tendering their own shares will derive a financial benefit that is not available to all Unocal stockholders. Thus, it is Mesa's ultimate contention that Unocal cannot establish that the exchange offer is fair to all shareholders, and argues that the Court of Chancery was correct in concluding that Unocal was unable to meet this burden.

Unocal answers that it does not owe a duty of "fairness" to Mesa, given the facts here. Specifically, Unocal contends that its board of directors reasonably and in good faith concluded that Mesa's $54 two-tier tender offer was coercive and inadequate, and that Mesa sought selective treatment for itself. Furthermore, Unocal argues that the board's approval of the exchange offer was made in good faith, on an informed basis, and in the exercise of due care. Under these circumstances, Unocal contends that its directors properly employed this device to protect the company and its stockholders from Mesa's harmful tactics.

[**Authority to Adopt Defensive Measures**] We begin with the basic issue of the power of a board of directors of a Delaware corporation to adopt a defensive measure of this type. Absent such authority, all other questions are moot. Neither issues of fairness nor business judgment are pertinent without the basic underpinning of a board's legal power to act.

The board has a large reservoir of authority upon which to draw. Its duties and responsibilities proceed from the inherent powers conferred by 8 Del.C. § 141(a), respecting management of the corporation's "business and affairs". Additionally, the powers here being exercised derive from 8 Del.C. § 160(a), conferring broad authority upon a corporation to deal in its own stock. From this it is now well established that in the acquisition of its shares a Delaware corporation may deal selectively with its stockholders, provided the directors have not acted out of a sole or primary purpose to entrench themselves in office. *Cheff v. Mathes.*

Finally, the board's power to act derives from its fundamental duty and obligation to protect the corporate enterprise, which includes stockholders, from harm reasonably perceived, irrespective of its source. Thus, we are satisfied that in the broad context of corporate governance, including issues of fundamental corporate change, a board of directors is not a passive instrumentality.

[**Enhanced Business Judgment Rule**] Given the foregoing principles, we turn to the standards by which director action is to be measured. In *Pogostin v. Rice*, we held that the business judgment rule, including the standards by which director conduct is judged, is applicable in the context of a takeover. * * *

When a board addresses a pending takeover bid it has an obligation to determine whether the offer is in the best interests of the corporation and its shareholders. In that respect a board's duty is no different from any other responsibility it shoulders, and its decisions should be no less entitled to the respect they otherwise would be accorded in the realm of business judgment. There are, however, certain caveats to a proper exercise of this function. Because of the omnipresent specter that a board may be acting primarily in its own interests, rather than those of the corporation and its shareholders, there is an enhanced duty which calls for judicial examination at the threshold before the protections of the business judgment rule may be conferred. * * *

In the face of this inherent conflict directors must show that they had reasonable grounds for believing that a danger to corporate policy and effectiveness existed because of another person's stock ownership. *Cheff v. Mathes*, 199 A.2d.548 (Del. 1964). However, they satisfy that burden "by showing good faith and reasonable investigation * * *." Furthermore, such proof is materially enhanced, as here, by the approval of a board comprised of a majority of outside independent directors who have acted in accordance with the foregoing standards. * * *

A further aspect is the element of balance. If a defensive measure is to come within the ambit of the business judgment rule, it must be reasonable in relation to the threat posed. This entails an analysis by the directors of the nature of the takeover bid and its effect on the corporate enterprise. Examples of such concerns may include: inadequacy of the price offered, nature and timing of the offer, questions of illegality, the impact on "constituencies" other than shareholders (i.e., creditors, customers, employees, and perhaps even the community generally), the risk of nonconsummation, and the quality of securities being offered in the exchange. While not a controlling factor, it also seems to us that a board may reasonably consider the basic stockholder interests at stake, including those of short term speculators, whose actions may have fueled the coercive aspect of the offer at the expense of the long term investor. Here, the threat posed was viewed by the Unocal board as a grossly inadequate two-tier coercive tender offer coupled with the threat of greenmail.

Specifically, the Unocal directors had concluded that the value of Unocal was substantially above the $54 per share offered in cash at the front end. Furthermore, they determined that the subordinated securities to be exchanged in Mesa's announced squeeze out of the remaining shareholders in the "back-end" merger were "junk bonds" worth far less than $54. It is now well recognized that such offers are a classic coercive measure designed to stampede shareholders into tendering at the first tier, even if the price is inadequate, out of fear of what they will receive at the back end of the transaction. Wholly beyond the coercive aspect of an inadequate two-tier tender offer, the threat was posed by a corporate raider with a national reputation as a "greenmailer." [21]

In adopting the selective exchange offer, the board stated that its objective was either to defeat the inadequate Mesa offer or, should the offer still succeed, provide the 49% of its stockholders, who would otherwise be forced to accept "junk bonds," with $72 worth of senior debt. We find that both purposes are valid.

However, such efforts would have been thwarted by Mesa's participation in the exchange offer. * * *

Thus, we are satisfied that the selective exchange offer is reasonably related to the threats posed. * * *

[**Discrimination among Stockholders**] Mesa contends that it is unlawful, and the trial court agreed, for a corporation to discriminate in this fashion against one shareholder. * * * However, as we have noted earlier, the principle of selective stock repurchases by a Delaware corporation is neither unknown nor unauthorized. *Cheff v. Mathes.* The only difference is that heretofore the approved transaction was the payment of "greenmail" to a raider or dissident posing a threat to the corporate enterprise. [*See Cheff v. Mathes.* finding that in causing the corporation to repurchase its stock from a raider, the board did not act "solely or primarily because of the desire to perpetuate themselves in office,"

21. The term "greenmail" refers to the practice of buying out a takeover bidder's stock at a premium that is not available to other shareholders in order to prevent the takeover. The Chancery Court noted that "Mesa has made tremendous profits from its takeover activities although in the past few years it has not been successful in acquiring any of the target companies on an unfriendly basis." * * *

and therefore, in making the discriminatory repurchase, the board was not liable for a breach of fiduciary duty.] * * *

Thus, while the exchange offer is a form of selective treatment, given the nature of the threat posed here the response is neither unlawful nor unreasonable. If the board of directors is disinterested, has acted in good faith and with due care, its decision in the absence of an abuse of discretion will be upheld as a proper exercise of business judgment. * * *

In conclusion, there was directorial power to oppose the Mesa tender offer, and to undertake a selective stock exchange made in good faith and upon a reasonable investigation pursuant to a clear duty to protect the corporate enterprise. Further, the selective stock repurchase plan chosen by Unocal is reasonable in relation to the threat that the board rationally and reasonably believed was posed by Mesa's inadequate and coercive two-tier tender offer. Under those circumstances the board's action is entitled to be measured by the standards of the business judgment rule. Thus, unless it is shown by a preponderance of the evidence that the directors' decisions were primarily based on perpetuating themselves in office, or some other breach of fiduciary duty such as fraud, overreaching, lack of good faith, or being uninformed, a Court will not substitute its judgment for that of the board. * * *

Notes and Questions

1. The discriminatory self tender used by Unocal is now prohibited by the best price, all holders rule applicable under the Williams Act provisions of the Securities Exchange Act of 1934. The prohibition applies both to self-tenders [*see* Rule 13e–4(f)(10) and Chapter 21] and to third party tenders [*see* Rule 14d–10 and Chapter 20]. Thus, although Delaware law does not prohibit a discriminatory tender offer, such transactions are illegal under the federal securities law.

2. State precisely the enhanced business judgment rule adopted by the court in *Unocal*. What is the first prong of the test and how is it satisfied? What is the second prong of the test and how is it satisfied? Although, discriminatory self-tenders are now prohibited, the *Unocal* standard governs other types of defensive actions. The *Unitrin* case, which elaborates on the second prong of the *Unocal* test, is set out in Section 3.18.E.5, and other cases illustrating the application of *Unocal* are set out in Chapter 23, which deals with defensive tactics.

E. Application of the Business Judgment Rule to the Adoption of a Poison Pill: The First Delaware Decision—*Moran*, Decided in 1985

Moran v. Household International, Inc.

Delaware Supreme Court, 1985 500 A.2d 1346

McNeilly, Justice:

This case presents to this Court for review the most recent defensive mechanism in the arsenal of corporate takeover weaponry—the Preferred Share Purchase Rights Plan ("Rights Plan" or "Plan"). The validity of this mechanism has attracted national attention. * * *

In a detailed opinion, the Court of Chancery upheld the Rights Plan as a legitimate exercise of business judgment by Household. We agree, and therefore, affirm the judgment below. * * *

[**Basic Facts**] On August 14, 1984, the Board of Directors of Household International, Inc. adopted the Rights Plan by a fourteen to two vote.[22] * * * Basically, the Plan provides that Household common stockholders are entitled to the issuance of one Right per common share under certain triggering conditions. There are two triggering events that can activate the Rights. The first is the announcement of a tender offer for 30 percent of Household's shares ("30% trigger") and the second is the acquisition of 20 percent of Household's shares by any single entity or group ("20% trigger").

If an announcement of a tender offer for 30 percent of Household's shares is made, the Rights are issued and are immediately exercisable to purchase 1/100 share of new preferred stock for $100 and are redeemable by the Board for $.50 per Right. If 20 percent of Household's shares are acquired by anyone, the Rights are issued and become non-redeemable and are exercisable to purchase 1/100 of a share of preferred. [These provisions are referred to as "flip-ins" because they give the shareholder the right to buy shares of the target.] If a Right is not exercised for preferred, and thereafter, a merger or consolidation occurs, the Rights holder can exercise each Right to purchase $200 of the common stock of the tender offeror for $100. This "flip-over" provision of the Rights Plan is at the heart of this controversy. [The term flip-over reflects the fact that the target's shareholders can purchase at a bargain shares of the acquiror.] * * *

Household did not adopt its Rights Plan during a battle with a corporate raider, but as a preventive mechanism to ward off future advances. The Vice-Chancellor found that as early as February 1984, Household's management became concerned about the company's vulnerability as a takeover target and began considering amending its charter to render a takeover more difficult. After considering the matter, Household decided not to pursue a fair price amendment.

In the meantime, appellant Moran, one of Household's own Directors and also Chairman of the Dyson-Kissner-Moran Corporation, ("D-K-M") which is the largest single stockholder of Household, began discussions concerning a possible leveraged buy-out of Household by D-K-M. * * *

Concerned about Household's vulnerability to a raider in light of the current takeover climate, Household secured the services of Wachtell, Lipton, Rosen and Katz ("Wachtell, Lipton") and Goldman, Sachs & Co. ("Goldman, Sachs") to formulate a takeover policy for recommendation to the Household Board at its August 14 meeting. After a July 31 meeting with a Household Board member and a pre-meeting distribution of material on the potential takeover problem and the proposed Rights Plan, the Board met on August 14, 1984.

Representatives of Wachtell, Lipton and Goldman, Sachs attended the August 14 meeting. The minutes reflect that Mr. Lipton explained to the Board that his recommendation of the Plan was based on his understanding that the Board was concerned about the increasing frequency of "bust-up"[23] takeovers, the increasing takeover activity in the financial service industry. * * * Against this factual background, the Plan was approved.

Thereafter, Moran and the company of which he is Chairman, D-K-M, filed this suit. * * * The trial was held, and the Court of Chancery ruled in favor of Household. Appellants now appeal from that ruling to this Court.

---

22. Household's Board has ten outside directors and six who are members of management. * * *

23. "Bust-up" takeover generally refers to a situation in which one seeks to finance an acquisition by selling off pieces of the acquired company.

[**The Issues**] The primary issue here is the applicability of the business judgment rule as the standard by which the adoption of the Rights Plan should be reviewed. Much of this issue has been decided by our recent decision in *Unocal Corp.*, [Section 3.14.D]. * * *

[H]ere we have a defensive mechanism adopted to ward off possible future advances and not a mechanism adopted in reaction to a specific threat. This distinguishing factor does not result in the Directors losing the protection of the business judgment rule. To the contrary, pre-planning for the contingency of a hostile takeover might reduce the risk that, under the pressure of a takeover bid, management will fail to exercise reasonable judgment. Therefore, in reviewing a pre-planned defensive mechanism it seems even more appropriate to apply the business judgment rule.

Of course, the business judgment rule can only sustain corporate decision making or transactions that are within the power or authority of the Board. Therefore, before the business judgment rule can be applied it must be determined whether the Directors were authorized to adopt the Rights Plan.

[**Authority to Adopt the Pill**] Appellants vehemently contend that the Board of Directors was unauthorized to adopt the Rights Plan. First, appellants contend that no provision of the Delaware General Corporation Law authorizes the issuance of such Rights. Secondly, appellants, along with the SEC, contend that the Board is unauthorized to usurp stockholders' rights to receive hostile tender offers. Third, appellants and the SEC also contend that the Board is unauthorized to fundamentally restrict stockholders' rights to conduct a proxy contest. We address each of these contentions in turn.

While appellants contend that no provision of the Delaware General Corporation Law authorizes the Rights Plan, Household contends that the Rights Plan was issued pursuant to 8 Del.C. § 151(g) and § 157. It explains that the Rights are authorized by § 157 and the issue of preferred stock underlying the Rights is authorized by § 151. Appellants respond by making several attacks upon the authority to issue the Rights pursuant to § 157.

Appellants begin by contending that § 157 cannot authorize the Rights Plan since § 157 has never served the purpose of authorizing a takeover defense. Appellants contend that § 157 is a corporate financing statute, and that nothing in its legislative history suggests a purpose that has anything to do with corporate control or a takeover defense. Appellants are unable to demonstrate that the legislature, in its adoption of § 157, meant to limit the applicability of § 157 to only the issuance of Rights for the purposes of corporate financing. Without such affirmative evidence, we decline to impose such a limitation upon the section that the legislature has not. * * *

Secondly, appellants contend that § 157 does not authorize the issuance of sham rights such as the Rights Plan. They contend that the Rights were designed never to be exercised, and that the Plan has no economic value. In addition, they contend the preferred stock made subject to the Rights is also illusory.

Appellants' sham contention fails in both regards. * * *

Household contends, *inter alia*, that the Rights Plan is analogous to "anti-destruction" or "anti-dilution" provisions which are customary features of a wide variety of corporate securities. * * *

"Anti-destruction" clauses generally ensure holders of certain securities of the protection of their right of conversion in the event of a merger by giving them the right to convert their securities into whatever securities are to replace the stock of their company. The fact that the rights here have as their purpose the prevention of coercive two-tier tender offers does not invalidate them. * * *

Having concluded that sufficient authority for the Rights Plan exists in 8 Del.C. § 157, we note the inherent powers of the Board conferred by 8 Del.C. § 141(a), concerning the management of the corporation's "business and *affairs*" (emphasis added), also provides the Board additional authority upon which to enact the Rights Plan.

[**Shareholders Right to Receive Tender Offer**] Appellants contend that the Board is unauthorized to usurp stockholders' rights to receive tender offers by changing Household's fundamental structure. We conclude that the Rights Plan does not prevent stockholders from receiving tender offers, and that the change of Household's structure was less than that which results from the implementation of other defensive mechanisms upheld by various courts.

Appellants' contention that stockholders will lose their right to receive and accept tender offers seems to be premised upon an understanding of the Rights Plan which is illustrated by the SEC *amicus* brief which states: "The Chancery Court's decision seriously understates the impact of this plan. In fact, as we discuss below, the Rights Plan will deter not only two-tier offers, but virtually all hostile tender offers."

The fallacy of that contention is apparent when we look at the recent takeover of Crown Zellerbach, which has a similar Rights Plan, by Sir James Goldsmith. The evidence at trial also evidenced many methods around the Plan ranging from tendering with a condition that the Board redeem the Rights, tendering with a high minimum condition of shares and Rights, tendering and soliciting consents to remove the Board and redeem the Rights, to acquiring 50% of the shares and causing Household to self-tender for the Rights. One could also form a group of up to 19.9% and solicit proxies for consents to remove the Board and redeem the Rights. These are but a few of the methods by which Household can still be acquired by a hostile tender offer.

In addition, the Rights Plan is not absolute. When the Household Board of Directors is faced with a tender offer and a request to redeem the Rights, they will not be able to arbitrarily reject the offer. They will be held to the same fiduciary standards any other board of directors would be held to in deciding to adopt a defensive mechanism, the same standard as they were held to in originally approving the Rights Plan. *See Unocal.* * * *

[**Proxy Contests**] Appellants' third contention is that the Board was unauthorized to fundamentally restrict stockholders' rights to conduct a proxy contest. Appellants contend that the "20% trigger" effectively prevents any stockholder from first acquiring 20% or more shares before conducting a proxy contest and further, it prevents stockholders from banding together into a group to solicit proxies if, collectively, they own 20% or more of the stock. * * *

We conclude that there was sufficient evidence at trial to support the Vice-Chancellor's finding that the effect upon proxy contests will be minimal. Evidence at trial established that many proxy contests are won with an insurgent ownership of less than 20%, and that very large holdings are no guarantee of success. There was also testimony that the key variable in proxy contest success is the merit of an insurgent's issues, not the size of his holdings.

[**Business Judgment Rule**] Having concluded that the adoption of the Rights Plan was within the authority of the Directors, we now look to whether the Directors have met their burden under the business judgment rule.

[I]n *Unocal* we held that when the business judgment rule applies to adoption of a defensive mechanism, the initial burden will lie with the directors. The "directors must show that they had reasonable grounds for believing that a danger to corporate policy and effectiveness existed * * * [T]hey satisfy that burden 'by showing good faith and reasonable investigation* * *'" *Unocal.* In addition, the directors must show that the defensive mechanism was "reasonable in relation to the threat posed." Moreover, that proof is materially enhanced, as we noted in *Unocal*, where, as here, a majority of the board favoring the proposal consisted of outside independent directors who have acted in accordance with the foregoing standards. Then, the burden shifts back to the plaintiffs who have the ultimate burden of persuasion to show a breach of the directors' fiduciary duties.

There are no allegations here of any bad faith on the part of the Directors' action in the adoption of the Rights Plan. There is no allegation that the Directors' action was taken for entrenchment purposes. Household has adequately demonstrated, as explained above, that the adoption of the Rights Plan was in reaction to what it perceived to be the threat in the market place of coercive two-tier tender offers. Appellants do contend, however, that the Board did not exercise informed business judgment in its adoption of the Plan. * * *

To determine whether a business judgment reached by a board of directors was an informed one, we determine whether the directors were grossly negligent. *Smith v. Van Gorkom,* [Section 3.14.C] Upon a review of this record, we conclude the Directors were not grossly negligent. * * *

In addition, to meet their burden, the Directors must show that the defensive mechanism was "reasonable in relation to the threat posed". The record reflects a concern on the part of the Directors over the increasing frequency in the financial services industry of "boot-strap" and "bust-up" takeovers. The Directors were also concerned that such takeovers may take the form of two-tier offers. In addition, on August 14, the Household Board was aware of Moran's overture on behalf of D-K-M. In sum, the Directors reasonably believed Household was vulnerable to coercive acquisition techniques and adopted a reasonable defensive mechanism to protect itself.

In conclusion, the Household Directors receive the benefit of the business judgment rule in their adoption of the Rights Plan. * * *

While we conclude for present purposes that the Household Directors are protected by the business judgment rule, that does not end the matter. The ultimate response to an actual takeover bid must be judged by the Directors' actions at that time, and nothing we say here relieves them of their basic fundamental duties to the corporation and its stockholders. Their use of the Plan will be evaluated when and if the issue arises. * * *

Note and Questions

1. Explain precisely how the poison pill in *Moran* works. What is the court's approach in determining (1) whether the poison pill can be legally adopted, (2) whether the board acted properly in adopting the pill, and (3) the standards that will apply to the board in determining whether to redeem the pill?

2. Chapter 23, which deals with defensive tactics, examines poison pills in greater detail.

F. The Quasi Auction Standard—*Revlon,* Decided in 1986

Revlon, Inc. v. MacAndrews & Forbes Holdings

Delaware Supreme Court, 1986 506 A.2d 173

Moore, Justice:

[**Basic Facts**] In this battle for corporate control of Revlon, Inc. (Revlon), the Court of Chancery enjoined certain transactions designed to thwart the efforts of Pantry Pride,

Inc. (Pantry Pride) to acquire Revlon. [Pantry Pride made an unsolicited tender offer for Revlon at a price the Revlon board found to be inadequate. As a defensive measure Revlon entered into an agreement with Forstman Little & Co., a white knight, pursuant to which Forstman would acquire Revlon in an LBO. A bidding war resulted with Forstmann increasing its offer to $57.25 and Pantry Pride increasing to $56.25. As part of Revlon's agreement with Forstmann, Forstmann agreed to support the value of certain notes that had been issued by Revlon and had fallen in value, thereby raising a possibility of personal liability for the Revlon board. Also, Revlon granted Forstmann an asset lock-up option, a no shop restriction, and a cancellation fee.] The defendants are Revlon, its board of directors, and Forstmann Little & Co. and the latter's affiliated limited partnership (collectively, Forstmann). The injunction barred consummation of an option granted Forstmann to purchase certain Revlon assets (the lock-up option), a promise by Revlon to deal exclusively with Forstmann in the face of a takeover (the no-shop provision), and the payment of a $25 million cancellation fee to Forstmann if the transaction was aborted. The Court of Chancery found that the Revlon directors had breached their duty of care by entering into the foregoing transactions and effectively ending an active auction for the company. The trial court ruled that such arrangements are not illegal per se under Delaware law, but that their use under the circumstances here was impermissible. We agree. * * *

In our view, lock-ups and related agreements are permitted under Delaware law where their adoption is untainted by director interest or other breaches of fiduciary duty. The actions taken by the Revlon directors, however, did not meet this standard. Moreover, while concern for various corporate constituencies is proper when addressing a takeover threat, that principle is limited by the requirement that there be some rationally related benefit accruing to the stockholders. We find no such benefit here.

Thus, under all the circumstances we must agree with the Court of Chancery that the enjoined Revlon defensive measures were inconsistent with the directors' duties to the stockholders. Accordingly, we affirm. * * *

[**The Poison Pill**] The first relevant defensive measure adopted by the Revlon board was the Rights Plan, which would be considered a "poison pill" in the current language of corporate takeovers * * *.

* * * On October 12, the board unanimously passed a resolution redeeming the Rights in connection with any cash proposal of $57.25 or more per share. Because all the pertinent offers eventually equaled or surpassed that amount, the Rights clearly were no longer any impediment in the contest for Revlon. This mooted any question of their propriety under *Moran* or *Unocal.*

[**Exchange Offer**] The second defensive measure adopted by Revlon to thwart a Pantry Pride takeover was the company's own exchange offer for 10 million of its shares. The directors' general broad powers to manage the business and affairs of the corporation are augmented by the specific authority conferred under 8 Del.C. § 160(a), permitting the company to deal in its own stock. However, when exercising that power in an effort to forestall a hostile takeover, the board's actions are strictly held to the fiduciary standards outlined in *Unocal,* [Section 3.14.D] * * *.

The Revlon directors concluded that Pantry Pride's $47.50 offer was grossly inadequate. In that regard the board acted in good faith, and on an informed basis, with reasonable grounds to believe that there existed a harmful threat to the corporate enterprise. The adoption of a defensive measure, reasonable in relation to the threat posed, was proper and fully accorded with the powers, duties, and responsibilities conferred upon directors under our law.

[**The Auction Requirement**] However, when Pantry Pride increased its offer to $50 per share, and then to $53, it became apparent to all that the break-up of the company was inevitable. The Revlon board's authorization permitting management to negotiate a merger or buyout with a third party was a recognition that the company was for sale. The duty of the board had thus changed from the preservation of Revlon as a corporate entity to the maximization of the company's value at a sale for the stockholders' benefit. This significantly altered the board's responsibilities under the *Unocal* standards. It no longer faced threats to corporate policy and effectiveness, or to the stockholders' interests, from a grossly inadequate bid. The whole question of defensive measures became moot. The directors' role changed from defenders of the corporate bastion to auctioneers charged with getting the best price for the stockholders at a sale of the company.

[**The Lock-up**] This brings us to the lock-up with Forstmann and its emphasis on shoring up the sagging market value of the Notes in the face of threatened litigation by their holders. Such a focus was inconsistent with the changed concept of the directors' responsibilities at this stage of the developments. The impending waiver of the Notes covenants had caused the value of the Notes to fall, and the board was aware of the noteholders' ire as well as their subsequent threats of suit. The directors thus made support of the Notes an integral part of the company's dealings with Forstmann, even though their primary responsibility at this stage was to the equity owners.

The original threat posed by Pantry Pride—the break-up of the company—had become a reality which even the directors embraced. Selective dealing to fend off a hostile but determined bidder was no longer a proper objective. Instead, obtaining the highest price for the benefit of the stockholders should have been the central theme guiding director action. Thus, the Revlon board could not make the requisite showing of good faith by preferring the noteholders and ignoring its duty of loyalty to the shareholders. The rights of the former already were fixed by contract. The noteholders required no further protection, and when the Revlon board entered into an auction-ending lock-up agreement with Forstmann on the basis of impermissible considerations at the expense of the shareholders, the directors breached their primary duty of loyalty.

The Revlon board argued that it acted in good faith in protecting the noteholders because *Unocal* permits consideration of other corporate constituencies. Although such considerations may be permissible, there are fundamental limitations upon that prerogative. A board may have regard for various constituencies in discharging its responsibilities, provided there are rationally related benefits accruing to the stockholders. However, such concern for non-stockholder interests is inappropriate when an auction among active bidders is in progress, and the object no longer is to protect or maintain the corporate enterprise but to sell it to the highest bidder. * * *

Under such circumstances we must conclude that the merger agreement with Forstmann was unreasonable in relation to the threat posed.

A lock-up is not per se illegal under Delaware law. * * * Such options can entice other bidders to enter a contest for control of the corporation, creating an auction for the company and maximizing shareholder profit. * * * However, while those lock-ups which draw bidders into the battle benefit shareholders, similar measures which end an active auction and foreclose further bidding operate to the shareholders' detriment. * * *

While Forstmann's $57.25 offer was objectively higher than Pantry Pride's $56.25 bid, the margin of superiority is less when the Forstmann price is adjusted for the time value of money. In reality, the Revlon board ended the auction in return for very little actual improvement in the final bid. The principal benefit went to the directors, who avoided personal liability to a class of creditors to whom the board owed no further duty under the circumstances. Thus, when a board ends an intense bidding contest on an insubstantial basis, and where a significant by-product of that action is to protect the directors against a perceived threat of personal liability for consequences stemming from the adoption of previous defensive measures, the action cannot withstand the enhanced scrutiny which *Unocal* requires of director conduct. In addition to the lock-up option, the Court of Chancery enjoined the no-shop provision as part of the attempt to foreclose further bidding by Pantry Pride. The no-shop provision, like the lock-up option, while not per se illegal, is impermissible under the *Unocal* standards when a board's primary duty becomes that of an auctioneer responsible for selling the company to the highest bidder. The agreement to negotiate only with Forstmann ended rather than intensified the board's involvement in the bidding contest. * * *

The court below similarly enjoined the payment of the cancellation fee, pending a resolution of the merits, because the fee was part of the overall plan to thwart Pantry Pride's efforts. We find no abuse of discretion in that ruling. * * *

The measures were properly enjoined. * * *

Question

When does the auction standard adopted in *Revlon* apply? What is the relationship between *Revlon* and *Unocal*? Other cases elaborating on *Revlon* are set out below and in Chapter 23, which deals with defensive tactics.

G. The Compelling Justification Test—*Blasius*, Decided in 1988

Blasius Industries, Inc. v. Atlas Corp.

Delaware Court of Chancery, 1988 564 A2d 651

ALLEN, Chancellor.

[This case pits] the directors of Atlas Corporation against that company's largest (9.1%) shareholder, Blasius Industries. * * * [The case] ultimately requires the court to determine who is entitled to sit on Atlas' board of directors. * * *

[Blasius] challenges the validity of board action taken at a telephone meeting of December 31, 1987 that added two new members to Atlas' seven member board. That action was taken as an immediate response to the delivery to Atlas by Blasius the previous day of a form of stockholder consent that, if joined in by holders of a majority of Atlas' stock, would have increased the board of Atlas from seven to fifteen members and would have elected eight new members nominated by Blasius.

As I find the facts, they present the question whether a board acts consistently with its fiduciary duty when it acts, in good faith and with appropriate care, for the primary purpose of preventing or impeding an unaffiliated majority of shareholders from expanding the board and electing a new majority. For the reasons that follow, I conclude that, even though defendants here acted on their view of the corporation's interest and not selfishly, their December 31 action constituted an offense to the relationship between corporate directors and shareholders that has traditionally been protected in courts of equity. As a consequence, I conclude that the board action taken on December 31 was invalid and must be voided.

[**Basic Facts**] Blasius is a new stockholder of Atlas. It began to accumulate Atlas shares for the first time in July, 1987. On October 29, it filed a Schedule 13D with the Securities Exchange Commission disclosing that, with affiliates, it then owed 9.1% of Atlas' common stock. It stated in that filing that it intended to encourage management of Atlas to consider a restructuring of the Company or other transaction to enhance shareholder values. * * *

Immediately after filing its 13D on October 29, Blasius' representatives sought a meeting with the Atlas management. * * *

At that meeting, Messrs. Lubin and Delano [acting for Blasius] suggested that Atlas engage in a leveraged restructuring and distribute cash to shareholders.

This written proposal was distributed to the Atlas board on December 9 and Goldman Sachs was directed to review and analyze it.

The proposal met with a cool reception from management. On December 9, Mr. Weaver issued a press release expressing surprise that Blasius would suggest using debt to accomplish what he characterized as a substantial liquidation of Atlas at a time when Atlas' future prospects were promising. * * *

On December 30, 1987, Blasius caused Cede & Co. (the registered owner of its Atlas stock) to deliver to Atlas a signed written consent (1) adopting a precatory resolution recommending that the board develop and implement a restructuring proposal, (2) amending the Atlas bylaws to, among other things, expand the size of the board from seven to fifteen members, the maximum number under Atlas' charter, and (3) electing eight named persons to fill the new directorships. * * *

The reaction was immediate. Mr. Weaver conferred with Mr. Masinter, the Company's outside counsel and a director, who viewed the consent as an attempt to take control of the Company. They decided to call an emergency meeting of the board, even though a regularly scheduled meeting was to occur only one week hence, on January 6, 1988. The point of the emergency meeting was to act on their conclusion (or to seek to have the board act on their conclusion) "that we should add at least one and probably two directors to the board * * * "A quorum of directors, however, could not be arranged for a telephone meeting that day. A telephone meeting was held the next day. At that meeting, the board voted to amend the bylaws to increase the size of the board from seven to nine and appointed John M. Devaney and Harry J. Winters, Jr. to fill those newly created positions. Atlas' Certificate of Incorporation creates staggered terms for directors; the terms to which Messrs. Devaney and Winters were appointed would expire in 1988 and 1990, respectively.

In increasing the size of Atlas' board by two and filling the newly created positions, the members of the board realized that they were thereby precluding the holders of a majority of the Company's shares from placing a majority of new directors on the board through Blasius' consent solicitation, should they want to do so. Indeed the evidence establishes that was the principal motivation in so acting. * * *

I conclude that, while the addition of these qualified men would, under other circumstances, be clearly appropriate as an independent step, such a step was in fact taken in order to impede or preclude a majority of the shareholders from effectively adopting the course proposed by Blasius. * * *

[**Issues**] Plaintiff attacks the December 31 board action as a selfishly motivated effort to protect the incumbent board from a perceived threat to its control of Atlas. Their conduct is said to constitute a violation of the principle, applied in such cases as *Schnell v. Chris Craft Industries*, [Section 3.8] that directors hold legal powers subjected to a supervening duty to exercise such powers in good faith pursuit of what they reasonably believe to be in the corporation's interest. The December 31 action is also said to have been taken in a grossly negligent manner, since it was designed to preclude the recapitalization from being pursued, and the board had no basis at that time to make a prudent determination about the wisdom of that proposal, nor was there any emergency that required it to act in any respect regarding that proposal before putting itself in a position to do so advisedly.

Defendants, of course, contest every aspect of plaintiffs' claims. They claim the formidable protections of the business judgment rule. * * *

The real question the case presents, to my mind, is whether, in these circumstances, the board, even if it is acting with subjective good faith (which will typically, if not always, be a contestable or debatable judicial conclusion), may validly act for the principal purpose of preventing the shareholders from electing a majority of new directors. The question thus posed is not one of intentional wrong (or even negligence), but one of authority as between the fiduciary and the beneficiary (not simply legal authority, *i.e.*, as between the fiduciary and the world at large).

[**The Compelling Justification Test**] It is established in our law that a board may take certain steps, such as the purchase by the corporation of its own stock, that have the effect of defeating a threatened change in corporate control, when those steps are taken advisedly, in good faith pursuit of a corporate interest, and are reasonable in relation to a threat to legitimate corporate interests posed by the proposed change in control. *See Unocal.* Does this rule—that the reasonable exercise of good faith and due care generally validates, in equity, the exercise of legal authority even if the act has an entrenchment effect—apply to action designed for the primary purpose of interfering with the effectiveness of a stockholder vote? Our authorities, as well as sound principles, suggest that the central importance of the franchise to the scheme of corporate governance, requires that, in this setting, that rule not be applied and that closer scrutiny be accorded to such transaction. * * *

Plaintiff argues for a rule of *per se* invalidity once a plaintiff has established that a board has acted for the primary purpose of thwarting the exercise of a shareholder vote. * * *

A *per se* rule that would strike down, in equity, any board action taken for the primary purpose of interfering with the effectiveness of a corporate vote would have the advantage of relative clarity and predictability. * * *

In two recent cases dealing with shareholder votes, this court struck down board acts done for the primary purpose of impeding the exercise of stockholder voting power. In doing so, a *per se* rule was not applied. Rather, it was said that, in such a case, the board bears the heavy burden of demonstrating a compelling justification for such action. * * *

In my view, our inability to foresee now all of the future settings in which a board might, in good faith, paternalistically seek to thwart a shareholder vote, counsels against the adoption of a *per se* rule invalidating, in equity, every board action taken for the sole or primary purpose of thwarting a shareholder vote, even though I recognize the transcending significance of the franchise to the claims to legitimacy of our scheme of corporate governance. It may be that some set of facts would justify such extreme action. This, however, is not such a case. * * *

The board was not faced with a coercive action taken by a powerful shareholder against the interests of a distinct shareholder constituency (such as a public minority). It was presented with a consent solicitation by a 9% shareholder. Moreover, here it had time (and understood that it had time) to inform the shareholders of its views on the merits of the proposal subject to stockholder vote. The only justification that can, in such a situation, be offered for the action taken is that the board knows better than do the shareholders what is in the corporation's best interest. While that premise is no doubt true for any number of matters, it is irrelevant (except insofar as the shareholders wish to be guided by the board's recommendation) when the question is who should comprise the board of directors. * * *

I therefore conclude that, even finding the action taken was taken in good faith, it constituted an unintended violation of the duty of loyalty that the board owed to the shareholders. * * *

Question

What standard does the Court adopt in *Blasius*, and in what circumstances does the standard apply?

§ 3.15 Elaboration on the Business Judgment Rule in Arm's Length Negotiated Mergers

A. Introduction

This section builds on *Van Gorkom*, Section 3.14.C, by focusing on the applicability of the business judgment rule in negotiated mergers and acquisition that do not present duty of loyalty issues. The *Revlon* doctrine, which is examined in greater detail subsequently, may also apply in these transactions, and for this reason, this section starts with a look at Chancellor Strine's discussion in *Dollar Thrifty* of the link between *Van Gorkom* and *Revlon*.

If the business judgment rule applies, a shareholder action against directors will be dismissed pursuant to a summary motion, such as a motion to dismiss on the pleadings, thus avoiding the need for a trial. This section does not deal with situations where the directors of a target are on both sides of a transaction and, therefore, are not disinterested and independent. Subsequent sections examine the applicable fiduciary duty standards in other contexts, such as interested party mergers and the employment of defensive tactics.

B. Review *Van Gorkom*, Section 3.14.C

C. The Link between *Revlon* and *Van Gorkom*—*Dollar Thrifty*

1. The *Dollar Thrifty* Case

In Re Dollar Thrifty Shareholder Litigation

Court of Chancery of Delaware, 2010 Del. Ch. LEXIS 192

STRINE, Vice Chancellor.

Introduction. The plaintiffs seek a preliminary injunction preventing the consummation of a merger under a merger agreement under which Hertz Global Holdings, Inc. will buy all the shares of its smaller rental car industry rival Dollar Thrifty Automotive Group, Inc. for $ 32.80 per share in cash (including a $ 200 million special dividend that will only be paid in the event of the merger) and 0.6366 shares of Hertz stock for each share of Dollar Thrifty stock (the "Merger," and the "Merger Agreement" respectively). The Merger consideration was worth $ 41 per share as of signing. The plaintiffs criticize the

Dollar Thrifty board (the "Board") for failing to conduct a pre-signing auction and for signing up a Merger Agreement that yielded only a modest premium over the closing price of Dollar Thrifty's stock on the last trading day before the Merger Agreement was signed. Even worse, the plaintiffs say, the Merger Agreement included a termination fee and matching rights that the plaintiffs believe have a quelling effect on any topping bidder. [The court indicated that Avis was interested in acquiring Dollar Thrifty, but unlike Hertz, Avis refused to agree to a reverse termination fee (RTF). *See* Section 15.14 for a discussion of these fees. An RTF would require Avis to pay a fee to Dollar Thrifty in the event the transaction was blocked on antitrust grounds.] * * *

[This case presented issues under the *Revlon* standard, and in finding that the Dollar Thrifty board satisfied its *Revlon* duties, Chancellor Strine described those duties as follows, linking *Revlon* to *Van Gorkom*.]

Overview Of The *Revlon* Obligations of The Board. When the Dollar Thrifty Board decided to enter into a transaction that involved the sale of the company in a change of control transaction, it was charged with the obligation to secure the best value reasonably attainable for its shareholders, and to direct its fiduciary duties to that end. As is well known, *Revlon* does not require that a board, in determining the value-maximizing transaction, follow any specific plan or roadmap in meeting its duty to take reasonable steps to secure—i.e., actually attain—the best immediate value. Instead, *Revlon* commands that directors, consistent with their traditional fiduciary duties, act reasonably, "by undertaking a sound process to get the best deal available." Indeed, the question posed by a board's action (or inaction) in a sales context is "whether the directors made a reasonable decision, not a perfect decision." Thus, although the level of judicial scrutiny under *Revlon* is more exacting than the deferential rationality standard applicable to run-of-the-mill decisions governed by the business judgment rule, at bottom *Revlon* is a test of reasonableness; directors are generally free to select the path to value maximization, so long as they choose a reasonable route to get there. Specifically, this form of enhanced judicial scrutiny involves two "key features":

(a) a judicial determination regarding the adequacy of the decisionmaking process employed by the directors, including the information on which the directors based their decision; and

(b) a judicial examination of the reasonableness of the directors' action in light of the circumstances then existing. The directors have the burden of proving that they were adequately informed and acted reasonably. * * *

The Board Diligently Attended To Its Duties. [T]he *Revlon* standard demands that the court look closely to ensure that the Board was diligently attending to its duties. [Citing *Barkan*, 567 A.2d at 1286 ("The need for adequate information is central to the enlightened evaluation of a transaction that a board must make.").] *Van Gorkom*, [Section 3.14.C] after all, was really a *Revlon* case. [Citing *See e.g., Gagliardi v. Trifoods Int'l, Inc.* 683 A.2d 1049, 1051 n.4 ("I count [*Van Gorkom*] not as a 'negligence' or due care case involving no loyalty issues, but as an early, and as of its date, not yet fully rationalized, '*Revlon*' or 'change of control' case."); Bernard Black & Reiner Kraakman, Delaware's Takeover Law: *The Uncertain Search for Hidden Value*, 96 NW. U. L. REV. 521, 522 (2002) ("*Van Gorkom* should be seen not as a business judgment rule case but as a takeover case that was the harbinger of the then newly emerging Delaware jurisprudence on friendly and hostile takeovers, which included the almost contemporaneous *Unocal* and *Revlon* decisions.").]

Here, the record reveals that the Board was closely engaged at all relevant times in making decisions about how to handle the negotiations with Hertz and whether to try to bring Avis into the process. The deposition testimony of the independent directors reflects their deep involvement and their substantial experience in finance and business; each of the directors deposed gave cogent, uncoached testimony reflecting an impressive knowledge of the company, the industry, and the benefits and risks that different approaches entailed. Put simply, it may be that a well-motivated and careful board made an unreasonable judgment about how to maximize value, but that is the stark question that must be answered. The defendants have convinced me that the entire Board was subjectively well motivated and exercised due care. Even in the realm of heightened scrutiny, judicial (law-trained) second guessing of the means chosen by such a (business-experienced) board to maximize value should, one would think, be rare. * * *

2. Post-*Dollar Thrifty* Case Developments

Notwithstanding Chancellor Strine's refusal in *Dollar Thrifty* to issue an injunction against the acquisition by Hertz of Dollar Thrifty, the shareholders of Dollar Thrifty rejected the transaction. After the abandonment of this merger, on August 26, 2012, Hertz and Dollar Thrifty entered into another merger agreement, which required Hertz to (1) make an any and all tender offer for control of Dollar Thrifty, and (2) follow the tender offer with an acquisition of the non-tendered shares in a second-step freeze out merger. Hertz was required to pay $87.50 per share in both the tender offer and the second-step merger. Interestingly, the price at the time of the signing of the first merger agreement between Hertz and Dollar Thrifty, which was at issue in the above *Dollar Thrifty* case, was $41.00 per share.

Hertz's tender offer for the shares of Dollar Thrifty was made pursuant to its Offer to Purchase for Cash, dated August 10, 2012. The following is an excerpt from Hertz's detailed description in that Offer to Purchase of how the transaction got from $41.00 per share in the original merger agreement, which was signed on April 25, 2010, to $87.50 per share in the final merger agreement, which was signed on August 26, 2012:

> Beginning in 2007, Hertz and Dollar Thrifty have held periodic discussions regarding a potential business combination transaction. These discussions culminated in the entry into the 2010 Merger Agreement by Hertz, Purchaser and Dollar Thrifty on April 25, 2010. Pursuant to the 2010 Merger Agreement, Hertz agreed to acquire Dollar Thrifty for $41.00 per share of Dollar Thrifty common stock * * * consisting of an 80% cash / 20% Hertz common stock consideration mix.
>
> On July 28, 2010, Avis sent a letter to Dollar Thrifty offering to acquire Dollar Thrifty for $39.25 in cash and 0.6543 shares of Avis stock (then valued at $7.25) per share.
>
> On August 3, 2010, Dollar Thrifty notified Avis that Avis's offer did not satisfy all of the prongs of the "Superior Proposal" requirement under the 2010 Merger Agreement.
>
> On September 2, 2010, Avis issued a press release announcing that it had increased the cash portion of its offer from $39.25 to $40.75 per share. * * *
>
> On September 10, 2010, Hertz, Purchaser and Dollar Thrifty entered into an amendment to the previously executed 2010 Merger Agreement. The amendment provided for a $10.80 increase in the per share cash consideration to be paid by Hertz to Dollar Thrifty stockholders from $32.80 * * * to $43.60. * * *
>
> On September 23, 2010, Avis announced that it was increasing the cash portion of its offer from $40.75 to $45.79 per share. * * *

On September 24, 2010, Hertz affirmed that its offer to acquire Dollar Thrifty at a purchase price equivalent to $50.25 (based on the then-current value of Hertz common stock and including the special per share amount) was Hertz's final offer.

On September 30, 2010, at a special meeting of Dollar Thrifty stockholders, such stockholders did not approve the proposal to adopt the 2010 Merger Agreement. As a result, on October 1, 2010, Hertz terminated the 2010 Merger Agreement. Also, on October 1, 2010, Hertz withdrew its application under the HSR Act with the FTC and the U.S. Department of Justice. * * *

On May 9, 2011, Hertz filed its registration statement on Form S-4 with the SEC and filed a press release announcing its intent to commence an exchange offer at a price per share of Dollar Thrifty common stock of (i) $57.60 in cash * * *, and (ii) 0.8546 shares of Hertz common stock, and to consummate a second-step merger following completion of the proposed exchange offer.

On May 18, 2011, Dollar Thrifty adopted a stockholder rights plan. * * *

On September 6, 2011, J.P. Morgan, on behalf of Dollar Thrifty, sent a letter to each of Mr. Frissora and Mr. Nelson outlining the process for Dollar Thrifty's solicitation of acquisition proposals. * * *

On August 2, 2012, Dollar Thrifty and Hertz executed a confidentiality agreement that included an exclusivity agreement. The confidentiality agreement provided that, during the exclusivity period, Dollar Thrifty would not (i) solicit or initiate, seek, participate in or otherwise knowingly encourage or knowingly take any action to facilitate the submission of, any expression of interest, inquiry, proposal or offer from any third party relating to a business combination transaction or (ii) knowingly participate in any negotiations or discussions with any third party regarding, or furnish any nonpublic information to any third party with respect to, or otherwise pursue, enter into, accept or consummate, any proposed business combination transaction involving any third party. Dollar Thrifty further agreed to terminate or suspend any then existing negotiations with any third party regarding a business combination transaction during the exclusivity period. The agreement provided that the exclusivity period would run from August 2, 2012 until terminated by either Hertz or Dollar Thrifty, provided that neither party could terminate the exclusivity period until August 16, 2012. * * *

During the afternoon of August 17, 2012, Hertz's board of directors convened a meeting to discuss the proposed transaction. Following this meeting, Mr. Frissora and Mr. Thompson again spoke by telephone. During this call, Mr. Frissora told Mr. Thompson that Hertz was prepared to increase its offer from $86.00 per share to $86.50 per share in cash. Mr. Thompson responded that in his view the Dollar Thrifty Board would also find a proposal of $86.50 to be inadequate. Later in the call, Mr. Thompson told Mr. Frissora that Dollar Thrifty may be willing to consider an all cash transaction of $88.00 per share. * * *

Following these discussions and until the entry into the definitive merger agreement, representatives of Cravath and representatives of Cleary held discussions regarding the terms of the proposed transaction.

On August 22, 2012, * * * Mr. Frissora told Mr. Thompson that Hertz would be willing to consider * * * an all cash transaction of $87.50 per share. * * *

On August 22, 2012, Mr. Thompson contacted Mr. Frissora and informed him that the Dollar Thrifty Board authorized Dollar Thrifty to pursue a transaction with Hertz at a price of $87.50 per share, in cash.

Later in the evening on August 26, 2012, the merger agreement was executed by officers of Dollar Thrifty, Hertz and Purchaser. * * *

On September 10, 2012, Hertz commenced the Offer.

D. Fiduciary Duties of Officers and the Availability of Exculpation under § 102(b)(7)—*Gantler* and *Hampshire*

In *Gantler v. Stephens*, 965 A.2d 695 (Del. 2009), the Delaware Supreme Court said the following regarding the fiduciary duties of officers:

> The Court of Chancery has held, and the parties do not dispute, that corporate officers owe fiduciary duties that are identical to those owed by corporate directors. That issue—whether or not officers owe fiduciary duties identical to those of directors—has been characterized as a matter of first impression for this Court. In the past, we have implied that officers of Delaware corporations, like directors, owe fiduciary duties of care and loyalty, and that the fiduciary duties of officers are the same as those of directors.[24] We now explicitly so hold.[25] The only question presented here is whether the complaint alleges sufficiently detailed acts of wrongdoing by Stephens and Safarek to state a claim that they breached their fiduciary duties as officers. We conclude that it does. * * *

Vice Chancellor, now Chief Justice, Strine in his decision in *Hampshire Group Limited v. Kuttner*, 2010 Del. Ch. LEXIS 144, addressed this issue as follows:

> As officers and key employees of Hampshire, both Clayton and Clark owed certain fiduciary duties to the company and its stockholders. As a general matter, our Supreme Court has found that the duties of corporate officers are similar to those of corporate directors. Generally, like directors, Clayton and Clark were expected to pursue the best interests of the company in good faith (*i.e.*, to fulfill their duty of loyalty) and to use the amount of care that a reasonably prudent person would use in similar circumstances (*i.e.*, to fulfill their duty of care). [Citing *inter alia*, *Disney*, *infra*]
>
> There are important and interesting questions about the extent to which officers and employees should be more or less exposed to liability for breach of fiduciary duty than corporate directors. The parties in this case have not delved into any of those issues, and I see no justifiable reason for me to do so myself. Indeed, Hampshire embraces the notion that the standard of liability that should apply to Clayton and Clark as to its due care claim requires proof that Clayton

---

24. *See, e.g.*, In re Walt Disney Co., Deriv. Litig., 2004 Del. Ch. LEXIS 132, 2004 WL 2050138, at *3 (Del. Ch. September 10, 2004) ("To date, the fiduciary duties of officers have been assumed to be identical to those of directors.") (citations omitted).

25. That does not mean, however, that the consequences of a fiduciary breach by directors or officers, respectively, would necessarily be the same. Under 8 Del. C. § 102(b)(7), a corporation may adopt a provision in its certificate of incorporation exculpating its directors from monetary liability for an adjudicated breach of their duty of care. Although legislatively possible, there currently is no statutory provision authorizing comparable exculpation of corporate officers.

> and Clark acted with gross negligence. That is the standard used for corporate directors. [Citing *Van Gorkom*] The reason for that standard is well-known. If corporate fiduciaries were held responsible in damages because a fact-finder, subject to hindsight bias, found they were negligent and caused preventable harm, useful risk-taking would be reduced. Hampshire does not fight with that justification here, and I apply the gross negligence standard. * * *

If an officer causes a corporation harm by acting negligently (but not grossly negligently), should the corporation be able to recover from the officer in the absence of a provision in the officer's employment agreement?

E. The Business Judgment Rule Generally and the Exception to Section 102(b)(7) for Acts Not in Good Faith—*Disney*

In Re The Walt Disney Company Derivative Litigation

Delaware Supreme Court, 2006 Del. LEXIS 307

JACOBS, Justice:

In August 1995, Michael Ovitz ("Ovitz") and The Walt Disney Company ("Disney" or the "Company") entered into an employment agreement under which Ovitz would serve as President of Disney for five years. In December 1996, only fourteen months after he commenced employment, Ovitz was terminated without cause, resulting in a severance payout to Ovitz valued at approximately $130 million.

In January 1997, several Disney shareholders brought derivative actions in the Court of Chancery, on behalf of Disney, against Ovitz and the directors of Disney who served at the time of the events complained of (the "Disney defendants"). The plaintiffs claimed that the $130 million severance payout was the product of fiduciary duty and contractual breaches by Ovitz, and breaches of fiduciary duty by the Disney defendants, and a waste of assets. * * * In August 2005, the Chancellor handed down a well-crafted 174 page Opinion and Order, determining that "the director defendants did not breach their fiduciary duties or commit waste." The Court entered judgment in favor of all defendants on all claims alleged in the amended complaint.

The plaintiffs have appealed from that judgment, claiming that the Court of Chancery committed multitudinous errors. We conclude, for the reasons that follow, that the Chancellor's factual findings and legal rulings were correct and not erroneous in any respect. Accordingly, the judgment entered by the Court of Chancery will be affirmed.

[As a result of the Section 102(b)(7) provision of Disney's charter, the directors would only be liable for violations of their duty of loyalty or for acts not in good faith. There was no loyalty issue in *Disney*, and only the treatment of the good faith issue is addressed here.]

The Good Faith Determinations **[Regarding the Hiring]**. The Court of Chancery held that the business judgment rule presumptions protected the decisions of the compensation committee and the remaining Disney directors, not only because they had acted with due care but also because they had not acted in bad faith. That latter ruling, the appellants claim, was reversible error because the Chancellor formulated and then applied an incorrect definition of bad faith.

In its Opinion the Court of Chancery defined bad faith as follows:

> Upon long and careful consideration, I am of the opinion that the concept of *intentional dereliction of duty*, a *conscious disregard for one's responsibilities*, is

> an appropriate (although not the only) standard for determining whether fiduciaries have acted in good faith. Deliberate indifference and inaction *in the face of a duty to act* is, in my mind, conduct that is clearly disloyal to the corporation. It is the epitome of faithless conduct. * * *

The precise question is whether the Chancellor's articulated standard for bad faith corporate fiduciary conduct-intentional dereliction of duty, a conscious disregard for one's responsibilities—is legally correct. In approaching that question, we note that the Chancellor characterized that definition as "*an* appropriate (*although not the only*) standard for determining whether fiduciaries have acted in good faith." That observation is accurate and helpful, because as a matter of simple logic, at least three different categories of fiduciary behavior are candidates for the "bad faith" pejorative label.

The first category involves so-called "subjective bad faith," that is, fiduciary conduct motivated by an actual intent to do harm. That such conduct constitutes classic, quintessential bad faith is a proposition so well accepted in the liturgy of fiduciary law that it borders on axiomatic. We need not dwell further on this category, because no such conduct is claimed to have occurred, or did occur, in this case.

The second category of conduct, which is at the opposite end of the spectrum, involves lack of due care—that is, fiduciary action taken solely by reason of gross negligence and without any malevolent intent. In this case, appellants assert claims of gross negligence to establish breaches not only of director due care but also of the directors' duty to act in good faith. Although the Chancellor found, and we agree, that the appellants failed to establish gross negligence, to afford guidance we address the issue of whether gross negligence (including a failure to inform one's self of available material facts), without more, can also constitute bad faith. The answer is clearly no.

From a broad philosophical standpoint, that question is more complex than would appear, if only because (as the Chancellor and others have observed) "issues of good faith are (to a certain degree) inseparably and necessarily intertwined with the duties of care and loyalty * * * ." But, in the pragmatic, conduct-regulating legal realm which calls for more precise conceptual line drawing, the answer is that grossly negligent conduct, without more, does not and cannot constitute a breach of the fiduciary duty to act in good faith. The conduct that is the subject of due care may overlap with the conduct that comes within the rubric of good faith in a psychological sense,[26] but from a legal standpoint those duties are and must remain quite distinct. Both our legislative history and our common law jurisprudence distinguish sharply between the duties to exercise due care and to act in good faith, and highly significant consequences flow from that distinction.

The Delaware General Assembly has addressed the distinction between bad faith and a failure to exercise due care (*i.e.*, gross negligence) in two separate contexts. The first is Section 102(b)(7) of the DGCL, which authorizes Delaware corporations, by a provision

26. An example of such overlap might be the hypothetical case where a director, because of subjective hostility to the corporation on whose board he serves, fails to inform himself of, or to devote sufficient attention to, the matters on which he is making decisions as a fiduciary. In such a case, two states of mind coexist in the same person: subjective bad intent (which would lead to a finding of bad faith) and gross negligence (which would lead to a finding of a breach of the duty of care). Although the coexistence of both states of mind may make them indistinguishable from a psychological standpoint, the fiduciary duties that they cause the director to violate—care and good faith—are legally separate and distinct.

in the certificate of incorporation, to exculpate their directors from monetary damage liability for a breach of the duty of care. That exculpatory provision affords significant protection to directors of Delaware corporations. The statute carves out several exceptions, however, including most relevantly, "for acts or omissions not in good faith * * *." Thus, a corporation can exculpate its directors from monetary liability for a breach of the duty of care, but not for conduct that is not in good faith. To adopt a definition of bad faith that would cause a violation of the duty of care automatically to become an act or omission "not in good faith," would eviscerate the protections accorded to directors by the General Assembly's adoption of Section 102(b)(7).

A second legislative recognition of the distinction between fiduciary conduct that is grossly negligent and conduct that is not in good faith, is Delaware's indemnification statute, found at 8 *Del. C.* § 145. To oversimplify, subsections (a) and (b) of that statute permit a corporation to indemnify (*inter alia*) any person who is or was a director, officer, employee or agent of the corporation against expenses (including attorneys' fees), judgments, fines and amounts paid in settlement of specified actions, suits or proceedings, where (among other things): (i) that person is, was, or is threatened to be made a party to that action, suit or proceeding, and (ii) that person "acted in good faith and in a manner the person reasonably believed to be in or not opposed to the best interests of the corporation * * * ." Thus, under Delaware statutory law a director or officer of a corporation can be indemnified for liability (and litigation expenses) incurred by reason of a violation of the duty of care, but not for a violation of the duty to act in good faith.

Section 145, like Section 102(b)(7), evidences the intent of the Delaware General Assembly to afford significant protections to directors (and, in the case of Section 145, other fiduciaries) of Delaware corporations. To adopt a definition that conflates the duty of care with the duty to act in good faith by making a violation of the former an automatic violation of the latter, would nullify those legislative protections and defeat the General Assembly's intent. There is no basis in policy, precedent or common sense that would justify dismantling the distinction between gross negligence and bad faith.[27]

That leaves the third category of fiduciary conduct, which falls in between the first two categories of (1) conduct motivated by subjective bad intent and (2) conduct resulting from gross negligence. This third category is what the Chancellor's definition of bad faith—intentional dereliction of duty, a conscious disregard for one's responsibilities—is intended to capture. The question is whether such misconduct is properly treated as a non-exculpable, non-indemnifiable violation of the fiduciary duty to act in good faith. In our view it must be, for at least two reasons.

First, the universe of fiduciary misconduct is not limited to either disloyalty in the classic sense (*i.e.*, preferring the adverse self-interest of the fiduciary or of a related person to the interest of the corporation) or gross negligence. Cases have arisen where corporate

---

27. Basic to the common law of torts is the distinction between conduct that is negligent (or grossly negligent) and conduct that is intentional. And in the narrower area of corporation law, our jurisprudence has recognized the distinction between the fiduciary duties to act with due care, with loyalty, and in good faith, as well as the consequences that flow from that distinction. Recent Delaware case law precludes a recovery of rescissory (as distinguished from out-of-pocket) damages for a breach of the duty of care, but permits such a recovery for a breach of the duty of loyalty. *See* Cinerama, Inc. v. Technicolor, Inc., 663 A.2d 1134, 1147–1150 (Del. Ch. 1994), aff'd., 663 A.2d 1156 (Del. 1995).

directors have no conflicting self-interest in a decision, yet engage in misconduct that is more culpable than simple inattention or failure to be informed of all facts material to the decision. To protect the interests of the corporation and its shareholders, fiduciary conduct of this kind, which does not involve disloyalty (as traditionally defined) but is qualitatively more culpable than gross negligence, should be proscribed. A vehicle is needed to address such violations doctrinally, and that doctrinal vehicle is the duty to act in good faith. The Chancellor implicitly so recognized in his Opinion, where he identified different examples of bad faith as follows:

> The good faith required of a corporate fiduciary includes not simply the duties of care and loyalty, in the narrow sense that I have discussed them above, but all actions required by a true faithfulness and devotion to the interests of the corporation and its shareholders. A failure to act in good faith may be shown, for instance, where the fiduciary intentionally acts with a purpose other than that of advancing the best interests of the corporation, where the fiduciary acts with the intent to violate applicable positive law, or where the fiduciary intentionally fails to act in the face of a known duty to act, demonstrating a conscious disregard for his duties. There may be other examples of bad faith yet to be proven or alleged, but these three are the most salient.

Those articulated examples of bad faith are not new to our jurisprudence. Indeed, they echo pronouncements our courts have made throughout the decades.

Second, the legislature has also recognized this intermediate category of fiduciary misconduct, which ranks between conduct involving subjective bad faith and gross negligence. Section 102(b)(7)(ii) of the DGCL expressly denies money damage exculpation for "acts or omissions not in good faith or which involve intentional misconduct or a knowing violation of law." By its very terms that provision distinguishes between "intentional misconduct" and a "knowing violation of law" (both examples of subjective bad faith) on the one hand, and "acts * * * not in good faith," on the other. Because the statute exculpates directors only for conduct amounting to gross negligence, the statutory denial of exculpation for "acts * * * not in good faith" must encompass the intermediate category of misconduct captured by the Chancellor's definition of bad faith.

For these reasons, we uphold the Court of Chancery's definition as a legally appropriate, although not the exclusive, definition of fiduciary bad faith. * * *

F. The Business Judgment Rule and the Financial Crisis—*Citigroup*

In Re Citigroup Inc. Shareholder Derivative Litigation

Delaware Chancery Court, 964 A.2d 106, 2009

CHANDLER, Chancellor

This is a shareholder derivative action brought on behalf of Citigroup Inc. ("Citigroup" or the "Company"), seeking to recover for the Company its losses arising from exposure to the subprime lending market. Plaintiffs, shareholders of Citigroup, brought this action against current and former directors and officers of Citigroup, alleging, in essence, that the defendants breached their fiduciary duties by failing to properly monitor and manage the risks the Company faced from problems in the subprime lending market and for failing to properly disclose Citigroup's exposure to subprime assets. Plaintiffs allege that there were extensive "red flags" that should have given defendants notice of the problems that were brewing in the real estate and credit markets and that defendants ignored these warnings in the pursuit of short term profits and at the expense of the Company's long term viability. * * *

DEMAND FUTILITY REGARDING PLAINTIFFS' FIDUCIARY DUTY CLAIMS. [After discussing *Caremark*, the court went on to say:] In *Stone v. Ritter*, [Section 3.11.E], the Delaware Supreme Court approved the *Caremark* standard for director oversight liability and made clear that liability was based on the concept of good faith, which the *Stone* Court held was embedded in the fiduciary duty of loyalty and did not constitute a freestanding fiduciary duty that could independently give rise to liability. As the *Stone* Court explained:

> *Caremark* articulates the necessary conditions predicate for director oversight liability: (a) the directors utterly failed to implement any reporting or information system or controls; or (b) having implemented such a system or controls, consciously failed to monitor or oversee its operations thus disabling themselves from being informed of risks or problems requiring their attention. In either case, imposition of liability requires a showing that the directors knew that they were not discharging their fiduciary obligations. Where directors fail to act in the face of a known duty to act, thereby demonstrating a conscious disregard for their responsibilities, they breach their duty of loyalty by failing to discharge that fiduciary obligation in good faith.

Thus, to establish oversight liability a plaintiff must show that the directors knew they were not discharging their fiduciary obligations or that the directors demonstrated a conscious disregard for their responsibilities such as by failing to act in the face of a known duty to act. The test is rooted in concepts of bad faith; indeed, a showing of bad faith is a necessary condition to director oversight liability.

CONCLUSION [In dismissing the plaintiffs' fiduciary duty claims on the grounds that they failed to adequately plead demand futility, the court reasoned:] Citigroup has suffered staggering losses, in part, as a result of the recent problems in the United States economy, particularly those in the subprime mortgage market. It is understandable that investors, and others, want to find someone to hold responsible for these losses, and it is often difficult to distinguish between a desire to blame someone and a desire to force those responsible to account for their wrongdoing. Our law, fortunately, provides guidance for precisely these situations in the form of doctrines governing the duties owed by officers and directors of Delaware corporations. This law has been refined over hundreds of years, which no doubt included many crises, and we must not let our desire to blame someone for our losses make us lose sight of the purpose of our law. Ultimately, the discretion granted directors and managers allows them to maximize shareholder value in the long term by taking risks without the debilitating fear that they will be held personally liable if the company experiences losses. This doctrine also means, however, that when the company suffers losses, shareholders may not be able to hold the directors personally liable.

G. Applicability of Business Judgment Rule to Decision of Target's Directors to Not Consider a Merger Proposal—*Gantler*

Gantler v. Stephens

Delaware Supreme Court, 2009 965 A.2d 695

Jacobs Justice:

The plaintiffs in this breach of fiduciary duty action, who are certain shareholders of First Niles Financial, Inc. ("First Niles" or the "Company"), appeal from the dismissal of their complaint by the Court of Chancery. The complaint alleges that the defendants, who are officers and directors of First Niles, violated their fiduciary duties by rejecting a valuable opportunity to sell the Company, deciding instead to reclassify the Company's shares in order to benefit themselves, and by disseminating a materially misleading proxy statement to induce shareholder approval. We conclude that the complaint pleads sufficient facts to overcome the business judgment presumption, and to state substantive fiduciary duty and disclosure claims. We therefore reverse the Court of Chancery's judgment of dismissal and remand the case for further proceedings consistent with this Opinion. * * *

The Court of Chancery Misapplied the Business Judgment Standard. The plaintiffs next claim that the legal sufficiency of Count I should have been reviewed under the entire fairness standard. * * *

A board's decision not to pursue a merger opportunity is normally reviewed within the traditional business judgment framework. [Citing *TW Services*, *infra* Section 3.18.E.3.] In that context the board is entitled to a strong presumption in its favor, because implicit in the board's statutory authority to propose a merger, is also the power to decline to do so.

Our analysis of whether the Board's termination of the Sales Process merits the business judgment presumption is two pronged. First, did the Board reach its decision in the good faith pursuit of a legitimate corporate interest? Second, did the Board do so advisedly? For the Board's decision here to be entitled to the business judgment presumption, both questions must be answered affirmatively. We consider first whether Count I alleges a cognizable claim that the Board breached its duty of loyalty. In *TW Services v. SWT Acquisition Corporation*, the Court of Chancery recognized that a board's decision to decline a merger is often rooted in distinctively corporate concerns, such as enhancing the corporation's long term share value, or "a plausible concern that the level of debt likely to be borne by [the target company] following any merger would be detrimental to the long term function of th[at] [c]ompany." A good faith pursuit of legitimate concerns of this kind will satisfy the first prong of the analysis.

Here, the plaintiffs allege that the Director Defendants had a disqualifying self-interest because they were financially motivated to maintain the status quo. A claim of this kind must be viewed with caution, because to argue that directors have an entrenchment motive solely because they could lose their positions following an acquisition is, to an extent, tautological. By its very nature, a board decision to reject a merger proposal could always enable a plaintiff to assert that a majority of the directors had an entrenchment motive. For that reason, the plaintiffs must plead, in addition to a motive to retain corporate control, other facts sufficient to state a cognizable claim that the Director Defendants acted disloyally.

The plaintiffs have done that here. At the time the Sales Process was terminated, the Board members were Stephens, Kramer, Eddy, Zuzolo and Gander. Only Gander voted to accept the First Place merger bid. The pled facts are sufficient to establish disloyalty of at least three (i.e., a majority) of the remaining directors, which suffices to rebut the business judgment presumption. * * *

In summary, the plaintiffs have alleged facts sufficient to establish, for purposes of a motion to dismiss, that a majority of the First Niles Board acted disloyally. Because a cognizable claim of disloyalty rebuts the business judgment presumption, we need not reach the separate question of whether, in deciding to terminate the Sales Process, the Director Defendants acted advisedly (i.e., with due care). Because the claim of disloyalty was subject to entire fairness review, the Court of Chancery erred in dismissing Count I as to the Director Defendants on the basis of the business judgment presumption. * * *

H. Applicability of Business Judgment Rule to Acquiror's Directors

1. Allegation That Acquiror's Directors Ignored Warning Signs—*Ash*

Ash v. McCall

Delaware Court of Chancery, 2000 Del. Ch. LEXIS 144

CHANDLER, Chancellor

Shareholder plaintiffs * * * assert derivative claims on behalf of McKesson HBOC, Inc. ("McKesson HBOC" or the "Company"), a Delaware corporation, which was formed through the merger of McKesson Corporation ("McKesson") [the acquiring company] and HBOC & Co. ("HBOC") [the target company] on January 12, 1999. Approximately 3 1/2 months after McKesson's acquisition of HBOC became effective, McKesson HBOC issued the first of what appears to be three downward revisions of revenues, earnings, net income, and other financial information, for financial years 1996–1998. The complaint generally asserts claims related to these revisions. Pending before me is defendants' motion to dismiss. * * *

Generally, plaintiffs allege [*inter alia*] that the * * * McKesson directors breached their duty of care in the course of investigating HBOC's books and records before the merger; and, finally, that McKesson's acquisition of HBOC constituted an act of corporate waste. * * *

Analysis * * *

Are the Director Defendants Disinterested and Independent? * * * Plaintiffs have not made a single factual allegation that ten of twelve [McKesson] board members, all of whom were non-management, outside directors, had any material self-interest in the merger. Nor have they alleged particularized facts that would establish that * * * the two allegedly interested directors * * * dominated the ten non-management, outside directors, neutralizing their ability to make a good faith judgment with respect to the merger transaction. * * *

Is There a Reasonable Doubt that Approval of the Merger was the Product of a Valid Exercise of Business Judgment? Under *Aronson's* second prong, the Court must determine whether the complaint raises a reasonable doubt that the "directors exercised proper business judgment in the transaction." * * *

The Due Care Claim. Here lies the heart of the lawsuit against former McKesson directors. * * * Plaintiffs contend that the directors missed several "red flags" that should have alerted them to the accounting problems, in the course of full-scale due diligence, before they approved the merger. Plaintiffs then allege that the directors failed to identify the accounting defects, with some degree of mental culpability ranging from actual knowledge to gross recklessness, reckless disregard, just plain recklessness and, finally, gross negligence.

The notion that McKesson directors had actual knowledge of HBOC's earnings overstatements and nonetheless proceeded with the merger finds no support in the amended complaint. Moreover, it is simply illogical to presume that McKesson directors would knowingly cause McKesson to acquire a company with significant, undisclosed earnings misstatements. * * *

Taking all the facts in the complaint as true, and reading every conceivable inference in plaintiffs' favor, inexorably leads to the conclusion that plaintiffs' claims sound in negligence, at most. The McKesson board determined that it was in McKesson's strategic interests to enter the healthcare information technology business. It then acted on that objective by pursuing a business combination with HBOC—one of the leading companies in the field. It hired expert accounting and financial advisors to perform due diligence on HBOC—DeLoitte & Touche and Bear Stearns, respectively. After DeLoitte and Bear Stearns completed their due diligence reviews, with the participation of McKesson management, they waived "green flags" to the McKesson board, in effect saying, "This merger is financially and strategically sound." The McKesson directors approved the merger. * * *

Plaintiffs have not alleged facts creating a reasonable doubt that the McKesson directors did not act in accordance with any of these guidelines. * * *

2. Allegation That Acquiror Overpaid to Keep CEO in Office—*J.P. Morgan*

In Re J.P. Morgan Chase & Co. Shareholder Litigation

Delaware Court of Chancery, 2005 WL 1076069

LAMB, Vice Chancellor.

In 2004, two banks [J.P. Morgan Chase (JPMC), the acquiror, and Bank One, the target] agreed to a business combination that was expected to create the second largest financial institution in the country. One bank paid a premium over the market share price for the other bank, effectively making one bank the acquirer and the other bank the target.

After the merger was completed, the stockholders of the acquirer sued its directors, alleging breaches of fiduciary duty with regard to the acquisition. Their claims stem from the allegation that the directors paid too much for the acquired bank. Specifically, the plaintiffs claim that the CEO of the target proposed a no-premium merger if he were immediately promoted to CEO of the resulting entity. The CEO of the acquirer allegedly refused that offer, choosing instead to pay the premium for the target's stock and retain his title.

The plaintiffs bring this class action in an effort to recover damages for what they contend are direct claims. The defendants move to dismiss the complaint on the basis that the claims are derivative, not direct, and that demand was not excused. For the reasons below, that motion is granted. * * *

The plaintiffs seek damages in the amount of the merger exchange ratio premium, approximately $7 billion. They allege that the JPMC board of directors, by approving the unfavorable merger exchange ratio and the unnecessary premium, harmed them directly by diluting their interests in JPMC. If the JPMC board had approved a no-premium merger exchange ratio, the argument goes, the plaintiffs would have a greater stake in the resulting company. Instead, the stockholders of the pre-merger JPMC now have less of a stake in the post-merger JPMC. * * *

Procedure. The defendants move to dismiss, arguing that the claims asserted are derivative and that demand is not excused. * * *

Direct Or Derivative Analysis. The court begins by analyzing whether the stated claims are direct or derivative. The Delaware Supreme Court recently revised the standard for determining whether a claim is direct or derivative to "turn solely on the following questions: (1) who suffered the alleged harm (the corporation or the suing stockholders, individually); and (2) who would receive the benefit of any recovery or other remedy (the corporation or the stockholders, individually)?" [citing *Tooley v. Donaldson, Lulkin & Jenrette, Inc.*, Section 3.11.C] "[U]nder *Tooley*, the duty of the court is to look at the nature of the wrong alleged, not merely at the form of words used in the complaint." "Instead the court must look to all the facts of the complaint and determine for itself whether a direct claim exists." * * *

Who Suffered the Alleged Harm? In order to show a direct injury under *Tooley,* a "stockholder must demonstrate that the duty breached was owed to the stockholder and that he or she can prevail without showing an injury to the corporation."

By describing the harm as a dilution of their stockholder interests, the plaintiffs attempt to allege a harm to them that does not affect the corporation. But their argument fails to acknowledge the context in which they were allegedly harmed. "[A] complaint that 'directly challenges the fairness of the process and the price' of a merger suggests * * * that the corporation suffered harm * * * and that the harm suffered by stockholders is only a natural and foreseeable consequence of the harm to the corporation." At the heart of their complaint, the plaintiffs claim that JPMC overpaid for Bank One. If JPMC had paid cash for Bank One, the plaintiffs' claim would clearly be derivative. JPMC would have suffered the alleged harm by paying too much money for Bank One. Any such cash overpayment would not have harmed the stockholders of JPMC directly. The only harm to the stockholders would have been the natural and foreseeable consequence of the harm to JPMC.

The fact that this transaction was effectuated by issuing stock and not by paying cash does not change the result. The harm, if any, was still suffered by JPMC. Although "dilution claims emphasizing the diminishment of voting power have been categorized as direct claims," "[they] are individual in nature [only] where a significant stockholder's interest is increased at the sole expense of the minority." "[T]o the extent that any alleged decrease in the asset value and voting power of plaintiffs' shares * * * results from the issuance of new equity to a third party * * *, plaintiffs' dilution theory as a basis for a direct claim fails and any individual claim for dilution must be dismissed." * * *

Putting the 14% premium payment in the proper context, the court finds that any alleged harm was suffered by JPMC, regardless of whether the payment was in cash or in stock. The plaintiffs, if they were harmed at all, were harmed indirectly and only because of their ownership in JPMC. Therefore, under the first prong of *Tooley,* the court concludes that the plaintiffs' claim is derivative.

Who Would Receive the Benefit of Any Recovery or Other Remedy? Under the second prong of *Tooley,* in order to maintain a direct claim, stockholders must show that they will benefit from the remedy. Here, the plaintiffs seek a return of the "proper interest" of JPMC to stockholders who owned pre-merger JPMC stock, but they offer no explanation of what such a proper interest might be. Additionally, the plaintiffs are unable to demonstrate why they, and not JPMC, should receive the benefit of any remedy. * * *

As discussed above, if there was harm suffered by payment of a merger premium, JPMC suffered it. Thus, if the defendants are found liable, the remedy will accrue to JPMC. Although the plaintiffs go to great lengths to define the class in a way that would allow them to argue for a direct class benefit, their effort to make the claim direct fails. The plaintiffs' argument that the previous Bank One stockholders, who ostensibly have already benefited from any misconduct, should be excluded from the remedy is not persuasive. Any remedy from the alleged harm would necessarily accrue to JPMC and not to a subset of stockholders. Therefore, the plaintiffs' claims are derivative under the second question of *Tooley.* * * *

Demand Futility. The plaintiffs argue that if their claims are derivative, demand is excused because it would be futile. * * *

The plaintiffs are unable to meet either prong of the *Aronson* test. They have failed to show that a majority of the board is either interested or not independent. They have also not shown why the board's decision is not protected by the business judgment rule. Thus, the plaintiffs' derivative claim must be dismissed because demand is not excused.

Questions and Note

Assume that it is ultimately determined that JPMC over paid by $7 billion and a recovery goes to JPMC in a derivative action. What shareholders would receive the economic benefit of the recovery? Should the benefit go exclusively to the pre-merger JPMC shareholders or to both the pre-merger JPMC shareholders and the Bank One shareholders who received stock in JPMC in the merger?

The disclosure claim in this case under Delaware law is set out in Section 3.15.H.2.

3. Allegation that Acquiror's Directors Entered Merger Agreement without a Financing Condition and Failed to Properly Supervise—*Dow*

In Re The Dow Chemical Company Derivative Litigation

Court of Chancery, Delaware, 2010 Del. Ch. LEXIS 2

CHANDLER, Chancellor

This is a shareholder derivative action brought on behalf of the Dow Chemical Company ("Dow" or the "Company"), seeking to recover for the Company its losses arising from the difficulties with the Rohm & Haas Company ("R&H") transaction. [Dow had entered into a merger agreement pursuant to which it was to acquire R&H, and prior to the closing Dow experienced some unexpected financial setbacks.] Plaintiffs, stockholders of Dow, brought this action against current directors and officers of the Company, alleging that the defendants breached their fiduciary duties to the company by (1) approving the R&H transaction, (2) misrepresenting the relationship between the R&H transaction and a joint venture with a Kuwaiti company, and (3) failing to detect and prevent a variety of alleged wrongs, including bribery, misrepresentation, insider trading, and wasteful compensation.

Pending before the Court is defendants' motion to dismiss the complaint for failure to properly plead demand futility under Chancery Court Rule 23.1. For the reasons set forth below, the motion to dismiss is granted as to all claims. * * *

Plaintiffs' Claims. Plaintiffs primarily allege that director defendants breached their fiduciary duties by entering a merger agreement with the specialty chemical maker Rohm & Haas for $18.8 billion that unconditionally obligated Dow to consummate the merger. * * * Since plaintiffs in this action challenge a board decision, they must show that demand was futile under the two-pronged *Aronson* test.

Plaintiffs also seek to hold the directors liable under a *Caremark* theory for a variety of alleged monitoring failures. Under this theory, plaintiffs must demonstrate that the defendant directors acted in bad faith and consciously disregarded their fiduciary duties and thus face a "substantial likelihood" of liability for the alleged bribery, misrepresentations, insider trading, and wasteful and excessive compensation. * * *

ANALYSIS. * * *

Demand Futility Regarding Plaintiffs' Breach of Fiduciary Duty Claims. Plaintiffs' complaint pleads three derivative claims. * * * Count II pleads breaches of fiduciary duty by the director defendants by: (a) approving the R&H Transaction, (b) misrepresenting the relationship between the R&H and K-Dow transactions, (c) failing to detect and prevent alleged bribery in connection with the K-Dow transaction, (d) failing to detect and prevent the alleged misrepresentations, (e) failing to detect and prevent insider trading, and (f) failing to prevent the payment of allegedly excessive and wasteful compensation. * * *

Approval of R&H Transaction—Count II. To satisfy *Aronson* plaintiffs must plead particularized facts that raise a reasonable doubt either (i) that a majority of the directors who approved the transaction in question were disinterested and independent, or (ii) that the transaction was the product of the board's good faith, informed business judgment.

First Prong of *Aronson*. [The meaning of "Disinterested" and "Independence"] Plaintiffs argue that demand is excused because it would be futile. According to plaintiffs, at least half of the board members, or six of the board's twelve directors, fail the test of being disinterested and independent. Disinterested "means that directors can neither appear on both sides of a transaction nor expect to derive any personal financial benefit from it in the sense of self-dealing, as opposed to a benefit which devolves upon the corporation or all stockholders generally." "Independence means that a director's decision is based on the corporate merits of the subject before the board rather than extraneous considerations or influences." One such influence occurs when a director is "dominated and controlled" by someone who is interested; an entrenchment motive can provide another such influence. But where there is no director who is interested in the transaction, there is no need to consider the independence of the remaining directors.

Here, none of the outside directors stood on both sides of the transaction; nor are they alleged to have received a personal financial benefit from it other than one devolved on all Dow stockholders alike. Moreover, *no* directors are alleged to have been interested in the deal. Thus, there is no issue regarding any directors' interest. Rather, the thrust of plaintiffs' allegations is that the Dow directors were not independent because of various business or personal relationships with Liveris [Dow's CEO], which allegedly left at least seven directors beholden to Liveris, and thus unable to act independently of his influence. [The court rejected this theory, and found:] Upon review of the plaintiffs' allegations, I find that plaintiffs fail to meet their burden under Rule 23.1 with respect to any of the outside directors. The majority of the Dow board was disinterested and independent.

Second Prong of *Aronson*. Plaintiffs argue that demand is also excused under the second prong of the *Aronson* test. In order to succeed, "plaintiffs must allege particularized facts that raise doubt about whether the challenged transaction is entitled to protection of the business judgment rule."[28] Specifically, the "plaintiffs must plead particularized facts sufficient to raise (1) a reason to doubt that the action was taken honestly and in good faith or (2) a reason to doubt that the board was adequately informed in making the decision."

Nothing in the complaint indicates the Dow board was not adequately informed about the transaction with R&H. * * *

Simply put, plaintiffs take issue with the substantive decisions of the R&H Transaction, instead of the process the board followed. This Court made clear in *Citigroup* that substantive second-guessing of the merits of a business decision, like what plaintiffs ask the Court to do here, is precisely the kind of inquiry that the business judgment rule prohibits.[29] Both of plaintiffs' attempts to distinguish *Citigroup* fail. * * *

Turning to plaintiffs' allegations of bad faith, I am unconvinced that the directors acted in any way other than honestly and in good faith. To show that a disinterested and independent board acted outside the bounds of business judgment, plaintiffs must show that directors acted in bad faith.[30] Recently, the Supreme Court clarified the concept of bad faith in *Lyondell Chemical Co. v. Ryan*, noting that "[i]n the transactional context, [an]

---

28. J.P. Morgan, 906 A.2d at 824 (citing In re Walt Disney Co. Derivative Litig., 825 A.2d 275, 286 (Del. Ch. 2003)).

29. Citigroup, 964 A.2d at 122 ("[S]o long as the court determines that the process employed was either rational or employed in a good faith effort to advance corporate interests" the court will not second-guess a board's business decisions.).

30. Lyondell Chem. Co. v. Ryan, 970 A.2d 235, 2009 WL 1024764 at *7 (Del. 2009).

extreme set of facts [is] required to sustain a disloyalty claim premised on the notion that disinterested directors were intentionally disregarding their duties."[31] Plaintiffs must show that defendants completely and "utterly failed" to even attempt to meet their duties.[32] * * *

Plaintiffs thus are unable to meet either prong of *Aronson*. They have failed to show that a majority of the board is either interested or lacks independence. They also have failed to establish a reasonable doubt that the board's decision was anything other than a valid business judgment. Plaintiffs' derivative claim for breach of fiduciary duties regarding the R&H Transaction must be dismissed because demand is not excused. Pursuant to Rule 15(aaa), this claim is dismissed with prejudice.

Caremark Failure to Supervise Claims—Count II. Plaintiffs allege that demand is futile as to their failure to supervise claims because the director defendants are not able to exercise disinterested business judgment in responding to a demand because their failure of oversight subjects them to a substantial likelihood of personal liability. According to plaintiffs, the directors face a substantial threat of liability because their conscious disregard of their duties and lack of proper supervision and oversight caused the Company to be exposed to (1) bribery allegations in relation to the K-Dow transaction, (2) misrepresentation allegations regarding the relationship between the K-Dow and R&H transactions, and (3) insider trading allegations.

A board's unconscious failure to act is governed by *Rales*.[33] Under *Rales*, the only demand futility issue is whether "the board that would be addressing the demand can impartially consider its merits without being influenced by improper considerations." Again, plaintiffs must plead particularized factual allegations that create a reasonable doubt that the board could have, at the time the complaint is filed, validly exercised its independent and disinterested business judgment when responding to a demand. Under *Rales*, defendant directors who face a "substantial likelihood of personal liability" are deemed interested in the transaction and thus cannot make an impartial decision. But "[d]emand is not excused solely because the directors would be deciding to sue themselves."[34] Rather, "demand will be excused based on a possibility of personal director liability only in the rare case when a plaintiff is able to show director conduct that is 'so egregious on its face that board approval cannot meet the test of business judgment, and a substantial likelihood of director liability therefore exists.' "

Substantial Likelihood of Personal Directorial Liability. As in *Citigroup*, plaintiffs' arguments are "based on a theory of director liability famously articulated by former-Chancellor Allen in *In re Caremark*."[35] That theory is oversight liability. Under *Citigroup*, "to establish oversight liability a plaintiff must show that the directors *knew* they were not discharging their fiduciary obligations or that the directors demonstrated a *conscious* disregard for their responsibilities such as by failing to act in the face of a known duty to act."[36] Furthermore, the test is "rooted in concepts of bad faith; indeed, a showing of bad faith is a *necessary condition* to director oversight liability." Only an "utter failure" will

31. Id. (quoting In re Lear Corp. S'holder Litig., 967 A.2d 640, 2008 WL 4053221 at *11 (Del. Ch. 2008)).

32. Lyondell, 970 A.2d 235, [WL]at *7.

33. See Rales, 634 A.2d at 930.

34. Citigroup, 964 A.2d at 121 (citing Jacobs v. Yang, 2004 Del. Ch. LEXIS 117, 2004 WL 1728521, at *6 n.31 (Del. Ch. Aug. 2, 2004).

35. Citigroup, 964 A.2d at 121 (citing In re Caremark Int'l Inc. Derivative Litig., 698 A.2d 959 (Del. Ch. 1996)).

36. Citigroup, 964 A.2d at 123 (emphasis supplied) (footnotes omitted).

satisfy a showing of bad faith.[37] Moreover, because Dow has adopted a Section 102(b)(7) provision in its charter, plaintiffs must plead particularized facts showing bad faith in order to establish a substantial likelihood of personal directorial liability.[38] * * * [The court found that the plaintiffs did not meet this standard.]

§ 3.16 Elaboration on Applicability of the Entire Fairness Standard in Mergers between a Controlling Shareholder and the Controlled Corporation, such as in a Parent Corporation's Merger with a Less Than Wholly-Owned Subsidiary and in a Management Buyout

A. Introduction

This section explores the Delaware entire fairness doctrine, which is generally applicable when a controlling shareholder acquires, through a long form merger transaction, shares of a controlled corporation from shareholders that are not affiliated with the controller. Thus, this section examines, *inter alia*, the three most important Delaware cases dealing with this topic: *Weinberger*, *Lynch*, and *MFW*. In its 2014 decision in *MFW*, the Delaware Supreme Court held that the business judgment rule, and not the entire fairness rule, applies in these transactions where there is fully empowered special committee with an effective majority of minority shareholder vote on the transaction.

This section also explores the tender offer followed by short form merger examined in *Pure Resources*, which may avoid the application of the entire fairness standard of review.

B. Review *Weinberger*, Section 3.14.B

C. When Is a Substantial Shareholder in Control?—*Lynch*

Kahn v. Lynch Communications System, Inc.

Delaware Supreme Court, 1994 638 A.2d 1110

* * * The action, instituted by Kahn in 1986, originally sought to enjoin the acquisition of the defendant-appellee, Lynch Communication Systems, Inc. ("Lynch"), by the defendant-appellee, Alcatel U.S.A. Corporation ("Alcatel"), pursuant to a tender offer and cash-out merger. * * *

Kahn alleged that Alcatel was a controlling shareholder of Lynch and breached its fiduciary duties to Lynch and its shareholders. * * *

This Court has held that "a shareholder owes a fiduciary duty only if it owns a majority interest in or exercises control over the business affairs of the corporation." *Ivanhoe Partners*

37. Lyondell, 970 A.2d 235, 2009 WL 1024764 at *7 (quoting In re Lear Corp. S'holder Litig., 967 A.2d 640, 2008 WL 4053221 at *11).

38. See Stone v. Ritter, 911 A.2d 362, 369–70 (Del. 2006); Citigroup, 964 A.2d at 125.

v. Newmont Mining Corp., Del. Supr., 535 A.2d 1334, 1344 (1987). With regard to the exercise of control, this Court has stated:

> [A] shareholder who owns less than 50% of a corporation's outstanding stocks does not, without more, become a controlling shareholder of that corporation, with a concomitant fiduciary status. For a dominating relationship to exist in the absence of controlling stock ownership, a plaintiff must allege domination by a minority shareholder through actual control of corporation conduct.

Alcatel held a 43.3 percent minority share of stock in Lynch. Therefore, the threshold question to be answered by the Court of Chancery was whether, despite its minority ownership, Alcatel exercised control over Lynch's business affairs. Based upon the testimony and the minutes of the August 1, 1986 Lynch board meeting, the Court of Chancery concluded that Alcatel did exercise control over Lynch's business decisions. * * *

The record supports the Court of Chancery's underlying factual finding that "the non-Alcatel [independent] directors deferred to Alcatel because of its position as a significant stockholder and not because they decided in the exercise of their own business judgment that Alcatel's position was correct." The record also supports the subsequent factual finding that, notwithstanding its 43.3 percent minority shareholder interest, Alcatel did exercise actual control over Lynch by dominating its corporate affairs. The Court of Chancery's legal conclusion that Alcatel owed the fiduciary duties of a controlling shareholder to the other Lynch shareholders followed syllogistically as the logical result of its cogent analysis of the record. * * *

D. Amplification on *Weinberger* Test—*Lynch*

Kahn v. Lynch Communications Systems, Inc.

Delaware Supreme Court, 1994 638 A.2d 1110

HOLLAND, Justice:

* * * The action, instituted by Kahn in 1986, originally sought to enjoin the acquisition of the defendant-appellee, Lynch Communication Systems, Inc. ("Lynch"), by the defendant-appellee, Alcatel U.S.A. Corporation ("Alcatel"), pursuant to a tender offer and cash-out merger. * * *

* * * Kahn alleged that Alcatel was a controlling shareholder of Lynch and breached its fiduciary duties to Lynch and its shareholders. According to Kahn, Alcatel dictated the terms of the merger; made false, misleading, and inadequate disclosures; and paid an unfair price.

The Court of Chancery concluded that Alcatel was, in fact, a controlling shareholder that owed fiduciary duties to Lynch and its shareholders. It also concluded that Alcatel had not breached those fiduciary duties. Accordingly, the Court of Chancery entered judgment in favor of the defendants. * * *

This Court has concluded that the record supports the Court of Chancery's finding that Alcatel was a controlling shareholder. However, the record does not support the conclusion that the burden of persuasion shifted to Kahn. Therefore, the burden of proving the entire fairness of the merger transaction remained on Alcatel, the controlling shareholder. Accordingly, the judgment of the Court of Chancery is reversed. The matter is remanded for further proceedings in accordance with this opinion.

[**Facts**] * * * In 1981, Alcatel acquired 30.6 percent of Lynch's common stock pursuant to a stock purchase agreement. As part of that agreement, Lynch amended its certificate of incorporation to require an 80 percent affirmative vote of its shareholders for approval of any business combination. In addition, Alcatel obtained proportional representation on the Lynch board of directors and the right to purchase 40 percent of any equity securities offered by Lynch to third parties. The agreement also precluded Alcatel from holding more than 45 percent of Lynch's stock prior to October 1, 1986. By the time of the merger which is contested in this action, Alcatel owned 43.3 percent of Lynch's outstanding stock; designated five of the eleven members of Lynch's board of directors; two of three members of the executive committee; and two of four members of the compensation committee.

In the spring of 1986, Lynch determined that in order to remain competitive in the rapidly changing telecommunications field, it would need to obtain fiber optics technology to complement its existing digital electronic capabilities. Lynch's management identified a target company, Telco Systems, Inc. ("Telco"), which possessed both fiber optics and other valuable technological assets. The record reflects that Telco expressed interest in being acquired by Lynch. Because of the supermajority voting provision, which Alcatel had negotiated when it first purchased its shares, in order to proceed with the Telco combination Lynch needed Alcatel's consent. * * * [Alcatel refused to give its consent.] Alcatel made * * * an offer to acquire the entire equity interest in Lynch, constituting the approximately 57 percent of Lynch shares not owned by Alcatel. The offering price was $14 cash per share.

On November 7, 1986, the Lynch board of directors revised the mandate of the Independent Committee. It authorized Kertz, Wineman, and Beringer to negotiate the cash merger offer with Alcatel. At a meeting held that same day, the Independent Committee determined that the $14 per share offer was inadequate. The Independent's Committee's own legal counsel, Skadden, Arps, Slate, Meagher & Flom ("Skadden Arps"), suggested that the Independent Committee should review alternatives to a cash-out merger with Alcatel, including a "white knight" third party acquiror, a repurchase of Alcatel's shares, or the adoption of a shareholder rights plan.

On November 12, 1986, Beringer, as chairman of the Independent Committee, contacted Michiel C. McCarty ("McCarty") of Dillon Read, Alcatel's representative in the negotiations, with a counteroffer at a price of $17 per share. McCarty responded on behalf of Alcatel with an offer of $15 per share. When Beringer informed McCarty of the Independent Committee's view that $15 was also insufficient, Alcatel raised its offer to $15.25 per share. The Independent Committee also rejected this offer. Alcatel then made its final offer of $15.50 per share.

At the November 24, 1986 meeting of the Independent Committee, Beringer advised its other two members that Alcatel was "ready to proceed with an unfriendly tender at a lower price" if the $15.50 per share price was not recommended by the Independent Committee and approved by the Lynch board of directors. * * * After meeting with its financial and legal advisors, the Independent Committee voted unanimously to recommend that the Lynch board of directors approve Alcatel's $15.50 cash per share price for a merger with Alcatel. The Lynch board met later that day. With Alcatel's nominees abstaining, it approved the merger.

[**Control Test**] This Court has held that "a shareholder owes a fiduciary duty only if it owns a majority interest in or exercises control over the business affairs of the corporation." With regard to the exercise of control, this Court has stated:

> [A] shareholder who owns less than 50% of a corporation's outstanding stocks does not, without more, become a controlling shareholder of that corporation, with a concomitant fiduciary status. For a dominating relationship to exist in

> the absence of controlling stock ownership, a plaintiff must allege domination by a minority shareholder through actual control of corporation conduct.

The record * * * supports the * * * factual finding that, notwithstanding its 43.3 percent minority shareholder interest, Alcatel did exercise actual control over Lynch by dominating its corporate affairs. * * *

[Entire Fairness Test] A controlling or dominating shareholder standing on both sides of a transaction, as in a parent-subsidiary context, bears the burden of proving its entire fairness. *Weinberger v. UOP, Inc.*, [*See* 3.14.B] * * *

[T]his Court recognized that it would be inconsistent with its holding in *Weinberger* [which rejected the business purpose test] to apply the business judgment rule in the context of an interested merger transaction which, by its very nature, did not require a business purpose. *See Rosenblatt v. Getty Oil Co.*, 493 A.2d at 937. Consequently, in *Rosenblatt*, in the context of a subsequent proceeding involving a parent-subsidiary merger, this Court held that the "approval of a merger, as here, by an informed vote of a majority of the minority stockholders, while not a legal prerequisite, shifts the burden of proving the unfairness of the merger entirely to the plaintiffs."

Entire fairness remains the proper focus of judicial analysis in examining an interested merger, irrespective of whether the burden of proof remains upon or is shifted away from the controlling or dominating shareholder, because the unchanging nature of the underlying "interested" transaction requires careful scrutiny. The policy rationale for the exclusive application of the entire fairness standard to interested merger transactions has been stated as follows:

> Parent-subsidiary mergers, unlike stock options, are proposed by a party that controls, and will continue to control, the corporation, whether or not the minority stockholders vote to approve or reject the transaction. The controlling stockholder relationship has the potential to influence, however subtly, the vote of [ratifying] minority stockholders in a manner that is not likely to occur in a transaction with a noncontrolling party. Even where no coercion is intended, shareholders voting on a parent-subsidiary merger might perceive that their disapproval could risk retaliation of some kind by the controlling stockholder. * * *
>
> Consequently, in a merger between the corporation and its controlling stockholder—even one negotiated by disinterested, independent directors—no court could be certain whether the transaction terms fully approximate what truly independent parties would have achieved in an arm's length negotiation. Given that uncertainty, a court might well conclude that even minority shareholders who have ratified a * * * merger need procedural protections beyond those afforded by full disclosure of all material facts. One way to provide such protections would be to adhere to the more stringent entire fairness standard of judicial review.

Citron v. E.I. Du Pont de Nemours & Co., 584 A.2d at 502.

Once again, this Court holds that the exclusive standard of judicial review in examining the propriety of an interested cash-out merger transaction by a controlling or dominating shareholder is entire fairness. *Weinberger*. The initial burden of establishing entire fairness rests upon the party who stands on both sides of the transaction. However, an approval of the transaction by an independent committee of directors or an informed majority of minority shareholders shifts the burden of proof on the issue of fairness from the controlling or dominating shareholder to the challenging shareholder-plaintiff. Nevertheless, even when an interested cash-out merger transaction receives the informed approval of a majority of minority stockholders or an independent committee of disinterested directors, an entire fairness analysis is the only proper standard of judicial review. * * *

[**Analysis of the Independent Committee**] The same policy rationale which requires judicial review of interested cash-out mergers exclusively for entire fairness also mandates careful judicial scrutiny of a special committee's real bargaining power before shifting the burden of proof on the issue of entire fairness. A recent decision from the Court of Chancery articulated a two-part test for determining whether burden shifting is appropriate in an interested merger transaction. *Rabkin v. Olin Corp.* In *Olin*, the Court of Chancery stated:

> The mere existence of an independent special committee * * * does not itself shift the burden. At least two factors are required. First, the majority shareholder must not dictate the terms of the merger. Second, the special committee must have real bargaining power that it can exercise with the majority shareholder on an arms length basis. * * *

The Court of Chancery's determination that the Independent Committee "appropriately simulated a third-party transaction, where negotiations are conducted at arm's-length and there is no compulsion to reach an agreement," is not supported by the record.

Conclusion.

Accordingly, the judgment of the Court of Chancery is reversed. This matter is remanded for further proceedings consistent herewith, including a redetermination of the entire fairness of the cash-out merger to Kahn and the other Lynch minority shareholders with the burden of proof remaining on Alcatel, the dominant and interested shareholder.

Questions and Note

Lynch Communications employed an independent negotiating committee as was suggested in *Weinberger*. In a freezeout merger, what does the controlling shareholder gain by employing an independent negotiating structure? What would have been the result in *Lynch* if an independent negotiating structure had not been employed?

On remand the court found that the entire fairness test had bee satisfied, and this decision was affirmed on appeal. *Kahn v. Lynch*, 669 A.2d 79 (Del. 1997).

E. The Possibility of Business Judgment Rule Application in a Freezeout Merger—*MFW*

Kahn v. M&F Worldwide Corp.

Delaware Supreme Court, 2014 Del. LEXIS 115 (Del. S.C. March 14, 2014)

Opinion

HOLLAND, Justice:

This is an appeal from a final judgment entered by the Court of Chancery in a proceeding that arises from a 2011 acquisition by MacAndrews & Forbes Holdings, Inc. ("M&F" or "MacAndrews & Forbes")—a 43% stockholder in M&F Worldwide Corp. ("MFW")—of the remaining common stock of MFW (the "Merger"). From the outset, M&F's proposal to take MFW private was made contingent upon two stockholder-protective procedural conditions. First, M&F required the Merger to be negotiated and approved by a special committee of independent MFW directors (the "Special Committee"). Second, M&F required that the Merger be approved by a majority of stockholders unaffiliated with

M&F. The Merger closed in December 2011, after it was approved by a vote of 65.4% of MFW's minority stockholders.

The Appellants initially sought to enjoin the transaction. [After] extensive discovery * * * [t]he Defendants * * * moved for summary judgment, which the Court of Chancery granted.

Court of Chancery Decision. The Court of Chancery found that the case presented a "novel question of law," specifically, "what standard of review should apply to a going private merger conditioned upfront by the controlling stockholder on approval by both a properly empowered, independent committee and an informed, uncoerced majority-of-the-minority vote." * * *

The Court of Chancery held that, rather than entire fairness, the business judgment standard of review should apply "if, but only if: (i) the controller conditions the transaction on the approval of both a Special Committee and a majority of the minority stockholders; (ii) the Special Committee is independent; (iii) the Special Committee is empowered to freely select its own advisors and to say no definitively; (iv) the Special Committee acts with care; (v) the minority vote is informed; and (vi) there is no coercion of the minority."

The Court of Chancery found that those prerequisites were satisfied and that the Appellants had failed to raise any genuine issue of material fact indicating the contrary. The court then reviewed the Merger under the business judgment standard and granted summary judgment for the Defendants.

Appellants' Arguments. The Appellants raise two main arguments on this appeal. First, they contend that the Court of Chancery erred in concluding that no material disputed facts existed regarding the conditions precedent to business judgment review. The Appellants submit that the record contains evidence showing that the Special Committee was not disinterested and independent, was not fully empowered, and was not effective. The Appellants also contend, as a legal matter, that the majority-of-the-minority provision did not afford MFW stockholders protection sufficient to displace entire fairness review.

Second, the Appellants submit that the Court of Chancery erred, as a matter of law, in holding that the business judgment standard applies to controller freeze-out mergers where the controller's proposal is conditioned on both Special Committee approval and a favorable majority-of-the-minority vote. Even if both procedural protections are adopted, the Appellants argue, entire fairness should be retained as the applicable standard of review.

Defendants' Arguments. The Defendants argue that the judicial standard of review should be the business judgment rule, because the Merger was conditioned ab initio on two procedural protections that together operated to replicate an arm's-length merger: the employment of an active, unconflicted negotiating agent free to turn down the transaction; and a requirement that any transaction negotiated by that agent be approved by a majority of the disinterested stockholders. The Defendants argue that using and establishing pretrial that both protective conditions were extant renders a going private transaction analogous to that of a third-party arm's-length merger under Section 251 of the Delaware General Corporation Law. That is, the Defendants submit that a Special Committee approval in a going private transaction is a proxy for board approval in a third-party transaction, and that the approval of the unaffiliated, noncontrolling stockholders replicates the approval of all the (potentially) adversely affected stockholders.

[BASIC FACTS] MFW and M&F. MFW is a holding company incorporated in Delaware. Before the Merger that is the subject of this dispute, MFW was 43.4% owned by MacAndrews & Forbes, which in turn is entirely owned by Ronald O. Perelman. * * *

The Taking MFW Private Proposal. In May 2011, Perelman began to explore the possibility of taking MFW private. At that time, MFW's stock price traded in the $20 to $24 per share range. MacAndrews & Forbes engaged a bank, Moelis & Company, to advise it. After preparing valuations based on projections that had been supplied to lenders by MFW in April and May 2011, Moelis valued MFW at between $10 and $32 a share.

On June 10, 2011, MFW's shares closed on the New York Stock Exchange at $16.96. The next business day, June 13, 2011, Schwartz sent a letter proposal ("Proposal") to the MFW board to buy the remaining MFW shares for $24 in cash. The Proposal stated, in relevant part:

> The proposed transaction would be subject to the approval of the Board of Directors of the Company [i.e., MFW] and the negotiation and execution of mutually acceptable definitive transaction documents. It is our expectation that the Board of Directors will appoint a special committee of independent directors to consider our proposal and make a recommendation to the Board of Directors. We will not move forward with the transaction unless it is approved by such a special committee. In addition, the transaction will be subject to a non-waivable condition requiring the approval of a majority of the shares of the Company not owned by M & F or its affiliates....
>
> ... In considering this proposal, you should know that in our capacity as a stockholder of the Company we are interested only in acquiring the shares of the Company not already owned by us and that in such capacity we have no interest in selling any of the shares owned by us in the Company nor would we expect, in our capacity as a stockholder, to vote in favor of any alternative sale, merger or similar transaction involving the Company. If the special committee does not recommend or the public stockholders of the Company do not approve the proposed transaction, such determination would not adversely affect our future relationship with the Company and we would intend to remain as a long-term stockholder.
>
> ....
>
> In connection with this proposal, we have engaged Moelis & Company as our financial advisor and Skadden, Arps, Slate, Meagher & Flom LLP as our legal advisor, and we encourage the special committee to retain its own legal and financial advisors to assist it in its review.

MacAndrews & Forbes filed this letter with the U.S. Securities and Exchange Commission ("SEC") and issued a press release disclosing substantially the same information.

The Special Committee Is Formed. The MFW board met the following day to consider the Proposal. At the meeting, Schwartz presented the offer on behalf of MacAndrews & Forbes. Subsequently, Schwartz and Bevins, as the two directors present who were also directors of MacAndrews & Forbes, recused themselves from the meeting, as did Dawson, the CEO of HCHC, who had previously expressed support for the proposed offer.

The independent directors then invited counsel from Willkie Farr & Gallagher—a law firm that had recently represented a Special Committee of MFW's independent directors in a potential acquisition of a subsidiary of MacAndrews & Forbes—to join the meeting. The independent directors decided to form the Special Committee, and resolved further that:

> [T]he Special Committee is empowered to: (i) make such investigation of the Proposal as the Special Committee deems appropriate; (ii) evaluate the terms of

> the Proposal; (iii) negotiate with Holdings [i.e., MacAndrews & Forbes] and its representatives any element of the Proposal; (iv) negotiate the terms of any definitive agreement with respect to the Proposal (it being understood that the execution thereof shall be subject to the approval of the Board); (v) report to the Board its recommendations and conclusions with respect to the Proposal, including a determination and recommendation as to whether the Proposal is fair and in the best interests of the stockholders of the Company other than Holdings and its affiliates and should be approved by the Board; and (vi) determine to elect not to pursue the Proposal....
>
> ....
>
> ... [T]he Board shall not approve the Proposal without a prior favorable recommendation of the Special Committee....
>
> ... [T]he Special Committee [is] empowered to retain and employ legal counsel, a financial advisor, and such other agents as the Special Committee shall deem necessary or desirable in connection with these matters.... * * *

ANALYSIS. What Should Be The Review Standard? * * * This appeal presents a question of first impression: what should be the standard of review for a merger between a controlling stockholder and its subsidiary, where the merger is conditioned ab initio upon the approval of both an independent, adequately-empowered Special Committee that fulfills its duty of care, and the uncoerced, informed vote of a majority of the minority stockholders. The question has never been put directly to this Court.

Almost two decades ago, in *Kahn v. Lynch*, we held that the approval by either a Special Committee or the majority of the noncontrolling stockholders of a merger with a buying controlling stockholder would shift the burden of proof under the entire fairness standard from the defendant to the plaintiff. *Lynch* did not involve a merger conditioned by the controlling stockholder on both procedural protections. The Appellants submit, nonetheless, that statements in Lynch and its progeny could be (and were) read to suggest that even if both procedural protections were used, the standard of review would remain entire fairness. However, in Lynch and the other cases that Appellants cited, *Southern Peru* and *Kahn v. Tremont*, the controller did not give up its voting power by agreeing to a non-waivable majority-of-the-minority condition. That is the vital distinction between those cases and this one. The question is what the legal consequence of that distinction should be in these circumstances.

The Court of Chancery held that the consequence should be that the business judgment standard of review will govern going private mergers with a controlling stockholder that are conditioned ab initio upon (1) the approval of an independent and fully-empowered Special Committee that fulfills its duty of care and (2) the uncoerced, informed vote of the majority of the minority stockholders.

The Court of Chancery rested its holding upon the premise that the common law equitable rule that best protects minority investors is one that encourages controlling stockholders to accord the minority both procedural protections. A transactional structure subject to both conditions differs fundamentally from a merger having only one of those protections, in that:

> By giving controlling stockholders the opportunity to have a going private transaction reviewed under the business judgment rule, a strong incentive is created to give minority stockholders much broader access to the transactional structure that is most likely to effectively protect their interests.... That structure,

> it is important to note, is critically different than a structure that uses only one of the procedural protections. The "or" structure does not replicate the protections of a third-party merger under the DGCL approval process, because it only requires that one, and not both, of the statutory requirements of director and stockholder approval be accomplished by impartial decisionmakers. The "both" structure, by contrast, replicates the arm's-length merger steps of the DGCL by "requir[ing] two independent approvals, which it is fair to say serve independent integrity-enforcing functions."

Before the Court of Chancery, the Appellants acknowledged that "this transactional structure is the optimal one for minority shareholders." Before us, however, they argue that neither procedural protection is adequate to protect minority stockholders, because "possible ineptitude and timidity of directors" may undermine the special committee protection, and because majority-of-the-minority votes may be unduly influenced by arbitrageurs that have an institutional bias to approve virtually any transaction that offers a market premium, however insubstantial it may be. Therefore, the Appellants claim, these protections, even when combined, are not sufficient to justify "abandon[ing]" the entire fairness standard of review.

With regard to the Special Committee procedural protection, the Appellants' assertions regarding the MFW directors' inability to discharge their duties are not supported either by the record or by well-established principles of Delaware law. As the Court of Chancery correctly observed:

> Although it is possible that there are independent directors who have little regard for their duties or for being perceived by their company's stockholders (and the larger network of institutional investors) as being effective at protecting public stockholders, the court thinks they are likely to be exceptional, and certainly our Supreme Court's jurisprudence does not embrace such a skeptical view.

Regarding the majority-of-the-minority vote procedural protection, as the Court of Chancery noted, "plaintiffs themselves do not argue that minority stockholders will vote against a going private transaction because of fear of retribution." Instead, as the Court of Chancery summarized, the Appellants' argued as follows:

> [Plaintiffs] just believe that most investors like a premium and will tend to vote for a deal that delivers one and that many long-term investors will sell out when they can obtain most of the premium without waiting for the ultimate vote. But that argument is not one that suggests that the voting decision is not voluntary, it is simply an editorial about the motives of investors and does not contradict the premise that a majority-of-the-minority condition gives minority investors a free and voluntary opportunity to decide what is fair for themselves.

Business Judgment Review Standard Adopted. We hold that business judgment is the standard of review that should govern mergers between a controlling stockholder and its corporate subsidiary, where the merger is conditioned ab initio upon both the approval of an independent, adequately-empowered Special Committee that fulfills its duty of care; and the uncoerced, informed vote of a majority of the minority stockholders. We so conclude for several reasons.

First, entire fairness is the highest standard of review in corporate law. It is applied in the controller merger context as a substitute for the dual statutory protections of disinterested board and stockholder approval, because both protections are potentially undermined by the influence of the controller. However, as this case establishes, that undermining influence does not exist in every controlled merger setting, regardless of the circumstances.

The simultaneous deployment of the procedural protections employed here create a countervailing, offsetting influence of equal—if not greater—force. That is, where the controller irrevocably and publicly disables itself from using its control to dictate the outcome of the negotiations and the shareholder vote, the controlled merger then acquires the shareholder-protective characteristics of third-party, arm's-length mergers, which are reviewed under the business judgment standard.

Second, the dual procedural protection merger structure optimally protects the minority stockholders in controller buyouts. As the Court of Chancery explained:

> [W]hen these two protections are established up-front, a potent tool to extract good value for the minority is established. From inception, the controlling stockholder knows that it cannot bypass the special committee's ability to say no. And, the controlling stockholder knows it cannot dangle a majority-of-the-minority vote before the special committee late in the process as a deal-closer rather than having to make a price move.

Third, and as the Court of Chancery reasoned, applying the business judgment standard to the dual protection merger structure:

> ... is consistent with the central tradition of Delaware law, which defers to the informed decisions of impartial directors, especially when those decisions have been approved by the disinterested stockholders on full information and without coercion. Not only that, the adoption of this rule will be of benefit to minority stockholders because it will provide a strong incentive for controlling stockholders to accord minority investors the transactional structure that respected scholars believe will provide them the best protection, a structure where stockholders get the benefits of independent, empowered negotiating agents to bargain for the best price and say no if the agents believe the deal is not advisable for any proper reason, plus the critical ability to determine for themselves [20] whether to accept any deal that their negotiating agents recommend to them. A transactional structure with both these protections is fundamentally different from one with only one protection.

Fourth, the underlying purposes of the dual protection merger structure utilized here and the entire fairness standard of review both converge and are fulfilled at the same critical point: price. Following *Weinberger v. UOP, Inc.*, this Court has consistently held that, although entire fairness review comprises the dual components of fair dealing and fair price, in a non-fraudulent transaction "price may be the preponderant consideration outweighing other features of the merger." The dual protection merger structure requires two price-related pretrial determinations: first, that a fair price was achieved by an empowered, independent committee that acted with care; and, second, that a fully-informed, uncoerced majority of the minority stockholders voted in favor of the price that was recommended by the independent committee.

The New Standard Summarized. To summarize our holding, In controller buyouts, the business judgment standard of review will be applied if and only if: (i) the controller conditions the procession of the transaction on the approval of both a Special Committee and a majority of the minority stockholders; (ii) the Special Committee is independent; (iii) the Special Committee is empowered to freely select its own advisors and to say no definitively; (iv) the Special Committee meets its duty of care in negotiating a fair price; (v) the vote of the minority is informed; and (vi) there is no coercion of the minority.

If a plaintiff that can plead a reasonably conceivable set of facts showing that any or all of those enumerated conditions did not exist, that complaint would state a claim for relief that would entitle the plaintiff to proceed and conduct discovery. If, after discovery, triable issues of fact remain about whether either or both of the dual procedural protections were established, or if established were effective, the case will proceed to a trial in which the court will conduct an entire fairness review.

This approach is consistent with *Weinberger*, *Lynch* and their progeny. A controller that employs and/or establishes only one of these dual procedural protections would continue to receive burden-shifting within the entire fairness standard of review framework. Stated differently, unless both procedural protections for the minority stockholders are established prior to trial, the ultimate judicial scrutiny of controller buyouts will continue to be the entire fairness standard of review.

Having articulated the circumstances that will enable a controlled merger to be reviewed under the business judgment standard, we next address whether those circumstances have been established as a matter of undisputed fact and law in this case.

Dual Protection Inquiry * * *

Both Procedural Protections Established. Based on a highly extensive record, the Court of Chancery concluded that the procedural protections upon which the Merger was conditioned—approval by an independent and empowered Special Committee and by a uncoerced informed majority of MFW's minority stockholders—had both been undisputedly established prior to trial. We agree and conclude the Defendants' motion for summary judgment was properly granted on all of those issues.

Business Judgment Review Properly Applied. We have determined that the business judgment rule standard of review applies to this controlling stockholder buyout. Under that standard, the claims against the Defendants must be dismissed unless no rational person could have believed that the merger was favorable to MFW's minority stockholders. In this case, it cannot be credibly argued (let alone concluded) that no rational person would find the Merger favorable to MFW's minority stockholders.

F. Entire Fairness in Negotiated Tender Offer and Merger Going Private Transaction—*Emerging Communications*

In Re Emerging Communications, Inc. Shareholders Litigation

Delaware Court of Chancery, 2004 Del. Ch. LEXIS 70

Jacobs, Justice:[39]

Addressed in this Opinion are the merits of consolidated statutory appraisal and class actions for breach of fiduciary duty. These actions all arise out of the two-step "going private" acquisition of the publicly owned shares of Emerging Communications, Inc. ("ECM") [a corporation operating in the Virgin Islands], by Innovative Communications Corporation, L.L.C. ("Innovative"), ECM's majority stockholder. The first step tender offer was commenced on August 18, 1998 by Innovative for 29% of ECM's outstanding shares at a price of $10.25 per share. The balance of ECM's publicly held shares were acquired in a second-step cash-out merger of ECM into an Innovative subsidiary, at the same price, on October 19, 1998.

At the time of this two-step transaction (the "Privatization"), 52% of the outstanding shares of ECM, and 100% of the outstanding shares of Innovative, were owned by

39. Sitting by designation as vice Chancellor under DEL. CONST., art. IV, § 13(2).

Innovative Communication Company, LLC ("ICC"). ICC, in turn, was wholly owned by ECM's Chairman and Chief Executive Officer, Jeffrey J. Prosser ("Prosser"). Thus, Prosser had voting control of both of the parties to the Privatization transaction.

In June 1998, shortly after the Privatization proposal was announced, a fiduciary duty class action was brought on behalf of the former public shareholders of ECM by Brickell Partners, an ECM shareholder. * * *

The Burden of Proof Issue. The final threshold issue is which side has the burden of proof. Both sides agree that because the Privatization is a self-dealing transaction of which the majority stockholder stands on both sides, entire fairness is the standard of review *ab initio.* The only question is whether the burden of proof, which normally falls upon the defendants, has shifted to the plaintiffs in this particular case.

The defendants argue that the burden of establishing that the merger was not entirely fair has shifted to the plaintiffs, because the merger was approved by both an informed independent committee of disinterested directors and an informed majority of minority stockholders. [*Citing Kahn v. Lynch*] The short answer is that the merger was not approved by a committee of independent directors who were properly informed or independent of Prosser, nor was it approved by an informed vote of a majority of ECM's minority stockholders. * * *

The defendants argue that the burden must shift, nonetheless, because the minimum tender condition, *i.e.,* the condition that a majority of the minority shareholders tender into the offer, was the functional equivalent of a shareholder ratification of the transaction. But no Delaware case has held that burden-shifting can be accomplished by a tender of shares rather than by an actual vote. Nor should a tender be treated as the equivalent of an informed vote. Shareholders cannot be deemed to have ratified board action unless they are afforded the opportunity to express their approval of the precise conduct being challenged. Stockholders have materially different interests at stake when tendering, as opposed to voting their shares. In considering whether to tender, stockholders must evaluate the risk of being left worse off, *i.e.,* left vulnerable to being frozen out at an even lower price, if the other stockholders were to tender into an inadequate offer. As Vice Chancellor Strine incisively observed in *In re Pure Resources S'holders Litig:*

> Indeed, many commentators would argue that the tender offer form is more coercive than a merger vote. In a merger vote, stockholders can vote no and still receive the transactional consideration if the merger prevails. In a tender offer, however, a non—tendering shareholder faces an uncertain fate. That stockholder could be one of the few who holds out, leaving herself in an even more thinly traded stock with little hope of liquidity and subject to a § 253 merger at a lower price or at the same price or * * * at a later (and, given the time value of money, a less valuable) time.

Accordingly, the burden of proving fair dealing remains with the defendants.

The preliminary issues having been decided, the Court turns next to the substantive fair dealing questions.

[The court found that a fair price had not been paid.]

THE DEFENDANTS' FIDUCIARY DUTY BREACHES AND LIABILITY THEREFOR. Having concluded that the Privatization was not entirely fair, the Court must next determine the nature of the fiduciary duty violation—whether of care, loyalty, or good faith—that resulted in the unfair transaction. Under *Emerald Partners v. Berlin,* that is necessary to enable the Court to adjudicate which (if any) of the director defendants is liable for money damages, because ECM's Section 102(b)(7) charter provision exculpates those directors found to have violated *solely* their duty of care from liability for money damages. * * *

The liability of the directors must be determined on an individual basis because the nature of their breach of duty (if any), and whether they are exculpated from liability for that breach, can vary for each director.

Prosser is liable in his capacity as a director for breach of his duty of loyalty, conduct that is not exculpated under Article Seventh. Prosser is also liable on the basis that he "derived an improper personal benefit" from the Privatization transaction—which is another exception to the exculpatory coverage of Article Seventh.

Raynor also is liable for breaching his fiduciary duty of loyalty—conduct that is excluded from the exculpatory shield of Article Seventh. Raynor did not personally and directly benefit from the unfair transaction (as did Prosser), but Raynor actively assisted Prosser in carrying out the Privatization, and he acted to further Prosser's interests in that transaction, which were antithetical to the interests of ECM's minority stockholders. * * *

The Court also concludes, albeit with reluctance, that Muoio is similarly liable, even though Muoio's conduct was less egregious than that of Prosser and Raynor. Unlike Raynor, Muoio did nothing affirmatively to assist Prosser in breaching his fiduciary duties of loyalty and good faith. Like his fellow directors, Muoio was also not independent of Prosser.

Muoio is culpable because he voted to approve the transaction even though he knew, or at the very least had strong reasons to believe, that the $10.25 per share merger price was unfair. Muoio was in a unique position to know that. He was a principal and general partner of an investment advising firm, with significant experience in finance and the telecommunications sector. From 1995 to 1996, Muoio had been a securities analyst for, and a vice president of, Lazard Freres & Co. in the telecommunications and media sector. From 1985 to 1995, he was a securities analyst for Gabelli & Co., Inc., in the communications sector, and from 1993 to 1995, he was a portfolio manager for Gabelli Global Communications Fund, Inc.

Hence, Muoio possessed a specialized financial expertise, and an ability to understand ECM's intrinsic value, that was unique to the ECM board members (other than, perhaps, Prosser). Informed by his specialized expertise and knowledge, Muoio conceded that the $10.25 price was "at the low end of any kind of fair value you would put," and expressed to Goodwin his view that the Special Committee might be able to get up to $20 per share from Prosser. In these circumstances, it was incumbent upon Muoio, as a fiduciary, to advocate that the board reject the $10.25 price that the Special Committee was recommending. As a fiduciary knowledgeable of ECM's intrinsic value, Muoio should also have gone on record as voting against the proposed transaction at the $10.25 per share merger price. Muoio did neither. Instead he joined the other directors in voting, without objection, to approve the transaction.

ECM's directors other than Prosser and Raynor could plausibly argue that they voted for the transaction in reliance on Houlihan's opinion that the merger term price was fair. In Muoio's case, however, that argument would be implausible. * * *

The conduct of [the other] four directors differs from that of Raynor and Muoio, in that there is no evidence that any of those four affirmatively colluded with Prosser to effectuate the Privatization, or that they otherwise deliberately engaged in conduct disloyal to the minority stockholders' interests. Nor have the plaintiffs shown that any of those directors knew or had reason to believe, that the merger price was unfair.

This is not intended to suggest that these directors covered themselves in glory, or merit commendation, for the manner in which they discharged their responsibility as fiduciaries. But it is to say, and this Court after considerable reflection finds, that there is no persuasive evidence that the fiduciary violations of the ECM directors other than Prosser, Raynor, and Muoio implicated conduct more egregious than breaches of their duty of care. * * *

There is no evidence that Goodwin, Ramphal and Vondras intentionally conspired with Prosser to engage in a process that would create the illusion, but avoid the reality, of arm's length bargaining to obscure the true purpose of benefiting Prosser at the expense of the minority stockholders. * * *

Nor, in these circumstances, did those directors' conduct amount to a breach of their fiduciary duty to act in good faith. * * *

The foregoing analysis and conclusion are equally applicable to the seventh director, Todman. The circumstance that differentiates Todman from Goodwin, Ramphal and Vondras is that Todman played no role in the negotiation of the merger terms, his sole involvement being to cast his vote as a director in favor of the Privatization. Because (unlike Muoio) there is no evidence that Todman knew or had reason to suspect that the price was unfair, it may fairly be concluded that he voted for the transaction in reliance upon the pronouncements by Houlihan and the Special Committee that the merger price was fair. * * *

Part VI. CONCLUSION. For the reasons set forth above: * * *

(2) In the fiduciary duty action, defendants Innovative, ICC, Prosser, Raynor and Muoio are jointly and severally liable to the plaintiff class. * * *

G. Constituency Directors and Sale of Portfolio Company where PE Firm Holds Preferred Stock—*Trados*[40]

In *In Re Trados Incorporated Shareholders Litigation*, 2013 Del. Ch. Lexis 207 (Del. Ch. August 16, 2013), Venture Capital (VC) firms purchased preferred stock in Trados Inc. (Trados), which allowed them to designate directors of the Trados board. As hopes of an IPO became bleak and the VC firms became antsy, the board adopted a plan to incentivize the management to sell Trados. The plan would compensate management for the sale of Trados even if common stock holders got nothing. The next year the board approved an acquisition of Trados in a merger, and the VC firms and directors owned enough common stock to push the merger through. As a result of the merger, (1) the management cashed-out pursuant to their incentive arrangement, (2) as preferred stockholders, the VC firms got paid the balance of the purchase price pursuant to a liquidation preference in Trados certificate of incorporation, and (3) the common stockholders received nothing. The common stockholders brought a breach of duty claim against the directors and an appraisal action for fair value.

Vice Chancellor Laster found that the entire fairness test applied because the directors were not disinterested and independent. He explained that three of the directors faced dual fiduciary issues as fiduciaries for the VC funds who were preferred shareholders. *Id.* at 71, 78–80, 110–112.

These three directors were dual directors because they were elected only by certain preferred shareholder constituencies. The Chancellor explained that the duty of loyalty

40. This section is adapted from Thompson, *Mergers, Acquisitions and Tender Offers, supra* Section 1.10, at Section 5:5.7.

is not diluted for constituency directors who continue to owe fiduciary duties to the company's common stock holders at large:

> If the interests of the beneficiaries to whom the dual fiduciary owes duties are aligned, then there is no conflict. But if the interests of the beneficiaries diverge, the fiduciary faces an *inherent* conflict of interest. (emphasis added)

Id. at 83.

Despite the fact that six of the seven directors were deemed to be conflicted, the Chancellor held that the directors had shown entire fairness by showing fair price even when the directors could not show fair dealing in initiation, negotiation, or structure of the transaction. *Id.* at 113–129.

Vice Chancellor Laster found that a determination of fair merger price does not necessarily moot the appraisal proceeding. The Chancellor reasoned that, "[a] court could conclude that a price fell within the range of fairness and would not support fiduciary liability, yet still find that the point calculation demanded by the appraisal statute yields an award in excess of the merger price." *Id.* at 179–180. However, the Chancellor held that the fair value of Trados's common stock was zero.

§ 3.17 Does the Entire Fairness Standard Apply in a Tender Offer by a Controlling Shareholder for the Minority Held Shares of Its Sub Where the Tender Offer Is Followed by a Second Step Merger?

A. Introduction

This section addresses the fiduciary duty principles applicable when a controlling shareholder of a target makes a tender offer for shares of the target held by the minority shareholders, with an intent by the controlling shareholder to follow the tender offer with a second-step merger, such as a short form merger.

B. Background—*Pure Resources*

In Re Pure Resources, Inc., Shareholders Litigation

Delaware Court of Chancery, 2002 Del. Ch. Lexis 112

STRINE, Vice Chancellor.

This is the court's decision on a motion for preliminary injunction. The lead plaintiff in the case holds a large block of stock in Pure Resources, Inc., 65% of the shares of which are owned by Unocal Corporation. The lead plaintiff and its fellow plaintiffs seek to enjoin a now-pending exchange offer (the "Offer") by which Unocal hopes to acquire the rest of the shares of Pure in exchange for shares of its own stock. * * *

The Plaintiffs' Demand For A Preliminary Injunction. The Merits.* * * The primary argument of the plaintiffs is that the Offer should be governed by the entire fairness standard of review. In their view, the structural power of Unocal over Pure and its board, as well as Unocal's involvement in determining the scope of the Special Committee's authority, make the Offer other than a voluntary, non-coercive transaction. In the plaintiffs' mind, the Offer poses the same threat of (what I will call) "inherent coercion" that motivated the Supreme Court in *Kahn v. Lynch Communication Systems, Inc.* [Section 3.16.C] to impose the entire fairness standard of review on any interested merger involving a controlling stockholder, even when the merger was approved by an independent board majority, negotiated by an independent special committee, and subject to a majority of the minority vote condition.

In support of their argument, the plaintiffs contend that the tender offer method of acquisition poses, if anything, a greater threat of unfairness to minority stockholders and should be subject to the same equitable constraints. More case-specifically, they claim that Unocal has used inside information from Pure to foist an inadequate bid on Pure stockholders at a time advantageous to Unocal. * * *

In response to these arguments, Unocal asserts that the plaintiffs misunderstand the relevant legal principles. Because Unocal has proceeded by way of an exchange offer and not a negotiated merger, the rule of *Lynch* is inapplicable. Instead, Unocal is free to make a tender offer at whatever price it chooses so long as it does not: i) "structurally coerce" the Pure minority by suggesting explicitly or implicitly that injurious events will occur to those stockholders who fail to tender; or ii) mislead the Pure minority into tendering by concealing or misstating the material facts. This is the rule of law articulated by, among other cases, *Solomon v. Pathe Communications Corp.* [*See also Siliconix*, 2001 Del. Ch. LEXIS 83, 2001 WL 716787] Because Unocal has conditioned its Offer on a majority of the minority provision and intends to consummate a short-form merger at the same price, it argues that the Offer poses no threat of structural coercion and that the Pure minority can make a voluntary decision. Because the Pure minority has a negative recommendation from the Pure Special Committee and because there has been full disclosure (including of any material information Unocal received from Pure in formulating its bid), Unocal submits that the Pure minority will be able to make an informed decision whether to tender. For these reasons, Unocal asserts that no meritorious claim of breach of fiduciary duty exists against it or the Pure directors.

This case therefore involves an aspect of Delaware law fraught with doctrinal tension: what equitable standard of fiduciary conduct applies when a controlling shareholder seeks to acquire the rest of the company's shares? * * *

I begin with negotiated mergers. In *Kahn v. Lynch Communication Systems, Inc.*, the Delaware Supreme Court addressed the standard of review that applies when a controlling stockholder attempts to acquire the rest of the corporation's shares in a negotiated merger pursuant to 8 *Del. C.* 251. The Court held that the stringent entire fairness form of review governed regardless of whether: i) the target board was comprised of a majority of independent directors; ii) a special committee of the target's independent directors was empowered to negotiate and veto the merger; and iii) the merger was made subject to approval by a majority of the disinterested target stockholders.

The Supreme Court concluded that even a gauntlet of protective barriers like those would be insufficient protection because of (what I will term) the "inherent coercion" that exists when a controlling stockholder announces its desire to buy the minority's shares.* * *

The policy balance struck in *Lynch* continues to govern negotiated mergers between controlling stockholders and subsidiaries. If anything, later cases have extended the rule in *Lynch* to a broader array of transactions involving controlling shareholders.

The second strand of cases involves tender offers made by controlling stock-holders—*i.e.*, the kind of transaction Unocal has proposed. The prototypical transaction addressed by this strand involves a tender offer by the controlling stockholder -addressed to the minority stockholders. In that offer, the controlling stockholder promises to buy as many shares as the minority will sell but may subject its offer to certain conditions. For example, the controlling stockholder might condition the offer on receiving enough tenders for it to obtain 90% of the subsidiary's shares, thereby enabling the controlling stockholder to consummate a short-form merger under 8 *Del. C.* § 253 at either the same or a different price.

As a matter of statutory law, this way of proceeding is different from the negotiated merger approach in an important way: neither the tender offer nor the short-form merger requires any action by the subsidiary's board of directors. The tender offer takes place between the controlling shareholder and the minority shareholders so long as the offering conditions are met. And, by the explicit terms of § 253, the short-form merger can be effected by the controlling stockholder itself, an option that was of uncertain utility for many years because it was unclear whether § 253 mergers were subject to an equitable requirement of fair process at the subsidiary board level. That uncertainty was recently resolved in *Glassman v. Unocal Exploration Corp.*, [Section 2.16.B.2] an important recent decision, which held that a short-form merger was not reviewable in an action claiming unfair dealing, and that, absent fraud or misleading or inadequate disclosures, could be contested only in an appraisal proceeding that focused solely on the adequacy of the price paid.

Before *Glassman*, transactional planners had wondered whether the back-end of the tender offer/short-form merger transaction would subject the controlling stockholder to entire fairness review. *Glassman* seemed to answer that question favorably from the standpoint of controlling stockholders, and to therefore encourage the tender offer/short-form merger form of acquisition as presenting a materially less troublesome method of proceeding than a negotiated merger.

Why? Because the legal rules that governed the front end of the tender offer/short-form merger method of acquisition had already provided a more flexible, less litigious path to acquisition for controlling stockholders than the negotiated merger route. Tender offers are not addressed by the Delaware General Corporation Law ("DGCL"), a factor that has been of great importance in shaping the line of decisional law addressing tender offers by controlling stockholders—but not, as I will discuss, tender offers made by third parties.

Because no consent or involvement of the target board is statutorily mandated for tender offers, our courts have recognized that "in the case of totally voluntary tender offers * * * courts do not impose any right of the shareholders to receive a particular price. Delaware law recognizes that, as to allegedly voluntary tender offers (in contrast to cash-out mergers), the determinative factors as to voluntariness are whether coercion is present, or whether there are materially false or misleading disclosures made to stockholders in connection with the offer." In two recent cases, this court has followed *Solomon's* articulation of the standards applicable to a tender offer, and held that the "Delaware law does not impose a duty of entire fairness on controlling stockholders making a non-coercive tender or exchange offer to acquire shares directly from the minority holders."[41]

The differences between this approach, which I will identify with the *Solomon* line of cases, and that of *Lynch* are stark. To begin with, the controlling stockholder is said to have no duty to pay a fair price, irrespective of its power over the subsidiary. Even more striking is the different manner in which the coercion concept is deployed. In the tender offer context addressed by *Solomon* and its progeny, coercion is defined in the more traditional sense as a wrongful threat that has the effect of forcing stockholders to tender

---

41. *In re Aquila Inc.*, 805 A.2d 184, 2002 WL 27815, at *5 (Del. Ch. 2002); *In re Siliconix Inc. S'holders Litig.*, 2001 Del. Ch. LEXIS 83, 2001 WL 716787, *6 (Del. Ch. June 19, 2001) ("unless coercion or disclosure violations can be shown, no defendant has the duty to demonstrate the entire fairness of this proposed tender transaction").

at the wrong price to avoid an even worse fate later on, a type of coercion I will call structural coercion. The inherent coercion that *Lynch* found to exist when controlling stockholders seek to acquire the minority's stake is not even a cognizable concern for the common law of corporations if the tender offer method is employed.

This latter point is illustrated by those cases that squarely hold that a tender is not actionably coercive if the majority stockholder decides to: (i) condition the closing of the tender offer on support of a majority of the minority and (ii) promise that it would consummate a short-form merger on the same terms as the tender offer. In those circumstances, at least, these cases can be read to bar a claim against the majority stockholder even if the price offered is below what would be considered fair in an entire fairness hearing ("fair price") or an appraisal action ("fair value"). That is, in the tender offer context, our courts consider it sufficient protection against coercion to give effective veto power over the offer to a majority of the minority. Yet that very same protection is considered insufficient to displace fairness review in the negotiated merger context.

The parties here cross swords over the arguable doctrinal inconsistency between the *Solomon* and *Lynch* lines of cases, with the plaintiffs arguing that it makes no sense and Unocal contending that the distinction is non-foolish in the Emersonian sense. * * *

The potential for coercion and unfairness posed by controlling stockholders who seek to acquire the balance of the company's shares by acquisition requires some equitable reinforcement, in order to give proper effect to the concerns undergirding *Lynch.* In order to address the prisoner's dilemma problem, our law should consider an acquisition tender offer by a controlling stockholder non-coercive only when: 1) it is subject to a non-waivable majority of the minority tender condition; 2) the controlling stockholder promises to consummate a prompt § 253 merger at the same price if it obtains more than 90% of the shares; and 3) the controlling stockholder has made no retributive threats. Those protections—also stressed in this court's recent *Aquila* decision—minimize the distorting influence of the tendering process on voluntary choice. They also recognize the adverse conditions that confront stockholders who find themselves owning what have become very thinly traded shares. These conditions also provide a partial cure to the disaggregation problem, by providing a realistic non-tendering goal the minority can achieve to prevent the offer from proceeding altogether.

The informational and timing advantages possessed by controlling stockholders also require some countervailing protection if the minority is to truly be afforded the opportunity to make an informed, voluntary tender decision. In this regard, the majority stockholder owes a duty to permit the independent directors on the target board both free rein and adequate time to react to the tender offer, by (at the very least) hiring their own advisors, providing the minority with a recommendation as to the advisability of the offer, and disclosing adequate information for the minority to make an informed judgment. For their part, the independent directors have a duty to undertake these tasks in good faith and diligently, and to pursue the best interests of the minority.

When a tender offer is non-coercive in the sense I have identified and the independent directors of the target are permitted to make an informed recommendation and provide fair disclosure, the law should be chary about superimposing the full fiduciary requirement of entire fairness upon the statutory tender offer process. Here, the plaintiffs argue that the Pure board breached its fiduciary duties by not giving the Special Committee the power to block the Offer by, among other means, deploying a poison pill. Indeed, the plaintiffs argue that the full board's decision not to grant that authority is subject to the entire fairness standard of review because a majority of the full board was not independent of Unocal.

That argument has some analytical and normative appeal, embodying as it does the rough fairness of the goose and gander rule. I am reluctant, however, to burden the common law of corporations with a new rule that would tend to compel the use of a device that our statutory law only obliquely sanctions and that in other contexts is subject to misuse, especially when used to block a high value bid that is not structurally coercive. When a controlling stockholder makes a tender offer that is not coercive in the sense I have articulated, therefore, the better rule is that there is no duty on its part to permit the target board to block the bid through use of the pill. Nor is there any duty on the part of the independent directors to seek blocking power. But it is important to be mindful of one of the reasons that make a contrary rule problematic—the awkwardness of a legal rule requiring a board to take aggressive action against a structurally non-coercive offer by the controlling stockholder that elects it. * * *

Turning specifically to Unocal's Offer, I conclude that the application of these principles yields the following result. The Offer, in its present form, is coercive because it includes within the definition of the "minority" those stockholders who are affiliated with Unocal as directors and officers. It also includes the management of Pure, whose incentives are skewed by their employment, their severance agreements, and their Put Agreements. This is, of course, a problem that can be cured if Unocal amends the Offer to condition it on approval of a majority of Pure's unaffiliated stockholders. Requiring the minority to be defined exclusive of stockholders whose independence from the controlling stockholder is compromised is the better legal rule (and result). Too often, it will be the case that officers and directors of controlled subsidiaries have voting incentives that are not perfectly aligned with their economic interest in their stock and who are more than acceptably susceptible to influence from controlling stockholders. Aside, however, from this glitch in the majority of the minority condition, I conclude that Unocal's Offer satisfies the other requirements of "non-coerciveness." Its promise to consummate a prompt § 253 merger is sufficiently specific, and Unocal has made no retributive threats. * * *

For all these reasons, therefore, I find that the plaintiffs do not have a probability of success on the merits of their attack on the Offer, with the exception that the majority of the minority condition is flawed.

* * *

C. Delaware Chancery Court's Unified Standard for Applying the Business Judgment Rule to a Controlling Party's Tender Offer Followed by Second Step Merger—*CNX*

In Re CNX Gas Corporation Shareholders Litigation

Delaware Chancery Court, 2010 Del. Ch. LEXIS 119

LASTER, Vice Chancellor.

Representatives of a putative class of minority stockholders have challenged a controlling stockholder freeze-out structured as a first-step tender offer to be followed by second-step short-form merger. * * *

[**The Basic Facts**] ***The Tender Offer.*** [CONSOL owned 83.5% of the stock of CNX Gas and the balance of the stock was held by the public, with T. Rowe Price, an investment company owning 6.3% of the outstanding stock and 37% of the public float. T. Rowe Price also owned approximately 6% of the stock of CONSOL. T. Rowe Price agreed to tender its shares of CNX to CONSOL for a price of $38.25.] On April 28, 2010, CONSOL commenced a tender offer to acquire the outstanding public shares of CNX Gas at a price of $38.25 per share in cash (the "Tender Offer"). The price represents a premium of 45.83% over the closing price of CNX Gas's common stock on the day before CONSOL announced * * * its intent to acquire the shares of CNX Gas that it did not already own ($26.23). * * *

CONSOL has committed to effect a short-form merger promptly after the successful consummation of the Tender Offer. In the merger, remaining stockholders will receive the same consideration of $38.25 per share in cash. Consummation of the Tender Offer is subject to a non-waivable condition that a majority of the outstanding minority shares be tendered, excluding shares owned by directors or officers of CONSOL or CNX Gas. The T. Rowe Price shares are included in the majority-of-the-minority calculation. With the T. Rowe Price shares locked up, CONSOL only needs to obtain an additional 3,006,316 shares, or approximately 12% of the outstanding stock, to satisfy the condition. * * *

LEGAL ANALYSIS. ***The Plaintiffs Have Shown A Reasonable Likelihood Of Success On The Merits Of Their Fairness Claim.*** The plaintiffs contend that the Tender Offer should be reviewed for entire fairness. This argument requires that I weigh in on a critical and much debated issue of Delaware law: the appropriate standard of review for a controlling stockholder freeze-out.

The Appropriate Standard Of Review For The Tender Offer. As knowledgeable readers understand all too well, Delaware law applies a different standard of review depending on how a controlling stockholder freeze-out is structured. Under *Kahn v. Lynch Communications Systems, Inc.*, 638 A.2d 1110 (Del. 1994) [hereinafter, "*Lynch*"], a negotiated merger between a controlling stockholder and its subsidiary is reviewed for entire fairness. [As a result of the Delaware Supreme Court's decision in *MFW*, Section 3.16.E, the business judgment rule standard of review may be applicable.] But under *In re Siliconix Inc. Shareholders Litigation,* 2001 Del. Ch. LEXIS 83, 2001 WL 716787 (Del. Ch. June 19, 2001), a controller's unilateral tender offer followed by a short-form merger is reviewed under an evolving standard far less onerous than *Lynch.* The tension created by the different fiduciary standards has been discussed at length by Vice Chancellor Strine [*see Pure Resources*] and generated reams of scholarly and practitioner commentary. I will set forth my own views in more abbreviated fashion.

I question the soundness of the twin cornerstones on which *Siliconix* rests. The first cornerstone is the statutory distinction between mergers and tender offers and the lack of any explicit role in the General Corporation Law for a target board of directors responding to a tender offer. For reasons explained at length in *Pure Resources,* the statutory distinction fails to justify adequately the divergent fiduciary approaches. *See Pure Resources,* 808 A.2d at 433–44, 439–41. Scholars have joined in criticizing the statutory distinction. *See, e.g., Fixing Freezeouts, supra,* at 24–25; Gilson & Gordon, *supra,* at 820–21.

The second cornerstone has been *Solomon v. Pathe Communications Corp.,* 672 A.2d 35 (Del. 1996) [hereinafter, "*Solomon II*"], which has been cited repeatedly for the rule that a tender offeror has no duty to provide a fair price. But *Solomon II* did not involve a freeze-out. * * *

Solomon II ... does not hold that controllers never owe fiduciary duties when making tender offers, nor does it eliminate the possibility of entire fairness review for a two-step freeze-out transaction. "[T]he *Solomon* line of cases does not eliminate the fiduciary duties of controlling stockholder or target boards in connection with tender offers made by controlling stockholders. Rather, the question is the contextual extent and nature of those duties...." *Pure Resources,* 808 A.2d at 444. Put differently, the question is: What transactional structures result in the controlling stockholder not standing on both sides of a two-step freeze-out?

Pure Resources sought to answer this question and move towards harmonizing the *Siliconix* and *Lynch* lines of authority. The decision did not establish immutable rules for tender offer freeze-outs, as the defendants contend. * * * As confirmed by his subsequent decision in *Cox Communications,* Vice Chancellor Strine did not regard *Pure Resources* as the final word on *Siliconix* tender offers. * * *

Pure Resources set out a series of requirements for a controlling stockholder tender offer.

> In order to address the prisoner's dilemma problem, our law should consider an acquisition tender offer by a controlling stockholder non-coercive only when: 1) it is subject to a non-waivable majority of the minority tender condition; 2) the controlling stockholder promises to consummate a prompt § 253 merger at the same price if it obtains more than 90% of the shares; and 3) the controlling stockholder has made no retributive threats. 808 A.2d at 445. The decision also imposed a duty on the controlling stockholder to permit the independent directors on the target board both free rein and adequate time to react to the tender offer, by (at the very least) hiring their own advisors, providing the minority with a recommendation as to the advisability of the offer, and disclosing adequate information for the minority to make an informed judgment.

Id.

Pure Resources was an evolutionary decision that raised the bar for two-step squeeze-outs. The transaction structures approved in the two preceding Court of Chancery decisions—*Siliconix* and *Aquila*—would not have passed muster under the *Pure Resources* test. * * *

Cox Communications rendered the *Lynch* and *Siliconix* standards coherent by explaining that the business judgment rule should apply to any freeze-out transaction that is structured to mirror *both* elements of an arms' length merger, *viz.* approval by disinterested directors *and* approval by disinterested stockholders. *Id.* at 606. [This principle has now been adopted by the Delaware Supreme Court in *MFW*, Section 3.16.E.]

[U]nder the *Cox Communications* framework, if a first-step tender offer is both (i) negotiated and recommended by a special committee of independent directors and (ii) conditioned on the affirmative tender of a majority of the minority shares, then the business judgment standard of review presumptively applies to the freeze-out transaction. *Id.* at 607. As with a merger, if both requirements are not met, then the transaction is reviewed for entire fairness. [In a footnote the Vice Chancellor explains:]

> The animating principle underlying the unified approach is to give judicial deference to processes that simulate arms' length third-party transactional approvals. In a merger, directors must approve and recommend the transaction before it is submitted to stockholders. 8 Del. C. § 251(b). Therefore an affirmative recommendation is required for entire fairness not to apply. The *Cox Communications* case elsewhere described the approval requirement in these terms. 879 A.2d at 646 (providing for business judgment review if "the tender offer was recommended by an independent special committee"). * * *

I recognize that by applying the unified standard [*i.e.*, (1) board negotiation and recommendation, and (2) majority of minority vote], I reach a different conclusion than the recent *Cox Radio* decision, which opted to follow *Pure Resources. See Cox Radio,* 2010 Del. Ch. LEXIS 102, 2010 WL 1806616, at *10–12 (approving settlement of litigation challenging *Siliconix* transaction). The choice among *Lynch*, *Pure Resources*, and *Cox Communications* implicates fundamental issues of Delaware law and public policy that only the Delaware Supreme Court can resolve. Until the Delaware Supreme Court has the opportunity to address *Lynch* and *Siliconix* definitively, I believe the unified standard from *Cox Communications* offers the coherent and correct approach.

Applying The Unified Standard To This Case. The Tender Offer does not pass muster under the unified standard. First and most obviously, the Special Committee did not recommend in favor of the transaction. That fact alone is sufficient to end the analysis and impose an obligation on CONSOL to pay a fair price.

Second, the Special Committee was not provided with authority comparable to what a board would possess in a third-party transaction. * * *

Third, the plaintiffs have raised sufficient questions about the role of T. Rowe Price to undercut the effectiveness of the majority-of-the-minority tender condition. * * *

T. Rowe Price as a whole owns 6.5% of CONSOL's outstanding common stock versus 6.3% of CNX Gas. T. Rowe Price's roughly equivalent equity interests leave it fully hedged and indifferent to the allocation of value between CONSOL and CNX Gas. * * * T. Rowe Price's has materially different incentives than a holder of CNX Gas common stock, thereby calling into question the effectiveness of the majority-of-the-minority condition. * * *

The absence of Special Committee approval imposes an obligation on the defendants to show that the Tender Offer price is fair. The defendants are free to argue at a later stage of the proceeding and on a fuller record that (i) the negotiations with T. Rowe Price were truly at arms' length and untainted by cross-ownership, and (ii) the majority-of-the-minority condition was effective.

§ 3.18 Elaboration on the Enhanced Business Judgment Rule for Defensive Tactics and Introduction to Poison Pills

A. Introduction

This section examines the fiduciary duties applicable in Delaware to a target's board that employs defensive tactics to avoid a takeover offer. The two most important cases dealing with this topic are the Delaware Supreme Court's decisions in (1) *Unocal*, which is one of the "Big Six" discussed previously, and (2) *Unitrin*, which is examined in this section. Since the "rights plan," commonly known as the "poison pill," is the most employed and effective defensive tactic, this section also elaborates on the poison pill, which was first introduced in the discussion of *Moran*, which is one of the "Big Six." This section also discusses the *Airgas* decision, which illustrates the limits on the use of a poison pill. Other aspects of defensive tactics, such as the classified board, are examined in Chapter 23, which deals generally with defensive tactics.

B. Review *Unocal*, Section 3.14.D

C. Note on Two-Tier Coercive Offers: The Prisoners' Dilemma

The *Unocal* court talks about the coercive nature of the Mesa two-tier tender offer. In the first tier Mesa offered cash of $54 per share for 37% of Unocal's outstanding stock.

Completion of this purchase would have made Mesa a 51% shareholder of Unocal. The second step was a freezeout merger with junk bonds. The bonds had a value of less than $54 per share, say, $40 per share. Unocal's board on the other hand, valued the Unocal shares at $70 per share. This presents the shareholder with a classic prisoners' dilemma.

For example, assume that there were just two shareholders of Unocal, A and B, and each held 50% of the shares. Assume also that Mesa offers to buy 50% of the shares at $54 per share and then to acquire the balance of the shares in a freezeout merger at a price of $40 per share. Assume that Mesa could force a freezeout merger with only 50% of the shares. Further, assume that the Unocal shares are in fact worth $70 per share.

If neither A nor B sell their shares, they will both hold shares worth $70 per share. If, however, A sells to Mesa and B does not, A will receive $54 per share and B will be forced to sell in the freezeout for $40 per share. The reverse is true if B sells to Mesa but A does not. On the other hand, if A and B each sell half their shares to Mesa for $54 and then have the balance of their shares purchased for $40 in the freezeout, they will each receive an average price per share of $47 (*i.e.*, half sold for $54 per share and half sold for $40 per share).

Under the above scenario, it is likely that both A and B will tender so that each will avoid the worst possible outcome, that is receiving $40 per share.

D. Introduction to Poison Pills: The Principal Defensive Tactic Scrutinized under *Unocal*

1. Description of a Poison Pill Plan

Description of Poison Pill Plan

Excerpt from Wachtell, Lipton, Rosen & Katz, The Share Purchase Rights Plan (1995)

THE SHARE PURCHASE RIGHTS PLAN

[**Background**] The basic objectives of the rights plan are to deter abusive takeover tactics by making them unacceptably expensive to the raider and to encourage prospective acquirors to negotiate with the board of directors of the target rather than to attempt a hostile takeover.

The plan includes a "flip-in" feature designed to deter creeping accumulations of a company's stock. The "flip-in" feature is structured to be available from a 10% to a 20% ownership threshold. If triggered, the flip-in feature would give shareholders, other than the holder triggering the flip-in, the right to purchase shares of the company at a discount to market price (thereby diluting the triggering shareholder). The plan also has a "flip-over" feature which provides shareholders protection against a squeeze-out. The flip-over feature would give shareholders the right to purchase shares of the acquiring company at a discount in the event of a freezeout merger or similar transaction (thereby diluting the acquiring company).

The rights issued pursuant to the plan are redeemable for a nominal amount prior to the acquisition of a large block of the target's shares. Thus, the effect of the plan is to force potential acquirors to deal with the company's board of directors (or conduct a proxy contest to replace directors) before acquiring shares in excess of the threshold levels. This increases the negotiating power of the Board.

The rights plan was designed not to interfere, and has not interfered, with the day-to-day operations of the companies that have adopted it. Prior to its being activated by an acquisition of a large block of the target company's shares, it has no effect on a company's balance sheet or income statement and it has no tax effect on the company or the shareholders. Companies have split their stock, issued stock dividends and combined their stock without interference from the plan. While the plan requires special care in such transactions, it has not hindered public offerings of common stock or SEC clearance of pooling of interests mergers.

The efficacy of the rights plan has made it a common feature among U.S. corporations. Over 1,700 companies have adopted a rights plan, including approximately half of the Business Week 1000 companies and Fortune 500 companies and approximately two-thirds of the Fortune 200 companies. Indeed, in upholding the adoption of a rights plan as a proportionate response to a tender offer in the recent *Unitrin* case [Section 3.18.E.5], the Delaware Supreme Court commented that the rights plan is an "effective takeover device" that has resulted in a "remarkable transformation in the market for corporate control."

Rights plans are also now well established in case law and statutory law. Starting with the Delaware Supreme Court's 1985 decision in the *Household* case, [Section 3.14.E] upholding one of the first rights plans to be adopted, the Delaware courts and courts in other jurisdictions have widely recognized the legality and legitimate uses of a variety of rights plans. In each of the few jurisdictions in which a rights plan has been held invalid under the state's corporation law (because of the discriminatory flip-in feature), the state legislature has amended the corporation law to establish clearly the legality of the flip-in feature of the rights plan.

The *Household* case and subsequent case law establish that adoption of a plan does not change the fiduciary standards to be followed by a board of directors in responding to a takeover bid. In the event of a specific takeover bid, the plan and its operation will have to be assessed in light of the response that the board decides is appropriate based on the advice at that time of the company's financial advisors and legal counsel. * * *

The rights plan combines the flip-over with a flip-in that is triggered by acquisition at the 20% level. The flip-in at a 20% threshold provides protections against takeover abuses involving partial and creeping accumulations. The plan also allows the board of directors to lower the threshold to not less than 10% if appropriate in light of specific circumstances.

If the flip-in is triggered, each holder of rights (other than the raider, whose rights become void) will be able to exercise the rights for common stock of the target having a market value, at the time the raider crosses the 20% threshold, of twice the right's exercise price. This would result in dilution to the raider both economically and in terms of its percentage ownership of the target's shares. The exact level of the dilution would depend on the market value of the target's common stock in relation to the exercise price of the rights.

The rights plan also contains a feature that gives the board of directors the option, after the flip-in is triggered by an acquisition at the 20% level (or such lower threshold down to 10% as has been set by the board) but before there has been a 50% acquisition, to exchange one new share of common stock of the company for each then-valid right (which would exclude rights held by the raider that have become void). This provision will have an economically dilutive effect on the acquiror, and provide a corresponding benefit to the remaining rights holders, that is comparable to the flip-in without requiring shareholders to go through the process and expense of exercising their rights. * * *

2. Description of MCI, Inc.'s Poison Pill

Read the annotated description of the poison pill adopted by MCI in 2004, which is Documentary Appendix J of *M&A Statutes, Rules, and Documents*, supra Section 1.1. The description discusses how (1) the MCI board adopted the pill unilaterally, (2) the flip-in provision (*i.e.*, the right of the target's shareholders, other than the acquiror, to buy stock of the target at a bargain price) works if an unapproved acquiror exceeds a 15% stock ownership trigger, and (3) the flip-over provision (*i.e.*, the right of the target's shareholders to buy stock of the acquiror at a bargain price) works if there is a merger between the unwanted acquiror and the target.

3. Flip-In Developed after the Crown Zellerbach Defect in the Flip-Over

The Flip-Over pill was developed first, and the Flip-In provision was added after a defect with the Flip-Over became apparent in Sir James Goldsmith's 1985 acquisition of the Crown Zellerbach corporation, which had a Flip-Over but no Flip-In.

To trigger Crown's Flip-Over pill, a hostile acquirer would have to (1) own more than 20% of the stock of Crown, and (2) acquire Crown in some type of second-step business combination. At the time of the second step, the shareholders of Crown, other than the hostile acquiror would have the right to acquire shares of the hostile acquiror at a bargain price, thereby diluting the interest of the hostile acquiror's pre-acquisition shareholders.

Goldsmith satisfied the first condition, that is, he acquired more than 20% of Crown's stock, but he did not satisfy the second condition, that is, he did not propose to acquire Crown in a business combination. However, Goldsmith continued to acquire shares of Crown on the market until he was above the 50% ownership level, at which time the incumbent management of Crown relinquished control of Crown.

If in addition to its Flip-Over, Crown had a Flip-In provision with a 20% trigger, once Goldsmith passed the 20% mark, the shareholders of Crown, other than Goldsmith, would have had the right to acquire additional shares of Crown at a bargain price, thereby diluting Goldsmith's interest.

4. Delaware Supreme Court Reaffirms *Moran—Hilton*

Leonard Loventhal v. Hilton Hotels Corporation

Delaware Supreme Court, 2001
2001 Del. LEXIS 386

Walsh, Justice:

In this appeal from the Court of Chancery, we revisit the question of whether the board of directors of a Delaware corporation may unilaterally adopt a poison pill rights plan. * * * The plaintiff shareholders rejected participation in the plan and thereafter commenced an action in the Court of Chancery seeking to invalidate its issuance. The Court of Chancery rejected that effort, ruling that under the principle of *stare decisis,* Hilton's entitlement to implement the rights plan was not subject to challenge. We agree and affirm. * * *

[**Analysis**]

It is indisputable that *Moran* established a board's authority to adopt a rights plan. As the Chancellor pointed out below, "There is simply no legal requirement that the Hilton shareholder must be a party to the Rights Plan or formally vote to accept the Rights Plan to ensure that the Plan is enforceable." * * *

The power recognized in *Moran* would have been meaningless if the rights plan required shareholder approval. Indeed it is difficult to harmonize *Moran's* basic holding with a contention that questions a Board's prerogative to unilaterally establish a rights plan. * * *

5. The Legality of Flip-In Provisions in Georgia, New York and Maine

In *West-Point Pepperell, Inc. v. Farley*, 711 F. Supp 1088 (N.D. Georgia 1988), the court held that a flip-in plan was *ultra vires* because of its discriminatory nature. Also, in *Bank of New York Co. v. Irving Bank Corp.* 536 N.Y.S. 2d 923 (N.Y.Supp. 1988), the court reached a similar conclusion under New York law. The legislatures in both of these states have overridden these decisions and permit discriminatory plans. *See* Georgia Business Corporation Code § 14–2–624 and New York Business Corporation Law § 505. A U.S. District Court has found that Maine would follow Delaware: "The Court has found nothing in its examination of the pertinent statutes and case law interpreting similar statutes in other jurisdictions to indicate that the Maine Law Court, if called upon to do so, would construe section 501 of the [Maine Business Corporation Act] so as to invalidate the flip-in provision of Great Northern's rights plan as illegally discriminatory." *Georgia-Pacific Corp. v. Great Northern Nekoosa Corp.*, 728 F.Supp. 807 (D.C. Maine, 1990).

6. The "Dead Hand" and "No Hand" Pill in Delaware—*Quickturn*

Quickturn Design Systems, Inc. v. Shapiro

Delaware Supreme Court, 761 A.2d 1281 1998

HOLLAND, Justice:

[**Essential Facts and Issue**] * * * In response to Mentor's tender offer and proxy contest to replace the Quickturn board of directors, as part of Mentor's effort to acquire Quickturn, the Quickturn board enacted two defensive measures. First, it amended the Quickturn shareholder rights plan ("Rights Plan") by adopting a "no hand" feature of limited duration (the "Delayed Redemption Provision" or "DRP"). * * *

Mentor filed actions for declarative and injunctive relief in the Court of Chancery challenging the [DRP]. * * * The Court of Chancery * * * concluded * * * that the DRP is invalid on fiduciary duty grounds. * * *

We have concluded that, as a matter of Delaware law, the Delayed Redemption Provision was invalid. Therefore, on that alternative basis, the judgment of the Court of Chancery is affirmed. * * *

After hearing the presentations [of Quickturn's investment banker], the Quickturn board concluded that Mentor's offer was inadequate, and decided to recommend that Quickturn shareholders reject Mentor's offer. * * *

At the August 21 board meeting, * * * the board amended Quickturn's shareholder Rights Plan by eliminating its "dead hand" feature and replacing it with the Deferred Redemption Provision, under which no newly elected board could redeem the Rights Plan for six months after taking office, if the purpose or effect of the redemption would be to facilitate a transaction with an "Interested Person" (one who proposed, nominated or financially supported the election of the new directors to the board).[42] * * *

---

42. The amended Rights Plan pertinently provides that: "[I]n the event that a majority of the Board of Directors of the Company is elected by stockholder action at an annual or special meeting of stockholders, then until the 180th day following the effectiveness of such election (including any postponement or adjournment thereof), the Rights shall not be redeemed if such redemption is reasonably likely to have the purpose or effect of facilitating a Transaction with an Interested Person."

An "Interested Person" is defined under the amended Rights Plan as "any Person who (i) is or will become an Acquiring Person if such Transaction were to be consummated or an Affiliate or Associate of such a Person, and (ii) is, or directly or indirectly proposed, nominated or financially supported, a director of [Quickturn] in office at the time of consideration of such Transaction who was elected at an annual or special meeting of stockholders."

The effect of the DRP would be to delay the ability of a newly-elected, Mentor-nominated board to redeem the Rights Plan or "poison pill" for six months, in any transaction with an Interested Person. * * *

At the time Mentor commenced its bid, Quickturn had in place a Rights Plan that contained a so-called "dead hand" provision. That provision had a limited "continuing director" feature that became operative only if an insurgent that owned more than 15% of Quickturn's common stock successfully waged a proxy contest to replace a majority of the board. In that event, only the "continuing directors" (those directors in office at the time the poison pill was adopted) could redeem the rights. * * *

[T]he Quickturn board amended the Rights Plan to eliminate its "continuing director" feature, and to substitute a "no hand" or "delayed redemption provision" into its Rights Plan. The Delayed Redemption Provision provides that, if a majority of the directors are replaced by stockholder action, the newly elected board cannot redeem the rights for six months if the purpose or effect of the redemption would be to facilitate a transaction with an "Interested Person."

It is undisputed that the DRP would prevent Mentor's slate, if elected as the new board majority, from redeeming the Rights Plan for six months following their election, because a redemption would be "reasonably likely to have the purpose or effect of facilitating a Transaction" with Mentor, a party that "directly or indirectly proposed, nominated or financially supported" the election of the new board. Consequently, by adopting the DRP, the Quickturn board built into the process a six month delay period in addition to the 90 to 100 day delay mandated by the By-Law Amendment. * * *

[**Analysis**] Our analysis of the Delayed Redemption Provision in the Quickturn Rights Plan is guided by the prior precedents of this Court with regard to a board of directors authority to adopt a Rights Plan or "poison pill." In *Moran* [Section 3.14.E], this Court held that the "inherent powers of the Board conferred by 8 Del.C. Section 141(a) concerning the management of the corporation's 'business and affairs' provides the Board additional authority upon which to enact the Rights Plan." Consequently, this Court upheld the adoption of the Rights Plan in *Moran* as a legitimate exercise of business judgment by the board of directors. In doing so, however, this Court also held "the rights plan is not absolute."

When the Household Board of Directors is faced with a tender offer and a request to redeem the Rights [Plan], they will not be able to arbitrarily reject the offer. They will be held to the same fiduciary standards any other board of directors would be held to in deciding to adopt a defensive mechanism, the same standards as they were held to in originally approving the Rights Plan.

In *Moran*, this Court held that the "ultimate response to an actual takeover bid must be judged by the Directors' actions at the time and nothing we say relieves them of their fundamental duties to the corporation and its shareholders." Consequently, we concluded that the use of the Rights Plan would be evaluated when and if the issue arises.

One of the most basic tenets of Delaware corporate law is that the board of directors has the ultimate responsibility for managing the business and affairs of a corporation. Section 141(a) requires that any limitation on the board's authority be set out in the certificate of incorporation. The Quickturn certificate of incorporation contains no provision purporting to limit the authority of the board in any way. The Delayed Redemption Provision, however, would prevent a newly elected board of directors from completely discharging its fundamental management duties to the corporation and its stockholders for six months. While the Delayed Redemption Provision limits the board of directors' authority in only one respect, the suspension of the Rights Plan, it nonetheless restricts the board's power in an area of fundamental importance to the shareholders—negotiating a possible sale of the corporation. Therefore, we hold that the Delayed Redemption Provision is invalid under Section 141(a), which confers upon any newly elected board of directors full power to manage and direct the business and affairs of a Delaware corporation. * * *

The Delayed Redemption Provision would prevent a new Quickturn board of directors from managing the corporation by redeeming the Rights Plan to facilitate a transaction that would serve the stockholders' best interests, even under circumstances where the board would be required to do so because of its fiduciary duty to the Quickturn stockholders. Because the Delayed Redemption Provision impermissibly circumscribes the board's statutory power under Section 141(a) and the directors' ability to fulfill their concomitant fiduciary duties, we hold that the Delayed Redemption Provision is invalid.

Note

In *Carmody v. Toll Brothers, Inc.*, Del.Ch., C.A. No. 15983, Jacobs, V.C., 1998 WL 418896 (July 24, 1998), which was decided before *Quickturn*, Vice Chancellor upheld a challenge to a dead hand pill under Delaware corporate law, reasoning:

[T]he Court concludes that the complaint states legally sufficient claims that the "dead hand" provision of the Toll Brothers Rights Plan violates 8 Del. C. Section 141(a) and (d). There are three reasons.

First, it cannot be disputed that the Rights Plan confers the power to redeem the pill only upon some, but not all, of the directors. But under Section 141(d), the power to create voting power distinctions among directors exists only where there is a classified board, and where those voting power distinctions are expressed in the certificate of incorporation. * * *

Second, Section 141(d) mandates that the "right to elect 1 or more directors who shall * * * have such [greater] voting powers" is reserved to the stockholders, not to the directors or a subset thereof. Absent express language in the charter, nothing in Delaware law suggests that some directors of a public corporation may be created less equal than other directors, and certainly not by unilateral board action.

Third, the complaint states a claim that the "dead hand" provision would impermissibly interfere with the directors' statutory power to manage the business and affairs of the corporation. That power is conferred by 8 Del. C. Section 141(a), which mandates:

> The business and affairs of every corporation organized under this chapter shall be managed by or under the direction of a board of directors, except as may be otherwise provided in this chapter or in its certificate of incorporation. * * *

The "dead hand" provision would jeopardize a newly-elected future board's ability to achieve a business combination by depriving that board of the power to redeem the pill without obtaining the consent of the "Continuing Directors," who (it may be assumed) would constitute a minority of the board. In this manner, it is claimed, the "dead hand" provision would interfere with the board's power to protect fully the corporation's (and its shareholders') interests in a transaction that is one of the most fundamental and important in the life of a business enterprise.

The statutory analysis employed, and the result reached here, are consistent with and supported by *Bank of New York Co. v. Irving Bank Corp,* [Section 3.18.D.5]. * * *

For these reasons, the statutory invalidity claims survive the motion to dismiss.[43] * * *

---

43. The defendants rely upon *Invacare Corp. v. Healthdyne Technologies, Inc.*, [Section 3.18.D.5]

[The court further concluded that both the plaintiff's *Blasius* and *Unocal/Unitrin* fiduciary] claims are cognizable under Delaware law.

E. When Must a Pill Be Redeemed?

1. Obligation to Redeem in View of All Cash Offer, *Interco*

City Capital Associates Limited Partnership v. Interco Inc.

Delaware Court of Chancery, 1988 551 A.2d 787

Allen, Chancellor.

[In *Interco*, the acquiring entity, CCA, made an all cash tender offer for the target, Interco, with a proposal for a freeze-out merger at the tender offer price. The initial tender offer price of $70 was raised to $72 and then to $74. Interco's board responded with a restructuring plan, which would have given the shareholders an extraordinary dividend of cash and securities, and would have left the stockholders with a stub equity interest in Interco. Interco's investment banker estimated that the value of the restructuring was $76, with the value of the stub estimated at $10. CCA's investment banker, Drexel, estimated the value of the restructuring between $68 and $70 per share with the value of the stub being between $4.53 and $5.45. Interco's board intended to keep its pill in place in order to protect the restructuring.]

This case, before the court on an application for a preliminary injunction, involves the question whether the directors of Interco Corporation are breaching their fiduciary duties to the stockholders of that company in failing to now redeem certain stock rights originally distributed as part of a defense against unsolicited attempts to take control of the company. * * *

[**Analysis**] I turn * * * to the analysis contemplated by *Unocal* . * * *

Turning to the first element of the *Unocal* form of analysis, it is appropriate to note that, in the special case of a tender offer for all shares, the threat posed, if any, is not importantly to corporate policies (as may well be the case in a stock buy-back case such as *Cheff v. Mathes*, or a partial tender offer case such as *Unocal* itself), but rather the threat, if any, is most directly to shareholder interests. Broadly speaking, threats to shareholders in that context may be of two types: threats to the voluntariness of the choice offered by the offer, and threats to the substantive, economic interest represented by the stockholding.

1. *Threats to voluntariness.* It is now universally acknowledged that the structure of an offer can render mandatory in substance that which is voluntary in form. The so-called "front-end" loaded partial offer already a largely vanished breed is the most extreme example of this phenomenon. An offer may, however, be structured to have a coercive effect on a rational shareholder in any number of different ways. Whenever a tender offer is so structured, a board may, or perhaps should, perceive a threat to a stockholder's interest in exercising choice to remain a stockholder in the firm. The threat posed by structurally coercive offers is typically amplified by an offering price that the target board responsibly concludes is substantially below a fair price.

That case is distinguishable and inapposite. *** The relevant Delaware corporate statutory scheme, like New York's, differs materially from that of Georgia.

Each of the cases in which our Supreme Court has addressed a defensive corporate measure under the *Unocal* test involved the sharp and palpable threat to shareholders posed by a coercive offer. *See Unocal*, [Section 3.14.D], and *Moran*, [Section 3.14.E].

2. *Threats from "inadequate" but noncoercive offers.* The second broad classification of threats to shareholder interests that might be posed by a tender offer for all shares relates to the "fairness" or "adequacy" of the price. * * *

Our cases * * * also indicate that in the setting of a noncoercive offer, absent unusual facts, there may come a time when a board's fiduciary duty will require it to redeem the rights and to permit the shareholders to choose.

In this instance, there is no threat of shareholder coercion. The threat is to shareholders' economic interests posed by an offer the board has concluded is "inadequate." If this determination is made in good faith (as I assume it is here) it alone will justify leaving a poison pill in place, even in the setting of a noncoercive offer, for a period while the board exercises its good faith business judgment to take such steps as it deems appropriate to protect and advance shareholder interests in light of the significant development that such an offer doubtless is. That action may entail negotiation on behalf of shareholders with the offeror, the institution of a *Revlon*-style auction for the Company, a recapitalization or restructuring designed as an alternative to the offer, or other action.

Once that period has closed, and it is apparent that the board does not intend to institute a *Revlon*-style auction, or to negotiate for an increase in the unwanted offer, and that it has taken such time as it required in good faith to arrange an alternative value-maximizing transaction, then, in most instances, the legitimate role of the poison pill in the context of a noncoercive offer will have been fully satisfied. The only function then left for the pill at this end-stage is to preclude the shareholders from exercising a judgment about their own interests that differs from the judgment of the directors, who will have some interest in the question. What then is the "threat" in this instance that might justify such a result? Stating that "threat" at this stage of the process most specifically, it is this: *Wasserstein Perella may be correct in their respective valuations of the offer and the restructuring but a majority of the Interco shareholders may not accept that fact and may be injured as a consequence.*

Perhaps there is a case in which it is appropriate for a board of directors to in effect permanently foreclose their shareholders from accepting a noncoercive offer for their stock by utilization of the recent innovation of "poison pill" rights. If such a case might exist by reason of some special circumstance, a review of the facts here show this not to be it. The "threat" here, when viewed with particularity, is far too mild to justify such a step in this instance. * * *

I thus conclude that the board's decision not to redeem the rights following the amendment of the offer to $74 per share cannot be justified in the way *Unocal* requires. * * *

2. Obligation to Redeem in View of All Cash Offer Notwithstanding Recapitalization Plan, *Grand Met*

Grand Metropolitan PLC v. The Pillsbury Company

Delaware Court of Chancery, 1988 558 A.2d 1049

Duffy, Justice (Retired):

[In *Grand Metropolitan*, the acquiring corporation made an all cash all shares tender offer for the target, Pillsbury, at $63 per share, with a commitment to complete a second-step freeze-out merger at the same price. Pillsbury responded with a proposed spin-off of Burger King, which was expected to have a combined value of $68 per share. Pillsbury's board intended to keep its pill in place.] * * *

[**Analysis**] I turn to the central issue in the case: What is to be done about the Pill? Shall it remain in status quo and thus a legal and financial barrier to Grand Met and, consequently, an immovable road block to the Pillsbury stockholders who would tender in? Or, should the Pillsbury Directors, who alone put the Pill in place, be ordered to remove it so that their stockholders may have a free choice to accept or refuse the Tender Offer? * * *

Certain it is that a Pillsbury shareholder, seeking to make a determination as to what is in his/her best interest, could conclude that $63 in present cash is preferable to the possibility of $68 if all of the "ifs" in Pillsbury's plan disappear and its hopes for the future become realities. But a stockholder in Pillsbury cannot make that choice unless the Rights are redeemed.

What about *Unocal*'s element of balance? Is the Board's defensive measure—the Rights and the Pill—"reasonable in relation to the threat posed?" I say again, and I emphasize, that the only "threat posed" here is to shareholder value—nothing whatsoever affects the corporate entity or any other constituency. But the real threat to shareholder value, as I see it, is not the spread between $63 and $68 per share. It is, rather, what will probably happen if the Pill remains in place and Grand Met's Offer is withdrawn. That threat of "loss," measured in dollars as to all Pillsbury shareholders, could amount to $1.5 billion and perhaps as much as $1.9 billion (assuming the price of the stock returns to its September 1988 level).

It is undisputed that Grand Met's Offer is the only factor supporting the present price (about $62) of Pillsbury's stock. Pillsbury implicitly argues that Grand Met will not walk but the Court must decide this case on the present record, not on the basis of speculation as to what Grand Met may do if the Pill is not redeemed. If the Pill remains at the end of this litigation and if the Tender Offer is withdrawn, the uncontested affidavits show that the price of Pillsbury's stock will fall into the high $30—a drop of about $25 per share for some 76,000,000 shares.

Faced with the possibility of such a dramatic and costly decline in value, it is little wonder that about 87% of the Pillsbury shares have been tendered into the Offer. * * *

I conclude that the Board's decision to keep the Pill in place was not reasonable in relationship to any threat posed and, therefore, the Board's decision is not protected by the business judgment rule. And since Pillsbury's Rights plan and its Poison Pill serve no purpose under the facts of this case, other than to preclude shareholder acceptance of the Offer, plaintiffs are entitled to appropriate relief. * * *

3. No Obligation to Redeem Poison Pills in Response to Merger Offer, *TW Services*

TW Services Inc. v. SWT Acquisition Corporation

Delaware Court of Chancery, 1989 CCH Fed. Sec. Law Rep. Para 94,334

Allen, Chancellor.

[**Essential Facts and Issue**] Pending is a motion by SWT Acquisition Corp. ("SWT") seeking a preliminary mandatory injunction requiring TW Services, Inc. ("TW") to redeem certain stock rights, authorized by the TW board of directors without action by shareholders, on September 19, 1988. It is asserted that the refusal of TW's board to redeem these rights precludes SWT from buying TW stock tendered to it pursuant to a public tender offer commenced on October 28, 1988. That offer, as amended, is for all shares and offers $29 per share cash. SWT, or entities affiliated with it, owned at the time it commenced its offer 19.09% of TW's outstanding stock. It reports that sufficient shares have been tendered to it so that, should it now close its offer, it would own approximately 88% of TW's common stock (85.7% on a fully diluted basis). * * *

The fact that the TW board has not redeemed the Company's poison pill in the face of this all cash, all shares offer that a preponderant proportion of TW shareholders wish to accept is said to constitute a breach of duty. This action cannot, it is said, be reasonable in relationship to a threat to shareholders or to the Company posed by this offer. * * *

The board does not attempt to defend its action as an attempt to maximize current share values. Rather, the directors say that they have looked at the overall situation and have concluded that the circumstances surrounding the SWT offer—including the history of SWT's principals, the course of the offer and the conditions in it—indicate that the offer is not a bona fide offer to purchase all TW shares but is either a ruse designed to put TW "in play" so that a quick profit might be made by SWT on its recently acquired TW position, or is designed to provide a setting in which "greenmail" might be paid. With that view of the matter—which the directors claim is taken in utter good faith and not as a pretext to enable themselves to remain in office—the directors have concluded that they are under no duty to even address the question whether it is appropriate to redeem the pill or to take other action to maximize short term shareholder values.

[**Analysis**] For the reasons that follow—having importantly to do with the particularities of this offer—I conclude that the proportionality test of *Unocal* does not, in this instance, apply to the TW board's decision not to divert this Company from its long term business plan in order to facilitate or propose an extraordinary transaction designed to maximize current share value. Having also concluded for the purpose of this motion that the board appears to be acting in the good faith pursuit of legitimate corporate interests in so deciding and with due care, I am unable to ascertain a basis to grant the remedy now sought. * * *

Here, I understand the board's motivation to include a plausible concern that the level of debt likely to be borne by TW following any merger would be detrimental to the long term functioning of the Company. * * * Concern with such long run implications is obviously legitimate, at least until a board turns away from long term management concerns and is required to focus upon the maximization of current share value. * * *

Nor is there any basis to question the board's due care in reaching the decision not to pursue merger discussions now. * * *

By conditioning the closing of its tender offer upon the execution of a merger agreement, SWT has implicated not simply the self-conferred power arising from the stock Rights Plan, but the board's Section 251 power. * * * The exercise of the board's power under that Section is, where there is no interested merger involved, subject to a traditional business judgment review, not the proportionality review of *Unocal*. Since SWT has chosen to proceed in a way that does require exercise of the TW board's Section 251 power, it cannot complain if the board's decision with respect to it is reviewed under the traditional business judgment approach.

In the circumstances as they now exist, the board is, in my opinion, justified in not further addressing the question whether it should deviate from its long term management mode in order to do a current value maximizing transaction; and surely before it has considered that question, it cannot be thought to have reached that stage at which it is under a duty to shareholders to dismantle its stock rights defense and permit the SWT offer to close.

The pending motion will be denied.

4. Impact of *Time Warner* on Pill Redemptions

In the 1989 *Time Warner* case, *infra*, Section 3.19.F, the Delaware Supreme Court addressed the above decisions in *Interco*, *Grand Met* and *TW Services* in the following paragraph:

> Plaintiffs' position represents a fundamental misconception of our standard of review under *Unocal* principally because it would involve the court in substituting its judgment as to what is a "better" deal for that of a corporation's board of directors. To the extent that the Court of Chancery has recently done so in certain of its opinions, we hereby reject such approach as not in keeping with a proper *Unocal* analysis. *See, e.g., Interco*, Section 3.18.E.1, [holding that a board was required to redeem its pill] and its progeny [*e.g., Grand Met*, Section 3.18.E.2 the same]; *but see TW Services* Section 3.18.E.3 holding that a board did not have to redeem its pill].

Vice Chancellor Strine has addressed the impact of this statement as follows:

> There [was] a period of ferment during which the Court of Chancery undertook to define the circumstances under which a board's use of a poison pill would be reasonable. The high-water mark of this intellectually innovative period occurred when Chancellor Allen decided *City Capital Associates Ltd. Partnership v. Interco Inc.* In *Interco*, he suggested that there were limits to a board's fiduciary power to stymie a fully funded, all-shares cash tender offer. When such an offer was made, it was (Chancellor Allen held) permissible for the board to use the pill as a delaying mechanism, giving the board time to develop an alternative option or to inform the stockholders why the board believed the tender offer should not be accepted. Once those purposes had been achieved, however, the board had exhausted the proper limits of its authority to maintain the pill, at which point the stockholders had the ultimate right to decide whether to accept the offer.
>
> *Interco* seemed to point to a clear, bright-line limitation on the authority of directors to use a rights plan. While directors could deploy a pill to hold off a noncoercive offer for a discrete, if undefined, period of time, in the end they had to let the stockholders decide, even if the directors reasonably and in good faith believed that the offer was too low and should not be accepted. Because *Moran* had held that there was a statutory basis for the issuance of a rights plan, this was an equitable (or fiduciary) limitation on director power, albeit a highly nontraditional one, because it constrained action taken even by well-motivated and well-informed independent directors.
>
> This period of development soon came to a halt, in no small part because of powerful dictum contained in the *Time-Warner* opinion. That case, the reader may recall, did not involve the issue of whether the Time board's use of a poison pill was proper. Despite that, the Delaware Supreme Court expressed a dim view of *Interco* and other Chancery pill decisions, in terms that made clear the Time-Warner panel's emphatic disapproval of those decisions.
>
> Equally important, Time-Warner also appeared to reflect the view that directors have the fiduciary discretion to reject a lucrative acquisition proposal and instead pursue a long-term corporate strategy, if they believe that strategy will generate even greater wealth for the persevering stockholder who retains his shares. Nonetheless, the absence of any frontal attack on the poison pill's use in Time-Warner left the full extent of that view's legal force in the netherworld of dicta and, therefore, uncertain. * * *

Since *Time-Warner*, the Delaware courts have not addressed, in the preliminary injunction context, any case seeking to overturn a corporate board's decision to block a tender offer by use of a poison pill. The tenor of the *Time-Warner* decision undoubtedly contributed to this dearth of cases.[44] * * *

5. Refining the Application of *Unocal* to Poison Pill and Repurchase Transaction — *Unitrin*

Unitrin, Inc. v. American General Corp.

Delaware Supreme Court, 1995 651 A.2d 1361

[The facts were summarized as follows in the lower court decision: These lawsuits come before the Court on motions for a preliminary injunction to prevent Unitrin, Inc., a Delaware corporation with its headquarters in Chicago, Illinois, from implementing its plan to repurchase ten million of its shares in the open market. American General Corporation ("American General"), a large consumer financial service organization that holds stock in Unitrin, and a group of stockholders purporting to represent all stockholders similarly situated (the "stockholder plaintiffs," and together with American General, the "plaintiffs") both seek to preliminarily enjoin Unitrin's repurchase program. Stockholder plaintiffs also ask the Court to remove a poison pill adopted by the board of directors of Unitrin (the "board") unless the board agrees to negotiate with American General.] * * *

The first aspect of the *Unocal* [Section 3.14.D] burden, the reasonableness test, required the Unitrin Board to demonstrate that, after a reasonable investigation, it determined in good faith, that American General's Offer presented a threat to Unitrin that warranted a defensive response. This Court has held that the presence of a majority of outside independent directors will materially enhance such evidence. * * *

[**Unocal**] The Unitrin Board identified two dangers it perceived the American General Offer posed: inadequate price and antitrust complications. The Court of Chancery characterized the Board's concern that American General's proposed transaction could never be consummated because it may violate antitrust laws and state insurance regulations as a "makeweight excuse" for the defensive measure. It determined, however, that the Board reasonably believed that the American General Offer was inadequate and also reasonably concluded that the Offer was a threat to Unitrin's uninformed stockholders.

The Court of Chancery held that the Board's evidence satisfied the first aspect or reasonableness test under Unocal. * * *

The second aspect or proportionality test of the initial *Unocal* burden required the Unitrin Board to demonstrate the proportionality of its response to the threat American General's Offer posed. The record reflects that the Unitrin Board considered three options as defensive measures: the poison pill, the advance notice bylaw, and the Repurchase Program. * * *

The Court of Chancery concluded that Unitrin's Board believed in good faith that the American General Offer was inadequate and properly employed a poison pill as a proportionate defensive response to protect its stockholders from a "low ball" bid.

No cross-appeal was filed in this expedited interlocutory proceeding. Therefore, the Court of Chancery's ruling that the Unitrin Board's adoption of a poison pill was a proportionate response to American General's Offer is not now directly at issue. * * *

---

44. Strine, *The Professorial Bear Hug: The ESB Proposal as a Conscious Effort to Make the Delaware Courts Confront the Basic "Just Say No" Question,* 55 Stan. L. Rev. 863, 869–74 (2002).

The Court of Chancery * * * made two factual findings: first, the Repurchase Program went beyond what was "necessary" to protect the Unitrin stockholders from a "low ball" negotiating strategy; and second, it was designed to keep the decision to combine with American General within the control of the members of the Unitrin Board, as stockholders, under virtually all circumstances. Consequently, the Court of Chancery held that the Unitrin Board failed to demonstrate that the Repurchase Program met the second aspect or proportionality requirement of the initial burden *Unocal* ascribes to a board of directors. * * *

Before the Repurchase Program began, Unitrin's directors collectively held approximately 23% of Unitrin's outstanding shares. Unitrin's certificate of incorporation already included a "shark-repellent" provision barring any business combination with a more-than-15% stockholder unless approved by a majority of continuing directors or by a 75% stockholder vote ("Supermajority Vote"). Unitrin's shareholder directors announced publicly that they would not participate in the Repurchase Program and that this would result in a percentage increase of ownership for them, as well as for any other shareholder who did not participate.

The Court of Chancery found that by not participating in the Repurchase Program, the Board "expected to create a 28% voting block to support the Board's decision to reject [a future] offer by American General." From this underlying factual finding, the Court of Chancery concluded that American General might be "chilled" in its pursuit of Unitrin * * *.

We begin our examination of Unitrin's Repurchase Program mindful of the special import of protecting the shareholder's franchise within *Unocal*'s requirement that a defensive response be reasonable and proportionate. *Stroud v. Grace.* * * *

The record reflects that the Court of Chancery's decision to enjoin the Repurchase Program is attributable to a continuing misunderstanding, *i.e.*, that in conjunction with the longstanding Supermajority Vote provision in the Unitrin charter, the Repurchase Program would operate to provide the director shareholders with a "veto" to preclude a successful proxy contest by American General. * * *

The Court of Chancery's subjective determination that the stockholder directors of Unitrin would reject an "excellent offer," unless it compensated them for giving up the "prestige and perquisites" of directorship, appears to be subjective and without record support. It cannot be presumed. * * *

The first objective premise relied upon by the Court of Chancery, unsupported by the record, is that the shareholder directors needed to implement the Repurchase Program to attain voting power in a proxy contest equal to 25%. * * *

The Court of Chancery and all parties agree that proxy contests do not generate 100% shareholder participation. The shareholder plaintiffs argue that 80–85% may be a usual turnout. Therefore, without the Repurchase Program, the director shareholders' absolute voting power of 23% would already constitute actual voting power greater than 25% in a proxy contest with normal shareholder participation below 100%.

The second objective premise relied upon by the Court of Chancery, unsupported by the record, is that American General's ability to succeed in a proxy contest depended on the Repurchase Program being enjoined because of the Supermajority Vote provision in Unitrin's charter. * * *

As American General acknowledges, a less than 15% stockholder bidder need not proceed with acquiring shares to the extent that it would ever implicate the Supermajority Vote provision. In fact, it would be illogical for American General or any other bidder to acquire more than 15% of Unitrin's stock because that would not only trigger the poison pill, but also the constraints of 8 Del.C. § 203. [The Section 203 limitation is addressed in Section 22.5.B.1.] If American General were to initiate a proxy contest before acquiring 15% of Unitrin's stock, it would need to amass only 45.1% of the votes assuming a 90% voter turnout. If it commenced a tender offer at an attractive price contemporaneously with its proxy contest, it could seek to acquire 50.1% of the outstanding voting stock. * * *

American General's two predicate assumptions are a 90% stockholder turnout in a proxy contest and a bidder with 14.9% holdings, *i.e.*, the maximum the bidder could own to avoid triggering the poison pill and the Supermajority Vote provision. American General also calculated the votes available to the Board or the bidder with and without the Repurchase Program: Assuming no Repurchase [Program], the [shareholder directors] would hold 23%, the percentage collectively held by the [directors] and the bidder would be 37.9%, and the percentage of additional votes available to either side would be 52.1%. Assuming the Repurchase [Program] is fully consummated, the [shareholder directors] would hold 28%, the percentage collectively held by the bidder and the [directors] would be 42.9%, and the percentage of additional votes available to either side would be 47.1%.

American General then applied these assumptions to reach conclusions regarding the votes needed for the 14.9% stockholder bidder to prevail: first, in an election of directors; and second, in the subsequent vote on a merger. With regard to the election of directors, American General made the following calculations: Assume 90% stockholder turnout. To elect directors, a plurality must be obtained; assuming no abstentions and only two competing slates, one must obtain the votes of 45.1% of the shares. The percentage of additional votes the bidder needs to win is: 45.1%–14.9% (maximum the bidder could own and avoid the poison pill, § 203 and supermajority) = 30.2%. A merger requires approval of a majority of outstanding shares, 8 Del.C. § 251, not just a plurality. In that regard, American General made the following calculations: Assume 90% stockholder turnout. To approve a merger, one must obtain the favorable vote of 50.1% of the shares. The percentage of additional votes the bidder needs to win is 50.1%–14.9% = 35.2%.

Consequently, to prevail in a proxy contest with a 90% turnout, the percentage of additional shareholder votes a 14.9% shareholder bidder needs to prevail is 30.2% for directors and 35.2% in a subsequent merger. The record reflects that institutional investors held 42% of Unitrin's stock and 20 institutions held 33% of the stock. * * *

The conclusion of the Court of Chancery that the Repurchase Program would make a proxy contest for Unitrin a "theoretical" possibility that American General could not realistically pursue may be erroneous * * * . * * *

The key variable in a proxy contest would be the merit of American General's issues, not the size of its stockholdings. If American General presented an attractive price as the cornerstone of a proxy contest, it could prevail, irrespective of whether the shareholder directors' absolute voting power was 23% or 28%. * * *

[Types of Threats] Pursuant to the *Unocal* proportionality test, the nature of the threat associated with a particular hostile offer sets the parameters for the range of permissible defensive tactics. Accordingly, the purpose of enhanced judicial scrutiny is to determine whether the Board acted reasonably in "relation * * * to the threat which a particular bid allegedly poses to stockholder interests." * * *

Courts, commentators and litigators have attempted to catalogue the threats posed by hostile tender offers. Commentators have categorized three types of threats: (i) opportunity loss * * * [where] a hostile offer might deprive target shareholders of the opportunity to select a superior alternative offered by target management [or, we would add, offered by another bidder]; (ii) structural coercion, * * * the risk that disparate treatment of non-tendering shareholders might distort shareholders' tender decisions; and (iii) substantive coercion, * * * the risk that shareholders will mistakenly accept an underpriced offer because they disbelieve management's representations of intrinsic value.

This Court has held that the "inadequate value" of an all cash for all shares offer is a "legally cognizable threat." [*Time-Warner*, Section 3.19.F] In addition, this Court has specifically concluded that inadequacy of value is not the only legally cognizable threat from "an all-shares, all-cash offer at a price below what a target board in good faith deems to be the present value of its shares." In making that determination, this Court held that the Time board of directors had reasonably determined that inadequate value was not the only threat that Paramount's all cash for all shares offer presented, but was also reasonably concerned that the Time stockholders might tender to Paramount in ignorance or based upon a mistaken belief, *i.e.*, yield to substantive coercion.

The record reflects that the Unitrin Board perceived the threat from American General's Offer to be a form of substantive coercion. * * * The Board determined that Unitrin's stock was undervalued by the market at current levels and that the Board considered Unitrin's stock to be a good long-term investment. * * *

The record appears to support Unitrin's argument that the Board's justification for adopting the Repurchase Program was its reasonably perceived risk of substantive coercion, *i.e.*, that Unitrin's shareholders might accept American General's inadequate Offer because of "ignorance or mistaken belief" regarding the Board's assessment of the long-term value of Unitrin's stock. * * *

[**Range of Reasonableness**] The Court of Chancery applied an incorrect legal standard when it ruled that the Unitrin decision to authorize the Repurchase Program was disproportionate because it was "unnecessary."* * *

In *QVC*, [Section 3.19.G] this Court recently elaborated upon the judicial function in applying enhanced scrutiny, citing *Unocal* as authority, albeit in the context of a sale of control and the target board's consideration of one of several reasonable alternatives. That teaching is nevertheless applicable here: a court applying enhanced judicial scrutiny should be deciding whether the directors made a reasonable decision, not a perfect decision. If a board selected one of several reasonable alternatives, a court should not second guess that choice even though it might have decided otherwise or subsequent events may have cast doubt on the board's determination. Thus, courts will not substitute their business judgment for that of the directors, but will determine if the directors' decision was, on balance, within a range of reasonableness. *See Unocal.* The Court of Chancery did not determine whether the Unitrin Board's decision to implement the Repurchase Program fell within a "range of reasonableness." *See Unocal.* * * *

The Court of Chancery's determination that the Unitrin Board's adoption of the Repurchase Program was unnecessary constituted a substitution of its business judgment for that of the Board, contrary to this Court's "range of reasonableness" holding in *Paramount Communications, Inc. v. QVC Network, Inc.* * * *

[**Draconian: Coercive or Preclusive**] In assessing a challenge to defensive actions by a target corporation's board of directors in a takeover context, this Court has held that the Court of Chancery should evaluate the board's overall response, including the justification for each contested defensive measure, and the results achieved thereby. Where all of the target board's defensive actions are inextricably related, the principles of *Unocal* require that such actions be scrutinized collectively as a unitary response to the perceived threat. Thus, the Unitrin Board's adoption of the Repurchase Program, in addition to the poison pill, must withstand *Unocal*'s proportionality review. * * *

An examination of the cases applying *Unocal* reveals a direct correlation between findings of proportionality or disproportionality and the judicial determination of whether a defensive response was draconian because it was either coercive or preclusive in character. * * *

If a defensive measure is not draconian, however, because it is not either coercive or preclusive, the *Unocal* proportionality test requires the focus of enhanced judicial scrutiny to shift to "the range of reasonableness." *Paramount Communications, Inc. v. QVC*. * * *

The *ratio decidendi* for the "range of reasonableness" standard is a need of the board of directors for latitude in discharging its fiduciary duties to the corporation and its shareholders when defending against perceived threats. The concomitant requirement is for judicial restraint. Consequently, if the board of directors' defensive response is not draconian (preclusive or coercive) and is within a "range of reasonableness," a court must not substitute its judgment for the board's. *QVC*.

[**Was the Repurchase Program Draconian?**] * * * We begin * * * by ascertaining whether the Repurchase Program, as an addition to the poison pill, was draconian by being either coercive or preclusive.

A limited nondiscriminatory self-tender, like some other defensive measures, may thwart a current hostile bid, but is not inherently coercive. Moreover, it does not necessarily preclude future bids or proxy contests by stockholders who decline to participate in the repurchase. A selective repurchase of shares in a public corporation on the market, such as Unitrin's Repurchase Program, generally does not discriminate because all shareholders can voluntarily realize the same benefit by selling. Here, there is no showing on this record that the Repurchase Program was coercive.

We have already determined that the record in this case appears to reflect that a proxy contest remained a viable (if more problematic) alternative for American General even if the Repurchase Program were to be completed in its entirety. Nevertheless, the Court of Chancery must determine whether Unitrin's Repurchase Program would only inhibit American General's ability to wage a proxy fight and institute a merger or whether it was, in fact, preclusive because American General's success would either be mathematically impossible or realistically unattainable. If the Court of Chancery concludes that the Unitrin Repurchase Program was not draconian because it was not preclusive, one question will remain to be answered in its proportionality review: whether the Repurchase Program was within a range of reasonableness? * * *

[**Remand**] In this case, the Court of Chancery erred by substituting its judgment, that the Repurchase Program was unnecessary, for that of the Board. The Unitrin Board had the power and the duty, upon reasonable investigation, to protect Unitrin's shareholders from what it perceived to be the threat from American General's inadequate all-cash for all-shares Offer. The adoption of the poison pill and the limited Repurchase Program was not coercive and the Repurchase Program may not be preclusive. Although each made a takeover more difficult, individually and collectively, if they were not coercive or preclusive the Court of Chancery must determine whether they were within the range of reasonable defensive measures available to the Board.

If the Court of Chancery concludes that individually and collectively the poison pill and the Repurchase Program were proportionate to the threat the Board believed American General posed, the Unitrin Board's adoption of the Repurchase Program and the poison pill is entitled to review under the traditional business judgment rule. The burden will then shift "back to the plaintiffs who have the ultimate burden of persuasion [in a preliminary injunction proceeding] to show a breach of the directors' fiduciary duties." In order to rebut the protection of the business judgment rule, the burden on the plaintiffs will be to demonstrate, "by a preponderance of the evidence that the directors' decisions were primarily based on [(1)] perpetuating themselves in office or [(2)] some other breach of fiduciary duty such as fraud, overreaching, lack of good faith, or [(3)] being uninformed." *Unocal.* * * *

Questions

How does *Unitrin* relate to *Unocal*? You have been asked by a target's board to explain the *Unocal* standard as amplified by *Unitrin.* Also, the board wants to know how *Revlon* fits into the scheme.

6. Use of Poison Pill to Prevent Sale of Stock of Target Held by Controlling Shareholder—*Hollinger*

a. The Chancery Court Decision

Hollinger International, Inc., v. Black

Delaware Court of Chancery, 2004 844 A.2d 1022

STRINE, Vice Chancellor

[I]n this case, defendant Conrad M. Black, the ultimate controlling stockholder of Hollinger International, Inc. ("International"), a Delaware public company, has repeatedly behaved in a manner inconsistent with the duty of loyalty he owed the company. Black faced potentially serious accusations of self-dealing on his own behalf, and on behalf of an intermediate holding company he dominates and controls, at the expense of International. He sued for peace realizing that International's independent directors might strip him of all his corporate offices and refer certain matters to the Securities and Exchange Commission before Black could take steps to remove them (and knowing that he faced serious personal repercussions if he took that aggressive step). The indignity Black faced was galling to him, as the International board was largely filled with outside directors Black had hand-selected and with whom he had a personal relationship.

To calm the roiled waters, Black made a formal contract, the "Restructuring Proposal," involving many key features. They included his agreement to resign as Chief Executive Officer and to repay certain funds without any admission of wrongdoing. Critically, Black also agreed to stay on as Chairman and devote his principal time and energy to leading a "Strategic Process" involving the development of a value-maximizing transaction for International, such as the sale of the company or some of its assets. Black told the International directors that this Process would be for the "equal and ratable" benefit of all of International's stockholders, and that he would refrain from consummating transactions at the level of the intermediate holding company he dominated, except under strict conditions.

But, Black immediately violated his newly undertaken obligations by diverting to himself a valuable opportunity presented to International—the possible sale of one of its flagship newspapers, the Daily Telegraph, or the company as a whole to the Barclays, English brothers who own newspapers, hotels and other businesses. Black accomplished this diversion in a cunning and calculated way, fully detailed in this opinion. During the course of his dealings, Black misrepresented facts to the International board, used confidential company information for his own purposes without permission, and made threats, as he would put it, of "multifaceted dimensions" towards International's independent directors.

As the culmination of his misconduct, Black unveiled a transaction involving the sale of the holding company [Hollinger, Inc. (Inc.)] through which Black wields voting control of International to the Barclays. The "Barclays Transaction," if consummated, would prevent International from realizing the benefits of the Strategic Process Black had contractually promised to lead with fidelity and energetic commitment. Effectively, the Barclays Transaction would end the Strategic Process before the bidding even began. The Barclays Transaction was also one that Black had, by contractual promise in the Restructuring Proposal, agreed not to effect.

When the International board took measures to stop the Barclays Transaction by considering a shareholder rights plan, Black caused the holding company he controlled to file a written consent enacting "Bylaw Amendments" requiring unanimous action by the International board for any significant decision, abolishing a committee that had been created to consider how International should respond to the Barclays Transaction, and thereby effectively permitting himself to disable International's independent directors from obstructing the completion of Black's injurious course of conduct. Believing the Bylaw Amendments to be unlawful and inequitable, the International independent directors, through a committee previously authorized to take such action, adopted a shareholder rights plan (the "Rights Plan") to prevent Black from consummating the Barclays Transaction, contingent on a judicial declaration that their decision was permissible. International then brought this suit seeking 1) a preliminary injunction against the Barclays Transaction and further breaches of the Restructuring Proposal; 2) a declaration that the Bylaw Amendments were ineffective because they were, among other things, adopted for an inequitable purpose; and 3) a determination that the Rights Plan was properly adopted. * * *

In this opinion, I conclude that Black breached his fiduciary and contractual duties persistently and seriously. His conduct threatens grave injury to International and its stockholders by depriving them of the benefits that might flow from the Strategic Process's search for a value-maximizing transaction. In the course of his improper dealings, Black acted functionally as both principal and agent for his holding companies, without restraint from the boards of those companies, which he dominated. To rectify the irreparable harm Black's wrongdoing obviously threatens, an injunction will issue against the Barclays Transaction and further breaches of the Restructuring Proposal.

The Bylaw Amendments Black proximately caused to be adopted were designed to cement into place the Barclays Transaction, by disabling the International board from protecting the company from his wrongful acts. Thus, I conclude that the Bylaw Amendments are inequitable and ineffective.

Finally, in these extraordinary circumstances, the International board has satisfied its burden under *Unocal* to justify the time-limited use of the Rights Plan to permit the completion of the Strategic Process in the contractually contemplated manner. The unique circumstances here involving serious breaches of duty by Black as a controlling stockholder and a concomitantly dangerous threat of imminent injury to International justify as proportionate the use of the Rights Plan to restore the independent directors' leverage and authority so that International may preserve its contractual expectations under the Restructuring Proposal and seek to help itself recover from Black's subversion of the Strategic Process.

The rich factual history of this dispute, the legal complexities that arise from it, and my resolution of them now follow. [Only the poison pill issue is addressed below.] * * *

Is the Rights Plan Permissible? * * * The defendants attack the Rights Plan on several fronts. As a preliminary matter, the defendants argue that the DGCL does not authorize the adoption of a rights plan that would be triggered by the sale of an upstream corporation that owns a controlling voting block in the underlying corporation adopting that rights plan.

Alternatively, the defendants argue that the CRC [the Corporate Review Committee, which consisted of all independent directors] did not satisfy its *Unocal* [Section 3.14.D] duties in adopting the Rights Plan. Even more assertively, the defendants insist that the Rights Plan must be addressed, not under *Unocal,* but instead under *Blasius.* [Section 3.14.G] The justification for this is said to exist in the combined effect of the Rights Plan and the Consent Order, which, when taken together, the defendants believe work a purposeful disenfranchisement of Inc.'s voting rights as a controlling stockholder.

International counters each of these arguments. It seeks a declaration that the Rights Plan was permissibly adopted and has made the effectiveness of the Rights Plan contingent on a judicial declaration to that effect. * * *

The Rights Plan Is Not Inconsistent With The DGCL. I begin with the defendants' claim that the Rights Plan is legally impermissible. This claim only has force if the Delaware Supreme Court's decision in *Moran v. Household International, Inc.* [Section 3.14.E] is no longer binding precedent. But the *Moran* decision was recently reaffirmed as good law by the Delaware Supreme Court. [Citing *Hilton Hotels*, Section 3.18.D.4]

In this case, I invited the defendants to tell me what provision of the DGCL prohibits the Rights Plan adopted by the CRC. They provided no argument of that sort. * * *

Put bluntly, the permissibility of the Rights Plan hinges on the equities.

The International Board Has Met Its Unocal Burden And The Rights Plan Is Permissible. The traditional test for examining whether a Rights Plan was permissibly adopted is that set forth in *Unocal.* Under *Unocal,* a defensive measure such as a rights plan may only be adopted if the board reasonably identified a threat to the corporation to which the rights plan is a proportionate response. Here, the defendants say that the CRC's decision to adopt the Rights Plan cannot satisfy *Unocal* because its knowledge of the Rights Plan's complex workings is grossly inadequate, the CRC identified no legitimate threat to International, and the Rights Plan is a disproportionate response. I do not accept these arguments and believe that International has sustained its affirmative duties under *Unocal.*

The CRC's determination that the Barclays Transaction thwarted the Strategic Process, denies International the bargained-for benefits of the Restructuring Proposal, and is a serious threat to International is a reasonable one. If consummated, the Barclays Transaction will prevent International from conducting the full market and transactional exploration contemplated by the Proposal. The Barclays, as buyers, seek the "once in a life-time opportunity" to control the Telegraph, and can hardly be expected to have an interest in turning around and selling that control or in competing in an auction.

The CRC also identified other threats. * * * I believe that the proportionality of the CRC's adoption of a rights plan must be measured against one primary threat: the injury that the Barclays Transaction poses to the board's ability to complete the contractually "bargained" for Strategic Process. This threat is a potent one justifying a strong response, arising as it does out of a course of improper conduct by Black that subverted the corporation's business strategy. * * *

In this case, the CRC's deployment of the Rights Plan is proportionate, in view of the extraordinary circumstances International confronts. The most direct way that International can protect itself and pursue the Strategic Process Black promised to support is by using the Rights Plan. * * *

Once the board has completed the Strategic Process and developed its preferred option, the further use of the Rights Plan would be suspect, absent further misconduct justifying its continued use. * * *

The time-limited use of the Rights Plan for this purpose is, in many ways, the most narrowly tailored remedy for Black's misbehavior. * * *

The defendants [also] argue that *Blasius* applies because they believe that the Rights Plan, working in concert with the Consent Order, precludes removal of the board and thereby disenfranchises Inc. stockholders.

I am not persuaded by this argument. * * *

As important, even if *Blasius* did apply to the Rights Plan, a sufficiently compelling justification exists for any incidental burden on Inc.'s voting rights. * * *

b. The Delaware Supreme Court's Decision

Black v. Hollinger International, Inc.

Delaware Supreme Court, 2005 Del. LEXIS 156

[In *Black v. Hollinger* the Delaware Supreme Court affirmed Chancellor Strine's decision, saying:]

Black and Inc. claim that the Court of Chancery erred in upholding the Rights Plan. They claim that the Rights Plan is statutorily invalid under 8 *Del. C.*§§ 157 and 203; and in any event, is equitably invalid under *Unocal* and *Blasius.* The appellees argue, in response, that the Court of Chancery correctly held that the Rights Plan was not statutorily invalid; that the Rights Plan satisfied the "threat" and "proportionality" standards of *Unocal*; that the *Blasius* standard of review did not apply; and that even if *Blasius* did apply, a sufficiently compelling justification existed for any incidental burden on Inc.'s voting rights.

We have considered carefully, and in depth, the multitudinous arguments advanced by the parties in their extensive briefs on their appeal and cross-appeal.

We conclude that the Court of Chancery did not err in any respect in its findings of fact or its conclusions of law. * * *

7. The Triggering of an NOL Pill—*Selectica*

Versata Enterprises, Inc. v. Selectica, Inc.

Supreme Court of Delaware, 2010 5 A.3d 586

HOLLAND, Justice:

This is an appeal from a final judgment entered by the Court of Chancery. On November 16, 2008 the Board of Directors of Selectica, Inc. ("Selectica") reduced the trigger of its "poison pill" Shareholder Rights Plan from 15% to 4.99% of Selectica's outstanding shares and capped existing shareholders who held a 5% or more interest to a further increase of only 0.5% (the "NOL Poison Pill"). Selectica's reason for taking such action was to protect the company's net operating loss carryforwards ("NOLs"). When Trilogy, Inc. ("Trilogy") subsequently purchased shares above this cap, Selectica filed suit in the Court of Chancery on December 21, 2008, seeking a declaration that the NOL Poison Pill was valid and enforceable. On January 2, 2009, Selectica implemented the dilutive exchange provision (the "Exchange") of the NOL Poison Pill, which reduced Trilogy's interest from 6.7% to 3.3%, and adopted another Rights Plan with a 4.99% trigger (the "Reloaded NOL Poison Pill"). Selectica then amended its complaint to seek a declaration that the Exchange and the Reloaded NOL Poison Pill were valid.

Trilogy and its subsidiary Versata Enterprises, Inc. ("Versata") counterclaimed that the NOL Poison Pill, the Reloaded NOL Poison Pill, and the Exchange were unlawful on the grounds that, before acting, the Board failed to consider that its NOLs were unusable or that the two NOL poison pills were unnecessary given Selectica's unbroken history of losses and doubtful prospects of annual profits. Trilogy and Versata also asserted that the NOL Poison Pill and the Reloaded NOL Poison Pill were impermissibly preclusive of a successful proxy contest for Board control, particularly when combined with Selectica's staggered director terms. After trial, the Court of Chancery held that the NOL Poison Pill, the Reloaded NOL Poison Pill, and the Exchange were all valid under Delaware law.

Trilogy and Versata now appeal and assert two claims of error. First, they contend that the Court of Chancery erred in applying the *Unocal* test for enhanced judicial scrutiny when confronting what they frame as a question of first impression. The issue (as framed by them) is: "what are the minimum requirements for a reasonable investigation before the board of a never-profitable company may adopt a [Rights Plan with a 4.99% trigger] for the ostensible purpose of protecting NOLs from an 'ownership change' under Section 382 of the Internal Revenue Code?" Second, they submit that the Court of Chancery erred in holding that the two NOL poison pills, either individually or in combination with a charter-based classified Board, did not have a preclusive effect on the shareholders' ability to pursue a successful proxy contest for control of the Company's board. We conclude that both arguments are without merit. * * *

[The following discussion of the Supreme Court's decision[45] is based on the discussion in Section 5:5.2[B][16] of Thompson, *Mergers, Acquisitions and Tender Offers*, *supra* Section 1.10.] * * *

Applying the two prong *Unocal*, *supra*, test, the Supreme Court first agreed with the Chancery Court's decision that Selectica had acted reasonably in identifying a threat as required by the first prong of Unocal. On this point, the court reasoned:

> The Court of Chancery found the record "replete with evidence" that, based upon the expert advice it received, the Board was reasonable in concluding that Selectica's NOLs were worth preserving and that Trilogy's actions presented a serious threat of their impairment. The Court of Chancery explained those findings, as follows:
>
> > The threat posed by Trilogy was reasonably viewed as qualitatively different from the normal corporate control dispute that leads to the adoption of a shareholder rights plan. In this instance, Trilogy, a competitor with a contentious history, recognized that harm would befall its rival if it purchased sufficient shares of Selectica stock, and Trilogy proceeded to act accordingly. It was reasonable for the Board to respond, and the timing of Trilogy's campaign required the Board to act promptly. Moreover, the 4.99% threshold for the NOL Poison Pill was driven by our tax laws and regulations; the threshold, low as it is, was measured by reference to an external standard, one created neither by the Board nor by the Court [of Chancery]. Within this context, it is not for the Court [of Chancery] to second-guess the Board's efforts to protect Selectica's NOLs.
>
> Those findings are not clearly erroneous. They are supported by the record and the result of a logical deductive reasoning process. Accordingly, we hold that the Selectica directors satisfied the first part of the *Unocal* test by showing "that

45. Versata Enterprises, Inc. v. Selectica, Inc., 5 A.3d 586 (Del. 2010).

they had reasonable grounds for believing that a danger to corporate policy and effectiveness existed because of another person's stock ownership."[46]

Turning to the second prong of *Unocal*, which requires that the defensive measure be reasonable in relation to the threat posed, the Supreme Court agreed with the Chancery Court that Selectica's actions in adopting both the NOL Pill and the Reloaded Pill, which was adopted after the triggering of the first pill, satisfied the second prong. Under *Unitrin, supra*, to meet the second prong, the defensive measure must not be coercive or preclusive and must fall within a range of reasonableness. In addressing whether Selectica's actions were preclusive, the Supreme Court reasoned:

> The Court of Chancery concluded that the NOL Poison Pill and Reloaded NOL Poison Pill were not preclusive. For a measure to be preclusive, it must render a successful proxy contest realistically unattainable given the specific factual context. The record supports the Court of Chancery's factual determination and legal conclusion that Selectica's NOL Poison Pill and Reloaded NOL Poison Pill do not meet that preclusivity standard.[47]

And, in addressing whether Selectica's actions were within a range of reasonableness, the Supreme Court indicated that "context determines reasonableness"[48] and elaborated as follows:

> Under a *Unocal* analysis, the reasonableness of a board's response is determined in relation to the "specific threat," at the time it was identified. Thus, it is the specific nature of the threat that "sets the parameters for the range of permissible defensive tactics" at any given time. The record demonstrates that a longtime competitor sought to increase the percentage of its stock ownership, not for the purpose of conducting a hostile takeover but, to intentionally impair corporate assets, or else coerce Selectica into meeting certain business demands under the threat of such impairment. Only in relation to that specific threat have the Court of Chancery and this Court considered the reasonableness of Selectica's response.[49]

Finally, the Supreme Court agreed with the conclusion of the Court of Chancery that Selectica's actions were reasonable in relation to the threat posed:

> Under part two of the *Unocal* test, the Court of Chancery found that the combination of the NOL Poison Pill, the Exchange, and the Reloaded NOL Poison Pill was a proportionate response to the threatened loss of Selectica's NOLs. Those findings are not clearly erroneous. They are supported by the record and the result of a logical deductive reasoning process. Accordingly, we hold that the Selectica directors satisfied the second part of the Unocal test by showing that their defensive response was proportionate by being "reasonable in relation to the threat" identified.[50]

In closing its opinion, the Supreme Court issued two caveats. First, in elaborating on the context theme, the Supreme Court said: "The fact that the NOL Poison Pill was reasonable under the specific facts and circumstances of this case, should not be construed as generally approving the reasonableness of a 4.99% trigger in the Rights Plan of a

46. *Id.* at 600–01.
47. *Id.* at 603.
48. *Id.* at 606.
49. *Id.* at 606–07.
50. *Id.* at 606.

corporation with or without NOLs."[51] Second, the Court issued the same caveat it issued at the end of the *Moran*, *supra*, decision, which first found that pills are permissible:

> To reiterate *Moran*, "the ultimate response to an actual takeover bid must be judged by the Directors' actions at that time." If and when the Selectica Board "is faced with a tender offer and a request to redeem the [Reloaded NOL Poison Pill], they will not be able to arbitrarily reject the offer. They will be held to the same fiduciary standards any other board of directors would be held to in deciding to adopt a defensive mechanism." The Selectica Board has no more discretion in refusing to redeem the Rights Plan than it does in enacting any defensive mechanism." Therefore, the Selectica Board's future use of the Reloaded NOL Poison Pill must be evaluated if and when that issue arises.[52]

8. The Delaware Chancery Court Addresses Pill with 30% Limit for Old Shareholders and 20% Limit for New Shareholders— *Yucaipa*

Yucaipa American Alliance Fund II, L.P. v. Riggio

Court of Chancery of Delaware, 2010 Del. Ch. LEXIS 172

STRINE, Vice Chancellor.

I. Introduction.

Less than two years ago, billionaire investor Ronald Burkle called Leonard Riggio, the founder of Barnes & Noble, Inc., to indicate that Burkle's funds * * * (collectively, "Yucaipa"), were going to invest in Barnes & Noble. * * * [Burkle was angry] when he learned in August 2009 that Barnes & Noble was to acquire a college bookstore chain that had been wholly-owned by Riggio. Burkle communicated his disappointment with how Barnes & Noble was governed, and his fund, Yucaipa, began to increase its stake in the company. Over a four day period in November 2009, Yucaipa approximately doubled its stake in Barnes & Noble to nearly 18%.

In response to the rapid accumulation of shares in Barnes & Noble by Yucaipa, the Barnes & Noble board of directors adopted a poison pill. That pill is triggered when a shareholder acquires over 20% of Barnes & Noble's outstanding stock, or when two or more shareholders, who combined own over 20%, enter into an "agreement, arrangement or understanding ... for the purpose of acquiring, holding, voting ... or disposing of any voting securities of the Company." Notably, however, the pill's 20% threshold does not apply to Riggio or his family, whose approximately 30% stake was grandfathered under the terms of the pill. The pill, however, also limited Riggio from further increasing that stake. * * *

Yucaipa then brought this action against the Barnes & Noble directors, claiming that the adoption of the pill, and the board's refusal to amend the pill per Burkle's specific suggestions, was a breach of the directors' fiduciary duties. [This excerpt focuses on the court's analysis of the 20% cap.] * * *

III. Legal Analysis.

Addressing Yucaipa's challenge to the Rights Plan is complicated by the evolving nature of Yucaipa's arguments and the multiple standards of review it advocates as being relevant to the consideration of its arguments. * * *

51. *Id.* at 607.
52. *Id.*

A. *Unocal Provides The Appropriate Standard Of Review In This Case*

Seeking to reverse decades of settled law, Yucaipa argues that the standard of review to evaluate whether the board's adoption and amendment of the Rights Plan complied with its fiduciary duties is subject not to the *Unocal* standard used in *Moran* and its progeny, but to either: (1) entire fairness review; or (2) *Blasius's* "compelling justification" standard. I reject that argument. * * * [The court found that *Unocal* applied.]

a. Although Its Process Was Not Ideal, The Board Made A Good Faith And Reasonable Determination That Yucaipa Posed A Threat. * * *

b. The Rights Plan Was A Proportional Response To The Threat The Company Faced. * * *

Here, the key issue is whether the Rights Plan unreasonably inhibits the ability of Yucaipa to run an effective proxy contest. In addressing that question, it is of course critical to confront the reality that the Riggios own nearly 30% of Barnes & Noble's outstanding stock, the rest of the board and the officers owns another 3.26%, and the Barnes & Noble employees own another 6%. Although I am dubious that it is appropriate to treat the employees as a part of a management bloc, and although I recognize that the other directors' equity holdings might give them a self-interest under certain conditions to break with Riggio, I accept for present purposes the notion that in a contested proxy contest the shares held by the board, company officers, and employees will be voted for the slate the board proposes. Thus, I accept the basic idea—which the board's and Yucaipa's experts agree upon—that the management slate would go into a proxy fight in which a turnout of around 91% is expected, with around 37% to 38% of the expected vote. Therefore, to win, Yucaipa would have to garner a strong super-majority of the remaining vote to get a majority. That is obviously a lift. But it is not a herculean lift. It is one that a reasonably fit proxy fighter can pull off, especially if it can get nearly half of the necessary votes just from one other stockholder, Aletheia.

Indeed, Yucaipa now admits that the Rights Plan is not preclusive. The Rights Plan is not preclusive because, as Yucaipa's own experts indicated, there is good reason to believe that Yucaipa will succeed in a proxy contest if it puts together a platform and a slate of candidates that are attractive to Aletheia and the leading institutional proxy advisors, particularly Risk Metrics. * * *

The reasons why Yucaipa can prevail despite the Riggios' bloc are several. First, the Rights Plan cap of 20% is high and allows Yucaipa to ensure itself 20% of the vote. Relatedly, that cap allows Aletheia to purchase up to 20% itself.

Second, if, as is clearly possible and even likely, Aletheia supports a Yucaipa slate that advocates a plausible value-maximizing platform and is comprised of distinguished business persons, Yucaipa almost immediately levels, if not exceeds, the Riggio advantage.

Third, and importantly, all of the experts in the case make a point that might make the object of their commentary blush. All say that one of the key factors in the outcome of a proxy contest will be the recommendation of the firms that provide institutional investors with recommendations about how to vote, the so-called "proxy advisory firms." * * *

For all these reasons, Barnes & Noble has convinced me that the Rights Plan is not an unreasonable device that "fundamentally restricts" Yucaipa from winning a proxy contest. To the contrary, the record shows that if Yucaipa makes a good merits case, it is likely to win. * * *

In this respect, it is critical that the board used a 20% trigger rather than a 15% cap. With the Riggios' ownership, that threshold was reasonable because setting the threshold any higher would have only made Yucaipa's creeping acquisition of control more likely. It may be that options other than a pill with a 20% trigger were available, but the 20% pill was certainly a reasonable alternative and that is the requirement under *Unocal,* not perfection. * * *

9. The Use of a Pill by a Closely Held Corporation—*eBay*

eBay Domestic Holdings, Inc. v. Newmark

Delaware Court of Chancery, 2010 16 A.3d 1

CHANDLER, Chancellor

On June 29, 2007, eBay launched the online classifieds site www.Kijiji.com in the United States. eBay designed Kijiji to compete with www.craigslist.org, the most widely used online classifieds site in the United States, which is owned and operated by craigslist, Inc. ("craigslist" or "the Company"). At the time of Kijiji's launch, eBay owned 28.4% of craigslist and was one of only three craigslist stockholders. The other two stockholders were Craig Newmark ("Craig") and James Buckmaster ("Jim"), who together own a majority of craigslist's shares and dominate the craigslist board. eBay purchased its stake in craigslist in August 2004 pursuant to the terms of a stockholders' agreement between Jim, Craig, craigslist, and eBay that expressly permits eBay to compete with craigslist in the online classifieds arena. Under the stockholders' agreement, when eBay chose to compete with craigslist by launching Kijiji, eBay lost certain contractual consent rights that gave eBay the right to approve or disapprove of a variety of corporate actions at craigslist. Another consequence of eBay's choice to compete with craigslist, however, was that the craigslist shares eBay owns were freed of the right of first refusal Jim and Craig had held over the shares, and the shares became freely transferable.

Notwithstanding eBay's express right to compete, Jim and Craig were not enthusiastic about eBay's foray into online classifieds. Accordingly, they asked eBay to sell its stake in craigslist, indicating a preference that eBay either sell its craigslist shares back to the Company or to a third party who would be compatible with Jim, Craig, and craigslist's unique corporate culture. When eBay refused to sell, Jim and Craig deliberated with outside counsel for six months about how to respond. Finally, on January 1, 2008, Jim and Craig, acting in their capacity as directors, responded by [*inter alia*] adopting a rights plan that restricted eBay from purchasing additional craigslist shares and hampered eBay's ability to freely sell the craigslist shares it owned to third parties. * * *

eBay asserts that, in approving and implementing [the rights plan], Jim and Craig, as directors and controlling stockholders, breached the fiduciary duties they owe to eBay as a minority stockholder of the corporation. * * * I conclude that Jim and Craig breached the fiduciary duties they owe to eBay by adopting the rights plan. * * *

The Rights Plan. The Rights Plan implemented on January 2, 2008 contains some standard terms frequently seen in rights plans and some not-so-standard terms. The Rights Plan pays a dividend to craigslist stockholders of one right per share of craigslist stock. Each right allows its holder to purchase two shares of craigslist stock at $ 0.00005 per share if the rights are triggered. There are two triggers. The first trigger involves acquisitions by Jim, Craig, or eBay. If any of these three becomes the "Beneficial Owner" of 0.01% of additional craigslist stock, the rights are triggered. The second trigger involves anyone other than Jim, Craig, or eBay. Should any such person become the "Beneficial Owner" of 15% or more of craigslist's outstanding shares, the rights are triggered. "Beneficial Ownership" is defined broadly. Specifically, a stockholder is deemed to "beneficially own" not only the shares he or she actually owns, but also shares owned by the stockholder's affiliates, associates, or persons with whom the stockholder has "any agreement, arrangement or understanding (whether or not in writing), for the purpose of acquiring, holding, voting ... or disposing of any voting securities of [craigslist]...."

Certain transfers do not trigger the rights. Specifically, the rights are not triggered if Jim or Craig transfers shares to his heirs by will or intestate succession, to a trust established for estate planning purposes, or to a charitable organization. eBay Holdings may transfer its shares to eBay, Inc. or to any successor in interest by merger (provided the successor remains a wholly owned direct or indirect subsidiary of eBay, Inc.) without triggering the rights.

The Rights Plan gives the craigslist board four options if the rights are triggered: (1) the board can redeem the rights at $ 0.00001 per right within ten days, and the rights will not become exercisable; (2) the board may amend the Rights Plan within ten days to make the Rights Plan inapplicable to the transaction that triggered the rights; (3) the board may leave the choice of whether to exercise the rights in the hands of the individual stockholders; or (4) within ten days of the rights being triggered, the board may unilaterally exchange the rights for shares of stock, at a rate of two shares of common stock per right. * * *

ANALYSIS. Jim and Craig owe fiduciary duties to eBay because they are directors and controlling stockholders of craigslist, and eBay is a minority stockholder of craigslist. All directors of Delaware corporations are fiduciaries of the corporations' stockholders. Similarly, controlling stockholders are fiduciaries of their corporations' minority stockholders. Even though neither Jim nor Craig individually owns a majority of craigslist's shares, the law treats them as craigslist's controlling stockholders because they form a control group, bound together by the Jim-Craig Voting Agreement, with the power to elect the majority of the craigslist board. eBay's complaint asserts that Jim and Craig breached the fiduciary duties they owed to eBay by [*inter alia*, adopting the rights plan].

The Rights Plan. I will review Jim and Craig's adoption of the Rights Plan using the intermediate standard of enhanced scrutiny, typically referred to as the *Unocal* test. * * *

This case involves a unique set of facts heretofore not seen in the context of a challenge to a rights plan. To my knowledge, no decision under Delaware law has addressed a challenge to a rights plan adopted by a privately held company with so few stockholders. The ample case law addressing rights plans almost invariably involves publicly traded corporations with a widely dispersed, potentially disempowered, and arguably vulnerable stockholder base. In cases involving rights plans to date, Delaware courts have typically and understandably approved the use of rights plans to remedy the collective action problems that stockholders face, including but not limited to the classically coercive prisoner's dilemma imposed by a two-tiered offer. At the same time, Delaware courts have guarded against the overt risk of entrenchment and the less visible, yet more pernicious risk that incumbents acting in subjective good faith might nevertheless deprive stockholders of value-maximizing opportunities.

In this unique case, I do not face those same concerns. Jim and Craig are not dispersed, disempowered, or vulnerable stockholders. They are the majority. Jim and Craig are not using the Rights Plan improperly to preclude craigslist stockholders from considering and opting for a value-maximizing transaction. As the majority, Jim and Craig can consider and opt-for a value-maximizing transaction whenever they want.

Nor are Jim and Craig using the Rights Plan to protect their board seats. Together Jim and Craig own an overwhelming majority of craigslist's voting power, and they have entered into the Jim-Craig Voting Agreement which ensures that each votes the other onto the board. If eBay were to sell its entire interest in craigslist to some third party, that third party would not be able to unseat either Jim or Craig because, like eBay, it would only own a minority interest. Neither eBay nor any third party who might purchase eBay's craigslist shares could threaten Jim or Craig with a proxy fight. Under their voting agreement, Jim cannot grant a proxy to unseat Craig, and Craig cannot grant a proxy to unseat Jim. Furthermore, as rationally self-interested actors, Jim and Craig will not give someone a proxy to unseat themselves.

These unique factors do not, however, eliminate *Unocal's* usefulness. * * *

First, did Jim and Craig properly and reasonably perceive a threat to craigslist's corporate policy and effectiveness? Second, if they did, is the Rights Plan a proportional response to that threat? * * *

Jim and Craig contend that they identified a threat to craigslist and its corporate policies that will materialize after they both die and their craigslist shares are distributed to their heirs. At that point, they say, "eBay's acquisition of control [via the anticipated acquisition of Jim or Craig's shares from some combination of their heirs] would fundamentally alter craigslist's values, culture and business model, including departing from [craigslist's] public-service mission in favor of increased monetization of craigslist." To prevent this unwanted potential future reality, Jim and Craig have adopted the Rights Plan now so that their vision of craigslist's culture can bind future fiduciaries and stockholders from beyond the grave. Having given new meaning to the concept of a "dead-hand pill," Jim and Craig ask this Court to validate their attempt to use a pill to shape the future of the space-time continuum.

It is true that on the unique facts of a particular case—*Paramount Communications, Inc. v. Time Inc.*—this Court and the Delaware Supreme Court accepted defensive action by the directors of a Delaware corporation as a good faith effort to protect a specific corporate culture. * * *

Time did not hold that corporate culture, standing alone, is worthy of protection as an end in itself. * * *

Ultimately, defendants failed to prove that craigslist possesses a palpable, distinctive, and advantageous culture that sufficiently promotes stockholder value to support the indefinite implementation of a poison pill. * * *

I find that there is nothing about craigslist's corporate culture that *Time* or *Unocal* protects. The existence of a distinctive craigslist "culture" was not proven at trial. It is a fiction, invoked almost talismanically for purposes of this trial in order to find deference under *Time's* dicta.

The defendants also failed to prove at trial that when adopting the Rights Plan, they concluded in good faith that there was a sufficient connection between the craigslist "culture" (however amorphous and intangible it might be) and the promotion of stockholder value. No evidence at trial suggested that Jim or Craig conducted any informed evaluation of alternative business strategies or tactics when adopting the Rights Plan. * * *

Jim and Craig's defense of the Rights Plan thus fails the first prong of *Unocal* both factually and legally. I find that defendants failed to prove, as a factual matter, the existence of a distinctly protectable craigslist culture and further failed to prove, both factually and legally, that they actually decided to deploy the Rights Plan because of a craigslist culture. I find, instead, that Jim and Craig acted to punish eBay for competing with craigslist. Directors of a for-profit Delaware corporation cannot deploy a rights plan to defend a business strategy that openly eschews stockholder wealth maximization—at least not consistently with the directors' fiduciary duties under Delaware law.

Up to this point, I have evaluated the Rights Plan primarily though the lens of the first prong of *Unocal*. To the extent I assume for purposes of analysis that a craigslist culture was something that Jim and Craig reasonably could seek to protect, the Rights Plan nonetheless does not fall within the range of reasonable responses. * * * I rescind the Rights Plan in its entirety.

10. The Non-Redemption of the *Airgas* Pill

Introduction to *Airgas*. This section discusses the February 2011 decision of Chancellor Chandler of the Delaware Chancery Court in *Air Products and Chemical, Inc. v. Airgas, Inc.*,[53] where he upheld the poison pill used by Airgas in deterring a hostile acquisition by Air Products. The discussion is based on Section 5:5.2[B][19] of Thompson, *Mergers, Acquisitions and Tender Offers*, *supra* Section 1.10.]

The decision had an immediate and significant impact on the long-running hostile offer, because rather than appealing the decision to the Delaware Supreme Court, Air Products immediately announced that it was abandoning its efforts to takeover Airgas. Air Products explained in a news release:

> Air Products ... today commented on the decision by the Delaware Chancery Court to uphold the Airgas, Inc.... poison pill.
>
> John E. McGlade, Air Products chairman, president and chief executive officer, said, "We are disappointed by the court's decision. We believe the Airgas Board of Directors has done a great disservice to Airgas shareholders by never allowing them to decide for themselves whether they want to accept our $70 per share all-cash offer. It is abundantly clear that the Airgas Board is thoroughly entrenched in its position, so we have decided to withdraw our offer and move on."[54]

On the announcement of the decision, there was an immediate drop in the price of the shares of Airgas from just under $64 a share to just over $62 a share. Five days after the decision, the shares were trading around $64 a share.

This poison pill decision is completely separate from Chancellor Chandler's decision and the Delaware Supreme Court's reversal of the decision in *Airgas, Inc. v. Air Products and Chemical Inc.*[55] There the Supreme Court held that the terms of a staggered board must approximate a year, rejecting a bylaw proposed by Air Products and accepted by the Airgas shareholders, that would have reduced the term of the directors who were next up for election to 4 months. The staggered board decision is discussed infra. Also, the suit by Airgas against Cravath, the attorneys for Air Products in the transaction, is discussed in Chapter 26, which addresses ethical issues. Cravath had previously represented Airgas. Because of the significance of this case, the following discussion is more detailed than normal.

The Basic Facts in *Airgas*. The basic facts in Chancellor Chandler's 153 page poison pill decision are as follows. Air Products first attempted to convince Airgas to agree to a negotiated transaction at $60 a share in stock. When Air Products made its first approach, Airgas, had a nine-member staggered board of directors, divided into three equal classes with one class of directors up for election each year. All of the directors were independent outside directors, other than McCausland, the founder, CEO and major shareholder.

---

53. Air Products and Chemical, Inc. v. Airgas, Inc., 2011 Del. Ch. LEXIS 22 (Del. Ch. Feb. 15, 2011).

54. Air Products, *Air Products Withdraws Offer for Airgas* (News Rel. Feb. 15, 2011).

55. Airgas, Inc. v. Air Products and Chemical Inc., 8 A.3d 1182 (Del. 2010).

After Airgas rejected this offer, Air Products launched a hostile tender offer at $60 per share, and began a proxy contest to replace the members of the staggered board of Airgas who were up for election at the September 2010 annual meeting. [Some of the documents used in the proxy contest are set out in Documentary Appendix HH, *Documents Relating to the Air Products 2010 Proxy Contest to Elect Directors to the Board of Airgas.* This Appendix is discussed further in Chapter 16, which deals with proxy contests.]

The proxy contest also included the bylaw that reduced the term of the directors up for reelection in 2011 to 4 months, providing that the election would be held in January 2011. Air Products was successful in both aspects of the proxy contest: its slate was elected and the bylaw was accepted. As indicated the Delaware Supreme Court found that the bylaw was illegal. Air Products put on the table its "best and final" offer at $70 per share, which was the offer price at the time the decision was rendered. The Airgas board unanimously rejected the $70 offer as inadequate. Thus, a very important fact here is that even the directors elected on Air Products slate voted against accepting the offer.

In this regard, it is important to focus on the court's description of the facts surrounding the decision to reject the offer. First, at the request of the Air Products Nominees, the board of Airgas agreed to (1) retain independent counsel for the Nominees, and (2) retain a third investment banker, Credit Suisse, to render an opinion on Air Products offer. The Airgas board was at the time represented by both the Goldman Sachs and Bank of America Merrill Lynch investment banking firms. The court describes as follows the background on these decisions:

> [O]n December 10, the Airgas board (minus McCausland [the CEO]) held a telephonic meeting. The nine independent directors unanimously agreed to retain Credit Suisse as a third independent financial advisor to represent the full board. The three new directors were satisfied with the choice of Credit Suisse, and Air Products' own representatives harbored no reason to doubt Credit Suisse's qualifications or independence. In addition, the Air Products Nominees retained their own independent counsel—Skadden, Arps, Slate, Meagher & Flom, LLP—and the board agreed to reimburse the reasonable costs of Skadden's past work for the new directors and to pay Skadden's fees going forward.[56]

The court discussed as follows the actions of the board of Airgas in considering Air Product's "best and final" offer of $70:

> On December 21, the Airgas board met to consider Air Products' "best and final" offer. Management kicked off the meeting by presenting an updated five-year plan to the board.... This was followed by presentations by the three financial advisors.... Both Bank of America Merrill Lynch and Goldman Sachs "were of the opinion that the Air Products' $70 offer was inadequate from a financial point of view."

Then they turned the floor over to David DeNunzio of Credit Suisse, Airgas's newly-retained third independent financial advisor. DeNunzio explained how Credit Suisse had performed its analysis, and how its analysis differed from that of Goldman Sachs and Bank of America Merrill Lynch.... In summary, DeNunzio said that Air Products' offer "was only slightly above what [Airgas] should trade at, was below most selected transactions and was well below the value of the Company on the basis of a DCF analysis, which was the analysis to which Credit Suisse gave the most weight." In the end, Credit Suisse "easily concluded that the $70 offer was inadequate from a financial point of view."

---

56. *Air Products*, 2011 Del. Ch. LEXIS 22, at *92.

After considering Airgas's updated five-year plan and the inadequacy opinions of all three of the company's financial advisors, the Airgas board unanimously—including the Air Products Nominees—rejected the $70 offer. Interestingly, the Air Products Nominees were some of the most vocal opponents to the $70 offer.[57]

The decision of the Airgas board to oppose the offer by Air Products was communicated to the Airgas shareholders by an amendment to Schedule 14D-9, which the Airgas board is required to file under the SEC's tender offer rules. The court described as follows the amended 14D-9:

> The next day, December 22, 2010, Airgas filed another amendment to its 14D-9, announcing the board's unanimous rejection of Air Products' $70 offer as "clearly inadequate" and recommending that Airgas stockholders not tender their shares. The board reiterated once more that the value of Airgas in a sale is at least $78 per share. In this filing, Airgas listed numerous reasons for its recommendation, in two pages of easy-to-read bullet points. These reasons included the Airgas board's knowledge and experience in the industry.... ; and the inadequacy opinions of its financial advisors. All three of the outside financial advisors' written inadequacy opinions were attached to the filing.[58]

The court went on to conclude that the "Airgas stockholders are a sophisticated group, and that they had an extraordinary amount of information available to them with which to make an informed decision about Air Products' offer."[59]

The Issue in *Airgas*. Chancellor Chandler provided the following summary of the state of facts at the time of his decision and the issue he faced:

> So, we are at a crossroads. Air Products has made its "best and final" offer—apparently its offer to acquire Airgas has reached an end stage. Meanwhile, the Airgas board believes the offer is clearly inadequate and its value in a sale transaction is at least $78 per share. At this stage, it appears, neither side will budge. Airgas continues to maintain its defenses, blocking the bid and effectively denying shareholders the choice whether to tender their shares. Air Products and Shareholder Plaintiffs now ask this Court to order Airgas to redeem its poison pill and other defenses that are stopping Air Products from moving forward with its hostile offer, and to allow Airgas's stockholders to decide for themselves whether they want to tender into Air Products' (inadequate or not) $70 "best and final"offer.[60]

The Standard of Review in *Airgas*. As would be expected, the court applied the *Unocal* standard of review, and the court set out the following succinct summary of this standard:

> Because of the "omnipresent specter" of entrenchment in takeover situations, it is well-settled that when a poison pill is being maintained as a defensive measure and a board is faced with a request to redeem the rights, the *Unocal* standard of enhanced judicial scrutiny applies. Under that legal framework, to justify its defensive measures, the target board must show (1) that it had "reasonable grounds for believing a danger to corporate policy and effectiveness existed" (i.e., the board must articulate a legally cognizable threat) and (2) that any board action taken in response to that threat is "reasonable in relation to the threat posed."

57. *Id.* at *102–*103.
58. *Id.* at *106–*107.
59. *Id.* at *107–*108.
60. *Id.* at *7–*8.

> The first hurdle under *Unocal* is essentially a process-based review: "Directors satisfy the first part of the *Unocal* test by demonstrating good faith and reasonable investigation." Proof of good faith and reasonable investigation is "materially enhanced, as here, by the approval of a board comprised of a majority of outside independent directors."
>
> But the inquiry does not end there; process alone is not sufficient to satisfy the first part of *Unocal* review—"under *Unocal* and *Unitrin* the defendants have the burden of showing the reasonableness of their investigation, the reasonableness of their process and also of the result that they reached." That is, the "process" has to lead to the finding of a threat. Put differently, no matter how exemplary the board's process, or how independent the board, or how reasonable its investigation, to meet their burden under the first prong of *Unocal* defendants must actually articulate some legitimate threat to corporate policy and effectiveness.
>
> Once the board has reasonably perceived a legitimate threat, *Unocal* prong 2 engages the Court in a substantive review of the board's defensive actions: Is the board's action taken in response to that threat proportional to the threat posed? In other words, "[b]ecause of the omnipresent specter that directors could use a rights plan improperly, even when acting subjectively in good faith, *Unocal* and its progeny require that this Court also review the use of a rights plan objectively." This proportionality review asks first whether the board's actions were "draconian, by being either preclusive or coercive." [Citing *Unitrin.*] If the board's response was not draconian, the Court must then determine whether it fell "within a range of reasonable responses to the threat" posed). [Citing *Unitrin.*]

In reaching this conclusion on the application of *Unocal*, the court rejected the argument of the Airgas board that because the board has presented "overwhelming evidence that the directors—particularly now including the three new Air Products Nominees—are independent and have acted in good faith, the 'theoretical specter of disloyalty does not exist' and therefore '*Unocal's* heightened standard of review does not apply here.'"[61] Chancellor Chandler strongly rejected this argument, reasoning in part:

> [D]efendants are wrong. The *Unocal* standard of enhanced judicial scrutiny—not the business judgment rule—is the standard of review that applies to a board's defensive actions taken in response to a hostile takeover. This is how Delaware has always interpreted the *Unocal* standard. There has never been any doubt about this, and as recently as four months ago the Delaware Supreme Court reaffirmed this understanding in *Selectica.*[62]

A Brief Poison Pill Primer from *Airgas*. In a section of the opinion entitled "A Brief Poison Pill Primer—*Moran* and Its Progeny," Chancellor Chandler reviewed the major cases dealing with pills and discussed the Delaware Supreme Court's rejection in *Time Warner* of an early case, *Interco*, in which the Chancery Court ordered redemption of a pill. *Time Warner*'s discussion of *Interco* is discussed *infra* in Section 5:5.2.G. Chancellor Chandler explained that at the time *Interco* was decided by Chancellor Allen, he referred to an article by Professors Gilson and Kraakman, in which they argued that there are three types of threats under *Unocal*:

61. *Id.* at *115.
62. *Id.* at *119.

> (1) structural coercion—"the risk that disparate treatment of non-tendering shareholders might distort shareholders' tender decisions" (*i.e.*, the situation involving a two-tiered offer where the back end gets less than the front end);
>
> (2) opportunity loss—the "dilemma that a hostile offer might deprive target shareholders of the opportunity to select a superior alternative offered by target management;" and
>
> (3) substantive coercion—"the risk that shareholders will mistakenly accept an underpriced offer because they disbelieve management's representations of intrinsic value."[63]

The Chancellor goes on to explain that the concept of substantive coercion contemplated by Professors Gilson and Kraakman was "intended to be a very carefully monitored 'threat' requiring close judicial scrutiny of any defensive measures taken in response to such a threat."[64] In this connection, Chancellor Chandler set out the following quote of Vice Chancellor Strine in *Chesapeake v. Shore*:[65]

> One might imagine that the response to this particular type of threat might be time limited and confined to what is necessary to ensure that the board can tell its side of the story effectively. That is, because the threat is defined as one involving the possibility that stockholders might make an erroneous investment or voting decision, the appropriate response would seem to be one that would remedy that problem by providing the stockholders with adequate information.
>
> Once the stockholders have access to such information, the potential for stockholder "confusion" seems substantially lessened. At that point, "[o]ur law should [] hesitate to ascribe rube-like qualities to stockholders. If the stockholders are presumed competent to buy stock in the first place, why are they not presumed competent to decide when to sell in a tender offer after an adequate time for deliberation has been afforded them?"[66]

Chancellor Chandler went on to explain that the approach suggested by Vice Chancellor Strine in *Chesapeake* was essentially the approach taken by Chancellor Allen in ordering the redemption of the pill in *Interco* and that this approach would lead to an ordering of the redemption of the pill in this situation were it not for Delaware Supreme Court precedent. Chancellor Chandler explains:

> [In *Interco*,] Chancellor Allen found it "significant" that the question of the board's responsibility to redeem or not to redeem the poison pill ... arose at the "end-stage" of the takeover contest. He explained:
>
>> [T]he negotiating leverage that a poison pill confers upon this company's board will, it is clear, not be further utilized by the board to increase the options available to shareholders or to improve the terms of those options. Rather, at this stage of this contest, the pill now serves the principal purpose of ... precluding the shareholders from choosing an alternative ... that the board finds less valuable to shareholders.

63. *Id.* at *125.
64. *Id.* at *135.
65. 771 A.2d 293 (Del. Ch. 2000).
66. *Air Products*, 2011 Del. Ch. LEXIS 22, at *135–*136.

> Similarly, here, the takeover battle between Air Products and Airgas seems to have reached an "end stage." Air Products has made its "best and final" offer. Airgas deems that offer to be inadequate. And we're not "talking nickels and quarters here"—an $8 gulf separates the two. The Airgas stockholders know all of this. At this stage, the pill is serving the principal purpose of precluding the shareholders from tendering into Air Products' offer. As noted above, however, the Supreme Court rejected the reasoning of *Interco* in *Paramount*. Thus, while I agree theoretically with former-Chancellor Allen's and Vice Chancellor Strine's conception of substantive coercion and its appropriate application, the Supreme Court's dictum in *Paramount* (which explicitly disapproves of *Interco*) suggests that, unless and until the Supreme Court rules otherwise, that is not the current state of our law.[67]

Note on *TW Services* from *Airgas*. In a section of his opinion entitled "A Note on *TW Services*," Chancellor Chandler discussed the impact of *TW Services, Inc. v. SWT Acquisition Corp.*,[68] where a board rejected a tender offer that was conditioned on the board entering into a merger agreement. As discussed in Section 3.18.E.3, in *TW Services*, Chancellor Allen applied the business judgment rule rather than *Unocal* because the tender offer was conditioned on the target's board entering into a merger agreement, which was within the board's discretion under Section 251 of the DGCL. Chancellor Chandler came to the following conclusion regarding the meaning of *TW Services*:

> [I]t seemed, [Chancellor Allen] endorsed the view that so long as a corporation is not for sale, it is not in *Revlon* mode and is free to pursue its long run goals. In essence, *TW Services* appeared to support the view that a well-informed board acting in good faith in response to a reasonably perceived threat may, in fact, be able to "just say no" to a hostile tender offer.[69]

Analyzing the Threat Prong of *Unocal* in *Airgas*. In analyzing the threat prong of *Unocal*, Chancellor Chandler first found that the "Airgas board's process easily passes the smell test"[70] in view of the fact that, *inter alia*, the board of Airgas was comprised of a majority of outside independent directors and the board relied on three outside independent financial advisors in reaching its conclusion that Air Products' offer is "clearly inadequate."[71] Turning to the question of whether there was an actual threat, after a long and detailed analysis, Chancellor Chandler concluded:

> I find that the Airgas board acted in good faith and relied on the advice of its financial and legal advisors in coming to the conclusion that Air Products' offer is inadequate. And as the Supreme Court has held, a board that in good faith believes that a hostile offer is inadequate may "properly employ[] a poison pill as a proportionate defensive response to protect its stockholders from a 'low ball' bid." [Citing *Unitrin.*]

In reaching this decision, Chancellor Chandler rejected the argument of Airgas concerning the impact of the ownership by arbs, short term investors, of a substantial amount of Airgas stock. Specifically, Airgas argued that the arbs present a threat to Airgas and its shareholders—"the threat that, because it is likely that the arbs would support the $70 offer, 'shareholders will be coerced into tendering into an inadequate offer.'"[72] In

67. *Id.* at *136–*137.
68. 1989 WL 20290 (Del. Ch. Mar. 2, 1989). *See* §3.18.E.3.
69. *Air Products*, 2011 Del. Ch. LEXIS 22, at *143.
70. *Id.* at *146.
71. *Id.* at *145.
72. *Id.* at *159.

dismissing this argument, Chancellor Chandler said: "The defendants do not appear to have come to grips with the fact that the arbs bought their shares from long-term stockholders who viewed the increased market price generated by Air Products' offer as a good time to sell.[73]

Analyzing the Proportionate Prong of *Unocal* in *Airgas*. As set out in *Unitrin*, discussed *supra*, to satisfy the proportionate prong of *Unocal*, the defensive measure must not be coercive or preclusive and must fall within a range of reasonableness.

Chancellor Chandler quickly found that the employment of the pill by Airgas was not coercive. The court then did an elaborate analysis of whether the pill was preclusive, that is, making Air Products' "ability to wage a successful proxy contest and gain control [of the [Airgas] board] ... 'realistically unattainable.'"[74] Although the Chancellor found that it was realistically unattainable for Air Products to dismantle Airgas's defenses by calling a special meeting to remove the Airgas board by a 67% supermajority vote, the Chancellor found that Airgas's defensive measures are not preclusive because Air Products could run a successful proxy contest to replace the members of the board who are up for relection. On this point, the court reasoned:

> Air Products ... had actually intended to run an insurgent slate at Airgas's 2011 annual meeting—when everyone thought that meeting was going to be held in January. The Supreme Court has now held, however, that each annual meeting must take place "approximately" one year after the last annual meeting. If Air Products is unwilling to wait another eight months to run another slate of nominees, that is a business decision of the Air Products board, but as the Supreme Court has held, waiting until the next annual meeting "delay[s]—but [does] not prevent—[Air Products] from obtaining control of the board." I thus am constrained to conclude that Airgas's defensive measures are not preclusive.[75]

In finding that the defensive measures employed by Airgas are within the range of reasonableness, the court explained:

> Here, the record demonstrates that Airgas's board, composed of a majority of outside, independent directors, acting in good faith and with numerous outside advisors concluded that Air Products' offer clearly undervalues Airgas in a sale transaction. The board believes in good faith that the offer price is inadequate by no small margin. Thus, the board is responding to a legitimately articulated threat.[76]

Pills, Policy and Professors (and Hypotheticals) from *Airgas*. In the last section of his opinion, entitled *Pills, Policy and Professors (and Hypotheticals)*, Chancellor Chandler made it clear that this case does not endorse a "just say never" defense and is consistent with Supreme Court precedent:

> To be clear ... this case does not endorse "just say never." What it does endorse is Delaware's long-understood respect for reasonably exercised managerial discretion, so long as boards are found to be acting in good faith and in accordance with their fiduciary duties (after rigorous judicial fact-finding and enhanced scrutiny of their defensive actions). The Airgas board serves as a quintessential example.

---

73. Id. at *160–*161.
74. *Id.* at *175.
75. *Id.* at *197.
76. Id. at *200.

> Directors of a corporation still owe fiduciary duties to all stockholders—this undoubtedly includes short-term as well as long-term holders. At the same time, a board cannot be forced into *Revlon* mode any time a hostile bidder makes a tender offer that is at a premium to market value. The mechanisms in place to get around the poison pill—even a poison pill in combination with a staggered board, which no doubt makes the process prohibitively more difficult—have been in place since 1985, when the Delaware Supreme Court first decided to uphold the pill as a legal defense to an unwanted bid. That is the current state of Delaware law until the Supreme Court changes it.[77]

Chancellor Chandler's Lament in *Airgas*. As indicated, on the basis of the application of Supreme Court precedent to the facts, Chancellor Chandler did not order the redemption of the Airgas pill. However, in a lament set out in the early part of the opinion, he indicated that, in his personal view, the time had come for Airgas to redeem the pill. In other words, he was criticizing the current state of Delaware corporate law as it applies to poison pills. In this regard, he first expressed the view that notwithstanding Supreme Court precedent, there was no cognizable threat here:

> Although I have a hard time believing that inadequate price alone (according to the target's board) in the context of a non-discriminatory, all-cash, all-shares, fully financed offer poses any "threat"—particularly given the wealth of information available to Airgas's stockholders at this point in time—under existing Delaware law, it apparently does. Inadequate price has become a form of "substantive coercion" as that concept has been developed by the Delaware Supreme Court in its takeover jurisprudence. That is, the idea that Airgas's stockholders will disbelieve the board's views on value (or in the case of merger arbitrageurs who may have short-term profit goals in mind, they may simply ignore the board's recommendations), and so they may mistakenly tender into an inadequately priced offer. Substantive coercion has been clearly recognized by our Supreme Court as a valid threat.
>
> Trial judges are not free to ignore or rewrite appellate court decisions. Thus, for reasons explained in detail below, I am constrained by Delaware Supreme Court precedent to conclude that defendants have met their burden under *Unocal* to articulate a sufficient threat that justifies the continued maintenance of Airgas's poison pill.[78]

He went on to elaborate on his view that in this situation the pill has served its purpose and the Airgas shareholders have been fully apprised of all information needed to make a decision:

> In my personal view, Airgas's poison pill has served its legitimate purpose. Although the "best and final" $70 offer has been on the table for just over two months (since December 9, 2010), Air Products' advances have been ongoing for over sixteen months, and Airgas's use of its poison pill—particularly in combination with its staggered board—has given the Airgas board over a full year to inform its stockholders about its view of Airgas's intrinsic value and Airgas's value in a sale transaction. It has also given the Airgas board a full year to express its views to its stockholders on the purported opportunistic timing of Air Products' repeated advances and to educate its stockholders on the inadequacy of Air

77. *Id.* at *220–*221.
78. *Id.* at *10–*11.

> Products' offer. It has given Airgas more time than any litigated poison pill in Delaware history—enough time to show stockholders four quarters of improving financial results, demonstrating that Airgas is on track to meet its projected goals. And it has helped the Airgas board push Air Products to raise its bid by $10 per share from when it was first publicly announced to what Air Products has now represented is its highest offer. The record at both the October trial and the January supplemental evidentiary hearing confirm that Airgas's stockholder base is sophisticated and well-informed, and that essentially all the information they would need to make an informed decision is available to them. In short, there seems to be no threat here—the stockholders know what they need to know (about both the offer and the Airgas board's opinion of the offer) to make an informed decision.[79]

Notwithstanding these laments, he explains as follows why Delaware Supreme Court precedent requires for him not to order the redemption of the pill:

> [A]s I understand binding Delaware precedent, I may not substitute my business judgment for that of the Airgas board. [Citing *inter alia Paramount Commc'ns, Inc. v. Time, Inc.*, 571 A.2d 1140, 1154 (Del. 1990).] The Delaware Supreme Court has recognized inadequate price as a valid threat to corporate policy and effectiveness. [Citing *inter alia Unitrin, Inc. v. Am. Gen. Corp.*, 651 A.2d 1361, 1384 (Del. 1995).] The Delaware Supreme Court has also made clear that the "selection of a time frame for achievement of corporate goals ... may not be delegated to the stockholders." [Citing *Paramount.*] Furthermore, in powerful dictum, the Supreme Court has stated that "[d]irectors are not obliged to abandon a deliberately conceived corporate plan for a short-term shareholder profit unless there is clearly no basis to sustain the corporate strategy." [Citing *Paramount.*] Although I do not read that dictum as eliminating the applicability of heightened *Unocal* scrutiny to a board's decision to block a non-coercive bid as underpriced, I do read it, along with the actual holding in *Unitrin*, as indicating that a board that has a good faith, reasonable basis to believe a bid is inadequate may block that bid using a poison pill, irrespective of stockholders' desire to accept it.[80]

The Reaction to *Airgas* of the Pill's Inventor, Martin Lipton. In a posting on the Harvard Corp. Gov. Forum, *infra* Table of References, Martin Lipton, the founder of the pill, praised as follows Chancellor Chandler's decision in *Airgas*:

> The Chancellor could not have been clearer that "the power to defeat an inadequate hostile tender offer ultimately lies with the board of directors." And it is up to directors, not raiders or short-term speculators, to decide whether a company should be sold: "a board cannot be forced into Revlon mode any time a hostile bidder makes a tender offer that is at a premium to market value." The Chancellor concluded: "in order to have any effectiveness, pills do not—and can not—have a set expiration date." The poison pill lives.[81]

Some Early Thoughts on *Airgas*. Chancellor Chandler has done an excellent job in discussing and applying the law in Delaware regarding poison pills. I think he has it right under the current state of the law, particularly in view of the fact that the Air Products

79. *Id.* at *11–*13.
80. *Id.* at *13.
81. *Delaware Court Reaffirms the Poison Pill and Directors' Power to Block Inadequate Offers*, Harvard Corp. Gov. Forum (Feb. 17, 2011).

Nominees to the board and the newly hired investment banker were of the same view on the transaction as the incumbent directors. If there had been a split on the board on the fundamental value of Airgas and whether the Air Products' offer was inadequate, the result in the case could have been very different. And, it is likely that in other cases there will be such disputes.

Turning to the question of whether the decision is wise from a policy perspective, I am in general agreement with Chancellor's lament. The shareholders have all the relevant information, and as a consequence, they should have the power to decide for themselves. Also, this approach of having a searching inquiry into whether there is a threat and proportionate response is cumbersome, time consuming, and subject to error. Consequently, from a pure policy perspective, I think the better approach would be to ban pills, except to the extent they are (1) used for the purpose of facilitating an auction or generating another bid, or (2) approved my a majority of non-affiliated shareholders. Thus, I think the U.K. and E.U. prohibition against defensive measures (*see* Chapter 26) is correct from a policy perspective.

11. State Law Governing Shareholder Bylaw Proposals Restricting the Board's Power to Issue a Poison Pill

a. Poison Pill Redemption Bylaw—*Fleming*

International Brotherhood of Teamsters General Fund v. Fleming Companies, Inc.

Supreme Court of Oklahoma, 1999 WL 35227

SIMMS, J:

[**Issue**] The United States Court of Appeals, Tenth Circuit * * * certified to the Oklahoma Supreme Court the following question of law:

Does Oklahoma law [A] restrict the authority to create and implement shareholder rights plans exclusively to the board of directors, or [B] may shareholders propose resolutions requiring that shareholder rights plans be submitted to the shareholders for vote at the succeeding annual meeting?

[**Analysis**] We answer the first part of the question in the negative and the second part affirmatively. We hold under Oklahoma law there is no exclusive authority granted boards of directors to create and implement shareholder rights plans, where shareholder objection is brought and passed through official channels of corporate governance. We find no Oklahoma law which gives exclusive authority to a corporation's board of directors for the formulation of shareholder rights plans and no authority which precludes shareholders from proposing resolutions or bylaw amendments regarding shareholder rights plans. We hold shareholders may propose bylaws which restrict board implementation of shareholder rights plans, assuming the certificate of incorporation does not provide otherwise.

The International Brotherhood of the Teamsters General Fund [Teamsters] owns sixty-five shares of Fleming Companies, Inc. [Fleming or the company] stock. In 1986, Fleming implemented a shareholder's rights plan with the term of the plan to expire in 1996. * * * Because the rights plans make the merger of companies more painful for the suitor and assist incumbent management in maintaining control, the plans are often called "poison pill rights plans" or "poison pills." * * *

Teamsters were critical of Fleming's rights plan, seeing it as a means of entrenching the current Fleming board of directors in the event Fleming became the target of a takeover. In 1996, the Teamsters organized and introduced a non-binding resolution for the annual shareholders meeting. The 1996 resolution called on the Fleming board to redeem the existing rights plan. The then current rights plan had been in effect since 1986 and was scheduled for renewal. The Teamsters proposal was met with apparent hostility from Fleming's board and the rights plan remained intact, despite a majority shareholder vote in agreement with the Teamsters' resolution to redeem it.

The following year, 1997, Teamsters mounted a more organized effort to change the continued implementation of the rights plan. Teamsters prepared a proxy statement for inclusion in the proxy materials for the 1997 annual shareholder's meeting. With the proxy effort, the Teamsters proposed an amendment to the company's bylaws which would require any rights plan implemented by the board of directors to be put to the shareholders for a majority vote. * * *

Fleming refused to include the resolution in its 1997 proxy statement, declaring the proposal was not a subject for shareholder action under Oklahoma law. Teamsters then brought an action in the Federal District Court for the Western District of Oklahoma. The district court ruled in favor of the Teamsters, the court finding that "shareholders, through the devise of bylaws, have a right of review." Fleming appealed to the 10th Circuit Court of Appeals, which submitted the certified question to this Court.

Fleming sought to postpone any shareholder vote on the 1997 proxy issue until after the resolution of this case. But the U.S. District Court and later the 10th Circuit denied Fleming's motion to suspend the injunction. Fleming was then forced to allow its shareholders to vote on the Teamsters' proxy. The Teamsters' resolution passed with approximately 60% of the voted shares.

Fleming's position is that Section 1038 [of the Oklahoma Corporation Law] gives the board of directors authority to create and issue shareholder rights plans, subject only to limits which might exist in the corporation's certificate of incorporation; and that shareholders cannot through bylaws restrict the board's powers to implement a rights plan. The Teamsters' position is that Section 1013 gives shareholders of a publicly traded corporation, such as Fleming, the authority to adopt bylaws addressing a broad range of topics from a corporation's business, corporate affairs, and rights and powers of shareholders and directors. It is this apparent conflict which brings this federal certified question to this Court.

This is a case of first impression in Oklahoma and there is little guidance from other states. Oklahoma and Delaware have substantially similar corporation acts, especially with regard to Sections 1013 & 1038 which are of primary concern here. 8 *Del.C.* Sections 109(a) & (b); 8 *Del.C.* Section 157. However, a review of Delaware decisions revealed no comparable case from that state. * * *

Fleming's argument relies on this passage, Section 1038:

> Subject to any provisions in the certificate of incorporation, every corporation may create and issue ... rights or options entitling the holders thereof to purchase from the corporation any shares of its capital stock of any class or classes, such rights or options to be evidenced by or in such instrument or instruments as shall be approved by the board of directors.

In making its argument, Fleming asserts that the word "corporation" is synonymous with "board of directors" as the term is used in Section 1038. Therefore, according to Fleming, "every corporation may create and issue ... rights and options[.]", can actually be read to say "[every corporation's board of directors] may create and issue ... rights and options[.]" However, in light of the fact that both terms, "corporation" and "board of directors", are used distinctly throughout the General Corporation Act and within the text of Section 1038 itself, this assertion is flawed. * * *

We find nothing in the Oklahoma General Corporation Act or existing case law which indicates the shareholder rights plan is somehow exempt from shareholder adopted bylaws. * * * We find no authority to support the contention that a certificate of incorporation which is silent with regard to shareholder rights plans precludes shareholder enacted bylaws regarding the implementation of rights plans.

A number of states have taken affirmative steps to ensure their domestic corporations, and in many instances the board of directors itself, are able to implement shareholder rights plans to protect the company from takeover. The legislation is typically called a shareholders rights plan endorsement statute. However, the Oklahoma legislature has not passed such legislation. There are at least twenty-four states with these share rights plan endorsement statutes.

[These] * * * shareholders rights plan endorsement statutes * * * give explicit authority to directors of the corporation [to adopt such plans]. * * *

[A] board of directors can operate with relative autonomy when a rights plan endorsement statute applies. This does not suggest the absence of a share rights plan endorsement statute in Oklahoma precludes the implementation of such a takeover defense. We merely find that without the authority granted in such an endorsement statute, the board may well be subject to the general procedures of corporate governance, including the enactment of bylaws which limit the board's authority to implement shareholder rights plans. * * *

[W]e find shareholders may, through the proper channels of corporate governance, restrict the board of directors authority to implement shareholder rights plans.

Question

What would be the result in a similar case brought under Delaware law?

b. ISS Proxy Advisor Position on Such Proposals

Institutional Shareholder Services (ISS) has taken the following position on shareholder bylaw proposals to limit the board's ability to issue a pill:

New Policy Position: ISS will generally recommend voting FOR shareholder proposals requesting that the company submit its poison pill to a shareholder vote or redeem it, unless the company has: (1) A shareholder approved poison pill in place; or (2) The company has adopted a policy concerning the adoption of a pill in the future specifying that the board will only adopt a shareholder rights plan if either:

Shareholders have approved the adoption of the plan; or

The board, in its exercise of its fiduciary responsibilities, determines that it is in the best interest of shareholders under the circumstances to adopt a pill without the delay in adoption that would result from seeking stockholder approval (*i.e.* the "fiduciary out" provision). A poison pill adopted under this fiduciary out will be put to a shareholder ratification vote within twelve months of adoption or expire. If the pill is not approved by a majority of the votes cast on this issue, the plan will immediately terminate. * * *

Rationale for Update: Shareholders should have the right to vote on shareholder rights plans. It is understandable, that, under certain circumstances, a board adopts a pill without shareholder approval to ensure negotiations with a potential acquirer take place. However, even pills adopted under these circumstances should be put to a vote within a reasonable period of time. Less than a twelve month period may require the board to incur additional costs by calling a special meeting just for this purpose or force a vote while the board may still be in delicate negotiations with the acquirer.

F. Policy Perspective on Poison Pills

1. SEC's Study of Poison Pills

Excerpts from a Study of the Economics of Poison Pills by SEC Office of Chief Economist

(1985)

* * * We find that although all pills have not been invincible, their adoption has not been well received by the capital markets. Announcements of poison pill plans in the midst of takeover speculation have resulted in on average 2.4 percent net of market price declines for firms adopting the plans. The stock-returns evidence suggests that the effect of poison pills to deter prospective hostile takeover bids outweighs the beneficial effects that come from increased bargaining leverage of the target management. * * *

[A] simple glance at target returns upon announcement of poison pill plans is not sufficient to judge right and wrong in a public policy context. Even if poison pills are used to elicit higher bids from an acquiror, this may not be desirable from an economic efficiency or fairness perspective. If acquirors are to realize returns on the information they generate, they must be able to make some profit (capital gain) on the shares of a corporation they acquire. The introduction of poison pill rights plans may make this more difficult for acquirors. Fears that such plans will be "sprung" on acquirors may make investment in valuable takeover information less attractive than is socially optional. * * *

2. Effect of Outside Directors in Adopting Pills

A 1994 study examined the effect of outside directors on the shareholder wealth effects of the adoption of a poison pill. *See* James A. Brickley, Jeffery L. Coles and Rory L. Terry, *Outside Directors and the Adoption of Poison Pills*, 35 J. of Fin. Eco. 371 (1994). The study reaches the following conclusion:

> We find a statistically significant, positive relation between the stock-market reaction to the adoption of poison pills and the fraction of outside directors on the board. In addition, we find that the average stock-price reaction to poison-pill adoptions is significantly negative [when there is an absence of outside directors.] Correspondingly, for firms that have adopted poison pills, the probability that a subsequent control contest is associated with an auction among competing bidders is higher when the board is controlled by outsiders. These results are consistent with the hypothesis that outside directors represent shareholder interests. *Id.* at 389. * * *

3. Studies of Premiums Paid for Targets with Pills

Studies by Georgeson & Co., a proxy solicitation firm, and J. P. Morgan Securities have found that targets with pills on balance receive higher prices in takeovers. Investment Dealers Digest reports that the Georgeson study showed that "[p]remiums paid to purchase target companies bearing poison pills were eight percentage points higher, on average, than those without." *Study: Poison Pills May be Good for You*, Investment Dealers Digest,

13 (Dec. 1997). Also, the Mergers and Acquisitions Report explains that a study by J. P. Morgan Securities showed that the "presence of a pill had a notable presence on the acquisition price tag." *Poison Pills Add Premium to Deal Pricing*, Merger and Acquisitions Report, 2 (Aug. 1997). Both these premium studies, which support the pill, and the event studies discussed above, which in some cases have challenged the pill, are evaluated by Professor Coates in the next Section.

4. Professor Coates' Evaluation of the Empirical Evidence on the Pill

John C. Coates IV, Empirical Evidence on Structural Takeover Defenses: Where Do We Stand?

54 U. Miami L. Rev. 783 (2000)

* * * Until recently, empirical research on takeover defenses has centered on event studies of poison pills. It is fair to say that event studies have provided the principal evidence supporting legal academic views of the effects of defenses on shareholder wealth and social welfare. Easterbrook & Fischel rely on such studies as the primary evidence for asserting that "*every* device giving managers the power to delay or prevent an acquisition makes shareholders worse off." Romano states that "event studies of defensive tactics find significant negative returns on their adoption" and cites those studies to support the statement that poison pills "are most likely to defeat [takeover] bids and *therefore* to diminish shareholder wealth."

Even taken at face value, however, pill event studies produced little reliable evidence (either way) on the wealth effects of takeover defenses. * * *

A second set of empirical studies on defenses ("premium studies") have produced results that are stronger and more consistent than those produce by pill event studies. However, the flaws that afflict poison pill event studies afflict premium studies as well. Thus, although the results of premium studies are interesting and worthy of further analysis, they do not on their own provide good evidence that defenses improve firm value, as practitioners have sometimes claimed.

§ 3.19 Elaboration on *Revlon*, the Requirement to Get the Best Price Reasonably Available, the Quasi Auction Duty

A. Introduction

This section examines various aspects of the *Revlon*, which is one of the "Big Six." The *Revlon* doctrine requires that in certain acquisition transactions the target's board must get the best price reasonably available. Many of the cases in this section deal with leveraged buyouts (LBOs) or management buyouts (MBOs). In these transactions a private equity firm, such as KKR (many times in partnership with the management of a target), acquires the target in a cash acquisition. The transaction is financed by (1) an equity contribution from the private equity firm and the management, and (2) the issuance of a significant amount of debt, sometimes secured by the target's assets. In general, the same fiduciary duty rules apply to a sale of a target for cash without respect to whether the transaction is an LBO, an MBO, or a strategic or other form of acquisition. Other aspects of LBOs and MBOs are discussed in Chapter 14.

B. Review *Revlon*, Section 3.14.F

C. Traditional Business Judgment Rule Analysis Where Directors Are Independent in a *Revlon* Transaction: *RJR-Nabisco*

RJR Nabisco, Inc. Shareholders Litigation

Delaware Chancery Court, 1989 CCH Fed. Sec. Law. Rep. at ¶ 94, 194

ALLEN, Chancellor:

[**Facts**] These consolidated actions, which are said to be brought on behalf of the shareholders of RJR Nabisco, Inc., a Delaware corporation, seek to enjoin the closing of a pending tender offer for up to 74% of the outstanding stock of RJR Nabisco (RJR). The offer is extended by entities organized for that purpose by the investment firm Kohlberg Kravis Roberts & Co. (KKR) and presently has been extended so as to close on February 6, 1989. The tender offer, if consummated, is intended to be followed promptly by a merger. The blended consideration to be received by each shareholder should these transactions be effectuated will consist of cash and securities valued, by the Company's investment bankers, at approximately $108 to $108.50 per share. The value of the total transaction is by all measures extraordinary—approximately $25 billion.

The terms of the transaction have been negotiated with and endorsed by the board of directors of RJR. No member of the RJR board appears to have a present or prospective financial interest in the KKR entities involved. Thus, the transaction appears to be wholly arm's-length.

The decision of the RJR board to endorse the KKR tender offer and to enter into a merger agreement with respect to a second step merger was made following the board's instigation of a public auction for the Company which is detailed below. In that auction, two other responsible bidders submitted proposals. The only serious competition for KKR, however, came, in the end, from a series of proposals advanced by a group including senior management of RJR, including most importantly F. Ross Johnson, the Company's President and CEO, Shearson Lehman Company and Salomon Brothers, Inc. (the Management Group). Notably, the auction was conducted so that the Company's CEO had no role in the selection of the membership of the Special Committee or its legal or investment advisors. Nor did the board permit management to occupy an insider role in the auction process itself. *Cf. Mills Acquisition Co. v. Macmillan, Inc.*, [*See* Section 3.19.D].

The concluding bid by the Management Group was claimed by it to have a value of $112 per share and included a higher proportion of cash than did the KKR proposal. The Company's bankers, however, were of the view that the Management Group's bid had a value of approximately $108.50–$109 per share and that the two bids were, so far as financial analysis could determine, substantially equivalent.

[**Issue**] When, on November 30, 1988, the Special Committee received these "substantially equivalent" bids, it did not seek to inquire again of the bidders whether they wished to increase their offers. Rather, the Committee and the Board opted to accept the KKR proposal and it is this decision that I am now called upon to address. * * *

[**Analysis**] I am of the opinion that (1) the *Revlon* case does not establish a basis for director liability or for the issuance of the protective remedy of injunction independent of the traditional bases for such liability or such relief: a breach of the duty of loyalty or of the duty of care with resulting injury; (2) that there is not sufficient evidence to permit the conclusion that plaintiffs have a reasonable probability of establishing that the Special Committee was motivated to favor KKR and impede the Management Group; and (3) that the decision to enter into a merger agreement with KKR appears at this time to represent a decision made with due care. Directors in a similar position could have decided without being grossly negligent that the bids in hand were substantially equivalent in value; that KKR's bid had non-financial aspects that permitted a reasonable person to prefer it; and that effectively testing at that stage of this contest whether some additional amount could be extracted entailed risks that one could prudently decide in the circumstances should be avoided. The pending motion will therefore be denied. * * *

The Business Judgment Form of Judicial Review [*Independence*] This aspect of the matter requires scant attention. The sort of "interest" that qualifies to disarm a board at the outset of the benefits of a business judgment approach is a financial interest in the transaction adverse to that of the corporation or its shareholders. * * * Here, there is no allegation that the members of the Special Committee had any direct financial interest in the sale of the Company to KKR that was adverse to or even differed from the interests of all of the stockholders of the Company. * * *

[*Good Faith*] The argument—alluded to above—is that the Special Committee was not motivated in good faith to seek the best available transaction regardless of whose deal it was, but rather, was motivated to see that the Management Group did not succeed even if it would, marginally at least, pay more. This motivation is explained by a posited desire by the members of the Special Committee to disassociate themselves from public criticism directed against Mr. Johnson and the avarice his initial proposal was said to represent. This inappropriate desire resulted, it is claimed, in (1) the premature termination of the auction, and (2) the choice of a demonstratively lower bid. * * *

[T]he fact that the board was faced with what it could reasonably believe were bids that were essentially equivalent from a financial point of view is a relevant circumstance in assessing its good faith in acting as it did. * * *

In the light of these circumstances, the decision not to attempt to break the tie but to accept one of the bids at that point and thus avoid the risk of the loss of that bid—no matter that my personal view might be that the risk was rather small—can in no event be seen as justifying an inference that those who made such a choice must have had some motivation other than the honest pursuit of the corporation's welfare. * * *

[*Due Care*] I cannot conclude that plaintiffs have demonstrated a reasonable likelihood that this theory of liability will be sustained. In connection with it, their burden of course will be to establish at final hearing that in electing to sign the KKR proposed merger agreement, the directors were grossly negligent. *Smith v. Van Gorkom*, [Section 3.14.C] * * * There appears to have been no neglect of duty of any sort in this instance. * * *

[*Revlon*] The claim is that the *Revlon* case establishes an exception to the business judgment form of judicial review in the context of a "sale" of a corporation. In this setting, it is claimed that even a fully independent board has a duty, distinct from its omnipresent duty, to act in good faith and with due care, to conduct a fair (or alternatively an effective) "auction." Thus, that case is said to create distinctive "*Revlon* duties" that exist not as a subset of traditional duties of loyalty and care but independently. Under this view, if on a post hoc review an auction is said to be unfair (presumably to shareholders to whom the board owes its fiduciary duty) or ineffective or "unauction-like" in some material respect, the results may be set aside even if no breach of directorial duty of care or loyalty is involved.

This is an interpretation of *Revlon* that I do not share. * * * Effectiveness cannot mean perfection. Moreover, there is no very persuasive record here that the auction did not result in the best deal prevailing. * * *

Question

Is the approach to *Revlon* by Chancellor Allen in *RJR* consistent with the approach to *Revlon* by the Delaware Supreme Court in *Mill* and *QVC*, which are set out below? When reading *Mills* and *QVC* try to distinguish the facts there from the facts in *RJR*.

D. Applicability of the Entire Fairness Test Due to Breach of Loyalty in *Revlon* Transaction—*Mills*

Mills Acquisition Co. v. Macmillan, Inc.

Delaware Supreme Court, 1988 559 A.2d 1261

Moore, Justice:

In this interlocutory appeal from the Court of Chancery, we review the denial of injunctive relief to Mills Acquisition Co., a Delaware corporation, and its affiliates Tendclass Limited and Maxwell Communications Corp., PLC, both United Kingdom corporations substantially controlled by Robert Maxwell. Plaintiffs sought control of Macmillan, Inc. ("Macmillan" or the "company"), and moved to enjoin an asset option agreement-commonly known as a "lockup" between Macmillan and Kohlberg Kravis Roberts & Co. (KKR), an investment firm specializing in leveraged buyouts. The lockup was granted by Macmillan's board of directors to KKR, as the purported high bidder, in an "auction" for control of Macmillan. [KKR had proposed a leveraged buyout of Macmillan, with Macmillan's senior management participating as part owners of the resulting company.]

Although the trial court found that the conduct of the board during the auction was not "evenhanded or neutral," it declined to enjoin the lockup agreement between KKR and Macmillan. That action had the effect of prematurely ending the auction before the board had achieved the highest price reasonably available for the company. Even though the trial court found that KKR had received improper favor in the auction, including a wrongful "tip" of Maxwell's bid by Macmillan's chairman of the board and chief executive officer, and that Macmillan's board was uninformed as to such clandestine advantages, the Vice Chancellor nevertheless concluded that such misconduct neither misled Maxwell nor deterred it from submitting a prevailing bid.

[W]e find that the legal conclusions of the trial court, refusing to enjoin the KKR lockup agreement, are inconsistent with its factual findings respecting the unfairness of the bidding process. Our decision in *Revlon,* [Section 3.14.F] requires the most scrupulous adherence to ordinary standards of fairness in the interest of promoting the highest values reasonably attainable for the stockholders' benefit. When conducting an auction for the sale of corporate control, this concept of fairness must be viewed solely from the standpoint of advancing general, rather than individual, shareholder interests. Here, the record reflects breaches of the duties of loyalty and care by various corporate fiduciaries which tainted the valuative and deliberative processes of the Macmillan board, thus adversely affecting general stockholder interests. With the divided loyalties that existed on the part of certain directors, and the absence of any serious oversight by the allegedly independent directors, the governing standard was one of intrinsic fairness. *Weinberger*, [Section 3.14.B]. The record here does not meet that rigorous test, and the Court of Chancery failed to apply it. We take it as a cardinal principle of Delaware law that such conduct of an auction for corporate control is insupportable. Accordingly, we reverse. * * *

[Facts] Macmillan's financial and legal advisors, originally chosen by Evans, [the CEO of Macmillan] independently constructed and managed the process by which bids for the company were solicited. * * * [T]he directors wholly delegated the creation and administration of the auction to an array of Evans' hand-picked investment advisors. It is undisputed that Wasserstein, who was originally retained as an investment advisor to Macmillan's senior management, was a principal, if not the primary, "auctioneer" of the company. * * * [I]t appears that Lazard Frères, allegedly the investment advisor to the independent directors, was a far more appropriate candidate to conduct this process on behalf of the board. Yet, both the board and Lazard acceded to Wasserstein's, and through him Evans', primacy. * * *

Clearly, this auction was clandestinely and impermissibly skewed in favor of KKR. The record amply demonstrates that KKR repeatedly received significant material advantages to the exclusion and detriment of Maxwell to stymie, rather than enhance, the bidding process.

As for any "negotiations" between Macmillan and Maxwell, they are noteworthy only for the peremptory and curt attitude of Macmillan, through its self-interested chief executive officer Evans, to reject every overture from Maxwell. * * * [N]ot only was Maxwell ignored, but Evans convinced Wasserstein, Perella and Lazard, contrary to their June 7 opinions, ascribing a maximum value to the company of $80 per share, to declare Maxwell's August 12 bid of $80 inadequate.[82] * * *

The tone and substance of the communications between Macmillan and Maxwell dispel any further doubt that Maxwell was seen as an unwelcome, unfriendly and unwanted bidder. Evans, a self-interested fiduciary, repeatedly stated that *he* had no intention of considering a merger with Maxwell, and that *he* would do everything to prevent Maxwell from acquiring Macmillan. * * *

This continuing hostility toward Maxwell cannot be justified after the Macmillan board actually decided on September 10–11 to abandon any further restructuring attempts, and to sell the entire company. Although Evans had begun negotiations with KKR on July 14, the board's action in September formally initiated the auction process. Further discriminatory treatment of a bidder, without any rational benefit to the shareholders, was unwarranted.

[**Analysis**] The proper objective of Macmillan's fiduciaries was to obtain the highest price reasonably available for the company, provided it was offered by a reputable and responsible bidder. *Revlon.* * * *

In examining the actual conduct of this auction, there can be no justification for the telephonic "tip" to KKR of Maxwell's $89 all-cash offer following the first round of bidding held on September 26th. * * *

Directors are not required by Delaware law to conduct an auction according to some standard formula, only that they observe the significant requirement of fairness for the purpose of enhancing general shareholder interests. * * *

We recognize that the conduct of a corporate auction is a complex undertaking both in its design and execution. We do not intend to limit the broad negotiating authority of the directors to achieve the best price available to the stockholders. * * *

We stated in *Revlon*, and again here, that in a sale of corporate control the responsibility of the directors is to get the highest value reasonably attainable for the shareholders. Beyond that, there are no special and distinct "*Revlon* duties." Once a finding has been made by a court that the directors have fulfilled their fundamental duties of care and loyalty under the foregoing standards, there is no further judicial inquiry into the matter.

82. Yet, on May 30 these same advisors had found management's $64.15 restructuring to be fair.

For the foregoing reasons, the judgment of the Court of Chancery, denying Maxwell's motion for a preliminary injunction, is REVERSED.

E. The Impact of a Passive Auction—*Barkan*

Barkan v. Amsted Industries, Inc.

Delaware Supreme Court, 1989 567 A.2d 1279

WALSH, Justice:

This is an appeal from a Court of Chancery decision that approved the settlement of several class action lawsuits. The litigation arose out of a management-sponsored leveraged buyout (MBO) of all of the common stock of Amsted Industries, Inc. (Amsted) by members of Amsted's management and a newly formed employee stock ownership plan (ESOP). * * *

[**Issue**] Barkan charges that the directors of Amsted breached their fiduciary duties of loyalty and due care by overseeing a selling process that was not designed to maximize the price paid to shareholders. In short, Barkan contends that the directors neglected their duties under the auction standard announced in *Revlon*. * * *

[**Analysis**] There is some dispute among the parties as to the meaning of *Revlon* [Section 3.14.F], as well as its relevance to the outcome of this case. We believe that the general principles announced in *Revlon*, in *Unocal* [Section 3.14.D] and in *Moran* [Section 3.14.E] govern this case and every case in which a fundamental change of corporate control occurs or is contemplated. However, the basic teaching of these precedents is simply that the directors must act in accordance with their fundamental duties of care and loyalty. * * *

* * * *Revlon* does not demand that every change in the control of a Delaware corporation be preceded by a heated bidding contest. *Revlon* is merely one of an unbroken line of cases that seek to prevent the conflicts of interest that arise in the field of mergers and acquisitions by demanding that directors act with scrupulous concern for fairness to shareholders. When multiple bidders are competing for control, this concern for fairness forbids directors from using defensive mechanisms to thwart an auction or to favor one bidder over another. When the board is considering a single offer and has no reliable grounds upon which to judge its adequacy, this concern for fairness demands a canvas of the market to determine if higher bids may be elicited. When, however, the directors possess a body of reliable evidence with which to evaluate the fairness of a transaction, they may approve that transaction without conducting an active survey of the market. * * * Here, the Chancellor found that the advice of the Special Committee's investment bankers, when coupled with the special circumstances surrounding the negotiation and consummation of the MBO, supported a finding that Amsted's directors had acted in good faith to arrange the best possible transaction for shareholders. Our own review of the record leads us to rule that the Chancellor's finding was well within the scope of his discretion.

Several factors provide the basis for the Chancellor's finding. First, the investment community had been aware that Amsted was a likely target for a takeover or an MBO from the moment that Hurwitz announced his sizeable interest in the corporation. In the parlance of the market, Hurwitz's actions put Amsted "in play." Yet in the ten months that passed between Hurwitz's appearance on the scene and the closing of the Exchange Offer, not one bidder emerged to make an offer for control of Amsted. Of course, Amsted was shielded by its stock purchase rights plan during much of this period. Nevertheless, the spate of takeover litigation that has confronted Delaware courts in recent years readily demonstrates that such "poison pills" do not prevent rival bidders from expressing their interest in acquiring a corporation. * * *

We certainly do not condone in all instances the imposition of the sort of "no-shop" restriction that bound Amsted's Special Committee. Where a board has no reasonable basis upon which to judge the adequacy of a contemplated transaction, a no-shop restriction gives rise to the inference that the board seeks to forestall competing bids. * * * It must be clear that the board had sufficient knowledge of relevant markets to form the basis for its belief that it acted in the best interests of the shareholders. The situations in which a completely passive approach to acquiring such knowledge is appropriate are limited. The Chancellor found this to be such a situation, however, and we believe his finding to be within the scope of his discretion. * * *

F. The "Just Say No" Defense in the Time-Warner Transaction: Do *Unocal* or *Revlon* Apply?—*Time-Warner*

Paramount Communications, Inc. v. Time Inc.

Delaware Supreme Court, 1989 571 A.2d 1140

Horsey, Justice:

Paramount Communications, Inc. ("Paramount") and two other groups of plaintiffs ("Shareholder Plaintiffs"), shareholders of Time Incorporated ("Time"), a Delaware corporation, separately filed suits in the Delaware Court of Chancery seeking a preliminary injunction to halt Time's tender offer for 51% of Warner Communication, Inc.'s ("Warner") outstanding shares at $70 cash per share. * * * [T]he Chancellor refused to enjoin Time's consummation of its tender offer, concluding that the plaintiffs were unlikely to prevail on the merits. * * *

Following briefing and oral argument, on July 24 we concluded that the decision below should be affirmed. * * *

The principal ground for reversal, asserted by all plaintiffs, is that Paramount's June 7, 1989 uninvited all-cash, all-shares, "fully negotiable" (though conditional) tender offer for Time triggered duties under *Unocal Corp.*, [Section 3.14.D] and that Time's board of directors, in responding to Paramount's offer, breached those duties. As a consequence, plaintiffs argue that in our review of the Time board's decision of June 16, 1989 to enter into a revised merger agreement with Warner, Time is not entitled to the benefit and protection of the business judgment rule.

Shareholder Plaintiffs also assert a claim based on *Revlon* [Section 3.14.F]. They argue that the original Time-Warner merger agreement of March 4, 1989 resulted in a change of control which effectively put Time up for sale, thereby triggering *Revlon* duties. Those plaintiffs argue that Time's board breached its *Revlon* duties by failing, in the face of the change of control, to maximize shareholder value in the immediate term.

Applying our standard of review, we affirm the Chancellor's ultimate finding and conclusion under *Unocal*. We find that Paramount's tender offer was reasonably perceived by Time's board to pose a threat to Time and that the Time board's "response" to that threat was, under the circumstances, reasonable and proportionate. Applying *Unocal*, we reject the argument that the only corporate threat posed by an all-shares, all-cash tender offer is the possibility of inadequate value.

We also find that Time's board did not by entering into its initial merger agreement with Warner come under a *Revlon* duty either to auction the company or to maximize short-term shareholder value, notwithstanding the unequal share exchange. Therefore, the Time board's original plan of merger with Warner was subject only to a business judgment rule analysis. *See Smith v. Van Gorkom*, [Section 3.14.C].

[**Facts**] Time is a Delaware corporation, * * * [and its] board consisted of sixteen directors. Twelve of the directors were "outside," nonemployee directors. * * *

The board's consensus was that a merger of Time and Warner was feasible, but only if Time controlled the board of the resulting corporation and thereby preserved a management committed to Time's journalistic integrity. To accomplish this goal, the board stressed the importance of carefully defining in advance the corporate governance provisions that would control the resulting entity. * * *

Time's board had recognized the potential need to pay a premium in the stock ratio in exchange for dictating the governing arrangement of the new Time-Warner. Levin [the time CEO] and outside director Finkelstein were the primary proponents of paying a premium to protect the "Time Culture." * * * The parties ultimately agreed upon an exchange rate [pursuant to which] Warner stockholders would have owned approximately 62% of the common stock of Time-Warner.

On March 3, 1989, Time's board, with all but one director in attendance, met and unanimously approved the stock-for-stock merger with Warner. Warner's board likewise approved the merger. The agreement called for Warner to be merged into a wholly-owned Time subsidiary with Warner becoming the surviving corporation. [This was a reverse subsidiary merger. *See* Documentary Appendix A of *M&A Statutes, Rules and Documents, supra* Section 1.1] The common stock of Warner would then be converted into common stock of Time at the agreed upon ratio. Thereafter, the name of Time would be changed to Time-Warner, Inc.

[Because Time would be issuing its stock in an amount equal to more than 20% of its outstanding stock before the merger, the] rules of the New York Stock Exchange required that Time's issuance of shares to effectuate the merger be approved by a vote of Time's stockholders. [*See* Section 3.19.F] The Delaware General Corporation Law required approval of the merger by a majority of the Warner stockholders. Delaware law did not require any vote by Time stockholders. [*See* Section 3.19.F] * * *

The resulting company would have a 24-member board, with 12 members representing each corporation. The company would have co-CEO's, at first Ross [CEO of Warner] and Munro [CEO of Time], then Ross and Nicholas [an executive of Time], and finally, after Ross' retirement, by Nicholas alone. The board would create an editorial committee with a majority of members representing Time. A similar entertainment committee would be controlled by Warner board members. A two-thirds supermajority vote was required to alter CEO successions * * * .

At its March 3, 1989 meeting, Time's board adopted several defensive tactics. Time entered an automatic share exchange agreement with Warner. Time would receive 17,292,747 shares of Warner's outstanding common stock (9.4%) and Warner would receive 7,080,016 shares of Time's outstanding common stock (11.1%). Either party could trigger the exchange. Time sought out and paid for "confidence" letters from various banks with which it did business. In these letters, the banks promised not to finance any third-party attempt to acquire Time. Time argues these agreements served only to preserve the confidential relationship between itself and the banks. The Chancellor found these agreements to be inconsequential and futile attempts to "dry up" money for a hostile takeover. Time also agreed to a "no-shop" clause, preventing Time from considering any other consolidation proposal, thus relinquishing its power to consider other proposals, regardless of their merits. Time did so at Warner's insistence. Warner did not want to be left "on the auction block" for an unfriendly suitor, if Time were to withdraw from the deal. * * *

Time representatives lauded the lack of debt [in financing the merger] to the United States Senate and to the President of the United States. Public reaction to the announcement of the merger was positive. * * * The board scheduled the stockholder vote for June 23; and a May 1 record date was set. On May 24, 1989, Time sent out extensive proxy statements to the stockholders regarding the approval vote on the merger. * * * [B]y the end of the day, the Time-Warner merger appeared to be an accomplished fact.

On June 7, 1989, these wishful assumptions were shattered by Paramount's surprising announcement of its all-cash offer to purchase all outstanding shares of Time for $175 per share. The following day, June 8, the trading price of Time's stock rose from $126 to $170 per share. Paramount's offer was said to be "fully negotiable."[83]

Time found Paramount's "fully negotiable" offer to be in fact subject to at least three conditions. First, Time had to terminate its merger agreement and stock exchange agreement with Warner, and remove certain other of its defensive devices, including the redemption of Time's shareholder rights. Second, Paramount had to obtain the required cable franchise transfers from Time in a fashion acceptable to Paramount in its sole discretion. Finally, the offer depended upon a judicial determination that section 203 of the General Corporate Law of Delaware (The Delaware Anti-Takeover Statute) [*see* Section 22.5.B] was inapplicable to any Time–Paramount merger. While Paramount's board had been privately advised that it could take months, perhaps over a year, to forge and consummate the deal, Paramount's board publicly proclaimed its ability to close the offer by July 5, 1989. Paramount executives later conceded that none of its directors believed that July 5th was a realistic date to close the transaction. * * *

[Time's] board viewed Paramount's offer as inadequate and concluded that its proposed merger with Warner was the better course of action. Therefore, the board declined to open any negotiations with Paramount and held steady its course toward a merger with Warner. * * *

Time's financial advisors informed the board that, on an auction basis, Time's per share value was materially higher than Warner's $175 per share offer. After this advice, the board concluded that Paramount's $175 offer was inadequate. * * *

In mid-June, Time sought permission from the New York Stock Exchange to alter its rules and allow the Time-Warner merger to proceed without stockholder approval. Time did so at Warner's insistence. The New York Stock Exchange rejected Time's request on June 15; and on that day, the value of Time stock reached $182 per share. * * *

Time's board decided to recast its consolidation with Warner into an outright cash and securities acquisition of Warner by Time; and Time so informed Warner. Time accordingly restructured its proposal to acquire Warner as follows: Time would make an immediate all-cash offer for 51% of Warner's outstanding stock at $70 per share. The remaining 49% would be purchased at some later date for a mixture of cash and securities worth $70 per share. To provide the funds required for its outright acquisition of Warner, Time would assume 7–10 billion dollars worth of debt, thus eliminating one of the principal transac-

83. Subsequently, it was established that Paramount's board had decided as early as March 1989 to move to acquire Time. However, Paramount management intentionally delayed publicizing its proposal until Time had mailed to its stockholders its Time-Warner merger proposal along with the required proxy statements.

tion-related benefits of the original merger agreement. Nine billion dollars of the total purchase price would be allocated to the purchase of Warner's goodwill.

Warner agreed.

On June 23, 1989, Paramount raised its all-cash offer to buy Time's outstanding stock to $200 per share. Paramount still professed that all aspects of the offer were negotiable. Time's board met on June 26, 1989 and formally rejected Paramount's $200 per share second offer. The board reiterated its belief that, despite the $25 increase, the offer was still inadequate. The Time board maintained that the Warner transaction offered a greater long-term value for the stockholders and, unlike Paramount's offer, did not pose a threat to Time's survival and its "culture." Paramount then filed this action in the Court of Chancery.

[**The Issues**] The Shareholder Plaintiffs first assert a *Revlon* claim. They contend that the March 4 Time-Warner agreement effectively put Time up for sale, triggering *Revlon* duties, requiring Time's board to enhance short-term shareholder value and to treat all other interested acquirors on an equal basis. The Shareholder Plaintiffs base this argument on two facts: (i) the ultimate Time-Warner exchange ratio of .465 favoring Warner, resulting in Warner shareholders' receipt of 62% of the combined company; and (ii) the subjective intent of Time's directors as evidenced in their statements that the market might perceive the Time-Warner merger as putting Time up "for sale" and their adoption of various defensive measures.

The Shareholder Plaintiffs further contend that Time's directors, in structuring the original merger transaction to be "takeover-proof," triggered *Revlon* duties by foreclosing their shareholders from any prospect of obtaining a control premium. * * *

Paramount asserts only a *Unocal* claim in which the shareholder plaintiffs join. Paramount contends that the Chancellor, in applying the first part of the *Unocal* test, erred in finding that Time's board had reasonable grounds to believe that Paramount posed both a legally cognizable threat to Time shareholders and a danger to Time's corporate policy and effectiveness. Paramount also contests the court's finding that Time's board made a reasonable and objective investigation of Paramount's offer so as to be informed before rejecting it. Paramount further claims that the court erred in applying *Unocal*'s second part in finding Time's response to be "reasonable." Paramount points primarily to the preclusive effect of the revised agreement which denied Time shareholders the opportunity both to vote on the agreement and to respond to Paramount's tender offer. Paramount argues that the underlying motivation of Time's board in adopting these defensive measures was management's desire to perpetuate itself in office.

The Court of Chancery posed the pivotal question presented by this case to be: Under what circumstances must a board of directors abandon an in-place plan of corporate development in order to provide its shareholders with the option to elect and realize an immediate control premium? As applied to this case, the question becomes: Did Time's board, having developed a strategic plan of global expansion to be launched through a business combination with Warner, come under a fiduciary duty to jettison its plan and put the corporation's future in the hands of its shareholders?

While we affirm the result reached by the Chancellor, we think it unwise to place undue emphasis upon long-term versus short-term corporate strategy. Two key predicates underpin our analysis. First, Delaware law imposes on a board of directors the duty to manage the business and affairs of the corporation. 8 Del.C. § 141(a). This broad mandate includes a conferred authority to set a corporate course of action, including time frame, designed to enhance corporate profitability. Thus, the question of "long-term" versus "short-term" values is largely irrelevant because directors, generally, are obliged to chart a course for a corporation which is in its best interests without regard to a fixed investment horizon. Second, absent a limited set of circumstances as defined under *Revlon*, a board of directors, while always required to act in an informed manner, is not under any *per se* duty to maximize shareholder value in the short term, even in the context of a takeover.[84] In our view, the pivotal question presented by this case is: "Did Time, by entering into the proposed merger with Warner, put itself up for sale?" A resolution of that issue through application of *Revlon* has a significant bearing upon the resolution of the derivative *Unocal* issue.

[***Revlon***] We first take up plaintiffs' principal *Revlon* argument, summarized above. In rejecting this argument, the Chancellor found the original Time-Warner merger agreement not to constitute a "change of control" and concluded that the transaction did not trigger *Revlon* duties. The Chancellor's conclusion is premised on a finding that "[b]efore the merger agreement was signed, control of the corporation existed in a fluid aggregation of unaffiliated shareholders representing a voting majority—in other words, in the market." The Chancellor's findings of fact are supported by the record and his conclusion is correct as a matter of law. However, we premise our rejection of plaintiffs' *Revlon* claim on different grounds, namely, the absence of any substantial evidence to conclude that Time's board, in negotiating with Warner, made the dissolution or break-up of the corporate entity inevitable, as was the case in *Revlon*.

Under Delaware law there are, generally speaking and without excluding other possibilities, two circumstances which may implicate *Revlon* duties. The first, and clearer one, is when a corporation initiates an active bidding process seeking to sell itself or to effect a business reorganization involving a clear break-up of the company. *See e.g., Mills Acquisition* [Section 3.19.D) However, *Revlon* duties may also be triggered where, in response to a bidder's offer, a target abandons its long-term strategy and seeks an alternative transaction also involving the breakup of the company. Thus, in Revlon, when the board responded to Pantry Pride's offer by contemplating a "bust-up" sale of assets in a leveraged acquisition, we imposed upon the board a duty to maximize immediate shareholder value and an obligation to auction the company fairly. If, however, the board's reaction to a hostile tender offer is found to constitute only a defensive response and not an abandonment of the corporation's continued existence, *Revlon* duties are not triggered, though *Unocal.* * * *

The plaintiffs insist that even though the original Time-Warner agreement may not have worked "an objective change of control," the transaction made a "sale" of Time inevitable. Plaintiffs rely on the subjective intent of Time's board of directors and principally upon certain board members' expressions of concern that the Warner transaction might be viewed as effectively putting Time up for sale. Plaintiffs argue that the use of a lock-up agreement, a no-shop clause, and so-called "dry-up" agreements prevented shareholders from obtaining a control premium in the immediate future and thus violated *Revlon*.

We agree with the Chancellor that such evidence is entirely insufficient to invoke *Revlon* duties; and we decline to extend *Revlon*'s application to corporate transactions simply because they might be construed as putting a corporation either "in play" or "up for sale." The adoption of structural safety devices alone does not trigger *Revlon*. Rather, as the Chancellor stated, such devices are properly subject to a *Unocal* analysis.

---

84. Thus, we endorse the Chancellor's conclusion that it is not a breach of faith for directors to determine that the present stock market price of shares is not representative of true value or that there may indeed be several market values for any corporation's stock. We have so held in another context. *See Van Gorkom*, [Section 3.14.C].

Finally, we do not find in Time's recasting of its merger agreement with Warner from a share exchange to a share purchase a basis to conclude that Time had either abandoned its strategic plan or made a sale of Time inevitable. * * * The legal consequence is that *Unocal* alone applies to determine whether the business judgment rule attaches to the revised agreement. * * *

[***Unocal***] We turn now to plaintiffs' *Unocal* claim. * * * We find ample evidence in the record to support the Chancellor's conclusion that the Time board's decision to expand the business of the company through its March 3 merger with Warner was entitled to the protection of the business judgment rule.

The Chancellor reached a different conclusion in addressing the Time-Warner transaction as revised three months later. He found that the revised agreement was defense-motivated and designed to avoid the potentially disruptive effect that Paramount's offer would have had on consummation of the proposed merger were it put to a shareholder vote. Thus, the court declined to apply the traditional business judgment rule to the revised transaction and instead analyzed the Time board's June 16 decision under *Unocal*. The court ruled that *Unocal* applied to all director actions taken, following receipt of Paramount's hostile tender offer, that were reasonably determined to be defensive. Clearly that was a correct ruling and no party disputes that ruling. * * *

Paramount and the individual plaintiffs extrapolate a rule of law that an all-cash, all-shares offer with values reasonably in the range of acceptable price cannot pose any objective threat to a corporation or its shareholders. Thus, Paramount would have us hold that only if the value of Paramount's offer were determined to be clearly inferior to the value created by management's plan to merge with Warner could the offer be viewed objectively as a threat.

Implicit in the plaintiffs' argument is the view that a hostile tender offer can pose only two types of threats: the threat of coercion that results from a two-tier offer promising unequal treatment for no tendering shareholders; and the threat of inadequate value from an all-shares, all-cash offer at a price below what a target board in good faith deems to be the present value of its shares. Since Paramount's offer was all-cash, the only conceivable "threat," plaintiffs argue, was inadequate value. We disapprove of such a narrow and rigid construction of *Unocal*, for the reasons which follow.

Plaintiffs' position represents a fundamental misconception of our standard of review under *Unocal* principally because it would involve the court in substituting its judgment as to what is a "better" deal for that of a corporation's board of directors. To the extent that the Court of Chancery has recently done so in certain of its opinions, we hereby reject such approach as not in keeping with a proper *Unocal* analysis. *See, e.g., Interco*, Section 3.18.E.1, [holding that a board was required to redeem its pill]. and its progeny [*e.g., Grand Met*, Section 3.18.E.2 the same]; *but see TW Services* Section 3.18.E.3 [holding that a board did not have to redeem its pill]. * * *

The usefulness of *Unocal* as an analytical tool is precisely its flexibility in the face of a variety of fact scenarios. *Unocal* is not intended as an abstract standard; neither is it a structured and mechanistic procedure of appraisal. Thus, we have said that directors may consider, when evaluating the threat posed by a takeover bid, the "inadequacy of the price offered, nature and timing of the offer, questions of illegality, the impact on 'constituencies' other than shareholders* * *the risk of nonconsummation, and the quality of securities being offered in the exchange." The open-ended analysis mandated by *Unocal* is not intended to lead to a simple mathematical exercise: that is, of comparing the discounted value of Time-Warner's expected trading price at some future date with Paramount's offer and determining which is the higher. Indeed, in our view, precepts underlying the business judgment rule militate against a court's engaging in the process of attempting to appraise and evaluate the relative merits of a long-term versus a short-term investment goal for shareholders. * * *

In this case, the Time board reasonably determined that inadequate value was not the only legally cognizable threat that Paramount's all-cash, all-shares offer could present. Time's board concluded that Paramount's eleventh hour offer posed other threats. One concern was that Time shareholders might elect to tender into Paramount's cash offer in ignorance or a mistaken belief of the strategic benefit which a business combination with Warner might produce. Moreover, Time viewed the conditions attached to Paramount's offer as introducing a degree of uncertainty that skewed a comparative analysis. Further, the timing of Paramount's offer to follow issuance of Time's proxy notice was viewed as arguably designed to upset, if not confuse, the Time stockholders' vote. Given this record evidence, we cannot conclude that the Time board's decision of June 6 that Paramount's offer posed a threat to corporate policy and effectiveness was lacking in good faith or dominated by motives of either entrenchment or self-interest.

Paramount also contends that the Time board had not duly investigated Paramount's offer. * * * [T]he record does, in our judgment, demonstrate that Time's board was adequately informed of the potential benefits of a transaction with Paramount. * * * Time's failure to negotiate cannot be fairly found to have been uninformed. The evidence supporting this finding is materially enhanced by the fact that twelve of Time's sixteen board members were outside independent directors. *Unocal.*

We turn to the second part of the *Unocal* analysis. The obvious requisite to determining the reasonableness of a defensive action is a clear identification of the nature of the threat. As the Chancellor correctly noted, this "requires an evaluation of the importance of the corporate objective threatened; alternative methods of protecting that objective; impacts of the 'defensive' action, and other relevant factors." It is not until both parts of the *Unocal* inquiry have been satisfied that the business judgment rule attaches to defensive actions of a board of directors. As applied to the facts of this case, the question is whether the record evidence supports the Court of Chancery's conclusion that the restructuring of the Time-Warner transaction, including the adoption of several preclusive defensive measures, was a reasonable response in relation to a perceived threat.

Paramount argues that, assuming its tender offer posed a threat, Time's response was unreasonable in precluding Time's shareholders from accepting the tender offer or receiving a control premium in the immediately foreseeable future. Once again, the contention stems, we believe, from a fundamental misunderstanding of where the power of corporate governance lies. Delaware law confers the management of the corporate enterprise to the stockholders' duly elected board representatives. * * *

Here, on the record facts, the Chancellor found that Time's responsive action to Paramount's tender offer was not aimed at "cramming down" on its shareholders a management-sponsored alternative, but rather had as its goal the carrying forward of a pre-existing transaction in an altered form. Thus, the response was reasonably related to the threat. The Chancellor noted that the revised agreement and its accompanying safety devices did not preclude Paramount from making an offer for the combined Time-Warner company or from changing the conditions of its offer so as not to make the offer dependent upon the nullification of the Time-Warner agreement. Thus, the response was proportionate. We affirm the Chancellor's rulings as clearly supported by the record. Finally, we note that although Time was required, as a result of Paramount's hostile offer, to incur a heavy debt to finance its acquisition of Warner, that fact alone does not render the board's decision unreasonable so long as the directors could reasonably perceive the debt load not to be so injurious to the corporation as to jeopardize its well being.

[**Conclusion**] Applying the test for grant or denial of preliminary injunctive relief, we find plaintiffs failed to establish a reasonable likelihood of ultimate success on the merits. Therefore, we affirm.

Questions and Note

Does the *Revlon* standard apply in *Paramount v. Time*? Should it? Does the *Unocal* standard apply? Should it? Does the Court properly apply the first and second prongs of the *Unocal* standard? After taking into account stock splits effectuated by Time-Warner, Paramount's $200 offer in 1989 translated into a $50 offer in 1999. The price of Time-Warner shares did not reach the level of the Paramount 1989 offer until 1997. *See* Abelson's, *When Boards Say 'No Deal' to Holders*, The New York Times, p. c1 (Oct. 6, 1996). Who was the winner here?

G. Enhanced Judicial Scrutiny in Sale of Control Transaction—*QVC*

Paramount Communications, Inc. v. QVC Network, Inc.

Delaware Supreme Court, 1994 637 A.2d 34

Veasey, Chief Justice.

In this appeal we review an order of the Court of Chancery dated November 24, 1993 (the "November 24 Order"), preliminarily enjoining certain defensive measures designed to facilitate a so-called strategic alliance between Viacom Inc. ("Viacom") and Paramount Communications Inc. ("Paramount") approved by the board of directors of Paramount (the "Paramount Board" or the "Paramount directors") and to thwart an unsolicited, more valuable, tender offer by QVC Network Inc. ("QVC"). [Viacom, Paramount, and QVC are publicly held Delaware corporations.] In affirming, we hold that the sale of control in this case, which is at the heart of the proposed strategic alliance, implicates enhanced judicial scrutiny of the conduct of the Paramount Board under *Unocal Corp.*, [Section 3.14.D] and *Revlon* [Section 3.14.F] We further hold that the conduct of the Paramount Board was not reasonable as to process or result.

* * * This action arises out of a proposed acquisition of Paramount by Viacom through a tender offer followed by a second-step merger (the "Paramount–Viacom transaction"), and a competing unsolicited tender offer by QVC. The Court of Chancery granted a preliminary injunction. * * *

The Court of Chancery found that the Paramount directors violated their fiduciary duties by favoring the Paramount–Viacom transaction over the more valuable unsolicited offer of QVC. The Court of Chancery preliminarily enjoined Paramount and the individual defendants (the "Paramount defendants") from amending or modifying Paramount's stockholder rights agreement (the "Rights Agreement"), including the redemption of the Rights, or taking other action to facilitate the consummation of the pending tender offer by Viacom or any proposed second-step merger, including the Merger Agreement between Paramount and Viacom dated September 12, 1993 (the "Original Merger Agreement"), as amended on October 24, 1993 (the "Amended Merger Agreement"). Viacom and the Paramount defendants were enjoined from taking any action to exercise any provision of the Stock Option Agreement between Paramount and Viacom dated September 12, 1993 (the "Stock Option Agreement"), as amended on October 24, 1993. The Court of Chancery did not grant preliminary injunctive relief as to the termination fee provided for the benefit of Viacom in Section 8.05 of the Original Merger Agreement and the Amended Merger Agreement (the "Termination Fee").

Under the circumstances of this case, the pending sale of control implicated in the Paramount–Viacom transaction required the Paramount Board to act on an informed basis to secure the best value reasonably available to the stockholders. Since we agree with the Court of Chancery that the Paramount directors violated their fiduciary duties, we have AFFIRMED the entry of the order of the Vice Chancellor granting the preliminary injunction and have REMANDED these proceedings to the Court of Chancery for proceedings consistent herewith. * * *

[**Basic Facts**] * * * There are 15 persons serving on the Paramount Board. Four directors are officer-employees of Paramount, [including] Martin S. Davis ("Davis"), Paramount's Chairman and Chief Executive Officer since 1983; * * * . Paramount's 11 outside directors are distinguished and experienced business persons. * * * Viacom is controlled by Sumner M. Redstone ("Redstone"), its Chairman and Chief Executive Officer, who owns indirectly approximately 85.2 percent of Viacom's voting Class A stock and approximately 69.2 percent of Viacom's nonvoting Class B stock through National Amusements, Inc. ("NAI"), an entity 91.7 percent owned by Redstone. Viacom has a wide range of entertainment operations * * * . * * *

[After significant negotiations between Viacom and Paramount,] on September 12, 1993, the Paramount Board * * * unanimously approved the Original Merger Agreement whereby Paramount would merge with and into Viacom. The terms of the merger provided that each share of Paramount common stock would be converted into 0.10 shares of Viacom Class A voting stock, 0.90 shares of Viacom Class B nonvoting stock, and $9.10 in cash. In addition, the Paramount Board agreed to amend its "poison pill" Rights Agreement to exempt the proposed merger with Viacom. The Original Merger Agreement also contained several provisions designed to make it more difficult for a potential competing bid to succeed. We focus, as did the Court of Chancery, on three of these defensive provisions: a "no-shop" provision (the "No-Shop Provision"), the Termination Fee, and the Stock Option Agreement.

First, under the No-Shop Provision, the Paramount Board agreed that Paramount would not solicit, encourage, discuss, negotiate, or endorse any competing transaction unless: (a) a third party "makes an unsolicited written, bona fide proposal, which is not subject to any material contingencies relating to financing"; and (b) the Paramount Board determines that discussions or negotiations with the third party are necessary for the Paramount Board to comply with its fiduciary duties.

Second, under the Termination Fee provision, Viacom would receive a $100 million termination fee if: (a) Paramount terminated the Original Merger Agreement because of a competing transaction; (b) Paramount's stockholders did not approve the merger; or (c) the Paramount Board recommended a competing transaction.

The third and most significant deterrent device was the Stock Option Agreement, which granted to Viacom an option to purchase approximately 19.9 percent (23,699,000 shares) of Paramount's outstanding common stock at $69.14 per share if any of the triggering events for the Termination Fee occurred. In addition to the customary terms that are normally associated with a stock option, the Stock Option Agreement contained two provisions that were both unusual and highly beneficial to Viacom: (a) Viacom was permitted to pay for the shares with a senior subordinated note of questionable marketability instead of cash, thereby avoiding the need to raise the $1.6 billion purchase price (the "Note Feature"); and (b) Viacom could elect to require Paramount to pay Viacom in cash a sum equal to the difference between the purchase price and the market price of Paramount's stock (the "Put Feature"). Because the Stock Option Agreement was not "capped" to limit its maximum dollar value, it had the potential to reach (and in this case did reach) unreasonable levels. * * *

Despite these attempts to discourage a competing bid, Diller [the CEO of QVC] sent a letter to Davis on September 20, 1993, proposing a merger in which QVC would acquire Paramount for approximately $80 per share, consisting of 0.893 shares of QVC common stock and $30 in cash. * * *

On October 21, 1993, QVC filed this action and publicly announced an $80 cash tender offer for 51 percent of Paramount's outstanding shares (the "QVC tender offer"). Each remaining share of Paramount common stock would be converted into 1.42857 shares of QVC common stock in a second-step merger. The tender offer was conditioned on, among other things, the invalidation of the Stock Option Agreement, which was worth over $200 million by that point.[85] QVC contends that it had to commence a tender offer because of the slow pace of the merger discussions and the need to begin seeking clearance under federal antitrust laws.

Confronted by QVC's hostile bid, which on its face offered over $10 per share more than the consideration provided by the Original Merger Agreement, Viacom realized that it would need to raise its bid in order to remain competitive. * * * [A bidding contest broke out with both Viacom and Paramount raising their bids.]

[**Sale of Control**] When a majority of a corporation's voting shares are acquired by a single person or entity, or by a cohesive group acting together, there is a significant diminution in the voting power of those who thereby become minority stockholders. Under the statutory framework of the General Corporation Law, many of the most fundamental corporate changes can be implemented only if they are approved by a majority vote of the stockholders. Such actions include elections of directors, amendments to the certificate of incorporation, mergers, consolidations, sales of all or substantially all of the assets of the corporation, and dissolution. 8 Del.C. §§ 242, 251–258, 263, 271, 275. Because of the overriding importance of voting rights, this Court and the Court of Chancery have consistently acted to protect stockholders from unwarranted interference with such rights.[86]

In the absence of devices protecting the minority stockholders, stockholder votes are likely to become mere formalities where there is a majority stockholder. * * *

In the case before us, the public stockholders (in the aggregate) currently own a majority of Paramount's voting stock. Control of the corporation is not vested in a single person, entity, or group, but vested in the fluid aggregation of unaffiliated stockholders. In the event the Paramount–Viacom transaction is consummated, the public stockholders will receive cash and a minority equity voting position in the surviving corporation. Following such consummation, there will be a controlling stockholder who will have the voting power to: (a) elect directors; (b) cause a break-up of the corporation; (c) merge it with another company; (d) cash-out the public stockholders; (e) amend the certificate of incorporation; (f) sell all or substantially all of the corporate assets; or (g) otherwise alter

85. By November 15, 1993, the value of the Stock Option Agreement had increased to nearly $500 million based on the $90 QVC bid.

86. [Citing, *inter alia*, *Schnell*, Section 3.15.A, and *Blasius*, Section 3.15.B]

materially the nature of the corporation and the public stockholders' interests. Irrespective of the present Paramount Board's vision of a long-term strategic alliance with Viacom, the proposed sale of control would provide the new controlling stockholder with the power to alter that vision.

Because of the intended sale of control, the Paramount–Viacom transaction has economic consequences of considerable significance to the Paramount stockholders. Once control has shifted, the current Paramount stockholders will have no leverage in the future to demand another control premium. As a result, the Paramount stockholders are entitled to receive, and should receive, a control premium and/or protective devices of significant value. There being no such protective provisions in the Viacom–Paramount transaction, the Paramount directors had an obligation to take the maximum advantage of the current opportunity to realize for the stockholders the best value reasonably available.

[**Directors' Obligations in Sale of Control**] The consequences of a sale of control impose special obligations on the directors of a corporation. In particular, they have the obligation of acting reasonably to seek the transaction offering the best value reasonably available to the stockholders. The courts will apply enhanced scrutiny to ensure that the directors have acted reasonably. * * *

The Paramount defendants and Viacom assert that the fiduciary obligations and the enhanced judicial scrutiny discussed above are not implicated in this case in the absence of a "break-up" of the corporation, and that the order granting the preliminary injunction should be reversed. This argument is based on their erroneous interpretation of our decisions in *Revlon* [Section 3.14.F] and *Time-Warner* [Section 3.19.F] * * *

[***Revlon* and *Time-Warner***] It is true that one of the circumstances bearing on [the] holdings [in *Revlon*] was the fact that "the break-up of the company* * *had become a reality which even the directors embraced." It does not follow, however, that a "break-up" must be present and "inevitable" before directors are subject to enhanced judicial scrutiny and are required to pursue a transaction that is calculated to produce the best value reasonably available to the stockholders. In fact, we stated in *Revlon* that "when bidders make relatively similar offers, or dissolution of the company becomes inevitable, the directors cannot fulfill their enhanced *Unocal* duties by playing favorites with the contending factions." *Revlon* thus does not hold that an inevitable dissolution or "break-up" is necessary.

The decisions of this Court following *Revlon* reinforced the applicability of enhanced scrutiny and the directors' obligation to seek the best value reasonably available for the stockholders where there is a pending sale of control, regardless of whether or not there is to be a break-up of the corporation. * * *

In our affirmance of the Court of Chancery's well-reasoned decision [in *Time-Warner*], this Court held that "The Chancellor's findings of fact are supported by the record and his conclusion is correct as a matter of law." Nevertheless, the Paramount defendants here have argued that a break-up is a requirement and have focused on the following language in our *Time-Warner* decision:

> However, we premise our rejection of plaintiffs' Revlon claim on different grounds, namely, the absence of any substantial evidence to conclude that Time's board, in negotiating with Warner, made the dissolution or break-up of the corporate entity inevitable, as was the case in *Revlon*.
>
> Under Delaware law there are, generally speaking and without excluding other possibilities, two circumstances which may implicate Revlon duties. The first,

> and clearer one, is when a corporation initiates an active bidding process seeking to sell itself or to effect a business reorganization involving a clear break-up of the company. However, Revlon duties may also be triggered where, in response to a bidder's offer, a target abandons its long-term strategy and seeks an alternative transaction involving the breakup of the company.

The Paramount defendants have misread the holding of *Time-Warner*. Contrary to their argument, our decision in *Time-Warner* expressly states that the two general scenarios discussed in the above-quoted paragraph are not the only instances where "*Revlon* duties" may be implicated. The Paramount defendants' argument totally ignores the phrase "without excluding other possibilities." Moreover, the instant case is clearly within the first general scenario set forth in *Time-Warner*. The Paramount Board, albeit unintentionally, had "initiate[d] an active bidding process seeking to sell itself" by agreeing to sell control of the corporation to Viacom in circumstances where another potential acquiror (QVC) was equally interested in being a bidder.

The Paramount defendants' position that both a change of control and a break-up are required must be rejected. * * *

Accordingly, when a corporation undertakes a transaction which will cause: (a) a change in corporate control; or (b) a break-up of the corporate entity, the directors' obligation is to seek the best value reasonably available to the stockholders. This obligation arises because the effect of the Viacom–Paramount transaction, if consummated, is to shift control of Paramount from the public stockholders to a controlling stockholder, Viacom. Neither *Time-Warner* nor any other decision of this Court holds that a "break-up" of the company is essential to give rise to this obligation where there is a sale of control.

[**Fiduciary Duties of Paramount's Board**] We now turn to duties of the Paramount Board under the facts of this case and our conclusions as to the breaches of those duties which warrant injunctive relief.

Under the facts of this case, the Paramount directors had the obligation: (a) to be diligent and vigilant in examining critically the Paramount–Viacom transaction and the QVC tender offers; (b) to act in good faith; (c) to obtain, and act with due care on, all material information reasonably available, including information necessary to compare the two offers to determine which of these transactions, or an alternative course of action, would provide the best value reasonably available to the stockholders; and (d) to negotiate actively and in good faith with both Viacom and QVC to that end.

Having decided to sell control of the corporation, the Paramount directors were required to evaluate critically whether or not all material aspects of the Paramount–Viacom transaction (separately and in the aggregate) were reasonable and in the best interests of the Paramount stockholders in light of current circumstances, including: the change of control premium, the Stock Option Agreement, the Termination Fee, the coercive nature of both the Viacom and QVC tender offers, the No-Shop Provision, and the proposed disparate use of the Rights Agreement as to the Viacom and QVC tender offers, respectively. * * *

Since the Paramount directors had already decided to sell control, they had an obligation to continue their search for the best value reasonably available to the stockholders. * * *

By November 12, 1993, the value of the revised QVC offer on its face exceeded that of the Viacom offer by over $1 billion at then current values. This significant disparity of value cannot be justified on the basis of the directors' vision of future strategy, primarily because the change of control would supplant the authority of the current Paramount Board to continue to hold and implement their strategic vision in any meaningful way. * * *

[*Viacom's* **Vested Rights Claim Rejected, See Section 3.19.G**]

[**Conclusion**] The realization of the best value reasonably available to the stockholders became the Paramount directors' primary obligation under these facts in light of the change of control. That obligation was not satisfied, and the Paramount Board's process was deficient. * * *

For the reasons set forth herein, the November 24, 1993, Order of the Court of Chancery has been AFFIRMED, and this matter has been REMANDED for proceedings consistent herewith, as set forth in the December 9, 1993, Order of this Court. * * *

H. Does *Revlon* Apply in an Arm's Length Stock for Stock Merger?

1. The Principal Case—*Arnold*

Arnold v. Society for Savings Bancorp, Inc.

Delaware Supreme Court, 1994 650 A.2d 1270

[In a friendly transaction, the board of directors of Society for Savings Bancorp, Inc., the target, negotiated a merger of the target into a subsidiary of the Bank of Boston (BoB), the acquiror, in exchange for stock of the acquiror.]

[**Revlon Claim**] Plaintiff [a shareholder of Bancorp, the target,] argues that the Court of Chancery erred in holding that *Revlon* [Section 3.14.F] was not "triggered" under the facts of this case because (i) Bancorp was seeking to sell itself and (ii) the Merger constituted a change in control. He contends that the board breached its "*Revlon* duties." Defendants contend that *Revlon* was not implicated and, even if it were, they fulfilled their duties. They further argue that, even if their conduct fell short of the requirements of *Revlon*, Bancorp stockholders ratified any improprieties by voting in favor of the Merger. The Court of Chancery held that *Revlon* was inapplicable under the facts of this case because the Merger did not involve a change in control. We agree.

The Court need not apply enhanced scrutiny under the circumstances of this case. The directors of a corporation "have the obligation of acting reasonably to seek the transaction offering the best value reasonably available to the stockholders," *Paramount Communications, Inc. v. QVC Network, Inc.*, [Section 3.19.G] in at least the following three scenarios: (1) "when a corporation initiates an active bidding process seeking to sell itself or to effect a business reorganization involving a clear break-up of the company," *Paramount Communications, Inc. v. Time Inc.*, [Section 3.19.F] [*Time-Warner*]; (2) "where, in response to a bidder's offer, a target abandons its long-term strategy and seeks an alternative transaction involving the break-up of the company," *Id.*; or (3) when approval of a transaction results in a "sale or change of control," *QVC*. In the latter situation, there is no "sale or change in control" when "[c]ontrol of both [companies] remain[s] in a large, fluid, changeable and changing market."[87] * * *

Plaintiff emphasizes Time-Warner's language "seeking to sell itself" in arguing that *Revlon* was implicated, but that argument fails because, to fall within that category, the target must have "initiate[d] an active bidding process." He also focuses on the board's subjective intent, a basis for enhancing director's duties which was rejected in *Time-Warner*.

---

87. *See also* Marcel Kahan, *Paramount or Paradox: The Delaware Supreme Court's Takeover Jurisprudence*, 19 J.Corp.L. 583, 595 (1994) ("What is important about the fact that control remains in the hands of unaffiliated shareholders, 'in the market,' is that all these unaffiliated shareholders have virtually identical interests with respect to the company: to maximize the value of their shares.").

Alternatively, plaintiff argues that there was a "sale or change in control" of Bancorp because its former stockholders are now relegated to minority status in BoB, losing their opportunity to enjoy a control premium. As a continuing BoB stockholder, plaintiff's opportunity to receive a control premium is not foreclosed. Thus, plaintiff's claim that enhanced scrutiny is required under the circumstances of this case lacks merit and the Court of Chancery did not err in so holding.

Note

The court in *In Re Lukens Inc. Shareholders Litigation*, 757 A.2d 720 (Del. Ch. 1999), addressed in footnote 25 when the *Revlon* doctrine applies in a merger in which both stock and cash is the consideration:

> The defendants argue that because over 30% of the merger consideration [was] shares of Bethlehem common stock, a widely held company without any controlling shareholder, *Revlon* and *QVC* [Section 3.19.G] do not apply. * * * The Supreme Court has not set out a black line rule explaining what percentage of the consideration can be cash without triggering *Revlon*. I take for granted, however, that a cash offer for 95% of a company's shares, for example, even if the other 5% will be exchanged for the shares of a widely held corporation, will constitute a change of corporate control. Until instructed otherwise, I believe that purchasing more than 60% achieves the same result.

2. The "Last Period" Problem—*Reis* and *Steinhart*

This section is adapted from Thompson, *Mergers, Acquisitions and Tender Offers, supra* Section 1.10, at Section 5:5.5.[L].

In *Steinhardt v. Howard-Anderson*,[88] a 2011 decision, Vice Chancellor Laster in a transcript decision applied the *Revlon* standard of review to a transaction in which the consideration was 50% cash and 50% stock, and the target's shareholders ended up with 15% of the stock of the acquirer. Presumably he would have also applied *Revlon* to the transaction even if the consideration had been all stock and the target's shareholders ended up with a significant minority position in the acquirer, which was the situation in *Arnold, supra*, where the Delaware Supreme Court held that *Revlon* did not apply. The Vice Chancellor gave as his explanation for this position the "last period" problem, which he addressed as follows:

> There was a lot of debate in the briefing over whether this was an enhanced scrutiny [*i.e., Revlon*] transaction or business judgment rule analysis. This is a deal where the consideration was approximately 50 percent cash floating based on the market price..., and the public will end up holding approximately 15 percent of the post-transaction entity after the fact.
>
> We tend to focus, in our jurisprudence, on change of control and the change of control test [*see Arnold, supra*]. So there was a lot of debate over whether this, in fact, was sufficient cash to merit a change of control. I think what people need to remember is that the change of control test is ultimately a derivative test.
>
> The point is that when enhanced scrutiny applies is when you have a final stage transaction. The reason enhanced scrutiny applies to a change of control is because it's a constructive final stage transaction. You're giving up control to a person who could then cash you out because he's the new controller.

---

88. Steinhardt v. Howard-Anderson, C.A.No 5878–VCL (Del. Ch. Jan. 24, 2011).

> This is a situation where the target stockholders are in the end stage in terms of their interest in Occam [the target]. This is the only chance they have to have their fiduciaries bargain for a premium for their shares as the holders of equity interests in that entity.
>
> It's easy to see here in two ways. First, it's easy to see in terms of the amount of cash. If you want more cash for your shares, this is the only time you have to get it. But it's also easy to see in terms of the amount of interest you're going to have in the post-transaction entity.
>
> We often talk about, oh, well, but the stockholders can get a future control premium. That's all well and good for the future entity, but what you're bargaining over now is how much of that future premium you're going to get.
>
> So let's say that Calix [the acquirer] is some day sold, and let's all hope that it does very well and becomes an attractive acquisition target, and that one of the big boys picks it up at some point for a healthy premium.
>
> The target stockholders today are bargaining for what their share of that premium will be. They're going to only get 15 percent, and obviously there could be more acquisitions that dilute everybody, *et cetera*. I get that.
>
> But as between the Calix stockholders and the Occam stockholders, now is the time; when the target fiduciaries are bargaining for how much of that future control premium their folks will get. This is it. This is the end. This is the only opportunity where you can depend upon your fiduciaries to maximize your share of that value.
>
> I think back in 1989, it made sense for people to be worried over the line between *Revlon* and non-*Revlon*. It was three years after that landmark case. That case was a Cunian paradigm shift if there ever was one. We had language in there like "auction duty, radically altered state," really seemingly heavy duty stuff.
>
> We now know it's a reasonableness standard. There's no single blueprint. A target board doesn't have to take the facially higher cash price. It can consider the strength of the currency. It can take a stock deal if it believes that the stock offers better long-term appreciation and more potential synergies.
>
> That's why I said at the outset in this case it's just not worth having the dance on the head of a pin as to whether it's 49 percent cash or 51 percent cash or where the line is. This is the only chance that Occam stockholders have to extract a premium, both in the sense of maximizing cash now, and in the sense of maximizing their relative share of the future entity's control premium. This is it.
>
> So I think it makes complete sense that you would apply a reasonableness review, enhanced scrutiny to this type of transaction.[89]

Although Vice Chancellor Laster applied the reasonableness standard of review, he did not enjoin the transaction on those grounds; he did, however, require certain enhanced disclosures.

Vice Chancellor Laster elaborated more fully on the "last period" problem in *Reis v. Hazelett Strip-Casting Corp.*,[90] another 2011 decision. As discussed more fully in Section 5:5.7[M], *Reis* dealt with a reverse stock split, a mechanism for a controlling shareholder to acquire the stock of the minority. As pointed out in that section, Vice Chancellor Laster

89. *Id.* at 3–7.
90. Reis v. Hazelett Strip-Casting Corp, 2011 Del. Ch. LEXIS 11 (Jan. 21, 2011).

held that the entire fairness standard of review applied to the transaction. The Vice Chancellor also indicated in *dictum* that he was of the view that enhanced scrutiny of *Revlon* should also apply to transactions presenting the "last period" problem. He discussed these transactions as follows:

> Final stage transactions for stockholders provide another situation where enhanced scrutiny applies. [citing *McMullin, supra* and *Revlon, supra*] Final stage transactions give rise to what economists refer to as the last period problem. "Simply put, in a situation where parties expect to have repeated transactions, the recognition that a party who cheats in one transaction will be penalized by the other party in subsequent transactions reduces the incentive to cheat. However, when a transaction is the last (or only) in a series—that is, the final period—the incentive to cheat reappears because, by definition, the penalty for doing so has disappeared." Ronald J. Gilson & Bernard S. Black, *The Law and Finance of Corporate Acquisitions* 720 (2d ed. 1995). *See generally* Sean J. Griffith, *Deal Protection Provisions in the Last Period of Play*, 71 Fordham L. Rev. 1899, 1942–53 (2003) (describing divergence of interests resulting from last period problem).
>
> In the corporate context, the ability of managers to shirk or self-deal ordinarily is constrained not only by legal duties but also by a range of markets, including the product markets, capital markets, employment markets, and the market for corporate control. But when managers are in their final period, market consequences have less traction, making managers more likely to favor their own interests. In connection with a final stage transaction,
>
>> the target corporation's board and management may demand side payments from the acquiror, thus effectively diverting a portion of the merger consideration from the shareholders to the management team. If the management team is able to protect the self-serving transaction with deal protection provisions, it will be further insulated from the disciplinary effect of the market for corporate control, leaving the outgoing management team free to serve their own self-interest with relative impunity.
>>
>> In addition to the unrestrained pursuit of their own self-interest, directors and managers in the last period may depart from the best interests of the corporation and its shareholders due to a variety of non-pecuniary, but equally selfish, motivations. Directors and managers may favor one deal over another because it is more in line with their self image and view of the world or because it is more likely to cause them to be remembered fondly by employees or the business press.
>
> *Griffith, supra*, at 1947 (internal footnotes omitted).
>
> Fiduciaries need not consciously pursue self-interest. "[T]he last period signals a time when otherwise common behavioral biases may lead to serious deviations from the welfare of the corporation and its shareholders." *Id.* at 1948; see id. at 1949–53 (discussing overconfidence, over-optimism, groupthink, reactive devaluation, and in-group/out-group thinking). The human psyche has a powerful ability "to rationalize as right that which is merely personally beneficial." *City Capital Assocs. v. Interco Inc.*, 551 A.2d 787, 796 (Del. Ch. 1988) (Allen, C.); *see eBay Domestic Hldgs., Inc. v. Newmark*, 2010 Del. Ch. LEXIS 187, 2010 WL 3516473, at *20 (Del. Ch. Sept. 9, 2010) ("Human judgment can be clouded by subtle influences like the prestige and perquisites of board membership, personal relationships with management, or animosity towards a bidder."). In recognition

> that potentially subtle conflicts can affect director decision-making, enhanced scrutiny places the burden on the defendant fiduciaries who approved the final stage transaction to show that they acted reasonably to obtain for their beneficiaries the best value reasonably available under the circumstances. *See Paramount Commc'ns Inc. v. QVC Network, Inc.*, 637 A.2d 34, 48–49 (Del. 1994). Enhanced scrutiny likewise extends to defensive measures that have the potential to insulate last period decision-making from market forces or undermine the ability of stockholders to reject the transaction. [*Citing e.g., Omnicare, Inc. v. NCS Healthcare, Inc.*, 818 A.2d 914, 934 (Del. 2003); *Paramount Commc'ns, Inc. v. Time, Inc.*, 571 A.2d 1140, 1151 (Del. 1989); and *ACE Ltd. v. Capital Re Corp.*, 747 A.2d 95, 106 (Del. Ch. 1999)].[91]

Vice Chancellor Laster has it right on this "last period" problem. It is not sensible to apply (1) the *Revlon* standard of review to the actions of a target's board in a transaction where the target is sold for cash, and (2) the business judgment rule standard of review to the actions of the target's board where the target is sold for stock representing a minor interest in the acquirer, as was the situation in *Arnold, supra.* In both of these transactions, the target's board should have to get the best price reasonably available as required by *Revlon.* One situation where the *Revlon* standard should not apply and where the business judgment rule standard of review should apply is where the transaction is a merger of equals with the shareholders of both the target and the acquirer having a substantial and essentially equal equity interest in the resulting firm.

I. Impact of Target's Decision to Seek a Private Equity, and Not a Strategic, Buyer — *Netsmart*

In Re Netsmart Technologies, Inc. Shareholders Litigation

Court of Chancery of Delaware, 2007 Del. Ch. LEXIS 35

STRINE, Vice Chancellor.

Introduction. This case literally involves a microcosm of a current dynamic in the mergers and acquisitions market. Netsmart Technologies, Inc. has entered into a "Merger Agreement" with two private equity firms, Insight Venture Partners ("Insight") and Bessemer Venture Partners ("Bessemer"). If the $ 115 million "Insight Merger" (or "Merger") is consummated, Netsmart's stockholders will receive $ 16.50 per share and the buyers will take the micro-cap company, whose shares are currently listed on the NASDAQ, private. * * *

The Merger Agreement prohibits the Netsmart board from shopping the company but does permit the board to consider a superior proposal. A topping bidder would only have to suffer the consequence of paying Insight a 3% termination fee. No topping bidder has emerged to date and a stockholder vote is scheduled to be held next month, on April 5, 2007.

A group of shareholder plaintiffs now seeks a preliminary injunction against the consummation of this Merger. As a matter of substance, the plaintiffs argue that the Merger Agreement flowed from a poorly-motivated and tactically-flawed sale process during which the Netsmart board made no attempt to generate interest from strategic buyers. The motive for this narrow search, the plaintiffs say, is that Netsmart's management only wanted to do a deal involving their continuation as corporate officers and their retention

---

91. *Id.* at *26–*30.

of an equity stake in the company going forward, not one in which a strategic buyer would acquire Netsmart and possibly oust the incumbent management team. The plaintiffs also insinuate that Netsmart's Chief Executive Officer, James L. Conway, was beguiled by the riches being received by CEOs of larger companies in private equity deals and sought to emulate their success. At the end of a narrowly-channeled search, the Netsmart directors, the plaintiffs say, landed a deal that was unimpressive, ranking at the low end of William Blair's valuation estimates. * * *

The defendant directors respond by arguing that they acted well within the bounds of the discretion afforded them by Delaware case law to decide on the means by which to pursue the highest value for the company's stockholders. They claim to have reasonably sifted through the available options and pursued a course that balanced the benefits of a discrete market canvass involving only a select group of private equity buyers (e.g., greater confidentiality and the ability to move quickly in a frothy market) against the risks (e.g., missing out on bids from other buyers). In order to stimulate price competition, the Special Committee encouraged submissions of interest from the solicited bidders with the promise that only bidders who made attractive bids would get to move on in the process. At each turning point during the negotiations with potential suitors, the Special Committee pursued the bidder or bidders willing to pay the highest price for the Netsmart equity. In the end, the directors argue, the board secured a deal with Insight that yielded a full $ 1.50 more per share than the next highest bidder was willing to pay.

Moreover, in order to facilitate an implicit, post-signing market check, the defendants say that they negotiated for relatively lax deal protections. Those measures included a break-up fee of only 3%, a "window shop" provision that allowed the board to entertain unsolicited bids by other firms, and a "fiduciary out" clause that allowed the board to ultimately recommend against pursuing the Insight Merger if a materially better offer surfaced. The directors argue that the failure of a more lucrative bid to emerge since the Merger's announcement over three months ago confirms that they obtained the best value available. Furthermore, the directors note that, unlike certain other private equity acquisitions, the Insight Merger is not one in which the selling company's CEO came out with a huge monetary win. Conway did all right for himself but not in any way that suggests that he received a windfall or had any particular reason to favor Insight over the other private equity bidders. * * *

Was The Board's Limited Action A Reasonable Approach To Maximizing Sale Value Given Netsmart's Circumstances? The plaintiffs' second argument has much more force. That argument is that the Special Committee and Netsmart board did not have a reliable basis to conclude that the Insight deal was the best one because they failed to take any reasonable steps to explore whether strategic buyers might be interested in Netsmart.

I believe on this score that the plaintiffs are, if this preliminary record is indicative of the ultimate record in the case, likely to be successful on this point. For reasons I have noted, the board's consideration of whether to seek out strategic buyers was cursory and poorly documented at best. * * *

I do not mean to imply in any way that Netsmart management or William Blair consciously pursued objectives at odds with getting the best price. Rather, I simply point out the reality that the Netsmart board rapidly narrowed its options to a channel consistent with those incentives. By the time the Special Committee began its work, the inertial energy of the sales process was already clearly directed at a private equity deal. The record evidence regarding the consideration of an active search for a strategic buyer is more indicative of an after-the-fact justification for a decision already made, than of a genuine and reasonably-informed evaluation of whether a targeted search might bear fruit. For all these reasons, I believe the plaintiffs have demonstrated a reasonable probability that they will later prove that the board's failure to engage in any logical efforts to examine the universe of possible strategic buyers and to identify a select group for targeted sales overtures was unreasonable and a breach of their *Revlon* duties. * * *

J. Delaware Supreme Court's Elaboration on *Revlon* Duties— *Lyondell*

Lyondell Chemical Company v. Ryan

Delaware Supreme Court, 2009, 970 A.2d 235

BERGER, Justice:

We accepted this interlocutory appeal to consider a claim that directors failed to act in good faith in conducting the sale of their company. The Court of Chancery decided that "unexplained inaction" permits a reasonable inference that the directors may have consciously disregarded their fiduciary duties. The trial court expressed concern about the speed with which the transaction was consummated; the directors' failure to negotiate better terms; and their failure to seek potentially superior deals. But the record establishes that the directors were disinterested and independent; that they were generally aware of the company's value and its prospects; and that they considered the offer, under the time constraints imposed by the buyer, with the assistance of financial and legal advisors. At most, this record creates a triable issue of fact on the question of whether the directors exercised due care. * * *

The Court of Chancery identified several undisputed facts that would support the entry of [summary] judgment in favor of the Lyondell directors: the directors were "active, sophisticated, and generally aware of the value of the Company and the conditions of the markets in which the Company operated." They had reason to believe that no other bidders would emerge, given the price Basell had offered and the limited universe of companies that might be interested in acquiring Lyondell's unique assets. Smith negotiated the price up from $ 40 to $ 48 per share—a price that Deutsche Bank opined was fair. Finally, no other acquiror expressed interest during the four months between the merger announcement and the stockholder vote.

Other facts, however, led the trial court to "question the adequacy of the Board's knowledge and efforts...." After the Schedule 13D was filed [indicating that the acquirer was a more than 5% shareholder and had intentions to acquire Lyondell] in May, the directors apparently took no action to prepare for a possible acquisition proposal. The merger was negotiated and finalized in less than one week, during which time the directors met for a total of only seven hours to consider the matter. The directors did not seriously press Blavatnik for a better price, nor did they conduct even a limited market check. Moreover, although the deal protections were not unusual or preclusive, the trial court was troubled by "the Board's decision to grant considerable protection to a deal that may not have been adequately vetted under *Revlon*."

The trial court found the directors' failure to act during the two months after the filing of the Basell Schedule 13D critical to its analysis of their good faith. The court pointedly referred to the directors' "two months of slothful indifference despite *knowing* that the Company was in play," and the fact that they "languidly awaited overtures from potential suitors...." In the end, the trial court found that it was this "failing" that warranted denial of their motion for summary judgment:

> [T]he Opinion clearly questions whether the Defendants "engaged" in the sale process.... This is where the 13D filing in May 2007 and the subsequent two months of (apparent) Board inactivity become critical.... [T]he Directors made *no apparent effort* to arm themselves with *specific knowledge* about the present value of the Company in the May through July 2007 time period, despite *admittedly knowing* that the 13D filing..effectively put the Company "in play," and, therefore, presumably, also knowing that an offer for the sale of the Company could occur at any time. It is these facts that raise the specter of "bad faith" in the present summary judgment record ...

The problem with the trial court's analysis is that *Revlon* duties do not arise simply because a company is "in play."[92] The duty to seek the best available price applies only when a company embarks on a transaction—on its own initiative or in response to an unsolicited offer—that will result in a change of control.[93] Basell's Schedule 13D did put the Lyondell directors, and the market in general, on notice that Basell was interested in acquiring Lyondell. The directors responded by promptly holding a special meeting to consider whether Lyondell should take any action. The directors decided that they would neither put the company up for sale nor institute defensive measures to fend off a possible hostile offer. Instead, they decided to take a "wait and see" approach. That decision was an entirely appropriate exercise of the directors' business judgment. The time for action under *Revlon* did not begin until July 10, 2007, when the directors began negotiating the sale of Lyondell.

The Court of Chancery focused on the directors' two months of inaction, when it should have focused on the one week during which they considered Basell's offer. During that one week, the directors met several times; their CEO tried to negotiate better terms; they evaluated Lyondell's value, the price offered and the likelihood of obtaining a better price; and then the directors approved the merger. The trial court acknowledged that the directors' conduct during those seven days might not demonstrate anything more than lack of due care. But the court remained skeptical about the directors' good faith—at least on the present record. That lingering concern was based on the trial court's synthesis of the *Revlon* line of cases, which led it to the erroneous conclusion that directors must follow one of several courses of action to satisfy their *Revlon* duties.

There is only one *Revlon* duty—to "[get] the best price for the stockholders at a sale of the company." No court can tell directors exactly how to accomplish that goal, because they will be facing a unique combination of circumstances, many of which will be outside their control. As we noted in *Barkan v. Amsted Industries, Inc.*, "there is no single blueprint that a board must follow to fulfill its duties. That said, our courts have highlighted both the positive and negative aspects of various boards' conduct under *Revlon*.[94] The trial court drew several principles from those cases: directors must "engage actively in the sale process," and they must confirm that they have obtained the best available price either by conducting an auction, by conducting a market check, or by demonstrating "an impeccable knowledge of the market."

---

92. *Paramount Communications, Inc. v. Time, Inc.*, 571 A.2d 1140, 1151 (Del. 1989).

93. *In re Santa Fe Pac. Corp. S'holder Litig.*, 669 A.2d 59, 71 (1995).

94. *See, e.g.: Barkan v Amsted Industries, Inc.*, 567 A.2d at 1287 (Directors need not conduct a market check if they have reliable basis for belief that price offered is best possible.); *Paramount Communications, Inc. v. QVC Network, Inc.*, 637 A.2d 34,49 (Del. 1994) (No-shop provision impermissibly interfered with directors' ability to negotiate with another known bidder); *In re Netsmart Technologies, Inc., Shareholders Litig.*, 924 A.2d 171, 199 (Del. Ch. 2007) (Plaintiff likely to succeed on claim based on board's failure to consider strategic buyers.)

The Lyondell directors did not conduct an auction or a market check, and they did not satisfy the trial court that they had the "impeccable" market knowledge that the court believed was necessary to excuse their failure to pursue one of the first two alternatives. As a result, the Court of Chancery was unable to conclude that the directors had met their burden under *Revlon*. In evaluating the totality of the circumstances, even on this limited record, we would be inclined to hold otherwise. But we would not question the trial court's decision to seek additional evidence if the issue were whether the directors had exercised due care. Where, as here, the issue is whether the directors failed to act in good faith, the analysis is very different, and the existing record mandates the entry of judgment in favor of the directors.

As discussed above, bad faith will be found if a "fiduciary intentionally fails to act in the face of a known duty to act, demonstrating a conscious disregard for his duties." The trial court decided that the *Revlon* sale process must follow one of three courses, and that the Lyondell directors did not discharge that "known set of *[Revlon]* 'duties'." But, as noted, there are no legally prescribed steps that directors must follow to satisfy their *Revlon* duties. Thus, the directors' failure to take any specific steps during the sale process could not have demonstrated a conscious disregard of their duties. More importantly, there is a vast difference between an inadequate or flawed effort to carry out fiduciary duties and a conscious disregard for those duties.

Directors' decisions must be reasonable, not perfect.[95] * * * [I]f the directors failed to do all that they should have under the circumstances, they breached their duty of care. Only if they knowingly and completely failed to undertake their responsibilities would they breach their duty of loyalty. The trial court approached the record from the wrong perspective. Instead of questioning whether disinterested, independent directors did everything that they (arguably) should have done to obtain the best sale price, the inquiry should have been whether those directors utterly failed to attempt to obtain the best sale price. Viewing the record in this manner leads to only one possible conclusion. [T]he Lyondell directors did not breach their duty of loyalty by failing to act in good faith. In concluding otherwise, the Court of Chancery reversibly erred.

CONCLUSION. Based on the foregoing, the decision of the Court of Chancery is reversed and this matter is remanded for entry of judgment in favor of the Lyondell directors. Jurisdiction is not retained.

K. Consider the Impact of *MFW*, Section 3.16.E, in LBO and MBO Transactions

§ 3.20 Elaboration on Issues with "No Solicitations," "Lock-Ups," "Break-Up Fees" and Other Deal Protection Measures in *Revlon* and Other Transactions

A. Introduction

Many merger agreements in which a publicly-held target is acquired will contain provisions designed to protect the deal from third party interlopers. A range of devices may be utilized, including (1) a "no shop" restricting the target's directors from seeking

95. *Paramount Communications, Inc. v. QVC Network, Inc.*, 637 A.2d at 45.

another deal, (2) a "no talk" restricting the target's directors from talking to another possible acquiror except in certain circumstances, and (3) a termination or break-up fee that will compensate the acquiror if the target terminates the deal and is acquired by another party.

This section focuses on the law in Delaware on the fiduciary duty standards that apply when reviewing a board's use of deal protection devices. Although a consensual transaction may implicate principally the business judgment rule standard of review, as will be seen below, the use of deal protection devices may raise issues under the *Unocal* standard of review. And, of course, any consensual deal may become hostile, in which case *Unocal* would apply to any defensive tactics employed by the target, such as a poison pill, examined previously. Further, although the business judgment rule applied in *Van Gorkom* in the context of a cash acquisition of a public target, as a result of the *Revlon* case, *Revlon* duties now apply to any cash acquisition of the target, because such a transaction involves a change of control. However, as pointed out in *Arnold*, *Revlon* duties do not arise in an acquisition of a publicly held target for stock of a publicly held acquiror, because such a transaction is not a change of control.

To give the reader a basic understanding of how standard deal protection devices work, Documentary Appendix K of *M&A Statutes, Rules, and Documents*, *supra* Section 1.1 sets out with commentary the deal protection devices in the 2005 merger agreement between Verizon and MCI, pursuant to which Verizon acquired MCI after MCI rejected a competing offer from Quest.

The deal protection provisions of a merger agreement are generally found in (1) the "Additional Agreements," section of the agreement, which sets out certain covenants or undertakings by the parties between the signing and closing of the deal, and (2) the termination provisions of the agreement, which specify the conditions under which the agreement may be terminated and the consequences of a termination, such as the obligation of the target to pay a termination fee to the acquirer. (*See* Chapter 15, which deals with the drafting of acquisition agreements for a general discussion of the various provisions of an acquisition agreement.) In many public company deals the deal protection devices apply to both the target and the acquiror, especially in mergers of equals or near equals. In other deals, the provisions apply only to the target, especially if the target is significantly smaller than the acquiror, as in the case of the acquisition of MCI. The MCI–Verizon merger agreement follows the standard model with the deal protection provisions applying only to MCI.

The use of a reverse termination fee, which is paid by an acquiror to a target if the acquiror does not close the transaction does not raise the type of fiduciary duty issues presented with direct termination fees, which are paid by a target to an acquirer. Consequently, reverse termination fees are examined in Chapter 15. On the other hand, this section and not Chapter 15, addresses the deal protection portions of an acquisition agreement, which present fiduciary duty issues.

B. Does the Acquiror Have a Vested Right in Deal Protection Devices?—*QVC*

Paramount Communications, Inc. v. QVC Network, Inc.

Delaware Supreme Court, 1994 637 A.2d 34

[The facts and other issues are addressed in Section 3.19.F]

[**Viacom's Vested Rights Claim**] Viacom argues that it had certain "vested" contract rights with respect to the No-Shop Provision and the Stock Option Agreement [with Paramount]. In effect, Viacom's argument is that the Paramount directors could enter into an agreement in violation of their fiduciary duties and then render Paramount, and ultimately its stockholders, liable for failing to carry out an agreement in violation of those duties. Viacom's protestations about vested rights are without merit. This Court has found that those defensive measures were improperly designed to deter potential bidders, and that such measures do not meet the reasonableness test to which they must be subjected. They are consequently invalid and unenforceable under the facts of this case.

The No-Shop Provision could not validly define or limit the fiduciary duties of the Paramount directors. To the extent that a contract, or a provision thereof, purports to require a board to act or not act in such a fashion as to limit the exercise of fiduciary duties, it is invalid and unenforceable. Despite the arguments of Paramount and Viacom to the contrary, the Paramount directors could not contract away their fiduciary obligations. Since the No-Shop Provision was invalid, Viacom never had any vested contract rights in the provision.

As discussed previously, the Stock Option Agreement contained several "draconian" aspects, including the Note Feature and the Put Feature. While we have held that lock-up options are not *per se* illegal, *see Revlon*, [Section 3.14.F] no options with similar features have ever been upheld by this Court. Under the circumstances of this case, the Stock Option Agreement clearly is invalid. Accordingly, Viacom never had any vested contract rights in that Agreement.

Viacom, a sophisticated party with experienced legal and financial advisors, knew of (and in fact demanded) the unreasonable features of the Stock Option Agreement. It cannot be now heard to argue that it obtained vested contract rights by negotiating and obtaining contractual provisions from a board acting in violation of its fiduciary duties. As the Nebraska Supreme Court said in rejecting a similar argument in *ConAgra, Inc. v. Cargill, Inc.* "To so hold, it would seem, would be to get the shareholders coming and going." Likewise, we reject Viacom's arguments and hold that its fate must rise or fall, and in this instance fall, with the determination that the actions of the Paramount Board were invalid.

C. Termination Fees as Liquidated Damages Provisions—*Bell Atlantic*

Brazen v. Bell Atlantic Corporation

Delaware Supreme Court, 1997 695 A.2d. 43

Veasey, Chief Justice:

In this appeal, the issues facing the Court surround the question of whether a two-tiered $550 million termination fee in a merger agreement is a valid liquidated damages provision or whether the termination fee was an invalid penalty and tended improperly to coerce stockholders into voting for the merger. * * *

[**Facts**] In 1995, defendant below-appellee, Bell Atlantic Corporation, and NYNEX Corporation entered into merger negotiations. * * *

Representatives of Bell Atlantic and NYNEX agreed that a two-tiered $550 million termination fee was reasonable for compensating either party for damages incurred if the merger did not take place because of certain enumerated events. The termination fee was divided into two parts. First, either party would be required to pay $200 million if there were both a competing acquisition offer for that party and either (a) a failure to obtain stockholder approval, or (b) a termination of the agreement. Second, if a competing transaction were consummated within eighteen months of termination of the merger agreement, the consummating party would be required to pay an additional $350 million to its disappointed merger partner. * * *

Bell Atlantic and NYNEX decided that $550 million, which represented about 2% of Bell Atlantic's approximately $28 billion market capitalization, would serve as a "reasonable proxy" for the opportunity cost and other losses associated with the termination of the merger. In addition, senior management advised Bell Atlantic's board of directors that the termination fee was at a level consistent with percentages approved by Delaware courts in earlier transactions, and that the likelihood of a higher offer emerging for either Bell Atlantic or NYNEX was very low. * * *

[**Issue**] * * * Plaintiff [a shareholder of Bell] alleged that the termination fee was not a valid liquidated damages clause because it failed to reflect an estimate of actual expenses incurred in preparation for the merger. Plaintiffs alleged that the $550 million payment was "an unconscionably high termination or 'lockup' fee," employed "to restrict and impair the exercise of the fiduciary duty of the Bell Atlantic board and coerce the shareholders to vote to approve the proposed merger. * * *"

The parties filed cross-motions for summary judgment. * * *

Plaintiff argued below and argues again here that the proper analysis for determining the validity of the termination fee * * * is to analyze it as a liquidated damages clause employing a test different from the business judgment rule. We agree.

The express language in * * * the agreement unambiguously states that the termination fee provisions "constitute liquidated damages and not a penalty." * * *

[W]e find no compelling justification for treating the termination fee in this agreement as anything but a liquidated damages provision, in light of the express intent of the parties to have it so treated.

[**Analysis**] In *Lee Builders v. Wells*, [103 A.2d 918 (Del. Ch. 1954)], a case involving a liquidated damages provision equal to 5% of the purchase price in a contract for the sale of land, the Court of Chancery articulated the following two-prong test for analyzing the validity of the amount of liquidated damages: "Where the damages are uncertain and the amount agreed upon is reasonable, such an agreement will not be disturbed."

Plaintiff argues that the termination fee, if properly analyzed as liquidated damages, fails the *Lee Builders* test because both portions of the fee are punitive rather than compensatory, having nothing to do with actual damages but instead being designed to punish Bell Atlantic stockholders and the subsequent third-party acquirer if Bell Atlantic were ultimately to agree to merge with another entity. We find, however, that the termination fee safely passes both prongs of the *Lee Builders* test.

To be a valid liquidated damages provision under the first prong of the test, the damages that would result from a breach of the merger agreement must be uncertain or incapable of accurate calculation. Plaintiff does not attack the fee on this ground. * * *

Plaintiff contends, however, that the $550 million fee violates the second prong of the *Lee Builders* test, *i.e.*, that it is not a reasonable forecast of actual damages, but rather a penalty intended to punish the stockholders of Bell Atlantic for not approving the merger. Plaintiff's attack is without force. * * * [T]o fail the second prong of *Lee Builders*, the amount at issue must be unconscionable or not rationally related to any measure of damages a party might conceivably sustain.

Here, in the face of significant uncertainty, Bell Atlantic and NYNEX negotiated a fee amount and a fee structure that take into account the following: (a) the lost opportunity costs associated with a contract to deal exclusively with each other; (b) the expenses incurred during the course of negotiating the transaction; * * *. The parties then settled on the $550 million fee as reasonable given these factors. Moreover, the $550 million fee represents 2% of Bell Atlantic's market capitalization of $28 billion. This percentage falls well within the range of termination fees upheld as reasonable by the courts of this State. We hold that it is within a range of reasonableness and is not a penalty.

This is not strictly a business judgment rule case. If it were, the Court would not be applying a reasonableness test. * * * Plaintiff further argues that the termination fee provision was coercive. * * * We find plaintiff's arguments unpersuasive. * * * In light of the foregoing, we affirm, albeit on somewhat different grounds, the judgment of the Court of Chancery.

D. Will a Market Check Satisfy *Revlon* Duties in a Cash Merger?—*Pennaco*

In Re Pennaco Energy, Inc. Shareholders Litigation

Delaware Court of Chancery, 2001 Del. Ch. LEXIS 19

STRINE, Vice Chancellor:

Shareholder plaintiffs seek a preliminary injunction against the February 5, 2001 closing of a tender offer by an acquisition subsidiary of Marathon Oil ("Marathon") for all the shares of Pennaco Energy, Inc. ("Pennaco"). The tender offer price is $19 per share and Marathon intends to consummate a back-end merger at the same price to cash-out any shares it does not acquire. The offer price is at a substantial premium to Pennaco's pre-offer trading price. [The tender offer and back-end merger was negotiated by the Pennaco board, dealing exclusively with Marathon.]

[B]ecause the Pennaco board did not actively shop the company and relied solely on a post-agreement market check, the plaintiffs assert that the directors' efforts were so deficient as to justify the entry of an injunction. * * *

Legal Analysis * * **Revlon Issue.* The Marathon Transaction is * * * an end-game transaction that represents the final opportunity for Pennaco's stockholders to realize value from their investment in the company. * * * Having decided to sell the enterprise, the directors became charged with the fiduciary responsibility to attempt to get the best price. * * * [*Citing QVC*, Section 3.19.G]

[T]he Pennaco board's knowledge of the company has not been seriously challenged. * * * [T]he court cannot say that it was unreasonable for the Pennaco board to deal with Marathon on an exclusive basis. Marathon was a major industry player with great financial clout. As all of the investment banks seeking Pennaco's business pointed out, there is no risk-free approach to selling a company, and dealing with one bidder at a time has its own advantages. Thus, the mere fact that the Pennaco board decided to focus on negotiating a favorable price with Marathon and not to seek out other bidders is not one that alone supports a breach of fiduciary duty claim.

Nor does the record support the inference that the Pennaco board's negotiating strategy was unreasonable and perfunctory. * * *

On the other hand, there is little doubt that the validity of the Pennaco board's decision to proceed in the manner it did would be subject to great skepticism had the board acceded to demands to lock up the transaction from later market competition. That is, if the merger agreement with Marathon contained onerous deal protection measures that presented a formidable barrier to the emergence of a superior offer, the Pennaco board's failure to canvass the market earlier might tilt its actions toward the unreasonable.

But it appears that the Pennaco board was careful to balance its single buyer negotiation strategy by ensuring that an effective post-agreement market check would occur. The merger agreement's provisions leave Marathon exposed to competition from rival bidders, with only the modest and reasonable advantages of a 3% termination fee and matching rights [*i.e.*, the right of Marathon to match any other offer]. The plaintiffs' attack on the termination fee's level is make-weight and at odds with precedent upholding the validity of fees at this level.

The board also retained significant flexibility to deal with any later-emerging bidder and ensured that the market would have a healthy period of time to digest the proposed transaction. As such, no substantial barriers to the emergence of a higher bid existed. Indeed, the fact that no higher bid has come forth in these circumstances is itself "evidence that the directors, in fact, obtained the highest and best transaction reasonably available." * * *

For all these reasons, I conclude that the plaintiffs are not likely to succeed on their *Revlon* claim. * * *

E. No Solicitation with a Match Provision and Break-Up Fee in an Auction—*Toys "R" Us*

In Re Toys "R" Us, Inc. Shareholder Litigation

Delaware Court of Chancery, 2005 877 A.2d 975

STRINE, Vice Chancellor:

Introduction. This opinion addresses a motion to enjoin a vote of the stockholders of Toys "R" Us, Inc. (the "Company") tomorrow to consider approving a merger with an acquisition vehicle formed by a group led by Kohlberg Kravis Roberts & Co. ("the KKR Group"). If the merger is approved, the Toys "R" Us stockholders will receive $26.75 per share for their shares. The proposed merger resulted from a lengthy, publicly-announced search for strategic alternatives that began in January 2004, when the Company's shares were trading for only $12.00 per share. The $26.75 per share merger consideration constitutes a 123% premium over that price. During the strategic process, the Toys "R" Us board of directors, nine of whose ten members are independent, had frequent meetings to explore the Company's strategic options. The board, with the support of its one inside member, the company's CEO, reviewed those options with an open mind, and with the advice of expert advisors.

Eventually, the board settled on the sale of the Company's most valuable asset, its toy retailing business, and the retention of the Company's baby products retailing business, as its preferred option. It did so after considering a wide array of options, including a sale of the whole Company.

The Company sought bids from a large number of the most logical buyers for the toy business, and it eventually elicited attractive expressions of interest from four competing bidders who emerged from the market canvass. When due diligence was completed, the board put the bidders through two rounds of supposedly "final bids" for the toys business. In the midst of this process, one of the bidders expressed a serious interest in buying the whole company for a price of $23.25 per share, and then $24.00. The board decided to stick by its original option until that bidder made an offer to pay $25.25 per share and signaled it might bid even a dollar more.

When that happened, the board was presented with a bid that was attractive compared with its chosen strategy in light of the valuation evidence that its financial advisors had presented, and in light of the failure of any strategic or financial buyer to make any serious expression of interest in buying the whole Company—even a non-binding one conditioned on full due diligence or a friendly merger—despite the board's openly expressed examination of its strategic alternatives. Recognizing that the attractive bids it had received for the toys business could be lost if it extended the process much longer, the "Executive Committee" of the board, acting in conformity with direction given to it by the whole board, approved the solicitation of bids for the entire Company from the final bidders for the toys business, after a short period of due diligence.

When those whole Company bids came in, the winning bid of $26.75 per share from the KKR Group topped the next most favorable bid by $1.50 per share. The bidder that offered $25.25 per share did not increase its bid. After a thorough examination of its alternatives and a final reexamination of the value of the Company, the board decided that the best way to maximize stockholder value was to accept the $26.75 bid. That was a reasonable decision given the wealth of evidence that the board possessed regarding the Company's value and the improbability of another bidder emerging.

In its proposed merger agreement containing the $26.75 offer, the KKR Group asked for a termination fee of 4% of the implied equity value of the transaction to be paid if the Company terminated to accept another deal, as opposed to the 3% offered by the company in its proposed draft. Knowing that the only other bid for the company was $1.50 per share or $350 million less, the Company's negotiators nonetheless bargained the termination fee down to 3.75% the next day, and bargained down the amount of expenses the KKR Group sought in the event of a naked no vote.

In their motion, the plaintiffs fault the Toys "R" Us board, arguing that it failed to fulfill its duty to act reasonably in pursuit of the highest attainable value for the Company's stockholders. They complain that the board's decision to conduct a brief auction for the full Company from the final bidders for the toys business was unreasonable, and that the board should have taken the time to conduct a new, full-blown search for buyers. Relatedly, they complain that the board unreasonably locked up the $26.75 bid by agreeing to draconian deal termination measures that preclude any topping bid.

In this opinion, I reject those arguments. A hard look at the board's decisions reveals that it made reasonable choices in confronting the real world circumstances it faced. That the board was supple in reacting to new circumstances and adroit in responding to a new development that promised, in its view, greater value to the stockholders is not evidence of infidelity or imprudence; it is consistent with the sort of difficult business decisions that corporate fiduciaries are required to make all the time. Having taken so much time to educate itself and having signaled publicly at the outset an openness to strategic alternatives, the Toys "R" Us board was well-positioned to make a reasoned decision to accept the $26.75 per share offer.

Likewise, the choice of the board's negotiators not to press too strongly for a reduction of the KKR Group's desired 4% termination fee all the way to 3% was reasonable, given that the KKR Group had topped the next best bid by such a big margin. To refuse to risk a reduction in the top bid, when the next best alternative was so much lower, can hardly be said to be unreasonable, especially when the board's negotiators did negotiate to reduce the termination fee from 4% to 3.75%. Furthermore, the size of the termination fee and the presence of matching rights in the merger agreement do not act as a serious barrier to any bidder willing to pay materially more than $26.75 per share.

For these and other reasons that I discuss below, the plaintiffs' motion for a preliminary injunction is denied. * * *

The Merits: Is It Probable That The Board Breached Its Revlon Duties? * * * In its most summary form, the plaintiffs' claim is that the directors did not fulfill their duties under the landmark case of *Revlon.* * * *

Critically, in the wake of *Revlon,* Delaware courts have made clear that the enhanced judicial review *Revlon* requires is not a license for law-trained courts to second-guess reasonable, but debatable, tactical choices that directors have made in good faith. For example, the Supreme Court has held that the duty to take reasonable steps to secure the highest immediately available price does not invariably require a board to conduct an auction process or even a targeted market canvass in the first instance, emphasizing that there is "no single blue-print" for fulfilling the duty to maximize value. [Citing *Barkan v. Amsted*] Nor does a board's decision to sell a company prevent it from offering bidders deal protections, so long as its decision to do so was reasonably directed to the objective of getting the highest price, and not by a selfish or idiosyncratic desire by the board to tilt the playing field towards a particular bidder for reasons unrelated to the stockholders' ability to get top dollar.

Thus, this Court has been "mindful that its task [under *Revlon*] is to examine whether the directors have undertaken reasonable efforts to fulfill their obligation to secure the best available price, and not to determine whether the directors have performed flawlessly." [Citing *Pennaco*] * * *

Overview Of The Plaintiffs' Argument That The Board Supposedly Breached Its Revlon Duties. The plaintiffs make two major arguments as to why the Toys "R" Us board failed in their duty to act reasonably in pursuit of the highest attainable value.

First, they contend that the board acted too hastily once it recognized that a sale of the whole Company, rather than the sale of just Global Toys, might be the best strategic option. * * * [The court's finding that the board satisfied its *Revlon* duties is not set out here.]

Relatedly, the plaintiffs argue that the board compounded the unreasonableness of its initial process by agreeing to deal protection measures that precluded the emergence of a later, topping bid. * * *

The Board Did Not Act Unreasonably In Agreeing To The Deal Protection Measures. The plaintiffs' other major argument is that the board acted unreasonably by signing a merger agreement with the KKR Group that, in their view, includes deal protection measures that preclude other bidders from making a topping offer. * * *

The plaintiffs posit that the board should have refused to sign the merger agreement with the KKR Group until the termination fee was reduced to some less onerous level and the matching rights were removed. In fact, the board did negotiate the termination fee down to 3.75% from the 4.0% that KKR had proposed on March 15, putting the $350 million bid differential at some risk to do so. The plaintiffs, however, assume that the board should have pressed harder and that the KKR Group would have yielded further, but still kept its bid at $26.75.

But what if the KKR Group had said, "if you want to cut the termination fee to 3%,[96] our offer is only $25.75 per share?" What was the board to do then? Even worse, suppose

96. Frankly, I cannot, as someone who has done a lot of negotiation, imagine retracting the 3% and matching rights offer. That sort of "oh, by the way ..." should only be put on the table when it is necessary to protect a client against a material disadvantage. For the sake of analysis, I have indulged the idea of pulling the matching rights offer back, although it seems a less-than-credible posture.

the KKR Group had asked, "what did the other groups bid?" What was First Boston supposed to say, knowing that the KKR Group had topped Cerberus by a full $1.50 per share or $350 million? In that dynamic, only the reckless would have been insensitive to the worry that the KKR Group's bid might drop if it were asked to give up the matching rights or to accept a termination fee of less than 3%. * * *

Given the Company's lengthy search for alternatives, the obvious opportunity that unsolicited bidders had been afforded to come forward over the past year, and the large gap between the Cerberus and the KKR Group bids, the board could legitimately give more weight to getting the highest value bid out of the KKR Group, and less weight to the fear that an unlikely higher-value bid would emerge later. After all, anyone interested had had multiple chances to present, however politely, a serious expression of interest—none had done so.

Nor was the level of deal protection sought by the KKR Group unprecedented in magnitude. In this regard, the plaintiffs ignore that many deals that were jumped in the late 1990s involved not only termination fees and matching rights but also stock option grants that destroyed pooling treatment, an additional effect that enhanced the effectiveness of the barrier to prevent a later-emerging bidder. In cases like *McMillan v. Intercargo* and *Pennaco Energy,* this court approved deal protection measures in the *Revlon* context that were nearly as substantial, taking all factors into account, as those here.[97] In *Pennaco Energy,* this court upheld an informed board's decision to sign up a sales deal, after negotiating with a single bidder that included a 3% termination fee and matching rights. The court did so because the board was well-informed, clearly desired the best price, and because any serious bidder who wanted to present a materially higher bid could still do so.[98]

In view of this jurisprudential reality, the board was not in a position to tell the KKR Group that they could not have any deal protection. The plaintiffs admit this and therefore second-guess the board's decision not to insist on a smaller termination fee, more like 2.5% or 3%, and the abandonment of the matching right. But that, in my view, is precisely the sort of quibble that does not suffice to prove a *Revlon* claim.

To begin with, the plaintiffs' assertion that the deal protection package here would deter a bidder willing to pay materially more than the KKR Group does not convince me at all. I have no doubt that it operates to deter someone who would want to make a bid that is trivially larger than the KKR Group's bid. But it is not the concern of our law to set up a system that promotes endless incremental bidding. To do so risks creating an incentive for lower initial deal prices because initial buyers will have less closing certainty.

---

97. *McMillan v. Intercargo Corp.*, 768 A.2d 492, 505 (Del.Ch.2000) (opining that it was "difficult to see how a 3.5% fee would have deterred a rival bidder who wished to pay materially more !!!"); *In re Pennaco Energy, Inc.*, 787 A.2d 691 (Del.Ch.2001) (termination fee of 3% and matching rights did not unreasonably preclude emergence of a later bid). Among other precedents of this court upholding deal protections comparable in strength to those in this case are: *Goodwin v. Live Entm't, Inc.*, 1999 WL 64265 (Del.Ch. Jan.25, 1999), aff'd,741 A.2d 16 (Del.1999) (finding reasonable a payment of a total of 4.167% to the original merger partner if a topping bidder got the company); *Lewis v. Leaseway Transp. Corp.*, 1990 WL 67383 (Del.Ch. May 16, 1990) (dismissing claim challenging a transaction involving a 3% break up fee).

98. Indeed, in his own scholarly work with Professor Coates, Subramanian reported that termination fees exceeding 3% of enterprise or deal value were relatively common. *Coates & Subramanian*, 53 Stan. L.Rev. at 347.

Furthermore, there are actual examples that prove that a package of this kind would not deter a fervent bidder intent on paying a materially higher price for the Company. In the recent struggle for control of MCI, Qwest bid repeatedly to try to top Verizon, despite its possession of matching rights. In *Capital Re*, the case was triggered by a bid that topped an initial merger partner protected by a termination fee and matching rights. Examples like these are simply not that unusual.

The plaintiffs attempt to strengthen their claim by focusing on the fact that financial buyers are typically more deterred by termination fees than strategic buyers because financial buyers can't reap gains from operational synergies. But these were exactly the same universe of buyers that had already been broadly solicited at the commencement of the strategic review, and were therefore least likely to have missed out on the opportunity to bid. * * *

It would be hubris ... for the court to conclude that the board acted unreasonably by assenting to a compromise 3.75% termination fee in order to guarantee $26.75 per share to its stockholders, and to avoid the substantial risk that the KKR Group might somehow glean the comparatively large margin by which it had outbid Cerberus. * * *

In sum, I conclude that the board's decision to assent to the deal protection measures was reasonable. In so ruling, I do not imply that those measures will not "rebuff a bidder who wishe[s] to top [the KKR Group's bid] by a relatively insubstantial amount that would not have been substantially more beneficial to [the Company's] stockholders, but to call such an insubstantial obstacle "draconian" is inconsistent with the very definition of the term."[99] Deal protections, of course, do provide a bidding cushion for merger partners that makes small, margin-topping bids non-viable. When that cushion results, as it did here, from a good faith negotiation process in which the target board has reasonably granted these protections in order to obtain a good result for the stockholders, there is no grounds for judicial intrusion. * * *

If the marginal cost to a second bidder of the difference between a 2.5% termination fee without matching rights and a 3.75% termination fee with matching rights really raises a reasonable concern that any material higher bid would be economically irrational, then that suggests that the board got close to the Company's maximum economic value, when measured by fundamental measures of its earning power.

This is not to say that this court is, or has been, willing to turn a blind eye to the adoption of excessive termination fees, such as the 6.3% termination fee in *Phelps Dodge* that Chancellor Chandler condemned, that present a more than reasonably explicable barrier to a second bidder, or even that fees lower than 3% are always reasonable.[100] But it is to say that *Revlon's* purpose is not to set the judiciary loose to enjoin contractual provisions that, upon a hard look, were reasonable in view of the benefits the board obtained in the other portions of an integrated contract. * * *

---

99. *Intercargo*, 768 A.2d at 506. In that regard, I close my consideration of the plaintiffs' argument that the deal protections presented an unreasonable barrier to a topping bid for the entire Company by commenting on the experts' reference to second bidders' fear of a "winner's curse" when faced with winning an auction over an initial merger partner. This idea, again, is the notion that the over bidder will pay too much, and emerge having over-leveraged itself and likely the target, too.

100. Nor, I believe, should we be entirely immune to the preclusive differences between termination fees starting with a "b" rather than an "m."

F. Break-Up Fee: Measured against Equity Value or Enterprise Value—*Cogent*[101]

In *Cogent*,[102] Vice Chancellor Parsons of the Delaware Chancery Court concluded that in determining the validity of a termination fee, the fee should be measured against equity value (*i.e.*, the cost of purchasing the equity of the target in the market) and not enterprise value (*i.e.*, the equity value, plus the value of debt, minus the cash on the target's balance sheet). He explained the plaintiffs' position as follows:

> 'Plaintiffs also take issue with the size of the $ 28.3 million Termination Fee. In the circumstances of this case, the Termination Fee represents 3% of equity value but 6.6% of enterprise value. While Plaintiffs implicitly acknowledge that a termination fee of 3% of the appropriate metric would be acceptable under this Court's precedent, they argue that the enterprise value, and not the equity value, is the proper metric against which to measure the reasonableness of the Termination Fee. Plaintiffs agree that the equity value of Cogent was $ 943 million, but note that its enterprise value was only $ 430 million because of the Company's large net cash position. They argue that any acquirer will be able to use the cash on Cogent's balance sheet to defray the effective cost of its bid and, therefore, would need only to kick in $ 430 million of "new" money. Therefore, Plaintiffs contend that $ 430 million plus the $ 28.3 million Termination Fee is the minimum amount of cash that a potential acquirer would have to put in play for Cogent, not $ 943 million. Plaintiffs further assert that a termination fee representing 6.6% of enterprise value is unreasonably high.[103]

In rejecting the plaintiffs' position and analyzing the fee as a percentage of equity value, Vice Chancellor Parsons reasoned as follows:

> A termination fee of 3% is generally reasonable. [Citing *Dollar Thrifty*, discussed infra and *Topps*, discussed infra] ... Ultimately, I conclude that it was not unreasonable for the Board to assent to a Termination Fee of 3% of the equity or transaction value in this case. Termination fees are not unusual in corporate sale or merger contexts, and, as Plaintiffs recognize, the reasonableness of such a fee "depends on the particular facts surrounding the transaction." Nothing in the record suggests that the Termination Fee here has deterred or will deter any buyer.... In addition, numerous Delaware cases have found reasonable termination fees of 3% or more of the equity or transaction value of a deal. [Citing e.g., *Toys*, discussed supra][104]

---

101. This section is adapted from Thompson, *Mergers, Acquisitions and Tender Offers*, *supra* Section 1.10, at Section 5:5.4[H][6][c].

102. *In re Cogent, Inc. S'holder Litig.*, 7 A.3d 487, 503 (Del. Ch. 2010).

103. *Id.* at 503–04.

104. *Id.* at 503.

G. Delaware Supreme Court's Divided Approach to Lock-Up by Target's Controlling Shareholder—*Omnicare*

Omnicare Inc. v. NCS Healthcare, Inc.

Delaware Supreme Court, 2003, 818 A.2d 914

HOLLAND, Justice, for the majority:

NCS Healthcare, Inc. ("NCS"), a Delaware corporation, was the object of competing acquisition bids, one by Genesis Health Ventures, Inc. ("Genesis"), a Pennsylvania corporation, and the other by Omnicare, Inc. ("Omnicare"), a Delaware corporation. * * *

Overview of Opinion. The board of directors of NCS, an insolvent publicly traded Delaware corporation, agreed to the terms of a merger with Genesis. Pursuant to that agreement, all of the NCS creditors would be paid in full and the corporation's stockholders would exchange their shares for the shares of Genesis, a publicly traded Pennsylvania corporation. Several months after approving the merger agreement, but before the stockholder vote was scheduled, the NCS board of directors withdrew its prior recommendation in favor of the Genesis merger.

In fact, the NCS board recommended that the stockholders reject the Genesis transaction after deciding that a competing proposal from Omnicare was a superior transaction. The competing Omnicare bid offered the NCS stockholders an amount of cash equal to more than twice the then current market value of the shares to be received in the Genesis merger. The transaction offered by Omnicare also treated the NCS corporation's other stakeholders on equal terms with the Genesis agreement.

The merger agreement between Genesis and NCS contained a provision authorized by Section 251(c) of Delaware's corporation law [a force the vote provision]. It required that the Genesis agreement be placed before the corporation's stockholders for a vote, even if the NCS board of directors no longer recommended it. At the insistence of Genesis, the NCS board also agreed to omit any effective fiduciary clause from the merger agreement. In connection with the Genesis merger agreement, two stockholders of NCS, who held a majority of the voting power, agreed unconditionally to vote all of their shares in favor of the Genesis merger. Thus, the combined terms of the voting agreements and merger agreement guaranteed, *ab initio*, that the transaction proposed by Genesis would obtain NCS stockholder's approval.

The Court of Chancery ruled that the voting agreements, when coupled with the provision in the Genesis merger agreement requiring that it be presented to the stockholders for a vote pursuant to 8 *Del. C.*§ 251(c), constituted defensive measures within the meaning of *Unocal Corp. v. Mesa Petroleum Co.* After applying the *Unocal* standard of enhanced judicial scrutiny, the Court of Chancery held that those defensive measures were reasonable. We have concluded that, in the absence of an effective fiduciary out clause, those defensive measures are both preclusive and coercive. Therefore, we hold that those defensive measures are invalid and unenforceable. * * *

LEGAL ANALYSIS. * * * *These Deal Protection Devices Unenforceable.* In this case, the Court of Chancery correctly held that the NCS directors' decision to adopt defensive devices to *completely*"lock up" the Genesis merger mandated "special scrutiny" under the two-part test set forth in *Unocal.* That conclusion is consistent with our holding in *Paramount v. Time* that "safety devices" adopted to protect a transaction that did not result in a change of control are subject to enhanced judicial scrutiny under a *Unocal* analysis. The record does not, however, support the Court of Chancery's conclusion that the defensive devices adopted by the NCS board to protect the Genesis merger were reasonable and proportionate to the threat that NCS perceived from the potential loss of the Genesis transaction.

Pursuant to the judicial scrutiny required under *Unocal's* two-stage analysis, the NCS directors must first demonstrate "that they had reasonable grounds for believing that a danger to corporate policy and effectiveness existed." * * * To satisfy that burden, the NCS directors are required to show they acted in good faith after conducting a reasonable investigation. The threat identified by the NCS board was the possibility of losing the Genesis offer and being left with no comparable alternative transaction.

The second stage of the *Unocal* test requires the NCS directors to demonstrate that their defensive response was "reasonable in relation to the threat posed." This inquiry involves a two-step analysis. The NCS directors must first establish that the merger deal protection devices adopted in response to the threat were not "coercive" or "preclusive," and then demonstrate that their response was within a "range of reasonable responses" to the threat perceived. In *Unitrin*, we stated:

- A response is "coercive" if it is aimed at forcing upon stockholders a management-sponsored alternative to a hostile offer.
- A response is "preclusive" if it deprives stockholders of the right to receive all tender offers or precludes a bidder from seeking control by fundamentally restricting proxy contests or otherwise.

This aspect of the *Unocal* standard provides for a disjunctive analysis. If defensive measures are either preclusive or coercive they are draconian and impermissible. In this case, the deal protection devices of the NCS board were *both* preclusive and coercive.

This Court enunciated the standard for determining stockholder coercion in the case of *Williams v. Geier.* A stockholder vote may be nullified by wrongful coercion "where the board or some other party takes actions which have the effect of causing the stockholders to vote in favor of the proposed transaction for some reason other than the merits of that transaction." In *Brazen v. Bell Atlantic Corporation*, [Section 3.20.C] we applied that test for stockholder coercion and held "that although the termination fee provision may have influenced the stockholder vote, there were 'no structurally or situationally coercive factors' that made an otherwise valid fee provision impermissibly coercive" under the facts presented.

In *Brazen*, we concluded "the determination of whether a particular stockholder vote has been robbed of its effectiveness by impermissible coercion depends on the facts of the case." In this case, the Court of Chancery did not expressly address the issue of "coercion" in its *Unocal* analysis. It did find as a fact, however, that NCS's public stockholders (who owned 80% of NCS and overwhelmingly supported Omnicare's offer) will be forced to accept the Genesis merger because of the structural defenses approved by the NCS board. Consequently, the record reflects that any stockholder vote would have been robbed of its effectiveness by the impermissible coercion that predetermined the outcome of the merger without regard to the merits of the Genesis transaction at the time the vote was scheduled to be taken. Deal protection devices that result in such coercion cannot withstand *Unocal's* enhanced judicial scrutiny standard of review because they are not within the range of reasonableness.

Although the minority stockholders were not forced to vote for the Genesis merger, they were required to accept it because it was *a fait accompli.* The record reflects that the defensive devices employed by the NCS board are preclusive and coercive in the sense that they accomplished *a fait accompli.* In this case, despite the fact that the NCS board has withdrawn its recommendation for the Genesis transaction and recommended its rejection by the stockholders, the deal protection devices approved by the NCS board operated in concert to have a preclusive and coercive effect. Those tripartite defensive measures—the Section 251(c) provision, the voting agreements, and the absence of an effective fiduciary out clause—made it "mathematically impossible" and "realistically unattainable" for the Omnicare transaction or any other proposal to succeed, no matter how superior the proposal.

The deal protection devices adopted by the NCS board were designed to coerce the consummation of the Genesis merger and preclude the consideration of any superior transaction. The NCS directors' defensive devices are not within a reasonable range of responses to the perceived threat of losing the Genesis offer because they are preclusive and coercive. Accordingly, we hold that those deal protection devices are unenforceable.

Effective Fiduciary Out Required. The defensive measures that protected the merger transaction are unenforceable not only because they are preclusive and coercive but, alternatively, they are unenforceable because they are invalid as they operate in this case. Given the specifically enforceable irrevocable voting agreements, the provision in the merger agreement requiring the board to submit the transaction for a stockholder vote and the omission of a fiduciary out clause in the merger agreement completely prevented the board from discharging its fiduciary responsibilities to the minority stockholders when Omnicare presented its superior transaction. "To the extent that a [merger] contract, or a provision thereof, purports to require a board to act or not act in such a fashion as to limit the exercise of fiduciary duties, it is invalid and unenforceable." * * *

Taking action that is otherwise legally possible, however, does not *ipso facto* comport with the fiduciary responsibilities of directors in all circumstances. The synopsis to the amendments that resulted in the enactment of Section 251(c) in the Delaware corporation law statute specifically provides: "the amendments are not intended to address the question of whether such a submission requirement is appropriate in any particular set of factual circumstances." Section 251 provisions, like the no shop provision examined in *QVC*, are "presumptively valid in the abstract." Such provisions in a merger agreement may not, however, "validly define or limit the directors' fiduciary duties under Delaware law or prevent the [NCS] directors from carrying out their fiduciary duties under Delaware law."

Genesis admits that when the NCS board agreed to its merger conditions, the NCS board was seeking to assure that the NCS creditors were paid in full and that the NCS stockholders received the highest value available for their stock. In fact, Genesis defends its "bulletproof" merger agreement on that basis. We hold that the NCS board did not have authority to accede to the Genesis demand for an absolute "lock-up."

The directors of a Delaware corporation have a continuing obligation to discharge their fiduciary responsibilities, as future circumstances develop, after a merger agreement is announced. Genesis anticipated the likelihood of a superior offer after its merger agreement was announced and demanded defensive measures from the NCS board that *completely* protected its transaction. Instead of agreeing to the absolute defense of the Genesis merger from a superior offer, however, the NCS board was required to negotiate a fiduciary out clause to protect the NCS stockholders if the Genesis transaction became an inferior offer. By acceding to Genesis' ultimatum for complete protection *in futuro*, the NCS board disabled itself from exercising its own fiduciary obligations at a time when the board's own judgment is most important, *i.e.* receipt of a subsequent superior offer. * * *

The NCS board was required to contract for an effective fiduciary out clause to exercise its continuing fiduciary responsibilities to the minority stockholders. * * *

In the context of this preclusive and coercive lock up case, the protection of Genesis' contractual expectations must yield to the supervening responsibility of the directors to discharge their fiduciary duties on a continuing basis. The merger agreement and voting agreements, as they were combined to operate in concert in this case, are inconsistent with the NCS directors' fiduciary duties. To that extent, we hold that they are invalid and unenforceable. * * *

VEASEY, Chief Justice, with whom STEELE, Justice, joins dissenting:

* * * Although it is debatable whether *Unocal* applies—and we believe that the better rule in this situation is that the business judgment rule should apply—we will, nevertheless, assume arguendo—as the Vice Chancellor did—that *Unocal* applies. * * *

In our view, the Majority misapplies the *Unitrin* concept of "coercive and preclusive" measures to preempt a proper proportionality balancing. * * *

In our view, the proportionality inquiry must account for the reality that the contractual measures protecting this merger agreement were necessary to obtain the Genesis deal. The Majority has not demonstrated that the director action was a disproportionate response to the threat posed. * * *

An Absolute Lock-up is not a Per Se Violation of Fiduciary Duty. We respectfully disagree with the Majority's conclusion that the NCS board breached its fiduciary duties to the Class A stockholders by failing to negotiate a "fiduciary out" in the Genesis merger agreement. * * *

Accordingly, we respectfully dissent.

STEELE, Justice, dissenting: * * *

I believe that the absence of a suggestion of self-interest or lack of care compels a court to defer to what is a business judgment that a court is not qualified to second guess. * * *

For the majority to articulate and adopt an inflexible rule where a board has discharged both its fiduciary duty of loyalty and care in good faith seems a most unfortunate turn. * * *

Therefore, I respectfully dissent.

H. Lock-Up with a Controlling Shareholder Is Permissible Where Not a *Fait Accompli*—*Cullman*

Orman v. Cullman

Delaware Court of Chancery, 2004 Del. Ch. LEXIS 150

CHANDLER, Chancellor:

This case is about a merger transaction in which one tobacco company, Swedish Match AB, purchased an equity stake in another tobacco company, General Cigar Holdings, Inc. Members of the Cullman family are the controlling shareholders of General Cigar. Swedish Match did not purchase control of General Cigar, as it wanted the Cullmans to continue managing the company after the merger.

Although Swedish Match paid a significant premium above the market price for the public shares in General Cigar, plaintiff Joseph Orman sued the General Cigar board of directors for breach of their fiduciary duties in negotiating the merger terms. * * * Defendants contend that a fully informed vote of a majority of the public shareholders in favor of the merger operates to extinguish plaintiff's claim. This contention raises the following question: Were the General Cigar public shareholders impermissibly coerced to vote for the merger because of a lock-up provision required by Swedish Match as part of the transaction?

The answer to this question, in my opinion, is no. The undisputed facts demonstrate that the lock-up did not coerce the public shareholders to approve the merger for reasons unrelated to its merits. Public shareholders of General Cigar retained full authority to veto the transaction, the board had negotiated an effective fiduciary out, and any interested third party was free to purchase the publicly owned shares of General Cigar. For these and other reasons set forth later in this Opinion, I will enter summary judgment in favor of defendants and against the plaintiff.

BACKGROUND. * * * Given the continuing interest of Swedish Match, General Cigar's board created a special committee to advise and make recommendations to the full board concerning any transaction with Swedish Match. * * * Although the special committee was charged with advising the board regarding any transaction with Swedish Match, it was not authorized to solicit offers by third parties. The special committee also did not negotiate directly with Swedish Match. * * *

During the negotiations that led to the merger, Swedish Match required that the Cullmans enter into a stockholders' voting agreement. "Under that agreement, the Cullmans agreed not to sell their shares, and to vote their shares against any alternative acquisition proposal for a specified period following any termination of the merger between Swedish Match and General Cigar." According to Swedish Match's CFO:

> A central purpose of the voting agreement was to protect Swedish Match against the risk that the Cullmans or General Cigar would "shop" Swedish Match's offer to other potential bidders. Because the Cullmans held a controlling interest in General Cigar, the voting agreement would prevent an alternative bidder from acquiring control of General Cigar during the specified period if the merger did not go forward. This protection was particularly important to Swedish Match because the merger agreement did not contain a termination fee or expense reimbursement provision.

Swedish Match originally asked that the Cullmans agree to a restricted period of three years. This was rejected. The restricted period was later negotiated down to one year.

Drafts of the merger agreement and the voting agreement were sent to the Cullmans and the special committee on January 18, 2000. These drafts reflected a potential transaction structure in which the Cullmans would sell approximately one third of their equity interest to Swedish Match at a price of $15.00 per share followed by a merger into a Swedish Match subsidiary in which public shareholders would also receive $15.00 per share. The voting agreement circulated on January 18 contained a requirement that the Cullmans not sell their shares, and to vote their shares against any alternative acquisition proposal, for one year following any termination of the merger agreement between Swedish Match and General Cigar. Following the merger, General Cigar would be owned 64% by Swedish Match and 36% by the Cullmans. The Cullmans, specifically Edgar Cullman Sr. and Edgar Cullman Jr., however, would remain in control of the Company. * * *

[T]he voting agreement between the Cullmans and Swedish Match required that the Cullmans vote their Class B shares, constituting a majority of the voting power of the Company, in favor of the merger and against any alternative acquisition of the Company for eighteen months after termination of the merger agreement. The voting agreement, however, reveals that the Cullmans were bound only in their capacities as shareholders and that nothing in the voting agreement limits or affects their actions as officers or directors of General Cigar. Moreover, the merger agreement permitted General Cigar's board to entertain unsolicited acquisition proposals from potential acquirers if the board, upon recommendation by the special committee, concluded that such a proposal was *bona fide* and would be more favorable to the pubic shareholders than the proposed merger with Swedish Match. The agreement also permitted the board to withdraw its recommendation of the merger with Swedish Match if the board concluded, upon consultation with outside counsel, that its fiduciary duties so required.

On April 10, 2000, almost three months after the public announcement of the Swedish Match transaction, General Cigar filed the proxy statement relating to the shareholder vote on the proposed merger. As expected, the proxy statement attached the merger agreement, the voting agreement, and contained the background relating to the proposed merger. The proxy statement also revealed (1) that the merger could not occur without the approval of the merger by the Class A shareholders and (2) that the Cullmans agreed to vote their shares of Class A common stock held by them pro rata in accordance with the vote of the Class A public shareholders. In other words, the merger could not proceed without approval by a "majority of the minority." The shareholder meeting was held on May 8, 2000. The public shareholders, *i.e.*, a majority of the minority, overwhelmingly approved the merger.

ANALYSIS. * * * **The Deal Protection Mechanisms.** * * * In *Omnicare*, the majority found that the NCS board's reasonable grounds for believing there was a danger to corporate policy and effectiveness were "the possibility of losing the Genesis offer and being left with no comparable alternative transaction." Nevertheless, the majority held that the deal protection devices were coercive and preclusive because they accomplished *a fait accompli, i.e.*, they "made it mathematically impossible—and realistically unattainable—for ... any other proposal to succeed, no matter how superior the proposal." * * * The Court reasoned that even though a majority of shareholders (via the voting agreement) had agreed to support the merger, the NCS board was nonetheless continually obligated to "exercise its continuing fiduciary responsibilities to the minority stockholders."

Applying the first stage of the *Unocal* analysis is simple in this case. During the negotiations that led to the merger, Swedish Match "required" some form of deal protection. If the special committee and full board had not approved the inclusion of the deal protection devices, they risked losing the Swedish Match transaction and being left with no comparable alternative transaction. As in *Omnicare* itself, this is reasonable grounds for believing that a danger to corporate policy and effectiveness existed.

Applying the second stage of the *Unocal* analysis is also straightforward. *Williams v. Geier* provides the standard for determining if deal protection measures are coercive. The measures are improper if they "have the effect of causing the stockholders to vote in favor of the proposed transaction for some reason other than the merits of that transaction." * * *

In *Brazen*, Bell Atlantic and NYNEX Corporation negotiated a merger agreement with a $550 million termination fee provision that could be triggered if Bell Atlantic's shareholders voted not to approve merger. The Supreme Court found that the termination fee was "an integral part of the merits of the transaction." The Court further stated "although the termination fee provision may have influenced the stockholder vote, there were no structurally or situationally coercive factors that made an otherwise valid fee provision impermissibly coercive in this setting."

Here, like *Brazen*, the deal would not have occurred without the inclusion of deal protection mechanisms, *i.e.*, the deal protection mechanisms were "an integral part of the merits of the transaction." * * * Furthermore, unlike the situation in *Omnicare*, the deal protection mechanisms at issue in this case were not tantamount to "*a fait accompli.*" The public shareholders were free to reject the proposed deal.

The last step of the *Unocal* analysis is a determination of whether the deal protection devices were within a range of reasonable responses to the danger to corporate policy and effectiveness. As mentioned, the danger in this case was the risk of losing the Swedish Match transaction and being left with no comparable alternative transaction. In fact, without the deal protection mechanisms "there would have been no merger." General Cigar's shareholders could have lost the significant premium that Swedish Match's offer carried, no small concern given the uncertain future of the tobacco business. In addition, "the latitude a board will have in either maintaining or using the defensive devices it has adopted to protect the merger it approved will vary according to the degree of benefit or detriment to the stockholders' interests that is presented by the value or terms of the subsequent competing transaction." Notably, there was no competing bid for General Cigar; no alternative transaction was available to its shareholders. General Cigar's board should therefore be afforded the maximum latitude regarding its decision to recommend the Swedish Match merger.

In sum, the argument that *Omnicare* applies in the circumstances here is misplaced. The General Cigar board retained a fiduciary out, allowing it to consider superior proposals and recommend against the Swedish Match deal. Importantly, a majority of the nonaffiliated public shareholders could have rejected the deal on its merits. Unlike *Omnicare*, nothing in the merger or stockholder agreements made it "mathematically certain" that the transaction would be approved. If the shareholders believed $15.25 per share (a 75% premium over the market price) did not reflect General Cigar's intrinsic value (and the market also misunderstood that value), they could have said, "no thanks, I would rather make an investment bet on the long term prospects of this company." These shareholders were fully informed about the offer. They knew that no other offer or potential buyer had appeared, although nothing prevented it. They knew that no termination fee would be paid if they rejected the proposal. It is true, as plaintiffs repeatedly point out, that the Cullman vote against any future, hypothetical deal was "locked-up" for 18 months. It was this deal or nothing, at least for that period of time. Again, however, no other suitor was waiting in the wings. And, assuming a shareholder believed that General Cigar's long term intrinsic value was greater than $15.25 per share, was an 18 month delay a meaningful "cost" that could be said realistically to "coerce" the shareholders' vote? The Cullman lock-up hardly seems unreasonable, given the absence of other deal protection devices in this particular transaction and given the buyer's understandable concern about transaction costs and market uncertainties. Unless being in a voting minority automatically means that the shareholder is coerced (because the minority shareholder's investment views or hopes have been precluded by a majority), plaintiff's concept of coercion is far more expansive than *Omnicare* or any other decisional authority brought to my attention. As a matter of law, therefore, the approval of the Swedish Match proposal by a fully informed majority of the minority public shareholders was not impermissibly coerced. As a result of that ratifying vote, plaintiff's remaining fiduciary duty claim is extinguished. * * *

I. Shareholder Consents Given After Signing of Merger Agreement—*Openlane and Optima*

Vice Chancellor Nobel's decision in *Openlane*[105] involved a sale of a publicly held company in a cash transaction subject to *Revlon*. The court found that although the target's board had not acted perfectly, it had acted reasonably, and therefore, the court denied the plaintiff's request for a preliminary injunction.

The court has an interesting analysis of whether consents (*see* Section 228 of Delaware General Corporation Law) supporting the merger filed by controlling shareholders of the

105. *In Re Openlane, Inc. Shareholders Lit.*, 2011 Del. Ch. LEXIS 156 (Del. Ch. Ct. Sept. 30, 2011).

target shortly after the signing of the merger agreement made the transaction a prohibited *fait accompli* under *Omnicare*. On this point, the court reasoned:

> The Merger, now before the Court, was not a *fait accompli*. Although the Merger Agreement contained a no-solicitation clause, there, evidently, was no shareholders' voting agreement entered into as part of the Merger. [The plaintiff] seems to suggest that "the lockup of the shareholder vote through the combined voting power of OPENLANE's directors and executive officers" was a defensive device, but the record, at least at this preliminary stage, merely suggests that, after the Board approved the Merger Agreement, the holders of a majority of shares quickly provided consents.
>
> Under the DGCL, a majority of a corporation's outstanding stock must support a merger, and stockholders are allowed to manifest their approval through written consent in this instance. If stockholders wish to submit their consents soon after the board has approved a transaction, they may do so. [Citing *Optima International of Miami v. WCI Steel*, 3833 VCL, Oral Argument (June 27, 2008)][106]

The court in *Optima* also found that *Omnicare* was not violated where a merger agreement contained a provision requiring that a vote of the target's shareholders approving the merger by consent take place shortly after the execution of the merger agreement. Thus, under this device, the controlling shareholders can vote by consent to immediately approve the merger. This can be utilized in both public and private company acquisitions; however, the transaction would have to satisfy *Revlon*, if applicable.

J. Investment Banker's Manipulation of the Sales Process, Stapled Financing—*Del Monte*[107]

The acquisition by three private equity firms (KKR, Centerview, and Vestar) of Del Monte, a publicly held Delaware corporation, illustrates how (1) a target's board should not deal with its investment banker, and (2) an investment banker should take care to avoid the creation of conflicts of interest in the course of its representation of a target in an M&A transaction. In this case, Vice Chancellor Laster of the Delaware Chancery Court rendered a scathing opinion in which, on a preliminary record, he concluded:

> (1) the Del Monte board had breached its fiduciary duties (a) in failing to properly supervise its investment banker, Barclays, and (b) by permitting Barclays to provide buy-side (*i.e.*, stapled) financing, which caused Del Monte to employ the services of a second investment banker for the purpose of rendering a second fairness opinion at a cost of $3 million to Del Monte;
>
> (2) Barclays had inappropriately promoted the sale of Del Monte by, *inter alia*, causing KKR and Vestar to cooperate in the acquisition of Del Monte in violation of a "no teaming" provision of confidentiality agreements; and
>
> (3) KKR had aided and abetted the Del Monte board's breach of fiduciary duty.[108]

---

106. *Id.* at *30–*32.

107. This section is adapted from Thompson, *Mergers, Acquisitions and Tender Offers*, *supra* Section 1.10, at Section 5:5.4[M].

108. In Re Del Monte Foods Company Shareholders Litigation, 2011 Del. Ch. LEXIS 30 (Del. Ch. Feb. 14, 2011).

In discussing the essential facts, the court explained:

> Barclays secretly and selfishly manipulated the sale process to engineer a transaction that would permit Barclays to obtain lucrative buy-side financing fees. On multiple occasions, Barclays protected its own interests by withholding information from the Board that could have led Del Monte to retain a different bank, pursue a different alternative, or deny Barclays a buy-side role. Barclays did not disclose the behind-the-scenes efforts of its Del Monte coverage officer to put Del Monte into play. Barclays did not disclose its explicit goal, harbored from the outset, of providing buy-side financing to the acquirer. Barclays did not disclose that in September 2010, without Del Monte's authorization or approval, Barclays steered Vestar [previously the high bidder] into a club bid with KKR, the potential bidder with whom Barclays had the strongest relationship, in violation of confidentiality agreements that prohibited Vestar and KKR from discussing a joint bid without written permission from Del Monte.
>
> Late in the process, at a time when Barclays was ostensibly negotiating the deal price with KKR, Barclays asked KKR for a third of the buy-side financing. Once KKR agreed, Barclays sought and obtained Del Monte's permission. Having Barclays as a co-lead bank was not necessary to secure sufficient financing for the Merger, nor did it generate a higher price for the Company. It simply gave Barclays the additional fees it wanted from the outset. In fact, Barclays can expect to earn slightly more from providing buy-side financing to KKR than it will from serving as Del Monte's sell-side advisor. Barclays' gain cost Del Monte an additional $3 million because Barclays told Del Monte that it now had to obtain a last-minute fairness opinion from a second bank.[109]

The court discussed as follows the approach Vice Chancellor Strine took in analyzing the handling of the investment banker's request to provide stapled financing in the *Toys "R" Us, Inc. Shareholder Litigation*:[110]

> In *Toys "R" Us*, Vice Chancellor Strine considered whether an investment banker's role in providing stapled financing created a conflict of interest that merited injunctive relief. At the outset of the sale process challenged in that case, the sell-side investment banker, First Boston, asked about possibly providing buy-side financing for purchasers of a subsidiary. "The board promptly nixed that idea." ... Then, following a lengthy process during which the form of the transaction shifted from a sale of the subsidiary to a sale of the whole company, and two months after the process culminated in an executed merger agreement, First Boston again asked to be permitted to provide a portion of the buy-side financing. This time the board agreed. Vice Chancellor Strine described that decision as "unfortunate, in that it tends to raise eyebrows by creating the appearance of impropriety, playing into already heightened suspicions about the ethics of investment banking firms." He suggested it would have been "[f]ar better, from the standpoint of instilling confidence, if First Boston had never asked for permission, and had taken the position that its credibility as a sell-side advisor was too important in this case, and in general, for it to simultaneously play on the buy-side in a deal when it was the seller's financial advisor." ... He likewise noted that "it might have been better, in view of First Boston's refusal

109. *Id.* at *4–*5.

110. *In re* Toys "R" Us, Inc. S'holder Litig., 877 A.2d 975 (Del. Ch. 2005).

> to refrain, for the board of the Company to have declined the request, even though the request came ... almost two months after the board had signed the merger agreement." ... Nevertheless, after reviewing in detail the public, year-long, multi-phase process that the board and its banker conducted, Vice Chancellor Strine concluded "upon close scrutiny" that First Boston's appearance of conflict did not have "a causal influence" on the board's process.... He cautioned that "[i]n general, however, it is advisable that investment banks representing sellers not create the appearance that they desire buy-side work, especially when it might be that they are more likely to be selected by some buyers for that lucrative role than by others."[111]

Vice Chancellor Laster then distinguished the actions of Barclays with respect to Del Monte from the actions of First Boston with respect to Toys:

> Applying these principles to the current case shows that Barclays' activities went far beyond what took place in Toys "R" Us. Barclays set out to provide acquisition financing, as established by the internal screening memos from January and March 2010. Barclays' Del Monte coverage officer pitched a Del Monte LBO to KKR, Apollo, and other private equity firms that would be likely to use Barclays for acquisition financing. Once it secured the sell-side role, Barclays structured a small, private process that maximized the likelihood that it could provide acquisition financing. Barclays never disclosed to the Board its interactions with the private equity shops or its desire to provide acquisition financing.[112]

The court also explained that Barclays ran the "go shop" provision of the merger agreement (see discussion of "go shops," supra) even though Goldman Sachs had made a bid to provide that service. The court discusses as follows the facts surrounding the reasons Goldman was not retained for that service:

> Upon learning of Goldman's interest, Barclays told KKR that Goldman was trying to "scare up competition." ... Brown of KKR told Barclays that he would "manage it" directly with Goldman.... He solved the problem by letting Goldman participate in 5% of the syndication rights for the acquisition financing, which "squared things away there." ... After that, Goldman dropped its efforts to conduct the go shop.[113]

If Goldman had been retained to run the "go shop" and had been successful in finding an acquirer that topped the bid of the KKR group, then Barclays may have lost the opportunity to provide the financing for the acquisition. Thus, Barclays had an incentive to see that the "go shop" did not result in a higher bid.

The court reasoned that the breach of fiduciary duties here was similar to the breach that occurred in the *Mills* case, discussed supra:

> By failing to provide the serious oversight that would have checked Barclays' misconduct, the directors breached their fiduciary duties in a manner reminiscent of *Mills Acquisition Co. v. Macmillan, Inc.*, 559 A.2d 1261 (Del. 1989). In that decision, the Delaware Supreme Court enjoined a transaction—ironically a leveraged buyout sponsored by KKR—when self-interested management and their financial advisor concealed information from the board. Like management's

111. *Id.* at *48–*50.
112. Id. at *50.
113. *Del Monte* , 2011 Del. Ch. LEXIS 30, at *36.

deal-specific, buy-side conflict in Mills, Barclays' deal-specific, buy-side conflict tainted the advice it gave and the actions it took.[114]

Because Del Monte's board appeared to act in good faith and did not become aware of Barclay's actions in promoting the sale of Del Monte until after discovery was taken in this case, the court concluded that it was highly unlikely that the directors would have any personal liability as a result of the breach of their fiduciary duties. The court explained:

> Unless further discovery reveals different facts, the one-two punch of exculpation under Section 102(b)(7) and full protection under Section 141(e) makes the chances of a judgment for money damages vanishingly small. The same cannot be said for the self-interested aiders and abetters [*i.e.*, KKR]. But while the directors may face little threat of liability, they cannot escape the ramifications of Barclays' misconduct. For purposes of equitable relief, the Board is responsible.[115]

The court went on to grant the following injunction:

> The defendants are enjoined preliminarily from proceeding with the vote on the Merger for a period of 20 days. Pending the vote on the Merger, the parties to the Merger Agreement are enjoined from enforcing the no-solicitation and match-right provisions in Section 6.5(b), (c) and (h), and the termination fee provisions relating to topping bids and changes of recommendation in Section 8.5(b). The injunction is conditioned on the plaintiffs posting a bond in the amount of $1.2 million.[116]

The *Del Monte* decision has valuable lessons for the boards of potential targets, investment bankers, and potential acquirers. The boards of targets should take measures to properly monitor the activities of their investment bankers to ensure that the bankers (1) are not acting inappropriately, (2) do not have any conflicts of interest or properly manage any conflicts, and (3) disclose fully all activities taken in connection with the representation of the target. The engagement letters should contain representations regarding any conflicts and a covenant requiring the disclosure of any subsequently developed conflict.

A target's board should also ensure that there is full disclosure to the shareholders of all aspects of its relationship with its investment banker. Vice Chancellor Laster elaborated on this point as follows:

> Because of the central role played by investment banks in the evaluation, exploration, selection, and implementation of strategic alternatives, this Court has required full disclosure of investment banker compensation and potential conflicts. This Court has not stopped at disclosure, but rather has examined banker conflicts closely to determine whether they tainted the directors' process.[117]

A target's board should not permit its investment banker to provide buy-side financing in the absence of a clear finding by the board that such financing provides a valuable benefit to the firm. In the words of Vice Chancellor Laster, buy side financing could be appropriate where it was "necessary to secure sufficient financing for the Merger,"[118] and "generate[d] a higher price for the Company."[119] A potential conflict could arise where, for example, there

---

114. *Id.* at *5–*6.
115. Id. at *6.
116. *Id.* at *7–*8.
117. *Id.*
118. *Id.* at *4–*5.
119. *Id.* at *5.

are strategic and financial buyers, and the strategic buyers do not need financing. On the other hand, the initial presence of stapled financing could facilitate the process of marketing the target by demonstrating the availability of financing. Along these same lines, a March 2011 analysis of *Del Monte* addresses the following question: "So, when should the financial adviser to a target company provide financing to potential buyers?"[120] The authors respond:

> Simply put, when doing so benefits the target company's stockholders. That benefit could be in the form of facilitating competition among bidders or providing greater financing certainty of more attractive terms to allow prospective buyers to bid more aggressively.... The record will need to show that the target's board carefully weighted the upside against the downside created by its financial adviser's conflict.[121]

In any situation in which stapled financing is provided, the board should consider retaining another, conflict free, investment banker to provide the (or a supplemental) fairness opinion, and of course, the board should take into account the cost of obtaining such an opinion when making the decision regarding stapled financing.

Investment banking firms should take care to ensure that (1) any conflicts are completely disclosed to the client, (2) their efforts are exclusively for the benefit of the client, (3) they receive clear instructions from the client, and (4) the client is fully aware of all actions taken by the bank in the course of the engagement, including any plans the bank has for requesting to provide buy-side financing.

Private equity firms and other potential acquirers should take steps to ensure that they are in full compliance with any confidentiality or other agreement relating to the transaction, such as a no teaming provision.

K. The Fight in Delaware Chancery Over "Don't Ask, Don't Waive" (DADW) — *Genomics, Ancestry,* and *NetSpend*[122]

Introduction to Don't Ask, Don't Waive (DADW) Provisions. As of May 21, 2013, the Delaware Chancery Court has considered "don't ask, don't waive" (DADW) provisions in three cases: Vice Chancellor Laster's November 27, 2012 transcript ruling in *Genomics*;[123] Chancellor Strine's December 17, 2013 transcript ruling in *Ancestry*,[124] and Vice Chancellor Glasscock's May 21, 2013 decision in *NetSpend*.[125]

DADW provisions may be included in the standstill provisions of a confidentiality agreement or in a separate standstill agreement, pursuant to which a potential acquirer, in exchange for confidential information on the target, agrees not to make an unwanted offer for the target. The DADW provision of a standstill could read as follows:

> During the two-year period commencing on the date of this standstill agreement, neither the Potential Acquirer or any of its representatives will in any

120. Peter D. Lyons, David P. Connolly, and Nathan Sawyer, *Sell-Side Financing After In re Del Monte Foods*, 15 The M&A Lawyer 1, 5 (March 2011).

121. *Id.* at 5.

122. This section is adapted from Thompson, *Mergers, Acquisitions and Tender Offers, supra* Section 1.10, at Section 5:5.4[P].

123. *In re Complete Genomics, Inc. Shareholder Litigation*, C.A. No. 7888–VCL (Del. Ch., Nov. 27, 2012) (transcript ruling), pp. 14–18.

124. *In re Ancestry.com.Inc Shareholder Litigation*, C.A. No. 7988–CS (Del. Ch., Dec. 17, 2012) (transcript ruling).

125. *Koehler v. NetSpend Holdings Inc.*, 2013 Del. Ch. LEXIS 131 (May 21, 2013).

> manner directly or indirectly [*inter alia*] request or propose that the target or any of its representatives amend, waive or consider an amendment to or waiver of any of the provisions of this standstill.

In some cases, a target will agree in a merger agreement not to waive or otherwise modify a DADW provision. For example, the "no solicitation" provision of the merger agreement in *Genomics* provided as follows:

> [The target] ... shall not ... waive, terminate, modify, fail to enforce or release any Person other than [the acquirer] from any provision of or grant any permission, waiver or request under any "standstill," confidentiality or similar agreement or obligation.... [126]

As discussed *infra*, the merger agreement in *NetSpend* also prohibited a waiver of the standstill. On the other hand, the merger agreement in *Ancestry* specifically provided that the target "may fail to enforce and waive any standstill or similar provision...."[127]

Vice Chancellor Laster's Transcript Ruling in *Genomics*.

In finding that the DADW provision in *Genomics* impermissible, Vice Chancellor Laster reasoned as follows:

> In my view, a Don't Ask, Don't Waive Standstill resembles a bidder-specific no-talk clause. In *Phelps Dodge Corporation v. Cyprus Amax*, [1999 Del. Ch. LEXIS 202 (Sept 27, 1999)] Chancellor Chandler considered whether a target board had breached its fiduciary duties by entering into a merger agreement containing a no-talk provision. Unlike a traditional no-shop clause, which permits a target board to communicate with acquirers under limited circumstances, a no-talk clause—and here I'm quoting from the Chancellor—"not only prevents a party from soliciting superior offers or providing information to third parties, but also from talking to or holding discussions with third parties." ...
>
> The Chancellor concluded that there was a reasonable probability that for the target board to have agreed to such a provision violated its ongoing—and again, I'm quoting—"duty to take care to be informed of all material information reasonably available." ... This was because the target board's agreement to disable itself from engaging in dialogue with a potential acquirer under any circumstances whatsoever was the legal equivalent of willful blindness.
>
> Subsequent Delaware decisions have endorsed the *Phelps Dodge* analysis....
>
> What these decisions and these authorities show is that the board has an ongoing statutory and fiduciary obligation with respect to the merger recommendation. So regardless of whether a no-talk provision, as in *Phelps Dodge*, or a Don't Ask, Don't Waive provision here, would create problems for the decision to negotiate, and certainly *Phelps Dodge* holds that it would, those provisions interfere with the target's ability to determine whether to change its merger recommendation because they absolutely preclude the flow of incoming information to the board.

---

126. Section 5.3(a), Agreement and Plan of Merger among BGI-Shenzhen, Beta Acquisition Corporation, and Complete Genomics, Inc., dated as of September 15, 2012.

127. Section 5.3(a) of Agreement and Plan of Merger by and among Global, Generations International, Inc. Global Generations Merger Sub Inc. and Ancestry .com. Inc., dated as of October 2012.

> So in my view, by analogy to *Phelps Dodge*, a Don't Ask, Don't Waive Standstill is impermissible because it has the same disabling effect as the no-talk clause, although on a bidder-specific basis. By agreeing to this provision, the Genomics board impermissibly limited its ongoing statutory and fiduciary obligations to properly evaluate a competing offer, disclose material information, and make a meaningful merger recommendation to its stockholders. With respect to the Don't Ask, Don't Waive Standstill provision, therefore, the plaintiffs have established a reasonable probability of success on the merits that that provision represents a promise by a fiduciary to violate its fiduciary duty, or represents a promise that tends to induce such a violation.[128]

It is clear that Vice Chancellor Laster's ruling was based on the fact that he had only recently learned that the target had agreed in the merger agreement not to waive the DADW provision of the confidentiality agreement. On this point, he explained:

> [On] November 21st, I denied the motion for reconsideration without argument. After the denial of the [plaintiff's] motion [for reconsideration], the defendants submitted a letter advising that the standstill agreement that binds the counterparty referred to as Party J in fact does contain a Don't Ask, Don't Waive provision. I appreciate the defendants making this clarification of the record because it is indeed true that I had misapprehended that fact. Because I misapprehended that fact, it is appropriate to reconsider this one aspect of my ruling under Rule 59. I am consequently enjoining Genomics pending trial from enforcing the standstill agreement.[129]

The letter referred to above contained the following description of the structure and status of the DADW provisions in that case:

> Each of the standstill provisions is the result of a negotiation between Complete Genomics and the counterparties thereto. Of the four standstill agreements, there are effectively three different formulations. The standstill with the party that was not named as a party in the 14D-9 only prohibits that party from "publicly request[ing] or propos[ing] that the Company or any of the Company's representatives amend, waive or consider the amendment or waiver of any provision set forth in this paragraph." The standstill with Party G contains no provision whatsoever limiting Party G's ability to request a waiver of that standstill. On the other hand, the standstill agreements with Parties I and J do prohibit them from request[ing] or propos[ing] that the Company or any of the Company's representatives amend, waive or consider the amendment or waiver of any provision set forth in this paragraph." As previously noted in the Company's Opposition to Plaintiff's Motion for Preliminary Injunction (at 23), Party 1 is signatory to a Tender and Support Agreement, effectively superseding its standstill agreement. Thus, in essence only one party, Party J, is currently restrained by a standstill but prohibited by the terms of that standstill from seeking to have those provisions waived.[130]

Chancellor Strine's Transcript Ruling in *Ancestry*. In his decision in *Ancestry*, Chancellor Strine appeared to take issue with Vice Chancellor Laster's approach in *Genomics* to DADW provisions. First, Chancellor Strine said:

---

128. *Genomics*, 14–18.

129. *Id.* at 12–13.

130. Letter dated Nov. 21, 2012 from Seitz, Ross, Aronstam & Moritz to Vice Chancellor Laster re *Genomics*.

> I'm giving you a bench ruling. Bench rulings are limited rulings. They're time-pressured ones.... [T]hey shouldn't make broad law....
>
> Per se rulings where judges invalidate contractual provisions across the bar [presumably he is talking about Vice Chancellor Laster's bench ruling in *Genomics*] are exceedingly rare in Delaware, and they should be. It's inconsistent with the model of our law....
>
> I know of no statute, I know of nothing, that says that these [DADW] provisions are per se invalid. And I don't think there has been a prior ruling of the Court to that effect. I know people have read a bench opinion [presumably Vice Chancellor's bench opinion in *Genomics*] that way. I think there was a lot going on in that case. Again, there is a role that bench opinions play, and I don't think it's to make per se rules.[131]

Chancellor Strine went on to say that he was "not prepared" to conclude that DADW provisions "can't be used for value-maximizing purposes,"[132] which are required by *Revlon*. He explained the value-maximizing purpose as follows:

> [T]o allow ... a well-motivated seller to use [the DADW] as a gavel, to impress upon the people that it has brought into the process the fact that the process is meaningful; that if you're creating an auction, there is really an end to the auction for those who participate. And therefore, you should bid your fullest because if you win, you have the confidence of knowing you actually won that auction at least against the other people in the process.[133]

Pointing out that the Ancestry board and CEO, and possibly the investment banker, were not aware of the DADW, Chancellor Strine concluded there was "probabilistically" a violation of the duty of care.[134] The DADW was later waived by the parties, and Chancellor Chandler went on to require disclosure of the provision and its waiver prior to the completion of the merger. On this point he reasoned:

> Well, at least when the electorate votes—if these things are going to be used, and they're used for a gavel, then the electorate should know that with respect to the comfort they should take in the ability to make a superior proposal, they should understand that there is a segment of the market where that segment cannot take advantage of that; that the board made the cost/benefit trade-off that the best way to get the value was to draw the highest bid out from those people while they were in the process; that in order to do that, it had to incur the cost of giving to the winner the right to enforce it. But what you as a stockholder know is, We invited these people in on the front end. That's how we tried to maximize value. You still have the ability of somebody we didn't test the market with coming in, but you shouldn't assume that these other people can come in.[135]

On the disclosure point, he added that the following should be part of the mix of information provided to the shareholders: (1) the DADW was "waived on December 11th," (2) until that waiver, the firms that were parties to the DADW "were precluded until then [from making a bid]."[136]

---

131. *Ancestry*, pp. 19–22.
132. *Id.* at 23.
133. *Id.*
134. *Id.* at 25–26.
135. *Id.* at 27–28.
136. *Id.* at 29.

The bottom line is that even though the DADW in *Ancestry* was not part of the merger agreement as in *Genomics*, the *Ancestry* DADW was waived.

Vice Chancellor Glasscock's Decision in *NetSpend*. In his May 2013 decision in *NetSpend*,[137] which is discussed more generally *infra*, in the context of the overall *Revlon* requirement, Vice Chancellor Glasscock addressed the use of a DADW provision of a standstill, which was also made non-waivable by the merger agreement. Thus, the situation in *NetSpend* was similar to the situation in *Genomics*. As indicated in the previous discussion, in *Ancestry* the DADW provision of the standstill was specifically made waivable by the merger agreement. Vice Chancellor Glasscock described as follows the DADW provisions in *NetSpend*:

> The DADW clauses originate in the standstill sections of the confidentiality agreements NetSpend entered into with Private Equity A and Private Equity B. The standstill provisions expressly prevent Private Equity A and Private Equity B from attempting to acquire NetSpend (as a whole) for a one- or two-year period. The DADW clauses prevent either Private Equity A or Private Equity B from asking NetSpend for a waiver of the standstill agreement....
>
> [T]he standstill agreements were expressly incorporated in the Merger Agreement—they may not be waived without the buyer's consent. The Merger Agreement forbad NetSpend from waiving the DADW provisions that prevent Private Equity A and Private Equity B from expressing any interest in bidding for the Company. Section 6.16 of the Merger Agreement provides that "neither the Company nor any of its Subsidiaries shall amend, modify or waive any provision of any confidentiality agreement relating to an Acquisition Proposal or standstill agreement to which the Company or any of its Subsidiaries is a party." Meanwhile, NetSpend contracted away its opportunity to solicit offers via the no-shop.[138]

The Vice Chancellor addressed the applicability of the fiduciary out provision of the merger agreement, which permits the board to consider an unsolicited superior proposal provided the board's fiduciary duties require such consideration. On this point he explained:

> Though Section 6.16 [on the Merger Agreement] has a fiduciary out, it is likely ineffective, because the standstill agreements themselves operated to preclude the communication of a superior offer. Without that communication, the Board would have no reason to invoke the fiduciary out and waive the standstills. Therefore, the fiduciary out provided only an illusory benefit.[139]

The Vice Chancellor rejected the argument that the DADWs used here were serving the purpose of a "gavel" as Chancellor Strine discussed in *Ancestry*. On this point Vice Chancellor Glasscock explained:

> As the Chancellor has pointed out, DADW provisions can have value, in that they produce pressures to bid high akin to those achieved in a sealed bid auction. *See In re Ancestry.com Inc. S'holder Litig.*, C.A. No. 7988–CS, at 225–26 (Del. Ch. Dec. 17, 2012) (TRANSCRIPT). Given that the clauses here are merely an artifact from an earlier Board strategy (to remain an independent entity), and given that they are here employed to lock up a single bidder sale, none of that utility can apply here.[140]

---

137. Koehler v. NetSpend Holdings Inc., 2013 Del. Ch. LEXIS 131 (May 21, 2013).
138. *Id.* at 66–68.
139. *Id.* at 68, note 229.
140. *Id.* at 71–72, note 235.

Finally, the Vice Chancellor noted that (1) shortly after oral argument, the acquirer consented to NetSpend's waiver of the DADW clauses in the standstill agreements, (2) NetSpend notified the private equity firms that were parties to the DADW that the clauses have been waived; and (3) disclosures regarding these matters were made to the shareholders.

My Take on DADWs. First, a DADW provision in a standstill seems silly, because it is prohibiting a potential acquirer from merely asking for a waiver of the standstill. What is the harm in asking for something? A fundamental common sense principle is "If you don't ask, you don't get." The DADW provision is designed to override this common sense principle.

Also, what would be the remedy for violation of a DADW where the acquirer was acting in good faith in making the request? A court of equity would likely find a remedy for a non-good faith request (such as a non-real bid designed to derail a transaction), but it seems inconceivable that a court of equity would provide the target with a meaningful remedy for a violation of a DADW by a potential acquirer that was making a real alternative bid that was significantly higher than the accepted bid. The important provision of a standstill is the power to prohibit an unsolicited bid, not the power to prevent a request for a waiver of that power.

So, as a practical matter, contrary to Chancellor Strine, I believe that it is appropriate for the Delaware Court of Chancery, a court of equity, to have a per se rule against DADW provisions, even when the target does not agree in the merger agreement not to waive the DADW.

Having concluded that DADW provisions of a standstill should be per se unenforceable, I obviously believe that any agreement between the target and the acquirer that prohibits the target from waiving the DADW should also be unenforceable. It is interesting to observe that both Vice Chancellor Laster in *Genomics* and Vice Chancellor Glasscock in *NetSpend* dealt with DADWs that were made part of the merger agreement and, therefore, were the most questionable types of restrictions. On the other hand, in *Ancestry*, Chancellor Strine, notwithstanding his criticism of per se rules, found illegal the least restrictive of the DADW provisions in these three cases.

Flawed Single Bidder Process, Including a DADW, But No Injunction—*NetSpend*

In *NetSpend*,[141] Vice Chancellor Glasscock was presented with a motion to enjoin a merger where the board of the target, NetSpend, was acquired in a transaction subject to the *Revlon* standard of review. The court specifically held that the board was not conflicted and, therefore, did not have a duty of loyalty issue. Although the Vice Chancellor concluded that "at trial the Board is likely to show that its initial decision to engage in a single-bidder process was reasonable,"[142] he indicated that this was "not the end of [the] analysis." [143] He explained the remaining issues as follows:

> Where a board decides to forgo a market check and focus on a single bidder, that decision must inform its actions regarding the sale going forward, which in toto must produce a process reasonably designed to maximize price. Thus, my review of the remainder of the sale process, including the reliance on BofA's Fairness Opinion, and the deal-protection devices, including the don't-ask-don't-

141. Koehler v. NetSpend Holdings Inc., 2013 Del. Ch. LEXIS 131 (May 21, 2013).
142. *Id.* at *55.
143. *Id.*

waive clauses, will assess whether the Board's actions were reasonable in light of the Board's awareness that it had no external market check.[144]

After an exhaustive review of the facts, Vice Chancellor Glasscock concluded that the "Defendants will fail to meet their burden at trial of proving that they acted reasonably to maximize share price,"[145] that is, satisfied their *Revlon* responsibilities. He explained:

> [T]he lack of a market check at any stage in this process; the Board's reliance on a weak fairness opinion [where the price was below the DCF (see chapter 11) range]; the deal protections, including the DADW clauses, which were incorporated into the Merger Agreement; and the lack of an anticipated leisurely post-agreement process which would give other suitors the opportunity to appear ... Though several of these facts, alone, are not outside the range of reasonable actions the Board could take, in their aggregate, these facts indicate a process that is unreasonable. In particular, in failing to waive the DADW [don't ask, don't waive, see discussion previously] provisions prior to entering the Merger Agreement, and in agreeing to forgo the right to waive them in the Merger Agreement, without considering or understanding the effect this would have on its duty to act in an informed manner, the Board acted unreasonably. The sale process, reviewed as a whole, was unreasonable.[146]

The Vice Chancellor distinguished the facts in this situation from those in *Pennaco*,[147] discussed previously, where the target also employed a single bidder strategy. On this point the court explained:

> [T]he Pennaco board intentionally conducted a single-bidder process similar to the process undertaken here. Then-Vice Chancellor Strine upheld the Pennaco board's sales process as reasonable. In that case, the Pennaco board had bargained hard for loose deal protections to ensure "that an effective post-agreement market check would occur." The board had negotiated to obtain a non-restrictive no-shop clause and to reduce the termination fee from 5% to 3%. Including matching rights, these were the only deal protections. Finally, despite the presence of the loose no-shop clause, Pennaco and its board contacted other potential bidders before the deal closed to see if any other entity was interested in acquiring Pennaco.[148]

Notwithstanding this finding of a likely breach of the board's *Revlon* duties, the Vice Chancellor refused to enjoin the merger because "the Plaintiff has failed to demonstrate that the equities of the matter favor injunctive relief."[149]

L. The Cumulative Effect of Deal Protection Provisions—*Orchid*[150]

In his 2011 decision in *Orchid Cellmark*,[151] Vice Chancellor Noble of the Delaware Chancery Court addressed, inter alia, the deal protection devices included in a merger

144. *Id.* at *55–*56.
145. *Id.* at *73.
146. *Id.* at *72–*73.
147. In re Pennaco Energy, Inc., 787 A.2d 691, 707 (Del. Ch. 2001).
148. *NetSpend*, at *73–*74.
149. *Id.* at *2.
150. This section is adapted from Thompson, *Mergers, Acquisitions and Tender Offers*, *supra* Section 1.10, at Section 5:5.4[H][6][d].
151. *In re Orchid Cellmark Inc. Shareholder Litigation*, letter to counsel, Vice Chancellor Noble, C.A. No. 6373–VCN (May 12, 2011).

agreement for a combination tender offer and second step merger in which Orchid, a publicly held Delaware corporation, would be acquired by Lab Corp. The Orchid board, which consisted of six directors, five of whom were independent and disinterested, engaged in significant negotiations prior to entering the merger agreement. The court described the deal protection measures as follows:

> The Merger Agreement includes a top-up option [*see* Chapter 2], a no-shop clause, provisions guaranteeing LabCorp the right to match offers and to receive the same information the Company shares with other bidders, and a termination fee payable either where the Company pulls out of the deal or where shareholders fail to tender a majority of shares. Finally, the Company has agreed to pull its poison pill with regard to LabCorp only. That is, the pill remains in place with respect to all other potential bidders, and, in fact, Section 5.2(a)(v) of the Merger Agreement prevents the Company from pulling the pill for other bidders without first terminating the Merger Agreement.[152]

The court points out that although Orchid is "allowed to respond to a 'Superior Offer' by furnishing the bidder with non-public information and by discussing and negotiating over such an offer, those provisions do not relieve [Orchid] of its commitment not to pull the pill for any suitor other than LabCorp."[153] The court also points out that Orchid could only redeem the pill in favor of a topping bid if it first terminated the merger agreement, which it could do if after receiving a Superior Offer, it changes its recommendation that its shareholder tender into the offer by LabCorp. In such case, Orchid would have to pay a termination fee.

In rejecting the plaintiffs' challenge to the termination fee and top-up option, the court reasoned:

> Plaintiffs describe the $2.5 million termination fee as 4.6% of the Company's enterprise value, that is, the Company's value after discounting its $19.8 million of cash on hand. Delaware's case law, however, teaches that such termination fees are generally measured according to a Company's equity value. [Citing *Cogent*, discussed *supra*] Measured on that basis, the termination fee represents less than 3% of the deal price and a termination fee of this size is generally deemed reasonable under Delaware law. [Citing *Cogent*] Finally, although top-up options have been challenged in the recent past, "[t]op-up options have become commonplace in two-step tender offer deals." [Citing *Cogent*][154]

The court addressed as follows the plaintiffs' claim that the court must consider the cumulative deterrent effect of the deal protection measures:

> The Plaintiffs ... correctly argue that the cumulative deterrent effect of all the deal protection measures in the Merger Agreement is greater than simply the sum of the effects of the individual provisions, and thus I must evaluate the cumulative effect of the deal protection devices in light of all the circumstances of the Proposed Transaction.[155]

The court found that in view of the "adequate" sales process run by Orchid's board, the cumulative effect of the deal protection measures withstood a reasonableness test.

---

152. *Id.* at *17–*18.
153. Id. at *19.
154. Id.
155. *Id.* at 21.

However, the court warned that in some subsequent case a court is going to find that the line has been crossed. The court reasoned as follows:

> Deal protection measures evolve. Not surprisingly, we do not have a bright line test to help us all understand when too much is recognized as too much. Moreover, it is not merely a matter of measuring one deal protection device; one must address the sum of all devices. Because of that, one of these days some judge is going to say "no more" and, when the drafting lawyer looks back, she will be challenged to figure out how or why the incremental enhancement mattered. It will be yet another instance of the straw and the poor camel's back. At some point, aggressive deal protection devices—amalgamated as they are—run the risk of being deemed so burdensome and costly as to render the "fiduciary out" illusory.
>
> In any event, the line has not been crossed here.... [156]

M. Introduction to "Go Shops"

1. Background

"Go shops" are provisions of acquisition agreements that specifically permit the target to seek a better deal for a specified period. For an illustration of a "go shop" provision of a merger agreement, *see* Sections 6.2 and 8.5 of the TXU merger agreement, Documentary Appendix Z of *M&A Statutes, Rules, and Documents, supra* Section 1.1. If the provision is "real" it should satisfy the target board's *Revlon* duties. Set out below are the first two Delaware cases addressing "go shops," *Topps* and *Lear*.

2. The "Go Shop" in *Topps*

In Re: The Topps Company Shareholders Litigation

Court of Chancery of Delaware, 2007 Del. Ch. LEXIS 82

STRINE, Vice Chancellor.

Introduction. The Topps Company, Inc. is familiar to all sports-loving Americans. Topps makes baseball and other cards (think Pokemon), this is Topps's so-called "Entertainment Business." It also distributes Bazooka bubble gum and other old-style confections, this is Topps's "Confectionary Business." Arthur Shorin, the son of Joseph Shorin, one of the founders of Topps and the inspiration for "Bazooka Joe," is Topps's current Chairman and Chief Executive Officer. Shorin has served in those positions since 1980 and has worked for Topps for more than half a century, though he owns only about 7% of Topps's equity. Shorin's son-in-law, Scott Silverstein, is his second-in-command, serving as Topps's President and Chief Operating Officer.

Despite its household name, Topps is not a large public company. Its market capitalization is less than a half billion dollars and its financial performance has, as a general matter, flagged over the past five years.

In 2005, Topps was threatened with a proxy contest. It settled that dispute by a promise to explore strategic options, including a sale of its Confectionary Business. Topps tried to auction off its Confectionary Business, but a serious buyer never came forward Insurgents reemerged the next year, in a year when Shorin was among the three directors up for re-

156. *Id.* at 22–23.

election to Topps's classified board. With the ballots about to be counted, and defeat a near certainty for the management nominees, Shorin cut a face-saving deal, which expanded the board to ten and involved his re-election along with the election of all of the insurgent nominees.

Before that happened, former Disney CEO and current private equity investor Michael Eisner had called Shorin and offered to be "helpful." Shorin understood Eisner to be proposing a going private transaction.

Once the insurgents were seated, an "Ad Hoc Committee" was formed of two insurgent directors and two "Incumbent Directors" to evaluate Topps's strategic direction. Almost immediately, the insurgent directors and the incumbent directors began to split on substantive and, it is fair to say, stylistic grounds. The insurgents then became "Dissident Directors."

In particular, the Ad Hoc Committee divided on the issue of whether and how Topps should be sold. The Dissident Directors waxed and waned on the advisability of a sale, but insisted that if a sale was to occur, it should involve a public auction process. The Incumbent Directors were also ambivalent about a sale, but were resistant to the idea that Topps should again begin an auction process, having already failed once in trying to auction its Confectionary Business.

From the time the insurgents were seated, Eisner was on the scene, expressing an interest in making a bid. Two other financial buyers also made a pass. But Topps's public message was that it was not for sale.

Eventually, the other bidders dropped out after making disappointingly low value expressions of interest. Eisner was told by a key Incumbent Director that the Incumbent Directors might embrace a bid of $10 per share. Eisner later bid $9.24 in a proposal that envisioned his retention of existing management, including Shorin's son-in-law. Eisner was willing to tolerate a post-signing Go Shop process, but not a pre-signing auction.

The Ad Hoc Committee split 2–2 over whether to negotiate with Eisner. Although offered the opportunity to participate in the negotiation process, the apparent leader of the Dissidents refused, favoring a public auction. One of the Incumbent Directors who was an independent director took up the negotiating oar, and reached agreement with Eisner on a merger at $9.75 per share. The "Merger Agreement" gave Topps the chance to shop the bid for 40 days after signing, and the right to accept a "Superior Proposal" after that, subject only to Eisner's receipt of a termination fee and his match right.

The Topps board approved the Merger Agreement in a divided vote, with the Incumbent Directors all favoring the Merger, and the Dissidents all dissenting. Because of the dysfunctional relations on the Ad Hoc Committee, that Committee was displaced from dealing with the Go Shop process by an Executive Committee comprised entirely of Incumbent Directors.

Shortly before the Merger Agreement was approved, Topps's chief competitor in the sports cards business, plaintiff The Upper Deck Company, expressed a willingness to make a bid. That likely came as no surprise to Topps since Upper Deck had indicated its interest in Topps nearly a year and half earlier. In fact, Upper Deck had expressed an unrequited ardor for a friendly deal with Topps since 1999, and Shorin knew that. But Topps signed the Merger Agreement with Eisner without responding to Upper Deck's overture. Shortly after the Merger was approved, Topps's investment banker began the Go Shop process, contacting more than 100 potential strategic and financial bidders, including Upper Deck, who was the only serious bidder to emerge.

Suffice it to say that Upper Deck did not move with the clarity and assiduousness one would ideally expect from a competitive rival seeking to make a topping bid. Suffice it also to say that Topps's own reaction to Upper Deck's interest was less than welcoming. Instead of an aggressive bidder and a hungry seller tangling in a diligent, expedited way over key due diligence and deal term issues, the story that emerges from the record is of a slow-moving bidder unwilling to acknowledge Topps's legitimate proprietary concerns about turning over sensitive information to its main competitor and a seller happy to have a bid from an industry rival go away, even if that bid promised the Topps's stockholders better value.

By the end of the Go Shop period, Upper Deck had expressed a willingness to pay $10.75 per share in a friendly merger, subject to its receipt of additional due diligence and other conditions. Although having the option freely to continue negotiations to induce an even more favorable topping bid by finding that Upper Deck's interest was likely to result in a Superior Proposal, the Topps board, with one Dissident Director dissenting, one abstaining, and one absent, voted not to make such a finding.

After the end of the Go Shop period, Upper Deck made another unsolicited overture, expressing a willingness to buy Topps for $ 10.75 without a financing contingency and with a strong come hell or high water promise to deal with manageable (indeed, mostly cosmetic) antitrust issues. The bid, however, limited Topps to a remedy for failing to close limited to a reverse break-up fee in the same amount ($ 12 million) Eisner secured as the only recourse against him. Without ever seriously articulating why Upper Deck's proposal for addressing the antitrust issue was inadequate and without proposing a specific higher reverse break-up fee, the Topps Incumbent Directors have thus far refused to treat Upper Deck as having presented a Superior Proposal, a prerequisite to putting the onus on Eisner to match that price or step aside.

In fact, Topps went public with a disclosure about Upper Deck's bid, but in a form that did not accurately represent that expression of interest and disparaged Upper Deck's seriousness. Topps did that knowing that it had required Upper Deck to agree to a contractual standstill (the "Standstill Agreement") prohibiting Upper Deck from making public any information about its discussions with Topps or proceeding with a tender offer for Topps shares without permission from the Topps board.

The Topps board has refused Upper Deck's request for relief from the Standstill Agreement in order to allow Upper Deck to make a tender offer and to tell its side of events. A vote on the Eisner Merger is scheduled to occur within a couple of weeks.

A group of "Stockholder Plaintiffs" and Upper Deck (collectively, the "moving parties") have moved for a preliminary injunction. They contend that the upcoming Merger vote will be tainted by Topps's failure to disclose material facts about the process that led to the Merger Agreement and about Topps's subsequent dealings with Upper Deck. Even more, they argue that Topps is denying its stockholders the chance to decide for themselves whether to forsake the lower-priced Eisner Merger in favor of the chance to accept a tender offer from Upper Deck at a higher price. Regardless of whether the Topps board prefers the Eisner Merger as lower risk, the moving parties contend that the principles animating *Revlon, Inc. v. MacAndrews & Forbes Holdings, Inc.* prevent the board from denying the stockholders the chance to make a mature, uncoerced decision for themselves. * * * [Only the *Revlon* issue and the go shop are addressed here.]

Factual Background. *The Eisner Merger Agreement.* * * * Eisner and Topps executed the Merger Agreement on March 5, 2006, under which Eisner will acquire Topps for $9.75 per share or a total purchase price of about $385 million. The Merger Agreement is not conditioned on Eisner's ability to finance the transaction, and contains a representation that Eisner has the ability to obtain such financing. But the only remedy against Eisner if he breaches his duties and fails to consummate the Merger is his responsibility to pay a $ 12 million reverse break-up fee.

The "Go Shop" provision in the Merger Agreement works like this. For a period of forty days after the execution of the Merger Agreement, Topps was authorized to solicit alternative bids and to freely discuss a potential transaction with any buyer that might come along. Upon the expiration of the "Go Shop Period," Topps was required to cease all talks with any potential bidders unless the bidder had already submitted a "Superior Proposal," or the Topps board determined that the bidder was an "Excluded Party," which was defined as a potential bidder that the board considered reasonably likely to make a Superior Proposal. If the bidder had submitted a Superior Proposal or was an Excluded Party, Topps was permitted to continue talks with them after the expiration of the Go Shop Period.

The Merger Agreement defined a Superior Proposal as a proposal to acquire at least 60% of Topps that would provide more value to Topps stockholders than the Eisner Merger. The method in which the 60% measure was to be calculated, however, is not precisely defined in the Merger Agreement, but was sought by Eisner in order to require any topping bidder to make an offer for all of Topps, not just one of its Businesses.

Topps was also permitted to consider unsolicited bids after the expiration of the 40-day Go Shop period if the unsolicited bid constituted a Superior Proposal or was reasonably likely to lead to one. Topps could terminate the Merger Agreement in order to accept a Superior Proposal, subject only to Eisner's right to match any other offer to acquire Topps.

The Eisner Merger Agreement contains a two-tier termination fee provision. If Topps terminated the Eisner Merger Agreement in order to accept a Superior Proposal during the Go Shop Period, Eisner was entitled to an $ 8 million termination fee (plus a $ 3.5 million expense reimbursement), in total, or approximately 3.0% of the transaction value. If Topps terminates the Merger Agreement after the expiration of the Go Shop Period, Eisner is entitled to a $ 12 million termination fee (plus a $ 4.5 million expense reimbursement), or approximately 4.6% of the total deal value. * * *

Resolution Of The Revlon Claims And Decision On The Scope Of The Injunction. * * * I do not believe that the substantive terms of the Merger Agreement suggest an unreasonable approach to value maximization. * * *

Critical, of course, to my determination is that the Topps board recognized that they had not done a pre-signing market check. Therefore, they secured a 40-day Go Shop Period and the right to continue discussions with any bidder arising during that time who was deemed by the board likely to make a Superior Proposal. Furthermore, the advantage given to Eisner over later arriving bidders is difficult to see as unreasonable. He was given a match right, a useful deal protection for him, but one that has frequently been overcome in other real-world situations. Likewise, the termination fee and expense reimbursement he was to receive if Topps terminated and accepted another deal—an eventuality more likely to occur after the Go Shop Period expired than during it—was around 4.3% of the total deal value. Although this is a bit high in percentage terms, it includes Eisner's expenses, and therefore can be explained by the relatively small size of the deal. At 42 cents a share, the termination fee (including expenses) is not of the magnitude that I believe was likely to have deterred a bidder with an interest in materially outbidding Eisner. In fact, Upper Deck's expression of interest seems to prove that point—the termination fee is not even one of the factors it stresses.

Although a target might desire a longer Go Shop Period or a lower break fee, the deal protections the Topps board agreed to in the Merger Agreement seem to have left reasonable room for an effective post-signing market check. For 40 days, the Topps board could shop like Paris Hilton. Even after the Go Shop Period expired, the Topps board could entertain an unsolicited bid, and, subject to Eisner's match right, accept a Superior Proposal. The 40-day Go Shop Period and this later right work together, as they allowed interested bidders to talk to Topps and obtain information during the Go Shop Period with the knowledge that if they needed more time to decide whether to make a bid, they could lob in an unsolicited Superior Proposal after the Period expired and resume the process. * * *

[However because] the Topps board is recommending that the stockholders cash out, its decision to foreclose its stockholders from receiving an offer from Upper Deck seems likely, after trial, to be found a breach of fiduciary duty. * * *

[T]he injunction I will issue will not allow Upper Deck to go backwards. * * * The Merger vote will be enjoined until after Topps has granted Upper Deck a waiver of the Standstill to: (1) make an all shares, non-coercive tender offer of $ 10.75 cash or more per share, on conditions as to financing and antitrust no less favorable to Topps than contained in Upper Deck's most recent offer; and (2) communicate with Topps stockholders about its version of relevant events. * * *

N. Fiduciary Duty Issues with Respect to the Use of Top-Up Options—*Cogent*

Top-up options, which are examined more fully in Section 20.10, may be employed in two-step acquisition transactions, where the first step is a consensual tender offer and the second step is a merger. The top-up option is used, if needed, after the first-step tender offer to get the acquiror over the 90% stock ownership threshold required for a short form merger. As pointed out in Section 20.10, with the enactment of Section 251(h) of the DGCL, top-up options are not needed in most two-step transactions.

§ 3.21 Elaboration on the *Blasius* Compelling Justification Test

A. Introduction

This section examines some of the cases that have considered the compelling justification test, which was first enunciated by Chancellor Allen in *Blasius*, one of the "Big Six."

B. Review *Blasius*, Section 3.14.G.

C. Delaware Supreme Court Clarifies *Blasius* Standard in *Unocal* Context—*Liquid Audio*

MM Companies, Inc. v. Liquid Audio, Inc.

Delaware Supreme Court, 2003 Del. Lexis 5

HOLLAND, Justice:

This is an expedited appeal [by MM, a shareholder of Liquid Audio, a Delaware corporation] from a final judgment entered by the Court of Chancery [permitting Liquid Audio's] incumbent board of directors to adopt defense measures which changed the size and composition of the board's membership. * * * [At an August 22, 2002 meeting, the Liquid Audio] Board expanded the size of the Board from five to seven members and [appointed] two new directors to those recently created vacancies. * * * On September 26, 2002, Liquid Audio held its 2002 annual meeting at which MM's two nominees were elected as Class III directors replacing [two] incumbent directors. * * *

Procedural Background. * * * [MM's] amended complaint * * * alleges that the Director Defendants' decision to expand the Board violated the principles established by *Blasius* and *Unocal.*

Chancery Court Denies Relief. * * * At the conclusion of the trial, the Court of Chancery ruled in favor of the defendants, holding that the Board expansion did not violate Delaware law under either *Blasius* or *Unocal.* The Court of Chancery rejected the plaintiff's independent *Blasius* claim on the basis that the addition of two new directors "did not impact the shareholder vote or the shareholder choices in any significant way." The Court of Chancery rejected the plaintiff's *Unocal* claim, on the basis that: plaintiff did "not contend that the board expansion was coercive," the expansion was not "preclusive," because the "choices that the shareholders had before the board action was taken were the same as they had after," and the plaintiff failed to make a showing that "the action that the board took falls outside a range of reasonable responses."

Issues on Appeal. MM has raised two issues on appeal. First, it contends that the Court of Chancery erred in ruling that the "compelling justification" standard, as enunciated in *Blasius,* was not applicable to the Board's action. In support of that argument, MM relies upon the finding by the Court of Chancery that the Director Defendants manipulated the size and composition of the Liquid Audio board during a contested election for directors *primarily* to interfere with and impede the success of MM's ability to gain two-of-five directorships on the Board, and, thus, to diminish the influence of MM's nominees on the Board.

Second, MM argues that the Court of Chancery erred in ruling that the precepts of this Court's holding in *Unocal* and its progeny were not violated by the Board's defensive action. According to MM, the Director Defendants never identified a legally cognizable threat to the corporate policy and effectiveness of Liquid Audio and, to the extent that a threat existed, never demonstrated that the "manipulation of the size and composition" of the Liquid Audio board was a reasonable response in relation to such threat. Based upon that asserted lack of record evidence, MM submits the Court of Chancery erred in concluding that this Court's holding in *Unocal* was not violated.

Background Facts. * * * ***Board's Primary Purpose: Impede Effective Vote.*** * * * During pretrial discovery, the Director Defendants identified the primary purpose of their action in expanding the Liquid Audio board from five to seven members. Their response to the following interrogatory request is illustrative:

> Summarize the complete reasons that support the decision of the Board to amend the Bylaws or to approve the Bylaw Amendment.
>
> Response: Subject to and without waiving the General Objections stated above, Defendants state that the Board of Directors, after receiving legal advice regarding their fiduciary duties, voted to expand the size of the board after a thorough and deliberate evaluation of the qualifications and expected contributions of Judith N. Frank and James D. Somes to Liquid's current operations and business plans. Furthermore, the Board of Directors believed that the Company would benefit from having seven directors instead of only five directors. In particular, the Company believed that it would benefit from creating new directorships and

> placing two additional outside directors on the board in light of the potential difficulties that may result from the addition of MM's nominees on the Board and in light of the possibility that one or more directors would decide to resign for a variety of reasons including, but not limited to, a reluctance to serve alongside a slate of directors proposed by MM * * *

By adding two additional directors, the board foreclosed * * * [t]he possibility of a deadlock or of MM taking control of the board. The reason is that even if MM's two nominees were elected at the 2002 annual meeting, the current directors would still constitute a majority of five. The result of the board's action was to *diminish the influence of any nominees of MM* that were elected, at least in numerical terms. Thus, based upon the evidence presented at trial * * * , the Court of Chancery concluded that the Director Defendants amended the bylaws to expand the Board from five to seven, appointed two additional members of the Board, and timed those actions for the *primary purpose* of diminishing the influence of MM's nominees, if they were elected at the annual meeting. * * *

Corporate Governance Review Standards. * * *In *Blasius*, Chancellor Allen set forth a cogent explanation of why judicial review under the deferential traditional business judgment rule standard is inappropriate when a board of directors acts for the *primary* purpose of impeding or interfering with the effectiveness of a shareholder vote, especially in the specific context presented in *Blasius* of a contested election for directors:

The ordinary considerations to which the business judgment rule originally responded are simply not present in the shareholder voting context. That is, a decision by the board to act for the primary purpose of preventing the effectiveness of a shareholder vote inevitably involves the question who, as between the principal and the agent, has authority with respect to a matter of internal corporate governance. That, of course, is true in a very specific way in this case which deals with the question who should constitute the board of directors of the corporation, but it will be true in every instance in which an incumbent board seeks to thwart a shareholder majority. * * *

In *Blasius*, the Chancellor set aside the board's action to expand the size of its membership for the primary purpose of impeding and interfering with the effectiveness of a shareholder vote in a contested election for directors. In this case, not only did the Liquid Audio board of directors take similar action in expanding the size of its membership and appointing two new directors to fill those positions, but it took that action for the same *primary* purpose.

Compelling Justification Within Unocal. The *Blasius* compelling justification standard of enhanced judicial review is based upon accepted and well-established legal tenets. This Court and the Court of Chancery have recognized the substantial degree of congruence between the rationale that led to the *Blasius* "compelling justification" enhanced standard of judicial review and the logical extension of that rationale *within* the context of the *Unocal* enhanced standard of judicial review. Both standards recognize the inherent conflicts of interest that arise when a board of directors acts to prevent shareholders from effectively exercising their right to vote either contrary to the will of the incumbent board members generally or to replace the incumbent board members in a contested election. * * *

The "compelling justification" standard set forth in *Blasius* is applied independently or within the *Unocal* standard only where "the primary purpose of the board's action is to interfere with or impede exercise of the shareholder franchise and the shareholders are not given a full and fair opportunity to vote effectively. Accordingly, this Court has noted that the non-deferential *Blasius* standard of enhanced judicial review, which imposes upon a board of directors the burden of demonstrating a compelling justification for such actions, is rarely applied either independently or within the *Unocal* standard of review.

In *Unitrin*, [Section 3.18.E.5], for example, although the board's action in adopting a repurchase program was a defensive measure that implicated the shareholders' franchise and called for an application of the *Unocal* standard of review, it did not require the board to demonstrate a compelling justification for that action. In *Unitrin*, the primary purpose of the repurchase program was not to interfere with or impede the shareholders' right to vote; the shareholders' right to vote effectively remained extant; and, in particular, we noted that the shareholders retained sufficient voting power to challenge the incumbent board by electing new directors with a successful proxy contest.

In this case, however, the Court of Chancery was presented with the ultimate defensive measure touching upon an issue of control. It was a defensive action taken by an incumbent board of directors for the primary purpose of interfering with and impeding the effectiveness of the shareholder franchise in electing successor directors. Accordingly, the incumbent board of directors had the burden of demonstrating a compelling justification for that action to withstand enhanced judicial scrutiny *within* the *Unocal* standard of reasonableness and proportionality.

Unocal Required Compelling Justification. This case presents a paragon of when the compelling justification standard of *Blasius* must be applied within *Unocal's* requirement that any defensive measure be proportionate and reasonable in relation to the threat posed. The *Unocal* standard of review applies because the Liquid Audio board's action was a "defensive measure taken in response to some threat to corporate policy and effectiveness which touches upon issues of control." The compelling justification standard of *Blasius* also had to be applied *within* an application of the *Unocal* standard to that specific defensive measure because the primary purpose of the Board's action was to interfere with or impede the effective exercise of the shareholder franchise in a contested election for directors.

The Court of Chancery properly decided to examine the Board's defensive action to expand from five to seven members and to appoint two new members in accordance with the *Unocal* standard of enhanced judicial review. Initially, the Court of Chancery concluded that defensive action was not preclusive or coercive. If a defensive measure is not draconian, because it is neither coercive nor preclusive, proportionality review under *Unocal* requires the focus of enhanced judicial scrutiny to shift to the range of reasonableness.

After the Court of Chancery determined that the Board's action was not preclusive or coercive, it properly proceeded to determine whether the Board's action was reasonable and proportionate in relation to the threat posed.[157] Under the circumstances presented in this case, however, the Court of Chancery did not "recognize the special [importance] of protecting the shareholder's franchise within *Unocal's* requirement that any defensive measure be proportionate and reasonable in relation to the threat posed." Since the Court of Chancery had already concluded that the *primary* purpose of the Liquid Audio board's defensive measure was to interfere with or impede an effective exercise of the shareholder's franchise in a contested election of directors, the Board had the burden of demonstrating a compelling justification for that action.

When the *primary purpose* of a board of directors' defensive measure is to interfere with or impede the effective exercise of the shareholder franchise in a contested election

157. In our review of the Court of Chancery's *Unocal* analysis, we have assumed without deciding that the Board was independent and had reasonable grounds for believing that there was a danger to corporate policy.

for directors, the board must first demonstrate a compelling justification for such action as a condition precedent to any judicial consideration of reasonableness and proportionately. As this case illustrates, such defensive actions by a board need not actually prevent the shareholders from attaining any success in seating one or more nominees in a contested election for directors and the election contest need not involve a challenge for outright control of the board of directors. To invoke the *Blasius* compelling justification standard of review *within* an application of the *Unocal* standard of review, the defensive actions of the board only need to be taken for the primary purpose of interfering with or impeding the effectiveness of the stockholder vote in a contested election for directors.

Board Expansion Invalid. The record reflects that the primary purpose of the Director Defendants' action was to interfere with and impede the effective exercise of the stockholder franchise in a contested election for directors. * * * Since the Director Defendants did not demonstrate a compelling justification for that defensive action, the bylaw amendment that expanded the size of the Liquid Audio board, and permitted the appointment of two new members on the eve of a contested election, should have been invalidated by the Court of Chancery. * * *

D. Vice Chancellor Strine's Suggested Modification of the *Blasius* Standard—*Mercier*

Mercier v. Inter-Tel (Delaware), Incorporated

Court of Chancery of Delaware, 2007 Del. Ch. LEXIS 119

STRINE, Vice Chancellor.

In this decision based on a preliminary injunction record, I conclude that well-motivated, independent directors may reschedule an imminent special meeting at which the stockholders are to consider an all cash, all shares offer from a third-party acquiror when the directors: (1) believe that the merger is in the best interests of the stockholders; (2) know that if the meeting proceeds the stockholders will vote down the merger; (3) reasonably fear that in the wake of the merger's rejection, the acquiror will walk away from the deal and the corporation's stock price will plummet; (4) want more time to communicate with and provide information to the stockholders before the stockholders vote on the merger and risk the irrevocable loss of the pending offer; and (5) reschedule the meeting within a reasonable time period and do not preclude or coerce the stockholders from freely deciding to reject the merger.

In the course of so deciding, I conclude that, consistent with the directional teaching of cases like *MM Companies, Inc. v. Liquid Audio, Inc.*, *In re MONY Group, Inc. S'holders Litig.* and *Chesapeake Corp. v. Shore*, the *Blasius* standard should be reformulated in a manner consistent with using it as a genuine standard of review that is useful for the determination of cases, rather than as an after-the-fact label placed on a result. Such a reformulation would be consistent with prior decisions recognizing the substantial overlap between and redundancy of the *Blasius* and *Unocal* standards, and would have the added benefit of creating a less prolix list of standards of review. Recognizing, however, that the Supreme Court's recent decision in Liquid Audio continued to employ the "compelling justification" language of *Blasius* within the context of an appropriate *Unocal* review of director conduct that affects a corporate election touching on corporate control, I also find that directors fearing that stockholders are about to make an unwise decision that poses the threat that the stockholders will irrevocably lose a unique opportunity to receive a premium for their shares have a compelling justification—the protection of their stockholders' financial best interests—for a short postponement in the merger voting process to allow more time for deliberation.

Therefore, the plaintiff's request for a preliminary injunction application based on the contrary assumption—that directors have no discretion as fiduciaries to reschedule a vote once a stockholder meeting is imminent and the directors know that the vote won't go their way if it is held as originally scheduled—is denied. * * *

[The following addresses only Vice Chancellor Strine's proposed standard of review that would replace *Blasius*.]

As is easy to grasp, the nettlesome problem here is what standard of review applies to the plaintiff's equitable claim. The plaintiff, of course, contends that this is a quintessential case calling for the application of the standard of review announced in the landmark decision of *Blasius Industries, Inc. v. Atlas Corp.* He says that the Inter-Tel Special Committee acted for the primary purpose of thwarting the opportunity for the majority of the stockholders of Inter-Tel to express their opposition to the Mitel Merger on June 29. Therefore, he contends that the Special Committee must demonstrate a compelling justification for flouting the majority will. * * *

For their part, the Special Committee argues that the plaintiff has failed to identify any self-interest on their part that would improperly motivate their support for the Mitel Merger. As the Special Committee points out, its members expect to lose their jobs as soon as the Mitel Merger is consummated. * * * [T]he Special Committee says it is impossible to attribute their motives to a desire to entrench themselves, and that their actions should be judged under the deferential business judgment rule standard. As they point out, this standard of review was applied to director action to postpone a merger vote and set a new record date in the recent *In re MONY Group, Inc. Shareholders Litigation* case, although only after a searching inquiry into the necessity and motivation for, as well as the reasonableness and effect of, the board's action.

It would hardly be indiscreet for me to acknowledge yet again the widely known reality that our law has struggled to define with certainty the standard of review this court should use to evaluate director action affecting the conduct of corporate elections. The results in the cases make sense, as the decisions do a good job of sorting between situations when directors have unfairly manipulated the electoral process to entrench themselves against insurgents and those when directors have properly used their authority over the election process for good faith reasons that do not compromise the integrity of the election process. The problem that remains though is that there is no certain prism through which judges are to view cases like this. The great strength of *Blasius*—its reminder of the importance of the director election process and the barrier the decision draws to the acceptance of the bizarre doctrine of "substantive coercion" as to the question of who should constitute the board—came along with some overbroad language that rendered the standard of review articulated in the case too crude a tool for regular employment. As has been noted elsewhere, the trigger for the test's application—director action that has the primary purpose of disenfranchisement—is so pejorative that it is more a label for a result than a useful guide to determining what standard of review should be used by a judge to reach an appropriate result. As a result, decisions in the wake of *Blasius* tended to involve threshold exertions in reasoning as to why director action influencing the ability of stockholders to act did not amount to disenfranchisement, thus obviating the need to apply *Blasius* at all. * * *

The Delaware Supreme Court's relatively recent decision in *MM Companies, Inc. v. Liquid Audio, Inc.* can be read as signaling that Court's recognition that a clearer approach to corporate election disputes was necessary, and that the stringency of the *Blasius* approach should be reserved largely for director election contests or election contests having consequences for corporate control. In that case, the Supreme Court strove to bring the *Blasius* and *Unocal* standards together in a workable manner. * * *

Although it does not use those precise words, *Liquid Audio* can be viewed as requiring the directors to show that their actions were reasonably necessary to advance a compelling corporate interest.

That formulation is an improved one but still a problematic one. The "compelling justification" standard remains, and no decision has, before today, found it satisfied. As a result, the temptation to avoid applying the standard as an actual means to make a decision rather than a post-hoc label will remain. * * *

Consistent with the directional impulse of *Liquid Audio,* I believe that the standard of review that ought to be employed in this case is a reasonableness standard consistent with the *Unocal* standard. * * *

To be specific, I believe that in this case, the burden should be on the Inter-Tel board as an initial matter to identify a legitimate corporate objective served by its decision to reschedule the June 29 special meeting on the Mitel Merger and to set a new record date. As part of meeting that burden, the directors should bear the burden of persuasion to show that their motivations were proper and not selfish. That showing, however, is not sufficient to ultimately prevail. To ultimately succeed, the directors must show that their actions were reasonable in relation to their legitimate objective, and did not preclude the stockholders from exercising their right to vote or coerce them into voting a particular way. If for some reason, the fit between means and end is not reasonable, the directors would also come up short. * * *

Unlike the Inter-Tel Special Committee, I am not troubled by the application of this form of reasonableness review to stockholder votes on mergers. For nearly a quarter of a century, Delaware law has subjected directors to reasonableness review as to much of their conduct in the M & A context. * * *

Because it would be impossible and inappropriate for me to ignore the existence of *Liquid Audio* and other Delaware Supreme Court decisions continuing to refer to a compelling justification standard, I will apply the analysis I have outlined, which I believe is consistent with the direction the teaching in *Liquid Audio* logically leads, but will also expressly set forth whether I conclude that the Inter-Tel Special Committee has demonstrated a compelling justification for its actions. * * *

§ 3.22 Issues in Sales of Publicly Held Controlled Corporations

A. Introduction

This section addresses other issues that can arise in the context of a sale of a controlled corporation, principally a publicly held, controlled corporation. This section does not address issues arising where a controlling shareholder acquires the stock of minority shareholders, a topic examined previously in connection with the discussion of the entire fairness doctrine. Also, this section does not address issues arising when a controlling shareholder of a closely held corporation sells its controlling shares. Those issues are addressed in Chapter 11, which deals with the acquisition of the stock of closely held corporations.

B. Controlling Shareholder's Responsibility in Structuring a Third-Party Tender Offer and Freezeout Merger of a Sub—*McMullin*

McMullin v. Beran

Delaware Supreme Court, 2000 Del. LEXIS 481

Justice HOLLAND.

The plaintiff-appellant, Mary E. McMullin, a purported shareholder of ARCO Chemical Company ("Chemical"), filed this putative class action against Chemical, its directors (the "Individual Defendants" or the "Chemical Directors") [and] Atlantic Richfield Company ("ARCO") * * * . ARCO owned 80% of Chemical's common stock. The Amended Complaint alleged that the Individual Defendants and ARCO * * * breached their fiduciary duties in connection with [the] acquisition of Chemical's shares at $57.75 per share [by a third party] (the "Transaction").

All defendants filed motions to dismiss the Amended Complaint. * * * The Court of Chancery granted the * * * defendants' motions to dismiss.

McMullin has raised three issues on appeal. Her first contention is that ARCO and the Chemical Directors were obligated to maximize value for all Chemical shareholders in the sale of the company to [the acquiror] Lyondell. Thus, according to McMullin, the Court of Chancery erred in holding that defendants' *Revlon* duty to maximize shareholder value was not "implicated" in this case. McMullin's second contention is that Chemical's Directors violated their fiduciary duties to manage the sale of Chemical by delegating control of the sale process to ARCO. According to McMullin, the Court of Chancery erred in holding that Chemical's Directors were justified in delegating their managerial responsibilities to ARCO simply because ARCO owned 80% of Chemical and no transaction could proceed without ARCO's approval. * * *

We have concluded that the Court of Chancery should not have granted the remaining defendant's motion to dismiss McMullin's Amended Complaint. Therefore, the judgment must be reversed.

Facts.* * * Before the Transaction, ARCO owned 80 million shares of Chemical's common stock, representing 80.1% of Chemical's outstanding shares. * * *

In mid-March, ARCO informed Chemical's Directors that it "had received indications of interest for an acquisition of all of the outstanding shares of the Common Stock." The Chemical Directors authorized ARCO to explore the sale of the entire company. * * *

[After several lower offers on] June 13, 1998, Lyondell made yet another revised bid, offering $57.75 in cash per share to purchase all of Chemical's outstanding stock. After negotiations, on June 17, 1998, Lyondell submitted a merger agreement and other related contracts. The Lyondell proposal contemplated a tender offer to purchase all outstanding shares of the Company for $57.75 per share, a commitment from ARCO to tender its 80 million shares of Chemical at the same $57.75 price paid to the minority, and a second-step merger whereby all untendered shares would be cashed out at the same time.

On June 18, 1998, Chemical's Board of Directors met to consider the Lyondell proposal. Representatives of ARCO and Salomon made presentations regarding the terms of the Lyondell proposal and the sale process. Merrill Lynch, Chemical's financial advisor, made a presentation and expressed its opinion that $57.75 per share was fair to Chemical's stockholders, other than ARCO, from a financial point of view. Chemical's Board of Directors unanimously approved the Transaction.

On June 24, 1998, Lyondell commenced its Tender Offer. The next day, Chemical filed its Schedule 14D-9. [This is a required SEC document setting out the position of the target's board on the transaction. *See* Chapter 20]. On July 23, 1998, the Tender Offer was completed, with 99% of Chemical's shares tendering to Lyondell. Shortly thereafter, Lyondell completed the second-step merger. None of the former Chemical shareholders sought to exercise their rights of appraisal. * * *

[**Discussion**] * * * McMullin does not dispute ARCO's right to sell its own 80% interest in Chemical for whatever consideration might have been acceptable to it, whether for cash or stock or a mixture of cash and stock. McMullin also acknowledges that this case does not involve a "change of control" of Chemical, as that concept has been described in the prior decisions of this Court. The Amended Complaint does contend that the Chemical Board's recommendation to approve the Lyondell Transaction implicated the directors' ultimate fiduciary duty that was described in *Revlon* and its progeny—to focus on whether shareholder value has been maximized. We agree with that contention because, rather than selling only its own 80% interest, ARCO negotiated for, with the Chemical Board's approval, the entire sale of Chemical to Lyondell.

The Amended Complaint would withstand a motion to dismiss if it successfully alleged facts that, if true, would rebut the procedural presumption of the business judgment rule. To do that, McMullin had to successfully allege that the Chemical Board had breached any one of its triad of fiduciary duties of care, loyalty or good faith. McMullin contends that the allegations in her Amended Complaint demonstrate that the Chemical Board breached both its duty of care and its duty of loyalty. If McMullin is correct with regard to either or both of her contentions, the Chemical Directors' motion to dismiss should have been denied.

Care Allegations. Under Section 251, a director is required "to act in an informed and deliberate manner in determining whether to approve an agreement of merger before submitting the proposal to the stockholders." A director's duty to exercise an informed business judgment implicates the duty of care. Director liability for breaching the duty of care "is predicated upon concepts of gross negligence." [*See Van Gorkom*, Section 3.14.C]

McMullin's Amended Complaint alleges that ARCO initiated and timed the Transaction to benefit itself because ARCO needed cash to fund the $3.3 billion cash acquisition of Union Texas Petroleum Holdings that ARCO announced on May 4, 1998. McMullin alleges that the Chemical Board authorized ARCO to unilaterally negotiate the merger agreement without establishing any procedural safeguards to protect the interests of the minority shareholders. * * *

One can reasonably infer from the factual allegations in McMullin's Amended Complaint that the Chemical Board compromised its deliberative process by seeking to accommodate ARCO's immediate need for cash. The Chemical Directors were obligated to determine whether the third-party Transaction with Lyondell that was being advanced by the majority shareholder, would maximize value for the minority shareholders in the sale of Chemical. The specific allegations contained in McMullin's Amended Complaint, if true, suggest that the directors of Chemical breached their duty of care by approving the merger with Lyondell without adequately informing themselves about the transaction and without determining whether the merger consideration equaled or exceeded Chemical's appraisal value as a going concern.

Loyalty Allegations. When the Chemical Board was considering a sale of the entire corporation, it was impermissible for the directors to allow any improper influence to compromise their evaluation of whether the proposed third party transaction with Lyondell would achieve maximum value for all Chemical shareholders. The ARCO officers and designees on Chemical's board owed Chemical's minority shareholders "an uncompromising duty of loyalty." There is no dilution of that obligation in a parent subsidiary context for the individuals who acted in a dual capacity as officers or designees of ARCO and as directors of Chemical. * * *

The allegations of loyalty to ARCO in McMullin's Amended Complaint challenge the independence of the Chemical Board. * * * The record reflects that the defendant directors should be required to file an answer to the well-pled loyalty allegations in McMullin's Amended Complaint, regarding the effects of the ARCO-related conflicts. * * *

C. Controlling Shareholder Receives Premium for High Vote Stock—*TCI*

In Re Tele-Communications, Inc. Shareholders Litigation

Delaware Court of Chancery, 2005 Del. Ch. Lexis 206

CHANDLER, Chancellor.

The plaintiffs in this purported class action are shareholders of Series A TCI Group Common Stock ("TCOMA"), a tracking stock reflecting the performance of the TCI Group division of Tele-Communications, Inc. ("TCI") [a Delaware corporation]. The TCOMA shareholders * * * alleg[e] breaches of fiduciary duties by the directors of TCI in relation to a merger with a subsidiary of AT&T Corp. ("AT&T"). [Specifically they allege that the board of TCI did not fulfill its fiduciary duties in agreeing to pay the Series B TCI Group Common Stock (TCOMB) a premium over what the TCOMA received in the merger.] Presently before this Court is the individual defendants' motion for summary judgment. Because the record raises triable issues of fact as to whether the merger was entirely fair to the TCOMA shareholders and in respect to certain disclosure claims, the motion for summary judgment is denied in respect to such claims. * * *

[**Basic Facts**] * * * [I]t appears that the persons most involved in the [merger] discussions on behalf of TCI were defendants Malone [Chairman and CEO of TCI] and Hindery [President of TCI]. The record is clear that Malone insisted from the outset that, in order to obtain his consent and approval for the transaction, the TCOMB [which he held a large percentage of] would have to receive a premium of ten percent over the consideration received by the TCOMA. * * *

ANALYSIS. * * *

Substantive Standard of Review.**Entire Fairness Applies to the Transaction.** * * * A plaintiff generally rebuts the business judgment rule by alleging (and then demonstrating at trial) a breach of fiduciary duty. In transactions where directors stand "on both sides of a transaction, they are required to demonstrate their utmost good faith and the most scrupulous inherent fairness of the bargain." A demonstration of fairness is also appropriate in evaluating transactions between the corporation and a third party when the directors of the corporation (and the affiliates of such directors) own significant non-majority stakes of the corporation's voting shares and have personal interests that significantly diverge from those of other equity holders. * * *

Evidence in the record suggests that a majority of the board of directors materially benefited from the TCOMB premium: Malone (over $100,000,000), Magness (over $90,000,000), Hindery (over $5,500,000), Gould (over $1,000,000) and Fisher (over $500,000). In light of what these directors actually received in the transaction, such interests in approving the TCOMB premium were substantial, and the benefits were material to each respective director. Therefore, a standard of entire fairness applies.

The Burden of Proving Entire Fairness Rests on Defendants. The initial burden of proof rests upon the director defendants to demonstrate the fairness of a particular transaction. Ratification of the transaction by disinterested directors or shareholders can have a powerful legal effect. Ratification by a majority of disinterested directors, generally serving on a special committee, can have the effect of shifting the burden onto the plaintiff shareholders to demonstrate that the transaction in question was unfair. [Citing *Lynch*, Section 3.16.D] In order to shift the burden, defendants must establish that the special committee was truly independent, fully informed, and had the freedom to negotiate at arm's length.

On this motion, where I must draw all reasonable inferences in favor of plaintiffs, facts in the record suggest that the Special Committee was not fully disinterested. * * *

CONCLUSION. * * * Because defendants have not demonstrated that the merger was entirely fair to the TCOMA holders, defendants' summary judgment motion is hereby denied.

D. Controlling Shareholder Sells Itself Rather Than a Controlled Sub—*Digex*

In Re Digex, Inc. Shareholders Litigation

Delaware Court of Chancery, 2000 Del. Ch. LEXIS 171

Chandler, Chancellor.

This is my decision on plaintiffs' motion to preliminarily enjoin the proposed merger between defendants WorldCom, Inc. ("WorldCom") [the acquiring corporation] and Intermedia Communications, Inc. ("Intermedia") [the target], the controlling shareholder of Digex, Inc. ("Digex") [the potential target a publicly held corporation]. Plaintiffs, minority shareholders of Digex, seek either of two alternative forms of relief: (1) an order enjoining the defendants from consummating the Agreement and Plan of Merger dated September 1, 2000, (the "merger"), or (2) an order enjoining the Digex board's waiver of 8 Del. C. § 203. [This Section 203 issue is addressed in Chapter 22.] * * *

Plaintiffs' first theory is that defendants usurped a corporate opportunity that (allegedly) fairly belonged to Digex by preventing Digex's sale to the highest bidder. * * * [The facts show that WorldCom was interested in acquiring Digex, but the transaction was structured instead as an acquisition of Intermedia, the controlling shareholder of Digex.]

The Corporate Opportunity Claim. Delaware Courts employ the following test to determine whether a corporate opportunity has been usurped by a fiduciary. The corporate opportunity will be found to have been usurped:

> If there is presented to a corporate officer or director a business opportunity which the corporation is financially able to undertake, [and that opportunity] is * * * in the line of the corporation's business and is of practical advantage to it, is one in which the corporation has an interest or a reasonable expectancy, and, by embracing the opportunity, the self-interest of the officer or director will be brought into conflict with that of his corporation . * * *

It is with this test in mind that I will evaluate the plaintiffs' claim that the defendants have usurped a corporate opportunity belonging to Digex.

Summary of the Arguments. The plaintiffs argue that they satisfy all elements of the test for the usurpation of a corporate opportunity and, thus, there is a likelihood that they will succeed on the merits at trial. The opportunity that plaintiffs insist they had was an "expectancy" in selling their Digex shares to a buyer for approximately $120.00 per share.

That expectancy, the plaintiffs urge, was created by Intermedia's alleged promise that any deal Intermedia brokered would include a sale of the Digex minority shareholders' shares. As the argument goes, the defendants breached their fiduciary duties when the Intermedia—affiliated Digex directors allegedly steered WorldCom away from a Digex deal and towards an Intermedia deal. * * *

The defendants * * * argue [*inter alia*] that there was no corporate opportunity to usurp because "Intermedia owns an absolute majority of Digex's voting rights and equity. Intermedia is entitled to sell or refuse to sell its Digex stock solely in its own interest; it is entitled to vote its shares in its own interest; and, neither the Digex board nor its shareholders can sell Digex without Intermedia's consent." * * *

Legal Analysis.* * * I conclude that Digex, as a corporation, had no legally cognizable "interest or expectancy" in a WorldCom–Digex deal. Thus, the plaintiffs will not be able to prove an element of the corporate opportunity doctrine and are unlikely to succeed on the merits. * * *

Why Digex had no "interest or expectancy" in a WorldCom–Digex deal. A claim that a director or officer improperly usurped a corporate opportunity belonging to the corporation is a derivative claim. * * *

Here, the plaintiffs contend that the defendants, by allegedly steering WorldCom away from a Digex deal and towards an Intermedia deal, appropriated an opportunity that belonged to the plaintiffs. That opportunity was the ability to sell Digex to the highest bidder.

The opportunity the plaintiffs identify, however, is not an "interest or expectancy" of Digex the corporation qua corporation. Rather, the purported opportunity is that of the Digex *shareholders* to sell their Digex shares to the highest bidder. Thus, the perceived corporate opportunity is not really a *corporate* opportunity at all, but more closely resembles an individual opportunity of the shareholders. Because the opportunity the plaintiffs identify was not one in which Digex as a corporation had an "interest or expectancy," plaintiffs do not have a reasonable likelihood of success on such a claim.

The present case also is strikingly similar to *Thorpe v. CERBCO, Inc.*,. * * * In *CERBCO*, the Supreme Court held that where a majority shareholder of a corporation can block any unacceptable transaction, the corporation cannot take advantage of the opportunity to enter into an unsanctioned transaction and, thus, there is no opportunity that fairly belongs to the corporation. * * *

I understand the Supreme Court's holding in *CERBCO* to require a finding that, while majority shareholders may breach their duty of loyalty on similar facts, the powers inherent in the majority status generally preclude a plaintiff from claiming that a corporate opportunity has been usurped where the majority shareholder could have blocked the transaction in any event. This is so because no "interest or expectation" fairly belonged to the corporation since the majority could block the transaction at any time. * * *

The Digex minority existed before the proposed merger and it will not change under the proposed transaction. What will change is the ownership of Digex's majority shareholder, Intermedia.[158]

---

158. It is noteworthy that the Supreme Court's recent decision in *McMullin* appears to indicate that even if Intermedia were selling its approximately 60% equity interest in Digex, rather than selling itself, that transaction also would not trigger *Revlon*. *See McMullin* [Section 3.22.B] ("The Amended Complaint does contend that the Chemical Board's recommendation to approve the Lyondell Transaction

[**Impact of *Revlon***] Finally, it is important to recognize that any effort to sell Digex in a *Revlon-style* auction would appear to be futile. As Vice Chancellor Lamb observed in *Odyssey Partners, L.P. v. Fleming Co., Inc.*: "*Revlon* duties do not arise where the directors do not have the power to control the terms on which a sale of the company takes place." Where, as here, a majority shareholder can block proposed transactions involving a sale of control, the courts will not require a board of directors to engage in 'a futile exercise, even though the board continues to owe requisite fiduciary duties to its shareholders. This claim thus has little chance of ultimate success. * * *

E. Controlling Shareholder Rejects Sale of Target in Favor of Investment by Third Party in Target—*Paxson*

In Re Paxson Communication Corporation Shareholders Litigation

Delaware Court of Chancery
2001 Del. Ch. LEXIS 95

CHANDLER, Chancellor.

This action arises out of the alleged rejection of a cash offer for Paxson Communications Corporation ("Pax" or the "Company") from Fox Network ("Fox") and the later acceptance by Pax of a series of agreements (the "NBC Transactions") with the National Broadcasting Company, Inc. ("NBC"). The plaintiffs allege that Fox made an all cash offer of $20 per share for Pax common stock (the "Fox Offer") that was summarily rejected by the directors and/or senior officers of Pax. Shortly after the alleged Fox Offer, NBC invested $415 million in Pax in exchange for convertible preferred stock, certain warrants, and the right to purchase certain shares owned by Pax's controlling stockholder, Lowell W. Paxson. * * *

Analysis * * * In this case, the plaintiffs assert that they have suffered two distinct, direct injuries that each bestow standing on the plaintiffs to bring direct claims against the defendants. Plaintiffs point to the dilution of their ownership interest, earnings per share and voting power due to the effect of the NBC Transactions. [Equity Dilution Claim] Additionally, plaintiffs argue that the Pax Board's failure to pursue the Fox Offer in favor of the NBC Transactions resulted in the loss of the opportunity for the shareholders to receive optimum value for their investment in Pax. I address each of these contentions in turn. * * *

[**Equity Dilution Claim**] First, the plaintiffs argue that "it is well-settled that equity dilution and diminution of one's voting power constitutes a direct injury to the shareholders and not the corporation." They contend that the NBC Transactions will dilute the equity and voting power of the plaintiff shareholders should NBC Sub I convert its 41,500 shares of preferred stock into 31,896,032 shares of common stock and NBC Sub II exercise its warrants to purchase a total of 32,032,127 shares of Pax common stock.

Plaintiffs point to two cases, *In re Tri-Star Pictures, Inc. Litigation*[634 A.2d 319 (Del 1993)] and *Oliver, et al. v. Boston University, et al.*[2000 Del. Ch. LEXIS 104] to support the proposition that their dilution claim is direct rather than derivative. Their reliance

---

implicated the directors' ultimate fiduciary duty that was described in *Revlon* and its progeny—to focus on whether shareholder value has been maximized. We agree with that contention because, rather than selling only its own 80% interest, ARCO negotiated for, with the Chemical Board's approval, the entire sale of Chemical to Lyondell." (emphasis added)).

on these two cases, however, is misplaced. In *Tri-Star,* the plaintiffs, former stockholders of Tri-Star Pictures, Inc. ("Tri-Star"), challenged an assets for stock transaction between Tri-Star and Coca-Cola Company ("Coca-Cola"), a 36.8% stockholder of Tri-Star before the transaction. The complaint alleged that Coca-Cola had wrongfully manipulated the transaction to receive an excessive amount of Tri-Star shares in exchange for assets having a lower value. As a result of the transaction, Coca-Cola obtained an 80% stock interest in Tri-Star and the public shareholders, who had formerly owned 43.4% of the common equity, now owned only 20% of Tri-Star's equity. Because Coca-Cola, a significant stockholder of Tri-Star before the transaction, did not suffer a similar dilution of their percentage ownership or their voting power as compared to the plaintiffs, the Supreme Court held that the plaintiffs had suffered a special injury not shared equally by all shareholders. This rendered the plaintiffs' claims direct and not derivative in nature.

[*Boston University* also dealt with a situation where] "the defendants engaged in self-dealing that resulted in reduced voting power and stock dilution."

Together, *Tri-Star and Boston University* stand for the proposition that dilution claims are individual in nature where a significant stockholder's interest is increased "at the sole expense of the minority." *Tri-Star* and *Boston University* have no application, in my opinion, where the entity benefiting from the allegedly diluting transaction, NBC, is a third party rather than an existing significant or controlling stockholder. * * *

[T]o the extent that any alleged decrease in the asset value and voting power of plaintiffs' shares of Pax results from the issuance of new equity to a third party (NBC), plaintiff's dilution theory as a basis for a direct claim fails and any individual claim for dilution must be dismissed. * * *

[***Revlon* Claim**] In the plaintiffs' second attempt to support a direct claim, they allege that the defendants' failure to properly explore the Fox Offer, and later engage in serious negotiations with Fox, deprived the plaintiffs of the opportunity to realize the optimum value for their Pax stock. This, according to the plaintiffs, caused them to suffer individual injury. In substance, the plaintiffs argue that as soon as the Pax Board announced that Pax had retained Salomon to "explore strategic alternatives," the plaintiffs were entitled to a reasonable inference that the individual defendants had engaged in an active bidding process seeking to sell Pax and were under a fiduciary obligation to maximize value for the Pax shareholders in accordance with *Revlon, Inc. v. McAndrews & Forbes Holdings, Inc.* [Section 3.14.F] This argument fails for at least two reasons.

First, the plaintiffs have failed to distinguish these facts from the numerous cases that have previously held that allegations that directors wrongfully failed to pursue business combinations are derivative in nature. * * *

Second, *Revlon* does not apply where the plaintiffs cannot allege that a sale or change of control has taken place or necessarily will take place such that the public shareholders of a corporation have been or will be deprived of a control premium. To the contrary, it is clear from the complaint that Mr. Paxson controls Pax through his ownership of 39.2% of the Company's Class A stock and 100% of the Company's class B stock. These holdings collectively represent 75% of Pax's voting power. * * * [T]he public shareholders of Pax will never be in the position to collectively control the corporation and therefore receive a control premium for their shares.

Conclusion Based on all the foregoing reasons, I conclude that the complaint in the present suit alleges claims that are solely derivative in nature. Due to the plaintiffs' failure to comply with the demand requirements of Court of Chancery Rule 23.1, the complaint is therefore dismissed.

F. Controlling Shareholder Causes Controlled Corp to Acquire in Exchange for Its Stock the Stock of a Sister Controlled Corp, $2 Billion of Damages, $304 Million of Attorneys' Fees—*Southern Peru*[159]

Chancellor Strine's 2011 decision in *Southern. Peru*[160] demonstrates the risk for a controller that engages in a transaction that is subject to the entire fairness standard of review. In this case, Grupo Mexico owned 54.17% of the outstanding stock (and 63.08% of the voting power) of Southern Peru, a Delaware corporation listed on the NYSE. Grupo Mexico also owned approximately 99% of the stock of Minera Mexico, a privately held company. Thus, Grupo Mexico was the controller of both the publicly held Southern Peru and the privately held Minera Mexico.

In response to a proposal from the controller, Grupo Mexico, Southern Peru acquired the target, Minera Mexico, in exchange for $3.1 billion of newly issued shares of Southern Peru. Thus, Grupo Mexico was the controller of both the acquirer, Southern Peru, and the target, Minera Mexico, and as a result of the transaction, Grupo Mexico increased its interest in the acquirer, Southern Peru.

Applying the entire fairness standard of review, the Chancellor found that "regardless of which party bears the burden of persuasion"[161] under *Kahn v. Lynch* (see *supra*), Southern Peru's Special Committee, which was appointed to review the transaction, breached its fiduciary duty in causing Southern Peru to overpay by approximately $2 billion in the acquisition of Minera Mexico.

The Delaware Supreme Court affirmed Chancellor Strine's decision in *Southern Peru*[162] to award more than $2 billion in damages and more than $304 million in attorneys' fees, which was 15% of the total award. The Delaware Supreme Court explained that Chancellor Strine held that the "controlling shareholder, and affiliate directors of Southern Peru ... breached their fiduciary duty of loyalty to Southern Peru and its minority stockholders by causing Southern Peru to acquire the controller's 99.15% interest in a Mexican mining company, Minera México..., for much more than it was worth, *i.e.*, at an unfair price."[163]

With regard to the Chancellor's application of the entire fairness doctrine to the transaction, the Supreme Court concluded:

> The Court of Chancery's post-trial determination of entire fairness must be accorded substantial deference on appeal. The Court of Chancery's factual findings are supported by the record and its conclusions are the product of an orderly and logical deductive reasoning process. Accordingly, the Court of Chancery's judgment, that the Merger consideration was not entirely fair, is affirmed.[164]

In addressing the damages issue, the Supreme Court explained that the "Court of Chancery awarded damages based on the difference in value between what was paid (the "give") and the value of what was received (the "get").[165] The court went on to conclude

159. This section is adapted from Thompson, *Mergers, Acquisitions and Tender Offers*, *supra* Section 1.10, at Section 5:5.7[P].

160. In re Southern. Peru Copper Corp. S'holder Derivative Litig., 30 A.3d 60 (Del. Ch. 2011).

161. *Id.* at 114.

162. *Americas Mining Corporation v. Theriault*, 51 A.3d 1213 (Del. 2012),

163. *Id.* at 1218.

164. *Id.* at 1248–1249.

165. *Id.* at 1252.

that "the record reflects that the Court of Chancery properly exercised its broad historic discretionary powers in fashioning a remedy and making its award of damages."[166]

§ 3.23 Pennsylvania's Approach to Fiduciary Duties in M&A Transactions

A. Introduction

As discussed previously, Pennsylvania and Delaware have a common border, and Philadelphia, the largest city in Pennsylvania is just 30 miles from Wilmington, the largest city in Delaware. Notwithstanding this geographic closeness, when it comes to fiduciary duties of directors of corporations, the two states could not be farther apart, particularly in change of control transactions.

Also, as will be seen in Chapter 22, which addresses state takeover laws, the approaches of Delaware and Pennsylvania to these laws are dramatically different. Chapter 22 discusses the impact of Pennsylvania's takeover law on the battle between CSX and Norfolk Southern to takeover Conrail, a Pennsylvania corporation. The purpose of this section is to highlight the basic approach of Pennsylvania to fiduciary duties in change of control transactions.

As demonstrated previously, Delaware's standards of review (*i.e.*, business judgment rule, *Unocal*, *Revlon*, *Blasius*, and Entire Fairness) were developed through the common law. As will be seen in the discussion in this section of *Simmons*, Pennsylvania has codified (1) the duty of care (see Section 1712 of the Pa. BCL), and (2) as seen in *Armstrong*, *infra*, an extremely permissive business judgment rule (*see* Section 1715). As *Simmons*, *infra*, points out, Section 1715 specifically rejects *Unocal* and *Revlon* (and, presumably, *Blasius*).

As demonstrated below in *AMP*, Pennsylvania's approach to "dead-hand" poison pills is completely the opposite of Delaware's approach.

As discussed below in *Mitchell*, the one place where there seems to be a convergence between Pennsylvania and Delaware law is in determining when appraisal is the exclusive remedy.[167]

B. Challenge to the Constitutionality of PA's Anti-Takeover Statute

Armstrong World Industries, Inc. v. Adams

United States Court of Appeals, Third Circuit, 1992 961 F.2d 405

Sirica, Circuit Judge:

This case involves a challenge to the constitutionality of the Pennsylvania anti-takeover act of 1990. Plaintiffs, shareholders of Armstrong World Industries, Inc., brought this action seeking declaratory and injunctive relief on behalf of themselves and Armstrong against the board of directors, state officials charged with implementing the Act, and Armstrong nominally. The district court dismissed plaintiffs' complaint for lack of subject

166. *Id.*

167. As indicated previously, I thank Taimoor Choudhry, a 2014 graduate of Penn State Law and my former research assistant, for his very helpful assistance in preparing the materials dealing with Pennsylvania law.

matter jurisdiction. Because we conclude that plaintiffs' claims are not ripe for judicial review, we will affirm.

[**Background**] On April 27, 1990, Act No. 36, 1990 Pa. Laws 129, became law. Considered one of the nation's toughest anti-takeover statutes, the Act enhances the ability of management of Pennsylvania corporations to fend off hostile takeover attempts. * * * Among other things, Act 36 revises directors' fiduciary duties, restricts the voting rights of shareholders who initiate control-share acquisitions, and empowers corporations to disgorge short-swing profits realized by bidders who place corporations "in play."

The fiduciary duties provision expands directors' discretion in determining the "best interests of the corporation." Directors may now consider whether the corporation's long-term interests and plans would be "best served by the continued independence of the corporation," as well as "the resources, intent and conduct (past, stated and potential) of any person seeking to acquire control of the corporation." [*See* § 1715(a)(2) & (3)] Moreover, "in considering the ... effects of any action," directors need not "regard any corporate interest or the interests of any particular group affected by such action as a dominant or controlling interest or factor." [*See* § 1715(b)].

The fiduciary duties provision also fortifies the presumption that directors' actions are in the "best interests of the corporation." Directors are under no "greater obligation to justify" their actions "relating to an acquisition or potential or proposed acquisition of control of the corporation" than in any other circumstances. [*See* § 1715(d)]. Furthermore, actions taken by disinterested directors in the change-of-control context are presumed to be in the "best interests of the corporation," except where it is proven that such actions were not taken "in good faith after reasonable investigation."

[As indicated the Third Circuit affirmed the dismissal of the plaintiffs' challenge to these fiduciary provisions and the other provisions of the PA Takeover statute discussed in Chapter 22, which deals generally with state takeover statutes.]

C. The Rejection of *Unocal* and *Revlon* in Pennsylvania—*Simmons*

Simmons v. Sutherland

Common Pleas Ct. of Luzerne Ct. Pa., 1998 Pa. Dist. & Cnty. Dec. LEXIS 200 (Nov. 12, 1998)

Opinion by: Thomas F. Burke, Jr.

Introduction. * * * The Lion Brewery, Inc. (the "Lion" or the "Company"), is a publicly held corporation, headquartered in Wilkes-Barre, PA. * * * Malt Acquiring, Inc. ("MAI"), is a privately held corporation owned and controlled by the current management of the Lion. [Plaintiffs include public shareholders of the Lion.]

[Plaintiffs assert] that the individual Defendants, acting in their collective role as the Board of Directors of the Lion (the "Board"), improperly practiced their influences in such a way as to ensure that MAI/Management would be the successful purchaser of the Company. The essence of the alleged impropriety, according to the Plaintiffs, was a breach of fiduciary duty by the Lion's directors, consisting of alleged self-dealing, dishonesty, and a lack of reasonable investigation in carrying out the auction process for the sale of the Company. * * *

[In rejecting the Plaintiffs' claims regarding a breach by the Board of its fiduciary duties, the court addressed as follows the impact of Sections 1712 and 1715 of the Pa. BCL. Before proceeding, read these two provisions in the *M&A Statutes, Rules, and Documents.*]

Breach of Fiduciary Duty: [W]e now examine the law in Pennsylvania which governs directors' duties in the context of a change in corporate control and also Plaintiffs' burden and the applicable standard of proof.

First, the law demonstrates that corporate directors in Pennsylvania enjoy the presumption of "the business judgment rule" which provides a considerable cloak of protection in regard to their decision-making. See *Cuker v. Mikalauskas,* 547 Pa. 600, 692 A.2d 1042 (1997), wherein the Pennsylvania Supreme Court stated:

> The business judgment rule insulates an officer or director of a corporation from liability for a business decision made in good faith if he is not interested in the subject of the business judgment, is informed with respect to the subject of the business judgment to the extent he reasonably believes to be appropriate under the circumstances, and rationally believes that the business judgment is in the best interests of the corporation.

Second, the Pennsylvania Legislature has established standards under the B.C.L. which allow broad protection to directors of Pennsylvania corporations, especially in the realm of change of control decision-making, as indicated in the analysis which follows.

A director of a Pennsylvania corporation stands in a fiduciary relation to a corporation and shall perform his duty as director "in good faith, in a manner he reasonably believes to be in the best interests of the corporation and with such care, including reasonable inquiry, skill and diligence, as a person of ordinary prudence would use under similar circumstances." 15 Pa.C.S.A. § 1712(a).

In the exercise of its general powers, a board of directors for a Pennsylvania corporation:

> [M]ay, in considering the best interests of the corporation, consider to the extent they deem appropriate:
>
> (1) The effects of any action upon any or all groups affected by such action, including shareholders, employees, suppliers, customers and creditors of the corporation, and upon communities in which offices or other establishments of the corporation are located.
>
> (2) The short-term and long-term interests of the corporation, including benefits that may accrue to the corporation from its long-term plans and the possibility that these interests may be best served by the continued independence of the corporation.
>
> (3) The resources, intent and conduct (past, stated and potential) of any person seeking to acquire control of the corporation.
>
> (4) All other pertinent factors.

15 Pa.C.S.A. § 1715.

In weighing these interests and factors, a board is not obliged to regard any one particular group or interest as dominant or controlling, and consideration of these interests and factors "shall not constitute a violation of section 1712." 15 Pa.C.S.A. § 1715(b).

In the merger or acquisition context, a board's decision is entitled to even greater deference than decisions in the ordinary course of business. 15 Pa.C.S.A. § 1502(a)(18). The fiduciary duty of directors does not require them to act or refrain from acting because of the effect it would have on a potential acquisition or the price to be paid to the shareholders. 15 Pa.C.S.A. § 1715(c)(3). Moreover, decisions concerning corporate control made by "disinterested directors"—a term defined in subsection e of section 1715, which encompasses the members of the Independent Committee—may only be overturned if "it is proven by clear and convincing evidence that the disinterested directors did not assent to such act in good faith after reasonable investigation." 15 Pa.C.S.A. § 1715(d).

In enacting Section 1715, the Pennsylvania legislature specifically intended that Courts defer to directors' decisions concerning mergers and acquisitions. "It is intended, therefore, that the directors' business conclusions with respect to the actions covered by the subsection would ordinarily not be subject to review". Draftsmen's Comment to 15 Pa.C.S.A. § 1715(c). Thus, "[in] particular, under this subsection, directors have the statutory authority to "just say no" with respect to a potential or proposed acquisition of the corporation's shares by … taking action that may have an effect on … the consideration offered to shareholders." *Id.* As a consequence, a Pennsylvania board's refusal to "pursue" an acquisition offer, or its refusal to be "amenable to other offers," cannot constitute a breach of fiduciary duty under Pennsylvania law. *B.T.Z., Inc. v. Grove,* 803 F. Supp. 1019, 1023, (M.D. Pa. 1992). *See also, AMP, Inc. v. Allied Signal, Inc.* Civ. A. Nos. 98–4405, 98–4058, 98–4109, 1998 U.S. Dist. LEXIS 15617 (E.D. Pa. Oct. 8, 1998).

The Court, upon consideration of the evidence, concludes that Plaintiffs have not shown a likelihood that they can prove either by a clear and convincing evidence standard or even by a preponderance of the evidence standard that the auction process for the sale of the Company was "rigged" or that the Defendants engaged in a course of conduct in selling the Company which was either in bad faith or fundamentally unfair. This is not to say that either the auction process for the sale of the Company or that the conduct and actions of the investment banker and the individual directors were in all instances fair. To the contrary, Plaintiffs have demonstrated several instances in which individual actions were, at least, inappropriate. However, in the context of the Board reaching its decision to enter into a merger agreement with Management on September 17, 1998, for the sale of the Company, taking into account the totality of the Board's actions and deliberations throughout the auction process, the Court concludes that it is unlikely that Plaintiffs can meet their burden of showing that the Board did not act in good faith after reasonable investigation.

Our review of the evidence indicates that the Board engaged an investment banker to assist with the sale of the Company, substantially relied upon the advice of the investment banker as well as independent counsel, and, after a protracted auction process, the Independent Committee of the Board appeared to reach its decision based on valid business considerations. Specifically, as to its ultimate decision to sell to Management, reached on September 17, 1998, the evidence shows that the Independent Committee took into account the prospect that the Management bid might be withdrawn should negotiations be reopened. * * *

In conclusion, while Plaintiffs produced evidence during the hearing which served to indicate that there was a bias on Sutherland's part in favor of Management, and, other indiscretions, we conclude that there is not a likelihood that Plaintiffs can sustain their burden to show that the independent Committee * * * failed to have the best interests of the corporation and its various constituencies (i.e. shareholders, employees, suppliers, and customers) in the forefront of its deliberations. Accordingly, we find it unlikely that the Plaintiffs will be able to demonstrate that the Independent Committee acted in bad faith, fundamentally unfairly, or without reasonable investigation.

In short, we conclude that Plaintiffs have failed to establish a "clear right of relief" which is, by itself, fatal to their case. However, because "[t]he harm which would warrant a preliminary injunction … must be viewed conjunctively with the existence or absence of a clear right to relief", Boehm v. University of Pennsylvania School of Veterinary Medicine, 392 Pa. Super. 502, 522, 573 A.2d 575, 585, alloc. denied,527 Pa. 596, 589 A.2d 687 (1990), we will also address the issue of "irreparable harm."

Irreparable Harm and No Adequate Remedy at Law: Plaintiffs contend that they will suffer irreparable harm and that they will have no adequate remedy at law if the Lion/MAI deal is allowed to be consummated. * * *

Plaintiffs have cited Delaware authority wherein injunctive relief was granted in two cases involving director misconduct (i.e. *Black & Decker Corp. v. American Standard, Inc.*, 682 F. Supp. 772 (D. Del. 1988) and *Robert M. Bass Group, Inc. v Evans,* 552 A.2d 1227 (Del. Ch. 1988). However, we consider Plaintiffs' reliance upon those cases to be misplaced, not only because of markedly different factual circumstances from the present case, but because Delaware law with respect to directors" duties in a change of control context are significantly different from those duties imposed on Pennsylvania corporate directors under the B.C.L. as discussed above.

Whereas Pennsylvania directors enjoy the protection of "the business judgment rule", as addressed in *Cuker,* and are entitled to act in accordance with §§ 1502(a)(18), 1712, 1715, 1716, and 1717 of the B.C.L., corporate directors in Delaware owe a fiduciary duty to *both* the shareholders and the corporation. *See Unocal Corp. v. Mesa Petroleum Co.,* 493 A.2d 946 (Del. 1985). Also, under Delaware law, directors have a heightened duty of awareness under a merger scenario and have an explicit duty to maximize price in conducting an auction sale of their company. *See Revlon, Inc. v. MacAndrews & Forbes Holdings, Inc.,* 506 A.2d 173 (Del. 1985), and *Unocal, supra.* No such "enhanced duty" exists for directors of Pennsylvania corporations. * * *

Conclusion. In conclusion, it is the Court's overall view that the foregoing analysis supports our ruling as contained in the attached Order that the Plaintiffs' Petition for Preliminary injunction should be denied. We also note that Plaintiffs have made an alternative prayer for relief in the nature of requesting that the Court void the break-up provision and/or other allegedly onerous conditions in the Lion/MAI definitive agreement. The Court concludes, however, upon consideration of the evidence, that the subject provisions, although somewhat unusual, were apparently placed in the definitive agreement for valid business reasons and that such relief as requested by Plaintiffs would be unwarranted.Bottom of Form

D. "Dead-Hand" Pill under Pennsylvania Law—*AMP*

AMP Incorporated v. Allied Signal, Inc.

United States District Court, Eastern District Pennsylvania, 1998 WL 778348 (E.D.Pa.)

[In *AMP Incorporated v. Allied Signal, Inc.* the court addressed the validity of a non-redeemable and non-amendable pill that was adopted by AMP Incorporated, a Pennsylvania corporation, in response to a hostile takeover offer by Allied Signal Inc. In upholding the provisions, the court reasoned:]

> 13. AMP's board had a poison pill with * * * a "dead-hand" provision which provided that, if a new majority was elected, only the directors who were on the board prior to the change in majority could vote to redeem the poison pill.
>
> 14. On August 20, 1998, in response to Allied Signal's proposed consent solicitations, AMP's board amended its poison pill to remove the "dead-hand" provision and to make the pill non-redeemable and non-amendable should

> AMP's disinterested board majority be replaced as a result of the acquisition of control of the board by a majority of directors nominated by an unsolicited acquiring company. The pill could remain non-redeemable and non-amendable until November 6, 1999, the date of the expiration of the shareholder rights plan. * * *
>
> 16. Allied Signal represents that by September 14, 1998, seventy-two percent (72%) of AMP's total outstanding shares had been tendered in response to its tender offer. * * *
>
> 48. Allied Signal requests declaratory judgment that the AMP board's poison pill amendments of August 20, 1998 and September 17, 1998 [making the pill non-redeemable and non-amendable] * * * are invalid.
>
> 49. Section 2513 [a pill validation provision] provides that a registered corporation may adopt poison pills, and may set forth "such terms as are fixed by the board of directors." Section 2513(a). Furthermore, the fiduciary duty of directors, provided in Section 1712, shall not require them to redeem any rights under, or modify or render inapplicable, any shareholder rights plan, including a plan adopted pursuant to Section 2513. Section 1715(c). * * * [T]he AMP board is not required to act solely because of the consideration that might be paid to shareholders in the event of an acquisition. Thus, in amending the poison pill and fixing it as non-amendable and non-redeemable, AMP did not act beyond the scope of its statutory authority. * * *

Note

In *Invacare Corporation v. Healthdyne Technologies, Inc.*, 1997 WL 399234 (U.S. Dist Ct. N.D. Georgia, 1997), the court upheld the issuance of a poison pill under Georgia's pill validation statute. There the court said the it was "satisfied that the concept of continuing directors is an integral part of a takeover defense and is not contrary to public policy in Georgia."

E. Fiduciary Duties of Acquiror's Nominee Directors in Combination Tender Offer Proxy Contest—*AMP*, Section 16.12

F. Exclusivity of Appriasal in the Face of Fraud or Fundamental Unfairness—*Mitchell*

Mitchell Partners, L.P. v. Irex Corp.

Supreme Court of Pennsylvania, 617 Pa. 423 (2012)

Opinion by: Saylor

We accepted certification from the United States Court of Appeals for the Third Circuit to address the exclusiveness of a statutory appraisal remedy provided, under Pennsylvania corporate law, to minority shareholders in certain merger scenarios.

Per Pennsylvania's Business Corporation Law, a shareholder of a domestic business corporation may have prescribed entitlements—termed "dissenter's rights"—upon the shareholder's objection to the corporation's participation in a merger(or some other transactions entailing fundamental corporate changes). See 15 Pa. C.S. § 1930(a). In certain of these scenarios, objecting shareholders are entitled to receive the fair value for their shares. *See id.* § 1571(a). Where there is a fair value dispute, the BCL provides for post-merger judicial valuation or appraisal of the shares. *See id.* § 1579(a). Furthermore, and of particular relevance to this appeal, the general provisions of the BCL impose the following constraint upon the rights of objecting and dissenting shareholders:

> § 1105. Restriction on equitable relief.
>
> A shareholder of a business corporation shall not have any right to obtain, in the absence of fraud or fundamental unfairness, an injunction against any proposed plan * * * authorized under any provision of this subpart, nor any right to claim the right to valuation and payment of the fair value of his shares because of the plan * * *, except that he may dissent and claim such payment if and to the extent provided in Subchapter D of Chapter 15[, 15 Pa. C.S. §§ 1571–1580,] (relating to dissenters rights) where this subpart expressly provides that dissenting shareholders shall have the rights and remedies provided in that subchapter. Absent fraud or fundamental unfairness, the rights and remedies so provided shall be exclusive. Structuring a plan or transaction for the purpose or with the effect of eliminating or avoiding the application of dissenters rights is not fraud or fundamental unfairness within the meaning of this section [that is, the de facto merger doctrine does not apply].

15 Pa. C.S. § 1105 (emphasis added).

Mitchell Partners, L.P., was a minority shareholder of Irex Corporation, a privately-held Pennsylvania business corporation. In 2006, Irex participated in a merger transaction structured so that some minority shareholders would be "cashed out" and would not receive an equity interest in the surviving corporation, a wholly owned subsidiary of North Lime Holdings Corporation. Mitchell objected to the acquisition, as it viewed the transaction as a "squeeze out" of minority interests at an unfair price. The merger proceeded nonetheless, and Irex commenced valuation proceedings in state court, per Section 1579 of the BCL, to address the dispute with Mitchell.

Meanwhile, Mitchell pursued common law remedies in a diversity action in federal court, naming as defendants Irex, its directors, most of its officers, and North Lime. The complaint asserted claims for breach of fiduciary duties, aiding and abetting breach of fiduciary duties, and unjust enrichment. The defendants sought dismissal on the ground that, under Section 1105 of the BCL, judicial valuation is the sole remedy available to dissenting shareholders in the post-merger time frame.

The district court agreed, relying on *In re Jones & Laughlin Steel Corporation*, 488 Pa. 524, 412 A.2d 1099 (1980) (holding that, under Section 1105's predecessor, an appraisal court lacks jurisdiction to determine the validity of a merger). The court believed that *Jones* confirmed that post-merger remedies available to dissenting shareholders are limited to appraisal in a judicial forum. * * * In terms of policy implications, the district court highlighted that the *Jones Court* "was not unmindful of the import of its decision and the limits it placed on minority shareholders." * * * In this regard, the court quoted from *Jones*, as follows:

> We wish to emphasize that today's decision does not condone the manner in which the appellants and other minority shareholders were deprived of their equitable interest.... We are not unmindful of the grave unfairness and fraud frequently present in mergers of this type, especially where there is a "cash-out" of the minority shareholders. Our concern, however, does not change the view that appellants' post-merger remedies were limited to the appraisal of the fair market value of their stock.

While the district court appreciated that several decisions of the Third Circuit Court of Appeals and of the Pennsylvania Superior Court sanctioned remedies beyond appraisal, *see, e.g., Herskowitz v. Nutri/System, Inc.*, 857 F.2d 179 (3d Cir. 1988), *Warden v. McLelland*, 288 F.3d 105 (3d Cir. 2002), and *In re Jones & Laughlin Steel Corp.*, 328 Pa. Super. 442, 477 A.2d 527 (1984), it distinguished these on the ground that they involved separate litigation that was filed before the consummation of merger transactions. * * * .

On appeal, a divided three-judge panel of the Third Circuit reversed. * * * Initially, the majority recognized that Section 1105 "clearly imposes some restrictions on the relief available to a dissenting shareholder outside of the appraisal remedy proceeding[.]" *Id.* at 209. The majority disagreed, however, with the district court's position that the statute precludes all other remedies. Acknowledging that some of the broader language from *Jones* supported the defendants' position, the majority nonetheless highlighted that *Jones* arose in the context of a statutory valuation proceeding, such that "the narrow issue of whether a suit for damages based on breach of fiduciary duties may be brought post-merger was not directly presented to the Supreme Court." *Id.* at 212. * * *

[T]he majority explained that other jurisdictions permit separate suits for fiduciary breaches, because even the expanded appraisal remedy "may not be adequate in certain cases, particularly where fraud, misrepresentation, self-dealing, deliberate waste of corporate assets, or gross and palpable overreaching are involved." Id. at 214 (quoting *Weinberger v. UOP, Inc.*, [Section 3.14.B]). In particular, the majority noted that Delaware courts have appreciated that the valuation remedy and suits for self-dealing "serve different purposes and are designed to provide different, and not interchangeable, remedies." *Id.* (quoting *Cede & Co. v. Technicolor, Inc.*, [see Chapter 2]. Additionally, the majority expressed the concern that, if exclusivity were the rule, a shareholder who was deceived by the majority into voting for a merger would have no remedy at all for the breach of fiduciary duty (since such a shareholder will have foregone an assertion of dissenter's rights).

Finally, the majority highlighted that Section 1105 provides that when there is "fraud or fundamental unfairness" the valuation remedy is not exclusive. * * * The majority concluded:

> We predict that the Supreme Court of Pennsylvania would hold that Pennsylvania's appraisal statute does not exclude separate, post-merger suits for damages alleging that majority shareholders breached their fiduciary duties to minority shareholders in the process of consummating a freeze out merger.... As we held in Herskowitz, "it is a clear holding that in Pennsylvania the statutory appraisal cause of action coexists with common law causes of action. Indeed no other rule makes sense, for the appraisal remedy is available even absent misconduct of corporate officials. It was hardly enacted to provide a shield for misconduct." * * *

[T]he defendants posited that Delaware law is not an appropriate polestar for interpreting Pennsylvania law, particularly since Delaware's appraisal statute does not make valuation an exclusive remedy. They developed that there are many ways in which Pennsylvania corporate law differs from that of Delaware and urged the court to honor the Pennsylvania Legislature's policy choice to limit the scope of post-merger remedies, thus affording strong protection to management discretion in critical business decision-making. * * *

Exceptions to exclusivity of the appraisal remedy based on fraud, illegality, or fundamental unfairness are common in the state corporate law of many jurisdictions and, indeed, are reflected in the Model Business Corporations Act in current and prior formulations. * * *

The primary impediment raised to our enforcement of Section 1105 as written is the *Jones* decision, since the *Jones* Court pronounced that the statutory appraisal remedy was an exclusive one. * * * We have emphasized many times, however, that a decision is to be read against its facts and will not be applied uncritically to subjects which were not directly before the Court. * * * As the Third Circuit aptly developed, Jones arose in the context of an appraisal proceeding and was concerned with the jurisdiction of the appraisal court. * * * Accordingly, like our federal colleagues, we also conclude that *Jones* is not controlling in the context of Mitchell's distinct action pursued in federal court. * * *

[W]e believe that the General Assembly did intend for the notion of exclusivity—as modified by the exception for fraud or fundamental unfairness—to curtail actions outside the appraisal context. Such qualified preclusion is suggested by the language of exclusivity appearing in Section 1105 and is supported by the general policy of reducing the burdensomeness of fundamental corporate changes. * * *

In light of such purposes, we also take this opportunity to observe that the fraud or fundamental unfairness exception may not be invoked lightly. For example, the Legislature has made clear that the exception does not apply merely by virtue of the character of a cash-out transaction. See 15 Pa. C.S. § 1105 ("Structuring a plan or transaction for the purpose or with the effect of eliminating or avoiding the application of dissenters rights is not fraud or fundamental unfairness within the meaning of this section."). It is also well established elsewhere, and should pertain in Pennsylvania, that mere inadequacy in price is not sufficient to implicate the exception. * * * Plainly, appraisal is intended as the usual remedy in the absence of exceptional circumstances.

In summary, in response to the certified question, Section 1105 precludes post-merger remedies other than appraisal only in the absence of fraud or fundamental unfairness.

§ 3.24 The MBCA Approach to the Business Judgment Rule and Entire Fairness

Section 8.01(b) of the MBCA, which is similar to Section 141(a) of the Delaware General Corporation Law (DGCL), provides that except as otherwise provided in the certificate of incorporation or a shareholder agreement, "[a]ll corporate powers shall be exercised by or under the authority of the board of directors of the corporation, and the business and affairs of the corporation shall be managed by or under the direction, and subject to the oversight, of its board of directors. (The sections of the MBCA and the DGCL discussed in this section are contained in the *M&A Statutes, Rules, and Documents, supra* Section 1.1)

The MBCA sets out "standards of conduct of directors" in Section 8.30. Section 8.30(a) requires each director to act in "(1) good faith, and (2) in a manner the director reasonably believes to be in the best interest of the corporation." Pursuant to Section 8.30(b) directors are required when becoming informed or in conducting their oversight function to "discharge their duties with the care that a person in a like position would reasonably believe appropriate under similar circumstances." Section 8.30(c) requires the director to disclose material information to other board members unless otherwise prohibited by law, contract, or ethical rule. Sections 8.30(d), (e), and (f) deal with reliance by directors on the acts of others. There are no comparable provisions to Section 8.30 in the DGCL, except for the provision on reliance in Section 141(e). All of the other concepts addressed in Section 8.30 are dealt with in the common law of corporations in Delaware.

Section 8.31 of the MBCA sets out standards of liability for directors, and Section 8.31(a)(2) sets out principles that are similar to the common law business judgment rule in Delaware. The MBCA does not have an enhanced business judgment rule as in Delaware under *Unocal.*

Sections 8.60 through 8.63 of the MBCA contain rules governing "directors conflicting interest transactions." These are transactions that raise duty of loyalty issues under Delaware common law and are also addressed in Section 144 of the DGCL. The principles of Section 144 can be applicable in considering loyalty issues in merger cases. Under Section 8.61(b), a director's conflicting interest transaction is permitted if it (1) is approved by either independent director action under Section 8.62 or independent shareholder action under Section 8.63, or (2) is fair to the corporation as defined in Section 8.60(b). This is similar to the structure of Section 144 and the common law entire fairness test in Delaware. The MBCA does not have a compelling justification test as in Delaware under *Blasius.*

Finally, the director exculpation provision in Section 2.02(b)(4) of the MBCA is similar to Section 102(b)(7) of the DGCL.

§3.25 The ALI's Proposed Rules Relating to the Business Judgment Rule

The ALI *Corporate Governance Project, supra* Section 1.10, contains proposals on director's duties. *See generally* Thompson, *The M&A Provisions of the ALI Corporate Governance Project, supra* Section 1.10, which explains:

[**Business Judgment Rule**] The business judgment rule, which is set out in Section 4.01(c) of the ALI Project, provides that a director or officer who makes a business judgment in "*good faith*" fulfills the duty under Section 4.01 if the director or officer:

> (1) is *not interested* [§ 1.23] in the subject of the business judgment [that is, is not a party to the transaction and has no business, financial or familial type interest in the transaction];
>
> (2) is *informed* with respect to the subject of the business judgment to the extent the director or officer reasonably believes to be appropriate under the circumstances; and
>
> (3) *rationally believes* that the business judgment is in the best interests of the corporation. (emphasis added).

Section 4.01(d) provides that the person challenging the conduct of a director or officer under Section 4.01 has the burden of proving a breach of the duty of care, including the inapplicability of the provisions of Section 4.01(b), relating to delegation, and Section 4.01(c), relating to the business judgment rule. Thus, the burden of proving that the business judgment rule is not applicable is on the challenging party.

Section 4.01(d) also provides that in a damage action, the challenging party has the "burden of proving that the breach was the legal cause of damage suffered by the corporation." This is not the rule in Delaware; in the event the plaintiff establishes that the business judgment does not apply, Delaware law places the burden on the directors to establish that the transaction is entirely fair. *See e.g., Technicolor*, Section 3.10.E.1.

[**Defensive Tactics**] Section 6.02(a) of the ALI *Project*, which applies only to publicly held corporations, governs the actions of a target's directors in defending against a tender offer by an unwanted acquiror for the stock of the target. Under Section 6.02(a), a target's board "may take an action that has the foreseeable effect of blocking an unsolicited tender offer, if the action is a reasonable response to the offer."

Section 6.02(b) provides that in determining whether its action is a reasonable response to the offer, the board may take into account "all factors relevant to the best interests of the corporation and [its] shareholders* * *." Such factors include the issue of whether the offer is legal and whether the offer would, if successful "threaten the corporation's essential economic prospects." In addition, the board may give consideration to the interests of non-shareholder groups for which the corporation has a "legitimate concern if to do so would not significantly disfavor the long-term interests of shareholders." Thus, to a limited extent the interests of other constituencies may be considered. * * *

Section 6.02(d) contemplates that a blocking action taken by a target's disinterested directors may not be a reasonable response to an offer as required by Section 6.02, but may still satisfy the business judgment rule of Section 4.01(c). * * *

References

ALI, *Corporate Governance Project, supra* Section 1.10, at Sections 4.01, 6.01 and 6.02.

Balotti and Finkelstein, *Delaware Corporate Law, supra* Section 1.10.

Block et al., *Business Judgment Rule, supra* Section 1.10.

Fleisher and Sussman, *Takeover Defense, supra* Section 1.10.

Folk on Delaware Corporate Law, supra Section 1.10.

Lipton and Steinberger, *Takeovers and Freezeouts, supra* Section 1.10.

Thompson, *Mergers, Acquisitions and Tender Offers, supra* Section 1.10, Chapter 5.

Chapter 4

Introduction to Securities Regulation

§4.1 Scope

This chapter provides a broad introduction to the federal securities laws embodied in the Securities Act of 1933 (the 33 Act or the Securities Act) and the Securities Exchange Act of 1934 (the 34 Act or the Exchange Act). Both the 33 and 34 Acts apply to "securities," which are defined broadly in both Acts to include stocks, bonds, and similar interests. The 33 Act is principally implicated when securities are initially issued. This Act applies, for example, when a closely-held corporation issues its stock in an initial public offering (IPO) and an acquiring corporation issues its stock in the acquisition of the stock or assets of a target corporation. The 34 Act deals with the regulation of the trading of securities after initial issuance. It applies principally to publicly-traded companies that are required to register under that Act and file periodic reports with the SEC and their shareholders. Subsequent chapters amplify and extend upon many of the concepts introduced here, and these and other securities issues are discussed in Chapters 6–8 of Thompson, *Mergers, Acquisitions and Tender Offers*, *supra* Section 1.10.

Section 4.2 presents introductory problems, and Section 4.3 provides an introduction to the liability provisions of the 33 and 34 Acts. Section 4.4 explores Rule 10b-5 under the 34 Act, an overarching provision prohibiting, *inter alia*, fraud in the purchase or sale of securities, whether publicly-held or closely-held. Section 4.5 explores the concept of "materiality" under both the 33 and 34 Acts; this concept is important because liability can arise if, for example, all material information about a security is not fully disclosed prior to the purchase or sale of the security.

We then turn to an examination in Section 4.6 of the registration requirements under Section 5 of the 33 Act. This section explores the SEC's 2005 Securities Offering Reform project, which significantly modified many of the rules under Section 5 and related provisions of the 33 Act. Section 4.7 introduces the state securities laws, that is, "blue sky" laws; these laws no longer apply to offerings that are listed on an exchange. Section 4.8 discusses issues that can arise in drafting a registration statement, including "gun jumping" in violation of Section 5(c) of the 33 Act. This topic is also addressed in Chapter 13, which deals with acquisitions of publicly-held corporations in negotiated transactions, in connection with an examination of the SEC's 1999 rules regarding regulation of takeovers and security holder communications. Section 4.9 illustrates the impact of the liability rules of Section 11 of the 33 Act and explores the due diligence defense by reference to the 2005 and 2006 decisions in the *WorldCom* litigation. Section 4.10 provides introductory problems on public offerings. Section 4.11 introduces the following issues that arise once a company goes public: (1) the Reg. FD disclosure rules, (2) certain disclosure provisions of the Sarbanes-Oxley Act, and (3) the "say on pay" provisions of the Dodd-Frank Act.

The chapter then turns to exempt offerings, with Section 4.12 providing an introduction to the exemptions to the registration requirements of Section 5 of the 33 Act. Section 4.13 provides a guide for completing a statutory private offering under Section 4(2) of the 33 Act, and Section 4.14 discusses the Regulation D exemption, which, in essence, provides a safe harbor private offering exemption. This section briefly discusses the amendments to Reg D made by the JOBS Act. Section 4.15 discusses Rule 144, which provides a safe harbor for the resale of restricted securities, and Section 4.16 discusses the Section 4(1-1/2) exemption for such resales. Finally, Section 4.17 introduces Rule 144A, which has provided for an exclusive public market among certain institutional shareholders for unregistered shares.

The provisions of the 33 Act and 34 Act discussed in this chapter are set out in *M&A Statutes, Rules, and Documents*, *supra* Section 1.1.

§ 4.2 Introductory Problems

Acquiring Corporation (AC) is negotiating to acquire all of the stock of Closely-Held Target Corporation (TC) from the ten shareholders of TC. If AC acquires the stock of TC for cash, is the 33 Act implicated and, if so, how? What if AC acquires the stock of TC in exchange for AC stock?

Assume that TC is publicly-held and AC makes a cash tender offer for the stock of TC. Is the 33 Act implicated and, if so, how? What if AC offers the TC shareholders stock of AC?

§ 4.3 Introduction to the Liability Provisions of the 33 Act and 34 Act

Before examining the technical requirements for complying with the 33 Act's registration and exemption rules, it is important to be aware of the potential liability that could arise from violating the 33 or 34 Acts.

If a registration statement contains an untrue statement of material fact or omits to state a material fact required to be stated or necessary to make the statements made not misleading, Section 11 of the 33 Act provides for strict liability for the issuer and strict liability, subject to a due diligence defense, for the directors of the issuer and for certain other persons. The concept of "materiality," which is important under both the 33 and 34 Acts is examined below.

Section 12(a)(2) of the 33 Act imposes liability, subject to a reasonable care defense, on any person who offers or sells a security through the use of a written or oral untrue statement of material fact or omission to state a material fact.

Section 12(a)(1) of the 33 Act imposes strict liability for the sale of a security in violation of the registration requirements of Section 5; thus, for example, a sale of securities in violation of the gun jumping rules discussed below could give rise to liability under Section 12(a)(1).

Rule 10b-5 under the 34 Act contains broad prohibitions against the use of fraud in connection with the "purchase" or "sale" of securities. Section 17(a) of the 33 Act provides for similar prohibitions against the use of fraud in the "sale" of securities. There is a private right of action under Rule 10b-5 but not under Section 17(a) of the 33 Act.

Rule 14a-9 under the 34 Act provides that no solicitation for a proxy for a publicly held firm subject to the 34 Act shall be made by any means (oral or written) that contains any statement that "is false or misleading with respect to any material fact, or which omits to state any material fact necessary in order to make the statements therein not false or misleading * * *."

§ 4.4 Introduction to Rule 10b-5

A. General Requirement of Scienter

Ernst & Ernst v. Hochfelder

United States Supreme Court, (1976) 96 S. Ct. 1375

Mr. Justice Powell:

The issue in this case is whether an action for civil damages may lie under § 10(b) of the Securities Exchange Act of 1934, and Securities and Exchange Commission Rule 10b-5, in the absence of an allegation of intent to deceive, manipulate, or defraud on the part of the defendant.

Petitioner, Ernst & Ernst, is an accounting firm. From 1946 through 1967 it was retained by First Securities Company of Chicago (First Securities), a small brokerage firm and member of the Midwest Stock Exchange and of the National Association of Securities Dealers, to perform periodic audits of the firm's books and records. In connection with these audits Ernst & Ernst prepared for filing with the Securities and Exchange Commission (Commission) the annual reports required of First Securities under § 17(a) of the 1934 Act. It also prepared for First Securities responses to the financial questionnaires of the Midwest Stock Exchange (Exchange).

Respondents were customers of First Securities who invested in a fraudulent securities scheme perpetrated by Leston B. Nay, president of the firm and owner of 92% of its stock. Nay induced the respondents to invest funds in "escrow" accounts that he represented would yield a high rate of return. Respondents did so from 1942 through 1966, with the majority of the transactions occurring in the 1950s. In fact, there were no escrow accounts as Nay converted respondents' funds to his own use immediately upon receipt. * * *

This fraud came to light in 1968 when Nay committed suicide, leaving a note that described First Securities as bankrupt and the escrow accounts as "spurious." Respondents subsequently filed this action for damages against Ernst & Ernst in the United States District Court for the Northern District of Illinois under § 10(b) of the 1934 Act. The complaint charged that Nay's escrow scheme violated § 10(b) and Commission Rule 10b-5, and that Ernst & Ernst had "aided and abetted" Nay's violations by its "failure" to conduct proper audits of First Securities. As revealed through discovery, respondents' cause of action rested on a theory of negligent nonfeasance. The premise was that Ernst & Ernst had failed to utilize "appropriate auditing procedures" in its audits of First Securities, thereby failing to discover internal practices of the firm said to prevent an effective audit. * * *

Section 10(b) makes unlawful the use or employment of "any manipulative or deceptive device or contrivance" in contravention of Commission rules. The words "manipulative or deceptive" used in conjunction with "device or contrivance" strongly suggest that § 10(b) was intended to proscribe knowing or intentional misconduct. * * *

[W]hen the Commission adopted the Rule it was intended to apply only to activities that involved scienter. * * * [W]e think the Commission's original interpretation of Rule

10b-5 was compelled by the language and history of § 10(b) and related sections of the Acts. When a statute speaks so specifically in terms of manipulation and deception, and of implementing devices and contrivances—the commonly understood terminology of intentional wrongdoing—and when its history reflects no more expansive intent, we are quite unwilling to extend the scope of the statute to negligent conduct. * * *

B. Aiding and Abetting Liability

In its 1994 decision in *Central Bank of Denver v. First Interstate Bank of Denver*, 114 S. Ct. 1439 (1994), the Supreme Court held that there is no aiding and abetting liability in a private action under Rule 10b-5. The Supreme Court reasoned in part:

"Because the text of § 10(b) does not prohibit aiding and abetting, we hold that a private plaintiff may not maintain an aiding and abetting suit under § 10(b). The absence of § 10(b) aiding and abetting liability does not mean that secondary actors in the securities markets are always free from liability under the securities Acts. Any person or entity, including a lawyer, accountant, or bank, who employs a manipulative device or makes a material misstatement (or omission) on which a purchaser or seller of securities relies may be liable as a primary violator under 10b-5, assuming all of the requirements for primary liability under Rule 10b-5 are met. In any complex securities fraud, moreover, there are likely to be multiple violators; in this case, for example, respondents named four defendants as primary violators."

"Respondents concede that Central Bank did not commit a manipulative or deceptive act within the meaning of § 10(b). Instead, in the words of the complaint, Central Bank was 'secondarily liable under § 10(b) for its conduct in aiding and abetting the fraud.' Because of our conclusion that there is no private aiding and abetting liability under § 10(b), Central Bank may not be held liable as an aider and abettor."

C. Rule 10b-5 in Short Form Mergers

Santa Fe Industries, Inc. v. Green

United States Supreme Court, (1977) 97 S. Ct. 1292

Mr. Justice White:

The issue in this case involves the reach and coverage of § 10(b) of the Securities Exchange Act of 1934 and Rule 10b-5 thereunder in the context of a Delaware short-form merger transaction used by the majority stockholder of a corporation to eliminate the minority interest.

In 1936, petitioner Santa Fe Industries, Inc. (Santa Fe), acquired control of 60% of the stock of Kirby Lumber Corp. (Kirby), a Delaware corporation. Through a series of purchases over the succeeding years, Santa Fe increased its control of Kirby's stock to 95%; the purchase prices during the period 1968–1973 ranged from $65 to $92.50 per share. In 1974, wishing to acquire 100% ownership of Kirby, Santa Fe availed itself of § 253 of the Delaware Corporation Law, known as the "short-form merger" statute. Section 253 permits a parent corporation owning at least 90% of the stock of a subsidiary to merge with that subsidiary, upon approval by the parent's board of directors, and to make payment in cash for the shares of the minority stockholders. The statute does not require the consent of, or advance notice to, the minority stockholders. However, notice of the merger must be given within 10 days after its effective date, and any stockholder who is dissatisfied with the terms of the merger may petition the Delaware Court of Chancery for a decree ordering the surviving corporation to pay him the fair value of his shares, as determined by a court-appointed appraiser subject to review by the court. Del.Code Ann., Tit. 8, §§253, 262.

Santa Fe obtained independent appraisals of the physical assets of Kirby land, timber, buildings, and machinery and of Kirby's oil, gas, and mineral interests. These appraisals, together with other financial information, were submitted to Morgan Stanley & Co. (Morgan Stanley), an investment banking firm retained to appraise the fair market value of Kirby stock. Kirby's physical assets were appraised at $320 million (amounting to $640 for each of the 500,000 shares); Kirby's stock was valued by Morgan Stanley at $125 per share. Under the terms of the merger, minority stockholders were offered $150 per share.

The provisions of the short-form merger statute were fully complied with. The minority stockholders of Kirby were notified the day after the merger became effective and were advised of their right to obtain an appraisal in Delaware court if dissatisfied with the offer of $150 per share. They also received an information statement containing, in addition to the relevant financial data about Kirby, the appraisals of the value of Kirby's assets and the Morgan Stanley appraisal concluding that the fair market value of the stock was $125 per share.

Respondents, minority stockholders of Kirby, objected to the terms of the merger, but did not pursue their appraisal remedy in the Delaware Court of Chancery. Instead, they brought this action in federal court on behalf of the corporation and other minority stockholders, seeking to set aside the merger or to recover what they claimed to be the fair value of their shares. The amended complaint asserted that, based on the fair market value of Kirby's physical assets as revealed by the appraisal included in the information statement sent to minority shareholders, Kirby's stock was worth at least $772 per share. The complaint alleged further that the merger took place without prior notice to minority stockholders; that the purpose of the merger was to appropriate the difference between the "conceded pro rata value of the physical assets," and the offer of $150 per share to "freez(e) out the minority stockholders at a wholly inadequate price," and that Santa Fe, knowing the appraised value of the physical assets, obtained a "fraudulent appraisal" of the stock from Morgan Stanley and offered $25 above that appraisal "in order to lull the minority stockholders into erroneously believing that [Santa Fe was] generous." This course of conduct was alleged to be "a violation of Rule 10b-5" because defendants employed a "device, scheme, or artifice to defraud" and engaged in an "act, practice or course of business which operates or would operate as a fraud or deceit upon any person, in connection with the purchase or sale of any security." Morgan Stanley assertedly participated in the fraud as an accessory by submitting its appraisal of $125 per share although knowing the appraised value of the physical assets. * * *

We granted the petition for certiorari challenging this holding because of the importance of the issue involved to the administration of the federal securities laws. We reverse.

Section 10(b) of the 1934 Act makes it "unlawful for any person * * * to use or employ * * * any manipulative or deceptive device or contrivance in contravention of [Securities and Exchange Commission rules];" Rule 10b-5, promulgated by the SEC under § 10(b), prohibits, in addition to nondisclosure and misrepresentation, any "artifice to defraud" or any act "which operates or would operate as a fraud or deceit." The court below construed the term "fraud" in Rule 10b-5 by adverting to the use of the term in several of this Court's decisions in contexts other than the 1934 Act and the related Securities Act of 1933. The Court of Appeals' approach to the interpretation of Rule 10b-5 is inconsistent with that taken by the Court last Term in *Ernst & Ernst v. Hochfelder*, 425 U.S. 185 (1976). * * *

The language of § 10(b) gives no indication that Congress meant to prohibit any conduct not involving manipulation or deception. Nor have we been cited to any evidence in the legislative history that would support a departure from the language of the statute. "When a statute speaks so specifically in terms of manipulation and deception * * * and when its history reflects no more expansive intent, we are quite unwilling to extend the scope of the statute. * * *" Thus the claim of fraud and fiduciary breach in this complaint states a cause of action under any part of Rule 10b-5 only if the conduct alleged can be fairly viewed as "manipulative or deceptive" within the meaning of the statute.

It is our judgment that the transaction, if carried out as alleged in the complaint, was neither deceptive nor manipulative and therefore did not violate either § 10(b) of the Act or Rule 10b-5. * * *

D. Misappropriation Theory under Rule 10b-5

United States v. O'Hagan

Supreme Court of the United States, (1997) U.S. Lexis 4033

[The portion of this opinion dealing with Rule 14e-3 is set out in Section 20.6.B]

Justice GINSBURG:

This case concerns the interpretation and enforcement of Section 10(b) and Section 14(e) of the Securities Exchange Act of 1934, and rules made by the Securities and Exchange Commission pursuant to these provisions, Rule 10b-5 and Rule 14e-3(a). Two prime questions are presented. The first relates to the misappropriation of material, nonpublic information for securities trading; the second concerns fraudulent practices in the tender offer setting. In particular, we address and resolve these issues: (1) Is a person who trades in securities for personal profit, using confidential information misappropriated in breach of a fiduciary duty to the source of the information, guilty of violating Section 10(b) and Rule 10b-5? (2) Did the Commission exceed its rulemaking authority by adopting Rule 14e-3(a), which proscribes trading on undisclosed information in the tender offer setting, even in the absence of a duty to disclose? Our answer to the first question is yes, and to the second question, viewed in the context of this case, no.

[**Facts**] Respondent James Herman O'Hagan was a partner in the law firm of Dorsey & Whitney in Minneapolis, Minnesota. In July 1988, Grand Metropolitan PLC (Grand Met), a company based in London, England, retained Dorsey & Whitney as local counsel to represent Grand Met regarding a potential tender offer for the common stock of the Pillsbury Company, headquartered in Minneapolis. Both Grand Met and Dorsey & Whitney took precautions to protect the confidentiality of Grand Met's tender offer plans. O'Hagan did no work on the Grand Met representation. Dorsey & Whitney withdrew from representing Grand Met on September 9, 1988. Less than a month later, on October 4, 1988, Grand Met publicly announced its tender offer for Pillsbury stock.

On August 18, 1988, while Dorsey & Whitney was still representing Grand Met, O'Hagan began purchasing call options for Pillsbury stock. Each option gave him the right to purchase 100 shares of Pillsbury stock by a specified date in September 1988. Later in August and in September, O'Hagan made additional purchases of Pillsbury call options. * * * O'Hagan also purchased, in September 1988, some 5,000 shares of Pillsbury common stock, at a price just under $39 per share. When Grand Met announced its tender offer in October, the price of Pillsbury stock rose to nearly $60 per share. O'Hagan then sold his Pillsbury call options and common stock, making a profit of more than $4.3 million.

[**Previous Disposition**] The Securities and Exchange Commission (SEC or Commission) initiated an investigation into O'Hagan's transactions, culminating in a 57-count indictment. The indictment alleged that O'Hagan defrauded his law firm and its client, Grand Met, by using for his own trading purposes material, nonpublic information regarding Grand Met's planned tender offer. * * * O'Hagan was charged with * * * securities fraud, in violation of Section 10(b) of the Securities Exchange Act of 1934 (Exchange Act), and SEC Rule 10b-5; [and] * * * fraudulent trading in connection with a tender offer, in violation of Section 14(e) of the Exchange Act, and SEC Rule 14e-3(a). * * * A jury convicted O'Hagan on all 57 counts, and he was sentenced to a 41-month term of imprisonment.

A divided panel of the Court of Appeals for the Eighth Circuit reversed all of O'Hagan's convictions. Liability under Section 10(b) and Rule 10b-5, the Eighth Circuit held, may not be grounded on the "misappropriation theory" of securities fraud on which the prosecution relied. The Court of Appeals also held that Rule 14e-3(a)—which prohibits trading while in possession of material, nonpublic information relating to a tender offer—exceeds the SEC's Section 14(e) rulemaking authority because the rule contains no breach of fiduciary duty requirement. * * *

[**Analysis**] Under the "traditional" or "classical theory" of insider trading liability, Section 10(b) and Rule 10b-5 are violated when a corporate insider trades in the securities of his corporation on the basis of material, nonpublic information. Trading on such information qualifies as a "deceptive device" under Section 10(b), we have affirmed, because "a relationship of trust and confidence [exists] between the shareholders of a corporation and those insiders who have obtained confidential information by reason of their position with that corporation." *Chiarella v. United States*, 445 U.S. 222, 228 (1980). That relationship, we recognized, "gives rise to a duty to disclose [or to abstain from trading] because of the 'necessity of preventing a corporate insider from * * * taking unfair advantage of * * * uninformed * * * stockholders.'" The classical theory applies not only to officers, directors, and other permanent insiders of a corporation, but also to attorneys, accountants, consultants, and others who temporarily become fiduciaries of a corporation. *See Dirks v. SEC*, 463 U.S. 646, 655, n. 14 (1983).

The "misappropriation theory" holds that a person commits fraud "in connection with" a securities transaction, and thereby violates Section 10(b) and Rule 10b-5, when he misappropriates confidential information for securities trading purposes, in breach of a duty owed to the source of the information. Under this theory, a fiduciary's undisclosed, self-serving use of a principal's information to purchase or sell securities, in breach of a duty of loyalty and confidentiality, defrauds the principal of the exclusive use of that information. In lieu of premising liability on a fiduciary relationship between company insider and purchaser or seller of the company's stock, the misappropriation theory premises liability on a fiduciary-turned-trader's deception of those who entrusted him with access to confidential information. * * *

In this case, the indictment alleged that O'Hagan, in breach of a duty of trust and confidence he owed to his law firm, Dorsey & Whitney, and to its client, Grand Met, traded on the basis of nonpublic information regarding Grand Met's planned tender offer for Pillsbury common stock. This conduct, the Government charged, constituted a fraudulent device in connection with the purchase and sale of securities.

We agree with the Government that misappropriation, as just defined, satisfies Section 10(b)'s requirement that chargeable conduct involve a "deceptive device or contrivance" used "in connection with" the purchase or sale of securities. * * *

In sum, considering the inhibiting impact on market participation of trading on misappropriated information, and the congressional purposes underlying Section 10(b), it makes scant sense to hold a lawyer like O'Hagan a Section 10(b) violator if he works for a law firm representing the target of a tender offer, but not if he works for a law firm representing the bidder. The text of the statute requires no such result. The misappropriation at issue here was properly made the subject of a Section 10(b) charge because it meets the statutory requirement that there be "deceptive" conduct "in connection with" securities transactions. * * *

§ 4.5 Materiality under the 33 and 34 Acts

A. The Supreme Court's View under Section 14(a) of the 34 Act

TSC Industries, Inc. v. Northway

United States Supreme Court (1976) 96 S. Ct. 2126

Mr. Justice Marshall:

The proxy rules promulgated by the Securities and Exchange Commission under the Securities Exchange Act of 1934 bar the use of proxy statements that are false or misleading with respect to the presentation or omission of material facts. [*See* Rule 14a-9] We are called upon to consider the definition of a material fact under those rules, and the appropriateness of resolving the question of materiality by summary judgment in this case.

[**Facts**] The dispute in this case centers on the acquisition of petitioner TSC Industries, Inc., by petitioner National Industries, Inc. In February 1969 National acquired 34% of TSC's voting securities by purchase from Charles E. Schmidt and his family. Schmidt, who had been TSC's founder and principal shareholder, promptly resigned along with his son from TSC's board of directors. Thereafter, five National nominees were placed on TSC's board; and Stanley R. Yarmuth, National's president and chief executive officer, became chairman of the TSC board, and Charles F. Simonelli, National's executive vice president, became chairman of the TSC executive committee. On October 16, 1969, the TSC board, with the attending National nominees abstaining, approved a proposal to liquidate and sell all of TSC's assets to National. The proposal in substance provided for the exchange of TSC common and Series 1 preferred stock for National Series B preferred stock and warrants. On November 12, 1969, TSC and National issued a joint proxy statement to their shareholders, recommending approval of the proposal. The proxy solicitation was successful, TSC was placed in liquidation and dissolution, and the exchange of shares was effected.

[**Plaintiff's Position**] This is an action brought by respondent Northway, a TSC shareholder, against TSC and National, claiming that their joint proxy statement was incomplete and materially misleading in violation of § 14(a) of the Securities Exchange Act of 1934 and Rules 14a-3 and 14a-9, promulgated thereunder. * * * The Rule 14a-9 claim, insofar as it concerns us, is that TSC and National omitted from the proxy statement material facts relating to the degree of National's control over TSC and the favorability of the terms of the proposal to TSC shareholders. * * *

[**Analysis**] As we have noted on more than one occasion, § 14(a) of the Securities Exchange Act "was intended to promote 'the free exercise of the voting rights of stockholders' by ensuring that proxies would be solicited with 'explanation to the stockholder of the real nature of the questions for which authority to cast his vote is sought.'" *Mills v. Electric Auto-Lite Co.*, [Section 13.17.A]. *See also J. I. Case Co. v. Borak*, [Section 13.16]. In *Borak*, the Court held that § 14(a)'s broad remedial purposes required recognition under § 27 of the Securities Exchange Act, of an implied private right of action for violations of the provision. And in *Mills*, we attempted to clarify to some extent the elements of a private cause of action for violation of § 14(a). In a suit challenging the sufficiency under § 14(a) and Rule 14a-9 of a proxy statement soliciting votes in favor of a merger, we held that there was no need to demonstrate that the alleged defect in the proxy statement actually had a decisive effect on the voting. So long as the misstatement or omission was material, the causal relation between violation and injury is sufficiently established, we concluded, if "the proxy solicitation itself * * * was an essential link in the accomplishment of the transaction." After *Mills*, then, the content given to the notion of materiality assumes heightened significance.

The question of materiality, it is universally agreed, is an objective one, involving the significance of an omitted or misrepresented fact to a reasonable investor. Variations in the formulation of a general test of materiality occur in the articulation of just how significant a fact must be or, put another way, how certain it must be that the fact would affect a reasonable investor's judgment.

The Court of Appeals in this case concluded that material facts include "all facts which a reasonable shareholder *might* consider important." This formulation of the test of materiality has been explicitly rejected by at least two courts as setting too low a threshold for the imposition of liability under Rule 14a-9. * * *

In arriving at its broad definition of a material fact as one that a reasonable shareholder *might* consider important, the Court of Appeals in this case relied heavily upon language of this Court in *Mills v. Electric Auto-Lite Co., supra*. That reliance was misplaced. The *Mills* Court did characterize a determination of materiality as at least "embod(ying) a conclusion that the defect was of such a character that it might have been considered important by a reasonable shareholder who was in the process of deciding how to vote." But if any language in *Mills* is to be read as suggesting a general notion of materiality, it can only be the opinion's subsequent reference to materiality as a "requirement that the defect have a significant *propensity* to affect the voting process." For it was that requirement that the Court said "adequately serves the purpose of ensuring that a cause of action cannot be established by proof of a defect so trivial, or so unrelated to the transaction for which approval is sought, that correction of the defect or imposition of liability would not further the interests protected by § 14(a)." * * *

The general standard of materiality that we think best comports with the policies of Rule 14a-9 is as follows: An omitted fact is material if there is a substantial likelihood that a reasonable shareholder would consider it important in deciding how to vote. This standard is fully consistent with *Mills* general description of materiality as a requirement that "the defect have a significant *propensity* to affect the voting process." It does not require proof of a substantial likelihood that disclosure of the omitted fact would have caused the reasonable investor to change his vote. What the standard does contemplate is a showing of a substantial likelihood that, under all the circumstances, the omitted fact would have assumed actual significance in the deliberations of the reasonable shareholder. Put another way, there must be a substantial likelihood that the disclosure of the omitted fact would have been viewed by the reasonable investor as having significantly altered the "total mix" of information made available. * * *

In summary, none of the omissions claimed to have been in violation of Rule 14a-9 were, so far as the record reveals, materially misleading as a matter of law, and Northway was not entitled to partial summary judgment. The judgment of the Court of Appeals is reversed, and the case is remanded for further proceedings consistent with this opinion.

B. The Supreme Court's View under Rule 10b-5 of the 34 Act

Basic, Inc. v. Levinson

United States Supreme Court, (1988) 108 S. Ct. 978

* * * The Court also explicitly has defined a standard of materiality under the securities laws, *see TSC Industries, Inc. v. Northway, Inc.*, [Section 4.5.A], concluding in the proxy-solicitation context that "[a]n omitted fact is material if there is a substantial likelihood that a reasonable shareholder would consider it important in deciding how to vote." Acknowledging that certain information concerning corporate developments could well be of "dubious significance," the Court was careful not to set too low a standard of materiality; it was concerned that a minimal standard might bring an overabundance of information within its reach, and lead management "simply to bury the shareholders in an avalanche of trivial information—a result that is hardly conducive to informed decision making." It further explained that to fulfill the materiality requirement "there must be a substantial likelihood that the disclosure of the omitted fact would have been viewed by the reasonable investor as having significantly altered the 'total mix' of information made available." We now expressly adopt the *TSC Industries* standard of materiality for the § 10(b) and Rule 10b-5 context.

C. Materiality under the 33 Act

Rule 405 under the 33 Act defines the term "material" as follows:

> The term "material," when used to qualify a requirement for the furnishing of information as to any subject, limits the information required to those matters to which there is a substantial likelihood that a reasonable investor would attach importance in determining whether to purchase the security registered.

D. SEC's View of Materiality in Financial Statements

Staff Accounting Bulletin No. 99

(August 19, 1999)

Facts: During the course of preparing or auditing year-end financial statements, financial management or the registrant's independent auditor becomes aware of misstatements in a registrant's financial statements. When combined, the misstatements result in a 4% overstatement of net income and a $.02 (4%) overstatement of earnings per share. Because no item in the registrant's consolidated financial statements is misstated by more than 5%, management and the independent auditor conclude that the deviation from generally accepted accounting principles ("GAAP") is immaterial and that the accounting is permissible.

Question: Each Statement of Financial Accounting Standards adopted by the Financial Accounting Standards Board ("FASB") states, "The provisions of this Statement need not be applied to immaterial items." In the staff's view, may a registrant or the auditor of its financial statements assume the immateriality of items that fall below a percentage threshold set by management or the auditor to determine whether amounts and items are material to the financial statements?

Interpretive Response: No. The staff is aware that certain registrants, over time, have developed quantitative thresholds as "rules of thumb" to assist in the preparation of their financial statements, and that auditors also have used these thresholds in their evaluation of whether items might be considered material to users of a registrant's financial statements. One rule of thumb in particular suggests that the misstatement or omission of an item that falls under a 5% threshold is not material in the absence of particularly egregious circumstances, such as self-dealing or misappropriation by senior management. The staff reminds registrants and the auditors of their financial statements that exclusive reliance on this or any percentage or numerical threshold has no basis in the accounting literature or the law. * * *

Under the governing principles, an assessment of materiality requires that one views the facts in the context of the "surrounding circumstances," as the accounting literature puts it, or the "total mix" of information, in the words of the Supreme Court [*see TSC*, Section 4.5.A]. * * *

§4.6 Introduction to (1) the Registration Requirements under Section 5 of the 1933 Act, (2) the SEC's 2005 Securities Offering Reform Rules, and (3) the 2012 JOBS Act

A. In General

When issuing shares or other securities a corporation must not only comply with the applicable state corporation law, it must also comply with the requirements of the Securities Act of 1933 (the 33 Act). Broadly speaking, the 33 Act applies to the issuance of any "security" through the use of interstate commerce. The term "security" is defined very broadly in Section 2 of the 33 Act to mean "any note, stock, treasury stock, bond, evidence of indebtedness, certificate of interest * * *" etc. It is clear that stock in business corporations, whether publicly traded or closely-held, constitutes a security under Section 2. *See Landreth Timber Company v. Landreth*, 471 U.S. 681 (1985) and *Gould v. Ruefenacht*, 471 U.S. 701 (1985). [*See* Chapter 11].

As will be seen below, the Act requires that prior to the sale or other issuance of securities, the securities must be either registered with the Securities and Exchange Commission (the SEC) or the securities or the transaction must be specifically exempted from the registration requirement. Section 3 of the 33 Act exempts certain securities, such as municipal bonds, and Section 4 of the 34 Act exempts certain transactions, such as a private offerings of securities.

Even though an issuance of shares may be in full compliance with state corporate law (*i.e.*, the corporation has sufficient authorized but unissued shares, legal consideration is paid for the shares, and the board acts properly in issuing the shares), the issuance of such shares must either be registered under the 33 Act or exempt from registration. This applies also to publicly-traded corporations that issue additional shares; any newly issued shares must be either registered or exempt under the 33 Act.

In any acquisition transaction in which the acquiring corporation issues its stock or debt securities in exchange for the target's stock or assets, it is necessary to determine whether (1) the acquiring corporation is required to register its stock or debt instruments prior to issuance, or (2) such stock or debt instruments can be issued pursuant to an exemption from registration.

In the case of a sale of an issuer's securities to the public, as distinguished from the issuance of an acquiror's securities in an acquisition transaction, underwriters will undertake to sell the issuer's securities through a group of broker-dealers. The underwriters act as wholesalers, and the broker-dealers (the selling group) act as retailers of the securities. There are two basic types of underwriting arrangements: the firm commitment and the best efforts. Under a firm commitment, the underwriters purchase the securities from the issuer at the designated price and then resell them at a markup. Under a best efforts, the underwriters put forward their best efforts to sell the securities on behalf of the issuer. Only the firm commitment underwriting, which is the most common, is examined further here.

B. Introduction to the Registration Requirement of Section 5

Section 5 is the heart of the 33 Act. Section 5(a) provides that unless a "registration statement" with respect to a security is effective, it is unlawful to sell the security. Under Section 12(a)(1), if a sale is made in violation of Section 5, the purchaser has an absolute right to put the securities back to the seller, without regard to whether there was any material misrepresentation or fault on the part of the seller.

A "registration statement" is a document filed with the SEC. As will be seen in Section 4.8.C, registration statements are generally filed on Forms S-1, S-3, or S-4. The S-4 is generally used in a merger or acquisition transaction and is examined in detail in Chapter 13, which deals with negotiated acquisitions. The S-1 and S-3 are examined further in this chapter. The S-1 requires full disclosure of all information regarding the issuer and the transaction and is used, for example, in IPOs. Certain publicly traded companies can use the less onerous disclosure required by the S-3, which requires full disclosure about the transaction, but allows "incorporation by reference" to publicly available information about the issuer. The registration statement discloses the facts concerning the security and the issuer. It does not become effective until full disclosure has been made to the satisfaction of the SEC. It contains a "prospectus," which is distributed to prospective purchasers (the offerees).

The period before the registration statement is filed is referred to as the pre-filing period; the period after filing but before the registration statement becomes effective is referred to as the waiting period; and the period after a registration statement becomes effective is referred to as the post-effective period. These three periods, which are governed by Section 5, are examined below after an introduction to (1) the SEC's 2005 Securities Offering Reform Rules, and (2) the 2012 JOBS Act, which made changes in the rules under Section 5.

C. Introduction to the SEC's 2005 Securities Offering Reform Rules

1. In General

In December of 2005 the SEC adopted new Securities Offering Reform rules, which substantially modified the rules and regulations issued under the 33 Act regarding registered offerings of securities. The greatest impact of these rules is for issuances of securities by public companies whose securities are widely traded. These companies are known as "well-known seasoned issuers" or WKSIs. The following excerpt from the adopting release explains the background of the rules. In dealing with these new rules, it is important to first determine whether the issuer is a WKSI or a non-WKSI. For purposes of this chapter, non-WKSIs encompass only an issuer engaging in an initial public offering (IPO), that is, a closely-held company issuing its shares to the public in a registered offering, and this chapter focuses mainly on non-WKSIs.

2. The Adopting Release Generally

Securities and Exchange Commission, Securities Offering Reform, Release No. 33–8591

(August 3, 2005)

Overview * * * We are adopting the proposed revisions to the registration, communications, and offering processes for registered transactions under the Securities Act with certain modifications. We believe the rules we are adopting, while limited in scope, properly address the areas that are in need of modernization. The adopted rules involve three main areas: Communications related to registered securities offerings; Registration and other procedures in the offering and capital formation processes; and Delivery of information to investors, including delivery through access and notice, and timeliness of that delivery. * * *

We believe that the rule changes we adopt today will: Facilitate greater availability of information to investors and the market with regard to all issuers; Eliminate barriers to open communications that have been made increasingly outmoded by technological advances; Reflect the increased importance of electronic dissemination of information, including the use of the Internet; Make the capital formation process more efficient; and Define more clearly both the information and the timeliness of the availability of information against which a seller's statements are evaluated for liability purposes. * * *

Well-Known Seasoned Issuers. [*Introduction*] We are modifying the framework for communications in connection with public offerings for all issuers and the framework of the registration process for most issuers that report under the Exchange Act [*i.e.*, public companies that are registered under the 34 Act and file periodic reports under that Act]. As we explained in the Proposing Release, we believe that the most far-reaching revisions of our communications rules and registration processes should be considered for issuers that have a reporting history under the Exchange Act and are presumptively the most widely followed in the marketplace [i.e., WKSIs].

Today, the largest issuers are followed by sophisticated institutional and retail investors, members of the financial press, and numerous sell-side and buy-side analysts that actively seek new information on a continual basis. * * * The communications of these well-known seasoned issuers are subject to scrutiny by investors, the financial press, analysts, and others who evaluate disclosure when it is made.

Definition of Well-Known Seasoned Issuer. [Rule 405 of the 33 Act] We are adding a new category of issuer—a "well-known seasoned issuer"—that will be permitted to benefit to the greatest degree from the modifications to our rules we are adopting today regarding communications and the registration processes. We are defining a well-known seasoned issuer as an issuer that is required to file reports pursuant to Section 13(a) or Section 15(d) the Exchange Act and satisfies the following requirements as of the date on which its status as a well-known seasoned issuer is determined: The issuer must meet the registrant requirements of Form S-3 or Form F-3 [for foreign issuers]; The issuer either: As of a date within 60 days of its eligibility determination date must have a worldwide market value of its outstanding voting and non-voting common equity held by non-affiliates of $700 million or more; or As of a date within 60 days of its eligibility determination date, must have issued in the last three years, at least $1 billion aggregate principal amount of non-convertible securities, other than common equity, in primary offerings for cash, not exchange. * * *

D. Introduction to the 2012 JOBS Act and Its Applicability to Registered Offerings

The Jumpstart Our Business Startups Act (JOBS Act) is a federal law passed in 2012 with the hope of increasing "American job creation and economic growth by improving access to the public capital markets for emerging growth companies." (Preamble to JOBS Act). Among other things, this legislation, which amended both the 33 and 34 Acts, added the concept of an "emerging growth company," which generally means a company with revenues of less than $1,000,000,000.

The SEC summarized as follows the provisions of the bill dealing with emerging growth companies:

> Title I provides scaled disclosure provisions for emerging growth companies, including, among other things, [1] two years of audited financial statements in the Securities Act registration statement [*i.e.*, Form S-1] for an initial public offering of common equity securities, [2] the smaller reporting company version of Item 402 of Regulation S-K [*see* discussion *infra*], and [3] no requirement for Sarbanes-Oxley Act Section 404(b) auditor attestations of internal control over financial reporting [*see* discussion *infra*]. Title I also [1] enables emerging growth companies to use test-the-waters communications [*see* discussion *infra*] with [Qualified Institutional Buyers] and institutional accredited investors and [2] liberalizes the use of research reports on emerging growth companies.[1]

Other provision of the JOBS Act deal with (1) when a company becomes a '34 Act reporting company under Section 12(g) of the 34 Act, (2) exemptions from registration, including the Crowdfunding exemption, and (3) the relaxation of the "no general solicitation" ban in private offerings. Each of these provisions is examined further in this chapter.

E. The Pre-Filing Period

1. The Pre-Filing Period before the 2005 SEC Reforms and 2012 JOBS Act Changes

Sections 5(c) of the Act makes it unlawful to "offer to sell" or "offer to buy" any security through the use of a prospectus or otherwise, unless a registration statement has been filed. The period prior to the filing of a registration statement is referred to as the "pre-filing period." Any offers to sell or buy during this period are referred to as "jumping the gun." The term "offer to sell" is defined very broadly in Section 2(a)(3) to include "every attempt or offer to dispose of, or solicitation of an offer to buy, a security * * * for value." Section 2(a)(3) exempts from the scope of the terms "offer to sell" or "offer to buy" preliminary negotiations between an issuer and an underwriter or a group of underwriters.

The pre-filing period is discussed as follows in SEC Release No. 33-4697 (1964):

> It should be borne in mind that publicity about an issuer, its securities or the proposed offering prior to the filing of a registration statement may constitute

---

1. SEC, *Jumpstart Our Business Startups Act, Frequently Asked Questions Generally Applicable Questions on Title I of the JOBS Act* (May 3, 2012).

an illegal offer to sell. Thus, announcement of the underwriter's identity should be avoided during this period. Experience shows that such announcements are very likely to lead to illegal offers to buy. * * *

These principles, however, are not intended to restrict the normal communications between an issuer and its stockholders or the announcement to the public generally of information with respect to important business and financial developments. Such announcements are required in the listing agreements used by stock exchanges, and the Commission is sensitive to the importance of encouraging this type of communication. In recognition of this requirement of certain stock exchanges, the Commission adopted Rule 135, which permits a brief announcement of [certain proposed registered] offerings * * * as not constituting an offer of a security for the purposes of Section 5 of the Act. [Thus, Rule 135 permits, for example, a press release announcing the offering limited to the information set out in the rule.]

2. The Pre-Filing Period after the 2005 SEC Reforms

Securities Offering Reform, Release No. 33–8591 (August 3, 2005), provides the following summary of the reforms that are applicable to the pre-filing period (read and study the referenced rules):

Overview of Communications Rules. Today, we are adopting rules that relate to the following: Regularly released factual business information; Regularly released forward-looking information; Communications made more than 30 days before filing a registration statement; Communications by well-known seasoned issuers [WKSIs] during the 30 days before filing a registration statement; [and] Written communications made in accordance with the safe harbor in Securities Act Rule 134 * * *:

The cumulative effect of the rules under the gun-jumping provisions is the following:

- Well-known seasoned issuers are permitted to engage at any time in oral and written communications, including use at any time of a free writing prospectus, subject to enumerated conditions (including, in specified cases, filing with us). [Rule 163] [A "free writing prospectus" is defined in Rule 405 to mean "except as otherwise provided specifically or otherwise required by the context, a written communication that constitutes an offer to sell or a solicitation of an offer to buy securities that are or will be the subject of a registration statement" and is not: A prospectus satisfying the requirements of Securities Act Section 10(a) (*i.e.*, a final prospectus); A prospectus satisfying our rules permitting the use of preliminary or summary prospectuses or prospectuses subject to completion (*e.g.*, a red herring preliminary prospectus); * * * A prospectus because a final prospectus meeting the requirements of Section 10(a) was sent or given with or prior to the written communication (a free writing accompanied by a final prospectus).]
- All reporting issuers are permitted, at any time, to continue to publish regularly released factual business information and forward-looking information. [Rule 168]
- Non-reporting issuers are permitted, at any time, to continue to publish regularly released factual business information that is intended for use by persons other than in their capacity as investors or potential investors. [Rule 169]
- Communications by issuers more than 30 days before filing a registration statement are not prohibited offers so long as they do not reference a securities offering that is or will be the subject of a registration statement. [Rule 163A] * * *

3. The Pre-Filing Period after the 2012 JOBS Act, "Test the Waters"

The JOBS Act added Section 5(d) to the 33 Act, which in certain cases permits a company to "test the waters" for a potential securities offering before (and after) the filing of a registration statement for the offering. Section 5(d) provides:

> (d) Limitation- Notwithstanding any other provision of this section, an emerging growth company or any person authorized to act on behalf of an emerging growth company may engage in oral or written communications with potential investors that are qualified institutional buyers or institutions that are accredited investors, as such terms are respectively defined in section 230.144A and section 230.501(a) of title 17, Code of Federal Regulations, or any successor thereto, to determine whether such investors might have an interest in a contemplated securities offering, either prior to or following the date of filing of a registration statement with respect to such securities with the Commission, subject to the requirement of subsection (b)(2).

Note that an "emerging growth company" can only test the waters with qualified institutional buyers (QIBs) and accredited investors, which, as will be seen below, are sophisticated and wealthy investors.

4. The Pre-Filing Period: Confidential Filings of an S-1—Twitter

Under pre-JOBS Act rules, IPO and other 33 Act registration statements generally could not be filed on a confidential basis. However, the JOBS Act added Section 6(e)(1) to the 33 Act, which permits an emerging growth company to file on a confidential basis a registration statement for an IPO. This section reads as follows:

> (1) IN GENERAL- Any emerging growth company, prior to its initial public offering date, may confidentially submit to the Commission a draft registration statement, for confidential nonpublic review by the staff of the Commission prior to public filing, provided that the initial confidential submission and all amendments thereto shall be publicly filed with the Commission not later than 21 days before the date on which the issuer conducts a road show, as such term is defined in section 230.433(h)(4) of title 17, Code of Federal Regulations, or any successor thereto.

Twitter, a San Francisco-based non-public company announced in the following Tweet that it was using this confidential filing process for its IPO:

> Twitter @twitter
>
> We've confidentially submitted an S-1 to the SEC for a planned IPO. This Tweet does not constitute an offer of any securities for sale.

In his September 12, 2013 New York Times, DealBook article entitled*An Initial Filing, in Fewer Than 140 Characters*, Professor Davidoff explains as follows the purpose of the confidentiality provision:

> One of the major benefits of the JOBS Act is that Twitter does not have to disclose publicly its registration statement for its filing. Section 106 of the law states that a registration statement for an emerging growth company can be filed and reviewed by the Securities and Exchange Commission confidentially. According to Ernst & Young, in the first year of the JOBS Act, 63 percent of eligible companies filed their statements confidentially, making this one of the new law's most popular provisions. * * *

The idea behind this provision is to allow companies to test the waters. The S.E.C. will review the companies' filings confidentially so that the company can decide whether to proceed with an offering without the public knowing. Additionally, this allows the company to work out any problems with the regulator outside of the glare of the public eye.

F. The Waiting Period

1. The Waiting Period before the 2005 SEC Reforms

Pursuant to Section 5(b)(1) of the 33 Act, a preliminary prospectus meeting the requirements of Section 10(b) of the 33 Act may be distributed during the period between the filing of a registration statement and the date it becomes effective. This interim period is known as the "waiting period." The preliminary prospectus, which is issued pursuant to Rule 430, is referred to as a "red herring" because of the statement it must contain that a registration statement has been filed but has not become effective. Specifically, Item 501 of Regulation S-K, which is discussed below, requires that the preliminary prospectus contain a prominent legend, generally in red, to the following effect:

> The information in this prospectus is not complete and may be changed. We may not sell these securities until the registration statement filed with the [SEC] is effective. This prospectus is not an offer to sell these securities and it is not soliciting an offer to buy these securities in any state where the offer or sale is not permitted.

The preliminary prospectus usually does not contain any information concerning the price at which the securities are to be sold.

The waiting period is discussed as follows in SEC Release 33-4697 (1964):

> After the registration statement is filed, and before its effective date, offers to sell the securities are permitted but no written offer may be made except by means of a statutory prospectus. For this purpose the statutory prospectus includes the preliminary prospectus provided for in Rule [430]. In addition the so-called 'tombstone' advertisement permitted by Rule 134 may be used. [The information in the tombstone is limited to that specified in Rule 134(a) and the tombstone must contain a legend as required by Rule 134(b) unless the information is limited to that set out in Rule 134(c).]
>
> During the period after the filing of a registration statement, the freedom of an underwriter or dealer expecting to participate in the distribution, to communicate with his customers is limited only by the antifraud provisions of the Securities Act and the Securities Exchange Act, and by the fact that written offering material other than a statutory prospectus or tombstone advertisement may not be used. In other words, during this period "free writing" is illegal. The dealer, therefore, can orally solicit indications of interest or offers to buy and may discuss the securities with his customers and advise them whether or not in his opinion the securities are desirable or suitable for them. [As will be seen below, free writing prospectuses may now be used during this period.] In this connection a dealer proposing to discuss an issue of securities with his customers should obtain copies of the preliminary prospectus in order to have a reliable source of information. This is particularly important where he proposes to recommend the securities, or where information concerning them has not been generally available. The corollary of the dealer's obligation to secure the copy is the obligation of the

issuer and managing underwriters to make it readily available. Rule 460 provides that as a condition to acceleration of the effective date of a registration statement [*i.e.*, the SEC declaring the registration effective upon the request of the issuer], the Commission will consider whether the persons making the offering have taken reasonable steps to make the information contained in the registration statement available to dealers who may participate in the distribution.

It is a principal purpose of the so-called "waiting period" between the filing date and the effective date to enable dealers and, through them, investors to become acquainted with the information contained in the registration statement and to arrive at an unhurried decision concerning the merits of the securities. [Thus, the SEC wants the preliminary prospectus to be distributed widely to potential investors.] Consistently with this purpose, no contracts of sale can be made during this period, the purchase price may not be paid or received and offers to buy [*i.e.*, indications of interest] may be cancelled.

During the waiting period, to generate interest in the securities, the underwriters will often go around the country (or world) putting on "road shows" for professional investors. Road shows are explored further below.

2. The Waiting Period after the 2005 SEC Reforms: "Free Writing Prospectuses" and "Electronic Road Shows"

Securities Offering Reform, Release No. 33–8591 (August 3, 2005), provides the following summary of the reforms that are applicable to the waiting period (read and study the referenced rules):

Overview of Communications Rules. * * *

- All issuers and offering participants are permitted to use *free writing prospectuses* after the filing of the registration statement, subject to enumerated conditions (including, in specified cases, filing with us). [Rules 164 and 433]
- A broader category of routine communications regarding issuers, offerings, and procedural matters, such as communications about the schedule for an offering or about account-opening procedures, are excluded from the definition of "prospectus." [Amendments to Rule 134] * * *

Road Shows. Definition of Electronic Road Show. [*See* Rule 433(h)(4) and (5)] Issuers and underwriters frequently conduct presentations known as "road shows" to market their offerings to the public. These road shows are a primary means by which issuers are involved directly and actively in a selling effort to investors. Historically, these presentations were conducted in person and limited to institutional investors. Today, due to advances in electronic media, road shows also are being conducted or re-transmitted over the Internet or other electronic media and in some cases to broader audiences.

We indicated in the Proposing Release that we intended to clarify the treatment of all electronic communications, including electronic road shows, as graphic communications [*see* Rule 405] under the Securities Act. Under the proposed rules, all electronic road shows would have been written offers and prospectuses, but also would have been permitted subject to conditions, as free writing prospectuses.

[W]e have revised the definition of graphic communication from the proposal to exclude a communication that, at the time of the communication, originates live, in real-time to a live audience and does not originate in recorded form or otherwise as a graphic communication, although it may be transmitted through graphic means. This revision applies in the context of road shows. Under the definition, a live, in real-time road show to a live audience that is transmitted graphically will not be a graphic communication, and therefore not a written communication, or a free writing prospectus. It will still, however, be an offer subject to Securities Act Section 12(a)(2) and the other liability provisions of the federal securities laws. Thus, * * * information that is presented as part of the live, in real-time road show to a live audience will not be a free writing prospectus. * * *

Road shows that do not originate live, in real-time to a live audience and are graphically transmitted are electronic road shows that will be considered written communications and, therefore, free writing prospectuses. * * *

Treatment of Electronic Road Shows. Electronic road shows have to date proceeded in reliance on a series of no-action letters granted by the staff of the Division of Corporation Finance. The rules we are adopting today permit the use of electronic road shows without many of the conditions in the electronic road show no-action letters. As we discussed in the Proposing Release, the electronic road show no-action letters for registered public offerings are withdrawn as of the effective date of Rule 433.

For road shows that are free writing prospectuses, the filing conditions of Rule 433 do not apply, with one exception. In the case of an issuer that is not required to file reports under Exchange Act Section 13 or Section 15(d) at the time of filing the registration statement [*e.g.*, an issuer engaging in an IPO] and is registering an offering of common equity or convertible equity securities, the filing condition applies to a road show that is a free writing prospectus unless the issuer makes at least one version of a *bona fide* electronic road show [*see* Rule 433(h)(5)] for the offering in question readily available without restriction electronically to any potential investor. [*See* Rule 433(d)(8)(ii)] . * * *

Whether or not road shows are written communications, all road shows that are offers are subject to Securities Act Section 12(a)(2) liability. In addition, all road shows that are offers that are written communications are free writing prospectuses, whether or not required to be filed.

3. The Waiting Period after the 2012 JOBS Act, "Test the Waters"

As discussed in connection with the pre-filing period, the JOBS Act added Section 5(d), which in certain cases permits a company to "test the waters" for a potential securities offering during both the pre-filing and waiting periods.

F. The Post-Effective Period

1. The Post-Effective Period before the 2005 SEC Reforms

Section 5(b)(2) of the Act makes it unlawful to transport in interstate commerce any security for sale, unless such security is accompanied or preceded by a prospectus complying with Section 10(a) (a final or statutory prospectus). The term "prospectus" is defined broadly in Section 2(a)(10) as any "notice, circular, advertisement, letter communication, written or by radio or television, which offers any security for sale * * *."

The interaction between Section 5(a) and Section 5(b)(2) requires that a registration statement be effective prior to any sale and that the purchaser receive a copy of the statutory prospectus. Pursuant to Section 2(a)(10), selling literature (free writing) concerning the securities and issuer may accompany a statutory prospectus. Also, under Section 2(a)(10), the statutory prospectus must precede or accompany the confirmation of sale. As discussed below, the Securities Offering Reform rules have relaxed this rule.

2. The Post-Effective Period after the 2005 SEC Reforms

Securities Offering Reform, Release No. 33–8591 (August 3, 2005), provides the following summary of the reforms that are applicable to the post-effective period (read and study the referenced rules):

> **Prospectus Delivery Reforms** *Current Prospectus Delivery Requirements.* The Securities Act requires delivery of a prospectus meeting the requirements of Securities Act Section 10(a), known as a "final prospectus," to each investor in a registered offering. After the effective date of a registration statement, a written communication that offers a security for sale or confirms the sale of a security may be provided if a final prospectus is sent or given previously or at the same time [Section 2(a)(10)].
>
> Otherwise, such a communication is a prospectus and may not be provided unless it meets the requirements of Securities Act Section 10(a). A written confirmation is not designed to meet these requirements. Therefore, a final prospectus must accompany or precede a written confirmation. In addition, Securities Act Section 5(b)(2) makes it unlawful to deliver a security "unless accompanied or preceded" by a final prospectus.
>
> Under these requirements, in the current system, if no preliminary prospectus or written selling materials are distributed, the final prospectus is the only prospectus received by investors. However, an investor's purchase commitment and the resulting contract of sale of securities to the investor in the offering generally occur before the final prospectus is required to be delivered under the Securities Act. * * *
>
> At this time, we believe that Internet usage has increased sufficiently to allow us to adopt a final prospectus delivery model for issuers and their intermediaries that relies on timely access to filed information and documents. Issuers, brokers, and dealers can satisfy their final prospectus delivery obligations if a final prospectus is or will be on file with us within the time required by the new rules, including the cure period.

[*See* Rules 172, 173 and 174 under the 33 Act.]

G. Summary of Operation of Section 5

The operation of Section 5, taking account of the 2005 Securities Offering Reforms and the 2012 JOBS Act, may be summarized as follows:

(1) **Pre-Filing Period.** During the period before the filing of a registration statement, no offer to buy or sell the security may be made [*see* Section 5(c)]; the issuer, however, may negotiate with the underwriters [*see* Section 2(3)]. Also, under Rule 135 the issuer may make a public announcement concerning certain terms of the proposed offering. The 2005 SEC Reforms provided several safe harbors for issuer communications prior to the filing of a registration statement, and the JOBS Act added the "test the waters" provision for emerging growth companies.

(2) **Waiting Period.** During the period between the filing of the registration statement and the effective date, a preliminary prospectus (red herring) may be distributed [*see* Section 5(b)(1)], but no sales may be made [*see* Section 5(a)]. During this period oral offers may be made and the underwriters may receive indications of interest from prospective

purchasers. As a result of the 2005 SEC Reforms, (1) issuers and offering participants are permitted to use *free writing prospectuses* during this period [*see* Rules 164 and 433], and (2) electronic road shows are permissible. Also, the JOBS Act "test the waters" provision applies during this period as well as during the pre-filing period.

(3) **Post-Effective Period.** After a registration statement has become effective, securities may be sold provided the securities are accompanied or preceded by a statutory prospectus [*see* Section 5(a) and 5(b)(2)]. Section 2(a)(10) permits the use of free writing during the post-effective period. Also, free writing prospectuses during this period are permitted by the 2005 SEC Reforms. [*See* Rules 164 and 433] In addition the 2005 SEC Reforms liberalized the prospectus delivery requirements by permitting certain electronic access to satisfy the delivery requirement.

§ 4.7 Compliance with State Blue Sky Laws

Under Section 18 of the 33 Act, federal law preempts states from regulating the issuance of securities that are, *inter alia*, listed on the New York Stock Exchange, the American Stock Exchange or the NASDAQ Stock Market. Also, states are prohibited from regulating the sale of securities to "qualified purchasers" as defined by the SEC, and the SEC has the power to adopt rules under the private offering exemption, Section 4(2), that prohibit states from adopting their own exemptions. For purposes of this chapter, it is assumed that any securities issued, whether in a public or private offering, are exempt from state regulation.

§ 4.8 Introduction to Issues Involved in the Preparation of Registration Statements

A. Introduction to Integration of Disclosure under the Securities Act of 1933 and the Securities Exchange Act of 1934

The Securities Act of 1933 deals with the issuance of new securities. As seen in Section 4.2, Section 5 of the 33 Act requires that newly issued securities be registered with the SEC, unless an exemption from registration applies.

Prior to the enactment of the JOBS Act, under Section 12(g) and Rule 12g-1 of the 34 Act, issuers with more than $10 million of assets and 500 security holders were required to register their securities with the SEC. The JOBS Act amended Section 12(g) in several ways, including a modification to the 500 security holder rule. The SEC describes as follows this modification:

> The holders of record threshold for triggering Section 12(g) registration for issuers ... has been raised from 500 or more persons to either (1) 2,000 or more persons or (2) 500 or more persons who are not accredited investors [see the discussion *infra* of the meaning of the term accredited investor].[2]

Under, Sections 13 and 14 of the 34 Act, reporting companies are required to file periodic disclosure reports with the SEC and shareholders. Under Section 13, (1) an annual report is required to be filed with the SEC on Form 10-K, (2) a quarterly report

2. SEC, *Jumpstart Our Business Startups Act, Frequently Asked Questions Generally Applicable Questions on Title I of the JOBS Act* (May 3, 2012).

is required to be filed on Form 10-Q, and (3) periodic reports regarding significant events are required to be filed on Form 8-K. These forms are set out in *M&A Statutes, Rules, and Documents, supra* Section 1.1.

Under Section 14, shareholders must be given an annual report and an annual proxy statement. Proxy statements are also required for certain transactions, such as mergers. Proxy statements are covered in Chapter 13, which deals with the acquisition of publicly-held target corporations in mergers.

As indicated in the next section, the SEC has integrated the periodic disclosures required under the 34 Act with the registration disclosures required under the 33 Act. Regulation S-K provides guidance for disclosure under both Acts.

If a closely-held company is engaging in an IPO it will not have any 34 Act reports at the time it goes public, but it will begin filing those reports after it completes the IPO.

B. Background on Forms 10-K, 10-Q, and 8-K under the 34 Act

1. Accelerated Filing Changes

Acceleration of Periodic Report Filing Dates and Disclosure Concerning Website Access to Reports SEC Release No. 34-46464

(April 8, 2003)

The Exchange Act Reporting System. The Exchange Act requires public companies to make information publicly available to investors on an ongoing basis to aid in their investment and voting decisions. Issuers that have been subject to the reporting requirements for a certain period of time also can incorporate information from their Exchange Act reports into their registration statements under the Securities Act. Investors purchasing securities in public offerings therefore also rely on Exchange Act disclosure.

The Commission's rules under the Exchange Act now require disclosure at quarterly [10-Q] and annual [10-K] intervals, with specified significant events reported on a more current basis [8-K]. Specifically, a domestic issuer subject to the Exchange Act must, among other obligations, file the following reports:

- An annual report on Form 10-K (or Form 10-KSB in the case of a small business issuer) no later than 90 calendar days after the end of its fiscal year;
- Quarterly reports on Form 10-Q (or Form 10-QSB in the case of a small business issuer) no later than 45 calendar days after the end of the first three quarters of its fiscal year; and
- Current reports on Form 8-K for a number of specified events generally within five or 15 days after their occurrence. * * *

Summary: We are adopting amendments to our rules and forms to accelerate the filing of quarterly and annual reports under the Securities Exchange Act of 1934 by [certain large reporting companies]. * * *

2. The 2004 Amendments to Form 8-K

Additional Form 8-K Disclosure Requirements and Acceleration of Filing Date
SEC Release No. 34–49424
(March 16, 2004)

Background. * * * Form 8-K is the Exchange Act form for current reports. * * * Under the previous Form 8-K regime, companies were required to report very few significant corporate events. The limited number of Form 8-K disclosure items permitted a public company to delay disclosure of many significant events until the due date for its next periodic report. During such a delay, the market was unable to assimilate such undisclosed information into the value of a company's securities. The revisions that we adopt today will benefit markets by increasing the number of unquestionably or presumptively material events that must be disclosed currently. They will also provide investors with better and more timely disclosure of important corporate events.

On July 29, 2002, Congress enacted the Sarbanes-Oxley Act of 2002. Section 409 of this Act requires public companies to disclose "on a rapid and current basis" material information regarding changes in a company's financial condition or operations as we, by rule, determine to be necessary or useful for the protection of investors and in the public interest. These amendments also further the goals of Section 409 of the Sarbanes-Oxley Act. * * *

Reorganization of Form 8-K Items. Because we are adding a number of new items to the form, we believe it is appropriate to organize the required reportable items into topical categories. Commenters generally supported such reorganization. The amendments organize the Form 8-K items under the following section headings and with the following new numbering system [only the items directly related to M&A are set out here]:

Section 1 Registrant's Business and Operations

Item 1.01 Entry into a Material Definitive Agreement [such as a merger agreement] * * *

Section 2 Financial Information

Item 2.01 Completion of Acquisition or Disposition of Assets * * *

Section 5 Corporate Governance and Management

Item 5.01 Changes in Control of Registrant * * *

C. Introduction to the S-1 and S-3 Registration Statements

Excerpt from Securities Act Release No. 33–6383
(March 3, 1982)

The concept of integrating the various disclosure systems under the Federal securities laws has been the subject of theoretical discussion for quite some time. It was long clear that the transaction-oriented framework of the Securities Act and the disclosure system which developed thereunder often overlap with, and produce disclosure duplicative of, that prepared independently in response to the status-oriented framework of the Exchange Act and the continuous disclosure system operating thereunder. The Commission's program to integrate the two disclosure systems has focused on two principal objectives: first, a comprehensive evaluation of the disclosure policies and procedures under both Acts to identify the information which is material to security holders and investors in both the distribution process and the trading markets, such as the minimum information package; and, second, a determination of the circumstances under which information should be disseminated to security holders, investors and the marketplace. The goal of the Commission's integrated disclosure program has been to revise or eliminate overlapping or unnecessary disclosure and dissemination requirements wherever possible, thereby reducing burdens on registrants while at the same time ensuring that security holders, investors and the marketplace have been provided with meaningful, nonduplicative information upon which to base investment decisions. * * *

The registration and report forms under the Securities Act and the Exchange Act provide the starting point for registrants complying with the integrated disclosure system. Each of the various Securities Act registration forms establishes the type and amount of disclosure required by registrants able to use the form. The Exchange Act forms establish the type and amount of disclosure required to be provided in the Exchange Act reports which registrants must file.

1. *Forms S-1, S-2 and S-3. Operation of the three-tier registration system.* [The SEC's 2005 Securities Offering Reform eliminated Form S-2. The S-1 and S-3 are set out in the *Selected Forms under the Securities Act of 1933* section of *M&A Statutes, Rules, and Documents, supra* Section 1.1.] New Forms S-1, S-2 and S-3 provide the basic framework for the registration of securities under the Securities Act. [While the S-1 and S-3 are used for the issuance of securities by a company or its shareholders directly to the public, the S-4 registration statement, which is examined in Chapter 13, is used by an acquiring corporation in the issuance of its securities in an M&A transaction.] These Forms establish three categories for registration statements. The same information will be required to be part of Securities Act registration statements in all categories, either presented in, or delivered with, the prospectus or incorporated by reference from another document. Differences among the three Forms reflect the Commission's determination as to (1) when this required information must be presented in full in the prospectus delivered to investors, (2) when certain of the delivered information may be presented on a streamlined basis and supplemented by documents incorporated by reference, and (3) when certain information may be incorporated by reference from documents in the Exchange Act continuous reporting system without delivery to investors.

Generally, it is the registrant-oriented portion of the information relating to a public offering, as opposed to the transaction-specific information, which sometimes may be satisfied otherwise than through full prospectus presentation. Much of this registrant-oriented information is the same as that which is required to be presented in annual reports to the Commission on Form 10-K and in annual reports to security holders, as well as in quarterly and current reports on Forms 10-Q and 8-K, respectively. Information about the offering, however, will not have been reported on in any other disclosure document or otherwise have been publicly disseminated and thus will be required to be presented in the prospectus in all cases.

The registration statement for the first category is Form S-1. It requires complete disclosure to be set forth in the prospectus and permits no incorporation by reference. Form S-1 is to be used by registrants in the Exchange Act reporting system for less than three years and also may be used by any registrants who choose to do so or for whom no other form is available. [Thus, the S-1 is used for IPOs.] * * *

Form S-3, in reliance on the efficient market theory [*i.e.*, the theory that the market will quickly internalize in the price of securities all public information], allows maximum use of incorporation by reference of Exchange Act reports and requires the least disclosure to be presented in the prospectus and delivered to investors. Generally, the Form S-3 prospectus will present the same transaction-specific information as will be presented in a Form S-1 * * * prospectus. Information concerning the registrant will be incorporated by reference from Exchange Act reports. The prospectus will not be required to present any information concerning the registrant unless there has been a material change in the registrant's affairs which has not been reported in an Exchange Act filing or the Exchange Act reports incorporated by reference do not reflect certain restated financial statements or other financial information. * * * [As a result of amendments made by the 2005 Securities Offering Reform, incorporation by reference is now permitted in S-1 forms filed by publicly-held companies that are not eligible to use Form S-3. This does not apply, however, to IPOs.]

D. Illustration of the S-3 Incorporation by Reference Process

Item 12 of Form S-3 sets out the incorporation by reference requirements. *See e.g.*, the discussion of "WHERE YOU CAN FIND MORE INFORMATION" in the S-4 for the J.P. Morgan Chase—Bank One Merger, Documentary Appendix E of *M&A Statutes, Rules, and Documents*, *supra* Section 1.1.

E. Shelf Registrations under Rule 415

1. Introduction

Under Rule 415, which is referred to as the "shelf registration" provision, securities can be used for registration of an offering to be made on a continuous or delayed basis. Two of the many types of securities that can be registered under Rule 415 are (1) securities that are to be issued in connection with business combination transactions (Rule 415(a)(1)(vii)), and (2) securities registered on Form S-3 that are to be offered and sold on an "immediate, continuous or delayed basis" (Rule 415(a)(1)(x)). Under this latter provision, an S-3 issuer could, for example, file a shelf registration statement and then immediately offer debt securities when market conditions are attractive.

2. Impact of 2005 Securities Offering Reform

Securities and Exchange Commission, Securities Offering Reform Release No. 33–8591

(August 3, 2005)

Automatic Shelf Registration for Well-Known Seasoned Issuers. * * * [W]e are adopting rules to establish a significantly more flexible version of shelf registration for offerings by well-known seasoned issuers. This version of shelf registration, which we refer to as "automatic shelf registration," [*see* the definition in Rule 405] involves filings on Form S-3 or Form F-3. The automatic shelf registration rules * * * will allow eligible well-known seasoned issuers substantially greater latitude in registering and marketing securities. The automatic shelf registration process will continue to enable the issuer, as with other shelf registrants, to take down securities off a shelf registration statement from time to time. Automatic shelf registration is not mandatory; a well-known seasoned issuer may continue to file any other registration statement it is eligible to use or engage in any exempt offering or offerings of exempt securities available to it. * * *

Under our automatic shelf registration process, eligible well-known seasoned issuers may register unspecified amounts of different specified types of securities on immediately effective Form S-3 or Form F-3 registration statements. [*See* Rules 415 and 430B] * * *

F. Preparation of the S-1 Registration Statement

As indicated above, Form S-1 is utilized in, for example, initial public offerings, whereas Form S-3 is utilized by seasoned publicly-traded companies to sell additional securities in the public markets. The structure of Forms S-1 and S-3 is similar. Each starts with a requirement that information with respect to the issuance be set forth and then contains a section entitled General Instructions. Part I of each form then sets out the information required in the prospectus portion of the registration statement. Each of the Items refers to a particular provision of (1) Regulation S-K, which sets out general rules regarding disclosures under both the 33 and 34 Acts, or (2) Regulation S-X, discussed in Chapter 6, which sets out general rules of accounting disclosure under both Acts. Excerpts from Reg. S-K are set out in *M&A Statutes, Rules, and Documents, supra* Section 1.1.

Obviously, S-1 requires more complete information than S-3. As a general matter S-1 requires full disclosures concerning both the issuer and the transaction, whereas, S-3 requires full disclosure only with respect to the transaction and new developments since the filing of the last disclosure documents incorporated by reference into the S-3.

In preparing a registration statement, the attorney will follow closely the directions set out in the applicable Form and the related disclosure requirements in Regulations S-K and S-X. Reg. S-X, of course, will be the primary responsibility of the accountants. For example, Item 1 of Part I of Form S-1, which addresses the *Forepart of Registration Statement and Outside Front Cover Page of Prospectus*, requires compliance with Item 501 of Reg. S-K, which sets out in great specificity the required disclosures. The reader should review the disclosures required in Part I of Form S-1 in connection with a review of the 2004 IPO prospectus for Greenhill. & Co. Inc., which is Documentary Appendix T of *M&A Statutes, Rules, and Documents, supra* Section 1.1.

Greenhill is an investment banking firm focused mainly on advising on M&A transactions; therefore, a review of this prospectus will provide a guide to how one such firm operates. In reviewing the Greenhill prospectus, particular attention should be given to (1) the following Items in Form S-1 and related S-K disclosure requirements, and (2) how these requirements were addressed in the prospectus:

- Item 3—*Summary Information, Risk Factors * * **, set out in the front part of the Greenhill prospectus (the SEC's plain English requirement, which is discussed below, applies to this part of the registration statement);
- Item 4—*Use of Proceeds*;
- Item 6—*Dilution*;
- Item 8—*Plan of Distribution*, set out in the rear portion of the Greenhill prospectus under Underwriting (this is a standard firm commitment underwriting);
- Item 11(a)—*Business*; and
- Item 11(h)—*Management's Discussion and Analysis* (an SEC release on the MD&A requirements is set out below).

In 2006, the SEC adopted rule changes regarding disclosures related to compensation, related party transactions, and corporate governance, and these proposed changes are introduced below. An issuer may include in a registration statement information that is "forward-looking," that is, non-historic information, such as a prediction about a future event, and as indicated below, both the 33 and 34 Acts contain safe harbors against liabilities for such information. However, the 33 Act safe harbor does not extend to IPOs and is generally only available to seasoned issuers. Nevertheless, many IPO issuers, as was the case with Greenhill [*see Forward Looking Information* section in its prospectus], will include in the prospectus forward looking information and rely on the "bespeaks caution" doctrine, which is discussed below, as a basis for avoiding liability if the forward looking information does not come true. As indicated above a person subject to the 33 and 34 Acts is required to disclose "material" information, and this is particularly true in registration statements.

G. Plain English Disclosure

The following SEC directive requires that certain parts of the registration statement be written in plain English:

Excerpt from SEC Division of Corporation Finance: Updated Staff Legal Bulletin No. 7, "Plain English Disclosure"

(June 7, 1999)

As of October 1, 1998, companies filing registration statements under the Securities Act of 1933 must:

- write the forepart of these registration statements in plain English;
- write the remaining portions of these registration statements in a clear, understandable manner; and
- design these registration statements to be visually inviting and easy to read. * * *

[Under Rule 421(d)], [i]ssuers must use plain English writing principles in the organization, language, and design of the front and back cover pages, the summary, and the risk factors section. Also, when drafting the language in these parts of the prospectus, issuers must substantially comply with these plain English principles:

- short sentences;
- definite, concrete everyday language;
- active voice;
- tabular presentation of complex information;
- no legal jargon; and
- no multiple negatives.

In designing these and other parts of the prospectus, issuers may include pictures, logos, charts, graphs, or other design elements so long as the design is not misleading and the required information is clear. * * *

[Under Rule 421(b)], [w]hen writing the remaining portions of their registration statements, issuers must use these standards:

- clear, concise sections, paragraphs, and sentences * * *; and
- descriptive headings and subheadings.

Questions and Answers: Q: Which filings do the new plain English rule and amendments apply to? **A:** They apply only to prospectuses filed under the Securities Act of 1933.

H. The MD&A

1. Introduction

One of the most important sections of Form S-1 is Item 11(h), which requires disclosures under Item 303 of Reg. S-K. This Item requires "management's discussion and analysis of financial condition and results of operation," which is referred to as the MD&A. The following

SEC release provides guidance on the preparation of the MD&A. The MD&A is also required in both Forms 10-Q and 10-K under the 34 Act. Thus, a firm filing an S-3 registration statement will incorporate its MD&A discussions by reference to its 34 Act filings.

2. SEC Guidance on the MD&A

Commission Guidance Regarding Management's Discussion and Analysis of Financial Condition and Results of Operations, Securities Act Release No. 33-8350

(December 19, 2003)

Summary: The Commission is publishing interpretive guidance regarding the disclosure commonly known as Management's Discussion and Analysis of Financial Condition and Results of Operations, or MD&A, which is required by Item 303 of Regulation S-K * * *. This guidance is intended to elicit more meaningful disclosure in MD&A in a number of areas, including the overall presentation and focus of MD&A, with general emphasis on the discussion and analysis of known trends, demands, commitments, events and uncertainties, and specific guidance on disclosures about liquidity, capital resources and critical accounting estimates. * * *

Overview. *Purpose.* This release interprets requirements for Management's Discussion and Analysis of Financial Condition and Results of Operations ("MD&A"). It provides guidance to assist companies:

- in preparing MD&A disclosure that is easier to follow and understand; and
- in providing information that more completely satisfies our previously enunciated principal objectives of MD&A.

We believe that management's most important responsibilities include communicating with investors in a clear and straightforward manner. MD&A is a critical component of that communication. The Commission has long sought through its rules, enforcement actions and interpretive processes to elicit MD&A that not only meets technical disclosure requirements but generally is informative and transparent. We believe and expect that when companies follow the guidance in this release, the overall quality of their MD&A will improve. * * *

Approach to MD&A. The purpose of MD&A is not complicated. It is to provide readers information "necessary to an understanding of [a company's] financial condition, changes in financial condition and results of operations." The MD&A requirements are intended to satisfy three principal objectives:

- to provide a narrative explanation of a company's financial statements that enables investors to see the company through the eyes of management;
- to enhance the overall financial disclosure and provide the context within which financial information should be analyzed; and
- to provide information about the quality of, and potential variability of, a company's earnings and cash flow, so that investors can ascertain the likelihood that past performance is indicative of future performance.

MD&A should be a discussion and analysis of a company's business as seen through the eyes of those who manage that business. * * *

I. 2006 Changes in Disclosures Related to Compensation, Related Party Transactions, and Corporate Governance

Executive Compensation and Related Person Disclosure
SEC Release No. 33-8732A
(January 27, 2006)

SUMMARY: The Securities and Exchange Commission is adopting amendments to the disclosure requirements for executive and director compensation [Item 402 of Reg. S-K], related person transactions [Item 404 of Reg. S-K], director independence and other corporate governance matters [Item 407 of Reg. S-K] and security ownership of officers and directors [Item 403 of Reg. S-K]. These amendments apply to disclosure in proxy and information statements, periodic reports, current reports and other filings under the Securities Exchange Act of 1934 and to registration statements under the Exchange Act and the Securities Act of 1933. We are also adopting a requirement that disclosure under the amended items generally be provided in plain English. The amendments are intended to make proxy and information statements, reports and registration statements easier to understand. They are also intended to provide investors with a clearer and more complete picture of the compensation earned by a company's principal executive officer, principal financial officer and highest paid executive officers and members of its board of directors. In addition, they are intended to provide better information about key financial relationships among companies and their executive officers, directors, significant shareholders and their respective immediate family members. * * *

Background and Overview. * * * The amendments that we publish today require that all elements of compensation must be disclosed. We also have sought to structure the revised requirements sufficiently broadly so that they will continue to operate effectively as new forms of compensation are developed in the future. Under the amendments, compensation disclosure will now begin with a narrative providing a general overview. Much like the overview that we have encouraged companies to provide with their Management's Discussion and Analysis of Financial Condition and Results of Operations (MD&A), the new Compensation Discussion and Analysis [Item 402(b) of Reg. S-K] calls for a discussion and analysis of the material factors underlying compensation policies and decisions reflected in the data presented in the tables. This overview addresses in one place these factors with respect to both the separate elements of executive compensation and executive compensation as a whole. We are adopting the overview substantially as proposed, but, in response to comments, we are requiring a separate report of the compensation committee similar to the report required of the audit committee, which will be considered furnished and not filed.

Following the Compensation Discussion and Analysis, we have organized detailed disclosure of executive compensation into three broad categories:

- compensation with respect to the last fiscal year (and the two preceding fiscal years), as reflected in an amended Summary Compensation Table that presents compensation paid currently or deferred (including options, restricted stock and similar grants) and compensation consisting of current earnings or awards that are part of a plan, and as supplemented by a table providing back-up information for certain data in the Summary Compensation Table;
- holdings of equity-related interests that relate to compensation or are potential sources of future gains, with a focus on compensation-related equity interests that

were awarded in prior years and are "at risk," whether or not these interests are in-the-money, as well as recent realization on these interests, such as through vesting of restricted stock or the exercise of options and similar instruments; and

- retirement and other post-employment compensation, including retirement and deferred compensation plans, other retirement benefits and other post-employment benefits, such as those payable in the event of a change in control. * * *

We believe that executive and director compensation is closely related to financial transactions and relationships involving companies and their directors, executive officers and significant shareholders and respective immediate family members. * * * Today's amendments update, clarify and somewhat expand the related party transaction disclosure requirements [Item 404 of Reg. S-K]. The amendments fold into the disclosure requirements for related party transactions what had been a separate disclosure requirement regarding indebtedness of management and directors. Further, we are adopting a requirement that calls for a narrative explanation of the independence status of directors under a company's director independence policies [Item 407 of Reg. S-K]. We intend this requirement to be consistent with recent significant changes to the listing standards of the nation's principal securities trading markets. We also are consolidating this and other corporate governance disclosure requirements regarding director independence and board committees, including new disclosure requirements about the compensation committee, into a single expanded disclosure item.

In order to ensure that these amended requirements result in disclosure that is clear, concise and understandable for investors, we are adding Rules 13a-20 and 15d-20 under the Exchange Act to require that most of the disclosure provided in response to the amended items be presented in plain English. * * *

J. Forward-Looking Statements

Conference Report to the Private Securities and Litigation Reform Act of 1995

See § 27A of the 33 Act and § 21E of the 34 Act

Safe Harbor for Forward-Looking Statements. Fear that inaccurate projections will trigger the filing of securities class action lawsuits has muzzled corporate management. One study found that over two-thirds of venture capital firms were reluctant to discuss their performance with analysts or the public because of the threat of litigation. Anecdotal evidence similarly indicates corporate counsel advise clients to say as little as possible, because "legions of lawyers scrub required filings to ensure that disclosures are as milquetoast as possible, so as to provide no grist for the litigation mill." * * *

The Conference Committee has adopted a statutory "safe harbor" to enhance market efficiency by encouraging companies to disclose forward-looking information. This provision adds a new section 27A to the 1933 Act and a new section 21E of the 1934 Act which protects from liability in private lawsuits certain "forward-looking" statements made by persons specified in the legislation.

The Conference Committee has crafted a safe harbor that differs from the safe harbor provisions in the House and Senate passed bills. The Conference Committee safe harbor, like the Senate safe harbor, is based on aspects of SEC Rule 175 and the judicial created "bespeaks caution" doctrine. It is a bifurcated safe harbor that permits greater flexibility to those who may avail themselves of safe harbor protection. There is also a special safe harbor for issuers who make oral forward-looking statements.

The first prong of the safe harbor protects a written or oral forward-looking statement that is: (i) identified as forward-looking and (ii) accompanied by meaningful cautionary statements identifying important factors that could cause actual results to differ materially from those projected in the statements.

Under this first prong of the safe harbor, boilerplate warnings will not suffice as meaningful cautionary statements identifying important factors that could cause actual results to differ materially from those projected in the statement. The cautionary statements must convey substantive information about factors that realistically could cause results to differ materially from those projected in the forward-looking statement, such as, for example, information about the issuer's business. * * *

Courts may continue to find a forward-looking statement immaterial and thus not actionable under the 1933 Act and the 1934 act on other grounds. To clarify this point, the Conference Committee includes language in the safe harbor provision that no liability attaches to forward-looking statements that are "immaterial." * * *

The second prong of the safe harbor provides an alternative analysis. This safe harbor also applies to both written and oral forward-looking statements. Instead of examining the forward- looking and cautionary statements, this prong of the safe harbor focuses on the state of mind of the person making the forward-looking statement. A person or business entity will not be liable in a private lawsuit for a forward-looking statement unless a plaintiff proves that person or business entity made a false or misleading forward-looking statement with actual knowledge that it was false or misleading. The Conference Committee intends for this alternative prong of the safe harbor to apply if the plaintiff fails to prove the forward-looking statement (1) if made by a natural person, was made with the actual knowledge by that person that the statement was false or misleading; or (2) if made by a business entity, was made by or with the approval of an executive officer of the entity with actual knowledge by that officer that the statement was false or misleading. * * *

This legislation permits covered issuers, or persons acting on the issuer's behalf, to make oral forward-looking statements within the safe harbor. The person making the forward-looking statement must identify the statement as a forward-looking statement and state that results may differ materially from those projected in the statement. The person must also identify a "readily available" written document that contains factors that could cause results to differ materially. The written information identified by the person making the forward-looking statement must qualify as a "cautionary statement" under the first prong of the safe harbor (*i.e.*, it must be a meaningful cautionary statement or statements that identify important factors that could cause actual results to differ materially from those projected in the forward-looking statement.) For purposes of this provision, "readily available" information refers to SEC filed documents, annual reports and other widely disseminated materials, such as press releases.

The safe harbor provision protects written and oral forward-looking statements made by issuers and certain persons retained or acting on behalf of the issuer. The Conference Committee intends the statutory safe harbor protection to make more information about a company's future plans available to investors and the public. The safe harbor covers underwriters, but only insofar as the underwriters provide forward looking information that is based on or "derived from" information provided by the issuer. * * *

The Conference Committee adopts the SEC's present definition, as set forth in Rule 175, of forward-looking information, with certain additions and clarifying changes. The definition covers: (i) certain financial items, including projections of revenues, income and earnings, capital expenditures, dividends, and capital structure; (ii) management's statement of future business plans and objectives, including with respect to its products or services; and (iii) certain statements made in SEC required disclosures, including management's discussion and analysis and results of operations; and (iv) any statement disclosing the assumptions underlying the forward-looking statement.

The Conference Committee has determined that the statutory safe harbor should not apply to certain forward-looking statements. Thus, the statutory safe harbor does not protect forward-looking statements: (1) included in financial statements prepared in accordance with generally accepted accounting principles (2) contained in an initial public offering registration statement; (3) made in connection with a tender offer; (4) made in connection with a partnership, limited liability company or direct participation program offering; or (5) made in beneficial ownership disclosure statements filed with the SEC under Section 13(d) of the 1934 Act. * * *

[T]he Committee has determined to extend the statutory safe harbor only to forward-looking information of certain established issuers subject to the reporting requirements of section 13(a) or section 15(d) of the 1934 Act. * * *

Question

Can a forward-looking statement included in a merger proxy statement qualify for the safe harbor in Section 27A of the 33 Act and Section 21E of the 34 Act?

K. Illustration of the "Bespeaks Caution" Doctrine in a Merger

Grossman v. Novell, Inc., et al.

United States District Court, District of Utah, (1995) 909 F.Supp 845

Benson District Judge:

This class-action securities fraud suit, brought by and on behalf of Novell stockholders, is before the Court on defendants' motion to dismiss. * * *

This case concerns statements made by the defendants concerning Novell, Inc.'s merger with WordPerfect Corporation ("WordPerfect"). Novell, Inc. ("Novell") is a publicly traded Utah corporation engaged in the creation and marketing of computer networking software. WordPerfect was a privately held Utah corporation engaged in software development and sales. * * *

Plaintiff Brad Grossman ("Grossman") is a shareholder of Novell common stock, which is publicly traded on the NASDAQ. * * *

In his complaint, Grossman alleges that between April 27, 1994 and August 19, 1994 (the "class period"), Novell, together with the individual defendants, issued a series of false and misleading statements which, in light of the circumstances under which they were made, had become false or misleading over time. Those statements concerned Novell's financial condition and its expectations for the near-term revenues and earnings to be posted by Novell. Those statements, according to the complaint, were false and misleading in that they "overstated the progress and purported success that had been achieved by Novell in its attempts to integrate the operations of two entities purchased by Novell in March 1994 * * * and falsely assured investors that the two acquisitions would not have a negative effect on Novell's near term earnings."

The complaint also alleges the defendants made "overly positive public statements" * * *.

The asserted causes of action arise under Section 10(b) of the Exchange Act and Rule 10b-5 * * *.

The third reason that the complaint fails to state a claim under the first element of a 10b-5 claim is that Novell in fact disclosed the risks behind the WordPerfect merger. The purpose of Rule 10b-5's "omission of a material fact" language is to allow plaintiffs to sue companies that fail to disclose risks to potential investors. This language is satisfied at the pleading stage by facts supporting an allegation of non-disclosure of certain risks which the company had a duty to reveal. Courts dismiss securities fraud claims where a company has disclosed the risks affecting future performance. *See, e.g.*, *In re Donald Trump Sec. Litig.*, 7 F.3d 357, 368 (3d. Cir. 1993). Securities fraud claims cannot be maintained where defendants have issued detailed cautionary warnings.

The "bespeaks caution" doctrine "provides a mechanism by which a court can rule as a matter of law (typically in a motion to dismiss * * *) that defendants' forward-looking representations contained enough cautionary language or risk disclosure to protect the defendant against claims of securities fraud." *In re Worlds of Wonder Sec. Litig.*, 35 F.3d 1407, 1413 (9th Cir. 1994). The *In re Worlds of Wonder* Court held that optimistic forward-looking representations are not actionable when cautionary language found elsewhere adequately discloses the risks. It does not matter "if the optimistic statements are later found to have been inaccurate or based on erroneous assumptions when made, provided that the risk disclosure was conspicuous, specific, and adequately disclosed the assumptions upon which the optimistic language was based." The Tenth Circuit applied this doctrine in *In re Storage Technology Corp. Sec. Litig.*, 147 F.R.D. 232, 237 (D.Colo. 1993).

Grossman's allegations of fact fail to state a claim because Novell issued cautionary language adequately disclosing the risks of the merger. Novell's SEC registration statement, filed on April 22, 1994, warned investors that, because of the "inherent difficulties" involved in completing a large merger, "there can be no assurance that * * * the integration of the respective businesses will be successful." * * *

§4.9 Illustration of Impact of Section 11 of the 33 Act

A. The Underwriters' Due Diligence and Reliance Defenses in *WorldCom*

In Re WorldCom, Inc. Securities Litigation

United States District Court, Southern District Of New York, (2004)
U.S. Dist. LEXIS 25155

DENISE COTE, District Judge:

This Opinion addresses issues related to an underwriter's due diligence obligations. Following the conclusion of fact discovery, several of the parties in this consolidated securities class action arising from the collapse of WorldCom, Inc. ("WorldCom") have filed for summary judgment. This Opinion resolves * * * [claims] by the underwriters for [two WorldCom] bond offerings [a 2000 and 2001 offering], who seek a declaration that they have no liability for any false statements in the WorldCom financials that accompanied the registration statements. * * *

It is undisputed that at least as of early 2001 WorldCom executives engaged in a secretive scheme to manipulate WorldCom's public filings concerning WorldCom's financial condition. Because those public filings were incorporated into the registration statements for the two bond offerings, the underwriters are liable for those false statements unless they can show that they were sufficiently diligent in their investigation of WorldCom in connection with the bond offerings. [T]he Lead Plaintiff emphasizes that the underwriters did almost no investigation of WorldCom in connection with their underwriting of the bond offerings for the company, and because they did essentially no investigation, will be unable to succeed with their defense that they were diligent. The Lead Plaintiff contends moreover that there were "red flags" that should have led the underwriters to question even the audited financials filed by WorldCom. * * *

[Citigroup, Inc., and related parties, including its subsidiary Salomon Smith Barney Inc. ("SSB"), which together with J.P. Morgan Chase, was one of the lead underwriter, settled the class action law suit for $2.575 billion.] * * *

Section 11. Section 11 of the Securities Act provides that any signer, director of the issuer, preparing or certifying accountant, or underwriter may be liable if "any part of the registration statement, when such part became effective, contained an untrue statement of a material fact or omitted to state a material fact required to be stated therein or necessary to make the statements therein not misleading." Purchasers of securities issued pursuant to a registration statement may sue if they purchased at the time of the initial public offering, or if they are "aftermarket purchasers who can trace their shares to an allegedly misleading registration statement." * * *

In determining whether a registration statement is materially misleading, the "central inquiry" is "whether defendants' representations, taken together and in context, would have misled a reasonable investor about the nature of the investment." * * *

Section 11 provides two affirmative defenses. First, the statute provides an affirmative defense where a defendant can prove that the loss in value of a security is due to something other than misleading statements within a registration statement. [Section 11(e)].

In addition, Section 11 provides an affirmative defense of "due diligence," which is available to defendants other than the issuer of the security. The standard that applies to this defense varies depending on whether the misleading statement in the registration statement is or expressly relies on an expert's opinion. The due diligence defense is discussed further below.

Section 12. Section 12(a)(2) of the Securities Act allows a purchaser of a security to bring a private action against a seller that "offers or sells a security * * * by means of a prospectus or oral communication, which includes an untrue statement of a material fact or omits to state a material fact necessary in order to make the statements * * * not misleading." * * *

Section 12(a)(2) provides affirmative defenses that parallel those available for a Section 11 claim. First, the statute prohibits recovery to the extent that defendant proves that the loss is attributable to other factors. In addition, Section 12(a)(2) provides an affirmative defense of reasonable care. * * *

The Underwriter Defendants' Motion for Summary Judgment: The Financial Statements. The Underwriter Defendants move for summary judgment with respect to the financial statements that were incorporated into the Registration Statements. They assert that there is no dispute that they acted reasonably in relying on Andersen's audits and comfort letters. The Underwriter Defendants contend that they were entitled to rely on WorldCom's audited financial statements and had no duty to investigate their reliability so long as they had "no reasonable ground to believe" that such financial statements contained a false statement. They also assert that they were entitled to rely in the same way on Andersen's comfort letters for the unaudited quarterly financial statements incorporated into the Registration Statements. * * *

Role of the Underwriter. An underwriter is commonly understood to be a "person who buys securities directly or indirectly from the issuer and resells them to the public, or performs some act (or acts) that facilitates the issuer's distribution." As the SEC has observed, in enacting Section 11, "Congress recognized that underwriters occupied a unique position that enabled them to discover and compel disclosure of essential facts about the offering." * * *

The "Due Diligence" Defenses. The phrase "due diligence" does not appear in the Securities Act, but two of the affirmative defenses available under Section 11(b) are collectively known as the "due diligence" defense. The first such defense provides that "as regards any part of the registration statement not purporting to be made on the authority of an expert," a defendant will not be liable upon a showing that he had, after reasonable investigation, reasonable ground to believe and did believe, at the time such part of the registration statement became effective, that the statements therein were true and that there was no omission to state a material fact required to be stated therein or necessary to make the statements therein not misleading. [Section 11(b)(3)(A)] * * *

There is a different standard that applies when a Section 11 defendant is entitled to rely upon the opinion of an expert. "As regards any part of the registration statement purporting to be made on the authority of an expert," a defendant other than that expert will not be liable if he demonstrates that he had no reasonable ground to believe and did not believe, at the time such part of the registration statement became effective, that the statements therein were untrue or that there was an omission to state a material fact required to be stated therein or necessary to make the statements therein not misleading. [Section 11(b)(3)(C)]

Although the requirements of due diligence vary depending on whether the registration statement has been made in part or in whole on the authority of an expert, the standard for determining what constitutes a reasonable investigation and reasonable ground for belief is the same: "The standard of reasonableness shall be that required of a prudent man in the management of his own property." [Section 11(c)]

Courts have distinguished between these two standards by labeling them the due diligence defense and the reliance defense, referring in the latter case to the reliance permitted by the statute on an expert's statement.

Section 12(a)(2) has a defense of reasonable care that is less demanding than the duty of due diligence imposed under Section 11. Section 12(a)(2) provides that a defendant shall not be liable if he "sustains the burden of proof that he did not know, and in the exercise of reasonable care could not have known, of such untruth or omission" which is "necessary in order to make the statements, in the light of the circumstances under which they were made, not misleading."

Thus, while Section 11 imposes a duty to conduct a reasonable investigation as to any portion of a registration statement not made on the authority of an expert, Section 12(a)(2) does not make any distinction based upon "expertised" statements and only requires the defendant to show that it used reasonable care. This difference is attributable to the emphasis placed on the importance of registration statements and the underwriter's vital role in assuring their accuracy. Because Section 11 imposes a more exacting standard, this Opinion principally addresses the law that applies to Section 11.

Accountants as Experts. Although Section 11(b) furnishes different standards, depending on whether a statement is made on the authority of an expert, the statute does not define the term "expert." Section 11(a)(4) lists professions that give a person authority to make a statement, which on consent can be included in a registration statement. [Section 11(a)(4)] The list of professions includes an accountant. Thus, while Section 11(b) does not define the term expert or explain what sort of documents and/or work constitutes that "made on an expert's authority," it is settled that an accountant qualifies as an expert, and audited financial statements are considered expertised portions of a registration statement.

Not every auditor's opinion, however, qualifies as an expert's opinion for purposes of the Section 11 reliance defense. * * * When a public company files a registration statement for a sale of securities, the auditor is customarily asked by underwriters to provide a comfort letter. The comfort letter will contain representations about the auditor's review of the interim financial statements. * * * There is frequently more than one comfort letter for a transaction: an initial comfort letter and a second or "bring down" comfort letter issued closer to the time of closing. * * *

In sum, underwriters can rely on an accountant's audit opinion incorporated into a registration statement in presenting a defense under Section 11(b)(3)(C). Underwriters may not rely on an accountant's comfort letters for interim financial statements in presenting such a defense. * * *

Integrated Disclosure, Shelf Registration, and Rule 176. * * * [The] SEC recognized [that the adoption of Form S-3 and incorporation by reference] affected the time in which underwriters could perform their investigations of an issuer. Underwriters had weeks to perform due diligence for traditional registration statements. By contrast, under a short-form registration regime, "preparation time is reduced sharply" thanks to the ability to incorporate by reference prior disclosures.

These two innovations triggered concern among underwriters. Members of the financial community worried about their ability "to undertake a reasonable investigation with respect to the adequacy of the information incorporated by reference from periodic reports filed under the Exchange Act into the short form registration statements utilized in an integrated disclosure system." * * *

[Consequently] the SEC introduced Rule 176 in 1981 "to make explicit what circumstances may bear upon the determination of what constitutes a reasonable investigation and reasonable ground for belief as these terms are used in Section 11(b)." * * *

Although "no court has ever been called upon to interpret Rule 176," the SEC's own commentary on the rule makes clear that Rule 176 did not alter the fundamental nature of underwriters' due diligence obligations. At the time Rule 176 was finalized, the SEC took care to explain that integrated disclosure was intended to "simplify disclosure and reduce unnecessary repetition and redelivery of information," not to "modify the responsibility of underwriters and others to make a reasonable investigation." * * *

Case Law: Reliance Defense. Over thirty-five years ago, the Honorable Edward C. McLean of this District observed that "there is little or no judicial authority" on how a defendant can successfully establish his affirmative defenses under Section 11. *Escott v. BarChris Constr. Corp.*, 283 F. Supp. 643, 683 (S.D.N.Y. 1968). This remains true today. Neither the Supreme Court nor the Second Circuit has explored this area of law in any significant way. * * *

It is * * * important to note that what constitutes a red flag depends on the facts and context of a particular case. * * *

Case Law: Due Diligence Defense. Just as there is little judicial elaboration of the reliance defense, so too there is "little judicial gloss" on the due diligence defense afforded to underwriters for non-expertised portions of a registration statement. * * *

Faced with "no judicial decision defining the degree of diligence which underwriters must exercise to establish their defense under Section 11," in 1968, the *BarChris* court contemplated whether "it is sufficient [for an underwriter] to ask questions, to obtain answers which, if true, would be thought satisfactory, and to let it go at that, without seeking to ascertain from the records whether the answers in fact are true and complete." The lead underwriter or its counsel read annual reports and prospectuses of other companies within the industry; perused the issuer's prior prospectuses, annual reports, and most recent unaudited interim financial statements, as well as its minutes from the previous five years and its major contracts; and attended several meetings with the issuer at which underwriter and underwriters' counsel asked "pertinent questions and received answers which satisfied them" and in which "extensive, successive proofs of the prospectus were considered and revised."

Rendering his opinion following a bench trial, Judge McLean noted the impossibility of establishing "a rigid rule suitable for every case defining the extent to which such verification must go. It is a question of degree, a matter of judgment in each case." Nonetheless, he held the underwriters had not conducted a "reasonable investigation of the truth of those portions of the prospectus which were not made on the authority of [the auditor] as an expert" because they made "almost no attempt to verify management's representations." In determining that an underwriter's due diligence obligations include efforts to verify information supplied by the issuer, the *BarChris* court relied heavily on the purpose of Section 11 and underwriters' role within the statutory scheme. * * *

Three years later, the Honorable Jack B. Weinstein further expounded on the due diligence defense in *Feit*. [*Feit v. Leasco Data Processing Equipment Co.*, 332 F. Supp 544 (D.C. N.Y. 1971)] Like the *BarChris* opinion before it, which refused to set forth a "rigid rule" for reasonable investigation, *Feit* insists that "what constitutes 'reasonable investigation' and a 'reasonable ground to believe' will vary with the degree of involvement of the individual, his expertise, and his access to the pertinent information and data." Yet *Feit* places great emphasis on the underwriters' role in a securities offering, observing that "the underwriter is the only participant in the registration process who, as to matters not certified by the accountant, is able to make the kind of investigation which will protect the purchasing public."

Given the underwriter's independence from the issuer, Judge Weinstein affirmed that while an underwriter is not "expected to possess the intimate knowledge of corporate affairs of inside directors," his obligation is to conduct a meaningful investigation, "not merely * * * listen[] to management's explanations of the company's affairs." "Tacit reliance on management assertions is unacceptable; the underwriters must play devil's advocate." Rendering his decision following a bench trial, Judge Weinstein found that the Feit underwriters had "just barely" satisfied this standard by completing a "thorough review of all available financial data," including an examination of the issuer's audit, "searching inquiries" of the issuer's major bank, and a study of the issuer's corporate minutes, records, and major agreements; attending due diligence meetings at which the proposed registration statement was reviewed "line by line"; reviewing correspondence pertinent to the omission at issue; and remaining in "constant contact" with the issuer.

The years following *BarChris* and *Feit* have been marked by considerable change in the regulatory framework governing securities registration. Specifically, short-form registration, the expansion of shelf registration, and Rule 176 were each introduced well after these two cases were decided. Recent Section 11 case law, however, shows no signs of abandoning the early courts' demand that underwriters employ "a high degree of care in investigation and independent verification of the company's representations." * * *

Where district courts have granted summary judgment for underwriters in recent years, the underwriters have demonstrated extensive due diligence efforts. As one court recounted in granting summary judgment,

> The underwriters had over twenty meetings with various management personnel, covering all aspects of the company's business. Company personnel were specifically questioned about the development and scheduled availability of products, related operating systems and applications software. The underwriters also contacted many of [the issuer's] suppliers, customers, and distributors, who were asked extensive questions about the company's operations. The underwriters reviewed company documents including operating plans, product literature, corporate records, financial statements, contacts, and lists of distributors and customers. They examined trade journals and other industry-related publications to ascertain industry trends, market trends and competitive information. * * * When any negative or questionable information was developed as a result of their investigation, the underwriters discussed it with the appropriate persons and arrived at informed decisions and opinions.

Weinberger v. Jackson, 1990 U.S. Dist. LEXIS 18394, at *7–8 (N.D. Cal. Oct. 11, 1990) * * *

Section 11(b) plainly commands that underwriters conduct an investigation as to portions of a registration statement not made on the authority of an expert. "When a word is not defined by statute, we normally construe it in accord with its ordinary or natural meaning." Today, as in 1933 when Section 11 became law, the word "investigation" connotes a "thorough" or "searching inquiry." Then and now, it can also mean the process of investigating. Under this latter definition, an investigation is no less demanding, as the word "investigate" is defined as "to inquire and examine into with systematic attention to detail and relationship."

The Application of the Law to This Motion. * * * The Underwriter Defendants contend that they are entitled to summary judgment on their affirmative defenses of reliance and due diligence because they were entitled to rely on Andersen's audits and comfort letters. The analysis that follows distinguishes between the expertised and non-expertised statements which are the subject of this motion.

Audited Financial Statements. The Underwriter Defendants contend that they were entitled to rely on Andersen's unqualified "clean" audit opinions for WorldCom's 1999 and 2000 Form 10-Ks as expertised statements under Section 11(b)(3)(C). Their motion for summary judgment on their reliance defense is denied. * * *

2000 Registration Statement. The Lead Plaintiff points to one issue that it contends gave the Underwriter Defendants a reasonable ground to question the reliability of WorldCom's 1999 Form 10-K. According to the computations presented by the Lead Plaintiff, WorldCom's reported E/R ratio [*i.e.*, the ratio of line cost expense to its revenue] was significantly lower than that of the equivalent numbers of its two closest competitors, Sprint and AT&T. The Lead Plaintiff argues that, in the extremely competitive market in which WorldCom operated, that discrepancy triggered a duty to investigate such a crucial measurement of the company's health. The Lead Plaintiff has shown that there are issues of fact as to whether the Underwriter Defendants had reasonable grounds to believe that the 1999 Form 10-K was inaccurate in the lines related to the E/R ratio reflected in that filing. * * *

If a "prudent man in the management of his own property," [§ 11(c)], upon reading the 1999 Form 10-K and being familiar with the other relevant information about the issuer's competitors would have questioned the accuracy of the figures, then those figures constituted a red flag and imposed a duty of investigation on the Underwriter Defendants. A jury would be entitled to find that this difference was of sufficient importance to have triggered a duty to investigate the reliability of the figures on which the ratio was based even though the figures had been audited. * * *

Interim Financial Statements. The Underwriter Defendants contend that, pursuant to Sections 11(b)(3)(A) and 12(a)(2), they were entitled to rely on Andersen's comfort letters for WorldCom's unaudited interim financial statements for the first quarter of 2000 and 2001 so long as the Lead Plaintiff is unable to show that the Underwriter Defendants were on notice of any accounting red flags. They argue that this statement of the due diligence defense is particularly appropriate because WorldCom was a seasoned issuer and the Registration Statements were part of the integrated disclosure system that allowed the Exchange Act periodic reports to be incorporated by reference. * * * [The court rejected this argument for the reasons stated above]

To prevail on their due diligence defense at trial, the Underwriter Defendants must show that they conducted a reasonable investigation and that after such an investigation that they had reasonable ground to believe that the statements in the Registration Statements, including the information in the unaudited interim financial statements, were true. [Section 11(b)(3)(A)] In judging that investigation, a jury will have to consider the non-exclusive list of factors enumerated in Rule 176. * * *

B. The Directors' Due Diligence and Reliance Defense in *WorldCom*

In Re WorldCom, Inc. Securities Litigation

United States District Court Southern District of New York, (2005)
U.S. Dist. LEXIS 4193

Denise Cote, District Judge:

This Opinion describes the standards for imposing liability on directors of public companies under Section 11 of the Securities Act of 1933 ("Securities Act"). * * * Bert C. Roberts, Jr. ("Roberts"), the former chairman of the board of WorldCom, Inc. ("WorldCom"), has moved for summary judgment in the consolidated securities class action arising from WorldCom's collapse, relying principally upon the affirmative defenses available under [Section 11]. [The] lead Plaintiff does not contend that Roberts knew of the accounting fraud which it alleges occurred at WorldCom. * * *

The Section 11 affirmative defense of due diligence. As a director of WorldCom, Roberts is named as a defendant in the Complaint's Section 11 claim. As already noted, the Section 11 claim is premised on the Registration Statements filed by WorldCom for the 2000 and 2001 Offerings. Roberts asserts principally that he relied and was entitled to rely on the integrity of WorldCom's officers and the work of WorldCom's auditor in connection with the contents of the Registration Statements. * * * [The court here discusses the due diligence and reliance defenses under Section 11 along the lines discussed in the above case relating to the liability of the underwriters.]

Application of the Law to Roberts' Motion. In his motion for summary judgment, Roberts argues that with respect to the expertised portions of the registration statements, he is entitled to summary judgment on the Section 11 claim against him because he relied on the financial statements prepared by Andersen and believed them to be correct. * * * Turning to the non-expertised portions of the registration statements, Roberts again phrases his argument in terms of reliance, contending that he "reasonably relied on the organization, the management personnel, and the obvious compliance by [WorldCom] with modern corporate governance standards," and pointing to Rule 176(f) as support for his actions. * * *

Roberts' motion is premised on several erroneous statements of law, not the least of which is his argument, stated most clearly within his reply brief, that "whether audited or unaudited," all of the financial statements reviewed by Andersen are expertised within the meaning of Section 11. The Summary Judgment Opinion addressed this issue squarely, finding that as a matter of statutory interpretation and SEC regulation, unaudited financial information is not expertised, and thus, Section 11 defendants may not claim the reliance defense with respect to unaudited financial information and must show that they conducted a reasonable investigation of all portions of a registration statement except the audited financial statements.

Even as to the audited financial statements, where a reliance defense is appropriate, Roberts' motion must fail. The Lead Plaintiff has pointed to information, most notably the decline in WorldCom's line costs as a percentage of revenue, that a jury may find should have raised a red flag for Roberts and caused him to question his reliance on the audited financial statements. This is particularly true given Roberts' history within and expertise in the telecommunications industry. * * * If the line cost data was a red flag, then Roberts had an obligation to inquire until satisfied as to the integrity of the line cost data.

Aside from Roberts' significant errors of law, he has also not fulfilled his burden of proof with respect to his due diligence defense. A defendant's assertion of the due diligence defense requires an exquisitely fact intensive inquiry into all of the circumstances surrounding the facts upon which the Section 11 claim is premised, including the factors set out in Rule 176. * * *

Here, the parties dispute whether Roberts should be considered an inside or outside director, a classification that weighs heavily on any evaluation of Roberts' argument that he is entitled to summary judgment on his due diligence defense. Even assuming that Roberts were able to show that he is properly considered an outside director, however, Roberts has not shown that he is entitled to summary judgment. He has not shown that he conducted any sort of investigation, much less a reasonable investigation in light of all relevant circumstances. * * * While reliance on management's presentations to the Board, after a careful examination of the materials provided to the Board, may suffice in some cases, the assertions in this case raise questions as to whether it was incumbent on Roberts to engage in a more active dialogue with management and perhaps even with the Company's auditors and underwriters. A motion for summary judgment requires a defendant to present evidence that establishes the absence of a genuine issue of fact; Roberts has not done that.

§4.10 Introductory Problems on Public Offerings

1. John, president of Closely-Held Corporation (CHC), has decided to explore the possibility of taking CHC public. John has entered negotiations with Morgan-Boston (M-B), an investment banking firm, concerning a possible firm commitment underwriting. M-B has sent John a letter of intent setting forth the terms and conditions of the underwriting. Can John sign the letter without violating Section 5?

2. After M-B and John reach agreement, can CHC make a public announcement of the planned offering before the registration statement is filed, and if so, what can be said in

the announcement? Also, what kind of public communications can CHC make prior to the filing of the registration statement?

3. After the registration statement has been filed, a broker at M-B calls a prospective customer and discusses the CHC offering. Is this a violation of Section 5? Suppose the broker sends the prospective customer a letter briefly summarizing the offering, together with a copy of the preliminary prospectus? Is this a violation of Section 5?

4. After the registration statement becomes effective, a broker at M-B sends to a customer who had expressed an interest in purchasing stock of CHC an electronic confirmation of sale. Is this a violation of Section 5? Suppose the confirmation also contained link to the prospectus and a copy of a brochure summarizing the offering?

5. What are the consequences of violating Section 5?

6. What if the registration statement contains a material misstatement of fact?

7. After becoming public, describe the periodic filings the CHC is required to make.

§ 4.11 Special Issues Once a Company Becomes Public

A. Applicability of Reg FD to Public Companies

Selective Disclosure and Insider Trading, Securities Act Release No. 33-7881

(Aug. 15, 2000)

Executive Summary. * * * Regulation FD (Fair Disclosure) is a new issuer disclosure rule that addresses selective disclosure. The regulation provides that when an issuer, or person acting on its behalf, discloses material nonpublic information to certain enumerated persons (in general, securities market professionals and holders of the issuer's securities who may well trade on the basis of the information), it must make public disclosure of that information. The timing of the required public disclosure depends on whether the selective disclosure was intentional or non-intentional; for an intentional selective disclosure, the issuer must make public disclosure simultaneously; for a non-intentional disclosure, the issuer must make public disclosure promptly. Under the regulation, the required public disclosure may be made by filing or furnishing a Form 8-K, or by another method or combination of methods that is reasonably designed to effect broad, non-exclusionary distribution of the information to the public. * * *

B. Financial Disclosure and Related Provisions of the Sarbanes-Oxley Act of 2002

1. Introduction to the Act

This section reviews the following provisions of the Sarbanes-Oxley Act, which is introduced in Chapter 1: (1) the rules regarding management assessment of internal controls, (2) the rules requiring officer certification of financial reports, and (3) the rules dealing with enhanced disclosure of beneficial interest under Section 16 of the 34 Act. Other provisions of the Act are addressed in Chapter 3.

2. Management Assessment of Internal Controls

a. SEC's Final Rules

SEC Final Rule on Disclosures Re Internal Controls, Release No. 34–47986

(June 5, 2003)

In this release, we implement Section 404 of the Sarbanes-Oxley Act of 2002 (the "Sarbanes-Oxley Act"), which requires us to prescribe rules requiring each annual report that a company, other than a registered investment company, files pursuant to Section 13(a) or 15(d) of the Exchange Act to contain an internal control report: (1) stating management's responsibility for establishing and maintaining an adequate internal control structure and procedures for financial reporting; and (2) containing an assessment, as of the end of the company's most recent fiscal year, of the effectiveness of the company's internal control structure and procedures for financial reporting. Section 404 also requires every registered public accounting firm that prepares or issues an audit report on a company's annual financial statements to attest to, and report on, the assessment made by management. The attestation must be made in accordance with standards for attestation engagements issued or adopted by the Public Company Accounting Oversight Board ("PCAOB"). Section 404 further stipulates that the attestation cannot be the subject of a separate engagement of the registered public accounting firm.

b. Applicability of Internal Controls Report Regarding a New Acquired Target

Division of Corporation Finance FAQs on Internal Controls (Relating to M&A)

(October 6, 2004)

* * * Question 3

Q: If a registrant consummates a material purchase business combination during its fiscal year, must the internal control over financial reporting of the acquired business be included in management's report on internal control over financial reporting for that fiscal year?

A: As discussed above, we would typically expect management's report on internal control over financial reporting to include controls at all consolidated entities. However, we acknowledge that it might not always be possible to conduct an assessment of an acquired business's internal control over financial reporting in the period between the consummation date and the date of management's assessment. In such instances, we would not object to management referring in the report to a discussion in the registrant's Form 10-K or 10-KSB regarding the scope of the assessment and to such disclosure noting that management excluded the acquired business from management's report on internal control over financial reporting. If such a reference is made, however, management must identify the acquired business excluded and indicate the significance of the acquired business to the registrant's consolidated financial statements. Notwithstanding management's exclusion of an acquired business's internal controls from its annual assessment, a registrant must disclose any material change to its internal control over financial reporting due to the acquisition pursuant to Exchange Act Rule 13a-15(d) or 15d-15(d), whichever applies. * * * In addition, the period in which management may omit an assessment of an acquired business's internal control over financial reporting from its assessment of the registrant's internal control may not extend beyond one year from the date of acquisition, nor may such assessment be omitted from more than one annual management report on internal control over financial reporting. * * *

3. Officer Certification of Financial Reports

SEC Final Rules on Certification, Release No. 34–46427

(August 29, 2002)

Summary: As directed by Section 302(a) of the Sarbanes-Oxley Act of 2002, we are adopting rules to require an issuer's principal executive and financial officers each to certify the financial and other information contained in the issuer's quarterly [10-Qs] and annual reports [10-Ks]. The rules also require these officers to certify that: they are responsible for establishing, maintaining and regularly evaluating the effectiveness of the issuer's internal controls; they have made certain disclosures to the issuer's auditors and the audit committee of the board of directors about the issuer's internal controls; and they have included information in the issuer's quarterly and annual reports about their evaluation and whether there have been significant changes in the issuer's internal controls or in other factors that could significantly affect internal controls subsequent to the evaluation. In addition, we are adopting previously proposed rules to require issuers to maintain, and regularly evaluate the effectiveness of disclosure controls and procedures designed to ensure that the information required in reports filed under the Securities Exchange Act of 1934 is recorded, processed, summarized and reported on a timely basis. [Section 906 of Sarbanes Oxley provides for harsh criminal penalties for false certifications.]

4. Enhanced Reporting of Beneficial Interest under Section 16

SEC Final Rules under Section 16 of the 34 Act, Release No. 34–46421

(August 27, 2003)

Executive Summary and Background. Section 16 applies to every person who is the beneficial owner of more than 10% of any class of equity security registered under Section 12 of the Exchange Act, and each officer and director (collectively, "reporting persons" or "insiders") of the issuer of such security. Upon becoming a reporting person, or upon the Section 12 [of the 34 Act] registration of that security [because, for example, shares are issued in an IPO], Section 16(a) requires a reporting person to file an initial report with the Commission disclosing his or her beneficial ownership of all equity securities of the issuer. To keep this information current, Section 16(a) also requires reporting persons to report changes in such ownership, or the purchase or sale of a security-based swap agreement involving such equity security. Previously, Section 16(a) provided for such transactions to be reported on a monthly basis within 10 days after the close of each calendar month in which such a change in ownership or purchase or sale of a security-based swap agreement occurs.

On July 30, 2002, the Sarbanes-Oxley Act of 2002 (the "Act") was enacted. Section 403(a) of the Act amends Section 16(a) to require reports of such a change in ownership or purchase or sale of a security-based swap agreement "before the end of the second business day following the day on which the subject transaction has been executed, or at such other time as the Commission shall establish, by rule, in any case in which the Commission determines that such 2-day period is not feasible." [*See* Form 4.]

C. The Provisions on Say on Pay and Golden Parachutes in the 2010 Dodd-Frank Act[3]

1. Introduction

Section 951 of the 2010 Dodd–Frank Wall Street Reform and Consumer Protection Act, which was enacted as a result of the financial crisis, added Section 14A to the 34 Act. Section 14A(a) gives the shareholders of 34 Act companies an advisory vote on executive compensation in certain circumstances. Section 14A(a) provides for both a shareholder advisory vote on pay and a shareholder vote on the frequency of such advisory votes:

> (1) IN GENERAL.—Not less frequently than once every 3 years, a proxy or consent or authorization for an annual or other meeting of the shareholders for which the proxy solicitation rules of the Commission require compensation disclosure shall include a separate resolution subject to shareholder vote to approve the compensation of executives, as disclosed pursuant to [Item 402 of Reg. SK], or any successor thereto.
>
> (2) FREQUENCY OF VOTE.—Not less frequently than once every 6 years, a proxy or consent or authorization for an annual or other meeting of the shareholders for which the proxy solicitation rules of the Commission require compensation disclosure shall include a separate resolution subject to shareholder vote to determine whether votes on the resolutions required under paragraph (1) will occur every 1, 2, or 3 years.

Thus, under Section 14A(a)(1), the advisory vote on compensation (the Compensation Vote) must occur at least once every 3 years. Also, under Section 14A(a)(2), at least once every 6 years, an advisory vote must be taken on whether the Compensation Vote will occur every 1, 2, or 3 years.

Section 14A(b), which sets out rules governing shareholder approval of certain golden parachute and similar provisions (*i.e.*, bonus payments to a target's management), is examined in Chapter 13.

2. Remarks on "Say on Pay" by SEC Chair White, December 2013, *See* Chapter 25

§ 4.12 Introduction to Exemptions from Registration

A. In General

The 1933 Act specifically exempts certain classes of securities and certain classes of transactions in securities from the registration requirement of Section 5.

Sections 3(a)(1) to (8) exempt from the registration requirement certain specialized securities, such as insurance or endowment policies and annuity contracts. Section 3(a)(9) exempts transactions in which existing security holders exchange their outstanding securities for new securities of the issuer. This exemption applies to recapitalizations. Section 3(a)(10) exempts certain transactions involving exchanges of securities if there has been

3. This section is adapted from Thompson, *Mergers, Acquisitions and Tender Offers, supra* Section 1.10, at Section 6:10.5[B].

a hearing on the fairness of the exchange. Section 3(a)(11) exempts transactions in which securities are sold within a single state. This is known as the intrastate exemption and is governed by Rule 147. If a single offer is made to a resident of another state, the exemption is broken. For this and other reasons, the exemption is of limited utility.

B. Reg A and Simplified Registration for Certain Small Issues

Section 3(b)(1) provides a simplified registration process, known as Regulation A, for certain small issues. Reg A issues cannot exceed $5 million.

Section 401 of the JOBS Act amends section 3(b) of the 33 Act by providing for a new small issuer exemption. To fall within this exemption, among other things, the offering cannot exceed $50 million in any 12-month period, and the securities cannot be restricted securities. *See* JOBS Act § 401. This section provides that on a biannual basis, the Commission will review the offering amount limitation involved here and increase it as the Commission thinks appropriate.

These provisions are not discussed further here.

C. The JOBS Act Crowdfunding Exemptions

Title III of the JOBS Act is the Capital Raising Online While Deterring Fraud and Unethical Non-Disclosure Act of 2012 or the "CROWDFUND Act." JOBS Act § 301. The Crowdfunding exemption amends Section 4 of the 33 Act by providing for this new exemption from registration under Section 4(a)(6). There are a number of requirements for an issuance to fall within this exemption. For example, the total amount of securities sold by an issuer to all investors within a 12-month period may not exceed $1,000,000. Moreover, there are limits on the amount of securities that can be sold to an investor. For example, for an investor with less than $100,000 of income or $100,000 of net worth, the aggregate amount sold to such investor must not exceed the greater of $2,000 or 5% of the investor's annual income or net worth, as applicable. Also, the transaction must be conducted through either a broker or a funding portal which complies with the requirements found in section 4A(a) of the 33 Act. This Crowdfunding exemption is not likely going to be used in M&A transactions, and for that reason it is not explored further here.

D. Introduction to the Private Offering Exemption

Section 4(a)(2) of the 1933 Act exempts "transactions by an issuer not involving a public offering." This is known as the private offering exemption. It permits a corporation to issue its stock or securities to a small number of informed investors without registering the stock. The principal manner in which this exemption is utilized is through compliance with Regulation D. Section 4(a)(1) exempts transactions by a person other than an issuer, underwriter, or dealer. The purpose of this exemption is to allow "routine trading transactions between individual investors with respect to securities already issued ..." [*see* SEC Rule 144 Preliminary Note]. The principal manner in which this exemption is utilized is through compliance with Rule 144.

In acquisitions of closely-held target corporations in exchange, in whole or in part, for the stock or other securities of the acquiring corporation, the securities are generally issued pursuant to a Regulation D exemption, and the target's shareholders generally resell the securities pursuant to the exemption provided by Rule 144. Thus, Regulation D and Rule 144 can be of crucial importance in the acquisition of a closely-held target corporation in exchange for stock or other securities of the acquiring corporation. However, in a cash acquisition, no security is issued and the 33 Act does not apply to the acquiror.

The availability of the private offering exemption of § 4(a)(2) of the 33 Act is basically dependent upon two factors: first, the number and the nature of the offerees, and second, the purpose for which purchasers acquire the securities. The offerees must be few in number and have "access" to the important investment information concerning the issuer. The purchasers must acquire the securities for the purpose of investment, not for resale to the public. In other words, the purchasers must not be conduits between the issuer and the public. If a purchaser acts as a conduit, he will be deemed an "underwriter," which is defined broadly in § 2(a)(11) as any person who purchases a security "with a view" to distribution. If deemed an "underwriter," a purchaser breaks the issuer's exemption under § 4(a)(2) and is himself denied the routine sale exemption of § 4(a)(1), which applies to a person who is not an "issuer, underwriter or dealer." Regulation D provides a regulatory safe harbor for the § 4(a)(2) private offering exemption, and Rule 144 provides a regulatory safe harbor for the routine resale exemptions of § 4(a)(1).

Regulation D provides four exceptions from registration. First, under Rule 504, an issuer can sell up to $1,000,000 of its securities in a 12-month period to an unlimited number of investors. Second, under Rule 505, an issuer can sell up to $5,000,000 of its securities in a 12-month period to not more than 35 non-accredited investors and to an unlimited number of accredited investors. Third, under Rule 506(a) and (b), which is referred to here as the "Traditional Rule 506," an issuer can sell an unlimited amount of its securities to not more than 35 non-accredited investors and to an unlimited number of accredited investors. As discussed subsequently, a number of requirements must be satisfied for each of these exemptions, including a "no general solicitation" requirement for an offering under Rule 505 and the Traditional Rule 506.

The JOBS Act added a fourth exemption, which has been implemented by Rule 506(a) and (c). This is referred to here as the JOBS Act Rule 506. Under this exemption an issuer can sell an unlimited amount of its securities to accredited investors without complying with the "no general solicitation requirement" applicable to Rule 505 and the Traditional Rule 506. This exemption is not likely to be used in an M&A transaction and, therefore, is explored only briefly below.

The Traditional Rule 506 exempt offering is often used in the acquisition of a privately held target and, therefore, is explored in greater detail below. If for some reason compliance with Regulation D is not feasible, as discussed *infra*, an offering may still qualify as a statutory Section 4(2) private offering.

E. Introduction to the Rule 144 Resale Exemption

Rule 144 specifies conditions under which a person who has purchased unregistered securities may sell them without being deemed engaged in a distribution of such securities and, therefore, an underwriter thereof. In general, Rule 144 requires that (1) the securities of a publicly held issuer that are acquired in a private offering be held for six months, and (2) the securities of a privately held issuer that are acquired in a private offering be held for one year. As will be seen, other limitations may be applicable.

Unregistered securities may also be sold pursuant to a registration statement in compliance with Section 5 of the 33 Act and in what is known as a section 4(a)(1) exempt offering. Section 4(a)(1) is explored *infra*. Finally, under Rule 144A, securities purchased by "qualified institutional buyers" (QIBs) in a private offering may be resold without restrictions to other QIBs. Rule 144A is introduced *infra*.

§ 4.13 Guide for Completing a Statutory Section 4(a)(2) Private Placement

ABA Federal Regulation of Securities Committee, Section 4(2) and Statutory Law

31 Bus Lawyer 485, 486–489, 491, 495, 497–499(1975)

Offers and sales of securities by an issuer which do not involve any public offering and therefore come within the scope of Section 4(2), are exempt from the registration and prospectus requirements of Section 5. * * *

The legislative history of Section 4(2) [now § 4(a)(2)] is scanty, as is apparent from the present confused state of the law, and is susceptible of widely differing interpretations. There have been relatively few published administrative interpretations of Section 4(2) by the Commission. * * *

Sources of Statutory Law. In our search for Statutory Law, there are several sources upon which we can draw. First, there is the legislative history, which referred to:

> [A] specific or isolated sale ... to a particular person.
>
> [W]here there is no practical need for the bill's application.
>
> [W]here the public benefits are too remote.
>
> [U]nless the stockholders are so small in number that the sale to them does not constitute a public offering.

An early opinion of the SEC General Counsel sets the interpretative stage for many years. This opinion focused on the number of offerees as a prime consideration, indicating that under ordinary circumstances an offering to approximately 25 or fewer persons would presumably not involve a public offering. It went on to enumerate the following factors as being relevant:

> The number of offerees;
>
> The relationship of the offerees to each other;
>
> The relationship of the offerees to the issuer;
>
> The number of units offered;
>
> The size of the offering; and
>
> The manner of the offering. * * *

From the standpoint of framing precise or objective standards, qualification of offerees is probably the most troublesome of all the attributes of the exemption. We believe that offerees in a private placement should be deemed qualified on any one of several bases. They may be qualified on the basis of their ability to understand the risk. This attribute is sometimes called "sophistication." They may be qualified on the basis of their ability to assume the investment risk, so called "wealth." Or, they may be qualified on the basis of a personal relationship to the issuer or a promoter. * * *

A second general attribute relates to the scope and manner of disclosure of information. It is generally considered necessary that each offeree have some information about the issuer, or at least access to that information, prior to the sale. * * *

The third general attribute of a proper private placement under Statutory Law relates to the manner of offering. In general, the offering should be made through direct communication with qualified offerees or their representatives, whether by the issuer itself or through an agent of the issuer. All forms of general advertising and mass media circulation should be avoided. The number of offers made may have evidentiary significance, as discussed below, in determining whether the manner of an offering was proper. * * *

A fourth general attribute of a proper private placement under Statutory Law is the absence of an immediate redistribution by the first-tier purchasers which would transform the overall transaction into a public offering. Query if it is still necessary for the purchaser to have "investment intent" of the type frequently discussed prior to the adoption of Rule 144. Investment intent was legal shorthand intended to reflect the absence of an intention to resell or distribute the security. * * *

Under the law as interpreted prior to the adoption of Rule 144, if an investor were to ask his lawyer shortly after the private placement when he could sell the stock, under a strict interpretation of the doctrine arguably the lawyer's answer should have been: "Now that you ask, the answer is never! The very fact that you raised the question shows that you lack adequate investment intent." Of course, there was an exception recognized, "the change of circumstance" doctrine, which was equally elusive. Hopefully, Rule 144 gave the *coup de grace* to all of this metaphysical nonsense. If no distribution is made, the exemption should not be jeopardized today by an unsuitable subjective state of mind on the purchaser's part.

Statutory Law does not require any mechanical procedures to avoid redistribution, such as the endorsement of legends on certificates, investment (non-distribution) letters or stop transfer instructions to transfer agents, although these devices are very useful to evidence the absence of distributive purpose or intent (and they may be required under applicable state law). As long as no redistribution occurs in fact, the absence of these mechanical procedures does not render the exemption unavailable.

Use of the three mechanical procedures, however, should be encouraged, at least where the class of security involved is, or is expected to become, publicly owned, or where the issuer has a number of "outside investors." * * *

If all the foregoing attributes are met—qualification of the offerees, availability of information, manner of the offering and absence of a redistribution—the exemption should apply to the transaction notwithstanding the failure of that transaction to meet some of the other tests sometimes articulated in the traditional sources.

§ 4.14 Regulation D—Exemptions for Transactions Involving Limited Offers and Sales

A. Introduction

Regulation D provides a safe harbor exemption under Section 4(a)(2) of the 33 Act, which sets forth the private offering exemption. Thus, if an issuance of securities falls within Regulation D, the securities do not have to be registered under Section 5. Regulation

D will be used in an acquisition context in situations where an acquiror is acquiring a closely-held target corporation in exchange, in whole or in part, for securities. Regulation D can be utilized in the acquisition of a closely-held target in (1) a stock acquisition, (1) an asset acquisition, and (3) a merger. Although asset acquisitions and mergers are covered by Rule 145, which is examined in Chapter 13, the notes to Rule 145 make it clear that Regulation D can be utilized in the issuance of stock of the acquiring corporation in the acquisition of a closely-held target corporation by merger or sale of assets.

In studying the following materials on Regulation D, attempt to identify those issues that are most likely to be present in an acquisition context. Will counsel for the acquiror or counsel for the target be most concerned about Regulation D? Prior to exploring Regulation D, however, Section 4.6.B illustrates how the private offering exemption may be implicated in the acquisition context.

B. Illustration of the Impact of the Private Offering Exemption in Acquisition Transactions

Klapmeier v. Telecheck International, Inc.

United States Court of Appeals, Eighth Circuit (1973) 482 F.2d 247

Bright, Circuit Judge:

[**Facts and Issue**] The stockholders of Boatel, Inc. (Boatel) agreed to exchange all of the capital stock of their corporation * * * for stock of Telecheck, Inc. (Telecheck)[.] James E. Klapmeier, plaintiff-appellee, the president and principal stockholder of Boatel, for himself and the other Boatel stockholders, negotiated with defendant-appellant, Harry M. Flagg, Klapmeier's friend and fraternity brother of his earlier college days at MIT. On May 10, 1969, the parties executed an agreement having the effect of merging Boatel into Telecheck. Thereafter, the old school ties proved too fragile to withstand business disagreements. [Klapmeier and other shareholders of Boatel brought an action against Telecheck and others for violation of Section 5 of the 33 Act in failing to register the Telecheck stock. Under Section 12[a](1) of the 33 Act, if securities are sold in violation of the registration requirements of Section 5, the purchaser has the right to put the securities back to the seller]. * * *

[**Discussion**] The parties concede that Telecheck did not register its stock prior to the signing of the agreement between the parties in accordance with the requirement of § 5 of the Securities Act of 1933. However, appellants vigorously press the argument that the trial court erred when it declined to rule the transfer of Telecheck stock to be an exempt private offering of securities under § 4(1) [now § 4(2)] of the Securities Act of 1933. Both sides agree that *Securities and Exchange Commission v. Ralston Purina Co.*, 346 U.S. 119 (1953), is the controlling authority. In the *Ralston Purina* case, a corporation sold nearly $2,000,000 worth of its stock to employees without registering the sale. The Court held these transactions to be nonexempt, stating:

> Exemption from the registration requirements of the Securities Act is the question. The design of the statute is to protect investors by promoting full disclosure of information thought necessary to informed investment decisions. The natural way to interpret the private offering exemption is in light of the statutory purpose. Since exempt transactions are those as to which "there is no practical need for [the bill's] application," the applicability of § 4(1) should turn on whether the particular class of persons affected needs the protection of the Act. An offering to those who are shown to be able to fend for themselves is a

> transaction "not involving any public offering." [346 U.S. at 124–125, 73 S.Ct. at 984 (brackets in original; footnote omitted)]

The Court added:

> The focus of inquiry should be on the need of the offerees for the protections afforded by registration. The employees here were not shown to have access to the kind of information which registration would disclose. [346 U.S. at 127, 73 S.Ct. at 985]

We think it doubtful that the registration provisions apply to the instant transaction, for the record undisputedly discloses a stock-for-stock exchange for investment purposes between Telecheck and only seven stockholder-owners of Boatel, who permitted Klapmeier to negotiate the merger agreement. Klapmeier received all published financial statements of Telecheck, plus the opportunity to explore fully the operations of Telecheck and its subsidiaries * * * . * * *

Questions

What are the fundamental differences between an action under Section 11 and an action under Section 12(a)(1)? What is the difference between an action under Sections 12(a)(1) and 12(a)(2)? What is the difference between an action under Section 11 and Section 12(a)(2)? What would have been the result in *Telecheck* if the court had found the transaction was a public offering?

C. Notice of Adoption of Regulation D; Provisions Relevant to Rule 505 and Traditional Rule 506

Securities Act Release No. 33-6389

(March 8, 1982)

Regulation D is a series of six rules, designated Rules 501–506, that establishes three [now four with the JOBS Act Rule 506] exemptions from the registration requirements of the Securities Act. * * *

Rules 501–503 set forth definitions, terms, and conditions that apply generally throughout the regulation. The exemptions of Regulation D are contained in Rules 504–506. * * *

Preliminary Notes. Regulation D contains six preliminary notes. The first preliminary note reminds issuers that Regulation D offerings, although exempt from Section 5 of the Securities Act, are not exempt from antifraud or civil liability provisions of the federal securities laws. The note also reminds issuers conducting Regulation D offerings of their obligation to furnish whatever material information may be needed to make the required disclosure not misleading.

Note 2 underscores an issuer's obligation to comply with applicable state law and highlights certain areas of anticipated differences between Regulation D at the federal and state levels.

Note 3 makes clear that reliance on any particular exemption in Regulation D does not act as an election. An issuer may always claim the availability of any other applicable exemption. Several commentators believed this note should address specifically the availability of an exemption under Section [4(a)(2)] of the Securities Act. The Commission has reworded the note by including language that appeared in proposed Rule 506(a) and clarified the specific availability of Section [4(a)(2)].

The fourth note specifies that Regulation D is available only to the issuer of the securities and not to its affiliates or others for resales of the issuer's securities. The note further provides that Regulation D exemptions are only transactional. * * *

Preliminary Note 5 * * * confirms the availability of Regulation D for business combinations [*i.e.*, Reg. D may be used in, for example, the issuance by an acquiring corporation of its securities in a merger].

The sixth note provides that the regulation is not available for use in a plan or scheme to evade the registration requirements of the Securities Act.

Rule 501—Definitions and Terms Used in Regulation D. Rule 501 sets forth, alphabetically, definitions that apply to the entire regulation. * * *

1. *Accredited investor.* * * * The following subsections review the eight categories of accredited investors in Rule 501(a). * * *

d. *Rule 501(a)(4)—Directors, Executive Officers and General Partners.* Rule 501(a)(4) provides that certain insiders of the issuer are accredited investors. As proposed, the category pertained only to directors and executive officers. A number of comment letters recommended that the provision be modified to cover general partners of limited partnerships. The category thus has been revised to include general partners of issuers, as well as directors, executive officers and general partners of those general partners. * * *

f. *Rule 501(a)([5])—$1,000,000 Net Worth Test.* This category extends accredited investor status to any natural person whose net worth at the time of purchase is $1,000,000. Net worth may be either the individual worth of the investor or the joint net worth of the investor and the investor's spouse. [A person's primary residence is not included as an asset.]

g. *Rule 501(a)([6])—$200,000 Income Test.* [Also the accredited investor concept includes any natural person who had an individual income in excess of $200,000 in each of the two most recent years or joint income with that person's spouse in excess of $300,000 in each of those years and has a reasonable expectation of reaching the same income level in the current year.] * * *

The rule as adopted does not define the term "income." Rather than adopting a definition, the Commission has determined to utilize a flexible approach, thereby avoiding the issues raised by inclusion in the rule of federal tax law concepts. * * *

3. *Aggregate offering price.* Rule 501(c) defines the method for calculating the aggregate offering price. * * *

4. *Business Combination.* [Rule 501(d) defines business combination as "any transaction of the type specified in paragraph (a) of Rule 145 * * * and any transaction involving the acquisition by one issuer, in exchange for all or a part of its own or its parent's stock, of stock of another issuer if, immediately after the acquisition, the acquiring issuer has control of the other issuer (whether or not it had control before the acquisition)."]

5. *Calculation of number of purchasers.* Rule 501(e) sets forth principles that govern the calculation of the number of purchasers in offerings under Rules 505 and 506. * * *

8. *Purchaser representative.* In response to comments, the definition of purchaser representative in Rule 501[(h)] has been revised in three respects. First, the introductory language to the paragraph has been reformulated. As adopted, the definition includes any person who satisfies the conditions of the term in fact, as well as any person the issuer reasonably believes falls within the category. A second change incorporated the categories set forth in Rule 501(e)(1)(ii) and (iii) into subparagraphs (ii) and (iii). Thirdly, paragraph (2) was revised to permit the purchaser representative to make the requisite evaluation of the prospective investment "with the purchaser."

C. *Rule 502—General Conditions to be Met.* Rule 502 sets forth general conditions that relate to all offerings under Rules 504 through 506. These cover guidelines for determining whether separate offers and sales constitute part of the same offering under principles of integration, requirements as to specific disclosure requirements in Regulation D offerings, and limitations on the manner of conducting the offering and on the resale of securities acquired in the offering. * * *

1. *Integration.* Rule 502(a) provides that all sales that are part of the same Regulation D offering must be integrated. The rule provides a safe harbor for all offers and sales that take place at least six months before the start of or six months after the termination of the Regulation D offering, so long as there are no offers and sales, excluding those to employee benefit plans, of the same securities within either of these six-month periods. * * *

2. *Information Requirements.* Rule 502(b) provides when and what type of disclosure must be furnished in Regulation D offerings. If an issuer sells securities under Rule 504 or only to accredited investors, then Regulation D does not mandate any specific disclosure. * * *

3. *Manner of offering.* Rule 502(c) prohibits the use of general solicitation or general advertising in connection with Regulation D offerings, except in certain cases under Rule 504. * * *

4. *Limitations on resale.* Securities acquired in a Regulation D offering, with the exception of certain offerings under Rule 504, have the status of securities acquired in a transaction under Section 4(2) of the Securities Act. As further provided in Rule 502(d), the issuer shall exercise reasonable care to assure that purchasers of securities are not underwriters, which reasonable care will include certain inquiry as to investment purpose, disclosure of resale limitations and placement of a legend on the certificate.

D. *Rule 503—Filings of Notice of Sales* * * * Rule 503 sets forth the filing requirements for Form D. The notice is due 15 days after the first sale of securities in an offering under Regulation D. Subsequent notices are due every six months after first sale and 30 days after the last sale. * * *

F. *Rule 505—Exemption for Offers and Sales Not Exceeding $5,000,000*

Rule 505 * * * provides an exemption under Section 3(b) of the Securities Act for offers and sales to no more than 35 purchasers that are not accredited where the aggregate offering price over 12 months does not exceed $5,000,000. As with Rule 504, the aggregate offering price includes proceeds from offers and sales under Section 3(b) or in violation of Section 5(a) of the Securities Act. * * *

Rule 505 is available to any issuer that is not an investment company. * * *

Finally, Rule 505 is not available to issuers that are subject to any of the disqualification provisions contained in Rule 262(c), (d), (e) or (f) of Regulation A. [These are the so-called "bad-boy" restrictions].

G. [*Traditional Rule 506—Exemption for Offers and Sales Without Regard to Dollar Amount*

Rule 506 relates to transactions that are deemed to be exempt under Section [4(a)(2)] of the Securities Act. * * * [Traditional] Rule 506 exempts offers and sales to no more than 35 purchasers. * * * [Traditional] Rule 506 excludes accredited investors in computing the number of purchasers. More significantly, [Traditional] Rule 506 modifies the offeree qualification principles of Rule 146 in two ways. First, Rule 506 requires that only purchasers meet the sophistication standard. Second, the rule eliminates the economic risk test. Commentators endorsed both modifications. * * *

D. Interpretative Release on Regulation D Relating to Rule 505 and Traditional Rule 506

Securities Act Release No. 33-6455

(March 3, 1983)

(23) Question: May a purchaser include unrealized capital appreciation in calculating income for purposes of Rule 501(a)(7)?

Answer: Generally, no. * * *

Purchaser Representative—Rule 501[(i)]. A purchaser representative is any person who satisfies, or who the issuer reasonably believes satisfies, four conditions enumerated in Rule 501(h). Beyond the obligations imposed by that rule, any person acting as a purchaser representative must consider whether or not he is required to register as a broker-dealer under section 15 of the Securities Exchange Act of 1934 (the "Exchange Act") or as an investment adviser under section 203 of the Investment Advisers Act of 1940. * * *

(39) Question: May the issuer in a Regulation D offering pay the fees of the purchaser representative?

Answer: Yes. Nothing in Regulation D prohibits the payment by the issuer of the purchaser representative's fees. Rule 501(h)(4), however, requires disclosure of this fact.

Disclosure Requirements—Rule 502(b). Rule 502(b)(1) sets forth the circumstances when disclosure of the kind specified in the regulation must be delivered to investors. The regulation requires the delivery of certain information 'during the course of the offering and prior to sale' if the offering is conducted in reliance on Rule 505 or 506 and if there are unaccredited investors. If the offering is conducted in compliance with Rule 504 or if securities are sold only to accredited investors, Regulation D does not specify the information that must be disclosed to investors. * * *

(49) Question: The issuer in a Regulation D offering of $7,000,000 is a corporation. That corporation is acquiring a business. The issuer is unable to obtain the financial statements for that business without unreasonable effort or expense. What are the relevant considerations under Regulation D?

Answer: Rule 502(b)(2)(i)(B) provides that if the issuer is not a limited partnership and "cannot obtain audited financial statements without unreasonable effort or expense, then only the issuer's balance sheet, which shall be dated within 120 days of the start of the offering, must be audited." The staff has interpreted this provision in the context of Rule 3–05 of Regulation S-X to apply to the financial statements of the business being acquired. Thus, if the business being acquired is other than a limited partnership, and if the issuer cannot obtain audited financial statements of that business without unreasonable effort or expense, then the issuer may provide the relevant financial statements for the business being acquired on an unaudited basis so long as it also provides an audited balance sheet for that business dated within 120 days of the start of the offering, or, if appropriate, as of the date of acquisition of the business. * * *

Limitations on Resale—Rule 502(d). Rule 502(d) makes it clear that Regulation D securities have limitations on transferability and requires that the issuer take certain precautions to restrict the transferability of the securities.

(61) Question: An investor in a Regulation D offering wishes to resell his securities within a year after the offering. The issuer has agreed to register the securities for resale. Will the proposed resale under the registration statement violate Rule 502(d)?

Answer: No. The function of Rule 502(d) is to restrict the unregistered resale of securities. Where the resale will be registered, however, such restrictions are unnecessary. * * *

Questions Relating to [Rule] 505. [Rule 505(b)(2)(i) require[s] that the offering not exceed a specified aggregate offering price. The allowed aggregate offering price, however, is reduced by the aggregate offering price for all securities sold within the last twelve months in reliance on section 3(b) or in violation of section 5(a) of the Securities Act.

(67) Question: An issuer preparing to conduct an offering of equity securities under Rule 505 raised $2,000,000 from the sale of debt instruments under Rule 505 eight months earlier. How much may the issuer raise in the proposed equity offering?

Answer: $3,000,000. A specific condition to the availability of Rule 505 for the proposed offering is that its aggregate offering price not exceed $5,000,000 less the proceeds for all securities sold under section 3(b) within the last 12 months. * * *

Rule 506. (72) Question: May an issuer of securities with a projected aggregate offering price of $3,000,000 rely on [Traditional] Rule 506?

Answer: Yes. The availability of [Traditional] Rule 506 is not dependent on the dollar size of an offering.

(73) Question: [Traditional] Rule 506 requires that the issuer shall reasonably believe that each purchaser who is not an accredited investor either alone or with a purchaser representative has such knowledge and experience in financial and business matters that he is capable of evaluating the merits and risks of the prospective investment. Former Rule 146 required the issuer to make a similar determination with respect to each offeree. Rule 506 is not an exclusive basis for satisfying the requirements of the private offering exemption in section 4[(a)](2). [*See* Preliminary Note 3 to Regulation D] What is the Commission's view of the relevance of the nature of the offerees in an offering that relies exclusively on section 4[(a)](2) as its basis for exemption from registration?

Answer: Clearly, in an offering relying exclusively on section 4[(a)](2) for an exemption from registration, all offerees who purchase must possess the requisite level of sophistication. The sophistication of each of those to whom the securities are offered who do not purchase is not a fact that in and of itself should determine mechanically the availability of the exemption; the number and the nature of the offerees, however, are relevant in determining whether an issuer has engaged in a general solicitation or general advertising that would preclude reliance on the exemption in section 4[(a)](2).

Questions Relating to Rules [505]–506. (74) Question: If an issuer relies on one exemption, but later realizes that exemption may not have been made available, may it rely on another exemption after the fact?

Answer: Yes, assuming the offering met the conditions of the new exemption. No one exemption is exclusive of another. * * *

E. Private Placement Guidelines

Marc H. Morgenstern, Private Placement Guidelines— A Lawyer's Letter to a First-Time Issuer

48 Bus. Lawyer 257(1992)

What follows, is an example of a letter explaining the compliance obligation in a specific private placement transaction. * * *

This document is governed by attorney-client privilege.

President

ABC Corporation

Re: Private Placement (Private Placement) of Common Stock (Stock) of ABC Corporation, a Delaware corporation (Company) pursuant to [Traditional] Rule 506 of Regulation D

Dear Client:

We have met with you, discussed the basic state and federal securities laws governing your offering of Stock, and determined how to structure the offering. Because the Regulation D exemptions under rules 504 and 505 of the Securities Act of 1933 (Securities Act) are unavailable to you due to, among other things, the aggregate offering price, we agreed to structure the offering to comply with [Traditional Rule 506] of Regulation D. The principal federal securities law issues applicable to this offering are summarized in this letter. The state securities law issues are examined in detail in a separate blue sky memorandum, but also are addressed briefly in Section 9. This letter confirms the substance of our discussions in nontechnical terms and outlines our respective responsibilities. Despite its foreboding length, this letter is not all-inclusive, and is not a legal opinion.

1. REGULATION OF SECURITIES-AN OVERVIEW. The sale of securities, such as common stock, is regulated by each state as well as the federal government. The regulation focuses on three key variables: the security (or transaction) itself, the persons and entities who sell the security, and the disclosures made to investors about the security.

Every security sold in the United States either must be registered with the Securities and Exchange Commission (SEC) or qualify for an exemption from registration. In addition, the security either must be registered or exempt from registration in all applicable states, *i.e.*, states in which investors are offered or sold the securities, or that have sufficient contacts with the sales process. Unfortunately, state registration exemptions differ dramatically from state to state. A federal exemption does *not* guarantee a state exemption (or vice versa), nor does an exemption in one state mean that a comparable exemption will be available in another.

In addition, the person selling the securities must be registered with the state and federal government as a broker-dealer or agent *unless* an applicable exemption from registration in those capacities is available. * * *

An exemption from registration for the sale of the Stock at either the state or federal level does not mean that the *person* selling the securities is exempt from registration as a broker-dealer. Similarly, exemption from registration does not relieve the Company of the state and federal antifraud provisions, which require the Company to provide all material information about the Company and the investment to allow investors to make an informed investment decision.

2. HOW DO I AVOID REGISTERING THE STOCK? Registration of the Stock with the SEC is expensive and time consuming. To avoid both problems, you are attempting to comply with an exemption from registration. The Company will be conducting a "private placement," either under rule 506 or the statutory provisions of section 4[(a)](2) of the Securities Act, each of which permits the raising of unlimited funds without registering the security with the SEC.

The requirements for the section 4[(a)](2) exemption are vague and uncertain. * * * Under section 4[(a)](2) and rule 506, the Stock must be acquired for investment purposes and may not be resold for an indefinite period of time, which for persons not closely associated with the Company is generally not less than one year. If the Stock is resold by an original investor in the Private Placement, the stock being resold either must be registered or exempt from registration at that time.

The availability of a private placement under section 4[a](2) further hinges on the number and sophistication of offerees. This is in sharp contrast to rule 506, which primarily deals with purchasers. * * *

The Company has the burden of establishing an exemption from registration.[4] The failure to satisfy even one element of the exemption (*e.g.*, under rule 506 selling to more than thirty-five nonaccredited investors) could destroy the availability of the exemption for the entire offering—*not just the single offer or sale in question.* * * *

3. WHO CAN BUY THE STOCK? We have recommended rule 506 because it has clearer and more objective standards than section 4[(a)](2). This is especially true with respect to the number and suitability of investors. For example, under rule 506, the Stock can be sold to no more than thirty-five nonaccredited *purchasers.* Investors either are accredited or nonaccredited for purposes of rule 506. Generally, each nonaccredited investor is counted as a purchaser while accredited investors and foreign investors are excluded in calculating the number of purchasers. Assuming compliance with the prohibitions against advertising and general solicitation, the Stock theoretically may be sold to an unlimited number of accredited investors.

Whether an investor is considered "accredited" depends on the investor's classification and whether the investor meets the requirements for that classification. [*See* Rule 501(a)] * * *

An investor who does not come within one of the accredited investor categories is a non accredited investor. There can be no more than thirty-five such investors [*See* Rule 506(b)(2)(i)] and you must "reasonably believe" that each of these investors (either individually, or with a "purchaser representative") has enough knowledge and experience in financial and business matters to evaluate the merits and risks of the investment. [*See* Rule 506(b)(2)(ii)] An accredited investor, however, does not need to satisfy any such sophistication standards.

4. WHO CAN SELL THE STOCK? You told us that the Company will sell the Stock without a broker-dealer. The Company and the individuals selling the Stock will avoid registering as broker-dealers or agents by complying with a federal exemption available to issuers and related individuals. [*See* Rule 3a4-1 under the 34 Act] This exemption usually is referred to as the "issuer" exemption and is available to individuals who are not engaged in the business of effecting transactions in securities.* * *

5. HOW DO I SATISFY DISCLOSURE OBLIGATIONS? State and federal securities laws require the Company to provide investors with full, fair, and complete disclosure of all "material" facts about the offering and the Company. * * *

Because the securities will be sold to both accredited and non-accredited investors, under rule 506 the Company must provide written disclosures that contain substantially the same information as disclosure statements from companies that are registering their securities with the SEC. [*See* Rule 502(b)(2)]

Even though the Stock is not required to be registered with the SEC, you must comply with state and federal antifraud provisions. The federal antifraud provisions arise primarily

4. *SEC v. Ralston Purina Co.*, 346 U.S. 119, 126 (1953).

from the well known section 10(b) and rule 10b-5 of the Securities Exchange Act of 1934 (Exchange Act). Failure to comply with these provisions can result in civil liabilities (*i.e.*, money damages). * * *

To satisfy the disclosure requirements and comply with the antifraud provisions, a Private Placement Memorandum (PPM) must be prepared. * * *

The PPM functionally serves two purposes which are inherently in sharp conflict with each other. First, the PPM is a marketing tool to sell the Stock. Because selling the Stock is your primary goal, your tendency will be to create a PPM that describes the company in an overly-positive way. The PPM, however, also is a document that protects you from being sued by disappointed investors if the investment is not successful. Because protecting you is our primary goal, our tendency will be to create a PPM that discloses as much as possible to investors, even if it causes the PPM to be a less effective marketing tool. * * *

6. WHAT OTHER LIMITS ARE THERE ON MY CONDUCT? A short document, called a Form D, must be filed with the SEC within fifteen days after the first "sale" of securities. [*See* Rule 503] * * *

Another important precondition to the availability of the exemption under section 4[(a)](2) and rule 506 is the prohibition against the Company, or any person acting on its behalf, offering or selling securities by any form of "general solicitation or general advertising." [*See* Rule 502(c)] * * *

7. WHAT INFORMATION AND COMMITMENTS DO I NEED FROM THE INVESTOR? The Company must have a reasonable basis for believing that the investor satisfies the suitability standards enunciated in the PPM and that the investor understands the risks of the offering and the information presented to him. [*See* Rule 506(b)(2)(ii)] This depends upon information that only can be provided by the prospective investor. In addition, the prospective investor must acknowledge the limited resaleability of the Stock. The Stock cannot be resold by the investor without registration under the Securities Act or an exemption from registration. [*See* Rule 502(d)] * * *

The investor questionnaire and the other subscription documents, which each prospective investor must complete and sign, are designed to elicit this information and other appropriate representations from investors. The maintenance of contemporaneous records, such as the confidential purchaser questionnaires, especially will be valuable if the registration exemption ever is challenged. * * *

10. WHY AM I READING THIS LETTER? The penalty for violating the registration or anti-fraud provisions of the securities laws is that, at a minimum, investors can rescind their purchase and receive a refund of their investment. [*See* § 12 of the 33 Act] * * * The first rule of securities law is that investors never sue when they make money—only when they lose it. * * *

F. Liability under Section 12(a)(2) in Private Offering

Glamorgan Coal Corp. v. Ratner's Group PLC

United States District Court, SDNY (1995) 1995 WL 406167

Owen, District Judge:

Pursuant to Fed. R. Civ. P. 12(c), defendants move to dismiss the three causes of action in the complaint that rely on § 12[a](2) of the 1933 Securities Act, arguing that under a recent Supreme Court ruling their dismissal is mandated as a matter of law.

In 1991, First Boston solicited plaintiff to buy stock in Ratners, an English company, for an upcoming "private" placement of the stock. The securities are identified as "Series D" and "Series E" Ratners APS. "APS" stands for "Auction Preferred Stock" which is stock whose dividend is reset periodically through a "Dutch auction" process. Plaintiff bought $6.3 million of the stock at the initial placement on July 25, 1991.

For the initial placement, First Boston and Goldman fashioned and sent out a "Final Private Placement Memorandum," a 275 page document containing information similar to that found in a public offering prospectus (e.g., financial data, analysis of financial condition, management discussion). Hundreds of copies of the Offering Memorandum were provided to potential investors throughout the United States.

After the initial solicitation and purchase, the plaintiff reset the dividend rates on the stock by selling and repurchasing them at the Dutch auctions, first in September, 1991 and then in October, 1991. On October 3, 1991, the stock was downgraded by Moody's, following public disclosure of Ratners' disappointing operating results through August 3, 1991. The market for the shares collapsed five days later.

The complaint sought rescission of purchases, a return of consideration, compensatory damages, and interests and costs. Plaintiff's first three causes of action are based on § 12[a](2) of the 1933 Securities Act. * * *

In the April 28, 1994 Second Amended Complaint, the plaintiff contends that defendants' "prospectus" contained misrepresentations and omissions of material fact leading to violations of the Act. Count 1 is based on the initial offering, Count 2 on the September, 1991 auction, and Count 3 on the October, 1991 auction.

As earlier observed, the Supreme Court in *Gustafson v. Alloyd Co.*, U.S., 115 S. Ct. 1061 (1995), 63 U.S.L.W. 4165 (Feb. 28, 1995), was presented with the following situation: in 1989, Gustafson contracted with the sole shareholders of Alloyd, Inc. to purchase substantially all of Alloyd's shares, issued some twenty-eight years earlier in 1961. The parties privately negotiated a contract of sale, pursuant to which a purchase price of $18 million was negotiated with a warranty that the financial statements "present fairly the company's financial condition." After Alloyd suffered lower than expected earnings, the purchasers sought rescission of the contract under § 12[a](2), contending that their private contract of sale was a "prospectus" so that misstatements therein gave rise to a § 12[a](2) right of rescission.

The Supreme Court in a 5–4 decision stated "the question presented is whether this right of rescission extends to a private, secondary transaction, on the theory that recitations in the purchase agreement are part of a 'prospectus.'" The Court began its analysis with § 10 [of the 33 Act], the section setting forth information that must be contained in a prospectus. From that section, the Court distilled the following: "[s]ave for the explicit and well-defined exemptions for securities listed under § 3 (exempting certain classes of securities from the coverage of the Act), its mandate is unqualified: "a prospectus ... shall contain the information contained in the registration statement." Although the Court acknowledged that § 10 does not define the universe of documents which are "prospectuses" under the Act, the section does reveal what a prospectus cannot be. "[A] document is not a prospectus within the meaning of the section if, absent an exemption, it need not comply with § 10's requirements in the first place." The Court then asserted "[b]y and large, only public offerings by an issuer of a security, or by controlling shareholders of an issuer, require the preparation and filing of registration statements. It follows, we conclude, that a prospectus under § 10 is confined to documents related to public offerings by an issuer or its controlling shareholders."

Every court since *Gustafson*, including this district, has held in light of *Gustafson*, that § 12[a](2) applies only to initial public offerings. * * *

In sum, if an offering document need not comply with § 10, and is not within a § 3 exemption, the document is not a prospectus and § 12[a](2) is inappropriate. Here the plaintiff concedes that the Ratners Offering Memorandum did not have to comply with the registration requirements of § 10 and that this was not because of a § 3 exemption. Further, in the Second Amended Complaint, the plaintiff refers to the sale of the Series D and E Ratners APS as occurring through a "private" placement. Accordingly, under *Gustafson* I dismiss all three § 12[a](2) causes of action alleged in the complaint. Leave to replead is denied because no matter how the plaintiff might word the claim, the document involved cannot be "silkenized" into a § 12(a)(2) "prospectus."

The foregoing is so ordered.

G. JOBS Act Relaxation of General Solicitation Ban for JOBS Act Rule 506 Transactions

Title II of the Jumpstart Our Business Startups Act (H.R. 3606) (JOBS Act) eliminates the prohibition against general solicitation and general advertising for offers and sales of private placements under Reg. D Rule 506, provided the offerings are sold to accredited investors. Obviously issuers will have to be careful to ensure that all purchasers are accredited investors. In July 2013, the SEC issued Release No 33-9415, implementing this provision. Excerpts from the release are set out here:

SEC Release on Reg D, Rule 506

SEC, Release No 33-9415, Eliminating the Prohibition Against General Solicitation and General Advertising in Rule 506 and Rule 144A Offerings

AGENCY: Securities and Exchange Commission.

ACTION: Final rules.

SUMMARY: We are adopting amendments to Rule 506 of Regulation D and Rule 144A [see discussion *infra*] under the Securities Act of 1933 to implement Section 201(a) of the Jumpstart Our Business Startups Act. The amendment to Rule 506 permits an issuer to engage in general solicitation or general advertising in offering and selling securities pursuant to Rule 506, provided that all purchasers of the securities are accredited investors and the issuer takes reasonable steps to verify that such purchasers are accredited investors. The amendment to Rule 506 also includes a non-exclusive list of methods that issuers may use to satisfy the verification requirement for purchasers who are natural persons. * * * We are also revising Form D to require issuers to indicate whether they are relying on the provision that permits general solicitation or general advertising in a Rule 506 offering.

Also today, in a separate release, to implement Section 926 of the Dodd-Frank Wall Street Reform and Consumer Protection Act, we are adopting amendments to Rule 506 to disqualify issuers and other market participants from relying on Rule 506 if "felons and other 'bad actors'" are participating in the Rule 506 offering. We are also today, in a separate release, publishing for comment a number of proposed amendments to Regulation D, Form D and Rule 156 under the Securities Act that are intended to enhance the Commission's ability to evaluate the development of market practices in Rule 506 offerings and address certain comments made in connection with implementing Section 201(a)(1) of the Jumpstart Our Business Startups Act. * * *

H. Problem on Use of Rule 505 and Traditional Rule 506 in Acquisition of Closely-Held Target

Closely-Held Target Corporation (CHTC), which has 1,000 shares of common stock outstanding, is owned by 45 shareholders as follows:

Shareholder	# of Shares	Position
A	400	President, Chairman of Board
B	50	Vice-President, Member of Board
C	50	Chief Financial Officer, Member of Board
D	50	Chief Operations Officer, Member of Board
E	50	Insurance Company, Investor
40 Other Individuals (10 Shares Each)	400	Employees
TOTAL SHARES	**1,000**	

Closely-Held Acquiring Corporation (CHAC), which has not issued any securities within the past five 5 years, is considering the acquisition of CHTC in exchange for stock of CHAC with a value of $4.5 Million. The transaction is proposed to be structured as a stock acquisition, with CHAC issuing its stock to each of the shareholders of CHTC in exchange for the stock of CHTC. The CHAC stock would be allocated among the CHTC shareholders in accordance with their proportionate stock interests.

1. Can the transaction be structured to come within Regulation D; and, if so, what steps would have to be taken?

2. What result if in the above transaction, CHAC is a 34 Act reporting company?

3. Assuming that the original transaction otherwise qualifies under Rule 505, what result if eight months before the transaction described above, CHAC had issued $1,000,000 of securities in a Rule 504 transaction? Any suggestions?

4. Same as Question 3, except that the securities had been issued under Rule 506?

5. Assume that the transaction otherwise qualifies in the alternative under Rules 505 or 506. What result if, three months before the transaction described above, CHAC had issued $400,000 of its stock in the acquisition of the stock of another target corporation from its 12 shareholders?

6. Assume that the transaction otherwise qualifies in the alternative under Rules 505 or 506. What result if, three months before the transaction described above, CHAC had issued $400,000 of its bonds to raise cash to build a plant?

7. Returning to the original transaction, suppose the transaction is structured as a merger of CHTC into CHAC with the shareholders of CHTC receiving stock of CHAC. Can the transaction qualify under Reg. D? [*See* Rule 145]

8. Returning to the original transaction, suppose the transaction is structured as an acquisition by CHAC of all of the assets and liabilities of CHTC in exchange for stock of CHAC, and CHTC is subsequently liquidated distributing the CHAC stock to the CHTC shareholders. Can the transaction qualify under Reg. D? [*See* Rule 145]

9. Returning to the original transaction, assume that the transaction cannot be structured to come within Reg. D and CHAC now proposes to acquire the stock of CHTC for cash. Is Section 5 implicated in this transaction? Should it be?

10. An issuer issues securities in a transaction that is intended to come within Regulation D or Section 4(a)(2), but the transaction fails to qualify for such exemption. One of the purchasers would like to get out of the deal. What rights does the purchaser have?

11. An issuer issues securities in a transaction that is intended to come within Regulation D or Section 4(a)(2). The transaction qualifies under Section 4(a)(2). The purchaser would like to get out of the deal. What rights does the purchaser have? What defenses does the seller or the underwriter have?

§ 4.15 Sale of Restricted Securities under Rule 144

A. The Adopting Release and 2007 Amendments

Securities Act Release No. 5223

(Jan. 11, 1972)

[Rule 144 has been amended many times since its original promulgation in 1972, and in connection with your review of this adopting release you should read carefully the portions of the rule set out in *M&A Statutes, Rules, and Documents*, *supra* Section 1.1.] The Securities and Exchange Commission today announced the adoption of Rule 144 under the Securities Act of 1933 (Act). The new rule relates to the application of the registration provisions of the Act to the resale of securities acquired directly or indirectly from issuers or from affiliates of such issuers in transactions not involving any public offerings (restricted securities) and securities held by affiliates. * * *

In brief, the rule provides that any affiliate or other person who sells restricted securities of an issuer for his own account, or any person who sells restricted or any other securities for the account of an affiliate of the issuer, is not deemed to be engaged in a distribution of the securities, and therefore is not an underwriter as defined in Section 2[(a)](11) of the Act, if the securities are sold in accordance with all the terms and conditions of the rule. The rule requires, among other things, that the restricted securities must have been beneficially owned for a period of at least two years [now one year for non-publicly traded securities and six months for publicly traded securities] by the person for whose account they are sold; [and for affiliates] [1] that the amount sold shall not exceed one percent of the class outstanding; [2] that if traded on an exchange, the lesser of that amount or the average weekly volume on all such exchanges during the four weeks preceding the sale; and [3] that the securities must be sold in brokers' transactions. In addition, [for affiliates] there must be adequate information available to the public in regard to the issuer of the securities and notice of the sale (Form 144) must be filed with the Commission concurrently with the sale. * * *

Background and Purpose. Congress, in enacting the federal securities statutes, created a continuous disclosure system designed to protect investors and to assure the maintenance of fair and honest securities markets. The Commission in administering and implementing the objectives of these statutes has sought to coordinate and integrate this disclosure system, and the rule and other related rules and amendments are a further effort in this direction.

Rule 144 is designed to implement the fundamental purposes of the Act as expressed in its preamble:

> "To provide full and fair disclosure of the character of the securities sold in interstate commerce and through the mails, and to prevent fraud in the sale thereof * * *."

The rule would also operate to inhibit the creation of public markets in securities of issuers concerning which adequate current information is not available to the public. At the same time, where adequate current information concerning an issuer is available to the public, the rule would permit the public sale in ordinary trading transactions of limited quantities of securities owned by persons controlling, controlled by or under common control with the issuer (hereinafter "affiliate") * * *.

Resales of securities acquired in private placements are frequently made under claims of an exemption pursuant to Section 4[a](1) of the Act, that is, a transaction by a person other than an issuer, underwriter, or dealer. This Section was intended to exempt only trading transactions between individual investors with respect to securities already issued and not to exempt distributions by issuers or acts of other individuals who engage in steps necessary to such distributions.

Generally, the majority of questions arising under this Section have dealt with whether the seller is an "underwriter." The term underwriter is broadly defined in Section 2[(a)](11) of the Act to mean any person who has purchased from an issuer with a view to, or offers or sells for an issuer in connection with, the distribution of any security, or participates or has a direct or indirect participation in any such undertaking, or participates or has a participation in the direct or indirect underwriting of any such undertaking. The interpretation of this definition has traditionally focused on the words "with a view to" in the phrase "purchased from an issuer with a view to * * * distribution." Thus, an investment banking firm which arranges with an issuer for the public sale of its securities is clearly an "underwriter" under that Section. Not so well understood is the fact that individual investors who are not professionals in the securities business may be "underwriters" within the meaning of that term as used in the Act if they act as links in a chain of transactions through which securities move from an issuer to the public. It is difficult to ascertain the mental state of the purchaser at the time of his acquisition, and the staff has looked to subsequent acts and circumstances to determine whether such person took with a view to distribution at the time of his acquisition. Emphasis has been placed on factors such as the length of time the person has held the securities (holding period) and whether there has been an unforeseeable change in circumstances of the holder. Experience has shown, however, that reliance upon such factors as the above has not assured adequate protection of investors through the maintenance of informed trading markets and has led to uncertainty in the application of the registration provisions of the Act. * * *

Rule 144, together with the other related rules and amendments, is designed to provide full and fair disclosure of the character of securities sold in trading transactions and to create greater certainty and predictability in the application of the registration provisions of the Act by replacing subjective standards with more objective ones. * * *

In summary, if the sale in question is made in accordance with all the provisions of the rule, as outlined below, any person who sells restricted securities shall be deemed not to be engaged in a distribution of such securities and therefore not an underwriter thereof. The rule also provides that any person who sells restricted or other securities on behalf of a person in a control relationship with the issuer shall be deemed not to be engaged in a distribution of such securities and therefore not to be an underwriter thereof. * * *

Synopsis of the Rule. A preliminary note has been added to the rule in order to provide a convenient reference to assist in understanding and interpreting its provisions.

The term "restricted security" is defined to mean securities acquired directly or indirectly from an issuer, or from a person in a control relationship with such an issuer (an affiliate) in a transaction or chain of transactions not involving any public offering. * * *

Broadly speaking, the term "person" is defined to include certain relatives of the seller, certain trusts and estates in which the seller and such relatives collectively own 10 percent or more of the beneficial interest and corporations or other organizations in which the foregoing, collectively, are the beneficial owners of 10 percent or more of any class of the equity securities or 10 percent or more of the equity interest. * * *

[*Conditions to be met. See* **Rule 144(b)**] [Rule 144(b) applies to two sets of persons. First, it applies to "any affiliate or other person who sells restricted securities of the issuer for his own account ..." This applies to all sales of restricted securities for the person's own account. A person selling restricted securities with a view to, or in connection with, a distribution would be an underwriter under Section 2[(a)](11) and would not, therefore, qualify for the 4[(a)](1) trading exemption, which is not available to underwriters. Second, Rule 144(b) applies to "any person who sells restricted or any other securities for the account of any affiliate of the issuer of such securities." * * * Thus, it applies to sales of both restricted and nonrestricted securities, for example, sales by brokers for the account of an affiliate. This encompasses situations covered by the last sentence of Section 2[(a)](11), which defines underwriter as follows:

> As used in this paragraph [*i.e.*, for purpose of defining the term underwriter but not for purposes of Section 4[(a)](2)], the term issuer shall include, in addition to an issuer, any person directly or indirectly controlling or controlled by the issuer, or by a person under direct or indirect common control with the issuer.

Thus, any person who sells securities for the account of an affiliate with a view to or in connection with a distribution is an underwriter under Section 2[(a)](11) and, therefore, does not qualify for the 4[(a)](1) exemption.

Rule 144(b) goes on to provide, however, that if each of the conditions of the rule is satisfied, then the persons specified in first and second above "shall be deemed not to be engaged in a distribution of such securities and, therefore, not to be an underwriter within the meaning of Section 2[(a)](11)." * * * Consequently, the 4[(a)](1) trading exemption is available to such persons.]

Availability of Public Information. [*See* **Rule 144(c)**] The rule provides that there shall be available adequate current public information with respect to the issuer of the securities. This provision is deemed satisfied if an issuer has been subject to the reporting requirements of Section 13 or 15(d) of the Exchange Act for a period of at least 90 days immediately preceding the sale of the securities and has filed all reports required by that Act and the rules and regulations thereunder and in addition has filed the most recent annual report required to be filed thereunder.

Under concurrently adopted amendments to Forms 10-K and 10-Q, issuers are required to state in their annual and quarterly reports whether they have filed all the reports required by Section 13 or 15(d) of the Exchange Act during the 90-day period preceding the date of the report and in addition have filed the most recent annual report required to be filed. * * *

In case of companies which are not subject to the reporting requirements of Section 13 or 15(d) of the Exchange Act, the information requirement is deemed to be met if there is publicly available with respect to the issuer, the information required by clauses (1) to (14), inclusive, and clause (16) of paragraph (a)(4) of Rule 15c2-11 under the Exchange Act. [Thus, even a non-34 Act reporting company can satisfy this public information requirement by complying with these clauses of Rule 15c2-11.] * * *

Holding Period. [*See* **Rule 144(d)**] Securities sold in reliance upon the rule must have been beneficially owned and fully paid for by the seller for a holding period of at least

[one] year prior to his sale as specified below. [SEC Release No. 33-8869 (Dec. 6, 2007) amended Rule 144(d) to shorten the "holding period for restricted securities of Exchange Act reporting issuers [*i.e.*, publicly held companies] to six months for both affiliates and non-affiliates.] This condition is designed to assure that the registration provisions of the Act are not circumvented by persons acting, directly or indirectly, as conduits for an issuer in connection with resales of restricted securities. In order to accomplish this, the rule provides that such persons be subject to the full economic risks of investment during the holding period. * * *

Limitation on Amount of Securities Sold. [*See* **Rule 144(e)**] If the securities are traded on a registered national securities exchange, the amount which may be sold in any 1-month [now 3-month] period shall not exceed the greater of one percent of the amount of the class outstanding as shown in the most recent report or statement published by the issuer, or the average weekly reported volume of trading on all such exchanges over the four-week period prior to the date of the required notice of sale described below. * * * [As indicated below, this restriction is only applicable to affiliates.]

Manner of Sale. [*See* **Rule 144(f) and (g)**] The rule provides that the securities shall be sold in brokers' transactions within the meaning of Section 4[(a)](4) of the Act, and that the person selling the securities shall not solicit or arrange for the solicitation of buy orders or make any payment in connection with the sale other than to the broker who executes the sell order.

Brokers' transactions are defined in the rule to include transactions in which a broker does no more than execute a sell order as agent and receives no more than the usual and customary commission. The broker may not solicit buy orders, but he may inquire of other brokers or dealers who have indicated an interest in the securities within the preceding 60 days.

In addition, the rule provides that the broker shall make a reasonable inquiry to ascertain whether the seller is engaged in a distribution. * * *

[As indicated below, these restrictions are only applicable to affiliates.]

[***Limitation on Amount of Securities Sold and Manner of Sale Not Applicable to Non-Affiliates.*** SEC Release No. 33-8869 (December 6, 2007) amended Rule 144 to "[s]ignificantly reduce requirements applicable to non-affiliates of reporting and non-reporting issuers so that:"

- Non-affiliates of reporting issuers will be subject only to the current public information requirement after meeting the six-month holding period for restricted securities of these issuers and up until one year since the date they acquired the restricted securities from the issuer or affiliate of the issuer; and
- Non-affiliates of non-reporting issuers will be able to resell restricted securities of these issuers after satisfying a one-year holding period without having to comply with any other condition of Rule 144.]

[***Amendments Applicable to Affiliates.*** For affiliate sales, SEC Release No. 33-8869 (Dec. 6, 2007) amended Rule 144 to:

- Revise the "manner of sale" limitations,
- Eliminate the "manner of sale" limitations with respect to debt securities,
- Raise the volume limitations for debt securities, and
- Increase the thresholds that trigger a Form 144[(h)] filing requirement.]

Notice of Offering. [See Rule 144(h)] The rule requires that a person desiring to sell securities in reliance upon the rule must file with the Commission a notice to that effect. * * *

Bona Fide Intention to Sell. In order to avoid persons filing any notice of offering "for the shelf," the rule provides that a person shall have a bona fide intention to sell the securities within a reasonable time after the filing of the notice. * * *

Applicability of the Anti-Fraud Provisions to Sales of Restricted Securities. Although private offerings are exempt from the registration provisions of the Act by virtue of Section 4[(a)](2), that exemption does not apply to a public resale of the securities by the purchaser. The Commission is particularly concerned about the position in which purchasers of such securities find themselves when they later desire to resell the securities. The anti-fraud provisions of the Securities Act, including Section 17(a) of the Act and Section 10(b) of the Exchange Act and Rule 10b-5 thereunder, make it unlawful, in connection with the purchase or sale of a security, to make misleading statements or to omit the disclosure of material facts, and prohibit other fraudulent or deceptive practices. The Commission is of the opinion that these provisions are violated when an issuer, an affiliate of the issuer, or other persons, in connection with a private placement of securities, fail to inform the purchaser fully as to the circumstances under which he is required to take and hold the securities and the limitations upon their resale. * * *

Use of Legends and Stop-Transfer Instructions. Precautions by issuers are essential to assure that a public offering does not result from resale of securities initially purchased in transactions claimed to be exempt under Section 4[(a)](2) of the Act. (Attention is directed to Securities Act Release No. 5121 which discusses the use of legends and stop-transfer instructions as evidence of a non-public offering.) Although such assurance cannot be obtained merely by the use of an appropriate legend on stock certificates or other evidences of ownership, or by appropriate instructions to transfer agents, these devices serve a useful policing function, and the use of such devices is strongly suggested by the Commission and will be considered a factor in determining whether in fact there has been a private placement.

Contractual Registration or Other Rights for Resale of Restricted Securities. Issuers, brokers, dealers, private placers and other holders of restricted securities are hereby put on notice that the Commission deems it appropriate that such persons when acquiring such securities, should consider contracting for registration or other rights, so that, if they desire to distribute their securities rather than resell in trading transactions pursuant to the rule, they can do so in a manner consistent with the provisions of the Act, *i.e.*, by filing a registration statement or a notification under Regulation A. If the issuer does not file reports pursuant to Sections 13 or 15(d) of the Exchange Act, such persons should consider obtaining an agreement by the issuer to register voluntarily under that Act so that Rule 144 may be available. * * *

B. Introductory Problems on Rule 144

1. The Regulation D offering contemplated in Section 4.14.H has been completed and all of the stock of Closely-Held Target Corporation (CHTC) has been acquired by Closely-Held Acquiring Corporation (CHAC) in exchange for shares of CHAC. It is now six months after the acquisition, and A, the former president of CHTC, wants to sell her CHAC shares. A is not a director or manager of CHAC. A owns approximately 5% of CHAC's shares. Under what circumstances can A sell? Suppose A has held the shares for

one year? Suppose CHAC is a 34 Act reporting company? Would your answers to any of these questions change if A is a director of CHAC?

2. In negotiating the original acquisition with CHAC, what should the shareholders of CHTC insist upon from CHAC to enable them to take advantage of Rule 144? Should the shareholders of CHTC negotiate for either demand registration rights (*i.e.*, the right to require registration) or piggy back registration rights (*i.e.*, the right to participate in any registration)? What impact would such rights have on the availability of Rule 144?

§ 4.16 Sale of Restricted Securities under Section 4(1-1/2)

ABA, Committee on Federal Regulation of Securities, The Section "4(1-1/2)" Phenomenon: Private Resales of "Restricted" Securities

34 Bus. Lawyer 1961, 1961–1963, 1975–1977 (1979)

The purpose of this Report is to consider the available methods by which a person may resell privately securities initially issued in a private placement (restricted securities) without registration under the Securities Act of 1933. This variety of sale has become popularly known as "section 4(1-1/2)" transactions, primarily because the SEC, in no-action letters and other pronouncements, frequently has required that such resales meet at least some of the established criteria for exemptions under both section 4(1) [now 4(a)(1)] and section 4(2) [now 4(a)(2)]. In this Report the term "Holder" is used to refer to a person who holds restricted securities and the term "Purchaser" to refer to a person who purchases restricted securities from a Holder. * * *

OVERVIEW OF THE 4(1-1/2) PHENOMENON. Private sales of Restricted Securities are fairly common. Despite the absence of a clear articulation of the statutory basis of the exemption for such sales, neither the Commission nor the securities bar has been very troubled by them. From a practical point of view, this feeling of relative security probably results from the recognition that registration of such sales would be an unnecessary burden to the Holder and of little practical benefit to the Purchaser.

Our initial inquiry in analyzing the scope of permissible sales of Restricted Securities is to determine what subsection within section 4 is applicable. Section 4(3), 4(4) and 4(5) may be ruled out summarily, because section 4(2) exempts only "transactions *by an issuer*" and a sale by a Holder is not a basis for an exemption.[1] Of necessity, one then must turn to section 4(1), which exempts "transactions by any person other than an issuer, underwriter, or dealer." Recognizing that the Holder, by hypothesis, is not an "issuer" (as defined in section 2(4)) and assuming that he is not a "dealer," the critical inquiry is whether he or his Purchaser may be deemed an "underwriter", as defined in section 2(11) of the 1933 Act. To avoid "underwriter" status, the Holder (i) must not have purchased the shares from the issuer "with a view to" their "distribution" and (ii) must not offer or sell the shares "for an issuer in connection with, the distribution." * * *

---

1. Although an affiliate is deemed an "issuer" for purposes of making a person to or through whom he sells an "underwriter" under § 2(11), the affiliate does not have independent status as an "issuer" for purposes of § 4(1). Alternatively, it has been suggested that a Holder may somehow be the "agent" of the issuer, and be continuing the initial nonpublic sale of the issuer, so that § 4(2) is applicable. However, this "agent" (or "conduit") theory seems somewhat artificial, at least where the Holder has purchased the security for his own account and assumed the investment risk.

GENERAL GUIDELINES: THEORY AND PRACTICE. Initially, we conclude that the only proper statutory basis for section 4(1) sales is section 4(1). We consider that the limiting phrase "by an issuer" is an affirmative basis for the exemption of section 4(1) sales. As discussed below, however, we consider it appropriate to apply certain section 4(2) criteria to limit the manner in which some varieties of section 4(1) transactions may otherwise be effected.

Where a nonaffiliate proposes to sell Restricted Securities, the critical inquiries in determining his status as an "underwriter" are whether his acquisition was made "with a view to ... distribution" and whether his sale is to be made "for an issuer in connection with" a "distribution." Because these phrases appear in the disjunctive in section 2(11), strict statutory analysis indicates that if either question is answered in the affirmative, the Holder would not be entitled to rely on section 4(1). As discussed below, however, even a purchase made subjectively "with a view to ... distribution" may under certain conditions be made under section 4(1). Each of these phrases in section 2(11) focuses, first, on the status of the shares in the hands of the Holder (specifically, have they "come to rest") and second, whether his sales constitute a "distribution."

Under the traditional (prerule 144) approach, the prevailing view of securities law practitioners was that once restricted securities had "come to rest" (in the sense that the resales would not be a further step in the issuer's distributive process), there should be no restriction on the manner of resale. Analytically, such resales by definition would not vitiate the issuer's 4(2) exemption and would be sufficiently removed from the original placement that (i) the Holder's resale would not be deemed "for" the issuer and (ii) the Holder's original purchase would not be deemed to have been made with the proscribed view. We think that this traditional approach has continuing validity and that the section 4(1) exemption should be available if the Holder can demonstrate (i) that he did not acquire the restricted securities from the issuer or an affiliate "with a view to" distribution *and* (ii) that the resale is not being made "for an issuer" (or in the case of the resale of restricted securities acquired from an affiliate, for the affiliate). The best objective evidence on these questions will be the length of time the Holder has owned the securities. If he has established a sufficiently long holding period, this alone should demonstrate conclusively that (i) his original acquisition was not "with a view" to distribution and (ii) that the resale is not being made "for the issuer." With respect to each of these standards, the mere length of the holding period should be sufficient. In this regard, we suggest that a Holder who subjectively intended, when he acquired the Restricted Securities, to "distribute" them, may nevertheless thereafter resell them in reliance on section 4(1) if his actual retention of them has been consistent with the opposite intent.

In the case of restricted securities that have not "come to rest," the Holder may nevertheless sell them if the sale does not constitutes a "distribution" (unless, as discussed below, the sale may be considered part of the original placement). In determining whether a "distribution" will result from the Holder's sale, we consider the better view to be that only the manner of sale and the number of purchasers are relevant. In short, only the quantitative aspects of the term "distribution" should be considered. We find no basis in the language or legislative history of the 1933 Act to impose the requirements that the Purchaser be sophisticated or have access to registration-type information. Accordingly, a Holder should be able to dispose of restricted securities provided there are few purchasers and the securities are not offered by means of mass communications. Nor, analytically, should there be any particular limit on the amount that may be sold. Obviously, some reasonable limitations must be observed on these points but there are no hard and fast rules. * * *

If the restricted securities have been acquired from the issuer under circumstances in which it cannot be concluded that the shares have come to rest after their sale in the section 4(2) transaction, it is appropriate for section 4(2) requirements of offeree sophistication and access to be applied to the Holder resales. But this is appropriate only for the purpose of assuring that the issuers original section 4(2) exemption for its sale to the Holder is not lost.

As a theoretical matter, a Purchaser of restricted securities can resell immediately so long as he adheres to the standards discussed above for the Holder's sale (*i.e.*, "privately") and his resales (and all others occurring around the same time) do not result in a "distribution" or otherwise vitiate the issuer's original section 4(2) exemption. The Purchaser thus is essentially in the same position as the Holder and should be able to make resales in the same fashion described herein for Holders. * * *

Questions

1. Returning to question 1 in Section 4.14.H, under what circumstances can A, the former president of CHTC sell her CHAC shares four months after the acquisition of CHTC by CHAC?

2. Under what circumstances may the shareholders of CHTC sell their shares to CHAC without registering those shares?

§ 4.17 Introduction to Rule 144A

Although Rule 144 generally applies to sales of restricted securities, a certain class of restricted securities can be resold without restriction under Rule 144A. This rule permits unregistered sales to and by qualified institutional buyers (QIBs), which are defined under the rule to include only sophisticated institutions with significant assets. [*See* Rule 144A(a)] The initial sale to QIBs will be structured as an exempt offering under Section 4(2) or Reg. D, because Rule 144 does not apply to sales by issuers. [*See* Rule 144A(b)] Subsequent sales to a QIB can qualify for exemption under Rule 144A if three basic conditions are satisfied [*See* Rule 144A(d)]: (1) the sale is to a QIB; (2) the seller takes steps to insure that the buyer is aware that the seller is relying on Rule 144A; (3) the securities are not publicly-traded in the U.S. (*e.g.*, a corporation with only common stock traded issues preferred stock or bonds in a Rule 144A transaction); and (4) if the issuer does not file periodic reports under the 34 Act, certain basic information on the issuer must be provided.

As a result of the JOBS Act, Rule 144A has been amended to provide that "securities may be offered pursuant to Rule 144A to persons other than qualified institutional buyers, provided that the securities are sold only to persons that the seller and any person acting on behalf of the seller reasonably believe are qualified institutional buyers." *See* SEC Release No 33-9415 (July 2013).

Rule 144A has led to the creation of an institutional market that exists virtually side-by-side with the public market. One SEC study showed that in 1997 Rule 144A offerings constituted 17% of all offerings on a dollar basis, amounting to 21% of all equity and 16% of all debt.

References

Hazen, *Securities Regulation*, *supra* Section 1.10.

Loss and Seligman, *Securities Regulation*, *supra* Section 1.10.

Thompson, *Mergers, Acquisitions and Tender Offers*, *supra* Section 1.10, Chapters 6–8.

Chapter 5

Introduction to the Tax Aspects of Mergers and Acquisitions

§ 5.1 Scope

This chapter introduces the federal income taxation of taxable and tax-free mergers and acquisitions under the Internal Revenue Code (Code). Unless otherwise indicated, all references in this chapter are to the Code. This is just an introduction to this very complex topic, and the purpose is to give the non-tax lawyer an understanding of some of the fundamental concepts. All of the topics covered here are addressed in greater detail in (1) Chapters 9, 21, and 22 of Thompson, *Mergers, Acquisitions and Tender Offers, supra* Section 1.10, and (2) Thompson, *Corporate Taxation Through the Lens of Mergers and Acquisitions, supra* Section 1.10.

Section 5.2 provides an introductory problem, and Section 5.3 introduces the taxation of C corporations and the realization and recognition concepts. Section 5.4 presents an overview of the tax treatment of mergers and acquisitions, including a discussion of the impact of Section 382, which limits the ability of the parties to utilize a target's net operating losses after an acquisition, whether taxable or tax-free.

Section 5.5 contains a summary of taxable asset and stock acquisitions of a target that is not a subsidiary; Section 5.6 deals with the treatment of a target's shareholders in a taxable acquisition; Section 5.7 deals with the treatment of the target corporation; and Section 5.8 examines the treatment of the acquiror. Section 5.9 compares the double level tax in a taxable asset acquisition with the single level tax in a taxable stock acquisition. Section 5.10 focuses on taxable reverse and forward subsidiary or triangular mergers. Section 5.11 focuses on the acquisition of a target that is a subsidiary of a parent corporation, and Section 5.12 introduces some of the tax considerations that arise in leveraged buyouts (LBOs), transactions in which significant debt is incurred in acquiring the target. The non-tax and tax aspects of LBOs are examined in detail in Chapter 14. Section 5.13 addresses the proxy disclosures in an acquisition of a publicly held corporation in a taxable reverse subsidiary merger. Finally on taxable acquisitions, Section 5.14 contains summary problems.

Sections 5.15 through 5.19 deal with the treatment of tax-free acquisitive reorganizations. Section 5.15 provides an introduction to acquisitive reorganizations; Section 5.16 addresses asset reorganizations, that is, reorganizations in which the acquiror acquires the assets of the target, and Section 5.17 discusses stock reorganizations, that is, reorganizations in which the acquiror acquires the stock of the target. This section also examines the use of Section 351 and the "horizontal double dummy" in acquisition transactions, such as Oracle's acquisition of Seibel. Section 5.18 refers to a proxy statement discussion of the federal income tax treatment of a reverse subsidiary merger reorganization. Section 5.19 provides a set of introductory problems on reorganizations. Finally, Section 5.20 briefly addresses acquisitions of S corporations. Two related issues, the tax treatment of golden parachute payments and greenmail payments, are addressed in Sections 23.5 and 23.6, respectively.

§ 5.2 Basic Introductory Problem

J.P. Morgan Chase & Co. (J.P. Morgan) is planning to acquire The Goldman Sachs Group, Inc. (Goldman Sachs) in a reverse subsidiary merger in which J.P. Morgan will form a new subsidiary ("Sub") that will merge into Goldman Sachs. Pursuant to the merger, the merger consideration will be paid to the Goldman Sachs shareholders, and the stock of Sub will be converted into stock of Goldman Sachs so that Goldman Sachs becomes a wholly-owned subsidiary of J.P. Morgan.

What is the federal income tax treatment to the various parties if the merger consideration is common stock of J.P. Morgan? What if the merger consideration is cash?

§ 5.3 Introduction to C Corporations and Realization and Recognition Concepts

A. Taxation of C Corporations and Their Shareholders

1. Basic Principles

A C corporation, which is subject to federal income tax under subchapter C of the Code, Section 301 *et seq.*, is a separate taxable entity distinct from its shareholders. C corporations are distinguished from "S corporations," which generally are not subject to taxation; the income or loss of an S corporation is passed through to its shareholders, as is the case with partnerships.

Section 11 of the Code imposes a tax on the "taxable income" of a subchapter C corporation; a maximum rate of 35% applies to taxable income (including both ordinary income and capital gain) in excess of $10 million. As with any taxpayer, the "taxable income" [*see* § 63] of a corporation is computed by first determining the corporation's "gross income" under Section 61 and then subtracting the allowed deductions. Gross income includes all income without regard to how such income arose, with certain specific exceptions, such as the exception for interest on state and local bonds, which is "excluded" from gross income under Section 103 of the Code. Deductions include "ordinary and necessary" business expenses under Section 162 and depreciation with respect to equipment under Section 168, which deals with the accelerated cost recovery system (ACRS). Under straight-line depreciation, which a taxpayer can elect instead of ACRS, the cost of business property is depreciated over the useful life of the property. For example, assume that a corporation pays $10K for a machine that has an expected useful life of ten years and a zero salvage value after the ten years. With straight-line depreciation, the taxpayer would deduct in computing its taxable income $1K per year for each of the ten years. Thus, the taxpayer would "recover" the cost incurred in acquiring the machine by taking deductions in computing its taxable income over the ten-year useful life period. The depreciation for property subject to the ACRS rules is at a faster, and, therefore, more beneficial, rate than straight-line depreciation.

Distributions by a "C corporation" out of its "earnings and profits" or "E&P," which are its after tax earnings (similar to the accounting concept of retained earnings) are included in the gross income of the shareholders as dividends. [*See* §§ 301, 316(a), and

61(a)(7)] Dividends received by shareholders are subject to a separate tax imposed under Section 1 for individual shareholders and under Section 11 for corporate shareholders. For individuals, the maximum rate on dividends and capital gains is 20%.

Corporate shareholders receive the benefit of a "dividends received deduction" (DRD) in the amount of 70%, 80% or 100% of the dividends received. *See* § 243. The 100% DRD applies to companies filing consolidated returns, which is generally the case with a group of commonly controlled (*i.e.*, at least 80% owned) corporations, such as a parent corporation and its subsidiaries. The purpose of this DRD is to mitigate the effect of multiple corporate level taxes on the same income.

2. Medicare Net Investment Income Tax[1]

As a result of the enactment of the Affordable Care Act (Obamacare), commencing January 1, 2013, Section 1411 of the Internal Revenue Code imposes a 3.8% tax on certain net investment income (NII) of individuals, estates and trusts that have income above the statutory threshold amounts. NII includes investment income, such as interest, dividends, and capital gains, reduced by certain expenses that are properly allocable to such income.

For example, married individuals filing jointly are subject to this Net Investment Income Tax (NIIT) when they have NII and also have modified adjusted gross income in excess of a threshold amount of $250,000, which is not indexed for inflation. Modified adjusted gross income is adjusted gross income adjusted for certain amounts under Section 911, relating to exclusions for income earned abroad.

Many of the examples in this chapter focus on the computation of the double tax by reference to (1) the 35% maximum income tax at the corporate level on ordinary income and capital gains, and (2) the 20% maximum income tax on dividends and capital gains at the individual shareholder level. In each of these examples, consideration will also have to be given to the impact of the NIIT. However, while for income tax purposes it may be advantageous to structure the sale of a C corporation as a stock sale rather than an asset sale, the presence of the NIIT should not normally have an impact on the structuring decision.

3. Illustration of the Combined Shareholder and Corporate Level Taxes

The combined maximum corporate and individual rates can result in an aggregate tax rate of approximately 48% on the distributed earnings of a subchapter C corporation, which is illustrated as follows:

> Individual *A* forms a corporation (*C*). *C* earns $100 million of taxable income for the taxable year and pays a corporate tax of $35 million (.35 X $100 million). *C* then distributes the $65 million after-tax earnings to *A* as a dividend. Under Section 1(h), *A* is taxed at a 20% rate on the dividend and, therefore, has a tax liability of $13 million (.20% X $65 million). Thus, the combined corporate and shareholder tax is $48 million ($35 million + $13 million). This is an aggregate 48% rate of tax on the distributed corporate income. In addition the 3.8% NIIT would be applicable at the shareholder level.

1. This section is adapted from Thompson, *Mergers, Acquisitions and Tender Offers, supra* Section 1.10, at Section 9:3.2.

B. Federal Income Taxation of Sales or Exchanges of Property

See § 1001, § 1011, § 1012, § 1016, and § 1221

Many business transactions involve either (1) a sale of property, such as the sale of the stock of a target corporation for cash, or (2) an exchange of property, such as an exchange of the stock of a target corporation for the stock of an acquiror. This section addresses the federal income tax treatment of a sale or exchange.

The starting point for determining the tax consequences upon the sale, exchange, or other disposition of property is Section 1001(a) of the Code, which provides that gain or loss on a sale or other disposition of property shall be the difference between the "amount realized" and the "adjusted basis" of the property transferred. This is known as the gain or loss realized. The "amount realized" on a sale or other disposition of property is defined in Section 1001(b) as "the sum of money received plus the fair market value of property (other than money) received." Under the case law reflected in *Crane*, a transferor's amount realized includes any liabilities, recourse or nonrecourse, attributable to property transferred. Thus, for example, assume that a target corporation sells for $60K in cash a plant that has a fair market value of $100K and a nonrecourse liability (*i.e.*, no personal liability) of $40K reflected as a mortgage on the plant. The target's amount realized is not only the cash of $60K but also the $40K liability that is transferred with the plant, or $100K.

Under Section 1011, the "adjusted basis" of property for purposes of determining gain or loss is, in general, the taxpayer's cost of the property as provided in Section 1012, less depreciation, if any, and plus or minus certain other adjustments, all as provided in Section 1016. Thus, for example, assume that a corporation purchases a machine for $100K and for each of the next three years takes $10K of depreciation with respect to the machine. The taxpayer's initial cost basis for the property under Section 1012 is $100K and at the beginning of the fourth year, the taxpayer's adjusted basis for the machine under Section 1011 is the $100K cost minus the $30K of aggregate depreciation, or $70K. Thus, if the taxpayer sold the machine for, say, $110K, the taxpayer would have a realized gain of $40K ($110K–$70K). On the other hand, if a taxpayer purchases stock in a corporation for $100K and later sells the stock, the adjusted basis of the stock is the cost of $100K because depreciation is not allowed on stock. Thus, if the stock is sold for $110K, the taxpayer has a gain realized of $10K.

Pursuant to Section 1001(c), realized gain or loss is "recognized" (*i.e.*, included in the taxpayer's gross income under Section 61), except as otherwise provided in the Code.

Section 1001 provides:

> (a) COMPUTATION OF GAIN OR LOSS.—The gain from the sale or other disposition of property shall be the excess of the amount realized [*see* (b)] therefrom over the adjusted basis provided in section 1011 for determining gain [*e.g.*, cost minus depreciation], and the loss shall be the excess of the adjusted basis provided in such section for determining loss over the amount realized.
>
> (b) AMOUNT REALIZED.—The amount realized from the sale or other disposition of property shall be the sum of any money received plus the fair market value of the property (other than money) [including liabilities transferred with the property] received.
>
> (c) RECOGNITION OF GAIN OR LOSS.—Except as otherwise provided in [the Code], the entire amount of the gain or loss [realized] on the sale or exchange of property shall be recognized [included in gross income].

It is necessary to determine if recognized gain or loss is capital gain or loss or ordinary income or loss. I focus here only on capital gain, which is the gain from the sale of a "capital asset." This term is defined in Section 1221 to include, for example, stock of a corporation. Thus, stock of IBM held by an individual is a capital asset, and therefore, any gain on the sale of such stock is capital gain. Gain from the sale of a capital asset held for more than a year is treated as "long term capital gain" [*see* § 1222], and the long term capital gains of individuals generally are subject to a maximum rate of 20% [*see* § 1(h)], the same rate that applies to dividends. Capital gains of corporations are taxed at regular ordinary income rates and, thus, are subject to a maximum rate of $35%.

The corporate provisions of the Code contain several exceptions to the general rule of recognition in Section 1001(c), particularly for an exchange of stock of a target for stock of an acquiror in a "reorganization" transaction. [*See* Sections 5.14 to 5.17] Many of these nonrecognition provisions are analogous to the nonrecognition rule of Section 1031 that applies to "like kind" exchanges of property.

To preserve (defer) the gain or loss not recognized in a transaction governed by an exception to the rule of recognition, the basis of the property received is, generally, either the basis of the property exchanged or the basis of the property received, depending on the taxpayer. Where the basis of property received is the basis of the property exchanged, the transaction is said in tax parlance to produce a *substituted basis*. On the other hand, where the basis of the property received by a taxpayer is the transferor's basis of the property, the transaction is said in tax parlance to produce a *carryover basis*. Both the *substituted basis* and the *carryover basis* are exceptions to the cost basis rule of Section 1012. Thus, if a transaction is excepted from the rule of recognition, there will also be an exception to the cost basis rule for the property received in the transaction.

A C corporation may participate in either a taxable or tax-free acquisition. Tax-free acquisitions are known as reorganizations. Taxable acquisitions may be taxable at either or both the target corporate level and the target shareholder level.

§ 5.4 Overview of Taxable and Tax-Free Acquisition

A. General Principles

Corporate acquisitions of stand-alone (*i.e.*, nonsubsidiary) domestic target corporations fall into two broad categories: (1) taxable acquisitions, and (2) tax-free acquisitive reorganizations under Section 368. Although Section 368 also encompasses non-acquisitive reorganizations, the focus here is on acquisitive reorganizations. Within each of these broad categories there can be either taxable or tax-free mergers, stock acquisitions, or asset acquisitions. Thus, the transactions addressed in Chapter 2, which focuses on the voting and dissenting rules for various forms of acquisitions and mergers, can be structured as either taxable or tax-free. Leveraged buyouts (LBOs) are taxable stock or asset acquisitions in which a substantial part of the consideration paid in the transaction is either debt or cash raised through the issuance of debt. The acquiring entity in an LBO is generally a private equity firm, such as KKR. [*See* Chapter 14] Thus, LBOs are a subset of taxable acquisitions.

The principal distinguishing feature between a taxable acquisition and a tax-free acquisitive reorganization is the consideration paid by the acquiring corporation. The consideration paid in a taxable acquisition generally consists of cash or debt instruments of the acquiring corporation or a combination of the two. Also, in certain cases, stock may be used in taxable acquisitions. If a substantial portion (and in certain cases all) of the consideration paid by the acquiring corporation consists of its stock or stock of its parent corporation, the acquisition may (assuming certain other conditions are satisfied) qualify as a tax-free acquisitive reorganization.

B. Treatment of a Target's Net Operating Losses (NOLs)

In an acquisition, a target may have net operating losses (NOLs), which are losses from prior years that can be carried forward to future years under Section 172. In stock acquisitions, whether taxable or tax-free, and in asset acquisitions that are reorganizations, the target's NOLs can be utilized in years after the acquisition, subject to limitation under Section 382. In a taxable sale of assets, the target can utilize its NOLs to offset taxable gain.

Section 382 is triggered by a "change of ownership" of a target (*i.e.*, the "loss corporation"), and any acquisition of all of the stock of a loss corporation would constitute a "change of ownership" of the loss corporation. Under Section 382, in each year after an acquisition that results in a "change of ownership" of a loss corporation, the NOLs of the loss corporation that otherwise carryover after the acquisition are deductible but in an amount not exceeding (1) the value of the stock of the loss corporation, multiplied by (2) the long term tax exempt rate, which is periodically published by the IRS. Thus, for example, if the value of the stock of a loss corporation is $100M, and the long term tax exempt rate is 5%, then $5M of the NOLs that carryover are, in essence, deductible by the acquiror in each year after the acquisition, until the carryover period, which is 20 years under Section 172, expires. Thus, the target's NOLs do not disappear as a result of the acquisition, but there are significant restrictions on the use of them after an acquisition.

As indicated in *Selectica*, Section 3.18.E.7, a poison pill (referred to as an NOL pill) may be issued for the purpose of preventing a "change of ownership" of a target corporation under Section 382.

§ 5.5 Summary of Taxable Acquisitions of Nonsubsidiary (Stand-Alone) Target

A. Taxable Asset Acquisitions

In this first pattern, the acquiring corporation purchases for cash or debt instruments the assets of an unrelated domestic target that is not a subsidiary, followed by the liquidation of the target (*i.e.*, an asset acquisition). The acquiror also generally assumes specified liabilities of the target. These transactions are examined in both Chapter 2 and Chapter 12. For the reasons outlined below, the taxable asset acquisition of a stand-alone target is generally not utilized. A taxable asset acquisition may be diagramed as follows:

Acquisition of Assets

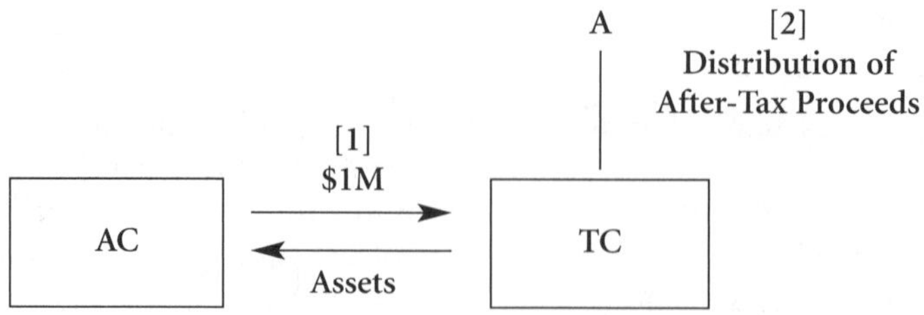

As discussed below, the taxable asset acquisition may also be effectuated by merging, pursuant to state law, the target into the acquiring corporation.

B. Taxable Stock Acquisitions

In this second pattern, the acquiring corporation purchases for cash or debt instruments the target's stock directly from the target's shareholders. These transactions are examined in detail in Chapter 11. A taxable stock acquisition may be diagramed as follows:

Stock Acquisition

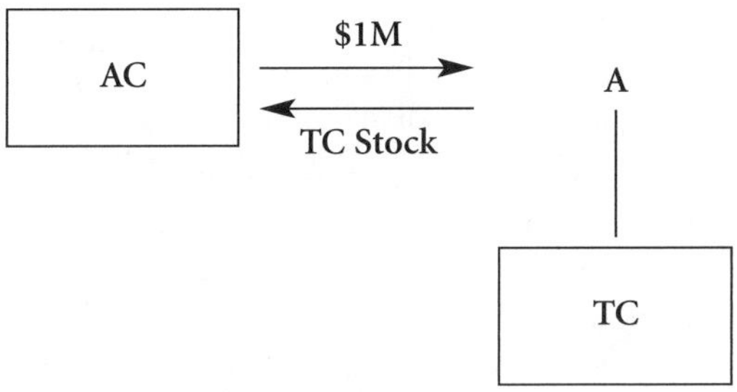

The taxable stock acquisition can be effectuated by a taxable reverse triangular (or subsidiary) merger, which is discussed below.

§ 5.6 Treatment of Target's Shareholders in a Taxable Acquisition of a Nonsubsidiary Target

The treatment of the target's shareholders is the same in each of these transactions. The shareholders have capital gain or possibly capital loss: (1) on the receipt of the sales proceeds upon the liquidation of the target after a direct sale of the target's assets, or after a taxable forward merger of the target into the acquiring corporation or its subsidiary [*see* § 331 providing that shareholders have sale treatment on receipt of liquidation proceeds], and (2) on the sale of their stock in either a stock purchase or a taxable reverse subsidiary merger [*see* § 1001]. As indicated, the maximum rate of tax on capital gains of individuals is 20%, which is also the maximum rate on dividends. [*See* § 1(h)]. Corporations do not receive a reduced rate on capital gains.

If the target's stock is nontradable and the target's shareholders receive nontradable debt instruments of the acquiror, such instruments may qualify for installment sale treatment under Section 453. If this section applies, the target's shareholders have nonrecognition until actual cash payments are received. For example, assume that an individual shareholder (A) owns all of the stock of target corporation (TC), and A has a $10K basis for the stock. A sells the stock of TC for a $100K nontradable note payable in the amount of $10K per year over the next ten years, with adequate interest. In such case, under Section 453, A recognizes $9K of gain (*i.e.*, $10K of cash minus $1K of basis) in each of the ten years during which the note is paid.

If the consideration paid by the acquiror is stock of the acquiror, the transaction may qualify as a reorganization as discussed below.

§ 5.7 Treatment of a Nonsubsidiary Target in a Taxable Acquisition

The Tax Reform Act of 1986 repealed the *General Utilities* doctrine, which provided that corporations do not recognize gain on the distribution and in certain sales of appreciated property. As a result of this repeal, a domestic target has recognition treatment on the direct sale of its assets and on the disposition of its assets in a taxable forward merger into the acquiring corporation or a subsidiary of the acquiring corporation. Also, the target recognizes gain (and in some cases loss) under Section 336 upon the distribution of appreciated assets in liquidation. Section 336 provides in part:

> (a) GENERAL RULE.—Except as otherwise provided in this section or section 337 [relating to liquidations of subsidiaries], gain or loss shall be recognized to a liquidating corporation on the distribution of property in complete liquidation as if such property were sold to the distributee at its fair market value.

The target has nonrecognition upon the purchase of its stock and there is no change in the target's basis for its assets and other tax attributes, unless the acquiror elects under Section 338 to treat the transaction as an asset acquisition. If a Section 338 election is made, the target is treated as selling and then reacquiring its assets, thus recognizing gains and losses and taking a cost basis (*i.e.*, a stepped-up basis) for its assets. The stepped-up basis will give the target a new fair market value basis for its assets for depreciation and other purposes.

As a result of the repeal of the *General Utilities* doctrine, an acquisition of a nonsubsidiary target corporation with appreciated assets generally is structured as a stock acquisition without a Section 338 election, thereby avoiding the corporate level tax. The present value of the future tax benefits, such as the increased depreciation deductions, from a step-up in basis of the target's assets does not offset the detriment associated with an immediate tax paid by the target corporation with regard to the gain in its assets.

An exception to this general rule may apply if the target has NOLs that can be utilized to offset the corporate level tax that is otherwise due in an asset acquisition or a stock acquisition followed by a Section 338 election. NOLs are not limited on a sale of assets by a target or when an acquiror makes a Section 338 after the purchase of the stock of a target.

§ 5.8 Treatment of Acquiror in a Taxabale Acquisition of Nonsubsidiary Target

In a taxable asset acquisition, the acquiring corporation takes a cost basis for the target's assets. As indicated above, none of the target's tax attributes such as NOLs come over to the acquiror, but the NOLs can be used by the target to offset gain on the sale of assets. The acquiror gets a fresh start on depreciation; also under Section 197, the acquiror can amortize (*i.e.*, deduct in computing taxable income) on a straight-line basis over a 15-year period the cost allocated to goodwill and other purchased intangibles.

In a taxable stock acquisition, the acquiror takes a cost basis for the target's stock. If a Section 338 election is not made, which as indicated above will normally be the case, there is no change in the target's basis for its assets; thus, there is no fresh start for depreciation and there are no purchased intangibles to be written off under Section 197. Also, the target's NOLs continue to be available, subject to the limitations in Section 382.

If the acquiror makes a Section 338 election, as indicated above, the target has complete recognition treatment and takes a cost basis for its assets, including goodwill, which is amortizable over a 15-year period under Section 197. In a Section 338 election, all of the target's tax attributes disappear; NOLs may, however, be utilized to offset gain recognized. Since after the stock acquisition the acquiror owns more than 80% of the stock of the target, the acquiror could liquidate the target in a wholly tax free transaction. *See* § 332 (tax-free for parent) and § 337 (tax-free for sub).

As will be seen in Chapter 6, which deals with accounting aspects of M&A, an acquiror can have goodwill for financial accounting purposes in all types of acquisition transactions, including tax-free reorganizations, but for accounting purposes there is no amortization deduction for goodwill. Instead, the goodwill is periodically evaluated for an impairment charge.

§ 5.9 Comparing the Double Level Tax in a Taxable Asset Acquisition with the Single Level Tax in a Taxable Stock Acquisition

The maximum potential double tax from an asset sale or in a stock acquisition with a Section 338 election is 48%, illustrated as follows:

> Assume that target corporation has assets with a fair market value of $100 million and with a zero tax basis. The target has no net operating losses or tax credits. The target has a sole individual shareholder who has a zero basis for her stock. If the target's assets are sold for $100 million, the target will have a realized and recognized gain of $100 million (*i.e.*, $100 million amount realized minus -0- adjusted basis for the assets), and the target will incur a tax liability under Section 11 of $35 million (*i.e.*, 35% of the taxable gain) on the sale. The after tax proceeds will be $65 million. The target distributes the after-tax proceeds to its sole shareholder, who has a capital gain realized and recognized under Section 331 of $65 million (*i.e.*, $65 million minus -0- adjusted basis for the stock). The shareholder incurs a 20% capital gains tax equal to $13. Thus, the total corporate and shareholder level taxes equal $48 million, or 48% of the $100 million sale proceeds, which means that the sole shareholder has only $52 million after all taxes.

This is significantly more than the 20% tax that would apply if the shareholder sold her stock, and the acquiror did not make a Section 338 election. Thus, the taxable acquisition of a non-subsidiary target corporation is generally structured as a stock acquisition without a Section 338 election. In these transactions, the acquiror will not pay the fair market value of the target's assets, because the acquiror will not receive the benefit of a fair market value basis for those assets. In determining the purchase price for the stock of the target, the acquiror should first determine the net fair market value of the target's assets (*i.e.*, fair market value of target's assets less target's liabilities). The acquiror's purchase price for the stock should be the net fair market value less the present value of the tax benefits the acquiror will lose because of the stock acquisition without a Section 338 election. This principle is illustrated by the following example:

> Acquiror and the sole shareholder of Target agree that Target has (1) assets with a fair market value of $100 million and a basis of zero, and (2) no NOLs. Consequently, in an asset acquisition, Acquiror would pay $100 million and take a $100 million basis for the assets. On the other hand, in a stock acquisition

without a Section 338 election, Target's basis for its assets will stay at zero. Therefore, from an income tax perspective, Acquiror should pay for target's stock (1) $100 million, less (2) the present value of the foregone tax benefits arising from the zero basis for Target's assets in the stock acquisition, which foregone tax benefits would not have occurred in an asset acquisition. The full amount of the foregone tax benefit is $35 million which is the tax savings that ultimately is possible with a $100 million basis for Target's assets (*i.e.*, $100 million of deductions saves $35 million in tax). Consequently, Acquiror's starting point in the negotiation may be $65 million for Target's stock. On the other hand, Target's shareholder will argue that because of the stretched out depreciation and other cost recoveries, the $35 million in foregone tax benefits from an asset acquisition would not be realized by Acquiror for a long time. Consequently, the present value of the foregone tax benefit is much less than $35 million. So, the parties settle on, say, an $80 million purchase price for the stock of Target. In any event, assuming, for example, that Target's shareholder has a zero basis for her stock, she would be better off after tax with an $80 million stock deal than a $100 million asset deal. As indicated in the preceding example, after the double level tax in the asset deal Target's shareholder has $52 million. On the other hand, after the single level shareholder tax in the $80 million stock deal Target's shareholder has $64 million, which is the $80 million purchase price less the $16 million capital gains tax (*i.e.*, 20% of $80 million).

Notwithstanding the tax benefit of a single level taxable stock acquisition over a double level taxable asset acquisition, there may be good business reasons for structuring the acquisition as an asset acquisition. For example, the acquiring corporation may only want to acquire certain of the target's assets and assume certain of its liabilities. This is possible in an asset acquisition. [*See* Chapter 12] In a stock acquisition, however, the target continues to hold all of its assets and liabilities. [*See* Chapter 11]

§ 5.10 Acquisition of a Nonsubsidiary Target in a Taxable Reverse and Forward Subsidiary (Triangular) Merger

A. Taxable Reverse Subsidiary Mergers

If the stock of a publicly held domestic corporation is being acquired, the acquisition can be structured as a taxable reverse subsidiary merger. In this transaction, an acquiring parent first forms a new wholly-owned subsidiary (acquiring sub) and transfers the merger consideration to acquiring sub. Acquiring sub then merges into the target with the following consequences: (1) the target survives the merger, (2) the target's shareholders receive the purchase price to be paid (cash or debt instruments) for their target shares, which are canceled, and (3) the acquiring parent's shares in the acquiring sub are converted into shares of target so that target becomes a wholly-owned subsidiary of acquiring parent. This transaction may be diagramed as follows:

Taxable Reverse Subsidiary Merger

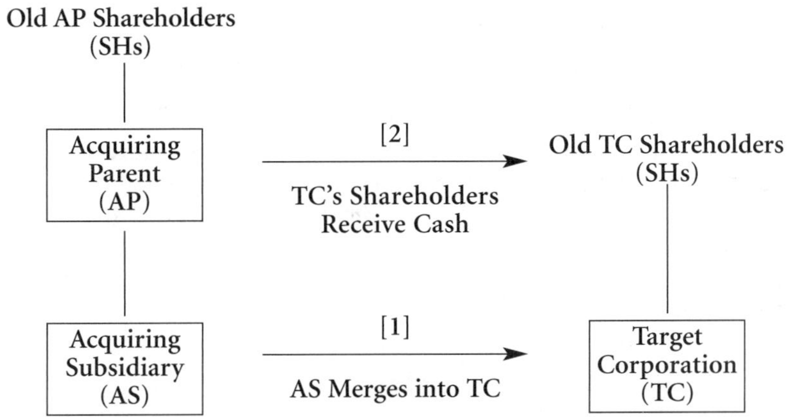

When the Dust Settles

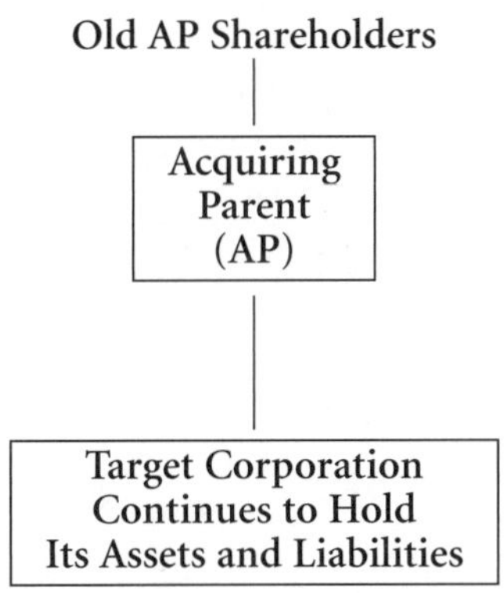

The consideration generally comes directly from AP, not AS.

The Internal Revenue Service treats this transaction as a purchase by the acquiring parent of the target's stock. *See* Rev. Rule. 90–95, 1990–2 C.B. 67. The target has non-recognition treatment and keeps the pre-acquisition basis for its assets, unless the acquiring parent makes a Section 338 election to trigger gain and step up the basis. The target's shareholders are subject to capital gains tax on the cash or debt they receive. The acquiring sub has no tax consequences. Thus, the reverse subsidiary merger produces the same tax results as a direct stock purchase.

The principal business advantage of the reverse subsidiary merger is that it allows the acquiring parent to acquire in one transaction all of the stock of the target without the target's shareholders having the right to retain their shares. Shareholders may, pursuant to the applicable state business corporation law, have the right to dissent from the transaction and be cashed out at the appraised value of their shares. *See* Chapter 2.

Most taxable acquisitions of a publicly held corporation are effectuated with a reverse subsidiary merger. In stock acquisitions of closely held corporations, the reverse subsidiary merger may also be used (in lieu of a straight stock purchase agreement) to force recalcitrant shareholders of the target to sell their stock.

If the consideration paid in a reverse subsidiary merger constitutes voting stock of the acquiror, the transaction may constitute a tax-free reorganization as indicated below. Thus, a reverse subsidiary merger may be either taxable or tax-free.

B. Taxable Forward Subsidiary Mergers

In a taxable forward subsidiary merger, an acquiring parent forms a new, wholly-owned subsidiary (acquiring sub) and transfers the merger consideration (which consists of cash or notes) to acquiring sub (alternatively a pre-existing sub may be used). The domestic target then merges into the acquiring sub with the acquiring sub surviving. The target's shareholders receive the merger consideration. A forward subsidiary merger may be diagramed as follows:

Taxable Forward Subsidiary Merger

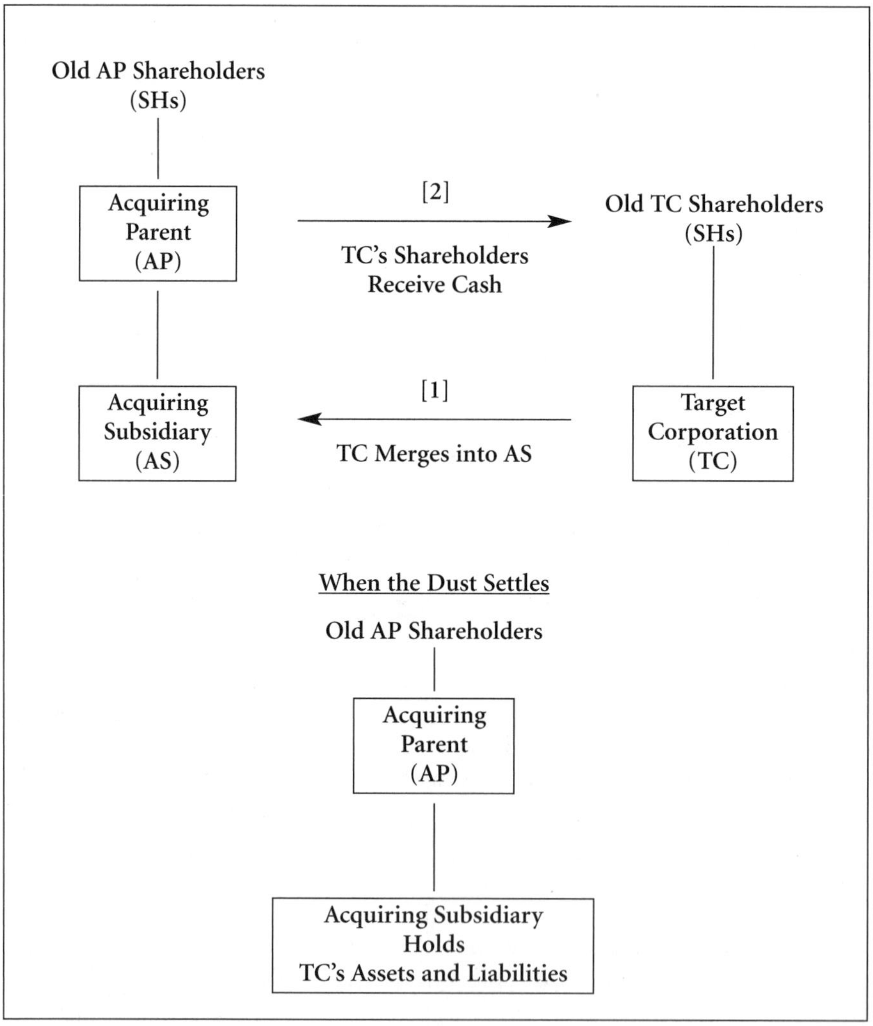

Under *West Shore Fuels, Inc. v. United States*, 598 F2d 1236 (2nd Cir. 1979), this transaction is treated as a sale by the target of its assets followed by a liquidating distribution of the merger consideration by the target to its shareholders. Both the target [*see* § 1001] and its shareholders [*see* § 331] are taxed on the transaction, but the acquiring sub has nonrecognition treatment. Thus, this transaction produces two levels of tax just like the direct asset acquisition. Consequently, generally a taxable forward merger is not used.

If the consideration paid in the acquisition of the target is stock of the acquiror, the transaction may qualify as a reorganization as discussed below. Thus, like the reverse subsidiary merger, the forward subsidiary merger may be either taxable or tax-free.

§ 5.11 Acquisition of a Target That Is a Subsidiary

The acquisition of a domestic subsidiary corporation that is a member of a consolidated group generally is structured as either (1) a direct acquisition of the sub's assets followed by the liquidation of the sub, or (2) an acquisition of the sub's stock with a Section 338(h)(10) election. In an acquisition of the sub's assets, (1) the sub has full taxable treatment under Section 1001, and (2) the parent has tax-free treatment under Section 332 on receipt of the sale proceeds as a result of the liquidation of the sub after the sale.

If a Section 338(h)(10) election is made for an acquisition of the sub's stock (the election must be made jointly by the acquiror and the selling parent), the actual stock acquisition is treated for tax purposes as an asset sale by the sub followed by a deemed liquidating distribution of the sale proceeds. The sub has gain or loss under Section 1001 on the deemed asset sale, and this is reported in the consolidated return of the selling parent corporation. Only one level of tax applies on the deemed sale of the sub's assets, because Section 332 provides for nonrecognition treatment to the parent corporation on the deemed receipt of liquidation proceeds from the sub.

It generally is prudent to file a Section 338(h)(10) election in a stock acquisition of a subsidiary. If, however, the parent's basis for the subsidiary's stock is substantially higher than the subsidiary's basis for its assets, the parent may not want to make the election, and therefore, the transaction generally is structured as a stock sale without a Section 338 election. In these situations, the parent's taxable gain on the sale of the stock is less than it would be with either an asset sale or a stock sale with a Section 338(h)(10) election.

As a general matter, if the parent has always owned the sub, as a result of the basis adjustment rules in the consolidated return regulations, it is likely that the parent's "outside basis" for the sub's stock will equal the "inside basis" of the sub's assets. In such case, the parent likely will be willing to make the Section 338(h)(10) election. If the sub was recently acquired, however, it is more likely that the outside basis (*i.e.*, the parent's basis for the stock of the sub) will exceed the inside basis (*i.e.*, the sub's basis for its assets), and the parent will not join the acquiror in making the Section 338(h)(10) election.

§ 5.12 Treatment of LBOs

Leveraged buy-outs (LBOs) are taxable acquisitions in which a substantial portion of the consideration is either debt or is raised by the issuance of debt. In many LBOs, such as KKR's acquisition in 1989 of RJR Nabisco, Inc., the acquisition vehicle is a shell corporation formed by a private equity firm for the sole purpose of effectuating the acquisition. The shell issues debt needed to complete the transaction. LBOs are generally structured as stock acquisitions (or reverse subsidiary mergers which are treated as stock acquisitions) for the same reason that other taxable acquisitions are so structured: to prevent the recognition of gain at the target corporate level. A major issue in any LBO is whether the debt is treated as debt for federal income tax purposes. Another issue is whether the interest on debt that is treated as debt for federal income tax purposes is disallowed under (1) Section 279, which disallows the interest deduction on certain convertible and subordinated corporate acquisition indebtedness, or (2) Section 163(i), which disallows the interest deduction on certain high yield discount obligations.

§ 5.13 Proxy Statement Discussion of the Federal Income Tax Consequences of the Acquisition of Toys "R" Us in a Taxable Reverse Subsidiary Merger

Proxy Statement on Schedule 14A for Toys "R" Us, Inc.

(May 23, 2005)

Q: What is the proposed transaction?

A: The proposed transaction is the acquisition of Toys "R" Us, Inc. ("Toys"), a publicly held corporation by an entity owned by an investment group consisting of entities advised by or affiliated with Bain Capital Partners LLC ("Bain"), Kohlberg Kravis Roberts & Co., L.P. ("KKR"), and Vornado Realty Trust ("Vornado," and together with Bain and KKR, the "Sponsors" [the sponsors are private equity firms]) pursuant to an Agreement and Plan of Merger (as may be amended from time to time, the "merger agreement") dated as of March 17, 2005 among [Toys], Global Toys Acquisition, LLC ("Parent") [owned by the private equity purchasers], and Global Toys Acquisition Merger Sub, Inc., a wholly owned subsidiary of Parent ("Acquisition Sub"). Once the merger agreement has been adopted by the [Toys's] stockholders and the other closing conditions under the merger agreement have been satisfied or waived, Acquisition Sub will merge with and into Toys (the "merger"). Toys will be the surviving corporation in the merger (the "surviving corporation") and will become a wholly owned subsidiary of Parent.

Q: What will I receive in the merger?

A: Upon completion of the merger, you will receive $26.75 in cash, without interest, for each share of our [Toys's] common stock that you own. For example, if you own 100 shares of our common stock, you will receive $2,675.00 in cash in exchange for your Toys shares. * * *

Material United States Federal Income Tax Consequences

U.S. Holders. The receipt of cash in the merger (or pursuant to the exercise of dissenters' rights) by U.S. holders of our common stock will be a taxable transaction for U.S. federal income tax purposes (and may also be a taxable transaction under applicable state, local and foreign tax laws). In general, for U.S. federal income tax purposes, a U.S. holder of our common stock will recognize gain or loss equal to the difference between:

- the amount of cash received in exchange for such common stock and
- the U.S. holder's adjusted tax basis in such common stock.

If the holding period in our common stock surrendered in the merger (or pursuant to the exercise of dissenters' rights) is greater than one year as of the date of the merger, the gain or loss will be long-term capital gain or loss. The deductibility of a capital loss recognized on the exchange is subject to limitations under the Code. If a U.S. holder acquired different blocks of our common stock at different times and different prices, such holder must determine its adjusted tax basis and holding period separately with respect to each block of our common stock.

Under the Code, a U.S. holder of our common stock may be subject, under certain circumstances, to information reporting on the cash received in the merger (or pursuant to the exercise of dissenters' rights) unless such U.S. holder is a corporation or other exempt recipient. * * *

§ 5.14 Summary Problems on Taxable Acquisitions

Closely-Held Target Corporation (CHTC) is owned as follows:

Shareholder	% Stock Interest	Adjusted Basis of Stock
A	33⅓	$15K
B	33⅓	$15K
C	33⅓	$15K

CHTC has assets with a fair market value of $100K and adjusted basis of -0-. CHTC has no net operating losses. Assume that the tax rate applicable to CHTC is 35% and the capital gains rate applicable to A, B, and C is 20%. Closely Held Acquiring Corporation (CHAC) is interested in acquiring the stock or assets of CHTC. CHTC and CHAC are incorporated in Delaware.

1. What result to A, B, C, CHTC, and CHAC if CHAC purchases CHTC's assets for $100K in cash and CHTC is liquidated?

2. What result to A, B, C, CHTC, and CHAC if CHAC purchases the stock of CHTC from A, B, and C? How much should CHAC pay? Should CHAC make a Section 338 election?

   a. What result if CHTC has $25K of net operating losses? The long-term tax-exempt rate is 10%.

   b. What result if CHTC has $100K of net operating losses?

3. A and B want to sell their shares to CHAC but C does not want to sell. To force C to sell, it has been proposed that CHAC form a subsidiary (CHAC-Sub) and that CHTC merge into CHAC-Sub with A, B, and C receiving the $100K in cash? What result to A, B, C, CHAC, CHAC-Sub, and CHTC? What result if instead of merging CHTC into CHAC-Sub, CHAC-Sub merges into CHTC?

4. Assume that both CHTC and CHAC are publicly held corporations, and that they are negotiating for CHAC's acquisition of CHTC in a cash merger. The trading price of CHTC's stock is significantly above CHTC's balance sheet net assets and adjusted basis for its assets. CHTC does not have any NOLs. How should the transaction be structured?

§ 5.15 Introduction to Acquisitive Reorganizations

In an acquisitive reorganization, a substantial portion of the consideration paid in the acquisition of the target is stock of the acquiror or the parent of the acquiror. These transactions are defined as "reorganizations" and are set forth in Section 368 of the Code. The acquisitive reorganizations in Section 368 are set out below and should be examined closely in connection with the following discussion of the specific reorganizations:

Sec. 368. Definitions Relating To Corporate Reorganizations

(a) REORGANIZATION.—

(1) IN GENERAL.—* * * [T]he term "reorganization" means—

(A) a statutory merger or consolidation [the (A)];

(B) the acquisition by one corporation [the acquiror], in exchange solely for all or a part of its voting stock (or in exchange solely for all or a part of the voting stock of a corporation which is in control of the acquiring corporation [acquiring parent]), of stock of another corporation [the target] if, immediately after the acquisition, the acquiring corporation has control [*i.e.*, at least 80% of the stock] of such other corporation (whether or not such acquiring corporation had control immediately before the acquisition) [the (B)];

(C) the acquisition by one corporation [the acquiror], in exchange solely for all or a part of its voting stock (or in exchange solely for all or a part of the voting stock of a corporation which is in control of the acquiring corporation [acquiring parent]), of substantially all of the properties of another corporation [the target], but in determining whether the exchange is solely for stock the assumption by the acquiring corporation of a liability of the other, or the fact that property acquired is subject to a liability, shall be disregarded [the (C)]; * * *

(2) SPECIAL RULES RELATING TO PARAGRAPH (1). * * *

(B) ADDITIONAL CONSIDERATION IN CERTAIN PARAGRAPH (1)(C) CASES. [This provision allows up to 20% non-voting stock consideration in a (C) reorganization] * * *

(D) USE OF STOCK OF CONTROLLING CORPORATION IN PARAGRAPH (1)(A) * * * CASE.—The acquisition by one corporation [acquiring sub], in exchange for stock of a corporation (referred to in this subparagraph as "controlling corporation") which is in control of the acquiring corporation [acquiring parent], of substantially all of the properties of another corporation [target] shall not disqualify a transaction under paragraph (1)(A) [the (A) merger] * * * if—

(i) no stock of the acquiring corporation is used in the transaction, and

(ii) in the case of a transaction under paragraph (1)(A), such transaction would have qualified under paragraph (1)(A) had the merger been into the controlling corporation. [The Section 368(a)(2)(D) forward subsidiary merger reorganization]

(E) STATUTORY MERGER USING VOTING STOCK OF CORPORATION CONTROLLING MERGED CORPORATION.—A transaction otherwise qualifying under paragraph (1)(A) [the (A) merger] shall not be disqualified by reason of the fact that stock of a corporation (referred to in this subparagraph as the "controlling corporation") [acquiring parent] which before the merger was in control of the merged corporation [acquiring sub] is used in the transaction, if—

(i) after the transaction, the corporation surviving the merger [target] holds substantially all of its properties and of the properties of the merged corporation [acquiring sub] (other than stock of the controlling corporation distributed in the transaction); and

(ii) in the transaction, former shareholders of the surviving corporation [target] exchanged, for an amount of voting stock of the controlling corporation [acquiring parent], an amount of stock in the surviving corporation [target] which constitutes control of such corporation. [The Section 368(a)(2)(E) reverse subsidiary merger reorganization] * * *

Courts have held that to qualify as an acquisitive reorganization there must be a continuity of interest (*i.e.*, the target's shareholders must receive a stock interest in the acquiror), a continuity of business enterprise (*i.e.*, a business previously conducted by the target must be continued), and a business purpose (as distinguished from a pure tax avoidance motive). As will be seen below, some of the forms of acquisitive reorganization have their own continuity of interest requirements, others do not.

In an acquisitive reorganization, the target's shareholders receive nonrecognition treatment on the exchange of their target stock or securities for stock or securities of the acquiror and take a substituted basis for the acquiror stock received. *See* §§354 and 358. If the target's shareholders receive other property (*i.e.*, boot) they recognize gain to the extent of the boot, and the gain is treated as a dividend if the transaction has the "effect of the distribution of a dividend." [*See* §356] Although capital gains and dividends are taxed at the same 20% rate, if the boot is treated as capital gain, the shareholder gets to recover some of the basis for the shares, whereas if the boot is treated as a dividend, there is no basis recovery. The target and the acquiror generally have nonrecognition treatment [*see* §§361 and 1032] with the acquiror taking a carryover basis in the target's stock or assets. [*See*§362]

There are seven basic forms of acquisitive reorganizations: (1) four reorganizations in which the assets of the target are acquired (asset reorganizations), and (2) three reorganizations in which the stock of the target is acquired (stock reorganizations). The stock or assets acquired in any of the above seven reorganizations may be pushed down to a subsidiary (over and down reorganizations). Also, Section 351, which provides tax-free treatment for contributions to corporations, may in certain circumstances be utilized as a tax-free acquisitive transaction.

§5.16 Acquisitive Asset Reorganizations

In the four asset reorganizations, the assets of the target corporation are acquired either by the acquiring corporation or by a subsidiary of the acquiring corporation. The following are the asset reorganizations:

A. The Direct Merger under §368(a)(1)(A)

The "(A)" reorganization under section 368(a)(1)(A) is a merger of a target directly into an acquiror with the target's shareholders receiving stock in the acquiror. The merger can be effectuated pursuant to state or foreign law. *See* Chapter 2 for the voting rules for mergers under state law. Although the statute does not set forth a continuity of interest requirement, a series of Supreme Court cases make it clear that there must be a continuity of interest, that is, the target's shareholders must receive a substantial stock interest in the acquiror. Pursuant to the regulations, the continuity of interest requirement will be satisfied if at least 40% of the consideration paid in an (A) reorganization is stock of the acquiror.

In general, tax-free treatment only applies to the receipt of an acquiror's common, not preferred, stock. [*See* §§354(a)(2)(C) and 351(g)] As a result of a 1998 amendment to the regulations under Section 368, pre-reorganization dispositions of stock of the target and post-reorganization dispositions of stock of the acquiror to unrelated persons are disregarded in determining whether the continuity of interest doctrine is satisfied. This principle applies to all forms of reorganizations. The Direct "A" Merger is diagramed as follows:

Direct "A" Merger Reorganization under Section 368(a)(1)(A)

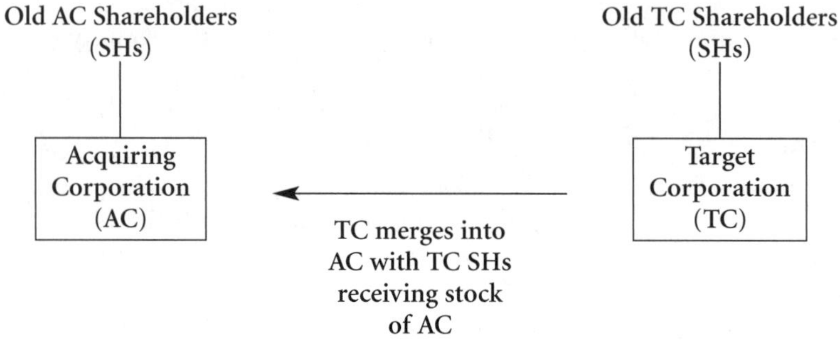

When the Dust Settles

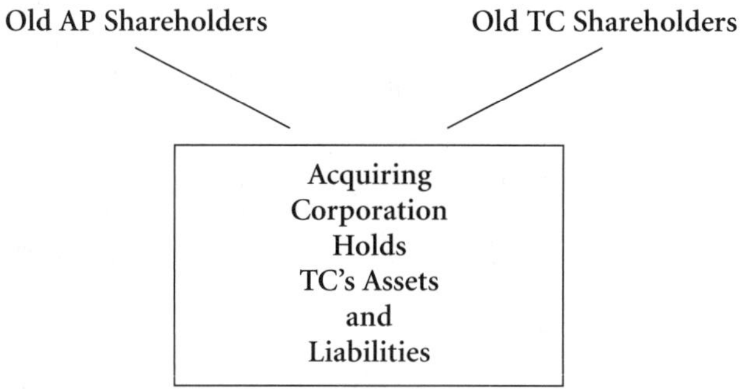

Under Section 354, the target's shareholders have tax-free treatment on the receipt of the acquiror's common stock, and under Section 358 they take a substituted basis for the acquiror's stock (*i.e.*, each shareholder substitutes as the basis for the acquiror stock received, the basis for target stock exchanged), thereby deferring the gain. Any boot received is subject to tax under Section 356, limited to the gain realized, as either a dividend or capital gain, which in either case will produce a maximum tax of 20%. [*See* § 1(h)] The gain is treated as a dividend only if the exchange has the "effect of a distribution of a dividend," a concept not explored here. Section 356 is referred to as the "boot gain rule." Sections 354, 356, and 358 are set out below:

Sec. 354. Exchanges of Stock and Securities in Certain Reorganizations

(a) GENERAL RULE.—

(1) IN GENERAL.—No gain or loss shall be recognized if stock or securities in a corporation a party to a reorganization [the target, *see* § 368(b)] are, in pursuance of the plan of reorganization, exchanged solely for stock or securities * * * in another corporation [the acquiror] a party to the reorganization. * * *

Sec. 356. Receipt of Additional Consideration

(a) GAIN ON EXCHANGES.—

(1) RECOGNITION OF GAIN.—If—

(A) section 354 * * * would apply to an exchange but for the fact that

(B) the property received in the exchange consists not only of property permitted by section 354 * * * to be received without the recognition of gain [*i.e.*, stock of the acquiror] but also of other property or money, then the gain, if any, to the recipient shall be recognized, but in an amount not in excess of the sum of such money and the fair market value of such other property. [the boot gain rule]

(2) TREATMENT AS DIVIDEND.—If an exchange is described in paragraph (1) but has the effect of the distribution of a dividend * * * then there shall be treated as a dividend to each distributee such an amount of the gain recognized under paragraph (1) as is not in excess of his ratable share of the undistributed earning and profits of the corporation . * * *

Sec. 358. Basis to Distributees

(a) GENERAL RULE.—In the case of an exchange to which section * * * 354 * * * applies—

(1) NONRECOGNITION PROPERTY.—The basis of the property permitted to be received under such section without the recognition of gain or loss [stock of acquiror] shall be the same as that of the property exchanged [stock of target]—

(A) decreased by—

(i) the fair market value of any other property (except money) received by the taxpayer,

(ii) the amount of any money received by the taxpayer, * * *, and

(B) increased by—

(i) the amount which was treated as a dividend, and

(ii) the amount of gain to the taxpayer which was recognized on such exchange . * * *

(2) OTHER PROPERTY.—The basis of any other property (except money) received by the taxpayer shall be its fair market value. * * *

The target has tax-free treatment under Section 361, and the acquiror has tax-free treatment under Section 1032 and takes a carryover basis for the target's assets (*i.e.*, takes the target's basis for the assets) under Section 362(b). These sections are set out below:

Sec. 361. Nonrecognition of Gain or Loss to Corporations; Treatment of Distributions

(a) GENERAL RULE.—No gain or loss shall be recognized to a corporation [the target] if such corporation is a party to a reorganization and exchanges property, in pursuance of the plan of reorganization, solely for stock or securities in another corporation [the acquiror] a party to the reorganization.

(b) EXCHANGES NOT SOLELY IN KIND.—[The target will not have gain on receipt of boot as long as the boot is distributed.] * * *

Sec. 1032. Exchange of Stock for Property

(a) NONRECOGNITION OF GAIN OR LOSS.—No gain or loss shall be recognized to a corporation [the acquiror] on the receipt of money or other property [stock of the target or the target's assets] in exchange for stock * * * of such corporation. * * *

Sec. 362. Basis to Corporations

(b) Transfers to Corporations.—If property was acquired by a corporation [the acquiror] in connection with a reorganization * * *, then the basis shall be the same as it would be in the hands of the transferor [the target in an asset reorganization or the target's shareholders in a stock reorganization], increased in the amount of gain recognized to the transferor on such transfer.

Under Section 381, other tax attributes, such as NOLs, carryover to the acquiror. However, the utilization by the acquiror of NOL carryovers is subject to limitation under Section 382.

J.P. Morgan Chase acquired Bank One in a direct merger. *See* The Merger Agreement and S-4 for this transaction in Documentary Appendices D and E of *M&A Statutes, Rules, and Regulations, supra* Section 1.1.

B. Forward Subsidiary Merger under Section 368(a)(2)(D)

This Section 368(a)(2)(D) reorganization is a merger of a target into a subsidiary (Acquiring Subsidiary) of the acquiring corporation (Acquiring Parent). Thus, this is the forward triangular reorganization discussed in Chapter 2. The Acquiring Subsidiary must acquire substantially all of the target's assets. Although there is no statutory continuity of interest requirement, as in the case of the (A) reorganization, a 40% continuity of interest is required. The transaction may be diagramed as shown on the following page.

The target has tax-free treatment under Section 361. The target's shareholders have tax-free treatment under Section 354 on the receipt of stock of the Acquiring Parent and take a substituted basis for the stock under Section 358. The boot gain rule of Section 356 applies. Both the Acquiring Sub and the Acquiring Parent have tax-free treatment under Section 1032 and the regulations thereunder, and under Section 362(b) the Acquiring Subsidiary takes a modified carryover basis for the target's assets. Also, under Section 381, the Acquiring Subsidiary will carry-over the target's other tax attributes, such as NOLs, subject to limitation under Section 382.

Because the basic requirements for a forward subsidiary merger are similar to the requirements for a straight (A) reorganization, in most acquisitions of publicly held corporations in reorganization transactions in which more than 20% of the consideration is boot, the transaction is structured as a forward subsidiary merger. This gives tax-free treatment to the target's shareholders who receive stock and keeps the target's assets and liabilities separate from the acquiror's assets and liabilities. If less than 20% of the consideration is boot, the reorganization transaction is generally structured as a reverse subsidiary merger under Section 368(a)(2)(E), which is discussed below. In addition to keeping the target's assets and liabilities in a separate entity, the reverse subsidiary merger does not require a transfer of the target's assets and liabilities. [*See* Chapter 2]

C. Direct Stock for Asset Reorganization under Section 368(a)(1)(C)

In this "(C)" reorganization under Section 368(a)(1)(C), an acquiring corporation acquires "substantially all" of a target's assets in exchange solely for voting stock of the acquiror. The acquiror can assume the target's liabilities. In certain limited circumstances the acquiror can pay up to 20% boot; this is known as the "boot relaxation rule." While there is some relaxation for the use of boot in a "(C)" reorganization, if any boot is in fact utilized in the

Forward Subsidiary Merger Reorganization under Section 368(a)(2)(D)

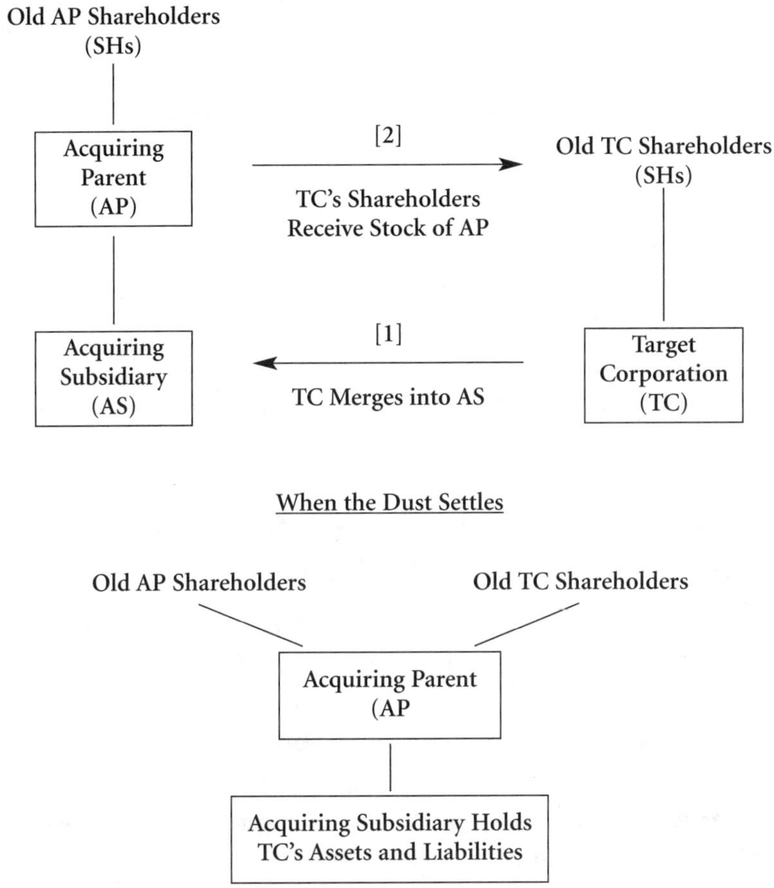

transaction, any liability assumed by the acquiror will constitute boot for purposes of calculating the 20% threshold. [*See* § 368(a)(2)(B)] Under Section 368(a)(2)(G), the target must liquidate, thereby distributing to the shareholders the stock received from the acquiror.

The target has tax-free treatment under Section 361. The target's shareholders have tax-free treatment under Section 354 and take a substituted basis under Section 358 for the acquiror's stock they receive. The boot gain rule of Section 356 applies. The acquiror has tax-free treatment under Section 1032 and takes a carryover basis for the target's assets under Section 362(b). Also, under Section 381, the acquiror carries over the target's other tax attributes, including NOLs, subject to limitation under Section 382. The (C) reorganization is not used as frequently as the (A), the forward subsidiary merger, and the reverse subsidiary merger reorganizations.

D. Triangular Stock for Asset Reorganization under Section 368(a)(1)(C)

The triangular (C) reorganization under Section 368(a)(1)(C), which is permitted by the parenthetical language in the statute, is essentially the same as the direct (C) reorganization described above, except the acquisition is made by an Acquiring Subsidiary and the consideration paid is voting stock of the Acquiring Parent.

The tax treatment to the target and the target's shareholders is the same as in the (C) reorganization. Both the Acquiring Parent and Acquiring Subsidiary have tax-free treatment under Section 1032 and the regulations thereunder. Under Section 362(b), the Acquiring Subsidiary takes a modified carryover basis for the target's assets, and under Section 381 the Acquiring Subsidiary carries over the target's other tax attributes, including NOLs, subject to limitation under Section 382. If a (C) is going to be used, it generally will be advantageous to utilize the triangular (C) because it will keep the target's assets and liabilities in a separate entity.

E. Summary of Acquisitive Asset Reorganizations

The four acquisitive asset reorganizations are (1) the direct (A) merger, (2) the forward triangular merger, (3) the stock for asset (C) reorganization, and (4) the triangular stock for asset (C) reorganization.

§ 5.17 Acquisitive Stock Reorganization and Acquisitive Section 351 Transactions

There are three types of reorganizations in which the stock of the target corporation is acquired by either the acquiring corporation or one of its subsidiaries.

A. Reverse Subsidiary Merger under § 368(a)(2)(E)

In the reverse triangular (or subsidiary) merger under Section 368 (a)(2)(E), an Acquiring Subsidiary merges into the target, with the target's shareholders receiving voting stock of the Acquiring Parent in exchange for at least 80% of the target's stock. The balance of the target's stock may be acquired for boot; thus, up to 20% of the consideration can be boot. When the dust settles, the target has become a wholly-owned subsidiary of the Acquiring Parent. [*See* Chapter 2.] The transaction is diagrammed on the next page.

In this transaction the target's shareholders receive tax-free treatment under Section 354 on receipt of stock of the acquiror, and under Section 358 they take a substituted basis for the acquiror stock received. Any boot received is subject to the boot gain rule of Section 356. The Acquiring Subsidiary, the target, and the Acquiring Parent also have nonrecognition treatment. The tax attributes of the target continue after the acquisition; however, any NOLs of the target are subject to limitation under Section 382. Most acquisitions of publicly-held corporations in either taxable or tax-free reorganizations are effectuated by the reverse subsidiary merger. As noted, if the boot is in excess of 20%, the transaction will generally be structured as a forward subsidiary merger.

B. Stock for Stock Reorganization under Section 368(a)(1)(B)

In this "(B)" reorganization under Section 368(a)(1)(B), an acquiring corporation acquires in exchange solely for its voting stock at least 80% of the stock of a target directly from the target's shareholders. The Supreme Court has held that "sole" means "solely" and, therefore, no boot can be used in the transaction. After the exchange, the target is a subsidiary of the acquiror.

Reverse Subsidiary Merger under Section 368(a)(2)(E)

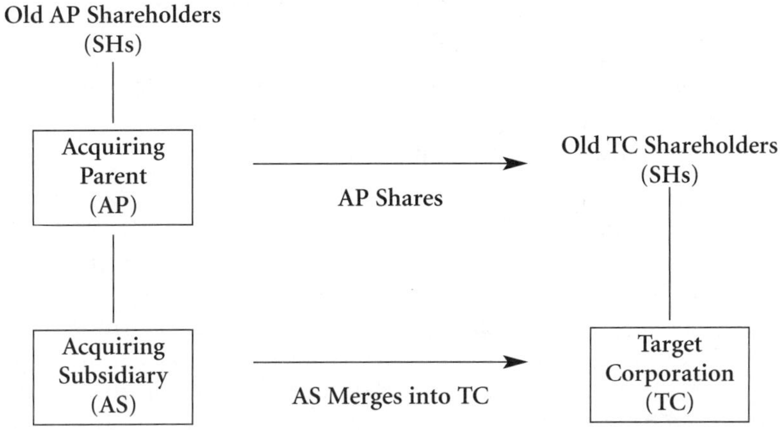

When the Dust Settles

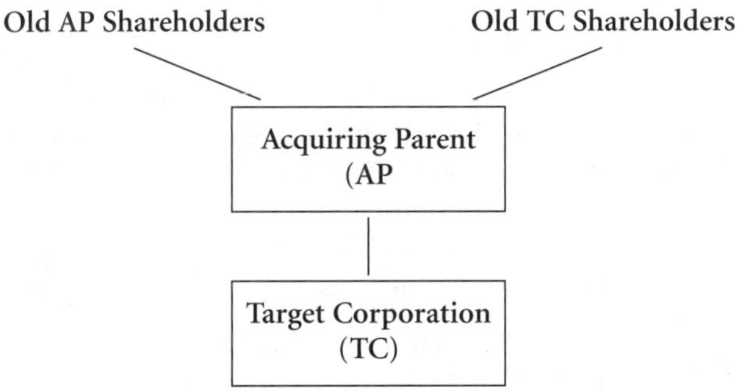

Under Section 354, the target's shareholders have tax-free treatment on receipt of the stock of the acquiror, and they take a substituted basis for that stock under Section 358. Under Section 1032 the acquiror has tax-free treatment, and under Section 362(b) the acquiror takes a carryover basis for the target's stock. The tax attributes of the target continue, but any NOLs are subject to limitation under Section 382. Because no boot can be used in a (B), this form of reorganization is seldom used.

C. Triangular (B) Reorganization under Section 368(a)(1)(B)

This triangular (B) reorganization under Section 368(a)(1)(B), which is permitted by the parenthetical language in the statute, is the same as the direct (B), except an Acquiring Subsidiary acquires the target's stock in exchange for stock of the Acquiring Parent. The tax treatment of the parties is the same as in a direct (B).

D. The Acquisitive Section 351 Transaction and the Horizontal Double Dummy

Section 351, which provides for tax-free treatment on certain transfers of property to a corporation in exchange for stock, can also be used (as a substitute for a reorganization) in effectuating certain tax-free acquisitions.

In one form of acquisitive Section 351 transaction the shareholders of a target corporation transfer their stock in the target to a newly formed holding company in exchange for common stock of the holding company. Simultaneously the shareholders of the acquiror transfer their stock in the acquiror to the holding company in exchange for common stock of the holding company. The shareholders of the acquiror end up with more than 50% of the stock of the holding company, but together the shareholders of the target and the acquiror must own at least 80% of the stock of the holding company. The transaction may be effectuated by causing the holding company to form two subs and have one of the subs merge into the acquiror while the other sub merges into the target in two reverse subsidiary mergers with the shareholders of the target and acquiror receiving stock of the holding company. This is known as the "horizontal double dummy" and was used in the 2005 acquisition by Oracle of Seibel. *See* Documentary Appendix H of *M&A Statutes, Rules, and Documents, Supra* Section 1.1.

In this transaction the shareholders of target and acquiror receive nonrecognition under Section 351 and take a substituted basis for their holding company shares under Section 358. Holding company has nonrecognition under Section 1032 and takes a carryover basis for the stock of target and acquiror under Section 362. The tax attributes of both the acquiror and the target continue; however, if the shareholders of the acquiror are in control of the holding company, the target's NOLs will be limited by Section 382.

One of the advantages of this transaction is that the continuity of interest doctrine does not apply, and consequently, any amount of the consideration paid to the target's shareholders can be boot. Thus, for example, in the Oracle–Seibel transaction, only 30% of the consideration paid to the Seibel shareholders was stock of the holding company; the balance was cash.

E. Summary of Acquisitive Stock Reorganizations and Acquisitive Section 351 Transactions

The three stock reorganizations are (1) the reverse subsidiary merger under Section 368(a)(2)(E), (2) the direct stock for stock (B) reorganization under Section 368(a)(1)(B), and (3) the triangular stock for stock (B) reorganization. In each of these transactions, the target ends up as a subsidiary of the acquiror or Acquiring Subsidiary, and assuming only voting stock consideration is paid, the target's shareholders have tax-free treatment under Section 354. The Section 351 holding company structure also involves the acquisition of stock and has as a similar result to these forms of stock reorganizations, except the acquiror and the target end up as subsidiaries of the holding company.

§5.18 Proxy Statement Discussion of the Federal Income Tax Consequences of the Acquisition by HP of Compaq in a Tax-Free Reverse Subsidiary Merger

Joint Proxy Statement of Hewlett Packard and Compaq and Prospectus of Hewlett Packard, As Filed on Form S-4

(November 15, 2001)

Hewlett-Packard Company and Compaq Computer Corporation have agreed to combine their businesses under the terms of an Agreement and Plan of Reorganization....

The Merger and the Merger Agreement* * * Under the terms of the merger agreement, a wholly-owned subsidiary of HP [Heloise Merger Corporation, a newly-formed, wholly-owned subsidiary of HP] will merge with and into Compaq and Compaq will survive the merger as a wholly-owned subsidiary of HP. Upon completion of the merger, holders of Compaq common stock will be entitled to receive 0.6325 of a share of HP common stock for each share of Compaq common stock they then hold. HP shareowners will continue to own their existing shares of HP common stock after the merger. HP currently intends to merge Compaq into HP as soon as reasonably practicable following the merger. * * *

United States Federal Income Tax Consequences of the Merger. The following summary discusses certain United States federal income tax consequences of the merger to Compaq shareowners. * * * The completion of the merger is conditioned upon the delivery by each of Wilson Sonsini Goodrich & Rosati, Professional Corporation, counsel to HP, and Skadden, Arps, Slate, Meagher & Flom LLP, counsel to Compaq, of its opinion to the effect that, on the basis of the facts, assumptions, and representations set forth in such opinion, the merger will constitute a "reorganization" for United States federal income tax purposes within the meaning of Section 368(a) of the Internal Revenue Code. As a result of the merger qualifying as a "reorganization:" Compaq shareowners will not recognize any gain or loss upon the receipt of HP common stock in exchange for Compaq common stock in connection with the merger, except for cash received instead of a fractional share of HP common stock; the aggregate tax basis of the HP common stock received by a Compaq shareowner in connection with the merger, including any fractional share of HP common stock not actually received, will be equal to the aggregate tax basis of the Compaq common stock surrendered in exchange for HP common stock; the holding period of the HP common stock received by a Compaq shareowner in connection with the merger will include the holding period of the Compaq common stock surrendered in connection with the merger; cash payments received by a Compaq shareowner for a fractional share of HP common stock will be treated as if such fractional share had been issued in connection with the merger and then redeemed by HP, and Compaq shareowners will recognize capital gain or loss with respect to such cash payment, measured by the difference, if any, between the amount of cash received and the tax basis in such fractional share; and HP, Heloise Merger Corporation and Compaq will not recognize gain or loss as a result of the merger. * * *

§5.19 Introductory Problems on Reorganizations

The following problems are designed to illustrate the basic operation of the reorganization provisions and the structure of taxable acquisitions.

Individuals *A* and *B* each own 50 percent of the outstanding stock of target corporation (*TC*). *A*'s basis for his stock is $50K, and *B*'s basis is $150K. The value of *TC*'s stock is

$200K, and, consequently, *A*'s and *B*'s shares are each worth $100K. The fair market value of *TC*'s assets is $220K, and the adjusted basis thereof is $100K. *TC* has liabilities of $20K and earnings and profits of $100K. Acquiring corporation (*AC*) is interested in acquiring *TC* in a nontaxable reorganization.

(a) What result to *A*, *B*, *TC* and *AC* if *TC* merges into *AC* in a transaction in which *A* and *B* each receive voting stock of *AC* with a fair market value of $100K? *See* § 368(a)(1)(A), § 368(b), § 354, §§ 356–358, § 361, § 362, and § 1032. What result if the merger consideration is cash?

(b) What if *AC* forms a subsidiary (*AC*-S) by transferring *AC* voting stock to it, and *TC* merges into *AC*-S with *A* and *B* receiving the *AC* stock? Focus only on the treatment of *A* and *B* and *AC*-S's basis for the *TC* assets. What if *AC*-S merges into *TC*? Focus only on the treatment of *A* and *B*. *See* § 368 (a)(1)(*A*), § (a)(2)(D), § (a)(2)(E), § 368(b), § 368(c), § 354, § 357, § 358, § 361, § 362, and § 1032. What result if the merger consideration is cash?

(c) What result to *A*, *B*, *TC* and *AC* if *AC* acquires the stock of *TC* from *A* and *B* in exchange for $200K of voting stock of *AC*? What result if *AC*-S makes the acquisition using *AC* voting stock? Focus only on the treatment of *A* and *B* and *AC*-S's basis for the *TC* stock. *See* § 368(a)(1)(B), § 368(b), § 368(c), § 354, § 357, § 358, § 361, § 362, and § 1032. What if the consideration paid in each case is cash?

(d) What results to *A*, *B*, *TC* and *AC* if *AC* acquires the assets and liabilities of *TC* in exchange for $200K of voting stock of *AC*, and *TC* is then liquidated? Suppose *AC*-S makes the acquisition using $200K of *AC* voting stock? *See* § 368(a)(1)(C), (a)(2)(B), § 368(b), § 354, §§ 356–358, § 361, § 362, and § 1032. What if the consideration paid in each case is cash?

§ 5.20 Acquisitions of S Corporations

An S corporation is a domestic corporation that (1) has no more than 100 shareholders, (who, except for certain trusts and estates, must be U.S. individuals), (2) meets certain other specific requirements, and (3) elects to be treated as an S corporation. *See* § 1361 and § 1362. An S corporation is generally not subject to tax; rather the shareholders include their relative shares of the S corporation's income or loss in their individual tax returns [*see* § 1366], and the shareholders increase the bases of their shares by the included income and decrease the bases of their shares by the included losses. [*See* 1367] Distributions are generally tax-free to the shareholders. [*See* § 1368]

If the S corporation was always an S corporation, there is only one level of tax on the acquisition of an S corporation's assets, because the gain realized by the S corporation passes through to the shareholders and increases the bases of their shares. Then, when the corporation makes a liquidating distribution of the proceeds, the shareholders have no gain or loss under Section 331, because the liquidating proceeds exactly equal the bases of their shares. Thus, a taxable asset acquisition is generally a tax efficient way to acquire an S corporation.

Also, under Treasury Regulation § 1.338(h)(10)–1, if the stock of an S corporation is acquired by an acquiring corporation in a qualified stock purchase, the selling shareholders and the acquiror can jointly elect to treat the stock acquisition as a taxable asset acquisition followed by a liquidation that will be tax-free under Section 331, because of the increase in the shareholders' bases for their shares.

S corporations generally may participate either as acquiror or target in acquisitive reorganizations.

References

Bittker and Eustice, *Corporate Tax, supra* Section 1.10.

Ginsburg and Levin, *Mergers and Acquisitions, supra* Section 1.10.

Thompson, *Corporate Taxation Through the Lens of Mergers and Acquisitions, supra* Section 1.10.

Thompson, *Mergers, Acquisitions and Tender Offers, supra* Section 1.10, Chapters 9, 21, and 22.

Chapter 6

Introduction to Accounting for Mergers and Acquisitions

§6.1 Scope

This chapter introduces accounting for mergers and acquisitions. Section 6.2 sets out an introductory problem presenting the basic questions raised in accounting for mergers and acquisitions. Section 6.3 provides an introduction to the core principles governing the balance sheet, income statement, and cash flow statement. Section 6.4 introduces the rules of the Financial Accounting Standards Board (FASB), the independent organization charged with setting accounting standards, adopted in 2001 and revised in 2007 for accounting for mergers and acquisitions. These rules eliminated both the pooling method and the amortization of goodwill. Section 6.5 discusses the SEC's Regulation S-X, which deals with accounting disclosure requirements in various SEC documents, such as S-4 registration statements and merger proxy statements. Thus, while FASB sets out the particular accounting rules for mergers and other transactions, the SEC specifies the accounting disclosure requirements relating to such transactions. Section 6.6 presents the proxy statement discussion of the accounting treatment of the acquisition by Hewlett Packard (HP) of Compaq in a tax-free reorganization. Section 6.7 addresses the huge goodwill impairment charge taken by AOL-Time Warner relating to the acquisition by AOL of Time Warner. Section 6.8 compares the treatment of goodwill under the tax and accounting rules. Section 6.9 first discusses "PE Magic," which was possible under the pooling of interest rules and then asks whether "PE Magic" is still possible under the current purchase rules. Section 6.10 contains summary problems. This topic is covered in greater detail in Chapter 10 of Thompson, *Mergers, Acquisitions and Tender Offers*, *supra* Section 1.10.

§6.2 Basic Introductory Problem on the Acquisition Method of Accounting

J.P. Morgan Chase & Co. (J.P. Morgan) has agreed to acquire The Goldman Sachs Group, Inc. (Goldman Sachs) in a reverse subsidiary merger with a subsidiary of J.P. Morgan Chase merging into Goldman Sachs. The Goldman Sachs shareholders are going to receive common stock of J.P. Morgan Chase equal to 45% of the J.P. Morgan Chase common stock after the transaction, and Goldman Sachs will become a subsidiary of J.P. Morgan Chase. What will the balance sheet and income statement of the acquiring corporation, J.P. Morgan Chase, look like after the acquisition?

Suppose the consideration paid in the reverse subsidiary merger is cash so that the Goldman Sachs shareholders receive cash for their shares and Goldman Sachs ends up as a subsidiary of J.P. Morgan Chase. What will the balance sheet and income statement of the acquiring corporation, J.P. Morgan Chase, look like after the acquisition?

§ 6.3 Introduction to Financial Accounting

SEC's Beginners' Guide to Financial Statements

http://www.sec.gov/investor/pubs/begfinstmtguide.htm

The Basics. If you can read a nutrition label or a baseball box score, you can learn to read basic financial statements. * * * Let's begin by looking at what financial statements do.

"Show me the money!" We all remember Cuba Gooding Jr.'s immortal line from the movie *Jerry Maguire*, "Show me the money!" Well, that's what financial statements do. They show you the money. They show you where a company's money came from, where it went, and where it is now.

There are four main financial statements. They are: (1) balance sheets; (2) income statements; (3) cash flow statements; and (4) statements of shareholders' equity. Balance sheets show what a company owns and what it owes at a fixed point in time. Income statements show how much money a company made and spent over a period of time. Cash flow statements show the exchange of money between a company and the outside world also over a period of time. The fourth financial statement, called a "statement of shareholders' equity," shows changes in the interests of the company's shareholders over time.

Let's look at each of the first three financial statements in more detail.

Balance Sheets. A balance sheet provides detailed information about a company's assets, liabilities and shareholders' equity.

Assets are things that a company owns that have value. This typically means they can either be sold or used by the company to make products or provide services that can be sold. Assets include physical property, such as plants, trucks, equipment and inventory. It also includes things that can't be touched but nevertheless exist and have value, such as trademarks and patents. And cash itself is an asset. So are investments a company makes. [*See* TC's assets on the balance sheet in Table 6.1]

Liabilities are amounts of money that a company owes to others. This can include all kinds of obligations, like money borrowed from a bank to launch a new product, rent for use of a building, money owed to suppliers for materials, payroll a company owes to its employees, environmental cleanup costs, or taxes owed to the government. Liabilities also include obligations to provide goods or services to customers in the future. [*See* TC's liabilities on the balance sheet in Table 6.1]

Shareholders' equity is sometimes called capital or net worth. It's the money that would be left if a company sold all of its assets and paid off all of its liabilities. This leftover money belongs to the shareholders, or the owners, of the company.

The following formula summarizes what a balance sheet shows:

ASSETS = LIABILITIES + SHAREHOLDERS' EQUITY

A company's assets have to equal, or "balance," the sum of its liabilities and shareholders' equity.

A company's balance sheet is set up like the basic accounting equation shown above. On the left side of the balance sheet, companies list their assets. On the right side, they list their liabilities and shareholders' equity. Sometimes balance sheets show assets at the top, followed by liabilities, with shareholders' equity at the bottom. [*See* TC's balance sheet in Table 6.1 in Section 6.10]

Assets are generally listed based on how quickly they will be converted into cash. Current assets are things a company expects to convert to cash within one year. A good example is inventory. Most companies expect to sell their inventory for cash within one year. Noncurrent assets are things a company does not expect to convert to cash within one year or that would take longer than one year to sell. Noncurrent assets include fixed assets. Fixed assets are those assets used to operate the business but that are not available for sale, such as trucks, office furniture and other property.

Liabilities are generally listed based on their due dates. Liabilities are said to be either current or long-term. Current liabilities are obligations a company expects to pay off within the year. Long-term liabilities are obligations due more than one year away. [TC's liabilities in Table 6.1 are only accounts payables, which are such items as accrued salaries and amounts owed for supplies. TC has no long term liabilities such as bonds or bank loans.]

Shareholders' equity is the amount owners invested in the company's stock plus or minus the company's earnings or losses since inception. [Shareholders' equity from the amounts shareholders invest in the company may, depending on the particular corporate law, be divided between par value and paid-in surplus. Par value is a minimum amount that must be paid for the shares, such as $1 per share, and paid-in-surplus is the amounts paid for the shares in excess of par value. Under some state statutes, including the Model Business Corporation Act, par value is completely optional. *See* Model Business Corporation Act § 2.02(b)(2)(4). TC's shares have a par value.] Sometimes companies distribute earnings, instead of retaining them. These distributions are called dividends.

A balance sheet shows a snapshot of a company's assets, liabilities and shareholders' equity at the end of the reporting period. It does not show the flows into and out of the accounts during the period.

Income Statements. An income statement is a report that shows how much revenue a company earned over a specific time period (usually for a year or some portion of a year). An income statement also shows the costs and expenses associated with earning that revenue. The literal "bottom line" of the statement usually shows the company's net earnings or losses. This tells you how much the company earned or lost over the period. [*See* TC's income statement in Table 6.2 in Section 6.11]

Income statements also report earnings per share (or "EPS"). [*See* the EPS calculations for TC and AC in Table 6.5 in Section 6.11] This calculation tells you how much money shareholders would receive if the company decided to distribute all of the net earnings for the period. (Companies almost never distribute all of their earnings. Usually they reinvest them in the business.)

To understand how income statements are set up, think of them as a set of stairs. You start at the top with the total amount of sales made during the accounting period. Then you go down, one step at a time. At each step, you make a deduction for certain costs or other operating expenses associated with earning the revenue. At the bottom of the stairs, after deducting all of the expenses, you learn how much the company actually earned or lost during the accounting period. People often call this "the bottom line."

At the top of the income statement is the total amount of money brought in from sales of products or services. This top line is often referred to as gross revenues or sales. * * *

The next line is money the company doesn't expect to collect on certain sales. This could be due, for example, to sales discounts or merchandise returns.

When you subtract the returns and allowances from the gross revenues, you arrive at the company's net revenues. * * *

Moving down the stairs from the net revenue line, there are several lines that represent various kinds of operating expenses. Although these lines can be reported in various orders, the next line after net revenues typically shows the costs of the sales. This number tells you the amount of money the company spent to produce the goods or services it sold during the accounting period.

The next line subtracts the costs of sales from the net revenues to arrive at a subtotal called "gross profit" or sometimes "gross margin." * * *

The next section deals with operating expenses. These are expenses that go toward supporting a company's operations for a given period—for example, salaries of administrative personnel and costs of researching new products. Marketing expenses are another example. Operating expenses are different from "costs of sales," which were deducted above, because operating expenses cannot be linked directly to the production of the products or services being sold.

Depreciation is also deducted from gross profit. Depreciation takes into account the wear and tear on some assets, such as machinery, tools and furniture, which are used over the long term. Companies spread the cost of these assets over the periods they are used. This process of spreading these costs is called depreciation or amortization. [Amortization applies to deductions attributable to intangible assets, while depreciation applies to tangible assets.] The "charge" for using these assets during the period is a fraction of the original cost of the assets.

After all operating expenses are deducted from gross profit, you arrive at operating profit before interest and income tax expenses. This is often called "income from operations."

Next companies must account for interest income and interest expense. Interest income is the money companies make from keeping their cash in interest-bearing savings accounts, money market funds and the like. On the other hand, interest expense is the money companies paid in interest for money they borrow. Some income statements show interest income and interest expense separately. Some income statements combine the two numbers. The interest income and expense are then added or subtracted from the operating profits to arrive at operating profit <u>before</u> income tax.

Finally, income tax is deducted and you arrive at the bottom line: net profit or net losses. (Net profit is also called net income or net earnings.) This tells you how much the company actually earned or lost during the accounting period. Did the company make a profit or did it lose money? [The net income or loss amount on the income statement has a direct effect on the equity section of the balance sheet. Net income increases equity and net loss decreases equity. Dividends also reduce shareholders' equity. Retained earnings are what is left in the corporation after increases in net equity for net income and decreases in net equity for net losses and dividends. Thus, if a corporation has net income for the year of $900K and pays dividends of $400K, retained earnings increases by $500K.]

Earnings Per Share or EPS. Most income statements include a calculation of earnings per share or EPS. This calculation tells you how much money shareholders would receive for each share of stock they own if the company distributed all of its net income for the period. To calculate EPS, you take the total net income and divide it by the number of outstanding shares of the company.

Cash Flow Statements. Cash flow statements report a company's inflows and outflows of cash. This is important because a company needs to have enough cash on hand to pay its expenses and purchase assets. While an income statement can tell you whether a company made a profit, a cash flow statement can tell you whether the company generated cash.

A cash flow statement shows changes over time rather than absolute dollar amounts at a point in time. It uses and reorders the information from a company's balance sheet and income statement.

The bottom line of the cash flow statement shows the net increase or decrease in cash for the period. Generally, cash flow statements are divided into three main parts. Each part reviews the cash flow from one of three types of activities: (1) operating activities; (2) investing activities; and (3) financing activities.

Operating Activities. The first part of a cash flow statement analyzes a company's cash flow from net income or losses. For most companies, this section of the cash flow statement reconciles the net income (as shown on the income statement) to the actual cash the company received from or used in its operating activities. To do this, it deducts from net income any non-cash items (such as depreciation expenses) and any cash that was used or provided by other operating assets and liabilities.

Investing Activities. The second part of a cash flow statement shows the cash flow from all investing activities, which generally include purchases or sales of long-term assets, such as property, plant and equipment, as well as investment securities. If a company buys a piece of machinery, the cash flow statement would reflect this activity as a cash outflow from investing activities because it used cash. If the company decided to sell off some investments from an investment portfolio, the proceeds from the sales would show up as a cash inflow from investing activities because it provided cash.

Financing Activities. The third part of a cash flow statement shows the cash flow from all financing activities. Typical sources of cash flow include cash raised by selling stocks and bonds or borrowing from banks. Likewise, paying back a bank loan would show up as a use of cash flow.

Read the Footnotes. A horse called "Read The Footnotes" ran in the 2004 Kentucky Derby. He finished seventh, but if he had won, it would have been a victory for financial literacy proponents everywhere. It's so important to *read the footnotes*. The footnotes to financial statements are packed with information. Here are some of the highlights: * * *

Read the MD&A. You can find a narrative explanation of a company's financial performance in a section of the quarterly or annual report entitled, "Management's Discussion and Analysis of Financial Condition and Results of Operations." MD&A is *management's* opportunity to provide investors with its view of the financial performance and condition of the company. It's management's opportunity to tell investors what the financial statements show and do not show, as well as important trends and risks that have shaped the past or are reasonably likely to shape the company's future.

The SEC's rules governing MD&A require disclosure about trends, events or uncertainties known to management that would have a material impact on reported financial information. The purpose of MD&A is to provide investors with information that the company's management believes to be necessary to an understanding of its financial condition, changes in financial condition and results of operations. It is intended to help investors to see the company through the eyes of management. It is also intended to provide context for the financial statements and information about the company's earnings and cash flows.

Financial Statement Ratios and Calculations. You've probably heard people banter around phrases like "P/E ratio," [*see* Table 6.5] "current ratio" and "operating margin." But what do these terms mean and why don't they show up on financial statements? Listed below are just some of the many ratios that investors calculate from information on financial statements and then use to evaluate a company. As a general rule, desirable ratios vary by industry.

Debt-to-equity ratio compares a company's total debt to shareholders' equity. Both of these numbers can be found on a company's balance sheet. To calculate debt-to-equity ratio, you divide a company's total liabilities by its shareholder equity, or

Debt-to-Equity Ratio = Total Liabilities/Shareholders' Equity

If a company has a debt-to-equity ratio of 2 to 1, it means that the company has two dollars of debt to every one dollar shareholders invest in the company. In other words, the company is taking on debt at twice the rate that its owners are investing in the company. * * *

P/E ratio compares a company's common stock price with its earnings per share. To calculate a company's P/E ratio, you divide a company's stock price by its earnings per share, or

P/E Ratio = Price per share/Earnings per share

If a company's stock is selling at $20 per share and the company is earning $2 per share, then the company's P/E Ratio is 10 to 1. The company's stock is selling at 10 times its earnings. * * *

Note on EBITDA

Chapter 7, which deals with valuation, shows that the concept of earnings before interest, taxes, depreciation and amortization (EBITDA) is an important valuation tool. EBITDA is a broad measure of income and is computed by removing from the income statement deductions for (1) all interest and dividends paid by the firm, (2) all income taxes paid by the firm, and (3) all depreciation and amortization, both non-cash deductions, taken by the firm.

§ 6.4 FASB Revision of the Accounting Treatment of Business Combinations

A. FASB Summary of Statement No. 141 Revised (2007), Requiring the "Acquisition Method" of Accounting for Business Combinations

Why Is the FASB Issuing This Statement? The objective of this Statement is to improve the relevance, representational faithfulness, and comparability of the information that a reporting entity provides in its financial reports about a business combination and its effects. To accomplish that, this Statement establishes principles and requirements for how the acquirer:

- Recognizes and measures in its financial statements the identifiable assets acquired, the liabilities assumed, and any noncontrolling interest in the acquiree

- Recognizes and measures the goodwill acquired in the business combination or a gain from a bargain purchase
- Determines what information to disclose to enable users of the financial statements to evaluate the nature and financial effects of the business combination.

What Is the Scope of This Statement? This Statement applies to all transactions or other events in which an entity (the acquirer) obtains control of one or more businesses (the acquiree), including those sometimes referred to as "true mergers" or "mergers of equals" * * *.

How Will This Statement Improve Current Accounting Practice? This Statement replaces FASB Statement No. 141, Business Combinations. This Statement retains the fundamental requirements in Statement 141 that the acquisition method of accounting (which Statement 141 called the purchase method) be used for all business combinations and for an acquirer to be identified for each business combination. This Statement defines the acquirer as the entity that obtains control of one or more businesses in the business combination and establishes the acquisition date as the date that the acquirer achieves control. * * *

This Statement retains the guidance in Statement 141 for identifying and recognizing intangible assets separately from goodwill. The main features of this Statement and the more significant improvements it makes to how the acquisition method was applied in accordance with Statement 141 are described below.

Recognizing and Measuring the Identifiable Assets Acquired, the Liabilities Assumed, and Any Noncontrolling Interest in the Acquiree. This Statement requires an acquirer to recognize the assets acquired, the liabilities assumed, and any noncontrolling interest in the acquiree at the acquisition date, measured at their fair values as of that date, with limited exceptions specified in the Statement. That replaces Statement 141's cost-allocation process, which required the cost of an acquisition to be allocated to the individual assets acquired and liabilities assumed based on their estimated fair values. * * * Statement 141 required the acquirer to include the costs incurred to effect the acquisition (acquisition-related costs) in the cost of the acquisition that was allocated to the assets acquired and the liabilities assumed. This Statement requires those costs to be recognized separately from the acquisition. In addition, in accordance with Statement 141, restructuring costs that the acquirer expected but was not obligated to incur were recognized as if they were a liability assumed at the acquisition date. This Statement requires the acquirer to recognize those costs separately from the business combination. Therefore, this Statement improves the relevance, completeness, and representational faithfulness of the information provided in financial reports about the assets acquired and the liabilities assumed in a business combination. * * *

Assets and Liabilities Arising from Contingencies. This Statement improves the completeness of the information reported about a business combination by changing the requirements for recognizing assets acquired and liabilities assumed arising from contingencies. Statement 141 permitted deferred recognition of preacquisition contingencies until the recognition criteria for FASB Statement No. 5, Accounting for Contingencies, were met. This Statement requires an acquirer to recognize assets acquired and liabilities assumed arising from contractual contingencies as of the acquisition date, measured at their acquisition-date fair values. * * *

Recognizing and Measuring Goodwill * * *. This Statement requires the acquirer to recognize goodwill as of the acquisition date, measured as a residual, which in most types of business combinations will result in measuring goodwill as the excess of the consideration transferred plus the fair value of any noncontrolling interest in the acquiree at the acquisition date over the fair values of the identifiable net assets acquired.

Statement 141 also required goodwill to be recognized and measured as a residual. However, as described below, this Statement improves the way in which an acquirer's obligations to make payments conditioned on the outcome of future events (often called contingent consideration) are recognized and measured, which in turn improves the measure of goodwill. * * *

B. FASB Statement 142 on Treatment of Goodwill and Other Intangibles in Business Combinations

Financial Accounting Standards Board, Summary of Statement No. 142 Goodwill and Other Intangible Assets

(June 2001)

Summary. This Statement addresses financial accounting and reporting for acquired goodwill and other intangible assets and supersedes APB Opinion No. 17, *Intangible Assets.* It addresses how intangible assets that are acquired individually or with a group of other assets (but not those acquired in a business combination) should be accounted for in financial statements upon their acquisition. This Statement also addresses how goodwill and other intangible assets should be accounted for after they have been initially recognized in the financial statements. * * *

Differences between This Statement and Opinion 17. This Statement changes the unit of account for goodwill and takes a very different approach to how goodwill and other intangible assets are accounted for subsequent to their initial recognition. Because goodwill and some intangible assets will no longer be amortized, the reported amounts of goodwill and intangible assets (as well as total assets) will not decrease at the same time and in the same manner as under previous standards. There may be more volatility in reported income than under previous standards because impairment losses are likely to occur irregularly and in varying amounts.

This Statement changes the subsequent accounting for goodwill and other intangible assets in the following significant respects:

Acquiring entities usually integrate acquired entities into their operations, and thus the acquirers' expectations of benefits from the resulting synergies usually are reflected in the premium that they pay to acquire those entities. However, the transaction-based approach to accounting for goodwill under Opinion 17 treated the acquired entity as if it remained a stand-alone entity rather than being integrated with the acquiring entity; as a result, the portion of the premium related to expected synergies (goodwill) was not accounted for appropriately. This Statement adopts a more aggregate view of goodwill and bases the accounting for goodwill on the units of the combined entity into which an acquired entity is integrated (those units are referred to as reporting units).

Opinion 17 presumed that goodwill and all other intangible assets were wasting assets (that is, finite lived), and thus the amounts assigned to them should be amortized in determining net income; Opinion 17 also mandated an arbitrary ceiling of 40 years for that amortization. This Statement does not presume that those assets are wasting assets. Instead, goodwill and intangible assets that have indefinite useful lives will not be amortized but rather will be tested at least annually for impairment. Intangible assets that have finite useful lives will continue to be amortized over their useful lives, but without the constraint of an arbitrary ceiling. * * *

Goodwill will be tested for impairment at least annually using a two-step process that begins with an estimation of the fair value of a reporting unit. The first step is a screen for potential impairment, and the second step measures the amount of impairment, if any. * * *

§ 6.5 SEC'S Financial Disclosure Requirements Relating to Mergers — Regulation S-X

Regulation S-X, Provisions Relating to Disclosures in Merger Registration Statements and Proxy Statements

17 CFR § 210.1.01 et seq.

Application of Regulation S-X (17 CFR Part 210)

Reg. § 210.1–01.

(a) This part * * * sets forth the form and content of and requirements for financial statements required to be filed as a part of:

(1) Registration statements under the Securities Act of 1933 [*e.g.*, the S-1, S-3 and S-4, *see* Chapters 4 and 13] * * * ; and

(2) [A]nnual or other reports under sections 13 [*e.g.*, the 8-K, 10-K and 10-Q, *see* Chapter 4] and * * * proxy and information statements under section 14 of the Securities Exchange Act of 1934 [*see* Chapter 13]. * * *

Consolidated Financial Statements of the Registrant and its Subsidiaries

Reg. § 210.3A–02.

In deciding upon consolidation policy, the registrant must consider what financial presentation is most meaningful in the circumstances and should follow in the consolidated financial statements [statements that include the parent corporation and all of its controlled subsidiaries] principles of inclusion or exclusion which will clearly exhibit the financial position and results of operations of the registrant. There is a presumption that consolidated statements are more meaningful than separate statements and that they are usually necessary for a fair presentation when one entity directly or indirectly has a controlling financial interest in another entity. * * * [With consolidated statements, which are presumed to be required where a parent corporation owns a majority of the stock of a sub, the assets, liabilities, and income of the controlled sub are simply added to such amounts on the parent's books. If an investment is made in a non-controlled corporation, the investment is carried on the parent's balance sheet as an "investment." Under certain circumstances, such an investment is adjusted for the parent's allocable share of the sub's income or loss. This is known as the equity method of accounting.]

Consolidated Balance Sheets

Reg. § 210.3–01. (a) There shall be filed, for the registrant and its subsidiaries consolidated, audited balance sheets as of the end of each of the two most recent fiscal years. * * * [In certain cases an unaudited interim balance sheet may be filed.]

Consolidated Statements of Income and Changes in Cash Flows

Reg. § 210.3–02. (a) There shall be filed, for the registrant and its subsidiaries consolidated and for its predecessors, audited statements of income and cash flow for each of the three fiscal years preceding the date of the most recent audited balance sheet being filed or such shorter period as the registrant (including predecessors) has been in existence. * * * [In certain cases an unaudited interim statements of income and changes in cash flow may be filed.]

Changes in Other Stockholders' Equity

Reg. § 210.3–04. An analysis of the changes in each caption of other stockholders' equity presented in the balance sheets shall be given in a note or separate statement. * * *

Financial Statements of Businesses Acquired or to be Acquired

Reg. § 210.3–05. (a) *Financial statements required.* (1) Financial statements prepared and audited in accordance with this regulation should be furnished for the periods specified in (b) below if any of the following conditions exist:

(i) Consummation of a business combination accounted for as a purchase has occurred or is probable * * *

(b) *Periods to be presented.* (1) If securities are being registered to be offered to the security holders of the business to be acquired, the financial statements specified in §§ 210.3–01 [consolidated balance sheet] and 210.3–02 [consolidated statement of income] shall be furnished for the business to be acquired, except as provided otherwise for filings on Form * * * S-4 or F-4. The financial statements covering fiscal years shall be audited except as provided in Item 14 of Schedule 14A with respect to certain proxy statements or in registration statements filed on Forms * * * S-4 or F-4.

(2) In all cases not specified in paragraph (b)(1) of this section, financial statements of the business acquired or to be acquired shall be filed for the periods specified in this paragraph (b)(2) or such shorter period as the business has been in existence. The periods for which such financial statements are to be filed shall be determined using the conditions specified in the definition of significant subsidiary [*i.e.*, a sub in which the parent has a more than 10% interest] in § 210.1–02(w) as follows:

(i) If none of the conditions exceeds 20 percent, financial statements are not required. * * *

(ii) If any of the conditions exceeds 20 percent, but none exceed 40 percent, financial statements shall be furnished for at least the most recent fiscal year and any interim periods specified in §§ 210.3–01 and 210.3–02.

(iii) If any of the conditions exceeds 40 percent, but none exceed 50 percent, financial statements shall be furnished for at least the two most recent fiscal years and any interim periods specified in §§ 210.3–01 and 210.3–02.

(iv) If any of the conditions exceeds 50 percent, the full financial statements specified in §§ 210.3–01 and 210.3–02 shall be furnished. However, financial statements for the earliest of the three fiscal years required may be omitted if net revenues reported by the acquired business in its most recent fiscal year are less than $25 million. * * *

Article 11—Pro Forma Financial Information

Presentation Requirements

Reg. § 210.11–01. [*See* the pro forma financial information provided in the HP-Compaq Merger, Section 6.6]

(a) Pro forma financial information shall be furnished when any of the following conditions exists:

(1) During the most recent fiscal year or subsequent interim period for which a balance sheet is required by § 210.3–01, a significant business combination accounted for as a purchase has occurred;

(2) After the date of the most recent balance sheet filed pursuant to § 210.3–01, consummation of a significant business combination to be accounted for by the purchase method * * * of accounting has occurred or is probable;

(3) Securities being registered by the registrant are to be offered to the security holders of a significant business to be acquired or the proceeds from the offered securities will be applied directly or indirectly to the purchase of a specific significant business;

(4) The disposition of a significant portion of a business either by sale, abandonment or distribution to shareholders by means of a spin-off, split-up or split-off [*see* Chapter 25] has occurred or is probable and such disposition is not fully reflected in the financial statements of the registrant included in the filing; * * *

(b) A business combination or disposition of a business shall be considered significant if:

(1) A comparison of the most recent annual financial statements of the business acquired or to be acquired and the registrant's most recent annual consolidated financial statements filed at or prior to the date of acquisition indicates that the business would be a significant subsidiary pursuant to the conditions specified in § 210.1–02(w), substituting 20 percent for 10 percent each place it appears therein; or

(2) The business to be disposed of meets the conditions of a significant subsidiary. * * *

Preparation Requirements

Reg. § 210.11–02. (a) *Objective.* Pro forma financial information should provide investors with information about the continuing impact of a particular transaction by showing how it might have affected historical financial statements if the transaction had been consummated at an earlier time. * * *

(b) *Form and content.* (1) Pro forma financial information shall consist of a pro forma condensed balance sheet, pro forma condensed statements of income, and accompanying explanatory notes. [*See* HP-Compaq Merger, Section 6.6] * * *

§ 6.6 SEC Disclosure Required by FASB Statements 141 and 142 in Merger Proxy Statement— The Acquisition by HP of Compaq in Exchange for HP Stock

Joint Proxy Statement of Hewlett Packard and Compaq and Prospectus of Hewlett Packard, As Filed on Form S-4

(November 15, 2001)

Hewlett-Packard Company and Compaq Computer Corporation have agreed to combine their businesses under the terms of an Agreement and Plan of Reorganization, which we refer to as the merger agreement, that is described in this joint proxy statement/prospectus. [The transaction was a tax-free reverse subsidiary merger (*see* Chapter 5) in which the shareholders of Compaq received shares of HP.]

Accounting Treatment of the Merger. In accordance with United States generally accepted accounting principles, HP will account for the merger using the purchase method [now acquisition method] of accounting. Under this method of accounting, HP will record the market value (based on an average of the closing prices of HP common stock for a range of trading days from two days before and after September 3, 2001, the announcement date) of its common stock issued in connection with the merger, the fair value of the options to purchase shares of Compaq common stock assumed in connection with the merger and the amount of direct transaction costs associated with the merger as the estimated purchase price of acquiring Compaq. [Note: transaction costs are now treated as an expense.] HP will allocate the estimated purchase price to the net tangible and amortizable intangible assets acquired (including developed and core technology and patents, customer contracts and lists, and distribution agreements), intangible assets with indefinite lives and in-process research and development, based on their respective fair values at the date of the completion of the merger. Any excess of the estimated purchase price over those fair values will be accounted for as goodwill.

Amortizable intangible assets, currently estimated at $4.1 billion, will generally be amortized over useful lives ranging from two to ten years, resulting in an estimated accounting charge for amortization attributable to these items of approximately $600 million on an annual basis. In-process research and development, which is currently estimated at $1 billion, will be expensed during the fiscal quarter in which the merger is completed. In accordance with the Statement of Financial Accounting Standards No. 142, "Goodwill and Other Intangible Assets," intangible assets with indefinite lives, and goodwill resulting from a business combination completed subsequent to June 30, 2001, will not be amortized but instead will be tested for impairment at least annually (more frequently if certain indicators are present). The amount of the estimated purchase price allocated to goodwill and intangible assets with indefinite lives is estimated to be approximately $10.7 billion.

In the event that the management of the combined company determines that the value of goodwill or intangible assets with indefinite lives has become impaired, the combined company will incur an accounting charge for the amount of impairment during the fiscal quarter in which the determination is made. In addition, in the event that the management of the combined company determines that the useful life of any intangible assets with indefinite lives has become definite, the intangible asset will be amortized over its remaining useful life, and the combined company will incur an accounting charge related to such amortization during each fiscal quarter of the intangible asset's remaining useful life. The amounts listed in the above paragraph are only preliminary estimates, however, actual amounts may differ from these estimates. * * *

Unaudited Pro Forma Condensed Combined Consolidated Financial Statements

The unaudited pro forma condensed combined consolidated balance sheet as of July 31, 2001 and the unaudited pro forma condensed combined consolidated statements of earnings for the nine months ended July 31, 2001 and for the year ended October 31, 2000 that follow are based on the historical financial statements of HP and Compaq after giving effect to the merger as a purchase of Compaq by HP using the purchase method of accounting. * * * [*See* next two pages.}

Notes to Unaudited Pro Forma Condensed Combined Consolidated Financial Statements

1. Basis of Pro Forma Presentation * * *

Under the purchase method of accounting, the total estimated purchase price [$24 billion] is allocated to Compaq's net tangible and intangible assets based on their estimated fair values as of the date of the completion of the merger. * * * [T]he preliminary estimated purchase price is allocated as follows (in millions): [*See* page 433.]

Unaudited Pro Forma Condensed Combined Consolidated Balance Sheet of HP and Compaq

July 31, 2001
(In millions)

	Historical			
	HP	Compaq	Pro Forma Adjustments	Pro Forma Combined
Assets				
Current Assets:				
Cash and cash equivalents	$2,727	$3,829	$ - -	$6,556
Short-term investments	513	- -	- -	513
Accounts receivable, net	4,900	5,104	- -	10,004
Financing Receivables, net	2,153	1,067	- -	3,220
Inventory	5,489	1,731	50	7,270
Other current assets	5,180	3,191	- -	8,371
Total current assets	20,962	14,922	50	35,934
Property, plant and equipment, net	4,613	3,300	1,100	9,013
Long-term investments and other assets	6,347	4,300	(1,989)	8,658
Amortizable intangible assets, net	36	1,492	2,608	4,136
Goodwill and intangible assets with indefinite lives	416	227	10,522	11,165
Total assets	$32,374	$24,241	$12,291	$68,906
Liabilities and stockholders' equity				
Current liabilities:				
Notes payable and short-term borrowings	$2,012	$1,209	$ - -	$3,221
Accounts payable	3,238	3,434	- -	6,672
Deferred revenue	1,879	1,249	(249)	2,879
Other accrued liabilities	6,821	4,546	150	11,517
Total current liabilities	13,950	10,438	(99)	24,289
Long-term debt	3,511	875	- -	4,386
Other liabilities	1,044	1,186	1,282	3,512
Total stockholders' equity	13,869	11,742	11,108	36,719
Total liabilities and stockholders' equity	$32,374	$24,241	$12,291	$68,906

Unaudited Pro Forma Condensed Combined Consolidated Statement of Earnings of HP and Compaq

Nine Months ended July 31, 2001

(In millions, except per share amounts)

	Historical			
	HP	Compaq	Pro Forma Adjustments	Pro Forma Combined
Net revenue:				
Products	$27,856	$23,999	$ - -	$51,855
Services	5,846	4,937	- -	10,783
	---------------		---------	--------
Total net revenue	33,702	28,936	- -	62,638
Cost and expenses:				
Cost of products sold and services/(1)/	24,890	22,374	95	47,359
Research and development	2,020	1,093	- -	3,113
Selling, general and administrative/(1)/	5,460	4,396	15	9,871
Restructuring and related charges	102	656	- -	758
Amortization of intangible assets	12	224	226	462
Amortization of goodwill	112	22	(22)	112
	---------------		---------	--------
Total cost and expenses	32,596	28,765	314	61,675
	---------------		---------	--------
Earnings from operations	1,106	171	(314)	963
Interest and other, net	(604)	(1,446)	- -	(2,050)
Earnings (loss) from continuing operations before taxes	502	(1,275)	(314)	(1,087)
Provision (benefit) for taxes	39	(402)	(110)	(473)
Net earnings (loss) from continuing operations/(2)/	$463	$(873)	$(204)	$(614)
	=====	=====	=====	=====
Net earnings (loss) per share from continuing operations/(2)/				
Basic	$0.24	$(0.52)		$(0.20)
Diluted	$0.24	$(0.52)		$(0.20)
Average number of shares and share equivalents				
Basic	1,935	1,690		3,004
Diluted	1,976	1,690		3,004

Preliminary estimated purchase price allocation:	
Net tangible assets	$10,275
Amortizable intangible assets:	
Customer contracts and lists, distribution agreements	2,400
Developed and core technology, patents	1,500
Other	200
Goodwill and intangible assets with indefinite lives	10,749
Net deferred tax liability	(2,124)
In-process research and development	1,000
Total preliminary estimated purchase price allocation	$24,000

Of the total estimated purchase price, a preliminary estimate of $10.3 billion has been allocated to net tangible assets acquired and approximately $4.1 billion has been allocated to amortizable intangible assets acquired. The depreciation and amortization related to the fair value adjustment to net tangible assets and the amortization related to the amortizable intangible assets are reflected as pro forma adjustments to the unaudited pro forma condensed combined consolidated statements of earnings. * * *

Of the total estimated purchase price, approximately $10.7 billion has been allocated to goodwill and intangible assets with indefinite lives. Goodwill represents the excess of the purchase price of an acquired business over the fair value of the underlying net tangible and intangible assets. * * *

In accordance with the Statement of Financial Accounting Standards No. 142, "Goodwill and Other Intangible Assets," goodwill and intangible assets with indefinite lives resulting from business combinations * * * will not be amortized but instead will be tested for impairment at least annually (more frequently if certain indicators are present). In the event that the management of the combined company determines that the value of goodwill or intangible assets with indefinite lives has become impaired, the combined company will incur an accounting charge for the amount of impairment during the fiscal quarter in which the determination is made. * * *

§ 6.7 Illustration of an Impairment Charge Resulting from a Merger — AOL-Time Warner

AOL Time Warner, Inc., SEC Form 10-K, for Fiscal Year Ending December 31, 2002, Discussing Impairment Charge Relating to the AOL-Time Warner Merger

Merger Accounting. The merger of America Online and Time Warner [which took place in 2000] has been accounted for by AOL-Time Warner as an acquisition of Time Warner under the purchase method of accounting for business combinations. Under the purchase method of accounting, the cost, including transaction costs, of approximately $147 billion to acquire Time Warner was allocated to the underlying net assets, based on their respective estimated fair values. The excess of the purchase price over the estimated fair values of the net assets acquired was recorded as goodwill. * * *

Accounting for Goodwill and Other Intangible Assets. * * * FAS142 requires that goodwill and certain intangible assets be assessed for impairment using fair value measurement techniques. Specifically, goodwill impairment is determined using a two-step process. The first step of the goodwill impairment test is used to identify potential impairment by comparing the fair value of a reporting unit (generally, the Company's operating segment) with its net book value (or carrying amount), including goodwill. If the fair value of a reporting unit exceeds its carrying amount, goodwill of the reporting unit is considered not impaired and the second step of the impairment test is unnecessary. If the carrying amount of a reporting unit exceeds its fair value, the second step of the goodwill impairment test is performed to measure the amount of impairment loss, if any. The second step of the goodwill impairment test compares the implied fair value of the reporting unit's goodwill with the carrying amount of that goodwill. If the carrying amount of the reporting unit's goodwill exceeds the implied fair value of that goodwill, an impairment loss is recognized in an amount equal to that excess. * * *

During the first quarter of 2002, the Company completed its initial impairment review and recorded a $54.235 billion non-cash pre-tax charge for the impairment of goodwill, substantially all of which was generated in the Merger. * * * [This means that $54 billion of the $147 billion in value of stock paid by AOL to acquire Time in 2000 had disappeared by 2002.]

§6.8 Comparing the Treatment of Goodwill under the Federal Income Tax and the Financial Accounting Rules

Under Code Section 197, an acquiring firm that acquires a target's assets in a taxable acquisition or makes a Section 338 election to step up the basis of the target's assets after an acquisition of the target's stock, receives an amortization deduction for the costs of goodwill and certain other intangibles. (*See* Chapter 5) The amortization deduction is taken on a pro rata basis over a fifteen-year period. No goodwill arises for federal income tax purposes in a taxable acquisition of the target's stock without a Section 338 election and in an acquisition of a target in a tax-free reorganization. However, goodwill will arise for financial accounting purposes in any type of acquisition, taxable or tax-free reorganization, where the purchase price exceeds the fair market value of the identifiable assets; in such case, there is no amortization deduction for goodwill under the financial accounting rules, but there is a possible future impairment charge.

§6.9 Price Earning Ratio Magic

Stephen D. Hogan and Marsha Cope Huie, Bigness, Junk and Bust-Ups: End of the Fourth Merger Wave?

Antitrust Bulletin/Winter 1992, 881 (Footnote 65) (1992)

Footnote 65 * * * Normally, if a company with a higher than average PE ratio of, say, 20 acquired a company whose PE was only 10 by exchanging its stock for stock in the target company, it is rational to expect that the combined firm would have a PE less than 20 but greater than 10.

Yet that is not what happened. During the middle 1960s at least, investors typically accorded the post-acquisition company the same PE of 20 as the acquiring firm enjoyed before the acquisition. Investors may have done so for any of several reasons, but two in particular stand out. First, they may have believed that the target firm's management was inferior and not able to achieve the target company's full potential. If true, combining the target firm with another whose management had proven its ability to realize company potential—why else the lofty PE ratio of 20?—and sacking the targeted firm's management would almost guarantee an improved performance for the targeted firm's operations. The combined operation would be managed by the acquiring management team that would presumably be able to continue realizing great potential. Hence, investors rationalized the lofty PE of 20 for the merged firm.

There also is a second possibility. If the acquiring firm were large and the target firm were small, operations and earnings of the smaller firm would doubtless be swallowed up and dominated by the larger firm. Investors might then rightly see that the smaller firm's impact on the combined firm's earnings would be small or even insignificant. In either case, it is plausible to suppose that investors would price the shares of the combined firm at the larger firm's historic PE of 20.

As long as this kind of magic worked, and it did through the mid-1960s, shareholders of both the acquiring company and the target company would benefit, sometimes handsomely. This was especially true if the acquisition were handled with a simple exchange of shares rather than with cash. For instance, suppose a high PE company had 1,000 shares outstanding, with each earning $5 and selling in the marketplace for $100. Total earnings would equal $5,000 and the PE would be 20. Suppose further that the 100 outstanding shares of a low PE firm also earned $5 each, but sold for a PE of only 5, or for $25.

In an effort to buy the low PE company, the high PE company might try to induce the low PE shareholders to sell by offering them one of its shares for every two shares of the low PE firm. The latter's shareholders would probably jump at the offer because they would be exchanging shares worth $50 for one worth $100. They would instantly receive a premium over prevailing market price of $50 and, by selling, would double their money.

The acquiring firm's shareholders would also benefit from the deal. In a simple stock transaction, the acquiring firm merely prints up the required 50 additional shares of stock and hands them over to the target shareholders, in the process retiring the target's old shares. There would be no exchange of cash. But total earnings for the post-acquisition firm would rise from $5,000 to $5,500, yielding per share earnings for each of the 1,050 shares of $5.23. Moreover, each of the shares would be priced at $104.60, an increase over the pre-acquisition price of $100. With this kind of financial alchemy, a high PE firm had merely to print up new stock certificates and everybody would make money. This was magic of the highest order.

Note

This type of PE magic was possible under the prior pooling of interest rules, because the target's income was not reduced by increased depreciation or amortization deductions. Is it possible today with the required purchase accounting rules? And if so, under what conditions?

§6.10 Summary Problems on Accounting Aspects of Acquisitions

Acquiring Corporation (AC) is planning to acquire Target Corporation (TC). Both AC and TC are calendar year corporations, and the acquisition is going to take place on January 1, 2017.

TC's balance sheet as of December 31, 2016 on a book value and a fair market value (FMV) basis is as set forth below in Table 6.1. The FMV basis was determined by an analysis by AC of the value of TC's assets.

Table 6.1

TC's BALANCE SHEET
December 31, 2016

		Book Value	FMV
A.	Assets	Book Value	FMV
1.	Cash	$10K	$10K
2.	Inventory	$50K	$75K
3.	Plant	$100K	$150K
4.	Goodwill	-0-	$65K
5.	Total	$160K	$300K
B.	**Liabilities and Shareholders' Equity**		
1.	Liabilities		
	a. Accounts Payable	$60K	$60K
2.	Shareholders' Equity		
	a. Par Value	$10K	
	b. Paid-in-Surplus	$10K	
	c. Retained Earnings	$80K	
	d. Total Shareholders' Equity (Net Worth)	$100K	$240K
3.	Total Liabilities and Shareholders' Equity	$160K	$300K

TC's income statement for calendar year 2016 is as follows:

Table 6.2

TC's INCOME STATEMENT
For 2016

Gross Sales	$210K
Deductions	$90K
Net Before Taxes	$120K
Taxes (50%)	$60K
Earnings	$60K

TC has 6000 common shares outstanding, and the market price per share is $40 for a total fair market value of $240K, which is equal to the Total Shareholders' Equity of $240K computed on a FMV basis. Since TC's earnings for 2016 were $60K, the earnings are $10 per share (*i.e.*, $60K ÷ 6000), and the Price-Earnings ratio is $40 to $10 or 4 to 1.

AC's balance sheet as of December 31, 2016 on a book value basis is set out in Table 6.3, as follows:

Table 6.3

AC's BALANCE SHEET
December 31, 2016

			Book Value
A.	**Assets**		
	1.	Cash	$350K
	2.	Inventory	$200K
	3.	Plant	$400K
	4.	Total	$950K
B.	**Liabilities and Shareholders' Equity**		
	1.	Liabilities Accounts Payable	$150K
	2.	Shareholders' Equity	
		a. Par Value	$100K
		b. Paid-in-Surplus	$300K
		c. Retained Earnings	$400K
		d. Total Shareholders' Equity (Net Worth)	$800K
	3.	Total Liabilities and Shareholders' Equity	$950K

AC has 20,000 shares outstanding. The shares were originally issued at $20 per share for an aggregate of $400K, which is the total of the par value of $5 per share (total par value of $100K) and the paid in surplus (*i.e.*, the excess of par value paid for the shares) of $15 per share (total paid in surplus of $300K). The current trading value of these shares is $1,600,000 or $80 per share. Thus, there is a premium of $800K over the book value of AC's Shareholders' Equity, that is, the par value of $100K, plus the paid in surplus of $300K, plus the retained earnings of $400K.

AC's income statement for calendar year 2016 is set out in Table 6.4

Table 6.4

AC's INCOME STATEMENT
For 2016

Gross Sales	$740K
Deductions	$340K
Net Before Taxes	$400K
Taxes (50%)	$200K
Earnings	$200K

AC's earnings per share are $10 (*i.e.*, $200K ÷ 20K) and the price to earnings ratio is $80 to $10, or 8 to 1.

Table 6.5 provides a summary of the earnings information for AC and TC:

Table 6.5
Summary of Earnings Information of AC and TC
For 2016

		AC	TC
a.	Number of Shares Outstanding	20,000	6,000
b.	Net Worth on a FMV Basis	$1,600,000	$240,000
c.	Market Price Per Share (b) a)	$80	$40
d.	Earnings	$200K	$60K
e.	Earnings Per Share (d ÷ a)	$10	$10
f.	Price-Earnings Ratio (c ÷ e)	$80 : $10 8 : 1	$40 : $10 4 : 1

TC's tangible assets have a useful life of 10 years and are to be written off on a straight line basis. None of TC's intangibles are amortizable for financial accounting purposes. Both AC's and TC's inventory turns over once a year.

1. AC purchases TC's assets for $240K in cash, plus the assumption of TC's $60K of liabilities. TC is liquidated, distributing the net after-tax proceeds to its shareholders.

a. Construct AC's post-acquisition balance sheet.

b. In 2017 the gross sales for the combined entity are equal to the sum of the gross sales for AC and TC in 2016. Also, the deductions for 2017 attributable to AC's pre-acquisition assets are the same as its deductions for 2016. In 2016 AC had net earnings of $200K and TC had net earnings of $60K, for a total net earnings of $260K. What are AC's net earnings for 2017? Assume a 50% combined state and federal income tax liability. Specify the additional deductions that result from the acquisition of TC.

c. Would the results above change if TC merged into AC with TC's shareholders receiving the net after tax cash proceeds?

d. In general, what are the federal income tax consequences of the above transactions?

2. AC purchases all of TC's stock for cash of $240K. AC does not make a Section 338 election [*see* Chapter 5].

a. Construct AC's post-acquisition consolidated balance sheet.

b. In 2017 the gross sales for the combined entity are equal to the sum of the gross sales for AC and TC in 2016. Also, the deductions for 2017 attributable to AC's pre-acquisition assets are the same as its deductions for 2016. In 2016, AC had net earnings of $200K and TC had net earnings of $60K, for a total net earnings of $260K. What are AC's net earnings for 2017? Assume a 50% combined state and federal income tax liability. Specify the additional deductions that result from the acquisition of TC.

c. Would the results above change if TC were acquired in a reverse triangular (subsidiary) merger with TC's shareholders receiving $240K in cash?

d. In general, what are the federal income tax consequences of the above transactions?

3. AC issues its stock with a $240K FMV (*i.e.*, 3,000 shares at $80 per share, with $5 dollars of par value per share and $75 of paid in capital per share) in exchange for all of TC's assets, plus the assumption of TC's liabilities. TC is liquidated, distributing the AC stock to the TC shareholders.

a. Construct AC's post-acquisition balance sheet.

b. In 2017 the gross sales for the combined entity are equal to the sum of the gross sales for AC and TC in 2016. Also, the deductions for 2017 attributable to AC's pre-acquisition assets are the same as in 2016. However, the deductions for TC's pre-acquisition assets must be adjusted for the acquisition. What are AC's net earnings for 2017? Assume a 50% combined state and federal income tax liability.

c. Would the results above change if TC merged into AC with TC's shareholders receiving $240K in AC stock?

d. In general, what is the federal income tax impact of the above transactions?

4. AC issues $240K of its stock to TC's shareholders for their stock.

a. Construct AC's post-acquisition consolidated balance sheet.

b. Would the results above change if TC were acquired in a reverse or forward triangular (subsidiary) merger with TC's shareholders receiving $240K in AC stock?

c. In general, what is the federal income tax impact of the above transactions?

5. Assume that AC makes the acquisition with $240K of AC stock. What can be expected to happen to the post-acquisition value of AC's stock assuming that the market values the AC stock at AC's pre-acquisition price-earnings ratio? First answer the question under the assumption that the transaction could have been accounted for as a pooling of interest with no write-up of TC's assets and no additional deductions attributable to TC; thus, TC's and AC's pre-acquisition incomes would have been added (pooled) with no adjustments. Is there earnings magic? Then assume that the stock acquisition is accounted for as a required purchase. Is there earnings magic? What would happen to price earnings magic if all of the purchase price over the book value of TC's assets were attributable to goodwill?

References

Fiflis, *Accounting for Mergers, Acquisitions, and Investments in a Nutshell: The Interrelationships of and Criteria for, Purchase or Pooling, the Equity Method, and Parent-Company-Only and Consolidated Statements*, 37 The Business Lawyer 94 (1981).

Kling and Nugent, *Negotiated Acquisitions*, *supra* Section 1.10, at Chapter 3.

Thompson, *Mergers, Acquisitions and Tender Offers*, *supra* Section 1.10, Chapter 10.

Chapter 7

Modern Valuation Techniques in Mergers and Acquisitions

§ 7.1 Scope

The starting point for both the buyer and the seller in any merger or acquisition transaction is to determine the value of the target corporation. For the buyer (*e.g.*, the acquiring corporation), this is a capital budgeting decision that is similar to any other investment decision, such as the decision to build a new plant. For the seller (*i.e.*, either the target corporation in a sale of assets or its shareholders in a sale of stock), the determination of the target's value sets the reservation price at which the seller will stop holding and sell.

There are many different techniques for determining the value of the assets or shares of a target corporation. This chapter focuses on three commonly used techniques:

1. Valuation based on comparable target corporations (the comparable companies technique).
2. Valuation based on comparable transactions (the comparable transactions technique). This technique looks to transactions that are similar to the one in which the stock or assets of the target are being acquired. This is similar to the traditional technique for valuing real estate.
3. Valuation based on the discounting to present value of the target's expected future cash flows through the use of the discounted cash flow (DCF) technique, with the discount rate determined by the use of (a) the capital asset pricing model (CAPM), (b) arbitrage pricing theory (APT), or (c) the weighted average cost of capital (WACC).

Sections 7.4 to 7.12 focus on DCF, CAPM, APT and WACC; these are modern valuation techniques based on economic models of valuation. The DCF model provides the mechanism for discounting to present value the target's expected future cash flows, and the CAPM model, the APT model, or the WACC model provides the discount rate to be used in the DCF model.

Both CAPM and APT are derived from the efficient capital markets hypothesis that holds that if information is easily available to investors in a securities market, security prices will reflect all relevant and ascertainable information.

Modern finance theory teaches that the value of an investment, such as a target corporation, is not determined by accounting conventions, but rather equals the present value of the cash flows expected to be produced by the investment, discounted at a rate that properly reflects the risk associated with the investment. Thus, cash flow, and not reported financial earnings, is one of the key elements in modern valuation techniques.

DCF, CAPM, APT and WACC are the principal tools for implementing this modern theory, and these tools are commonly used by investment bankers and other valuation specialists involved in the merger and acquisition process.

In many situations it may be appropriate to utilize multiple techniques in valuing a target; for that reason, Section 7.13 addresses the comparable transactions and comparable companies technique.

Section 7.2 presents an introductory problem on valuation of target companies, and Section 7.3 outlines various acquisition and other contexts in which knowledge of modern valuation concepts can be important to persons who are not valuation experts. This section also examines rules of FINRA relating to the independence of investment bankers rendering fairness opinions. Section 7.4 introduces the concepts of present value and net present value (NPV). These concepts are at the heart of the DCF technique. Section 7.4 also discusses the related concept of internal rate of return. Section 7.5 expands on the DCF and NPV techniques in situations involving multiple cash flows. Section 7.6 provides guidelines for estimating the free cash flows and terminal value used in the DCF technique. Section 7.7 explores the determination, through the use of CAPM, of the discount rate that is used in the DCF model, and Section 7.8 briefly discusses the use of the APT model for determining the discount rate. This APT model is based on multiple factors, many of which are difficult to identify and quantify, whereas CAPM is based on three factors, each of which generally can be easily determined.

Section 7.9 examines the interaction between the investment decision and the financing decision, that is, the manner in which the investment in the target will be financed by the acquiror. Section 7.10 discusses the weighted average cost of capital (WACC) approach for determining the discount rate. WACC is one way of taking account of the investment decision in determining the discount rate. Section 7.11 discusses the use of DCF in acquisitions that produce synergies. Synergies arise when the combination of the acquiror and the target result in reduced costs or increased revenue that could not be realized if the two firms remained independent. Section 7.12 illustrates the application of DCF and CAPM in determining the price of a target in a merger. Section 7.13 provides an introduction to two non-DCF valuation techniques: the comparable companies technique and the comparable transactions technique. Finally, Section 7.14 looks at the law governing investment bankers' fairness opinions.

Documentary Appendix C of *M&A Statutes, Rules and Documents, supra* Section 1.1, contains excerpts from the joint presentation in 1989 by the investment banking firms of Wasserstein Perella & Co., Inc. and Shearson Lehman Hutton, Inc. (Wasserstein/Shearson) to the board of directors of Time regarding the valuation of Warner. In that presentation Wasserstein/Shearson used the DCF, comparable companies, and comparable transactions techniques. This appendix is referred to throughout this chapter, which is based on Thompson, *A Lawyer's Guide to Modern Valuation Techniques in Mergers and Acquisitions*, 21 J. of Corporation Law 457 (1996) (with permission). *See also* Thompson, *Demystifying the Use of Beta in the Determination of the Cost of Capital and an Illustration of Its Use in Lazard's Valuation of Conrail*, 25 J. of Corporation Law 241 (1999). The techniques used by Wasserstein/Shearson are still in use today.

This chapter principally relies on several of the leading treatises and books dealing with corporate finance, valuation, and the financial aspects of mergers and acquisitions. *See, e.g.*, Richard A. Brealey and Stewart C. Myers, *Principles of Corporate Finance* (4th ed. 1991) [hereinafter Brealey & Myers]; Alfred Rappaport, *Creating Shareholder Value* (1986) [hereinafter Rappaport]; Alan C. Shapiro, *Modern Corporate Finance* (1990) [hereinafter

Shapiro]; and Bradford Cornell, *Corporate Valuation: Tools for Effective Appraisal and Decision Making* (1993) [hereinafter Cornell, *Corporate Valuations*]. For a collection of materials on valuation *see* Ronald J. Gilson, and Bernard S. Black, *The Law and Finance of Corporate Acquisitions* 62 to 154 (2nd Ed. 1995) [hereinafter Gilson and Black, *Law and Finance*], and Ronald J. Gilson and Bernard S. Black, *(Some of) the Essentials of Finance and Investment* (1993). *See also* Tom Copeland, Tim Koller, and Jack Murrin, *Valuation: Measuring and Managing the Value of Companies* (3rd Ed. 2000), Burton G. Malkiel, *A Random Walk Down Wall Street* (2003), and the latest editions of *Brealey & Myers* and *Shapiro*.

When consulting the above references, the most recent editions should be used. The materials in this chapter are covered in greater detail in Chapter 11 of Thompson, *Mergers, Acquisitions and Tender Offers, supra* Section 1.10. For example, that chapter has a more detailed discussion of the potential liability faced by investment bankers in M&A transactions.

§ 7.2 Introductory Problem on Valuation of Target Corporations

Time, Inc. is considering an acquisition of Warner Communications, Inc., and Time has asked its investment bankers (Wasserstein/Shearson) to provide Time with advice concerning the value of Warner. Wasserstein/Shearson is going to utilize three valuation techniques: DCF, comparable companies, and comparable transactions.

(1) Since this is a friendly acquisition, Warner has made available the projected cash flow statement set forth on page 2 of Documentary Appendix C. Does the cash flow statement have any significance in the comparable companies and comparable transactions models? Why does the cash flow statement not have a deduction for interest? Surely Warner has outstanding debt. How is depreciation treated on the cash flow statement? How are capital expenditures and working capital treated on the cash flow statement?

(2) Wasserstein/Shearson's DCF analysis of Warner is on page 2 of Documentary Appendix C. How did Wasserstein/Shearson determine the discount rates? Assuming the risk free rate of interest is 5%, the expected market return on equities is 15%, and the asset Beta for Warner's film entertainment division is 1.2, what is the appropriate discount rate using CAPM? How did Wasserstein/Shearson determine the estimated terminal values for the film entertainment business and the present value of the terminal values? Why did Wasserstein/Shearson use a range of discount rates and a range of estimated terminal values?

(3) Wasserstein/Shearson's summary comparable transactions and comparable companies analysis is set out on page 3 of Documentary Appendix C. Why did Wasserstein/Shearson use net sales and EBIT (earnings before interest and taxes) as measures of comparability? Why did they not use EBITDA (earnings before interest, taxes, depreciation and amortization)? Why did Wasserstein/Shearson add a 50% premium in their comparable companies analysis?

(4) Wasserstein/Shearson's summary of the pre-tax segment valuation of Warner is set out on page 5 of Documentary Appendix C. Why did Wasserstein/Shearson separately value each segment? Why did it not simply value Warner's equity?

(5) Wasserstein/Shearson's valuation of Warner's equity is set out on page 6 of Documentary Appendix C. Explain the rationale for the corporate adjustments, that is, the additions and the subtractions. For example, why are cash and cash equivalents an addition and why is debt a subtraction?

§7.3 Importance of Modern Valuation Concepts for Non-Valuation Experts

A. Impact in Appraisal: Introduction to the *Technicolor* and *Orchard* Appraisal Proceedings

The importance of modern valuation concepts is highlighted in the Delaware Supreme Court's decision in *Weinberger v. UOP, Inc.*, Section 3.14.B. There the court held that in determining the value of stock in appraisal proceedings, Delaware courts are no longer required to use the Delaware block method [*see* Section 2.10.F.1] exclusively, but may follow a more "liberal approach," including "proof of value by any techniques or methods which are generally considered acceptable in the financial community." * * * In *Weinberger*, the plaintiff's investment analyst used both the DCF technique and the comparable transactions approach in valuing the target company.

The *American Law Institute's Principles of Corporate Governance* project proposes that in appraisal proceedings involving arm's length transactions, "fair value should be determined using customary valuation concepts and techniques generally employed in the relevant securities and financial markets for similar businesses in the context of the transaction giving rise to appraisal." *See* §7.22(a).

B. Introduction to Valuation in the *Technicolor* Appraisal Proceeding

In the appraisal proceeding in *Cede & Co. v. Technicolor, Inc.*, 1990 WL161084 Del. Ch., the Delaware Chancery Court did a detailed analysis of the DCF techniques employed by the experts for each side. In introducing the DCF concept the court said:

> In many situations, the discounted cash flow technique is in theory the single best technique to estimate the value of an economic asset. Prior to our Supreme Court's decision in *Weinberger* * * *, however, that technique was not typically employed in appraisal cases in this jurisdiction. But with *Weinberger*'s implicit encouragement, this technique has become prominent.

The *Technicolor* court also gave the following general description of the DCF technique:

> The DCF model entails three basic components: an estimation of net cash flows that the firm will generate and, when, over some period; a terminal or residual value equal to the future value, as of the end of the projection period, of the firm's cash flows beyond the projection period; and finally a cost of capital with which to discount to a present value both the projected net cash flows and the estimated terminal or residual value.

Although both of the experts in the *Technicolor* case (one of whom was Professor Rappaport, whose book, *Creating Shareholder Value*, is cited throughout this chapter) used the DCF technique, the court said that their opinions of the value "cover an astonishing range." The court explained:

> Two experts looking at the same historic data and each employing a discounted cash flow valuation technique arrive at best estimates as different as $13.14 per share and $62.75 per share.

The *Technicolor* court correctly explains why it is possible to get such a difference in valuations using the DCF technique:

> While the basic three-part structure of the two DCF models of the same firm, as of the same date, will be the same, it is probably the case (and is certainly true here) that the details of the analysis may be quite different. That is, not only will assumptions about the future differ, but different methods may be used within the model to generate inputs.

Excerpts from this 1990 *Technicolor* case are used throughout this chapter to illustrate various concepts. The Delaware Supreme Court reversed the Chancery Court's 1990 decision in this case, but on grounds not pertinent to this chapter. The Supreme Court did not render a final decision in the appraisal action in this case, which involved a 1983 merger, until 2005. In that decision, the Supreme Court explained:

> This is the sixth appeal by Cinerama relating either to its statutory appraisal proceeding * * * or its shareholder rescissory damages lawsuit for fraud and unfair dealing . * * * As the Court of Chancery correctly noted, the history of this "sempiternal appraisal action" is thoroughly recorded in the annals of Delaware corporate law. * * *
>
> We remand this case with instructions to enter judgment consistent with this opinion so that this litigation, at long last, is brought to an end.

This *Technicolor* saga illustrates that valuation is complex and an art, not a science. Further, it may indicate that Delaware appraisal law is inefficient and should be amended, possibly along the lines of the MBCA, discussed in Chapter 2.

C. Introduction to Valuation in the *Orchard* Appraisal Proceeding

In the 2012 decision in *In Re: Appraisal of The Orchard Enterprises, Inc.*, 2012 Del. Ch. LEXIS 165 (Del. Ch. Ct. July 18, 2012), an appraisal action, Chancellor Strine of the Delaware Chancery Court addressed several valuation issues involving the use of the discounted cash flow model and the comparable companies model. Subsequent sections address the Chancellor's discussion of some of the issues presented in *Orchard* involving these models.

D. Impact of Fairness Opinions in SEC Disclosure Documents

The DCF technique is likely to be employed by investment bankers as one of the bases for the issuance of fairness opinions in a variety of contexts, including mergers, tender offers, and leveraged buyouts. Although investment bankers have no established industry guidelines for rendering fairness opinions, they generally use some form of DCF in conjunction with an analysis of comparable transactions and comparable companies. For example, Wasserstein/Shearson used DCF, comparable companies, and comparable transactions in valuing Warner.

Fairness opinions have become particularly important in mergers and acquisitions in view of the Delaware Supreme Court's opinion in *Smith v. Van Gorkom*, Section 3.14.C, where one of the bases of the court's decision, holding the directors liable, was the failure of the directors to follow the normal (although not legally required) practice of obtaining an opinion of an investment banker to the effect that the transaction was fair to the target's shareholders. The practical effect of the *Van Gorkom* decision is to force publicly-held firms to seek fairness opinions from investment bankers in merger, acquisition, and similar corporate change transactions.

Although a fairness opinion is not required in a going-private transaction (*i.e.*, certain acquisitions of publicly-held corporations by controlling shareholders, *see* Chapter 24) governed by SEC Rule 13e-3, the parties to such a transaction must indicate whether the transaction is fair or unfair to the target's shareholders and whether a fairness opinion was received in the transaction. If a fairness opinion is utilized in a going private transaction, which will virtually always be the case, Item 9 of Schedule 13E-3 requires the disclosures concerning fairness opinions required by Item 1015 of Regulation M-A.]*See* Chapter 13 for a discussion of Reg. M-A, which together with all other SEC provisions cited here are contained in the *M&A Statutes, Rules, and Documents, supra* Section 1.1] Item 1015 requires background information on the investment banker and a detailed description of the opinion including the procedures followed in preparing the opinion. Thus, this provision requires disclosure of the information in the "blue books" that are prepared by the investment bankers for presentation to the boards of directors. The blue book contains the analysis on which the fairness opinion is based. Blue books are required to be filed as an Exhibit to Schedule 13E-3, but are not required to be filed in arm's length transactions. This type of fairness opinion disclosure is illustrated in Documentary Appendix Q, Schedule TO and 13E-3 Offer to Purchase by Cox Communications at *Recommendation of the Special Committee; Fairness of the Offer*, of *M&A Statutes, Rules and Documents, supra* Section 1.1.

Although the above type of full disclosure was previously applicable to going private transactions only, the same type of comprehensive disclosure is now also required for arm's length acquisitions. Under Item 14(7)(b)(6) of Schedule 14A (the SEC proxy rules applicable to the target in a cash acquisition, *see* Chapter 13), if a fairness opinion is referred to in the proxy statement, the information required by Item 1015(b) of Reg. M-A is required. For an illustration of this type of disclosure in an arm's length cash merger *see* Documentary Appendix G, the Proxy Statement for Toys "R" Us, at *Opinions of the Company's Financial Advisors*, of *M&A Statutes, Rules, and Documents, supra* Section 1.1.

Also, under Item 4(b) of Form S-4 (the SEC's business combination registration statement, which applies when an acquiror is issuing its shares in a merger, *see* Chapter 13), if a fairness opinion is discussed in the registration statement, then the information required by Item 9 of Schedule 13E-3 is required. Item 9 refers in turn to Item 1015 of Reg. M-A. For an illustration of this type of disclosure in a stock merger *see* Documentary Appendix D, the J.P Morgan Chase S-4 Registration Statement and Joint Proxy Statements of J.P Morgan Chase and Bank One, at *Opinions of Financial Advisors* of Documentary Appendix E of *M&A Statutes, Rules, and Documents, supra* Section 1.1. Note particularly the use by the investment bankers for J.P. Morgan Chase of the "Dividend Discount Analysis," which is similar to the DCF model, and the "Contribution Analysis," which is only used in stock mergers. The cases involving this transaction are set out in Chapters 3 and 13.

The actual fairness opinion is attached to the applicable disclosure document, as indicated by the fairness opinion of Goldman Sachs, which is attached to Documentary Appendix Q, Schedule TO and 13E-3 Offer to Purchase by Cox Communications.

E. Impact in Other Contexts

DCF, CAPM, and WACC may also be employed in determining whether a fraudulent transfer has occurred in an LBO or similar transaction. *See* Chapter 14. For example, in LBO and similar transactions, it is common for the lenders to receive from an appraisal company an opinion to the effect that the target will be solvent after the acquisition.

F. Rule 5150, Fairness Opinions of the Financial Industry Regulatory Authority (FINRA)

1. Background and Discussion [From SEC Release Approving Predecessor of FINRA Rule 5150]

A fairness opinion addresses, from a financial point of view, the fairness of the consideration in a transaction. Fairness opinions are routinely used by directors of companies in connection with a change of control transaction, such as a merger or sale or purchase of assets, to satisfy their fiduciary duties to act with due care and in an informed manner.

Although not required by statute or regulation, fairness opinions have become commonplace in change of control transactions following the 1985 Delaware Supreme Court case of *Smith v. Van Gorkom* [*see* Section 3.14.C] in which a corporate board was held to have breached its fiduciary duty of care by approving a merger without adequate information on the transaction, including information on the value of the company and the fairness of the offering price.

In addition to providing a basis for the exercise of care by the board of directors, a fairness opinion, or information about a fairness opinion, is often provided to shareholders as a part of the proxy materials relating to a change of control transaction.

Fairness opinions express a conclusion as to the whether the consideration offered in a transaction is within the range of what would be considered "fair"; such opinions generally do not offer an opinion as to whether the consideration offered is the best price that could likely be attained or reach other matters, such as solvency issues, that may arise from the transaction.

Under the SEC's proxy rules, which apply to issuers, certain disclosures about potential conflicts of interest are provided to investor-shareholders. NASD Rule 2290 is a complementary rule that requires broker-dealers that render fairness opinions to inform investor-shareholders about the potential conflicts of interest that may exist between the firm rendering the fairness opinion and the issuer. The Rule also addresses specific procedures concerning the issuance of fairness opinions. * * *

2. Rule 5150 Fairness Opinions

5150. Fairness Opinions

(a) Disclosures

If at the time a fairness opinion is issued to the board of directors of a company the member [e.g., investment bank] issuing the fairness opinion knows or has reason to know that the fairness opinion will be provided or described to the company's public shareholders, the member must disclose in the fairness opinion:

(1) if the member has acted as a financial advisor to any party to the transaction that is the subject of the fairness opinion, and, if applicable, that it will receive compensation that is contingent upon the successful completion of the transaction, for rendering the fairness opinion and/or serving as an advisor;

(2) if the member will receive any other significant payment or compensation contingent upon the successful completion of the transaction;

(3) any material relationships that existed during the past two years or that are mutually understood to be contemplated in which any compensation was re-

ceived or is intended to be received as a result of the relationship between the member and any party to the transaction that is the subject of the fairness opinion;

(4) if any information that formed a substantial basis for the fairness opinion that was supplied to the member by the company requesting the opinion concerning the companies that are parties to the transaction has been independently verified by the member, and if so, a description of the information or categories of information that were verified;

(5) whether or not the fairness opinion was approved or issued by a fairness committee [*e.g.*, existing at the investment bank]; and

(6) whether or not the fairness opinion expresses an opinion about the fairness of the amount or nature of the compensation to any of the company's officers, directors or employees, or class of such persons, relative to the compensation to the public shareholders of the company.

(b) Procedures

Any member issuing a fairness opinion must have written procedures for approval of a fairness opinion by the member, including:

(1) the types of transactions and the circumstances in which the member will use a fairness committee to approve or issue a fairness opinion, and in those transactions in which it uses a fairness committee:

(A) the process for selecting personnel to be on the fairness committee;

(B) the necessary qualifications of persons serving on the fairness committee;

(C) the process to promote a balanced review by the fairness committee, which shall include the review and approval by persons who do not serve on the deal team to the transaction; and

(2) the process to determine whether the valuation analyses used in the fairness opinion are appropriate.

§7.4 Introduction to Present Value, Net Present Value, and Internal Rate of Return

A. The Basic Concept of Present Value

One of the basic principles of finance is that a dollar received today is worth more than a dollar received tomorrow. This is because a dollar received today can be invested today and begin earning an immediate return, whereas a dollar received tomorrow cannot be invested until tomorrow. This fundamental principle is at the heart of the present value concept: the present value (*i.e.*, today's value) of $1 to be received at some point in the future (*i.e.*, a future amount) is less than $1. Thus, the present value of a future amount can be determined by multiplying the future amount by a discount factor. The discount factor is naturally less than 1.

The present value concept can be expressed algebraically by the following formula, where PV means present value and FA means the future amount:

$$\text{PV} = \text{discount factor} \times \text{FA}_n$$

The n represents the particular period during which the FA is to be received. The discount factor is a fraction that is the reciprocal of 1 plus the required rate of return, raised to the power of n. This required rate of return, which is also known as the "discount rate," the "hurdle rate," or the "cost of capital," is represented by r. The discount factor is written as follows:

$$\frac{1}{(1 + r)^n}$$

The discount rate (r) is the reward that investors demand for making an investment today, and n represents the number of periods (*e.g.*, years) that must elapse before the particular payment (*i.e.*, FA) is received.[1] The discount factor can be obtained from standard charts which generally have on the vertical axis the number of years to run until the payment is to be received (*i.e.*, n) and on the horizontal axis the discount rate (*i.e.*, r). Such charts are generally provided as appendices to texts on corporate finance and are similar to the following chart:

Discount Factors

	Interest Rate Per Year (r)			
Number of Years (n)	1%	5%	10%	15%
1	.990	.952	.909	.870
2	.980	.907	.826	.756
3	.971	.864	.751	.658
5	.951	.784	.621	.497
10	.905	.614	.386	.247

The greater the number of years to run before the FA is to be received and the higher the interest rate, the lower the discount factor, and the lower the present value of the payment.

The greater the risk associated with an investment, the greater the reward investors will demand for making the investment. The present value of a future payment of a safe dollar is worth more than the present value of the future payment of a risky dollar. Therefore, the greater the risk, the greater the required return. One of the purposes of CAPM, APT and WACC is to determine the appropriate discount rate given the particular level of risk associated with the investment.

These concepts are illustrated as follows:

> *Example (1)*. Assume that acquiring corporation (AC) is considering the acquisition of all the stock of a closely-held target corporation (TC) and AC wants to determine how much it should pay for the stock of TC. Assume further that AC is confident that after operating TC for one year it can sell all the stock of TC for $1 million and that AC intends to make such a sale. Thus, in this situation n is 1 year because that is when the FA is to be paid. Also, assume that because TC is in a growth business TC will not be paying any dividends during the year that AC plans to hold the stock of TC. Thus, there is to be only one FA of $1 million. Finally, assume that AC has determined (through the use of CAPM, APT or WACC) that, given the risk associated with an investment in TC, the re-

1. In this chapter the compounding interval is assumed to be a year, which is the general interval used in valuing acquisition targets. Compounding can occur more frequently than once a year. For example, interest on bonds is generally compounded semiannually.

quired discount rate is 15% (*i.e.*, r is 15%). In such case, the present value of the stock of TC can be computed as follows (with the discount factor obtained from the above chart):

$$PV = \frac{1}{(1+r)^n} (\$1 \text{ million})$$

$$PV = \frac{1}{(1+.15)^1}$$

$$PV = .87\ (\$1 \text{ million})$$

$$PV = \$870{,}000$$

The present value of the expected $1 million payment on the sale of TC in one year is $870,000. Thus, as long as AC can purchase the stock of TC for no more than $870,000, AC will not have overpaid for TC.

The above example shows that there are two variables in measuring present value: first, an estimate of the FA, and second, the determination of r, the discount rate: the higher the estimate of the FA, the higher the PV, but the higher the r, the lower the PV.

In the above example there is just one FA; however, as a practical matter in most acquisition transactions it can be expected that there will be periodic FAs. An investment in a target can be expected to produce a current return (*e.g.*, dividends or free cash flow) and an expected terminal FA, which is an estimate of the final sale or liquidation value of the target. In order for the present value formula to work there must be either an estimate of the terminal FA or an infinite projection of free cash flows.

The present value can be computed on a calculator that has the capacity to compute present values by the following three-step process: First, enter each expected future payment (FA) for the period during which such payment is expected (n). Second, enter in the required rate of return (r). Finally, hit the PV button to determine the present value of such payments.

B. Basic Concept of Net Present Value

Net Present Value (NPV) is a way of determining if the cost of an investment is worth more or less than the value of the investment. Thus, NPV is found by subtracting from the PV of an investment the cost of the investment. The initial cost (IC) of an investment is the amount paid for the investment. NPV can be expressed as follows:

$$\text{NPV} = \text{IC} + \text{PV}$$

The algebraic formula for computing NPV can be written as follows:[2]

$$NPV = IC + \frac{1}{(1+r)^n} (FA_n)$$

2. Brealey & Myers, supra Chapter 7 Scope, at 13.

IC is a negative number because it represents a cash outflow and

$$\frac{1}{(1+r)^n} FA_n$$

is a positive number. Thus, if

$$\frac{1}{(1+r)^n} FA_n$$

is greater than IC, the NPV of the investment is positive. These concepts are illustrated as follows:

Example (2). Assume that in Example (1) AC is able to purchase the stock of TC for $800,000 even though the value of TC to AC is $870,000. In that case the investment has a positive NPV of $70,000 computed as follows:

$$NPV = IC + \frac{1}{(1+r)^n} FA_n$$

$$NPV = (-800{,}000) + \frac{1}{(1+.15)} (\$1 \text{ million})$$

$$NPV = (-800{,}000) + .870\ (\$1 \text{ million})$$

$$NPV = (-800{,}000) + \$870{,}000$$

$$NPV = \$70{,}000$$

Thus, the value of AC should be increased by $70,000 if it makes the acquisition.

C. Basic Concept of Internal Rate of Return

The internal rate of return (IRR) is the rate of return that discounts expected future amounts (FAs) to an amount equal to the initial cost (IC) of an investment. Therefore, the IRR is the discount rate that produces a zero NPV. The IRR is the same as the concept of the yield to maturity which is used in determining the interest rate that can be expected from an investment in bonds.

Although there are potential defects with the use of IRR, generally if the IRR of an investment exceeds the cost of capital (r) of the investment, it makes good economic sense to make the investment. This is similar to saying that if the NPV is positive it makes economic sense to make the investment. The reason for the similarity is the obvious point that if the IRR of the investment exceeds the cost of capital of the investment, then the NPV has to be positive. The more positive the NPV the greater the IRR exceeds the cost of capital (r) of an investment.

D. Relationship Between NPV and IRR

In general, there is an equivalence between the NPV rule and the IRR rule in investment decision making. Under the NPV rule, investments with a positive NPV are made. Under the IRR rule, investments with an IRR in excess of the cost of capital are made.

Notwithstanding the apparent equivalence between the NPV and IRR rules, it is commonly understood that the NPV method is superior to the IRR method and to other methods such as payback, average return on book value, and profitability index.

E. Reason for Use of NPV in Making Investment Decisions

1. In General

Shareholder wealth is enhanced if the firm invests in projects with positive NPVs. Such projects add value to the firm because the expected returns exceed the firm's cost of capital.

2. NPV and Economic Rents

Brealey and Myers explain that if a project has a "positive NPV then in a classical economic sense the project produces economic rents," that is, profits in excess of the firm's opportunity cost of capital.[3] These rents may be either persistent, indicating that the firm has monopoly or market power, or temporary (*i.e.*, quasi rents), indicating that the firm is not in long-run equilibrium.[4]

Therefore, as a practical matter whenever there is a positive NPV the firm should have some identifiable advantage over other firms in the market.

Thus, acquiring corporations should be careful to avoid the tendency to be overly optimistic in the preparation of cash flow estimates because such optimism can lead to an overstated NPV. This type of over optimism is apparently one of the principal reasons for unsuccessful acquisitions. Of course, an overstated NPV may also result from an underestimate of the cost of capital, but for reasons that will become clear later, the cost of capital is generally based on standard financial processes and, therefore, is less susceptible to errors in calculation.

This optimism in the preparation of cash flow projections can lead to the "winner's curse" which can occur in an auction. Even though the average bidder in an auction may accurately assess the value of the thing being sold (*e.g.*, the target), some bidders may underestimate the target's value and others may overestimate. The winner may be one who overestimates. Professor Roll argues that the winner's curse in acquisitions may result from hubris,[5] which is over confidence by the managers of an acquiring corporation that their valuation of a target is correct and that the lower market valuation does not fully reflect the economic value of the target. Hubris may manifest itself in an overestimate of free cash flows.

F. Capital Rationing and NPV

In many cases the capital available for acquisitions or other investments is limited. And, even if capital is not limited, management capacity may restrict the amount of a firm's

---

3. Brealy & Myers, supra Chapter 7 Scope, at 248.

4. Id.

5. Richard Roll, The Hubris Hypothesis in Corporate Takeovers, Journal of Business 197 (April, 1986).

new investments. A firm may have multiple acquisition or investment opportunities that have positive NPVs. In such cases the firm must decide which of the various opportunities to pursue. Thus, the firm is faced with choosing among several investment opportunities all of which produce a positive NPV. If capital and management resources were unlimited, the firm would invest in each project.

One way of solving this capital rationing problem is to choose the project or projects with the highest profitability index. The profitability index is the ratio of the present value of the project to the initial cost:

$$\text{Probability Index} = \frac{\text{Present Value of Project}}{\text{Initial Cost of Project}}$$

If the profitability index for a project is 1, the project has a zero NPV because the present value of the project equals the initial cost. The more the profitability index exceeds 1, the greater the profitability of the project.

§7.5 Present Value of Multiyear Income Flows: The Discounted Cash Flow and Net Present Value Formulas

A. Introduction

The formula for computing the present value of a cash flow is as follows:

$$\text{PV} = \text{Discount Factor} \times \text{FA}_\text{n}$$

$$PV = \frac{1}{(1 + r)^n} \times \text{FA}_\text{n}$$

This assumes that the required rate of return (r) is the same for each period (n), that is, the required rate for discounting an FA to be received in year two is the same as the required rate that is used for discounting an FA to be received in year 10. As will be seen in the discussion of CAPM, the r is generally the same for all periods. Although the r is the same, the discount factor,

$$\frac{1}{(1 + r)^n}$$

is different for each period. The greater the time to run to a particular payment date the lower the discount factor.

Assuming that future payments (FAs) are to be received at the end of years 1, 2 and 3, the present value or discounted cash flow (DCF) formula can be written as follows:

$$PV = \frac{FA_1}{(1+r)^1} + \frac{FA_2}{(1+r)^2} + \frac{FA_3}{(1+r)^3}$$

The shorthand expression for the DCF formula is:

$$PV = \sum \frac{FA_n}{(1+r)^n}$$

Interest is automatically compounded in the DCF formula. The assumption in the above model (which is very often the assumption in capital budgeting) is that cash flows (FAs) are paid at the end of the year.

The net present value (NPV) is determined by merely adding to the DCF formula the initial cost of the investment (IC) as follows:

$$NPV = IC + PV = IC + \sum \frac{FA_n}{(1+r)^n}$$

In essence, this involves subtracting from the present value of the cash flows the initial cost of the investment.

B. The Five Basic Steps in Using DCF and NPV

There are five basic steps in using the DCF and NPV concepts. First, the analyst must estimate the amount and timing of the income stream (*i.e.*, free cash flow, not accounting profits) or negative income stream (*i.e.*, negative cash flow) that will be generated by an investment for each year of the investment's life. This requires an estimate of the terminal value of the investment. This is the amount to be realized when the investment is liquidated or finally disposed of. The use of a terminal value simplifies the calculation of the present value of what is otherwise an infinite series of cash flows.

An investment may have a negative cash flow for a particular year because, for example, the required investment of cash for that year exceeds the net cash flow generated from operations for that year. This estimation process is explored further below in Section 7.6.

Second, the analyst must determine the appropriate discount rate for the particular investment. Although there are many techniques for determining the discount rate, three leading techniques are discussed here: (1) the capital asset pricing model (CAPM) [*see* Section 7.7], (2) arbitrage pricing theory [*see* Section 7.8], and (3) weighted average cost of capital (WACC) [*see* Section 7.10].

Third, the analyst discounts to present value using the DCF formula the free and negative cash flows for each period and the terminal value. The discounting of a negative cash flow results in a negative present value for that particular flow.

Fourth, the analyst determines the present value of the investment by adding together the positive present values of the free cash flows and the terminal value and subtracting the aggregate of the negative present values of the negative cash flows. This amount is represented algebraically as follows:

$$\sum \frac{FA_n}{(1 + r)^n}$$

FA_n represents both the free or negative cash flow for each period and the terminal value for the last period. The discount rate is r.

Finally, to compute the NPV of the investment, the analyst subtracts the initial cost (IC) of the investment from the present value of the investment as determined under paragraph Fourth. The NPV formula is as follows:

$$NPV = \text{IC} + \sum \frac{\text{FA}_\text{n}}{(1 + \text{r})^\text{n}}$$

$$NPV = \text{IC} + \frac{\text{FA}_1}{(1 + \text{r})^1} + \frac{FA_2}{(1 + r)^2} + \frac{FA_3}{(1 + r)^3} + \frac{\text{Terminal Value}}{(1 + r)^n}$$

If the result is positive, then the investment has a positive NPV and should be undertaken, unless there are other projects with positive NPVs and the firm's capital rationing technique, such as the profitability index, indicates that one or more of such other projects should be undertaken instead.

If the target has multiple lines of business this five-step process should be followed in valuing each line, with a separate discount rate determined for each line of business.

This process can be illustrated as follows.

Example (3). Acquiring corporation (AC) is considering the acquisition of all of the assets of target corporation (TC). TC is asking $1.5 million for all the assets and this is a firm non-negotiable price. TC has no outstanding debt. AC expects that it will dispose of the acquired assets three years after the acquisition. AC follows the following five-step process in determining whether to make this investment.

First, AC estimates that TC's assets will generate $100,000 of free cash flow at the end of the first year of operation and $400,000 at the end of the second year. At the end of the third year AC expects that it will sell TC for $2 million. AC does not expect any free cash flow from the operation of TC during the third year.

Second, using CAPM, APT or WACC, AC determines that the appropriate discount rate for an investment in TC's assets is 15%.

Third, AC determines the present value of each of the two free cash flows of $100,000 and $400,000 and of the $2 million terminal value. The computation is made pursuant to the following formula and the discount factors are obtained from the chart in Section 7.4.A above:

$$PV = \sum \frac{1}{(1+r)^n} \times FA_n$$

$$PV = .870(\$100{,}000) + .756(\$400{,}000) + .658(\$2 \text{ million})$$

$$PV = \$87{,}000 + \$302{,}400 + \$1{,}316{,}000$$

Fourth, AC adds the present values of the cash flows and the terminal value. This results in a present value of the investment of $1,705,400:

Present Value of $100,000	$87,000
Present Value of $400,000	$302,400
Present Value of $2 million	$1,316,000
Total Present Value	$1,705,4000

The same computation could be made on a calculator by entering each of the free cash flows and the terminal value for the applicable period and then discounting these amounts to present value at the 15% discount rate.

Finally, in order to compute the net present value (NPV) of the investment, AC subtracts from the present value of the investment ($1,705,400) the initial cost of the investment which is the $1.5 million asking price for the shares. Thus, the investment has an NPV of $205,400 and should be undertaken, unless there are other potential projects with positive NPVs and the firm's capital rationing model indicates that one or more of those other projects should be pursued instead of this one.

C. Use of DCF and Other Methodologies in Time's Acquistion of Warner

The use of the DCF methodology in Time's acquisition of Warner is illustrated in the Wasserstein/Shearson presentation to the Time board, Documentary Appendix C.

Page 2 of the Wasserstein/Shearson presentation, Documentary Appendix C, of *M&A Statutes, Rules, and Documents, supra* Section 1.1, sets forth the estimates of the free cash flows for Warner's Film Entertainment segment. This estimation process is discussed in detail in Section 7.6. Page 3 shows the computation of the present value of the Film Entertainment segment using three different discount rates and three different estimates of the terminal value. The appendix does not indicate how the range of discount rates was determined. The different terminal values are apparently determined by multiplying the projected free cash flow for the terminal year by one of four multipliers. A similar DCF process is followed for each of Warner's other business segments.

Wasserstein/Shearson also utilized the comparable transaction technique [*see e.g.*, Documentary Appendix C, page 4] and the comparable company technique [*see e.g.*, Documentary Appendix C, page 4] in valuing each of Warner's business segments.

The Wasserstein/Shearson summary of the pre-tax segment valuations of each of Warner's business segments utilizing DCF, comparable acquisitions and comparable companies is contained on page 5 of Documentary Appendix C. This is a valuation of the operating assets of each segment without taking account of associated debt. This point is discussed further in Section 7.6.E. Page 6 of Documentary Appendix C shows how the range of asset values for the various business segments are adjusted to produce an estimate of the equity value of Warner. On a per share basis, this estimate ranges from a low of $68.40 to a high of $77.12. In computing equity value, cash and investments, which are not included in the DCF analysis, are added to the asset value, and debt is subtracted. The reason for first valuing the assets and then valuing the equity, by, among other things, subtracting the outstanding debt is discussed further in Section 7.7.F.

§ 7.6 Estimating Free (or Negative) Cash Flows and Terminal Value

A. Introduction

There are two key elements in the DCF and NPV techniques: (1) estimation of the cash flows and terminal value, and (2) determination of the appropriate discount rate. This section provides some guidelines for estimating the periodic free or negative cash flows from the project and the terminal value of the project.

B. General Principles

Four general rules govern the preparation of a cash flow statement. First, the only relevant factor is cash flow; thus accounting earnings are irrelevant. Second, cash flow is estimated on an incremental basis, that is, only the cash flows resulting from the investment are taken into account. Third, the investment decision is separated from the financing decision. Fourth, inflation must be treated consistently. Each of these rules is explored below.

C. Estimating Cash Flows

Cash flow is the difference between dollars in and dollars out. Cash flow is different from the accounting earnings or profits of the firm. In computing profits accountants may defer reporting certain cash receipts to future periods or report in an earlier period certain expected future cash receipts. Also, accountants divide cash outflows between deductible expenses and capital expenditures which are recovered through depreciation deductions. Thus, accounting profits are not the same as cash flow.

Cash flow is determined on an after tax basis by deducting taxes in the year actually paid and not when the liability accrues. The taxes are computed as if the firm has no debt and, therefore, no deductible interest. Taxes are determined on the basis of the projected actual tax liability for an all equity financed transaction; not the book tax liability. Thus, cash flow is computed without taking account of the manner in which the project is financed. This is unleveraged cash flow, that is, cash flow that does not take account of any tax savings from interest deductions. This concept is illustrated on page 2 of the Wasserstein/Shearson cash flow statement for Warner in Documentary Appendix C.

The effect of any interest deduction is separately accounted for in one of two ways. First, under the adjusted net present value method (APV) [*see* Section 7.9], the taxes saved by the projected interest deductions are separately determined and then are discounted back to present value. This amount is then added to the NPV of the project to come up with APV. Second, if the discount rate is determined by the use of the weighted average cost of capital WACC [*see* Section 7.10], the effect of any tax savings from the use of debt is automatically accounted for by the use of a lower discount rate. Correctly used, these two methods should produce the same result.

Noncash deductions in computing earnings, such as depreciation deductions and amortization deductions for intangibles, are added back in computing cash flow, and cash expenditures which are not deductible in computing earnings, such as capital expenditures, are deducted in computing cash flow. Thus, computing cash flow is merely a process of subtracting from dollars coming in all dollars going out.

Also, the working capital needs of the firm should be recognized as a cash expenditure in estimating cash flows. Working capital, which includes the excess of investments in cash, accounts receivable and inventory, over accounts payable, increases with the growth of the firm.

The one exception to the dollars in rule is that the proceeds of debt and equity financing are not included as cash in, and the one exception to the dollars out rule is that interest payments to debt holders and dividends to shareholders are not deducted. As explained in Section 7.7.E., the reason for these two exceptions is that under the DCF model the financing decision is separated from the investment decision.

The above principles are set forth in the following equation:

Free Cash Flow (FCF) = (Revenue – Expense, including Depreciation, – Taxes + Depreciation – Working Capital – Capital Expenditures).

[Revenue – Expense, including Depreciation,] is the same as a firm's EBIT, earnings before interest and taxes.

A positive free cash flow indicates the funds available to pay the providers of capital (*i.e.*, the shareholders and creditors). A negative free cash flow indicates funds that must be made available to the firm by the providers of capital.

D. Estimate Cash Flows on an Incremental Basis

In projecting cash flows only additional flows that arise because of the project are considered. For example, even though accounting conventions may allocate part of the overhead cost of an acquiring corporation, such as supervisory salaries, rent, heat and lights, to a newly acquired target corporation, in projecting the cash flows expected to be generated by the target only the extra overhead cost that can be expected to result from the acquisition of the target should be included.

E. Separate the Investment Decision from the Financing Decision

The investment decision is separate from the financing decision in applying the DCF model, and, therefore, debt proceeds used to make the investment are ignored and interest and principal payments on debt are not treated as cash flows. Thus, the project is treated as if it were all equity-financed, with all cash outflows coming from shareholders and all cash inflows going to them. The financing decision is made only after a computation of NPV.

Although the impact of debt acquisition financing is ignored in applying the DCF methodology, the amount of debt that can be used to finance the transaction is in a real way constrained by the free cash flow that is available for the payment of interest and principal on the debt, taking into account, of course, the deductibility of interest, which reduces the tax liability.

The analysis of the debt repayment ability after an acquisition is often done by comparing (1) the operating cash flow, which can be estimated by earnings before depreciation, interest and taxes (EBDIT), with (2) the interest and debt repayment costs. Other analyses are undertaken, as well, including a comparison of the balance sheets, operating results, and earnings per share of the acquiring corporation after the acquisition under various financing proposals. For an illustration of this type of financing analysis in Time's acquisition of Warner *see* page 7 of the Wasserstein/Shearson presentation to Time's board (Documentary Appendix C). This page contains a portion of Wasserstein/Shearson's analysis of the financial effects of an all cash acquisition of Warner. Other analyses include the assumption of an acquisition with 50% cash and 50% stock.

The interaction between the investment decision and the financing decision is discussed further in Section 7.9.

F. Treat Inflation Consistently

The projected cash flows should reflect the projected effects of inflation because the discount rate generally reflects such effects. The discount rate is stated in terms of nominal rather than real (*i.e.*, rate minus expected inflation) terms, and it would be inconsistent to discount at a nominal rate cash flows that were stated in real (*i.e.*, noninflation adjusted) terms. Thus, it is important to state both the cash flows and the discount rate on a nominal basis. This means that an estimate of inflation is taken into account in making the cash flow projections.

G. Illustration of Estimation of Free (or Negative) Cash Flows

In estimating cash flows, the starting point is to estimate for each year running from the acquisition date to the termination date the target's inflation adjusted sales. This sales forecast is in many cases the most important element of a cash flow forecast. All other elements in the cash flow projection are driven by the projected sales.

The inflation adjusted cost of goods sold and other operating expenses are then subtracted from the sales to arrive at operating profit. This is equal to earnings before interest and taxes, or EBIT.

Next, taxes are subtracted from operating profit to reach an estimate of unleveraged net cash flow from operations, that is, cash flow without taking into account any debt. Any noncash deductions included in operating expenses, such as depreciation, amortization of goodwill and deferred taxes are added to this amount.

Finally, any needed inflation adjusted capital investments and inflation adjusted increases in working capital are subtracted. The resulting figure is unleveraged free cash flow. This is the process followed by Wasserstein/Shearson in their presentation to Time's board. [*See* page 2 of Documentary Appendix C] The process is illustrated in the following example:

> *Example (4)*. Acquiring corporation (AC) is considering the acquisition of target corporation (TC). AC has prepared the following inflation adjusted estimates of TC's free cash flow for the five-year period after the date of the acquisition. AC plans to dispose of TC at the end of the five-year period.

	Year	1	2	3	4	5
	(1) Sales	$1,600,000	$1,700,000	$1,800,000	$1,900,000	$2,100,000
–	(2) Costs of Goods Sold	350,000	475,000	500,000	575,000	650,000
–	(3) Other Operating Expenses (Including Depreciation)	150,000	125,000	100,000	75,000	50,000
=	(4) Operating Profit	1,100,000	1,100,000	1,200,000	1,250,000	1,400,000
–	(5) Taxes	300,000	300,000	350,000	350,000	350,000
=	(6) Unleveraged Net Cash Flow	800,000	800,000	850,000	900,000	1,050,000
+	(7) Depreciation	100,000	75,0000	50,0000	25,0000	—
+	(8) Amortization of Goodwill	10,000	10,000	10,000	10,000	10,000
+	(9) Deferred Taxes	—	—	—	—	—
+	(10) Any other Noncash Expenses	—	—	—	—	—
–	(11) Capital Expenditures	300,000	165,000	90,000	—	—
	(12) Increases in Working Capital and	10,000	20,000	10,000	10,000	10,000
–	(13) Any Other Non-Deductible Cash Expenditures	—	—	—	—	—
=	(14) Unleveraged Free Cash Flow	$600,000	$700,000	$800,000	$900,000	$1,000,000

H. Use of a Formula in Estimating Free Cash Flow

If specific projections of the elements of a target's free cash flows are not available, a projected cash flow statement may be prepared by using a formula which makes certain assumptions about (1) the expected growth in sales, (2) the operating profit margin, (3) the incremental fixed capital investment rate, and (4) the incremental working capital investment rate.[6] This method may be used, for example, when the acquiring corporation does not have access to the target's internal cash flow projections. Professor Rappaport gives the formula as follows:

Cash Flow = Cash In – Cash Out
= [(Sales in Prior Year) (1 + Sales Growth Rate) (Operating Profit Margin) (1 – Cash Income Tax Rate)] – [(Increase in Sales) (Incremental Fixed Capital Investment Rate) + (Increase in Sales) (Incremental Working Capital Investment Rate)][7]

The Cash In is determined as follows: Sales in the Prior Period multiplied by (1 + Sales Growth Rate) produces the expected sales for next year. This amount multiplied by the Operating Profit Margin produces the expected operating profit for the year. The Operating Profit Margin is the ratio of pre-interest, pre-tax operating profit to sales. For example, if sales are $10 million and all expenses except interest and taxes are $8 million, the operating profit is $2 million and the Operating Profit Margin is 20%. By focusing on pre-interest operating profit, the formula properly does not take interest expense into account in computing free cash flow.

6. Rappaport, supra Chapter 7 Scope, at 51–55.
7. Id.

The expected operating profit [*i.e.*, (Sales in Prior Year) (1 + Sales Growth Rate) (Operating Profit Margin)] includes allowances for depreciation, but depreciation is eliminated from the formula as discussed below.

The expected operating profit multiplied by (1 – Cash Income Tax Rate) gives the expected after-tax earnings for the year, or Cash In. The term (1 – Cash Income Tax Rate) gives the after-tax rate. For example, if the Cash Income Tax Rate is 34% the after-tax rate is 66%. The actual tax rate and not the book rate is used.

The sum of the following two Cash Out amounts is deducted from the expected after-tax earnings (Cash In) to come up with free cash flow. The first deductible amount is the Incremental Fixed Capital Investment, which is estimated by multiplying the expected Increase in Sales for the year by the historical Incremental Fixed Capital Investment Rate for the business, that is, by the historical relationship between increase in sales and increase in capital investment. Incremental Fixed Capital Investment takes into account capital expenditures minus depreciation expense, thereby eliminating depreciation from the formula. The Incremental Fixed Capital Investment Rate is computed by dividing Incremental Fixed Capital Investment by Incremental Sales:

$$\text{Incremental Fixed Capital Investment Rate (\%)} = \frac{\text{(Capital Expenditures)} - \text{(Depreciation Expense)}}{\text{Incremental Sales}}$$

$$\text{Incremental Fixed Capital Investment Rate (\%)} = \frac{\text{Incremental Fixed Capital Investment}}{\text{Incremental Sales}}$$

The second deductible amount is the Incremental Working Capital Investment, which is estimated by multiplying the expected Increase in Sales for the year by the historical Incremental Working Capital Investment Rate, that is, the historical relationship between the increase in sales and the increase in working capital. The Incremental Working Capital Investment, which "represents the net investment in accounts receivable, inventory, accounts payable and accruals that are required to support sales growth,"[8] is expressed as a percentage of sales:

$$\text{Incremental Working Capital Rate (\%)} = \frac{\text{Incremental Working Capital Investment}}{\text{Incremental Sales}}$$

Adjustments to this formula may be required for adding back amortization and other noncash deductions.

I. Estimating Free Cash Flows in *Orchard*[9]

In the 2012 appraisal decision in *Orchard*,[10] Chancellor Strine of the Delaware Chancery Court addressed the computation of free cash flows. Prior to the merger giving rise to

8. *Id.* at 54.

9. This section is adapted from Thompson, *Mergers, Acquisitions and Tender Offers*, *supra* Section 1.10, at Section 11:5.7[B].

10. In Re: Appraisal of The Orchard Enterprises, Inc., 2012 Del. Ch. LEXIS 165 (Del. Ch. Ct. July 18, 2012).

the appraisal rights, the company's management prepared three financial projections representing a "worst case," a "base case" and an "aggressive case" case.[11] At trial the valuation experts for the shareholders and the company used the same projections in computing free cash flows, but assigned different weights to them as indicated in the following table:

Valuation Expert	Worst Case	Base Case	Aggressive Case
Shareholders' Expert (Meinhart's), Assigned Weights:	0%	50%	50%
Company's Expert (Fesnak's), Assigned Weights:	NA	90%	10%

Obviously the weights assigned by the shareholder's expert produced greater free cash flow than the weights assigned by the company's expert. The Chancellor accepted the weights assigned by the company's expert, explaining:

> The special committee's representation that the base case was the most likely to occur is supported by Orchard's actual financial results for the last twelve months ("LTM") ended June 30, 2010, which are much closer to the base case projections than they are to the aggressive case projections. Orchard's revenues for 2010 in the base case projections used by [Orchard's expert] were forecasted to be $72.57 million; the actual LTM revenues as of June 30, 2010 were $67.12 million. Orchard's LTM EBITDA was $2.15 million; the base case projections used by [Orchard's expert] forecasted EBITDA of $2.9 million. Thus, Orchard's actual financial results were not even between the base and aggressive case projections—they were less than the base case projections. For these reasons, I adopt [Orchard's] approach and give 90% weight to the base case management projections and 10% weight to the aggressive case projections that were used in the fairness opinion and disclosed in Orchard's Schedule 13E.[12]

The Chancellor also addressed the impact of Orchard's net operating loss deductions (NOLs) on the computation of Orchard's estimated tax liability used in the free cash flow forecasts. As discussed above, taxes are deducted in computing free cash flows, and the availability of NOLs will reduce future taxes and thus increase free cash flow. Consequently, Orchard's expert has an incentive to understate the impact of NOLs, and the shareholder's expert has an incentive to overstate their impact. On this issue, the Chancellor concluded:

> As between Meinhart's NOL calculations and those prepared for the fairness opinion, I choose to accept the latter. Because I am accepting the projections prepared for the fairness opinion as the most accurate reflection of Orchard management's knowledge at the relevant time, I adopt the tax adjustments made in those projections by that same logic. Meinhart has not offered any reason to doubt the reliability of these tax adjustments, and therefore I do not see a reason to depart from management's view of what NOLs would be available to Orchard.[13]

11. *Id.* at *44.
12. *Id.* at *59–*60.
13. *Id.* at *51–*52.

The Chancellor also addressed as follows the impact on the DCF analysis of the "residual NOL," that is, the unused NOLs available after the forecast period:

> I also accept the value conclusion regarding leftover NOLs that Fesnak and Associates came to at the time of the fairness opinion, discounted at the court's chosen rate of 15.3% instead of Fesnak's 20%. This produces a present value for the residual NOL tax benefit of $824,000.[14]

J. Estimating Terminal Value

1. Introduction

The DCF model does not work unless there is either (1) an estimate of the final sale or liquidation value of the target, or (2) an infinite series of periodic cash flows. It appears that in most cases involving a target, the parties estimate the cash available from the final disposition of the target. As will be seen below, this was the method used by Wasserstein/Shearson in their valuation of Warner.

The terminal date is often chosen arbitrarily, and terminal (or residual or horizon) value is often the largest portion of the firm's value. For example, *see* page 3 of the Wasserstein/Shearson valuation in Documentary Appendix C, which shows that under all assumptions the present value of the terminal value exceeds the present value of the free cash flows. Professor Rappaport points out that "for most businesses only a small proportion of value can be reasonably attributed to its estimated cash flow for the next five or ten years."[15]

Brealey & Myers discuss two formulas and two rules of thumb for determining terminal value:[16]

(1) The constant growth model [*see* Section 7.6.I.2];

(2) The competitive equilibrium model [*see* Section 7.6.I.3];

(3) The price/earnings rule of thumb [*see* Section 7.6.I.4]; and

(4) The market/book rule of thumb [*see* Section 7.6.I.5].

As will be seen below, the different models for estimating terminal value can produce dramatically different results. On this point Professor Cornell says:

> Given the strengths and weaknesses of each procedure, it is wise to use more than one model to calculate the continuing value. If the different models produce similar continuing values, confidence in the estimate rises. If the different models produce different values, further research is suggested to reconcile the discrepancies.[17]

2. Estimating Terminal Value through the Constant Growth Model

The constant growth formula first requires an estimate of the free cash flow for the first year in which the target is likely to settle into a long-run growth rate, that is, the point at which the target can be expected to grow at a constant rate. The second element in the formula is an estimate of the rate of long-term growth of free cash flow. The terminal value is then determined pursuant to the following formula:

14. Id. at *52.
15. Rappaport, supra Chapter 7 Scope, at 59.
16. Brealey & Myers, supra Chapter 7 Scope, at 67.
17. Cornell, Corporate Valuation, supra Chapter 7 Scope, at 168.

$$\frac{\text{Free Cash Flow for First Year of Long-Run Growth (FCF)}}{\text{[Required Discount Rate (r)]} - \text{[Rate of Long-run Growth of Free Cash Flow (g)]}}$$

In order for this formula to work the required discount rate must exceed the long-term growth rate. This formula is similar to the constant-dividend growth valuation model that is often used by analysts in valuing marketable securities. In this model, the numerator is the expected dividend, and the denominator is the cost of equity capital minus the dividend growth rate.

The constant growth model is illustrated as follows:

Example (6). Acquiring corporation (AC) estimates that five years after the acquisition of the target corporation (TC), TC's inflation adjusted free cash flow will settle into a long-term growth pattern at an expected growth rate of 5%. The estimated free cash flow for year 5 is $1 million. Thus, in year 6, for example, free cash flow is expected to be $1,050,000 (*i.e.*, $1 million x 1.05). The required discount rate is 15%. The estimated terminal value (TV) of TC at the end of year 5, therefore, is $10 million computed as follows:

$$\frac{\text{Free Cash Flow in Year 5}}{\text{[Required Discount Rate]} - \text{[Rate of Long-Term Growth]}}$$

$$\frac{\$1{,}000{,}000}{.15 - .05}$$

$$\frac{\$1{,}000{,}000}{.10} = \$10{,}000{,}000$$

The denominator of .10 is the equivalent of a price/earning multiple of 10, that is, $1,000,000/.10 is the same as 10 times $1,000,000. The .10 is sometimes referred to as the capitalization rate, the rate used in determining the capital value of an investment.

3. Estimating Terminal Value through the Competitive Equilibrium Model

The competitive equilibrium model requires a determination of when the "industry is likely to settle into competitive equilibrium," that is, when competitors catch up and everyone is on an equal footing.[18] At that point the net present value of new growth opportunities is zero. The terminal value at this point is determined by the following formula:[19]

$$TV = \frac{\text{FCF for the Next Period After Termination Date}}{\text{Required Discount Rate (r)}}$$

This model is similar to the constant growth model. The model says that the terminal value in year five is equal to the capitalized value of the free cash flows for year six. The

18. Brealey & Myers, supra Chapter 7 Scope, at 66.

19. The numerator of the formula can also be the expected earnings for the next period after the termination date.

denominator, however, is the required discount rate rather than the discount rate minus the growth rate which applies in the constant growth model. This model is illustrated as follows:

Example (7). Assume that in Example 6 the estimate of earnings for year six is \$1,050,000. This is the year after the year in which the industry is expected to settle into competitive equilibrium. The discount rate is still 15%. The TV for year five is therefore \$7,000,000 computed as follows:

$$TV = \frac{\text{FCF for the Next Period After Termination Date}}{r}$$

$$TV = \frac{\$1{,}050{,}000}{.15}$$

$$TV = \$7{,}000{,}000$$

Professor Rappaport says that the competitive equilibrium model, which he refers to as the perpetuity method, is generally the best method to use in estimating terminal value.[20]

The differences between the constant growth model and the competitive equilibrium model can be summarized as follows: the numerator in the constant growth model is the FCF for the terminal year, whereas the numerator in the competitive equilibrium model is the FCF for the year after the terminal year, the year the industry is projected to settle into competitive equilibrium. Thus, the numerator in the competitive equilibrium model is larger. The denominator in the constant growth model is the cost of capital minus the growth rate, whereas the denominator in the competitive equilibrium model is the cost of capital. Thus, the denominator in the competitive equilibrium model is larger. In most cases, the competitive equilibrium model will produce a smaller terminal value than the constant growth model.

4. Estimating Terminal Value by Reference to Price/Earnings Ratios

The first rule of thumb suggested by Brealey & Myers is to look to the price/earnings ratio of companies whose "scale, risk, and growth prospects today roughly match those projected [for the target in the terminal year]."[21] Once the comparable price/earnings ratio is determined, that ratio is applied to the expected earnings of the target for the termination year to determine the estimated terminal value. This method is illustrated as follows:

Example (8). Assume that in Example 6 the terminal date is at the end of the fifth year, target's expected earnings (not free cash flow) for year 5 are \$1.1 million, and the price/earnings ratio of comparable companies is 10. As a consequence, the estimated terminal value of target at the end of year 5 is \$11 million, computed as follows:

$$10 \times \$1.1 \text{ million} = \$11 \text{ million}$$

The price/earnings method is one of the elements used in the comparable companies technique for valuing a target on the basis of present (not future) comparable compa-

20. Rappaport, supra Chapter 7 Scope, at 60–61.
21. Brealey & Myers, supra Chapter 7 Scope, at 65.

nies. This can be seen, for example, in Wasserstein/Shearson's valuation of Warner [*see* Documentary Appendix C, page 4].

5. Estimating Terminal Value by Reference to Market/Book Ratios

The second rule of thumb discussed by Brealey & Myers is to use the market book ratio, which is the ratio of stock price to book value per share. This method involves the determination of the market/book ratios of companies that are today comparable to the expected composition of the target on the terminal date, and the application of that ratio to the target's expected book value on the terminal date. This method is illustrated as follows:

> *Example (9).* Assume that in Example 6 the terminal date is at the end of the fifth year, the target's expected book value is $5 million and the market/book ratio of comparable companies is 2. In such case, the expected terminal value of the target is $10 million (*i.e.*, 2 times $5 million of book value).

6. Summary of the Results under the Four Methods

The following chart is a summary of (1) the estimated terminal values, and (2) the present value of the terminal values, under each of the above four methods of determining the terminal value.

Method	Terminal Value	Present Value of Terminal Value
Constant Growth Model	$10,000,000	$4,970,000
Competitive Equilibrium Model	7,000,000	3,479,000
Price/Earnings Rule of Thumb	11,000,000	5,467,000
Market to Book Rule of Thumb	10,000,000	4,970,000

Brealey & Myers say that although there is no "best" method for determining terminal value, generally most weight should be put on the competitive equilibrium method, which sets the terminal date at the point at which positive net present value disappears.[22] They say that the competitive equilibrium method "forces managers to remember that sooner or later the competition catches up."[23] They go on to say that it is not unusual for the various methods to produce a broad range of estimates of terminal value.[24]

7. Estimating Terminal Value in the Time-Warner Acquisition: Multiple of Cash Flow Method

Wasserstein/Shearson in their opinion to the Time board estimated the terminal value of Warner by multiplying the expected cash flow for the terminal period by a factor that presumably represents a likely multiple of cash flows for comparable companies.

In their presentation to Time's board, Wasserstein/Shearson used multiples of 10, 11, 12 and 13 in estimating the terminal value of Warner's film entertainment segment. [*See* Documentary Appendix C, page 3]

22. Id. at 67.
23. Id.
24. Id.

8. Estimating Terminal Value in *Orchard*[25]

As discussed previously, in the 2012 decision in *Orchard*,[26] an appraisal action, Chancellor Strine of the Delaware Chancery Court addressed several valuation issues, including the computation of terminal value used in the DCF model. The Chancellor explained as follows the challenge by the shareholder's expert (Meinhart) to the terminal value used by the company's expert (Fesnak):

> The petitioners contend that Fesnak included "excess depreciation and amortization expenses in his calculation of [Orchard's] terminal value." In 2014, the year that Fesnak used as the basis for determining Orchard's terminal year cash flow, Fesnak reduced Orchard's projected pre-tax income for both the aggressive and base cases by $654,993 in depreciation expenses and $875,942 in amortization expenses, but assumed capital expenditures for that year of only $500,000. According to the petitioners, depreciation and amortization expenses that are three times Orchard's capital expenditures are not sustainable on a normalized basis. In other words, going into perpetuity, capital expenditures and depreciation and amortization expenses must match up. As a solution, the petitioners suggest that the difference between $1.57 million in amortization and depreciation expenses and $500,000 in capital expenditures ($1.03 million) be added to Fesnak's projected cash flow for the terminal period.[27]

The Chancellor went on to indicate as follows that this challenge was consistent with finance theory:

> The petitioners' challenge is grounded in the sound valuation principle that because the terminal value is meant to capture the present value of all future cash flows of the company, typically the net cash flow figure used to generate the terminal value should be normalized, rather than "unrealistically extrapolate[] [a company's] short run circumstances into perpetuity." The Gordon growth model indicates the equity value of a firm assuming full distribution of its net earnings. One of the important implications of this assumption is that "[c]apital expenditures are equal to depreciation."[28]

Notwithstanding the Chancellor's conclusion that Meinhart's "analytical premise is sound," he went on to conclude that "a closer look at Fesnak's model reveals that the petitioners' challenge has no factual premise."[29]

K. Sensitivity Analysis

Uncertainty is inherent in the preparation of a cash flow forecast, and therefore, there is uncertainty in computing a single NPV of a project.

The effect of potential estimation errors may be analyzed through sensitivity analysis. This can involve, for example, the preparation of cash flow forecasts on the basis of the following three possible outcomes: (1) expected, (2) pessimistic, and (3) optimistic. Each

---

25. This section is adapted from Thompson, *Mergers, Acquisitions and Tender Offers*, *supra* Section 1.10, at Section 11:5.9[H].

26. In Re: Appraisal of The Orchard Enterprises, Inc., 2012 Del. Ch. LEXIS 165 (Del. Ch. Ct. July 18, 2012).

27. *Id.* at *53–*54.

28. *Id.* at *54.

29. *Id.* at *55.

outcome could be prepared on the basis of different variables in the cash flow projections, such as, size, market share, variable costs, sales growth, etc. Thus, for example, a range of NPVs for a project could be determined by setting each variable at its pessimistic, expected and optimistic value while holding all other variables equal to their expected values.

Wasserstein/Shearson used this type of sensitivity analysis in valuing Warner. As indicated on page 3 of Documentary Appendix C, Wasserstein/Shearson used three different discount rates and four different estimates of terminal value in valuing Warner's film entertainment business.

§ 7.7 Use of the Capital Asset Pricing Model (CAPM) in Determining the Appropriate Discount Rate

A. Introduction

The discount rate (r) in the NPV formula is the cost of capital, which is the minimum rate of return necessary to induce an acquiring firm to acquire the target. It is the rate at which the free cash flows and terminal value of an acquisition candidate are discounted to present value. This section examines the capital asset pricing model (CAPM), which provides a method for determining the discount rate. Two other methods for determining the discount rate, arbitrage pricing theory (APT) and weighed average cost of capital (WACC), are discussed in Sections 7.8 and 7.9, respectively.

The approach taken here is to separate the financing decision from the investment decision and to use CAPM to determine the discount rate (cost of capital) on the basis of the assumption of all equity financing. Under this method, the benefits or costs associated with the financing decision are separately determined and discounted to present value at the cost of capital. A similar approach is used with APT. This interaction between the investment and financing decisions is discussed in Section 7.9.

WACC provides a method for determining the cost of a firm's debt and equity financing. In determining the discount rate, WACC directly takes into account the financing decision and, therefore, the impact of the interest deduction on the debt. Thus, under WACC, the benefit of the interest deduction is not separately determined and discounted, but rather is reflected in a lower cost of capital. In using WACC to determine the cost of capital, as is the case in using CAPM or APT, the cash flows are projected on the basis of an all equity financing.

CAPM or APT is used in determining the cost of equity capital used in WACC. Thus, CAPM and APT have a role even in the use of WACC.

Both CAPM and APT are based on the market efficiency theory. This theory, which is only outlined here, posits that if investors have easy access to information about a security, the price of the security will properly reflect that information. Consequently, "[i]f capital markets are efficient, then purchase or sale of any security at the prevailing market price is never a positive NPV transaction,"[30] that is, the price of the security will equal the present value of the expected cash flows discounted at the appropriate cost of capital. As Brealey & Myers explain, "the capital asset pricing model boils down to the statement that the market portfolio [*i.e.*, a portfolio of all stocks] is efficient."[31] Thus, the purchase of the market portfolio would not create a positive NPV.

30. *Id.* at 289.
31. *Id.* at 164.

To understand the principles behind CAPM it is first necessary to consider the concepts of (1) systematic and unsystematic risk [*see* Section 7.7.H], (2) the measure of market risk, beta [*see* Section 7.7.C], and (3) the market risk premium [*see* Section 7.7.D]. After explanation of these concepts, CAPM is introduced in Section 7.7.E. A recent criticism of CAPM by Professors Fama and French is discussed in Section 7.7.G.

As explained more fully in Section 7.7.E, CAPM gives the rate of return (r) for a particular investment by a formula that takes account of the following variables: (1) the risk-free rate of return (r_f), (2) the market risk premium ($r_m - r_f$), which is the difference between the expected return on the market (r_m) and the risk-free rate (r_f), and (3) the beta (β) of the investment. The formula is as follows:[32]

$$r = r_f + \beta(r_m - r_f)$$

This CAPM formula states that the required discount rate for an investment is equal to the risk free rate plus an additional percentage equal to the beta for the investment multiplied by the market risk premium.

B. Systematic and Unsystematic Risk

There are two types of risk: systematic risk and unsystematic risk. Risk for this purpose means that future returns are uncertain. Systematic risk is a function of broad macroeconomic conditions that affect the prices of all assets. Thus, there is systematic risk in holding any asset. On the other hand, unsystematic risk is a function of the characteristics associated with a particular asset as opposed to broad market factors. For example, risk factors such as the rate of growth of GNP or interest rate levels "systematically affect all firms in the economy to a greater or lesser extent."[33] On the other hand, risk factors such as possible changes in consumer tastes, new product developments and changes in prices of raw materials affect particular firms and therefore, are referred to as unsystematic risks.

Diversification can reduce or eliminate unsystematic risk by balancing the losers with winners; such risk is often referred to as diversifiable risk, unique risk, residual risk, and specific risk. The specific risk of holding the stock of a particular company can be diversified away by investing in stocks of other companies, possibly in other industries. Diversification cannot, however, eliminate systematic risk, which is often referred to as undiversifiable risk or market risk. Since market risk results from the broad macroeconomic factors that threaten most businesses, stocks have a tendency to move in the same direction.

Brealey & Myers elaborate on the concepts of unique (or unsystematic) risk and market (or systematic) risk:

> "* * * If you only have a single stock, unique risk is very important, but once you have a portfolio of 20 or more stocks, diversification has done the bulk of its work. For a reasonably well-diversified portfolio, only market risk matters. Therefore, the predominant source of uncertainty for a diversified investor is that the market will rise or plummet, carrying the investor's portfolio with it."[34]

Graph A illustrates how total risk is a function of both systematic and unsystematic risk and how unsystematic risk reduces with diversification.

---

32. *Id.* at 190–197.
33. *Id.* at 108.
34. *Id.*

Graph A

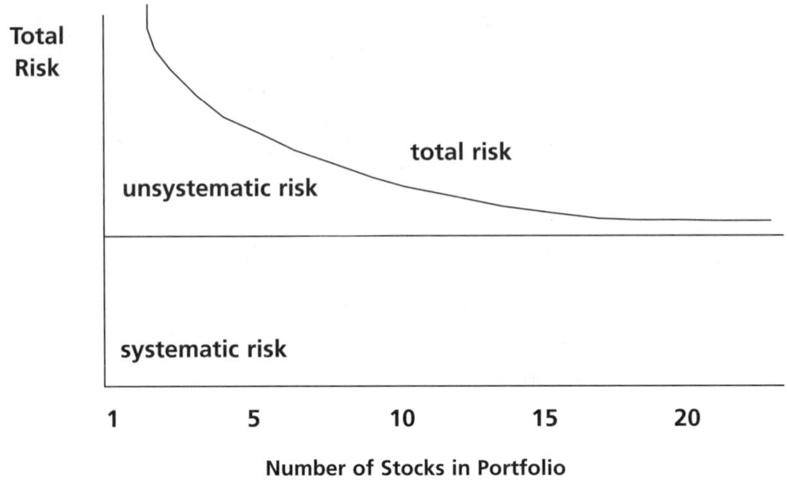

The above graph illustrates that the greater the diversification, which is illustrated on the horizontal axis, the less the total risk, which is measured on the vertical axis. Unsystematic risk is reduced by diversification, systematic risk is not. Diversification reduces unsystematic risk because the prices of different stocks move differently; the price movements are less than perfectly correlated and the decline in the prices of some stocks are offset by increases in the prices of others.

Brealey and Myers explain that "[w]ith more securities, and therefore better diversification, portfolio risk declines until all unique risk is eliminated and only the bedrock of market risk remains."[35]

C. Beta: The Measure of Market Risk

1. Introduction

Beta is the measure of the sensitivity of a security's return to market movements; thus, it is a measure of a systematic risk of a security. Beta is an indication of what the likely move for the particular stock will be for a given move in the market, that is, how sensitive a particular stock is to a move in the market. For a stock with a beta of 1, a 10% market rise would, on average, lead to a 10% rise in the price of the stock. For a stock with a beta of 1.5, a market rise of 10% would lead on average to a 15% rise in the price of the stock. Thus, beta "measures the marginal contribution of a stock to the risk of the market portfolio."[36]

The beta for a particular stock is calculated by running a linear regression between past returns for that stock and past returns of a market index, such as the Standard and Poor's 500; the statistical derivation of beta is not covered here.

35. *Id.* at 144.
36. *Id.* at 163.

2. Further Elaboration on Beta

Since the market has a beta of 1, a high beta stock is one with a beta of more than 1 and a low beta stock is one with a beta of less than 1. A high beta stock tends to move up by a greater percentage than the market moves up and tends to move down by a greater percentage than the market moves down. Thus, such stocks tend to "amplify the overall movements of the market."[37] On the other hand, "stocks with a beta between 0 and 1.0 tend to move in the same direction as the market, but not as far."[38]

Thus, betas estimate the amount by which investors expect the price of a particular stock to change as a result of a change in the market. A stock with a beta of greater than 1, such as the stock of a start-up telecom company, is generally sensitive to movements in the market, whereas a stock with a low beta, such as the stock of an established telecom company, is less sensitive to market moves. This is because the cash flows of the established telecom company are more certain than the cash flows of the start-up; that is, there is more risk associated with the start-ups cash flows.

Various investment services provide estimates of the betas of various companies. For example, Merrill Lynch publishes a Beta Book. Betas can also be estimated for particular projects or divisions of a larger firm by looking at betas for the particular industry involved. As indicated in Section 7.7.F, betas may have to be adjusted for financial risk (*i.e.*, leverage) employed by the firm. For a further discussion of beta *see* Thompson, *Demystifying the Use of Beta in the Determination of the Cost of Capital and an Illustration of Its Use in Lazard's Valuation of Conrail*, 25 J. of Corporation Law 241 (1999).

D. Risk Free Rate and Market Risk Premium

In addition to beta, in applying CAPM it is necessary to determine the risk free rate and the market premium. The risk free rate of return is measured by the return on Treasury bills or Treasury bonds. For purposes of the discussion here, Treasury bills will be used. Treasury bills have a risk free rate because there is no safer investment and the risk of default is in essence nonexistent. On the other hand, the rate of return offered by a well diversified portfolio of common stocks is the market return. The market return has to be greater over time than the return on Treasury bills for otherwise no one would invest in common stocks. Since the risk of holding common stocks is greater than the risk of holding Treasury bills, the reward for holding common stock must be greater than the reward for holding Treasury bills.

Historically the market risk premium, or the excess of the return on a diversified portfolio of common stocks over the Treasury bill rate has been approximately 8.4%.[39] Thus, if the Treasury bill rate is presently 7%, it can be expected that the rate of return (including dividends and capital gains) from holding a well diversified portfolio of common stock would be approximately 15.4%.

The market risk premium is written algebraically as follows, where r_m means the market return and r_f means the risk free rate on Treasury bills:

$$\text{Market Risk Premium} = (r_m - r_f)$$

37. *Id.* at 143.
38. *Id.*
39. *Id.* at 131.

E. The Capital Asset Pricing Model

The elements of CAPM are (1) the beta for the particular stock, (2) the risk free rate (r_f), and (3) the market risk premium, which is the expected return on the market portfolio, minus the risk free return ($r_m - r_f$). Since the beta for the market is 1, the expected return of holding the market portfolio is equal to the sum of (1) the risk free rate (r_f), and (2) the market risk premium ($r_m - r_f$), that is, $(r_f) + 1(r_m - r_f)$.

The expected risk premium on a particular stock can, therefore, be written as follows:

$$\begin{aligned} \text{Expected Risk Premium} &= \text{Beta} \times \text{Expected Risk Premium of Market} \\ &= \text{Beta} \times (r_m - r_f) \\ &= \beta(r_m - r_f) \end{aligned}$$

If a stock has a beta of 1 like the market, then the stock will require a market return. It follows that the expected rate of return (or the discount rate, or hurdle rate or cost of capital) can be derived from the following equation that is an algebraic statement of the CAPM:

Expected Rate of Return = Risk Free Rate of Return + Beta × Market Risk Premium

If the target is involved in several lines of business, it is appropriate to determine through the use of the CAPM a discount rate for each segment and to discount to present value using the DCF model the estimated free cash flows and terminal value of each line of business. In the words of Brealey & Myers, "[t]he true cost of capital depends on the use to which the capital is put."[40]

This is basically the method that was followed in valuing Warner's different business segments, by Wasserstein/Shearson in their opinion to Time's board [*see, e.g.*, pages 2 and 3 of Documentary Appendix C].

Some companies use different discount rates depending on the type of investment. For example, an investment that is an expansion of the firm's core business may be analyzed with a discount rate equal to the firm's cost of capital. A more risky venture may be analyzed with a higher discount rate, and a less risky venture may have a lower rate.

F. Asset and Equity Betas

A firm's cost of capital is a function of the firm's business risk, that is, the risk associated with the firm's investments or assets. In a firm with no debt, the shareholders of the common stock are faced only with this business risk. On the other hand, if the firm has debt (*i.e.*, is leveraged), the shareholders of the common shares are also faced with financial risk. This is the risk that the firm will not be able to service the debt and will, therefore, go into bankruptcy. Obviously, the more leverage the greater the risk to the common shareholders. Financial risk, however, has no effect on business risk; leverage has no effect on the firm's assets.

In determining the beta of a firm's equity, the beta must be adjusted to reflect the financial risk (*i.e.*, leverage) employed by the particular company: the higher the leverage, the higher the financial risk and the higher the beta. A firm's asset beta is the beta that would apply if the firm did not employ any leverage and, therefore, faced business risk but no financial risk. Brealey and Myers explain that because of the general low risk associated with debt of large blue-chip firms, financial analysts generally assume that the

40. *Id.* at 182.

beta of the debt of such firms is zero. This means that the debt is not sensitive to moves in the equity market.

If the beta of a firm's debt is zero, the beta of its stock will equal the firm's asset beta. The asset beta is equal to the sum of the weighted average of (1) the beta of the firm's debt (D), and (2) the beta of the firm's equity (E). Thus, the firm's asset beta can be expressed algebraically as follows:

$$\beta \text{ assets} = \frac{D}{V} \text{ Beta of debt} + \frac{E}{V} \text{ Beta of equity}$$

In this formula D/V is the portion of the firm's value attributable to debt and E/V is the portion of the value attributable to equity.

The following principles can be derived from the previous formula for determining the asset beta:

First, the lower the beta of debt, the lower the beta of equity, and if debt has a beta of zero, the beta of equity is equal to the asset beta.

Second, as the beta for debt increases, the beta for equity increases.

Third, the asset beta is the weighted average of the firm's debt and equity betas.

Fourth, the firm's asset beta does not change with leverage; that is, asset betas are not affected by financial risk.

In the acquisition context it is generally appropriate to use asset betas in determining the discount rate for the DCF model. If asset betas are used, any cost or benefits associated with the financing of the acquisition, such as the tax benefits from interest deductions, should be separately determined for each year and then discounted to present value with the other cash flows. This process is discussed further in Section 7.9, which deals with the interaction between the investment decision and the financing decision. In certain situations it may be appropriate to use equity betas. For example, the equity beta may be used in analyzing a partial stock investment in a leveraged firm and in determining the cost of equity capital when applying WACC [*see* Section 7.10].

If the asset beta is used to determine the value of a target's assets in the DCF model, the target's outstanding debt is subtracted to ascertain the value of the equity. This technique of valuing the equity by first determining the value of assets with DCF and then subtracting the outstanding debt was utilized by Wasserstein/Shearson in its presentation to Time's board [*see* page 7 of Documentary Appendix C].

G. Determination of the Discount Rate in *Orchard*—The Superiority of CAPM[41]

1. The Chancellor Finds CAPM Superior

As discussed previously, in the 2012 decision in *Orchard*,[42] an appraisal action, Chancellor Strine of the Delaware Chancery Court addressed several valuation issues, includ-

---

41. This section is adapted from Thompson, *Mergers, Acquisitions and Tender Offers*, *supra* Section 1.10, at Section 11:6.8.

42. In Re: Appraisal of The Orchard Enterprises, Inc., 2012 Del. Ch. LEXIS 165 (Del. Ch. Ct. July 18, 2012).

ing the computation of the discount rate used in the DCF model. In this part of the decision, the Chancellor accepted the use of CAPM (and rejected the use of the build-up rate model and the Duff & Phelps Risk Premium Report model) for purposes of determining the discount rate. The Chancellor reasoned:

> Both experts calculated a cost of equity for Orchard using three different methods: CAPM, the build-up rate model, and the Duff & Phelps Risk Premium Report model. The latter two methods are related, with the Duff & Phelps model being a variation of the build-up rate model.
>
> I am uncomfortable using the latter two methods for a few reasons. I begin with the important one that the build-up model is not, in my view, well accepted by mainstream corporate finance theory as a proper way to come up with a discount rate. Indeed, its components involve a great deal of subjectivity and expressly incorporate company-specific risk as a component of the discount rate. This is at odds with the CAPM, which excludes company-specific risk from inclusion in the discount rate, on the grounds that only market risk should be taken into account because investors can diversify away company-specific risk. Relatedly, corporate finance theory suggests that concern about the achievability of the company's business plan and thus its generation of cash flows should be taken into account by adjustments to the cash flow projections, and not by adjusting the discount rate. The build-up model, however, allows for a variety of risks to be poured into the discount rate, including so-called projection risk and other factors.[43]

2. The Chancellor Sets out the Elements of CAPM

After exploring in greater detail his conclusion on the superiority of CAPM, the Chancellor then discussed as follows the use of CAPM in determining the cost of equity:

> Cost of Equity = rf + β * (rm – rf), where rf is the risk-free rate of return, β is the beta of the company, which measures the risk and volatility of the company's securities relative to the overall market portfolio, and rm – rf is the equity risk premium, or risk differential between investment in a particular company and investment in a diversified stock portfolio. A size premium is a generally acceptable addition to the CAPM formula in the valuation of smaller companies to account for the higher rate of return that investors demand as compensation for the greater risk associated with small company equity. As noted, both parties agree that a size factor should be considered in applying the CAPM method to Orchard, based on empirical evidence regarding the performance of stocks of different market capitalizations.[44]

3. The Chancellor Explains the Disagreements between the Parties' Experts on the Elements of CAPM

The Chancellor went on to explain that the parties' "experts largely agree on the components of their CAPM estimates of the discount rate," and consequently he was focusing only on the "areas of disagreement," which he described as follows:

> (i) whether a historical or supply-side equity risk premium should be used; (ii) whether a 1% company-specific risk premium should be added to the CAPM; and

43. *Id.* at *60–*61.
44. *Id.* at *66.

(iii) whether the 6.3% size premium added to the CAPM by both experts should be adjusted if the supply-side equity risk premium is used instead of the historical equity risk premium.[45]

4. A Brief Introduction to the Supply-Side Equity Risk Premium

As discussed in the next section, in *Orchard*, Chancellor Strine discussed the concept of the "supply side" equity risk premium. Before considering this part of the Chancellor's opinion, it is helpful to briefly introduce this concept. An article entitled *Unraveling the Supply-Side Equity Risk Premium*, introduces the concept as follows:

> The equity risk premium (ERP) is arguably the most influential component of a company's cost of capital. So it is no surprise that it attracts much debate. The two most commonly used ERP models are the historical and the supply-side ERP. The latter has received a lot of attention and questions in the recent years. Its complicated nature creates a shroud of confusion, which can lead to a misinterpretation of the underlying theory and cause practitioners to shy away from using the premium in valuations.
>
> Those who do use the supply-side ERP choose it over the historical ERP because it incorporates a forward-looking assumption in its calculation. Also, the supply-side ERP usually generates a lower premium than the historical model. * * *
>
> *Theory of Supply-side*. The term "supply-side" sparks much confusion, since it is not referring to the economic supply and demand equilibrium of the market. In actuality, the supply-side ERP primarily takes into account the earnings that companies generate (supply). As such, it omits the expected premium or discount embedded within market price attributed to investor trading. On the other hand, a demand-side model's methodology would only consider this price divergence from fair value, which is investor-demand driven. While the words "supply" and "demand" portray images of economic equilibrium, they are really referring to a buildup of total return components.[46]

5. The Chancellor Accepts the Supply-Side Equity Risk Premium

The Chancellor found that the supply-side equity risk premium, which in this case resulted in a lower discount rate and a higher present value under the DCF model, has substantial support in the professional and academic valuation literature and therefore would be used here. The Chancellor explained:

> Fesnak [Orchard's expert] calculated a discount rate under a modified CAPM using the historical equity risk premium of 6.7% published in the 2010 Ibbotson SBBI Valuation Yearbook (the "Ibbotson Yearbook"). Meinhart [the shareholders' expert] relied on the Ibbotson Yearbook's supply-side equity risk premium of 5.2%. [Note that the higher the discount rate the lower the present value under the DCF Model.] Ibbotson's historical equity risk premium is generated using historical market returns from 1926 to the relevant valuation date. Ibbotson's supply-side equity risk premium uses the same historical data, but separates the

45. *Id.* at *67.

46. Magdalena Mroczek, *Unraveling the Supply-Side Equity Risk Premium*, Morningstar, The Value Examiner, 19 (Jan/Feb 2012), available at http://corporate.morningstar.com/ib/documents/Published Research/UnravelingSupplySideERP.pdf.

> components of the equity risk premium into those attributable to a stock's price-to-earnings ratio and those attributable to a stock's expected earnings growth, excluding the former and including the latter. This is because the supply-side premium assumes that actual equity returns will track real earnings growth, not the growth reflected in the price-to-earnings ratio.
>
> Meinhart's use of a 5.2% equity risk premium has substantial support in professional and academic valuation literature. I recently reviewed this literature and addressed the choice between the historical equity risk premium and the supply-side equity risk premium in *Global GT LP v. Golden Telecom, Inc.* [993 A.2d 497 (Del. Ch. 2010), aff'd, 11 A.3d 214 (Del. 2010). In Golden Telecom, although recognizing that the historical equity risk premium is the more traditional estimate, I concluded that the academic community has shifted toward greater support for equity risk premium estimates that are closer to the supply-side rate published by Ibbotson. I therefore determined that using an equity risk premium based on Ibbotson's supply-side rate in my DCF valuation of the subject company was appropriate. I noted that when academics and experts have "mined additional data and pondered the reliability of past practice and come, by a healthy weight of reasoned opinion, to believe that a different practice should become the norm, this court's duty is to recognize that practice if, in the court's lay estimate, the practice is the most reliable available for use in an appraisal."[47]

The Chancellor also pointed out that "*Golden Telecom's* default acceptance of the supply-side equity risk premium was recently embraced by this court in *Gearreald v. Just Care, Inc.* [2012 Del. Ch. LEXIS 91, 2012 WL 1569818 (Del. Ch. Apr. 30, 2012).]"[48] The Chancellor further explained:

> In [the *Just Care*] appraisal action, Vice Chancellor Parsons rejected the respondent's use of a historical equity risk premium under *Golden Telecom*, finding that the expert had provided "no persuasive substantive financial reason as to why the application of a supply side equity risk premium would be inappropriate." Like the respondent in *Just Care*, Orchard has not provided me with a persuasive reason to revisit the supply-side versus historical equity risk premium debate. I therefore find that the Ibbotson Yearbook's supply-side equity risk premium of 5.2% is an appropriate metric to be applied in valuing Orchard under the CAPM.[49]

6. The Chancellor Rejects a Company-Specific Risk Premium

The Chancellor explained that "Fesnak [Orchard's expert] included a 1% company-specific risk premium in his calculation of the discount rate under the CAPM "to account for the specific risks facing Orchard that were not otherwise captured within the other components of the cost of capital."[50] This increase in the discount rate would have the effect of reducing the present value of the projected cash flows. The Chancellor went on to explain that "[a]lthough Meinhart [the shareholders' expert] indicated in his report that a

47. *Orchard* at *68–*70.
48. *Id.* at *71–*72.
49. *Id.* at *72.
50. *Id.*

company-specific risk premium, if appropriate, is part of a modified CAPM, [Meinhart] concluded that addition of this factor is inappropriate here."[51]

The Chancellor explained that he did "not believe that a company-specific risk premium should be used in a CAPM calculation of a discount rate, especially in a case like this."[52] The Chancellor elaborated as follows:

> A company-specific risk premium is not an addition to the CAPM that is accepted by corporate finance scholars, but is sometimes added to the discount rate by practitioners valuing a company to reflect that the company has risk factors that they believe have not already been captured by the equity risk premium as modified by beta and (if applicable) the small company size premium. "Pure proponents of the CAPM argue that only systemic risk as measured by beta is relevant to the cost of capital and that company-specific risks should be addressed by appropriate revisions in cash-flow estimates."
>
> More generally, for a corporation that operates primarily in the United States and where there are sound projections, the calculation of a CAPM discount rate should not include company-specific risk for the obvious reason that it is inconsistent with the very theory on which the model is based. If there are concerns about projection risk because the projections were generated by an inexperienced management team, the company's track record is such that estimating future performance is difficult even for an experienced management team, or projections seems to be infected with a bias, it would be better for the expert to directly express his skepticism by adjusting the available projections directly in some way, to make plain his reasoning. Admittedly, this would involve as much subjectivity as heaping on to the discount rate, but it would also force more rigor and clarity about the expert's concern. Here, where management under the control of Dimensional came up with various scenarios and Orchard's expert gave overwhelming weight to management's base case scenario, no extra discounting is warranted and the CAPM method should be applied on its own terms, and not be infected by an ingredient from the build-up method.[53]

7. The Chancellor Accepts a Size Premium

The Chancellor describes as follows the positions of the experts on the appropriateness of a size premium, which would increase the discount rate and thereby decrease the present value of Orchard's free cash flows:

> Meinhart and Fesnak relied upon the same size premium of 6.3% in their respective CAPM calculations of Orchard's cost of capital, which is the size premium for the broader 10th decile published in the 2010 Ibbotson Yearbook. A size premium is an accepted part of CAPM because there is evidence in empirical returns that investors demand a premium for the extra risk of smaller companies. The petitioners describe the 6.3% premium as, if anything, too high, and Orchard argues it is conservative and is not justified if other inputs to the CAPM are modified, such as the equity risk premium.[54]

51. *Id.* at *72–*73.
52. *Id.* at *73.
53. *Id.* at *73–*76.
54. *Id.* at *81.

For the following reasons, the Chancellor rejected Orchard's argument that the size premium should be increased beyond the 6.3%:

> The use of a size premium with the CAPM model is already a nod in Orchards direction, and Orchard has not persuaded me that simply because I use the supply-side equity risk premium, I should add more to the size premium. By adding a hefty 6.3% into the CAPM formula for size, Orchard is treated fairly in my view, even though I acknowledge that academic and practitioner thinking in this area seems to be in a period of active evolution.[55]

H. FAMA and French Critique of CAPM

Although there had been criticisms of CAPM prior to 1992, most of the empirical studies reached similar conclusions which principally were (1) that "[s]ecurity returns appear to be linearly related to beta as predicted by the CAPM," and (2) "[t]here is a positive relationship between beta and past returns; that is, higher betas tend to lead to higher returns."[56]

In a 1992 empirical examination of beta, Professors Fama and French have, however, seriously questioned the validity of the "basic prediction" of CAPM that "average stock returns are positively related to market betas."[57] However, notwithstanding the finding of Fama and French, CAPM is still used as one way of determining an appropriate discount rate. For example, it was used by the Lazard investment banking firm in 2006 in its valuation of Time Warner for Carl Ichan. *See* The Lazard Report, Time Warner, Inc. (February 1, 2006).

§7.8 Use of Arbitrage Pricing Theory (APT) in Determining the Appropriate Discount Rate

CAPM provides an economic model for determining the discount rate; arbitrage pricing theory (APT) provides an alternative and more elaborate economic model for determining such rate.[58] CAPM is a unidimensional model that focuses only on return of the market. On the other hand, APT attempts to take into account all of the macroeconomic factors that can affect the price of a particular stock. The expected risk premium for each factor is measured and then the sensitivity of the stock to each factor is determined. Finally, the expected return is computed.[59] This, needless to say, is an extremely complicated process. It appears that most investment bankers do not use APT in valuing targets.

§7.9 Interaction Between Investment and Financing Decisions

Brealey & Myers suggest a methodology for analyzing the interactions between the investment decision (which employs DCF and CAPM) and the financing decision.[60]

---

55. *Id.* at *86.
56. Shapiro, supra Chapter 7 Scope, at 124.
57. Eugene F. Fama and Kenneth R. French, The Cross-Section of Expected Stock Returns, XLVII J. of Finance 427 (June 1992) [hereinafter cited as "Fama and French"].
58. For a discussion of APT, *see* Brealey & Myers, supra Chapter 7 Scope, at 169–173; Shapiro, supra Chapter 7 Scope at 128–130. For the seminal article on the topic, *see* Stephen A. Ross, The Arbitrage Theory of Capital Asset Pricing, J. of Economics Theory 341–360 (December 1976).
59. Brealey & Myers, supra Chapter 7 Scope, at 172–173.
60. Id. at Chapter 19.

Their approach is to first compute the NPV of the project on the assumption of all equity financing using the DCF model with the discount rate determined using CAPM with asset betas. Under this base-case, taxes are estimated assuming that there is no debt financing. The base case NPV is then adjusted to account for the effects of financing the project. The result is adjusted NPV or APV.[61] Brealey & Myers provide the following formula:[62]

APV = Base-case of NPV + NPV of Financing Decisions Caused by Acquisition of Target

Brealey & Myers give two illustrations of financing effects. The first shows that if stock is to be issued to finance the project the NPV of the issuance cost will cause APV to be less than the base case NPV. The second illustration shows that if part of the acquisition is to be financed by debt, the present value of the expected tax savings from the interest deductions will cause APV to exceed the base-case NPV.[63] They explain the process as follows:

> A series of present value calculations is made. * * * The first establishes a base-case value for the project: Its value as a separate, all-equity financed mini-firm. Then each side effect is traced out and the present value of its cost or benefit to the firm is calculated. Finally, all the present values are added together to estimate the project's total contribution to the value of the firm. Thus, in general, Project APV = Base-case NPV + Sum of the Present Values of the Side Effects of Accepting the Project.[64]

The APV concept performs a similar function to that performed by the weighted average cost of capital concept (WACC), suggested by Rappaport.[65] WACC takes account of the financing decision by considering the cost of both debt and equity financing. Brealey & Myers point out three mistakes commonly made with WACC.[66] First, the weighted average formula works only for a project that is the same as the business carried on by the firm.

Second, the application of the concept to a discrete project may lead to the assumption that more debt should be used in financing the project thereby lowering the discount rate and making the project look more attractive.

Third, using excessive debt in an acquisition will not necessarily reduce the cost of capital because the debt will increase the financial risk to shareholders, thereby increasing the required rate of return on equity, *i.e.*, the cost of equity.

§7.10 Use of the Weighted Average Cost of Capital (WACC) in Determining the Appropriate Discount Rate

In certain situations it may be appropriate to discount a target's cash flows at the target's weighted average cost of capital (WACC). The WACC is determined by summing:[67]

> (1) The *after-tax cost of debt*, multiplied by the *percentage of the value of the firm that is represented by debt*, and

61. *Id.* at 457–458.
62. *Id.* at 458.
63. *Id.* at 458–459.
64. *Id.* at 460.
65. *See* Section 7.8.
66. Brealey & Myers, supra Chapter 7 Scope, at 454–456.
67. This discussion is based in part on Brealey and Myers, supra Chapter 7 Scope, at 465–466.

(2) the *expected return on equity,* multiplied by the *percentage of the value of the firm represented by equity.*

Each of the italicized terms is defined below.

The after-tax cost of debt is determined by multiplying the firm's current borrowing rate (r^d) by 1 minus the corporate tax rate (t), that is, (1 – t). This is the reciprocal of the tax rate. If the corporate tax rate is 34%, (1 – t) is equal to 66% or .66. Thus, the after-tax cost of debt can be expressed as follows:

$$\text{After-tax cost of debt} = r^d (1 - t)$$
$$= r^d (.66)$$

The expected return on the firm's equity (r^e) is a function of the firm's business risk and financial risk, that is, the degree of leverage. The r^e can be computed by using CAPM and adjusting for financial risk as discussed in Section 7.7.F. Thus, the equity beta can be used in the WACC model for determining the cost of equity. Alternatively, the cost of equity can be determined by using APT as discussed in Section 7.8.

Shapiro suggests that in determining the cost of equity capital for the WACC formula the dividend growth model be used as a check on the cost of equity determined under CAPM or APT.[68] Under the dividend growth model, the cost of equity is determined by the following formula:[69]

$$\text{Cost of Equity} = \frac{\text{Current Dividend}}{\text{Current Stock Price}} + \text{Expected Growth in Dividend}$$

Thus, if the current dividend is $7, the current stock price is $100, and the expected growth in the dividend is 5%, the cost of equity is 12%, determined as follows:

$$\text{Cost of Equity} = \frac{\$7}{\$100} + 5\% = 7\% + 5\% = 12\%$$

The value of the firm (V) is equal to the sum of the value of the debt (D) and equity (E). Thus, WACC can be expressed algebraically as follows:

$$\text{WACC} = r^d (1 - \text{t}) \frac{D}{V} + r^e \frac{E}{V}$$

The following example illustrates the computation of WACC:[70]

Example (10). Acquiring corporation (AC) has a cost of debt (r^d) of 10% and its after-tax cost of debt [r^d (1 – .34)] is, therefore, 6.6%. AC's cost of equity using CAPM and adjusting the beta for financial risk is 15%. Target corporation (TC) is in the same line of business as AC. AC plans to finance its acquisi-

68. Shapiro, supra Chapter 7 Scope, at 283–284.
69. *Id.*
70. *See* e.g., Rappaport, supra Chapter 7 Scope, at 55.

tion of TC using AC's historic debt to equity ratio, which is 30% debt and 70% equity. Given these elements AC's WACC is computed as follows:

	Weight (%)	Cost of Capital (%)	Weighted Cost (%)
Debt	30	6.6	1.9
Equity	70	15	10.5
Cost of Capital			12.4

Brealey & Myers explain that the weighted average cost of capital is the correct discount rate for the firm as a whole but not necessarily for a particular project:

> The first thing to notice about the weighted-average formula is that all variables in it refer to the firm as a whole. As a result the formula gives the right discount rate only for projects that are just like the firm undertaking them. The formula works for the 'average' project. It is incorrect for projects that are safer or riskier than the average of the firm's existing assets. It is incorrect for projects whose acceptance would lead to an increase or decrease in the firm's debt ratio.[71]

§ 7.11 Application of DCF in Acquisitions That Produce Synergies

In applying the DCF and NPV techniques, any synergistic (or merger) gains resulting from the acquisition must be taken into account. Synergistic gains increase cash flow as a result of either an increase in revenues or a decrease in cost. Professor Rappaport says that synergistic gains fall into three principal categories: operating, financial and tax.[72]

§ 7.12 Illustration of the Application of DCF, NPV and CAPM in an Acquisition Context

Acquiring corporation (AC) is analyzing the proposed acquisition of target corporation (TC) through the use of DCF, NPV and CAPM. The asking price of TC is $6,000,000. AC follows the five steps set forth in Section 7.5.

First, AC estimates the amount and timing of the free cash flows and the terminal value of TC [*see* Documentary Appendix C, page 2]. The estimate of the free cash flow for the five-year period AC intends to operate TC is taken from the cash flow statement set forth in *Example (4)* in Section 7.6.G, as follows:

Estimated Free Cash Flows					
Year	1	2	3	4	5
	$600,000	$700,000	$800,000	$900,000	$1,000,000

71. Brealey & Myers, supra Chapter 7 Scope, at 465.
72. Rappaport, supra Chapter 7 Scope, at 207–215.

The terminal value of TC at the end of the fifth year is estimated to be $7,000,000 as computed in *Example (7)* in Section 7.6.J.3 using the competitive equilibrium formula. Thus, the cash flows are as follows:

	Free Cash Flow					
Year	1	2	3	4	5–Current Cash Flow	5–Cash Flow from Sale
	$600,00	$700,00	$800,00	$900,000	$1,000,000	$7,000,000

There are two expected cash flows in year five, because in that year it is anticipated that TC will throw off $1 million in operating cash and the balance of its assets will be sold for the terminal value of $7,000,000.

Second, AC determines the appropriate discount rate (r) by utilizing CAPM [*see* Documentary Appendix C, page 3]. Assume that AC is buying all the stock of TC, TC is debt free, and the acquisition will be financed with cash on hand. If the target has outstanding debt that is going to be assumed, the following methodology should still be utilized; however, after determining the value of the target, the value of the assumed debt is subtracted to determine the value of the equity. [*See* Documentary Appendix C, page 3] Also, the value of any marketable securities or other investment not taken into account in computing free cash flows and terminal value are added in computing the value of target. [*See* Documentary Appendix C, page 6]

Further, assume that TC operates one line of business. AC first determines the asset beta for the line of business operated by TC. This can be done through the use of a beta book. If only an equity beta is available, the beta will have to be adjusted (*i.e.*, unleveraged) to arrive at the asset beta. If there are multiple lines of business, a separate asset beta and separate discount rate would be determined for each business.

Assume that the asset beta is 1.2. TC then determines the risk free (r_f) rate, which is assumed to be 5%. AC takes as the market risk premium ($r_m - r_f$) the 8.4% historic premium. These elements are plugged into the CAPM model as follows:

$$r = r_f + \beta(r_m - r_f)$$

$$r = 5\% + 1.2(8.4)$$

$$r = 5\% + 10.08\%$$

$$r = 15.08\%$$

Thus, the appropriate discount rate is 15.08% (rounded to 15%).

This rate does not have to be adjusted because the acquisition is financed with available cash. If the acquisition were partially financed with debt, then at least two adjustment methods could be used. First, if TC is in the same line of business as AC and the acquisition is to be financed with the same proportions of debt and equity as AC has outstanding, then AC could use as the discount rate its weighted average cost of capital (WACC). [*See* Section 7.10] Second, the adjusted net present value (APV) method suggested by Brealey and Myers [*see* Section 7.9] could be utilized to bring to present value the expected benefits from the interest deduction on the debt. Each of these methods will increase the net present value of the project over the net present value produced with the asset beta. If each method is properly employed, the bottom line results (*i.e.*, NPV for the project) should be the same.

Under the third step in the process, the free cash flows and terminal value for each year are discounted to present value at the applicable discount rate using the DCF model (with the discount factors determined from the chart in Section 7.4.A) as follows:

DCF Model

$$PV = \frac{1}{(1+r)^1} FA_1 + \frac{1}{(1+r)^2} FA_2 + \frac{1}{(1+r)^3} FA_3 + \frac{1}{(1+r)^4} FA_4 + \frac{1}{(1+r)^5} FA_5 + \frac{1}{(1+r)^5} TV$$

$$PV = \frac{\$600{,}000}{1+.15} + \frac{\$700{,}000}{(1+.15)^2} + \frac{\$800{,}000}{(1+.15)^3} + \frac{\$900{,}000}{(1+.15)^4} + \frac{\$1{,}000{,}000}{(1+.15)^5} + \frac{\$7{,}000{,}000}{(1+.15)^5}$$

$$PV = .870(600{,}000) + .756(7{,}000{,}000) + .658(800{,}000) + .572(900{,}000) + .497(1{,}000{,}000) + .497(7{,}000{,}000)$$

$$PV = \$522{,}000 + \$529{,}200 + \$526{,}400 + \$514{,}600 + \$497{,}000 + \$3{,}479{,}000$$

The fourth step requires that the above amounts be added to determine the present value of all the cash flows and the terminal value. This amount is $6,068,200. This same amount can be derived through the use of a calculator by plugging in the cash flows and terminal value for each period and then discounting these amounts at the 15% rate.

Finally, AC computes the net present value (NPV) of the investment by subtracting the initial cost of TC, which would be the asking price of $6,000,000, from the present value of the cash flows and terminal value, which is $6,068,200, and determines that the proposed investment has a net present value of $68,200. Thus, this project could be undertaken by AC. Of course, AC would want to offer something less than $6,000,000 to possibly increase the NPV of the project.

If AC has other potential projects with positive NPVs, AC should select the project or projects indicated by AC's capital rationing model, such as the profitability index (Section 7.4.F). Before proceeding, however, AC may want to do a sensitivity analysis [*see* Section 7.6.K], particularly since the project only has a NPV of $68,200, assuming a $6,000,000 purchase price.

§ 7.13 Non-DCF Valuation Techniques: Comparable Companies and Comparable Transactions[73]

A. Introduction to the Direct Comparisons

Professor Cornell says that "[e]conomic theory and common sense agree on the basic principle that similar assets should sell at similar prices."[74] Consequently, the value of an asset (*i.e.*, a target) may be determined by reference to the value of a comparable asset (*i.e.*, a comparable company) that has recently been sold by a reasonably informed seller to a reasonably informed purchaser. Professor Cornell refers to this as the direct comparison approach.

If the size of the comparable company is not identical to the size of the target, which will normally be the case, then one way of adjusting for this size difference is to identify

73. This section is based on many of the concepts addressed in Bradford Cornell, Corporate Valuation, supra Chapter 7 Scope, at 56–99.

74. *Id.* at 56.

an observable variable that is related to the price or value of both the comparable company and the target. The fundamental assumption in the direct comparison approach is that the ratio of the price (P) of the comparable company to the observable variable (X) of the comparable company is approximately equal to the ratio of the value (V) of the target to the observable variable (X) of the target.

As will be seen below, this approach will work if both the price and observable variable are available for the comparable company and the observable variable is available for the target.

The above principle can be expressed mathematically as follows, where V_T is the value of the target, X_T is the observable variable of the target, P_C is the price of the comparable firm or firms and X_C is the observable variable of the comparable firm or firms.

$$\frac{V_T}{X_T} = \frac{P_C}{X_C}$$

The only unknown variable in the above equation is V_T, and, consequently, V_T can be determined as follows:

$$V_T = X_T \times \frac{P_C}{X_C}$$

For example, assume that (1) the trading price of the comparable company (P_C) is \$100 per share, (2) the observable variable (X_C) is earnings per share of \$20, and (3) the observable variable of the target (X_T) is earnings per share of \$10. In such case, the per share value of the target (V_T) is \$50, computed as follows:

$$V_T = \$10 \times \frac{\$100}{\$20}$$

$$V_T = \$10 \times 5$$

$$V_T = \$50$$

The above formula is merely deriving the per share value of the target by multiplying the target's earnings per share by the price earnings ratio of the comparable firm.

Professor Cornell points out that "a critical step in applying the direct comparison approach is choosing observable variables, X, that have a consistent relationship to value, V, [and price, P]."[75] He goes on to point out that in valuing companies observable variables, such as "cash flow and earnings are good choices because the ultimate sources of value are the net benefits received by investors."[76]

75. *Id.*
76. *Id.*

As demonstrated below, Wasserstein/Shearson used the direct comparison approach in valuing Warner.

B. Equivalence Between Direct Comparison and Direct Capitalization

In the direct comparison approach in determining the value of the target, the observable variable of the target (X_T) is multiplied by the ratio of the price of the comparable firm or firms (P_C) to the observable variable of the comparable firm or firms (X_C), as follows:

$$V_T = X_T \times \frac{P_C}{X_C}$$

An equivalent alternative approach to valuing the target is to use the direct capitalization method in which the observable variable of the target X_T is divided by the inverse of the ratio of the price of the comparable firm or firms (P_C) to the observable variable of the comparable firm or firms (X_C) as follows:

$$V_T = \frac{X_T}{X_c / P_c}$$

The denominator of the above equation is known as the capitalization rate. That is the rate at which the observable variable of the target is capitalized to ascertain the value of the target.

The equivalence of the direct comparison and direct capitalization methods can be demonstrated as follows under the assumption that X_T = \$10 per share, P_C = \$100 per share and X_C = \$20 per share.

Direct Comparison

$$V_T = X_T \times \frac{P_C}{X_C}$$

$$V_T = \$10 \times \frac{\$100}{\$20}$$

$$V_T = \$10 \times 5$$

$$V_T = \$50$$

Direct Capitalization

$$V_T = \frac{X_T}{X_c / P_c}$$

$$V_T = \frac{\$10}{\$20 / \$100}$$

$$V_T = \frac{\$10}{.2}$$

$$V_T = \$50$$

Professor Cornell points out that the capitalization rate should not be confused with the cost of capital that is used in the DCF model. [*See* Sections 7.7 and 7.8] He says that "situations in which the cost of capital can be used as a capitalization rate are extraordinarily rare."[77]

C. Selecting Comparable Companies and Determining Multiples

The selection of comparable companies invariably involves a matter of judgment. One approach is to focus on companies doing business in the same standard industrial classification (SIC) code, published in the Federal government's Standard Industrial Classification Manual. Another approach is to focus on reports of securities analysts, which often contain lists of comparable firms. Yet another approach is to review reports of investment research firms like Standard & Poor's, Moody's and Valueline. Also, industry experts, including operations personnel at both the target and the acquiror, may be of assistance in identifying comparable companies.

Once the comparable companies are selected, an analysis is made of the relationship between the price at which such companies are trading and the observable variable, such as the earnings. If, for example, the price to earnings (P:E) ratio is used, an average and median P:E ratio for the companies may be computed. In the P:E ratio, the value indicator (P) is the trading price of the equity of the comparable firms, and the observable variable (E) is the after tax earnings of such firms.

If a company has a significantly higher or lower P:E ratio than is representative of the group, such "outliers" may be eliminated.

The following example illustrates the above process:

Comparable Company	Equity Value × 2007 Earnings
1	20
2	25
3	25
4	15
5	15
Average 100/5	= 20
Median	= 20

If target's 2007 earnings are $10 million, then the implied value of the target's equity is $200 million, that is 20 times $10 million.

D. Selecting the Value Indicator and the Observable Variable

As indicated above, in the P:E ratio, the value of the common equity is the value indicator (P), and the earnings, net of interest, taxes and preferred dividends, is the observable variable (E). Although the P:E ratio is commonly used in valuing common equity, there are potential major defects with this method.

77. *Id.* at 58–59.

First, the capital structure of firms can vary significantly and this can have a significant impact on earnings, because if Firm A is financed with, say, 50% debt and Firm B has no debt, then other things being equal, Firm B will have higher earnings because it has no interest deduction. This can be illustrated as follows:

	Firm A	Firm B
Sales	$200K	$200K
Operating Expense	–40K	–40K
Interest	–50K	-0-
Income Before Taxes	110K	160K
Taxes (50%)	–55K	–80K
After Tax Earnings	$55K	$80K

Thus, use of the P:E ratio may produce distorted results if the capital structure of the comparable firms is different from the capital structure of the target.

Second, the accounting practices used by the comparable firms may be different from the practices used by the target. For example, firms may use different depreciation or amortization methods. Also, earnings may reflect extraordinary items.

An alternative to the use of the P:E ratio is the use of total firm value (TFV), that is, the value of the firm's debt and equity, as the Value Indicator and the use of a broad measure of earnings, such as earnings before interest, taxes, depreciation and amortization (EBITDA) as the Observable Variable.

The advantage of using the ratio of TFV to EBITDA can be illustrated as follows: Assume that firms A and B below have been identified as comparable firms to the target. Firm A is financed with 50% debt which has a value of $500K. The interest rate on the debt is 10% or $50K per year. The trading value of Firm A's common stock is $1 million. Firm B has no debt but has an amortization deduction attributable to an acquisition it made. This amortization deduction is not taken into account in computing Firm B's taxes. The trading value of Firm B's common stock is $1.5 million. The reported earnings of Firm A and Firm B are as follows:

	Firm A	Firm B
Sales	$200K	$200K
Operating Expense other than depreciation	–20K	–20K
Depreciation	–30K	–30K
Interest	–50K	-0-
Income Before Taxes	100K	150K
Taxes (50%)	–50K	–75K
After Tax Earnings	$40K	$75K
Amortization Deduction	-0-	10K
Reported Earnings	$50K	$65K

The P:E ratio of Firm A is 20 to 1, computed as follows:

Price of Common Stock $1 million	:	Reported Earnings $50K
= $1 million	:	$50K
= 20	:	1

The P:E ratio of Firm B is 23 to 1, computed as follows:

Price of Common Stock \$1.5 million	:	Reported Earnings \$65K
= \$1.5 million	:	\$65K
= 23.1	:	1

The EBITDA of Firms A and B are calculated as follows:

	Firm A	Firm B
Sales	\$200K	\$200K
Operating Expense other than depreciation	–20K	–20K
EBITDA	\$180K	\$180K

Thus, when this broader measure of earnings is used, the firms have comparable earnings.

At this point it is possible to consider the ratio of total firm value (TFV) as the Value Indicator and EBITDA as the Observable Variable. Since Firm A has debt with a value of \$500K and common equity with a value of \$1 million, the TFV of Firm A is \$1.5 million. Firm B has common stock with a value of \$1.5 million and no debt. Therefore, its TFV is \$1.5 million. Since both Firm A and Firm B have the same TFV and EBITDA, they each have an 8.3 to 1 ratio of TFV to EBITDA, computed as follows:

TVF (\$1.5 million)	:	EBITDA (\$180K)
= \$1.5 million	:	\$180K
= 8.3	:	1

If the target has EBITDA of \$100K, the estimated TFV of the target would be \$830K, computed as follows:

Target's EBITDA	\$100K
Multiplied by the TFV:EBIT ratio of Comparable firms	× 8.3
	\$830K

The value of the target's common stock is \$830K, minus the value of its debt and preferred stock.

In certain cases it may be appropriate to adjust whatever Observable Variable, such as earnings or EBITDA, is utilized to account for abnormalities.

E. Accounting for Control Premiums: The Comparable Transactions Approach

In identifying the Value Indicator, the current trading price of common equity of comparable firms may be used. However, this may understate the value of the target because the current trading price may not reflect a control premium. The price reflecting a control premium is probably a better value indicator in determining the value of the target in a change of control transaction. In focusing on a control premium, the task is to identify comparable companies that have undergone comparable transactions. Alternatively, a control premium may be added to the value determined using the trading value as the Value Indicator.

F. Applicability of the Direct Comparison Approach in Time-Warner

Wasserstein/Shearson used the direct comparison approach in valuing Warner; they used both comparable transactions and comparable companies.

Wasserstein/Shearson's use of the comparable transaction approach is illustrated on page 4 of Documentary Appendix C. One of the Value Indicators used was Transaction Value + Net Debt, which is the total firm value (TFV). Two Observable Variables were used: Net Sales and EBIT. Thus, two broad measures of economic activity were used. A mean, median, high, and low were computed in determining the multiple of Net Sales or EBIT to TFV, that is the ratio between TFV and Net Sales and TFV and EBIT. The implied value of the assets of the Filmed Entertainment segment was then determined by multiplying the 1989 Net Sales and EBIT for that segment by the mean, median, high, and low multipliers.

A similar procedure was followed with Wasserstein/Shearson's comparable companies analysis on page 4 of Documentary Appendix C, except that a 50% control premium was added to the implied asset values. The addition of a control premium to the trading value is one of the techniques suggested by Professor Cornell. [*See* Section 7.13.E]

G. Comparable Companies Rejected in *Orchard*[78]

In *Orchard*,[79] discussed previously, Chancellor Strine rejected the use of the comparable companies methodology by the expert for the company, Orchard, in an appraisal action. The Chancellor concluded:

> I do not know whether it would be possible for me to find an unbiased financial analyst to perform a ground-up comparables valuation of Orchard. But I do know that the one proffered by Orchard is not a reliable one that would be accepted by a disinterested mind.[80]

The Chancellor provided the following insightful discussion of the rationale behind, and conditions for the employment of, this methodology:

> A comparable, or market-based, approach to valuation is rooted in the same intuition as the DCF method. But rather than directly estimating the future cash flows of the subject company and reducing them to present value, the market-based methods draw inferences about the future expected cash flows from the market's expectations about comparable companies. The idea is that if the market expects comparable companies to grow at a certain rate, then one can infer the growth of the subject company by applying a multiple drawn from the comparables to a relevant metric, such as EBITDA or revenues.
>
> For obvious reasons, the utility of a market-based method depends on actually having companies that are sufficiently comparable that their trading multi-

---

78. This section is adapted from Thompson, *Mergers, Acquisitions and Tender Offers*, *supra* Section 1.10, at Section 11:12.6[E].

79. In Re: Appraisal of The Orchard Enterprises, Inc., 2012 Del. Ch. LEXIS 165 (Del. Ch. Ct. July 18, 2012).

80. *Id.* at *35.

> ples provide a relevant insight into the subject company's own growth prospects. When there are a number of corporations competing in a similar industry, the method is easiest to deploy reliably. For example, fast food restaurant chains, commercial banks, and automobile manufacturers might be seen as industries with a number of recognizable players who compete in the same markets. By generating a good set of comparables, one can obtain a sense of how the market perceives the growth prospects of the industry to be, and one can apply the resulting multiples to the relevant metric of the subject company to make a judgment about its value.
>
> When, by contrast, it is difficult to find companies that actually do the same thing as the subject company, the comparables method is less reliable. Reliance on a comparable companies or comparable transactions approach is improper where the purported "comparables" involve significantly different products or services than the company whose appraisal is at issue, or vastly different multiples. "At some point, the differences become so large that the use of the comparable company method becomes meaningless for valuation purposes."

Likewise, if a sample of comparables is identified by a party using this method, and that party determines not to use either the median or the mean of the multiples derived from her sample, but instead picks a multiple that has no logical relation to either, that party is indicating that her comparables are in fact not at all very comparable. She is in that case not deriving a value by inferring that the growth prospects of the subject company are like her sample of comparable companies, but rather she is inferring that they are materially different from her sample. In essence, the party simply picks her own multiple, throwing away her sample as being too different from the subject company to provide a reliable basis for determining its value.[81]

§ 7.14 The Role of the Investment Banker's Fairness Opinions in Mergers and Acquisitions

A. Illustration of a Court's Evaluation of Investment Banker's Fairness Opinion in the *Time-Warner* Case

Excerpt from In Re Time Incorporated Shareholder Litigation

Delaware Chancery Court 1989 Fed. Sec. L. Rep (CCH) 94, 914

Pending are motions in several related lawsuits seeking, principally, a preliminary injunction restraining Time Incorporated from buying stock under a June 16, 1989, offer to purchase 100 million shares of common stock (comprising 51% of the outstanding common stock) of Warner Communications Inc. at $70 per share cash. * * *

It was the view of Wasserstein, Perella that the stock of Time-Warner would trade at around $150 per share. They noted as well that the range might also be higher, citing a range of $160 to $175 per share. In the written presentation given to the board on June 16, the trading range given for the year 1990 is $106–$188, based on both cash flow and earnings per share analysis.

81. Id. at *30–*35.

In the longer term, Time's advisors have predicted trading ranges of $159–$247 for 1991, $230–$332 for 1992 and $208–$402 for 1993. The latter being a range that a Texan might feel at home on. * * *

Note

The court went on to find that Time's board had acted appropriately, and this decision was affirmed by the Delaware Supreme Court. *See* Section 3.14.B. As indicated in the note after the case, the price of Time-Warner shares did not reach the level of the Paramount 1989 offer until 1997.

B. Claim of Negligent Advice against Lazard in *RJR Nabisco* Case

Schneider v. Lazard Frères & Co.

New York Appellate Division, (1990) 552 N.Y.S. 2d 571

Plaintiffs, a group of shareholders in RJR Nabisco, Inc., a Delaware corporation, claim that an unfairly conducted auction of RJR stock resulted in the acceptance of a bid by the RJR Board of Directors more than a billion dollars less than what could have been obtained by a fair auction. They sued the RJR Board and the successful bidder, Kohlberg, Kravis, Roberts & Co., in the Delaware Court of Chancery for an injunction against consummation of the tender offer. * * * [I]n the alternative, the shareholders requested damages in the event an injunction against the tender offer was no longer feasible at the time of trial. The gist of the Delaware action is that the auction, which was run by a Special Committee of disinterested RJR directors, was prematurely terminated at a point when a management-led group of bidders should have been expected to respond to the Kohlberg bid declared as the winner. As the shareholders explain, the practical effect of the relief sought in the Delaware action would be to revive the auction. When a motion by the shareholders for a preliminary injunction in the Delaware action was denied, they brought the instant action in New York against the two investment bankers hired by the Special Committee to advise it in conducting the auction, Lazard Frères & Co. and Dillon Read & Co., Inc., the gist of which is that the Special Committee conducted the auction in the unfair manner it did because of faulty advice given to it by the bankers. More particularly, the shareholders allege that the bankers advised the Special Committee that the final bids submitted by Kohlberg and the Management Group were "substantially equivalent from a financial point of view" when, in fact, the latter was superior; alternatively, the shareholders allege that if the Management Group's bid was inferior, then, given the dynamics of the auction, the bankers should have advised the Special Committee to invite another bid from the Management Group, or, if the two bids were, as they were represented to be, substantially equivalent in value, then the bankers should have advised the Special Committee to solicit a set of tie-breaking bids. The failure to invite tie-breaking bids is presented only as the final and most egregious example of an auction that was throughout run in a way to give Kohlberg an unfair advantage over the Management Group.

The bankers * * * [moved] for an order dismissing the complaint for failure to state a cause of action, their main argument being that their advice was addressed to the Special Committee, not the shareholders, and that they therefore owed no duty to the shareholders to render non-negligent advice; in addition, the bankers argued that if they did owe a duty of care to the shareholders, the complaint does not allege how it was breached.

Turning to whether the bankers owed the shareholders a duty of care, the argument on this question is somewhat distractingly presented mainly in terms of whether the relationship between the shareholders and the bankers was or was not one "approaching privities." * * *

In determining whether the bankers owed the shareholders a duty of care, we think the question is not whether the relationship between them was one approaching privities, but whether the relationship between the shareholders and the Special Committee was one governed by the law of agency or the law of corporations. The bankers argue that well settled principles of corporate law make corporate management the responsibility and prerogative of the board, not the shareholders; that directors at all times, no more so in the present context than in others, act as fiduciaries for the shareholders, this being their reason for being; that it was for the RJR Board to decide, in the exercise of its business judgment and as the shareholders' fiduciary, whether the bankers were negligent, and, if so, whether RJR should sue them for it; and that to permit this action to go forward would be to permit shareholders to decide whether any lawyer, accountant or other professional hired by a board to advise it with respect to corporate business should be sued for malpractice. We reject this argument because we agree with the shareholders that sale of the control of a corporation is not corporate business of the type governed by traditional principles of corporate governance, and that the Special Committee stood in a relationship to the shareholders different from that which normally obtains between a corporation's board and shareholders. The Special Committee's purpose was not to judge transactions accruing to the benefit of the corporate treasury; nor was it concerned with any matters affecting RJR's internal affairs. Rather, its purpose was to advise the shareholders with respect to a transaction that contemplated RJR's demise and whose end and aim was to obtain for the shareholders the highest possible price for their stock. In this "buyout" context, if something less than the highest possible price was obtained, the loss was sustained by the shareholders, not the corporation, and, for that reason, we are of the view that the relationship between the shareholders and the Special Committee was essentially that of principal and agent on which principles of corporate law should not be superimposed [*see Wells v. Shearson Lehman/American Express, Inc.*, 127 A.D.2d 200, 203, 514 N.Y.S.2d 1, *red's on other grounds*, 72 N.Y.2d 11, 530 N.Y.S.2d 517, 526 N.E.2d 8].

We agree with the shareholders that the complaint gives adequate notice of how the bankers were negligent. With respect to the valuation of the bids, the financial facts allegedly disregarded by the bankers are set forth with particularity, and it will be the shareholders' burden to show that a failure to consider these facts was a failure to exercise that degree of care that a reasonably prudent investment banker would have exercised under the same circumstances. With respect to the conduct of the auction, it will be necessary for the shareholders to show that a reasonably prudent person, intent on obtaining the highest possible price for the shareholders' stock, would not have conducted the auction in the manner advised by the bankers. * * *

C. Investment Banker's Conflict: Manipulation of the Sales Process, Stapled Financing—*Del Monte*[82]

The acquisition by three private equity firms (KKR, Centerview, and Vestar) of Del Monte, a publicly held Delaware corporation, illustrates how (1) a target's board should

82. This section is adapted from Thompson, *Mergers, Acquisitions and Tender Offers*, *supra* Section 1.10, at Section 5:5.4[M].

not deal with its investment banker, and (2) an investment banker should take care to avoid the creation of conflicts of interest in the course of its representation of a target in an M&A transaction. In this case, Vice Chancellor Laster of the Delaware Chancery Court rendered a scathing opinion in which, on a preliminary record, he concluded:

> (1) the Del Monte board had breached its fiduciary duties (a) in failing to properly supervise its investment banker, Barclays, and (b) by permitting Barclays to provide buy-side (*i.e.*, stapled) financing, which caused Del Monte to employ the services of a second investment banker for the purpose of rendering a second fairness opinion at a cost of $3 million to Del Monte;
>
> (2) Barclays had inappropriately promoted the sale of Del Monte by, inter alia, causing KKR and Vestar to cooperate in the acquisition of Del Monte in violation of a "no teaming" provision of confidentiality agreements; and
>
> (3) KKR had aided and abetted the Del Monte board's breach of fiduciary duty.[83]

In discussing the essential facts, the court explained:

> Barclays secretly and selfishly manipulated the sale process to engineer a transaction that would permit Barclays to obtain lucrative buy-side financing fees. On multiple occasions, Barclays protected its own interests by withholding information from the Board that could have led Del Monte to retain a different bank, pursue a different alternative, or deny Barclays a buy-side role. Barclays did not disclose the behind-the-scenes efforts of its Del Monte coverage officer to put Del Monte into play. Barclays did not disclose its explicit goal, harbored from the outset, of providing buy-side financing to the acquirer. Barclays did not disclose that in September 2010, without Del Monte's authorization or approval, Barclays steered Vestar [previously the high bidder] into a club bid with KKR, the potential bidder with whom Barclays had the strongest relationship, in violation of confidentiality agreements that prohibited Vestar and KKR from discussing a joint bid without written permission from Del Monte.
>
> Late in the process, at a time when Barclays was ostensibly negotiating the deal price with KKR, Barclays asked KKR for a third of the buy-side financing. Once KKR agreed, Barclays sought and obtained Del Monte's permission. Having Barclays as a co-lead bank was not necessary to secure sufficient financing for the Merger, nor did it generate a higher price for the Company. It simply gave Barclays the additional fees it wanted from the outset. In fact, Barclays can expect to earn slightly more from providing buy-side financing to KKR than it will from serving as Del Monte's sell-side advisor. Barclays' gain cost Del Monte an additional $3 million because Barclays told Del Monte that it now had to obtain a last-minute fairness opinion from a second bank.[84]

The court discussed as follows the approach Vice Chancellor Strine took in analyzing the handling of the investment banker's request to provide stapled financing in the *Toys "R" Us, Inc. Shareholder Litigation*:[85]

83. *In Re* Del Monte Foods Company Shareholders Litigation, 25 A.3d 813 (Del. Ch. 2011).
84. *Id.* at 817–818.
85. *In re* Toys "R" Us, Inc. S'holder Litig., 877 A.2d 975 (Del. Ch. 2005).

> In *Toys "R" Us*, Vice Chancellor Strine considered whether an investment banker's role in providing stapled financing created a conflict of interest that merited injunctive relief. At the outset of the sale process challenged in that case, the sell-side investment banker, First Boston, asked about possibly providing buy-side financing for purchasers of a subsidiary. "The board promptly nixed that idea." ... Then, following a lengthy process during which the form of the transaction shifted from a sale of the subsidiary to a sale of the whole company, and two months after the process culminated in an executed merger agreement, First Boston again asked to be permitted to provide a portion of the buy-side financing. This time the board agreed. Vice Chancellor Strine described that decision as "unfortunate, in that it tends to raise eyebrows by creating the appearance of impropriety, playing into already heightened suspicions about the ethics of investment banking firms." He suggested it would have been "[f]ar better, from the standpoint of instilling confidence, if First Boston had never asked for permission, and had taken the position that its credibility as a sell-side advisor was too important in this case, and in general, for it to simultaneously play on the buy-side in a deal when it was the seller's financial advisor." ... He likewise noted that "it might have been better, in view of First Boston's refusal to refrain, for the board of the Company to have declined the request, even though the request came ... almost two months after the board had signed the merger agreement." ... Nevertheless, after reviewing in detail the public, year-long, multi-phase process that the board and its banker conducted, Vice Chancellor Strine concluded "upon close scrutiny" that First Boston's appearance of conflict did not have "a causal influence" on the board's process.... He cautioned that "[i]n general, however, it is advisable that investment banks representing sellers not create the appearance that they desire buy-side work, especially when it might be that they are more likely to be selected by some buyers for that lucrative role than by others."[86]

Vice Chancellor Laster then distinguished the actions of Barclays with respect to Del Monte from the actions of First Boston with respect to *Toys*:

> Applying these principles to the current case shows that Barclays' activities went far beyond what took place in Toys "R" Us. Barclays set out to provide acquisition financing, as established by the internal screening memos from January and March 2010. Barclays' Del Monte coverage officer pitched a Del Monte LBO to KKR, Apollo, and other private equity firms that would be likely to use Barclays for acquisition financing. Once it secured the sell-side role, Barclays structured a small, private process that maximized the likelihood that it could provide acquisition financing. Barclays never disclosed to the Board its interactions with the private equity shops or its desire to provide acquisition financing.[87]

The court also explained that Barclays ran the "go shop" provision of the merger agreement (see discussion of "go shops," supra) even though Goldman Sachs had made a bid to provide that service. The court discusses as follows the facts surrounding the reasons Goldman was not retained for that service:

> Upon learning of Goldman's interest, Barclays told KKR that Goldman was trying to "scare up competition." ... Brown of KKR told Barclays that he would "manage it" directly with Goldman.... He solved the problem by letting Gold-

86. 25 A.3d at 832–833.
87. *Id.* at 833.

> man participate in 5% of the syndication rights for the acquisition financing, which "squared things away there." ... After that, Goldman dropped its efforts to conduct the go shop.[88]

If Goldman had been retained to run the "go shop" and had been successful in finding an acquirer that topped the bid of the KKR group, then Barclays may have lost the opportunity to provide the financing for the acquisition. Thus, Barclays had an incentive to see that the "go shop" did not result in a higher bid.

The court reasoned that the breach of fiduciary duties here was similar to the breach that occurred in the *Mills* case, discussed supra:

> By failing to provide the serious oversight that would have checked Barclays' misconduct, the directors breached their fiduciary duties in a manner reminiscent of *Mills Acquisition Co. v. Macmillan, Inc.*, 559 A.2d 1261 (Del. 1989). In that decision, the Delaware Supreme Court enjoined a transaction—ironically a leveraged buyout sponsored by KKR—when self-interested management and their financial advisor concealed information from the board. Like management's deal-specific, buy-side conflict in Mills, Barclays' deal-specific, buy-side conflict tainted the advice it gave and the actions it took.[89]

Because Del Monte's board appeared to act in good faith and did not become aware of Barclay's actions in promoting the sale of Del Monte until after discovery was taken in this case, the court concluded that it was highly unlikely that the directors would have any personal liability as a result of the breach of their fiduciary duties. The court explained:

> Unless further discovery reveals different facts, the one-two punch of exculpation under Section 102(b)(7) and full protection under Section 141(e) makes the chances of a judgment for money damages vanishingly small. The same cannot be said for the self-interested aiders and abetters [*i.e.*, KKR]. But while the directors may face little threat of liability, they cannot escape the ramifications of Barclays' misconduct. For purposes of equitable relief, the Board is responsible.[90]

The court went on to grant the following injunction:

> The defendants are enjoined preliminarily from proceeding with the vote on the Merger for a period of 20 days. Pending the vote on the Merger, the parties to the Merger Agreement are enjoined from enforcing the no-solicitation and match-right provisions in Section 6.5(b), (c) and (h), and the termination fee provisions relating to topping bids and changes of recommendation in Section 8.5(b). The injunction is conditioned on the plaintiffs posting a bond in the amount of $1.2 million.[91]

The *Del Monte* decision has valuable lessons for the boards of potential targets, investment bankers, and potential acquirers. The boards of targets should take measures to properly monitor the activities of their investment bankers to ensure that the bankers (1) are not acting inappropriately, (2) do not have any conflicts of interest or properly manage any conflicts, and (3) disclose fully all activities taken in connection with the representation of the target. The engagement letters should contain representations regarding any conflicts and a covenant requiring the disclosure of any subsequently developed conflict.

---

88. *Id.* at 828.
89. *Id.* at 818.
90. *Id.*
91. *Id.* at 818–819.

A target's board should also ensure that there is full disclosure to the shareholders of all aspects of its relationship with its investment banker. Vice Chancellor Laster elaborated on this point as follows:

> Because of the central role played by investment banks in the evaluation, exploration, selection, and implementation of strategic alternatives, this Court has required full disclosure of investment banker compensation and potential conflicts. This Court has not stopped at disclosure, but rather has examined banker conflicts closely to determine whether they tainted the directors' process.[92]

A target's board should not permit its investment banker to provide buy-side financing in the absence of a clear finding by the board that such financing provides a valuable benefit to the firm. In the words of Vice Chancellor Laster, buy side financing could be appropriate where it was "necessary to secure sufficient financing for the Merger,"[93] and "generate[d] a higher price for the Company."[94] A potential conflict could arise where, for example, there are strategic and financial buyers, and the strategic buyers do not need financing. On the other hand, the initial presence of stapled financing could facilitate the process of marketing the target by demonstrating the availability of financing. Along these same lines, a March 2011 analysis of *Del Monte* addresses the following question: "So, when should the financial adviser to a target company provide financing to potential buyers?"[95] The authors respond:

> Simply put, when doing so benefits the target company's stockholders. That benefit could be in the form of facilitating competition among bidders or providing greater financing certainty of more attractive terms to allow prospective buyers to bid more aggressively.... The record will need to show that the target's board carefully weighted the upside against the downside created by its financial adviser's conflict.[96]

In any situation in which stapled financing is provided, the board should consider retaining another, conflict free, investment banker to provide the (or a supplemental) fairness opinion, and of course, the board should take into account the cost of obtaining such an opinion when making the decision regarding stapled financing.

Investment banking firms should take care to ensure that (1) any conflicts are completely disclosed to the client, (2) their efforts are exclusively for the benefit of the client, (3) they receive clear instructions from the client, and (4) the client is fully aware of all actions taken by the bank in the course of the engagement, including any plans the bank has for requesting to provide buy-side financing.

Private equity firms and other potential acquirers should take steps to ensure that they are in full compliance with any confidentiality or other agreement relating to the transaction, such as a no teaming provision.

References

The references for this chapter are set out in the Scope.

---

92. *Id.* at 832.
93. *Id.* at 818.
94. *Id.*
95. Peter D. Lyons, David P. Connolly, and Nathan Sawyer, *Sell-Side Financing After In re Del Monte Foods*, 15 The M&A Lawyer 1, 5 (March 2011).
96. *Id.* at 5.

Chapter 8

Introduction to Antitrust Law Aspects of Mergers and Acquisitions

§ 8.1 Scope

This chapter examines the antitrust aspects of mergers and acquisitions. The focus is primarily on horizontal mergers, which are mergers between competitors. Although the antitrust laws can prohibit conglomerate mergers (*i.e.*, mergers between firms in unrelated businesses) and vertical mergers (*i.e.*, mergers between firms at different levels in the production chain), very few of these mergers are challenged.

This chapter focuses on substantive antitrust law; Chapter 9 examines the Hart-Scott-Rodino law, which requires that the parties to certain acquisitions give prior notice of the acquisition to the federal antitrust enforcement agencies: The Antitrust Division of the Department of Justice and the Federal Trade Commission (FTC). As will be seen in Chapter 9, the parties may elect to give notification to the appropriate state antitrust official. Section 9.11 discusses the provisions of a merger agreement addressing the antitrust review of the transaction. The materials in this chapter are covered in greater detail in Chapter 12 of Thompson, *Mergers, Acquisitions and Tender Offers*, *supra* Section 1.10.

Part I, which provides an introduction, contains Sections 8.1 through 8.9. Section 8.2 presents an introductory problem, and Section 8.3 provides an introduction to the scope and purpose of the antitrust laws. Section 8.4 sets out Sections 1 (prohibition against certain agreements in restraint of trade) and 2 (prohibition against monopolization) of the Sherman Act and Section 7 of the Clayton Act, the principal weapon against anticompetitive mergers and acquisitions. Section 8.5 reviews the legislative history of Section 7, and Sections 8.6 through 8.9 set out four of the leading Supreme Court cases under Section 7: *Brown Shoe*, *Philadelphia National Bank*, *Vons*, and *General Dynamics*.

Part II, which consists of Section 8.10 through Section 8.19, presents an introduction to the microeconomic foundations of antitrust merger law. An appreciation of the core microeconomic principles of competition, monopoly, and oligopoly is key to understanding the approach of the antitrust laws to mergers and acquisitions.

Part III, which is introduced in a special Scope section in Section 8.20, presents an analysis of the 2010 Horizontal Merger Guidelines of the Justice Department and FTC. These Guidelines set out the enforcement standard these agencies follow in examining the antitrust aspects of mergers. Part III also examines some of the principal cases applying concepts set out in these Guidelines. This part, which consists of Sections 8.20 through 8.36, also introduces the 1993 Horizontal Merger Guidelines of the National Association of Attorneys General (NAAG). Many mergers, including mergers involving two U.S. firms, are subject to antitrust scrutiny in foreign jurisdictions, such as the European Union. The approach of the European Union's Competition Commission to the antitrust review of mergers is examined in Chapter 26.

Part IV, which consists of Sections 8.37 and 8.38, contains the Justice Department's 1984 Guidelines on Conglomerate and Vertical Mergers. Part V, which focuses on competitor and target standing, contains Sections 8.39 and 8.40.

Part I
Introduction

§ 8.2 Basic Introductory Problem on Antitrust Aspects of Mergers and Acquisitions

Time Entertainment, Inc. is contemplating an acquisition of an entertainment company, such as Warner Entertainment, Inc. or Paramount Entertainment, Inc. Time is also engaged in the entertainment business and there are likely to be substantial overlaps between the business operations of Time and those of the ultimate target. Indeed, Time would generally like to get as much overlap as possible, subject to avoiding an antitrust challenge to the acquisition.

To help in planning for the acquisition, Time's Chief of M & A asks you for a brief memo outlining the current approach of the antitrust authorities in enforcing Section 7 of the Clayton Act with regard to horizontal mergers.

§ 8.3 Introduction to the Scope and Purpose of the Antitrust Laws

General Accounting Office Report to House Judiciary Committee, Chairman on Changes in Antitrust Enforcement Policies and Activities of the Justice Department

(Dec. 7, 1990)

The Department of Justice's Antitrust Division is responsible for promoting and maintaining competition in the marketplace by enforcing the federal antitrust laws. It shares enforcement responsibility with the Federal Trade Commission (FTC) and state attorneys general. The Division may bring either civil or criminal suits against anticompetitive conduct. In addition, private individuals injured in business or property as a result of violations of the antitrust laws may also institute civil antitrust actions in federal district courts. * * *

The antitrust laws are based on a belief that a competitive market system provides optimum use of economic resources and maximizes consumer benefits. As such, the laws seek to both prevent anticompetitive behavior and preserve and promote competition. The Sherman Antitrust Act and the Clayton Antitrust Act make up the basic antitrust legislation. Each shares the objective of protecting and promoting competition in the marketplace.

Section 1 of the Sherman Act [*see* Section 8.4] makes illegal any contract, combination, or conspiracy that results in a "restraint of trade." The courts have construed the term to cover a variety of horizontal and vertical trade restraining agreements. Horizontal restraints are agreements among competitors at the same level of the production or distribution process (*e.g.*, among competing manufacturers or distributors). Vertical restraints are arrangements between persons or firms operating at different levels of the manufacturing or distribution chain (*e.g.*, between a manufacturer and a wholesaler) that restrict the conditions under which firms may purchase, sell, or resell. Section 2 of the Sherman Act [*see* Section 8.4] prohibits monopolization as well as attempts, combinations, or conspiracies to monopolize.

The Clayton Act, as amended, supplements the Sherman Act by proscribing certain types of market behavior that constitute an existing restraint of trade and other behavior that, if left as is, may restrain trade. Section 7 [*see* Section 8.4] expands on the general prohibitions of the Sherman Act by prohibiting certain mergers or acquisitions of stocks or assets of firms engaged in interstate or foreign commerce. In general, mergers and acquisitions covered by section 7 are unlawful if they would tend to create a monopoly or may substantially lessen competition.

The Hart-Scott-Rodino Antitrust Improvements Act of 1976, which added section 7A to the Clayton Act, [*see* Chapter 9] provides several mechanisms to assist the Division in investigating whether proposed mergers and acquisitions ("mergers") would be anticompetitive. * * * The Hart-Scott-Rodino Act requires enterprises that have sales or assets in excess of certain thresholds to submit information concerning the proposed transaction. After submission, the parties must wait a specified time (between 15 and 30 days, depending on the nature of the transaction) before the transaction can be consummated. * * *

To prevent duplication of activities, the Division and the FTC coordinate responsibility for investigations under a formal liaison or "clearance" agreement. Under this arrangement, either agency wishing to pursue an investigation requests clearance from the other to proceed. * * *

§ 8.4 Principal Antitrust Laws Governing Mergers and Acquisitions

A. The Principal Statutes

The principal substantive provision of the antitrust laws governing mergers and acquisitions is Section 7 of the Clayton Act. This provision was originally added to the law in 1914 as a supplement to Sections 1 and 2 of the Sherman Act, which was enacted in 1890. Section 7 was substantially revised in 1950. Prior to 1950 most merger cases arose under § 1 and § 2 of the Sherman Act. Section 7 is directed at the substantive issue of whether a merger or acquisition should be prohibited on antitrust grounds.

The Hart-Scott-Rodino Pre-merger Notification Law requires the parties to certain proposed mergers and acquisitions to file information with respect to the proposed transaction with the Justice Department and the Federal Trade Commission prior to completing the transaction. This law is examined in Chapter 9.

Section 5 of the Federal Trade Commission Act, which in many respects is a backstop to § 1 and § 2 of the Sherman Act, is not examined here.

SECTION 1 OF THE SHERMAN ACT

> Every contract, combination in the form of trust or otherwise, or conspiracy, in restraint of trade or commerce among the several States, or with foreign nations, is hereby declared to be illegal. Every person who shall make any contract or engage in any combination or conspiracy hereby declared to be illegal shall

be deemed guilty of a felony and, on conviction thereof, shall be punished by fine not exceeding one million dollars if a corporation, or, if any other person, one hundred thousand dollars, or by imprisonment not exceeding three years, or by both said punishments, in the discretion of the court.

SECTION 2 OF THE SHERMAN ACT

Every person who shall monopolize, or attempt to monopolize, or combine or conspire with any other person or persons, to monopolize any part of the trade or commerce among the several States, or with foreign nations, shall be deemed guilty of a felony, and, on conviction thereof, shall be punished by fine not exceeding one million dollars if a corporation, or, if any other person, one hundred thousand dollars, or by imprisonment not exceeding three years, or by both said punishments, in the discretion of the court.

SECTION 7 OF THE CLAYTON ACT

No person engaged in commerce or in any activity affecting commerce shall acquire, directly or indirectly, the whole or any part of the stock or other share capital and no person subject to the jurisdiction of the Federal Trade Commission shall acquire the whole or any part of the assets of another person engaged also in commerce or in any activity affecting commerce, where in any line of commerce or in any activity affecting commerce in any section of the country, the effect of such acquisition may be substantially to lessen competition, or to tend to create a monopoly. * * *

This section shall not apply to persons purchasing such stock solely for investment and not using the same by voting or otherwise to bring about, or in attempting to bring about, the substantial lessening of competition. * * *

B. Introduction to Antitrust Analysis under Sections 1 and 2 of the Sherman Act and Section 7 of the Clayton Act

Guide to the FTC, Bureau of Competition

FTC Web Site (June 27, 2006)

Nonmerger Enforcement. * * * The Commission's nonmerger enforcement efforts focus on business activities that significantly threaten competition and harm consumers. These involve direct competitors ("horizontal" arrangements), suppliers and customers ("vertical" arrangements), or single firms.

The Bureau focuses significant attention on horizontal restraints, or agreements between or among direct competitors, because these pose the greatest risk of harm to competition. Under the antitrust laws companies may not agree to limit competition in ways that hurt consumers. [*See* Section 1 of the Sherman Act and Section 5 of the Federal Trade Commission Act]

Horizontal restraints may take many different forms:

- An explicit agreement among competitors on price—price fixing—is illegal per se. Competitors must establish prices and terms independently.
- The legality of many other types of agreements is not as clear-cut [and thus such agreements are subject to a "rule of reason" analysis]. These cases often are complex and require a detailed and painstaking examination of the facts to determine whether the agreement violates antitrust laws. For example, an agreement among

manufacturers to adopt specifications requiring fire-resistant materials for certain products may have a beneficial effect on public safety that far outweighs any impact on competition.

Agreements among competitors to divide sales territories or allocate customers are generally illegal because they are essentially agreements not to compete. For example, an agreement between cable TV companies not to enter each other's territory would prevent the head-to-head competition that helps consumers. * * *

Restrictions agreed to by firms at different levels within an industry, known as vertical restraints, also can be harmful to consumers, although these restraints tend to be more beneficial than not.

The sale of one product on condition that a customer purchase a second product, which the customer may not want or can buy elsewhere at a lower price, is a "tie-in." Requirements like these are illegal if they harm competition. * * *

Practices of single firms may violate the antitrust laws' prohibition on monopolization or attempted monopolization. [*See* Section 2 of the Sherman Act and Section 5 of the FTC Act] Although it is not illegal to have a monopoly, a single company cannot monopolize or try to monopolize an industry through unfair practices—tactics that either unreasonably exclude firms from the market or significantly impair their ability to compete. For example, it would likely be illegal for a company with a monopoly in one market to attempt to use its power in that market to interfere with competition in another market.

Merger Enforcement. Most mergers actually benefit competition and consumers by allowing firms to operate more efficiently. In a competitive market, firms pass on these lower costs to consumers. But some mergers, by reducing competition, can cost consumers many millions of dollars every year in the form of higher prices and reduced product quality, consumer choice and innovation.

The Bureau of Competition reviews mergers to determine which ones have the potential to harm consumers; thoroughly investigates those that may be troublesome; and recommends enforcement action to the Commission when necessary to protect competition and consumers. [*See* Section 7 of the Clayton Act] While the FTC challenges only a small percentage of mergers, its merger enforcement actions typically save consumers hundreds of millions of dollars each year.

The Commission's merger enforcement activity focuses primarily on mergers between direct competitors ("horizontal" mergers), because these maybe most likely to harm consumers. The Commission also examines mergers involving firms at different levels of the same industry ("vertical" mergers) and those involving firms that exert a procompetitive influence because of the possibility of their entering a market ("potential competition" mergers).

In a *horizontal* merger, a direct competitor maybe eliminated, allowing the acquiring firm latitude to raise prices without losing sales.

A *vertical* merger, such as a manufacturer acquiring a supplier of component products, or a manufacturer merging with a distributor of its products, is less likely to be anticompetitive, because the parties do not compete with each other. A vertical merger may harm competition, however, by making it difficult for competitors to gain access to an important component product or to an important channel of distribution, such as cable TV networks for providers of television programming.

Various remedies may be suitable for transactions that pose antitrust concerns. These include settlement, litigation or abandonment of the transaction by the parties:

It often is possible to correct the antitrust problems raised by a merger through the divestiture of assets used in the affected markets. Divestiture is the most common but not the only remedy employed. Mergers of large companies usually involve many different markets, and a divestiture of a part of the company to another firm may protect competition while allowing the beneficial aspects of the merger to go forward.

In some cases, however, a divestiture remedy is insufficient, or the parties cannot agree on the scope of needed divestitures. Then, the Commission may seek to prevent the entire transaction by asking a federal court to block the merger from proceeding.

§ 8.5 The Supreme Court's Review of the Legislative History of the Amended Section 7

Brown Shoe Co. v. United States

United States Supreme Court, 1962 82 S. Ct. 1502

LEGISLATIVE HISTORY

This case is one of the first to come before us in which the Government's complaint is based upon allegations that the appellant has violated Section 7 of the Clayton Act, as that section was amended in 1950.[1] * * *

As enacted in 1914, § 7 of the original Clayton Act prohibited the acquisition by one corporation of the *stock* of another corporation when such acquisition would result in a substantial lessening of competition *between the acquiring and the acquired* companies, or tend to create a monopoly in any line of commerce. The Act did not, by its explicit terms, or as construed by this Court, bar the acquisition by one corporation of the *assets* of another. Nor did it appear to preclude the acquisition of stock in any corporation other than a direct competitor. * * *

The dominant theme pervading congressional consideration of the 1950 amendments was a fear of what was considered to be a rising tide of economic concentration in the American economy. Apprehension in this regard was bolstered by the publication in 1948 of the Federal Trade Commission's study on corporate mergers. Statistics from this and other current studies were cited as evidence of the danger to the American economy in unchecked corporate expansions through mergers. Other considerations cited in support of the bill were the desirability of retaining "local control" over industry and the protection of small businesses. Throughout the recorded discussion may be found examples of Congress' fear not only of accelerated concentration of economic power on economic grounds, but also of the threat to other values a trend toward concentration was thought to pose.

What were some of the factors, relevant to a judgment as to the validity of a given merger, specifically discussed by Congress in redrafting § 7?

First, there is no doubt that Congress did wish to "plug the loophole" and to include within the coverage of the Act the acquisition of assets no less than the acquisition of stock.

---

1. Material in italics was added by the amendments; material in brackets was deleted. "No corporation engaged in commerce shall acquire, directly or indirectly, the whole or any part of the stock or other share capital *and no corporation subject to the jurisdiction of the Federal Trade Commission shall acquire the whole or any part of the assets* of another corporation engaged also in commerce, where *in any line of commerce in any section of the country,* the effect of such acquisition may be [to] substantially *to* lessen competition [between the corporation whose stock is so acquired and the corporation making the acquisition, or to restrain such commerce in any section or community], or *to* tend to create a monopoly [of any line of commerce]." * * *

Second, by the deletion of the "acquiring-acquired" language in the original text, it hoped to make plain that §7 applied not only to mergers between actual competitors, but also to vertical and conglomerate mergers whose effect may tend to lessen competition in any line of commerce in any section of the country.

Third, it is apparent that a keystone in the erection of a barrier to what Congress saw was the rising tide of economic concentration, was its provision of authority for arresting mergers at a time when the trend to a lessening of competition in a line of commerce was still in its incipiency. * * *

Fourth, and closely related to the third, Congress rejected, as inappropriate to the problem it sought to remedy, the application to §7 cases of the standards for judging the legality of business combinations adopted by the courts in dealing with cases arising under the Sherman Act, and which may have been applied to some early cases arising under original §7.

Fifth, at the same time that it sought to create an effective tool for preventing all mergers having demonstrable anti-competitive effects, Congress recognized the stimulation to competition that might flow from particular mergers. When concern as to the Act's breadth was expressed, supporters of the amendments indicated that it would not impede, for example, a merger between two small companies to enable the combination to compete more effectively with larger corporations dominating the relevant market, nor a merger between a corporation which is financially healthy and a failing one which no longer can be a vital competitive factor in the market. The deletion of the word "community" in the original Act's description of the relevant geographic market is another illustration of Congress' desire to indicate that its concern was with the adverse effects of a given merger on competition only in an economically significant "section" of the country. Taken as a whole, the legislative history illuminates congressional concern with the protection of *competition*, not *competitors*, and its desire to restrain mergers only to the extent that such combinations may tend to lessen competition.

Sixth, Congress neither adopted nor rejected specifically any particular tests for measuring the relevant markets, either as defined in terms of product or in terms of geographic locus of competition, within which the anti-competitive effects of a merger were to be judged. Nor did it adopt a definition of the word "substantially," whether in quantitative terms of sales or assets or market shares or in designated qualitative terms, by which a merger's effects on competition were to be measured.

Seventh, while providing no definite quantitative or qualitative tests by which enforcement agencies could gauge the effects of a given merger to determine whether it may "substantially" lessen competition or tend toward monopoly, Congress indicated plainly that a merger had to be functionally viewed, in the context of its particular industry. * * *

Eighth, Congress used the words "*may* be substantially to lessen competition" (emphasis supplied), to indicate that its concern was with probabilities, not certainties. * * *

§8.6 Market Shares Are the Primary Index

Brown Shoe Co. v. United States

United States Supreme Court, 1962 82 S. Ct. 1502

Mr. Chief Justice Warren:

This suit was initiated in November 1955 when the Government filed a civil action in the United States District Court for the Eastern District of Missouri alleging that a contemplated merger between the G. R. Kinney Company, Inc. (Kinney) [the target] and the Brown Shoe Company, Inc. (Brown) [the acquiror], through an exchange of Kinney for Brown stock, would violate § 7 of the Clayton Act. * * *

[After finding] that the District Court correctly defined men's, women's, and children's shoes as the relevant lines of commerce [*i.e.*, product market] in which to analyze the * * * horizontal aspects of the merger [and] that the District Court properly defined the relevant geographic markets in which to analyze this merger as those cities with a population exceeding 10,000 and their environs in which both Brown and Kinney retailed shoes through their own outlets, [the court went on to reason:]

The Probable Effect of the Merger. Having delineated the product and geographic markets within which the effects of this merger are to be measured, we turn to an examination of the District Court's finding that as a result of the merger competition in the retailing of men's, women's and children's shoes may be lessened substantially in those cities in which both Brown and Kinney stores are located. * * *

[W]e believe the record is adequate to support the findings of the District Court. * * * An analysis of undisputed statistics of sales of shoes in the cities in which both Brown and Kinney sell shoes at retail, separated into the appropriate lines of commerce, provides a persuasive factual foundation upon which the required prognosis of the merger's effects may be built. * * * They show, for example, that during 1955 in 32 separate cities, ranging in size and location from Topeka, Kansas, to Batavia, New York, and Hobbs, New Mexico, the combined share of Brown and Kinney sales of women's shoes (by unit volume) exceeded 20%. In 31 cities some the same as those used in measuring the effect of the merger in the women's line the combined share of children's shoes sales exceeded 20%; in 6 cities their share exceeded 40%. In Dodge City, Kansas, their combined share of the market for women's shoes was over 57%; their share of the children's shoe market in that city was 49%. In the 7 cities in which Brown's and Kinney's combined shares of the market for women's shoes were greatest (ranging from 33% to 57%) each of the parties alone, prior to the merger, had captured substantial portions of those markets (ranging from 13% to 34%); the merger intensified this existing concentration. In 118 separate cities the combined shares of the market of Brown and Kinney in the sale of one of the relevant lines of commerce exceeded 5%. In 47 cities, their share exceeded 5% in all three lines.

The market share which companies may control by merging is one of the most important factors to be considered when determining the probable effects of the combination on effective competition in the relevant market. In an industry as fragmented as shoe retailing, the control of substantial shares of the trade in a city may have important effects on competition. If a merger achieving 5% control were now approved, we might be required to approve future merger efforts by Brown's competitors seeking similar market shares. * * * It is competition, not competitors, which the Act protects. But we cannot fail to recognize Congress' desire to promote competition through the protection of viable, small, locally owned business. Congress appreciated that occasional higher costs and prices might result from the maintenance of fragmented industries and markets. It resolved these competing considerations in favor of decentralization. We must give effect to that decision.

Other factors to be considered in evaluating the probable effects of a merger in the relevant market lend additional support to the District Court's conclusion that this merger may substantially lessen competition. One such factor is the history of tendency toward concentration in the industry. As we have previously pointed out, the shoe industry has, in recent years, been a prime example of such a trend. * * * As a result of this merger, Brown moved into second place nationally in terms of retail stores directly owned. Including the stores on its franchise plan, the merger placed under Brown's control almost 1,600 shoe outlets, or about 7.2% of the Nation's retail "shoe stores" as defined by the Census Bureau, and 2.3% of the Nation's total retail shoe outlets. We cannot avoid the mandate of Congress that tendencies toward concentration in industry are to be curbed in their incipiency, particularly when those tendencies are being accelerated through giant steps striding across a hundred cities at a time. In the light of the trends in this industry we agree with the Government and the court below that this is an appropriate place at which to call a halt. * * *

The judgment is affirmed.

§ 8.7 Supreme Court's Prima Facie Rule of Illegality

United States v. Philadelphia National Bank

United States Supreme Court, 1963 83 S. Ct. 1715

Mr. Justice Brennan:

The United States, appellant here, brought this civil action in the United States District Court for the Eastern District of Pennsylvania under § 4 of the Sherman Act, and § 15 of the Clayton Act, to enjoin a proposed merger of The Philadelphia National Bank (PNB) and Girard Trust Corn Exchange Bank (Girard), appellees here. The complaint charged violations of § 1 of the Sherman Act, 15 U.S.C. § 1, and § 7 of the Clayton Act, 15 U.S.C. § 18. * * * We reverse the judgment of the District Court. We hold that the merger of appellees is forbidden by § 7 of the Clayton Act and so must be enjoined; we need not, and therefore do not, reach the further question of alleged violation of § 1 of the Sherman Act. * * *

[**Facts**] The Philadelphia National Bank and Girard Trust Corn Exchange Bank are, respectively, the second and third largest of the 42 commercial banks with head offices in the Philadelphia metropolitan area, which consists of the City of Philadelphia and its three contiguous counties in Pennsylvania. The home county of both banks is the city itself; Pennsylvania law, however, permits branching into the counties contiguous to the home county, and both banks have offices throughout the four-county area. PNB, a national bank, has assets of over $1,000,000,000, making it (as of 1959) the twenty-first largest bank in the Nation. Girard a state bank is a member of the FRS and is insured by the FDIC; it has assets of about $750,000,000. Were the proposed merger to be consummated, the resulting bank would be the largest in the four-county area, with (approximately) 36% of the area banks' total assets, 36% of deposits, and 34% of net loans. It and the second largest (First Pennsylvania Bank and Trust Company, now the largest) would have between them 59% of the total assets, 58% of deposits, and 58% of the net loans, while after the merger the four largest banks in the area would have 78% of total assets, 77% of deposits, and 78% of net loans.

The present size of both PNB and Girard is in part the result of mergers. Indeed, the trend toward concentration is noticeable in the Philadelphia area generally, in which the number of commercial banks has declined from 108 in 1947 to the present 42. * * *

In November 1960 the boards of directors of the two banks approved a proposed agreement for their consolidation under the PNB charter. By the terms of the agreement, PNB's stockholders were to retain their share certificates * * * while Girard's stockholders would surrender their shares in exchange for shares in the consolidated bank. * * *

[**Statute**] The statutory test is whether the effect of the merger "may be substantially to lessen competition" "in any line of commerce in any section of the country." * * *

[**Product Market**] We have no difficulty in determining the "line of commerce" (relevant product or services market) and "section of the country" (relevant geographical market) in which to appraise the probable competitive effects of appellees' proposed merger. We agree with the District Court that the cluster of products (various kinds of credit) and services (such as checking accounts and trust administration) denoted by the term "commercial banking," composes a distinct line of commerce. * * *

[**Geographic Market**] We part company with the District Court on the determination of the appropriate "section of the country." The proper question to be asked in this case is not where the parties to the merger do business or even where they compete, but where, within the area of competitive overlap, the effect of the merger on competition will be direct and immediate. * * *

We think that the four-County Philadelphia metropolitan area, which state law apparently recognizes as a meaningful banking community in allowing Philadelphia banks to branch within it, and which would seem roughly to delineate the area in which bank customers that are neither very large nor very small find it practical to do their banking business, is a more appropriate 'section of the country' in which to appraise the instant merger than any larger or smaller or different area. We are helped to this conclusion by the fact that the three federal banking agencies regard the area in which banks have their offices as an "area of effective competition." * * *

[**Effects**] Having determined the relevant market, we come to the ultimate question under § 7: whether the effect of the merger "may be substantially to lessen competition" in the relevant market. Clearly, this is not the kind of question which is susceptible of a ready and precise answer in most cases. It requires not merely an appraisal of the immediate impact of the merger upon competition, but a prediction of its impact upon competitive conditions in the future; this is what is meant when it is said that the amended § 7 was intended to arrest anticompetitive tendencies in their "incipiency." * * *

We noted in *Brown Shoe Co.*, [Section 8.6], that "[t]he dominant theme pervading congressional consideration of the 1950 amendments (to § 7) was a fear of what was considered to be a rising tide of economic concentration in the American economy." This intense congressional concern with the trend toward concentration warrants dispensing, in certain cases, with elaborate proof of market structure, market behavior, or probable anticompetitive effects. Specifically, we think that a merger which produces a firm controlling an undue percentage share of the relevant market, and results in a significant increase in the concentration of firms in that market is so inherently likely to lessen competition substantially that it must be enjoined in the absence of evidence clearly showing that the merger is not likely to have such anticompetitive effects.

Such a test lightens the burden of proving illegality only with respect to mergers whose size makes them inherently suspect in light of Congress' design in § 7 to prevent undue concentration. Furthermore, the test is fully consonant with economic theory. That "(c)ompetition is likely to be greatest when there are many sellers, none of which has any significant market share," is common ground among most economists, and was undoubtedly a premise of congressional reasoning about the antimerger statute.

The merger of appellees will result in a single bank's controlling at least 30% of the commercial banking business in the four-county Philadelphia metropolitan area. Without attempting to specify the smallest market share which would still be considered to threaten undue concentration, we are clear that 30% presents that threat. Further, whereas presently the two largest banks in the area (First Pennsylvania and PNB) control between them approximately 44% of the area's commercial banking business, the two largest after the merger (PNB-Girard and First Pennsylvania) will control 59%. Plainly, we think, this increase of more than 33% in concentration must be regarded as significant. * * *

There is nothing in the record of this case to rebut the inherently anticompetitive tendency manifested by these percentages. * * *

We turn now to three affirmative justifications which appellees offer for the proposed merger. * * *

Second, it is suggested that the increased lending limit of the resulting bank will enable it to compete with the large out-of-state bank, particularly the New York banks, for very large loans. We reject this application of the concept of "countervailing power." If anticompetitive effects in one market could be justified by procompetitive consequences in another, the logical upshot would be that every firm in an industry could, without violating § 7, embark on a series of mergers that would make it in the end as large as the industry leader. * * *

This brings us to appellees' final contention, that Philadelphia needs a bank larger than it now has in order to bring business to the area and stimulate its economic development. We are clear, however, that a merger the effect of which "may be substantially to lessen competition" is not saved because, on some ultimate reckoning of social or economic debits and credits, it may be deemed beneficial. * * *

Reversed and remanded with direction.

§ 8.8 The Government's Most Significant Victory

United States v. Von's Grocery, Co.

United States Supreme Court, 1966 86 S. Ct. 1478

Mr. Justice Black:

On March 25, 1960, the United States brought this action charging that the acquisition by Von's Grocery Company of its direct competitor Shopping Bag Food Stores, both large retail grocery companies in Los Angeles, California, violated § 7 of the Clayton Act * * *.

The sole question here is whether the District Court properly concluded on the facts before it that the Government had failed to prove a violation of § 7.

The record shows the following facts relevant to our decision. The market involved here is the retail grocery market in the Los Angeles area. In 1958 Von's retail sales ranked third in the area and Shopping Bag's ranked sixth. In 1960 their sales together were 7.5% of the total two and one-half billion dollars of retail groceries sold in the Los Angeles market each year. * * * The merger of these two highly successful, expanding and aggressive competitors created the second largest grocery chain in Los Angeles. * * * In addition the findings of the District Court show that the number of owners operating single stores in the Los Angeles retail grocery market decreased from 5,365 in 1950 to 3,818 in 1961. By 1963, three years after the merger, the number of single-store owners had dropped still further to 3,590. * * * Moreover, a table prepared by the Federal Trade Commission * * * shows that acquisitions and mergers in the Los Angeles retail grocery market have continued at a rapid rate since the merger. These facts alone are enough to cause us to conclude contrary to the District Court that the Von's-Shopping Bag merger did violate § 7. Accordingly, we reverse. * * *

Mr. Justice Stewart, with whom Mr. Justice Harlan joins, dissenting.

[T]he Court pronounces its work consistent with the line of our decisions under § 7 since the passage of the 1950 amendment. The sole consistency that I can find is that in litigation under § 7, the Government always wins. * * * The merger between Von's and Shopping Bag produced a firm with 1.4% of the grocery stores and 7.5% of grocery sales in Los Angeles, and resulted in an increase of 1.1% in the market share enjoyed by the two largest firms in the market and 3.3% in the market share of the six largest firms. The former two figures are hardly the "undue percentage" of the market, nor are the latter two figures the "significant increase" in concentration, that would make this merger inherently suspect under the standard of *Philadelphia Nat. Bank*. Instead, the circumstances of the present merger fall far outside the simplified test established by that case for precisely the sort of merger here involved. * * *

§ 8.9 Rebutting the Supreme Court's Prima Facie Case

United States v. General Dynamics

United States Supreme Court, 1974 94 S. Ct. 1186

Mr. Justice Stewart:

On September 22, 1967, the Government commenced this suit in the United States District Court for the Northern District of Illinois, challenging as violative of § 7 of the Clayton Act, the acquisition of the stock of United Electric Coal Companies by Material Service Corp. and its successor, General Dynamics Corp. * * * [T]he District Court issued an opinion and judgment finding no violation of the Clayton Act. The Government appealed * * *.

[**Facts**] At the time of the acquisition involved here, Material Service Corp. was a large Midwest producer and supplier of building materials, concrete, limestone, and coal. All of its coal production was from deep-shaft mines operated by it or its affiliate, appellee Freeman Coal Mining Corp., and production from these operations amounted to 6.9 million tons of coal in 1959 and 8.4 million tons in 1967. In 1954, Material Service began to acquire the stock of United Electric Coal Companies. United Electric at all relevant times operated only strip or open-pit mines in Illinois and Kentucky; at the time of trial in 1970 a number of its mines had closed and its operations had been reduced to four mines in Illinois and none in Kentucky. In 1959, it produced 3.6 million tons of coal, and by 1967, it had increased this output to 5.7 million tons. Material Service's purchase of United Electric stock continued until 1959. At this point Material's holdings amounted to more than 34% of United Electric's outstanding shares and all parties are now agreed on this point. Material had effective control of United Electric. The president of Freeman was elected chairman of United Electric's executive committee, and other changes in the corporate structure of United Electric were made at the behest of Material Service.

Some months after this takeover, Material Service was itself acquired by the appellee General Dynamics Corp. General Dynamics is a large diversified corporation, much of its revenues coming from sales of aircraft, communications, and marine products to Government agencies. * * * In September 1966 the board of directors of General Dynamics authorized a tender offer to holders of the remaining United Electric stock. This offer was successful, and United Electric shortly thereafter became a wholly owned subsidiary of General Dynamics.

[**Issues**] The thrust of the Government's complaint was that the acquisition of United Electric by Material Service in 1959 violated § 7 of the Clayton Act because the takeover substantially lessened competition in the production and sale of coal in either or both of two geographic markets. It contended that a relevant "section of the country" within the meaning of § 7 was, alternatively, the State of Illinois or the Eastern Interior Coal Province Sales Area, the latter being one of four major coal distribution areas recognized by the coal industry and comprising Illinois and Indiana, and parts of Kentucky, Tennessee, Iowa, Minnesota, Wisconsin, and Missouri.

At trial controversy focused on three basic issues: the propriety of coal as a "line of commerce," the definition of Illinois or the Eastern Interior Coal Province Sales Area as a relevant "section of the country," and the probability of a lessening of competition within these or any other product and geographic markets resulting from the acquisition. The District Court decided against the Government on each of these issues. * * *

[**Government's Position**] The Government sought to prove a violation of § 7 of the Clayton Act principally through statistics showing that within certain geographic markets the coal industry was concentrated among a small number of large producers; that this concentration was increasing; and that the acquisition of United Electric would materially enlarge the market share of the acquiring company and thereby contribute to the trend toward concentration.

The concentration of the coal market in Illinois and, alternatively, in the Eastern Interior Coal Province was demonstrated by a table of the shares of the largest two, four, and 10 coal-producing firms in each of these areas for both 1957 and 1967 that revealed the following:

	Eastern Interior Coal Province		Illinois	
	1957	1967	1957	1967
Top 2 firms	29.6	48.6	37.8	52.9
Top 4 firms	43.0	62.9	54.5	75.2
Top 10 firms	65.5	91.4	84.0	98.0

These statistics, the Government argued, showed not only that the coal industry was concentrated among a small number of leading producers, but that the trend had been toward increasing concentration. Furthermore, the undisputed fact that the number of coal-producing firms in Illinois decreased almost 73% during the period of 1957 to 1967 from 144 to 39 was claimed to be indicative of the same trend. The acquisition of United Electric by Material Service resulted in increased concentration of coal sales among the leading producers in the areas chosen by the Government, as shown by the following table:

	1959			1967		
	Share of top 2 but for merger	Share of top 2 given merger	Percent Increase	Share of top 2 but for merger	Share of top 2 given merger	Percent Increase
Province	33.1	37.9	14.5	45.0	48.6	8.0
Illinois	36.6	44.3	22.4	44.0	52.9	20.2

Finally, the Government's statistics indicated that the acquisition increased the share of the merged company in the Illinois and Eastern Interior Coal Province coal markets by significant degrees:

	Province		Illinois	
	Rank	Share (percent)	Rank	Share (percent)
1959				
Freeman	2	7.6	2	15.1
United Electric	6	4.8	5	8.1
Combined	2	12.4	1	23.2
1967				
Freeman	5	6.5	2	12.9
United Electric	9	4.4	6	8.9
Combined	2	10.9	2	21.8

[**Analysis of Government's Position**] In prior decisions involving horizontal mergers between competitors, this Court has found prima facie violations of § 7 of the Clayton Act from aggregate statistics of the sort relied on by the United States in this case. [Citing *Brown Shoe Co. v. United States*, [Section 8.6] and *United States v. Philadelphia National Bank*, [Section 8.7].]

While the statistical showing proffered by the Government in this case, the accuracy of which was not discredited by the District Court or contested by the appellees, would under [the *Philadelphia National Bank*] approach have sufficed to support a finding of "undue concentration" in the absence of other considerations, the question before us is whether the District Court was justified in finding that other pertinent factors affecting the coal industry and the business of the appellees mandated a conclusion that no substantial lessening of competition occurred or was threatened by the acquisition of United Electric. We are satisfied that the court's ultimate finding was not in error.

In *Brown Shoe v. United States*, we cautioned that statistics concerning market share and concentration, while of great significance, were not conclusive indicators of anticompetitive effects * * * In this case, the District Court assessed the evidence of the "structure, history and probable future" of the coal industry, and on the basis of this assessment found no substantial probability of anticompetitive effects from the merger.

Much of the District Court's opinion was devoted to a description of the changes that have affected the coal industry since World War II. On the basis of more than three weeks of testimony and a voluminous record, the court discerned a number of clear and significant developments in the industry. First, it found that coal had become increasingly less able to compete with other sources of energy in many segments of the energy market. * * *

Second, the court found that to a growing extent since 1954, the electric utility industry has become the mainstay of coal consumption. While electric utilities consumed only 15.76% of the coal produced nationally in 1947, their share of total consumption increased every year thereafter, and in 1968 amounted to more than 59% of all the coal consumed throughout the Nation.

Third, and most significantly, the court found that to an increasing degree, nearly all coal sold to utilities is transferred under long-term requirements contracts, under which coal producers promise to meet utilities' coal consumption requirements for a fixed period of time, and at predetermined prices. * * *

Because of these fundamental changes in the structure of the market for coal, the District Court was justified in viewing the statistics relied on by the Government as insufficient to sustain its case. Evidence of past production does not, as a matter of logic, necessarily give a proper picture of a company's future ability to compete. In most situations, of course, the unstated assumption is that a company that has maintained a certain share of a market in the recent past will be in a position to do so in the immediate future. * * *

In the coal market, as analyzed by the District Court, however, statistical evidence of coal production was of considerably less significance. The bulk of the coal produced is delivered under long-term requirements contracts, and such sales thus do not represent the exercise of competitive power but rather the obligation to fulfill previously negotiated contracts at a previously fixed price. * * * In a market where the availability and price of coal are set by long-term contracts rather than immediate or short-term purchases and sales, reserves rather than past production are the best measure of a company's ability to compete.

The testimony and exhibits in the District Court revealed that United Electric's coal reserve prospects were "unpromising." United's relative position of strength in reserves was considerably weaker than its past and current ability to produce. While United ranked fifth among Illinois coal producers in terms of annual production, it was 10th in reserve holdings, and controlled less than 1% of the reserves held by coal producers in Illinois, Indiana, and western Kentucky. Many of the reserves held by United had already been depleted at the time of trial, forcing the closing of some of United's Midwest mines. Even more significantly, the District Court found that of the 52,033,304 tons of currently mineable reserves in Illinois, Indiana, and Kentucky controlled by United, only four million tons had not already been committed under long-term contracts. United was found to be facing the future with relatively depleted resources at its disposal, and with the vast majority of those resources already committed under contracts allowing no further adjustment in price. In addition, the District Court found that "United Electric has neither the possibility of acquiring more (reserves) nor the ability to develop deep coal reserves," and thus was not in a position to increase its reserves to replace those already depleted or committed.

Viewed in terms of present and future reserve prospects and thus in terms of probable future ability to compete rather than in terms of past production, the District Court held that United Electric was a far less significant factor in the coal market than the Government contended or the production statistics seemed to indicate. While the company had been and remained a "highly profitable" and efficient producer of relatively large amounts of coal, its current and future power to compete for subsequent long-term contracts was severely limited by its scarce uncommitted resources. * * *

The Government asserts that United Electric was a healthy and thriving company at the time of the acquisition and could not be considered on the brink of failure, and also that the appellees have not shown that Material Service was the only available acquiring company. These considerations would be significant if the District Court had found no violation of § 7 by reason of United Electric's being a failing company, but the District Court's conclusion was not, as the Government suggests, identical with or even analogous to such a finding. The failing-company defense presupposes that the effect on competition and the "loss to (the company's) stockholders and injury to the communities where its plants were operated," * * * will be less if a company continues to exist even as a party to a merger than if it disappears entirely from the market. [*See* Section 8.35] * * * The appellees' demonstration of United's weak reserves position, however, proved an entirely different point. Rather than showing that United would have gone out of business but for the merger with Material Service, the finding of inadequate reserves went to the heart of the Government's statistical prima facie case based on production figures and substantiated the District Court's conclusion that United Electric, even if it remained in the market, did not have sufficient reserves to compete effectively for long-term contracts. The failing-company defense is simply inapposite to this finding and the failure of the appellees to meet the prerequisites of that doctrine did not detract from the validity of the court's analysis. * * *

Since we agree with the District Court that the Government's reliance on production statistics in the context of this case was insufficient, it follows that the judgment before us may be affirmed without reaching the issues of geographic and product markets.

The judgment of the District Court is affirmed.

Question

The defense to the challenge to this merger is commonly referred to as the *General Dynamics* defense. What is the scope and content of this defense?

Part II
Introduction to Microeconomic Foundations of Antitrust Merger Law

§ 8.10 Scope of Part II

This part provides an introduction to microeconomic principles that are important to understanding the antitrust laws governing mergers. Section 8.11 introduces general principles regarding competition, monopoly and oligopoly; and Section 8.12 focuses on basic economic principles governing demand and supply. These principles are the foundation upon which the competition and monopoly models are based. Section 8.13 examines the pure competition model, under the assumption that ten firms of the same size are operating in a market. Section 8.14 focuses on the monopoly model; this section assumes that the ten firms in the competitive market merge to form a monopoly. The specific price and output decisions under these two models are examined.

Section 8.15 compares these two models and examines the welfare triangle, which represents the dead weight loss from monopoly. Section 8.16 considers the effects of a merger to monopoly that results in efficiency gains. Section 8.17 focuses on oligopoly. Section 8.18 presents summary problems on these concepts. Finally, Section 8.19 surveys the empirical evidence concerning the relationship between concentration and price.

This Part II is principally based on Thompson, *A Practitioner's Guide to the Economics of the Antitrust Merger Guidelines* (1997, ABA-ALI) (reprinted with permission).

§ 8.11 General Principles Regarding Competition, Monopoly and Oligopoly

A. Characteristics of Pure or Perfect Competition

Under pure or perfect competition the individual firm is unable to influence market price. There are four basic characteristics of perfect competition:

FIRST: The product sold by any one firm is the same for all other firms; that is, the product is homogeneous, such as bushels of wheat.

SECOND: Each firm in the market is so small in relation to the entire market that no firm can affect price.

THIRD: Resources are completely mobile.

FOURTH: Consumers and firms have perfect knowledge of all relevant economic and technological data.

To put it another way: the number of firms selling a homogeneous product is so large and each firm's market share is so small that, as a result, no firm is able to influence price by varying the quantity of the product it sells. Professor Scherer, one of the leading industrial economists, has said that a competitive market generally results when there are ten to twelve firms in the market.[2]

A competitive market can lead to a number of desirable effects, including: (1) efficient production at minimum possible cost, (2) efficient consumption because value equals marginal cost, (3) no profits above the marginal level (that is no economic profits or rents), and (4) a single price at which the amount demanded by consumers equals the amount firms want to supply.

Moreover, a competitive market may lead to technological innovation that results in cost savings, because the only way competitive firms can earn positive economic profits is through innovative superiority. Since a firm in a competitive market does not have power over price, that is, the firm is a price taker, additional profits can be earned only by taking steps, such as technological innovation, to lower costs. Schumpeter has argued, however, that monopoly facilitates technological innovation because more of the gains are appropriated by the firm.[3] On the other hand, a recent study by Michael Porter finds significant support for the theory that competition promotes innovation.[4]

B. Characteristics of a Monopoly

In a market that is a pure monopoly, one firm sells all of the product. Therefore, the firm is able to set the price. Consequently, to maximize profits under monopoly, output is lower and price higher than under competition.

Monopoly pricing is a matter of opportunity; the object of any firm is to maximize profits whether selling in a competitive or monopoly market. The difference is that under com-

---

2. F.M. Scherer and David Ross, *Industrial Market Structure and Economic Performance* 277 (3d ed. 1990) [hereinafter Scherer & Ross].
3. Joseph A. Schumpeter, *Capitalism, Socialism and Democracy* 88, 103 (1943).
4. Michael Porter, *The Competitive Advantage of Nations*, (1990).

petition the firm cannot alter its market price, but under monopoly it can. Thus, a monopolist is a price-setter, whereas a firm in a competitive market is a price-taker.

Monopoly power (*i.e.*, the power to alter price) is not a guarantor of profits; however, if demand is such to insure profitability under pure competition, then profits will be higher under monopoly pricing.

There are four basic characteristics of monopoly:

FIRST: The firm sets the price and determines the level of output.

SECOND: The firm sells a unique product (*i.e.*, there are no or very few substitutes); the product is differentiated.

THIRD: There are barriers to entry by other firms into the market.

FOURTH: Market knowledge is imperfect (*i.e.*, there is a lack of knowledge about the product and how to make it).

A monopolist need not be a large firm; a small firm may have monopoly power in a small market, and a large firm may have only a small share of a large market.

The principal complaint economists have with monopoly is that it leads to an inefficient allocation of resources, because more goods would be provided if the market were competitively organized. Scherer and Ross explain that, "[t]his seeming technicality, so trivial at first glance, is the basis of the economist's most general condemnation of monopoly: it leads to an allocation of resources that is inefficient in the sense of failing to satisfy consumer wants as completely as possible."[5]

Another significant effect of monopoly is that it reallocates income from consumers to producers. Professor Harberger explains that for many purposes "monopoly profits can be treated as a privately imposed and privately collected tax."[6]

C. Characteristics of Oligopoly

In an oligopoly two or more firms produce products in the market and each firm is able to influence but not determine price. There is some interdependence between the firms; sellers will take account of each other's reactions in setting the price and output. The four basic characteristics of oligopoly are:

FIRST: Several firms produce in the market, with each firm determining its own price and output.

SECOND: The firms may sell "differentiated" as opposed to homogeneous products (*i.e.*, one that is distinguishable from the product of any other firm).

THIRD: It is difficult for new firms to enter the market.

FOURTH: There is usually imperfect market knowledge.

One of the antitrust concerns with oligopoly is the possibility of collusion among the members of the market to increase price and lower output. Such actions, of course, would be violative of Section 1 of the Sherman Act. Professor Mansfield explains that,

---

5. Scherer & Ross, *supra* note 1, at 23.

6. Arnold C. Harberger, *Taxation and Welfare*, 17 (1974) [hereinafter Harberger, Taxation and Welfare].

"[c]onditions in oligopolistic industries tend to promote collusion, since the number of firms is small and ... [t]he advantages to the firms of collusion seems obvious: increased profits, decreased uncertainty, and a better opportunity to prevent entry."[7]

Professor Mansfield goes on to point out that cartels (*e.g.*, a group of firms that conspires to fix prices) are inherently unstable, because a participant may increase its profits by cheating on the agreement.[8]

Another concern with oligopoly is the potential for pricing above the competitive level by dominant firms in the market.

D. Theory of Contestable Markets

The economics of scale in some industries may lead to only one or a few firms in the market. Nonetheless the market may not perform as a monopoly or oligopoly if the market is "perfectly contestable." A perfectly contestable market has free entry into and exit from the market; there are no sunk costs (*i.e.*, non-recoverable costs). The theory, which was developed by Professors Baumol, Panzar and Willig,[9] predicts that the presence of potential competitors at the edge of the market keeps the firm or firms operating in the market from pricing above the competitive level.

§ 8.12 Basic Economic Principles for Constructing the Competitive and Monopoly Models

A. Demand Schedule and Demand Curve

1. Basic Law of Demand

The basic law of demand is that the lower the price the greater the quantity demanded; that is, the quantity demanded varies inversely with price. The factors that determine an individual consumer's demand schedule are:

(1) Taste of the consumer;

(2) Income of the consumer; and

(3) Prices of other competing products.

The market demand schedule is determined by the individual demand schedules of all the consumers in the market. In other words, the market demand schedule is merely the horizontal summation of the individual demand curves of all the consumers in the market.

2. Construction of Demand Schedule

The construction of a market demand schedule is illustrated in Chart 8.12-I on the next page, which shows the hypothetical number of widgets that would be purchased by each of three consumers in the market at a particular price for the good.

7. Edwin Mansfield, *Microeconomics, Theory/Applications* 307 (7th ed. 1991) [hereinafter Mansfield].

8. *Id.* at 308–10.

9. *See* William J. Baumol, John C. Panzar & Robert D. Willig, *Contestable Markets and the Theory of Industry Structure* (1982).

Chart 8.12-I
Quantity of Widgets Demanded by Individual Consumers

Price Per Unit of Widgets	Consumer #1	Consumer #2	Consumer #3	Market or Industry Demand Schedule
10	200	100	200	500
8	300	200	500	1000
6	400	400	700	1500
4	500	700	800	2000
2	600	1000	900	2500

Chart 8.12-I illustrates that for each of the three consumers in the market, the number of widgets that would be purchased goes up as the price of the product goes down; this is also true for the market demand schedule which is the summation of the demand schedules of the three consumers. Thus, Chart 8.12-II below summarizes the market demand schedule.

Chart 8.12-II
Widget Market Demand Schedule

Price Per Unit	Quantity Demanded
10	500
8	1000
6	1500
4	2000
2	2500

3. Plotting the Demand Curve

This market demand schedule can be plotted on a graph, with the quantity demanded on the horizontal axis and the possible prices on the vertical axis, as indicated on Graph 8.12-A [see next page].

Graph 8.12-A
Widget Demand Curve

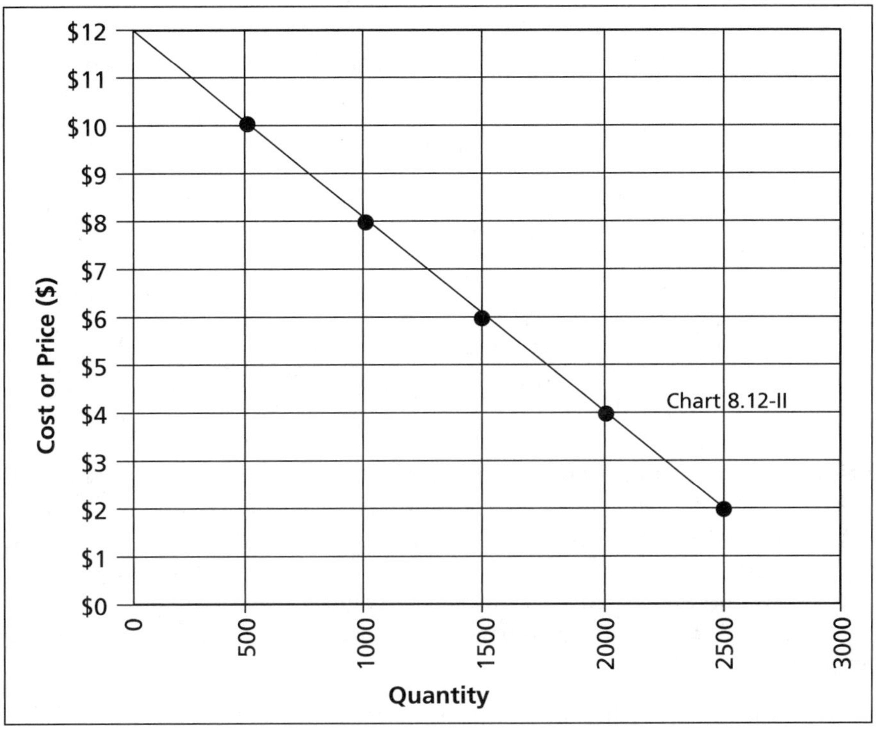

4. Shifts in the Demand Curve: Cross Elasticity of Demand

The demand curve expresses the complete functional relationship between price and quantity keeping the following factors constant: (1) income of consumers, (2) prices of other products, (3) number of consumers, and (4) consumers' taste. If any of these factors change, then the demand curve may shift to the right or left. The demand curve does not express actual purchases but only consumers' desires at a particular price. It indicates consumers' reservation prices, *i.e.*, the point at which consumers will get out of the market.

A rightward shift in the demand curve occurs if more quantity is demanded because of a change in factors other than the price of the product. An increase in consumers' taste for the product, an increase in consumer income, an increase in the prices of other goods, or an increase in the number of consumers would, other factors being the same, result in a rightward shift of the demand curve. For example, there could be a rightward shift in the demand curve for coal as a result of an increase in the price of oil. Alternatively, there could be a leftward shift in the demand curve (*i.e.*, less would be demanded) of coal because of a decrease in the price of oil. This means there is a "cross elasticity of demand" between coal and oil; that is, as a result of a change in the price of oil there is a change in demand for coal. This cross elasticity of demand is illustrated on Graph 8.12-B on the next page.

Graph 8.12-B
Shift in Demand Curve Due to Cross Elasticity of Demand

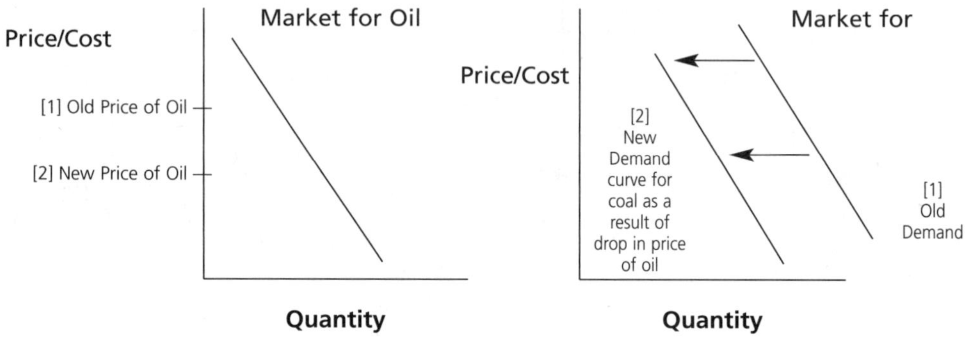

In Graph 8.12-B, a price drop in the market for oil gives rise to a leftward shift in the demand curve for coal, which means that for each particular price, less coal will be demanded after the drop in the price of oil than before the drop. This is referred to as a positive cross elasticity of demand, meaning the goods are substitutes. A negative cross elasticity of demand would indicate complimentary goods (*i.e.*, autos and oil). Cross elasticity of demand is a measure of demand side substitution. Supply side substitution is taken up below.

The cross elasticity of demand concept is generally used in defining the relevant market in Section 7 cases.

5. Demand Curve Is the Average Revenue Curve

The demand curve is the average revenue curve, because each vertical price point represents the average revenue received by the seller for the corresponding quantity of market sales. Unless the seller is able to discriminate between consumers in the price it charges, there is one price in the marketplace and this is the average revenue received from the sale of each unit. The assumption here is that the seller cannot engage in price discrimination.

6. Demand Curve of (1) a Monopolistic Firm and (2) Firms in a Competitive Market

The demand curve of the monopolist is the market demand curve. Since the monopolist is the only seller in the market, it faces the downward sloping market demand curve. The monopolist can decide where to set the price of its product.

On the other hand, the demand curve for a firm in a competitive market is perfectly flat as indicated on Graph 8.12-C [see next page].

Graph 8.12-C
Demand Curve of a Firm in a Competitive Market

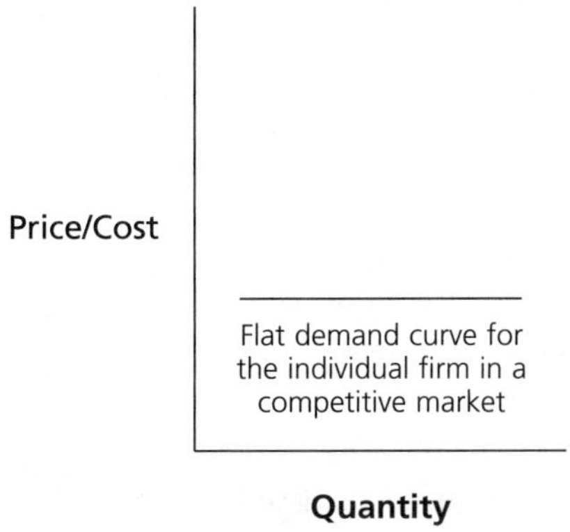

Graph 8.12-C presents a microscopic view of the market demand curve by the individual firm in a competitive market. Since the firm is an insignificant part of the market, it simply faces the prevailing market price.

B. Construction of the Supply Curve

1. In General

The supply curve represents the amount of a product sellers want to sell at a given price. In general, the supply curve increases as the price increases as indicated on Graph 8.12-D. Thus, there is a direct relationship between price and the quantity supplied.

Graph 8.12-D
Supply Curve

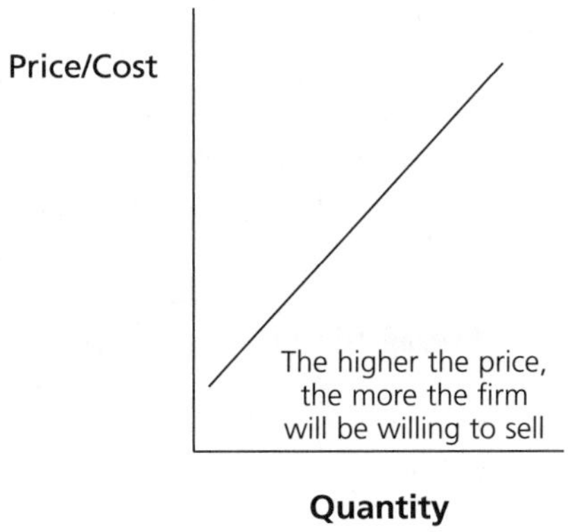

2. Relationship Between Marginal Cost Curve and the Supply Curve

An individual firm's supply curve is its incremental or marginal cost curve. This is so because a firm will not sell at a price that does not cover its marginal cost; that is, if the revenue received from a sale of an additional unit (*i.e.*, the price) does not exceed the marginal cost of producing the item, then it would not be economically beneficial to make the sale.

Just as the industry demand curve is the horizontal summation of each individual consumer's demand curve, the industry supply curve is the horizontal summation of each firm's marginal cost curve. This is illustrated below.

3. Construction of Marginal Cost Curve from the Firm's Cost Curves

a. The Firm's Cost in General

The firm's marginal cost curve is computed by reference to the firm's cost of operating. The firm incurs costs for land, labor and capital, which are the factors of production. Costs can be fixed (*i.e.*, they do not change over a specified range of production, such as the cost of constructing a plant), or variable (*i.e.*, they increase as output increases, such as the increase in labor cost as a plant moves from one shift to two shifts).

The total cost is the summation of the fixed and variable costs. The law of costs says that total cost goes up when the quantity produced increases.

The cost curves described below are based on the assumption that the costs of the various factors of production (*i.e.*, land, labor and capital) are held constant. If the costs of these factors increases, then the cost curves would shift up.

Before deriving marginal cost, we first determine average fixed cost ("AFC"), average variable cost ("AVC") and average total cost ("ATC"). One element of each of these costs is the cost of raising both the debt capital (*i.e.*, the interest expense) and equity capital (*i.e.*, the dividends) needed to finance the manufacture and sale of the good. Thus, a reasonable return on capital is built into the costs figures.

b. Average Fixed Cost

Average fixed cost is merely the total fixed cost ("TFC") divided by the quantity ("Q"):

$$AFC = \frac{TFC}{Q}$$

Average fixed cost constantly decreases as quantity increases.

Thus, it can be diagramed as indicated on Graph 8.12-E.

Graph 8.12-E
Average Fixed Cost (AFC)

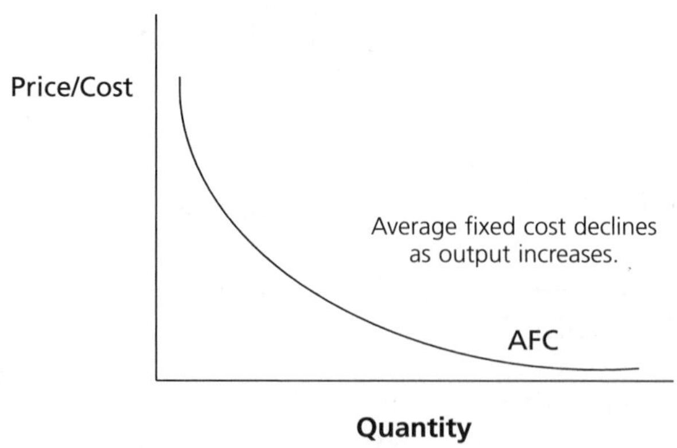

c. Average Variable Cost

Average variable cost is the total variable cost ("TVC") divided by the quantity (Q):

$$AVC = \frac{TVC}{Q}$$

Average variable cost first falls but then rises as the plant is operated at a greater and greater capacity and a second and third shift are added that increases labor costs over that incurred in the first shift. The average variable cost curve generally appears as indicated on Graph 8.12-F.

Graph 8.12-F
Average Variable Cost (AVC)

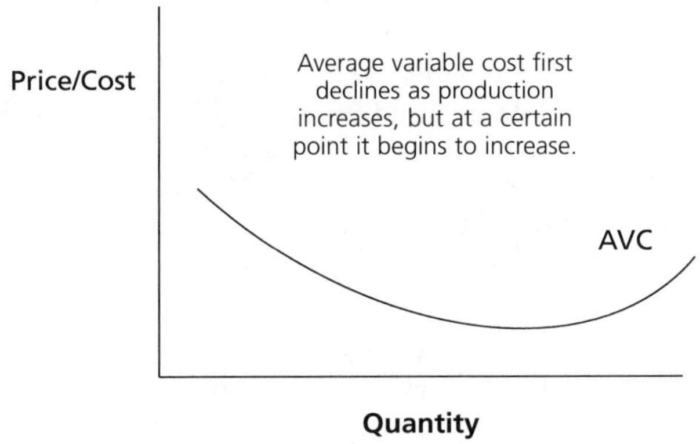

d. Average Total Cost

Average total cost is merely the summation of average variable cost and average fixed cost, or the total cost ("TC") divided by the quantity (Q):

$$ATC = \frac{TC}{Q}$$

The average total cost curve also declines at first but later rises, and it is above the average variable cost curve. It is diagramed on Graph 8.12-G on the next page.

Graph 8.12-G
Average Total Cost (ATC)

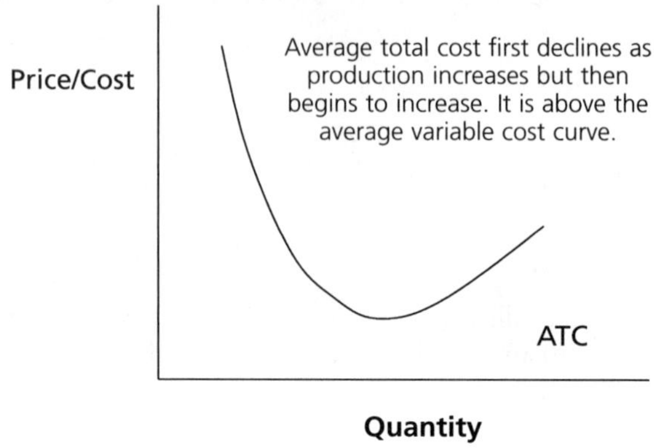

e. Marginal Cost

The marginal cost ("MC") is the incremental variable cost of producing one additional unit. Thus, the marginal cost is equal to the total variable cost of producing N units of an item minus the total variable cost of producing N-1 units. These concepts are explored further.

As indicated, average total cost and average variable cost first fall and then rise. The minimum values for average total cost and average variable cost equal the marginal cost at the particular level of output. The average variable cost minimum is reached before the average total cost minimum. Note that after a point, average total cost is pulled up by average variable cost and down by average fixed cost. Thus, the curves generally appear as indicated on Graph 8.12-H.

Graph 8.12-H
Graphs of AFC, AVC, ATC, and MC

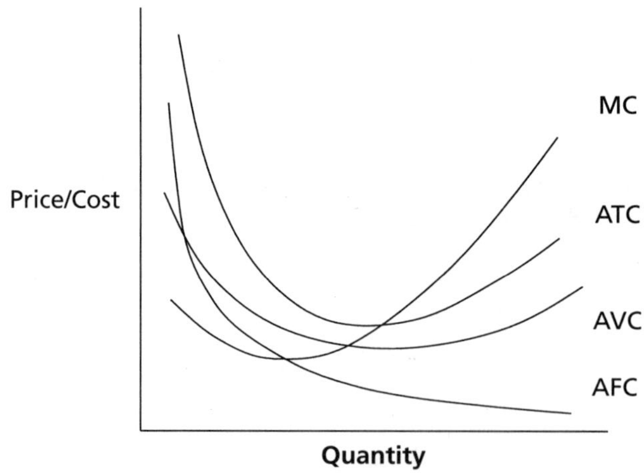

f. Illustration of the Construction of AFC, AVC, and ATC Curves

Assume that ten firms of equal size operate in the market for widgets. Each firm has the same production function; that is, the same cost for producing the same number of units. This information is summarized in Chart 8.12-III for each firm, and the average fixed cost, average variable cost, and average total cost are computed. Each firm has $50 of fixed costs, and each firm's variable costs starts at $250 for production of 50 units of output and rises to $1,000 for 250 units of output.

Chart 8.12-III
Cost Data of Each Firm in the Widget Market

[1]	[2]	[3]	[4]	[5]	[6]	[7]
Amount of Total Output	Fixed Cost*	Total Variable Cost*	Total Costs (2)+(3)	Average Fixed Cost (2)÷(1)	Average Variable Cost (3)÷(1)	Average TotalCost (4)÷(1)
50	$50	$ 250	$ 300	$1.00	$5.00	$6.00
100	$50	$ 400	$ 450	$ .50	$4.00	$4.50
150	$50	$ 500	$ 550	$ .33	$3.33	$3.66
200	$50	$ 700	$ 750	$ .25	$3.50	$3.75
250	$50	$1000	$1050	$ .20	$4.00	$4.20

* Includes cost of both debt and equity capital

Chart 8.12-IV summarizes the above cost data for the ten firms. This is the horizontal summation of the production functions of each of the firms.

Chart 8.12-IV
Aggregate Cost Data for all Firms in the Widget Market

[1]	[2]	[3]	[4]	[5]	[6]	[7]
Amount of Total Output	Fixed Cost	Total Variable Cost	Total Costs (2)+(3)	Average Fixed Cost (2)÷(1)	Average Variable Cost (3)÷(1)	Average TotalCost (4)÷(1)
500	$500	$ 2500	$ 3000	$1.00	$5.00	$6.00
1000	$500	$ 4000	$ 4500	$ .50	$4.00	$4.50
1500	$500	$ 5000	$ 5500	$ .33	$3.33	$3.66
2000	$500	$ 7000	$ 7500	$ .25	$3.50	$3.75
2500	$500	$10000	$10500	$ .20	$4.00	$4.20

The average fixed cost, average variable cost, and average total cost in Chart 8.12-IV for all of the firms in the market are the same as the respective amounts for each of the firms in the market as shown in Chart 8.12-III. This is because it is assumed in Chart 8.12-III that each firm has the same production function.

The average fixed cost, average variable cost, and average total cost curves for this industry are plotted on the Graph 8.12-I on the next page.

Graph 8.12-I
Graphs of AFC, AVC, and ATC

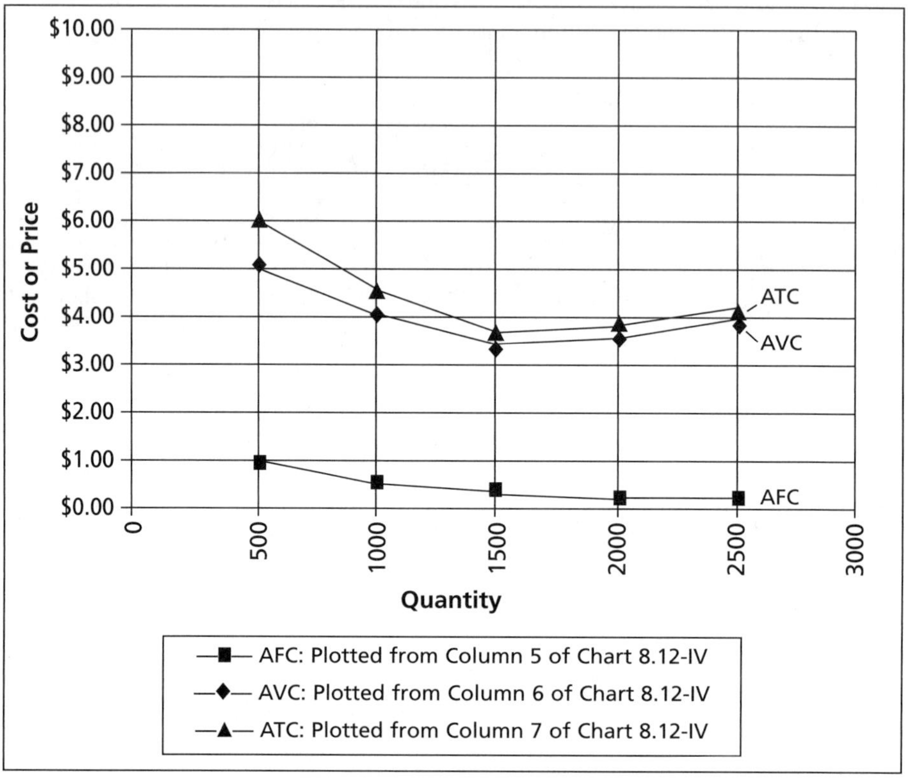

As indicated on Chart 8.12-III for each of the ten firms in the industry, the above curves indicate the average costs for the following levels of output: 50, 100, 150, 200 and 250.

g. Approximation of the Marginal Cost Curve and the Industry Supply Curve through Use of Arithmetic

The marginal cost curve can be approximated through the use of arithmetic. It could be determined precisely through the use of calculus, but that is not necessary for the purposes here. The marginal cost curve is constructed by dividing the increase in variable costs at each level of output by the increase in output at that level. This produces the incremental cost of producing the next level of output. Interpolation can be used to produce a more exact measure of marginal cost.

The marginal cost curve for an industry (a part of which, as will be seen below, is the industry supply curve) is the horizontal summation of each firm's marginal cost curve. Each firm's marginal cost for each marginal unit is computed on Chart 8.12-V, which utilizes the data on Chart 8.12-IV relating to each firm's variable output and variable costs.

The marginal cost per unit for the industry, which is the horizontal summation of each firm's marginal cost per unit, is computed on the Chart 8.12-VI from the data on Chart 8.12-V.

As noted, the costs shown on Chart 8.12-VI are for the ten firms in this industry. The industry marginal cost per marginal unit in column 6 of Chart 8.12-VI is the same as each firm's marginal cost per marginal unit in column 6 of Chart 8.12-V; it is assumed in Chart 8.12-V that each of the firms in the industry has the same production function.

Chart 8.12-V
Approximation of Each Firm's Marginal Cost

[1] Amount of Total Output	[2] Amount of Variable Output	[3] Total Variable Cost*	[4] Variable Cost of Next Lower Level of Output		[5] Increase in Variable Cost [3]–[4]	[6] Average Marginal Cost for Marginal Unit*** [5]÷[2]	[7] Mid-point of Output Range	[8] Marginal Cost of Midpoint of Output Range
50	50	250	0	=	250	$5	25	$5
100	50	400	250	=	150	$3	75	$3
150	50	500	400	=	100	$2	125	$2
200	50	700	500	=	200	$4	175	$4
250	50	1000	700	=	300	$6	225	$6

* From Column [3] of Chart 8.12-III.

** The next lower level of output here is 0 for 50 units of output, 50 for 100 units of output, 100 for 150 units of output, and so on.

*** This column computes the average marginal cost over a range of output as opposed to the additional cost of the last unit produced, which is the true marginal cost. The indicated marginal cost is a more accurate reflection of the midpoint of the output ranges, as computed in column [8]. For example, it would be more accurate to place a marginal cost of $6 at an output of 225 as opposed to 250, which is done in column [8].

Chart 8.12-VI
Approximation of Industry Marginal Cost Per Marginal Unit

[1] Amount of Total Output	[2] Amount of Variable Output	[3] Total Variable Cost*	[4] Variable Cost of Next Lower Level of Output		[5] Increase in Variable Cost [3]–[4]	[6] Average Marginal Cost for Marginal Unit*** [5]÷[2]	[7] Mid-point of Output Range	[8] Marginal Cost of Midpoint of Output Range
500	500	2500	0	=	$2500	$5	250	$5
1000	500	4000	2500	=	$1500	$3	750	$3
1500	500	5000	4000	=	$1000	$2	1250	$2
2000	500	7000	5000	=	$2000	$4	1750	$4
2500	500	10000	7000	=	$3000	$6	2250	$6

* From Column [3] of Chart 8.12-IV.

** The next lower level of output here is -0- for 500 units of output, 500 for 1000 units of output, 1000 for 1500 units of output, and so on.

*** This column computes the average marginal cost over a range of output as opposed to the additional cost of the last unit produced, which is the true marginal cost. The indicated marginal cost is a more accurate reflection of the midpoint of the output ranges, as computed in column [8]. For example, it would be more accurate to place a marginal cost of $6 at an output of 2250 as opposed to 2500, which is done in column [8].

The marginal cost curve using the marginal cost at the midpoint of the output range [*see* Chart 8.12-VI, column [8]], is plotted on Graph 8.12-J.

Graph 8.12-J
Approximate Industry Marginal Cost Curve*

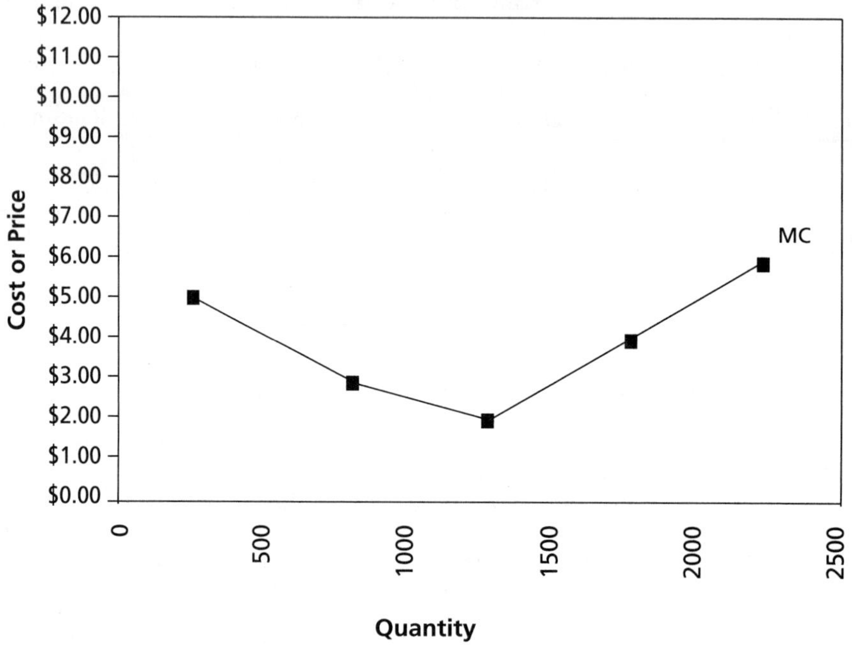

*Plotted from column [8] of Chart 8.12-VI

Thus the marginal cost curve initially falls and later begins to rise as the variable cost begins to rise.

The marginal cost curve intersects the average variable cost and average total cost curves at their respective minimums. The firm's supply curve is the firm's marginal cost curve above the average variable cost curve because if the price at which units are sold does not at least cover the firm's average variable cost, the firm would shut down and have no supply. The industry supply curve is, therefore, the summation of each individual firm's marginal cost curve above such firm's average variable cost curve. Thus, the supply curve of the widget industry is the portion of the industry marginal cost curve (Graph 8.12-J) to the right of 1600 units of output, which is the level at which the marginal cost curve and average variable cost curves intersect. The price at this point is approximately $3.20. The industry supply curve is diagramed on Graph 8.12-K [see next page].

Graph 8.12-K
Widget Industry Supply Curve

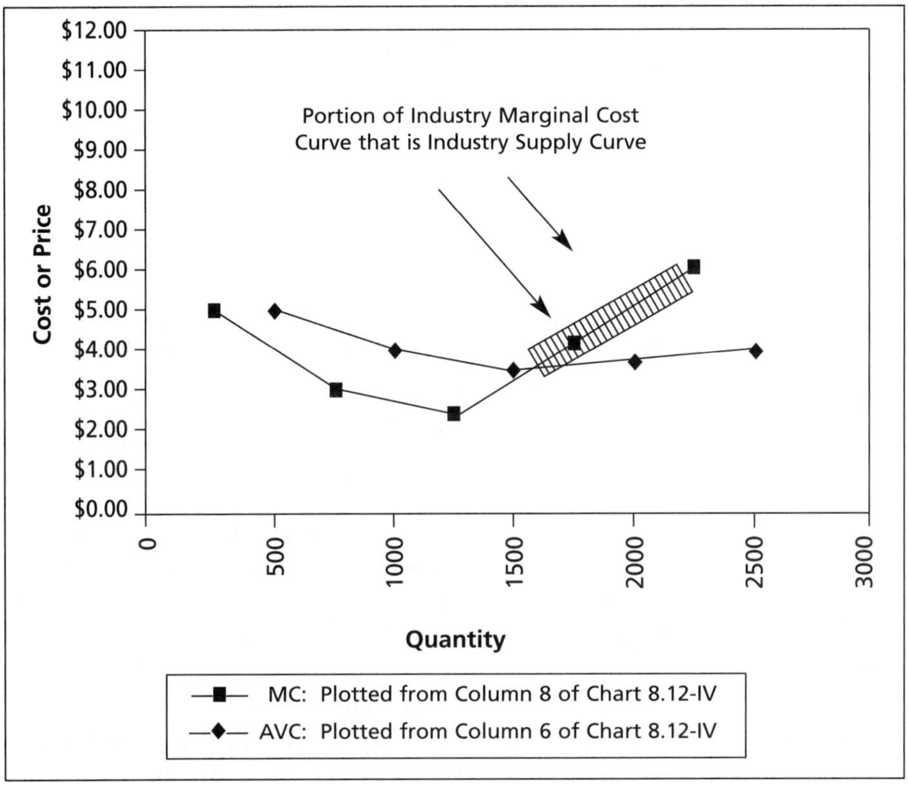

In the example here of the widget industry, Graph 8.12-K is the industry short run supply curve, which is the supply curve for the period of time during which individual firms may vary their output but neither entry nor exit may occur. Some costs are fixed in the short run, but in the long run all costs are variable. Section 8.12 demonstrates that this supply curve leads to production at a price level that exceeds average total cost, thus resulting in an economic return that is above the normal cost of capital that is built into average total cost.

h. Shifts in the Supply Curve: Supply Side Substitution

The supply curve is a function of two factors: (1) the level of input prices, and (2) the level of technology. The supply curve is drawn on the assumption that (1) the level of input prices and technology are constant, and (2) the price of the product is variable.

The higher the price of a good, the greater the incentive for potential competitors (potential entrants) to attempt to capture a part of the sales by (1) new entry, (2) expansion of present facilities, (3) the development of new substitutes through innovation, or (4) some combination of the above. The threat of potential entrants can cause firms in the market to restrain prices in order to reduce the risk of new competition.

This concept of competition from potential entrants has the effect of shifting the supply curve to the right as demonstrated in Graph 8.12-L [see next page].

Graph 8.12-L
Shifting of the Supply Curve for Widgets

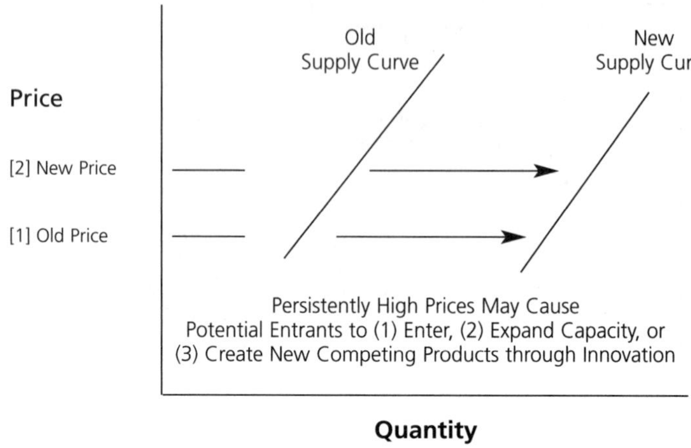

This shifting of the supply curve is referred to as supply side substitution. As a result of the increase in price, there is a shift to new production which causes input cost to be lowered and a rightward shift in the supply curve. For example, the addition of a new plant producing widgets will likely decrease the marginal costs of producing widgets.

The concept of supply side substitution has been used by courts in defining the relevant market. For example, in *Brown Shoe Co. v. United States,*[10] the Supreme Court said that "[t]he cross elasticity of production facilities may also be an important factor in defining a product market."[11]

C. Intersection of the Industry Supply and Demand Curves

As discussed more fully below, in a competitively organized industry the intersection of the industry supply and demand curves determines the price at which the product is sold. If price is below the equilibrium point, there is an excess of demand, and if prices are above the point, there is an excess of supply. When the price is at the intersection of the supply and demand curves, the market is in equilibrium; that is, there is a market clearing price. This is shown generally on Graph 8.12-M [see next page]. Thus, the market clearing price is at the intersection of the supply and demand curves.

10. 370 U.S. 294 (1962).
11. *Id.* at 325, n.42.

Graph 8.12-M
Intersection of the Supply and Demand Curve

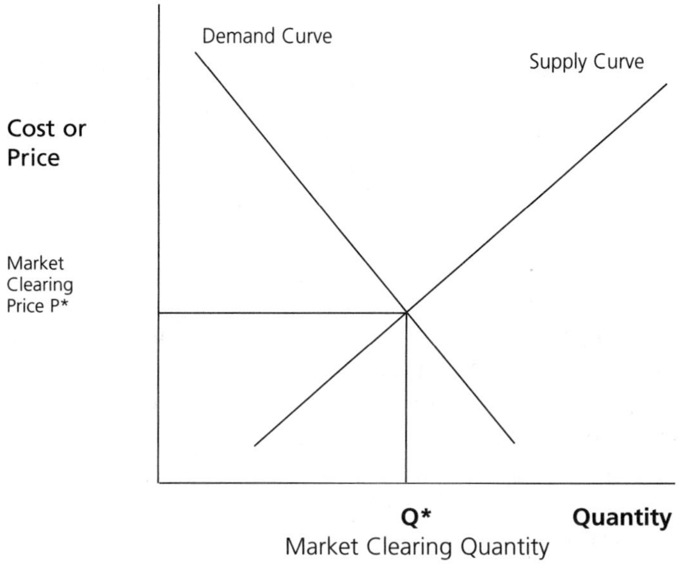

A rightward shift in the demand curve (resulting, for example, from an increase in consumer incomes) would cause an increase in the market clearing price, whereas a leftward shift in the demand curve (resulting, for example, from a decrease in consumer taste for the good) would cause a decrease in the market clearing price. On the other hand, a rightward shift in the supply curve (resulting, for example, from the entry of a new competitor) would cause a decrease in the market clearing price, whereas a leftward shift in the supply curve (resulting, for example, from the destruction of a major production facility) would cause an increase in the market clearing price.

D. Profit Maximizing Condition: Marginal Cost Equals Marginal Revenue

The firm produces as long as the last unit (the marginal unit) of production increases the firm's profits. Thus, the firm expands production until its increment to cost (*i.e.*, its marginal cost) equals its enhancement to revenue (*i.e.*, its marginal revenue). This makes intuitive sense; for example if a firm could produce one more unit at a marginal cost of $4 and sell that unit for $5 (the marginal revenue) then it makes good economic sense for the firm to produce the item. On the other hand, if the firm's marginal cost is $6 and its marginal revenue is only $5 it does not make economic sense to produce the item, other things being equal.

The demand curve is related to marginal revenue. If the demand curve is flat, then the demand curve is equal to the marginal revenue curve. On the other hand, if the demand curve slopes downward, then the marginal revenue curve also slopes downward and is lower than the demand curve because there is a loss of revenue effect associated with a move from a higher to a lower price. This point is explored further in Section 8.13.

§ 8.13 The Pure Competition Model

A. In General

Since the firm operating under pure competition is unable to influence market prices, it must sell the amount of its goods that produces the greatest profit at the externally determined price. Overlooking any non-economic motives, the firm will seek the output level at which profits are a maximum. At that output the firm is relieved of any incentive to either accelerate or curtail its output flow and seeks to maintain its production schedule. It expands production as long as its additional total revenue exceeds its additional total cost; that is, it expands production as long as its marginal revenue exceeds its marginal cost. In a competitive market, the firm sells at the point where its marginal revenue equals its marginal cost.[12] Since marginal revenue is equal to price, this necessarily means that under pure competition the firm produces to the point where price equals marginal cost. This is the necessary condition of output equilibrium under pure competition.

As noted above, for the firm selling in a competitive market, although the industry demand curve slopes downward, the demand curve faced by the individual firms in the market is flat. This is because the seller is insignificant in the market. The point at which the individual firm's demand curve, which is flat, intersects the industry supply curve determines the market equilibrium price. This is illustrated generally in Graph 8.13-A. Thus, each individual firm has only a microscopic view of the demand curve at the equilibrium point.

Graph 8.13-A
Market Equilibrium Price
Intersection of Supply and Demand Curves

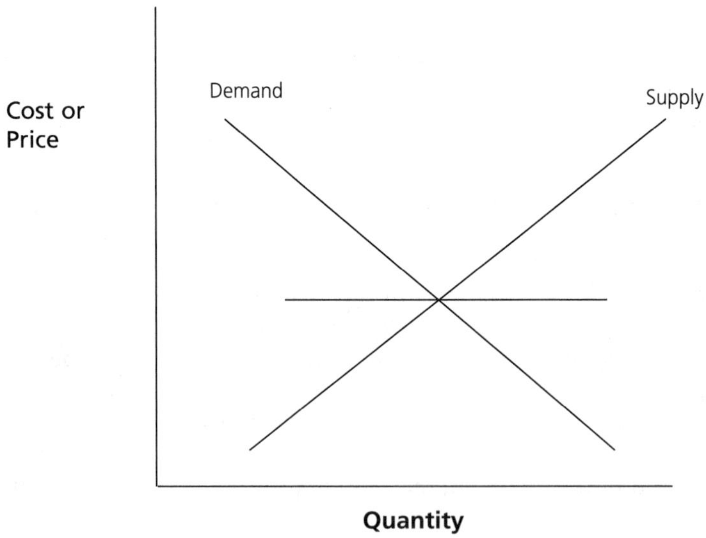

12. The monopolist also sells at the point where its marginal cost equals marginal revenue; however, the marginal revenue curve for the monopolist is different from the marginal revenue curve under competition. *See* Section 8.14.

When the individual firm's marginal cost curve is shown on a graph with the flat demand curve, it can be demonstrated that the firm produces to the point where price equals marginal cost. This is demonstrated on Graph 8.13-B below.

Graph 8.13-B
Intersection of the Individual Firm's Marginal Cost Curve with the Industry Demand Curve

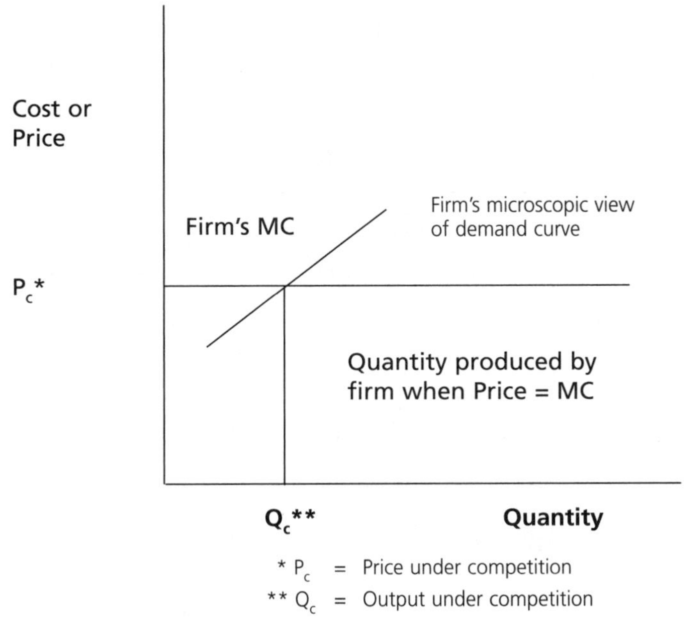

At any point to the left of Qc, the additional revenue (which is the marginal revenue and the price) received from the sale of an additional unit exceeds the marginal cost of producing the unit, and, consequently, it is economically beneficial for the firm to increase its production (as long as marginal cost is less than or equal to average variable cost). On the other hand, at any point to the right of Qc it is not economically beneficial for the firm to produce because the marginal cost exceeds the marginal revenue (*i.e.*, the price). By selling at the point where marginal cost equals marginal revenue (or price), the firm realizes normal profits because one of the factors of cost is the cost of equity and debt capital, the return required by the providers of capital to the firm.

B. Computation of the Price and Output in a Competitive Widget Market

1. The Basic Case

The widget industry, which is discussed above, is assumed to be competitive because it consists of 10 firms of equal size; Scherer and Ross say that once there are ten to twelve evenly matched firms in a market, the firms begin ignoring their individual influence on price.

The industry demand curve is the horizontal summation of consumers' individual demand curves, and the widget industry demand curve is plotted on Graph 8.13-C below from the information in Chart 8.12-II.

Graph 8.13-C
Intersection of Industry Demand and Supply Curves

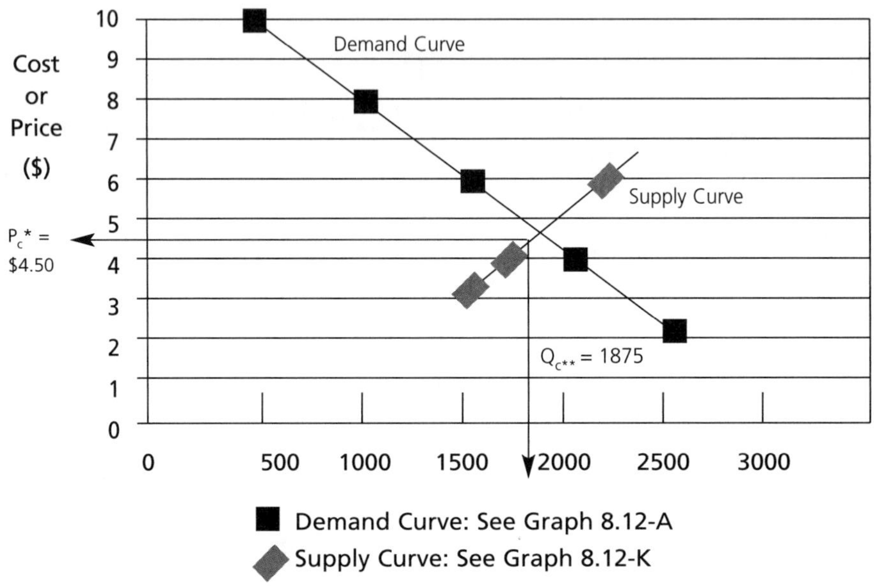

* P_c = Price under competition = $4.50
** Q_c = Quantity under competition = 1875

The industry supply curve, which is also plotted on Graph 8.13-C above from the information in Graph 8.12-K, is derived from the industry marginal cost curve, which is the horizontal summation of the individual firms' marginal cost curves. The industry supply curve is the portion of the industry marginal cost curve that is above the industry average variable cost curve. The intersection of these two curves indicates the price and output levels that prevail in a competitive widget market.

The price is $4.50 and the output is 1875 units. Each firm's marginal revenue and average revenue is equal to the $4.50 price. Each firm produces one tenth of the total production or 187.5 units. Each firm's average total cost per unit for producing 187.5 units is $3.70,[13] and therefore, the sales price under the competitive industry in this particular situation is approximately 80 cents above the average total cost of producing the items. Thus, an economic profit (*i.e.*, an economic rent) of 80 cents per unit is realized by the firms. This profit is in addition to the normal return on capital that is built into the average total cost curve.

13. *See* Chart 8.12–III.

2. The Long Run Adjustment

As a result of this economic profit of 80 cents per unit earned in the widget industry, the economic theory of competitive markets predicts that the industry supply curve is the short run supply curve. In the short run, firms in this market may vary their output but neither entry nor exit occurs. The theory holds that in the long run, which is the period during which entry or exit may occur and all costs are variable, this economic profit will attract new firms to the market and cause firms in the market to increase their production. As a result of this new entry and expansion, the long run supply curve will shift downward to the point where the intersection of the long run supply curve and the demand curve produces a price that is equal to the average total cost, thus eliminating the economic profit.

§ 8.14 The Monopoly Model

A. General Principles

In a monopoly market the firm has the opportunity to set price without respect to its competitors. It has power over price; it thus faces a downward sloping demand curve. The monopolist can set the price high and sell less or set the price low and sell more. As discussed earlier, the four basic characteristics of a monopoly are:

(1) A single seller;

(2) A differentiated product;

(3) Substantial barriers to entry; and

(4) Imperfect market information.

Since a monopolist faces a downward sloping demand curve, its marginal revenue curve also is downward sloping. And, since the profit maximizing assumption dictates that the firm sell at the point where marginal cost equals marginal revenue (*i.e.*, it would be unprofitable to sell where the marginal cost of producing the item (say $6) exceeds the marginal revenue from selling the item (say $5)), it is necessary to determine the marginal revenue curve of the monopolist.

B. The Marginal Revenue Curve of the Monopolist

Marginal revenue is the change in total revenue resulting from a one unit increment in sales volume. Thus, the Marginal Revenue curve is computed by assuming that production increases from 0 to 2500 in this example, and it depicts the change in total revenue resulting from one further sale. In the case of a competitive market, marginal revenue is equal to the price, because that is the addition to revenue from the sale of one additional item. On the other hand, in computing the marginal revenue curve of the monopolist, it is necessary to determine the impact on revenue of selling more items at a lower price.

For the downward sloping demand curve of a monopolist, marginal revenue is the change in total revenue resulting from the netting of the following two factors:

(1) The additional income earned from the sale of one additional unit at a lower, new price, and

(2) The loss of income due to the fact that all units saleable at a higher price now must be sold at a lower price. (This is because, generally, the monopolist cannot discriminate in price among consumers).

Marginal revenue is positive only if the income earned from the sale of the additional unit in paragraph (1) is greater than the income lost from the reduced price for all of the old units in paragraph (2).

Expressed more simply, marginal revenue is the difference between the revenue earned at the new price with the new quantity sold, and the revenue earned at the old price with the old quantity sold. This is diagrammed in Graph 8.14-A below.

Graph 8.14-A
Illustration of the Marginal Revenue of a Monopolist

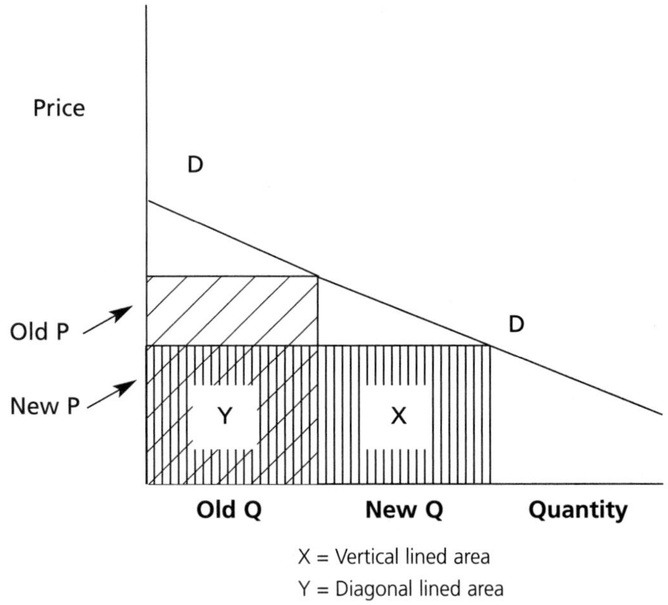

Marginal revenue in Graph 8.14-A is the difference between X and Y. The area shaded with the vertical lines (X) represents the total revenue earned at the new price with the sale of the new quantity and the area shaded by the crossed lines (Y) represents the total revenue earned at the old price with the sale of the old quantity. The resulting amount can be put on a per unit basis by dividing the resulting amount by the number of incremental units sold, as follows:

$$\frac{(\text{New Price} \times \text{New Quantity}) - (\text{Old Price} \times \text{Old Quantity})}{\text{Incremental Units}}$$

With a downward sloping demand curve, the marginal revenue is not equal to the price indicated by any particular point on the demand curve; it is always less than price. As a consequence, the marginal revenue curve is lower than the demand curve and can be generally diagrammed as indicated in Graph 8.14-B [see next page].

Graph 8.14-B
General Diagram of the Marginal Revenue Curve

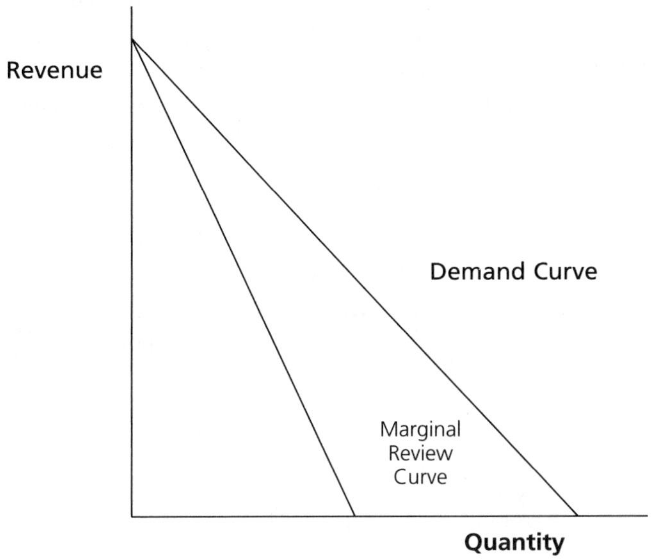

To reiterate, the marginal revenue curve depicts the marginal revenue earned on a per unit basis of producing the particular level of output, thus it shows the increment to revenue resulting from a level of output. The greater the output, the lower the marginal revenue because greater production will naturally bring lower prices.

C. Computation of the Marginal Revenue Curve in a Widget Industry That Has Merged to Monopoly

1. Approximation Using Arithmetic

This section approximates the marginal revenue curve using simple arithmetic and the information given about the demand curve. Calculus is needed to precisely compute the curve, and the next section shows the results of the precise computation. The purpose of this section is to provide an intuitive grasp of the concepts.

Assume that the ten firms in the widget industry decide to merge. There could be a variety of motivations for this merger, such as the desire to operate more efficiently or the hubris of the president of the acquiring firm. Another motivation could be the desire to attain the gains that would arise from the acquisition of market power.

This section demonstrates the computation of the marginal revenue curve after the merger of the ten firms.

The marginal revenue curve of the single firm resulting from the merger could be computed using the following methodology. Recall that marginal revenue is the increment to revenue added by an additional unit of sales. It can be approximated by the following formula:

$$\frac{(\text{New Price} \times \text{New Quantity}) - (\text{Old Price} \times \text{Old Quantity})}{\text{Incremental Units}}$$

The "New Price x New Quantity" is simply the total revenue realized at the new price and the "Old Price x Old Quantity" is the total revenue realized at the old price. Thus, the marginal revenue per incremental unit (determined at output levels of 500, 1000, 1500, 2000 and 2500) of the resulting monopoly firm is approximated in Chart 8.14-I .

Chart 8.14-I
Approximation of Marginal Revenue Per Unit

[1] Amount of Total Output	[2] New P	[3] New Q	[4] Total Revenue at New Price New P × New Q [2]×[3]	[5] Old P	[6] Old Q	[7] Total Revenue at Old Price Old P × Old Q [5]×[6]	[8] New P × New Q minus Old P× Old Q [4]−[7]	[9] Incremental Units	[10] Marginal Revenue Per Unit [8]÷[9]
500	$10	500	5000	12	0	0	5000	500	$10
1000	$ 8	1000	8000	10	500	5000	3000	500	$ 6
1500	$ 6	1500	9000	8	1000	8000	1000	500	$ 2
2000	$ 4	2000	8000	6	1500	9000	−1000	500	−$2
2500	$ 2	2500	5000	4	2000	8000	−3000	500	−$6

Using the above information, the approximation of the marginal revenue curve, together with the demand curve and the actual marginal revenue curve, as computed in the next section, are plotted on Graph 8.14-C [see next page].

Graph 8.14-C
Plotting of the Marginal Revenue Curve of the Monopolist

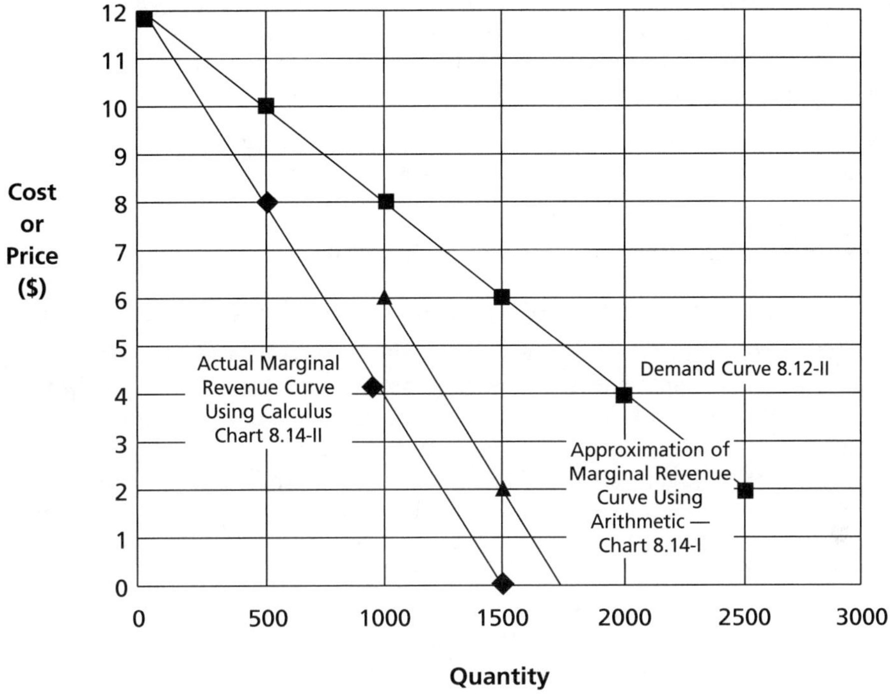

2. Derivation of the Marginal Revenue Curve by Use of Calculus

The precise marginal revenue curve, as derived from the demand curve by the use of algebra and elementary calculus, is set out in Chart 8.14-II below.

Chart 8.14-II
Computation of Actual Marginal Revenue Curve Using Calculus

Amount of Total Output	Marginal Revenue
-0-	$12
500	$ 8
1000	$ 4
1500	$ 0

The above data is plotted on Graph 8.14-C as the actual marginal revenue curve.

Since the marginal revenue is zero at 1500 units of output, any production above 1500 units will cause marginal revenue to become negative. This is because the revenue from the increased sales at any price lower than the $6 price that prevails at the 1500 level of output will be less than the revenue from the 1500 sales at the $6 price.

The difference between the approximation of the marginal revenue curve and the computation of the actual marginal revenue curve can be explained as follows. Marginal revenue at a particular point on the demand curve is the increment of total revenue from the production of one additional item. It is, therefore, a measure of the instantaneous rate of change in revenue at the particular level of production. On the other hand, the approximation of the marginal revenue curve with the use of arithmetic in Section C.1 was made on the basis of a change in marginal revenue averaged over increments of 500 units of production, that is from 0 to 500, from 500 to 1000, etc.

The smaller the number of units used in the arithmetic model, the more closely the derived marginal revenue curve will approximate the actual curve.

D. Profit Maximization for the Monopolist

1. Graphical Determination of Profit Maximization Output

The firm produces at the point where marginal cost equals marginal revenue; production at a higher point generates losses and production at a lower point fails to maximize profits. It is assumed that the merger of the ten firms in the widget industry does not result in any efficiency gains. Therefore, the marginal cost curve of the monopolist is the same as the widget industry marginal cost curve exhibited in Chart 8.12-VI and Graph 8.12-K. This marginal cost (or supply) curve for the monopolist is plotted on Graph 8.14-D, together with the actual marginal revenue curve and the demand curve.

Graph 8.14-D
Plotting the Monopolist's Marginal Revenue, Marginal (Supply) Cost and Demand Curves

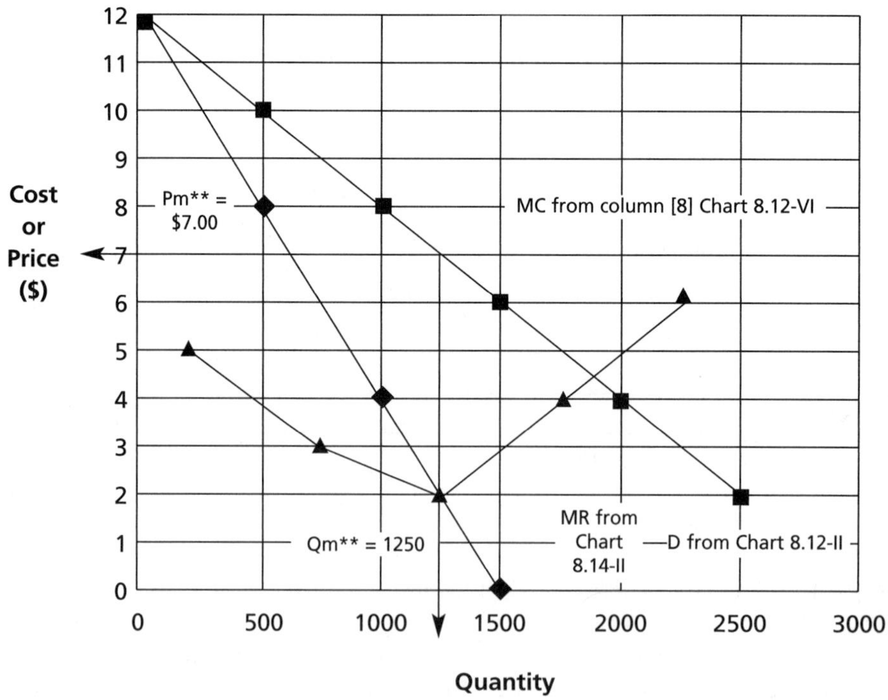

* Pm = Price under monopoly = $7.00
** Qm = Output under monopoly - 1250

Thus, after the merger of the ten firms in the widget industry, the single monopolist firm will produce approximately 1250 units, because those are the units indicated by the intersection of the marginal cost and marginal revenue curves. The price charged by the monopolist is determined by the price indicated on the demand curve for the approximately 1250 units. This is a price of $7 per unit.

The monopolist produces at that level in order to maximize profits; at that point and only at that point is marginal cost equal to marginal revenue.

The monopolist operates in the elastic part of the demand curve, which means that greater revenue would be spent on widgets with a price decrease. Firms in a competitive market operate at a point on the demand curve that is less elastic.

2. Comparison of the Price and Output Levels under Monopoly and Competition

Under monopoly, output is less and price is higher than in a competitive widget market. Chart 8.13-III below provides a comparison of the price and output of widgets under monopoly and under competition with the short run supply curve.

Chart 8.14-III
Comparison of Price and Output Under Monopoly and Competition

	Price	Output
Competitive Widget Market*	$4.50	1,875
Monopolized Widget Market**	$7.00	1,250

* From Graph 8.13-C
** From Graph 8.14-D

§ 8.15 Comparison of Monopoly Market with a Competitive Market: The Welfare Triangle and the Total Revenue and Cost Functions

A. Introduction to Concept of Consumer Surplus

Although the competitive and monopoly models are not necessarily a precise reflection of the real world, in general, the monopolist will produce less and charge more than would otherwise be the case under competitive conditions. Thus, under monopoly, consumers do not get the benefit of purchasing as much of the product as they would in a competitive market. The amount consumers would be willing to pay (assuming price discrimination were possible) above the amount actually charged by the producers is referred to as consumer surplus. This is a measure of the benefit consumers receive at a given price. Since price is higher under monopoly than under competition, consumer surplus is less under monopoly than under competition.

Consumer surplus is the amount under the demand curve and above the horizontal line connecting the price on the vertical axis and the demand curve. The amount of consumer welfare or surplus in the competitive widget industry is shown on Graph

8.15-A[1] below and in the monopolized widget industry is shown on Graph 8.15-A[2] [see next page].

Graph 8.15-A [1]
Consumer Welfare in Competitive Widget Industry

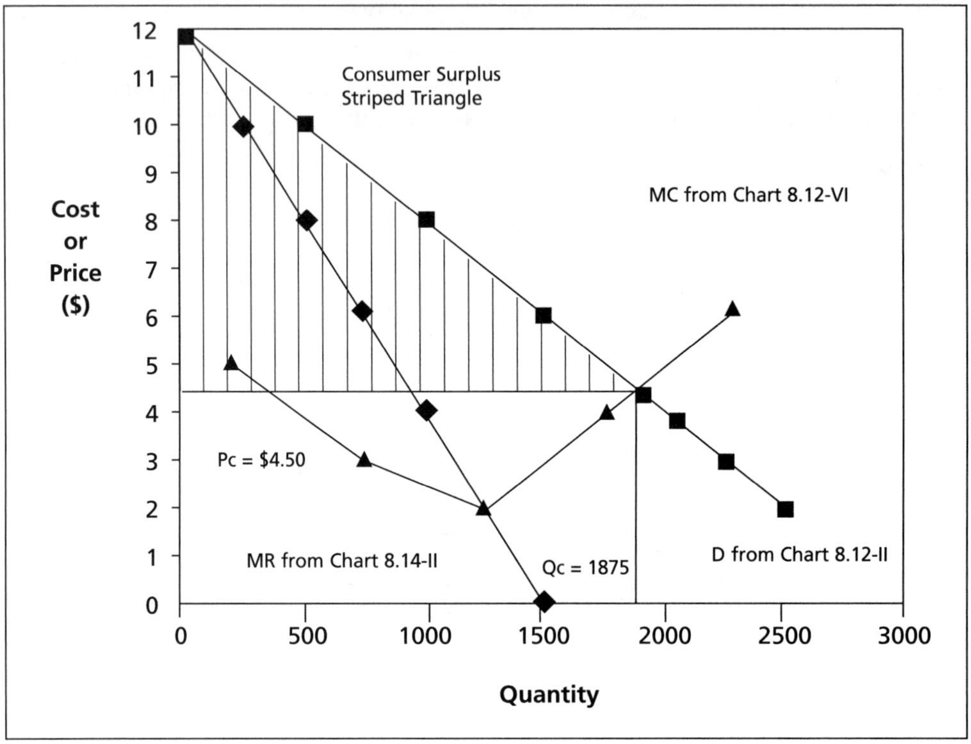

Graph 8.15-A [2]
Consumer Welfare in Monopolized Widget Industry

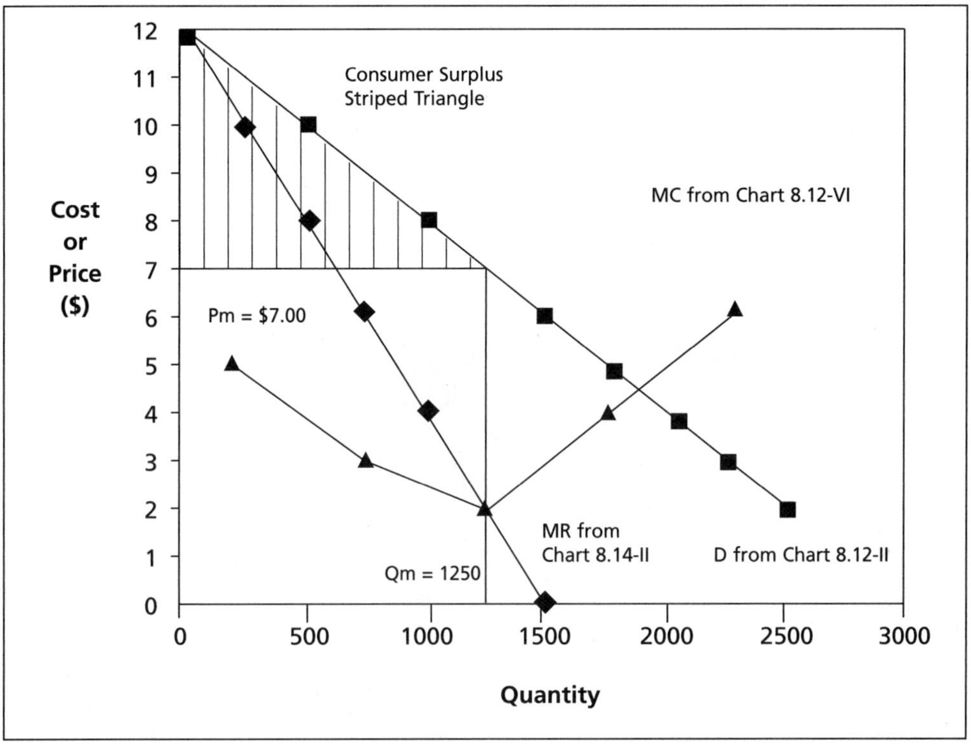

The total consumer welfare under competition is $7,031.25, which is one half of the product of the base of the triangle (1875) times the height of the triangle ($7.50). The total consumer welfare under monopoly is $3,125, which is one half of the product of the base of the triangle (1250) times the height of the triangle ($5). Thus, in moving from competition to monopoly, consumer welfare decreases by $3,906.25.

B. The Consumer Welfare Triangle and the Loss in Producer Surplus

In addition to leading to reduced consumer surplus, monopoly also leads to producer surplus that does not exist in the long run competitive model. The producer surplus is the amount charged above the marginal cost of the monopolist. Thus, when compared with the competitive model, monopoly decreases consumer surplus and creates producer surplus.

The increase in producer surplus under monopoly is not as great as the decrease in consumer surplus, and therefore, monopoly leads to an inefficient allocation of resources. The increase in producer surplus and the decrease in consumer surplus can be computed from Graph 8.15-B [see next page].

Graph 8.15-B
Consumer Welfare in Monopolized Widget Industry

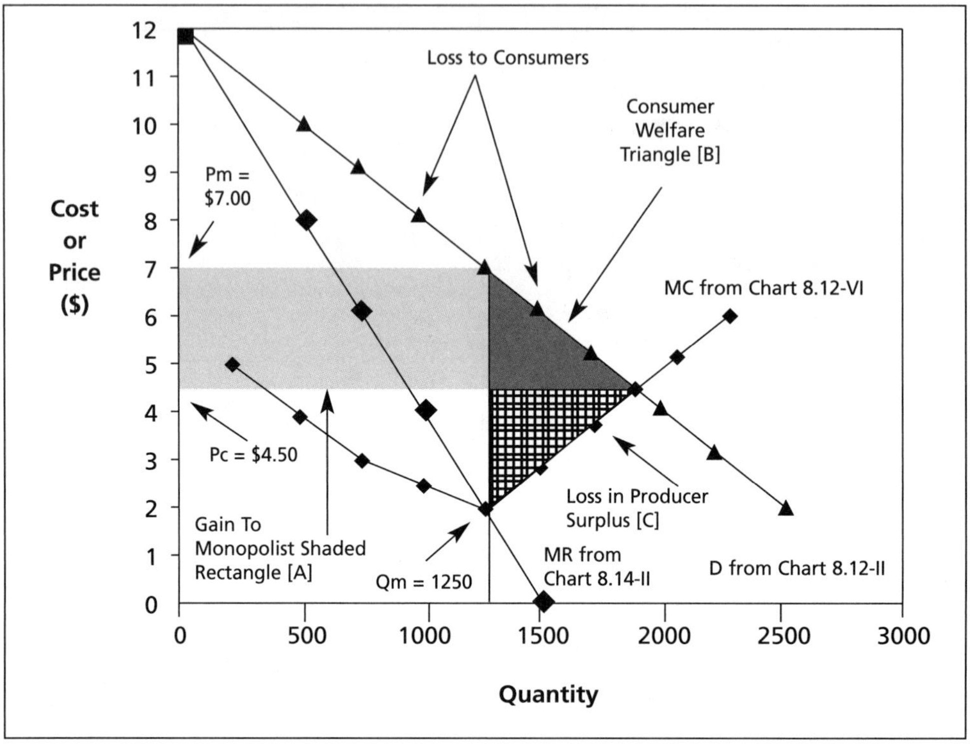

The loss in consumer surplus from monopoly is equal to the sum of (1) the amount of surplus that moves from consumers to the monopolist, which is represented by the shaded rectangle [A] on Graph 8.15-B, plus (2) the consumer welfare triangle [B], which is an amount of surplus that consumers lose but the monopolist does not gain. Thus, the consumer welfare triangle indicates a loss in total welfare or a deadweight loss.

The gain in welfare for the monopolist is not the full amount of rectangle [A], because the monopolist also experiences a loss in welfare in moving from competition to monopoly, and this loss is the triangle directly under the welfare triangle on Graph 8.15-B, which is designated loss in producer surplus [C]. Since surplus is the amount charged above the marginal cost, if the monopolist were to charge the competitive price, the monopolist would realize additional surplus in the amount of triangle [C]. Thus, the net gain in surplus realized by the monopolist in moving from competition to monopoly is equal to (1) the gain in surplus represented by rectangle [A], minus (2) the loss in surplus represented by triangle [C].

The gain to the monopolist represented by rectangle [A] is equal to $3,125, which is the product of (1) the increase in price under monopoly from the $4.50 competitive price to the $7 monopoly price (or $2.50) multiplied by (2) the units produced under monopoly (1250). That is, $2.50 multiplied by 1250 equals $3,125.

The decrease in consumer welfare resulting from monopoly is the sum of the amount represented by rectangle [A] ($3,125) plus the amount represented by welfare triangle [B].

The amount of surplus represented by welfare triangle [B] is $781.25, which is equal to one half the product of (1) the base of the welfare triangle or the number of reduced units under monopoly (*i.e.*, the 625 difference between the 1875 units produced under competition and the 1250 units produced under monopoly), multiplied by (2) the height of the welfare triangle or the $2.50 difference between the monopoly price ($7) and the competitive price ($4.50). That is, one half of 625 multiplied by $2.50 equals $781.25.

Thus, the loss in consumer welfare is $3,906.25 (*i.e.*, $3,125 plus $781.25), and producers gain only $3,125 of the loss. Thus, this $781.25 loss in welfare represented by triangle [B] is an allocative inefficiency or deadweight loss from monopoly.

The loss to producers represented by triangle [C] on Graph 8.15-B also represents a deadweight loss in welfare because it is a loss to producers that is not gained by anyone. Producers will voluntarily incur this loss because the loss is more than offset by the gain producers realize by capturing rectangle [A] from consumers. Triangle [C] is the same size as the welfare triangle (*i.e.*, the base is 625 and the height is $2.50) and, consequently, there is a $781.25 loss in allocative efficiency attributable to this loss in producer surplus that is not gained by anyone, that is a deadweight loss.

The net gain realized by the monopolist in moving from the competitive price to the monopoly price is, therefore, $2,343.75, which is the difference between the $3,125 in rectangle [A] and the $781.25 in triangle [C].

The total deadweight loss (*i.e.*, the sum of welfare triangle [B] and the loss to producers triangle [C]) is $1,562.50. Professor Mansfield explains that this total deadweight loss from monopoly, which "equals the amount the consumers' losses [*i.e.*, [A] + [B]] exceed the producer's gains [*i.e.*, [A]-[C]], is thus the loss in total surplus ... due to monopoly rather than perfect competition."

Many economics texts show the welfare loss from monopoly as being only the welfare triangle. This is the case, however, only if the marginal cost curve is flat. If the marginal cost curve slopes upward as in this situation, the deadweight loss equals the amount of the welfare triangle and the loss in producer surplus triangle.

To summarize: Welfare triangle [B] represents the loss in consumer surplus under monopoly that is not captured in producer surplus, and triangle [C] represents the loss in producer surplus under monopoly that is not captured by anyone. The combination of the welfare triangle [B] and the loss in producer surplus triangle [C] illustrates that there is a loss in allocative efficiency under monopoly. This loss in allocative efficiency is a "deadweight loss," that is a societal welfare loss.

In addition to the allocative inefficiency associated with monopoly, there is a significant transfer of wealth from consumers to the monopolist, and this redistribution of wealth can certainly have an impact on political power.

The Chicago School, however, ignores the wealth transfer effects and focuses on only deadweight or efficiency loss represented by the welfare triangle. This focus on the allocative effects of monopoly is premised on Professor Harberger's third basic postulate for applied welfare economics:

> [W]hen evaluating the net benefits or cost of a given action (project, program, or policy), the costs and benefits accruing to each member of the group (*e.g.* a nation) should normally be added without regard to the individual(s) to whom they accrue.[14]

14. Arnold C. Harberger, *Three Basic Postulates for Applied Welfare Economics*, IX J. Econ. Lit. 785 (1971) *reprinted in* Harberger, *Taxation and Welfare*, 5 (1974) [hereinafter *Taxation and Welfare*].

Professor Harberger goes on to argue that although income distributional effects "may be exceedingly important, perhaps even the dominant factors governing any policy decision[s] ... [such effects] are not a part of the package of expertise that distinguishes the professional economist from the rest of humanity."

Professors Richard and Peggy Musgrave take a different view from Professor Harberger on distributional issues:

Policy design ... inevitably involves distributional judgments.... [G]iven the close bearing of distributional issues on questions of economic policy and their major or even dominant weight in economic politics, economists who are concerned with public policy can hardly detach their thinking from equity issues.[15]

§ 8.16 Computation of Results of Productive Efficiency Gains from a Merger to Monopoly

A. Productive Efficiencies: Economies of Scale

Economies of scale may result from mergers, and this may be one of the principal business advantages of mergers. There appear to be four major types of economies of scale:

(1) Capital raising economies;

(2) Plant specific economies;

(3) Product specific economies; and

(4) Marketing economies.

Capital raising economies may result from the acquisition of a small firm by a larger firm. After such acquisitions, the smaller firm may benefit from the larger firm's lower cost of capital. This benefit may be offset, however, if the merger results in an increase in business risk, which generally occurred with conglomerate mergers in the 1960s. If a merger results in greater business risk for the firm, the cost of capital may increase after the merger.

Plant-specific and product-specific economies are more likely after horizontal mergers. In the short run, however, plant-specific economies of scale are unlikely after a horizontal merger, because the operation of the plants of the merging firms is likely to continue.

Marketing economies may result from better utilization of field sales forces, broader product lines, common advertising themes, and the sharing of any quantity discounts offered by advertising agencies or the media.

B. Impact of Productive Efficiencies

1. The General Case: The Graphical Presentation

Professor Williamson has developed the theory that in certain mergers that create monopoly power, productive efficiency gains can outweigh the loss in welfare.[16]

---

15. Richard & Peggy Musgrave, *Public Finance in Theory and Practice* 76 (5th ed. 1989).

16. Oliver Williamson, *Economies as an Antitrust Defense Revisited*, 125 U. PA. L. REV. 699 (1977) [hereinafter Williamson, *Economies Defense*]; *see also*, Oliver Williamson, *Economies as an Antitrust Defense: The Welfare Trade Offs*, 58 AM. ECON. REV. 18, 21–23 (1980).

His theory is that cost saving from an efficiency enhancing merger may offset the deadweight loss from the output restriction. In this situation, the argument goes as follows: if the overall effect of the merger on allocative efficiency is positive, the merger should be permitted even though it results in reduced output and higher prices to consumers. Others have argued that the proper antitrust approach is to permit an efficiency enhancing merger only if the price reducing effect of efficiencies offsets the price increasing effect of enhanced market power.

It is instructive to put Professor Williamson's theory to test in the monopolized market for widgets by assuming substantial efficiency gains (*i.e.*, productive efficiencies). For example, assume that after the merger of the ten firms, there are substantial cost savings (*i.e.*, productive efficiency gains) in the widget industry so that the total variable cost schedule of the new firm is as shown in Chart 8.16-I below.

Chart 8.16-I
Cost Savings

Amount of Total Output	Old Total Variable Cost	New Total Variable Cost
500	$2500	$2000
1000	$4000	$3000
1500	$5000	$3500
2000	$7000	$4500
2500	$10000	$6500

Thus, the cost savings for each level of output are equal to, or in excess of 20%, which are substantial cost savings.

With the new total variable cost, the new average total cost schedule would be as shown in Chart 8.16-II below.

Chart 8.16-II
Computation of New Average Total Cost

[1] Amount of Total Output	[2] Fixed Cost	[3] New Total Variable Cost	[4] New Total Cost [2]+[3]	[5] New Average Total Cost [4]÷[1]
500	$500	$2000	$2500	$5.0
1000	$500	$3000	$3500	$3.5
1500	$500	$3500	$4000	$2.6
2000	$500	$4500	$5000	$2.5
2500	$500	$6500	$7000	$2.8

The new marginal cost schedule would be as illustrated in Chart 8.16-III [see next page].

Chart 8.16-III
Computation of New Marginal Cost Per Marginal Unit

[1] Amount of Total Output	[2] Amount of Variable Output	[3] New Total Variable Costs	[4] Variable Cost of Next Lower Level of Output	[5] New Increase in Variable Cost [3]–[4]	[6] Average Marginal Costs per Marginal Unit*** [5]÷[2]	[7] Mid-point of Output Range	[8] Marginal Cost of Midpoint of Output Range
500	500	$2000	$0	$2000	$4	250	$4
1000	500	$3000	$2000	$1000	$2	750	$2
1500	500	$3500	$3000	$ 500	$1	1250	$1
2000	500	$4500	$3500	$1000	$2	1750	$2
2500	500	$6500	$4500	$2000	$4	2250	$4

The new marginal cost curve reflecting the productive efficiencies is plotted below on Graph 8.16-A with the demand curve and the marginal revenue curve also plotted.

Graph 8.16-A
New Output Levels and New Prices Resulting from Product Efficiency

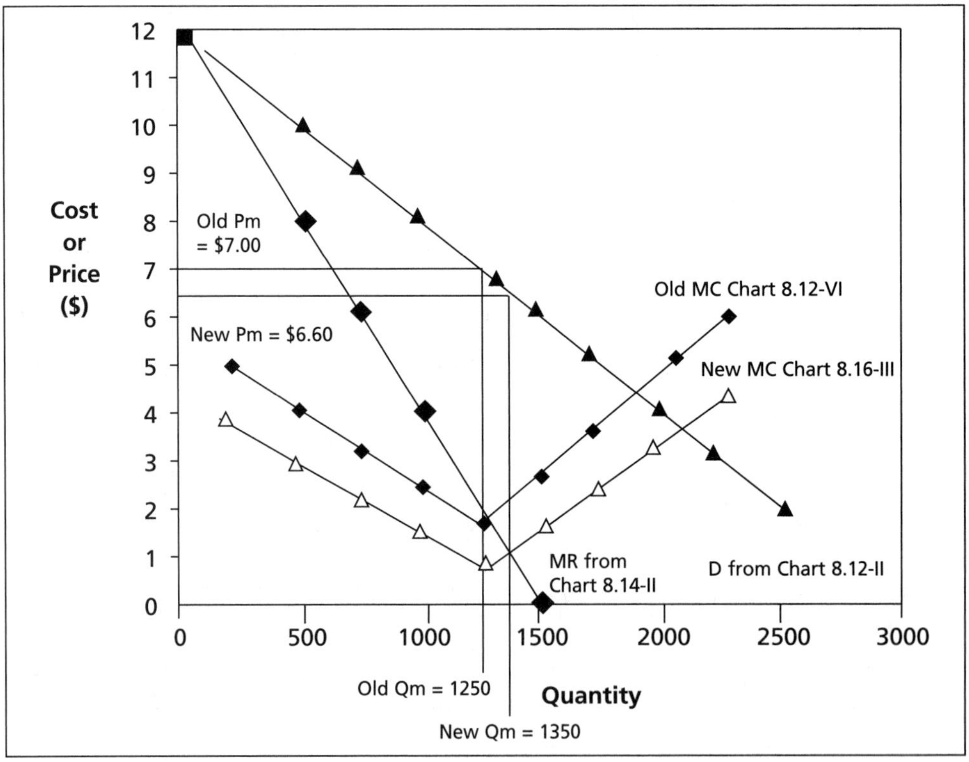

As a result of the substantial productive efficiencies, production would be increased to approximately 1350 units as compared to 1250 units without any productive efficiencies,[17] and price would be approximately $6.60, as compared with the $7 price without productive efficiencies.

2. Impact of Productive Efficiencies on the Welfare Triangle

Notwithstanding the substantial productive efficiencies, the output and price are not substantially different from that which occurs under monopoly without productive efficiencies. Also, the productive efficiencies reduce the size of both the welfare triangle and the triangle indicating the loss in producer surplus. These are triangles [B] and [C] on Graph 8.15-B, which indicates the deadweight loss from monopoly. The reductions, however, are relatively small. This can be seen on Graph 8.16-B below, which displays both triangles under monopoly without productive efficiency gains and demonstrates the effect the productive efficiencies have on the triangles.

Graph 8.16-B
Illustration of Impact on Welfare Triangle Resulting from Productive Efficiencies

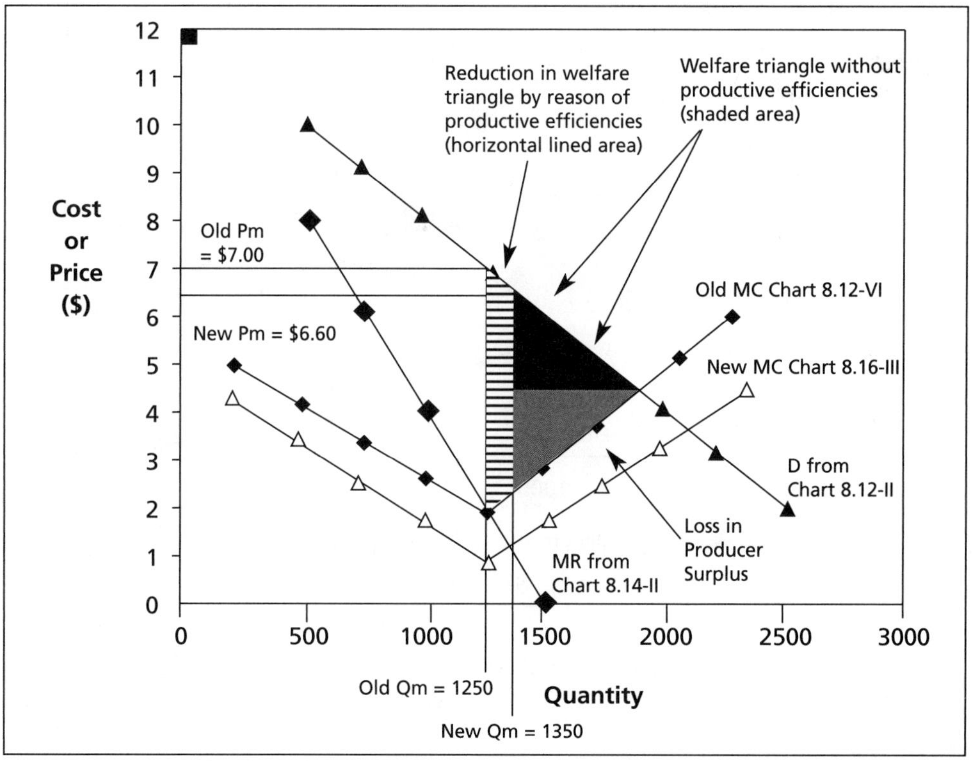

Graph 8.16-B demonstrates that the productive efficiencies only partially offset the welfare loss from monopoly. Therefore, even these substantial productive efficiencies, which as a practical matter are unlikely to be attained, do not substantially reduce the allocative inefficiency represented by both the welfare triangle and the loss in producer surplus triangle. It would appear from this example that only in rare circumstances could productive efficiency gains from monopoly outweigh the deadweight loss in allocative efficiency.

17. *See*, Graph 8.14-O.

Professor Williamson argues, however, that it is appropriate to compare the deadweight loss with the cost saving realized by the monopolist. He argues that the net allocative efficiency effect of the merger is positive if the cost savings realized by the monopolist exceeds the deadweight loss. The cost saving is demonstrated on Graph 8.16-C below, which also shows both the welfare triangle and the loss in producer surplus triangle, as reduced by efficiencies. The cost saving is determined by comparing the average total cost curves before and after the merger [*see* Charts 8.12-IV and 8.16-II] at the point where the old marginal cost curve intersects the marginal revenue curve.

Graph 8.16-C
Illustration of Impact of Cost Savings on Allocative Efficiency

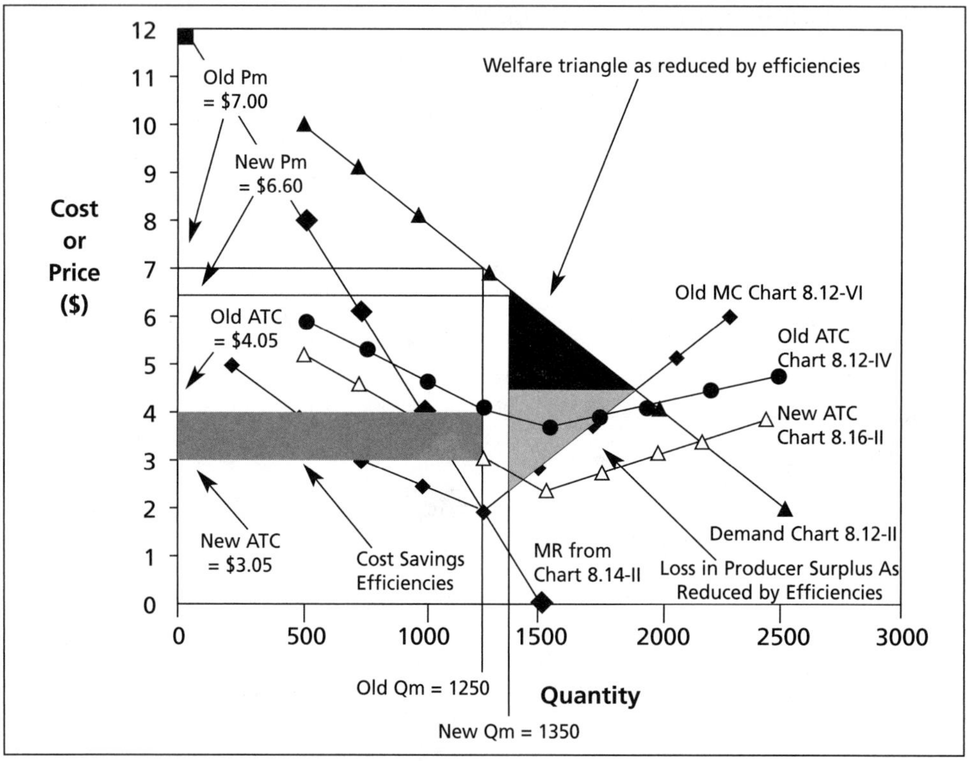

It can be demonstrated that the total cost savings is approximately $1,250, which is the number of units of output under monopoly without the productive efficiencies (1250), multiplied by the average cost savings of $1.00. On the other hand, both the welfare triangle and the loss in producer surplus triangle each represent a loss to society of approximately $551.25.

Under Professor Williamson's analysis, this type of merger results in a positive net allocative efficiency effect even with monopoly pricing. This is because the cost savings of $1,250 exceeds the welfare loss of $1,102.50. Professor Williamson explains, "a relatively modest cost reduction is sufficient to offset relatively large price increases even if the elasticity of demand is high."[18] He goes on to say that "a merger that promises nontrivial

18. *Id.* at 709.

economies—say greater than two percent—will generally yield a net allocative efficiency gain."[19]

It should be noted, however, that even with the approximately 20% cost savings in this case, the net gain in allocative efficiency is not that large. The reason for the significant difference between the results here and the predictions of Professor Williamson is that he assumes a flat marginal cost curve, both with and without efficiencies. With a flat marginal cost curve, the loss in welfare is equal to the welfare triangle, but with an upward sloping marginal cost curve, the welfare loss is equal to the aggregate of the welfare triangle and the loss in producer surplus triangle. Thus, with an upward sloping marginal cost curve the loss in welfare is significantly more (in this case double) than the loss in welfare with a flat marginal cost curve.

Although Professor Williamson's conclusion may appear sound, his reasoning is fundamentally flawed. There is a cost savings here only in the most narrow sense of the word. Consumers do not realize a cost savings. They suffer a price increase as a result of the merger. Thus, although there is a reduction in the costs of producing widgets that is attributable to the efficiency gains (such as reduced wages from jobs lost as a result of closing down overlapping factories), consumers do not get any benefit from this savings. Rather, the monopolist takes all of the savings plus more in the form of increased profits. These increased profits are the equivalent of a "privately imposed and privately collected tax" on consumers.[20]

As a policy matter, it is arguable that potential efficiencies should be taken into account only if the benefit of the efficiencies is likely to be passed on to consumers. This passing on requirement, which is essentially reflected in the 1993 NAAG Guidelines, has been criticized by Professor Pitofsky, a former Chairman of the Federal Trade Commission, on the grounds that with this requirement "efficiency defenses would only be permitted in highly competitive markets, and in such markets mergers would be unlikely to be challenged anyway."[21]

Professor Pitofsky makes the following proposal for an efficiencies defense:

> In any market where post-merger concentration is moderate, and the combined company after the merger would hold less than thirty-five percent of the market, a horizontal merger should be legal if the defendants can clearly support the claim that production efficiencies leading to a substantial reduction in unit cost will result and these efficiencies could not be achieved through a much less restrictive alternative.

§ 8.17 Oligopoly

A. Noncooperative Oligopoly

In a noncooperative oligopoly, the firms in the market act independently but take into account the potential reaction of rival firms. Although there is wide agreement among economists on the models of competition and monopoly discussed above, there is no such agreement on a model of noncooperative oligopoly. There is one point, however, on

19. *Id.*

20. Harberger, *Taxation and Welfare*, *supra*, note 16, at 17.

21. Robert Pitofsky, *Proposals for Revised United States Merger Enforcement in a Global Economy*, 81 GEO. L. J. 195,221 (1992).

which most of the models of noncooperative oligopoly are in agreement: the pricing and output decisions under noncooperative oligopoly lie somewhere between such decisions under monopoly and competition.

Although collusive oligopoly is a clear violation of Section 1 of the Sherman Act, it appears that noncooperative oligopoly generally is not illegal under either Section 1 of the Sherman Act or under Section 5 of the Federal Trade Commission Act.

B. Potential for Collusion in an Oligopolistic Market

The firms in a competitive market generally find it difficult to enter into explicit or tacit agreements to simulate a monopolist by jointly lowering output and increasing price. The large number of firms in a competitive market make such agreements practically unworkable. Thus, the firms in a competitive market take the price resulting from the intersection of the industry supply and demand curves as indicated in Graph 8.12-L. The firm in a competitive market, therefore, faces a horizontal demand curve as demonstrated in Graph 8.12-C.

Collusive agreements are, however, possible for firms operating in an oligopolistic market. This is because the firms realize their interdependence. Thus, one of the dangers of oligopoly is that the firms may be able through collusion to simulate the actions of a monopolist. This type of collusion (*e.g.*, price fixing or market division) is unlawful under Section 1 of the Sherman Act.

Collusive agreements are inherently unstable because the firms have an incentive to cheat. A firm can enhance its profits by cheating, provided the other colluders maintain the higher price and lower output. The cheater increases its profits by selling slightly below the agreed price thereby increasing its sales at a price that still exceeds marginal cost.

§ 8.18 Problems Illustrating the Microeconomic Principles of Monopoly and Competition

Problems

1. The Industry Demand Schedule in the widget industry is shown on Chart 8.12-II. Plot the Industry Demand Curve on a graph.

2. There are ten firms operating in this industry and each firm is the same size and has the same production function. Chart 8.12-IV summarizes the aggregate costs data (other than marginal cost) for these ten firms. Plot the curves for the Average Fixed Cost (AFC), Average Variable Cost (AVC), and Average Total Cost (ATC) on the graph drawn for question number 1.

Note that for any one of the ten firms in the industry the graph illustrates the average costs for the following levels of quantity: 50, 100, 150, 200 and 250; that is, one tenth of the industry quantity. *See* Chart 8.12-III.

3. The Marginal Cost per unit at each level of output is computed by dividing the increase in variable costs at each level by the increase in output at that level. Therefore, *Marginal Cost* is computed as indicated on Chart 8.12-VI.

The costs are for all of the ten firms in this industry. Plot the Marginal Cost curve on the graph that contains the various average cost curves. Does the Marginal Cost curve intersect the Average Variable Cost (AVC) curve and the Average Total Cost (ATC) curve at their respective minimums? Identify the industry supply curve.

4. Assuming a competitive widget industry, plot on the graph the industry demand and supply curves and determine the equilibrium price and output.

What will be each firm's marginal revenue (MR) and average revenue (AR) per unit? How much of the total quantity sold will each firm produce? What will be the industry's total revenue (*i.e.*, price x quantity sold)?

5. If the ten firms merged into one firm, what will be the quantity produced and the price paid assuming the resulting firm acts rationally? Assume that widgets are unique products, there are substantial barriers to entry, and market knowledge is imperfect. First, determine the firm's Marginal Revenue Curve. Recall that Marginal Revenue is the increment to revenue added by an additional unit of sales. It can be approximated by the following formula:

$$\frac{(\text{New Price} \times \text{New Quantity}) - (\text{Old Price} \times \text{Old Quantity})}{\text{Incremental Units}}$$

Thus, the Marginal Revenue Curve of the resulting firm can be approximated from the information on Chart 8.14-I.

The Marginal Revenue Curve could be precisely computed through the use of calculus. The results are indicated on Chart 8.14-II.

First plot the Demand Curve the firm will face, and the Marginal Revenue Curve. Then plot the Marginal Cost Curve of the firm assuming no changes in costs.

What is the level of output and the price? Note that the firm will produce to the point where Marginal Cost equals Marginal Revenue. Why? What will be the firm's total revenue (*i.e.* price x quantity sold)? How does the total revenue of the single firm under monopoly compare with total revenue in the competitive market? How much monopoly profit will the firm make (*i.e.*, the excess of the monopoly price times the monopoly quantity over Average Total Cost (ATC) times the monopoly quantity)? Identify the welfare triangle and the loss in producer surplus triangle.

6. What would be the price and output in the market if the ten firms did not merge, but entered into an effective (though illegal) price fixing conspiracy?

7. What result would obtain in the market if, after the merger of the ten firms, there were substantial cost savings (*i.e.*, efficiency gains), such that the Total Variable Cost schedule of the new firm was as indicated on Chart 8.16-I.

In such case, the new Average Total Cost schedule would be as indicated on Chart 8.16-II, and the new Marginal Cost Schedule would be as outlined in Chart 8.16-III.

Plot on a graph the Demand Curve, the Marginal Revenue Curve, the Old Marginal Cost Curve, and the New Marginal Cost Curve.

What will be the level of output and the price with the production efficiencies? Note that the firm will produce to the point where Marginal Cost equals Marginal Revenue. Why? How does the quantity produced and price charged under this efficiency enhancing merger compare with the price and quantity in the competitive market and in the monopoly market without efficiency gains. What is the impact of the efficiency gains on the welfare triangle and the loss in producer surplus triangle? How do the cost savings compare with the remaining welfare triangle and loss in producer surplus triangle?

§ 8.19 Analysis of Empirical Studies of Concentration-Price Relationship

Samuel C. Thompson, Jr., A Proposal for Antitrust Merger Enforcement Reform: Repudiating Judge Bork in Favor of Current Economic Learning

The Antitrust Bulletin, pp. 98–116 (Spring 1996)

The significance of the study of the relationship between concentration and anticompetitive market performance for purposes of merger analysis is illustrated in Judge Posner's opinion in *United States v. Rockford Memorial Corp.*[22] * * * [In this case,] Judge Posner * * * noted the presumption that present law applies upon a finding of a high level of concentration resulting from a merger:

> [O]nce the government showed that the merger would create a firm having market share approaching, perhaps exceeding, a common threshold of monopoly power two-thirds (*United States v. Aluminum Co. of America*, 148 F.2d 416, 424 (2d Cir. 1945) (L Hand, J) it behooved the defendants to present evidence that the normal inference to be drawn from such a market share would mislead.[23] * * *

Professor Mueller criticizes Judge Posner's adoption of the two-thirds rule from the *Alcoa* decision as the "common threshold of monopoly power":

> [This threshold] is rather dramatically inconsistent, however, with the empirical findings of industrial-organization economists as reported in standard text, ... that higher prices generally begin when the 4-firm concentration ratio reaches about 50% (CR4–50).

A review of the Mueller article shows that the number of surveyed economists that agree with the proposition that there is a relationship between concentration and price out number those who believe that there is no such relationship by a margin of almost two to one. Thus, there appears to be substantial agreement within the economic profession on this point. * * *

Part III
Department of Justice/FTC Horizontal Merger Guidelines

§ 8.20 Scope of Part III

Section 8.21 introduces both (1) the 1992 DOJ and FTC Horizontal Merger Guidelines (1992 DOJ/FTC Guidelines), and (2) the 2010 DOJ and FTC Horizontal Merger Guidelines (2010 DOJ/FTC Guidelines). As indicated previously, an understanding of the basic approach of the 1992 DOJ/FTC Guidelines can help with an understanding of the 2010 DOJ/FTC Guidelines. Section 8.22 briefly introduces the 1993 Horizontal Merger Guidelines of the National Association of Attorneys General (1993 NAAG Guidelines). A state attorney general has the authority to enforce Section 7 of the Clayton Act to protect the welfare and economy of his or her state, and the 1993 NAAG Guidelines

22. 898 F.2d 1278 (7th Cir. 1990).
23. *Id.* at 1285–1286.

explain the "general enforcement policy of the attorneys general ..." Thus, these Guidelines could become important if a state attorney general decides to take a careful look at an acquisition. After this introduction the focus is mainly on the 2010 DOJ/FTC Guidelines.

The EU's Competition Commission has also adopted Horizontal Merger Guidelines, and these Guidelines, which follow the structure of the 1992 DOJ/FTC Guidelines, are examined in Chapter 26, which deals with cross-border M&A. This part also contains cases illustrating the application of the principles in the Guidelines.

The basic enforcement standards under the 2010 DOJ/FTC Guidelines are explored in Section 8.23. Sections 8.24 and 8.25 focus on market definition under the pre-Guideline case law and the 2010 DOJ/FTC Guidelines. Sections 8.26 through 8.28 examine the approach of the 2010 DOJ/FTC Guidelines to the competitive effects analysis, which looks at concentration, unilateral effects, and coordinated interactions. Section 8.29 looks at the power buyer defense under both the case law and the Guidelines. Sections 8.30 and 8.31 consider the treatment of entry under the case law and the Guidelines, and Sections 8.32 through 8.34 explore the treatment of economic efficiencies under the case law and the Guidelines. Section 8.35 addresses the failing firm defense under the Guidelines, and Section 8.36 presents the *Evanston Hospital* case, which dealt with an FTC challenge to a completed merger on the basis of post-acquisition increases in price. Section 8.37 deals with the approach of the 2010 DOJ/FTC Guidelines to mergers of competing buyers and Section 8.38 addresses the Guidelines' treatment of partial acquisitions.

In this Part, the 2010 DOJ/FTC Guidelines are broken down into their essential elements, and the focus here is on the basic principles in these Guidelines. The Guidelines, which are long and intricate, are available on the websites of both the DOJ and the FTC and should be consulted in the analysis of any actual transaction. The sections in this part contain numerous references to the *Commentary on the Horizontal Merger Guidelines* (DOJ/FTC Commentary), which was published by the DOJ and the FTC in March 2006.

§ 8.21 Introduction to 1992 and 2010 DOJ/FTC Horizontal Merger Guidelines

A. Background

On April 2, 1992 the DOJ and FTC issued Horizontal Merger Guidelines. These Guidelines set forth the enforcement policy for these agencies under Section 7 of the Clayton Act and supersede the horizontal provisions of the DOJ's 1984 Merger Guidelines. The provisions of the 1984 Merger Guidelines dealing with conglomerate and vertical mergers continue to be in effect and are examined in Sections 8.39 and 8.40. The DOJ initially issued merger guidelines in 1968. As explained in a statement accompanying the 1992 DOJ/FTC Guidelines, the 1968 Guidelines "fell into disuse," and were superseded by revised merger guidelines issued by the DOJ in 1982. The statement explains that the 1982 Guidelines "departed dramatically" from the 1968 Guidelines and purportedly reflected current "developments in legal and economic thinking about mergers."

Although the FTC did not join with the DOJ in the issuance of the 1968, 1982 and 1984 Guidelines, it issued a statement accompanying the 1982 Guidelines setting forth its views on merger enforcement. The principal "economic thinking," reflected initially in the 1982 Guidelines and carried over to the 1984 and 1992 Guidelines, involves the application of microeconomic principles in analyzing mergers. The "analytical foundations" referred to in the 1992 DOJ/FTC Guidelines are the principles governing the microeconomic models of competition, monopoly, and oligopoly, discussed in Part II of this chapter.

An August 19, 2010 joint press release issued by the DOJ and FTC provides the following explanation of the reasons for adopting the 2010 DOJ/FTC Guidelines:

> The Department of Justice and the Federal Trade Commission (FTC) issued today revised Horizontal Merger Guidelines that outline how the federal antitrust agencies evaluate the likely competitive impact of mergers and whether those mergers comply with U.S. antitrust law. These changes mark the first major revision of the merger guidelines in 18 years, and will give businesses a better understanding of how the agencies evaluate proposed mergers.
>
> A primary goal of the 2010 guidelines is to help the agencies identify and challenge competitively harmful mergers while avoiding unnecessary interference with mergers that either are competitively beneficial or likely will have no competitive impact on the marketplace. To accomplish this, the guidelines detail the techniques and main types of evidence the agencies typically use to predict whether horizontal mergers may substantially lessen competition.
>
> The revised merger guidelines derive from the agencies' collective experience in assessing thousands of transactions focusing on the types of evidence the department and the FTC use to decide whether a merger of competitors may harm competition. Many of the proposed refinements and changes reflect issues previously identified in the "Commentary on the Horizontal Merger Guidelines," which the agencies jointly issued in 2006. In crafting the revisions, the agencies considered a wide range of opinions gathered through a series of joint public workshops, as well as hundreds of public comments submitted by attorneys, academics, economists, consumer groups and businesses.
>
> "The revised guidelines better reflect the agencies' actual practices," said Christine Varney, Assistant Attorney General in charge of the Department of Justice's Antitrust Division. * * *

B. Overview of the Five Steps in the 1992 DOJ/FTC Guidelines

The 1992 DOJ/FTC Guidelines set out a five-step process for answering the ultimate inquiry: Will the merger likely create or enhance market power or facilitate its exercise? Although the 2010 DOJ/FTC Guidelines do not explicitly set out a five-step process, as will be seen in the discussion below, these 2010 Guidelines contain each of the elements in the five steps of the 1992 Guidelines. For this reason, the five steps are discussed here.

First step. The first step is to determine whether the merger would significantly increase concentration and result in a concentrated market, properly defined. Thus, the starting point is the definition of the market and the determination of concentration levels in the market. This step is consistent with the approach of the case law discussed in Part I of this chapter.

The relevant market is determined by applying a formula that is premised on the microeconomic concept of cross elasticity of demand. Thus, market definition under the 1992 DOJ/FTC Guidelines focuses on the demand side of the market.

After determining the relevant market, the final part of the first step is to determine the level of concentration in the market. This involves an analysis of the productive capacities of both actual competitors and certain potential competitors (*i.e.*, "uncommitted entrants"). Uncommitted entrants are firms that could begin producing in the relevant market quickly without incurring significant "sunk" costs of entry or exit. Thus, these are the "hit and run" potential entrants of the contestable markets theory. [*See* Section 8.11.D]

Second step. The second step in the 1992 DOJ/FTC Guidelines is to determine whether, in view of market concentration and numerous other factors, the merger raises concerns about potential anticompetitive effects. Thus, in ascertaining whether there is any anticompetitive effect, consideration is given both to the concentration level in the market and to an examination of market structure to determine whether the market is likely to be characterized by either coordinated interactions or unilateral anticompetitive effects.

The Guidelines divide markets into three concentration levels depending on the post-merger Herfindahl-Hirschman index ("HHI"). The HHI is determined by squaring the market shares of the firms in the market and summing the squares. Thus, if one firm has 100% of a market, the HHI is 10,000, indicating a monopoly, and if each of 100 firms in a market has 1% of the market, the HHI is 100, indicating a competitive market.

Third step. The third step is to determine whether entry into the market by "committed entrants" would be timely, likely and sufficient to deconcentrate the market. Committed entrants are those potential entrants that could enter only by incurring significant sunk costs.

Even if the merger appears to be anticompetitive after an analysis of concentration levels and the other oligopoly factors, it may not be challenged if the possibility of new entry by committed entrants would prevent the exercise of market power.

Fourth step. If after considering entry the decision to challenge still holds, then the analysis proceeds to the fourth step: determining whether there are any efficiency gains that cannot be attained otherwise. Thus, the presence of efficiencies may lead to the decision not to challenge a merger.

Fifth step. If after going through the first four steps, a decision to challenge the merger is made, then the analysis turns to the fifth step: determining whether the failing firm exception applies.

C. Section 1, Overview, of the 2010 DOJ/FTC Guidelines

1. Overview.

These Guidelines outline the principal analytical techniques, practices, and the enforcement policy of the Department of Justice and the Federal Trade Commission (the "Agencies") with respect to mergers and acquisitions involving actual or potential competitors ("horizontal mergers") under the federal antitrust laws.[24] The relevant statutory provisions include Section 7 of the Clayton Act, 15 U.S.C. § 18, Sections 1 and 2 of the Sherman Act, 15 U.S.C. §§ 1, 2, and Section 5 of the Federal Trade Commission Act, 15

24. These Guidelines replace the Horizontal Merger Guidelines issued in 1992, revised in 1997. They reflect the ongoing accumulation of experience at the Agencies. The Commentary on the Horizontal Merger Guidelines issued by the Agencies in 2006 remains a valuable supplement to these Guidelines. These Guidelines may be revised from time to time as necessary to reflect significant changes in enforcement policy, to clarify existing policy, or to reflect new learning. These Guidelines do not cover vertical or other types of non-horizontal acquisitions.

U.S.C. § 45. Most particularly, Section 7 of the Clayton Act prohibits mergers if "in any line of commerce or in any activity affecting commerce in any section of the country, the effect of such acquisition may be substantially to lessen competition, or to tend to create a monopoly."

The Agencies seek to identify and challenge competitively harmful mergers while avoiding unnecessary interference with mergers that are either competitively beneficial or neutral. Most merger analysis is necessarily predictive, requiring an assessment of what will likely happen if a merger proceeds as compared to what will likely happen if it does not. Given this inherent need for prediction, these Guidelines reflect the congressional intent that merger enforcement should interdict competitive problems in their incipiency and that certainty about anticompetitive effect is seldom possible and not required for a merger to be illegal.

These Guidelines describe the principal analytical techniques and the main types of evidence on which the Agencies usually rely to predict whether a horizontal merger may substantially lessen competition. They are not intended to describe how the Agencies analyze cases other than horizontal mergers. These Guidelines are intended to assist the business community and antitrust practitioners by increasing the transparency of the analytical process underlying the Agencies' enforcement decisions. They may also assist the courts in developing an appropriate framework for interpreting and applying the antitrust laws in the horizontal merger context.

These Guidelines should be read with the awareness that merger analysis does not consist of uniform application of a single methodology. Rather, it is a fact-specific process through which the Agencies, guided by their extensive experience, apply a range of analytical tools to the reasonably available and reliable evidence to evaluate competitive concerns in a limited period of time. Where these Guidelines provide examples, they are illustrative and do not exhaust the applications of the relevant principle.[25]

The unifying theme of these Guidelines is that mergers should not be permitted to create, enhance, or entrench market power or to facilitate its exercise. For simplicity of exposition, these Guidelines generally refer to all of these effects as enhancing market power. A merger enhances market power if it is likely to encourage one or more firms to raise price, reduce output, diminish innovation, or otherwise harm customers as a result of diminished competitive constraints or incentives. In evaluating how a merger will likely change a firm's behavior, the Agencies focus primarily on how the merger affects conduct that would be most profitable for the firm.

A merger can enhance market power simply by eliminating competition between the merging parties. This effect can arise even if the merger causes no changes in the way other firms behave. Adverse competitive effects arising in this manner are referred to as "unilateral effects." A merger also can enhance market power by increasing the risk of coordinated, accommodating, or interdependent behavior among rivals. Adverse competitive effects arising in this manner are referred to as "coordinated effects." In any given case, either or both types of effects may be present, and the distinction between them may be blurred.

25. These Guidelines are not intended to describe how the Agencies will conduct the litigation of cases they decide to bring. Although relevant in that context, these Guidelines neither dictate nor exhaust the range of evidence the Agencies may introduce in litigation.

These Guidelines principally describe how the Agencies analyze mergers between rival suppliers that may enhance their market power as sellers. Enhancement of market power by sellers often elevates the prices charged to customers. For simplicity of exposition, these Guidelines generally discuss the analysis in terms of such price effects. Enhanced market power can also be manifested in non-price terms and conditions that adversely affect customers, including reduced product quality, reduced product variety, reduced service, or diminished innovation. Such non-price effects may coexist with price effects, or can arise in their absence. When the Agencies investigate whether a merger may lead to a substantial lessening of non-price competition, they employ an approach analogous to that used to evaluate price competition. Enhanced market power may also make it more likely that the merged entity can profitably and effectively engage in exclusionary conduct. Regardless of how enhanced market power likely would be manifested, the Agencies normally evaluate mergers based on their impact on customers. The Agencies examine effects on either or both of the direct customers and the final consumers. The Agencies presume, absent convincing evidence to the contrary, that adverse effects on direct customers also cause adverse effects on final consumers.

Enhancement of market power by buyers, sometimes called "monopsony power," has adverse effects comparable to enhancement of market power by sellers. The Agencies employ an analogous framework to analyze mergers between rival purchasers that may enhance their market power as buyers. See Section 12.

D. Section 2, Evidence of Adverse Competitive Effects, of the 2010 DOJ/FTC Guidelines

2. Evidence of Adverse Competitive Effects

The Agencies consider any reasonably available and reliable evidence to address the central question of whether a merger may substantially lessen competition. This section discusses several categories and sources of evidence that the Agencies, in their experience, have found most informative in predicting the likely competitive effects of mergers. The list provided here is not exhaustive. In any given case, reliable evidence may be available in only some categories or from some sources. For each category of evidence, the Agencies consider evidence indicating that the merger may enhance competition as well as evidence indicating that it may lessen competition.

2.1 Types of Evidence

2.1.1 Actual Effects Observed in Consummated Mergers * * *

2.1.2 Direct Comparisons Based on Experience

The Agencies look for historical events, or "natural experiments," that are informative regarding the competitive effects of the merger. * * *

2.1.3 Market Shares and Concentration in a Relevant Market

The Agencies give weight to the merging parties' market shares in a relevant market, the level of concentration, and the change in concentration caused by the merger. See Sections 4 and 5. Mergers that cause a significant increase in concentration and result in highly concentrated markets are presumed to be likely to enhance market power, but this presumption can be rebutted by persuasive evidence showing that the merger is unlikely to enhance market power.

2.1.4 Substantial Head-to-Head Competition * * *

2.1.5 Disruptive Role of a Merging Party [a "Maverick" Firm] * * *

2.2 Sources of Evidence

The Agencies consider many sources of evidence in their merger analysis. The most common sources of reasonably available and reliable evidence are the merging parties, customers, other industry participants, and industry observers. * * *

E. Section 3, Targeted Customers and Price Discrimination, of the 2010 DOJ/FTC Guidelines

3. Targeted Customers and Price Discrimination

When examining possible adverse competitive effects from a merger, the Agencies consider whether those effects vary significantly for different customers purchasing the same or similar products. Such differential impacts are possible when sellers can discriminate, e.g., by profitably raising price to certain targeted customers but not to others. * * *

F. DOJ/FTC Commentary on the 1992 DOJ/FTC Guidelines—Introduction

DOJ and FTC Comments on the Horizontal Merger Guidelines

(March 2006)

*Governing Legal Principles.** * * In applying the [1992] Guidelines to the transactions that each separately reviews, the Agencies strive to allow transactions unlikely substantially to lessen competition to proceed as expeditiously as possible. The Agencies focus their attention on quickly identifying those transactions that could violate the antitrust laws, subjecting those mergers to greater scrutiny. * * *

For more than 95% of the transactions reported under HSR, the Agencies promptly determine—*i.e.*, within the initial fifteen- or thirty-day waiting period that immediately follows HSR filings—that a substantial lessening of competition is unlikely. * * *

§ 8.22 Introduction to 1993 NAAG Horizontal Merger Guidelines

The purpose of the 1993 NAAG Guidelines is to "articulate an analytical framework the states apply in determining whether a merger is likely substantially to lessen competition ..." The purpose is not to describe how the states will conduct litigation. These Guidelines purport to be "grounded in and consistent with the purposes and meaning of Section 7 of the Clayton Act ... as reflected in its legislative history and interpretations of the Supreme Court." The 1993 NAAG Guidelines go on to say:

> The organizing principle of the Guidelines is the application of facts concerning the marketplace and widely accepted economic theory to these authoritative sources of the law's meaning. [*See* Section 1]

The 1993 NAAG Guidelines say that the "central purpose" of Section 7 is to "prevent firms from attaining either market or monopoly power" [*see* Section 2], which the Guidelines define as the "ability of one or more firms to maintain prices above a competitive level, or to prevent prices from decreasing to a lower competitive level, or to limit output or entry."(*See* Section 2) By raising prices above competitive levels, firms with monopoly power effectuate the "transfer of wealth from consumers to firms." [*See* Section 2] Thus, whereas the 1992 DOJ/FTC Guidelines appear to express equal concern with both the wealth transfer effect and the misallocation of resources effect (*i.e.*, the welfare triangle) of monopoly power, the 1993 NAAG Guidelines express primary concern with the wealth transfer effect. The analytical framework of the 1993 NAAG Guidelines can be broken down into four steps that are similar to the five-step process in the 1992 DOJ/FTC Guidelines.

§ 8.23 Section 5.3, Market Concentration, of the 2010 DOJ/FTC Horizontal Merger Guidelines

A. The Provisions of the Guidelines

5.3 Market Concentration

Market concentration is often one useful indicator of likely competitive effects of a merger. In evaluating market concentration, the Agencies consider both the post-merger level of market concentration and the change in concentration resulting from a merger. Market shares may not fully reflect the competitive significance of firms in the market or the impact of a merger. They are used in conjunction with other evidence of competitive effects. See Sections 6 and 7. * * *

The Agencies often calculate the Herfindahl-Hirschman Index ("HHI") of market concentration. The HHI is calculated by summing the squares of the individual firms' market shares,[26] and thus gives proportionately greater weight to the larger market shares. When using the HHI, the Agencies consider both the post-merger level of the HHI and the increase in the HHI resulting from the merger. The increase in the HHI is equal to twice the product of the market shares of the merging firms.[27]

Based on their experience, the Agencies generally classify markets into three types:

- Unconcentrated Markets: HHI below 1500
- Moderately Concentrated Markets: HHI between 1500 and 2500
- Highly Concentrated Markets: HHI above 2500

The Agencies employ the following general standards for the relevant markets they have defined:

- Small Change in Concentration: Mergers involving an increase in the HHI of less than 100 points are unlikely to have adverse competitive effects and ordinarily require no further analysis.

26. For example, a market consisting of four firms with market shares of thirty percent, thirty percent, twenty percent, and twenty percent has an HHI of 2600 ($30^2 + 30^2 + 20^2 + 20^2 = 2600$). The HHI ranges from 10,000 (in the case of a pure monopoly) to a number approaching zero (in the case of an atomistic market). Although it is desirable to include all firms in the calculation, lack of information about firms with small shares is not critical because such firms do not affect the HHI significantly.

27. For example, the merger of firms with shares of five percent and ten percent of the market would increase the HHI by 100 ($5 \times 10 \times 2 = 100$).

- Unconcentrated Markets: Mergers resulting in unconcentrated markets are unlikely to have adverse competitive effects and ordinarily require no further analysis.
- Moderately Concentrated Markets: Mergers resulting in moderately concentrated markets that involve an increase in the HHI of more than 100 points potentially raise significant competitive concerns and often warrant scrutiny.
- Highly Concentrated Markets: Mergers resulting in highly concentrated markets that involve an increase in the HHI of between 100 points and 200 points potentially raise significant competitive concerns and often warrant scrutiny. Mergers resulting in highly concentrated markets that involve an increase in the HHI of more than 200 points will be presumed to be likely to enhance market power. The presumption may be rebutted by persuasive evidence showing that the merger is unlikely to enhance market power.

The purpose of these thresholds is not to provide a rigid screen to separate competitively benign mergers from anticompetitive ones, although high levels of concentration do raise concerns. Rather, they provide one way to identify some mergers unlikely to raise competitive concerns and some others for which it is particularly important to examine whether other competitive factors confirm, reinforce, or counteract the potentially harmful effects of increased concentration. The higher the post-merger HHI and the increase in the HHI, the greater are the Agencies' potential competitive concerns and the greater the likelihood that the Agencies will request additional information to conduct their analysis.

Questions

(1) Each of the twenty firms in the widget market, including Acquiring Corporation (AC) and Target Corporation (TC), has 5% of the market. AC proposes to acquire TC. What action is the DOJ or FTC likely to take under the 2010 DOJ/FTC Guidelines?

(2) Each of the ten firms in the widget market, including AC and TC has 10% of the market. AC proposes to acquire TC. What action is the DOJ or FTC likely to take under the Guidelines?

(3) AC has 20% of the widget market and TC has 5%. The other 15 firms in the market have 5% of the market. AC proposes to acquire TC. What action is the DOJ or FTC likely to take under the Guidelines?

B. HHI Analysis of Some Leading Pre-1982 Horizontal Merger Cases

Eleanor M. Fox, The New Merger Guidelines a Blueprint for Microeconomic Analysis

Antitrust Bulletin 519, 590–591 (Fall 1982)

A comparison of the Supreme Court case law under Section 7 of the Clayton Act with the 1982 Merger Guidelines [which first set out the HHI approach], yields the following results.

In the following cases the Supreme Court held the merger illegal and the 1982 Guidelines indicate that the Government probably would not have sued: *Brown Shoe* [Section 8.6], and * * * *Von's* [Section 8.8]. * * *

In the following cases the Supreme Court held the merger illegal and the 1982 Guidelines indicate that the Government probably would have sued: *Philadelphia National Bank* [Section 8.7] * * *

In the following cases the Supreme Court held the merger not illegal and the 1982 Guidelines indicate that the Government probably would not have sued: *General Dynamics* [Section 8.9] * * *

C. Illustration of General Dynamics Defense: Boeing's Acquisition of McDonnell Douglas: Statement of Chairman Pitofsky

In the Matter of the Boeing Company/McDonnell Douglas Corporation

(July 1, 1997)

After an extensive and exhaustive investigation, the Federal Trade Commission has decided to close the investigation of The Boeing Company's proposed acquisition of McDonnell Douglas Corporation. * * *

On its face, the proposed merger appears to raise serious antitrust concerns. The transaction involves the acquisition by Boeing, a company that accounts for roughly 60% of the sales of large commercial aircraft, of a non-failing direct competitor in a market in which there is only one other significant rival, Airbus Industries, and extremely high barriers to entry. The merger would also combine two firms in the U.S. defense industry that develop fighter aircraft and other defense products. Nevertheless, for reasons we will now discuss, we do not find that this merger will substantially lessen competition in any relevant market. * * *

With respect to the commercial aircraft sector, our decision not to challenge the proposed merger was a result of evidence that (1) McDonnell Douglas, looking to the future, no longer constitutes a meaningful competitive force in the commercial aircraft market and (2) there is no economically plausible strategy that McDonnell Douglas could follow, either as a stand-alone concern or as part of another concern, that would change that grim prospect. * * *

Our decision not to challenge the proposed merger does not reflect a conclusion that McDonnell Douglas is a failing company or that Douglas Aircraft is a failing division [Section 8.35]. Nor does our decision not to challenge the proposed merger reflect a conclusion that Douglas Aircraft could maintain competitively significant sales, but has simply decided to redeploy or retire its assets. While McDonnell Douglas's prospects for future commercial aircraft sales are virtually non-existent, its commercial aircraft production assets are likely to remain in the market for the near future as a result of a modest backlog of aircraft orders. As a result, it is unlikely that the aircraft division would have been liquidated quickly. Moreover, the failing company defense comes into play only where the Commission first finds that the transaction is likely to be anticompetitive. Here, the absence of any prospect of significant commercial sales, combined with a dismal financial forecast, indicate that Douglas Aircraft is no longer an effective competitor, and there is no prospect that position could be reversed.

The merger also does not threaten competition in military programs. * * *

Note

See The European Commission's action in this matter at Section 26.19.I.

§ 8.24 Illustration of Principles of Market Definition: Elasticity of Demand

United States v. E.I. Du Pont de Nemours and Co.

United States Supreme Court, 1956 76 S.Ct. 994

Mr. Justice Reed:

The United States brought this civil action under § 4 of the Sherman Act against E. I. du Pont de Nemours and Company. The complaint * * * charged du Pont with monopolizing, attempting to monopolize and conspiracy to monopolize interstate commerce in cellophane * * * in violation of § 2 of the Sherman Act. * * * After a lengthy trial, judgment was entered for du Pont on all issues. * * *

During the period that is relevant to this action, du Pont produced almost 75% of the cellophane sold in the United States, and cellophane constituted less than 20% of all flexible packaging material sales. * * *

The Government contends that, by so dominating cellophane production, du Pont monopolized a "part of the trade or commerce" in violation of § 2. * * * The court below found that the "relevant market for determining the extent of du Pont's market control is the market for flexible packaging materials," and that competition from those other materials prevented du Pont from possessing monopoly powers in its sales of cellophane.

The Government asserts that cellophane and other wrapping materials are neither substantially fungible nor like priced. For these reasons, it argues that the market for other wrappings is distinct from the market for cellophane and that the competition afforded cellophane by other wrappings is not strong enough to be considered in determining whether du Pont has monopoly powers. Market delimitation is necessary under du Pont's theory to determine whether an alleged monopolist violates § 2. * * *

If cellophane is the "market" that du Pont is found to dominate, it may be assumed it does have monopoly power over that "market." Monopoly power is the power to control prices or exclude competition. It seems apparent that du Pont's power to set the price of cellophane has been limited only by the competition afforded by other flexible packaging materials. Moreover, it may be practically impossible for anyone to commence manufacturing cellophane without full access to du Pont's technique. However, du Pont has no power to prevent competition from other wrapping materials. The trial court consequently had to determine whether competition from the other wrappings prevented du Pont from possessing monopoly power in violation of § 2. * * *

The Relevant Market. When a product is controlled by one interest, without substitutes available in the market, there is monopoly power. * * *

The Government argues: "We do not here urge that in no circumstances may competition of substitutes negative possession of monopolistic power over trade in a product. The decisions make it clear at the least that the courts will not consider substitutes other than those which are substantially fungible with the monopolized product and sell at substantially the same price."

But where there are market alternatives that buyers may readily use for their purposes, illegal monopoly does not exist merely because the product said to be monopolized differs from others. If it were not so, only physically identical products would be a part of the market. To accept the Government's argument, we would have to conclude that the manufactures of plain as well as moisture proof cellophane were monopolists, and so with films such as Pliofilm, foil, glassine, polyethylene, and Saran, for each of these wrapping materials is distinguishable. * * * New wrappings appear, generally similar to cellophane, is each a monopoly? What is called for is an appraisal of the 'cross-elasticity' of demand in the trade. The varying circumstances of each case determine the result. In considering what is the relevant market for determining the control of price and competition, no more definite rule can be declared than that commodities reasonably interchangeable by consumers for the same purposes make up that "part of the trade or commerce", monopolization of which may be illegal. As respects flexible packaging materials, the market geographically is nationwide. * * *

Cellophane differs from other flexible packaging materials. From some it differs more than from others. * * *

It may be admitted that cellophane combines the desirable elements of transparency, strength and cheapness more definitely than any of the others. * * *

But, despite cellophane's advantages it has to meet competition from other materials in every one of its uses. * * *

An element for consideration as to cross-elasticity of demand between products is the responsiveness of the sales of one product to price changes of the other. [*See* Section 8.12.A.4] If a slight decrease in the price of cellophane causes a considerable number of customers of other flexible wrappings to switch to cellophane, it would be an indication that a high cross-elasticity of demand exists between them; that the products compete in the same market. The court below held that the "(g)reat sensitivity of customers in the flexible packaging markets to price or quality changes" prevented du Pont from possessing monopoly control over price. The record sustains these findings. * * *

We conclude that cellophane's interchangeability with the other materials mentioned suffices to make it a part of this flexible packaging material market.

The Government stresses the fact that the variation in price between cellophane and other materials demonstrates they are noncompetitive. * * * Cellophane costs two or three times as much, surface measure, as its chief competitors for the flexible wrapping market, glassine and greaseproof papers. * * * But the necessity for flexible wrappings is the central and unchanging demand. * * *

[We cannot] say that du Pont's profits, while liberal (according to the Government 15.9% net after taxes on the 1937–1947 average), demonstrate the existence of a monopoly without proof of lack of comparable profits during those years in other prosperous industries. Cellophane was a leader over 17%, in the flexible packaging materials market. * * *

[The] market is composed of products that have reasonable interchangeability for the purposes for which they are produced price, use and qualities considered. While the application of the tests remains uncertain, it seems to us that du Pont should not be found to monopolize cellophane when that product has the competition and interchangeability with other wrappings that this record shows.

On the findings of the District Court, its judgment is affirmed.

Question

The Court found that cellophane was more expensive than other flexible wrapping products, and du Pont's profits from cellophane sales were higher than profits from sales of other flexible wrapping products. What conclusion about the cross elasticity of demand between cellophane and other flexible wrapping products can be drawn from these two findings?

§ 8.25 Market Definition and Measurement under the 2010 DOJ/FTC Horizontal Merger Guidelines

A. Section 4, Market Definition, of the 2010 DOJ/FTC Horizontal Merger Guidelines

4. Market Definition

When the Agencies identify a potential competitive concern with a horizontal merger, market definition plays two roles. First, market definition helps specify the line of commerce and section of the country in which the competitive concern arises. In any merger enforcement action, the Agencies will normally identify one or more relevant markets in which the merger may substantially lessen competition. Second, market definition allows the Agencies to identify market participants and measure market shares and market concentration. See Section 5. The measurement of market shares and market concentration is not an end in itself, but is useful to the extent it illuminates the merger's likely competitive effects. * * *

Market definition focuses solely on demand substitution factors, i.e., on customers' ability and willingness to substitute away from one product to another in response to a price increase or a corresponding non-price change such as a reduction in product quality or service. The responsive actions of suppliers are also important in competitive analysis. They are considered in these Guidelines in the sections addressing the identification of market participants, the measurement of market shares, the analysis of competitive effects, and entry. * * *

Defining a market broadly to include relatively distant product or geographic substitutes can lead to misleading market shares. This is because the competitive significance of distant substitutes is unlikely to be commensurate with their shares in a broad market. * * *

Market shares of different products in narrowly defined markets are more likely to capture the relative competitive significance of these products, and often more accurately reflect competition between close substitutes. * * *

Section 4.1 describes the principles that apply to product market definition, and gives guidance on how the Agencies most often apply those principles. Section 4.2 describes how the same principles apply to geographic market definition. Although discussed separately for simplicity of exposition, the principles described in Sections 4.1 and 4.2 are combined to define a relevant market, which has both a product and a geographic dimension. In particular, the hypothetical monopolist test is applied to a group of products together with a geographic region to determine a relevant market.

4.1 Product Market Definition

When a product sold by one merging firm (Product A) competes against one or more products sold by the other merging firm, the Agencies define a relevant product market around Product A to evaluate the importance of that competition. Such a relevant product market consists of a group of substitute products including Product A. Multiple relevant product markets may thus be identified.

4.1.1 The Hypothetical Monopolist Test

The Agencies employ the hypothetical monopolist test to evaluate whether groups of products in candidate markets are sufficiently broad to constitute relevant antitrust markets. The Agencies use the hypothetical monopolist test to identify a set of products that are reasonably interchangeable with a product sold by one of the merging firms.

The hypothetical monopolist test requires that a product market contain enough substitute products so that it could be subject to post-merger exercise of market power significantly exceeding that existing absent the merger. Specifically, the test requires that a hypothetical profit-maximizing firm, not subject to price regulation, that was the only present and future seller of those products ("hypothetical monopolist") likely would impose at least a small but significant and non-transitory increase in price ("SSNIP") on at least one product in the market, including at least one product sold by one of the merging firms. For the purpose of analyzing this issue, the terms of sale of products outside the candidate market are held constant. The SSNIP is employed solely as a methodological tool for performing the hypothetical monopolist test; it is not a tolerance level for price increases resulting from a merger.

Groups of products may satisfy the hypothetical monopolist test without including the full range of substitutes from which customers choose. The hypothetical monopolist test may identify a group of products as a relevant market even if customers would substitute significantly to products outside that group in response to a price increase.

> Example 5: Products A and B are being tested as a candidate market. Each sells for $100, has an incremental cost of $60, and sells 1200 units. For every dollar increase in the price of Product A, for any given price of Product B, Product A loses twenty units of sales to products outside the candidate market and ten units of sales to Product B, and likewise for Product B. Under these conditions, economic analysis shows that a hypothetical profit-maximizing monopolist controlling Products A and B would raise both of their prices by ten percent, to $110. Therefore, Products A and B satisfy the hypothetical monopolist test using a five percent SSNIP, and indeed for any SSNIP size up to ten percent. This is true even though two-thirds of the sales lost by one product when it raises its price are diverted to products outside the relevant market. * * *

4.1.2 Benchmark Prices and SSNIP Size * * *

The SSNIP is intended to represent a "small but significant" increase in the prices charged by firms in the candidate market for the value they contribute to the products or services used by customers. * * *

The Agencies most often use a SSNIP of five percent of the price paid by customers for the products or services to which the merging firms contribute value. However, what constitutes a "small but significant" increase in price, commensurate with a significant loss of competition caused by the merger, depends upon the nature of the industry and the merging firms' positions in it, and the Agencies may accordingly use a price increase that is larger or smaller than five percent. * * *

4.1.3 Implementing the Hypothetical Monopolist Test

The hypothetical monopolist's incentive to raise prices depends both on the extent to which customers would likely substitute away from the products in the candidate market in response to such a price increase and on the profit margins earned on those products. * * *

When the necessary data are available, the Agencies also may consider a "critical loss analysis" to assess the extent to which it corroborates inferences drawn from the evidence noted above. Critical loss analysis asks whether imposing at least a SSNIP on one or more products in a candidate market would raise or lower the hypothetical monopolist's profits.

While this "breakeven" analysis differs from the profit-maximizing analysis called for by the hypothetical monopolist test in Section 4.1.1, merging parties sometimes present this type of analysis to the Agencies. A price increase raises profits on sales made at the higher price, but this will be offset to the extent customers substitute away from products in the candidate market. Critical loss analysis compares the magnitude of these two offsetting effects resulting from the price increase. The "critical loss" is defined as the number of lost unit sales that would leave profits unchanged. The "predicted loss" is defined as the number of unit sales that the hypothetical monopolist is predicted to lose due to the price increase. The price increase raises the hypothetical monopolist's profits if the predicted loss is less than the critical loss. * * *

4.2.1 Geographic Markets Based on the Locations of Suppliers

Geographic markets based on the locations of suppliers encompass the region from which sales are made. * * * .

The hypothetical monopolist test requires that a hypothetical profit-maximizing firm that was the only present or future producer of the relevant product(s) located in the region would impose at least a SSNIP from at least one location, including at least one location of one of the merging firms. In this exercise the terms of sale for all products produced elsewhere are held constant. A single firm may operate in a number of different geographic markets, even for a single product.

> Example 12: The merging parties both have manufacturing plants in City X. The relevant product is expensive to transport and suppliers price their products for pickup at their locations. Rival plants are some distance away in City Y. A hypothetical monopolist controlling all plants in City X could profitably impose a SSNIP at these plants. Competition from more distant plants would not defeat the price increase because supplies coming from more distant plants require expensive transportation. The relevant geographic market is defined around the plants in City X. * * *

4.2.2 Geographic Markets Based on the Locations of Customers

When the hypothetical monopolist could discriminate based on customer location, the Agencies may define geographic markets based on the locations of targeted customers. * * *

B. Section 5.1 and 5.2, Market Participants and Market Shares, of the 2010 DOJ/FTC Horizontal Merger Guidelines

5.1 Market Participants [and "Rapid Entrants"]

All firms that currently earn revenues in the relevant market are considered market participants. Vertically integrated firms are also included to the extent that their inclusion accurately reflects their competitive significance. Firms not currently earning revenues in the relevant market, but that have committed to entering the market in the near future, are also considered market participants.

[Rapid Entrants] Firms that are not current producers in a relevant market, but that would very likely provide rapid supply responses with direct competitive impact in the event of a SSNIP, without incurring significant sunk costs, are also considered market participants. These firms are termed "rapid entrants." Sunk costs are entry or exit costs that cannot be recovered outside the relevant market. Entry that would take place more slowly in response to adverse competitive effects, or that requires firms to incur significant sunk costs, is considered in Section 9.

Firms that produce the relevant product but do not sell it in the relevant geographic market may be rapid entrants. Other things equal, such firms are most likely to be rapid entrants if they are close to the geographic market.

> Example 16: Farm A grows tomatoes halfway between Cities X and Y. Currently, it ships its tomatoes to City X because prices there are two percent higher. Previously it has varied the destination of its shipments in response to small price variations. Farm A would likely be a rapid entrant participant in a market for tomatoes in City Y. * * *

5.2 Market Shares

The Agencies normally calculate market shares for all firms that currently produce products in the relevant market, subject to the availability of data. The Agencies also calculate market shares for other market participants if this can be done to reliably reflect their competitive significance.

Market concentration and market share data are normally based on historical evidence. However, recent or ongoing changes in market conditions may indicate that the current market share of a particular firm either understates or overstates the firm's future competitive significance. * * *

In most contexts, the Agencies measure each firm's market share based on its actual or projected revenues in the relevant market. * * *

In markets for homogeneous products, a firm's competitive significance may derive principally from its ability and incentive to rapidly expand production in the relevant market in response to a price increase or output reduction by others in that market. As a result, a firm's competitive significance may depend upon its level of readily available capacity to serve the relevant market if that capacity is efficient enough to make such expansion profitable. * * *

C. Market Definition and Impact of Concentration in the *Staples* Case

FTC v. Staples, Inc.

United States District Court, District of Columbia, 1997 WL 381901

Opinion by: Thomas F. Hogan.

Plaintiff, the Federal Trade Commission ("FTC" or "Commission"), seeks a preliminary injunction pursuant to Section 13(b) of the Federal Trade Commission Act, to enjoin the consummation of any acquisition by defendant Staples, Inc. of defendant Office Depot, Inc., pending final disposition before the Commission of administrative proceedings to determine whether such acquisition may substantially lessen competition in violation of Section 7 of the Clayton Act. * * * For the reasons set forth below, the Court will grant the plaintiff's motion. * * *

Defendants are both corporations which sell office products including office supplies, business machines, computers and furniture through retail stores, commonly described as office supply superstores, as well as through direct mail delivery and contract stationer operations. Staples is the second largest office superstore chain in the United States with approximately 550 retail stores located in 28 states and the District of Columbia, primarily in the Northeast and California. * * * Office Depot, the largest office superstore chain, operates over 500 retail office supply superstores that are located in 38 states and the District of Columbia, primarily in the South and Midwest. * * * OfficeMax, Inc., is the only other office supply superstore firm in the United States.

On September 4, 1996, defendants Staples and Office Depot * * * entered into an "Agreement and Plan of Merger" whereby Office Depot would become a wholly-owned subsidiary of Staples. * * *

On March 10, 1997, the Commission voted 4–1 to challenge the merger. * * *

[I]n a suit for preliminary relief, the FTC is not required to prove, nor is the Court required to find, that the proposed merger would in fact violate Section 7 of the Clayton Act. The determination of whether the acquisition actually violates the antitrust laws is reserved for the Commission and is, therefore, not before this Court. The only question before the Court is whether the FTC has made a showing which justifies preliminary injunctive relief. * * *

[**The Geographic Market**] One of the few issue about which the parties to this case do not disagree is that metropolitan areas are the appropriate geographic markets for analyzing the competitive effects of the proposed merger. * * * [T]he FTC identified forty-two such metropolitan areas as well as future areas which could suffer anti-competitive effects from the proposed merger. Defendants have not challenged the FTC's geographic market definition in this proceeding. Therefore, the Court will accept the relevant geographic markets identified by the Commission.

[**The Relevant Product Market**] In contrast to the parties' agreement with respect to the relevant geographic market, the Commission and the defendants sharply disagree with respect to the appropriate definition of the relevant product market or line of commerce. * * *

The Commission defines the relevant product market as "the sale of consumable office supplies through office superstores." * * * The defendants characterize the FTC's product market definition as "contrived" with no basis in law or fact, and counter that the appropriate product market within which to assess the likely competitive consequences of a Staples-Office Depot combination is simply the overall sale of office products, of which a combined Staples-Office Depot accounted for 5.5% of total sales in North America in 1996. In addition, the defendants argue that the challenged combination is not likely "substantially to lessen competition" however the product market is defined. * * * [T]he Court finds that the appropriate relevant product market definition in this case is, as the Commission has argued, the sale of consumable office supplies through office supply superstores.

The general rule when determining a relevant product market is that "[t]he outer boundaries of a product market are determined by the reasonable interchangeability of use [by consumers] or the cross-elasticity of demand between the product itself and substitutes for it." * * *

Whether there are other products available to consumers which are similar in character or use to the products in question may be termed "functional interchangeability." *See, e.g., E.I. Du Pont de Nemours*, [Section 8.24] (recognizing "functional interchangeability" between cellophane and other flexible wrappings). * * * This case, of course, is an example of perfect "functional interchangeability." The consumable office products at issue here are identical whether they are sold by Staples or Office Depot or another seller of office supplies. * * * No one disputes the functional interchangeability of consumable office supplies. However, as the government has argued, functional interchangeability should not end the Court's analysis.

The Supreme Court did not stop after finding a high degree of functional interchangeability between cellophane and other wrapping materials in the *E.I. Du Pont de*

Nemours case. Instead, the Court also found that "an element for consideration as to cross-elasticity of demand between products is the responsiveness of the sales of the one product to price changes of the other." For example, in that case, the Court explained, "[i]f a slight decrease in the price of cellophane causes a considerable number of customers of other flexible wrappings to switch to cellophane, it would be an indication that a high cross-elasticity of demand exists between [cellophane and other flexible wrappings], [and therefore] that the products compete in the same market." *Id.* Following that reasoning in this case, the Commission has argued that a slight but significant increase in Staples-Office Depot's prices will not cause a considerable number of Staples-Office Depot's customers to purchase consumable office supplies from other non-superstore alternatives such as Wal-Mart, Best Buy, Quill, or Viking. On the other hand, the Commission has argued that an increase in price by Staples would result in consumers turning to another office superstore, especially Office Depot, if the consumers had that option. Therefore, the Commission concludes that the sale of consumable office supplies by office supply superstores is the appropriate relevant product market in this case, and products sold by competitors such as Wal-Mart, Best Buy, Viking, Quill, and others should be excluded. * * *

[A] combined Staples-Office Depot would only have a 5.5% share of the overall market in consumable office supplies. * * *

The Supreme Court has recognized that within a broad market, well-defined submarkets may exist which, in themselves, constitute product markets for antitrust purpose." *Brown Shoe Co. v. United States* [Section 8.6] * * *

[T]he FTC focused on what it termed the "pricing evidence," which the Court finds corresponds with *Brown Shoe*'s "sensitivity to price changes" factor. First, the FTC presented evidence comparing Staples' prices in geographic markets where Staples is the only office superstore, to markets where Staples competes with Office Depot or OfficeMax, or both. Based on the FTC's calculations, in markets where Staples faces no office superstore competition at all, something which was termed a one firm market during the hearing, prices are 13% higher than in three firm markets where it competes with both Office Depot and OfficeMax. The data which underlie this conclusion make it compelling evidence. * * *

The FTC also pointed to internal Staples documents which present price comparisons between Staples' prices and Office Depot's prices and Staples' prices and OfficeMax's prices within different price zones. * * * [T]he FTC showed once again that Staples charges significantly higher prices, more than 5% higher, where it has no office superstore competition than where it competes with two other superstores. * * *

This evidence all suggests that office superstore prices are affected primarily by other office superstores and not by non-superstore competitors such as mass merchandisers. * * *

When assessing key trends and making long range plans, Staples and Office Depot focus on the plans of other superstores. In addition, when determining whether to enter a new metropolitan area, both Staples and Office Depot evaluate the extent of office superstore competition in the market and the number of office superstores the market can support. * * *

For the reasons set forth in the above analysis, the Court finds that the sale of consumable office supplies through office supply superstores is the appropriate relevant product market for purposes of considering the possible anti-competitive effects of the proposed merger between Staples and Office Depot. * * * In addition, the factors or "practical indicia' of Brown Shoe support a finding of a "submarket" under the facts of this case, and "submarkets," as Brown Shoe established, may themselves be appropriate product markets for antitrust purposes. * * *

[**Probable Effect on Competition**] After accepting the Commission's definition of the relevant product market, the Court next must consider the probable effect of a merger between Staples and Office Depot in the geographic markets previously identified. One way to do this is to examine the concentration statistics and HHIs within the geographic markets. If the relevant product market is defined as the sale of consumable office supplies through office supply superstores, the HHIs in many of the geographic markets are at problematic levels even before the merger. Currently, the least concentrated market is that of Grand Rapids-Muskegon-Holland, Michigan, with an HHI of 6,597, while the most concentrated is Washington, D.C. with an HHI of 6,944. In contrast, after a merger of Staples and Office Depot, the least concentrated area would be Kalamazoo-Battle Creek Michigan, with an HHI of 5,003, and many areas would have HHIs of 10,000. The average increase in HHI caused by the merger would be 2,715 points. * * *

[A]ccording to the Merger Guidelines, unless mitigated by other factors which lead to the conclusion that the merger is not likely to lessen competition, an increase in the HHI in excess of 50 points in a post-merger highly concentrated market [i.e., HHI in excess of 1800] may raise significant competitive concerns. * * * The Merger Guidelines, of course, are not binding on the Court, but, as this Circuit has stated, they do provide "a useful illustration of the application of the HHI," and the Court will use that guidance here. In addition, though the Supreme Court has established that there is no fixed threshold at which an increase in market concentration triggers the antitrust laws, see, *e.g.*, *United States v. Philadelphia National Bank* [Section 8.7], this is clearly not a borderline case. * * *

By showing that the proposed transaction between Staples and Office Depot will lead to undue concentration in the market for consumable office supplies sold by office superstores in the geographic markets agreed upon by the parties, the Commission establishes a presumption that the transaction will substantially lessen competition. * * *

[The court then rejected Staple's entry argument, which is set out in Section 8.31.B and its efficiencies argument, which is set out in Section 8.34.C]

[**Conclusion**] [T]he Court finds that the Commission has shown a likelihood that it will succeed in proving, after a full administrative trial on the merits, that the effect of the proposed merger between Staples and Office Depot "may be substantially to lessen competition" in violation of Section 7 of the Clayton Act. * * *

D. FTC 2013 Decision Not to Challenge Office Depot-OfficeMax Merger

Statement of the Federal Trade Commission Concerning the Proposed Merger of Office Depot, Inc. and OfficeMax, Inc.

FTC File No. 131-0104

November 1, 2013

The Commission has unanimously decided to close its seven-month investigation of Office Depot, Inc.'s proposed merger with OfficeMax, Inc., a transaction that aims to combine the country's second and third largest chains of office supply superstores (OSS).[28] Although sixteen years ago the Commission blocked a proposed merger between Staples, Inc. and Office Depot, the nation's two largest OSS, our current investigation has shown that the market for the sale of consumable office supplies has changed significantly in the

28. The Attorneys General of several states joined in the Commission's investigation.

intervening years. For the reasons discussed below, we conclude that Office Depot and OfficeMax should be permitted to move forward with their proposed transaction. In reaching this conclusion, we assessed the proposed merger's competitive effects in two distinct lines of commerce: the sale of office supplies to retail and contract customers. We discuss each in turn.

I. Retail Channel

In the 1997 *Staples* case,[29] the Commission successfully argued that the relevant product market was the sale of consumable office supplies through OSS and that the proposed merger of two of the three OSS would lead to competitive harm.[30] In finding an OSS-only market, the Staples court relied principally on qualitative and empirical evidence that OSS prices were set according to the number of competing OSS in a local area. Company documents revealed the merging parties' intense competitive focus on other OSS and general lack of concern with non-OSS rivals. The evidence also showed that the defendants grouped their stores into price zones specifically based on the number of nearby OSS, resulting in higher prices in local markets with fewer OSS, even if non-OSS competitors were present.

The current competitive dynamics are very different. The Commission's investigation shows that today's market for the sale of consumable office supplies is broader, due mainly to two significant developments. One is that customers now look beyond OSS for office supply products and rely more heavily on non-OSS brick-and-mortar retailers. Mass merchants like Wal-Mart and Target and club stores like Costco and Sam's Club have proliferated and expanded their product offerings and sales of office supplies. The result is that fewer consumers today shop OSS as a destination. Instead, consumers place a greater premium on convenience, preferring in many cases to purchase supplies at retailers that also offer other products that office supply customers purchase.

The other is the explosive growth of online commerce, which has had a major impact on this market. Online retailers stock a vast array of office supply products and can deliver them quickly anywhere in the country at nominal cost. Company documents show that OSS are acutely aware of, and feel threatened by, the continued growth of online competitors, most notably Amazon. OSS have lost, and continue to lose, substantial in-store sales to online competitors. This increased competition from online retailers has caused OSS to respond with new pricing practices and other strategies. For example, because online prices are often lower than in-store prices, and because many customers comparison shop in-store prices against online prices, OSS are often pressured to match these lower online prices in their stores. And, in-store and online channel boundaries are blurring as OSS seek to create a seamless customer experience by offering in-store pickup for online orders and using in-store Internet kiosks to order products online.

The merging parties' pricing policies and practices reflect these changes in customer behavior and now specifically factor in non-OSS competition. Price zones and retail pricing are no longer dictated by the number of local OSS. In fact, a majority of products sold by the merging parties are priced nationally, and the products priced locally take into ac-

29. FTC v. Staples, Inc., 970 F. Supp. 1066 (D.D.C. 1997).

30. "Consumable office supplies" refers to non-durable products that consumers use up, discard, and purchase on a recurrent basis. Examples included pens, paper, file folders, Post-it notes, and ink and toner cartridges. Id. at 1080.

count competition from non-OSS retailers. OSS closely monitor, and respond competitively to, other non-OSS retailers. This competitive interaction includes price-checking, price matching, and advertising and promotion designed specifically to compete effectively with non-OSS retailers.

The econometric analysis reflects the new competitive dynamics in the industry and shows that the proposed merger is unlikely to result in anticompetitive price effects. Commission staff replicated the type of econometric work performed in Staples and conducted an extensive amount of additional econometric analysis, including comparisons of prices in markets with varying numbers of OSS and "events studies" analyzing the impact of OSS store closings on the prices charged by remaining OSS in local areas. All of the econometrics, none of which assumed or depended on any particular definition of a relevant product or geographic market, indicate that the merger is unlikely to lead to anticompetitive price increases.

Altogether, the overwhelming evidence supports the conclusion that OSS today face significant competition and demonstrates that the proposed merger is unlikely to substantially lessen competition in the retail sale of consumable office supplies.

II. Contracting Channel

The Commission also examined the potential for competitive harm in the sale of consumable office supplies to businesses and other customers on a contract basis, a channel not at issue in Staples. Many businesses and public entities purchase office supplies under a contract. Unlike retail purchasers, contract customers typically receive discounted pricing based on actual or anticipated purchase volume. These contracts allow customers to order office products at previously negotiated prices. Because there are dozens, if not hundreds, of office suppliers that compete effectively to serve small and medium-sized businesses, the investigation focused on contracts for large multi-regional or national customers, which typically have the most demanding purchasing requirements and, as a result, fewer potential suppliers capable of meeting their needs.

A substantial body of evidence indicates that the merger is unlikely to substantially lessen competition or harm large contract customers. First, large customers use a variety of tools to ensure that they receive competitive pricing such as ordering certain products (like ink and toner) directly from manufacturers and sourcing (or threatening to source) certain categories of office supply products from multiple firms. Second, the merging parties' documents show that they are rarely each other's closest competitor for most large customers and that non-OSS competitors take business from the parties in a substantial number of contracting opportunities. Third, the parties will continue to face strong competition for such customers from Staples and a host of non-OSS competitors, such as W.B. Mason Co., Inc. Non-OSS competitors are growing in number and strength and have demonstrated the ability to win large multi-regional and national customer contracts. In particular, regional office supply competitors have developed and utilized various strategies to compete successfully for large national accounts, including working with office supply wholesalers and joining cooperatives of independent office supply dealers to create a distribution network capable of meeting the needs of large multi-regional and national customers. Finally, potential competitors in adjacent product categories, such as janitorial and industrial products, have existing contractual relationships with large office supply customers and can leverage those relationships to enter the office supply distribution market.

In light of the foregoing, there was little concern from contract customers about the proposed merger, and even the largest customers believe the merger would be either procompetitive or competitively neutral. We therefore find that the proposed merger is unlikely to result in competitive harm in the contract channel.[31]

III. Conclusion

Analyzing the likely competitive effects of a proposed transaction is always a fact specific exercise that must take into account the evolving nature of markets. Our decision highlights that yesterday's market dynamics may be very different from the market dynamics of today. In this case, significant developments in the market for consumable office supplies have led us to approve a merger when we had blocked a similar merger sixteen years ago. In so finding, we emphasize that our decision, including our view of the competitive interaction between brick-and-mortar retailers and Internet sellers, is limited to the facts before us in this particular matter.

E. DOJ/FTC 2006 Commentary on Guidelines—Market Definition

Excerpt from DOJ/FTC Commentary on Guidelines, Market Definition

(March 2006)

Market Definition* * * The Agencies * * * examine all plausible markets to determine whether an adverse competitive effect is likely to occur in any of them. The market definition process is not isolated from the other analytic components in the [1992] Guidelines. The Agencies do not settle on a relevant market definition before proceeding to address other issues. Rather, market definition is part of the integrated process by which the Agencies apply Guidelines principles, iterated as new facts are learned, to reach an understanding of the merger's likely effect on competition. * * *

Product market definition depends critically upon demand-side substitution—*i.e.*, consumers' willingness to switch from one product to another in reaction to price changes. The Guidelines' approach to market definition reflects the separation of demand substitutability from supply substitutability—*i.e.*, the ability and willingness, given existing capacity, of firms to substitute from making one product to producing another in reaction to a price change. Under this approach, demand substitutability is the concern of market delineation, while supply substitutability and entry are concerned with current and future market participants. * * *

§ 8.26 The Potential Adverse Competitive Effects of Mergers: The DOJ/FTC 2006 Commentary of Guidelines

Excerpt from DOJ/FTC Commentary on Guidelines, Adverse Competitive Effects

(March 2006)

Potential Adverse Competitive Effects of Mergers. Section 2 of the [1992] Guidelines identifies two broad analytical frameworks for assessing whether a merger between rival

---

31. We also assessed the potential for coordinated effects, but found that market conditions, including the number and diversity of competing firms, the complexity of contract terms, and the lack of transparency into the identity of bidders and terms of contracts and bids, would render post-merger coordination or market allocation difficult.

firms may substantially lessen competition: "coordinated interaction" and "unilateral effects." A horizontal merger is likely to lessen competition substantially through coordinated interaction if it creates a likelihood that, after the merger, competitors would coordinate their pricing or other competitive actions, or would coordinate them more completely or successfully than before the merger. A merger is likely to lessen competition substantially through unilateral effects if it creates a likelihood that the merged firm, without any coordination with non-merging rivals, would raise its price or otherwise exercise market power to a greater degree than before the merger. * * *

§ 8.27 Section 7, Coordinated Effects, of the 2010 DOJ/FTC Guidelines

7. Coordinated Effects

A merger may diminish competition by enabling or encouraging post-merger coordinated interaction among firms in the relevant market that harms customers. Coordinated interaction involves conduct by multiple firms that is profitable for each of them only as a result of the accommodating reactions of the others. These reactions can blunt a firm's incentive to offer customers better deals by undercutting the extent to which such a move would win business away from rivals. They also can enhance a firm's incentive to raise prices, by assuaging the fear that such a move would lose customers to rivals.

Coordinated interaction includes a range of conduct. Coordinated interaction can involve the explicit negotiation of a common understanding of how firms will compete or refrain from competing. Such conduct typically would itself violate the antitrust laws. Coordinated interaction also can involve a similar common understanding that is not explicitly negotiated but would be enforced by the detection and punishment of deviations that would undermine the coordinated interaction. Coordinated interaction alternatively can involve parallel accommodating conduct not pursuant to a prior understanding. Parallel accommodating conduct includes situations in which each rival's response to competitive moves made by others is individually rational, and not motivated by retaliation or deterrence nor intended to sustain an agreed-upon market outcome, but nevertheless emboldens price increases and weakens competitive incentives to reduce prices or offer customers better terms. Coordinated interaction includes conduct not otherwise condemned by the antitrust laws. * * *

7.1 Impact of Merger on Coordinated Interaction

The Agencies examine whether a merger is likely to change the manner in which market participants interact, inducing substantially more coordinated interaction. The Agencies seek to identify how a merger might significantly weaken competitive incentives through an increase in the strength, extent, or likelihood of coordinated conduct. * * *

Pursuant to the Clayton Act's incipiency standard, the Agencies may challenge mergers that in their judgment pose a real danger of harm through coordinated effects, even without specific evidence showing precisely how the coordination likely would take place.

[The Three Conditions] The Agencies are likely to challenge a merger if the following three conditions are all met: (1) the merger would significantly increase concentration and lead to a moderately or highly concentrated market; (2) that market shows signs of vulnerability to coordinated conduct (see Section 7.2); and (3) the Agencies have a credible basis on which to conclude that the merger may enhance that vulnerability. An ac-

quisition eliminating a maverick firm (see Section 2.1.5) in a market vulnerable to coordinated conduct is likely to cause adverse coordinated effects.

7.2 Evidence a Market is Vulnerable to Coordinated Conduct

The Agencies presume that market conditions are conducive to coordinated interaction if firms representing a substantial share in the relevant market appear to have previously engaged in express collusion affecting the relevant market, unless competitive conditions in the market have since changed significantly. * * *

A market typically is more vulnerable to coordinated conduct if each competitively important firm's significant competitive initiatives can be promptly and confidently observed by that firm's rivals. This is more likely to be the case if the terms offered to customers are relatively transparent. Price transparency can be greater for relatively homogeneous products. * * *

A firm is more likely to be deterred from making competitive initiatives by whatever responses occur if sales are small and frequent rather than via occasional large and long-term contracts or if relatively few customers will switch to it before rivals are able to respond. * * *

The Agencies regard coordinated interaction as more likely, the more the participants stand to gain from successful coordination. Coordination generally is more profitable, the lower is the market elasticity of demand.

Coordinated conduct can harm customers even if not all firms in the relevant market engage in the coordination, but significant harm normally is likely only if a substantial part of the market is subject to such conduct. * * *

§ 8.28 Section 6, Unilateral Effects, of the 2010 DOJ/FTC Guidelines

A. The 2010 DOJ/FTC Guidelines

6 Unilateral Effects

The elimination of competition between two firms that results from their merger may alone constitute a substantial lessening of competition. Such unilateral effects are most apparent in a merger to monopoly in a relevant market, but are by no means limited to that case. Whether cognizable efficiencies resulting from the merger are likely to reduce or reverse adverse unilateral effects is addressed in Section 10.

Several common types of unilateral effects are discussed in this section. Section 6.1 discusses unilateral price effects in markets with differentiated products. Section 6.2 discusses unilateral effects in markets where sellers negotiate with buyers or prices are determined through auctions. Section 6.3 discusses unilateral effects relating to reductions in output or capacity in markets for relatively homogeneous products. Section 6.4 discusses unilateral effects arising from diminished innovation or reduced product variety. These effects do not exhaust the types of possible unilateral effects; for example, exclusionary unilateral effects also can arise.

A merger may result in different unilateral effects along different dimensions of competition. For example, a merger may increase prices in the short term but not raise longer-term concerns about innovation, either because rivals will provide sufficient innovation competition or because the merger will generate cognizable research and development efficiencies. See Section 10.

6.1 Pricing of Differentiated Products

In differentiated product industries, some products can be very close substitutes and compete strongly with each other, while other products are more distant substitutes and compete less strongly. For example, one high-end product may compete much more directly with another high-end product than with any low-end product.

A merger between firms selling differentiated products may diminish competition by enabling the merged firm to profit by unilaterally raising the price of one or both products above the pre-merger level. Some of the sales lost due to the price rise will merely be diverted to the product of the merger partner and, depending on relative margins, capturing such sales loss through merger may make the price increase profitable even though it would not have been profitable prior to the merger.

The extent of direct competition between the products sold by the merging parties is central to the evaluation of unilateral price effects. Unilateral price effects are greater, the more the buyers of products sold by one merging firm consider products sold by the other merging firm to be their next choice. The Agencies consider any reasonably available and reliable information to evaluate the extent of direct competition between the products sold by the merging firms. * * *

Substantial unilateral price elevation post-merger for a product formerly sold by one of the merging firms normally requires that a significant fraction of the customers purchasing that product view products formerly sold by the other merging firm as their next-best choice. However, unless pre-merger margins between price and incremental cost are low, that significant fraction need not approach a majority. * * *

Adverse unilateral price effects can arise when the merger gives the merged entity an incentive to raise the price of a product previously sold by one merging firm and thereby divert sales to products previously sold by the other merging firm, boosting the profits on the latter products. * * *

A merger is unlikely to generate substantial unilateral price increases if non-merging parties offer very close substitutes for the products offered by the merging firms. In some cases, non-merging firms may be able to reposition their products to offer close substitutes for the products offered by the merging firms. Repositioning is a supply-side response that is evaluated much like entry, with consideration given to timeliness, likelihood, and sufficiency. See Section 9. * * *

6.2 Bargaining and Auctions

In many industries, especially those involving intermediate goods and services, buyers and sellers negotiate to determine prices and other terms of trade. In that process, buyers commonly negotiate with more than one seller, and may play sellers off against one another. Some highly structured forms of such competition are known as auctions. Negotiations often combine aspects of an auction with aspects of one-on-one negotiation, although pure auctions are sometimes used in government procurement and elsewhere.

A merger between two competing sellers prevents buyers from playing those sellers off against each other in negotiations. This alone can significantly enhance the ability and incentive of the merged entity to obtain a result more favorable to it, and less favorable to the buyer, than the merging firms would have offered separately absent the merger. The Agencies analyze unilateral effects of this type using similar approaches to those described in Section 6.1.

Anticompetitive unilateral effects in these settings are likely in proportion to the frequency or probability with which, prior to the merger, one of the merging sellers had been the runner-up when the other won the business. * * *

6.3 Capacity and Output for Homogeneous Products

In markets involving relatively undifferentiated products, the Agencies may evaluate whether the merged firm will find it profitable unilaterally to suppress output and elevate the market price. A firm may leave capacity idle, refrain from building or obtaining capacity that would have been obtained absent the merger, or eliminate pre-existing production capabilities. A firm may also divert the use of capacity away from one relevant market and into another so as to raise the price in the former market. The competitive analyses of these alternative modes of output suppression may differ.

A unilateral output suppression strategy is more likely to be profitable when (1) the merged firm's market share is relatively high; (2) the share of the merged firm's output already committed for sale at prices unaffected by the output suppression is relatively low; (3) the margin on the suppressed output is relatively low; (4) the supply responses of rivals are relatively small; and (5) the market elasticity of demand is relatively low. * * *

6.4 Innovation and Product Variety

Competition often spurs firms to innovate. The Agencies may consider whether a merger is likely to diminish innovation competition by encouraging the merged firm to curtail its innovative efforts below the level that would prevail in the absence of the merger. That curtailment of innovation could take the form of reduced incentive to continue with an existing product-development effort or reduced incentive to initiate development of new products. * * *

B. Unilateral Effects in Oracle-PeopleSoft Acquisition

United States of America v. Oracle Corporation

United States District Court, Northern District Of California, 2004 331 F. Supp. 2d 1098

VAUGHN R. WALKER:

FINDINGS OF FACT, CONCLUSIONS OF LAW AND ORDER THEREON. [This is a long and complex decision that has been edited substantially here.] The government, acting through the Department of Justice, Antitrust Division, and [several] states, * * * seeks to enjoin Oracle Corporation from acquiring, directly or indirectly, the whole or any part of the stock of PeopleSoft, Inc. Plaintiffs allege that the acquisition would violate section 7 of the Clayton Act. * * *

Oracle initiated its tender offer for the shares of PeopleSoft on June 6, 2003. Plaintiffs brought suit on February 26, 2004. * * * Based on the evidence presented and the applicable law, the court concludes that plaintiffs have failed to carry the burden of proof entitling them to relief and, therefore, orders that judgment be entered for defendant and against plaintiffs.

INTRODUCTORY FINDINGS: INDUSTRY OVERVIEW. ***Products at Issue.*** Of the many types of computer software, such as operating system software, database software, integration software (sometimes called "middleware" in software parlance) and utilities software, this case involves only one application software. And within this type, the present case deals with only applications that automate the overall business data processing of business and similar entities; these applications are called "enterprise application software" (EAS). There are three main kinds of EAS. Plaintiffs single out one.

Some EAS programs are mass market PC-based applications of fairly limited "functionality" (meaning capability). Other EAS programs are developed by or for a specific enterprise and its particular needs; most large organizations had such specially designed EAS (called "legacy software") prior to the advent of the products in suit. Plaintiffs focus their claims on the third, intermediate category of EAS enterprise resource planning (ERP) system software. ERP is packaged software that integrates most of an entity's data across all or most of the entity's activities. Oracle and PeopleSoft develop, produce, market and service ERP software.

These copyrighted software programs are licensed ("sold" is the term applied to these license transactions) to end users along with a continued right to use license which usually includes maintenance or upgrades of the software. * * *

Many ERP programs were developed to address the needs of particular industries, such as banking and finance, insurance, engineering, construction, healthcare, government, legal and so forth (in industry lingo, these are called "verticals"). * * *

ERP programs have been developed to handle the full range of an enterprise's activities; these include human relations management (HRM), financial management systems (FMS), customer relations management (CRM), supply chain management (SCM), Product Life Cycle Management, Business Intelligence (BI), among many others. These are called "pillars." Although ERP encompasses many pillars, plaintiffs assert claims with respect to only two pillars, HRM and FMS.

Within these two pillars, plaintiffs further limit their claims to only those HRM and FMS products able to meet the needs of large and complex enterprises with "high functional needs." Plaintiffs label HRM and FMS products capable of meeting these high function needs "high function HRM software" and "high function FMS software," respectively. ERP pillars incapable of meeting these high function needs are called "mid-market" software by plaintiffs.

"High function software" is a term adopted by plaintiffs to describe what they contend is the separate and distinct line of commerce in which they contend competition would be lessened by the proposed acquisition. Plaintiffs apply the term "high function" to both HRM and FMS. "High function software," as defined by plaintiffs, has no recognized meaning in the industry.

Rather, industry participants and software vendors use the terms "enterprise" software, "up-market" software and "Tier One" software to denote ERP that is capable of executing a wide array of business processes at a superior level of performance. Software vendors use these terms to focus sales and marketing initiatives. * * *

Customers at Issue. "Large Complex Enterprises" (LCE) is a term adopted by plaintiffs to describe the ERP customers that have "high function software" needs. Based on the testimony described hereafter, the court finds that industry participants and software vendors do not typically use this term and it has no widely accepted meaning in the industry. * * *

Vendors at Issue. Many firms develop, produce, market and maintain ERP software. Some ERP software vendors, notably Oracle, PeopleSoft and a German company, SAP AG, developed cross-industry applications or "suites" of "generalized integrated software that could be customized for virtually any large business," It is to the products of these three vendors that plaintiffs direct their allegations. Although not alone in the ERP business, these three firms have the most comprehensive ERP software offerings. [The other firms making ERP software include: Lawson, AMS, Microsoft and "best of breed" vendors.] * * *

Plaintiffs' Claim of Threatened Injury to Competition. Plaintiffs allege that the HRM and FMS sold by Oracle, PeopleSoft and SAP are the only HRM and FMS products that can appropriately be deemed "high function HRM and FMS."

Plaintiffs allege that these "high function" HRM and FMS products have the "scale and flexibility to support thousands of simultaneous users and many tens of thousands of simultaneous transactions and the ability to integrate seamlessly into bundles or 'suites' of associated HRM and FMS functions." Plaintiffs allege that "high function" HRM and FMS products compete in a market that is separate and distinct from that of all other ERP products, such as SCM, CRM or mid-market HRM and FMS, the latter being HRM or FMS products designed for organizations having less demanding needs. * * *

Moreover, plaintiffs allege that this competition is geographically confined to the United States. Within this narrowly defined product and geographic market, plaintiffs allege that with limited and specially explained exceptions, only Oracle, PeopleSoft and, to a lesser degree, SAP's United States arm, SAP America, are in effective competition. The proposed merger would therefore, in plaintiffs' view, constrict this highly concentrated oligopoly to a duopoly of SAP America and a merged Oracle/PeopleSoft.

Oracle, predictably enough, contends that plaintiffs' market definition is legally and practicably too narrow. Oracle contends that (1) "high function" HRM and FMS software does not exist; "high function" is simply a label created by plaintiffs; (2) there is just one market for all HRM and FMS ERP products; (3) many firms other than the three identified by plaintiffs compete in the business of developing, producing, marketing and maintaining HRM and FMS ERP software; (4) this competition plays out in many more products than those in the HRM and FMS pillars; (5) price competition comes from sources in addition to ERP software vendors and includes competition from firms that provide outsourcing of data processing, the integration layer of the "software stack" and from the durability and adaptability of enterprises' installed base or legacy systems; (6) the geographic area of competition is worldwide or, at the very least, the United States and Europe; (7) the knowledgeable and sophisticated customers of ERP software would impede the exercise of any market power by a merged Oracle/PeopleSoft; and (8) potential entrants are poised to enter into competition, so that the proposed merger will not have an anticompetitive effect. * * *

HORIZONTAL MERGER ANALYSIS * * * ***Unilateral Effects.*** There is little case law on unilateral effects merger analysis. Few published decisions have even discussed the issue, at least using the term "unilateral effects." *See, e g, Swedish Match.* 131 F Supp 2d at 168; *New York v. Kraft Gen Foods, Inc.*, 926 F Supp 321, 333–35 (SDNY 1995); Guidelines § 2.2. But, as the court demonstrates below, "unilateral effects" is primarily a new term to address antitrust issues that courts have in other contexts considered for quite some time.

Unilateral effects result from "the tendency of a horizontal merger to lead to higher prices simply by virtue of the fact that the merger will eliminate direct competition between the two merging firms, even if all other firms in the market continue to compete independently." * * *

The Guidelines provide some instruction on the necessary elements of a unilateral effects claim involving differentiated products under section 7. * * *

[I]t appears that four factors make up a differentiated products unilateral effects claim. First, the products controlled by the merging firms must be differentiated. * * * Second, the products controlled by the merging firms must be close substitutes. * * * Third, other products must be sufficiently different from the products controlled by the merging firms that a merger would make a small but significant and non-transitory price increase profitable for the merging firms. Finally, repositioning by the non-merging firms must be unlikely. In other words, a plaintiff must demonstrate that the non-merging firms are unlikely to introduce products sufficiently similar to the products controlled by the merging firms to eliminate any significant market power created by the merger. * * *

Relevant markets defined in terms of "localized competition" may be much narrower than relevant markets defined in typical cases in which a dominant position is required. Judicial experience cautions against the use of qualitative factors to define narrow markets. This judicial experience arises, in part, from the rise (and fall) of the "submarkets" doctrine. * * *

The Guidelines adopt a structural approach for addressing unilateral effects claims that closely mirrors traditional structural analysis. *See* Guidelines § 2.211. The biggest weakness in the Guidelines' approach appears to be its strong reliance on particular market share concentrations. Under the Guidelines, anticompetitive effects are presumed "where market concentration data fall outside the safe harbor regions of Section 1.5, the merging firms have a combined market share of at least thirty-five percent, and where data on product attributes and relative product appeal show that a significant share of purchasers of one merging firm's product regard the other as their second choice," unless "rival sellers likely would replace any localized competition lost through the merger by repositioning their product lines." *Id.* at §§ 2.211, 2.212.

A presumption of anticompetitive effects from a combined share of 35% in a differentiated products market is unwarranted. Indeed, the opposite is likely true. To prevail on a differentiated products unilateral effects claim, a plaintiff must prove a relevant market in which the merging parties would have essentially a monopoly or dominant position. In *Rebel Oil*, the Ninth Circuit noted that a market share of 30% is "presumptively insufficient to establish the power to control price." 51 F3d at 1438. * * *

CONTENTIONS, EVIDENCE AND FINDINGS. * * ****Plaintiffs' Proposed Product Market Definition.*** * * * Plaintiffs offer a product market of high function HRM and FMS and a geographic market of the United States.

Four elements constitute plaintiffs' definition of high function HRM software as alleged in the FAC: "[1] Human Resource Management (HRM) [2] software and accompanying services [3] that can be integrated into suites of associated functions from a single vendor [4] with performance characteristics that meet the demands of multifaceted organizations with high-level functional needs." * * *

Added together, plaintiffs propose a very restricted product market definition: HRM and FMS integrated suites sold to large complex enterprises ("high function FMS and HRM market"). * * * Plaintiffs contend that this product market does not include mid-market vendors, best-of-breed solutions, incumbent solutions or outsourcing.

Plaintiffs' Evidence of a High Function HRM & FMS Market.* * * ***Customer Witnesses.*** [Several witnesses from large companies testified essentially to the same effect concerning their needs for HRM and FMS software as represented by the following.] Michael Gorriz, Vice President of Information Technology Business at DaimlerChrysler (Daimler), testified about his company's large and complex needs regarding HRM software. * * * Gorriz stated that "only SAP, PeopleSoft or Oracle could serve [Daimler's] needs for the HR management." Gorriz stated that Daimler considered no other vendors. Daimler's legacy system was "too old" for the company seriously to consider upgrading. * * *

Plaintiffs' Expert: Elzinga. By far the most important of plaintiffs' witnesses was Professor Kenneth Elzinga of the University of Virginia. Elzinga is a well-known and highly regarded economist. The court finds Elzinga to be highly qualified to offer testimony on market definition. Elzinga was the only one of plaintiffs' witnesses who offered testimony from which the court could attempt to calculate market shares and apply the *Philadelphia Nat'l Bank* presumptions or perform the HHI calculations of the Guidelines.

In reaching his proposed market definition, Elzinga purported to follow the Guidelines approach. Elzinga concluded that the relevant market was limited to high function FMS and HRM software. Elzinga testified that a hypothetical monopolist could profitably impose a SSNIP in high function FMS and HRM. Elzinga posited that if a merged Oracle/PeopleSoft decided to increase the price of its high function FMS and HRM products, consumers would not substitute (1) mid-market solutions (such as those produced by ERP vendor Lawson), (2) best-of-breed solutions (such as those produced by vendor Kronos), (3) incumbent or legacy solutions or (4) the services of outsourcing firms (such as Fidelity and ADP). * * *

From his numbers, Elzinga calculated the following United States high function FMS market shares: SAP, 39 percent; PeopleSoft, 31 percent; and Oracle, 17 percent. A merged Oracle/PeopleSoft would, in Elzinga's view, possess a 48 percent market share. Using the same data, Elzinga calculated the HHI1 in the high function FMS market to be 2800. Based upon Elzinga's calculations, a merger between Oracle and PeopleSoft would increase the high function FMS HHI2 to 3800.

For high function HRM, Elzinga calculated PeopleSoft's market share at 50 percent, SAP at 30 percent and Oracle at 18 percent; hence, in Elzinga's view, a merged Oracle/PeopleSoft would have a market share approaching 70 percent. Elzinga calculated an HHI1 [premerger HHI] of 2800 in the high function HRM market. Post-merger, the HHI2 [postmerger HHI] would increase to 5700.

Plainly, the levels of concentration reflected in Elzinga's testimony exceed the thresholds for "significant competitive concerns" under the Guidelines. Guidelines § 1.51(c). Both HHI2 amounts exceed 1800, and [the change in] HHI amounts exceed 50 points. Likewise, of course, post-merger market shares of this magnitude would satisfy the conditions to raise the anticompetitive presumption described by the Supreme Court in *Philadelphia Nat'l Bank.*

But for reasons explained more fully following the discussion of Oracle's expert witnesses, the court finds that Elzinga failed to carry the plaintiffs' burden of (1) establishing an articulable product market and (2) providing post-merger market share and HHI measurements, in a properly defined market, invoking an anticompetitive presumption under *Philadelphia Nat'l Bank* or the Guidelines. * * *

Findings of Fact: Product Market Definition. In order to sustain plaintiffs' product market definition the court must find, by a preponderance of the evidence, that plaintiffs' have shown an articulable and distinct product market for HRM and FMS sold by Oracle, PeopleSoft and SAP only that does not include mid-market software, outsourcing solutions, best of breed solutions, legacy systems or the infrastructure layer.

Based upon a review of the law and the evidence, the court concludes that the plaintiffs have not met their burden of establishing that the relevant product market is limited to so-called high function FMS and HRM sold by Oracle, PeopleSoft and SAP. * * *

Accordingly, based upon the evidence presented at trial, the court concludes that the following products cannot be excluded from the relevant product market for purposes of analyzing the effects of this merger. *Outsourcing.* * * * *Mid-market vendors.* * * * *Microsoft.* * * * and *Best of Breed.* * * *

Accordingly, without a relevant market having been established, the court cannot conduct a burden-shifting statistical analysis under *Philadelphia National Bank*, much less hold that plaintiffs are entitled to such a presumption. Nor, of course, can the court apply the concentration methodology of the Guidelines. *See* Guidelines § 1.51.

Plaintiffs' Proposed Geographic Market. Assuming that high function FMS and HRM is the relevant product market, plaintiffs claimed that the relevant geographic market is the United States. Again, plaintiffs relied heavily on Elzinga's testimony. In reaching this market definition, Elzinga ironically enough did not rely upon the oft-used Elzinga-Hogarty (E-H) test, which he admitted has been used in "dozens and dozens of merger cases" and which he himself co-developed.

In informal terms, the E-H test "measures the accuracy of a market delineation by determining the amount of either imports into or exports from a tentative market. The test is based on the assumption that if an area has significant exports or imports, then that area is not a relevant geographic market. Under the [test], exports or imports greater than 10% suggest that the market examined is not a relevant market." *United States v. Country Lake Foods, Inc.*, 754 F. Supp 669, 672 n2 (D Minn 1990).

Elzinga stated that he did not believe the E-H test "fit this particular antitrust case." Instead, Elzinga relied solely upon the Guidelines "hypothetical monopolist" test in determining the geographic market. *See* Guidelines § 1.21. "I am persuaded that the United States [is the geographic market because] if someone were the sole supplier of high function FMS and HRM * * * in the US, and [he imposed a SNNIP], he would not be thwarted or undercut by economic * * * agents outside the United States." *Id.* * * *

Oracle's Proposed Geographic Market. Oracle asks the court to reject the plaintiffs' proposed geographic market. Oracle argues that the geographic market in this case is "so clearly [a global market] that reasonable people ought not be debating it." * * *

Accordingly, Oracle urged the court to look at concentration figures based upon a global market of all FMS and HRM software. Using these product and geographic market definitions, Oracle offered the following global FMS market shares: SAP, 19.2 percent; Oracle, 16.8 percent; and PeopleSoft, 2 percent. A merged Oracle/PeopleSoft would, in Oracle's view, possess a 28.8 percent market share in the FMS market.

For global HRM, Oracle offers the following market shares: SAP, 11.9 percent; PeopleSoft, 11.3 percent; and Oracle, 3.04 percent. A merged Oracle/PeopleSoft would possess only a 14.3 percent market share in the HRM market.

Findings of Fact: Geographic Market. The court finds that the relevant geographic market ("the area of effective competition") in this case is a worldwide market. * * *

Findings of Fact: Market Shares and Concentration. In addition to failing to meet their burden of proving a distinct product market, plaintiffs have failed to prove that the relevant product market in this case is geographically bound to the United States. Accordingly, the market share and concentration statistics presented by Elzinga are wholly inapplicable to the court's analysis. The court is left with a new product market definition which includes, at least: (1) ERP sold by Oracle, SAP, PeopleSoft, Lawson, AMS and Microsoft; (2) outsourcing solutions; and (3) best of breed solutions. Further, this product market must be analyzed as a global one. * * *

[I]t is plaintiffs, not defendant, who carry the burden of proving market shares and concentration in order to invoke the presumptions of the case law or to sustain a showing in accordance with the Guidelines. The court cannot furnish its own statistics.

Without the benefit of presumptions, the burden remains upon plaintiffs to come forward with evidence of actual anticompetitive effects. * * *

Plaintiffs' Evidence of Unilateral Effects. Plaintiffs rest their theory of anticompetitive effects on an attempt to prove that Oracle and PeopleSoft are in a "localized" competition sphere (a "node") within the high function FMS and HRM market. This sphere does not include SAP or any other vendors, and a merger of Oracle and PeopleSoft would, therefore, adversely affect competition in this localized market. Plaintiffs also offered evidence to show that SAP could not reposition itself to replace the localized competition that would allegedly be lost if Oracle and PeopleSoft merge. * * *

Findings of Fact: Unilateral Effects. The court finds that the plaintiffs have wholly failed to prove the fundamental aspect of a unilateral effects case they have failed to show a "node" or an area of localized competition between Oracle and PeopleSoft. In other words, plaintiffs have failed to prove that there are a significant number of customers (the "node") who regard Oracle and PeopleSoft as their first and second choices. If plaintiffs had made such a showing, then the court could analyze the potential for exercise of monopoly power over this "node" by a post-merger Oracle or the ability of SAP or Lawson to reposition itself within the node in order to constrain such an exercise of monopoly power. * * *

In sum, the court finds that plaintiffs have failed to show an area of localized competition between Oracle and PeopleSoft. * * *

C. DOJ/FTC 2006 Commentary on Guidelines—Unilateral Effects

Excerpt from DOJ/FTC Commentary on Guidelines, Unilateral Effects

(March 2006)

Unilateral Effects. Section 2.2 of the [1992] Guidelines states that "merging firms may find it profitable to alter their behavior unilaterally following the acquisition by elevating price and suppressing output." The manner in which a horizontal merger may generate unilateral competitive effects is straightforward: By eliminating competition between the merging firms, a merger gives the merged firm incentives different from those of the merging firms. The simplest unilateral effect arises from merger to monopoly, which eliminates all competition in the relevant market. Since the issuance of the Guidelines in 1992, a substantial proportion of the Agencies' merger challenges have been predicated at least in part on a conclusion that the proposed mergers were likely to generate anticompetitive unilateral effects. * * *

The Agencies' analysis of unilateral competitive effects draws on many models developed by economists. The simplest is the model of monopoly, which applies to a merger involving the only two competitors in the relevant market. One step removed from monopoly is the dominant firm model. That model posits that all competitors but one in an industry act as a "competitive fringe," which can economically satisfy only part of total market demand. The remaining competitor acts as a monopolist with respect to the portion of total industry demand that the competitive fringe does not elect to supply. This model might apply, for example, in a homogeneous product industry in which the fringe competitors are unable to expand output significantly.

In other models, two or more competitors interact strategically. These models differ with respect to how competitors interact. In the Bertrand model, for example, competitors interact in the choice of the prices they charge. Similar to the Bertrand model are auction models, in which firms interact by bidding. There are many auction models with many different bidding procedures. In the Cournot model, competitors interact in the choice of the quantities they sell. And in bargaining models, competitors interact through their choices of terms on which they will deal with their customers.

Formal economic modeling can be useful in interpreting the available data (even with natural experiments). One type of modeling the Agencies use is "merger simulation," which "calibrates" a model to match quantitative aspects (*e.g.*, demand elasticities) of the industry in which the merger occurs and uses the calibrated model to predict the outcome of the competitive process after the merger. Merger simulation can be a useful tool in determining whether unilateral effects are likely to constitute a substantial lessening of competition when a particular model mentioned above fits the facts of the industry under review and suitable data can be found to calibrate the model. The fit of a model is evaluated on the basis of the totality of the evidence. * * *

§ 8.29 The Power Buyer Defense under the Case Law and the 2010 DOJ/FTC Guidelines

8. Powerful Buyers

Powerful buyers are often able to negotiate favorable terms with their suppliers. Such terms may reflect the lower costs of serving these buyers, but they also can reflect price discrimination in their favor.

The Agencies consider the possibility that powerful buyers may constrain the ability of the merging parties to raise prices. This can occur, for example, if powerful buyers have the ability and incentive to vertically integrate upstream or sponsor entry, or if the conduct or presence of large buyers undermines coordinated effects. However, the Agencies do not presume that the presence of powerful buyers alone forestalls adverse competitive effects flowing from the merger. Even buyers that can negotiate favorable terms may be harmed by an increase in market power. The Agencies examine the choices available to powerful buyers and how those choices likely would change due to the merger. Normally, a merger that eliminates a supplier whose presence contributed significantly to a buyer's negotiating leverage will harm that buyer.

> Example 22: Customer C has been able to negotiate lower pre-merger prices than other customers by threatening to shift its large volume of purchases from one merging firm to the other. No other suppliers are as well placed to meet Customer C's needs for volume and reliability. The merger is likely to harm Customer C. In this situation, the Agencies could identify a price discrimination market consisting of Customer C and similarly placed customers. The merger threatens to end previous price discrimination in their favor.

Furthermore, even if some powerful buyers could protect themselves, the Agencies also consider whether market power can be exercised against other buyers.

> Example 23: In Example 22, if Customer C instead obtained the lower pre-merger prices based on a credible threat to supply its own needs, or to sponsor new entry, Customer C might not be harmed. However, even in this case, other customers may still be harmed.

§ 8.30 The Case Law on Ease of Entry: Rejection of the Government's "Quick and Effective Entry Test"

United States v. Baker Hughes Inc.

United States Court of Appeals, District of Columbia Circuit, 1990 908 F.2d 981
(Judge now Justice Thomas, writing)

Circuit Judge CLARENCE THOMAS:

Appellee Oy Tampella AB, a Finnish corporation, through its subsidiary Tamrock AG, manufactures and sells hard rock hydraulic underground drilling rigs (HHUDRs) in the United States and throughout the world. Appellee Baker Hughes Inc., a corporation based in Houston, Texas, owned a French subsidiary, Eimco Secoma, S.A. (Secoma), that was similarly involved in the HHUDR industry. In 1989, Tamrock proposed to acquire Secoma.

The United States challenged the proposed acquisition, charging that it would substantially lessen competition in the United States HHUDR market in violation of section 7 of the Clayton Act. * * * In February 1990, the district court held a bench trial and issued a decision rejecting the government's request for a permanent injunction and dismissing the section 7 claim. The government immediately appealed to this court. * * *

By presenting statistics showing that combining the market shares of Tamrock and Secoma would significantly increase concentration in the already highly concentrated United States HHUDR market, the government established a prima facie case of anticompetitive effect. The district court, however, found sufficient evidence that the merger would not substantially lessen competition to conclude that the defendants had rebutted this prima facie case. The government did not produce any additional evidence showing a probability of substantially lessened competition, and thus failed to carry its ultimate burden of persuasion.

In this appeal, the government assails the court's conclusion that the defendants rebutted the prima facie case. * * * The government argues that, as a matter of law, section 7 defendants can rebut a prima facie case *only by a clear showing that entry into the market by competitors would be quick and effective.* Because the district court failed to apply this standard, the government submits, the court erred in concluding that the proposed acquisition would not substantially lessen future competition in the United States HHUDR market.

We find no merit in the legal standard propounded by the government. It is devoid of support in the statute, in the case law, and in the government's own Merger Guidelines. Moreover, it is flawed on its merits in three fundamental respects. First, it assumes that ease of entry by competitors is the *only* consideration relevant to a section 7 defendant's rebuttal. Second, it requires that a defendant who seeks to show ease of entry bear the onerous burden of proving that entry will be "quick and effective." * * *

The existence and significance of barriers to entry are frequently, of course, crucial considerations in a rebuttal analysis. In the absence of significant barriers, a company probably cannot maintain supracompetitive pricing for any length of time. * * * The district court in this case reviewed the prospects for future entry into the United States HHUDR market and concluded that, overall, entry was likely, particularly if Tamrock's acquisition of Secoma were to lead to supracompetitive pricing. The government attacks this conclusion, asserting that, as a matter of law, the court should have required the defendants to show clearly that entry would be "quick and effective." We reject this novel and unduly onerous standard. The district court's factual findings amply support its determination that future entry into the United States HHUDR market is likely. This determination, in turn, supports the court's conclusion that the defendants successfully rebutted the government's prima facie case.

As authority for its "quick and effective" entry test, the government relies primarily on *United States v. Waste Management, Inc.*, 743 F.2d 976, 981–84 (2d Cir.1984). This reliance is misplaced. Neither *Waste Management* nor any other case purports to establish a categorical "quick and effective" entry requirement. The Second Circuit in *Waste Management* simply noted that the defendant had successfully rebutted the government's prima facie case by showing that entry into the Dallas/Fort Worth trash collection market was "easy." That a defendant *may* successfully rebut a prima facie case by showing quick and effective entry does not mean that successful rebuttal *requires* such a showing. * * *

Having rejected the "quick and effective" entry standard itself, we turn briefly to the government's more general argument that the district court's findings regarding ease of entry failed to support its conclusion that the defendants had rebutted the prima facie case. The district court in this case discussed a number of considerations that led it to conclude that entry barriers to the United States HHUDR market were not high enough to impede future entry should Tamrock's acquisition of Secoma lead to supracompetitive pricing. First, the court noted that at least two companies, Cannon and Ingersoll-Rand, had entered the United States HHUDR market in 1989, and were poised for future expansion. Second, the court stressed that a number of firms competing in Canada and other countries had not penetrated the United States market, but could be expected to do so if Tamrock's acquisition of Secoma led to higher prices. Because the market is small, "[i]t is inexpensive to develop a separate sales and service network in the United States." Third, these firms would exert competitive pressure on the United States HHUDR market even if they never actually entered the market. * * *

In sum, we see no error legal or factual in the district court's determination that entry into the United States HHUDR market would likely avert anticompetitive effects from Tamrock's acquisition of Secoma. The court's determination on entry, considered along with the findings discussed in section I of this opinion, suffices to rebut the government's prima facie case.

§ 8.31 Entry under the 2010 DOJ/FTC Guidelines

A. Section 9, Entry, of the 2010 DOJ/FTC Guidelines

9. Entry

The analysis of competitive effects in Sections 6 and 7 focuses on current participants in the relevant market. That analysis may also include some forms of entry. Firms that would rapidly and easily enter the market in response to a SSNIP are market participants and may be assigned market shares. See Sections 5.1 and 5.2. Firms that have, prior to the merger, committed to entering the market also will normally be treated as market participants. See Section 5.1. This section concerns entry or adjustments to pre-existing entry plans that are induced by the merger.

As part of their full assessment of competitive effects, the Agencies consider entry into the relevant market. The prospect of entry into the relevant market will alleviate concerns about adverse competitive effects only if such entry will deter or counteract any competitive effects of concern so the merger will not substantially harm customers.

The Agencies consider the actual history of entry into the relevant market and give substantial weight to this evidence. Lack of successful and effective entry in the face of non-transitory increases in the margins earned on products in the relevant market tends to suggest that successful entry is slow or difficult. Market values of incumbent firms greatly exceeding the replacement costs of their tangible assets may indicate that these firms have valuable intangible assets, which may be difficult or time consuming for an entrant to replicate.

A merger is not likely to enhance market power if entry into the market is so easy that the merged firm and its remaining rivals in the market, either unilaterally or collectively, could not profitably raise price or otherwise reduce competition compared to the level that would prevail in the absence of the merger. Entry is that easy if entry would be timely, likely, and sufficient in its magnitude, character, and scope to deter or counteract the competitive effects of concern.

The Agencies examine the timeliness, likelihood, and sufficiency of the entry efforts an entrant might practically employ. * * *

9.1 Timeliness

In order to deter the competitive effects of concern, entry must be rapid enough to make unprofitable overall the actions causing those effects and thus leading to entry, even though those actions would be profitable until entry takes effect.

Even if the prospect of entry does not deter the competitive effects of concern, post-merger entry may counteract them. This requires that the impact of entrants in the relevant market be rapid enough that customers are not significantly harmed by the merger, despite any anticompetitive harm that occurs prior to the entry.

The Agencies will not presume that an entrant can have a significant impact on prices before that entrant is ready to provide the relevant product to customers unless there is reliable evidence that anticipated future entry would have such an effect on prices.

9.2 Likelihood

Entry is likely if it would be profitable, accounting for the assets, capabilities, and capital needed and the risks involved, including the need for the entrant to incur costs that would not be recovered if the entrant later exits. Profitability depends upon (a) the output level the entrant is likely to obtain, accounting for the obstacles facing new entrants; (b) the price the entrant would likely obtain in the post-merger market, accounting for the impact of that entry itself on prices; and (c) the cost per unit the entrant would likely incur, which may depend upon the scale at which the entrant would operate.

9.3 Sufficiency

Even where timely and likely, entry may not be sufficient to deter or counteract the competitive effects of concern. For example, in a differentiated product industry, entry may be insufficient because the products offered by entrants are not close enough substitutes to the products offered by the merged firm to render a price increase by the merged firm unprofitable. * * *

B. The Entry Analysis in the *Staples* Case

[The following is the district court's discussion of the entry claim in the *Staples* case, which is set out in Section 8.25.D]

[**Entry into the Market**] "The existence and significance of barriers to entry are frequently, of course, crucial considerations in a rebuttal analysis [because] [i]n the absence of significant barriers, a company probably cannot maintain supra-competitive pricing for any length of time." *Baker Hughes*, [Section 8.30] Thus, the Court must consider whether, in this case, "entry into the market would likely avert anticompetitive effects from [Staples'] acquisition of [Office Depot]." If the defendants' evidence regarding entry showed that the Commission's market-share statistics give an incorrect prediction of the proposed acquisition's probable effect on competition because entry into the market would likely avert any anti- competitive effect by acting as a constraint on Staples-Office Depot's prices, the Court would deny the FTC's motion. The Court, however, cannot make such a finding in this case.

The defendants argued during the hearing and in their briefs that the rapid growth in overall office supply sales has encouraged and will continue to encourage expansion and entry. * * *

[W]hile it is true that all office superstore entrants have entered within the last 11 years, the recent trend for office superstores has actually been toward exiting the market rather than entering. * * * A new office superstore would need to open a large number of stores nationally in order to achieve the purchasing and distribution economies of scale enjoyed by the three existing firms. Sunk costs would be extremely high. Economies of scale at the local level, such as in the costs of advertising and distribution, would also be difficult for a new superstore entrant to achieve since the three existing firms have saturated many important local markets. For example, according to the defendants' own saturation analyses, Staples estimates that there is room for less than two additional superstores in the Washington, D.C. area and Office Depot estimates that there is room for only two more superstores in Tampa, Florida. * * *

For the reasons discussed above, the Court finds it extremely unlikely that a new office superstore will enter the market and thereby avert the anti-competitive effects from Staples' acquisition of Office Depot. * * * The Court also finds it unlikely that the expansions by U.S. Office Products and Wal-Mart would avert the anti-competitive effects which would result from the merger. * * *

C. DOJ/FTC 2006 Commentary on Guidelines—Entry

Excerpt from DOJ/FTC Commentary on Guidelines, Entry

(March 2006)

Entry may be considered successful if the entrant generates sufficient revenue to cover all costs apart from the sunk costs of entry. Such entry succeeds in the sense that the entrant becomes and remains a viable competitor in the market. Defined in this way, successful entry into some markets may require nothing more than the investment of time and money. In such a market, an anticompetitive merger nevertheless will not attract entry if the sunk cost is so great that the entry offers little prospect of a reasonable return on that investment. Significant sunk costs may be associated, for example, with building a manufacturing facility, developing a product, achieving regulatory approvals, and gaining customer acceptance. An anticompetitive merger also will not attract entry if the risk of failed entry, and the associated loss of the entry investment, is so great that potential rewards do not justify making that investment. The Agencies therefore examine the sunk costs and likely returns associated with entry. * * *

§ 8.32 The Warren Court's View of Efficiencies: Potential Competition in Market Extension Merger

FTC v. Proctor & Gamble Company

United States Supreme Court, 1967 87 S.Ct. 1224

Mr. Justice DOUGLAS:

This is a proceeding initiated by the Federal Trade Commission charging that respondent, Procter & Gamble Co., had acquired the assets of Clorox Chemical Co. in violation of § 7 of the Clayton Act. The charge was that Procter's acquisition of Clorox might substantially lessen competition or tend to create a monopoly in the production and sale of household liquid bleaches. [Proctor did not manufacture bleach] * * *

As noted by the Commission, this merger is neither horizontal, vertical, nor conglomerate. Since the products of the acquired company are complementary to those of the acquiring company and may be produced with similar facilities, marketed through the same channels and in the same manner, and advertised by the same media, the Commission aptly called this acquisition a "product-extension merger" * * * .

The anticompetitive effects with which this product-extension merger is fraught can easily be seen: (1) the substitution of the powerful acquiring firm for the smaller, but already dominant, firm may substantially reduce the competitive structure of the industry by raising entry barriers and by dissuading the smaller firms from aggressively competing; (2) the acquisition eliminates the potential competition of the acquiring firm. * * *

Possible economies cannot be used as a defense to illegality. Congress was aware that some mergers which lessen competition may also result in economies but it struck the balance in favor of protecting competition.

[The Court found that the merger violated Section 7]

§ 8.33 The Eleventh Circuit's View of Efficiencies Defense: Must Be Substantial and Be Passed on

FTC v. University Health, Inc.

United States Court of Appeals, Eleventh Circuit, 1991 938 F.2d 1206

TJOFLAT, Chief Judge:

The Federal Trade Commission (FTC) filed this action to obtain a preliminary injunction pursuant to section 13(b) of the Federal Trade Commission Act (FTCA), to prevent the appellees from consummating an asset acquisition, which the FTC plans to challenge as violative of section 7 of the Clayton Act. Following a hearing, the district court held that the FTC had failed to demonstrate a likelihood of ultimate success in proving that the intended acquisition would substantially lessen competition; accordingly, the court denied the FTC's request for a preliminary injunction. * * *

[T]he FTC established a strong prima facie case that the proposed acquisition would substantially lessen competition in violation of section 7 of the Clayton Act. Additionally, the FTC bolstered this prima facie case with evidence that substantial barriers to entry into the relevant market exist. To overcome the strong presumption of illegality to which the FTC is entitled, based on its showing, the appellees make three principal arguments, all of which the district court accepted. As we explain below, these arguments, or the appellees' evidence in support of them, are insufficient to overcome the FTC's case. * * *

[**Efficiencies Defense**] The appellees argue that the proposed acquisition would generate significant efficiencies and, therefore, would not substantially lessen competition. The FTC responds that the law recognizes no such efficiency defense in any form. We conclude that in certain circumstances, a defendant may rebut the government's prima facie case with evidence showing that the intended merger would create significant efficiencies in the relevant market. Here, however, the appellees have failed to introduce sufficient evidence to demonstrate that their transaction would yield any efficiencies, and the district court's factual finding to the contrary is clearly erroneous. Accordingly, the appellees may not rely on an efficiency defense.

The Supreme Court stated in *FTC v. Procter & Gamble Co.*, [Section 8.32] (*Clorox*), that "[p]ossible economies cannot be used as a defense to illegality" in Section 7 merger cases. *See also Philadelphia Nat'l Bank*, [Section 8.7] ("We are clear ... that a merger the effect of which 'may be substantially to lessen competition' is not saved because, on some ultimate reckoning of social or economic debits and credits, it may be deemed beneficial."). * * *

It is clear that whether an acquisition would yield significant efficiencies in the relevant market is an important consideration in predicting whether the acquisition would substantially lessen competition. Market share statistics, which the government uses to make out a prima facie case under section 7, are not an end in themselves; rather, they are used to estimate the effect an intended transaction would have on competition. Thus, evidence that a proposed acquisition would create significant efficiencies benefiting consumers is useful in evaluating the ultimate issue the acquisition's overall effect on competition. We think, therefore, that an efficiency defense to the government's prima facie case in section 7 challenges is appropriate in certain circumstances.

We recognize, however, that it is difficult to measure the efficiencies a proposed transaction would yield and the extent to which these efficiencies would be passed on to consumers. * * * Moreover, it is difficult to calculate the anticompetitive costs of an acquisition against which to compare the gains realized through greater efficiency; such a comparison is necessary, though, to evaluate the acquisition's total competitive effect. Because of these difficulties, we hold that a defendant who seeks to overcome a presumption that a proposed acquisition would substantially lessen competition must demonstrate that the intended acquisition would result in significant economies and that these economies ultimately would benefit competition and, hence, consumers. * * *

The appellees here have not presented sufficient evidence to support their claim that the intended acquisition would generate efficiencies benefiting consumers. * * * [A]lthough we hold that an efficiency defense may be used in certain cases to rebut the government's prima facie showing in a section 7 challenge, the appellees may not rely on this defense because they failed to demonstrate that their proposed acquisition would yield significant economies. * * *

§ 8.34 Efficiencies under the 2010 DOJ/FTC Guidelines

A. The Economic Case for an Efficiencies Defense

The economic case for an efficiencies defense, which was first developed by Professor Williamson, is discussed in Section 8.16.

B. Section 10, Efficiencies, of the 2010 DOJ/FTC Guidelines

10. Efficiencies

Competition usually spurs firms to achieve efficiencies internally. Nevertheless, a primary benefit of mergers to the economy is their potential to generate significant efficiencies and thus enhance the merged firm's ability and incentive to compete, which may result in lower prices, improved quality, enhanced service, or new products. For example, merger-generated efficiencies may enhance competition by permitting two ineffective competitors to form a more effective competitor, e.g., by combining complementary assets. In a unilateral effects context, incremental cost reductions may reduce or reverse any increases in the merged firm's incentive to elevate price. Efficiencies also may lead to new or improved products, even if they do not immediately and directly affect price. In a coordinated effects context, incremental cost reductions may make coordination less likely or effective by enhancing the incentive of a maverick to lower price or by creating a new maverick firm. Even when efficiencies generated through a merger enhance a firm's ability to compete, however, a merger may have other effects that may lessen competition and make the merger anticompetitive.

The Agencies credit only those efficiencies likely to be accomplished with the proposed merger and unlikely to be accomplished in the absence of either the proposed merger or another means having comparable anticompetitive effects. These are termed merger-specific efficiencies.[32] Only alternatives that are practical in the business situation faced by the merging firms are considered in making this determination. The Agencies do not insist upon a less restrictive alternative that is merely theoretical.

Efficiencies are difficult to verify and quantify, in part because much of the information relating to efficiencies is uniquely in the possession of the merging firms. Moreover, efficiencies projected reasonably and in good faith by the merging firms may not be realized. Therefore, it is incumbent upon the merging firms to substantiate efficiency claims so that the Agencies can verify by reasonable means the likelihood and magnitude of each asserted efficiency, how and when each would be achieved (and any costs of doing so), how each would enhance the merged firm's ability and incentive to compete, and why each would be merger-specific.

Efficiency claims will not be considered if they are vague, speculative, or otherwise cannot be verified by reasonable means. Projections of efficiencies may be viewed with skepticism, particularly when generated outside of the usual business planning process. By contrast, efficiency claims substantiated by analogous past experience are those most likely to be credited.

Cognizable efficiencies are merger-specific efficiencies that have been verified and do not arise from anticompetitive reductions in output or service. Cognizable efficiencies are assessed net of costs produced by the merger or incurred in achieving those efficiencies.

The Agencies will not challenge a merger if cognizable efficiencies are of a character and magnitude such that the merger is not likely to be anticompetitive in any relevant market.[33] To make the requisite determination, the Agencies consider whether cogniz-

---

32. The Agencies will not deem efficiencies to be merger-specific if they could be attained by practical alternatives that mitigate competitive concerns, such as divestiture or licensing. If a merger affects not whether but only when an efficiency would be achieved, only the timing advantage is a merger-specific efficiency.

33. The Agencies normally assess competition in each relevant market affected by a merger independently and normally will challenge the merger if it is likely to be anticompetitive in any relevant market. In some cases, however, the Agencies in their prosecutorial discretion will consider efficien-

able efficiencies likely would be sufficient to reverse the merger's potential to harm customers in the relevant market, e.g., by preventing price increases in that market.[34] In conducting this analysis, the Agencies will not simply compare the magnitude of the cognizable efficiencies with the magnitude of the likely harm to competition absent the efficiencies. The greater the potential adverse competitive effect of a merger, the greater must be the cognizable efficiencies, and the more they must be passed through to customers, for the Agencies to conclude that the merger will not have an anticompetitive effect in the relevant market. When the potential adverse competitive effect of a merger is likely to be particularly substantial, extraordinarily great cognizable efficiencies would be necessary to prevent the merger from being anticompetitive. In adhering to this approach, the Agencies are mindful that the antitrust laws give competition, not internal operational efficiency, primacy in protecting customers.

In the Agencies' experience, efficiencies are most likely to make a difference in merger analysis when the likely adverse competitive effects, absent the efficiencies, are not great. Efficiencies almost never justify a merger to monopoly or near-monopoly. Just as adverse competitive effects can arise along multiple dimensions of conduct, such as pricing and new product development, so too can efficiencies operate along multiple dimensions. Similarly, purported efficiency claims based on lower prices can be undermined if they rest on reductions in product quality or variety that customers value.

The Agencies have found that certain types of efficiencies are more likely to be cognizable and substantial than others. For example, efficiencies resulting from shifting production among facilities formerly owned separately, which enable the merging firms to reduce the incremental cost of production, are more likely to be susceptible to verification and are less likely to result from anticompetitive reductions in output. Other efficiencies, such as those relating to research and development, are potentially substantial but are generally less susceptible to verification and may be the result of anticompetitive output reductions. Yet others, such as those relating to procurement, management, or capital cost, are less likely to be merger-specific or substantial, or may not be cognizable for other reasons.

When evaluating the effects of a merger on innovation, the Agencies consider the ability of the merged firm to conduct research or development more effectively. Such efficiencies may spur innovation but not affect short-term pricing. The Agencies also consider the ability of the merged firm to appropriate a greater fraction of the benefits resulting from its innovations. Licensing and intellectual property conditions may be important to this enquiry, as they affect the ability of a firm to appropriate the benefits of its innovation. Research and development cost savings may be substantial and yet not be cognizable efficiencies because they are difficult to verify or result from anticompetitive reductions in innovative activities.

---

cies not strictly in the relevant market, but so inextricably linked with it that a partial divestiture or other remedy could not feasibly eliminate the anticompetitive effect in the relevant market without sacrificing the efficiencies in the other market(s). Inextricably linked efficiencies are most likely to make a difference when they are great and the likely anticompetitive effect in the relevant market(s) is small so the merger is likely to benefit customers overall.

34. The Agencies normally give the most weight to the results of this analysis over the short term. The Agencies also may consider the effects of cognizable efficiencies with no short-term, direct effect on prices in the relevant market. Delayed benefits from efficiencies (due to delay in the achievement of, or the realization of customer benefits from, the efficiencies) will be given less weight because they are less proximate and more difficult to predict. Efficiencies relating to costs that are fixed in the short term are unlikely to benefit customers in the short term, but can benefit customers in the longer run, e.g., if they make new product introduction less expensive.

C. The Efficiencies Analysis in the *Staples* Case

[The following is the district court's discussion of the efficiency claims in the *Staples* case, which is set out in Section 8.25.D]

[**Efficiencies**] Whether an efficiencies defense showing that the intended merger would create significant efficiencies in the relevant market, thereby offsetting any anti-competitive effects, may be used by a defendant to rebut the government's prima facie case is not entirely clear. The newly revised efficiencies section of the Merger Guidelines recognizes that, "mergers have the potential to generate significant efficiencies by permitting a better utilization of existing assets, enabling the combined firm to achieve lower costs in producing a given quality and quantity than either firm could have achieved without the proposed transaction." This coincides with the view of some courts that "whether an acquisition would yield significant efficiencies in the relevant market is an important consideration in predicting whether the acquisition would substantially lessen competition.... [T]herefore, ... an efficiency defense to the government's prima facie case in section 7 challenges is appropriate in certain circumstances." *FTC v. University Health.* The Supreme Court, however, in *FTC v. Proctor & Gamble Co.*, [Section 8.32], stated that "[p]ossible economies cannot be used as a defense to illegality in section 7 merger cases." There has been great disagreement regarding the meaning of this precedent and whether an efficiencies defense is permitted. * * * Assuming that it is a viable defense, however, the Court cannot find in this case that the defendants' efficiencies evidence rebuts the presumption that the merger may substantially lessen competition or shows that the Commission's evidence gives an inaccurate prediction of the proposed acquisition's probable effect. * * *

[T]he Court [does not] believe that the defendants must prove that efficiencies by "clear and convincing evidence" in order for those efficiencies to be considered by the Court. That would saddle Section 7 defendants with the nearby impossible task of rebutting a possibility with a certainty, a burden which was rejected in *United States v. Baker Hughes*, Inc., [Section 8.30]. Instead, like all rebuttal evidence in Section 7 cases, the defendants must simply rebut the presumption that the merger will substantially lessen competition by showing that the Commission's evidence gives an inaccurate prediction of the proposed acquisition's probable effect. Defendants, however, must do this with credible evidence, and the Court with respect to this issue did not find the defendants' evidence to be credible.

Defendants' submitted an "Efficiencies Analysis" which predicted that the combined company would achieve savings of between $4.9 and $6.5 billion over the next five years. In addition, the defendants argued that the merger would also generate dynamic efficiencies. For example, defendants argued that as suppliers become more efficient due to their increased sales volume to the combined Staples-Office Depot, they would be able to lower prices to their other retailers. Moreover, defendants argued that two-thirds of the savings realized by the combined company would be passed along to customers.

Evaluating credibility, as the Court must do, the Court credits the testimony and Report of the Commission's expert, David Painter, over the testimony and Efficiencies Study of the defendants' efficiencies witness, Shira Goodman, Senior Vice President of Integration at Staples. Mr. Painter's testimony was compelling, and the Court finds, based primarily on Mr. Painter's testimony, that the defendants' cost savings estimates are unreliable. * * * The cost savings claims submitted to the Court are also substantially greater than those represented in the defendants' Joint Proxy Statement/Prospectus "reflecting the best currently available estimate of management," and filed with the Securities and Exchange Commission on January 23, 1997, or referenced in the "fairness opinions" rendered by the defendants' investment bankers which are contained in the Proxy Statement. * * *

[T]he Court also finds that the defendants' projected pass through rate the amount of the projected savings that the combined company expects to pass on to customers in the form of lower prices is unrealistic. The Court has no doubt that a portion of any efficiencies achieved through a merger of the defendants would be passed on to customers. Staples and Office Depot have a proven track record of achieving cost savings through efficiencies, and then passing those savings to customers in the form of lower prices. However, in this case the defendants have projected a pass through rate of two-thirds of the savings while the evidence shows that, historically, Staples has passed through only 15–17%. * * * Based on the above evidence, the Court cannot find that the defendants have rebutted the presumption [of a violation]. * * *

D. Merger to Duopoly and Impact of Efficiencies—*Heinz*

Federal Trade Commission v. H.J. Heinz Co.

United States Court Of Appeals For The District of Columbia Circuit, 2001246 F.3d 708; 2001 U.S. App. LEXIS 7735

Karen Lecraft Henderson, *Circuit Judge:*

On February 28, 2000 H.J. Heinz Company (Heinz) and Milnot Holding Corporation (Beech-Nut) entered into a merger agreement. The Federal Trade Commission (Commission or FTC) sought a preliminary injunction pursuant to section 13(b) of the Federal Trade Commission Act (FTCA) to enjoin the consummation of the merger. The injunction was sought in aid of an FTC administrative proceeding which was subsequently instituted by complaint to challenge the merger as violative of, *inter alia,* section 7 of the Clayton Act. The district court denied the preliminary injunction and the FTC appealed to this court. For the reasons set forth below, we reverse the district court and remand for entry of a preliminary injunction against Heinz and Beech-Nut.

Background. Four million infants in the United States consume 80 million cases of jarred baby food annually, representing a domestic market of $865 million to $1 billion. The baby food market is dominated by three firms, Gerber Products Company (Gerber), Heinz and Beech-Nut. Gerber, the industry leader, enjoys a 65 per cent market share while Heinz and Beech-Nut come in second and third, with a 17.4 per cent and a 15.4 per cent share respectively. The district court found that Gerber enjoys unparalleled brand recognition with a brand loyalty greater than any other product sold in the United States. Gerber's products are found in over 90 per cent of all American supermarkets.

By contrast, Heinz is sold in approximately 40 per cent of all supermarkets. Its sales are nationwide but concentrated in northern New England, the Southeast and Deep South and the Midwest. Despite its second-place domestic market share, Heinz is the largest producer of baby food in the world with $1 billion in sales worldwide. Its domestic baby food products with annual net sales of $103 million are manufactured at its Pittsburgh, Pennsylvania plant, which was updated in 1991 at a cost of $120 million. The plant operates at 40 per cent of its production capacity and produces 12 million cases of baby food annually. Its baby food line includes about 130 SKUs (stock keeping units), that is, product varieties (*e.g.*, strained carrots, apple sauce, etc.). Heinz lacks Gerber's brand recognition; it markets itself as a "value brand" with a shelf price several cents below Gerber's.

Beech-Nut has a market share (15.4%) comparable to that of Heinz (17.4%), with $138.7 million in annual sales of baby food, of which 72 per cent is jarred baby food. Its jarred baby food line consists of 128 SKUs. Beech-Nut manufactures all of its baby food in Canajoharie, New York at a manufacturing plant that was built in 1907 and began manufacturing baby food in 1931. Beech-Nut maintains price parity with Gerber, selling at about one penny less. It markets its product as a premium brand. Consumers generally view its product as comparable in quality to Gerber's. Beech-Nut is carried in approximately 45 per cent of all grocery stores. Although its sales are nationwide, they are concentrated in New York, New Jersey, California and Florida.

At the wholesale level Heinz and Beech-Nut both make lump-sum payments called "fixed trade spending" (also known as "slotting fees" or "pay-to-stay" arrangements) to grocery stores to obtain shelf placement. Gerber, with its strong name recognition and brand loyalty, does not make such pay-to-stay payments. The other type of wholesale trade spending is "variable trade spending," which typically consists of manufacturers' discounts and allowances to supermarkets to create retail price differentials that entice the consumer to purchase their product instead of a competitor's. * * *

Analysis. * * * *Prima Facie Case.* * * * Sufficiently large HHI figures establish the FTC's prima facie case that a merger is anti-competitive. The district court found that the pre-merger HHI "score for the baby food industry is 4775" indicative of a highly concentrated industry. The merger of Heinz and Beech-Nut will increase the HHI by 510 points. This creates, by a wide margin, a presumption that the merger will lessen competition in the domestic jarred baby food market.

Here, the FTC's market concentration statistics are bolstered by the indisputable fact that the merger will eliminate competition between the two merging parties at the wholesale level, where they are currently the only competitors for what the district court described as the "second position on the supermarket shelves." Heinz's own documents recognize the wholesale competition and anticipate that the merger will end it. Indeed, those documents disclose that Heinz considered three options to end the vigorous wholesale competition with Beech-Nut: two involved innovative measures while the third entailed the acquisition of Beech-Nut. Heinz chose the third, and least pro-competitive, of the options.

Finally, the anticompetitive effect of the merger is further enhanced by high barriers to market entry. The district court found that there had been no significant entries in the baby food market in decades and that new entry was "difficult and improbable." This finding largely eliminates the possibility that the reduced competition caused by the merger will be ameliorated by new competition from outsiders and further strengthens the FTC's case.

As far as we can determine, no court has ever approved a merger to duopoly under similar circumstances.

Rebuttal Arguments. In response to the FTC's prima facie showing, the appellees make three rebuttal arguments, which the district court accepted in reaching its conclusion that the merger was not likely to lessen competition substantially. For the reasons discussed below, these arguments fail and thus were not a proper basis for denying the FTC injunctive relief. * * *

Post-Merger Efficiencies. The appellees' second attempt to rebut the FTC's prima facie showing is their contention that the anticompetitive effects of the merger will be offset by efficiencies resulting from the union of the two companies, efficiencies which they assert will be used to compete more effectively against Gerber. It is true that a merger's primary benefit to the economy is its potential to generate efficiencies. As the Merger

Guidelines now recognize, efficiencies "can enhance the merged firm's ability and incentive to compete, which may result in lower prices, improved quality, or new products."

Although the Supreme Court has not sanctioned the use of the efficiencies defense in a section 7 case, *see Procter & Gamble Co.*[35] [Section 8.32] the trend among lower courts is to recognize the defense. *See, e.g. FTC v. Tenet Health Care Corp.*; *University Health* [Section 8.33]; *FTC v. Staples* [Section 8.34.C]; *see also* ABA Antitrust Section, Mergers and Acquisitions: Understanding the Antitrust Issues 152 (2000) ("The majority of courts have considered efficiencies as a means to rebut the government's prima facie case that a merger will lead to restricted output or increased prices. These courts, however, generally have found inadequate proof of efficiencies to sustain a rebuttal of the government's case."). In 1997 the Department of Justice and the FTC revised their Horizontal Merger Guidelines to recognize that "mergers have the potential to generate significant efficiencies by permitting a better utilization of existing assets, enabling the combined firm to achieve lower costs in producing a given quantity and quality than either firm could have achieved without the proposed transaction." Horizontal Merger Guidelines, *supra,* § 4.

Nevertheless, the high market concentration levels present in this case require, in rebuttal, proof of extraordinary efficiencies, which the appellees failed to supply. *See* Universal Health ("[A] defendant who seeks to overcome a presumption that a proposed acquisition would substantially lessen competition must demonstrate that the intended acquisition would result in significant economies and that these economies ultimately would benefit competition and, hence, consumers."); Horizontal Merger Guidelines, supra, § 4 (stating that "efficiencies almost never justify a merger to monopoly or near-monopoly"); 4A Areeda, *et al., Antitrust Law* P 971f, at 44 (requiring "extraordinary" efficiencies where the "HHI is well above 1800 and the HHI increase is well above 100"). Moreover, given the high concentration levels, the court must undertake a rigorous analysis of the kinds of efficiencies being urged by the parties in order to ensure that those "efficiencies" represent more than mere speculation and promises about post-merger behavior. The district court did not undertake that analysis here.

In support of its conclusion that post-merger efficiencies will outweigh the merger's anticompetitive effects, the district court found that the consolidation of baby food production in Heinz's under-utilized Pittsburgh plant "will achieve substantial cost savings in salaries and operating costs." The court also credited the appellees' promise of improved product quality as a result of recipe consolidation. The only cost reduction the court quantified as a percentage of pre-merger costs, however, was the so-called "variable conversion cost": the cost of processing the volume of baby food now processed by Beech-Nut. The court accepted the appellees' claim that this cost would be reduced by 43% if the Beech-Nut production were shifted to Heinz's plant, a reduction the appellees' expert characterized as "extraordinary."

The district court's analysis falls short of the findings necessary for a successful efficiencies defense in the circumstances of this case. We mention only three of the most important deficiencies here. First, "variable conversion cost" is only a percentage of the total vari-

35. In *Proctor & Gamble*, the Supreme Court stated that "possible economies cannot be used as a defense to illegality" in section 7 merger cases. The issue is, however, not a closed book. See *Stables*, (collecting cases). Areeda and Turner explain that "in interpreting the Clorox language, moreover, observe that the court referred only to 'possible' economies and to economies that 'may' result from mergers that lessen competition. To reject an economies defense based on mere possibilities does not mean that one should reject such a defense based on more convincing proof." Phillip Areeda & Donald Turner, Antitrust Law P 941b, at 154 (1980). They conclude that "the Court's brief and unelaborated language [in Clorox] cannot reasonably be taken as a definitive disposition of so important and complex an issue as the role of economies in analyzing legality of a merger." Id.

able manufacturing cost. A large percentage reduction in only a small portion of the company's overall variable manufacturing cost does not necessarily translate into a significant cost advantage to the merger. Thus, for cost reduction to be relevant, we must at least consider the percentage of Beech-Nut's total variable manufacturing cost that would be reduced as a consequence of the merger. At oral argument, the appellees' counsel agreed. This correction immediately cuts the asserted efficiency gain in half since, according to the appellees' evidence, using total variable manufacturing cost as the measure cuts the cost savings from 43% to 22.3%.

Second, the percentage reduction in *Beech-Nut's* cost is still not the relevant figure. After the merger, the two entities will be combined, and to determine whether the merged entity will be a significantly more efficient competitor, cost reductions must be measured across the new entity's combined production not just across the pre-merger output of Beech-Nut. *See* 4A Areeda, et al., supra, P 976d at 93–94. The district court, however, did not consider the cost reduction over the merged firm's combined output. At oral argument the appellees' counsel was unable to suggest a formula that could be used for determining that cost reduction.

Finally, and as the district court recognized, the asserted efficiencies must be "merger-specific" to be cognizable as a defense, see Horizontal Merger Guidelines, supra, §4; 4A Areeda, *et al., supra,* P 973, at 49–62. That is, they must be efficiencies that cannot be achieved by either company alone because, if they can, the merger's asserted benefits can be achieved without the concomitant loss of a competitor. *See generally* 4A Areeda, *et al., supra,* P 973. Yet the district court never explained why Heinz could not achieve the kind of efficiencies urged without merger. As noted, the principal merger benefit asserted for Heinz is the acquisition of Beech-Nut's better recipes, which will allegedly make its product more attractive and permit expanded sales at prices lower than those charged by Beech-Nut, which produces at an inefficient plant. Yet, neither the district court nor the appellees addressed the question whether Heinz could obtain the benefit of better recipes by investing more money in product development and promotion say, by an amount less than the amount Heinz would spend to acquire Beech-Nut. At oral argument, Heinz's counsel agreed that the taste of Heinz's products was not so bad that no amount of money could improve the brand's consumer appeal. That being the case, the question is how much Heinz would have to spend to make its product equivalent to the Beech-Nut product and hence whether Heinz could achieve the efficiencies of merger without eliminating Beech-Nut as a competitor. The district court, however, undertook no inquiry in this regard. In short, the district court failed to make the kind of factual determinations necessary to render the appellees' efficiency defense sufficiently concrete to offset the FTC's prima facie showing. * * *

Although we recognize that, post-hearing, the FTC may accept the rebuttal arguments proffered by the appellees, including their efficiencies defense, and permit the merger to proceed, we conclude that the FTC succeeded in "raising questions going to the merits so serious, substantial, difficult and doubtful as to make them fair ground for thorough investigation, study, deliberation and determination by the FTC." * * *

E. DOJ/FTC 2006 Commentary on Guidelines—Efficiencies

Excerpt from DOJ/FTC Commentary on Guidelines, Efficiencies

(March 2006)

Efficiencies. Merging parties may reduce their costs by combining complementary assets, eliminating duplicate activities, or achieving scale economies. Mergers also may lead to enhanced product quality or to increased innovation that results in lower costs and prices or in more rapid introduction of new products that benefit consumers.

As the Guidelines state, efficiencies "can enhance the merged firm's ability and incentive to compete, which may result in lower prices, improved quality, enhanced service, or new products." Guidelines §4. Moreover, when a merged firm achieves such efficiencies, it may induce competitors to strive for greater efficiencies in order to compete more effectively. Consumers benefit from such increased competition. * * *

Sufficiency of Efficiencies. As noted in section 4 of the Guidelines, the Agencies seek to determine "whether cognizable efficiencies likely would be sufficient to reverse the merger's potential to harm consumers in the relevant market, *e.g.*, by preventing price increases in that market." Within the integrated analysis framework for evaluating competitive effects, "efficiencies are most likely to make a difference in merger analysis when the likely adverse competitive effects, absent the efficiencies, are not great." Efficiencies are a significant factor in the Agencies' decisions not to challenge some mergers that otherwise are likely to have, at most, only slight anticompetitive effects. * * *

"Out-of-Market" Efficiencies. In some cases, merger efficiencies are "not strictly in the relevant market, but so inextricably linked with it that a partial divestiture or other remedy could not feasibly eliminate the anticompetitive effect in the relevant market without sacrificing the efficiencies in the other market(s)." Guidelines §4 at n.36. If out-of-market efficiencies are not inextricably linked to the relevant market, the Agencies often find an acceptable narrowly tailored remedy that preserves the efficiencies while preventing anticompetitive effects. * * *

Inextricably linked out-of-market efficiencies, however, can cause the Agencies, in their discretion, not to challenge mergers that would be challenged absent the efficiencies. This circumstance may arise, for example, if a merger presents large procompetitive benefits in a large market and a small anticompetitive problem in another, smaller market. * * *

Fixed-Cost Savings. Merger-specific, cognizable efficiencies are most likely to make a difference in the Agencies' enforcement decisions when the efficiencies can be expected to result in direct, short-term, procompetitive price effects. Economic analysis teaches that price reductions are expected when efficiencies reduce the merged firm's marginal costs, *i.e.*, costs associated with producing one additional unit of each of its products. By contrast, reductions in fixed costs—costs that do not change in the short-run with changes in output rates—typically are not expected to lead to immediate price effects and hence to benefit consumers in the short term. Instead, the immediate benefits of lower fixed costs (*e.g.*, most reductions in overhead, management, or administrative costs) usually accrue to firm profits.

Exceptions to this general rule, however, exist. For example, under certain market or sales circumstances, fixed-cost savings may result in lower prices in the short term. Selling prices that are determined on a "cost-plus basis" (*e.g.*, cost-based contracts) can be influenced by changes in fixed costs. Contractual arrangements also may allow fixed-cost savings to be passed through.

The Agencies consider merger-specific, cognizable reductions in fixed costs, even if they cannot be expected to result in direct, short-term, procompetitive price effects because consumers may benefit from them over the longer term even if not immediately. As with any other type of efficiency, reductions in fixed costs must be substantiated by the parties and verified by reasonable means. * * *

§8.35 Section 11, Failure and Exiting Assets, of the 2010 DOJ/FTC Guidelines

11. Failure and Exiting Assets

Notwithstanding the analysis above, a merger is not likely to enhance market power if imminent failure, as defined below, of one of the merging firms would cause the assets of that firm to exit the relevant market. This is an extreme instance of the more general circumstance in which the competitive significance of one of the merging firms is declining: the projected market share and significance of the exiting firm is zero. If the relevant assets would otherwise exit the market, customers are not worse off after the merger than they would have been had the merger been enjoined.

The Agencies do not normally credit claims that the assets of the failing firm would exit the relevant market unless all of the following circumstances are met: (1) the allegedly failing firm would be unable to meet its financial obligations in the near future; (2) it would not be able to reorganize successfully under Chapter 11 of the Bankruptcy Act; and (3) it has made unsuccessful good-faith efforts to elicit reasonable alternative offers that would keep its tangible and intangible assets in the relevant market and pose a less severe danger to competition than does the proposed merger.[36]

Similarly, a merger is unlikely to cause competitive harm if the risks to competition arise from the acquisition of a failing division. The Agencies do not normally credit claims that the assets of a division would exit the relevant market in the near future unless both of the following conditions are met: (1) applying cost allocation rules that reflect true economic costs, the division has a persistently negative cash flow on an operating basis, and such negative cash flow is not economically justified for the firm by benefits such as added sales in complementary markets or enhanced customer goodwill;[37] and (2) the owner of the failing division has made unsuccessful good-faith efforts to elicit reasonable alternative offers that would keep its tangible and intangible assets in the relevant market and pose a less severe danger to competition than does the proposed acquisition.

§8.36 Impact of Post Merger Evidence of Elevated Prices—*Evanston Hospital*

In the Matter of Evanston Northwestern Healthcare Corporation

Federal Trade Commission, (2005) FTC LEXIS 146

STEPHEN J. MCGUIRE, Chief Administrative Law Judge:

INTRODUCTION Overview and Summary of Decision. In January 2000, Evanston Hospital ("Evanston") and Glenbrook Hospital ("Glenbrook") merged with Highland Park Hospital ("Highland Park") to form the Evanston Northwestern Healthcare Corporation ("ENH" or "Respondent"). Over four years later, on February 10, 2004, Com-

---

36. Any offer to purchase the assets of the failing firm for a price above the liquidation value of those assets will be regarded as a reasonable alternative offer. Liquidation value is the highest value the assets could command for use outside the relevant market.

37. Because the parent firm can allocate costs, revenues, and intra-company transactions among itself and its subsidiaries and divisions, the Agencies require evidence on these two points that is not solely based on management plans that could have been prepared for the purpose of demonstrating negative cash flow or the prospect of exit from the relevant market.

plaint Counsel for the Federal Trade Commission ("FTC") filed a Complaint challenging the merger under Section 7 of the Clayton Act, 15 U.S.C. § 18, asserting that the merger has substantially lessened competition.

This case presents a rare opportunity to examine "the actual effect of concentration on price in the hospital industry." *See United States v. Rockford Memorial Corp.*, 898 F.2d 1278, 1280 (7th Cir. 1990). Since the enactment of the Hart-Scott-Rodino Antitrust Improvements Act of 1976 (15 U.S.C. § 18a), most enforcement actions are initiated prior to the proposed merger. In those cases, courts must rely on predictions based on market concentration data. In this consummated merger case, however, there is significant post-acquisition evidence to evaluate in assessing whether the probable effect of the merger will be to "substantially lessen competition."

This opinion follows the traditional Clayton 7 approach in assessing whether there is a reasonable probability that the merger is likely to result in anticompetitive effects in a relevant market. First, the relevant product market and geographic market are determined. Then, the Court analyzes whether anticompetitive effects are probable, using both market concentration statistics and post-acquisition evidence. Finally, Respondent's procompetitive justifications and affirmative defense are assessed.

The relevant product market in this case is found to be general acute care inpatient services sold to managed care organizations, including primary, secondary, and tertiary inpatient services. The relevant geographic market is found to be the area encompassing the following seven hospitals: Evanston, Glenbrook, Highland Park, Lake Forest, Advocate Lutheran General, Rush North Shore, and St. Francis. The post-merger market concentration level, as measured by the Herfindahl-Hirschman Index ("HHI"), is found to be 2739, with an increase of 384. This corresponds to a "highly concentrated" market and the presumption that the merger is likely to "create or enhance market power." Horizontal Merger Guidelines, § 1.51 (1992, as amended 1997).

Contemporaneous and post-acquisition evidence establishes that ENH exercised its enhanced post-merger market power to obtain price increases significantly above its pre-merger prices and substantially larger than price increases obtained by other comparison hospitals. As a result of the elimination of Highland Park as a competitor, Respondent was able to convert existing price methodologies to managed care organizations to much more favorable post-merger terms than either Evanston or Highland Park could have achieved alone. The evidence further shows that Respondent, in 2002 and 2003, continued to unilaterally raise rates in its charge master, which significantly increased the prices paid by managed care organizations for ENH services. The empirical evidence presented by Complaint Counsel's expert ruled out explanations for the price increases other than market power.

Complaint Counsel's expert compared price increases implemented by ENH post-merger to price increases implemented by other hospitals in her control groups and found that, across all managed care plans, ENH's price increases exceeded the control groups by 11 to 18%, *i.e.*, if other hospitals raised their prices by 10%, ENH raised its prices by 21 to 28%. Even under Respondent's expert's calculations, ENH's post-merger price increases were 9 to 10% higher than price increases by hospitals in his control groups. This evidence confirms the predictive assessments made by the structural market analysis of market concentration.

The evidence presented by Respondent fails to rebut the government's prima facie case. Upon review, the Court has determined that Respondent's learning about demand theory [*i.e.*, that Evanston learned in the due diligence process that some of its contracts were below market] is flawed, is inconsistent with Respondent's contemporaneous actions, and is based upon unreliable empirical analysis. In addition, Respondent's few merger specific improvements to Highland Park do not constitute a sufficiently procompetitive justification to outweigh the competitive harm resulting from the merger. Thus, neither of Respondent's main defenses, the learning about demand theory, nor the quality of care improvements argument, justify the substantial post-merger price increases to managed care organizations and, ultimately, consumers. Respondent's other defenses, its nonprofit status, ease of entry, and that Highland Park was a failing firm, and Respondent's affirmative defense that Evanston and Highland Park were already a single entity at the time of the merger are similarly unpersuasive. The only viable explanation for Respondent's anticompetitive prices is that the merger, through elimination of a competitor, enhanced ENH's market power.

Complaint Counsel proved that the challenged merger has substantially lessened competition in the product market of general acute inpatient services and in the geographic market of the seven hospitals described above. Therefore, Complaint Counsel has established a violation of Section 7 of the Clayton Act under Count I of the Complaint. Count II of the Complaint, an alternate pleading, is not dispositive and therefore dismissed as moot.

The appropriate remedy for the violation is full divestiture of Highland Park from ENH, which, with ancillary relief, is specified more fully in the attached Order. This is the most effective remedy to restore competition to that which would have existed without the merger and which is necessary and in the public interest to eliminate the ill effects of the acquisition offensive to the statute. * * *

§ 8.37 Section 12, Mergers of Competing Buyers, "Monopsony," of the 2010 DOJ/FTC Guidelines

12. Mergers of Competing Buyers

Mergers of competing buyers can enhance market power on the buying side of the market, just as mergers of competing sellers can enhance market power on the selling side of the market. Buyer market power is sometimes called "monopsony power."

To evaluate whether a merger is likely to enhance market power on the buying side of the market, the Agencies employ essentially the framework described above for evaluating whether a merger is likely to enhance market power on the selling side of the market. In defining relevant markets, the Agencies focus on the alternatives available to sellers in the face of a decrease in the price paid by a hypothetical monopsonist.

Market power on the buying side of the market is not a significant concern if suppliers have numerous attractive outlets for their goods or services. However, when that is not the case, the Agencies may conclude that the merger of competing buyers is likely to lessen competition in a manner harmful to sellers. * * *

§ 8.38 Section 13, Partial Acquisitions, of the 2010 DOJ/FTC Guidelines

13. Partial Acquisitions

In most horizontal mergers, two competitors come under common ownership and control, completely and permanently eliminating competition between them. This elimination of competition is a basic element of merger analysis. However, the statutory provisions referenced in Section 1 also apply to one firm's partial acquisition of a competitor. The Agencies therefore also review acquisitions of minority positions involving competing firms, even if such minority positions do not necessarily or completely eliminate competition between the parties to the transaction.

When the Agencies determine that a partial acquisition results in effective control of the target firm, or involves substantially all of the relevant assets of the target firm, they analyze the transaction much as they do a merger. Partial acquisitions that do not result in effective control may nevertheless present significant competitive concerns and may require a somewhat distinct analysis from that applied to full mergers or to acquisitions involving effective control. The details of the post-acquisition relationship between the parties, and how those details are likely to affect competition, can be important. While the Agencies will consider any way in which a partial acquisition may affect competition, they generally focus on three principal effects.

First, a partial acquisition can lessen competition by giving the acquiring firm the ability to influence the competitive conduct of the target firm. * * *

Second, a partial acquisition can lessen competition by reducing the incentive of the acquiring firm to compete. * * *

Third, a partial acquisition can lessen competition by giving the acquiring firm access to non-public, competitively sensitive information from the target firm. * * *

Part IV
DOJ Guidelines for Conglomerate and Vertical Mergers

§ 8.39 1984 Justice Department Guidelines on Conglomerate Mergers

A. Introduction

The 1992 DOJ/FTC Horizontal Merger Guidelines did not replace the conglomerate and vertical provisions of the 1984 DOJ Merger Guidelines, which continue to apply.

B. Section 4 Horizontal Effect from Non-Horizontal Mergers

4. HORIZONTAL EFFECT FROM NON-HORIZONTAL MERGERS

4.0 By definition, non-horizontal mergers involve firms that do not operate in the same market. It necessarily follows that such mergers produce no immediate change in the level of concentration in any relevant market as defined in Section 2 of these Guidelines. Although non-horizontal mergers are less likely than horizontal mergers to create competitive problems, they are invariably innocuous. This section introduces the principal theories under which the Department is likely to challenge non-horizontal mergers.

4.1 Elimination of Specific Potential Entrants.

4.11 The Theory of Potential Competition. In some circumstances, the non-horizontal merger[38] of a firm already in a market (the "acquired firm") with a potential entrant to

38. Under traditional usage, such a merger could be characterized as either "vertical" or "conglomerate," but the label adds nothing to the analysis.

that market (the "acquiring firm") may adversely affect competition in the market. If the merger effectively removes the acquiring firm from the edge of the market, it could have either of the following effects:

4.111 Harm to "Perceived Potential Competition." By eliminating a significant present competitive threat that constrains the behavior of the firms already in the market, the merger could result in an immediate deterioration in market performance. The economic theory of limiting pricing suggests that monopolists and groups of colluding firms may find it profitable to restrain their pricing in order to deter new entry that is likely to push prices even lower by adding capacity to the market. If the acquiring firm had unique advantages in entering the market, the firms in the market might be able to set a new and higher price after the threat of entry by the acquiring firm was eliminated by the merger.

4.112 Harm to "Actual Potential Competition." By eliminating the possibility of entry by the acquiring firm in a more procompetitive manner, the merger could result in a lost opportunity for improvement in market performance resulting from the addition of a significant competitor. The more procompetitive alternatives include both new entry and entry through a "toehold" acquisition of a present small competitor. * * *

§ 8.40 1984 Justice Department Guidelines on Vertical Mergers

Section 4.2 Competitive Problems from Vertical Mergers

4.2 Competitive Problems from Vertical Mergers

4.21 Barriers to Entry from Vertical Mergers. In certain circumstances, the vertical integration resulting from vertical mergers could create competitively objectionable barriers to entry. Stated generally, three conditions are necessary (but not sufficient) for this problem to exist. First, the degree of vertical integration between the two markets must be so extensive that entrants to one market (the "primary market") also would have to enter the other market (the "secondary market") simultaneously. Second, the requirement of entry at the secondary level must make entry at the primary level significantly more difficult and less likely to occur. Finally, the structure and other characteristics of the primary market must be otherwise so conducive to non-competitive performance that the increased difficulty of entry is likely to affect its performance. * * *

Part V
Competitor and Target Standing under Section 7

§ 8.41 Competitor's Standing to Challenge Acquisition under Section 7

Cargill, Inc. v. Monfort of Colorado, Inc.

Supreme Court of United States, 1986 479 U.S. 104

Justice Brennan delivered the opinion of the Court.

Under § 16 of the Clayton Act, private parties "threatened [with] loss or damage by a violation of the antitrust laws" may seek injunctive relief. This case presents two questions: whether a plaintiff seeking relief under § 16 must prove a threat of antitrust injury, and, if so, whether loss or damage due to increased competition constitutes such injury.

[**Facts**] Respondent Monfort of Colorado, Inc. (Monfort), the plaintiff below, owns and operates three integrated beef-packing plants, that is, plants for both the slaughter of cattle and the fabrication of beef. Monfort operates in both the market for fed cattle (the input market) and the market for fabricated beef (the output market). These markets are highly competitive, and the profit margins of the major beef packers are low. The current markets are a product of two decades of intense competition, during which time packers with modern integrated plants have gradually displaced packers with separate slaughter and fabrication plants.

Monfort is the country's fifth-largest beef packer. Petitioner Excel Corporation (Excel), one of the two defendants below, is the second-largest packer. Excel operates five integrated plants and one fabrication plant. It is a wholly owned subsidiary of Cargill, Inc., the other defendant below, a large privately owned corporation with more than 150 subsidiaries in at least 35 countries.

On June 17, 1983, Excel signed an agreement to acquire the third-largest packer in the market, Spencer Beef, a division of the Land O'Lakes agricultural cooperative. Spencer Beef owned two integrated plants and one slaughtering plant. After the acquisition, Excel would still be the second-largest packer, but would command a market share almost equal to that of the largest packer, IBP, Inc. (IBP).

[**Issue**] Monfort brought an action under § 16 of the Clayton Act, to enjoin the prospective merger. Its complaint alleged that the acquisition would "violat[e] Section 7 of the Clayton Act because the effect of the proposed acquisition may be substantially to lessen competition or tend to create a monopoly in several different ways...." Monfort described the injury that it allegedly would suffer in this way:

> "(f) *Impairment of plaintiff's ability to compete.* The proposed acquisition will result in a concentration of economic power in the relevant markets which threatens Monfort's supply of fed cattle and its ability to compete in the boxed beef market." * * *

Excel moved for involuntary dismissal on the ground, *inter alia*, that Monfort had failed to allege or show that it would suffer antitrust injury as defined in *Brunswick Corp. v. Pueblo Bowl-O-Mat, Inc.*, 429 U.S. 477, (1977). * * *

This case requires us to decide, at the outset, a question we have not previously addressed: whether a private plaintiff seeking an injunction under § 16 of the Clayton Act must show a threat of antitrust injury. To decide the question, we must look first to the source of the antitrust injury requirement, which lies in a related provision of the Clayton Act, § 4, 15 U.S.C. § 15.

[**Analysis**] Like § 16, § 4 provides a vehicle for private enforcement of the antitrust laws. Under § 4, "any person who shall be injured in his business or property by reason of anything forbidden in the antitrust laws may sue therefore in any district court of the United States..., and shall recover threefold the damages by him sustained, and the cost of suit, including a reasonable attorney's fee." In *Brunswick Corp. v. Pueblo Bowl-O-Mat, Inc., supra*, we held that plaintiffs seeking treble damages under § 4 must show more than simply an "injury causally linked" to a particular merger; instead, "plaintiffs must prove antitrust injury, which is to say injury of the type the antitrust laws were intended to prevent and that flows from that which makes the defendants' acts unlawful." * * * It is plain that § 16 and § 4 do differ in various ways. * * * Section 16 requires a showing only of "threatened" loss or damage; similarly, § 4 requires a showing of injury to "business or property," while § 16 contains no such limitation. Although these differences do affect the nature of the injury cognizable under each section, the lower courts, including the courts below, have found that under both § 16 and § 4 the plaintiff must still allege an injury of the type the antitrust laws were designed to prevent. We agree.

[However,] the wording concerning the relationship of the injury to the violation of the antitrust laws in each section is comparable. Section 4 requires proof of injury "by reason of anything forbidden in the antitrust laws"; § 16 requires proof of "threatened loss or damage by a violation of the antitrust laws." * * *

Sections 4 and 16 are thus best understood as providing complementary remedies for a single set of injuries. Accordingly, we conclude that in order to seek injunctive relief under § 16, a private plaintiff must allege threatened loss or damage "of the type the antitrust laws were designed to prevent and that flows from that which makes defendants' acts unlawful." *Brunswick*, 429 U.S., at 489. We therefore turn to the question whether the proposed merger in this case threatened respondent with antitrust injury.

Initially, we confront the problem of determining what Monfort alleged the source of its injury to be. Monfort's complaint is of little assistance in this regard, since the injury alleged therein "an impairment of plaintiff's ability to compete" is alleged to result from "a concentration of economic power." * * *

[T]wo theories of injury to Monfort emerge: (1) a threat of a loss of profits stemming from the possibility that Excel, after the merger, would lower its prices to a level at or only slightly above its costs; (2) a threat of being driven out of business by the possibility that Excel, after the merger, would lower its prices to a level below its costs. * * *

We hold that a plaintiff seeking injunctive relief under § 16 of the Clayton Act must show a threat of antitrust injury, and that a showing of loss or damage due merely to increased competition does not constitute such injury. The record below does not support a finding of antitrust injury, but only of threatened loss from increased competition. Because respondent has therefore failed to make the showing § 16 requires, we need not reach the question whether the proposed merger violates § 7. * * *

§ 8.42 Target's Standing to Challenge Acquisition under Section 7

Anago, Inc. v. Tecnol Medical Products, Inc.

United States Court of Appeals, Fifth Circuit, (1992) 976 F.2d 248

Duhé, Circuit Judge:

Plaintiff-Appellant Anago, Inc. seeks review of the district court's denial of its request for a preliminary injunction under section 16 of the Clayton Act. Because we find that Anago has failed to allege an antitrust injury, we affirm.

[**Facts**] For the purposes of this appeal, the facts are undisputed. Anago and Tecnol both make disposable hospital supplies. * * *

In 1991, Tecnol began efforts to buy Anago, and eventually succeeded in purchasing all of Anago's preferred stock. After reaching agreements to purchase the common stock of several Anago shareholders, Tecnol publicly proposed a friendly merger. Anago immediately sued Tecnol for violations of the Williams Act, and moved for a preliminary injunction under the Clayton Act, 15 U.S.C.A. § 26 (Supp.1992). * * *

[**Analysis**] A plaintiff may seek either damages or injunctive relief for violations of the Clayton Act. 15 U.S.C.A. § 15, § 26. It must, however, prove that it has or will suffer an antitrust injury. *Cargill, Inc. v. Monfort of Colorado, Inc.*, [Section 8.41] The sole issue we face in this appeal is whether Anago, a target company, has alleged an antitrust injury.

The Supreme Court has defined antitrust injury as an injury "of the type the antitrust laws were intended to prevent and that flows from that which makes defendants' acts unlawful." As the Court explained in *Brunswick*, "The injury should reflect the anticompetitive effect either of the violation or of the anticompetitive acts made possible by the violation." *Brunswick*, 429 U.S. at 489, 97 S.Ct. at 697. Typical anticompetitive effects include increased prices and decreased output. This circuit has narrowly interpreted the meaning of antitrust injury, excluding from it the threat of decreased competition.

Before *Cargill* was announced, courts often granted target companies injunctions in the face of antitrust violations. * * *

In light of *Cargill*'s explicit antitrust injury requirement some courts have grown reluctant to grant injunctions to target companies. * * * The Second Circuit, in contrast, has not changed its position since the Supreme Court's decision. *Consolidated Gold Fields P.L.C. v. Minorco, S.A.*, 871 F.2d 252 (2nd Cir. 1989), *cert. dismissed*, 492 U.S. 939, 110 S.Ct. 29, 106 L.Ed.2d 639 (1989).

In *Gold Fields*, the Second Circuit addressed a situation almost identical to the case at hand. There, a target company, among others, sued to enjoin a takeover attempt. The target alleged that the takeover would destroy its ability to compete independently in the market. The Second Circuit reversed the district court's denial of the preliminary injunction. It reasoned:

> Surely Gold Fields' loss of independence is causally related to the injury occurring in the market place, where acquisition threatens to diminish competitive forces ... It is hard to imagine an injury to competition more clearly "of the type the antitrust laws were intended to prevent," than the elimination of a major competitor's power to determine its prices and output.

Id. at 258 (citation omitted).

Anago offered evidence that a takeover will dramatically decrease competition and raise prices in the American market. Anago also offered proof that it will lose its power of independent decision making should Tecnol buy its operations. Relying on *Gold Fields*, it argues that this showing is sufficient to establish an antitrust injury. If we were inclined to follow *Gold Fields*, we would agree. We prefer, however, to adhere to the line of cases predating *Cargill* that require antitrust injury, *see, e.g., Carter Hawley Hale Stores, Inc. v. Limited, Inc.*, 587 F.Supp. 246, 250 (C.D.Cal. 1984), and those cases postdating *Cargill* that narrowly interpret the meaning of antitrust injury. *See, e.g., Burlington Indus. Inc. v. Edelman*, 666 F.Supp. 799, 805–06 (M.D.N.C. 1987).

First, we are concerned that the Second Circuit's emphasis on a causal relationship between the loss of independence and the alleged antitrust violation does not comport with Supreme Court precedent. As the Court has stated, a plaintiff "must prove more than injury causally linked to an illegal presence in the market." *Brunswick*, 429 U.S. at 489, 97 S.Ct. at 697.

Second, we are not convinced, as is the Second Circuit, that the loss of independent decision making is the type of injury meant to be prevented by the antitrust laws. As we have stated, this court narrowly construes the meaning of antitrust injury. * * *

Proof that a plaintiff will be adversely affected by the merger itself will not suffice in this Court, unless the injuries are related to the anticompetitive effects of the merger. Although Anago presented evidence that the merger will have anticompetitive effects, such as higher prices and decreased competition, it did not show that either of these effects will cause its injury. In fact, Anago will suffer a loss of independence whether or not its takeover violates antitrust principles. Moreover, once the takeover is complete, Anago and its shareholders are likely to benefit from any increased prices or decreased competition that might result.

Because Anago's alleged injury is not "of the type the antitrust laws were intended to prevent," the order of the district court denying Anago's request for injunction relief is AFFIRMED.

References

ABA Mergers and Acquisitions, supra Section 1.10.

ABA The Merger Review Process, supra Section 1.10.

Areeda and Turner, *Antitrust, supra* Section 1.10.

Hoevenkamp, *Antitrust Policy, supra* Section 1.10.

Sullivan and Grimes, *Antitrust, supra* Section 1.10.

Thompson, *A Practitioner's Guide to Understanding the Microeconomics of Federal and State, supra* Section 8.10.

Thompson, *Mergers, Acquisitions and Tender Offers, supra* Section 1.10, Chapter 12.

Chapter 9

Hart-Scott-Rodino Pre-Merger Notification

§ 9.1 Scope

This chapter examines the pre-merger notification requirements under the Hart-Scott-Rodino Act (HSR), Section 7A of the Clayton Act, 15 USC § 18a. The rules under the Act are set out in 16 CFR § 801.1 et seq. Under HSR, before consummating certain mergers or acquisitions, the parties are required to file with the Federal Trade Commission (FTC) and the Antitrust Division of the Department of Justice (DOJ) certain information designed to permit the appropriate agency to properly examine the acquisition under the antitrust laws. Even if a transaction is below the threshold for HSR, there is no prohibition against an antitrust challenge. Although the Notification Form is filed with both agencies, only one of the agencies examines the particular acquisition, generally the agency with the greatest experience with the industry. The rules under HSR are quite voluminous, and the focus in this chapter is on those provisions that have general applicability. The materials in this chapter are covered in greater detail in Chapter 13 of Thompson, *Mergers, Acquisitions and Tender Offers*, *supra* Section 1.10.

Section 9.2 contains an introductory problem; Section 9.3 provides an introduction to HSR; and Section 9.4 sets forth an introduction to the 2000 amendments to the Act. Section 9.5 gives a statistical profile of activity under the Act during 2013. Section 9.6 sets out most of the statutory provisions as amended in 2000 and also discusses the annual adjustments that are required to be made to the thresholds and filing fees. Section 9.7 provides a guide to understanding the very complicated rules under HSR; selected HSR rules and selected provisions of the Instructions to the Notification Report Form are set out in *M&A Statutes, Rules, and Documents*, *supra* Section 1.1. The rules and Instructions to the form should be studied carefully in conjunction with the study of the guide in Section 9.7. Section 9.8 discusses the penalty provisions, and Section 9.9 provides summary problems. Section 9.10 deals with the role of state attorneys general under HSR. Section 9.11 discusses provisions commonly found in merger agreements relating to the antitrust clearance of the transaction, and Section 9.12 addresses the antitrust risk in exchanging competitively sensitive information during the due diligence process and post signing period. The HSR rules relating to foreign acquisitions are set out in Section 26.7.

§ 9.2 Introductory Problem on Hart-Scott-Rodino Pre-Merger Notification

On March 1, 2014, Time, Inc., and Warner Communications, Inc. both publicly-held Delaware corporations, enter into a merger agreement, pursuant to which Time will acquire Warner in a reverse subsidiary merger in exchange for Time common stock with a value of $2 billion. Time and Warner also enter into a Share Exchange Agreement pursuant to which, upon the happening of certain events, such as a hostile tender offer by a third party for either Time or Warner, Time would acquire, in exchange for 12% of its shares, 10% of Warner's shares.

Chris Craft, Inc., which owns 6% of the stock of Warner with a value of $220 million, is the largest shareholder of Warner and is Warner's only shareholder that is holding for other than purely investment reasons. Also, Warner owns 25% of the stock of BHC, Inc., with a value of $200 million. Ten days after entering into the Merger Agreement and Share Exchange Agreement, Paramount Communications Inc., a publicly-held Delaware corporation, makes a cash tender offer for any and all of Time's common shares at $175 per share. The aggregate value of the offer is $1.8 billion.

(1) What are the HSR filing and waiting period requirements with regard to the Time-Warner Merger Agreement?

(2) What is the treatment of Chris Craft under HSR?

(3) What is the treatment of BHC under HSR?

(4) Can the exchange of shares pursuant to the Share Exchange Agreement be implemented immediately upon the occurrence of the Paramount tender offer for Time?

(5) What are the HSR filing and waiting period requirements with regard to Paramount's tender offer for Time?

§ 9.3 Statement of Basis and Purpose of the Original Rules

Federal Trade Commission, Pre-Merger Notification; Reporting and Waiting Period Requirements

Federal Register, (July 31, 1978) part ii, pp. 33450

On September 30, 1976, President Gerald Ford signed into law the Hart-Scott-Rodino Antitrust Improvements Act of 1976. Section 201 of that statute added a new section 7A to the Clayton Act, (referred to in this Statement of Basis and Purpose as the act), relating to pre-merger notification.

The act creates a requirement that "persons" of specified size or larger, [*i.e.*, the size of person test], which intend to make voting securities or asset acquisitions of specified size or larger, [*i.e.*, the size of transaction test], must report their intentions in advance and provide information relevant to the transaction to the Antitrust Division of the Department of Justice and to the Federal Trade Commission. After reporting, those persons must wait a prescribed period of time before consummating the reported transaction. That waiting period may be extended by either enforcement agency by means of a request for additional information or documentary material. The act also contains 11 specific types of exemptions, along with a grant of rulemaking authority to define any terms used in the act, to create additional exemptions, and generally to carry out the purposes of the act.

The act provides for expedited consideration by a Federal district court in the event that either agency seeks a preliminary injunction to prevent consummation of an acquisition. It also contains penalty and enforcement provisions, a requirement that information filed by reporting persons not be made public except under certain circumstances, provisions clarifying the relationship between the act and certain substantive and procedural aspects of other antitrust laws, and the requirement of an annual report to the Congress. * * *

§9.4 Introduction to 2000 Amendments to the Act and 2001 Interim Rules

Pre-Merger Notification; Reporting and Waiting Period Requirements and Rules of Practice

Federal Register: (February 1, 2001)

Background. * * * The 2000 Amendments are the first significant changes to Section 7A since the passage of the HSR Act in 1976. These changes include: An increase in the size-of-transaction threshold to $50 million (in place of the previous $15 million threshold). Elimination of the 15 percent size-of-transaction threshold. Reportability of transactions valued at greater than $200 million without regard to "size-of-person." The current size-of-person test will continue in place for transactions valued between $50 million and $200 million. Adjustment to the size-of-transaction threshold each fiscal year, beginning with FY 2005, for changes in GNP during the previous year. * * *

Extension of the waiting period that follows substantial compliance with requests for additional information and documentary material to 30 days for most transactions. The 10-day post-compliance period for cash tender offers (and bankruptcy transactions) is not changed.

The end of any waiting period that would be on a Saturday, Sunday or legal public holiday shall be the next regular business day. * * *

§9.5 Background on the Act and Statistical Profile of the HSR Program in Fiscal 2012

FTC and DOJ Annual Report to Congress on HSR for Fiscal Year 2012

[*i.e.*, Oct. 1, 2012 to Sept. 30, 2013]

(February 2014)

The appendices to this report * * * [show] that the number of transactions reported in fiscal year 2012 decreased 1.4% from the number of transactions reported in fiscal year 2011. In fiscal year 2012, 1,429 transactions were reported, while 1,450 were reported in fiscal year 2011. The statistics in Appendix A also show that the number of merger investigations in which second requests were issued in fiscal year 2012 decreased 10.9% from the number of merger investigations in which second requests were issued in fiscal year 2011. Second requests were issued in 49 merger investigations in fiscal year 2012 (20 issued by the FTC and 29 issued by the Division). * * *

During fiscal year 2012, the Commission brought 25 merger enforcement actions, including three in which the Commission initiated administrative litigation; 15 in which it accepted consent orders for public comment, 14 of which resulted in final orders (with one still pending), and seven in which the transactions were abandoned or restructured as a result of antitrust concerns raised during the investigation. These enforcement actions preserved competition in numerous sectors of the economy, including pharmaceuticals, hospital and other health care providers, industrial and high tech goods, energy, and retailing. In two of the cases in which the Commission issued administrative complaints, the Commission sought preliminary injunctions in federal district court to enjoin the acquisitions pending resolution of the Commission's administrative litigation. * * *

During fiscal year 2012, the Antitrust Division challenged 19 merger transactions that it concluded might have substantially lessened competition if allowed to proceed as proposed. In eight of these challenges, the Antitrust Division filed a complaint in U.S. district court. In all eight court challenges, the parties filed settlement papers simultaneously with the complaint. Seven of these court challenges were ultimately settled by consent decree, and in the other court challenge, the parties abandoned the transaction and the Division filed a notice with the court withdrawing the complaint and proposed settlement. In the eleven challenges in which the Antitrust Division did not file a complaint during fiscal year 2012, when apprised of the Division's concerns regarding their proposed transactions, the parties in six instances abandoned the proposed transaction, in two instances restructured the proposed transaction and in three instances changed their conduct to avoid competitive problems, thus resolving the Division's concerns. * * *

§9.6 Section 7A of the Clayton Act as Amended December 21, 2000 and Adjusted Thresholds

A. The Statute

Sec. 7A. (a) [**Affected Transactions**] Except as exempted pursuant to subsection (c), no person shall acquire, directly or indirectly, any voting securities or assets of any other person, unless both persons (or in the case of a tender offer, the acquiring person) file notification pursuant to rules under subsection (d)(1) and the waiting period described in subsection (b)(1) has expired, if—

(1) the acquiring person, or the person whose voting securities or assets are being acquired, is engaged in commerce or in any activity affecting commerce; and

(2) as a result of such acquisition, the acquiring person would hold an aggregate total amount of the voting securities and assets of the acquired person-

(A) in excess of $200,000,000 (as adjusted and published for each fiscal year beginning after September 30, 2004, in the same manner as provided in section 8(a)(5) to reflect the percentage change in the gross national product for such fiscal year compared to the gross national product for the year ending September 30, 2003); or

(B) (i) in excess of $50,000,000 (as so adjusted and published) but not in excess of $200,000,000 (as so adjusted and published); and

(ii) (I) any voting securities or assets of a person engaged in manufacturing which has annual net sales or total assets of $10,000,000 (as so adjusted and published) or more are being acquired by any person which has total assets or annual net sales of $100,000,000 (as so adjusted and published) or more;

(II) any voting securities or assets of a person not engaged in manufacturing which has total assets of $10,000,000 (as so adjusted and published) or more are being acquired by any person which has total assets or annual net sales of $100,000,000 (as so adjusted and published) or more; or

(III) any voting securities or assets of a person with annual net sales or total assets of $100,000,000 (as so adjusted and published) or more are being acquired by any person with total assets or annual net sales of $10,000,000 (as so adjusted and published) or more.

In the case of a tender offer, the person whose voting securities are sought to be acquired by a person required to file notification under this subsection shall file notification pursuant to rules under subsection (d).

(b)

(1) [**Waiting Periods**] The waiting period required under subsection (a) shall—

(A) begin on the date of the receipt by the Federal Trade Commission and the Assistant Attorney General in charge of the Antitrust Division of the Department of Justice (hereinafter referred to in this section as the "Assistant Attorney General") of—

(i) the completed notification required under subsection (a), or

(ii) if such notification is not completed, the notification to the extent completed and a statement of the reasons for such noncompliance, from both persons, or, in the case of a tender offer, the acquiring person; and

(B) end on the thirtieth day after the date of such receipt (or in the case of a cash tender offer, the fifteenth day), or on such later date as may be set under subsection (e)(2) or (g)(2).

(2) [**Early Termination**] The Federal Trade Commission and the Assistant Attorney General may, in individual cases, terminate the waiting period specified in paragraph (1) and allow any person to proceed with any acquisition subject to this section, and promptly shall cause to be published in the Federal Register a notice that neither intends to take any action within such period with respect to such acquisition.

(3) [**Definitions**] As used in this section—

(A) The term "voting securities" mean any securities which at present or upon conversion entitle the owner or holder thereof to vote for the election of directors of the issuer or, with respect to unincorporated issuers, persons exercising similar functions.

(B) The amount or percentage of voting securities or assets of a person which are acquired or held by another person shall be determined by aggregating the amount or percentage of such voting securities or assets held or acquired by such other person and each affiliate thereof.

(c) [**Exemptions**] The following classes of transactions are exempt from the requirements of this section—

(1) acquisitions of goods or realty transferred in the ordinary course of business; * * *

(3) acquisitions of voting securities of an issuer at least 50 per centum of the voting securities of which are owned by the acquiring person prior to such acquisition; * * *

(6) transactions specifically exempted from the antitrust laws by Federal statute if approved by a Federal agency, if copies of all information and documentary material filed with such agency are contemporaneously filed with the Federal Trade Commission and the Assistant Attorney General; * * *

(9) acquisitions, solely for the purpose of investment, or voting securities, if, as a result of such acquisition, the securities acquired or held do not exceed 10 per centum of the outstanding voting securities of the issuer; * * *

(d) [**The Form**] The Federal Trade Commission, with the concurrence of the Assistant Attorney General and by rule in accordance with section 553 of title 5, United States Code, consistent with the purposes of this section—

(1) shall require that the notification required under subsection (a) be in such form and contain such documentary material and information relevant to a proposed acquisition as is necessary and appropriate to enable the Federal Trade Commission and the Assistant Attorney General to determine whether such acquisition may, if consummated, violate the antitrust laws; and

(2) may—

(A) define the terms used in this section;

(B) exempt, from the requirements of this section, classes of persons, acquisitions, transfers, or transactions which are not likely to violate the antitrust laws; and

(C) prescribe such other rules as may be necessary and appropriate to carry out the purposes of this section.

(e) [**Second Requests**]

(1) (A) The Federal Trade Commission or the Assistant Attorney General may, prior to the expiration of the 30-day waiting period (or in the case of a cash tender offer, the 15-day waiting period) specified in subsection (b)(1) of this section, require the submission of additional information or documentary material relevant to the proposed acquisition, from a person required to file notification with respect to such acquisition under subsection (a) of this section prior to the expiration of the waiting period specified in subsection (b)(1) of this section, or from any officer, director, partner, agent, or employee of such person.

(B) (i) The Assistant Attorney General and the Federal Trade Commission shall each designate a senior official who does not have direct responsibility for the review of any enforcement recommendation under this section concerning the transaction at issue, to hear any petition filed by such person to determine—

(I) whether the request for additional information or documentary material is unreasonably cumulative, unduly burdensome, or duplicative; or

(II) whether the request for additional information or documentary material has been substantially complied with by the petitioning person. * * *

(2) [**Extension of Second Requests**] The Federal Trade Commission or the Assistant Attorney General, in its or his discretion, may extend the 30-day waiting period (or in the case of a cash tender offer, the 15-day waiting period) specified in subsection (b)(1) of this section for an additional period of not more than 30 days (or in the case of a cash tender offer, 10 days) after the date on which the Federal Trade Commission or the Assistant Attorney General, as the case may be, receives from any person to whom a request is made under paragraph (1), or in the case of tender offers, the acquiring person, (A) all the information and documentary material required to be submitted pursuant to such a request, or (B) if such request is not fully complied with, the information and documentary material submitted and a statement of the reasons for such noncompliance. Such additional period may be further extended only by the United States district court, upon an application by the Federal Trade Commission or the Assistant Attorney General pursuant to subsection (g)(2).

(f) [**Enforcement Actions**] If a proceeding is instituted or an action is filed by the Federal Trade Commission, alleging that a proposed acquisition violates section 7 of this Act or section 5 of the Federal Trade Commission Act, or an action is filed by the United States, alleging that a proposed acquisition violates such section 7 or section 1 or 2 of the Sherman Act, and the Federal Trade Commission or the Assistant Attorney General (1) files a motion for a preliminary injunction against consummation of such acquisition pendente lite, and (2) certifies the United States district court for the judicial district within which the respondent resides or carries on business, or in which the action is brought, that it or he believes that the public interest requires relief pendente lite pursuant to this subsection, then upon the filing of such motion and certification, the chief judge of such district court shall immediately notify the chief judge of the United States court of appeals for the circuit in which such district court is located, who shall designate a United States district judge to whom such action shall be assigned for all purposes.

(g) [**Penalties**]

(1) Any person, or any officer, director, or partner thereof, who fails to comply with any provision of this section shall be liable to the United States for a civil penalty of not more than $10,000 for each day during which such person is in violation of this section. Such penalty may be recovered in a civil action brought by the United States. [Under the terms of the Act of April 26, 1996, Public Law 104–134, 110 Stat. 1321, Sec. 31001(s), and a conforming Federal Trade Commission regulation, the penalty is adjusted according to the cost of living approximately every four years] * * *

(h) [**Confidentiality**] Any information or documentary material filed with the Assistant Attorney General or the Federal Trade Commission pursuant to this section shall be exempt from the disclosure under section 552 of title 5, United States Code. * * *

(i) [**No Limitations**]

(1) Any action taken by the Federal Trade Commission or the Assistant Attorney General or any failure of the Federal Trade Commission or the Assistant Attorney General to take any action under this section shall not bar any proceeding or any action with respect to such acquisition at any time under any other section of this Act or any other provision of law. * * *

(k) [**End of Time Periods**] If the end of any period of time provided in this section falls on a Saturday, Sunday, or legal public holiday (as defined in section 6103(a) of title 5 of the United States Code), then such period shall be extended to the end of the next day that is not a Saturday, Sunday, or legal public holiday.

[**Provision of Related Law Prescribing Filing Fees**]

(a) [T]he Federal Trade Commission shall assess and collect filing fees established in subsection (b) which shall be paid by persons acquiring voting securities or assets who are required to file pre-merger notifications by section 7A of the Clayton Act (15 U.S.C. 18a) and the regulations promulgated thereunder. * * *

(b) The filing fees referred to in subsection (a) are—

(1) $45,000 if the aggregate total amount determined under section 7A(a)(2) of the Clayton Act (15 U.S.C. 18a(a)(2)) is less than $100,000,000 (as adjusted and published for each fiscal year beginning after September 30, 2004, in the same manner as provided in section 8(a)(5) of the Clayton Act (15 U.S.C. 19(a)(5)) to reflect the percentage change in the gross national product for such fiscal year compared to the gross national product for the year ending September 30, 2003) [as of February 2014, this $45,000 fee applied to acquisitions valued at $75.9 million but less than $151.7 million];

(2) $125,000 if the aggregate total amount determined under section 7A(a)(2) of the Clayton Act (15 U.S.C. 18a(a)(2)) is not less than $100,000,000 (as so adjusted and published) but less than $500,000,000 (as so adjusted and published) [as of February 2014, this $125,000 fee applied to acquisitions valued at $151.7 million or greater but less than $758.6 million]; and

(3) $280,000 if the aggregate total amount determined under section 7A(a)(2) of the Clayton Act (15 U.S.C. 18a(a)(2)) is not less than $500,000,000 (as so adjusted and published) [as of February 2014, this $280.000 fee applied to acquisitions valued at $758.6 million or greater].

B. Adjusted Thresholds Including Filing Fees

Introduction of Adjusted Jurisdictional Thresholds

70 FR 4987 (January 31, 2005)

Statement of Basis and Purpose. The 2000 amendments to Section 7A require the Commission to revise the Act's jurisdictional and filing fee thresholds annually, based on the change in gross national product, in accordance with Section 8(a)(5) for each fiscal year beginning after September 30, 2004. The Commission, with the concurrence of the Assistant Attorney General, is adopting these final rules to reflect the revised thresholds in the examples contained in the rules and to provide a method for future adjustments as required by the 2000 amendments. * * *

Note

Under the above adjustments as applicable on February 24, 2014, an acquisition was not potentially reportable unless it was above $75.9 million rather than the original $50 million, and an acquisition was not automatically reportable unless it was above $304.4 million rather than the original $200 million. The thresholds are amended each February.

§9.7 A Guide to the Pre-Merger Notification Rules under Hart-Scott-Rodino[1]

A. Introduction

This is a guide to pre-merger notification under Hart-Scott-Rodino (HSR or the Act) and the rules promulgated thereunder by the Federal Trade Commission (FTC). Section 9.7.B considers the impact of HSR in the pre-filing period. The principal consideration here is determining whether the parties are required to file under HSR. Section 9.7.C deals with the preparation of the report form. Section 9.7.D considers the impact of HSR in the post-filing period. That section considers, among other things, the waiting period that applies to the particular filing.

In reading the guide, the reader should also study the particular rules discussed. The rules and the Instructions to the Report Form are set out in *M&A Statutes, Rules, and Documents*, *supra* Section 1.1.

1. This is a modification of the descriptive portions of a Report by Samuel C. Thompson, Jr., prepared for the FTC's Pre-merger Notification Office, entitled *Evaluation of Pre-merger Notification Program* (May 1981).

B. Impact of HSR in Pre-Filing Period

1. Description of the Period

At this stage of an acquisition transaction, the target has been identified and the transaction is being structured. The terms of the transaction are being negotiated or the tender offer is being planned.

The first step is to determine whether the reporting requirements under HSR apply. This requires an analysis of the rules.

2. Determining the Acquiring and Acquired Persons

a. General Principles

The first step in determining whether HSR applies is to identify the "Acquiring Person" and the "Acquired Person" under "Section 801.2 of the rules."[2] This requires reference to the various defined terms and rules discussed below.

The term "*person*" is defined as the "*ultimate parent entity* [UPE] and all *entities* which it *controls* directly or indirectly."[3] "*Entity*" is defined as "any natural person, corporation, company, partnership, joint venture * * *."[4]

An "ultimate parent entity" (UPE) is "an entity which is not controlled by any other entity."[5] The term control is defined as:

(1) Either,

(i) Holding 50 percent or more of the outstanding voting securities of an issuer; or

(ii) In the case of an entity that has no outstanding voting securities, having the right to 50 percent or more of the profits of the entity, or having the right in the event of dissolution to 50 percent or more of the assets of the entity; or

(2) Having the contractual power presently to designate 50 percent or more of the directors of a corporation, or in the case of unincorporated entities, of individuals exercising similar functions.[6]

The application of the control concept in the case of a group of controlled corporations is illustrated by the following example in the rules:

> Example: 1. Corporation A holds 100% of the stock of corporation B, 75% of the stock of corporation C, 50% of the stock of corporation D, and 30% of the stock of corporation E. Corporation A controls corporations B, C and D, but not Corporation E. Corporation A is the ultimate parent entity of a person comprised of corporations A, B, C and D, and each of these corporations (but not corporation E) is 'included within the person.'[7]

---

2. The rules are contained in Part 801 of 16 CFR.
3. Sec. 801.1(a)(1).
4. Sec.801.1(a)(2).
5. Sec.801.1(a)(3).
6. Sec.801.1(b)(1),(2).
7. Sec.801.1(b) (Example 1).

The Rules set out specific guidance for identifying the Acquiring Person and the Acquired Person in various types of acquisitions, such as asset acquisitions, stock acquisitions, mergers, and tender offers. The following sections discuss these provisions.

Under the rules, an Acquiring Person is defined as any *person* (UPE and all controlled entities) who would hold voting securities or assets as a result of an acquisition.[8] Except as noted below, the Acquired Person is defined as the *person* (UPE and all controlled entities) within which the entity whose assets or voting securities are being acquired is included.[9] Thus, if acquiror acquires in a non-merger transaction for cash either the stock or assets of target corporation, the acquiror (together with its subsidiaries)[10] is the *Acquiring Person*, and the target (together with its subsidiaries) is the *Acquired Person*.

Under § 801.2(d), a merger or consolidation or other transaction combining all or any part of the business of two or more persons is treated as an acquisition subject to the Act and is treated as an acquisition of voting securities.[11]

b. When an Acquiring Person Can Also Be an Acquired Person

Under § 801.2(c), a person may be both an Acquiring Person and an Acquired Person.[12] Section 801.2(c) is described in the *Statement of Basis and Purpose* as follows:

> Amended paragraph 801.2(c) provides that a person may be both an acquiring and an acquired person in a single transaction. The amendment makes clear that a person is both an acquiring and an acquired person in a transaction when it occupies both roles in separate parts of the transaction. The example following the paragraph illustrates such a situation: 'Corporation A' (an entity within the person "A") plans to transfer certain of its assets to 'Corporation B' (an entity within person "B") in return for voting securities of 'B.' With respect to the transfer of assets, 'B' is an acquiring person and 'A' is an acquired person; with respect to the transfer of voting securities, 'A' is an acquiring person and 'B' is an acquired person. In the transaction as a whole, therefore, 'A' and 'B' are both acquiring and acquired persons.

Whenever voting securities are to be acquired from the Acquiring Person, the acquisition of the voting securities is separately subject to the Act.[13] For example, if target merges into acquiror with target's shareholders receiving acquiror's stock, then the acquisition by target's shareholders is separately subject to the Act. Thus, if corporation B is one of target's shareholders, B will be an Acquiring Person and acquiror will be an Acquired Person. If the Act applies because, for example, B acquires $150 million of the stock of the acquiror, then B will have to file as an Acquiring Person and the acquiror will have to file as an Acquired Person. The same rule could apply if acquiror made an exchange offer for the target's stock (*i.e.*, offered acquiror's stock to target's shareholders in exchange for their stock); the Act could apply to the acquisition of acquiror's stock by one or more of target's shareholders. Also, if acquiror acquires target's assets in exchange for acquiror's

---

8. Sec § 801.2(a).
9. Sec.801.2(b).
10. Subsidiaries here means at least 50% owned subsidiaries. [See Sec.801.2(b)].
11. Sec.801.2(d).
12. Sec.801.2(c).
13. Sec.801.2(e).

stock and target stays in existence and holds the stock, then acquiror is an Acquiring Person because it acquired target's assets, and acquiror is an Acquired Person because target acquired acquiror's stock. In addition to being an Acquired Person, target is an Acquiring Person.

If, however, acquiror makes the acquisition of target's assets or stock in exchange for cash, acquiror is not an Acquired Person and target and its shareholders are not Acquiring Persons.[14]

The practical significance of this rule can be illustrated as follows. Assume that (1) in a stock-for-asset acquisition the target stays alive and continues to hold the acquiror's stock, and (2) the thresholds are satisfied so that the HSR Act applies. In such case, the target will have to complete Items 5–8 of the Form with respect to all entities included within it, rather than just with respect to the assets disposed of.[15] Thus, for example, if acquiror acquired from target $300M of assets in exchange for $300M of acquiror's stock, then target would be an Acquiring Person and (absent an exemption) would be required to complete Items 5–8 of the Form with respect to the assets disposed of, plus all assets it continues to hold and all the assets held by any of its subsidiaries. On the other hand, if the sale had been for cash, target would report only with respect to the assets disposed of.[16] In the acquisition of assets for acquiror's stock, there is a continuing linkage between acquiror and target that does not exist in a cash acquisition, and the purpose of the rule is to provide the agencies with information regarding all possible overlaps and relationships between acquiror and target.

It should be noted that this type of transaction may be exempt under the investment exemption if target (or its shareholders) holds 10% or less of acquiror's stock.[17]

c. After the Identification of the Acquiring Person and Acquired Person

Once the Acquiring Person and Acquired Person have been identified, the next step is to determine whether the *Commerce* test, the *Size of Person* test and the *Size of Transaction* test are satisfied.

3. Determining Whether the Commerce Test Applies

There are few problems in determining whether the Acquiring Person or the Acquired Person are engaged in commerce.[18]

4. Determining Whether the Size of Person Test and the Size of Transaction Test Are Satisfied: Impact of the February 1, 2000 Interim Rules

The size of person test is now in Section 7A(a)(2)(B)(ii), which applies only for acquisitions that meet the $50 million to $200 million size of transaction test (as adjusted). (As previously indicated, as of the adjustments, which are made each February, as of

14. Sec.801.21(a).
15. Sec.803.2(b)(1)(i).
16. Sec.803.2(b)(1)(ii).
17. Sec.802.9.
18. See Sec.7A(a)(1) and Sec.802.3.

February 2014, the $50 million threshold was $75.9 million and the $200 million threshold was $304.4 million.) Thus, if the acquisition meets the more than $200 million size of transaction test in Section 7A(a)(2)(A), the size of person test in not applicable.

The size of person test for acquisitions between $50 million and $200 million is met if, for example, a target that is engaged in manufacturing has annual net sales or total assets (on a book value basis) of $10,000,000 (as adjusted) or more, and the acquiror has annual net sales or total assets (on a book value basis) of $100,000,000 (as adjusted) or more. *See* Section 7A(a)(2)(B). For transactions below $50 million (as adjusted), the size of transaction test is not satisfied regardless of the size of the persons, and therefore, no reporting is required.

5. Other Issues in Determining Whether the Acquiring Person Holds the Requisite Amount of Assets or Securities

In determining whether the Acquiring Person holds the requisite amount of assets or securities of the Acquired Person, it is necessary to determine what will be held "*as a result of*" the acquisition.[19]

After determining what is held as a result of the acquisition, the next step is to value the assets or securities so acquired. Section 801.10 provides the rules for valuing voting securities and assets for purposes of determining whether the $50M Size of Transaction test has been satisfied.

For example, if the securities are traded, and the acquisition price has been determined, then the value is the greater of the market price or the acquisition price.

The acquisition price includes the value of all consideration paid, including the assumption of liabilities.[20] Under Section 801.10(c)(3), if it is necessary to determine the FMV of assets or voting securities (because the acquisition price has not been determined), such determination must be made by the board of directors of the Acquiring Person or its designee (1) within 60 days prior to the filing, or (2) if filing is not required, within 60 days prior to consummation of the acquisition.

6. The Notification Threshold Provisions of the February 1, 2001 Interim Rules: Reporting and Waiting Period Requirements and Rules of Practice

Section 801.1(h): Notification Threshold

Federal Register: (February 1, 2001)

Section 801.1(h) of the rules defines the term "notification threshold." This term does not appear in the act, and its principal appearance in the rules is in connection with Section 802.21, an exemption for certain incremental acquisitions. In general, the notification thresholds specify the levels of ownership of the assets or voting securities of an acquired person that cannot be attained or exceeded without observing the filing and waiting period requirements of the Clayton Act. [The thresholds discussed below are subject to adjustment, *see* Section 9.6] * * *

19. Sec.801.13.
20. *See* Statement of Basis and Purpose, p. 33471.

The 2001 thresholds are: Assets and voting securities valued at greater than $50 million but less than $100 million; assets and voting securities valued at $100 million or greater but less than $500 million; assets and voting securities valued at $500 million or greater; 25 percent of the voting securities of an issuer if valued at greater than $1 billion; and 50 percent of the voting securities of an issuer if valued at greater than $50 million. [See Item 2(c) of the Form]

To understand the function of the notification thresholds in the rules, it is necessary to look closely at the requirements of the act. Under the act as amended, one must file notification and observe a waiting period if at least one of the parties is engaged in commerce or in any activity affecting commerce, in certain transactions if the size-of-person test is met, and if "as a result of such acquisition, the acquiring person would hold an aggregate total amount of voting securities and assets of the acquired person" in excess of $50 million [as adjusted]. The rules interpret this provision to mean that all prior acquisitions of voting securities of an issuer are held as a result of any subsequent acquisition of voting securities from that issuer. This means that once the $50 million level is reached, every acquisition of voting securities is potentially reportable, not just the one that first exceeds this amount.

This result is overly burdensome and serves no law enforcement purpose. To avoid this consequence, the drafters of the 1978 rules added the concept of notification thresholds and Section 802.21. The thresholds establish certain levels of acquisitions likely to be of competitive significance. Section 802.21 exempts all acquisitions between these levels not meeting or exceeding the next threshold for a period of five years after expiration or termination of the waiting period for the transaction which initially crossed the prior threshold. * * * The thresholds, in conjunction with Section 802.21, thus operate to inform the agencies that if a reported transaction is not challenged, the acquiring person can acquire up to the next highest threshold without having to file again. * * *

7. Secondary Acquisitions

Secondary acquisitions occur whenever, as a result of an acquisition (the primary acquisition), an acquiror obtains control of a target which itself holds a non-controlling block of voting securities of another corporation (Secondary-target). The secondary acquisition is separately subject to the Act.[21] A secondary acquisition is not exempt merely because the primary acquisition is exempt.

8. The Investment Exemption

Act Section 7A(c)(9) provides an exemption to the reporting requirements for acquisitions of 10% or less of a target's stock "solely for the purpose of investment." Section 801.1(i) defines solely for purpose of investment to require that the persons acquiring the securities have "no intention of participating in the formation, determination or direction of the basic business decisions of the issuer."[22]

9. Application of HSR to Unincorporated Entities

In 2005 the HSR rules were amended to make the rules applicable to unincorporated entities, including the formation of joint ventures in the form of partnerships and limited

21. Sec.801.4.
22. Sec.801.1(i)(1).

liability companies (LLCs). The rules had always applied to the formation of corporate joint ventures.

C. Preparation of the Report Form

1. In General and Items 1–4

Under § 803.2(a), the Notification and Report Form is to be filed by the preacquisition UPE or by any entity included within the person authorized by the UPE to file.[23]

An excerpt from the instructions to the Form is set out in *M&A Statutes, Rules, and Documents*, supra Section 1.1, and these instructions should be studied in connection with the reading of this section. Specific rules, discussed below, govern the completion of the Form by the Acquiring Person and the Acquired Person.

Items 1–4 deal generally with the parties and the transaction.

2. Item 4(c) and 4(d) Documents

Items 4(c) and 4(d) require that certain internal documents relating to the transaction be disclosed. Item 4(c) requires the filing of the following information:

> **Item 4(c)**—all studies, surveys, analyses and reports which were prepared by or for any officer(s) or director(s) (or, in the case of unincorporated entities, individuals exercising similar functions) for the purpose of evaluating or analyzing the acquisition with respect to market shares, competition, competitors, markets, potential for sales growth or expansion into product or geographic markets, and indicate (if not contained in the document itself) the date of preparation, and the name and title of each individual who prepared each such document.

Item 4(d), which was added to the Form in 2011, requires the filing of the following information:

> **Item 4(d)(i)**: Provide all Confidential Information Memoranda prepared by or for any officer(s) or director(s) * * * of the Ultimate Parent Entity of the Acquiring or Acquired Person or of the Acquiring or Acquired Entity(s) that specifically relate to the sale of the acquired entity(s) or assets. If no such Confidential Information Memorandum exists, submit any document(s) given to any officer(s) or director(s) of the buyer meant to serve the function of a Confidential Information Memorandum. * * *
>
> **Item 4(d)(ii)**: Provide all studies, surveys, analyses and reports prepared by investment bankers, consultants or other third party advisors ("third party advisors") for any officer(s) or director(s) * * * of the Ultimate Parent Entity of the Acquiring or Acquired Person or of the Acquiring or Acquired Entity(s) for the purpose of evaluating or analyzing market shares, competition, competitors, markets, potential for sales growth or expansion into product or geographic markets that specifically relate to the sale of the acquired entity(s) or assets. * * *
>
> **Item 4(d)(iii)**: Provide all studies, surveys, analyses and reports evaluating or analyzing synergies and/or efficiencies prepared by or for any officer(s) or director(s) ... for the purpose of evaluating or analyzing the acquisition. * * *

---

23. Sec.803.2(a).

The preamble to the Final Rule adopting Item 4(d)[24] explains as follows, the reasons behind the Item and the complimentary nature of Items 4(c) and 4(d):

> In proposing Item 4(d), the Commission noted that certain categories of documents are quite useful for the Agencies' initial substantive analysis of transactions but were not always provided because parties have differing interpretations as to whether they were called for under current Item 4(c). The Commission proposed new Item 4(d) to enumerate these discrete categories of documents and require their submission with the Form. * * *
>
> The Commission intends Items 4(c) and 4(d) to complement one another. For instance, if a filing party includes a document responsive to Item 4(d) * * * with its HSR filing, it need not submit that document separately in response to Item 4(c).[25]

3. Items 5–8

Items 5 through 8 require the companies to provide certain North American Industry Classification System (NAICS) data. Item 5 focuses on the product market by requiring "information by NAICS code regarding nonmanufacturing and manufacturing dollar revenues."

Item 6 requires certain geographical information and information on certain related parties. Item 7 asks for information concerning overlaps in the product and geographic markets. Whenever the acquiror or target has reason to believe that it derives dollar revenues from the same six digit NAICS industry code as the other party, such person must identify the geographic areas in which it derives those dollar revenues. Item 8 requires certain information concerning previous acquisitions made by the acquiror.

Under § 803.2(b)(1) and (2), Items 5–8 of the Form (*i.e.*, NAICS information, entities, dollar revenue and geographic markets, and prior acquisitions) must be completed as follows:

> (i) By acquiring persons, with respect to all entities included within the acquiring person;
>
> (ii) By acquired persons, in the case of an acquisition of assets, only with respect to the assets to be acquired;
>
> (iii) By acquired persons, in the case of an acquisition of voting securities, with respect to only the issuer whose voting securities are being acquired, and all entities controlled by such issuer; * * *

4. Associate (PE Firm) Reporting Rules, As Added by 2011 Amendments

In amendments to the HSR rules adopted in July 2011,[26] the FTC adopted new rules regarding the reporting obligations of "associates," which are entities that are not controlled by, or in control of, an acquiring person but who manage or are managed by an acquiring

---

24. Federal Trade Commission, Premerger Notification: Reporting and Waiting Period Requirements, Final Rule, 76 Fed. Reg. No. 138, p. 42471 (Tue. July 19, 2011).

25. *Id.* at 42474–75.

26. Federal Trade Commission, Premerger Notification: Reporting and Waiting Period Requirements, Final Rule, 76 Fed. Reg. No. 138, p. 42471 (Tue. July 19, 2011).

person. The preamble to the Final Rule gives the following explanation of the purpose of the "associates" concept:

> An acquiring person is required to provide information in its notification with respect to all entities included within it at the time of filing. In some instances, particularly with families of investment funds, entities that are commonly managed with the acquiring person are not included because these "associated" entities are not controlled, as defined in § 801.1(b) of the Rules [*i.e.*, not owned to the extent of 50% or more], by the acquiring Ultimate Parent Entity ("UPE"). As a result, the Agencies do not receive the information they need to get a complete picture of potential antitrust ramifications of an acquisition....
>
> To capture information on overlaps between entities commonly managed with the acquirer and the target, the Commission proposed three changes: introducing and defining the term associate, creating Item 6(c)(ii) [information provided for associates], and revising Item 7 to require the submission of information on minority and controlling interests of associates that overlap with the entity(s) or assets that are being acquired.
>
> These amendments are implemented by addition of the defined term "associate," and modifications to the Report Form and Instructions.

D. Impact of HSR in Post-Filing Period

1. In General

This is the period after the filing has been made. One of the principal concerns is the running of the waiting period. This section addresses the waiting period rules and the second request procedure.

2. Basic Waiting Period Rules

[**Negotiated Mergers**] Section 803.10(a)(3) provides that in negotiated mergers and asset acquisitions (*i.e.*, non-§ 801.30 acquisitions), the waiting period starts upon the filing by both parties. Under § 803.5(b), such a notification is required to contain an affidavit "attesting that a contract, agreement in principle, or letter of intent to merge or acquire, has been executed, and further attesting to the good faith intention of the person filing notification to complete the transaction." Thus, to start the waiting period the target and acquirer in a consensual deal must enter into an acquisition agreement or an agreement in principle or a letter of intent. Under § 803.10(b), the waiting period for negotiated deals ends 30 days after filing, unless earlier terminated or extended as noted below.

[**Tender Offers and Certain Other Acquisitions of Stock**] Section 801.30 specifies various types of transactions in which the waiting period will begin upon the receipt of acquiror's Notification Form.

The § 801.30 transactions include:

1) Open market purchases of target's voting securities.
2) Tender Offers; defined in § 801.1(g)(l) as a tender offer under § 14 of Securities Exchange Act.
3) Secondary acquisitions defined in § 801.4. *See* Section 9.7.B.7.

Under § 801.30(b), the waiting period in each of these transactions begins upon the filing of the Notification Form by acquiror, and target is required to file its notification within 15 days (or 10 days in the case of a cash tender offer) following the date of the filing by acquiror. These principles are illustrated in three examples contained in Rule § 801.30(b).

Under § 803.10(b), the waiting period ends on the 30th day after the beginning of the waiting period (or 15 days after commencement of a cash tender offer) unless:

1) Extended under § 7A(e) and § 803.20 (relating to Second Requests, *see* below);
2) Extended by court order under § 7A(g)(2) for failure to substantially comply; or
3) Early termination under § 7A(b)(2) and § 803.11.

3. Early Termination

Rule § 803.11 implements Act § 7A(b)(2), by setting forth the procedures by which the parties may request the early termination of the waiting period. In order for early termination to be granted, the FTC and DOJ must have determined that no additional information is required and that there is no intention to take further action during the waiting period. The Report form has a box where the parties indicate if they are requesting early termination.

4. Second Requests: Description of the Rule and Effect on Waiting Period

If under § 803.20 and § 7A(e)(1), the FTC or DOJ issues a second request, then under § 803.20(c), during the time period when the request for additional information remains outstanding to any person (other than, in the case of a tender offer, the target or any officer or directors of the target), the waiting period will remain in effect even though the 30- or 15-day initial period has elapsed. Under § 803.21, responses to a second request must be filed within a reasonable time.

Under § 803.10(b)(2), unless extended because of failure to substantially comply (§ 7A(g)(2)), any waiting period that is extended because of a second request shall expire 30 days after receipt of the information or, in the case of a cash tender offer, 10 days after such receipt.

The FTC and the DOJ have adopted a "quick look" procedure which gives the parties to a transaction for which a second request has been issued the option of furnishing limited information that might convince the agencies after a "quick look" to close the investigation and terminate the waiting period. *See The Merger Review Process, supra* Section 1.10, at 175–178.

The FTC has a Model Second Request that sets out information that is usually requested in a second request. *See* Request for Additional Information and Documentary Information on the FTC's website at www.ftc.gov. Also, both the FTC and the DOJ have appeal procedures pursuant to which merger parties can appeal a second request on the basis that it is overbroad. *See* FTC and DOJ websites.

5. Conduct of Merger Investigations

Both the FTC and the DOJ have guidelines regarding the conduct of merger investigations. *See Statement of the FTC's Bureau of Competition on Guidelines on Merger Investigations*; *FTC Bureau of Economics, Best Practices for Data, and Economics and Financial Analyses in Antitrust Investigations*; *Statement of the FTC's Bureau of Competition on Negotiating Merger Remedies*; and *DOJ Merger Review Initiative*. The current issues of these documents are available on the FTC and DOJ websites.

6. Table Summary of Waiting Period Rules

The *Waiting Period Scheme—Types of Transactions* table on the facing page summarizes the waiting period rules and the related concepts of substantial compliance, early termination and second requests.

§ 9.8 Impact of the Penalty Provision

A. HSR 2004 Annual Report Discussion of Penalties

FTC and DOJ, Annual Report to Congress

Fiscal Year 2004

Compliance. The Commission and the Antitrust Division continued to monitor compliance with the pre-merger notification program's filing and waiting period requirements and initiated a number of compliance investigations in fiscal year 2004. The agencies monitor compliance through a variety of methods, including the review of newspapers and industry publications for announcements of transactions that may not have been reported in accordance with the requirements of the Act. In addition, industry sources, such as competitors, customers and suppliers, and interested members of the public, often provide the agencies with information about transactions and possible violations of the Act's requirements.

Under Section 7A(g)(1) of the Act, any person that fails to comply with the Act's notification and waiting period requirements is liable for a civil penalty of up to $11,000 for each day the violation continues. The antitrust agencies examine the circumstances of each violation to determine whether penalties should be sought. During fiscal year 2004, 25 corrective filings for violations were received, and the agencies brought two enforcement actions, resulting in the payment of $1.8 million in civil penalties.

In *United States v. Gates*, the complaint alleged that Bill Gates, through his personal investment company, acquired more than $50 million of the voting securities of ICOS Corporation in 2002, without complying with HSR reporting requirements. According to the complaint, he did not qualify for the "solely for the purpose of investment" HSR Act exemption because he intended to participate in the basic business decisions of ICOS, a pharmaceutical company, through among other things, his longstanding membership on its board of directors. Under the terms of a consent decree filed simultaneously with the complaint, Gates agreed to pay a civil penalty of $800,000 to settle the charges. The case was not related to Gates' position in Microsoft Corporation or the Antitrust Division's antitrust litigation with the company. * * *

B. Illustration of Penalty for Violation of Item 4(c)

In a March 31, 1999 final judgment in the U.S. District Court, Blackstone Capital Partners II Merchant Banking Fund L.P. and Howard Lipson, the general partner of the fund, agreed to pay penalties of, respectively, $2.785 million and $50,000. The penalties were attributable to Lipson's failure to file documents required by Item 4(c) of the Report Form, *see M&A Statutes, Rules, and Documents*, *supra* Section 1.1. The FTC's position was that Lipson "knew or should have known that the filing was inaccurate" and that it was appropriate that he pay a "penalty for what was at a minimum his reckless disregard for his obligations under the HSR Act." *See* CCH, Trade Regulation Reports, para 24,582.

Waiting Period Scheme—Types of Transactions

Computation of Waiting Period	Negotiated Mergers and Asset Acquisitions	§801.30 Open Market Purchased and Negotiated Stock Acquisitions	Cash Tender Offers	Noncash Tender Offers
[1] Waiting Period Begins:	Upon filing by both parties. (§803.10(a)(3)).	Upon filing by AC (§§801.30(b)(1) and 803.10(a)(1)) AC must give TC notice (§803.5(1)).	Upon filing by AC (§803.10(a)(1)) AC must give TC notice and tender offer must be publicly announced (§803.5(a)(1)).	Upon filing by AC (§803.10(a)(1)). AC must give TC notice and tender offer must be publicly announced. (§803.5(a)(1)).
[2] TC Must File:	At the time AC files (in order to start waiting period (§803.10(a)(3)).	15 days after AC files (§801.30(b)(2)).	10 days after AC files (§801.30(b)(2)).	15 days after AC files (§801.30(b)(2)).
[3] Waiting Period Expires (Assuming no Second Request (§803.20), no change in terms of tender offer (§802.23), no action for failure to substantially comply (§7A(g)(2)), and no early termination (§803.11)):	30 days after filing by both parties (§803.10(b)(1)).	30 days after filing by AC (§803.10(b)(1)).	15 days after filing by AC (§803.10(b)(1)).	30 days after filing by AC (§803.20I).
[4] Filing of Second Request both parties respond (§803.20I):	Waiting Period continues until both parties respond §803.20I). (Note: TC required to respond within a reasonable time, §803.21).	Waiting Period continues until both parties respond (§803.20I) (Note: TC required to respond within a reasonable time, §803.21).	Waiting Period continues until AC responds (§803.20I). (Note: TC required to respond within a reasonable time, §803.21).	Waiting Period continues until AC responds. (§803.20I). (Note: TC required to respond within a reasonable time, §803.21).
[5] Waiting Period Expires After Receipt of Response to Second Request (Assuming not extended for failure to substantially comply (§7A(g)(2)), and not terminated early (§803.11)):	30 days after receipt of all additional info from both parties (§803.10(b)(2)(i)). Act §7A(e)(2)	30 days after receipt of all additional info from both parties (§803.10(b)(2)(i)). Act §7A(e)(2)	10 days after receipt of all additional information requested from AC (§803.10(b)(2)(i)) (Note that a Second Request to TC does not extend the waiting period under §803.20(c)).	30 days after receipt of all additional information requested from AC (§803.10(b)(2)(i)) Act §7A(e)(2)

The FTC says that the documents would have alerted it to antitrust problems associated with the acquisition.

§ 9.9 Summary Problems on Hart-Scott-Rodino

1. Acquiring Corporation (AC), a publicly owned corporation, owns all of the stock of Sub-1 and 50% of the stock of Sub-2. AC acquires all of the stock of Target Corporation (TC), a publicly held firm. TC owns 75% of the stock of Sub-3 and 25% of the stock of Sub-4. What firms are the ultimate parent entities? *See* § 801.1(a)(3). Who are the "acquiring person" and the "acquired person" under HSR? *See* §§ 801.2(a) and (b), § 801.1(a)(1) (definition of person), and § 801.1(b) (definition of control).

2. AC in Question 1 forms a partnership with Acquiring Corporation Two (AC-2) for the purpose of acquiring TC in Question 1. AC-2 is a publicly held corporation that owns no subsidiaries. AC and AC-2 each have a 50% interest in profits, losses and distributions. Who are the "acquiring person" and the "acquired person?" *See* §§ 801.2(a) and (b), § 801.1(a)(1) (definition of person) and § 801.1(b)(2).

3. Acquiring Corporation (AC), which has sales of $75 million and assets of $25 million, acquires all of the stock of Target Corporation (TC) for $95 million. TC has sales of $90 million and assets of $60 million. Both AC and TC are engaged in manufacturing. Is the transaction subject to HSR? *See* § 7A(a).

4. The facts are the same as in Question 3, except TC has sales of $180 million. Is the transaction subject to HSR? *See* § 7A(a).

5. Target Corporation (TC), a publicly held corporation, has over $500 million in sales. Acquiring Corporation (AC), a publicly held corporation, also has over $500 million in sales. AC is planning to purchase on the open market 4% of TC's stock, and AC expects that the purchase price will be about $95 million. Is the transaction subject to HSR? Does AC have to file before completing the acquisition? (This transaction is not subject to reporting under Section 13(d) of the Williams Act because AC has not acquired more than 5% of TC's stock.) *See* §§ 7A(a) and (c)(9), § 801.1(h), and § 801.30.

6. Same facts as in Question 5. Six months after purchasing 4% of TC's stock for $95 million, AC is planning to acquire an additional 8% for $200 million. Is this transaction subject to HSR? *See* § 801.1(h), § 801.20, § 801.30, and § 802.21.

7. Same facts as in Question 6, except that four months after acquiring 12% of TC's shares, AC is planning to make a tender offer for an additional 39% of TC's shares for $800 million, thereby bringing A's interest up to 51%. Is this transaction subject to HSR? *See* § 801.1(h), § 801.20, § 801.30, and § 802.21. What if after this tender offer AC makes additional open market purchases of TC's shares?

8. The boards of directors of AC and TC reach agreement on a merger in which TC will be merged into a subsidiary of AC with the shareholders of TC receiving cash. Assume that in this and in succeeding questions, the commerce test, the size of person test, and the size of transaction test are satisfied. What are the filing requirements and when does the waiting period expire? *See* § 801.2(d) (identification of the acquiring and acquired person in a merger); § 801.1(a)(3)

(ultimate parent entity), § 803.2 (notification form) and § 803.10 (running of time). What result if AC acquires TC in a tender offer? *See also* § 801.30.

9. The facts are the same as in Question 8, except the merger consideration is common stock of AC. Corporation X owns 30% of the stock of TC and will receive in the merger stock of AC with a value of $90 million. What are the filing requirements and when does the waiting period expire? *See* § 801.2(e).

10. The facts are the same as in question 8. TC owns 25% of the stock of Sub-1. The stock has a value of $120 million. What are the filing requirements and what are the waiting period requirements?

§ 9.10 Dealing with State Attorneys General

A. National Association of Attorneys General: Pre-Merger Disclosure Compact

NAAG Voluntary Pre-Merger Disclosure Compact

As Amended, (March 21, 1994)

The undersigned state and territorial Attorneys General who are empowered under federal and/or state antitrust law to enjoin corporate mergers and acquisitions which are likely substantially to lessen competition or tend to create a monopoly in any line of commerce in any section of the country hereby institute the "NAAG Voluntary Pre-Merger Disclosure Compact" (The Compact) which shall be governed according to the following rules and principles:

First, that the Attorney General members of The Compact agree that it is in the [public] interests * * * that state and federal government officials invested with authority to enforce the antitrust laws as they relate to mergers and acquisitions (mergers) analyze the same factual information when determining whether a merger is anticompetitive * * * .

Second, that any party to any proposed merger subject to the filing requirements of HSR may voluntarily file a photocopy of the first filing with the "liaison state" member of The Compact, as defined in the Third Proviso herein, simultaneous with the filing of the original with the federal enforcement agency. * * *

Third, the "liaison state" upon whom the voluntary filings specified in the Second and Fourth Provisos herein shall be made, shall be a member of The Compact determined in the following order of preference: First the Attorney General of the state which is the principal place of business of the acquiring party to the merger, next to the Attorney General of the state which is the principal place of business of the acquired party, next to the Attorney General of the state of incorporation of the acquiring party and next to the Attorney General of the state of incorporation of the acquired party. * * *

Fourth, the parties to The Compact agree to serve no other or further investigative subpoenas, Civil Investigative Demands or other compulsory pre-complaint demands for disclosure upon the merging party that makes the voluntary filing specified in the Second Proviso during the pendency of the Hart-Scott-Rodino waiting period. * * *

B. Coordination of Federal-State Merger Probes

Protocol for Coordinating Federal-State Merger Investigations between the Federal Enforcement Agencies and State Attorneys General

(March 11, 1998)

Some mergers and acquisitions may become subject to simultaneous federal and state investigations by either the Antitrust Division of the U.S. Department of Justice ("Antitrust Division") or the Federal Trade Commission ("FTC"), and one or more State Attorneys General. To the extent lawful, practicable and desirable in the circumstances of a particular case, the Antitrust Division or the FTC and the State Attorneys General will cooperate in analyzing the merger. This protocol is intended to set forth a general framework for the conduct of joint investigations with the goals of maximizing cooperation between the federal and state enforcement agencies and minimizing the burden on the parties. * * *

Agencies receiving confidential information from another agency ("the originating agency") will agree to take all appropriate steps to maintain its confidentiality. * * *

The Antitrust Division and the FTC will, with the consent of the merging parties, provide certain otherwise confidential information to State Attorneys General. * * *

§9.11 Provisions of Merger Agreements Addressing Antitrust Review Issues

It is common for acquisition agreements, such as merger agreements, to contain provisions relating to the antitrust clearance of the transaction. Such provisions often include (1) an undertaking by the parties to seek antitrust clearance and to file all required documents under applicable pre-merger notification law, (2) a specification of the party liable for payment of any pre-merger filing fee, such as the filing fee under HSR, (3) procedures for handing competitively sensitive information provided by the other party that could cause the parties to have "jumped the gun" on the acquisition, thereby giving rise to antitrust liability [*see* Section 9.12], (4) the conditioning of the closing on the receipt of, *inter alia*, antitrust clearance, and (5) the right to terminate the agreement if antitrust clearance is not received. In certain cases, the parties may also include in the agreement (1) a provision that clarifies whether the parties are required to agree to a divestiture as a condition of receiving antitrust clearance, and (2) a fee (known as a "reverse break-up fee") that the acquiror will have to pay to the target if the transaction does not close because of antitrust opposition to the transaction. The reverse break-up fee may be used if there is significant risk that the transaction will be prohibited on antitrust grounds, and the target has rejected other offers that are not as antitrust sensitive.

All of these provisions were included in the merger agreement pursuant to which Whirlpool Corporation acquired Maytag, a transaction ultimately approved by the antitrust authorities. The antitrust provisions of this merger agreement are set out in the in Documentary Appendix I of *M&A Statutes, Rules, and Documents, supra* Section 1.1. *See e.g.*, Flaum, *Antitrust Provisions: A Dealmaker's Guide*, The M&A Journal.

§9.12 Antitrust Risk in Exchanging Competitively Sensitive Information during the Due Diligence Process and Post-Signing Period—*Omnicare*[27]

The sharing of competitively sensitive information during the due diligence process and after the signing but before the closing can give rise to issues under Section 1 of the Sherman Act. In affirming the district court's dismissal of an antitrust claim asserting that two merger partners violated Section 1 by sharing information during the due diligence process, the Seventh Circuit[28] reasoned, in part, as follows:

> We agree with the district court that the nature of Omnicare's information-exchange contentions requires us to walk a fine line:
>
> > On the one hand, courts should not allow plaintiffs to pursue Sherman Act claims merely because conversations concerning business took place between competitors during merger talks; such a standard could chill business activity by companies that would merge but for a concern over potential litigation. On the other hand, the mere possibility of a merger cannot permit business rivals to freely exchange competitively sensitive information. This standard could lead to "sham" merger negotiations, or at least allow for periods of cartel behavior when, as here, there is a substantial period of time between the signing of the merger agreement and the closing of the deal.
>
> *Omnicare*, 594 F. Supp. 2d at 968. Looking at the pricing information that was exchanged, however, we cannot see how a reasonable jury could conclude that it is more consistent with action on the conspiratorial side of the line than with action on the innocuous due diligence side. * * *
>
> Viewed separately and collectively, Omnicare's evidence of information exchange would not enable reasonable jurors to infer that United and PacifiCare inappropriately shared information damaging to competition in and of itself (Omnicare's alleged standalone claim), nor that the information exchanged facilitated the development or advancement of a coordinated negotiating and pricing strategy.[29]

Omnicare illustrates that in any antitrust sensitive transaction, antitrust counsel should be consulted concerning the structuring of the exchange of sensitive information in the due diligence process and after the signing and prior to the closing.

References

The leading treatise on Hart-Scott-Rodino is Axinn, et al., *Acquisitions Under the Hart-Scott-Rodino*, *supra* Section 1.10. *See also ABA The Merger Review Process*, *supra* Section 1.10, and Thompson, *Mergers, Acquisitions and Tender Offers*, *supra* Section 1.10, Chapter 13.

---

27. This section is adapted from Thompson, *Mergers, Acquisitions and Tender Offers*, *supra* Section 1.10, at Section 13:7.1.

28. Omnicare, Inc. v. UnitedHealth Group, Inc, 629 F. 3d 697 (7th Cir. 2011).

29. *Id.* at 709–711. *See generally* Barry Nigro and Alexsandr Livshits, *Seventh Circuit Outlines Merger Discussion and Due Diligence Safeguards to Protect Against Antitrust Violations*, 15 The M&A Lawyer 7 (April 2011).

Chapter 10

Confidentiality Agreements, Exclusivity Agreements, Due Diligence and Letters of Intent

§ 10.1 Scope

The merger and acquisition process often starts with a confidentiality agreement between the acquiror and the target or its shareholders. The purpose of these agreements is to permit the parties to confidentially examine non-public information regarding the other party prior to entering into an acquisition agreement. The acquisition agreement may also contain confidentiality provisions or the confidentiality agreement may continue in effect after entering the acquisition agreement. The parties may also enter into an exclusivity agreement pursuant to which the parties agree to only negotiate with each other for a period of time. A confidentiality agreement and an exclusivity agreement may facilitate the due diligence process, pursuant to which the parties "kick the tires" on each other. Prior to negotiating the acquisition agreement, the drafting of which is addressed in Chapter 15, the parties may enter into a letter of intent outlining the basic terms of the transaction. The parties may, however, find it preferable to skip a letter of intent and move directly to the drafting of the acquisition agreement.

This chapter focuses on confidentiality agreements, exclusivity agreements, due diligence, and letters of intent. Section 10.2 sets out an introductory problem; Section 10.3 focuses on confidentiality agreements; Section 10.4 looks at exclusivity agreements, Section 10.5 introduces the due diligence process, and Section 10.6 addresses the question of when a letter of intent becomes a binding contract. The materials in this chapter are covered in greater detail in Chapter 3 of Thompson, *Mergers, Acquisitions and Tender Offers*, *supra* Section 1.10.

§ 10.2 Introductory Problem

The president (P) of Acquiring Corporation (AC) has indicated to the Chairman of the board and the sole shareholder (S) of Target Corporation (TC) that AC might be interested in acquiring TC. P wants to visit TC's premises and review certain information. How should S proceed? What are P's concerns? What if TC were a publicly-held corporation?

After P's review of TC, P and S come to a basic understanding of the terms under which AC would acquire TC. P has proposed that the terms be set forth in a letter of intent. How should S proceed? What are P's concerns?

§ 10.3 Negotiating the Confidentiality Agreement

A. Introduction

Excerpts from Henry Lesser, Ann Lederer and Charles Steinberg, Increasing Pressures for Confidentiality Agreements That Work

Mergers and Acquisitions, pp 23–27, (March/April, 1992)

[When reading this section also read the sample Confidentiality Agreement in Documentary Appendix CC.]

* * * In this article, we discuss the confidentiality agreement as the first step in the process that can lead to a possible corporate combination and address how it can be negotiated and structured, given current M&A market conditions. Although, we focus on the type of agreement often used in deals involving public companies, many of the same principles and practices are equally applicable to private company transactions.

It is important to stress that the confidentiality agreement is a method of reconciling the conflicting objectives of a target company that is negotiating a change-in-control transaction or a significant minority investment by an outsider. Once the target has decided to entertain acquisition or investment offers, it will be requested to provide sufficient information to enable bidders to make their best offers. However, the release of confidential information to interested buyers, many of whom might be direct competitors, poses obvious dangers that the target will want to minimize. * * *

Sellers sometimes fear that a potential bidder may be more interested in accessing the target's closely guarded information than seriously negotiating a transaction. And if a deal can't be struck an increasing possibility at a time when financing is hard to get there is danger that a potential buyer may leave with precious business secrets.

Besides dealing with these acute worries, the confidentiality agreement for a public company also must provide comfort that a bidder armed with confidential information won't be tempted to "end run" the seller's board. Unless restrained, the bidder can publicly issue an unsolicited proposal in an attempt to have stockholders pressure the board to make an unsolicited tender offer directly to shareholders. The bidder's aim would be to consummate the transaction at a lower price than the board would demand in direct negotiations.

The confidentiality agreement is a contractual device used to reconcile varying objectives and concerns by permitting the target company to provide confidential information to the bidder while protecting itself from the risks of misuse. The agreement typically contains:

> Confidentiality provisions to protect the company against the business risks of disclosure or misuse of information by competitors; and

> Standstill provisions to protect the company against unsolicited takeover attempts by bidders while providing for an orderly process of marketing the business.

Types of Information. The types of information of interest to a bidder include financial, technical, and human resource material. Each type of information has differing characteristics, and the relative importance of each to the two sides will shape the context of the negotiations. For example, financial information, such as projections, typically has a short "shelf life" of usefulness. On the other hand, technical information, such as manufacturing techniques, may have an indefinite shelf life and may be easily exploitable by competitors.

Financial Information. The bidder and its representatives generally need confidential financial information regarding the target, including both historical data, particularly for nonpublic companies, and projections. In addition, the bidder may want detailed business information, including pricing details and data on individual business units (such as stores, factories, divisions, profit centers, and other strategic business units). The seller and its advisers must be sensitive to antitrust concerns if the company intends to provide pricing and market information to competitors.

Technical Information. In the category of technical information, serious and complex issues may arise with regard to the scope of detailed information to be provided to competitors. The tensions, moreover, have increased, given the higher incidence of mergers and acquisitions in technology-driven industries.

This is an area in which the buyer can be as eager as the seller to protect the legal position. A competitor may request that confidential technical information be excluded from the material that is provided, and seek only information deemed "nonconfidential" in order to avoid any possible future claim that it misused the target's proprietary information. * * *

Access to Employees. It is good practice to require that all contacts be made through one source (usually, the target's investment banker) to control the number and identity of the employees being interviewed and to ensure that they are properly briefed. * * *

Disclosure of Negotiations. The agreement may prohibit a bidder from disclosing, unless the seller consents in writing. * * * The bidder in turn may ask for a reciprocal provision that prohibits the target from announcing the negotiations.

Discussions Among Bidders. The target also will try to control a bidder's ability to discuss the possible transaction with other potential acquirors. Without a prohibition on such talks, a bidder could reach a secret agreement with another party to submit a joint bid. * * *

Standstill Provisions in the Confidentiality Agreement. If the target is a public company, the confidentiality agreement typically contains "standstill" provisions setting forth the terms under which the bidder may acquire, vote, or dispose of stock of the target. * * *

Stock Acquisitions and Dispositions. When negotiations start, the target's opening position is usually to try to prohibit all acquisitions of the company's securities by the bidder. Sometimes the bidder may request a "basket" that would permit it to acquire up to a specified percentage of the company's stock. The appropriateness of this request depends upon the facts of each case. * * *

[T]he target usually will not want the bidder to acquire more than 5% of its stock, since that normally would trigger the filing of a Schedule 13D with the Securities and Exchange Commission. The Notification in turn would require disclosure of the bidder's plans and purposes with respect to the seller and the bidder's contracts with respect to the target's shares (including the confidentiality agreement). This disclosure may put the company "in play," *i.e.*, create public anticipation of a pending transaction and cause a run-up in the company's stock.

Note that the bidder, in any event, will need to be sensitive to the requirements of federal securities laws restricting trading while in the possession of material inside information. * * *

Proxy Solicitations. The target typically will try to prevent bidders from attempting to acquire control of the company through a proxy contest. * * *

Timing of Proposals. The target usually wants to restrict the ability of the bidder to offer proposals concerning the types of transactions cited above, as well as any transactions that can be effected only with the seller's cooperation, such as mergers, recapitalizations, and asset sales. Although the bidder may question how the target's interests are advanced by such prohibitions, this is, in fact, one of the most critical aspects of a standstill during an auction for a public company.

A variety of factors could force the target to publicly disclose any proposal it receives concerning a change-in-control transaction. The target could determine that its previous disclosures may become misleading without a follow-up statement, if it has not followed a strict "no comment" policy in the past. Or the target may feel obligated to make an announcement if there is a sudden increase in stock market activity based on rumors. Any public disclosure could put the company "in play" and reduce the chances of completing a negotiated deal. * * *

Enforceability of Standstill Provisions. Despite the prevalence of confidentiality agreements, relatively few court cases offer guidance on their enforceability. In one case, the Delaware Chancery Court condoned the use of confidentiality agreements with standstill provisions when the target conducted an auction after receiving an unsolicited bid. In another case, a federal district court held that a standstill provision provided the basis for issuing a preliminary injunction against an unsolicited tender offer. * * *

Survival of the Confidentiality Agreement. There are a variety of approaches to specifying time limits on a confidentiality agreement. The options include setting a specific term of duration, omitting a term, or specifying that only some provisions survive termination.

The standstill and nonsolicitation provisions typically will specify a term during which the bidder will be subject to restrictions. Other provisions, such as the obligation to keep records of confidential information, may be perpetual or may expire after a stated number of years or upon a stated event.

The target may be able to make a persuasive argument that certain proprietary information, such as technical know-how, has an indefinite life. Such information would remain proprietary until it is disclosed. If the information is proprietary, the seller may argue that the bidder should not dissolve or misuse it until it becomes public through another source.

Most-Favored Nation Clauses. A bidder sometimes may request "most-favored nation status," *i.e.*, the right to get the same preferential concessions granted to any other potential buyer. The target, on the other hand, can assert its need to respond with flexibility to bidders, depending upon their individual circumstances. * * *

Note

As indicated, a sample confidentiality agreement is included as Documentary Appendix CC. For other sample confidentiality agreements *see* Ancillary Documents No. 1 in *ABA Model Asset Purchase Agreement, supra* Section 1.10, and Ancillary Document No. 1 in *ABA Model Stock Purchase Agreement, supra* Section 1.10. The *ABA Model Asset Purchase Agreement* has a confidentiality provision in Section 12. The Comment to this section explains the relationship between confidentiality agreements and confidentiality provisions of asset acquisition agreements:

> Typically, a confidentiality agreement will have been signed by the time a buyer and seller are negotiating the terms of an asset acquisition agreement. [The drafting of asset acquisition agreements is examined in Chapter 15.] Most definitive asset acquisition agreements, therefore, give only passing treatment to confidentiality issues, typically by addressing the existing confidentiality agreement in the integration clause to provide either that the confidentiality agreement survives or does not survive execution of the agreement or closing of the transaction.

The above principle applies also to other acquisition agreements, such as stock purchase agreements and merger agreements.

B. Delaware Supreme Court's Interpretation of the "Stealth" Standstill in *Vulcan*[1]

Martin Marietta v. Vulcan[2] required the Delaware Chancery and Supreme Courts to interpret the meaning of (1) a confidentiality agreement, that is, a Nondisclosure Agreement (NDA), and (2) a joint defense agreement (JDA). Martin and Vulcan signed the NDA and the JDA in contemplation of a possible friendly merger.

Vulcan later pulled out of the negotiations, and Martin responded with the launch of a hostile exchange offer (*see* Chapter 20) for the shares of Vulcan and also initiated a proxy contest (*see* Chapter 16). Vulcan claimed that Martin's actions violated the NDA and the JDA. The Chancery Court agreed with Vulcan and enjoined Martin's hostile actions for four months. As a practical matter, as a result of the injunction, the proxy contest could not take place until Vulcan's next annual meeting, which was over 12 months away. Martin claimed that the Chancery Court's interpretation of these confidentiality provisions gave rise to a "stealth" standstill provision. The Supreme Court affirmed, and this discussion focuses on the Supreme Court's decision on the substantive issue but not its decision on the remedy.

The Supreme Court described as follows the alleged "stealth" standstill provisions in the NDA:

> [T]he NDA prohibited both the "use" and the "disclosure" of "Evaluation Material," except where expressly allowed. Paragraph 2 permitted either party to use the other party's Evaluation Material, but "solely for the purpose of evaluating a Transaction." Paragraph 2 also categorically prohibited either party from disclosing Evaluation Material to anyone except the receiving party's representatives. The NDA defined "Evaluation Material" as "any nonpublic information furnished or communicated by the disclosing party" as well as "all analyses, compilations, forecasts, studies, reports, interpretations, financial statements, summaries, notes, data, records or other documents and materials prepared by the receiving party ... that contain, reflect, are based upon or are generated from any such nonpublic information...." The NDA defined "Transaction" as "a possible business combination transaction ... between [Martin] and [Vulcan] or one of their respective subsidiaries."[3]

The alleged "stealth" standstill provisions of the JDA were described as follows by the Supreme Court:

> The JDA, like the NDA, prohibits and limits the use and the disclosure of information that the JDA describes as "Confidential Materials." The critical prohibitions and limitations are found in JDA Paragraphs 2 and 4. Paragraph 2 prohibits the disclosure of Confidential Materials without "the consent of all Parties who may be entitled to claim any privilege or confidential status with respect to such materials...." JDA Paragraph 4 relevantly provides that "Confidential Materials will be used, consistent with the maintenance of the privileged and confidential status

---

1. This section is adapted from Thompson, *Mergers, Acquisitions and Tender Offers*, *supra* Section 1.10, at Section 3:2.16[E].

2. Martin Marietta Materials, Inc. v. Vulcan Materials Co., 2012 Del. LEXIS 342 (Del. S. Ct. July 10, 2012).

3. *Id.* at *6–*7.

> of those materials, solely for purposes of pursuing and completing the Transaction." The JDA defines "Transaction" as "a potential transaction being discussed by Vulcan and Martin[] ... involving the combination or acquisition of all or certain of their assets or stock...."[4]

After the signing of the NDA and JDA, Vulcan provided Martin with confidential information relating to the proposed transaction. The Supreme Court explained that the "Court of Chancery found, and Martin does not dispute, that Martin used and disclosed Vulcan's nonpublic information in preparing its Exchange Offer and its Proxy Contest to oust some of Vulcan's board members (collectively, the 'hostile takeover bid')."[5] The Supreme Court described these disclosures as follows:

> Both before and after Martin commenced its hostile takeover bid, Martin disclosed Vulcan's nonpublic information, first to third party advisors (investment bankers, lawyers and public relations advisors), and later publicly [in the exchange offer document]. Martin did that without Vulcan's prior consent and without adhering to the Notice and Vetting Process mandated by the NDA."[6]

The Supreme Court explained that the Chancery Court found that the disclosures of the confidential information in the exchange offer documents were "tactical," "argumentative," "selective," and "exceeded the scope of what was legally required."[7]

Of course, Martin asserted that its use and disclosure of the nonpublic information was "not legally prohibited by the Confidentiality Agreements."[8]

The Supreme Court described as follows the Chancery Court's finding that Martin had breached the NDA and the JDA by impermissibly using and disclosing confidential information:

> Specifically, the Court of Chancery found that, although the Confidentiality Agreements did not contain a "standstill" provision, they did bar Martin (and Vulcan) from:
>
> - "Using the broad class of 'evaluation material' defined by the confidentiality agreements except for the consideration of a contractually negotiated business combination transaction between the parties, and not for a combination that was to be effected by hostile, unsolicited activity of one of the parties;"
> - "Disclosing either the fact that the parties had merger discussions or any evaluation material shared under the confidentiality agreements unless the party was legally required to disclose because: (i) it had received 'oral questions, interrogatories, requests for information or documents in legal proceedings, subpoena, civil investigative demand or other similar process;' and (ii) its legal counsel had, after giving the other party notice and the chance for it to comment on the extent of disclosure required, limited disclosure to the minimum necessary to satisfy the requirements of law; or"
> - "Disclosing information protected from disclosure by the confidentiality agreements through press releases, investor conference calls, and communications with journalists that were in no way required by law."[9]

---

4. *Id.* at *12–*13.
5. *Id.* at *14.
6. *Id.* at *17.
7. *Id.* at *21–*20.
8. *Id.* at *14.
9. *Id.* at *23–*24.

Martin asserted that "by interpreting the Confidentiality Agreements in the manner it did, the Court of Chancery 'stealthily' converted those two contracts into a standstill agreement, which neither party intended or agreed to."[10] In response, the Supreme Court discussed as follows the distinction between a standstill and a confidentiality agreement:

> Standstill agreements and confidentiality agreements are qualitatively different. A standstill agreement expressly prohibits specific conduct by a contracting party to acquire control of the other contracting party. Typically, a standstill agreement will prohibit a hostile bid in any form, including a hostile tender offer to acquire stock control of the other contracting party and/or a proxy contest to replace all or some of its directors. Standstill prohibitions do not require, or in any way depend upon, a contracting party's use or disclosure of the other party's confidential, nonpublic information. Rather, a standstill agreement is intended to protect a contracting party against hostile takeover behavior, as distinguished from the unauthorized use or disclosure of the other party's confidential nonpublic information.
>
> A confidentiality agreement, in contrast, is intended and structured to prevent a contracting party from using and disclosing the other party's confidential, non-public information except as permitted by the agreement. In that respect it is qualitatively distinguishable from a prohibition that precludes a party categorically from engaging in specified hostile takeover activity. Thus, a confidentiality agreement will not typically preclude a contracting party from making a hostile bid to acquire control of the other party, so long as the bid does not involve the use or disclosure of the other party's confidential, nonpublic information. A confidentiality agreement is intended to protect a contracting party's non-public information, not its corporate ownership and control.[11]

In affirming the Chancery Court's decision, the Supreme Court reasoned, in part, as follows:

> It is undisputed that the Confidentiality Agreements in this case were true confidentially agreements, not standstill agreements. They did not categorically preclude Martin from making a hostile takeover bid for Vulcan. What they did was preclude Martin from using and disclosing Vulcan's confidential, nonpublic information except insofar as the agreements themselves permitted. The Court of Chancery clearly understood that distinction. It interpreted and enforced the disputed agreements in this case as confidentiality agreements, using the appropriate tools of contract interpretation....
>
> The Chancellor determined that Martin, in making its hostile bid, both "used" and "disclosed" Vulcan Confidential Materials in violation of the JDA. That agreement (the trial court found) unambiguously prohibits the use of "Confidential Materials" without Vulcan's consent, except "for purposes of pursuing and completing the Transaction," which the JDA defines as "a potential transaction being discussed by Vulcan and Martin Marietta." The Court of Chancery found as fact that "the only transaction that was 'being discussed' at the time the parties entered into the JDA was a negotiated merger," and that "neither [the] Exchange Offer nor [the] Proxy Contest ... was 'the' transaction that was 'being discussed' at the time that the JDA was negotiated."[12]

---

10. *Id.* at *27.
11. *Id.* at *27–*30.
12. *Id.* at *31–*32..

Although the court says that there is a difference between a standstill agreement and a confidentiality agreement, as a practical matter the court's interpretation of the NDA and JDA in this case makes these agreements a standstill. In view of this case, it seems improbable that a party to a similar NDA or JDA would be permitted to make a hostile offer for the counterparty, because such an offer would necessarily require the use and disclosure of confidential information. If the parties to future similar confidentiality agreement intend that the agreement not be construed as a standstill, they should explicitly say so in the agreement.

C. Introduction to Don't Ask, Don't Waive (DADW) Provisions of a Standstill

As discussed more fully in Chapter 3, a DADW provision may be included in the standstill provisions of a confidentiality agreement, or in a separate standstill agreement. Pursuant to a DADW provision, a potential acquirer agrees not to "request or propose that the target or any of its representatives amend, waive or consider an amendment to or waiver of any of the provisions of standstill.

For the reasons discussed in Chapter 3, as of May 21, 2013, on fiduciary duty grounds, the Delaware Chancery Court has found such provisions to be unenforceable in the following three cases: Vice Chancellor Laster's November 27, 2012 transcript ruling in *Genomics*;[13] Chancellor Strine's December 17, 2013 transcript ruling in *Ancestry*,[14] and Vice Chancellor Glasscock's May 21, 2013 decision in *NetSpend*.[15]

D. No Teaming Provision of a Confidentiality Agreement— *Del Monte*[16]

Confidentiality agreements may contain a "no teaming" provision, which without the approval of the target, prohibits a potential acquirer from combining with any other party to make a joint bid for the target. In the *Del Monte*[17] case, the court found that KKR, with the assistance of Barclays, had violated a "no teaming" provision in a confidentiality agreement it had signed with Del Monte. The "no teaming" provision of the Del Monte confidentiality agreement was part of the provision prohibiting the disclosure of the confidential information, and the provision read as follows:

> In addition, you agree that, without the prior written consent of the Company [Del Monte], you and your Representatives will not disclose to any other person (other than your Representatives) the fact that you are considering a possible transaction with the Company, that this Agreement exists, that the Confidential Information has been made available to you, that discussions or negotiations are taking place concerning a possible transaction involving the Company or any of the terms, conditions, or other facts with respect thereto (including the status thereof).... Without limiting the generality of the foregoing, you further agree

---

13. *In re Complete Genomics, Inc. Shareholder Litigation*, C.A. No. 7888-VCL (Del. Ch., Nov. 27, 2012) (transcript ruling), pp. 14–18.

14. *In re Ancestry.com.Inc Shareholder Litigation*, C.A. No. 7988-CS (Del. Ch., Dec. 17, 2012) (transcript ruling).

15. *Koehler v. NetSpend Holdings Inc.*, 2013 Del. Ch. LEXIS 131 (May 21, 2013).

16. This section is adapted from Thompson, *Mergers, Acquisitions and Tender Offers, supra* Section 1.10, at Section 3:2.21.

17. In Re Del Monte Foods Company Shareholders Litigation, 2011 Del. Ch. LEXIS 30 (Del. Ch. Feb. 14, 2011).

> that you will not, directly or indirectly, share the Confidential Information with or enter into any agreement, arrangement or understanding, or any discussions which would reasonably be expected to lead to such an agreement, arrangement or understanding with any other person, including other potential bidders and equity or debt financing sources (other than your Representatives as permitted above) regarding a possible transaction involving the Company without the prior written consent of the Company and only upon such person executing a confidentiality agreement in favor of the Company with terms and conditions consistent with this Agreement.[18]

Pointing out that the confidentiality agreement also contained a two-year standstill, the court discussed as follows the effect of the "no teaming" provision:

> By securing this language, the Board ensured that Del Monte would have the contractual right to control the competitive dynamics of the process and determine whether any bidders would be allowed to work together on a joint bid.[19]

§ 10.4 Exclusivity Agreements

In some transactions the acquirer and target may enter into an exclusivity agreement or exclusive dealing agreement pursuant to which they agree to negotiate only with each other for a period of time, and as discussed previously these provisions may be included in letters of intent. These agreements are generally non-controversial. However, the exclusivity agreement entered into in September 2008 by Citigroup and Wachovia (Documentary Appendix FF, Exclusivity Agreement between Citigroup and Wachovia) became the subject of litigation between Citigroup, on the one hand, and Wachovia and Wells Fargo, on the other.

Pursuant to this exclusivity agreement Citigroup and Wachovia were negotiating regarding an acquisition by Citigroup of Wachovia's banking assets for consideration that amounted to approximately $2 per Wachovia share. During the period covered by the exclusivity agreement, Wachovia entered into a merger agreement with Wells Fargo pursuant to which Wachovia would be acquired by Wells Fargo for approximately $10 per share in stock of Wells Fargo. Citigroup immediately brought an action against Wachovia, Wells Fargo, and certain officers and directors of these firms asserting, *inter alia*, breach of contract by Wachovia and tortious interference with Citi's contractual rights by Wells Fargo. Although, Citigroup originally tried to block the merger, it subsequently decided to abandon its opposition, explaining in an October 8, 2008 press release:

> Citi believes that it has strong legal claims against Wachovia, Wells Fargo and their officers, directors, advisors and others for breach of contract and for tortious interference with contract. [Citi is seeking $30 billion in damages.] Citigroup plans to pursue these damage claims vigorously on behalf of its shareholders. However, Citigroup has decided not to ask that the Wells Fargo-Wachovia merger be enjoined.

The tortious interference claim against Wells Fargo is similar to the tortious interference claim brought against Texaco by Pennzoil in the *Texaco* case discussed below in connection with the examination of letters of intent. One of the issues in Citi's case was the absence

18. *Id.* at *14–*15.
19. *Id.*

of any type of "fiduciary out" for Wachovia in the exclusivity agreement and whether the agreement was required to have one. As discussed in Chapter 5, non-solicitation provisions in public company merger agreements generally must contain a fiduciary out that permits the target's board to enter into discussions with a third party who makes a proposal that is likely to lead to a superior proposal. Wachovia's board will undoubtedly argue that notwithstanding the exclusivity agreement, it had a fiduciary obligation to its shareholders to enter into the Wells Fargo deal because it was obviously superior to the Citi deal.

Although the law is not clear on this issue, it is the opinion of this author that since the "no solicitation" provision of any acquisition agreement that Citi and Wachovia could have entered would have been subject to a fiduciary out, the exclusivity agreement was required to have such an out. In this connection, the exclusive dealing provision in Section V.B of the Letter of Intent, PerfectData-Sona, Appendix 3-C, contains the following fiduciary out:

> Notwithstanding anything to the contrary in this [Exclusive Dealing] Paragraph, if, at any time prior to Closing, the Board of Directors of either party determines, based upon advice from outside legal counsel, that failure to act could reasonably be expected to be inconsistent with the Board's fiduciary duties under applicable law, such party may provide information with respect to such party to another person or entity that has made an unsolicited proposal for an Alternative Transaction and participate in discussions and negotiations with such person or entity relating to such Alternative Transaction.

Since the Citi–Wachovia exclusivity agreement did not have a fiduciary out, it is the author's opinion that a court likely would impute into the agreement such an "out." In this regard, the court in the *QVC* case discussed in Chapter 3 refused to enforce an acquirer's onerous deal protection devices because they were subject to the implicit fiduciary obligation of the target's directors to its shareholders. It appears to this author that there was no contractual right that Wells Fargo could have tortiously interfered with.

A fiduciary out in an exclusivity agreement clearly would not be required in a situation in which a closely held corporation is being acquired and all of the target's shareholders are participating in the transaction.

In determining whether to enter an exclusivity agreement, targets should weigh (1) the potential disadvantage of an exclusive dealing provision, which is the inability to shop the company, against (2) the advantage, which is the possibility of getting the focused attention of the acquirer.

§ 10.5 Due Diligence Investigation in Connection with Acquisitions

A. Introduction

In connection with your study of this section, read the Documentary Appendix CC, a Due Diligence Checklist.

In virtually every acquisition, the acquiring corporation will want to complete a due diligence investigation of the target, and if the consideration is anything other than cash, the sellers may want to undertake a due diligence investigation of the acquiring firm. The conduct of the due diligence investigation in an acquisition is similar to the due diligence investigation required to preserve the defense in Section 11(b)(3) of the Securities Act of 1933 for a material misstatement in a registration statement. [*See* Chapter 4]

The due diligence investigation begins before the decision to make the acquisition is made, continues through the preparation of the acquisition agreement, and then accelerates after the signing of the acquisition agreement and before the closing. The Section of Business Law of the ABA has published a *Manual on Acquisition Review* (1995) that discusses the principles that should be followed in examining a target's operations, including analyses of basic corporate documents, financial statements, environmental laws, intellectual property, and labor and employment matters. This manual should be consulted prior to undertaking a due diligence investigation. *See also* ABA Section of Business Law, Committee on Negotiated Acquisitions, *Purchasing the Stock of a Privately Held Company: The Legal Effect of an Acquisition Review*, 51 Bus. Lawyer 479 (1996) [hereinafter *Legal Effect of Acquisition Review*]. The following discussion, which is based on an article by William F. Wynne, Jr. entitled *Corporate Review in Connection with Mergers and Acquisitions*, PLI Course Handbook, Acquiring and Selling the Privately Held Company (1989) (modified with permission), discusses the due diligence investigation of a closely-held target corporation.

B. Purpose of Corporate Review

The primary purposes of a corporate review by the counsel for the Acquiring Corporation in connection with a proposed acquisition of a Target are:

(i) To assist the Acquiring Corporation in understanding and evaluating the information contained in the Acquisition Agreement and the Exhibits and Schedules related thereto and, in particular in assessing liabilities and other risk factors of a legal nature related to the Target;

(ii) To determine whether the information contained in the Acquisition Agreement and the Exhibits and Schedules related thereto is consistent with the corporate records and other documents of the Target and that such records and documents do not indicate that information important to an informed acquisition decision has been omitted from the Acquisition Agreement and the related Exhibits and Schedules; and

(iii) To identify legal and contractual impediments to the completion of the proposed acquisition, including required authorizations, consents and approvals.

The Acquisition Agreement and its related Exhibits and Schedules should provide at least the same information as the prospectus is meant to provide to potential investors in a public offering: information necessary to allow the Acquiring Corporation to make an *informed investment decision* with respect to the acquisition.

The primary purposes of the counsel for the Target in a corporate review are:

(i) To assist the Target or its shareholders in preparing the Schedules and other disclosure material responsive to the representations and warranties set forth in the Acquisition Agreement;

(ii) To insure that the information contained in the Acquisition Agreement and the Exhibits and Schedules related thereto is consistent with the corporate records and other documents of the Target;

(iii) To identify legal and contractual impediments to completion of the proposed acquisition, including required authorizations, consents and approvals; and

(iv) To establish a basis for the legal opinions which are generally required of the Target's or Shareholders' counsel pursuant to the Acquisition Agreement. [*See* Section 15.16]

C. Procedure for Corporate Review

If the Acquisition Agreement has been executed and all Exhibits and Schedules thereto have been delivered prior to the commencement of the corporate review by counsel to the Acquiring Corporation, the reviewing attorney should examine the certificate of incorporation and by-laws of the Target and the financial statements, Exhibits and Schedules delivered pursuant to the Acquisition Agreement. The reviewing attorney should contact the attorney for the Target and set up a mutually convenient time for the review session. At such time as the appointment is made, the reviewing attorney should send his or her counterpart a letter setting forth the documents he or she wishes to examine. Such documents should include:

(i) The minutes of meetings of the Board of Directors, Executive Committee and other Committees of the Board of Directors and of shareholders of the Target from the date of incorporation or, if agreed to by the client, a date not less than five years preceding the proposed acquisition, plus organizational minutes and all minutes which show share authorizations since the date of incorporation;

(ii) The minutes of the meetings of the Board of Directors of the Target's principal subsidiaries since the later of the date of incorporation or a date not less than five years preceding the proposed acquisition, plus organizational minutes and all minutes which show share authorizations since the date of incorporation;

(iii) The Target's stock records; and

(iv) All documents and other materials relating to the Target and its subsidiaries which are listed or referred to on the Schedules.

In the event the Exhibits and Schedules to the Acquisition Agreement have not been completed prior to the commencement of the corporate review or the Acquisition Agreement has very limited representations and warranties, the reviewing attorney should provide counsel for the Target with a more detailed list of documents as a starting point for the corporate review. A similar list, tailored to the particular transaction and company to be acquired, can also be utilized by counsel for the Target or the selling shareholders to assist the Target or the selling shareholders in the preparation of disclosure Schedules, to identify consents and approvals necessary for the completion of the acquisition, and to establish the foundation for the legal opinion required of such counsel.

The right to undertake a complete and unfettered review of the Target should be clearly established in the Acquisition Agreement. [*See* § 5.4 of the Time-Warner Merger Agreement, Documentary Appendix A]

Minutes of all meetings of the Target's Board of Directors and any other committees and of shareholders should be reviewed as to:

(i) Authorizations and issuances of capital stock, convertible securities, any options or warrants to acquire stock and preemptive rights granted with respect to any class of capital stock. This is undertaken to determine that all (or the acquired portion) of the shares of capital stock of the Target will be owned by the Acquiring Corporation after the completion of the acquisition and not subject to dilution.

(ii) References to, and proper authorization of, material contracts and transactions including employment contracts, pension and other employee benefit plans, leases, loans, acquisitions or other transactions, and any pending or threatened litigation, which in the nature of the business of the Target may be material or to which officers, directors or principal shareholders of the Target are parties.

(iii) Adherence to proper corporate procedures (*i.e.* regular Board and shareholder meetings, proper notice of such meetings or waivers thereof).

Also a review should be made of the actual stock books and a record made of all issuances and transfers of stock. This should be compared with a current stockholder list. Any shares that have been cancelled should have been earmarked as such and be found in the stock book or, alternatively, there should be some evidence that all cancelled shares have been returned to the Target.

All contracts listed on the related Schedule to the Acquisition Agreement and all merger or acquisition agreements entered into since the Target's date of incorporation should be reviewed. Further, all contracts referred to in minutes and which are or may be material to the ownership of the Target or the business, properties, assets or operations of the Target should be reviewed.

The scope of the review of subsidiaries' records necessarily will depend upon (i) the relative importance of subsidiary operations as compared to the direct operations of the Target, and (ii) the number of subsidiaries and their relative importance as among themselves and with respect to the Target. The consolidated financial statements of the Target and its subsidiaries provided pursuant to the Acquisition Agreement should furnish a guide to the relative significance of the subsidiaries.

The minutes of meetings of the Board of Directors or committees of any subsidiary contributing more than 10% of the consolidated sales or net income or owning more than 10% of the consolidated assets of the Target and its subsidiaries should be examined. Review of the minutes of meetings of the Board of Directors or committees of other subsidiaries will necessarily depend upon their proportion of consolidated sales, net income and assets and the feasibility of effecting a spot-check rather than a detailed review of their provisions.

The stock books of all material subsidiaries should be examined to confirm that, except as the Schedules to the Acquisition Agreement otherwise disclose, no shares are outstanding in names other than that of the Target. Appropriate notes should be made of any outstanding directors' qualifying shares or other minority interests.

Any company that has been acquired by the Target in exchange for stock or convertible securities of the Target through a statutory merger or an exchange of stock should be examined in the same manner as the Target to determine (i) the validity of its outstanding stock at the time of the acquisition, (ii) the due authorization and valid issuance of Target debt or equity securities in connection with the acquisition, and (iii) the nature of any material contracts or other obligations or liabilities which may have been assumed in connection with the acquisition. Where the Target has acquired assets of another company in exchange for stock, access to the other company's books and records (especially when less than all of its assets have been conveyed) may not be practicable. If access is so restricted, the review may be limited to examination of the validity of the corporate authorization for the sale of the assets to the Target. Where information is limited or unavailable with respect to the stock of predecessor companies, counsel to the Acquiring Corporation may, depending on the assessment of the competency of such predecessor's counsel and the adequacy of back-up documentation, rely upon opinions of such other counsel with respect to the stock of such predecessor companies.

D. Corporate Review Memorandum

After the review of all requested documents has been completed, the reviewing attorney should compare the information reviewed with the information contained in the Acquisition

Agreement and the Exhibits and Schedules thereto. The purpose of the comparison is to determine whether any material matter that should have been disclosed in the Acquisition Agreement or the Exhibits and Schedules thereto has been omitted, and whether, based on the results of the corporate review, the information provided to the Acquiring Corporation as the basis for its acquisition decision is consistent with the information and documents reviewed.

In appropriate circumstances, the reviewing attorney should prepare a memorandum providing the following information:

(a) The date and place of the review and specific identification of the documents reviewed;

(b) Names of the persons contacted with regard to information about the documents or the Target;

(c) A general review of the history of the Target and its subsidiaries including place and date of incorporation, any foreign qualifications and predecessor companies;

(d) A general discussion of the securities of the Target, due authorization, etc.;

(e) General discussion of outstanding debt and material contracts, including material leases;

(f) Specific description and discussion of consents, authorizations or approvals required by the terms of the documents reviewed or other problems, rights or forfeitures triggered by the proposed acquisition and specific recommendations for dealing with such matters;

(g) Specific discussion of all pending material, legal proceedings to which the Target or any of its subsidiaries is a party or to which any of their property is subject;

(h) Specific discussion of any variance between the material reviewed and the information contained in the Acquisition Agreement and the Exhibits and Schedules thereto; and

(i) Any other information the reviewer deems relevant to the client in assessing the acquisition.

Significant problems capable of resolution and discovered in the course of the corporate review should be raised, in writing, with the Target as soon as possible. Required consents, authorizations, or approvals, whether governmental or third party, are best handled in a cooperative fashion to avoid postponement of the completion of the acquisition. If, in the course of the corporate review, a transaction-threatening issue is discovered, for instance a certain antitrust obstacle, a material undisclosed liability or any other matter which would jeopardize or preclude the Target's satisfaction of the conditions precedent to the closing of the transaction, the issue should be brought to the attention of the client so that an appropriate strategy dealing with the issue may be developed.

§ 10.6 When Does a Letter of Intent Become a Binding Contract?

A. Introduction

In many situations the parties to a merger or acquisition may enter into a letter of intent or agreement in principle setting out the basic terms of the deal. For an illustration of a letter of intent read Documentary Appendix FF, a Letter of Intent.

One issue with letters of intent is whether such a document will be considered a binding contract. The following case illustrates this issue.

B. Illustration

Texaco, Inc. v. Pennzoil Co.

Court of Appeals of Texas, 1987 729 S.W.2d 768

WARREN, Justice:

This is an appeal from a judgment awarding Pennzoil damages for Texaco's tortious interference with a contract between Pennzoil and the "Getty entities" (Getty Oil Company, the Sarah C. Getty Trust, and the J. Paul Getty Museum).

[**Lower Court**] The jury found, among other things, that:

(1) At the end of a board meeting on January 3, 1984, the Getty entities intended to bind themselves to an agreement providing for the purchase of Getty Oil stock, whereby the Sarah C. Getty Trust would own 4/7th of the stock and Pennzoil the remaining 3/7th; * * *

(2) Texaco knowingly interfered with the agreement between Pennzoil and the Getty entities;

(3) As a result of Texaco's interference, Pennzoil suffered damages of $7.53 billion;

(4) Texaco's actions were intentional, willful, and in wanton disregard of Pennzoil's rights; and,

(5) Pennzoil was entitled to punitive damages of $3 billion.

[**Issues**] The main questions for our determination are: (1) whether the evidence supports the jury's finding that there was a binding contract between the Getty entities and Pennzoil, and that Texaco knowingly induced a breach of such contract; (2) whether the trial court properly instructed the jury on the law pertinent to the case; (3) whether the evidence supported the jury's damage awards; * * *.

[**Facts**]* * * There is evidence that for several months in late 1983, Pennzoil had followed with interest the well-publicized dissension between the board of directors of Getty Oil Company and Gordon Getty, who was a director of Getty Oil and also the owner, as trustee, of approximately 40.2% of the outstanding shares of Getty Oil. On December 28, 1983, Pennzoil announced an unsolicited, public tender offer for 16 million shares of Getty Oil at $100 each.

Soon afterwards, Pennzoil contacted both Gordon Getty and a representative of the J. Paul Getty Museum, which held approximately 11.8% of the shares of Getty Oil, to discuss the tender offer and the possible purchase of Getty Oil. In the first two days of January 1984, a "Memorandum of Agreement" was drafted to reflect the terms that had been reached in conversations between representatives of Pennzoil, Gordon Getty, and the Museum.

Under the plan set out in the Memorandum of Agreement, Pennzoil and the Trust (with Gordon Getty as trustee) were to become partners on a 3/7-to-4/7 basis respectively, in owning and operating Getty Oil. Gordon Getty was to become chairman of the board, and Hugh Liedtke, the chief executive officer of Pennzoil, was to become chief executive officer of the new company.

The Memorandum of Agreement further provided that the Museum was to receive $110 per share for its 11.8% ownership, and that all other outstanding public shares were to be cashed in by the company at $110 per share. Pennzoil was given an option to buy an additional 8 million shares to achieve the desired ownership ratio. The plan also provided that Pennzoil and the Trust were to try in good faith to agree upon a plan to restructure Getty Oil within a year, but if they could not reach an agreement, the assets of Getty Oil were to be divided between them, 3/7ths to Pennzoil and 4/7ths to the Trust.

The Memorandum of Agreement stated that it was subject to approval of the board of Getty Oil, and it was to expire by its own terms if not approved at the board meeting that was to begin on January 2. Pennzoil's CEO, Liedtke, and Gordon Getty, for the Trust, signed the Memorandum of Agreement before the Getty Oil board meeting on January 2, and Harold Williams, the president of the Museum, signed it shortly after the board meeting began. Thus, before it was submitted to the Getty Oil board, the Memorandum of Agreement had been executed by parties who together controlled a majority of the outstanding shares of Getty Oil. * * *

The board voted to reject recommending Pennzoil's tender offer to Getty's shareholders, then later also rejected the Memorandum of Agreement price of $110 per share as too low. Before recessing at 3 a.m., the board decided to make a counter-proposal to Pennzoil of $110 per share plus a $10 debenture. Pennzoil's investment banker reacted to this price negatively. In the morning of January 3, Getty Oil's investment banker, Geoffrey Boisi, began calling other companies, seeking a higher bid than Pennzoil's for the Getty Oil shares.

When the board reconvened at 3 p.m. on January 3, a revised Pennzoil proposal was presented, offering $110 per share plus a $3 "stub" that was to be paid after the sale of a Getty Oil subsidiary ("ERC"), from the excess proceeds over $1 billion. Each shareholder was to receive a *pro rata* share of these excess proceeds, but in any case, a minimum of $3 per share at the end of five years. During the meeting, Boisi briefly informed the board of the status of his inquiries of other companies that might be interested in bidding for the company. He reported some preliminary indications of interest, but no definite bid yet.

The Museum's lawyer told the board that, based on his discussions with Pennzoil, he believed that if the board went back "firm" with an offer of $110 plus a $5 stub, Pennzoil would accept it. After a recess, the Museum's president (also a director of Getty Oil) moved that the Getty board should accept Pennzoil's proposal provided that the stub be raised to $5, and the board voted 15 to 1 to approve this counter-proposal to Pennzoil. The board then voted themselves and Getty's officers and advisors indemnity for any liability arising from the events of the past few months. * * * There was evidence that during another brief recess of the board meeting, the counter-offer of $110 plus a $5 stub was presented to and accepted by Pennzoil. After Pennzoil's acceptance was conveyed to the Getty board, the meeting was adjourned, and most board members left town for their respective homes.

That evening, the lawyers and public relations staff of Getty Oil and the Museum drafted a press release describing the transaction between Pennzoil and the Getty entities. The press release, announcing an agreement in principle on the terms of the Memorandum of Agreement but with a price of $110 plus a $5 stub, was issued on Getty Oil letterhead the next morning, January 4, and later that day, Pennzoil issued an identical press release.

On January 4, Boisi continued to contact other companies, looking for a higher price than Pennzoil had offered. After talking briefly with Boisi, Texaco management called several meetings with its in-house financial planning group, which over the course of the day studied and reported to management on the value of Getty Oil, the Pennzoil offer terms, and a feasible price range at which Getty might be acquired. Later in the day, Texaco hired an investment banker, First Boston, to represent it with respect to a possible acquisition of Getty Oil. Meanwhile, also on January 4, Pennzoil's lawyers were working on a draft of a formal "transaction agreement" that described the transaction in more detail than the outline of terms contained in the Memorandum of Agreement and press release.

On January 5, the Wall Street Journal reported on an agreement reached between Pennzoil and the Getty entities, describing essentially the terms contained in the Memorandum of Agreement. The Pennzoil board met to ratify the actions of its officers in negotiating an agreement with the Getty entities. * * *

The board of Texaco also met on January 5, authorizing its officers to make an offer for 100% of Getty Oil and to take any necessary action in connection therewith. Texaco first contacted the Museum's lawyer, Lipton, and arranged a meeting to discuss the sale of the Museum's shares of Getty Oil to Texaco. Lipton instructed his associate, on her way to the meeting in progress of the lawyers drafting merger documents for the Pennzoil/Getty transaction, to not attend that meeting, because he needed her at his meeting with Texaco. At the meeting with Texaco, the Museum outlined various issues it wanted resolved in any transaction with Texaco, and then agreed to sell its 11.8% ownership in Getty Oil.

That evening, Texaco met with Gordon Getty to discuss the sale of the Trust's shares. He was informed that the Museum had agreed to sell its shares to Texaco. Gordon Getty's advisors had previously warned him that the Trust shares might be "locked out" in a minority position if Texaco bought, in addition to the Museum's shares, enough of the public shares to achieve over 50% ownership of the company. Gordon Getty accepted Texaco's offer of $125 per share and signed a letter of his intent to sell his stock to Texaco, as soon as a California temporary restraining order against his actions as trustee was lifted.

At noon on January 6, Getty Oil held a telephone board meeting to discuss the Texaco offer. The board voted to withdraw its previous counter-proposal to Pennzoil and unanimously voted to accept Texaco's offer. Texaco immediately issued a press release announcing that Getty Oil and Texaco would merge.

Soon after the Texaco press release appeared, Pennzoil telexed the Getty entities, demanding that they honor their agreement with Pennzoil. Later that day, prompted by the telex, Getty Oil filed a suit in Delaware for declaratory judgment that it was not bound to any contract with Pennzoil. The merger agreement between Texaco and Getty Oil was signed on January 6; the stock purchase agreement with the Museum was signed on January 6; and the stock exchange agreement with the Trust was signed on January 8, 1984.

[**Sufficiency of Evidence**] Texaco contends that the evidence at trial was legally and factually insufficient to support the jury's answers to Special Issues 1 and 2.

The parties agree that in our review, we are required to apply the substantive law of New York and the procedural law of Texas.

There are two standards of review for questions attacking the sufficiency of the evidence: (1) legal insufficiency and (2) factual insufficiency review. * * *

[**Special Issue No. 1: Was there a Contract?**] Texaco contends that under controlling principles of New York law, there was insufficient evidence to support the jury's finding that at the end of the Getty Oil board meeting on January 3, the Getty entities intended to bind themselves to an agreement with Pennzoil.

Pennzoil responds that the question of the parties' intent is a fact question, and the jury was free to accept or reject Texaco's after-the-fact testimony of subjective intent. Pennzoil contends that the evidence showed that the parties intended to be bound to the terms in the Memorandum of Agreement plus a price of $110 plus a $5 stub, even though the parties may have contemplated a later, more formal document to memorialize the agreement already reached. Pennzoil also argues that the binding effect of the Memorandum of Agreement was conditioned only upon approval of the board, not also upon execution of the agreement by a Getty signature.

Under New York law, if parties do not intend to be bound to an agreement until it is reduced to writing and signed by both parties, then there is no contract until that event occurs. If there is no understanding that a signed writing is necessary before the parties will be bound, and the parties have agreed upon all substantial terms, then an informal agreement can be binding, even though the parties contemplate evidencing their agreement in a formal document later. * * *

Thus, under New York law, the parties are given the power to obligate themselves informally or only by a formal signed writing, as they wish. The emphasis in deciding when a binding contract exists is on intent rather than on form.

It is the parties' expressed intent that controls which rule of contract formation applies. To determine intent, a court must examine the words and deeds of the parties, because these constitute the objective signs of such intent. Only the outward expressions of intent are considered secret or subjective intent is immaterial to the question of whether the parties were bound. * * *

Pennzoil and Texaco presented conflicting evidence at trial on the common business usage and understanding of the term "agreement in principle." Texaco's witnesses testified that the term is used to convey an invitation to bid or that there is no binding contract. Pennzoil's witnesses testified that when business people use "agreement in principle," it means that the parties have reached a meeting of the minds with only details left to be resolved. * * *

The jury was the sole judge of the credibility of the witnesses and was entitled to accept or reject any testimony it wished, as well as to decide what weight to give the testimony. There was sufficient evidence at trial on the common business usage of the expression "agreement in principle" and on its meaning in this case for the jury reasonably to decide that its use in the press release did not necessarily establish that the parties did not intend to be bound before signing a formal document. * * *

It was the jury's task to judge the credibility of the witnesses, to resolve conflicts in the factual evidence, and to decide which inferences to draw from the evidence presented. The reviewing court may not substitute its own opinion for that of the jury on these matters. We find that there was sufficient evidence to support the jury's finding that at the end of the Getty Oil board meeting on January 3, the parties had reached agreement on Getty's purchase of the Museum's shares. * * *

[**Special Issue No. 2: Did Texaco Interfere?**] Texaco's next points of error concern the jury's finding in Special Issue No. 2 that Texaco knowingly interfered with the agreement, if so found, between Pennzoil and the Getty entities. Texaco contends that the evidence is legally and factually insufficient to show that Texaco had actual knowledge of any agreement, that it actively induced breach of the alleged contract, and that the alleged contract was valid and capable of being interfered with. * * *

As discussed above, Texaco assembled its in-house financial planning group, which worked all day on January 4 to study Getty and the Pennzoil situation and then reported to management. The evidence of Texaco's strong motivation to acquire Getty's reserves, given Texaco's own declining reserves and high finding costs, is also relevant here. * * *

The evidence discussed above on Texaco's calculated formulation and implementation of its ideal strategy to acquire Getty is also inconsistent with its contention that it was merely the passive target of Getty's aggressive solicitation campaign and did nothing more than to accept terms that Getty Oil and the Museum had proposed. * * *

Texaco argues that its testimony shows that Getty Oil and the Museum were the real moving forces that eventually led to the Texaco contract. However, we find that there is legally and factually sufficient evidence in the record to support the jury's finding that Texaco actively induced the breach of the Getty entities' agreement with Pennzoil.

Texaco also contends that Getty's shopping for bids constituted a breach of an implied "no-shop" provision of Pennzoil's alleged contract before Texaco ever entered the picture. We reject this contention. It was no defense that Getty was not happy with the Pennzoil price, or might have been dissatisfied with the agreement. We overrule Points of Error 48 and 50, contending that there was no evidence or factually insufficient evidence to support the jury's finding that Texaco knowingly induced the breach of Pennzoil's agreement. * * *

Questions and Note

(1) Target and Acquiror enter into a letter of intent that sets forth the price and basic structure of a transaction in which Acquiror will acquire Target. Acquiror #2 is thinking of making an acquisition proposal to Target's board at a price higher than that offered by Acquiror. How should Acquiror #2 proceed? What type of "outs" does the Target want in the letter of intent? What "outs" does the Acquiror want?

(2) For a sample letter of intent with commentary *see* Ancillary Document No. 2 of *ABA Model Stock Purchase Agreement, supra* Section 1.10. The sample contains non-binding provisions in Part One and binding provisions in Part Two. Section 14 provides in part that "[t]he paragraphs and provisions of Part One * * * do not constitute an will not give rise to any legally binding obligation on the part of any of the parties * * *." *See also*, Ancillary Document No. 2 of *ABA Model Asset Purchase Agreement, supra* Section 1.10.

References

ABA Asset Purchase Agreement, supra Section 1.10, Ancillary Document No.1, Confidentiality Agreement, and Ancillary Document No. 2, Letter of Intent.

ABA Model Stock Purchase Agreement, supra Section 1.10, Ancillary Document No.1, Confidentiality Agreement, and Ancillary Document No. 2, Letter of Intent.

Kling and Nugent Simon, *Negotiated Acquisitions, supra* Section 1.10, at Chapter 9 (confidentiality agreements) and Chapter 6 (letters of intent).

Thompson, *Mergers, Acquisitions and Tender Offers, supra* Section 1.10, Chapter 3.

Chapter 11

Acquisition of Stock of Closely-Held Corporations, Including Acquisition of a Controlling Interest

§ 11.1 Scope

This chapter deals with acquisitions of stock of closely-held corporations. The chapter covers both (1) acquisitions by an acquiror of all of the stock of a target, and (2) acquisitions by an acquiror of a controlling stock interest that is less than all of the stock of a target. Many of the principles discussed here also apply in the acquisition of stock of publicly-held corporations.

Section 11.2 provides an introductory problem that raises many of the issues addressed in this chapter and in other relevant chapters, such as Chapter 4, dealing with securities regulation; Chapter 5, dealing with federal income tax; Chapter 6, dealing with accounting; and Chapter 9, dealing with pre-merger notification. Section 11.3 addresses certain federal securities law issues relevant to stock acquisitions, while Sections 11.4, 11.5, and 11.6 refer respectively to the federal income tax aspects in Chapter 5, the accounting aspects in Chapter 6, and the pre-merger notification aspects in Chapter 9.

Sections 11.7 through 11.10 deal with issues that can rise where an acquiror acquires a controlling interest that is less than all of a target's stock. Section 11.7 examines whether there is an equal opportunity doctrine that requires that all shareholders of a target share in any premium paid for a controlling interest in the target's shares. Section 11.8 considers the rules regarding the sale of corporate office in connection with a sale of stock, and Section 11.9 addresses the obligation to investigate before selling stock to avoid a sale to a looter. Section 11.10 examines the rules in the *ALI's Corporate Governance Project* governing the sale of a controlling stock interest. Chapter 3 of this book contains several other cases involving controlling shareholders in various types of public M&A transactions. Finally, Section 11.11 deals with a parent corporation's potential derivative liability for its sub's direct environmental liability.

For a discussion of the many issues that can arise in a stock acquisition *see ABA Model Stock Purchase Agreement, supra* Section 1.10, and various chapters of Thompson, *Mergers, Acquisitions and Tender Offers, supra* Section 1.10.

This chapter does not address labor and employee rights issues, such as compliance with ERISA and the Worker Adjustment and Retraining Notification Act (the WARN Act).

§ 11.2 Introductory Problem on Stock Acquisition

Target Corporation (TC), which is incorporated in a state with the Model Business Corporation Act, is owned by 16 shareholders as follows:

Shareholder	**Interest**
A	25%
Other 15 Shareholders	5% each

Shareholder A is the President and Chairman of the three-person board of TC. TC operates a coal mine, and TC has assets with a book value and fair market value of $80 million. TC has liabilities of $30 million. Thus, the net fair market value (*i.e.*, fair market value less liabilities) of TC's assets and stock is $50 million. Also, TC has sales of $90 million. Acquiring corporation (AC), a large publicly-held corporation with over $200 million in assets, needs coal for its business and would like to acquire a controlling interest in TC for the purpose of insuring itself an adequate supply of coal. AC is not interested, however, in acquiring all of the stock or assets of TC.

AC has proposed to acquire shareholder A's 25% stock interest for $25 million in cash or in AC stock. The offer is conditioned upon AC replacing TC's directors with AC's designees. This would be accomplished pursuant to TC's by-laws by having the seriatim resignation of TC's directors and the election by the remaining directors of the AC designees until the full board consists of AC designees. (For an example of a bylaw provision providing for the filing of vacancies by current directors, *see* Section 2.2 of the Goldman By-laws, Documentary Appendix W of *M&A Statutes, Rules, and Documents, supra* Section 1.1.) AC has also offered to pay Shareholder A $5 million for a covenant from A not to compete with TC.

Since the net fair market value of TC's assets and stock is $50 million, the net fair market value of A's 25% stock interest is, therefore, $12.5 million. Thus, AC is offering A a 50% premium over the net fair market value of the assets standing behind those shares. Within the past month, one of TC's other shareholders purchased her 5% stock interest for the book value of such interest, that is $2.5 million (5% of $50 million). It is normally expected that the stock of coal companies like TC will sell for approximately book value. The transaction will be effectuated pursuant to a Stock Purchase Agreement between AC and A. A sample stock purchase agreement is contained in Documentary Appendix U of *M&A Statutes, Rules, and Documents, supra* Section 1.1.

1. Questions with regard to A:
   a. What action is A required to take in considering AC's offer? Is A required to make the offer known to the other shareholders and to TC's Board of Directors?
   b. Is there a problem under the federal securities laws or state law with the seriatim resignation of TC's directors?
   c. Is A required to urge AC to purchase all of TC's shares?
   d. Does A have any potential liability to the non-selling shareholders under the federal securities laws or state laws?
   e. Is A required to share any premium with either TC or the non-selling shareholders of TC?
   f. What measures should A take in order to minimize his potential liability to the non-selling shareholders upon a sale of the shares to AC?
   g. If AC makes the purchase using its stock, can A resell the stock?
   h. What is the federal income tax impact to A from the receipt of cash? Stock?
   i. In general, what types of representations, covenants, and conditions would A want in the stock acquisition agreement? *See* Chapter 15.

2. Questions with respect to AC:
   a. In general, what type of representations from A would AC want in its stock purchase agreement with A? Does A have any potential liability under the federal securities law for breach of those representations? *See* Chapter 15.
   b. If AC's acquisition is made for cash, does AC have any potential liability to A under the federal securities law?
   c. If AC makes the purchase using its stock, what are the potential implications to AC under the federal securities law?
   d. Will AC have any potential liability under state or federal law to either TC or the non-selling shareholders of TC?
   e. Is the transaction subject to reporting under Hart-Scott-Rodino?
   f. What are the federal income tax and accounting aspects to AC if the acquisition consideration is cash? Stock?
   g. After the acquisition by AC of A's shares what will be the impact of AC's purchase of coal from TC?
   h. What corporate and shareholder action is required by AC to effectuate the transaction?

Assume that the proposed purchase by AC of A's shares is abandoned and that AC now proposes to purchase all of the shares of TC for $105 million in cash. The transaction will be effectuated pursuant to a Stock Purchase Agreement between AC and all the shareholders of TC. A sample stock purchase agreement is contained in Documentary Appendix U of *M&A Statutes, Rules, and Documents, supra* Section 1.1.

3. Questions with regard to TC and its shareholders:
   a. Suppose that one of TC's 5% shareholders refuses to go along with the deal. Can a transaction that would be treated as a stock acquisition for federal income tax purposes be structured to force this shareholder to sell his shares?
   b. In general, what representations, covenants and conditions will TC's shareholders want? *See* Chapter 15.
   c. Is this transaction subject to reporting under Hart-Scott-Rodino?
   d. If AC makes the purchase using its stock can the TC shareholders resell the stock?
   e. What is the federal income tax impact to the TC shareholders upon receipt of cash? Stock?

4. Questions with respect to AC:
   a. In general, what representations, covenants and conditions will AC want in the stock acquisition agreement? *See* Chapter 15.
   b. What should be the scope of AC's due diligence investigation? *See* Chapter 10.
   c. If AC makes the purchase using its stock, what are the potential implications to AC under the federal securities laws?
   d. Is the transaction reportable under Hart-Scott-Rodino?
   e. What is the impact on AC under the federal income tax laws and the accounting rules from the use of cash in the acquisition? Stock?
   f. What steps can AC take to ensure that it does not become subject to any of TC's liabilities?

§11.3 Securities Law Impact

A. Acquisitions of Closely-Held Target's Stock for Acquiror's Securities

1. Qualifying Transaction under Reg. D

Regulation D, which is explored in Chapter 4, may be utilized for exempting from registration an acquisition by an acquiring corporation of the stock of a closely-held target corporation in exchange for stock of the acquiror. Note that Reg D can be used by both closely-held and publicly-held acquirors.

2. Resale under Rule 144 of Securities Received in Reg. D Offering

As indicated in Chapter 4, any stock received by the target's shareholders in a transaction that is exempt under Regulation D can only be resold under Rule 144, in a registered offering, or in a §4(1½) transaction.

B. Impact of Rule 10b-5

1. Do the Non-Selling Shareholders Have a Cause of Action against the Sellers under Rule 10b-5?

a. The Origin of the Purchaser/Seller Doctrine

Birnbaum v. Newport Steel Corp.

United States Court of Appeals, Second Circuit, 1952 193 F.2d 461

Augustus N. Hand, Circuit Judge.

The appellants are stockholders of the Newport Steel Corporation who brought suit on behalf of that corporation and as the representatives of all similarly situated stockholders. The complaint alleges a violation of Section 10(b) of the Securities Exchange Act of 1934, and Rule 10b-5. * * * The defendants * * * moved in the court below to dismiss the complaint for failure to state a cause of action. That court granted the motion and directed judgment accordingly. * * *

Prior to the sale in controversy, the Newport Steel Corporation manufactured steel which it sold to manufacturers of finished steel products. The defendant Feldmann owned approximately forty percent of the common stock of Newport, which was sufficient for voting control, and was its president and chairman of its board of directors; the remaining stock of Newport was publicly-held and scattered among thousands of small investors. * * * During this period Follansbee Steel Corporation and Newport were negotiating for a merger of the two corporations, which merger, on the terms offered by Follansbee, would have been highly profitable to all the stockholders of Newport. However, in August of 1950, Feldmann, acting in his official capacity as president of Newport, rejected the Follansbee offer, and on August 31, 1950, sold his stock to the defendant Wilport Company at a price of approximately $22 per share which was twice the then market value of the stock. * * * [I]n a letter to the Newport stockholders on August 3, 1950, Feldmann stated that the negotiations with Follansbee had been suspended because of the "uncertain international situation." And in a letter dated September 14, 1950, Gibson, the new president of Newport, reported the sale of Feldmann's stock but failed to state the selling price or that Newport was to become a "captive" subsidiary of Wilport.

It is claimed by the appellants that these misrepresentations operated as a fraud upon the stockholders of Newport in connection with the sale of Feldmann's stock, and that SEC Rule 10b-5 was thereby violated. The district court, however, viewed the Rule in question as aimed only at "a fraud perpetrated upon the purchaser or seller" of securities and as having no relation to breaches of fiduciary duty by corporate insiders resulting in fraud upon those who were not purchasers or sellers. We are in accord with the district court's interpretation of the Rule. * * *

The appellants contend that the applicability of the rule is not limited to the actual purchasers or sellers of securities, but that the general proscription of fraud "upon any person" includes and supplements the common law liability of those who abuse the trust of their corporate positions. They contend that this construction is further supported by the use of the words "in connection with" the purchase or sale of securities; for, if the intent had been to deal with just the purchase or sale of securities, the words "in connection with" are superfluous and would not have been added.

While the Rule may have been somewhat loosely drawn, its meaning and scope are not difficult to ascertain when reference is had to the scheme of SEC Regulation and the purpose underlying the adoption of 10b-5. Prior to its adoption the only prohibitions against fraud in the sale or purchase of securities were contained in Section 17(a) of the 1933 Act, and § 15(c) of the 1934 Act. Section 17(a) of the 1933 Act only made it unlawful to defraud or deceive *purchasers* of securities, and Section 15(c) of the 1934 Act dealt only with fraudulent practices by security brokers or dealers in over-the-counter markets. No prohibition existed against fraud on a seller of securities by the purchaser if the latter was not a broker or a dealer. Consequently, on May 21, 1942 the SEC adopted Rule 10b-5 to close this * * * "loophole in the protections against fraud administered by the Commission by prohibiting individuals or companies from buying securities if they engage in fraud in their purchase." The SEC's press release, above quoted, which announced the Commission's adoption of Rule 10b-5, shows that the Commission was attempting only to make the same prohibitions contained in Section 17(a) of the 1933 Act applicable to purchasers as well as to sellers. * * *

[T]he judgment of the district court was correct and is accordingly affirmed.

b. The Supreme Court's Ratification of the Purchaser/Seller Doctrine under Rule 10b-5

Blue Chip Stamps v. Manor Drug Stores

United States Supreme Court, 1975 95 S. Ct. 1917

Mr. Justice Rehnquist delivered the opinion of the Court.

This case requires us to consider whether the offerees of a stock offering, made pursuant to an antitrust consent decree and registered under the Securities Act of 1933, may maintain a private cause of action for money damages where they allege that the offeror has violated the provisions of Rule 10b-5, but where they have neither purchased nor sold any of the offered shares. *See Birnbaum v. Newport Steel Corp.*, Section 11.3.B.1.a. * * *

Three principal classes of potential plaintiffs are presently barred by the *Birnbaum* rule. First are potential purchasers of shares, either in a new offering or on the Nation's post-distribution trading markets, who allege that they decided not to purchase because of an unduly gloomy representation or the omission of favorable material which made the issuer appear to be a less favorable investment vehicle than it actually was. Second are actual shareholders in the issuer who allege that they decided not to sell their shares because of an unduly rosy representation or a failure to disclose unfavorable material.

Third are shareholders, creditors, and perhaps others related to an issuer who suffered loss in the value of their investment due to corporate or insider activities in connection with the purchase or sale of securities which violate Rule 10b-5. It has been held that shareholder members of the second and third of these classes may frequently be able to circumvent the *Birnbaum* limitation through bringing a derivative action on behalf of the corporate issuer if the latter is itself a purchaser or seller of securities. * * *

There has been widespread recognition that litigation under Rule 10b-5 presents a danger of vexatiousness different in degree and in kind from that which accompanies litigation in general. * * *

Thus we conclude that what may be called considerations of policy, which we are free to weigh in deciding this case, are by no means entirely on one side of the scale. Taken together with the precedental support for the *Birnbaum* rule over a period of more than 20 years, and the consistency of that rule with what we can glean from the intent of Congress, they lead us to conclude that it is a sound rule and should be followed. * * *

2. Does the Purchaser of the Stock of a Closely-Held Target Have a Cause of Action against the Seller under Rule 10b-5

Landreth Timber Company v. Landreth

United States Supreme Court, 1985 105 S. Ct. 2297

Justice Powell delivered the opinion of the Court.

This case presents the question whether the sale of all of the stock of a company is a securities transaction subject to the antifraud provisions of the federal securities laws (the Acts).

[**Facts**] Respondents Ivan K. Landreth and his sons owned all of the outstanding stock of a lumber business they operated in Tonasket, Washington. The Landreth family offered their stock for sale through both Washington and out-of-state brokers. Before a purchaser was found, the company's sawmill was heavily damaged by fire. Despite the fire, the brokers continued to offer the stock for sale. Potential purchasers were advised of the damage, but were told that the mill would be completely rebuilt and modernized.

Samuel Dennis, a Massachusetts tax attorney, received a letter offering the stock for sale. On the basis of the letter's representations concerning the rebuilding plans, the predicted productivity of the mill, existing contracts, and expected profits, Dennis became interested in acquiring the stock. * * * After having an audit and an inspection of the mill conducted, a stock purchase agreement was negotiated, with Dennis the purchaser of all of the common stock in the lumber company. * * *

After the acquisition was completed, the mill did not live up to the purchasers' expectations. Rebuilding costs exceeded earlier estimates, and new components turned out to be incompatible with existing equipment. Eventually, petitioner sold the mill at a loss and went into receivership. Petitioner then filed this suit seeking rescission of the sale of stock and $2,500,000 in damages, alleging that respondents had widely offered and then sold their stock without registering it as required by the Securities Act of 1933. [*See* Chapter 4] Petitioner also alleged that respondents had negligently or intentionally made misrepresentations and had failed to state material facts as to the worth and prospects of the lumber company, all in violation of the Securities Exchange Act of 1934. *See* Rule 10b-5.

[**Issue**] Respondents moved for summary judgment on the ground that the transaction was not covered by the Acts because under the so-called "sale of business" doctrine, petitioner had not purchased a "security" within the meaning of those Acts. The District Court granted respondents' motion and dismissed the complaint for want of federal jurisdiction. It acknowledged that the federal statutes include "stock" as one of the instruments constituting a "security," and that the stock at issue possessed all of the characteristics of conventional stock. Nonetheless, it joined what it termed the "growing majority" of courts that had held that the federal securities laws do not apply to the sale of 100% of the stock of a closely-held corporation. Relying on *United Housing Foundation, Inc. v. Forman*, 421 U.S. 837, (1975), and *SEC v. W.J. Howey Co.*, 328 U.S. 293, the District Court ruled that the stock could not be considered a "security" unless the purchaser had entered into the transaction with the anticipation of earning profits derived from the efforts of others. Finding that managerial control of the business had passed into the hands of the purchasers, and thus that the transaction was a commercial venture rather than a typical investment, the District Court dismissed the complaint.

The United States Court of Appeals for the Ninth Circuit affirmed the District Court's application of the sale of business doctrine. * * * Because the Courts of Appeals are divided over the applicability of the federal securities laws when a business is sold by the transfer of 100% of its stock, we granted certiorari. We now reverse.

[**Analysis**] It is axiomatic that "[t]he starting point in every case involving construction of a statute is the language itself." Section 2[(a)](1) of the 1933 Act, as amended, defines a "security" as including "any note, stock, treasury stock, bond, debenture, evidence of indebtedness, certificate of interest or participation in any profit-sharing agreement, * * *."[1]

As we have observed in the past, this definition is quite broad, and includes both instruments whose names alone carry well-settled meaning, as well as instruments of "more variable character [that] were necessarily designated by more descriptive terms," such as "investment contract" and "instrument commonly known as a 'security.'" *SEC v. C.M. Joiner Leasing Corp.*, 320 U.S. 344, (1943). The face of the definition shows that "stock" is considered to be a "security" within the meaning of the Acts. As we observed in *United Housing Foundation, Inc. v. Forman, supra*, most instruments bearing such a traditional title are likely to be covered by the definition.

As we also recognized in *Forman*, the fact that instruments bear the label "stock" is not of itself sufficient to invoke the coverage of the Acts. Rather, we concluded that we must also determine whether those instruments possess "some of the significant characteristics typically associated with" stock, recognizing that when an instrument is both called "stock" and bears stock's usual characteristics, "a purchaser justifiably [may] assume that the federal securities laws apply." We identified those characteristics usually associated with common stock as (i) the right to receive dividends contingent upon an apportionment of profits; (ii) negotiability; (iii) the ability to be pledged or hypothecated; (iv) the conferring of voting rights in proportion to the number of shares owned; and (v) the capacity to appreciate in value.

Under the facts of *Forman*, we concluded that the instruments at issue there were not "securities" within the meaning of the Acts. That case involved the sale of shares of stock

1. We have repeatedly ruled that the definitions of "security" in § 3(a)(10) of the 1934 Act and § 2[(a)](1) of the 1933 Act are virtually identical and will be treated as such in our decisions dealing with the scope of the term.

entitling the purchaser to lease an apartment in a housing cooperative. The stock bore none of the characteristics listed above that are usually associated with traditional stock. * * *

In contrast, it is undisputed that the stock involved here possesses all of the characteristics we identified in *Forman* as traditionally associated with common stock. * * * Under the circumstances of this case, the plain meaning of the statutory definition mandates that the stock be treated as "securities" subject to the coverage of the Acts.* * *

We also perceive strong policy reasons for not employing the sale of business doctrine under the circumstances of this case. By respondents' own admission, application of the doctrine depends in each case on whether control has passed to the purchaser. It may be argued that on the facts of this case, the doctrine is easily applied, since the transfer of 100% of a corporation's stock normally transfers control. We think even that assertion is open to some question, however, as Dennis and Bolten had no intention of running the sawmill themselves. * * *

More importantly, however, if applied to this case, the sale of business doctrine would also have to be applied to cases in which less than 100% of a company's stock was sold. This inevitably would lead to difficult questions of line-drawing. * * * As we explain more fully in *Gould v. Ruefenacht*, 471 U.S. 701 (1985), decided today as a companion to this case, coverage by the Acts would in most cases be unknown and unknowable to the parties at the time the stock was sold. * * *

In sum, we conclude that the stock at issue here is a "security" within the definition of the Acts, and that the sale of business doctrine does not apply. The judgment of the United States Court of Appeals for the Ninth Circuit is therefore ***Reversed.***

Notes and Questions

1. In *Gould v. Ruefenacht*, 471 U.S. 701 (1985), the Court held that the sale of 50% of the stock of a closely-held corporation was the sale of a security under the 33 Act and 34 Act.

2. What are the implications of the Court's holding? What potential liability does a seller of closely-held stock have under Sections 12(a)(1) and 12(a)(2) of the 1933 Act and under Rule 10b-5 of the 34 Act?

3. Required Disclosure under Rule 10b-5 upon Purchase of Stock of a Closely-Held Corporation

Jordan v. Duff and Phelps, Inc.

United States Court of Appeals, Seventh Circuit, 1987 815 F.2d 429

EASTERBROOK, Circuit Judge.

* * * *Michaels v. Michaels*, 767 F.2d 1185, 1194–97 (7th Cir.1985), holds that a closely-held firm must disclose material information to investors from whom it purchases stock, and that a decision to seek another firm with which to merge may be the sort of material information that must be disclosed to the investor selling his shares, even though the firm has not reached agreement in principle on the price and structure of a deal. * * *

[**Facts**] Duff and Phelps, Inc., evaluates the risk and worth of firms and their securities. * * * Jordan started work at Duff & Phelps in May 1977 and was viewed as a successful securities analyst. In 1981 the firm offered Jordan the opportunity to buy some stock. By November 1983 Jordan had purchased 188 of the 20,100 shares outstanding. He was making installment payments on another 62 shares. Forty people other than Jordan held stock in Duff & Phelps.

Jordan purchased his stock at its "book value" (the accounting net worth of Duff & Phelps, divided by the number of shares outstanding). Before selling him any stock, Duff & Phelps required Jordan to sign a "Stock Restriction and Purchase Agreement" (the Agreement). This provided in part:

> Upon the termination of any employment with the Corporation * * * for any reason, * * * the individual whose employment is terminated or his estate shall sell to the Corporation, and the Corporation shall buy, all Shares of the Corporation then owned by such individual or his estate [at adjusted book value.] * * *

While Jordan was accumulating stock, Hansen, the chairman of the board, was exploring the possibility of selling the firm. Between May and August 1983 Hansen and Francis Jeffries, another officer of Duff & Phelps, negotiated with Security Pacific Corp., a bank holding company. The negotiators reached agreement on a merger, in which Duff & Phelps would be valued at $50 million, but a higher official within Security Pacific vetoed the deal on August 11, 1983. As of that date, Duff & Phelps had no irons in the fire.

On November 16, 1983, Jordan told Hansen that he was going to resign and accept [other] employment. Jordan did not ask Hansen about potential mergers; Hansen did not volunteer anything. Jordan delivered a letter of resignation, which Duff & Phelps accepted the same day. By mutual agreement, Jordan worked the rest of the year for Duff & Phelps even though his loyalties had shifted. He did this so that he could receive the book value of the stock as of December 31, 1983—for under the Agreement a departure in November would have meant valuation as of December 31, 1982. Jordan delivered his certificates on December 30, 1983, and the firm mailed him a check for $23,225, the book value (at $123.54 per share) of the 188 shares of stock. Jordan surrendered, as worthless under the circumstances, the right to buy the remaining 62 shares.

Before Jordan cashed the check, however, he was startled by the announcement on January 10, 1984, of a merger between Duff & Phelps and a subsidiary of Security Pacific. Under the terms of the merger Duff & Phelps would be valued at $50 million. If Jordan had been an employee on January 10, had quickly paid for the other 62 shares, and the merger had closed that day, he would have received $452,000 in cash and the opportunity to obtain as much as $194,000 more in "earn out * * *." Jordan refused to cash the check and demanded his stock back; Duff & Phelps told him to get lost. He filed this suit in March 1984, asking for damages measured by the value his stock would have had under the terms of the acquisition.

The public announcement on January 10 explained that the boards of the two firms had reached an agreement in principle on January 6. The definitive agreement was signed on March 23. Because Security Pacific is a bank holding company, the acquisition required the approval of the Board of Governors of the Federal Reserve. The Fed granted approval, but with a condition so onerous that the firms abandoned the transaction. * * * The agreement was formally cancelled on January 9, 1985. Duff & Phelps quickly asked the district court to dismiss Jordan's suit, on the ground that he could not establish damages. Jordan responded by amending his complaint, with Judge Hart's permission, to ask for rescission rather than damages.

Throughout 1985 Duff & Phelps continued looking for a partner; finding none, it decided to dance with itself. The firm's management formed an "Employee Stock Ownership Trust", which was able to borrow $40 million against the security of the firm's assets and business. The Trust acquired Duff & Phelps through a new firm, Duff Research, Inc. This transaction occurred in December 1985. The employees at the time * * * received cash, notes, and beneficial interests in the Trust. Jordan asserts that the package was worth almost $2000 per share, or $497,000 if he had held 250 shares in December 1985. * * *

[**Analysis**]*Michaels* holds that close corporations that purchase their own stock must disclose to the sellers all information that meets the standard of "materiality" set out in *TSC Industries, Inc. v. Northway, Inc.*, [Section 4.5.A] A jury would be free under *Michaels* to conclude that the board's decision of November 14 to seek a buyer for Duff & Phelps—coupled with the fact that at least one putative buyer thought Duff & Phelps worth $50 million, which casts an important light on the prospect of a profitable conclusion to the search—was "material" under the standard of *TSC Industries*. * * *

The "duty" in question is the fiduciary duty of corporate law. Close corporations buying their own stock, like knowledgeable insiders of closely-held firms buying from outsiders, have a fiduciary duty to disclose material facts. * * *

The timing of the sale and the materiality of the information Duff & Phelps withheld on November 16 are for the jury to determine. Our dissenting colleague stresses that businesses would be shocked to learn that they must disclose valuable corporate information to fickle employees. If disclosure is unthinkable, however, Jordan may have trouble establishing that Duff & Phelps acted with intent to defraud, a necessary element of a case under Rule 10b-5. * * *

4. Impact of an Anti-Reliance Clause on a Rule 10b-5 Action

It is common for acquisition agreements to contain an "anti-reliance" or "non-reliance" representation. Pursuant to this type of provision, the acquiror (and sometimes the target) represents, for example, that "except for the representations and warranties contained in the acquisition agreement, the acquiror acknowledges that the target and its shareholders make no other express or implied representation or warranty with respect to the target and any other information provided to the acquiror."

In *Harsco Corp. v. Segui*, 91 F.3d 337 (2nd Cir. 1996), the contract of sale contained an anti-reliance clause providing that the only representations and warranties made by the seller were those set out in the contract. Because of the clause, the court found that the purchaser could not bring a Rule 10b-5 action against the seller on the basis of representations purportedly made outside of the stock purchase agreement.

On the other hand, in *AES Corp. v. Dow Chemical Company*, 325 F.3d 174 (3d Cir.), *cert denied*, 540 U.S. 1068 (2003), the Third Circuit rejected *Harsco* and concluded that an anti-reliance clause in an acquisition agreement cannot prevent a Rule 10b-5 claim.

Both the Rule 10b-5 and contract law issues with anti-reliance clauses are examined in Section 2:10.6[AE] of Thompson, *Mergers, Acquisitions and Tender Offers*, *supra* Section 1.10.

§ 11.4 Tax Aspects

Chapter 5 addresses both taxable and tax-free acquisitions. This section addresses only the acquisition by an acquiror of all of the stock of a stand-alone target. As indicated in Chapter 5, an acquisition of the stock of a stand-alone target in a taxable acquisition results in a single shareholder level tax, unless the acquiror makes a Section 338 election to step-up the basis of the target's assets. As indicated in Chapter 5, a Section 338 election generally will not be made. If the consideration paid is voting stock of the acquiror, the transaction may be treated as a tax-free reorganization under Section 368(a)(1)(B).

In general, in a taxable acquisition of stock of a target, should the acquiror be willing to pay for the target's stock an amount equal to the full fair market value (less liabilities) of the target's assets?

§ 11.5 Accounting Aspects

As indicated in Chapter 6, for accounting purposes the acquisition of all of the stock of a target is treated under the "acquisition" method without respect to the consideration issued by the acquiror. Consequently, goodwill may arise as a result of the acquisition.

§ 11.6 Hart-Scott-Rodino Aspects

The Hart-Scott-Rodino pre-merger notification rules are examined in Chapter 9. In general, any acquisition in excess of $50 million (adjusted for inflation) is reportable.

§ 11.7 Is There an Equal Opportunity Doctrine?

A. Possibly

Perlman v. Feldmann

United States Court of Appeal, Second Circuit, 1955 219 F.2d 173

Clark, Chief Judge.

This is a derivative action brought by minority stockholders of Newport Steel Corporation to compel accounting for, and restitution of, allegedly illegal gains which accrued to defendants as a result of the sale in August, 1950, of their controlling interest in the corporation. The principal defendant, C. Russell Feldmann, who represented and acted for the others, members of his family, was at that time not only the dominant stockholder, but also the chairman of the board of directors and the president of the corporation. Newport, an Indiana corporation, operated mills for the production of steel sheets for sale to manufacturers of steel products, first at Newport, Kentucky, and later also at other places in Kentucky and Ohio. The buyers, a syndicate organized as Wilport Company, a Delaware corporation, consisted of end-users of steel who were interested in securing a source of supply in a market becoming ever tighter in the Korean War. Plaintiffs contend that the consideration paid for the stock included compensation for the sale of a corporate asset, a power held in trust for the corporation by Feldmann as its fiduciary. This power was the ability to control the allocation of the corporate product in a time of short supply, through control of the board of directors; and it was effectively transferred in this sale by having Feldmann procure the resignation of his own board and the election of Wilport's nominees immediately upon consummation of the sale. * * *

Plaintiffs argue here, as they did in the court below, that in the situation here disclosed the vendors must account to the non-participating minority stockholders for that share of their profit which is attributable to the sale of the corporate power. Judge Hincks denied the validity of the premise, holding that the rights involved in the sale were only those normally incident to the possession of a controlling block of shares, with which a dominant stockholder, in the absence of fraud or foreseeable looting, was entitled to deal according to his own best interests. Furthermore, he held that plaintiffs had failed to satisfy their burden of proving that the sales price was not a fair price for the stock *per se*. Plaintiffs appeal from these rulings of law which resulted in the dismissal of their complaint.

The essential facts found by the trial judge are not in dispute. Newport was a relative newcomer in the steel industry with predominantly old installations which were in the process of being supplemented by more modern facilities. Except in times of extreme shortage Newport was not in a position to compete profitably with other steel mills for customers not in its immediate geographical area. Wilport, the purchasing syndicate, consisted of geographically remote end-users of steel who were interested in buying more steel from Newport than they had been able to obtain during recent periods of tight supply. The price of $20 per share was found by Judge Hincks to be a fair one for a control block of stock, although the over-the-counter market price had not exceeded $12 and the book value per share was $17.03. But this finding was limited by Judge Hincks' statement that "[w]hat value the block would have had if shorn of its appurtenant power to control distribution of the corporate product, the evidence does not show." It was also conditioned by his earlier ruling that the burden was on plaintiffs to prove a lesser value for the stock.

Both as director and as dominant stockholder, Feldmann stood in a fiduciary relationship to the corporation and to the minority stockholders as beneficiaries thereof. His fiduciary obligation must in the first instance be measured by the law of Indiana, the state of incorporation of Newport. Although there is no Indiana case directly in point, the most closely analogous one emphasizes the close scrutiny to which Indiana subjects the conduct of fiduciaries when personal benefit may stand in the way of fulfillment of trust obligations. * * *

[T]he same rule should apply to his fiduciary duties as majority stockholder, for in that capacity he chooses and controls the directors, and thus is held to have assumed their liability. This, therefore, is the standard to which Feldmann was by law required to conform in his activities here under scrutiny.

It is true, as defendants have been at pains to point out, that this is not the ordinary case of breach of fiduciary duty. We have here no fraud, no misuse of confidential information, no outright looting of a helpless corporation. But on the other hand, we do not find compliance with that high standard which we have just stated and which we and other courts have come to expect and demand of corporate fiduciaries. * * *

The corporate opportunities of whose misappropriation the minority stockholders complain need not have been an absolute certainty in order to support this action against Feldmann. * * *

[Consideration must be given to] the benefits which Newport might have derived from the steel shortage. In the past Newport had used and profited by its market leverage by operation of what the industry had come to call the "Feldmann Plan." This consisted of securing interest-free advances from prospective purchasers of steel in return for firm commitments to them from future production. The funds thus acquired were used to finance improvements in existing plants and to acquire new installations. In the summer of 1950 Newport had been negotiating for cold-rolling facilities which it needed for a more fully integrated operation and a more marketable product, and Feldmann plan funds might well have been used toward this end.

Further, as plaintiffs alternatively suggest, Newport might have used the period of short supply to build up patronage in the geographical area in which it could compete profitably even when steel was more abundant. Either of these opportunities was Newport's, to be used to its advantage only. Only if defendants had been able to negate completely any possibility of gain by Newport could they have prevailed. * * *

Defendants seek to categorize the corporate opportunities which might have accrued to Newport as too unethical to warrant further consideration. * * * In any event, it ill becomes the defendants to disparage as unethical the market advantages from which they themselves reaped rich benefits.

We do not mean to suggest that a majority stockholder cannot dispose of his controlling block of stock to outsiders without having to account to his corporation for profits or even never do this with impunity when the buyer is an interested customer, actual or potential, for the corporation's product. But when the sale necessarily results in a sacrifice of this element of corporate good will and consequent unusual profit to the fiduciary who has caused the sacrifice, he should account for his gains. So in a time of market shortage, where a call on a corporation's product commands an unusually large premium, in one form or another, we think it sound law that a fiduciary may not appropriate to himself the value of this premium. * * *

Hence to the extent that the price received by Feldmann and his codefendants included such a bonus, he is accountable to the minority stockholders who sue here. * * * And plaintiffs, as they contend, are entitled to a recovery in their own right, instead of in right of the corporation (as in the usual derivative actions), since neither Wilport nor their successors in interest should share in any judgment which may be rendered. * * *

The case will therefore be remanded to the district court for a determination of the question expressly left open below, namely, the value of defendants' stock without the appurtenant control over the corporation's output of steel. We reiterate that on this issue, as on all others relating to a breach of fiduciary duty, the burden of proof must rest on the defendants. Judgment should go to these plaintiffs and those whom they represent for any premium value so shown to the extent of their respective stock interests.

The judgment is therefore reversed and the action remanded for further proceedings pursuant to this opinion.

B. The Pervasive View

Zetlin v. Hanson Holding, Inc.

New York Court of Appeals, 1979 48 N.Y. 2d 684, 397 N.E. 2d 387

Plaintiff Zetlin owned approximately 2% of the outstanding shares of Gable Industries, Inc., with defendants Hanson Holdings, Inc., and Sylvestri, together with members of the Sylvestri family, owning 44.4% of Gable's shares. The defendants sold their interests to Flintkote Co. for a premium price of $15 per share, at a time when Gable stock was selling on the open market for $7.38 per share. It is undisputed that the 44.4% acquired by Flintkote represented effective control of Gable.

Recognizing that those who invest the capital necessary to acquire a dominant position in the ownership of a corporation have the right of controlling that corporation, it has long been settled law that, absent looting of corporate assets, conversion of a corporate opportunity, fraud or other acts of bad faith, a controlling stockholder is free to sell, and a purchaser is free to buy, that controlling interest at a premium price.

Certainly, minority shareholders are entitled to protection against such abuse by controlling shareholders. They are not entitled, however, to inhibit the legitimate interests of the other stockholders. It is for this reason that control shares usually command a premium price. The premium is the added amount an investor is willing to pay for the privilege of directly influencing the corporation's affairs.

In this action plaintiff Zetlin contends that minority stockholders are entitled to an opportunity to share equally in any premium paid for a controlling interest in the corporation. This rule would profoundly affect the manner in which controlling stock interests are now transferred. It would require, essentially, that a controlling interest be transferred only by means of an offer to all stockholders, *i.e.*, a tender offer. This would be contrary to existing law and if so radical a change is to be effected it would best be done by the Legislature. Order affirmed.

C. Controlling Shareholder's Refusal to Permit Corporation to Sell Subsidiary and Attempted Sale of Controlling Stock: Impact of Delaware Section 271

Thorpe v. CERBCO, Inc.

Delaware Supreme Court, 1996 676 A.2d. 436

WALSH, Justice:

In this appeal from the Court of Chancery we address the duties owed to a corporation by controlling shareholders who are also directors. The shareholder-plaintiff in this derivative suit, Merle Thorpe ("Thorpe") alleged that the controlling shareholders of CERBCO, Inc. had usurped an opportunity which belonged to the corporation. That opportunity was the potential sale of control of one of CERBCO's subsidiaries [East]. The Chancellor held that the defendants, George and Robert Erikson ("the Eriksons"), who were directors, officers and controlling shareholders of CERBCO, breached their duty of loyalty by failing to make complete disclosure to CERBCO of this corporate opportunity and by not removing themselves from consideration of the matter. [The Ericksons negotiated with INA, the acquiror, for the sale of their controlling interest in CERBCO.] The court concluded however that, as controlling shareholders, the Eriksons had the right under 8 Del.C. Sec 271 to veto any transaction which CERBCO would have entered into which constituted the sale of all or substantially all of the assets of the corporation. Thus, according to the Chancellor, the Eriksons' conduct caused no injury to CERBCO. * * *

In the opinion below, the Chancellor determined that the sale of East would constitute a radical transformation of CERBCO. In addition, CERBCO's East stock accounted for 68% of CERBCO's assets in 1990 and this stock was its primary income generating asset. We therefore affirm the decision that East stock constituted "substantially all" of CERBCO's assets as consistent with Delaware law.

Because the alternative transaction would have been covered by Section 271, the Eriksons had the statutory right as shareholders to veto this transaction. * * *

It is true that the Eriksons breached their fiduciary duties and that damages flowing from that breach are to be liberally calculated. Section 271 must, however, be given independent legal significance apart from the duty of loyalty. * * * Thus, the Section 271 rights, not the breach, were the proximate cause of the nonconsummation of the transaction. Accordingly, transactional damages are inappropriate. * * *

The Eriksons profited from their dealings with INA [they received $75,000 for extending the period of the letter of intent], and CERBCO incurred certain expenses in connection with these negotiations which it would not otherwise have incurred had the Eriksons not attempted to expropriate the INA sale opportunity.

Even though the corporation may not have been able to effectuate the transaction because of the Eriksons' rights under Section 271, some recovery is warranted because of the breach of fiduciary duty. * * *

Once disloyalty has been established, the standards evolved in *Oberly v. Kirby* and *Tri-Star* require that a fiduciary not profit personally from his conduct, and that the beneficiary not be harmed by such conduct. While there are no transactional damages in this case, we find the Eriksons liable for damages incidental to their breach of duty. Specifically the Eriksons are liable to CERBCO for the amount of $75,000 received from INA in connection with the letter of intent. * * * In addition, the Eriksons must reimburse CERBCO for any expenses, including legal and due diligence costs, that the corporation incurred to accommodate the Eriksons' pursuit of their own interests prior to the deal being abandoned by the Eriksons and INA.

D. Other Issues in Sales of Control

Section 3.22 contains several other cases involving controlling shareholders in various types of M&A transactions, including *Digex*, Section 3.22.D (controlling shareholder sells itself rather than a controlled sub); and *TCI*, Section 3.22.C (controlling shareholder receives premium for high vote stock).

E. The Policy Debate

1. Andrews' Equal Opportunity View

Excerpt from Andrews, The Stockholder's Right to Equal Opportunity in the Sale of Shares

78 Harv. L. Rev. 505, 505–506 (1965)

A stockholder is ordinarily free to hold or sell his shares solely according to the dictates of his own interests as he conceives them. Further, he is free to determine for himself the price at which he will sell, and below which he will not. It follows, according to some, that a controlling stockholder can sell his shares at any price he is offered, whether or not the offer is made to other stockholders. There are only two qualifications: (1) the stockholder may not receive anything as consideration for the sale of control itself, apart from the stock, as when part of the consideration paid is identified as compensation for his resignation as an officer or director or his participation in the election of successors nominated by the purchaser; (2) the controlling stockholder must not act in such a way as deliberately or negligently to harm his corporation, as, for example, by delivering it into the hands of thieves, or, perhaps, by depriving it of a favorable opportunity for corporate action. The scope of these qualifications is uncertain; indeed, they may embrace the field if one accepts the argument that control, even as it attaches to a block of shares, is a corporate asset. Careful practitioners have therefore been concerned about the risks in any sale of controlling shares at a premium over the price available on the market to other stockholders.

The problem can be approached by calling in question the general proposition that a stockholder is free to sell at a price not offered generally. I agree that a stockholder should be free to decide to sell or hold according to his own measure of his own interests. I agree further that he should be wholly free to determine for himself the price at which he will sell, and below which he will hold his shares. But it does not follow that a controlling stockholder (or any other stockholder) is free to sell on terms not generally available to other stockholders. A stockholder can be given complete freedom of choice in deciding to sell or hold, and in fixing his price, but still be required to exercise that freedom within the realm of a market where all stockholders are guaranteed an equal opportunity. Indeed, frequently the vitality of a free market, and the purposes that it serves, are enhanced rather than impaired by the prescription of minimal rules within which the participants must make and implement their choices.

I propose to consider the sale-of-control problem from the point of view of the proposition that a controlling stockholder should not be free to sell, at least to an outsider, except pursuant to a purchase offer made equally available to other stockholders; or, put in the affirmative, that one of the rights of the minority stockholders is to have an equal opportunity with all other stockholders to participate ratably in any sale of shares pursuant to a favorable offer for the purchase of controlling shares in their corporation. * * *

2. The Easterbrook and Fischel Unequal Opportunity View

Excerpt from Easterbrook and Fischel, Corporate Control Transactions

91 Yale L. Rev. 698, 715–719 (1982)

Investors' welfare is maximized by a legal rule that permits unequal division of gains from corporate control changes, subject to the constraint that no investor be made worse off by the transaction. In essence, this is a straightforward application of the Pareto principle of welfare economics. * * *

Sales of controlling blocs of shares provide a good example of transactions in which the movement of control is beneficial. The sale of control may lead to new offers, new plans, and new working arrangements with other firms that reduce agency costs and create other gains from new business relationships. The premium price received by the seller of the control bloc amounts to an unequal distribution of the gains. For the reasons we have discussed, however, this unequal distribution reduces the costs to purchasers of control, thereby increasing the number of beneficial control transfers, and increasing the incentive for inefficient controllers to relinquish their positions.

Numerous academic commentators, however, argue for some form of sharing requirement. Adolph Berle, for example, has argued that control is a "corporate asset" requiring that premiums paid for control go into the corporate treasury. Another well-known proposal is the "equal opportunity" rule advocated by Professors Jennings and Andrews. This proposal would entitle the minority shareholders to sell their shares on the same terms as the controlling shareholder.

Both of these proposed treatments of the control premium would stifle transfers of control. If the premium must be paid into the corporate treasury, people may not consent to the sale of a controlling bloc; if minority shareholders may sell on the same terms as the controlling shareholder, bidders may have to purchase more shares than necessary, possibly causing the transaction to become unprofitable. Minority shareholders would suffer under either rule, as the likelihood of improvements in the quality of management declined.

The mountain of academic commentary calling for some type of sharing requirement has not been influential, and the legal treatment of control sales is largely along the lines of wealth maximization. Sales at a premium are lawful, and the controlling shareholder generally has no duty to spread the bounty. The rhetoric of the cases, however, is not uniform. In particular the famous case of *Perlman v. Feldmann* [Section 11.7.A] suggests that the gains may have to be shared in some circumstances. * * *

F. The Equal Opportunity-Mandatory Bid Provision of the EU's Takeover Code and Other Examples of Equal Opportunity

As discussed in Chapter 26, the U.K.'s Takeover Code has a mandatory bid provision that is an equal opportunity doctrine. Pursuant to this provision, if an acquiror purchases more than 30% of the stock of a publicly-held target, the acquirior is obligated to make a mandatory bid to all of the other shareholders of the target at the highest price paid in the acquisition of the stock that triggered the mandatory bid. The effect of this provision is to prevent the payment of a control premium for more than 30% of the stock of a target. Also as noted in Chapter 26, the EU's Takeover Directive, which all EU countries are obligated to follow, has a mandatory bid provision.

As will be seen in Chapter 20, which deals with tender offers, an equal opportunity doctrine applies under the SEC rules to purchases made pursuant to a tender offer.

As seen in Chapter 3, one of the purposes of the poison pill is to prevent two-tier freeze-out acquisitions in which one price is paid on the first end for the control shares and a lower price is paid in the second step merger. Thus, the poison pill can be used by a board to adopt a *de facto* equal opportunity doctrine.

Given these examples of the equal opportunity at work in the case of publicly-held corporations, why should the doctrine not apply as a general matter to all corporations? Would the adoption of this doctrine have an adverse effect on the alienability of the stock of closely-held corporations?

§ 11.8 Sale of Corporate Office in Conjunction with a Sale of Stock

A. Sale of 3% of Stock Followed by Election of New Board Members

Caplan v. Lionel Corp.

Supreme Court, Appellate Division, First Department, 1964 246 N.Y.S.2d 913

STEUER, J.

On March 8, 1963, Defiance Industries, Inc. entered into a transaction with Roy Cohn which, though unusual in form, amounted to a deferred sale of 55,000 shares of Lionel Corporation then owned by Cohn. Half of the stock was to be delivered one year from date, the balance two years from date. Payment was made at the rate of $5 per share, but Cohn gave two promissory notes each for half of the purchase price he had received, the due dates of the notes corresponding with the delivery dates of the stock. In the event the stock was selling at the purchase price or less, the notes were to be cancelled on delivery. If it was selling for more, the difference was to be paid in addition to cancellation. In the event Cohn was unable to deliver the stock, the notes were to be paid. The voting rights of the stock were transferred immediately to Defiance. The 55,000 shares constituted 3% of the outstanding stock of Lionel Corporation.

The board of directors of Lionel consisted of ten directors, of whom Cohn was one. Six of the other directors were his nominees. Just how his holdings, amounting to 3%, enabled him to have this representation does not appear. Immediately after making the contract, these six directors resigned and their places were filled by nominees of Defiance.

On October 9, 1963, Defiance sold its interest in the above-described contract to A. M. Sonnabend, the transaction to close October 23, 1963. It was a condition of that agreement that prior to closing the six Defiance directors should be replaced by nominees of Sonnabend. On October 16 this was done. On November 14, 1963, Cohn resigned as a director and was replaced by a Sonnabend nominee. All of these changes in the board were effected by the directors filling the vacancy as each was created by resignation.

This proceeding is brought by a stockholder of Lionel to set aside and vacate the elections of the seven directors so elected. Special Term found the elections to be illegal and vacated them. With this finding and disposition we are in accord. The underlying principle is that the management of a corporation is not the subject of trade and cannot be bought apart from actual stock control. Where there has been a transfer of the majority of the stock, or even such a percentage as gives working control, a change of directors by resignation and filling of vacancies is proper. Here no claim was made that the stock interest which changed hands even approximated the percentage necessary to validate the substitution. * * *

B. Sale of 28% of Stock Followed by Election of New Board Members

Essex Universal Corp. v. Yates

United States Court of Appeals, Second Circuit, 1962 305 F.2d 572

LUMBARD, Chief Judge.

This appeal from the district court's summary judgment in favor of the defendant raises the question whether a contract for the sale of 28.3 percent of the stock of a corporation is, under New York law, invalid as against public policy solely because it includes a clause giving the purchaser an option to require a majority of the existing directors to replace themselves, by a process of seriatim resignation, with a majority designated by the purchaser. Despite the disagreement evidenced by the diversity of our opinions, my brethren and I agree that such a provision does not on its face render the contract illegal and unenforceable, and thus that it was improper to grant summary judgment. * * *

[**Facts**] The defendant Herbert J. Yates, a resident of California, was president and chairman of the board of directors of Republic Pictures Corporation, a New York corporation which at the time relevant to this suit had 2,004,190 shares of common stock outstanding. Republic's stock was listed and traded on the New York Stock Exchange. In August 1957, Essex Universal Corporation, a Delaware corporation owning stock in various diversified businesses, learned of the possibility of purchasing from Yates an interest in Republic. Negotiations proceeded rapidly, and on August 28 Yates and Joseph Harris, the president of Essex, signed a contract in which Essex agreed to buy, and Yates agreed "to sell or cause to be sold" at least 500,000 and not more than 600,000 shares of Republic stock. The price was set at eight dollars a share, roughly two dollars above the then market price on the Exchange. Three dollars per share was to be paid at the closing on September 18, 1957 and the remainder in twenty-four equal monthly payments beginning January 31, 1958. The shares were to be transferred on the closing date, but Yates was to retain the certificates, endorsed in blank by Essex, as security for full payment. In addition to other provisions not relevant to the present motion, the contract contained the following paragraph:

> "6. Resignations.
>
> Upon and as a condition to the closing of this transaction if requested by Buyer at least ten (10) days prior to the date of the closing:

(a) Seller will deliver to Buyer the resignations of the majority of the directors of Republic.

(b) Seller will cause a special meeting of the board of directors of Republic to be held, legally convened pursuant to law and the by-laws of Republic, and simultaneously with the acceptance of the directors' resignations set forth in paragraph 6(a) immediately preceding will cause nominees of Buyer to be elected directors of Republic in place of the resigned directors."

Before the date of the closing, as provided in the contract, Yates notified Essex that he would deliver 566,223 shares, or 28.3 per cent of the Republic stock then outstanding, and Essex formally requested Yates to arrange for the replacement of a majority of Republic's directors with Essex nominees pursuant to paragraph 6 of the contract. This was to be accomplished by having eight of the fourteen directors resign seriatim, each in turn being replaced by an Essex nominee elected by the others; such a procedure was in form permissible under the charter and by-laws of Republic, which empowered the board to choose the successor of any of its members who might resign.

On September 18, the parties met as arranged for the closing at Republic's office in New York City. Essex tendered bank drafts and cashier's checks totaling $1,698,690, which was the 37 per cent of the total price of $4,529,784 due at this time. The drafts and checks were payable to one Benjamin C. Cohen, who was Essex's banker and had arranged for the borrowing of the necessary funds. Although Cohen was prepared to endorse these to Yates, Yates upon advice of his lawyer rejected the tender as "unsatisfactory" and said, according to his deposition testimony, "Well, there can be no deal. We can't close it."

[**Issue**] Essex began this action in the New York Supreme Court, and it was removed to the district court on account of diversity of citizenship. Essex seeks damages of $2,700,000, claiming that at the time of the aborted closing the stock was in actuality worth more than $12.75 a share. Yates' answer raised a number of defenses, but the motion for summary judgment now before us was made and decided only on the theory that the provision in the contract for immediate transfer of control of the board of directors was illegal *per se* and tainted the entire contract. We have no doubt, and the parties agree, that New York law governs. * * *

[**Analysis**][W]e hold the provision regarding directors inseparable from the sale of shares, and proceed to a consideration of its legality.

Up to this point my brethren and I are in agreement. The following analysis is my own, except insofar as the separate opinions of Judges Clark and Friendly may indicate agreement.

It is established beyond question under New York law that it is illegal to sell corporate office or management control by itself (that is, accompanied by no stock or insufficient stock to carry voting control). The same rule apparently applies in all jurisdictions where the question has arisen. The rationale of the rule is undisputable: persons enjoying management control hold it on behalf of the corporation's stockholders, and therefore may not regard it as their own personal property to dispose of as they wish. Any other rule would violate the most fundamental principle of corporate democracy, that management must represent and be chosen by, or at least with the consent of, those who own the corporation.

Essex was, however, contracting with Yates for the purchase of a very substantial percentage of Republic stock. If, by virtue of the voting power carried by this stock, it could have elected a majority of the board of directors, then the contract was not a simple agreement for the sale of office to one having no ownership interest in the corporation, and the question of its legality would require further analysis. Such stock voting control would incontestably belong to the owner of a majority of the voting stock, and it is commonly known that equivalent power usually accrues to the owner of 28.3% of the stock. For the purpose of this analysis, I shall assume that Essex was contracting to acquire a majority of the Republic stock, deferring consideration of the situation where, as here, only 28.3% is to be acquired. * * *

There is no question of the right of a controlling shareholder under New York law normally to derive a premium from the sale of a controlling block of stock. In other words, there was no impropriety *per se* in the fact that Yates was to receive more per share than the generally prevailing market price for Republic stock.

The next question is whether it is legal to give and receive payment for the immediate transfer of management control to one who has achieved majority share control but would not otherwise be able to convert that share control into operating control for some time. I think that it is. * * *

[A] holder of corporate control will not, as a fiduciary, be permitted to profit from facilitating actions on the part of the purchasers of control which are detrimental to the interests of the corporation or the remaining shareholders. There is, however, no suggestion that the transfer of control over Republic to Essex carried any such threat to the interests of the corporation or its other shareholders. * * *

I can see no reason why a purchaser of majority control should not ordinarily be permitted to make his control effective from the moment of the transfer of stock.

Thus if Essex had been contracting to purchase a majority of the stock of Republic, it would have been entirely proper for the contract to contain the provision for immediate replacement of directors. Although in the case at bar only 28.3 per cent of the stock was involved, it is commonly known that a person or group owning so large a percentage of the voting stock of a corporation which, like Republic, has at least the 1,500 shareholders normally requisite to listing on the New York Stock Exchange, is almost certain to have share control as a practical matter. If Essex was contracting to acquire what in reality would be equivalent to ownership of a majority of stock, *i.e.*, if it would as a practical certainty have been guaranteed of the stock voting power to choose a majority of the directors of Republic in due course, there is no reason why the contract should not similarly be legal. Whether Essex was thus to acquire the equivalent of majority stock control would, if the issue is properly raised by the defendants, be a factual issue to be determined by the district court on remand. * * *

Reversed and remanded for further proceedings not inconsistent with the judgment of this court. * * *

Friendly, Circuit Judge (concurring).

* * * I have no doubt that many contracts, drawn by competent and responsible counsel, for the purchase of blocks of stock from interests thought to "control" a corporation although owning less than a majority, have contained provisions like paragraph 6 of the contract *sub judice*. However, developments over the past decades seem to me to show that such a clause violates basic principles of corporate democracy. * * * A mass seriatim resignation directed by a selling stockholder, and the filling of vacancies by his henchmen at the dictation of a purchaser and without any consideration of the character of the latter's nominees, are beyond what the stockholders contemplated or should have been expected to contemplate. This seems to me a wrong to the corporation and the other

stockholders which the law ought not countenance, whether the selling stockholder has received a premium or not. * * *

Hence, I am inclined to think that if I were sitting on the New York Court of Appeals, I would hold a provision like Paragraph 6 violative of public policy save when it was entirely plain that a new election would be a mere formality—*i.e.*, when the seller owned more than 50% of the stock. * * *

C. Impact of Federal Securities Laws

See § 14(f) of the 1934 Act and Rule 14f-1.

§ 11.9 Is There an Obligation to Investigate the Intention of the Purchaser? The Looting Situation

A. The New York View

Gerdes v. Reynolds

Supreme Court, Special Term, New York County, 1941 28 N.Y.S.2d 622

WALTER, Justice.

[**Facts**]* * * Defendants * * * were the officers and directors of Reynolds Investing Company, Inc. [the target], a Delaware corporation of the kind commonly known as an investment trust. They were also stockholders, and, with members of their families, owned a majority of its common stock. Ownership of such majority of the common stock was sold, and the [defendants] resigned their offices and directorships and elected as their successors four persons designated by the purchaser. Assets of the [Reynolds] were then wasted and improperly applied, and the plaintiffs * * * seek to hold accountable therefore * * * those who sold and those who * * * aided the transaction. * * *

[**Analysis**] There is not a scintilla of evidence that any of the defendants in this group in any way participated in or knew of any of the transactions respecting [the purchaser], or that they ever heard of any of the persons connected with [the purchaser]. Neither is there a scintilla of evidence that any of such defendants in any way participated in or knew of the use made of the assets of Reynolds Investing Company after December 31, 1937. Liability is asserted against them upon the grounds (a) that the sale of the stock, accompanied by their resignations and the election of successors nominated by the purchaser, was itself an illegal transaction because in violation of fiduciary duties owed to the corporation and the holders of its debentures and preferred stock and its minority common stockholders; and (b) that even if the transaction were not illegal in itself, it is made so because the selling defendants negligently or in bad faith failed to make proper investigation of the purchaser or to give advance notice to the other stockholders of an impending change of management, especially so inasmuch as what is claimed to be the excessive price paid was itself sufficient to put those defendants upon notice that some wrongful act was intended. Those contentions present interesting and important and difficult questions of law.

Inherent in the very nature of stock corporations as constituted by our law are the settled principles that the shares of stock are the property of the stockholders, that the stockholders may sell their shares when and to whom they please and for such price as they can get, that they may sell to buyers of whose identity and integrity and responsibility they are unaware (as is the common practice in the multitudinous sales through brokers on and off exchanges), that the purchase price paid upon such sales belongs to the sellers, and that these same rights exist even where the stockholders hold a majority of the stock and where the sellers are a group who together own and sell such a majority. * * *

Clearly, therefore, in the matter of selling their stock the holders of a majority thereof, whether one or a group, act for themselves alone and not as trustees, either technically or substantially, for the other stockholders, and no fiduciary duty is violated by such a sale, even though such sale ultimately bring about a change in the directorate. * * *

In this case, however, it indisputably was a condition of the sale that all the officers and directors then in office should forthwith resign and that under their power to fill vacancies they should forthwith elect an entirely new directorate chosen wholly by the purchaser of the stock, and all the officers and directors then in office did so resign and did so elect as directors persons designated by the purchaser. * * *

It is obvious, of course that it would be illegal for officers and directors to resign and elect as their successors persons who they knew intended to loot the corporation's treasury. Even stockholders, despite their right to sell their stock to whom they please, could not legally do that. Liability for such an act would not have to be predicated upon breach of a fiduciary relation, for the act would amount to a willful and malicious injury to property, tortious in its very nature. * * * I here find as a fact that none of the sellers of the stock of Reynolds Investing Company had any knowledge that the purchasers thereof, or any one acting for them, had any intention to loot the corporation or to pay any part of the purchase price out of the corporation's own assets. Whether or not the resigning officers and directors nevertheless are chargeable with notice of such an intention—whether or not it was, under all the circumstances, a risk reasonably to be perceived—is, of course, another question.

The questions determinative of the liability of corporate officers and directors in such a situation as is here disclosed thus appear to me to be these: (1) Are the circumstances such that, despite actual ignorance of unlawful plans and designs on the part of the purchasers, they are chargeable with notice of such plans and designs, or, perhaps more accurately, with notice that unlawful plans and designs are a risk reasonably to be perceived? "The risk reasonably to be perceived defines the duty to be obeyed." *Palsgraf v. Long Island R. R. Co.*, 248 N.Y. 339, 344, (2) Is the price paid in reality a price paid for the stock, or is it, in part at least, a price paid for the resignations of the existing officers and directors and the election of the buyer's nominees? And the principal factors which must supply the answers to these questions are the nature of the assets which are to pass into the possession and control of the purchasers by reason of the transaction, the method by which the transaction is to be consummated, and the relation of the price paid to the value of the stock. * * *

Viewing all the elements which the fiduciary obligations of the officers and directors of Reynolds Investing Company required them to view I am convinced that $2,110,000 was so grossly in excess of the value of the stock that it carried upon its face a plain indication that it was not for the stock alone but partly for immediate en masse resignations and immediate election of the purchasers' nominees as successors. The transaction was not one in which there was merely a sale of stock, with the right to elect directors passing to the purchasers as a legal incident of the sale, and I think it proper to add that these officers and directors did not submit to the lawyers whom they retained in the matter the question of the price paid or its significance. They had their eyes and minds so centered upon the personal interests of themselves and their families and associates as stockholders and upon a desire to get what they could for what they regarded as theirs, that they failed to consider their position as officers and directors, and the consequent duty they owed as such to the corporation itself and its creditors and other stockholders.

It thus becomes necessary to determine what part of the $2,110,000 was paid for the 1,055,000 shares of stock, and what part was paid for resignations and election of successors. * * * [I conclude that] $791,250 [was] the price paid for 1,055,000 shares of stock, and $1,318,750 [was] the price paid for the resignations of the officers and directors and their election of the buyer's nominees as their successors, or, in other words, for what is termed the turning over of control.

The conclusion ordinarily to be drawn from the foregoing is that, having violated their fiduciary duty, these officers and directors must account to the corporation or to its duly appointed trustees for the sum of $1,318,750, and for all damages naturally resulting from their official misconduct. * * *

B. The Fourth Circuit's View

Swinney v. Keebler Company

United States Court of Appeals, Fourth Circuit, 1973 480 F.2d 573

WINTER, Circuit Judge:

* * * The district court found that, in connection with the successive sales of Meadors' [the target] stock from Keebler to Atlantic to Flora Mir Distributing, Meadors had been looted by Atlantic and its corporate assets dissipated, with the result, among others, that the interest and principal of the debentures were in default. Although the district court made no finding that Keebler had looted Meadors and, indeed, made no finding of any intentional wrongdoing on the part of Keebler, it nevertheless held Keebler liable for violation of its obligation to Meadors and Meadors' debenture holders "[i]n light of all the circumstances known to Keebler * * * to conduct such investigation of the purchaser [Atlantic] as would convince a reasonable man that the sale was legitimate, or to refrain from making the sale."

We disagree that the circumstances were such as to give rise to an obligation on the part of Keebler to conduct an investigation of Atlantic beyond that which was actually conducted or to refrain from making the sale. Accordingly, we reverse and direct the entry of judgment for Keebler. * * *

[**The Law**] The parties do not seriously dispute the applicable law. The district court, correctly, we think, drew upon the leading case of *Insuranshares Corporation v. Northern Fiscal Corporation*, which held the sellers of a controlling interest in a corporation liable to the corporation when the buyers proceeded to loot it after their acquisition of control. Liability was predicated upon breach of a duty not to transfer control since the circumstances surrounding the transfer were "such as to awaken suspicion and put a prudent man on his guard—unless a reasonably adequate investigation discloses such facts as would convince a reasonable person that no fraud is intended or likely to result."

In *Insuranshares*, the suspicious circumstances included (1) the defendants' probable knowledge that the purchase was to be financed by a pledge of the corporation's assets, (2) the corporation's president's clear predisposition to allow a sale to be financed by pledging those assets as security, (3) defendants' awareness of the purchasers' plan to have a large part of the corporation's assets converted into cash prior to the sale, (4) the inflated price or premium paid for control, especially given the nature of the business which was an investment trust with no physical assets but only the ready equivalent of cash in the form of marketable securities, (5) warnings from the sellers' attorneys as to their potential liabilities for dealing with little-known purchasers, and (6) the fact that the corporation had been looted five years before by a different group who had gained control by using the same method of financing.

The standard of conduct to which *Insuranshares* holds controlling transferors had been widely accepted. Generally, the owner of corporate stock may dispose of his shares as he sees fit. A dominant or majority stockholder does not become a fiduciary for other stockholders *merely* by owning stock. In selling their stock, the stockholders necessarily act for themselves, and not as trustees for the other stockholders. *Gerdes v. Reynolds*, [Section 11.9.A] But majority stockholders who assume the management of the corporation, as Keebler did here, can be said to stand in fiduciary relation to the minority under certain circumstances. Thus, while the majority is not an absolute insurer against any wrongs which may be done to the corporation after the transfer of control or against any decisions by the new owners that may not be in the best interest of the minority, if the sellers of control are in a position to foresee the likelihood of fraud on the corporation, including its creditors, or on the remaining stockholders, at the hands of the transferee, their fiduciary duty imposes a positive duty to investigate the motives and reputation of the would-be purchaser; and unless such a reasonable investigation shows that to a reasonable man no fraud is intended or likely to result, the sellers must refrain from the transfer of control.

[**Analysis**] In light of the facts and applicable law, plaintiffs' right to recover turns on whether Keebler had sufficient knowledge to foresee the likelihood of fraud so as to give rise to a duty to conduct a further investigation and to satisfy itself, by the test of a reasonable man, that no fraud was intended or likely to result before it consummated the sale of control. The district court identified essentially seven circumstances which "might have indicated [to Keebler] that Atlantic Services had no intention of operating Meadors * * *." These factors were: (1) no one from Atlantic had any experience in the candy business, (2) at the time the contract was executed no one from Atlantic had inspected the "Meadors operation," (3) by the time of the closing, only Atlantic's accountant had examined Meadors to "any appreciable extent and he was interested principally in the books and inventory," (4) Meadors had no market of its own and the "profit as shown could not have been accepted at face value by an outsider," (5) prior to the closing Atlantic had no negotiations with Meadors' key employees concerning the continuation of the business, (6) the sale was consummated with dispatch, and (7) Atlantic had inquired as to the availability of Meadors' funds for payment of the purchase price. Although the district court concluded that the first five factors were "not necessarily inconsistent with a legitimate sale of a business the size of Meadors," it held that when coupled with facts six and seven, they "were more than sufficient to arouse the suspicion of Keebler." * * *

Overall, we conclude that the seven factors considered singly or in concert, were not sufficient to suggest to Keebler that Atlantic did not intend to operate Meadors, but rather intended to loot it. As our discussion of the findings relied on to support the contrary conclusion discloses, there were many positive indications that Atlantic intended to operate Meadors and to operate it profitably. * * * [T]here was * * * no basis to impose liability on Keebler. **Reversed.**

§ 11.10 The ALI's Proposed Rules Relating to the Sale of a Controlling Stock Interest

Section 5.16 of the ALI Corporate Governance Project, *supra* Section 1.10, provides that a controlling shareholder has, subject to certain exceptions, the same right to dispose of its shares as any other shareholder and may dispose of its shares for "a price that is not made proportionately available to other shareholders * * *." Thus, the controlling shareholder has the right to a control premium on the sale of its shares. An exception in Section 5.16(b) relating to likelihood of a violation of the duty of fair dealing is consistent with such cases as *Swinney v. Keebler Co.* [Section 11.9.B] which hold generally that a controlling shareholder cannot sell to a known looter. *See* Thompson, *The M&A Provisions of the ALI Corporate Governance Project, supra* Section 1.10.

§ 11.11 Parent's Potential Liability for Sub's CERCLA Liability

United States v. Bestfoods

United States Supreme Court, 1998 524 U.S. 51

Opinion by: SOUTER

The United States brought this action for the costs of cleaning up industrial waste generated by a chemical plant. The issue before us, under the Comprehensive Environmental Response, Compensation, and Liability Act of 1980 (CERCLA), 94 Stat. 2767, as amended, 42 U.S.C. § 9601 et seq., is whether a parent corporation that actively participated in, and exercised control over, the operations of a subsidiary may, without more, be held liable as an operator of a polluting facility owned or operated by the subsidiary. We answer no, unless the corporate veil may be pierced. But a corporate parent that actively participated in, and exercised control over, the operations of the facility itself may be held directly liable in its own right as an operator of the facility.

I. [CERCLA] In 1980, CERCLA was enacted in response to the serious environmental and health risks posed by industrial pollution. * * * "As its name implies, CERCLA is a comprehensive statute that grants the President broad power to command government agencies and private parties to clean up hazardous waste sites." * * * If it satisfies certain statutory conditions, the United States may, for instance, use the "Hazardous Substance Superfund" to finance cleanup efforts, which it may then replenish by suits brought under § 107 of the Act against, among others, "any person who at the time of disposal of any hazardous substance owned or operated any facility." 42 U.S.C. § 9607(a)(2). So, those actually "responsible for any damage, environmental harm, or injury from chemical poisons [may be tagged with] the cost of their actions," S. Rep. No. 96-848, p. 13 (1980). The term "person" is defined in CERCLA to include corporations and other business organizations, and the term "facility" enjoys a broad and detailed definition as well. The phrase "owner or operator" is defined only by tautology, however, as "any person owning or operating" a facility, § 9601(20)(A)(ii), and it is this bit of circularity that prompts our review. * * * .

II [Facts] In 1957, Ott Chemical Co. (Ott I) began manufacturing chemicals at a plant near Muskegon, Michigan, and its intentional and unintentional dumping of hazardous substances significantly polluted the soil and ground water at the site. In 1965, respondent CPC International Inc. [later renamed Best Foods] incorporated a wholly owned subsidiary to buy Ott I's assets in exchange for CPC stock.[**This was the first stock acquisition of the target, Ott.**] The new company, also dubbed Ott Chemical Co. (Ott II), continued chemical manufacturing at the site, and continued to pollute its surroundings. CPC kept the managers of Ott I, including its founder, president, and principal shareholder, Arnold Ott, on board as officers of Ott II. Arnold Ott and several other Ott II officers and directors were also given positions at CPC, and they performed duties for both corporations.

In 1972, CPC sold Ott II to Story Chemical Company, which operated the Muskegon plant until its bankruptcy in 1977.[**This was the second stock acquisition of the target, Ott.**] Shortly thereafter, when respondent Michigan Department of Natural Resources (MDNR) examined the site for environmental damage, it found the land littered with thousands of leaking and even exploding drums of waste, and the soil and water saturated with noxious chemicals. MDNR sought a buyer for the property who would be willing to contribute toward its cleanup, and after extensive negotiations, respondent Aerojet-General Corp. arranged for transfer of the site from the Story bankruptcy trustee in 1977. Aerojet created a wholly owned California subsidiary, Cordova Chemical Company (Cordova/California), to purchase the property [**this is the acquisition of Ott's assets**], and Cordova/California in turn created a wholly owned Michigan subsidiary, Cordova Chemical Company of Michigan (Cordova/Michigan), which manufactured chemicals at the site until 1986.[2]

By 1981, the federal Environmental Protection Agency had undertaken to see the site cleaned up, and its long-term remedial plan called for expenditures well into the tens of millions of dollars. To recover some of that money, the United States filed this action under § 107 in 1989, naming five defendants as responsible parties: CPC, Aerojet, Cordova/California, Cordova/Michigan, and Arnold Ott. (By that time, Ott I and Ott II were defunct.) * * *

The District Court said that operator liability may attach to a parent corporation both directly, when the parent itself operates the facility, and indirectly, when the corporate veil can be pierced under state law. * * *

[T]he District Court held both [1] CPC [which acquired Ott in a stock acquisition], and [2] Aerojet [whose subsidiary acquired Ott in an asset acquisition], liable under § 107(a)(2) as operators. As to CPC, the court found it particularly telling that CPC selected Ott II's board of directors and populated its executive ranks with CPC officials, and that a CPC official, G.R.D. Williams, played a significant role in shaping Ott II's environmental compliance policy. * * *

Applying Michigan veil-piercing law, the Court of Appeals decided that neither CPC nor Aerojet was liable for controlling the actions of its subsidiaries, since the parent and subsidiary corporations maintained separate personalities and the parents did not utilize the subsidiary corporate form to perpetrate fraud or subvert justice.

We granted certiorari * * * to resolve a conflict among the Circuits over the extent to which parent corporations may be held liable under CERCLA for operating facilities ostensibly under the control of their subsidiaries. We now vacate and remand.

III [Viel Piercing]

It is a general principle of corporate law deeply "ingrained in our economic and legal systems" that a parent corporation (so-called because of control through ownership of another corporation's stock) is not liable for the acts of its subsidiaries. * * * Thus it is hornbook law that the exercise of the 'control' which stock ownership gives to the stock-

2. Cordova/California and MDNR entered into a contract under which Cordova/California agreed to undertake certain cleanup actions, and MDNR agreed to share in the funding of those actions and to indemnify Cordova/California for various expenses. The Michigan Court of Appeals has held that this agreement requires MDNR to indemnify Aerojet and its Cordova subsidiaries for any CERCLA liability that they may incur in connection with their activities at the Muskegan facility. See Cordova Chemical Co. v. MDNR, 212 Mich. App. 144, 536 N.W.2d 860 (1995), appeal denied, 554 N.W.2d 319 (1996).

holders ... will not create liability beyond the assets of the subsidiary. That 'control' includes the election of directors, the making of by-laws ... and the doing of all other acts incident to the legal status of stockholders. Nor will a duplication of some or all of the directors or executive officers be fatal." * * * Although this respect for corporate distinctions when the subsidiary is a polluter has been severely criticized in the literature, * * * nothing in CERCLA purports to reject this bedrock principle, and against this venerable common-law backdrop, the congressional silence is audible. * * * The Government has indeed made no claim that a corporate parent is liable as an owner or an operator under § 107 simply because its subsidiary is subject to liability for owning or operating a polluting facility.

But there is an equally fundamental principle of corporate law, applicable to the parent-subsidiary relationship as well as generally, that the corporate veil may be pierced and the shareholder held liable for the corporation's conduct when, *inter alia*, the corporate form would otherwise be misused to accomplish certain wrongful purposes, most notably fraud, on the shareholder's behalf. * * * Nothing in CERCLA purports to rewrite this well-settled rule, either. CERCLA is thus like many another congressional enactment in giving no indication "that the entire corpus of state corporation law is to be replaced simply because a plaintiff's cause of action is based upon a federal statute," * * * and the failure of the statute to speak to a matter as fundamental as the liability implications of corporate ownership demands application of the rule that "in order to abrogate a common-law principle, the statute must speak directly to the question addressed by the common law[.]" * * * The Court of Appeals was accordingly correct in holding that when (but only when) the corporate veil may be pierced, may a parent corporation be charged with derivative CERCLA liability for its subsidiary's actions.

IV [Direct Liability]

If the act rested liability entirely on ownership of a polluting facility, this opinion might end here; but CERCLA liability may turn on operation as well as ownership, and nothing in the statute's terms bars a parent corporation from direct liability for its own actions in operating a facility owned by its subsidiary. As Justice (then-Professor) Douglas noted almost 70 years ago, derivative liability cases are to be distinguished from those in which "the alleged wrong can seemingly be traced to the parent through the conduit of its own personnel and management" and "the parent is directly a participant in the wrong complained of." * * * In such instances, the parent is directly liable for its own actions. * * * The fact that a corporate subsidiary happens to own a polluting facility operated by its parent does nothing, then, to displace the rule that the parent "corporation is [itself] responsible for the wrongs committed by its agents in the course of its business," * * *, and whereas the rules of veil-piercing limit derivative liability for the actions of another corporation, CERCLA's "operator" provision is concerned primarily with direct liability for one's own actions. * * *

B * * *

[In imposing direct liability,] the District Court wrongly assumed that the actions of the joint officers and directors are necessarily attributable to CPC. The District Court emphasized the facts that CPC placed its own high-level officials on Ott II's board of directors and in key management positions at Ott II, and that those individuals made major policy decisions and conducted day-to-day operations at the facility. * * *

In imposing direct liability on these grounds, the District Court failed to recognize that " it is entirely appropriate for directors of a parent corporation to serve as directors of its subsidiary, and that fact alone may not serve to expose the parent corporation to liability for its subsidiary's acts." * * *

This recognition that the corporate personalities remain distinct has its corollary in the "well established principle [of corporate law] that directors and officers holding positions with a parent and its subsidiary can and do 'change hats' to represent the two corporations separately, despite their common ownership." * * *

In sum, the District Court's focus on the relationship between parent and subsidiary (rather than parent and facility), combined with its automatic attribution of the actions of dual officers and directors to the corporate parent, erroneously, even if unintentionally, treated CERCLA as though it displaced or fundamentally altered common law standards of limited liability. * * *

The critical question is whether, in degree and detail, actions directed to the facility by an agent of the parent alone are eccentric under accepted norms of parental oversight of a subsidiary's facility.

There is, in fact, some evidence that CPC engaged in just this type and degree of activity at the Muskegon plant. * * *

Prudence * * * counsels us to remand, on the theory of direct operation set out here, for reevaluation of Williams's role, and of the role of any other CPC agent who might be said to have had a part in operating the Muskegon facility.

References

ABA Model Stock Purchase Agreement, supra Section 1.10.

ALI, *Corporate Governance Project, supra* Section 1.10, at Section 5.16.

Easterbrook and Fischel, *The Economic Structure of Corporate Law*, 109–134, 140–144 (1991).

Elhauge, *The Triggering Function of Sale of Control Doctrine*, 59 Univ. of Chicago L. Rev. 1465 (1992).

Kling and Nugent Simon, *Negotiated Acquisitions, supra* Section 1.10.

Thompson, *Mergers, Acquisitions and Tender Offers, supra* Section 1.10.

Chapter 12

Acquisition of Assets of a Closely-Held Corporation

§ 12.1 Scope

This chapter focuses on the acquisition of the assets of a closely-held corporation. Many of the principles here would also apply to the acquisition of the assets of a division or of a subsidiary. Section 12.2 sets out a problem dealing with the many aspects of this type of transaction. Section 12.3 refers to Chapter 2 for the rules regarding (1) the votes required by the target's shareholders to effectuate a sale of all or substantially all of a target's assets, and (2) the appraisal rights, if any, of the target's shareholders in such transactions. Section 12.4 focuses on the impact of federal securities laws on an acquisition of a target's assets in exchange for the acquiror's securities. This section refers in substantial part to many of the principles covered in Chapter 4. Sections 12.5, 12.6, and 12.7, refer respectively to Chapter 5 for federal income tax aspects, Chapter 6 for accounting aspects, and Chapter 9 for Hart-Scott-Rodino aspects. Section 12.8 focuses on the due diligence investigation.

Section 12.9 deals with potential successor liability in asset acquisitions, in which case an acquiring firm may be liable for the torts and other liabilities of the target corporation even though the acquiring firm does not explicitly assume those liabilities. Section 12.10 deals with the right of the acquiror to assume a target's indebtedness in an asset acquisition, thereby preventing the acceleration of the principal payments on such debt. Finally, Section 12.11 addresses the bulk sale provisions of the UCC.

For a discussion of the many issues that can arise in an asset acquisition *see ABA Model Asset Purchase Agreement, supra* Section 1.10, and various chapters of Thompson, *Mergers, Acquisitions and Tender Offers, supra* Section 1.10.

This chapter does not address labor and employee rights issues, such as compliance with ERISA and the Worker Adjustment and Retraining Notification Act (the WARN Act).

§ 12.2 Introductory Problem on Sale of Substantially All of the Assets of a Closely-Held Target

The basic facts are similar to the facts in Section 11.2, as follows:

Target Corporation (TC), a Delaware corporation, is owned by 16 shareholders as follows

Shareholder	Interest
A	25%
Other 15 Shareholders	5% each

Shareholder A is the President and Chairman of the three-person board of TC. TC operates a coal mine, and TC has assets with a fair market value of $80 million. TC has liabilities of $30 million. Thus, the net fair market value (*i.e.*, fair market value less liabilities) of TC's assets and stock is $50 million. Also, TC has sales of $90 million. Acquiring corporation (AC), a large publicly-held corporation with over $200 million in assets, needs coal for its business and would like to acquire a controlling interest in TC for the purpose of insuring itself an adequate supply of coal. AC is not interested, however, in acquiring all of the stock or assets of TC.

In the course of doing its due diligence on the proposed stock acquisition set out in the problem in Section 11.2, AC discovered that TC has a potential liability for unpaid federal income taxes and also a contingent liability for violation of certain environmental laws. As a consequence, the proposed stock acquisition has been abandoned, and it is now proposed that AC acquire TC's assets and certain specified liabilities. As indicated above, TC has $30 million of liabilities, and $25 million is attributable to TC's outstanding bonds, which have a favorable interest rate. The $5 million balance is owed to various trade creditors.

It is proposed that AC acquire all of TC's assets and assume the obligation on TC's $25 million of outstanding bonds. AC will pay either $100 million in cash or $100 million in its stock. Immediately after the transaction, TC will pay off its creditors and make a liquidating distribution to its shareholders on a pro rata basis. AC will specifically not assume any of TC's obligations to its trade creditors, to the state or federal taxing authorities, to any party with respect to a violation by TC of environmental laws, or to any other party relating to any other contingent or non-specified liability of TC. The transaction will be effectuated pursuant to an Asset Acquisition Agreement between AC and TC. A sample asset acquisition agreement is contained in Documentary Appendix V of *M&A Statutes, Rules, and Documents*, *supra* Section 1.1.

1. Questions with regard to TC:
   a. What corporate and shareholder action is required by TC in order to effectuate the transaction? Suppose one of TC's 5% shareholders does not want to go along with the deal? What result if TC is incorporated in a state that has adopted the Model Business Corporation Act?
   b. What are the tax consequences of the transaction for TC and TC's shareholders if the consideration is $100 million in cash?
   c. What are the tax consequences of the transaction for TC and TC's shareholders if the consideration is $100 million in AC voting common stock?
   d. What are the federal securities laws implications of the transaction for TC and its shareholders if the consideration is in the alternative cash and AC voting stock? In particular, what rights and obligations do TC and its shareholders have under the federal securities laws when the consideration is in the alternative stock and cash?
      i. Can the TC shareholders resell any stock they receive in the transaction?
      ii. What potential causes of action will the TC shareholders have against AC under the federal securities laws if the consideration is stock? Cash?
      iii. Do the TC shareholders have any liability under the federal securities laws if the assets are sold for cash? For stock?
   e. Is the transaction reportable under the Hart-Scott-Rodino pre-merger notification law?
   f. What type of representations, covenants and conditions, will TC and its shareholders want in the Asset Acquisition Agreement? *See* Chapter 15. Should AC require that the shareholders of TC sign the Asset Acquisition Agreement?

2. Questions with respect to AC:
   a. What corporate and shareholder action is required by AC to effectuate the transaction? What if AC is incorporated in a state with the MBCA?
   b. What are the tax and accounting consequences to AC if it makes the acquisition with cash? Stock?
   c. What are the federal securities laws implications to AC from the use of cash? Stock? In particular, what is the potential liability of AC under the federal securities laws?
   d. Is the transaction reportable under the Hart-Scott-Rodino pre-merger notification law?
   e. Is there any problem with AC assuming TC's obligations to TC's outstanding bondholders?
   f. What action does AC want to take with respect to TC's trade creditors?
   g. Is AC potentially liable for TC's unpaid taxes, and if so, how should AC deal with this potential liability?
   h. Is AC potentially liable for TC's environmental obligations, and if so, how should AC deal with this potential liability?
   i. Suppose that after completion of the acquisition by AC, one of TC's former employees develops an illness associated with the TC work environment. Is AC potentially liable to this employee, and if so, what measures should AC have taken to avoid that type of liability? In particular, are there any alternatives to AC's direct acquisition of TC's assets?
   j. What type of representations, covenants and conditions will AC and its shareholders want in the Asset Acquisition Agreement? *See* Chapter 15.
3. Substantial opposition has developed among the shareholders of TC to the proposed acquisition, and it is expected that 40% of the shareholders will vote against the transaction, seek appraisal rights, if available, and otherwise challenge the transaction. The shareholders of AC are enthusiastic about the transaction. As a result of this opposition, AC is contemplating restructuring the transaction into an acquisition by TC of all of the assets and liabilities of AC in exchange for stock of TC. AC will liquidate as part of the transaction, transferring the TC stock to the AC shareholders. After the transaction, the AC shareholders will own 85% of the stock of TC. TC has sufficient authorized and unissued shares to complete the acquisition without a shareholder vote.
   a. Does AC gain anything by restructuring the transaction as proposed assuming that the consideration to be paid by AC to TC in the basic transaction was, in the alternative, cash and stock?
   b. Assuming TC is incorporated in a state that gives a corporation's shareholders appraisal rights on a sale of substantially all of the corporation's assets followed by a liquidation, does AC gain anything by restructuring the transaction as proposed, assuming that the consideration to be paid by AC to TC in the basic transaction was, in the alternative, cash and stock? The former MBCA provided for a similar rule.

§ 12.3 Voting and Dissenting by Target's and Acquiror's Shareholders in Asset Sales

Chapter 2 discusses the corporate mechanics for effectuating a sale of all or of substantially all of a target's assets, including the voting and appraisal rights of the target's shareholders. Chapter 3 addresses the fiduciary duties of directors in such transactions.

§ 12.4 Federal Securities Impact of Acquisition of Closely-Held Target's Assets for Acquiror's Securities

A. Qualifying Transaction under Regulation D

Regulation D, which is explored in Chapter 4, may be utilized for exempting from registration an acquisition by an acquiring corporation (whether public or private) of the assets of a closely-held target corporation in exchange for stock of the acquiror.

B. Resale under Rule 144 of Securities Received under Regulation D Offering

As indicated in Chapter 4, any stock received by the target's shareholders in a transaction that is exempt under Regulation D can only be resold under Rule 144, in a registered offering, or in a § 4(1½) transaction.

C. Applicability of Rule 10b-5 on a Sale of Assets for Stock

Nationwide Cellular Service, Inc. v. American Mobile Communications, Inc.

United States District Court, Southern District New York, 1991 Fed. Sec. Law. Rep. ¶ 96,435

Opinion of SAND, District Judge.

[**Facts**] This dispute * * * involves an agreement to exchange the stock of one member of the cellular telephone industry for the assets of another. * * * Nationwide [the acquiring corporation] alleges that American Mobile Communications (AMC) [the target corporation] and several AMC shareholders (collectively the AMC defendants), and Chester Watson and the accounting firm of BDO Seidman (collectively the BDO defendants), fraudulently induced the sale of Nationwide's stock by misrepresenting the value of AMC's assets and liabilities. Nationwide claims that the defendants violated Section 10(b). * * *

On July 27, 1989, after months of negotiation, the parties entered into an "Assets Acquisition Agreement" (the Agreement). Pursuant to that document, Nationwide agreed to exchange 250,000 shares of its stock at a price of $9.75 per share for AMC's assets and additional cash and promissory notes. * * * [The transaction closed with Nationwide transferring its restricted stock to AMC in exchange for its assets.]

[**Issue**] In its complaint, Nationwide alleges that AMC and the AMC shareholders fraudulently induced the transfer of Nationwide's stock by misrepresenting the value of AMC's net assets, which constituted the bulk of the consideration for the exchange. * * *

Nationwide alleges, *inter alia*, that such conduct establishes violations of Section 10(b) and Rule 10b-5, as well as a claim of common law fraud.

[T]he AMC defendants have moved to dismiss Nationwide's 10(b) claim on the ground that it fails to state a claim for which relief may be granted. * * * For the reasons discussed below, the AMC defendants' motion is denied in all respects.

[**Analysis**] In order to state a cause of action under Rule 10b-5, a plaintiff must demonstrate the existence of six elements. Plaintiff must allege (1) a misstatement or omission by the defendant; (2) as to a material fact; (3) upon which plaintiff relied; (4)

and which caused plaintiff to suffer damage. In addition, the plaintiff must show that (5) defendant acted with scienter; and that (6) the misstatement or omission was made in connection with the purchase or sale of securities.

In its complaint, Nationwide has made allegations aimed at satisfying each of those elements. The complaint identifies a number of allegedly false statements in both the June 1989 financial statements and in the Agreement itself, and alleges that those statements were false despite AMC's and the AMC shareholders' express warranties and representations in section 5 of the Agreement that they were fair and accurate. The complaint alleges that the misrepresentations were material to the transaction; that Nationwide relied on the financial statements and the AMC defendants' warranties regarding their accuracy in negotiating the amount of stock to be sold and whether to close the transaction; and that Nationwide suffered substantial damage as a result. Nationwide further alleges that the AMC defendants either knowingly misrepresented AMC's financial condition in the financial statements and representations and warranties in the Agreement, or acted with reckless disregard as to the truth or falsity of the statements in those documents. Finally, the complaint alleges that its fraud claim arises from the sale of Nationwide securities pursuant to the Agreement.

In the face of plaintiff's numerous allegations of fraud, the AMC defendants nonetheless insist that Nationwide has failed to meet the requirement that the fraud be committed "in connection with" a purchase or sale of securities; to plead reliance; or to allege scienter. None of these claims has any merit.

While the AMC defendants' "in connection with" argument is a bit muddled, the heart of their claim seems to be that fraudulent representations must relate to more than the "mechanics" of a deal to be "in connection with" the sale of securities and that "the alleged fraud or misrepresentations must relate to the value of the securities purchased or sold, not just to the underlying transaction embodying their sale." Since the alleged misrepresentations in this case pertain only to the financial condition of AMC and not to the value of Nationwide's stock, the AMC defendants argue, the fraudulent misrepresentations would not be actionable under 10(b) even if provable at trial.

While AMC is certainly correct in suggesting that the mere incidental involvement of securities in a transaction does not satisfy the "in connection with" requirement, numerous cases—including some of those cited by the AMC defendants themselves—make clear that fraud pertaining to the consideration for a securities transaction does satisfy the requirement. * * * Thus, since Nationwide's complaint clearly states that the AMC defendants misrepresented the value of AMC's assets, and that those assets were the primary consideration for the transfer of its 250,000 shares of stock, Nationwide has satisfied its burden of pleading a fraud "in connection with" the purchase or sale of a security. * * *

Question

What result in *Nationwide Cellular* if Nationwide had paid in cash? Promissory notes?

§ 12.5 Tax Aspects

As indicated in Chapter 5, an acquisition of the assets of a stand-alone target in a taxable acquisition followed by the liquidation of the target results in a double tax. If the consideration paid is voting stock of the acquiror, the transaction may be treated as a tax-free reorganization under Section 368(a)(1)(C).

In general, in a taxable acquisition of assets, should the acquiror be willing to pay the full fair market value (less liabilities assumed) of the target's assets?

§ 12.6 Accounting Aspects

As indicated in Chapter 6, for accounting purposes the transaction is treated under the "acquisition" method without respect to the consideration issued by AC. Consequently, good will may arise as a result of the acquisition.

§ 12.7 Hart-Scott-Rodino Aspects

The Hart-Scott-Rodino pre-merger notification rules are examined in Chapter 9. In general, any acquisition in excess of $50 million (adjusted for inflation) is reportable.

§ 12.8 Due Diligence Investigation

Chapter 10 addresses steps needed to conduct a proper due diligence investigation.

§ 12.9 Potential Successor Liability in Asset Acquisitions

A. Extension of De Facto Merger Concept to Products Liability Situations

Knapp v. North American Rockwell Corp.

United States Court of Appeal, Third Circuit, 1974 506 F.2d 361

OPINION OF THE COURT

Adams, Circuit Judge.

The principal question here is whether it was error to grant summary judgment on the ground that one injured by a defective machine may not recover from the corporation that purchased substantially all the assets of the manufacturer of the machine because the transaction was a sale of assets rather than a merger or consolidation.

[Facts] Stanley Knapp, Jr., an employee of Mrs. Smith's Pie Co., was injured on October 6, 1969, when, in the course of his employment, his hand was caught in a machine known as a "Packomatic." The machine had been designed and manufactured by Textile Machine Works (TMW) and had been sold to Mrs. Smith's Pie Co. in 1966 or 1967.

On April 5, 1968, TMW entered into an agreement with North American Rockwell whereby TMW exchanged substantially all its assets for stock in Rockwell. TMW retained only its corporate seal, its articles of incorporation, its minute books and other corporate records, and $500,000 in cash intended to cover TMW's expenses in connection with the transfer. TMW also had the right, prior to closing the transaction with Rockwell, to dispose of land held by TMW or its subsidiary. Among the assets acquired by Rockwell was the right to use the name "Textile Machine Works." TMW was to change its name on the closing date, then to distribute the Rockwell stock to its shareholders and to dissolve TMW "[a]s soon as practicable after the last of such distributions."

The accord reached by Rockwell and TMW also stipulated that Rockwell would assume specified obligations and liabilities of TMW, but among the liabilities not assumed were:

"(a) liabilities against which TMW is insured or otherwise indemnified to the extent of such insurance or indemnification unless the insurer or indemnitor agrees in writing to insure and indemnify (Rockwell) to the same extent as it was so insuring and indemnifying TMW."

Closing took place pursuant to the agreement on August 29, 1968. Plaintiff sustained his injuries on October 6, 1969. TMW was dissolved on February 20, 1970, almost 18 months after the bulk of its assets had been exchanged for Rockwell stock.

[**Issue**] Plaintiff filed this suit against Rockwell in the district court on March 22, 1971. He alleged that his injuries resulted from the negligence of TMW in designing and manufacturing the machine and that Rockwell, as TMW's successor, is liable for such injuries. * * *

Rockwell moved for summary judgment in the district court on June 19, 1973. On September 6, 1973, the district court granted the motion, ruling that Rockwell had neither merged nor consolidated with TMW, that Rockwell was not a continuation of TMW, and that Rockwell had not assumed TMW's liability to Knapp. Therefore, the court concluded, Rockwell was not responsible for the obligations of TMW. * * * Knapp appealed to this Court on December 11, 1973.

Both parties agree that this case is controlled by the following principle of law:

> The general rule is that "a mere sale of corporate property by one company to another does not make the purchaser liable for the liabilities of the seller not assumed by it." * * * There are, however, certain exceptions to this rule. Liability for obligations of a selling corporation may be imposed on the purchasing corporation when (1) the purchaser expressly or impliedly agrees to assume such obligations; (2) the transaction amounts to a consolidation or merger of the selling corporation with or into the purchasing corporation; (3) the purchasing corporation is merely a continuation of the selling corporation; or (4) the transaction is entered into fraudulently to escape liability for such obligations.

In light of this language, Knapp contends that the transaction in question "amounts to a consolidation or merger of (TMW) with or into the purchasing corporation (Rockwell)" or, alternatively, that Rockwell is a "continuation" of TMW. Although the TMW corporation technically continued to exist until its dissolution approximately 18 months after the consummation of the transaction with Rockwell, TMW was, Knapp argues, a mere shell during that period. It had none of its former assets, no active operations, and was required by the contract with Rockwell to dissolve itself "as soon as practicable." Knapp urges in effect that the transaction between TMW and Rockwell should be considered a de facto merger.

Rockwell asserts, in defense of the district court's grant of summary judgment, that a merger, a consolidation and a continuation all require that the corporation being merged, consolidated or continued cease to exist. TMW, Rockwell claims, did not go out of existence at the time of the exchange with Rockwell, but continued its corporate life for 18 months thereafter. Further, Rockwell argues, TMW until its dissolution possessed assets of substantial value, in the form of Rockwell stock.

[**Analysis**] In a diversity case, the federal court must apply the rule of law which would govern if suit were brought in a court of the forum state. We must, therefore, determine how this case would be decided by a Pennsylvania court.

All jurisdictions which have considered the question appear to have accepted not only the general rule that a corporation which purchases the assets of a second corporation is not thereby liable for the obligations of the selling corporation, unless there exists one of the exceptions set out [above] * * * .

[T]he first of the four exceptions rendering the purchasing corporation liable for duties of the seller is a transaction amounting to a merger or consolidation. In a merger a corporation absorbs one or more other corporations, which thereby lose their corporate identity. "A merger of two corporations contemplates that one will be absorbed by the other and go out of existence, but the absorbing corporation will remain." * * * Another * * * exception to the general rule of nonliability arises when there is a continuation. In a continuation, a new corporation is formed to acquire the assets of an extant corporation, which then ceases to exist. "There is in effect but one corporation which merely changes its form and ordinarily ceases to exist upon the creation of the new corporation which is its successor."

No prior cases decided under Pennsylvania law have addressed the problem presently before this Court. However, when courts from other jurisdictions have considered similar questions, they have ascertained the existence *vel non* of a merger, a consolidation or a continuation on the basis of whether, immediately after the transaction, the selling corporation continued to exist as a corporate entity and whether, after the transaction, the selling corporation possessed substantial assets with which to satisfy the demands of its creditors. * * *

The cases * * * decided under the law of jurisdictions other than Pennsylvania, may suggest that the arrangement between Rockwell and TMW should be considered a sale rather than a merger or a continuation, since TMW did not officially terminate its corporate existence for 18 months after the exchange, and throughout that period possessed valuable assets with which to respond to tort claims similar to the one now advanced. However, a number of considerations indicate the insubstantiality of the continued existence of TMW, including the brevity of the corporation's continued life, the contractual requirement that TMW be dissolved as soon as possible, the prohibition on engaging in normal business transactions, and the character of the assets TMW controlled. Although each of these factors was present in one or more of the above cases, the present appeal is unique in combining all these elements. In addition, the better-reasoned result would be to conclude that, for the purpose of determining liability to tortuously injured parties, the Rockwell-TMW transaction should be treated as a merger, thereby subjecting Rockwell to liability for injuries caused by defective products distributed by TMW prior to the transaction.

We must, of course, apply the rule we believe a Pennsylvania appellate tribunal would adopt if the case arose in the state courts. In resolving issues relating to the recognition of a cause of action in favor of an injured party, the Pennsylvania courts have emphasized the public policy considerations served by imposing liability on the defendant rather than formal or technical requirements.

The Pennsylvania Supreme Court has held, in the context of the rights of dissenting shareholders, that if an agreement between two corporations bears the essential character of a merger, the failure of the contracting parties to follow the statutory merger procedures should not deprive third parties of relief otherwise available to them. * * * *Farris v. Glen Alden Corp.*, [**Section 2.13.B**] * * *

The present case, like *Farris*, involves a transaction which resembles a merger but does not possess all the formal characteristics of one. It seems appropriate to infer from *Farris* that in deciding whether to treat such an arrangement as a merger the Pennsylvania courts would consider the purposes which would be served by imposing liability on Rockwell for the tortious conduct of TMW.

In the present case, Knapp is confronted with the melancholy prospect of being barred from his day in court unless Rockwell is held subject to suit. And quite significantly, if

Knapp had been injured more than two years after the dissolution of TMW, Knapp would never have had any opportunity to recover at law, since under Pennsylvania law a dissolved corporation is subject to suit for only two years after the date of dissolution. * * *

If we are to follow the philosophy of the Pennsylvania courts that questions of an injured party's right to seek recovery are to be resolved by an analysis of public policy considerations rather than by a mere procrustean application of formalities, we must, in considering whether the TMW-Rockwell exchange was a merger, evaluate the public policy implications of that determination. * * *

In resolving, where the burden of a loss should be imposed, the Pennsylvania Supreme Court has considered which of the two parties is better able to spread the loss. In *Ayala v. Philadelphia Board of Education*, a student who had been injured by a shredding machine during an upholstery class sued the Board of Education. The Court, in abolishing the doctrine of immunity in suits against local government, observed that the Board was in a better position than the student to have avoided the injury, and that "The city is a far better loss-distributing agency than the innocent and injured victim." The Court, quoting the Supreme Court of Illinois, decried the injustice of imposing upon an injured party the entire burden of his injuries, rather than distributing the responsibility throughout the community "where it could be borne without hardship upon any individual." * * *

Interpreting all the allegations in the light most favorable to Knapp, as we must on a motion for summary judgment, neither Knapp nor Rockwell was ever in a position to prevent the occurrence of the injury, inasmuch as neither manufactured the defective device. As between these two parties, however, Rockwell is better able to spread the burden of the loss. Prior to the exchange with Rockwell, TMW had procured insurance that would have indemnified TMW had it been held liable to Knapp for his injuries. Rockwell could have protected itself from sustaining the brunt of the loss by securing from TMW an assignment of TMW's insurance. There is no indication in the record that such an assignment would have placed a burden on either Rockwell or TMW since TMW had already purchased the insurance protection, and the insurance was of no continuing benefit to TMW after its liability to suit was terminated by Pennsylvania statute. Rockwell has adduced no explanation, either in its brief or at oral argument, why it agreed in the contract not to take an assignment of TMW's prepaid insurance. Rockwell therefore should not be permitted to impose the weight of the loss upon a user of an allegedly defective product by delaying the formal dissolution of TMW. In the absence of contrary controlling decisions by the Pennsylvania courts, we conclude that the state judiciary would adopt the rule of law that appears to be better reasoned and more consistent with the social policy set forth in recent Pennsylvania cases.

The judgment of the district court will therefore be reversed and the case remanded for further proceedings consistent with this opinion. * * *

Questions

In *Knapp* the consideration paid by the acquiring corporation was its stock. Would the court have reached the same decision if the consideration paid had been cash? How can an acquiring corporation protect itself from the type of liability incurred in *Knapp*?

B. The California Strict Liability Approach

Rosales v. Thermex-Thermatron, Inc.

Court of Appeals of California, 1998 78 Cal.Rptr.2d 861

GILBERT, Associate Justice.

In this product liability case, judgment was awarded to plaintiff for injuries she suffered from a product manufactured by defendant's corporate predecessor 24 years earlier. Defendant [Thermex-Thermatron] had continued to distribute the same products of the corporation it had acquired. Its acquisition of the predecessor corporation had destroyed plaintiff's remedy against that corporation.

Liability was based on *Ray v. Alad Corp.* (1977) 19 Cal.3d 22, 136 Cal.Rptr. 574, 560 P.2d 3 in which our Supreme Court held that under these, and other circumstances, the acquiring company is strictly liable for defects in the products manufactured by the predecessor company. The circumstances of Ray are applicable here.

Defendant argues that the Ray doctrine of "product line liability" should be overruled. It points out that only one published decision affirmed a judgment based on *Ray's* theory of successor liability.

This is the second case. * * *

Thermex-Thermatron contends it should not be held liable for the obligations of its predecessor. The ordinary rule is that where a corporation purchases the assets of another corporation for adequate consideration, the purchaser does not become liable for the obligations of the seller. The question presented by the parties here is whether the exception to that rule stated in *Ray v. Alad Corp* applies to this case.

In *Ray*, plaintiff claimed he was injured by a defective ladder. He sued Alad Corporation (Alad II) alleging strict tort liability. Alad II, however, had not manufactured the ladder. The ladder had been manufactured by another corporation with the same name (Alad I). Prior to the accident Alad II had purchased all of the assets of Alad I, including plant, equipment, inventory, trade name and good will. Alad II continued to manufacture the same line of ladders using the same name, the same equipment, designs, personnel and solicited Alad I's customers. There was no outward indication of any change in the ownership of the business.

In holding Alad II liable our Supreme court stated: "Justification for imposing strict liability upon a successor to a manufacturer under the circumstances here presented rests upon (1) the virtual destruction of the plaintiff's remedies against the original manufacturer caused by the successor's acquisition of the business, (2) the successor's ability to assume the original manufacturer's risk-spreading role, and (3) the fairness of requiring the successor to assume a responsibility for defective products that was a burden necessarily attached to the original manufacturer's good will being enjoyed by the successor in the continued operation of the business." (*Ray v. Alad Corp.*, *supra*, 19 Cal.3d at p. 31, 136 Cal.Rptr. 574, 560 P.2d 3) * * *

First, the sale of [the assets of the predecessor corporation] to Thermex-Thermatron virtually destroyed Rosales' remedies against the original manufacturer. * * *

The next question is whether Thermex-Thermatron had the ability to assume its predecessor's risk-spreading role. The new Thermex-Thermatron corporation obtained the physical plant and manufacturing equipment of its predecessor. It also obtained its predecessor's knowledge of the business. The new corporation's owners were employees of the Solidyne subsidiary. Thermex-Thermatron had essentially the same ability as its predecessor to assess the risks. It also had the ability to continue manufacturing the machines to spread the risks. These were the factors used by the court in Ray to conclude the successor corporation had the ability to assume the risk spreading role.

Finally, it is fair to require Thermex-Thermatron to assume responsibility for its predecessor's defective products. Thermex-Thermatron continues to benefit from its predecessor's good will. It uses the name of Solidyne and its former divisions in advertising and, in particular, in telephone books. It continues to use customer lists compiled by Solidyne. Even the name Thermex-Thermatron is composed of the names of former Solidyne divisions and is the same name as the former Solidyne subsidiary. * * *

Questions and Note

How can an acquiring corporation avoid the type of liability incurred in *Rosales*? For a similar approach *see Ramirez v. Amsted Industries, Inc.*, 431 A.2d 811 (NJ 1981), which held: "[W]here one corporation acquires all or substantially all the manufacturing assets of another corporation, even if exclusively for cash, and undertakes essentially the same manufacturing operation as the selling corporation, the purchasing corporation is strictly liable for injuries caused by defects in units of the same product line, even if previously manufactured and distributed by the selling corporation or its predecessor."

C. A Restrained Approach

Bernard v. Kee Mfg. Co., Inc.

Supreme Court of Florida, 1982 409 So.2d 1047

Sundberg, Chief Justice.

The issue we confront in this case is whether the purchaser of the assets of a manufacturing firm which continues under the same trade name the general product line of the seller can be liable for a defective product manufactured by the seller, even though the traditional corporate law rule would impose no liability. We adhere to the traditional rule.

Petitioners, the Bernards, brought a products liability claim against respondent Kee Manufacturing Company, Inc. (Kee, Inc.). They claimed that a lawn mower manufactured and sold in 1967 by Kee Manufacturing Company (Kee), the predecessor business to Kee, Inc., caused an injury in 1976 to James Bernard, Jr., who with his mother sought recovery based on negligence, implied warranty and strict liability. Kee, Inc. had incorporated in 1972 when it had acquired for cash the assets of Kee from the owner, Flechas J. Kee, who did business as Kee Manufacturing Company. These assets included the manufacturing plant, inventory, good will, and the right to use the name "Kee Manufacturing Company." Kee, Inc., by the terms of this acquisition, had not assumed liabilities or obligations of its predecessor, Kee. The former owner of the business had no interest in the new company. Kee, Inc. used these assets to continue the manufacture of lawn mowers, maintaining the same factory personnel and using the trade name of Kee Mowers. The entire manufacturing process was effectively continued, but under a new owner and management. Kee, Inc. still provides replacement parts for the model of lawn mower involved here, though it has discontinued manufacturing the model. The brochure of Kee, Inc. states that it has been manufacturing lawn mowers since 1948. The Bernards have also sought separate recovery from Flechas J. Kee, individually, and from the retailer who sold the lawn mower.

The trial court granted Kee, Inc.'s motion for summary judgment, and this was affirmed by the District Court of Appeal, Second District, which refused to consider the financial responsibility of the predecessor to determine potential liability of a successor company * * * .

The vast majority of jurisdictions follow the traditional corporate law rule which does not impose the liabilities of the selling predecessor upon the buying successor company unless (1) the successor expressly or impliedly assumes obligations of the predecessor, (2) the transaction is a *de facto* merger, (3) the successor is a mere continuation of the predecessor, or (4) the transaction is a fraudulent effort to avoid liabilities of the predecessor.

Courts in a few jurisdictions have begun to extend products liability to the successor corporation in an effort to effectuate an acknowledged purpose of strict liability for defective products, that the costs of a defective product should be included in that product. * * *

We choose not to join this vanguard of courts, due in part to the threat of economic annihilation that small businesses would face under such a rule of expanded liability. Because of their limited assets, small corporations would face financial destruction from imposition of liability for their predecessor's products * * * .

> The economy as a whole suffers when small successor corporations lose such cases since corporate acquisitions are discouraged due to business planners' fears of being held so liable. Furthermore, the marketability of on-going corporations is diminished * * * . * * *

Although we do not consider that the legislature is alone suited to make the determination of whether successor corporate liability should be extended, we do perceive other legitimate policy considerations for refusing to expand such liability. Extending liability to the corporate successor is not consistent with at least one major premise of strict liability, which is to place responsibility for a defective product on the manufacturer who placed that product into commerce. The corporate successor has not created the risk, and only remotely benefits from the product. The successor has not invited usage of the product or implied its safety. Since the successor was never in a position to eliminate the risk, a major purpose of strict liability in modifying a manufacturer's behavior is also lost.

For these reasons we adhere to the traditional corporate law rule, and approve the decision of the District Court of Appeal, Second District, in this case, other than its deference to the legislature. * * *

Question

Is the Court's policy analysis concerning the harm to small business resulting from a product line or similar liability rule persuasive?

D. Liability of Successor Corporations under CERCLA

Memorandum of Assistant Administrator for Enforcement and Compliance Monitoring, United States Environmental Protection Agency

(June 13, 1984)

THE LIABILITY OF SUCCESSOR CORPORATIONS UNDER CERCLA

Background.Section 107(a)(2) of CERCLA extends liability for response costs to "any person who at the time of disposal of any hazardous substance owned or operated any facility at which such hazardous substances were disposed of." Situations may arise, however, where a corporation, which previously had owned or operated a hazardous waste facility, now transfers corporate ownership to another corporation. In such cases, it is important to determine whether the liability of the predecessor corporation's action regarding the disposal of hazardous waste is also transferred to the successor corporation.

Issue. What is the extent of liability for successor corporations under CERCLA?

Discussion. The liability of a successor corporation, according to traditional corporation law, is dependent on the structure of the corporate acquisition. Corporate ownership may be transferred in one of three ways: 1) through the sale of stock to another corporation; 2) by a merger or consolidation with another corporation; or 3) by the sale of its assets to another corporation. Where a corporation is acquired through the "purchase of all of its outstanding stock, the corporate entity remains intact and retains its liabilities, despite the change of ownership." By the same token, a purchasing corporation retains liability for claims against the predecessor company if the transaction is in the form of a merger or consolidation. Where, however, the acquisition is in the form of a sale or other transference of all of a corporation's assets to a successor corporation, the latter is not liable for the debts and liabilities of the predecessor corporation.

There are four exceptions to this general rule of non-liability in asset acquisitions. A successor corporation is liable for the actions of its predecessor corporation if one of the following is shown:

1) The purchaser expressly or impliedly agrees to assume such obligations;

2) The transaction amounts to a "*de facto*" consolidation or merger;

3) The purchasing corporation is merely a continuation of the selling corporation; or

4) The transaction is entered into fraudulently in order to escape liability.

The application of the traditional corporate law approach to successor liability has in many instances led to particularly harsh and unjust results, especially with respect to product liability cases. Therefore, in an effort to provide an adequate remedy and to protect injured consumers, courts have broadened the exemptions to the general rule by either modifying or recasting the "*de facto*" and "mere continuation" exemptions to include an element of public policy.

More recently, however, the general rule has been abandoned altogether by several jurisdictions and, in essence, a new theory for establishing successor liability has evolved based upon the similarity of business operations. * * *

This theory of establishing successor liability differs from the "*de facto*" and "mere continuation" exemptions in that the new approach does not examine whether there is a continuity of corporate structure or ownership (*e.g.*, whether the predecessor and successor corporation share a common director or officer). Instead, according to the new theory, liability will be imposed if the successor corporation continues essentially the same manufacturing or business operation as its predecessor corporation, even if no continuity of ownership exists between them.

Until recently, this new approach for establishing successor liability was confined mostly to product liability cases. However, a recent New Jersey decision extended its application to the area of environmental torts. The Superior Court of New Jersey, in *N.J. Transportation Department v. PSC Resources, Inc.*,[1] rejected the traditional corporate approach to successor liability where the defendant and its predecessor corporation had allegedly discharged hazardous wastes. The court reasoned that the underlying policy rationale for abandonment of the traditional approach in defective product cases is applicable to environmental torts.

1. 175 N.J. Super. 447, 419 A.2d 1151 (Super. Ct. Law Dir. 1980).

Therefore, the court held that a corporation which purchased assets of another corporation and engaged in the practice of discharging hazardous waste into a state-owned lake is strictly liable for present and previous discharges made by itself and the predecessor corporation because the successor continued the same waste disposal practice as its predecessor.

A similar "continuity of business operation" approach has been used in cases involving statutory violations. The Ninth Circuit, for example, held in a case involving the Federal Insecticide, Fungicide, and Rodenticide Act (FIFRA), that "EPA's authority to extend liability to successor corporations stems from the purpose of the statute it administers, which is to regulate pesticides to protect the national environment." Furthermore, the court noted that "[t]he agency may pursue the objectives of the Act by imposing successor liability where it will facilitate enforcement of the Act. After establishing that there had been violations of FIFRA by the predecessor corporation, the court found that there was substantial continuity of business operation between the predecessor and successor corporations to warrant imposition of successor liability.

Although CERCLA is not primarily a regulatory statute, public policy considerations and the legislative history of the Act clearly indicate that federal law would be applicable to CERCLA situations involving successor liability. Therefore, it is reasonable to assume that courts would similarly adopt the federal "continuity of business operation approach" in cases involving CERCLA. * * *

Note

See the *Bestfoods* case in Section 11.11 for a discussion of a parent corporation's potential derivative liability for a sub's direct CERCLA liability.

E. Potential Liability for State Sales and Other Taxes

In addition to potential successor liability under the common law doctrines discussed above, some states impose by statute successor liability for certain taxes, such as sales taxes. Section 212.10 of the Florida Statutes (which has recently been replaced with a more expansive requirement) is such a provision. Under this section, in an asset acquisition, the seller is required to pay any sales tax within 15 days of the closing, and the buyer is required to withhold a sufficient portion of the purchase price to cover the amount of such taxes. Further, if the buyer fails to withhold a sufficient amount of the purchase proceeds to cover the liability, the buyer "shall be personally liable for the payment of the taxes, interest, and penalties accruing and unpaid on account of the operation of business by [the seller]." *See generally* Peter L. Faber, *State and Local Income and Franchise Tax Aspects of Corporate Acquisitions,* Negotiation Business Acquisitions, J14 to J15 (ABA-CLE, 1998).

F. Use of an Acquiring Sub to Reduce Potential Successor and Other Liabilities

It is obvious from the materials in this Section 12.9 that in an asset acquisition an acquiror must be concerned about bringing the specifically assumed and other potential liabilities (*i.e.*, "bad" liabilities) of the target into the corporate entity that holds the acquiror's "good" assets. To minimize this problem, the acquiror should consider having a subsidiary of the target acquire the target's assets and assume the specifically assumed liabilities. The acquiror would want to ensure that the sub was adequately capitalized and properly operated so as to avoid potential piercing of the corporate veil. This veil piercing issue is discussed in the *Bestfoods* case, in Section 11.11.

§ 12.10 Purchasing Corporation's Right to Assume Target's Debt: Impact of Successor Obligor Clause in Bond Indenture

Sharon Steel Corp. v. Chase Manhattan Bank, N.A.

United States Court of Appeals, Second Circuit, 1982 691 F.2d 1039, cert. denied 103 S.Ct. 1253

[Sharon Steel Corp. (Sharon) purchased certain assets from UV Industries, Inc. (UV), a corporation that was in the process of making liquidating sales to Sharon and to others. UV had debt outstanding that had been issued pursuant to various indentures. The indentures contained "successor obligor" clauses that permitted UV's debt to be assumed by an acquiring firm in certain cases. Sharon argued that as a result of its purchase of part of UV's assets, Sharon had the right to assume UV's debt and that the debt did not, therefore, become due and payable as a result of the purchase by Sharon.]

Between 1965 and 1977, UV issued debt instruments pursuant to five separate indentures, the salient terms of which we briefly summarize. In 1965, UV issued approximately $23 million of 5% subordinated debentures due in 1995, under an indenture naming The Chase Manhattan Bank, N.A. (Chase) as the trustee (First Chase Indenture). The current principal amount of the debentures outstanding under that indenture is approximately $14 million. * * *

The debentures, notes and guaranties are general obligations of UV. * * * The First Chase Indenture * * * contains a "successor obligor" provision allowing UV to assign its debt [to an acquiror in certain mergers and sales of all or substantially all of UV's assets] * * *.

Accepting Sharon's position [that the successor obligor clause applies] would severely impair the interests of lenders. Sharon's view would allow a borrowing corporation to engage in a piecemeal sale of assets, with concurrent liquidating dividends to that point at which the asset restrictions of an indenture prohibited further distribution. A sale of "all or substantially all" of the remaining assets could then be consummated, a new debtor substituted, and the liquidation of the borrower completed. The assignment of the public debt might thus be accomplished, even though the last sale might be nothing more than a cash for cash transaction in which the buyer purchases the public indebtedness. The UV/Sharon transaction is not so extreme, but the sale price paid by Sharon did include a cash for cash exchange of $107 million. Twenty-three percent of the sale price was, in fact, an exchange of dollars for dollars. Such a transaction diminishes the protection for lenders in order to facilitate deals with little functional significance other than substituting a new debtor in order to profit on a debenture's low interest rate. We hold, therefore, that boilerplate successor obligor clauses do not permit assignment of the public debt to another party in the course of a liquidation unless "all or substantially all" of the assets of the company at the time the plan of liquidation is determined upon are transferred to a single purchaser.

The application of this rule to the present case is not difficult. The plan of liquidation was approved by UV's shareholders on March 26, 1978. Since the Indenture Trustees make no claim as to an earlier time, *e.g.*, the date of the Board recommendation, we accept March 26 as the appropriate reference date. The question then is whether "all or substantially all" of the assets held by UV on that date were transferred to Sharon. That is easily answered. The assets owned by UV on March 26 and later transferred to Sharon were Mueller Brass, certain metals mining property, and substantial amounts of cash and other liquid assets. UV's Form 10-K and Sharon's Form S-7 state that Mueller Brass and the metals mining properties were responsible for only 38% of UV's 1978 operating revenues and 13% of its operating profits. They constitute 41% of the book value of UV's operating properties. When the cash and other liquid assets are added, the transaction still involved only 51% of the book value of UV's total assets.

Since we do not regard the question in this case as even close, we need not determine how the substantiality of corporate assets is to be measured, what percentage meets the "all or substantially all" test or what role a jury might play in determining those issues. Even when the liquid assets (other than proceeds from the sale of Federal and the oil and gas properties) are aggregated with the operating properties, the transfer to Sharon accounted for only 51% of the total book value of UV's assets. In no sense, therefore, are they "all or substantially all" of those assets. The successor obligor clauses are, therefore, not applicable. UV is thus in default on the indentures and the debentures are due and payable. For that reason, we need not reach the question whether the April Document was breached by UV. * * *

§ 12.11 Introduction to the Impact of Bulk Sale Provision

A. Basic Principles

Article 6 of the Uniform Commercial Code may apply upon the sale of a division or the sale of substantial assets of a business. Under this provision, the trade creditors of the seller-transferor must be given advance notice that the sale will be consummated. If the notice requirements are not satisfied, then under UCC § 1–107(3), the sale is deemed ineffective against the seller's creditors. As a result, the creditors can treat the property transferred to the buyer as that of the seller and available for satisfaction of the seller's debts. The buyer may be liable even though it attempted compliance in good faith. The creditor must bring its action within six months of the sale. *See* UCC § 1–111.

The bulk sale rules are governed by state law and in a case of a sale of assets located in multiple states, the bulk sale laws of each of the states will have to be considered.

B. The Revised Article 6 Official Comment to § 6–101, the Revised Article 6 of the Uniform Commercial Code

Official Comment

Rationale for Revision of the Article. Article 6 (1987 Official Text) imposes upon transferees in bulk several duties toward creditors of the transferor. These duties include the duty to notify the creditors of the impending bulk transfer and, in those jurisdictions that have adopted optional Section 1–106, the duty to assure that the new consideration for the transfer is applied to pay debts of the transferor.

Compliance with the provisions of Article 6 can be burdensome, particularly when the transferor has a large number of creditors. When the transferor is actively engaged in business at a number of locations, assembling a current list of creditors may not be possible. Mailing a notice to each creditor may prove costly. When the goods that are the subject of the transfer are located in several jurisdictions, the transferor may be obligated to comply with Article 6 as enacted in each jurisdiction. The widespread enactment of nonuniform amendments makes compliance with Article 6 in multiple-state transactions problematic. Moreover, the Article requires compliance even when there is no reason to believe that the transferor is conducting a fraudulent transfer, *e.g.*, when the transferor is scaling down the business but remaining available to creditors.

Article 6 imposes strict liability for noncompliance. Failure to comply with the provisions of the Article renders the transfer ineffective, even when the transferor has attempted compliance in good faith, and even when no creditor has been injured by the noncompliance. The potential liability for minor noncompliance may be high. If the transferor should enter bankruptcy before the expiration of the limitation period, Bankruptcy Code § 544(b), § 550(a), § 11 U.S.C., § 544(b), § 550(a), may enable the transferor's bankruptcy trustee to set aside the entire transaction and recover from the noncomplying transferee all the goods transferred or their value. The trustee has this power even though the noncompliance was with respect to only a single creditor holding a small claim.

The benefits that compliance affords to creditors do not justify the substantial burdens and risks that the Article imposes upon good faith purchasers of business assets. The Article requires that notice be sent only ten days before the transferee takes possession of the goods or pays for them, whichever happens first. Given the delay between sending the notice and its receipt, creditors have scant opportunity to avail themselves of a judicial or nonjudicial remedy before the transfer has been consummated.

In some cases Article 6 may have the unintended effect of injuring, rather than aiding, creditors of the transferor. Those transferees who recognize the burdens and risks that Article 6 imposes upon them sometimes agree to purchase only at a reduced price. Others refuse to purchase at all, leaving the creditors to realize only the liquidation value, rather than the going concern value, of the business goods.

As a response to these inadequacies and others, the National Conference of Commissioners on Uniform State Laws has completely revised Article 6. This revision is designed to reduce the burdens and risks imposed upon good-faith buyers of business assets while increasing the protection afforded to creditors. Among the major changes it makes are the following:

—this Article applies only when the buyer has notice, or after reasonable inquiry would have had notice, that the seller will not continue to operate the same or a similar kind of business after the sale (Section 1–102(1)(c)).

—this Article does not apply to sales in which the value of the property otherwise available to creditors is less than $10,000 or those in which the value of the property is greater than $25,000,000 (Section 1–103(3)(l)).

—the choice-of-law provision (Sections 1–103(1)(b) and 1–103(2)) limits the applicable law to that of one jurisdiction.

—when the seller is indebted to a large number of persons, the buyer need neither obtain a list of those persons nor send individual notices to each person but instead may give notice by filing (Sections 1–105(2) and 1–104(2)).

—the notice period is increased from 10 days to 45 days (Section 1–105(5)), and the statute of limitations is extended from six months to one year (Section 1–110).

—the notice must include a copy of a "schedule of distribution," which sets forth how the net contract price is to be distributed (Sections 1–105(3) and 1–106(1)).

—a buyer who makes a good faith effort to comply with the requirements of this Article or to exclude the sale from the application of this Article, or who acts on the good faith belief that this Article does not apply to the sale, is not liable for noncompliance (Section 1–107(3)).

—a buyer's noncompliance does not render the sale ineffective or otherwise affect the buyer's title to the goods; rather, the liability of a noncomplying buyer is for damages caused by the noncompliance (Sections 1–107(1) and 1–107(8)).

In addition to making these and other major substantive changes, revised Article 6 resolves the ambiguities that three decades of law practice, judicial construction, and scholarly inquiry have disclosed.

References

Kling and Nugent, *Negotiated Acquisitions, supra* Section 1.10.

ABA Model Asset Purchase Agreement, supra Section 1.10.

Various chapters of Thompson, *Mergers, Acquisitions and Tender Offers, supra* Section 1.10.

Chapter 13

Acquisition of a Publicly-Held Target in a Negotiated Merger

§ 13.1 Scope

This chapter, which builds on prior chapters, particularly Chapter 3, directors' duties, and Chapter 4, SEC rules and regulations, addresses various issues that can arise in the acquisition of a publicly-held target corporation in a negotiated merger. Section 13.2 sets out a problem that addresses issues examined in this chapter. Section 13.3 deals with structuring issues such as the voting and dissenting rights of the target's and the acquiror's shareholders and builds on concepts addressed in Chapter 2. Section 13.4 addresses the federal income tax aspects of these transactions by referring to Chapter 5; Section 13.5 addresses the accounting aspects by referring to Chapter 6; and Section 13.6 addresses the pre-merger notification rules and the related antitrust standards by referring to Chapters 9 and 8, respectively. Section 13.7 examines the rules governing the actions of the target's and the acquiror's boards of directors in structuring a negotiated acquisition. This section refers to many of the cases in Chapter 3, which deals with directors' duties, particularly cases dealing with deal protection devices such as "no talks," "fiduciary outs," and "break-up fees."

Section 13.8 explores what can be publicly said under Rule 10b-5 under the 34 Act about a potential merger or acquisition prior to a formal press release announcing the transaction, and Section 13.9 looks at the Delaware law on this issue. Section 13.10 deals with the federal securities laws and rules governing the issuance of securities in a merger transaction. Thus, this section deals with transactions in which the merger consideration is stock or other securities and therefore, focuses on Rule 145 and Form S-4 under the 33 Act. This section discusses the 2007 amendments to Rule 145. Section 13.11 addresses gun-jumping issues that can arise in an acquisition of a publicly-held target corporation and explores the SEC's 1999 rules on shareholder communications, which significantly reduce gun-jumping concerns. Section 13.12 examines the impact of the federal proxy rules in consensual transactions and considers (1) the SEC's 1999 amendments to the proxy rules, (2) the adoption of Regulation M-A, and (3) the golden parachute voting requirements enacted by Dodd-Frank Act. Section 13.13 discusses the SEC's views on lock-ups in which a target's shareholders agree to vote their shares for a transaction. Section 13.14 examines Reg. M under the 34 Act, which governs trading in securities during the period in which the securities are being issued, for example, an IPO or M&A transaction, and Section 13.15 focuses on Rule 10b-18 under the 34 Act, which sets out a safe harbor for certain repurchase activity during a distribution of securities, including M&A distributions.

Sections 13.16 through 13.20 address various issues concerning liability for violation of the federal proxy rules. Section 13.21 deals with the merger proxy requirements under Delaware law, and Section 13.22 introduces the impact of Section 16(b) of the 34 Act, which governs certain purchases and sales of stock within a six month period, in the context of mergers and acquisitions. Section 13.23 introduces the two-step negotiated tender offer followed by a second step merger. This transaction is discussed further at the end of the study of the rules governing third-party tender offers in Chapter 20.

The issues covered in this chapter are addressed in various chapters of Thompson, *Mergers, Acquisitions and Tender Offers, supra* Section 1.10, including Chapter 5, Directors' Duties, and Chapters 6, 7, and 8, which deal with securities laws issues in M&A.

§ 13.2 Introductory Problem on Acquisition of Publicly-Held Target in a Negotiated Merger

Publicly Held Acquiring Corporation (PHAC), a Delaware corporation, listed on the NYSE, is negotiating to acquire Publicly Held Target Corporation (PHTC), a Delaware Corporation, listed on the NYSE. PHAC has proposed to issue two of its shares for each share of PHTC. At current prices this would provide the PHTC shareholders with a 20% premium over the current trading value of the PHTC shares, and the shares issued to PHTC shareholders would amount to 25% of the outstanding shares of PHAC after the transaction. PHAC has sufficient authorized but unissued shares to complete this transaction. The negotiations have been going on for several weeks. Recently there has been increased trading activity in the PHTC stock, and the price has begun to rise.

PHTC's board wants the transaction to be tax-free to the PHTC shareholders. For business reasons, it is important to keep PHTC as a free-standing corporation, and for that reason the parties are planning a reverse subsidiary merger in which PHAC will form a subsidiary (PHAC-Sub), which will merge into PHTC. Pursuant to the merger, the PHTC shareholders will receive stock of PHAC and PHTC will become a subsidiary of PHAC.

Five of PHTC's officers are members of PHTC's board of directors and each of these five individuals has a substantial stock interest in PHTC. It is contemplated however, that only one of these five officers, the President of PHTC (Pres), will have a management role after the acquisition. The other officers of PHTC will exchange their stock in PHTC for stock in PHAC and will retire after the transaction. On the other hand Pres, who owns 20% of the stock of PHTC, will end up owning 5% of the stock of PHAC and will become a board member of PHAC.

To dissuade other potential acquirors, (1) PHTC will agree to a standard no solicitation with a fiduciary out for a superior proposal, and (2) PHAC will receive a break-up fee (termination fee) of 4.5% of the transaction price in the event PHTC is taken over by another company.

After the transaction is announced, Risk Arbitrage, Inc., (RA), which specializes in purchasing shares in takeover candidates, acquires a significant stock interest in PHTC through open market purchases. RA purchases stock in PHTC at three different times within two weeks after the announcement of the transaction. In the first purchase, RA ended up with 4.5% of the stock of PHTC; in the second purchase, RA ended up with 11% of the stock of PHTC; and in the third purchase, RA ended up with 16% of the stock of PHTC.

1. What are the voting and appraisal rights of the PHAC and PHTC shareholders in the proposed reverse subsidiary merger? What would be the voting and appraisal rights of the PHTC and PHAC shareholders if the consideration for the merger is cash? What if the PHTC shareholders can elect either cash or stock, without any limit on either election?

2. What conditions will have to be satisfied for the transaction to be treated as non-taxable for federal income tax purposes? [*See* Section 13.3] What would be the federal income tax treatment of the transaction if the merger consideration is cash? What is the accounting treatment of the transaction? [*See* Section 13.5]

3. What are the pre-merger notification requirements for this transaction, including the purchases by RA?

4. What standard governs the actions of the boards of directors of PHAC and PHTC in negotiating the transaction and entering into the no solicitation clause and break-up fee?

5. Prior to completion of the merger negotiations, a reporter from the *Wall Street Journal* calls PHTC inquiring about rumors that PHTC is in merger negotiations and also inquiring about a recent increase in activity in PHTC shares. How should PHTC respond?

6. PHTC is planning a previously scheduled public offering of debt. The offering takes place before the finalization of the merger negotiations. Does PHTC have an obligation to discuss the merger negotiations in the registration statement for the debt?

7. PHAC and PHTC have successfully negotiated a merger agreement reflecting the terms discussed above. In general, what representations, conditions and covenants, should PHAC and PHTC insist upon in the merger agreement? [*See* Chapter 15]

8. After the merger agreement is entered into, PHTC would like very much to issue a press release. Can it, and if so what can the press release contain? What if the consideration is cash?

9. What SEC rules and regulations relating to registration statements and proxy statements must be complied with in order to complete the proposed transaction?

10. When and under what circumstances can the following shareholders of PHTC sell their PHAC stock?
    a. The public shareholders?
    b. The officers of PHTC who do not become officers of PHAC?
    c. Pres of PHTC who becomes a director of PHAC?

11. What federal and state rules govern the potential liability for the preparation of an inaccurate proxy statement?

12. What is the treatment to RA under the following circumstances?
    a. RA swaps its shares in PHTC for shares in PHAC pursuant to the merger which takes place three months after the announcement of the merger.
    b. Prior to the consummation of the merger, RA sells all of its shares at a profit on the NYSE.
    c. Prior to the consummation of the transaction, RA first sells sufficient shares to reduce its interest to 9% and then sells the balance of its shares.

§ 13.3 Structuring the Transaction: Voting and Dissenting by Target's and Acquiror's Shareholders

A. In General

The rules governing the right of the shareholders of the target and the acquiror to vote and seek appraisal in mergers and other acquisitions are covered in Chapter 2.

B. Use of the Reverse Subsidiary Merger

Most acquisitions of publicly-held target firms are effectuated by a reverse subsidiary merger. For example, this was the form of the transaction in (1) Time's initially proposed merger with Warner [*see* Documentary Appendix A of M&A Statutes, Rules, and Documents, *supra* Section 1.1], and (2) the acquisition of Toys "R" Us in an LBO transaction [*see* Documentary Appendix G of M&A Statutes, Rules, and Documents, *supra* Section 1.1].

In a reverse subsidiary merger, the Acquiror forms a subsidiary (Acquiror Sub), and Acquiror Sub merges into Target, with Target surviving. Target's shareholders receive the merger consideration, and Acquiror's shares in Acquiror Sub are converted into shares of Target, so that Target becomes a wholly-owned subsidiary of Acquiror. The voting and appraisal rights arising in this transaction are explored in Chapter 2.

C. Mergers-of-Equals (MOE)

A merger-of-equals (MOE) involves a merger of publicly-held corporations in which neither the target's nor the acquiror's shareholders receive a premium. The *Mergers and Acquisitions and Takeover Preparedness 1996 Update*, p.56, of Wachtell, Lipton, Rosen & Katz, explains:

> "[C]ontrol is shared between the parties. The exchange ratio is set to reflect the relative asset, earnings and capital contributions and market capitalizations of the two merging parties—typically resulting in a market-to-market exchange. * * * Common goals and vision are critical and cooperation must begin at the highest levels of the company * * *.
>
> * * * It is critical that a positive stock market reaction to the transaction be obtained in order to reduce both parties' vulnerability to shareholder unrest and/or a competing offer following the announcement of the deal. While cross stock options can provide some economic and structural protection against competing offers, the protection must often be incomplete, especially for smaller transactions. * * * "

A balanced management structure, with possibly an even split of the board of the resulting firm between members from the two merging firms, is a key to a successful MOE. Also, there often will be a split between the Chairman and the CEO of the resulting firm with the head person at one of the merging firms becoming Chairman and the head person at the other becoming the CEO.

The legal issues arising in MOEs are essentially the same as the legal issues arising in any other negotiated merger. For example, see *Tracinda*, Section 13.20, addressing a Rule 10b-5 claim in the MOE between Chrysler and Daimler-Benz of Germany.

D. SEC's Overview of the Regulatory Regime for Consensual and Hostile Public Company Acquisitions

Notice of Proposed Rules, Regulation of Takeovers and Security Holder Communications, Overview of the Regulatory Scheme, Securities Act Release No. 33-7607

(December 4, 1998)

This release discusses two primary business combination methods: tender offers and mergers. Tender offers may be made either by the issuer of the securities sought [*see* Chapter 21] or by a third party. [*See* Chapter 20] The essence of a tender offer is that the offeror, or bidder, can go directly to security holders of the target company with an offer to buy their shares. Each security holder makes an individual decision whether or not to tender. A tender offer may or may not have the cooperation of the target company's board of directors. Even if the tender offer is successful, the bidder is unlikely to receive 100% of the shares. In contrast, a merger is a collective, voting decision. The acquiror acquires the entire company if security holders of the target company approve the merger. The acquiror generally needs the approval of the target's board of directors in order to present the transaction for a security holder vote. [*See* Chapter 2]

In either a tender offer or a merger, the offeror may offer cash, securities, or a combination. [*See* Chapter 2] If the consideration consists all or partly of securities, the offeror generally will have to register them under the Securities Act. [*See* Chapters 4 and Section 13.10] The offeror will have to give more information to security holders of the target company than if it were offering cash, since the investment decision is more complex. Security holders of the target need information about the issuer whose securities they will receive if the transaction is consummated, which really means information about the surviving, combined entity (the issuer plus the acquired company).

The following summarizes the regulatory process for the four basic business combination methods. * * *

Cash tender offer—either issuer or third party. [*See* Chapters 19, 20, and 21] The bidder commences the offer by disseminating tender offer material to security holders, including a request that they tender their shares. On the same day, the bidder files this material publicly with the Commission, along with a tender offer schedule that contains additional information. Unlike the other three transactions discussed below, the Commission staff does not have the opportunity to review the tender offer material until after the tender offer has begun. If the staff decides to review the filed material, and has comments, the staff gives comments to the bidder during the tender offer and the bidder addresses the comments appropriately. (For example, the bidder may need to send additional information to the security holders of the target and the offer may have to be extended.) The offer must remain open for at least 20 business days, and then the bidder can purchase the shares if all conditions to the offer have been satisfied or waived.

Exchange offer (stock tender offer)—either issuer or third party. [*See* Chapters 20 and 21] [Prior to the adoption of the new rules that permit an exchange offer to begin at the time of the filing of the tender offer statement, exchange offers were commenced as follows.] The bidder files a Securities Act registration statement containing a preliminary prospectus covering the securities it is offering to security holders of the target in exchange for their shares. The prospectus also contains the information about the exchange offer required by the tender offer rules. * * * [The bidder] usually does not [distribute the preliminary prospectus] because it cannot request tenders or buy any shares until the registration statement is declared effective. [*See* Chapter 4] * * * [As a result of the new rules, which are designed to put exchange offers on the same basis as cash tender offers, exchange offers can commence as early as the filing of a registration statement. *See* Chapter 20]

Cash merger. [*See* Section 13.12] The offeror files a preliminary proxy statement with the Commission that describes the transaction. This is usually a public document, but the offeror can request that the preliminary merger proxy statement be treated confidentially, with some exceptions. The offeror may mail the preliminary proxy statement to security holders, but often waits until the proxy statement is final, or "definitive." This is because the offeror can send the proxy card only with the definitive proxy statement. The offeror may mail the definitive proxy statement ten days after the preliminary proxy statement is filed. However, if the staff decides to review the proxy material, in most cases offerors wait to receive staff comments before mailing. Once all comments have been resolved, the offeror mails the definitive proxy statement along with a proxy card for security holders to mark and return. There is no federally mandated time period between the date the offeror mails the proxy material and the date of the security holder meeting, but state law generally requires security holder notice of the meeting a specified time before the meeting. If the vote at the meeting is to approve the merger and all conditions have been met, the merger can close.

Stock merger. [*See* Chapters 4 and 13] The offeror files a Securities Act registration statement with the Commission that contains a preliminary prospectus as well as the information required in a proxy statement. Registration statements are filed publicly, but the material may be filed as a confidential proxy statement if the offeror so chooses. The registration statement is then filed as a "wrap around" the proxy statement when the offeror is ready to make the information public. The offeror may disseminate the preliminary prospectus/proxy statement, but ordinarily will not do so because the offeror may not include the proxy card. If the staff decides to review the filing, it gives comments to the offeror. After comments are resolved, the offeror requests that the staff declare the registration statement effective. Once the registration statement is effective, the offeror can mail the combined final prospectus/definitive proxy statement along with a proxy card. The process then continues as it would for a cash merger.

Any of the above transactions also could be a "going-private" transaction if it meets the criteria set forth in the "going-private" rule. [*See* Chapter 14] In this case, the offeror and any other party engaging in the transaction must file another schedule and provide additional information to the Commission and security holders, in addition to complying with the other regulatory requirements discussed. Usually this information is combined into a single disclosure document with the proxy statement, tender offer material or prospectus.

§ 13.4 Federal Income Tax Aspects

The federal income tax treatment of the acquisition of a publicly-held target firm is covered in Chapter 5. That chapter discusses, *inter alia*, the federal income tax consequences of a reverse subsidiary merger. If the merger consideration is cash, the transaction is treated as a taxable purchase by Acquiror of the stock of Target, and Target has no gain or loss. If the merger consideration is voting stock of Acquiror and certain other conditions are satisfied, the transaction is treated as a non-taxable reorganization under Code Section 368(a)(2)(E).

§ 13.5 Accounting Aspects

The accounting treatment of acquisitions of publicly-held targets is covered in Chapter 6. Such transactions are treated under the "acquisition" method without respect to whether the transaction is taxable or tax-free, and goodwill can arise.

§ 13.6 Hart-Scott-Rodino and Antitrust Aspects

The pre-merger notification rules and the antitrust rules governing mergers of publicly-held firms are explored in Chapters 9 and 8, respectively.

§ 13.7 Responsibilities of Target's and Acquiror's Boards in Structuring Transactions and Deal Protection Devices

A. General Principles Regarding the Business Judgment Rule, the Entire Fairness Doctrine and the Enhanced Business Judgment Rule

This chapter builds on many of the fiduciary duty concepts discussed in Chapter 3, in particular the business judgment rule standard of review under *Van Gorkom*, the enhanced business judgment rule standard of review under *Unocal*, and the duty to auction under *Revlon*. Thus, the reader should be familiar with the concepts addressed in Chapter 3. An understanding of these concepts is particularly important when advising the board of a target or an acquiror in an acquisition of a public company.

Although a consensual transaction may implicate principally the business judgment rule standard of review, as will be seen below, the use of deal protection devices may raise issues under the *Unocal* standard of review. And, of course, any consensual deal, may become hostile, in which case *Unocal* would apply to any defensive tactics employed by the target, such as a poison pill. Further, although the business judgment rule applied in *Van Gorkom* in the context of a cash acquisition of a public target, as a result of the *Revlon* case, *Revlon* duties now apply to any cash acquisition of the target, because such a transaction involves a change of control. However, as pointed out in *Arnold*, *Revlon* duties do not arise in an acquisition of a target for stock of the acquiror, because such a transaction is not a change of control.

The student should first review the above mentioned cases and then review the other materials in Chapter 3 referenced below.

B. Directors' Duties in Using Deal Protection Devices — Asset Lock-Ups, Stock Warrants, No Shops, No Talk, and Good Bye Fees — In Consensual Transactions

Many merger agreements in which a publicly-held target is acquired will contain provisions designed to protect the deal from third party interlopers. A range of devices may be utilized, including a "no shop" restricting the target's directors from seeking another deal, a "no talk" restricting the target's directors from talking to another possible acquiror except in certain circumstances, and a termination or break-up fee that will compensate the acquiror if the target terminates the deal and is acquired by another party.

To give the reader a basic understanding of how standard deal protection devices work, Documentary Appendix K of *M&A Statutes, Rules, and Documents, supra* Section 1.1 sets out with commentary the deal protection devices in the 2005 merger agreement between Verizon and MCI, pursuant to which Verizon acquired MCI after MCI rejected a competing offer from Quest.

The deal protection provisions of a merger agreement are generally found in (1) the "Additional Agreements" section of the agreement, which sets out certain covenants or undertakings by the parties between the signing and closing of the deal, and (2) the termination provisions of the agreement, which specify the conditions under which the agreement may be terminated and the consequences of a termination, such as the obligation to pay a termination fee. [*See* Chapter 15, which deals with the drafting of acquisition agreements.] In many public company deals the deal protection devices apply to both the target and the acquiror, especially in mergers of equals or near equals. In other deals, the provisions apply only to the target, especially if the target is significantly smaller than the acquiror, as in the case of MCI. The MCI-Verizon merger agreement follows the standard model with the deal protection provisions applying only to MCI.

Some of the materials referenced below deal with deal protection measures.

C. Reverse Termination Fees

Reverse termination fees, which are fees paid by the acquiror to the target if the acquiror walks from the deal, do not present the fiduciary duty issues that arise with direct termination fees. In many cases reverse termination fees will be payable if the transaction does not receive antitrust clearance, and for that reason, reverse termination fees are covered in Chapter 9, which addresses premerger notification.

D. Elaboration on the Business Judgment Rule in Arm's Length Negotiated Mergers, Section 3.15, particularly *Dollar Thrifty*, Section 3.15.C; and *Dow*, Section 3.15.H.3

E. Elaboration on the Enhanced Business Judgment Rule for Defensive Tactics and Introduction to Poison Pills, Section 3.18, Particularly Section 3.18.D

F. Elaboration on *Revlon*, the Requirement to Get the Best Price Reasonably Available, the Quasi Auction Duty, Section 3.19, Particularly *Time-Warner*, Section 3.19.F; *QVC*, Section 3.19.G; and *Lyondell*, Section 3.19.J

G. Elaboration on Issues with "No Solicitations," "Lock-Ups," "Break-Up Fees" and Other Deal Protection Measures in *Revlon* and Other Transactions, Section 3.20, Particularly *QVC*, Section 3.20.B; *Pennaco*, Section 3.20.D; *Toys "R" Us*, Section 3.20.E;

Cogent, Section 3.20.F and N; *Omnicare*, Section 3.20.G; *Cullman*, Section 3.20.H; and *Topps*, Section 3.20.M.2

§ 13.8 Impact of Rule 10b-5 on Disclosure of Merger Negotiations

A. The SEC's Position on Disclosure of Merger Negotiations

In the Matter of Carnation Company, Exchange Act Release No. 22214

(July 8, 1985)

In the view of the Commission, based upon the staff's investigation, certain public statements by Carnation Company ('Carnation') were materially false and misleading in violation of Section 10(b) of the Securities Exchange Act of 1934 ('Exchange Act') and Rule 10b-5 thereunder. * * *

[**Facts**] In early June, 1984, a major Carnation [the target] shareholder, Dwight Stuart, (D. Stuart) informed Carnation's chairman of the board, H. Everett Olson (Olson), and president, Tim F. Crull (Crull), that he had recently discussed with an investment banking firm the possibility of arranging a sale of the company [to Nestle]. * * *

In early July, certain articles reported rumors that D. Stuart was considering selling his Carnation stock and that Nestle, among others, was a possible acquiror of Carnation. By early August, numerous press articles had noted unusual activity in Carnation stock and had reported market rumors that Carnation was a takeover candidate. * * *

On August 7, 1984, Carnation's stock price increased 4 to 66. In a story appearing on the Dow Jones newswire at 2:55 p.m., Carnation treasurer Michael Malone was quoted as saying: "There is no news from the company and no corporate developments that would account for the stock action." Malone's responsibilities included responding to financial press inquiries. However, Malone was not informed of the discussions between Carnation and Nestle and did not discuss his August 7 statement with anyone else at Carnation prior to its issuance.

[Carnation and Nestle negotiated over a possible acquisition.] * * *

On August 21, 1984, while Crull [was] meeting with Nestle in Switzerland, a Dow Jones newswire story at 10:59 A.M. reported that Malone, late on the previous day, had said that Carnation knew "of no corporate reason for the recent surge in its stock price." After noting that Carnation's stock was trading at a twelve month high of 71 on August 21, the story also stated the following:

> Malone said he had been informed of rumors in the market that Carnation is about to be acquired by Nestle S.A. or be taken private in a leveraged buyout by Kohlberg Kravis Roberts. "But to the best of my knowledge there is nothing to substantiate either one of them" said Malone. "We are not negotiating with anyone." * * *

On August 31, 1984, the Carnation board and the Stuart family shareholders each received a written offer from Nestle. The Nestle offer to Carnation provided for a cash tender offer by a Nestle subsidiary at $82 per share. The related offer to the Stuart family provided for the sale of the Stuart family holdings to the Nestle subsidiary at the same price. * * *

From Friday, August 31, through Sunday September 2, three-way negotiations continued among representatives of Nestle, the Stuart family shareholders, and Carnation's investment banking firm. These negotiations resulted in agreement among the three parties upon a price of $83 per share. * * *

These agreements were presented to and approved by the Carnation and Nestle boards on September 3. * * *

[**Analysis**] Section 10(b) of the Exchange Act and Rule 10b-5 thereunder prohibit an issuer from making public statements that are false or that fail to include material facts necessary to make the statements made, in light of the circumstances under which they are made, not misleading. This prohibition is triggered whenever the issuer speaks, regardless of whether the issuer is trading in its own securities or is otherwise required to disclose material facts.

The importance of accurate and complete issuer disclosure to the integrity of the securities markets cannot be overemphasized. * * *

Whenever an issuer makes a public statement or responds to an inquiry from a stock exchange official concerning rumors, unusual market activity, possible corporate developments or any other matter, the statement must be materially accurate and complete. If the issuer is aware of nonpublic information concerning acquisition discussions that are occurring at the time the statement is made, the issuer has an obligation to disclose sufficient information concerning the discussions to prevent the statements made from being materially misleading.[1]

When an issuer makes a public statement, information concerning preliminary acquisition discussions is material and must be disclosed if the information assumes "actual significance in the deliberation of" and significantly alters 'the total mix of information available [to]' the reasonable shareholder. *TSC Industries, Inc. v. Northway* [Section 4.5.A]. Thus, in the Commission's view, an issuer statement that there is no corporate development that would account for unusual market activity in its stock, made while the issuer is engaged in acquisition discussions, may be materially false and misleading.

Applying these principles here, Carnation, in commenting publicly on takeover rumors and unusual market activity in its stock, was required to make statements which were truthful and not materially misleading. In the Commission's view, Carnation's public statements on August 7, 1984 and August 21, 1984 failed to satisfy these requirements in that the August 7 statement was materially misleading and the August 21 statement was materially false and misleading. * * *

[**Conclusion**] Issuers that make public statements are required under Section 10(b) of the Exchange Act and Rule 10b-5 thereunder to speak truthfully and to include all material facts necessary to make the statements made, in light of the circumstances under which they are made, not materially misleading. This requirement applies to issuers engaged in preliminary acquisition discussions.

---

1. The Commission encourages public companies to respond promptly to market rumors concerning material corporate developments. * * * However, an issuer that wants to prevent premature disclosure of nonpublic preliminary merger negotiations can, in appropriate circumstances, give a "no comment" response to press inquiries concerning rumors or unusual market activity. A "no comment" response would not be appropriate where, *inter alia*, the issuer has made a statement that has been rendered materially false or misleading as a result of subsequent events or market rumors are attributable to leaks from the issuer. * * *

B. The Supreme Court's Position on Disclosure of Merger Negotiations and Materiality Standard under Section 10b-5

Basic Inc. v. Levinson

United States Supreme Court, 1988 108 S.Ct. 978

Justice BLACKMUN:

This case requires us to apply the materiality requirement of § 10(b) of the Securities Exchange Act of 1934, (1934 Act), and the Securities and Exchange Commission's Rule 10b-5, promulgated thereunder, in the context of preliminary corporate merger discussions.

[**Facts**] Prior to December 20, 1978, Basic Incorporated was a publicly traded company primarily engaged in the business of manufacturing chemical refractories for the steel industry. As early as 1965 or 1966, Combustion Engineering, Inc., a company producing mostly alumina-based refractories, expressed some interest in acquiring Basic, but was deterred from pursuing this inclination seriously because of antitrust concerns it then entertained. In 1976, however, regulatory action opened the way to a renewal of Combustion's interest. The "Strategic Plan," dated October 25, 1976, for Combustion's Industrial Products Group included the objective: "Acquire Basic Inc. $30 million."

Beginning in September 1976, Combustion representatives had meetings and telephone conversations with Basic officers and directors, including petitioners here, concerning the possibility of a merger. During 1977 and 1978, Basic made three public statements denying that it was engaged in merger negotiations. On December 18, 1978, Basic asked the New York Stock Exchange to suspend trading in its shares and issued a release stating that it had been "approached" by another company concerning a merger. On December 19, Basic's board endorsed Combustion's offer of $46 per share for its common stock, and on the following day publicly announced its approval of Combustion's tender offer for all outstanding shares.

[**Issue**] Respondents are former Basic shareholders who sold their stock after Basic's first public statement of October 21, 1977, and before the suspension of trading in December 1978. Respondents brought a class action against Basic and its directors, asserting that the defendants issued three false or misleading public statements and thereby were in violation of § 10(b) of the 1934 Act and of Rule 10b-5. Respondents alleged that they were injured by selling Basic shares at artificially depressed prices in a market affected by petitioners' misleading statements and in reliance thereon. * * *

On the merits * * * the District Court granted summary judgment for the defendants. It held that, as a matter of law, any misstatements were immaterial: there were no negotiations ongoing at the time of the first statement, and although negotiations were taking place when the second and third statements were issued, those negotiations were not "destined, with reasonable certainty, to become a merger agreement in principle."

The United States Court of Appeals for the Sixth Circuit * * * reversed the District Court's summary judgment, and remanded the case. * * * The court reasoned that while petitioners were under no general duty to disclose their discussions with Combustion, any statement the company voluntarily released could not be "so incomplete as to mislead." In the Court of Appeals' view, Basic's statements that no negotiations were taking place, and that it knew of no corporate developments to account for the heavy trading activity, were misleading. With respect to materiality, the court rejected the argument that preliminary merger discussions are immaterial as a matter of law, and held that "once a statement is made denying the existence of any discussions, even discussions that might not have been material in absence of the denial are material because they make the statement made untrue." * * *

[The portion of the Court's opinion that adopts for Rule 10b-5 purposes the *TCS Northway* definition of materiality is set out in Section 4.5.B] * * *

[**Analysis**] The application of this materiality standard to preliminary merger discussions is not self-evident. Where the impact of the corporate development on the target's fortune is certain and clear, the *TSC Industries* materiality definition admits straightforward application. Where, on the other hand, the event is contingent or speculative in nature, it is difficult to ascertain whether the "reasonable investor" would have considered the omitted information significant at the time. Merger negotiations, because of the ever-present possibility that the contemplated transaction will not be effectuated, fall into the latter category.

Petitioners urge upon us a Third Circuit test for resolving this difficulty. Under this approach, preliminary merger discussions do not become material until "agreement-in-principle" as to the price and structure of the transaction has been reached between the would-be merger partners. *See Greenfield v. Heublein, Inc.*, 742 F.2d 751, 757 (CA3 1984), *cert. denied*, 469 U.S. 1215, (1985). By definition, then, information concerning any negotiations not yet at the agreement-in-principle stage could be withheld or even misrepresented without a violation of Rule 10b-5. * * *

We * * * find no valid justification for artificially excluding from the definition of materiality information concerning merger discussions, which would otherwise be considered significant to the trading decision of a reasonable investor, merely because agreement-in-principle as to price and structure has not yet been reached by the parties or their representatives.

The Sixth Circuit explicitly rejected the agreement-in-principle test, as we do today, but in its place adopted a rule that, if taken literally, would be equally insensitive, in our view, to the distinction between materiality and the other elements of an action under Rule 10b-5:

> "When a company whose stock is publicly traded makes a statement, as Basic did, that 'no negotiations' are underway, and that the corporation knows of 'no reason for the stock's activity,' and that 'management is unaware of any present or pending corporate development that would result in the abnormally heavy trading activity,' information concerning ongoing acquisition discussions becomes material *by virtue of the statement denying their existence.* * * *
>
> [O]nce a statement is made denying the existence of any discussions, even discussions that might not have been material in absence of the denial are material because they make the statement made untrue."

This approach, however, fails to recognize that, in order to prevail on a Rule 10b-5 claim, a plaintiff must show that the statements were *misleading* as to a *material* fact. It is not enough that a statement is false or incomplete, if the misrepresented fact is otherwise insignificant. * * *

Even before this Court's decision in *TSC Industries*, the Second Circuit had explained the role of the materiality requirement of Rule 10b-5, with respect to contingent or speculative information or events, in a manner that gave that term meaning that is independent of the other provisions of the Rule. Under such circumstances, materiality "will depend at any given time upon a balancing of both the indicated probability that the event will occur and the anticipated magnitude of the event in light of the totality of the company activity." *SEC v. Texas Gulf Sulphur Co.*, 401 F.2d, at 849. Interestingly, neither the Third Circuit decision adopting the agreement-in-principle test nor petitioners here take issue with this general standard. Rather, they suggest that with respect to preliminary merger discussions, there are good reasons to draw a line at agreement on price and structure.

In a subsequent decision, the late Judge Friendly, writing for a Second Circuit panel, applied the *Texas Gulf Sulphur* probability/magnitude approach in the specific context of preliminary merger negotiations. After acknowledging that materiality is something to be determined on the basis of the particular facts of each case, he stated:

> "Since a merger in which it is bought out is the most important event that can occur in a small corporation's life, to wit, its death, we think that inside information, as regards a merger of this sort, can become material at an earlier stage than would be the case as regards lesser transactions—and this even though the mortality rate of mergers in such formative stages is doubtless high." *SEC v. Geon Industries, Inc.*, 531 F.2d 39, 47–48 (1976).

We agree with that analysis.

Whether merger discussions in any particular case are material therefore depends on the facts. Generally, in order to assess the probability that the event will occur, a factfinder will need to look to indicia of interest in the transaction at the highest corporate levels. Without attempting to catalog all such possible factors, we note by way of example that board resolutions, instructions to investment bankers, and actual negotiations between principals or their intermediaries may serve as indicia of interest. To assess the magnitude of the transaction to the issuer of the securities allegedly manipulated, a factfinder will need to consider such facts as the size of the two corporate entities and of the potential premiums over market value. No particular event or factor short of closing the transaction need be either necessary or sufficient by itself to render merger discussions material.[2] * * *

Because the standard of materiality we have adopted differs from that used by both courts below, we remand the case for reconsideration of the question whether a grant of summary judgment is appropriate on this record. * * *

---

2. To be actionable, of course, a statement must also be misleading. Silence, absent a duty to disclose, is not misleading under Rule 10b-5. "No comment" statements are generally the functional equivalent of silence. *See In re Carnation Co.*, [Section 13.8.A] * * * .

It has been suggested that given current market practices, a "no comment" statement is tantamount to an admission that merger discussions are underway. *See Flamm v. Eberstadt*, 814 F.2d, at 1178. That may well hold true to the extent that issuers adopt a policy of truthfully denying merger rumors when no discussions are underway, and of issuing "no comment" statements when they are in the midst of negotiations. There are, of course, other statement policies firms could adopt; we need not now advise issuers as to what kind of practice to follow, within the range permitted by law. Perhaps more importantly, we think that creating an exception to a regulatory scheme founded on a pro-disclosure legislative philosophy, because complying with the regulation might be "bad for business," is a role for Congress, not this Court. *See also Id.*, at 1182 (opinion concurring in judgment and concurring in part).

C. SEC Guidance Concerning Inclusion of Merger Negotiations in the Management Discussion and Analysis Section of Disclosure Documents

Item 303 of Regulation SK under the 1933 Act Section 501.06d of SEC Interpretive Release No. 6835

(May 18, 1986)

501.06.d. Preliminary Merger Negotiations. While Item 303 could be read to impose a duty to disclose otherwise nondisclosed preliminary merger negotiations, as known events or uncertainties reasonably likely to have material effects on future financial condition or results of operations, the Commission did not intend to apply, and has not applied, Item 303 in this manner. As reflected in the various disclosure requirements under the Securities Act and Exchange Act that specifically address merger transactions, the Commission historically has balanced the informational need of investors against the risk that premature disclosure of negotiations may jeopardize completion of the transaction. * * *

[W]here a registrant registers securities for sale under the Securities Act, the Commission requires disclosure of material probable acquisitions and dispositions of businesses, including the financial statements of the business to be acquired or sold. Where the proceeds from the sale of the securities being registered are to be used to finance an acquisition of a business, the registration statement must disclose the intended use of proceeds. Again, accommodating the need for confidentiality of negotiations, registrants are specifically permitted not to disclose in registration statements the identity of the parties and the nature of the business sought if the acquisition is not yet probable and the board of directors determines that the acquisition would be jeopardized. The Commission's interpretation of Item 303, as applied to preliminary merger negotiations, incorporates the same policy determinations. Accordingly, where disclosure is not otherwise required, and has not otherwise been made, the MD&A need not contain a discussion of the impact of such negotiations where, in the registrant's view, inclusion of such information would jeopardize completion of the transaction. Where disclosure is otherwise required or has otherwise been made by or on behalf of the registrant, the interests in avoiding premature disclosure no longer exist. In such case, the negotiations would be subject to the same disclosure standards under Item 303 as any other known trend, demand, commitment, event or uncertainty. These policy determinations also would extend to preliminary negotiations for the acquisition or disposition of assets not in the ordinary course of business.

§ 13.9 Materiality of Merger Negotiations under Delaware Law—*Alessi*

Alessi v. Beracha

Delaware Court of Chancery, 2004 849 A.2d 939

Chandler, Chancellor:

Plaintiff, Margaret Alessi, was a small investor in The Earthgrains Company. She owned less than 100 shares. On May 18, 2001, Earthgrains issued a press release announcing a program that would allow its shareholders holding less than 100 shares to sell or buy shares at the current market value (around $25) for a below normal brokerage fee. Seizing the opportunity, Alessi sold her shares. Shortly thereafter, Earthgrains announced that

Sara Lee Corporation had agreed to purchase the Company for almost double the price that Alessi received for her shares. As it turns out, Earthgrains had been negotiating intensely with Sara Lee before Alessi sold her shares. Alessi believes Earthgrains' board of directors should have informed Earthgrains' stockholders about those negotiations. Defendants have moved to dismiss Alessi's complaint. Because I believe that Alessi has stated a viable claim for disclosure violations, I deny defendants' motion to dismiss her complaint. * * *

Materiality of Merger Negotiations. Defendants assert that, accepting all the allegations in the complaint as true, the information allegedly withheld from shareholders was immaterial as a matter of law under the Delaware Supreme Court's decision in *Bershad v. Curtiss-Wright Corporation.* [535 A.2d 840 (Del. 1987)] In *Bershad,* Curtiss-Wright Corporation effectuated a cash-out merger of one its subsidiaries, Dorr-Oliver Incorporated. One of the issues in the case was whether defendant directors breached their fiduciary duties of disclosure by failing to disclose "certain casual inquiries" for Dorr-Oliver in the proxy statement seeking shareholder approval of the merger. In *Bershad,* the evidence indicated that the defendants informed inquiring parties that "Dorr-Oliver was not for sale." In addition, the one inquiring party that the plaintiff specifically identified "did not have detailed, non-public financial data on Dorr-Oliver and never seriously considered making an offer." The Court held that "since it is undisputed that: (1) Dorr-Oliver was not for sale, and (2) no offer was ever made for Dorr-Oliver, the defendants were not obligated to disclose preliminary discussions regarding an unlikely sale."

In my opinion, the *Bershad* holding does not require dismissal of the complaint in this case. The allegations here establish that Earthgrains was for sale, the discussions were substantive and advanced, an offer was made, and the sale was actually consummated. * * *

After *Bershad* was decided, the United States Supreme Court grappled with whether it would adopt a bright-line rule that all merger discussions before agreement on "price and structure" are immaterial. [Citing *Basic*] The United States Supreme Court rejected the bright-line rule, concluding:

> We ... find no valid justification for artificially excluding from the definition of materiality information concerning merger discussions, which would otherwise be considered significant to the trading decision of a reasonable investor, merely because agreement-in-principle as to price and structure has not yet been reached by the parties or their representatives.

The Supreme Court stated that "whether merger discussions in any particular case are material * * * depends on the facts." * * *

The United States Supreme Court provided meaningful standards to assess whether merger discussions should be disclosed. * * *

Application of [the *Basic*] standards leads to only one conclusion: Alessi's complaint should not be dismissed. The complaint alleges "indicia of interest in the transaction at the highest corporate levels." The pending Sara Lee transaction was arguably the most important event in Earthgrains' short life: "to wit, its death." Further, the complaint alleges that the Sara Lee acquisition was at a significant premium over market value. Importantly, the information regarding Earthgrains' merger discussions with Sara Lee was allegedly withheld from those shareholders who sold their Earthgrains' stock under the buy-sell program sponsored by defendants. As such, I cannot find "that the plaintiff would not be entitled to relief under any set of facts that could be proven to support the claim."

I am convinced that the Delaware Supreme Court, if presented with these facts, would agree with me for two reasons. First, as I have already mentioned, the facts as alleged are categorically different than the facts presented in *Bershad*. * * * Second, federal law on the subject has matured since the *Bershad* decision. At the time *Bershad* was decided, the United States Supreme Court had yet to express its opinion that the reasoning supporting a bright-line rule to address the inherently fact-sensitive inquiry into materiality is infirm. * * *

§ 13.10 Issuance of Securities in Reclassifications, Mergers, Consolidations and Asset Acquisitions: 33 Act Rule 145 and Form S-4

A. Introduction

Read Rule 145 and Form S-4 in connection with your study of the following materials. These provisions deal with the impact of the Securities Act of 1933 on the issuance by a publicly-held acquiror of its securities in an acquisition of a publicly-held target. The impact of the proxy rules under the Securities Exchange Act of 1934 on these transactions is examined in Section 13.12. The rules adopted by the SEC in 1999 regarding communications with shareholders participating in an acquisition are set out in Section 13.11.B. Sections 13.10 through 13.12 should be studied together.

B. 1972 Notice of Adoption of Rule 145 and Notice of 2007 Amendments to the Presumptive Underwriter Rule

1. 1972 Notice of Adoption of Rule 145

Excerpt from Securities Act Release No. 33–5316

(October 6, 1972)

The Securities and Exchange Commission today announced the adoption of Rule 145 under the Securities Act of 1933 (Act) and several related proposals and the prospective rescission of Rule 133 under that Act. The effect of this action will be to subject transactions involving business combinations of types described in the new rule to the registration requirements of the Act. Rule 145 is designed to implement the purpose and policies underlying the Act and is based on the Commission's experience in administering Rule 133. * * *

Congress, in enacting the federal securities statutes, created a continuous disclosure system designed to protect investors and to assure the maintenance of fair and honest securities markets. The Commission in administering and implementing the objectives of these statutes has sought to coordinate and integrate this disclosure system, and the rescission of Rule 133 and adoption of Rule 145 and related matters are further steps in this direction.

The rescission of Rule 133 and adoption of Rule 145 are designed to implement the fundamental purposes of the Act as expressed in its preamble:

> "To provide full and fair disclosure of the character of the securities sold in interstate commerce and through the mails, and to prevent fraud in the sale thereof * * *."

Rule 145 is also intended to inhibit the creation of public markets in securities of issuers about which adequate current information is not available to the public. This approach is consistent with the philosophy underlying the Act, that a disclosure law provides the best protection for investors. If a security holder who is offered a new security in a Rule

145 business combination transaction has available to him the material facts about the transaction, he will be in a position to make an informed investment judgment. In order to provide such information in connection with public offerings of these securities, Rule 145 will require the filing of a registration statement with the Commission and the delivery to security holders of a prospectus containing accurate and current information concerning the proposed business combination transaction.

Explanation and Analysis

Rescission of Rule 133. Definition for Purposes of Section 5 of "Sale," "Offer to Sell," and "Offer for Sale." Rule 133 provides that for purposes only of Section 5 of the Act, the submission to a vote of stockholders of a corporation of a proposal for certain mergers, consolidations, reclassifications of securities or transfers of assets is not deemed to involve a "sale", "offer", "offer to sell", or "offer for sale" of the securities of the new or surviving corporation to the security holders of the disappearing corporation. [Thus, under Rule 133, a publicly held acquirer could issue its securities in the acquisition of a publicly held target pursuant to a merger agreement without registering the securities.] That rule further provides that persons who are affiliates of the constituent corporation are deemed to be underwriters within the meaning of the Section [2(a)(11)] of the Act, and except for certain limited amounts cannot sell their securities in the surviving corporation without registration.

The "no-sale" theory embodied in Rule 133 is based on the rationale that the types of transactions specified in the rule are essentially corporate acts, and the volitional act on the part of the individual stockholder required for a "sale" was absent. The basis of this theory was that the exchange or alteration of the stockholder's security occurred not because he consented thereto, but because the corporate action, authorized by a specified majority of the interests affected, converted his security into a different security.

Based on the Commission's experience in administering the provisions of the Act and Rule 133 thereunder, and having given consideration to the Disclosure Policy Study Report, to the comments received on the Commission's published proposed revision of Rule 133 and to the comments received on the proposed adoption of Rule 145, the Commission is of the view that the "no-sale" approach embodied in Rule 133 overlooks the substance of the transactions specified therein and ignores the fundamental nature of the relationship between the stockholders and the corporation. The fact that such relationships are in part controlled by statutory provisions of the state of incorporation does not preclude as a matter of law the application of the broad concepts of "sale," "offer," "offer to sell," and "offer for sale" in Section [2(a)(3)] of the Act which are broader than the commercial or common law meanings of such terms.

Transactions of the type described in Rule 133 do not, in the Commission's opinion, occur solely by operation of law without the element of individual stockholder volition. A stockholder faced with a Rule 133 proposal must decide on his own volition whether or not the proposal is one in his own best interest. The basis on which the "no-sale" theory is predicated, namely, that the exchange or alteration of the stockholder's security occurs not because he consents thereto but because the corporation by authorized corporate action converts his securities, in the Commission's opinion, is at best only correct in a formalistic sense and overlooks the reality of the transaction. The corporate action, on which such great emphasis is placed, is derived from the individual consent given by each stockholder in voting on a proposal to merge or consolidate a business or reclassify a security. In voting, each consenting stockholder is expressing his voluntary and individual acceptance of the new security, and generally the disapproving stockholder is deferring his decision as to whether to accept the new security or, if he exercises his dissenter's rights, a cash payment. The corporate action in these circumstances, therefore, is not some type of independent fiat, but is only the aggregate effect of the voluntary decisions made by the individual stockholders to accept or reject the exchange. Formalism should no longer deprive investors of the disclosure to which they are entitled.

The Commission also is aware that Rule 133 has caused anomalous applications of the provisions of the securities laws. * * *

In view of the above, the Commission is of the opinion that transactions covered by Rule 133 involve a "sale," "offer," "offer to sell," or "offer for sale" as those terms are defined in Section [2(a)(3)] of the Act. The Commission no longer sees any persuasive reason why, as a matter of statutory construction or policy, in light of the broad remedial purposes of the Act and of public policy which strongly supports registration, this should not be the interpretative meaning.

Adoption of Rule 145. Reclassifications of Securities, Mergers, Consolidations and Acquisitions of Assets. A preliminary note has been added to the rule in order to provide a convenient reference to assist in understanding and interpreting its provisions.

Paragraph (a) of Rule 145 provides that the submission to a vote of security holders of a proposal for certain reclassifications of securities, mergers, consolidations, or transfers of assets, is deemed to involve an "offer," "offer to sell," "offer for sale," or "sale" of the securities to be issued in the transaction. The effect of the Rule is to require registration of the securities to be issued in connection with such transactions, unless an exemption from registration is available. * * *

In response to comments received from the public, several textual changes have been made in Rule 145(a) as proposed. As noticed for comment, the rule by its literal language only applied to business combinations involving "corporations." Rule 133 was intended to apply to business combinations involving corporations as well as other entities, such as partnerships and real estate investment trusts. Accordingly, the rule has been revised to read "corporation or other person" in order to make clear that it applies to all issuers, without distinction as to the form of business organization. Also, the phrase "certificate of incorporation" has been revised to read "certificate of incorporation or similar controlling instruments."

A number of comments focused upon the question of whether foreign issuers should be included within the scope of Rule 145. * * * Rule 145 will apply to foreign issuers making offers or sales of securities to United States investors, unless an exemption is available under the Securities Act. * * * To clarify the applicability of Rule 145 to foreign issuers, the phrase "state of incorporation" has been changed to read "jurisdiction."

Also in response to public comments, Rule 145 has been revised to make clear that it covers transactions involving action taken upon security holder approval. The words "or consent" have been added to the word "vote" wherever it appears.

Rule 145(a), as proposed, covered any reclassification "other than a stock split or reverse stock split which involves the substitution of a security for another security." The rule has been revised to also exclude any reclassification which involves only a change in par value.

Rule 145(a)(2). Mergers or Consolidations. Rule 145(a)(2) has been revised in three respects. The first revision adds the phrase "or similar plan of acquisition" after the words "merger or consolidation" because a number of similar transactions do not fit precisely within the terms "merger or consolidation." The second revision adds the phrase "held by such security holders" to describe those securities which will become or be exchanged for other securities. This revision is designed to clarify that in a transaction of the character described in Rule 145(a), an offer occurs under the rule only as to security holders who are entitled to vote or consent to the matter, and who hold securities which become or will be exchanged for new securities. The third revision adds an exception to indicate that registration is not required where a merger or consolidation is effected solely to change an issuer's domicile.

Several commentators suggested that the applicability of Rule 145 to short-form mergers should be clarified. In certain instances, state law allows a merger of a parent and its 85 to 90 percent owned subsidiary to be consummated without shareholder approval. Because Rule 145(a) is couched in terms of offers arising in connection with a submission for the vote or consent of security holders, short-form mergers not requiring such vote or consent are not within the scope of the Rule. However, if a security is to be issued in such short-form mergers, the Commission is of the opinion that the transaction involves an "offer," "offer to sell," "offer for sale" or "sale," within the meaning of Section [2(a)(3)] of the Act, and accordingly such transactions are subject to the registration provisions of the Act unless an exemption is available.

Rule 145(a)(3). Transfers of Assets. Rule 145(a)(3) has been revised to clarify those conditions under which Rule 145 is applicable to a stock for assets transaction. As revised, the rule applies only if: (1) the matter voted upon provides for dissolution of the corporation receiving the securities; (2) the matter voted upon provides for a *pro rata* distribution by the corporation receiving the securities; (3) the directors of the corporation receiving the securities adopt resolutions relative to (1) or (2) within one year after the vote; or (4) a subsequent dissolution or distribution is part of a pre-existing plan for distribution. However, if the securities acquired in the transaction are distributed after one year, notwithstanding the absence of a plan, such securities must be registered unless a statutory exemption from registration is then available.

With regard to the third condition above, if the vote of the stockholders of the selling corporation is taken to authorize the sale, and the selling corporation thereafter decides to dissolve or distribute the securities within one year after the transaction, the sale of assets and the dissolution or distribution by the selling corporation are deemed to be portions of the same transaction and to involve a sale for value of the purchasing corporation's stock to the shareholders of the selling corporation. Accordingly, the transaction should be registered on Form [S-4] at the time the plan or agreement for the sale of assets is submitted to shareholders for their vote or consent if it is contemplated that the corporation receiving the securities will adopt resolutions within one year for dissolution or distribution of the securities received. If the transaction is not registered at the time of submission of the plan or agreement for the vote or consent of security holders, but a resolution for dissolution or distribution of the securities received is adopted within one year, the issuer should file a registration statement covering the dissolution or distribution of securities on the appropriate form other than Form [S-4], unless an exemption is available.

Rule 145(b). Communications Not Deemed to be a "Prospectus" or "Offer to Sell." Notice of a proposed action or of a meeting of security holders for voting on transactions of the character specified in Rule 145 is generally sent or furnished to security holders. Because the Rule will make the registration provisions of the Act applicable to these transactions, questions have been raised as to whether such notices will constitute statutory prospectuses or involve an offer for sale of a security. Paragraph (b) of Rule 145 is designed to resolve these questions by providing that any written communication which contains no more than the information specified in paragraph (b) of the Rule shall not be deemed a prospectus for purposes of Section [2(a)(10)] of the Act and shall not be deemed an "offer for sale" of the security involved for the purposes of Section 5 of the Act. [Rule 145(b) has been revised as noted in Section 13.11.B] * * *

Rule 145(c). Persons and Parties Deemed to be Underwriters. ***[Together with Rule 145(c) the Presumptive Underwriter Provision, which as indicated below was modified in 2007]*** Rule 145(c), as proposed, contained specific criteria designed to clarify the underwriter status of persons who acquire substantial amounts of securities in a business combination registered on Form S-4, and who desire to resell such securities. * * *

Revised paragraph (c) of the Rule provides that any party to any transaction specified in Rule 145(a), other than the issuer, or any person who is an affiliate of such party at the time any such transaction is submitted for vote or consent, who offers or sells securities acquired in such transaction, shall be deemed to be engaged in a distribution and therefore an underwriter, except with respect to the limited resales permitted pursuant to paragraph (d) of Rule 145. Moreover, from a practical standpoint, because such persons usually are in a position to verify the accuracy of information set forth in the registration statement, and usually are in a position to influence the transaction, the Commission believes that this provision is not unreasonably burdensome.

Rule 145(c) includes a definition of the term "party" with respect to the phrase "any party to any transaction specified in paragraph (a) ..." The term is defined to mean the corporations, business entities, or other persons, other than the issuer, whose assets or capital structure are affected by the transaction specified in paragraph (a).

The securities received in a Rule 145 transaction by persons who are neither affiliates of the acquired company nor of the acquiring company are registered securities without restriction on resale.

Rule 145(d). Resale Provisions For Persons and Parties Deemed Underwriters. ***[Together with Rule 145(c) the Presumptive Underwriter Provision, which as indicated below was modified in 2007]*** Rule 145(d) provides that a person or party specified in paragraph (c) shall not be deemed to be engaged in a distribution if he sells in accordance with certain provisions of Rule 144; paragraph (c) (Current Public Information); (e) (Limitation on Amount of Securities Sold); (f) (Manner of Sale); and (g) (Brokers' Transactions). This provision is designed to permit public sale by such persons or parties in ordinary trading transactions of limited quantities of securities. Such resales are permissible within successive [three]-month periods, but no accumulation is permitted, *i.e.*, the person cannot skip [three] months and then sell an accumulated amount in the following [three] months.

The volume limitations of Rule 144(e) for resales of securities listed on a national securities exchange may be determined by reference to the average weekly trading volume for the four weeks preceding receipt of the order by the broker to execute the transaction. It should be noted that the holding period requirement of Rule 144(d), and the requirement to file a Form 144 pursuant to Rule 144(h) are not applicable. In addition to resales permitted by Rule 145(d), the amended Form [S-4] may be used for the registration under the Act of distributions by persons or parties who are deemed underwriters.

Rule 145(e). Definition of "Person." Paragraph (e) of Rule 145 provides that the term "person" in paragraphs (c) and (d) of the rule when used with reference to a person for whose account securities are to be sold, shall have the same meaning as the definition of that term in paragraph (a)(2) of Rule 144 under the Act.

Rule 153A. Definition of "Preceded by a Prospectus" as used in Section 5(b)(2) of the Act, in Relation to Certain Transactions Requiring Approval of Security Holders. Rule 153A defines the phrase "preceded by a prospectus" in connection with transactions of the type subject to Rule 145. The rule has been revised in two respects. First, the word "delivery" has been substituted for the word "sending" to conform the Rule to the General Instructions in Form S-4. Second, the Rule has been revised to apply the delivery requirement when action is taken by consent.

The persons entitled to vote on or consent to a Rule 145 transaction will usually be determined either: (1) by the fixing of a record date for shareholders so entitled, or (2) by the closing of the stock transfer records of the acquired company. The group of persons thus determined may, because of interim transfers, vary somewhat from the group of persons ultimately entitled to receive the securities issued in the transaction. Thus, Rule 153A provides that the delivery of the final prospectus to security holders entitled to vote on or consent to the transaction shall be deemed to satisfy the prospectus delivery requirements of Section 5(b)(2) of the Act. * * *

Amendments to [Form S-4]. The Commission believes that registration of securities issued in transactions of the character specified in Rule 145 is practical and not unduly burdensome. However, the Commission is aware that registration of such securities imposes some additional burdens on issuers, and, in order to minimize these burdens to the extent feasible, particularly for small businesses, Form [S-4] provides that the prospectus to be used shall consist of a proxy or information statement that meets the requirements of the Commission's proxy or information rules under Section 14 of the Exchange Act. In the case of companies subject to those rules the filing of the registration statement on Form [S-4] satisfies the requirement for filing a proxy statement and form of proxy or information statement pursuant to those rules. [*See* Rule 14a-6(j)] Thus, registration will involve little additional work on the part of the companies subject to those rules who are required to solicit votes from their security holders, because the informational requirements will be the same for both. * * *

Registration for Transactions of the Type Specified in Rule 145. Form [S-4] is not the exclusive form available for the registration under the Act of securities to be issued in a transaction of the type specified in Rule 145. Form S-1 is available for registration of such transactions * * *. If Form S-1 is used, the information set forth therein should generally follow the format utilized for exchange offers, including a complete description of the parties, together with pro forma information on the resulting business entity.

2. 2007 Notice of Amendments to the Presumptive Underwriter Provisions of Rule 145

Securities Act Release No. 8869, Amendments to Rule 145

December 6, 2007

SUMMARY: * * * [W]e are eliminating the presumptive underwriter provision in Securities Act Rule 145, except for transactions involving a shell company, and revising the resale requirements in Rule 145(d). We believe that the amendments will increase the liquidity of privately sold securities and decrease the cost of capital for all issuers without compromising investor protection. * * *

Amendments to Rule 145. Securities Act Rule 145 provides that exchanges of securities in connection with reclassifications of securities, mergers or consolidations or transfers of assets that are subject to shareholder vote constitute sales of those securities. Unless an exemption from the registration requirement is available, Rule 145(a) requires the registration of these sales. Rule 145(c) deems persons who were parties to such a transaction, other than the issuer, or affiliates of such parties to be underwriters. Rule 145(d) permits the resale, subject to specified conditions, of securities received in such transactions by persons deemed underwriters. In the 1997 Proposing Release, we proposed to eliminate the presumed underwriter and resale provisions in Rule 145(c) and (d). * * *

In the 2007 Proposing Release, we proposed amendments to Rule 145(c) and (d) that would:

- Eliminate the presumed underwriter provision in Rule 145(c), except with regard to Rule 145(a) transactions that involve a shell company (other than a business combination related shell company); and
- Harmonize the requirements in Rule 145(d) with the proposed provisions in Rule 144 that would apply to securities of shell companies.

[These rules with regard to shell companies are not addressed further here. *See* Rule 145(c) and (d).] * * *

The presumptive underwriter provision in Rule 145 is no longer necessary in most circumstances. However, based on our experience with transactions involving shell companies that have resulted in abusive sales of securities, we believe that there continues to be a need to apply the presumptive underwriter provision to reporting and non-reporting shell companies and their affiliates and promoters. We are amending Rule 145 to eliminate the presumptive underwriter provision except when a party to the Rule 145(a) transaction is a shell company. * * *

3. Presumed SEC Interpretations of Rule 145 after Repeal of the Presumptive Underwriter Provisions of Rule 145

In Securities Act Release No. 33-5463 (February 28, 1974), the SEC set out its interpretations of various aspects under Rule 145, including the application of the presumptive underwriter rule. These interpretations are set out below with the modifications the author thinks would be applicable to a non-shell target in view of the repeal of the presumptive underwriter rule.

Securities Act Release No. 33-5463, Interpreting Rule 145
(February 28, 1974)

[5]*Facts*: X Company filed a registration statement on Form S-1 covering the proposed issuance of its common stock (but not covering the resale thereof) in connection with a proposed acquisition of Y Company [which is not a shell company] in a Rule 145 type statutory merger which, if approved by Y Company's stockholders, would result in Y Company's stockholders receiving common stock of X Company. * * *

Question A-1: Assuming for the purposes of this question only that A is a controlling person of X Company and also owns common stock of Y Company, would his resales of the X Company common stock which he receives in this transaction be [freely tradable as a result of the repeal of the presumptive underwriter rule]?

Interpretative Response: No. Inasmuch as A controls X Company, he is already deemed to be an affiliate of X Company and is subject to the provisions of Rule 144. Accordingly, the resale of any additional shares of X Company common stock, which he acquires in a Rule 145 transaction or otherwise, is subject to the provisions of Rule 144.

Question A-2: Assuming for the purposes of this question only that B does not own any common stock of X Company but is a controlling person of Y Company and that after the merger he will become a controlling person of X Company, would his resales of the X Company common stock which he receives in this transaction be [freely tradable as a result of therepeal of the presumptive underwriter rule]?

Interpretative Response: No. Inasmuch as B will become a controlling person of X Company, he would be deemed to be an affiliate of X Company. By virtue of his becoming an affiliate of X Company, B would become subject to Rule 144 and the resale of all of his X Company common stock would be subject to the provisions of Rule 144.

Question A-3: Assuming for the purposes of this question only that C is an affiliate of Y Company but not of X Company; [as a result of the repeal of the presumptive underwriter rule], what restrictions are imposed on C's public resale of the X Company common stock which he receives in the Rule 145 transaction?

Interpretative Response: [As a result of the repeal of the presumptive underwriter rule, C could] resell X Company securities received in the Rule 145 transaction [without restriction.] * * *

Question A-4: Assuming for the purposes of this question only that D is not an affiliate of X Company or of Y Company and that his only relationship to the transaction is that he owns Y Company common stock, some of which was purchased previously in a private offering, would D be immediately free to resell publicly all of the X Company common stock which he receives in the transaction?

Interpretative Response: Yes. * * * D is immediately free to resell publicly all of the X Company common stock which he receives in the transaction regardless of whether some of his Y Company common stock was restricted. [Note that the presumptive underwriter rule would not have applied to D because he was not an affiliate of Y.] * * *

4. Illustration of Disclosures in S-4 Dealing with Resales in View of Repeal of the Presumptive Underwriter Provisions of Rule 145

A Proxy Statement/Prospectus on Form S-4 was issued on January 24, 2014 by New Endo, a newly formed Irish holding company, relating to its acquisition of (1) in exchange for stock of New Endo, all the stock of Endo Health Solutions, Inc. (Endo), a U.S. corporation, and (2) in exchange for stock of New Endo and cash, all of the stock of Paladin Labs Inc., a Canadian corporation. Reflecting the repeal of the presumptive underwriter rule, the Proxy Statement/Prospectus contains the following disclosure with regard to the ability of the shareholders of Endo to resell their shares:

> **Restrictions on Resales**
>
> All New Endo ordinary shares received by Endo shareholders in the merger will be freely tradable, except that New Endo ordinary shares received in the merger by persons who become affiliates of New Endo for purposes of Rule 144 under the Securities Act may be resold by them only in transactions permitted by Rule 144, or as otherwise permitted under the Securities Act. Persons who may be deemed affiliates of New Endo generally include individuals or entities that control, are controlled by or are under common control with, New Endo and may include the executive officers and directors of New Endo as well as its principal shareholders.

C. Other SEC Interpretations of Rule 145

Securities Act Release No. 33-5463, Interpreting Rule 145

(February 28, 1974)

[1]*Facts*: X Company proposes to issue common stock in exchange for the assets of Y Company after Y Company obtains the approval of its several stockholders, as required by state law, with respect to an agreement setting forth the terms and conditions of the exchange and providing for a distribution of the X Company common stock to the Y Company stockholders. X Company has determined that the private offering exemption afforded by Section [4(a)(2)] of the Act would be available for the transaction.

Question: In light of Rule 145, may X Company choose between relying upon the private offering exemption available under Section [4(a)(2)] and registering the securities to be issued in the transaction on Form S-[4]?

Interpretative Response: Yes, X Company may choose between relying upon the private offering exemption available under Section [4(a)(2)] and registering the securities to be issued in the transaction on Form S-[4] [discussed *infra*]. Rule 145 does not affect statutory exemptions which are otherwise available. However, * * * X Company may register the securities to be issued in the transaction on Form S-[4] so that an affiliate of Y Company would be able to resell immediately his securities pursuant to the registration statement * * *.

[3]*Facts*: X Company proposes to acquire at least 80% of the outstanding common stock of Y Company by offering its common stock to the stockholders of Y Company in exchange for their Y Company common stock in a transaction intended to qualify as a tax-free reorganization pursuant to Section 368(a)(1)(B) of the Internal Revenue Code of 1954, as amended. [*See* Chapter 5]

Question: Is Rule 145 applicable to such an exchange offer so that X Company can utilize Form S-[4]?

Interpretative Response: No. Rule 145 [is] not applicable to "B" type reorganizations. Absent a statutory exemption, the securities issued in the transaction would have to be registered under the Act on Form S-1 or on another form if applicable. [Form S-4 is now available. *See* General Instruction A] * * *

[6]*Facts*: X Company intends to effect a short-form merger pursuant to state law whereby its ninety percent owned subsidiary, Y Company, would be merged into X Company without a vote or consent of Y Company's minority stockholders, who would receive common stock of X Company.

Question C-1: Is this transaction subject to the registration requirements set forth in Section 5 of the Act?

Interpretative Response: Yes. The issuance of X Company common stock to the stockholders of Y Company would involve a "sale" within the meaning of Section 2(3) of the Act and, absent a statutory exemption, registration would be required.

Question C-2: May the securities to be issued in this transaction be registered pursuant to the Act on a Form S-[4]?

Interpretative Response: Yes. Although Rule 145 is not applicable because a short-form merger does not involve a vote or consent of all the stockholders, the Division will not object to the use of Form S-[4] for the registration of the securities to be issued in this transaction.

D. Notice of Adoption of Form S-4 for Business Combination Transactions

Excerpt from Securities Act Release No. 6578

(April 23, 1985)

SUMMARY: The Commission announces the adoption of a new form to be used to register securities under the Securities Act of 1933 in connection with business combination transactions. The form applies the principles of the integrated disclosure system to disclosure in the context of mergers and exchange offers. The form is designed to improve the effectiveness of the business combination prospectus by requiring that information be presented in a more accessible and meaningful format. * * *

Form S-4, as adopted, is available for registration under the Securities Act of 1933 (Securities Act) of securities issued in: (i) transactions of the type specified in Rule 145(a); (ii) mergers in which the applicable state law would not require the solicitation of the votes or consents of all of the security holders of the company being acquired [*e.g.*, short form mergers]; (iii) exchange offers for securities of the issuer or another entity; and (iv) reoffers or resales of securities registered on this Form. Form S-4 employs the principles underlying the integrated disclosure system and, thus, permits incorporation by reference of information from reports filed pursuant to the continuous reporting requirements under the Securities Exchange Act of 1934 (Exchange Act) to the same extent as is permitted when a company registers securities under the Securities Act in a primary offering not involving a business combination. [*See* Chapter 4] * * *

Availability and Use of Form. Form S-4 is available for the registration of securities in connection with Rule 145 transactions as well as other mergers,[3] exchange offers and reoffers or resales of securities registered on the Form.[4] In addition, registrants that choose to use the incorporation by reference feature of the Form must send the prospectus twenty business days prior to the date of the meeting of security holders or, where no such meeting is held, the date the investment decision would become final.[5] For example, in a consent solicitation the prospectus would have to be disseminated at least twenty business days before the consents could be used to effect the proposal. * * *

---

3. Merger transactions to which General Instruction A.1.(2) of Form S-4 would apply include short form mergers pursuant to state corporation laws similar to Section 253 of the Delaware General Corporation Law (the "DGCL") and merger by consent provisions like those found in Section 228 of the DGCL. * * *

4. Form S-1 will remain available for mergers and exchange offers. For example, registrants may choose to use Form S-1 and to have the company being acquired prepare its own proxy statement so that the company being acquired will assume liability for the information in its own proxy statement. Of course, [Form S-3], which [is] not available for business combination transactions, will remain unavailable for such transactions because registrants qualifying for use of those forms may use the respective forms' disclosure approaches through the use of Form S-4. Form S-4 also will be available for registration of securities in connection with issuer exchange offers.

5. Form S-4 also contains two related provisions: (1) The requirement in Item 2 of a legend in the prospectus to inform investors that they need to make prompt requests for documents incorporated by reference; and (2) A requirement in Item 22 for an undertaking by registrants to respond to requests for documents within one business day and to furnish the requested documents by first class mail or other equally prompt means. Where the registration statement incorporates by reference documents at the S-3 level, a request for such documents would include documents filed subsequent to the effective date of the registration statement up to the date of the response to the request. The undertaking would not require delivery of incorporated documents filed subsequent to such request.

Relationship with Exchange Act Rules. The Form S-4 prospectus may serve as the proxy or information statement used in connection with the transaction. It would be deemed to meet the informational and filing requirements of the proxy or information statement rules under section 14 of the Exchange Act and Regulations 14A and 14C thereunder, where applicable to the transaction. [*See* Form S-4, General Instruction E, Compliance with Exchange Act Rules.] All other provisions of those regulations also apply.

In addition, General Instruction E.3 of the Form provides that if the transaction in which the securities being registered are to be issued is subject to sections 13(e) [a going private transaction under Rule 13-e-3, Chapter 14], 14(d) or 14(e) [a tender offer, Chapter 20] of the Exchange Act, the disclosure and other provisions of those sections and the rules and regulations thereunder shall apply to the transaction in addition to the provisions of Form S-4. Thus, the provision calling for the more extensive disclosure will prevail, as will the time periods and other substantive provisions of the Williams Act and the Commission's going private and tender offer rules and schedules thereunder.[6] * * *

The two-part structure of Form S-4, separating the information which must be included in the prospectus (Part I) and that which need not (Part II), is the same as other Securities Act forms. [*See* Form S-1 and S-3] Part I of the Form is divided into four separate sections in order to set forth clearly the requirements relating to the transaction, the companies involved, voting and management information.

Information Required in the Prospectus—Part I

Information about the Transaction—Section A. Section A calls for information about the transaction. This information must be presented in the prospectus instead of being incorporated by reference. The items in section A include: Items 1 and 2, information called for by Items 501 and 502 of Regulation S-K; Item 3, risk factors, ratio of earnings to fixed charges and other information; Item 4, terms of the transaction; Item 5, pro forma financial information; Item 6, material contacts between the companies; Item 7, additional information related to resales; and Items 8 and 9, information called for by Items 509 and 510 of Regulation S-K. These items are adopted substantially as proposed; there follows a discussion of areas where changes have been made from the proposal, or that otherwise are highlighted.

Risk Factors, Ratio of Earnings to Fixed Charges and Other Information—Item 3. Item 3 is adopted with modifications and additional items that reflect commentators' suggestions. First, the Item has been redesignated "Risk Factors, Ratio of Earnings to Fixed Charges and Other Information," to clarify that the information set forth in this part of the prospectus is not a summary of all material information concerning the transaction. The Item requires the registrant to furnish information required by Item 503 of Regulation S-K * * *.

Based upon commentators' suggestions, Item 3 has been revised further to require (1) a statement as to whether any federal or state regulatory requirements must be complied with or approvals must be obtained in connection with the transaction, and if so, the status of such compliance or approvals; and (2) a requirement to furnish the information required by Item 301 of Regulation S-K (condensed financial data for five year trend information) for (1) the registrant; (2) the company being acquired; and (3) if material with respect to the registrant, pro forma data giving effect to the transaction. * * *

Terms of the Transaction—Item 4. Item 4 calls for a description of the terms of the transaction, including information about the acquisition agreement, reasons for and con-

6. For example, if the transaction is an exchange offer subject to Regulation 14D, the registrant is required to disseminate material changes pursuant to Rule 14d-4(c) (17 CFR 240.14d-4(c)). * * *

sequences of the transaction, description of securities and differences in the rights of security holders. * * *

[Note: The information required by this Item is similar to the information required by Item 14 (*Mergers, Consolidations, Acquisitions and Similar Matters*) of Schedule 14A, discussed *infra*, which applies to cash mergers. Paragraph 1 of the Instructions to Item 14 of Schedule 14A says that in a transaction covered by Form S-4, the registrant should "furnish the information required by Form S-4 * * * instead of this Item."]

Item 4 also has been revised to codify existing administrative practice in the area of investment banking and other opinions. The Item requires that if the registrant or the company being acquired has obtained a report, opinion or appraisal from an outside party as to the transaction and refers to such opinion in the prospectus, then the information called for by Item 9(b)(1) of Schedule 13E-3 must be furnished. The Item does not require that such a report be obtained or that there be an affirmative statement as to whether one was obtained. The Item applies only where a report has been obtained and reference to it is made in the prospectus.

In addition, pursuant to commentators' suggestions, a requirement to furnish a brief statement as to the accounting treatment of the transaction has been added. * * *

Pro Forma Financial Information—Item 5. * * * The pro forma financial information relating to the transaction pursuant to which a Form S-4 is filed, like other transaction information, must be presented in the prospectus and may not be incorporated by reference. However, pro forma information relating to other business combinations besides the transaction pursuant to which this registration statement is filed, is treated like company information and, therefore, may be presented in the prospectus or incorporated by reference therein.

Material Contacts Between Companies—Item 6. Item 6 of Form S-4, which has been adopted as proposed, calls for information relating to any past, present or proposed material contracts, negotiations, transactions or similar contacts between the registrant and the company being acquired. * * * The Item is designed to elicit information about: (1) Possible conflicts of interest and (2) facts relating to transactions such as pre-takeover transactions or purchases by the registrant of significant blocks of the securities of the company being acquired. * * *

Information About the Registrant—Section B.

Reporting Companies. If a registrant is subject to either section 13(a) or 15(d) of the Exchange Act [*see* Chapter 4], the information it would have to present in the prospectus about itself is the same as that required by Form S-1 * * * or S-3 if it were making a primary offering of securities not involving a business combination. Registrants eligible to use Form * * * S-3 are not required to present information at the most streamlined level available, but may elect instead to comply with provisions of the Form calling for greater prospectus presentation. * * *

Non-Reporting Companies. For registrants that are not subject to the reporting requirements of the Exchange Act, Form S-4 requires disclosure of company information at the level prescribed by Form S-1. * * *

Information About the Company Being Acquired—Section C.

Reporting Companies. Form S-4 generally provides for the same prospectus presentation about a reporting company being acquired that would be required by Form S-1 * * * or S-3 were such company making a primary offering of securities not involving a business combination. Thus, Form S-4 for the most part requires registrants to provide information about the company being acquired as if that company were the registrant. * * *

Item 17(b)(7) [sets out the financial statement requirements for a non-reporting company that is being acquired.] * * *

Voting and Management Information — Section D.

Voting Information. If a proxy, consent or authorization is to be solicited. Form S-4 requires registrants to present in the prospectus information concerning (1) the vote needed for approval, (2) dissenters' rights of appraisal, (3) revocability of proxies, (4) interest of certain persons in the transaction, (5) persons making the solicitation and (6) the registrant's relationship with independent public accountants. * * *

Management Information. Whether or not proxies are to be solicited. Form S-4 requires information concerning voting securities and the principal holders of such shares with respect to all directors and executive officers of both entities and, with regard to the directors and executive officers of the surviving or acquiring company, information about directors and executive officers, certain relationships and related transactions, and executive compensation. * * *

Information Not Required in the Prospectus — Part II

Part II of Form S-4 prescribes information called for by: (1) Item 702 of Regulation S-K indemnification of directors and officers; (2) Item 601 of Regulation S-K, exhibits; and (3) Item 512 of Regulation S-K, undertakings.

This information would be included in the registration statement, but could be omitted from the prospectus. * * *

§ 13.11 Gun-Jumping under the 33 Act: The Impact of the New SEC Rules Governing Increased Communications

A. Traditional Concern with Gun-Jumping, *see* Chapter 4

B. SEC's Final M&A Release and Rules Regarding Increased Communications in Mergers That Also Involve Offers of the Acquiror's Securities [*See* Rules 135, 145(b), 165, 166, and 425]

Final M&A Release, Regulation of Takeovers and Security Holders Communications, Discussion of New Regulatory Regime, Securities Act Release No. 33-7760

(October 22, 1999)

[**Background**] Today, merger and acquisition transactions are occurring at a faster pace, due in part to the rapid development of new technologies and advancements in communications. As a result of economic and regulatory pressures, many companies are releasing more information to the market before a registration, proxy or tender offer statement is filed publicly with us. In many cases, parties are releasing information on proposed transactions including pro forma financial information for the combined entity, estimated cost savings and synergies. As we noted in the Proposing Release, parties to business combination transactions provide several reasons for the need to disclose information early, including the duty under Rule 10b-5 to disclose material information in a manner that is not misleading.[7] We also recognize that parties may be subject to other regulatory requirements to disclose information to the markets early.

Existing restrictions on communications result primarily from the broad concepts of "offer"[8] and "prospectus"[9] under the Securities Act, "solicitation"[10] under the Exchange Act proxy rules, and "commencement"[11] under the Williams Act tender offer rules. We recognize that restricting communications to one document may actually impede, rather than promote, informed investing and voting decisions.

We are adopting, as proposed, non-exclusive exemptions under the Securities Act, proxy rules and tender offer rules that permit communications for an unrestricted length of time without a cooling-off period between the end of communications and filing. Written communications made in reliance on the exemptions must be filed. * * *

One major benefit of permitting earlier communications is that more information will be available generally to all security holders, not simply to a limited audience of analysts and financially sophisticated market participants. Because the new rules do not require oral communications to be reduced to writing and filed, some selective disclosure may continue to occur. Nevertheless, the rules adopted today are designed to reduce selective disclosure by permitting widespread dissemination of information through a variety of media calculated to inform all security holders about the terms, benefits and risks of a planned extraordinary transaction. * * * Although this release does not impose new requirements on oral communications, we remain extremely troubled by the selective disclosure of material information. The staff is considering broader regulatory approaches to limit or inhibit written and oral selective disclosure by issuers in all contexts, including those addressed in this release. * * *

The scheme we adopt today provides the maximum amount of flexibility to disclose information to security holders and the markets. This new communications scheme, however, does not change the current requirement that security holders receive a mandated disclosure document before they are asked to make a voting or investment decision (*e.g.*, a prospectus, proxy statement, or tender offer statement setting forth complete and balanced information). * * *

---

7. We have long recognized the needs of issuers to communicate with security holders regarding important business and financial developments. In addition, the Division of Corporation Finance has previously recognized the needs of bidders to disclose information regarding a contemplated "back-end" transaction (i.e., a subsequent transaction in which the bidder acquires any remaining securities outstanding). Disclosure of information required by Schedule 14D-1 regarding a "back-end" transaction generally will not result in "gun-jumping" because the information is not designed to prime the market for a subsequent registered offering of securities. Instead, the information aids investors in evaluating the terms of a tender offer and deciding whether to tender for cash or wait for securities in a back-end transaction. See Release No.33–5927 [Section 20.4.O].

8. Section 2(a)(3) of the Securities Act broadly defines "offer" as including every attempt or offer to dispose of, or solicitation of an offer to buy, a security or interest in a security, for value. Offers are currently prohibited during the pre-filing period and restricted during the waiting period.

9. The term "prospectus" is defined in Section 2(a)(10) to include any prospectus, notice, circular, advertisement, letter of communication, written or by radio or television, that offers any security for sale or confirms the sale of the security, except for communications that are preceded or accompanied by a statutory prospectus.

10. "Solicitation" is broadly defined to include "the furnishing of a form of proxy or other communication to security holders under circumstances reasonably calculated to result in the procurement, withholding or revocation of a proxy." *See* Rule 14a-1(l).

11. The Williams Act provides that only very limited information can be announced without either commencing a cash tender offer or requiring the filing of a registration statement in a stock offer. *See* Rule 14d-2(c) and (d).

Our long-held concern regarding communications that could condition the market before dissemination of a mandated disclosure document is mitigated by the continuing requirement to deliver a disclosure document before any voting or investment decision can be made, and the attendant liability for false or misleading statements. Communications made in reliance on the new exemptions would, of course, be subject to Section 10(b) liability. We remind persons relying on the exemptions that fraudulent statements in these communications could not be cured by subsequent filings. * * *

Our proposals did not make distinctions based on size and seasoned status. Due to the extraordinary nature of business combination transactions, security holders and the markets need full and timely information regarding those transactions regardless of the size or seasoned status of the companies involved. * * *

We also asked whether the exemptions should be limited to the parties to the transaction or available to others who may be acting on behalf of the parties to the transaction. * * * [W]e are adopting the exemptions to cover all persons acting on the parties' behalf.

We are adopting, as proposed, a condition to the communications exemptions that all written communications in connection with or relating to a business combination transaction be filed on or before the date of first use. In addition, all written communications must include a prominent legend advising investors to read the registration, proxy or tender offer statement, as applicable. We believe that a prompt filing requirement is necessary to protect security holders and assure that these communications are available to all investors on a timely basis. In most cases, this information will need to be filed electronically via the EDGAR System, and thus will be rapidly disseminated to the marketplace. * * *

The filing requirement applies to written communications that are made public or are otherwise provided to persons that are not a party to the transaction.[12] As a general matter, this would include, for example, scripts used by parties to the transaction to communicate information to the public and other written material (*e.g.*, slides) relating to the transaction that is shown to investors. In contrast, internal written communications provided solely to parties to the transaction, legal counsel, financial advisors, and similar persons authorized to act on behalf of the parties to the transaction would not need to be filed. Also, as explained in the Proposing Release, business information that is factual in nature and relates solely to ordinary business matters, and not the pending transaction, would not need to be filed. We expect that filing persons will apply traditional legal principles in determining whether a particular written communication is made in connection with or relates to a proposed business combination transaction. * * *

[**Securities Act Exemption and Filing Rules**] * * * [W]e adopt new Rules 165, 166 and 425 and amend Rules 135 and 145. These new and amended rules permit parties to communicate freely about a planned business combination transaction before a registration statement is filed, as well as during the waiting period and post-effective periods, so long as their written communications used in connection with or relating to the transaction are filed beginning with the first public announcement and ending with the close of the proposed transaction. As noted in the Proposing Release, these communications are not

---

12. Oral communications are covered by the exemptions, but they do not need to be reduced to writing or filed. Oral communications, as proposed, will be subject to liability under the applicable regulatory scheme. For example, pre-filing oral communications regarding a proposed offering of securities in connection with a business combination transaction will be subject to Section 12(a)(2) liability.

excluded from the definition of "offer" in the Securities Act,[13] as no content restriction is imposed on the communications. Instead, new Rule 165 exempts persons making these communications from Sections 5(b)(1) and (c) of the Securities Act.[14]

New Rules 165 and 166 are available only for business combination transactions. New Rule 165 defines a business combination transaction as a transaction specified in Rule 145(a) or an exchange offer. Thus, either the proxy rules or the tender offer rules must be applicable to the transaction. We have added a preliminary note to Rules 165 and 166 to state that the exemption is not available to communications that may technically comply with the rule, but have the primary purpose or effect of conditioning the market for a capital-raising or resale transaction.

[**Liability for Communications**] As proposed, both oral and written communications made in reliance on the Securities Act exemption would be offers subject to Section 12(a)(2) liability, based on the belief that this level of liability would adequately protect investors without chilling communications. * * *

We are adopting the proposed regulatory scheme. To the extent that these communications constitute offers, they currently would be subject to Section 12(a)(2) liability. As a result, we do not believe that the adopted rules alter the current liability levels for these communications. In light of the extensive pre-filing communications that are ongoing in the marketplace now with respect to business combination transactions, we believe that a Section 12(a)(2) standard of liability would not significantly chill communications. * * *

[W]e are revising the filing requirement in new Rule 165 to state that an immaterial or unintentional failure to file or delay in filing will not result in a loss of the exemption from Section 5(b)(1) or (c), so long as a good faith and reasonable attempt to file the written communication is made and the communication is filed as soon as practicable after discovery of the failure to file. [New Rule 165(e)]

[**Rules 135 and 145**] Currently, Rule 135 provides that disclosure of certain limited information in notice form will not be deemed an "offer" for purposes of Section 5 of the Securities Act.[15] A Rule 135 notice is typically made upon announcement of a proposed securities offering before a registration statement is filed.[16] Rule 145(b)(1) contains a similar provision regarding the information in a stock merger that will not be deemed a "prospectus" or "offer."

We proposed several revisions to Rules 135 and 145 in the Proposing Release and the Securities Act Reform Release. In particular, we proposed moving the substance of Rule

13. A communication that contains no more information than that specified in Rule 135 will not be an offer, as is currently the case.

14. New Rule 166 provides that communications before the first public announcement of a transaction will not be offers, so long as parties to the transaction take reasonable steps to prevent further distribution or publication until the first public announcement or the registration statement is filed.

15. Rule 135 generally permits prospective offerors to issue notices that include the following information: (1) the name of the issuer; (2) the title, amount and basic terms of the securities to be offered, the amount of the offering, if any, by selling security holders, the anticipated time of the offering, and a brief statement of the manner and purpose of the offering, without naming the underwriters; and (3) any statement or legend required by state law. Other limited information also is permitted under the rule for rights offerings, exchange offers and offers to employees of the issuer or an affiliate.

16. Cash tender offers and cash mergers do not involve the Securities Act, and thus no reliance on Rule 135 is necessary.

145(b)(1) to Rule 135, as both rules contain similar provisions regarding the information that will not be deemed an offer. We are adopting those revisions.

In addition to the changes proposed, we asked whether Rule 135 notices should be filed. Although Rule 135 does not currently require these notices to be filed, in many cases the 135 notice would be the first written communication relating to a proposed business combination transaction. We believe it is important for this information to reach the marketplace promptly and on a widespread basis. * * *

We are adopting a filing requirement that encompasses Rule 135 notices. These notices must be filed under new Rule 425 because they are written communications relating to a proposed transaction. Even though we are requiring these notices to be filed, our rules provide that they will not constitute offers and therefore will not have Section 12(a)(2) prospectus liability. In addition, subsequent notices or announcements made under Rule 135 that do not contain new or different information are not required to be filed. This approach is consistent with the filing requirement under each of the three regulatory schemes.

[**Public Announcement**] Under the terms of the exemptions, written communications must be filed beginning with the first public announcement of the business combination transaction. Today we are adopting a specific definition of "public announcement" that encompasses all communications that put the market on notice of a proposed transaction. For purposes of determining when a filing obligation is incurred under the exemptions, "public announcement" means any communication by a party to the transaction, or any person authorized to act on a party's behalf, that is reasonably designed to, or has the effect of, informing the public or security holders in general about the transaction.[17] * * *

§ 13.12 The Federal 34 Act Proxy Rules and Form S-4 in Negotiated Transactions

A. Introduction to the Provisions of the Proxy Rules and Form S-4 Relating to the Preparation of a Merger Proxy Statement and Prospectus

1. Introduction to the Proxy Rules

Section 14(a) of the Securities Exchange Act of 1934 (34 Act) makes it unlawful for any person through the use of interstate commerce to solicit any proxy or consent or other authorization in respect to any security registered under Section 12 of the 34 Act [*i.e.*, a publicly held corporation] in contravention of any of the rules or regulations promulgated under Section 14(a). Corporations that are required to register under Section 12 include corporations that have total assets exceeding $10 million and a class of equity securities held by either (1) 2,000 or more persons or (2) 500 or more persons who are not accredited investors. [*See* Section 12(g)]

The SEC has promulgated Regulation 14A that deals with the solicitation of proxies and related matters. Regulation 14A consists of:

17. New Rule 165(f)(3). A similar definition of "public announcement" is included in revised Rules 13e-4(c) and 14d-2(b).

(1) Rules 14a-1 et seq., and

(2) Schedule 14A, setting forth information required in a proxy statement.

Thus, in summary, Regulation 14A deals with proxy statements generally, including proxy statements issued in the context of mergers and acquisitions, and Regulation 14C deals with the informational distribution requirement in merger transactions in which the target's minority shareholders are not required to vote.

2. Form-S-4 and Its Relationship to the Proxy Rules

As discussed previously, Form S-4 is a registration statement under the Securities Act of 1933 (33 Act). The form can be used for registering securities to be issued (1) in a transaction of a type specified in paragraph (a) of Rule 145, that is, in a merger or acquisition of substantially all of a target's assets, (2) in a merger in which the applicable state law does not require the solicitation of the votes or consents of the target's shareholders, and (3) in an exchange offer in which the acquiring corporation (the issuer) proposes to exchange its stock for the stock of a target corporation. *See* Form S-4, General Instructions A.l.

It is important to understand the relationship between Form S-4 and the proxy rules. If in an acquisition of a publicly traded target in a merger or purchase of assets, the acquiring corporation does not issue its securities but rather merely pays cash, then the target corporation will have to comply with Regulation 14A under the proxy rules, but the acquiring corporation will not. Since the acquiring corporation is only paying cash in the acquisition, it will not have to comply with the proxy rules because its shareholders will not have a right to vote on the transaction under state law. On the other hand, if the acquiring corporation issues its securities in an acquisition of a publicly-held target corporation, then those securities must be registered under the 33 Act as required by Rule 145 [Section 13.10], unless the issuance qualifies as a private offering or other exempt offering. An acquisition of a publicly-held target for stock of an acquiring corporation could not qualify as a private offering.

Depending on the amount of securities issued, the acquiring corporation may also have to solicit proxies from its shareholders in which case the acquiring corporation will have to comply with Regulation 14A, assuming it is a publicly-held firm. However, without respect to whether the acquiring corporation must itself comply with Regulation 14A, in most cases the target will have to comply with Regulation 14A, and since the acquiring corporation is issuing securities it will have to register those securities. The registration will be made on Form S-4 [Section 13.10.B]. Thus, where an acquiring corporation's securities are issued in an acquisition of a publicly-held target corporation, the transaction will have to comply with both Form S-4 and Regulation 14A. However, Form S-4 provides that the prospectus required under that form "may be in the form of a proxy or information statement and may contain the information required by [Form S-4] in lieu of that required by [the proxy rules.]" *See* Form S-4 General Instructions E.1.

3. Introduction to Section 14(c) Information Statement

Prior to the completion of certain transactions, such as short form mergers, that do not require a vote of the public shareholders, an issuer must, pursuant to Section 14(c) of the 34 Act, provide to its security holders information that is substantially similar to the information supplied in a proxy statement. Regulation 14C, which requires an information statement in Section 14(c) transactions, is examined in Chapter 14, which deals with going private transactions.

4. Form S-4: Joint Proxy Statement and Prospectus, and Joint Information Statement and Prospectus in Time-Warner Transaction

The combined proxy statement and Form S-4 is illustrated in the Time/Warner Joint Proxy Statement and Time Prospectus, Documentary Appendix B of *M&A Statutes, Rules, and Documents, supra* Section 1.1. This document complies with Regulation 14A for both Time and Warner since the shareholders of both companies were required to vote on the transaction. Time shareholders were required to vote because its articles were amended and the NYSE rules required a shareholder vote, and the Warner shareholders were required to vote because Warner, the target, was a constituent corporation under Section 251 under the Delaware General Corporation Law. Also, the document included Time's prospectus prepared under Form S-4, relating to the stock of Time to be issued to the Warner shareholders in the merger. *See also* the J.P. Morgan Chase-Bank One S-4, Documentary Appendix E.

B. Overview of Proxy Rules As They Relate to Long Form Mergers and Purchases of Assets

1. Introduction to the Proxy Rules of General Applicability in M&A

The discussion in this section focuses principally on the provisions of the proxy rules under the 34 Act (Rule 14a-1 et seq.) that have an impact on proxy statements prepared for consensual mergers and acquisitions. The next two sections deal with the following provisions of the proxy rules that have an impact on M&A: (1) Rule 14a-12 governing oral and written communications prior to filing of a proxy statement, and (2) Rule 14a-21(c) dealing with the golden parachute disclosure provisions added by the Dodd-Frank Act. Section 16.6 focuses on the provisions of these rules that impact upon proxy contests and other solicitations by persons that are not parties to a merger or acquisition.

1. **Rule 14a-1.** Rule 14a-1 sets forth certain definitions that govern Regulation 14A. The following are some of the more important definitions. The term "proxy" is defined to include "every proxy, consent or authorization within the meaning of Section 14(a) of the [34] Act." Rule 14a-1(f). The term "proxy statement" is defined as a "statement required by Rule 14a-3(a), whether or not contained in a single document." Rule 14a-1(g). The term "registrant" is defined as the "issuer of the securities in respect of which proxies are to be solicited." Rule 14a-l(j).

The terms "solicit" and "solicitation" are defined very broadly to include: "(i) Any request for a proxy whether or not accompanied by or included in a form of proxy; (ii) Any requests to execute or not to execute or to revoke a proxy; or (iii) The furnishing of a form of proxy or other communication to security holders under circumstances reasonably calculated to result in the procurement, withholding or revocation of a proxy." Rule 14a-1(1)(1).

Rule 14a-1(1)(2) exempts certain acts from the definition of solicitation, including certain communications by a security holder who does not otherwise engage in a proxy solicitation. Rule 14 a-l(l)(2)(iv).

2. **Rule 14a-2.** Rule 14a-2 specifies the solicitations to which Rules 14a-3 to 14a-12 apply. In general, Rule 14a-2 provides that the rules apply to "every solicitation of a proxy with respect to securities, registered pursuant to section 12 of the [34] Act ..." Thus, the rules apply to securities of publicly-traded corporations, and they apply to solicitations by both the issuer and any shareholder or shareholder groups in a proxy contest. [*See* Chapter 16, relating to proxy contests] Rules 14a-2(a) and (b) set forth certain circumstances

under which the rules do not apply, such as a solicitation by a person in respect of securities carried in his name.

Rule 14a-2(b)(1) provides that certain rules do not apply to certain solicitations by a person who does not seek the power to act as a proxy. This exception does not apply to solicitations by, *inter alia*, (1) the registrant, (2) an officer or director of the registrant, (3) a nominee for whose election as a director proxies are solicited, (4) any person soliciting in opposition to a merger or acquisition recommended by the registrant's board which person is proposing an alternative transaction, or (5) any more-than-5% shareholder who is required to file a schedule 13D under Section 13(d) of the Williams Act. Rule 14a-2(b)(1).

Rule 14a-2(b)(2) provides that certain of the rules do not apply to "[a]ny solicitation made otherwise than on behalf of the registrant where the total number of persons solicited is not more than ten." The exemptions in Rule 14a-2(b) are explored further in Section 16.6.

3. **Rule 14a-3.** Rule 14a-3 sets forth the information to be furnished to security holders and provides that no solicitation may be made unless each person solicited is "concurrently furnished or has previously been furnished with a publicly-filed preliminary or definitive written proxy statement containing the information specified in Schedule 14A or with a preliminary or definitive written proxy statement included in a registration statement filed * * * on Form S-4." Rule 14a-3(a). Thus, the proxy statement or the proxy statement and registration statement must be distributed to the security holders before they can be solicited.

Rule 14a-3(b) provides that if the solicitation is made in connection with an annual meeting of security holders, then the proxy statement must be accompanied by an annual report to security holders (ARS), which provides the information set forth in paragraphs 1–13 of Rule 14a-3(b). Rule 14a-3(c) provides that the ARS is to be sent to the SEC at the time it is sent to security holders. The ARS is solely for the information of the SEC and is not deemed to be "soliciting materials" or to be filed with the SEC. Rule 14a-3(c). Rules 14a-3(d) and (e) set forth certain additional rules governing the ARS, and Rule 14a-3(f) provides that the proxy delivery requirements of Rule 14a-3 do not apply to certain public communications.

4. **Rule 14a-4.** Rule 14a-4 sets forth the requirements for a proxy, such as the form of the proxy and the voting procedures to be contained in the proxy.

5. **Rule 14a-5.** Rule 14a-5 sets forth the rules governing the presentation of information in a proxy statement. The information must be clearly presented and the material must be divided into groups according to subject matter with appropriate heading.

6. **Rule 14a-6.** Rule 14a-6 sets forth the filing requirements. Under Rule 14a-6(a) five copies of the proxy statement and other soliciting materials must be filed with the SEC at least ten calendar days prior to sending the material to security holders. This prefiling requirement is relaxed in the case of certain annual meetings that do not involve controversial matters.

Rule 14a-6 was amended in 1999 as indicated below:

Final M&A Release, Regulation of Takeovers and Security Holders Communications under the Proxy Rules, Securities Act Release No. 33-7760

(October 22, 1999)

[**Timing of Filings**] Rule 14a-6(b) requires that definitive proxy materials be "filed with, or mailed for filing to, the Commission not later than the date such material is first sent or given to security holders." Similar language appears in several other proxy and information statement filing rules. [*See* Rules 14a-4(f), 14a-6(c), 14a-11(c), 14a-12(b) and 14c-5(b)] The mailing alternative, however, is no longer an option because companies must file electronically. Therefore, we are amending the proxy and information statement filing rules as proposed to require filing no later than the date the materials are first sent or given to security holders. [Rule 14a-6(b)] * * *

[**Limited Confidential Treatment of Merger Proxy Materials**] Today, a proxy statement relating to a merger, consolidation, acquisition or similar matter may be filed confidentially with the Commission. * * * We proposed to eliminate the provision for confidential treatment. * * *

We have decided to retain confidential treatment under limited circumstances. Where the parties to a merger or other business combination transaction limit their public communications to those specified in Rule 135, confidential treatment will continue to be available for the proxy materials. If, however, the parties elect to publicly disclose, either orally or in writing, information relating to the transaction that goes beyond Rule 135, confidential treatment will not be available. [Revised Rules 14a-6(e)(2) and 14c-5(c)(2)] * * *

Other provisions under this rule govern (1) personal solicitation materials (c), (2) release dates (d), (3) publicly available information (e), (4) communications not required to be filed (f), (5) solicitations subject to Rule 14a-2(b)(1),(g), (6) revised material (h), (7) fees (i), and (8) computation of time periods (k).

Also, Rule 14a-6(j) sets forth certain requirements regarding merger proxies. Under this rule, any proxy statement or other soliciting material required to be filed by Rule 14a-6 that is also included in a registration statement filed on Form S-4 is deemed filed both for the purposes of the 1933 Act and the 1934 Act. Consequently, separate copies need not be filed with the SEC. However, if any additional soliciting material is used after the effective date of the registration statement on Form S-4, then such information must be filed, unless such information is filed as an amendment to the registration statement.

7. **Rule 14a-7.** Rule 14a-7 sets forth the requirements for mailing the proxy material to security holders. * * *

8. **Rule 14a-8.** Rule 14a-8 governs proposals of security holders that are included in proxy statements. This provision is not examined further here.

9. **Rule 14a-9.** Rule 14a-9 prohibits false or misleading statements in connection with the distribution of a proxy statement. This rule should be read very carefully. Case law interpretations of this rule are examined in Sections 13.16 through 13.19.

10. **Rule 14a-10.** Rule 14a-10 prohibits solicitations with, among other things, undated or postdated proxies.

11. **Rule 14a-11.** Former Rule 14a-11, which set forth provisions applicable to election contests, that is, proxy contests, has been eliminated and folded into Rule 14a-12 as indicated below.

2. Rule 14a-12 Regarding Written and Oral Communications before Filing a Proxy Statement

Rule 14a-12, which has a significant impact on M&A transactions, was significantly modified in 1999 as explained in the following release:

Final M&A Release, Regulation of Takeovers and Security Holders Communications under the Proxy Rules, Securities Act Release No. 33-7760

(October 22, 1999)

[**Rule 14a-12 Expanded**] We are revising Rule 14a-12, substantially as proposed, to permit both written and oral communications before the filing of a proxy statement so long as all written communications related to the solicitation are filed on the date of first use. [The expansion of Rule 14a-12 to cover all solicitations eliminates the need for many of the provisions in Rule 14a-11. As a result, we are rescinding Rule 14a-11 and moving paragraphs (d) and (f) of Rule 14a-11 to new Rule 14a-12. * * * Revised Rule 14a-12 makes it clear that these provisions are limited to election contests.] [Written communications by soliciting parties before a proxy statement is furnished to security holders must be filed on the date of first use and must provide information regarding the participants and their interests or include a legend advising security holders where they can obtain this information. *See* revised Rule 14a-12(a)(1). Once a proxy statement is furnished to security holders, any additional soliciting materials used must be filed on the date of first use but need not include participant information or a legend advising where to obtain that information. *See* revised Rule 14a-6(b)]

This is the same filing requirement adopted for the communications exemption under the Securities Act. [*See* Rule 165] This exemption is not limited to business combination transactions, but is available regardless of the subject matter of the solicitation. Oral communications do not need to be reduced to writing and filed. In revising Rule 14a-12, we retain substantially all the proposed conditions to reliance on the exemption. These conditions are that no form of proxy is furnished until a proxy statement is delivered, the obligation to disclose participant information, and the requirement to file all written communications with a prominent legend advising security holders to read the proxy statement.

As a result of these changes to Rule 14a-12, management can communicate more freely with security holders about significant corporate events, including a proposed merger or acquisition, or other significant corporate governance matters that may require a security holder vote. Likewise, security holders are able to communicate more freely with one another. The revised rule does not, however, expand a company's or security holder's ability to secure promises to vote a certain way before a proxy statement is provided. The expansion of Rule 14a-12 to non-contested matters is premised on the same rationale for increasing communications related to business combination transactions under the Securities Act. * * *

We believe that the requirement to file all written communications, the condition that no proxy or form of proxy be furnished to security holders before a written proxy statement is delivered, and the requirement to include a legend on all written communications advising security holders to read the proxy statement and where to find participant information should be sufficient to protect against misleading solicitations. Together with the antifraud provisions of Rule 14a-9, these requirements should maintain the integrity of the solicitation process and adequacy of information disseminated to security holders. In addition to these safeguards, security holders will receive a complete proxy statement before they can vote.

In the Proposing Release we solicited comment on whether a federally mandated proxy solicitation period would be appropriate for mergers and similar transactions in light of the free communications permitted under the exemption. * * * We are not adopting a minimum solicitation period at this time. * * *

[The "As Soon as Practicable" Requirement] Many of the commenters urged us to revise the current and proposed condition in Rule 14a-12 that a written proxy statement meeting the requirements of Regulation 14A be sent or given to solicited security holders at the earliest practicable date. * * *

In view of these concerns, current practice, and the overall approach to communications adopted today, we are eliminating the current "as soon as practicable" requirement. As revised, Rule 14a-12 requires that a definitive proxy statement be furnished to security holders when a form of proxy is either given to or requested from security holders. [Revised Rule 14a-12(a)(2)] * * *

[**Participant Information**] We are modifying the current requirement to disclose participant information in proxy materials. Instead, the revised rule requires a prominent legend on written communications advising security holders where they can obtain a detailed list of the names, affiliations and interests of participants in the solicitation. Of course, the soliciting materials could include the participant information in full, as currently required, instead of a legend. * * *

13. **Rule 14a-13.** Rule 14a-13 sets forth the obligations of the issuer in communicating with the beneficial owners of securities.

14. **Rule 14a-14.** Rule 14a-14 provides rules with respect to certain modified or superseded documents.

3. Introduction to the Golden Parachute Disclosure Requirement Added by the Dodd-Frank Act, Rule14a-21(c) and Related Rules[18]

Rule 14a-21(c) of the proxy rules requires a shareholder vote on golden parachutes as part of the merger proxy, unless a prior shareholder vote with regard to the golden parachutes has occurred. This golden parachute requirement was added by the Dodd-Frank Act, which added Section 14A to the 34 Act. Section 14A(a), which is discussed in Chapter 4, gives the shareholders of 34 Act reporting companies an advisory vote on executive compensation in certain circumstances, and Section 14A(b) sets out rules governing shareholder approval of certain golden parachute and similar provisions.

Section 14A(b)(1) sets out the following disclosure requirements with regard to golden parachutes arrangements:

> (1) DISCLOSURE.—In any proxy or consent solicitation material (the solicitation of which is subject to the rules of the Commission pursuant to subsection (a)) for a meeting of the shareholders ... at which shareholders are asked to approve an acquisition, merger, consolidation, or proposed sale or other disposition of all or substantially all the assets of an issuer, the person making such solicitation shall disclose in the proxy or consent solicitation material, in a clear and simple form in accordance with regulations to be promulgated by the Commission, any agreements or understandings that such person has with any named executive officers of such issuer (or of the acquiring issuer, if such issuer is not the acquiring issuer) concerning any type of compensation (whether present, deferred, or contingent) that is based on or otherwise relates to the ac-

18. This section is adapted from Thompson, *Mergers, Acquisitions and Tender Offers*, *supra* Section 1.10, at Section 6:10.5[B].

> quisition, merger, consolidation, sale, or other disposition of all or substantially all of the assets of the issuer and the aggregate total of all such compensation that may (and the conditions upon which it may) be paid or become payable to or on behalf of such executive officer.

The disclosures required by Section 14A(b)(1) are in addition to the existing rules under Item 402(j) of Reg. SK, *Potential Payments upon Termination or Change-In-Control*, which require disclosures "[r]egarding [*inter alia*] each contract, agreement, plan or arrangement, whether written or unwritten, that provides for payment(s) to a named executive officer at, following, or in connection with any ... change in control of the registrant...."

Section 14A(b)(2) requires, in connection with a merger or acquisition transaction, a shareholder vote approving any parachute arrangements that have not been subject to an advisory vote under Section 14A(a). Section 14A(b)(2) provides:

> (2) SHAREHOLDER APPROVAL.—Any proxy or consent or authorization relating to the proxy or consent solicitation material containing the disclosure required by paragraph (1) shall include a separate resolution subject to shareholder vote to approve such agreements or understandings and compensation as disclosed, unless such agreements or understandings have been subject to a shareholder vote under subsection (a) [relating to say on pay vote].

Section 14A(c) makes it clear that the votes on pay in Section 14A(a) and on golden parachutes in Section 14A(b) are advisory only.

The SEC implemented the golden parachute provisions of Section 14A(b) principally by adding:

> (1) section (t), Golden Parachute Compensation, to Item 402, Executive Compensation, of Reg. SK;
>
> (2) a new paragraph (b) to Item 1011, Additional Information, of Reg MA, which requires the disclosures set out in Item 402(t);
>
> (3) new Rule 14a-21(c), requiring a shareholder vote on golden parachutes as part of the merger proxy, unless a prior shareholder vote with regard to the golden parachutes has occurred; and
>
> (4) related amendments to Schedule 14A, relating to proxy statements, Schedule 14D-9, relating to a target's position on a tender offer, Schedule 13E-3, relating to going private transactions, and Schedule TO, relating to tender offers.

Section (t)(1) of Item 402 sets out the disclosure requirements relating to golden parachute payments:

> (1) In connection with any proxy or consent solicitation material providing the disclosure required by section 14A(b)(1) of the Exchange Act [relating to golden parachute disclosures] or any proxy or consent solicitation that includes disclosure under Item 14 of Schedule 14A pursuant to Note A of Schedule 14A, with respect to each named executive officer of the acquiring company and the target company, provide the information specified in paragraphs (t)(2) and (3) of this section regarding any agreement or understanding, whether written or unwritten, between such named executive officer and the acquiring company or target company, concerning any type of compensation, whether present, deferred or contingent, that is based on or otherwise relates to an acquisition, merger, consolidation, sale or other disposition of all or substantially all assets of the issuer, [pursuant to the] Golden Parachute Compensation [Table].

Section (t)(2) of Item 402 specifies certain information to be included in the Golden Parachute Compensation Table, and Section (t)(3) requires "a succinct narrative description of any material factors necessary to an understanding of each [golden parachute] contract, agreement, plan or arrangement and the payments quantified in the tabular disclosure [in the Golden Parachute Compensation Table]."

Rule 14a-21(c) sets out the rules regarding the required shareholder advisory votes on golden parachute payments:

> (c) [*General Rule Regarding Shareholder Advisory Votes in an M&A Transaction*] If a solicitation is made by a registrant for a meeting of shareholders at which shareholders are asked to approve an acquisition, merger, consolidation or proposed sale or other disposition of all or substantially all the assets of the registrant, the registrant shall include a separate resolution subject to shareholder advisory vote to approve any agreements or understandings and compensation disclosed pursuant to Item 402(t) of Regulation S-K, unless such agreements or understandings have been subject to a shareholder advisory vote under paragraph (a) [*General Rule Regarding Shareholder Advisory Votes Prior to an M&A Transaction*] of this section. Consistent with section 14A(b) of the Exchange Act, any agreements or understandings between an acquiring company and the named executive officers of the registrant, where the registrant is not the acquiring company, are not required to be subject to the separate shareholder advisory vote under this paragraph.

The last sentence of Rule 14a-21(c) makes it clear, for example, that an advisory vote of the target's shareholders is not required for arrangements between an acquirer and the employees of the target.

4. Illustration of Golden Parachute Disclosure

A Proxy Statement/Prospectus on Form S-4 was issued on January 24, 2014 by New Endo, a newly formed Irish holding company, relating to its acquisition of (1) all the stock of Endo Health Solutions, Inc. (Endo), a U.S. corporation, in exchange for New Endo Stock, and (2) all of the stock of Paladin Labs Inc., a Canadian corporation, in exchange for New Endo Stock. The Proxy Statement/ Prospectus contains the following disclosure regarding the advisory vote on golden parachutes:

Q: Why am I being asked to approve, on a non-binding advisory basis, certain merger-related compensatory arrangements between Endo and its named executive officers?

A: Under the Dodd-Frank Wall Street Reform and Consumer Protection Act, which is referred to in this proxy statement/prospectus as the "Dodd-Frank Act," and section 14A of the Securities Exchange Act of 1934, as amended, which is referred to in the proxy statement/prospectus as the "Exchange Act", Endo shareholders are entitled to vote to approve, on an advisory basis, the compensation of the named executive officers of Endo that is based on or otherwise relates to the merger as disclosed in this registration statement. See "*Shareholder Advisory Vote on Certain Compensatory Arrangements*" beginning on page 143.

Approval by the Endo shareholders of merger-related compensation to the Endo named executive officers is not a condition to completion of the merger. In addition, because the vote is advisory in nature, it will not be binding on Endo. Regardless of the outcome of this advisory vote, such compensation may be payable, subject only to the Endo board of directors' discretion and the conditions applicable thereto, if the merger is approved. The terms of the merger-related compensation is described under "*The Merger and the*

Arrangement—Interests of Certain Persons in the Merger—Golden Parachute Compensation" beginning on page 87 and "*Shareholder Advisory Vote on Certain Compensatory Arrangements*" beginning on page 143.

C. Overview of Schedule 14A as It Relates Principally to M&A

1. **Introduction.** Schedule 14A sets forth the information required to be included in a proxy statement. The schedule contains several "Notes." Note A provides that if a solicitation is for the purpose of approving the authorization of additional securities which are to be used in the acquisition of a target company, and the registrant's stockholders will not have a separate opportunity to vote on the acquisition, then the solicitation for the additional securities is also a solicitation with respect to the acquisition. Schedule 14A contains several items relating to various types of information required to be included in the proxy statement. The following is a discussion of the items that are most relevant to a merger proxy statement.

2. **Item 3.** Item 3 requires that dissenter or appraisal rights be set forth in the proxy statement. *See* for example, paragraph [12] of the Time-Warner Joint Proxy Statement and Time Prospectus, Documentary Appendix B of *M&A Statutes, Rules, and Documents, supra* Section 1.1.

3. **Item 4.** Item 4 requires information with respect to the persons making the solicitation. Item 4(a) relates to solicitations by the issuer, and Item 4(b) relates to solicitations by proxy contestants.

4. **Item 5.** Item 5 requires that the interest of certain persons in the matters to be acted upon be set forth. Item 5(a) relates to solicitations in non-proxy contests, and Item 5(b) relates to solicitations in proxy contests.

5. **Item 6.** Item 6 requires certain information with respect to voting securities and the principal holders thereof. Under Item 6(e), specific information with respect to any change in control of the registrant must be provided.

6. **Item 11.** Item 11 requires certain information concerning the purposes for which new shares are authorized, including a brief description of the transaction in which the securities are to be issued.

7. **Item 14.** Item 14 sets forth the information required for mergers, consolidations, and similar transactions. As discussed in connection with the section addressing Form S-4, the information required by Item 14 is similar to the information required in Form S-4, which applies to mergers and other acquisitions in which the acquirer issues its stock. (For example, compare Item 4, Terms of the Transaction, of Form S-4 with Item 14 of Schedule 14A.) Paragraph 1 of the Instructions to Item 14 of Schedule 14A says that in a transaction covered by Form S-4, the registrant should "furnish the information required by Form S-4 * * * instead of this Item." Thus, Item 14 applies in cash mergers, and Form S-4 applies in stock for stock mergers.

Item 14(b) requires information about the transaction. Such information includes a summary term sheet and the terms of the proposed transaction [*see* Items 14(b)(1) and (4)].

Also, Item 14(b)(6) provides that "if a report, opinion, or appraisal materially relating to the transaction has been received from an outside party and such report, opinion or appraisal is referred to in the proxy statement, furnish the information required by Item 1015(b) of Regulation M-A [*see* Section 13.12.E.1 and Section 20.4.M]." Item 1015(b) of

Regulation M-A requires a full disclosure of the background of any person providing an appraisal and a complete report on the appraisal methods utilized. For an illustration of the type of disclosures required by this provision *see* the discussion of the opinions of the financial advisors for J.P. Morgan Chase in the S-4 for its acquisition of Bank One, Documentary Appendix E of *M&A Statutes, Rules, and Documents, supra* Section 1.1.

Item 14(c) requires information about the parties to the transaction. The information requirements vary depending upon whether the registrant is an S-1 or S-3 company. Item 14(e) provides guidance regarding information to be incorporated by reference.

8. **Item 15.** Item 15 deals with matters relating to the acquisition or disposition of property.

9. **Item 19.** Item 19 requires information with respect to any amendment of the registrant's charter, by-laws, or other documents as to which information is not required to be filed under any other item.

D. An Overview of Form S-4

Form S-4 is discussed in Section 13.10.D.

E. New Unified Disclosure Requirements in Tender Offers and Mergers—Regulation M-A and Streamlined Disclosure

1. Regulation M-A

Final M&A Release, Regulation of Takeovers and Security Holders Communications, Disclosure Requirements for Tender Offers and Mergers, Regulation M-A, Securities Act Release No. 33-7760

(October 22, 1999)

We are adopting Regulation M-A substantially as proposed. This series of disclosure items incorporates all the current disclosure requirements for issuer [Chapter 21] and third-party [Chapter 20] tender offers, tender offer recommendation statements [Chapter 20] and going-private transactions [Chapter 14]. The new regulation includes some disclosure items for cash merger proxy statements as well. [Regulation M-A is discussed further in Section 20.4.M]

2. "Plain English" Summary Term Sheet

Final M&A Release, Regulation of Takeovers and Security Holder Communications, Plain English Summary Term Sheet, Securities Act Release No. 33-7760

(October 22, 1999)

[**"Plain English" Summary Term Sheet**] We proposed to require a plain English summary term sheet in all cash tender offers and all cash mergers, as well as going-private transactions. [*See also* the discussion of this issue in Section 20.4.M.2, relating to tender offers] The disclosure documents in these transactions often can be difficult to understand, especially in the context of a business combination transaction where a vast amount of information may be available. We believe security holders should be provided with a concise, easy to read term sheet that highlights the most important and relevant information regarding an extraordinary transaction.

Accordingly, we are adopting the plain English summary term sheet requirement as proposed. [Item 1001 of Regulation M-A] We are not adopting a plain English summary term sheet for transactions involving the registration of securities because these transactions already are required to have a plain English summary [*see* Form S-4], although the format may be somewhat different from the summary term sheet approach. [Item 1001 of Regulation M-A] The summary term sheet must begin on the first or second page of the disclosure document, and must highlight the most important or material features of a proposed transaction. This requirement applies to all issuer and third-party cash tender offers, cash mergers and going-private transactions. We believe the disclosure in these transactions can be improved through the use of a plain English summary term sheet. * * *

As for merger proxy statements, we believe a summary term sheet should provide a brief outline of the particular matters proposed, the material terms of the proposals, including the parties to the proposed transaction, the consideration to be received by security holders, the board's recommendation on how to vote or their position regarding the transaction, the effect of a vote for and against each matter presented, including the effects of not voting, the procedures for voting and changing or revoking a vote, and the existence of appraisal rights. * * * Of course, we do not attempt to provide an exhaustive list in this release of all the matters or issues that may be material to security holders warranting inclusion in a plain English summary term sheet. * * * [For the plain English presentation in the J.P. Morgan Chase-Bank One S-4, *see Summary of Transaction*, in Documentary Appendix E of *M&A Statutes, Rules, and Documents, supra* Section 1.1.]

3. Harmonization of Cash Mergers and Cash Tender Offers under Item 14 of Schedule 14A

Final M&A Release, Regulation of Takeovers and Security Holder Communications, Amendments to Schedule 14A, Securities Act Release No. 33-6670

(October 22, 1999)

[Item 14 of Schedule 14A Revised to Clarify Requirements and Harmonize Cash Merger and Cash Tender Offer Disclosure] Item 14 of Schedule 14A specifies the information required in proxy and information statements relating to extraordinary transactions. We are revising Item 14 substantially as proposed, [and the] revised item refers filers to the applicable disclosure requirements in Forms S-4 and F-4. This approach should make the item easier to understand, and harmonize the proxy and registration statement disclosure requirements. Since the disclosure and incorporation by reference requirements in Forms S-4 and F-4 are essentially the same as in current Item 14, this streamlined approach will not greatly modify the disclosure required in a merger proxy statement. * * *

In addition, we are adopting several substantive changes regarding the information required for acquirors and targets under Item 14. * * * We continue to believe that in certain circumstances the disclosure requirements in Item 14 may be unnecessarily burdensome and inconsistent with the level of information that would be required if the same transaction was structured as an all-cash, all-share tender offer. Therefore, we are adopting the following proposed revisions:

Item 14 is revised to clarify that financial statement and other information about the acquiror is required in a cash merger only if that information is material to voting security holders' evaluation of the transaction. [Revised Instruction 2(a) to Item 14 of Schedule

14A] Similar to the need for a bidder's financial statements in a cash tender offer, information about the acquiror in a merger is generally not needed when target security holders are receiving cash and the acquiror has demonstrated its financial ability to satisfy the terms of the offer.

In cases where financial statement information for the acquiror would be material to a security holder's voting decision, acquiror information is required for only two years and not three, consistent with the treatment of tender offers. [Revised Item 14(c)(1) to Schedule 14A]

The requirement to provide information about the target in a cash merger is eliminated when the acquiror's security holders are not voting on the transaction. * * *

The changes adopted today do not change the current requirement to provide financial statements of the target and other company information when the acquiror's security holders are voting on the transaction, since those security holders may not know anything about the target. * * *

4. Reduced Financial Statement Requirements for Mergers and Stock Tender Offers

Final M&A Release, Regulation of Takeovers and Security Holder Communications, Reduced Financial Statement Requirements for Mergers and Stock Tender Offers, Securities Act Release No. 33-6670

(October 22, 1999)

[**Reduced Financial Statement Requirements for Mergers and Stock Tender Offers**]* * * We also have examined financial statement requirements in the context of stock mergers and stock tender offers. As we noted in the Proposing Release, financial statements of the target generally are required when registered securities are being offered. The rules currently provide special treatment when the target is not subject to the Commission's reporting requirements, but we believe these requirements can be further relaxed. Currently, the rules require the filing person (the acquiror) to provide financial statements of the non-reporting target going back three years. We noted that providing three years of financial statements prepared in accordance with Regulation S-X for a non-reporting company can be costly and burdensome to prepare. In some cases they may not be available. Therefore, we proposed to reduce the financial statements required for non-reporting targets when the acquiror's security holders are not being asked to vote on the transaction. * * *

Accordingly, we are eliminating the requirement to provide financial statements for the non-reporting target altogether when the acquiror's security holders are not voting on the transaction and the non-reporting target is not significant to the acquiror above the 20% level. [*See* Form S-4, Item 17(b)(7). Determination of the significance of an acquisition to the acquiror is made in accordance with Rule 3-05 of Regulation S-X. * * *] * * *

The current requirement to provide "audited" financial statements for the non-reporting target remains the same. Financial statements for the latest fiscal year must be audited only to the extent practicable. Audited financial statements are not required for years before the most recent fiscal year if the target's financial statements were not previously audited.

We are not changing the current requirement that a resale registration statement include audited financial statements in accordance with Rule 3-05 of Regulation S-X. Also, to the extent that a transaction is significant to the acquiror, audited financial statements would ultimately need to be provided under Item 7 of Form 8-K. Of course, if the acquiror's security holders are voting on the transaction, then the current financial statement requirements apply.

F. Unbundling of Merger Related Proxy Proposals

SEC Manual of Publicly Available Telephone Interpretations Fifth Supplement

(September 2004)

Proxy Rules and Schedule 14A, Rule 14a-4(a)(3). Questions have arisen concerning the application of Rule 14a-4(a)(3) in the context of mergers, acquisitions, and similar transactions. This rule is commonly referred to as the Commission's "unbundling rule." We are providing this guidance to assist companies in determining when charter, bylaw or similar provisions need to be set out separately on the form of proxy in the context of mergers, acquisitions, and similar transactions and to establish a uniform approach by companies in applying Rule 14a-4(a)(3).

Rule 14a-4(a)(3) requires that the form of proxy "identify clearly and impartially each separate matter intended to be acted upon, whether or not related to or conditioned on the approval of other matters." Rule 14a-4(b)(1) further requires that the form of proxy provide separate boxes for shareholders to choose between approval, disapproval or abstention "with respect to each separate matter referred to therein as intended to be acted upon ..." These rules are intended to provide a means for shareholders to communicate their views to the board of directors on each matter to be acted upon.

Applying the Unbundling Rule to Merger and Acquisition Transactions. Merger and acquisition transactions can raise complex issues in the application of Rule 14a-4(a)(3). It is sometimes necessary in merger and acquisition transactions to determine when charter, bylaw or similar provisions that will become applicable as a result of a transaction need to be set out as separate proposals. Unless the company whose shareholders are voting on a merger or acquisition transaction determines that the affected provisions in question are immaterial, those provisions should be set out as separate proposals apart from the merger or acquisition transaction where: the provisions in question were not previously part of the company's charter or bylaws; the provisions in question were not previously part of the charter or bylaws of a public acquiring company; and state law, securities exchange listing standards, or the company's charter or by-laws would require shareholder approval of the proposed changes if they were presented on their own. * * *

§ 13.13 Treatment under the 33 Act of Agreements Pursuant to Which Certain Target Shareholders Agree to Vote Their Shares for a Proposed Merger—Lock-Ups

A. The Aircraft Carrier Release

Notice of Proposed Rulemaking Regarding the Regulation of Securities Offerings, Securities Act Release No. 33-7606A

(December 4, 1998) (the Aircraft Carrier Release)

Lock-up Agreements Under Proposed Rule 159 [not adopted] The use of lock-up agreements in business combinations has become common. [For example, a lock-up of Kirk Kerkorian's shares was utilized in the DaimlerChrysler transaction discussed in Section 13.20.] As part of the negotiations for these combinations, the acquiring party usually requires that management and principal security holders of the company to be acquired commit to vote for the acquisition. These so-called "lock-up" agreements are made when the acquisition agreement is finalized, before any action by the public security holders. These agreements could be considered investment decisions under the Securities Act. If they are, the offers and sales of securities were made to persons who entered into those agreements before the business combination is presented to the non-affiliated security holders for their vote. Under this reasoning, those offers and sales could not be included in the registration statement for the offering to the persons not entering into lock-up agreements. In recognition of the legitimate business reasons underlying the practice, the staff has permitted the registration of offers and sales under certain circumstances where lock-up agreements have been signed. We propose a rule that codifies this position. Our proposed rule would allow registration of those offers and sales when:

(i) The lock-up agreements involve only executive officers, directors, affiliates, founders and their family members, and holders of 5% or more of the voting equity securities of the company being acquired;

(ii) The persons signing the agreements own less than 100% of the voting equity securities of the company being acquired; and

(iii) Votes will be solicited from shareholders of the company being acquired who have not signed the agreements and who would be ineligible to purchase in an offering under Section 4(2) or 4(6) of the Securities Act or Rule 506 of Regulation D. * * *

[This rule has not been adopted.]

B. The Current Issues Outline

SEC Division of Corporation Finance, Current Issues and Rulemaking Projects

(November 14, 2000)

[**Lock-up Agreements**] The use of "lock-up agreements" in business combination transactions is common. What is not common or consistent is the extent to which these agreements may be used to lock up target shareholders beyond key executives and "blocking" shareholders of the target. While the signing of a lock-up agreement may constitute the making of an investment decision, the staff, noting the realities of these transactions, traditionally has not raised issues with respect to these agreements in connection with acquisitions of public companies. However, the staff has raised issues concerning recently filed acquisition registration statements where 100% of the target shares are locked up or the "lock-up" group is expanded to include non-traditional "members" such as middle management.

§ 13.14 Introduction to the Impact of 34 Act Reg M: Restrictions on Trading During a Distribution in Connection with M&A

SEC Staff Legal Bulletin No. 9 (Regulation M)

Introduction. Regulation M was adopted by the Commission on December 10, 1996. * * *

[Before turning to the Qs and As in the Bulletin, the following is an excerpt from adopting Release No 38067, December 20, 1996:]

Regulation M is intended to preclude manipulative conduct by persons with an interest in the outcome of an offering. Regulation M significantly eases regulatory burdens on offering participants by eliminating the trading restrictions for underwriters of actively-traded securities; reducing the scope of coverage for other securities; reducing restrictions on issuer plans; providing a more flexible framework for stabilizing transactions; and deregulating rights offerings. * * *

INTRODUCTION AND SUMMARY OF NEW REGULATION M. A fundamental goal of the federal securities laws is the prevention of manipulation. * * * [T]he Commission has focused on the market activities of persons participating in a securities offering, and determined that securities offerings present special opportunities and incentives for manipulation that require specific regulatory attention. * * *

Regulation M contains six rules covering the following activities during a securities offering: (1) activities by underwriters or other persons who are participating in a distribution (*i.e.*, distribution participants) and their affiliated purchasers; (2) activities by the issuer or selling security holder and their affiliated purchasers; (3) NASDAQ passive market making; (4) stabilization [*e.g.*, purchases during a distribution] transactions to cover syndicate short positions, and penalty bids; and (5) short selling in advance of a public offering. A separate rule under Regulation M, Rule 100, contains definitional provisions. * * *

The provisions of Regulation M that are analogous to Rule 10b-6 are contained in Rules 101 and 102, which cover distribution participants, and issuers and selling security holders, respectively. Rules 101 and 102 apply only during a "restricted period" that commences one or five business days before the day of the pricing of the offered security and continues until the distribution is over. The restricted periods are based on the trading volume value of the offered security and the public float value of the issuer, rather than the price per share and public float criteria used in Rule 10b-6, and generally are of a shorter duration than the cooling-off periods under Rule 10b-6. Furthermore, the restricted periods of Regulation M focus on the time of pricing. * * *

Rule 102 covers issuers, selling security holders, and related persons. The rule allows issuers and selling security holders to engage in market activities prior to the applicable restricted period. It also gives issuers greater flexibility in conducting their dividend reinvestment and stock purchase plans and odd-lot repurchase programs. * * *

Rule 104, which replaces Rule 10b-7, regulates stabilizing and other activities related to a distribution. The rule provides a more flexible framework for stabilizing transactions than Rule 10b-7. Rule 104 allows underwriters to initiate and change stabilizing bids based on the current price in the principal market (whether U.S. or foreign), as long as the bid does not exceed the offering price. Also, by providing for greater disclosure and recordkeeping of transactions that can influence market prices immediately following an offering, Rule 104 addresses the fact that underwriters now engage in substantial syndicate-related market activity, and enforce penalty bids in order to reduce volatility in the market for the offered security.

Rule 105 recodifies Rule 10b-21 governing short selling in connection with a public offering. * * *

The following questions and answers regarding Regulation M have been compiled by the staff of the Division of Market Regulation to assist in the understanding and application of this regulation. * * *

Questions and Answers * * *

Rule 101 * * * **Mergers/Exchange Offers**

Q: Have restrictions on purchases of target company securities by an acquiror during an exchange offer been eliminated?

A: Regulation M generally does not apply to purchases of the target security by an acquiror or target during a merger or exchange offer. Purchases of the target stock are restricted, however, where the acquiror's securities have a feature that ties its value directly to the price of the target securities. We also note that Rule 14e-5 under the Exchange Act generally will prohibit purchases of the target security by the bidder during an exchange offer. [*See* Chapter 20] * * *

Rule 102 * * * **Concurrent Distributions**

Q: An issuer conducts different but concurrent distributions of the same securities, such as an offering of its common stock for cash while it is offering its common stock to security holders of another company in connection with a merger or exchange offer. Is the issuer (or distribution participant) permitted to solicit investors to purchase the common stock in the cash distribution without violating Rule 102 (or Rule 101 in the case of a distribution participant) as it applied to the merger or exchange offer distribution, and vice versa, or would selling activity in one distribution be deemed an impermissible inducement to purchase with regard to the other distribution?

A: Paragraph (b)(5) of Rule 102 provides an exception for "offers to sell or the solicitation of offers to buy the securities being distributed." Similarly, Rule 101(b)(9) allows distribution participants and their affiliated purchasers to conduct bona fide selling activities in connection with the securities being distributed. However, neither Rule 101(b)(9) nor Rule 102(b)(5) explicitly allows any inducements to purchase otherwise than for offers to sell the securities in a specific distribution. Accordingly, these provisions do not extend to inducements to purchase in one distribution while the issuer or distribution participant is engaged in another distribution of the same security or a reference security. We do not believe, however, that solicitation activity qualifying for the Rule 101(b)(9) and Rule 102(b)(5) exceptions necessarily creates an impermissible inducement to purchase in a concurrent distribution. Therefore, absent additional factors, bona fide offers to sell or the solicitation of offers to buy the securities being distributed in one distribution would not be impermissible inducements with respect to a concurrent distribution.

For example, Company A conducts an offering of A common stock for cash. At the same time, Company A conducts an exchange offer in which it distributes A common stock and purchases Company B's common stock. Assuming the cash offering and exchange offer are distributions of A's common stock, Company A may solicit offers to purchase the common stock in the cash offering at same time it solicits offers to exchange securities in the exchange offer, and vice versa.

However, a distribution may rise to the level of an impermissible inducement to purchase when a distribution participant engages in sales efforts that go beyond bona fide offers to sell or the solicitation of offers to buy the securities in distribution. * * *

§ 13.15 Introduction to 34 Act Rule 10b-18: Restrictions on Repurchases in Connection with M&A

Purchases of Certain Equity Securities by the Issuer and Others under Rule 10b-18 Securities Act Release No. 8335

(November 10, 2003)

Summary: We are adopting amendments to Rule 10b-18 under the Securities Exchange Act of 1934 (Exchange Act), which provides issuers with a "safe harbor" from liability for manipulation when they repurchase their common stock in the market in accordance with the Rule's manner, timing, price, and volume conditions. The amendments are intended to simplify and update the safe harbor provisions in light of market developments since the Rule's adoption. To enhance the transparency of issuer repurchases, we also are adopting amendments to a number of regulations and forms to require disclosure of all issuer repurchases (open market and private transactions), regardless of whether the repurchases are effected in accordance with the safe harbor rule. * * *

Introduction. On December 10, 2002, we proposed amendments to Rule 10b-18, Regulations S-K and S-B, Forms 10-Q, 10-QSB, 10-K, 10-KSB, 20-F, and N-CSR, which would [*inter alia*] * * * clarify the scope of the exclusion for purchases effected "pursuant to a merger, acquisition, or similar transaction involving a recapitalization." * * *

Overview of Current Rule 10b-18. Rule 10b-18 as a "Safe Harbor." In 1982, the Commission adopted Rule 10b-18 which provides that an issuer will not be deemed to have violated Sections 9(a)(2) and 10(b) of the Exchange Act, and Rule 10b-5 under the Exchange Act, solely by reason of the manner, timing, price, or volume of its repurchases, if the issuer repurchases its common stock in the market in accordance with the safe harbor conditions. Rule 10b-18's safe harbor conditions are designed to minimize the market impact of the issuer's repurchases, thereby allowing the market to establish a security's price based on independent market forces without undue influence by the issuer.

Although the safe harbor conditions are intended to offer issuers guidance when repurchasing their securities in the open market, Rule 10b-18 is not the exclusive means of making non-manipulative issuer repurchases. As the Rule states, there is no presumption that bids or purchases outside of the safe harbor violate Sections 9(a)(2) or 10(b) of the Exchange Act, or Rule 10b-5 under the Exchange Act. Given the widely varying characteristics in the market for the stock of different issuers, it is possible for issuer repurchases to be made outside of the safe harbor conditions and not be manipulative. * * *

Amendments to Rule 10b-18. Amendments Concerning the Scope of the Safe Harbor. * * *

Availability of Rule 10b-18 once a Merger, Acquisition, or Similar Transactions Involving a Recapitalization is Announced. We proposed to amend the definition of "Rule 10b-18 purchase" to clarify that the current exception for purchases effected "pursuant to a merger, acquisition, or similar transaction involving a recapitalization" includes purchases effected during the period from the time of public announcement of the merger, acquisition, or similar transaction involving a recapitalization, until the completion of such transaction. Once a merger or acquisition is announced, an issuer has considerable incentive to support or raise the market price of its stock in order to facilitate the merger or acquisition. For example, in a recent contested takeover, several news articles suggested that the banks repurchased their respective securities in order to boost their stock price to enhance the value of their competing merger proposals.

Some of the commenters, however, argued that the proposed amendment would drastically expand the scope of the current exclusion and that Regulation M's restricted periods and other federal and state laws adequately address any manipulative concerns. These commenters also argued that, because regulatory approvals for mergers may take several months, the proposed merger exclusion would keep issuers out of the market far longer than necessary. Other commenters argued that the proposed amendment should not apply to all cash mergers; after the shareholder vote in a merger; after the exchange ratio is fixed; or after the valuation period expires.

After considering the comments, and in view of the fact that we are limiting the amount that can be repurchased within the safe harbor * * *, we have determined that it is not necessary to exclude from the safe harbor all issuer repurchase activity following the announcement of a merger, acquisition, or similar transaction involving a recapitalization. Instead, as adopted in 10b-18(a)(13)(iv), the merger exclusion applies to purchases that are effected during the period from the time of public announcement of a merger, acquisition, or similar transaction involving a recapitalization, until the earlier of the completion of such transaction or the completion of the vote by target shareholders (including during any period where the market price of a security will be a factor in determining the consideration to be paid pursuant to a merger, acquisition, or similar transaction), with the following exceptions.

The exclusion does not extend to transactions in which the consideration is solely cash and there is no valuation period (*i.e.,* where the issuer has little or no incentive to manipulate the market price of its securities). We also recognize that some issuers may desire to carry out ordinary repurchases (*i.e.*, purchases not made in connection with or relating to the merger or other covered transaction) during what could be an extended period of time until completion of the transaction. Thus, we are modifying the proposed merger exclusion to allow ordinary Rule 10b-18 purchases to be effected after the announcement of a merger or covered transaction (subject to Regulation M's restricted period and any other applicable restrictions) so long as the total amount of the issuer's Rule 10b-18 purchases effected on any single day does not exceed [a specified limit]. * * *

Note

The Preliminary Notes to the rule explain:

> 1. Section 240.10b-18 provides an issuer (and its affiliated purchasers) with a "safe harbor" from liability for manipulation under sections 9(a)(2) of the Act and § 240.10b-5 under the Act *solely* by reason of the manner, timing, price, and volume of their repurchases when they repurchase the issuer's common stock in the market in accordance with the section's manner [only one broker can be

used], timing [limits are placed on the timing of orders], price [the price can not exceed, *e.g.*, the highest independent bid], and volume [daily purchases can not exceed 25% of the average daily trading volume (ADTV)] conditions. As a safe harbor, compliance with § 240.10b-18 is voluntary. To come within the safe harbor, however, an issuer's repurchases must satisfy (on a daily basis) each of the section's four conditions. Failure to meet any one of the four conditions will remove all of the issuer's repurchases from the safe harbor for that day. The safe harbor, moreover, is not available for repurchases that, although made in technical compliance with the section, are part of a plan or scheme to evade the federal securities laws.

2. Regardless of whether the repurchases are effected in accordance with § 240.10b-18, reporting issuers must report their repurchasing activity as required by Item 703 of Regulations S-K * * *.

§ 13.16 Implied Right of Action under 34 Act Section 14(a)

J.I. Case Company v. Borak

United States Supreme Court, 1964 84 S. Ct. 1555

Mr. Justice Clark:

This is a civil action brought by respondent, a stockholder of petitioner J. I. Case Company, charging deprivation of the pre-emptive rights of respondent and other shareholders by reason by a merger between Case and the American Tractor Corporation. It is alleged that the merger was effected through the circulation of a false and misleading proxy statement by those proposing the merger. * * *

The claims pertinent to the asserted violation of the Securities Exchange Act were predicated on diversity jurisdiction as well as on § 27 of the Act. They alleged: that petitioners, or their predecessors, solicited or permitted their names to be used in the solicitation of proxies of Case stockholders for use at a special stockholders' meeting at which the proposed merger with ATC was to be voted upon; that the proxy solicitation material so circulated was false and misleading in violation of § 14(a) of the Act and Rule 14a-9 which the Commission had promulgated thereunder; that the merger was approved at the meeting by a small margin of votes and was thereafter consummated; that the merger would not have been approved but for the false and misleading statements in the proxy solicitation material; and that Case stockholders were damaged thereby. The respondent sought judgment holding the merger void and damages for himself and all other stockholders similarly situated, as well as such further relief "as equity shall require." * * *

It appears clear that private parties have a right under § 27 to bring suit for violation of § 14(a) of the Act. Indeed, this section specifically grants the appropriate District Courts jurisdiction over "all suits in equity and actions at law brought to enforce any liability or duty created" under the Act. The petitioners make no concessions, however, emphasizing that Congress made no specific reference to a private right of action in § 14(a) * * *.

Private enforcement of the proxy rules provides a necessary supplement to Commission action. * * * The Commission advises that it examines over 2,000 proxy statements annually and each of them must necessarily be expedited. Time does not permit an independent examination of the facts set out in the proxy material and this results in the Commission's acceptance of the representations contained therein at their face value, unless contrary to other material on file with it. Indeed, on the allegations of respondent's complaint, the proxy material failed to disclose alleged unlawful market manipulation of the stock of ATC, and this unlawful manipulation would not have been apparent to the Commission until after the merger.

We, therefore, believe that under the circumstances here it is the duty of the courts to be alert to provide such remedies as are necessary to make effective the congressional purpose. * * *

§ 13.17 Causation under Section 14(a)

A. The Supreme Court's Rule

Mills v. Electric Auto-Lite Company

United States Supreme Court, 1970 90 S.Ct. 616

Mr. Justice HARLAN:

This case requires us to consider a basic aspect of the implied private right of action for violation of § 14(a) of the Securities Exchange Act of 1934, recognized by this Court, in *J.I. Case Co. v. Borak*, [Section 13.16]. As in *Borak* the asserted wrong is that a corporate merger was accomplished through the use of a proxy statement that was materially false or misleading. The question with which we deal is what causal relationship must be shown between such a statement and the merger to establish a cause of action based on the violation of the Act. * * *

In the present case there has been a hearing specifically directed to the causation problem. The question before the Court is whether the facts found on the basis of that hearing are sufficient in law to establish petitioners' cause of action, and we conclude that they are.

Where the misstatement or omission in a proxy statement has been shown to be "material," as it was found to be here, that determination itself indubitably embodies a conclusion that the defect was of such a character that it might have been considered important by a reasonable shareholder who was in the process of deciding how to vote. This requirement that the defect have a significant *propensity* to affect the voting process is found in the express terms of Rule 14a-9, and it adequately serves the purpose of ensuring that a cause of action cannot be established by proof of a defect so trivial, or so unrelated to the transaction for which approval is sought, that correction of the defect or imposition of liability would not further the interests protected by § 14(a). [For elaboration of the Supreme Court's materiality standard, *see TCS Industries, Inc. v. Northway,* Section 4.5.A]

There is no need to supplement this requirement, as did the Court of Appeals with a requirement of proof of whether the defect actually had a decisive effect on the voting. Where there has been a finding of materiality, a shareholder has made a sufficient showing of causal relationship between the violation and the injury for which he seeks redress if, as here he proves that the proxy solicitation itself, rather than the particular defect in the solicitation materials was an essential link in the accomplishment of the transaction. This objective test will avoid the impracticalities of determining how many votes were affected, and by resolving doubts in favor of those the statute is designed to protect, will effectuate the congressional policy of ensuring that the shareholders are able to make an informed choice when they are consulted on corporate transactions. * * *

B. The Supreme Court's Materiality Standard

See TSC Industries, Inc. v. Northway, Inc., Section 4.5.A.

C. The Supreme Court's Interpretation of the Essential Link Requirement

Virginia Bankshares, Inc. v. Sandberg

United States Supreme Court, 1991 111 S.Ct 2749

Justice Souter:

Section 14(a) of the Securities Exchange Act of 1934, authorizes the Securities and Exchange Commission (SEC) to adopt rules for the solicitation of proxies, and prohibits their violation. In *J.I. Case Co. v. Borak*, [Section 13.16], we first recognized an implied private right of action for the breach of § 14(a) as implemented by SEC Rule 14a-9, which prohibits the solicitation of proxies by means of materially false or misleading statements.

[**Issue**] The question before us [is] whether * * * causation of damages compensable under § 14(a) can be shown by a member of a class of minority shareholders whose votes are not required by law or corporate bylaw to authorize the corporate action subject to the proxy solicitation. * * *

[**Facts**] [First American Bankshares, Inc. (FABI), a bank holding company, owned all of the stock of Virginia Bankshares, Inc. (VBI). VBI owned 85% of the stock of First American Bank of Virginia (Bank), the target corporation. The 15% balance of Bank's shares was held by some 2,000 minority shareholders. VBI acquired Bank in a freeze-out merger.] * * *

FABI hired the investment banking firm of Keefe, Bruyette & Woods (KBW) to give an opinion on the appropriate price for shares of the minority holders, who would lose their interests in the Bank as a result of the merger. * * * KBW gave the Bank's executive committee an opinion that $42 a share would be a fair price for the minority stock. The executive committee approved the merger proposal at that price, and the full board followed suit.

Although Virginia law [did not require a shareholder vote on the transaction, the directors of Bank] nevertheless solicited proxies for voting on the proposal at the annual meeting set for April 21, 1987.[19] In their solicitation, the directors urged the proposal's adoption and stated they had approved the plan because of its opportunity for the minority shareholders to achieve a "high" value, which they elsewhere described as a "fair" price, for their stock.

Although most minority shareholders gave the proxies requested, respondent Sandberg did not, and after approval of the merger she sought damages in the United States District Court for the Eastern District of Virginia from VBI, FABI, and the directors of the Bank. She pleaded two counts, one for soliciting proxies in violation of § 14(a) and Rule 14a-9, and the other for breaching fiduciary duties owed to the minority shareholders under state law. Under the first count, Sandberg alleged, among other things, that the directors had not believed that the price offered was high or that the terms of the merger were fair, but had recommended the merger only because they believed they had no alternative if they wished to remain on the board. At trial, Sandberg invoked language from this Court's opinion in *Mills v. Electric Auto-Lite Co.*, [Section 13.17.A], to obtain an instruction that the jury could find for her without a showing of her own reliance on the alleged misstatements, so long as they were material and the proxy solicitation was an "essential link" in the merger process.

---

19. Had the directors chosen to issue a statement instead of a proxy solicitation, they would have been subject to an SEC antifraud provision analogous to Rule 14a-9. See 17 CFR § 240.14c-6 (1990).

[**Lower Courts**] The jury's verdicts were for Sandberg on both counts, after finding violations of Rule 14a-9 by all defendants and a breach of fiduciary duties by the Bank's directors. The jury awarded Sandberg $18 a share, having found that she would have received $60 if her stock had been valued adequately. * * *

On appeal, the United States Court of Appeals for the Fourth Circuit affirmed the judgments, holding that certain statements in the proxy solicitation were materially misleading for purposes of the Rule, and that respondents could maintain their action even though their votes had not been needed to effectuate the merger. We granted certiorari because of the importance of the issues presented. * * *

[**Issue**] The second issue before us, left open in *Mills v. Electric Auto-Lite Co.*, is whether causation of damages compensable through the implied private right of action under § 14(a) can be demonstrated by a member of a class of minority shareholders whose votes are not required by law or corporate bylaw to authorize the transaction giving rise to the claim. * * *

[**Analysis**] The *Mills* Court avoided [an] evidentiary morass that would have followed from requiring individualized proof that enough minority shareholders had relied upon the misstatements to swing the vote. Instead, it held that causation of damages by a material proxy misstatement could be established by showing that minority proxies necessary and sufficient to authorize the corporate acts had been given in accordance with the tenor of the solicitation, and the Court described such a causal relationship by calling the proxy solicitation an "essential link in the accomplishment of the transaction." In the case before it, the Court found the solicitation essential, as contrasted with one addressed to a class of minority shareholders without votes required by law or by law to authorize the action proposed, and left it for another day to decide whether such a minority shareholder could demonstrate causation.

[**Plaintiff's First Theory of an Essential Link**] In this case, respondents address *Mills*' open question by proffering two theories that the proxy solicitation addressed to them was an "essential link" under the *Mills* causation test. They argue, first, that a link existed and was essential simply because VBI and FABI would have been unwilling to proceed with the merger without the approval manifested by the minority shareholders' proxies, which would not have been obtained without the solicitation's express misstatements and misleading omissions. On this reasoning, the causal connection would depend on a desire to avoid bad shareholder or public relations, and the essential character of the causal link would stem not from the enforceable terms of the parties' corporate relationship, but from one party's apprehension of the ill will of the other.

[**Plaintiff's Second Theory of an Essential Link**] In the alternative, respondents argue that the proxy statement was an essential link between the directors' proposal and the merger because it was the means to satisfy a state statutory requirement of minority shareholder approval, as a condition for saving the merger from voidability resulting from a conflict of interest on the part of one of the Bank's directors, Jack Beddow, who voted in favor of the merger while also serving as a director of FABI. Under the terms of Va. Code Ann. § 13.1–691(A) (1989), minority approval after disclosure of the material facts about the transaction and the director's interest was one of three avenues to insulate the merger from later attack for conflict, the two others being ratification by the Bank's directors after like disclosure and proof that the merger was fair to the corporation. On this theory, causation would depend on the use of the proxy statement for the purpose of obtaining votes sufficient to bar a minority shareholder from commencing proceedings to declare the merger void.

[**Rejection of Plaintiff's Theories of an Essential Link**] Although respondents have proffered each of these theories as establishing a chain of causal connection in which the proxy statement is claimed to have been an "essential link," neither theory presents the proxy solicitation as essential in the sense of *Mills'* causal sequence, in which the solicitation links a directors' proposal with the votes legally required to authorize the action proposed. As a consequence, each theory would, if adopted, extend the scope of *Borak* actions beyond the ambit of *Mills* and expand the class of plaintiffs entitled to bring *Borak* actions to include shareholders whose initial authorization of the transaction prompting the proxy solicitation is unnecessary. * * *

This case does not * * * require us to decide whether § 14(a) provides a cause of action for lost state remedies, since there is no indication in the law or facts before us that the proxy solicitation resulted in any such loss. The contrary appears to be the case. Assuming the soundness of respondents' characterization of the proxy statement as materially misleading, the very terms of the Virginia statute indicate that a favorable minority vote induced by the solicitation would not suffice to render the merger invulnerable to later attack on the ground of the conflict. The statute bars a shareholder from seeking to avoid a transaction tainted by a director's conflict if, *inter alia*, the minority shareholders ratified the transaction following disclosure of the material facts of the transaction and the conflict. * * *

Questions

Does *Virginia Bankshares* mean that a controlling parent corporation has no liability under the federal securities laws even though, with clear intent, it makes a gross misstatement or omission of a material fact in a proxy statement in a freezeout merger for which the votes of the minority shareholders are not needed? What if the misstatement or a omission is in an information statement? [*See* Rule 14c-6] Even if a proxy statement is not used in the transaction, Section 14(c) requires that an information statement be distributed to the minority shareholders. Is the information statement, therefore, an "essential link" in the consummation of the merger?

§ 13.18 Generally Only Negligence Required under Section 14(a)

Blau v. William B. Harrison, Jr.

United States District Court, Northern District of Illinois, 2006 U.S. Dist. LEXIS 19795

William J. Hibbler:

* * * Plaintiffs allege that Defendants negligently failed to disclose material terms of the negotiation involving the merger between Bank One Corporation ("Bank One") and J.P. Morgan Chase & Co. ("J.P. Morgan") to J.P. Morgan shareholders in its proxy statement. Specifically, Plaintiffs contend that Defendants [including Harrison, CEO of J.P. Morgan Chase] failed to disclose Bank One's CEO's [Dimon's] offer to "do the deal for no premium if he could become chief executive immediately." [The facts are the same as those set out in the discussion of the Delaware due care issue in this matter. *See* Section 3.10.F.2] According to Plaintiffs, Defendants' actions amounted to negligence, and resulted in J.P. Morgan Shareholders approval of a 14 percent premium in favor of Bank One shares.

Defendants seek to dismiss Blau's Amended Class Action Complaint ("Complaint") for [*inter alia*] failure to state a claim upon which relief can be granted pursuant to Federal Rule of Civil Procedure 12(b)(6), for failure to plead fraud with particularity pursuant to Federal Rule of Civil Procedure 9(b), and for failure to meet the pleading standards set forth in the Private Securities Litigation Reform Act of 1995. * * *

ANALYSIS. The two-count Complaint in this case is premised on the alleged negligence of J.P. Morgan with regard to an alleged omission of a material fact in its proxy statement. In count one, Plaintiffs allege that Defendants violated Section 14(a) of the Securities and Exchange Act of 1934 ("the Exchange Act") and Rule 14a-9 promulgated by the SEC. Count two [is not addressed here.]

Count I—Section 14(a), Pleading. In order to state a claim under Section 14(a), Plaintiffs must allege that (1) a proxy statement contained a material misrepresentation or omission, which (2) caused plaintiffs injury, and (3) that the proxy solicitation itself, rather than the particular defect in the solicitation materials, was "an essential link" in the accomplishment of the transaction. *Mills v. Elec. Auto-Lite Co.*, [Section 13.17.A]. "The purpose of [Section] 14(a) is to prevent management or others from obtaining authorization for corporate action by means of deceptive or inadequate disclosure in proxy solicitations." *J. I. Case Co. v. Borak*, [Section 13.16]. Section 14(a) and Rule 14a-9 regulate the proxy solicitation process and "prohibit[] the solicitation of proxies by means of materially false or misleading statements." *Virginia Bankshares, Inc. v. Sandberg*, [13.17.C].

[**Does the Higher Standard for Pleading Fraud Apply?**] In enacting the Private Securities Litigation Reform Act, Congress raised the pleading standards for claims alleging private securities fraud, "to a very specific version of fact pleading—one that exceeds even the particularity requirements of Federal Rule of Civil Procedure 9(b). * * *

Plaintiffs respond that its Section 14(a) claims are sufficiently pled pursuant to Federal Rule of Civil Procedure 8(a). Plaintiffs argue that because the Complaint purports that Defendants acted with negligence, not fraud, the heightened pleading requirements of the PSLRA are not implicated. * * * Thus, Plaintiff contends that its Complaint is sufficiently pled in accordance with Fed. R. Civ. Pro. 8(a) as the Complaint neither alleges intentional conduct, nor does the Complaint "sound in fraud." * * *

Viewing, as the Court must, all the facts alleged in the Complaint, as well as any reasonable inferences drawn from those facts, in the light most favorable to Plaintiff. Plaintiffs' Complaint sets forth a Section 14(a) claim alleging that Defendants acted negligently; thus, they need not plead fraud at all, let alone fraud with particularity. Simply, Plaintiffs' Section 14(a) allegations are not required to meet the PSLRA particularity requirements because these claims are based on averments of negligence. * * *

Accordingly, the Court finds that Blau's Complaint sufficiently pled violations of Section 14(a).

Materiality. An omitted fact is material "if there is a substantial likelihood that a reasonable shareholder would consider it important in deciding how to vote." *TSC Indus., Inc.* [Section 4.5.A] * * *

The crux of Plaintiffs' Complaint is Defendants negligently failed to disclose a material fact during the proxy solicitation regarding Harrison's rejection of an offer to conduct the merger with no premium. According to the Complaint, after Harrison rejected this offer, the negotiations resulted in Bank One shareholders receiving a 14% premium for their stock and which ultimately cost J.P. Morgan shareholders over 7 billion dollars in unnecessary merger compensation. Defendants argue that the proxy statement was not required to disclose alleged negotiating positions. * * *

On a motion to dismiss, the Court must assume the truth of the facts asserted by Plaintiffs and all reasonable inferences in favor of the Plaintiff. The Proxy Statement indicated that the offer was "fair, from a financial point of view." If, as Plaintiffs allege, Dimon offered to consummate the transaction for no premium and the only reason Harrison rejected the offer was to retain a position as CEO of the merged company, this may be a fact a "reasonable shareholder would consider * * * important." *TSC Indus.*, [Section 4.5.A]. While it is not necessary to disclose all factors in a negotiation, failure to offer shareholders a more profitable exchange may have been important to shareholders in considering whether or not to approve the merger. For the purposes of the instant motion to dismiss, the Court concludes that the omission regarding an alleged "no premium" stock exchange is material.

Accordingly, Defendants' motion to dismiss Plaintiffs' Section 14(a) claim against them in Count I of the Complaint is DENIED. * * *

Note

For the treatment of the issues in this case under Delaware law, *see* Section 3.15.H.2.

§ 13.19 In Certain Cases Scienter May Be Required under Section 14(a)

In *Adams v. Standard Knitting*, 623 F.2d 422, (6th Cir. 1976), the Sixth Circuit held that an outside accountant is subject to a higher standard than negligence in a Section 14(a) action. The court reasoned:

> Federal courts created the private right of action under section 14, and they have a special responsibility to consider the consequences of their rulings and to mold liability fairly to reflect the circumstances of the parties. Although we are not called on in this case to decide the standard of liability of the corporate issuer of proxy material, we are influenced by the fact that the accountant here, unlike the corporate issuer, does not directly benefit from the proxy vote and is not in privity with the stockholder. * * * In contrast to section 12[a](2) of the 1933 Act which imposes liability for negligent misrepresentation in a prospectus, Rule 14a-9 does not require privity. In contrast to section 11 of the 1933 Act which imposes liability for negligent misrepresentation in registration statements, Rule 14a-9 does not require proof of actual investor reliance on the misrepresentation. Rule 14a-9, like 10b-5, substitutes the less exacting standard of materiality for reliance, *TSC Ind., Inc. v. Northway, Inc.*, [Section 4.5.A], and in the instant case there was no proof of investor reliance on the notes to the financial statements which erroneously described the restriction on payment of dividends. We can see no reason for a different standard of liability for accountants under the proxy provisions than under 10(b). * * *

In *Herskowitz v. Nutri/System, Inc.*, 857 F.2d 179 (3rd Cir. 1989), *cert. denied*, 109 S.Ct. 1315 (1989), the Third Circuit held that a negligence standard applies under Rule 14a-9 to both insiders and outsiders.

§ 13.20 Rule 10b-5 and Section 14(a) Action for Alleged Misrepresentation Regarding Merger of Equals—*DaimlerChrysler*

Tracinda Corp. v. DaimlerChrysler Ag.

United States District Court, District of Delaware, 2005 CCH FSLR ¶ 93,236

FARNAN, District Judge:

[Chrysler corporation merged with Daimler-Benz, a German corporation, to form DaimlerChrysler in what purported to be a "merger of equals."] This action was brought by Plaintiff, Tracinda Corporation, ("Tracinda") [the largest Chrysler shareholder] against Defendants, DaimlerChrysler AG, Daimler-Benz AG ("Daimler-Benz" or "Daimler"), Jürgen Schrempp [the CEO of Daimler-Benz] and Manfred Gentz (collectively, "Defendants") alleging violations of securities laws, common law fraud and conspiracy in connection with the November 1998 merger between Chrysler Corporation ("Chrysler") and Daimler-Benz AG ("Daimler-Benz"). * * *

FINDINGS OF FACT * * *

With respect to the term "merger of equals," the Proxy/Prospectus uses the term at least 13 times, but it is not expressly defined. The term "merger of equals" is first used as a broad description of the characteristics of the combination of the various constituencies of Daimler-Benz and Chrysler. This use of the term "merger of equals" is exemplified in Eaton's [the CEO of Chrysler] cover letter, which refers to "two companies of equal financial strength under joint leadership of both management groups with its common equity about evenly split between the two shareholder groups." The term "merger of equals" is next used to refer to the specific governance structure for DaimlerChrysler following the Merger. When used in this manner, the term "merger of equals" refers to that which is provided for in the BCA [the Business Combination Agreement]. * * *

The term "merger of equals" is also used in the context of the CSFB [Chrysler's investment banker] fairness opinion. In this regard, the term is used not only to refer to the Transactions contemplated by the BCA, but also to refer to "a strategic business combination not involving a sale of control" which includes precedent "merger of equals" transactions some of which involved equal representation from the constituent companies in the combined company's post-merger governance, and some of which did not. * * *

After reviewing the draft Proxy/Prospectus, the SEC sought clarification of the meaning of the term "merger of equals." In response, outside counsel for Chrysler and Daimler-Benz referred the SEC to the second paragraph in Eaton's cover letter to the Chrysler shareholders. * * *

Press Reports of the Changes [after the Merger]. * * * As the Management Board and other changes at DaimlerChrysler were made, they were widely reported in the press, along with speculation that the Merger was not a merger of equals. To address the press speculation, DaimlerChrysler hired the public relations firm of Bell Pottinger, and Eaton and Schrempp publicly maintained that these changes did not undermine the merger of equals.

Schrempp's *Financial Times* and *Barron's Magazine* Interviews. Before Holden's departure in November 2000, Schrempp agreed to an interview with the *London Financial Times* ("*Financial Times*"). On October 30, 2000, portions of that interview were published in an article in the *Financial Times* (the "October 30th Article"). In pertinent part, the October 30th Article read:

> In a wide-ranging interview ahead of this week's two-day meeting [of the DaimlerChrysler Management Board], he [Mr. Schrempp] delivered a passionate defense of both the merger and his ambition to create a global car maker.
>
> In doing so, however, he admitted that Chrysler had been relegated to a stand-alone division. Far from being a "merger of equals," as originally conceived, the deal has emerged as just one deal among several from the "executive war-room" of Daimler's Stuttgart headquarters.
>
> Now that most of Chrysler's old management board has resigned or retired, Mr. Schrempp sees no reason to maintain the fiction. "Me being a chess player, I don't normally talk about the second or third move. The structure we have now with Chrysler (as a standalone division) was always the structure I wanted," he says. "We had to go a roundabout way but it had to be done for psychological reasons. If I had gone and said Chrysler would be a division, everybody on their side would have said: "There is no way we'll do a deal."
>
> But it's precisely what I wanted to do. From the start structure, we have moved to what we have today.
>
> What DaimlerChrysler has today is a US division where vehicle design, procurement, production and marketing are being overhauled. Mr. Schrempp maintains this was always the plan following the initial post-merger integration, which generated about $1.4 bn (Pounds 970M) in savings.

Schrempp was also interviewed for an article in *Barron's Magazine* ("*Barron's*") which was published on November 4, 2000. The *Barron's* article quotes Schrempp as stating: "We said in spirit it was a merger of equals, but in our minds we knew how we wanted to structure the company, and today I have it. I have Daimler, and I have divisions." At trial, Schrempp did not deny any of the statements he made in the interviews, but contended that the interviewers misinterpreted his remarks. * * *

Kerkorian [the owner of Tracinda], Eaton and others testified that Schrempp's remarks to the press were upsetting. However, ten former Chrysler directors reaffirmed that they would still vote in favor of the Merger, knowing what they know today, including what the *Financial Times* reported. Indeed, Eaton testified that without the Merger, there is a "high probability that Chrysler would be in bankruptcy today...."

CONCLUSIONS OF LAW

Applicable Legal Standards. *Claims Under Section 10(b) and Rule 10b-5 of the Exchange Act.* Section 10(b) of the Exchange Act prohibits the use "in connection with the purchase or sale of any security [of] any manipulative or deceptive device or contrivance in contravention of such rules and regulations as the Commission may prescribe." Rule 10b-5 was promulgated in connection with Section 10(b) and "provides the framework for a private cause of action for violations involving false statements or omissions of material fact."

Section 10(b) claims are similar to common law fraud claims. To establish a violation of Section 10(b), the plaintiff must prove by a preponderance of the evidence that the defendant made (1) a misstatement or omission; (2) of a material fact, (3) with scienter; (4) in connection with the purchase or sale of a security; (5) upon which the plaintiff reasonably relied; and (6) that reliance was the proximate cause of plaintiff's injury.

Claims Under Section 14(a) and Rule 14a-9 of the Exchange Act. Rule 14a-9 prohibits the solicitation of a shareholder's vote by means of a proxy statement that "is false or misleading with respect to any material fact, or which omits to state any material fact necessary in order to make the statements therein not false or misleading. . . ." To establish a violation of Section 14(a) and Rule 14a-9, the plaintiff must prove by a preponderance of the evidence that (1) that the defendant made a material misrepresentation or omission in a proxy statement; (2) which caused the plaintiff injury and (3) the proxy solicitation was an essential link in effecting the proposed corporate action. * * *

Whether Tracinda Can Assert a Section 14(a) Claim Against Defendants. Defendants also contend, as a threshold matter, that Tracinda cannot assert a Section 14(a) claim against them as a matter of law, because Defendants did not issue the Proxy Statement. * * *

Whether Defendants Jointly Issued The Proxy/Prospectus And/Or Permitted Their Names To Be Used In Connection With The Chrysler Proxy Solicitation. * * * Courts interpreting [Section 14(a)] have recognized that a defendant who permits the use of his name in a manner substantially connected to the proxy solicitation may be held liable under Section 14(a) for misstatements and omissions contained in the proxy materials. * * *

Reviewing the documents filed in this case in light of the applicable law, the Court concludes that Defendants permitted the use of their names in a manner substantially connected to the Chrysler proxy solicitation such that Defendants are properly subject to liability under Section 14(a). * * *

Whether Tracinda Has Established by a Preponderance of the Evidence Its Claims for Common Law Fraud and Violations of Sections 10b and 14(a) of the Exchange Act And Rules 10b-5 and 14a-9 Promulgated Thereunder. * * * Considering the totality of the circumstances, in light of the applicable law and the evidence adduced at trial, the Court concludes that Tracinda was not fraudulently induced to enter in to the Stockholder Agreement, did not rely on any oral representations allegedly made by Eaton, and that, even if Tracinda relied on such oral representations, its reliance was unreasonable under the circumstances. * * *

Whether Tracinda Has Proven Actionable Written Misrepresentations in the Stockholder Agreement, the BCA, or the Proxy Prospectus. * * *

Tracinda contends that Defendants made five material misrepresentations based on the contents of the BCA, Eaton's letter and the Proxy/Prospectus. Specifically, Tracinda contends that (1) the transaction was represented to be a "merger of equals," but Defendants never intended the transaction to be equal; (2) the transaction was represented to entail joint management and control, but Defendants never intended to share management and control. * * *

The Merger of Equals and Joint Management and Control Representations. * * *

Reviewing the term "merger of equals" as it is used in these documents, the Court concludes that Tracinda has not established a misrepresentation based on the use of the term "merger of equals." Although the BCA and the Proxy/Prospectus set forth proposals concerning the numbers of individuals on the Management Board and the Supervisory Board from each side of the transaction, those documents do not require the proposed compositions to last for any specific period of time, reiterate that the proposed compositions are initial compositions, state that the proposed compositions are recommendations subject to the rights and approval of the shareholders and the Supervisory Board, and make clear that changes to the corporate governance structure are not barred after consummation of the transaction. * * *

CONCLUSION. For the reasons discussed, the Court concludes that Tracinda has failed to prove its claims of common law fraud and violations of the Exchange Act. Because the Court has concluded that Tracinda has not established the elements of its claims, specifically a material misrepresentation, and for its common law fraud and Section 10 claims in particular, the element of reasonable reliance, the Court will not address the remaining questions of scienter and damages. In sum, the Court will enter final judgment in favor of Defendants and against Tracinda on all claims.

§ 13.21 Merger Proxy Requirements under State Law

See the discussion of the duty of candor in Delaware, Section 3.9.

§ 13.22 Impact of Section 16(b)

A. Must Be a Beneficial Owner of 10% at Time of Purchase

Foremost-McKesson, Inc. v. Provident Securities Company

United States Supreme Court, 1976 423 U.S. 232

Mr. Justice Powell:

This case presents an unresolved issue under § 16(b) of the Securities Exchange Act of 1934 (Act). * * * The question presented here is whether a person purchasing securities that put his holdings above the 10% level is a beneficial owner "at the time of the purchase" so that he must account for profits realized on a sale of those securities within six months. The United States Court of Appeals for the Ninth Circuit answered this question in the negative. We affirm.

[**Facts**]* * * Provident and Foremost executed a purchase agreement embodying their deal on September 25, 1969. The agreement provided that Foremost would buy two-thirds of Provident's assets for $4.25 million in cash and $49.75 million in Foremost convertible subordinated debentures. The agreement further provided that Foremost would register under the Securities Act of 1933 $25 million in principal amount of the debentures and would participate in an underwriting agreement by which those debentures would be sold to the public. * * *

Provident's holdings in Foremost debentures as of October 20 were large enough to make it a beneficial owner of Foremost within the meaning of § 16. Having acquired and disposed of these securities within six months, Provident faced the prospect of a suit by Foremost to recover any profits realized on the sale of the debenture to the underwriters. Provident therefore sued for a declaration that it was not liable to Foremost under § 16(b). The District Court granted summary judgment for Provident, and the Court of Appeals affirmed. * * *

[**Analysis**] The Court of Appeals [addressed] the theory of nonliability based on the exemptive provision that we consider here. It held that in a purchase-sale sequence the phrase "at the time of the purchase," "must be construed to mean prior to the time when the decision to purchase is made." Thus, although Provident became a beneficial owner of Foremost by acquiring the debentures, it was not a beneficial owner "at the time of the purchase." Accordingly, the exemptive provision prevented any § 16(b) liability on Provident's part. * * *

* * * We reiterate that nothing suggests that the construction urged by Foremost would serve better to further congressional purposes. Indeed, the legislative history of § 16(b) indicates that by adding the exemptive provision Congress deliberately expressed a contrary choice. But even if the legislative record were more ambiguous, we would hesitate to

adopt Foremost's construction. It is inappropriate to reach the harsh result of imposing § 16(b)'s liability without fault on the basis of unclear language. * * *

B. The Unorthodox Transaction Exception

1. The Supreme Court's Rule

Kern County Land Co. v. Occidental Petroleum Corp.

United States Supreme Court, 1973 411 U.S. 582

Mr. Justice White:

Section 16(b) of the Securities Exchange Act of 1934, provides that officers, directors, and holders of more than 10% of the listed stock of any company shall be liable to the company for any profits realized from any purchase and sale or sale and purchase of such stock occurring within a period of six months. Unquestionably, one or more statutory purchases occur when one company, seeking to gain control of another, acquires more than 10% of the stock of the latter through a tender offer made to its shareholders. But is it a § 16(b) 'sale' when the target of the tender offer defends itself by merging into a third company and the tender offeror then exchanges his stock for the stock of the surviving company[.] * * *

[**Facts**] On May 8, 1967, after unsuccessfully seeking to merge with Kern County Land Co. (Old Kern), Occidental Petroleum Corp. (Occidental) announced an offer, to expire on June 8, 1967, to purchase on a first-come, first-served basis 500,000 shares of Old Kern common stock at a price of $83.50 per share plus a brokerage commission of $1.50 per share. By May 10, 1967, 500,000 shares, more than 10% of the outstanding shares of Old Kern, had been tendered. On May 11, Occidental extended its offer to encompass an additional 500,000 shares. At the close of the tender offer, on June 8, 1967, Occidental owned 887,549 shares of Old Kern.

Immediately upon the announcement of Occidental's tender offer, the Old Kern management undertook to frustrate Occidental's takeover attempt. * * * Old Kern undertook merger discussions with Tenneco, Inc. (Tenneco), and, on May 19, 1967, the Board of Directors of Old Kern announced that it had approved a merger proposal advanced by Tenneco. Under the terms of the merger, * * * [t]he shareholders of Old Kern would receive a share of Tenneco cumulative convertible preference stock in exchange for each share of Old Kern common stock which they owned. * * *

The Old Kern-Tenneco merger plan was presented to and approved by Old Kern shareholders at their meeting on July 17, 1967. Occidental refrained from voting its Old Kern shares, but in a letter read at the meeting Occidental stated that it had determined prior to June 2 not to oppose the merger and that it did not consider the plan unfair or inequitable. Indeed, Occidental indicated that, had it been voting, it would have voted in favor of the merger. * * *

The Old Kern-Tenneco merger transaction was closed on August 30. Old Kern shareholders thereupon became irrevocably entitled to receive Tenneco preference stock, share for share in exchange for their Old Kern stock. * * *

[**Issue**] On October 17, 1967, New Kern instituted a suit under § 16(b) against Occidental to recover the profits which Occidental had realized as a result of its dealings in Old Kern stock. The complaint alleged that * * * the exchange of Old Kern shares for shares of Tenneco to which Occidental became entitled pursuant to the merger closed on August 30, 1967, [was a] "sale" within the coverage of § 16(b). Since [the merger] took place within six months of the date on which Occidental became the owner of more than 10% of the stock of Old Kern, New Kern asserted that § 16(b) required surrender of the profits realized by Occidental. * * * [T]he District Court granted summary judgment in favor of New Kern. The District Court held that the * * * the exchange of Old Kern shares for shares of Tenneco on August 30, 1967, [was a] "sale" under § 16(b). The Court ordered Occidental to disgorge its profits plus interest. * * *

On appeal, the Court of Appeals reversed and ordered summary judgment entered in favor of Occidental. The Court held that * * * the exchange [did not] constitute a "sale" within the purview of § 16(b). We granted certiorari. We affirm. * * *

[**Analysis**] On August 30, 1967, the Old Kern-Tenneco merger agreement was signed, and Occidental became irrevocably entitled to exchange its shares of Old Kern stock for shares of Tenneco preference stock. Concededly, the transaction must be viewed as though Occidental had made the exchange on that day. But, even so, did the exchange involve a "sale" of Old Kern shares within the meaning of § 16(b)? We agree with the Court of Appeals that it did not, for we think it totally unrealistic to assume or infer from the facts before us that Occidental either had or was likely to have access to inside information, by reason of its ownership of more than 10% of the outstanding shares of Old Kern, so as to afford it an opportunity to reap speculative, short-swing profits from its disposition within six months of its tender-offer purchases. * * *

It cannot be contended that Occidental was an insider when, on May 8, 1967, it made an irrevocable offer to purchase 500,000 shares of Old Kern stock at a price substantially above market. * * *

Once the merger and exchange were approved, Occidental was left with no real choice with respect to the future of its shares of Old Kern. * * * The merger left no right in dissenters to secure appraisal of their stock. Occidental could, of course, have disposed of its shares of Old Kern for cash before the merger was closed. Such an act would have been a § 16(b) sale and would have left Occidental with a prima facie § 16(b) liability. It was not, therefore, a realistic alternative for Occidental as long as it felt that it could successfully defend a suit like the present one. We do not suggest that an exchange of stock pursuant to a merger may never result in § 16(b) liability. But the involuntary nature of Occidental's exchange, when coupled with the absence of the possibility of speculative abuse of inside information, convinces us that § 16(b) should not apply to transactions such as this one. * * *

2. Sale Pursuant to Tender Offer Not an Orthodox Transaction

Colan v. Mesa Petroleum Co.

United States Court of Appeals, Ninth Circuit, 1991 941 F.2d 933

ALARCON, Circuit Judge:

In this action for recovery of short-swing profits brought pursuant to § 16(b) of the Securities Exchange Act of 1934, Unocal Corporation appeals from the denial of its cross motion for summary judgment, and the order granting a motion for summary judgment in favor of Mesa Petroleum Company * * * (Mesa Defendants). We must decide whether an exchange by a beneficial owner of its common stock for non-convertible debt securities, in response to a self-tender offer, is a "sale" within the meaning of § 16(b) of the Securities Exchange Act of 1934. We reverse because we have concluded that an exchange of common stock for a negotiable debt security pursuant to a self-tender offer is a "sale" within section 16(b).

Unocal's contentions on appeal can be summarized as follows: * * * The district court erred in concluding that Mesa's exchange of Unocal common stock for negotiable debt securities in response to its self-tender offer was an "unorthodox transaction," and not a "sale" requiring a disgorgement by the Mesa Defendants of any profits that may have been realized as a result of this transaction.

[**Facts**] In October of 1984, Mesa Partners II was formed and began accumulating stock in Unocal. * * *

On February 14, 1985, Mesa Partners II filed a Schedule 13D statement with the Securities and Exchange Commission (SEC), in which it reported that it had acquired 7.3 percent of Unocal's common stock for investment purposes. By February 22, 1985, Mesa Partners II owned 17 million shares of Unocal's common stock, representing 9.7 percent of the outstanding shares.

Unocal initiated defensive measures in order to discourage a perceived takeover threat by Mesa Partners II. [*See Unocal*, Section 3.14.D]

On March 27, 1985, Mesa Partners II acquired a total of 6.7 million shares of Unocal common stock at $48.10 per share. This transaction increased Mesa Partners II's shares to 23.7 million and its ownership interest to 13.6 percent of Unocal's common stock. * * *

On April 8, 1985, Mesa Partners II made a tender offer to purchase 64 million shares of Unocal common stock at $54 per share. Unocal's Board of Directors recommended that Unocal's shareholders reject Mesa Partners II's tender offer as inadequate and not in their best interests. * * *

On April 16, 1985, Unocal offered to exchange "a package of its debt securities with an aggregate principal amount of $72 * * * for up to 87.2 million shares (approximately one-half) of Unocal's outstanding common stock." * * * Unocal expressly excluded Mesa Partners II from participating in its exchange offer. * * *

On May 17, 1985, the Delaware Supreme Court * * * held that Unocal was not prohibited by law from excluding Mesa Partners II from its tender offer.

Following the Delaware Supreme Court's decision, representatives of Mesa Partners II contacted Unocal and sought to reopen negotiations. After several rounds of negotiations, an agreement was reached on May 20, 1985.

Pursuant to the agreement, the "Mesa Entities" were allowed to participate in Unocal's self-tender offer. Mesa Partners II agreed to terminate its tender offer. In addition, Mesa Partners II agreed that it would not participate in any proxy solicitation and would not acquire any additional Unocal shares for a period of twenty-five years. Mesa Partners II also agreed that, for a period of ten years, it would vote its Unocal stock on all matters in the same way and "in the same proportion as the votes cast by holders of Shares other than the Mesa Entities." In addition, Mesa Partners II agreed to strict controls on its ability to sell its Unocal common stock.

On the same date, Mesa Partners II exchanged approximately 7.8 million shares of Unocal common stock for negotiable debt securities. * * *

[**Issue**] Unocal asks this court to direct the entry of a summary judgment in its favor on the ground that the exchange of the Mesa Defendants' common stock for negotiable debt securities was a "sale" within section 16(b). Unocal asserts that the "unorthodox transaction" defense to an action brought pursuant to section 16(b) is not applicable to a self-tender offer in which a beneficial owner exchanges his common stock for negotiable debt securities issued as a result of a recapitalization of the issuer. * * *

The district court concluded that "[a]lthough Mesa's tender of its Unocal stock in exchange for debt securities can be considered a 'sale,' the Court finds that the *Kern County* [Section 13.22.B.1] unorthodox transaction exception applies to the May 1985 exchange offer to exempt it from Section 16(b) liability." * * *

The Mesa Defendants contend that their exchange of stock for non-convertible debt securities on May 20, 1985, falls within the "unorthodox transaction" defense to section 16(b) liability established by the Supreme Court in *Kern County.* * * *

[**Analysis**] The exchange of Unocal stock for debt securities pursuant to Unocal's tender offer is factually distinguishable from the transaction in *Kern County.* The exchange of Occidental's stock for equity shares of the new corporation which was formed as the result of the merger in *Kern County* was involuntary and automatic. The May 20, 1985, exchange of stock for debt securities by the Mesa Defendants was not an involuntary or automatic transaction. Unocal did not merge into a new corporation so as to compel its shareholders to exchange their stock.

The Mesa Defendants not only were not compelled to exchange their stock for Unocal's debt securities, but Unocal expressly excluded them from its self-tender offer. The Mesa Defendants filed a suit in Delaware seeking an injunction to force Unocal to permit the Mesa Defendants to participate in Unocal's tender offer.

The Mesa Defendants had the choice of participating in the tender offer or holding onto their stock. * * *

Unlike the plight of the hapless beneficial owner in *Kern County*, the record conclusively shows that the Mesa Defendants voluntarily exchanged their common stock for negotiable debt securities. The exchange in the matter *sub judice* was not the inexorable consequence of corporate machinations that forced the stockholders to exchange their shares as the result of the dissolution of the corporation. Here, the beneficial owners controlled their own destiny and skillfully negotiated a result that Mr. Pickens characterized as a victory for his side. * * *

We conclude that the facts in this matter do not come within the holding of *Kern County* that an involuntary transaction that results from a merger is "unorthodox." * * *

§ 13.23 The Two Step Negotiated Tender Offer Followed by Merger

Many negotiated acquisitions will be structured in two steps, with a first-step tender offer, followed by a second step merger. This type of structure is examined further in Chapter 20, which deals with the rules governing third-party tender offers. These two-step transactions can have certain timing advantages over the one-step transaction that is the subject of this chapter.

References

Hazen, *Securities Regulation*, *supra* Section 1.10.

Kling and Nugent, *Negotiated Acquisitions*, *supra* Section 1.10.

Lorne, *Negotiated and Contested Transactions*, *supra* Section 1.10.

Thompson, *Mergers, Acquisitions and Tender Offers*, *supra* Section 1.10.

Chapter 14

Going Private in Freezeout Mergers and in Leveraged and Management Buyouts

§ 14.1 Scope

This chapter surveys various issues that can arise in freezeout mergers and in leveraged buyouts (LBOs), including management buyouts (MBOs). The emphasis is on publicly-held targets, but each of these transactions can occur with privately held targets. Freezeouts, LBOs, and MBOs are considered together here because they raise some of the same (1) fiduciary duty issues under state law, and (2) securities law issues under the SEC's Going Private rules.

Freezeout mergers occur when a controlling shareholder of a target corporation, whether publicly held or privately held, causes the shares of the minority shareholders to be acquired by a vehicle that is wholly-owned by the controlling shareholder. LBOs and MBOs are transactions in which a corporation, whether publicly held, privately held, or a subsidiary, is acquired in a transaction in which debt is issued to raise a significant part of the purchase price. Private equity (PE) firms, such as KKR and Cerberus, are involved in many LBOs, particularly LBOs involving public and substantial private companies and subsidiaries. In many LBOs the managers of the target become equity owners with the PE firm in the acquisition vehicle, thus making the transaction an MBO.

Section 14.2 presents an introductory problem dealing with the acquisition of a target in both a freezeout merger and an LBO/MBO. Section 14.3 introduces freezeout mergers, and Section 14.4 contains a brief introduction to the structure of an LBO/MBO. Section 14.5 addresses the standard of review applicable in Delaware, and in the ALI proposals, to freezeout mergers and LBOs/MBOs. Section 14.6 addresses the applicability of the SEC'S Going Private rules in freezeout mergers and MBOs. To illustrate both the Delaware and SEC approach to these transactions, Sections 14.5 and 14.6 discuss the LNR transaction.

Section 14.7 introduces Section 14(c) of the 34 Act, and Section 14.8 examines the potential impact of fraudulent conveyance law in an LBO transaction. Section 14.9 considers the potential of making an illegal corporate distribution in the context of an LBO. Section 14.10 examines the potential breach of implied covenants in a bond indenture of pre-LBO bondholders.

Section 14.11 addresses the impact of the Federal Reserve's margin rules in financing an LBO. Section 14.12 briefly introduces the potential liability of a PE's investment funds for unfunded pensions of a bankrupt portfolio company, and Section 14.13 discusses the potential antitrust liability for PE firms engaging in "club deals." Finally, Section 14.14 contains a summary problem on LBOs. For an illustration of the provisions of a merger agreement relating to the financing of an LBO, *see* Sections 5.2(e) of the TXU merger agreement, Documentary Appendix Z of *M&A Statutes, Rules, and Documents, supra* Section 1.1.

The issues covered in this chapter are addressed in greater detail in Chapter 14 of Thompson, *Mergers, Acquisitions and Tender Offers, supra* Section 1.10.

§ 14.2 Introductory Problem on Freezeout Mergers and LBOs

Target Corporation (TC) is a publicly held Delaware corporation. TC's stock has been trading around $10 per share. A controlling shareholder (CS) owns 35% of the stock of TC. CS has made a proposal to acquire all of the publicly held stock of TC in a merger in which CS would form a new corporation, which would merge into TC in a reverse subsidiary merger with the publicly held TC shareholders receiving $12 in cash for their shares. The top management (TM) of TC thinks CS has made a low-ball offer, and TM is considering joining with KRK, a private equity firm, in making a competing offer for an MBO at a price of $14 per share. What standard of review would apply to these two transactions under Delaware law, and how would the SEC's going private rules apply, if at all, to these two transactions?

§ 14.3 Introduction to Freezeout Transactions

A. Background on Freezeout Mergers

Brudney and Chirelstein, A Restatement of Corporate Freezeouts

87 Yale L.J. 1354, 1356–1358 (1978)

Freezeouts fall into three analytically distinct categories: (a) two-step, or integrated, mergers; (b) pure going-private transactions; and (c) mergers of long-held affiliates. * * *

The essence of a freezeout is the displacement of public investors by those who own a controlling block of stock of a corporation, whether individuals or a parent company, for cash or senior securities. The public investors are thus required to give up their equity in the enterprise, while the controllers retain theirs. Freezeouts most commonly take the form of a merger of a corporation into its existing parent or into a shell corporation newly formed for the purpose by those who control the merged entity.

Freezeouts, by definition, are coercive: minority stockholders are bound by majority rule to accept cash or debt in exchange for their common shares, even though the price they receive may be less than the value they assign to those shares. But this alone does not render freezeouts objectionable. Majority rule always entails coercion. It is, nonetheless, an acceptable rule of governance if all members of the voting constituency share a common goal and if all will be identically affected by the outcome of the vote. In the ordinary arm's-length merger negotiated by the managements of two unrelated corporations, stockholders of the merged entity are properly viewed as having a common interest in maximizing the returns on their stock, whether through periodic dividends or through sale or liquidation of the firm. Once approved by a statutory majority, the terms of such a merger will apply equally to each of the merging company's stockholders, and the common decision will satisfy the principle that all members of the class be treated alike. Majority rule is thus an appropriate means of deciding whether an arm's-length merger should be allowed. * * *

Freezeouts obviously differ from arm's-length mergers in that all the members of the same class of stockholders do not receive identical treatment: the controlling stockholders *retain* their equity but force the minority, the public investors, to accept cash or debt. In this context, majority rule does not protect the public investor from the danger that he will be denied his pro rata share of the value of the combined company. To be sure, this danger is present even when the outside stockholders receive new common *stock* in the surviving company and hence are not frozen out, for the amount of common stock they receive may be insufficient. But most agree that the likelihood that public investors will be treated unfairly is greater when, as outside common stockholders, they receive cash or debt, with the insiders in effect receiving or retaining the equity. One inevitably suspects that inequality of treatment underlies the distribution of different forms of participation or payoff to members of the same class, and experience suggests that payouts to the public in cash or senior securities often reflect a temptation to undercompensate the public investors. In any event, determining whether all members of the class have in fact been treated equally is necessarily more difficult when payouts are in different forms.

All freezeouts, then, involve the distinct possibility that a self-interested majority stockholder or control group has ruled unfairly, and all require special safeguards to ensure that minority stockholders receive equal though not identical treatment. * * *

Our own view is that mergers representing merely a second step in the takeover of a target firm by a previously unrelated company present the least need for protective regulation and can be dealt with largely through the familiar medium of advance disclosure. At the other extreme, pure going-private transactions are of small value and high risk and hence should be prohibited. Mergers between affiliated operating companies, though also susceptible to abuse, at the same time promise social benefits in varying degree, and in our opinion are best regulated by rules relating to fairness of price. * * *

B. Corporate Mechanics with Freezeout Mergers

1. Long Form Freezeout Mergers

The provisions relating to long form mergers discussed in Chapter 2 also apply to freezeout mergers unless the transaction can be effectuated under (1) the applicable short-form merger statute, which is introduced below, or (2) Section 251(h) under the Delaware General Business Corporation Law, *see* Section 20.10.

2. Short Form Mergers under the Model Business Corporation Act

See Section 2.16.A.

3. Short Form Mergers under Delaware General Business Corporation Law Section 253

See § 253 Delaware General Corporation Law.

4. Short Form Mergers under California Corporations Code Section 1110

See § 1110 California Corporations Code.

5. Right to Dissent under the Short Form Merger Statutes

See § 13.02 MBCA, § 262 Delaware General Corporation Law, and § 1300 California Corporation Code.

§ 14.4 Introduction to LBOs, Including MBOs

Principal Parties in LBOs

LBOs take a variety of forms, and the parties discussed in this section are present in most LBOs. The principles discussed here are illustrated by reference to the LBO/MBO in which LNR, a publicly held firm, was acquired by investment funds associated with Cerberus, a well-known private equity firm. *See* Documentary Appendix GG, Excerpts From Schedule 13E-3 and Proxy Statement for LNR's Freezeout Merger/MBO, *M&A Statutes, Rules, and Documents*, *supra* Section 1.1.

Shareholders of the Target Corporation

Some (but not necessarily all) of the shareholders of the target corporation want to receive cash or notes in exchange for the stock of the target corporation.

Management of the Target Corporation

Some of the senior employees of the target corporation, who may be shareholders of the target corporation, want to become major shareholders of the continuing corporation. In many cases the management will want to "roll-over" on a tax-free basis their stock in the target into stock in the acquiring entity. This type of roll-over is illustrated below in connection with the discussion of the acquisition vehicle, and the potential for roll-over in the LNR transaction is discussed in Section II of Appendix GG. The managers may also want to convert some of their stock in the target corporation into cash or notes.

Private Equity Firm and Its Investment Fund

A private equity (PE) firm raises funds from the issuance of limited partnership interests or LLC interests to institutional investors and high net worth individuals. The transactions generally qualify as private offerings under the Securities Act of 33. *See* Chapter 4. The limited partnerships or LLCs are generally referred to as Investment Funds. The PE firm acts as the general partner of the limited partnership or the manager of the LLC, and the PE firm takes an equity interest in the Fund. The Investment Fund, or a group of Investment Funds in what is known as a "club deal," contributes capital to an acquiring vehicle (*see* discussion below) in exchange for equity. The acquiring vehicle uses the contributed equity plus the proceeds of debt to acquire the target. *See* Section II.K of Appendix GG. The Investment Fund thereby becomes the owner of the target. The PE firm and the Fund investors are looking to realize substantial appreciation on their equity.

Financial Institution

A financial institution, such as an insurance company or bank, provides the debt financing for the acquisition. The financial institution's debt may be secured by the target's assets as described below. It may also receive an equity interest in the leveraged corporation in the form of common stock, convertible debt, options or warrants. *See* Section II.K of Appendix GG.

Junk Bonds

Publicly or privately issued "junk" bonds may be used to finance a portion of the acquisition proceeds. Junk bonds have a high degree of risk, as distinguished from investment grade bonds.

The Target and the Acquisition Vehicle

The acquisition of a stand-alone (*i.e.*, non-subsidiary) target corporation is generally effectuated through a taxable reverse subsidiary merger [*see* Chapter 5 and Section III.A of Appendix GG]. However, in some transactions, the assets of the target corporation are purchased by the acquiring corporation or acquired in a direct or forward merger.

The commonly used reverse subsidiary merger could take the following form. The private equity firm and the management team from the target corporation form a new corporation (Acquiring-Parent). The private equity firm contributes cash to Acquiring-Parent in exchange for its stock. The management team will generally transfer their target stock (or a significant portion thereof) to Acquiring-Parent in exchange for stock of Acquiring Parent in a tax-free rollover under Section 351 of the Code. *See* Chapter 5.

Acquiring-Parent then forms a subsidiary (Acquiring-Sub). The financial institution makes a loan to Acquiring-Sub of a substantial portion of the acquisition proceeds. The balance of the proceeds come from equity contributions made by the private equity firm to Acquiring-Parent and then by Acquiring-Parent to Acquiring-Sub. Acquiring-Sub may also issue junk bonds to raise a portion of the acquisition proceeds. Acquiring-Sub then merges into the target with the following results:

1. The target's shareholders (other than Acquiring-Parent, which continues to hold the target stock contributed by the target's management team) receive the acquisition proceeds in exchange for their target stock.
2. Acquiring-Sub disappears in the merger, and the target assumes all of the Acquiring-Sub's liabilities, principally its liabilities to the financial institution and to the junk bond holders. The target's assets may be pledged to secure the loan from the financial institution.
3. The stock of Acquiring-Sub that is held by Acquiring-Parent is converted into stock of target; as a result Acquiring-Parent becomes the sole shareholder of target. Note that (1) part of the target's stock held by Acquiring Parent is received in the contribution by the target's management, and (2) the balance is acquired in the reverse subsidiary merger.

For tax purposes the above transaction is treated as a purchase by Acquiring-Parent of the stock of target. Consequently, there is a capital gains tax at the target shareholder level, but not at the target level. The transaction, therefore, results in only one level of tax. [*See* Chapter 5]

If the target is a subsidiary corporation, the transaction could be structured as a direct purchase of the target's assets. Generally a double tax will not apply on the purchase of the assets of a subsidiary corporation. On the other hand, if the assets of a stand-alone target are purchased, and the target is then liquidated, two levels of tax apply. [*See* Chapter 5]

Acquiring-Parent and its shareholders will want to insure that the interest paid on the debt to the financial institution and to the junk bond holders is deductible for federal income tax purposes. Generally, the interest deduction will be allowed as long as the transaction is not overly leveraged. It is difficult to determine whether a transaction is overly leveraged, but as a general rule, the interest deduction should be allowed as long as at least 10% of the acquisition proceeds comes from equity contributions.

§ 14.5 What Standard of Review Applies in Freezeout Mergers and LBOs/MBOs?

A. The Delaware Law Approach

1. One Step Going Private Transactions

This section builds on fiduciary duty principles discussed in Chapter 3, and the student should review the cases in Chapter 3 discussed here.

As indicated in *Weinberger*, Section 3.14.B, the default standard of review in a freezeout merger is entire fairness. The entire fairness standard of review is examined in detail in Section 3.16, *Elaboration on Applicability of the Entire Fairness Standard in Mergers between a Controlling Shareholder and the Controlled Corporation, such as in a Parent Corporation's Merger with a Less than Wholly-Owned Subsidiary and in a Management Buyout.*

As shown in *Kahn v. Lynch*, Section 3.16.D, where the entire fairness standard of review applies, the burden of proof is on the defendant unless the transaction is approved by an independent committee of the board or a fully informed vote of a majority of the non-affiliated shareholders in which case the burden of proving unfairness is on the plaintiff.

Mills, Section 3.19.D, shows that these principles also apply in LBO/MBO transactions and that the transaction may also be subject to *Revlon*, Section 3.14.F.

However, as shown in the Delaware Supreme Court's 2014 decision in *MFW*, Section 3.16.E, in a freezeout merger, the business judgment rule and not the entire fairness rule applies if the transaction is approved in a fully informed non-coerced vote by both (1) the target's independent directors, and (2) a majority of the target's non-affiliated shareholders. This principle would also apparently apply to an LBO/MBO, which was essentially the result reached by Chancellor Allen in his 1989 decision in *RJR Nabisco*, Section 3.19.C.

2. Two Step Going Private Transactions

As indicated in Section 3.17, *Does the Entire Fairness Standard Apply in a Tender Offer by a Controlling Shareholder for the Minority Held Shares of Its Sub where the Tender Offer Is Followed by a Second Step Merger?*, the entire fairness standard of review may be avoided in a freezeout merger where the controlling shareholder makes a tender offer for the target's shares which is followed by a short form merger. *See e.g., Pure Resources*, Section 3.17.B, and *CNX*, Section 3.17.C. This avenue also should be available in an LBO/MBO transaction.

Documentary Appendix Q of *M&A Statutes, Rules, and Documents, supra* Section 1.1 contains the combined Schedule TO, tender offer statement [*see* Chapter 20], Schedule 13E-3, going private statement, and Schedule 13E-4, issuer tender offer statement [*see* Chapter 21], filed for the 2005 two-step going private transaction for Cox Communications, a Delaware corporation. The transaction was structured as a first step tender offer with a second step follow-up merger pursuant to a merger agreement. If in the tender offer the offeror was able to acquire at least 90% of the stock of Cox, then the second step would have been a short form merger; otherwise the merger would have been a long form merger. As *CNX*, Section 3.17.C, which discusses *Cox* indicates, this structure of a tender offer followed by a hoped for short form merger avoids the applicability of the entire fairness doctrine in Delaware.

Two step transactions are discussed further in Chapter 20.

B. Illustration of a Freezeout Merger in the Context of an MBO—*LNR*

In Re LNR Property Corp Shareholders Litigation

Delaware Court of Chancery, 2006 896 A.2d 169

LAMB, Vice Chancellor:

* * * This is a purported class action against a Delaware corporation, its former directors, and its former controlling shareholder, alleging breach of fiduciary duty in connection with a cash-out merger pursuant to which the controlling stockholder and other members of management exercised the right to purchase a 25% equity stake in the surviving entity. Specifically, the complaint alleges that the directors breached their fiduciary duties when they allowed the purportedly conflicted controlling shareholder to negotiate (and later vote to authorize) the merger on terms that were inadequate and unfair to the public stockholders.

All defendants moved to dismiss the complaint for failure to state a claim upon which relief can be granted. The principal issue raised by the individual defendants' motion is whether the standard of the court's review in examining the complaint is the deferential standard of the business judgment rule or the more intrusive standard of entire fairness. Because the complaint (although strikingly bare-boned in character) adequately alleges facts that, if true, could support a reasonable inference that the controlling stockholder had a disabling conflict and, in essence, stood on both sides of the transaction, the court concludes that the entire fairness standard may apply. [Therefore] the motion of the individual defendants to dismiss is denied. * * *

The Parties

LNR Property Corporation is a Delaware corporation with its corporate headquarters located in Miami Beach, Florida. LNR is a real estate investment, finance, and management company which owns and manages properties. As of May 30, 2004, LNR had 20,024,436 shares of common stock and 9,770,298 shares of Class B common stock outstanding. The common stock had one vote per share while the Class B common stock, convertible share-for-share into common stock, had ten votes per share. LNR had a nine-member board of directors[.] * * * The complaint makes factual allegations attacking the independence of only four of the nine LNR directors. The other five * * * * were presumably both disinterested and independent with respect to the challenged transaction.

Miller, LNR's controlling shareholder, was the chairman of the LNR board and beneficial owner of approximately 99.64% of LNR's outstanding Class B common stock and 2.71% of the company's common stock. Miller beneficially owned 31% of the LNR equity and held 77.35% of the company's voting power. Krasnoff was the president and CEO of LNR.

The plaintiffs * * * are former owners of LNR common stock who were cashed out in the merger.

The Sale of LNR

The complaint alleges that Miller and Krasnoff negotiated to sell LNR to Cerberus Capital Management L.P., a private investment firm [*i.e.*, a PE firm], for $ 63.10 per share in cash. As part of that same arrangement, Miller agreed to invest $ 150 million (approximately 25% of his cash proceeds) to acquire a 20.4% interest in the vehicle formed by Cerberus to effect that transaction. Similarly, Krasnoff and other members of LNR management agreed to invest approximately $ 34 million to acquire a 4.6% stake in that entity.

According to the complaint, the LNR board, which the plaintiffs allege was dominated and controlled by Miller, formed a Special Committee to evaluate the transaction, but that committee did not have authority either to engage in independent negotiations with Cerberus or Miller, or to pursue alternative transactions. Instead, the Special Committee was only permitted to review and approve [or disapprove] the merger on the terms negotiated by Miller and Krasnoff.

The Special Committee retained its own counsel but chose Greenhill & Co., which had worked with Miller and Krasnoff in negotiating the terms of the deal, as its financial advisor. On August 29, 2004, LNR announced that its board of directors had unanimously agreed, upon the recommendation of the Special Committee, to the proposed $ 63.10 per share cash merger involving LNR, Cerberus, and the acquisition vehicle, Riley Property Holdings LLC. The merger was valued at $ 3.8 billion including equity and debt. The merger agreement contained a no-shop provision, prohibiting the LNR board from soliciting any other bids. In addition, "Miller and partnerships and trusts he and his family control entered into a voting agreement under which he agreed to vote their shares in favor of the merger as long as the LNR board or Special Committee continued to recommend the transaction." On January 31, 2005, the stockholders (with Miller casting 77% of the voting power in favor) approved the transaction, which was consummated on February 3, 2005.

As a result of the merger, Miller sold his 31% interest in the company for $ 586 million and then reinvested $ 150 million to purchase a 20.4% interest in Riley Property. According to the complaint, "in effect, therefore, Miller sold 10.6% of his stock for a significant sum yet still retained the ability to participate in the Company's future profits and growth." Miller also received $ 6.4 million for his options, a $ 4 million change in control premium payment, and $2.5 million in tax reimbursement payments. Family trusts affiliated with Miller received an additional $ 42.1 million in cash. In sum, the complaint alleges, Miller and entities affiliated with him received $ 491 million in cash and a 20.4% stake in Riley Property.

In addition to their 4.6% equity stake in Riley Property, Krasnoff and other members of management allegedly received significant increases in their salaries and five-year employment contracts with Riley Property. The complaint further alleges that, under the terms of the agreement, Krasnoff was to become CEO of Riley Property and receive a 150% increase in salary, from $ 500,000 to $ 1.25 million per year. * * *

[*Analysis*] The complaint can be read to allege that the board improperly allowed Miller, owning 77% of the voting power of the company and acting as a buyer and seller in the transaction, to control the negotiations with Cerberus [a PE firm], as well as the outcome of the vote, resulting in an unfair and inadequate price for the stock in the cash-out. According to the complaint, Miller personally negotiated a one-sided deal that allowed him and select members of management to continue to reap the benefits of LNR's future growth while cutting out plaintiff and the class. Miller exchanged [in a tax-free roll-over transaction] his 31% interest in LNR shares for a 20.4% interest in the new company, thus enabling Miller to participate in the significant growth prospects of the Company going forward while selling only a fraction of his LNR shares and forcing out the public stockholders.

Despite Miller's conflicts of interest, the complaint alleges, the board permitted Miller and Krasnoff to negotiate the terms of the merger. Additionally, the complaint alleges that the board formed a "sham" Special Committee which "did not have the authority to engage in independent negotiations with Cerebrus or Miller, or to pursue alternative transactions." * * *

The defendants are correct that the complaint does not adequately allege either self-interest or a lack of independence on the part of a majority of the LNR directors. Nevertheless, as already discussed, the business judgment rule does not protect the board's decision to approve a merger (even where a majority of the directors are independent and disinterested) where a controlling shareholder has a conflicting self-interest. [Citing *Weinberger*] Instead, Delaware law imposes an entire fairness burden when the fiduciary charged with protecting the minority in a sale of the company does not have an undivided interest to extract the highest value for the shareholders. * * *

Note

Excerpts from the Schedule 13E-3, which is discussed in the next section, and related proxy statement for this transaction are set out in Appendix GG of *M&A Statutes, Rules, and Documents, supra* Section 1.1.

C. The ALI's Approach to Freezeout Mergers

The ALI *Project, supra* Section 1.10, contains proposals on freezeout mergers. *See generally* Thompson, *The M&A Provisions of the ALI Corporate Governance Project, supra* Section 1.10. The approach differentiates between majority controlled and non-majority controlled freezeouts.

D. The ALI's Approach to LBO/MBOs

The ALI *Corporate Governance Project, supra* Section 1.10 contains proposals on directors' duties in management buyouts. *See generally* Thompson, *The M&A Provisions of the ALI Corporate Governance Project*, supra Section 1.9. The approach encourages the use of independent directors.

§ 14.6 Applicability of the SEC's Going Private Rules in Freezeout Mergers and MBOs

A. Introduction to SEC's Going Private Rules

In Securities Exchange Act of 1934 Release No. 16,075 (August 2, 1979), the SEC adopted Rule 13e-3 and Schedule 13E-3, which govern going private transactions. These provisions were adopted under Section 13(e) of the 34 Act, which was part of the Williams Act amendments to the 34 Act. Section 13(e), which is examined in Chapter 17, provides:

> (e) Untrue statement of material fact or omission of fact with respect to tender offer. It shall be unlawful for any person to make any untrue statement of a material fact or omit to state any material fact necessary in order to make the statements made, in the light of the circumstances under which they are made, not misleading, or to engage in any fraudulent, deceptive, or manipulative acts or practices, in connection with any tender offer or request or invitation for tenders, or any solicitation of security holders in opposition to or in favor of any such offer, request, or invitation. The Commission shall, for the purposes of this subsection,

> by rules and regulations define, and prescribe means reasonably designed to prevent, such acts and practices as are fraudulent, deceptive, or manipulative.

Section 14.6.B and Section 14.6.C set out the SEC's explanation of the rule and schedule and the SEC's interpretative release relating to going private transactions under Rule 13e-3. Section 14.6.D sets out the SEC's *Current Issues Outline* regarding these matters. Section 14.6.E refers to the Schedule 14E-3 filed in the LNR transaction. Section 14.6.F contains a case illustrating the private right of action under Rule 13e-3, and Section 14.6.G addresses the materiality concept under Rule 13e-3. Finally, Section 14.6.H addresses the impact of *Virginia Bankshares* in Rule 13e-3 transactions.

B. SEC's Explanation of Rule 13e-3 and Schedule 13E-3

Securities Exchange Act Release No. 16,075

(1979)

[Rule 13e-3 was revised by the SEC's Final M&A Release, *see* Section 20.4.]

Discussion

[T]he application of [Rule 13e-3 and Schedule 13E-3] will depend on three factors: (1) whether the transaction involved is a Rule 13e-3 transaction [*The Rule 13e-3 Transaction and Effects Requirement*]; (2) if so, whether an exception from the application of Rule 13e-3 is available [*The Rule 13e-3 Exceptions*]; and (3) if no exception is available, whether the equity securities which are the subject of the Rule 13e-3 transaction are of a class which is registered pursuant to Section 12 of the Exchange Act or of a class of an issuer which is required to file periodic reports pursuant to Section 15(d) of the Exchange Act [*The Rule 13e-3 Public Company Requirement*].

[*The Rule 13e-3 Transaction and Effects Requirement*] A Rule 13e-3 transaction [*The Transaction Requirement*] is defined to mean any transaction or series of transactions involving one or more of the transactions specified in paragraph (a)[3](i) which has either a reasonable likelihood or purpose of producing, directly or indirectly, any of the effects [*The Effects Requirement*] specified in paragraph (a)[3](ii).

[*The Transaction Requirement*] The specified transactions are: (a) a purchase of any equity security by the issuer of such security **or by an affiliate** of such issuer; (b) a tender offer or request or invitation for tenders of any equity security made by the issuer of such class of securities **or by an affiliate** of such issuer; or (c) a solicitation or distribution [in connection with certain corporate events, that is] subject to [1] Regulation 14A [*i.e.*, the proxy solicitation rules] or [2] Regulation 14C [*i.e.*, the rules that require the distribution to the non-affiliated shareholders of an *information statement* regarding the transaction where the proxies or consents of such shareholders is not required for the corporate action]. The corporate events include a merger, consolidation, reclassification, recapitalization, reorganization or similar corporate transaction by an issuer or between an issuer (or its subsidiaries) and its affiliates; a sale by the issuer of substantially all of its assets to its affiliate; or a reverse stock split of any class of equity securities of the issuer involving the purchase of fractional interests. * * *

[*The Definition of Affiliate*. As indicated above, in determining if *The Transaction Requirement* is satisfied, it is important to determine if a person is an "affiliate" of an issuer. The term "affiliate" is defined broadly as follows in Rule 13e-3(a)(1):

> An affiliate of an issuer is a person that directly or indirectly through one or more intermediaries controls, is controlled by, or is under common control with

> such issuer. For the purposes of this section only, a person who is not an affiliate of an issuer at the commencement of such person's tender offer for a class of equity securities of such issuer will not be deemed an affiliate of such issuer prior to the stated termination of such tender offer and any extensions thereof[.]

An "affiliate" would include, for example, (1) a controlling parent corporation or other controlling shareholder in a freezeout merger, and (2) the top management of a target in an MBO.]

[*The Effects Requirement*] [Under the effects provision in (a)[3](ii)] Rule 13e-3 is triggered by a specified transaction which has either the reasonable likelihood or purpose of causing either (i) the termination of reporting obligations under the Exchange Act, by virtue of the class of securities being held of record by less than 300 persons, or (ii) the securities to be neither listed on any exchange nor authorized to be quoted on an inter-dealer quotation system of any registered national securities association. [Thus, the effect must be that a publicly-held firm is taken private.] * * *

The tests of "a reasonable likelihood" or "a purpose" that the transaction or series of transactions will produce a specified effect operate as alternative standards. * * *

If the requirements of a Rule 13e-3 transaction are present, the application of the rule would be triggered unless an exception is available. Accordingly, the second factor to be considered is the availability of the exceptions set forth in paragraph (g). * * *

[*The Rule 13e-3 Exceptions*] First, Rule 13e-3(g)(1) excepts second-step, clean-up transactions which occur within one year of a tender offer by or on behalf of a bidder who, as a result of such tender offer, became an affiliate, provided that the equal consideration, disclosure and other requirements of the rule are met. The Commission believes that if a transaction is structured to meet the conditions of that rule it may safely be viewed as a unitary transaction which is not within the purview of the purposes of Rule 13e-3. [This exception applies to an arm's length negotiated, two-step tender offer, which is followed by second step clean-up merger. These two step-transactions are examined in Chapter 20.]

Second, Rule 13e-3(g)(2) provides an exception for transactions, including recapitalizations, in which, *inter alia*, security holders are offered only an equity security which is either common stock or has essentially the same attributes as the equity security which is the subject of the Rule 13e-3 transaction. The Commission believes that such transactions are also outside the purpose of Rule 13e-3 since all holders of that class of security are on an equal footing and are permitted to maintain an equivalent or enhanced equity interest. [This exception is of limited utility in freezeout mergers and MBOs and is not examined further here.]

[*The Rule 13e-3 Public Company Requirement*]. The third factor to be considered in the application of Rule 13e-3 is the status under the Exchange Act of the issuer or the class of equity securities of the issuer. If the class of equity securities, which is subject to the Rule 13e-3 transaction, is registered pursuant to Section 12 of the Exchange Act (a "Section 12 issuer"), Rule 13e-3(b) would apply. [This discussion focuses only on a Section 12 issuer.] Rule 13e-3(b) is divided into two subparagraphs, the first of which defines fraudulent, deceptive or manipulative acts or practices in connection with a Rule 13e-3 transaction and the second of which prescribes means reasonably designed to prevent such acts and practices [i.e., compliance with the requirements of paragraphs (d) [*The Schedule 13E-3 Requirement*], (e) [*The Disclosure of Information Requirement*], and (f) [*The Disseminations Requirement*]. Thus, a Section 12 issuer or an affiliate of such issuer proposing to engage in a Rule 13e-3 transaction would be required to comply with the anti-fraud provisions of proposed Rule 13e-3(b). Compliance with these provisions would be in addition to compliance by a Section 12 issuer or affiliate of such issuer with the filing, disclosure and dissemination requirements of paragraphs (d), (e) and (f) of Rule 13e-3, respectively. * * *

Under Rule 13e-3(d)(1) [*The Schedule 13E-3 Requirement*], the issuer or affiliate engaging in a Rule 13e-3 transaction would be required to file a Rule 13e-3 Transaction Statement on Schedule 13E-3, including all exhibits thereto, with the Commission. The time for such an initial filing is set forth in General Instruction A to Schedule 13E-3. This instruction recognizes the variety of methods employed in such transactions. Consequently, the initial filing requirement for the proposed Schedule would depend on the type of Rule 13e-3 transaction involved. If the transaction involves the filing with the Commission of soliciting materials or an information statement pursuant to Regulations 14A or 14C, respectively, the Schedule 13E-3 would be filed concurrently with the filing of "Preliminary Copies" of such soliciting materials or information statement. If the transaction involves the filing of a registration statement under the Securities Act, the Schedule would be filed concurrently therewith. If the transaction involves a tender offer, the Schedule would be filed as soon as practicable on the date the tender offer is first published, sent or given to security holders of the class of equity securities which is the subject of the Rule 13e-3 transaction. * * *

Material changes in the information set forth in the initial filing of the Schedule would be required to be promptly filed with the Commission under Rule 13e-3(d)(2). These filings would be denominated as amendments on Schedule 13E-3.

A final amendment on Schedule 13E-3 disclosing the results of the Rule 13e-3 transaction would be required to be filed under Rule 13e-3(d)(3) promptly but not later than ten days after the termination of the transaction. * * *

Rule 13e-3(e) [*The Disclosure of Information Requirement*] establishes the information required to be included in the disclosure document furnished to holders of the class of equity securities which is the subject of the transaction. This disclosure provision consists of two elements: (1) the information required by Items 1 through 6 and 10 through 16 of Schedule 13E-3, or a fair and adequate summary thereof, and Items 7, 8 and 9 of the Schedule and (2) any other information required to be disclosed pursuant to any other applicable rule or regulation under the Federal securities laws.

Rule 13e-3(e)(3)[iii] requires the placement of a legend on the outside front cover page of the document which contains the information required by paragraph (e). The wording of the legend will depend on whether the Rule 13e-3 transaction involves a prospectus. If a prospectus is involved, the legend required by Rule 13e-3(e)(3)(ii)(B) shall be used in lieu of the legend set forth in Rule 425. * * *

The Commission believes that the legend will be of assistance to investors by clarifying the Commission's role in reviewing Rule 13e-3 transactions, and by assuring, to the extent possible, that they do not place false reliance upon such review. * * *

The Commission believes that certain of the required disclosures are particularly important to investors in the context of a Rule 13e-3 transaction and is therefore requiring that they be adequately highlighted. Thus, Rule 13e-3(e) requires the information called for by Items 7, 8 and 9 of Schedule 13E-3, relating to the purpose for and fairness of the transaction and certain reports, opinions, appraisals and negotiations, to be prominently set forth in a special factors section to be included in the forepart of the disclosure document furnished to security holders.

Rule 13e-3(f) [*The Disseminations Requirement*] prescribes the methods of dissemination of the information required to be disclosed to the security holders of the class of equity securities which is the subject of the Rule 13e-3 transaction. The method of dissemination applicable to a Rule 13e-3 transaction depends on the type of transaction involved.

If the Rule 13e-3 transaction is a purchase as described in Rule 13e-3(a)[3](i)(A) or a vote, consent or authorization or distribution of information statements, as described in proposed Rule 13e-3(a)[3](i)(C), Rule 13e-3(f)(1) would apply. While the disclosure would be disseminated in accordance with the provisions of applicable Federal or state law, in no event would such dissemination occur later than 20 days prior to: any such purchase; any such vote; consent or authorization; or with respect to the distribution of information statements, the meeting date, or if corporate action is to be taken by means of the written authorization or consent of security holders, the earliest date on which corporate action may be taken. Thus, Rule 13e-3(f)(1)(i)(A) would provide for a 20 day waiting period during which a Rule 13e-3 transaction could not be effected. Moreover, Rule 13e-3(f)(1)(i)(B) requires that the disclosure be disseminated to persons who are record holders as of the date not more than 20 days prior to the date of dissemination. For example, if the vote on a Rule 13e-3 transaction will occur on August 30, the disclosure would be disseminated not later than August 10. If August 10 is the date of dissemination, the disclosure would be transmitted to persons who are listed as record holders as of date not earlier than July 21. * * *

[*Elaboration on the Enhanced Disclosures*] Schedule 13E-3 establishes specific disclosure requirements for Rule 13e-3 transactions. [As indicated in Section 20.4.M, a Schedule TO can be filed in lieu of a Schedule 13E-3 in certain cases.] As noted in General Instruction [H] to the Schedule, these requirements are in addition to those of other applicable provisions of the Federal securities laws and supersede such requirements where there is a conflict. The Commission believes that the Schedule will provide more meaningful disclosures to investors in the context of a Rule 13e-3 transaction. * * *

[*Disclosure Regarding Fairness*] The most significant change in the items of the Schedule is with respect to disclosure of the fairness of the transaction. Item 8 requires the issuer or affiliate to state whether it reasonably believes the Rule 13e-3 transaction is fair or unfair to unaffiliated security holders. The issuer or affiliate is also required to provide a detailed discussion of the material factors upon which that belief is based. This discussion is required to address the extent to which the following factors were taken into account: (1) whether the transaction is structured so that approval of at least a majority of unaffiliated security holders is required; (2) whether the consideration offered to unaffiliated security holders constitutes fair value; (3) whether the majority of non-employee directors has retained an unaffiliated representative to act solely on behalf of unaffiliated security holders for the purposes of negotiating the terms of the transaction and/or preparing a report concerning the fairness of the transaction; (4) whether the Rule 13e-3 transaction was approved by a majority of the directors of the issuer who are not employees of the issuer; and (5) whether a report, opinion or appraisal of the type described in Item 9 of the Schedule was obtained. In order to minimize meaningless, boilerplate responses an instruction specifies that conclusory statements are not considered sufficient disclosure in responding to this requirement. * * *

[T]he Commission believes that increased discussion of factors bearing upon fairness to unaffiliated security holders is necessary in view of the potential for abuse which exists in a Rule 13e-3 transaction. The absence of arm's-length negotiations which is characteristic of going private transactions requires that unaffiliated security holders be furnished with detailed information so that they can determine whether their rights have been adequately protected. * * *

C. SEC Interpretative Release Relating to Going Private Transactions under Rule 13e-3

Securities Exchange Act Release No. 34–17,719

(April 13, 1981)

The purpose of this release is to provide guidance to the public and thereby assist issuers and their affiliates in complying with Rule 13e-3. * * *

1. *Question*: Rule 13e-3(a)(4)(i)(C) relates to transactions involving the solicitation of proxies or the distribution of information statements in connection with, among other things, "a merger, consolidation * * * reorganization * * * or similar corporate transaction of an issuer or between an issuer (or its subsidiaries) and its affiliate * * *." Is the merger of an issuer with a non-affiliate encompassed by this provision?

Response: No. The Rule is intended to apply to a merger, consolidation or similar multi-party reorganization transaction of an issuer only if an affiliate of the issuer is also a party to the transaction. Transactions between the issuer and a non-affiliate are ordinarily the product of arm's-length negotiations and therefore do not involve the potential for abuse and overreaching associated with the types of transactions intended to be covered by the Rule. * * *

2. *Question*: Is a short-form merger subject to the Rule?

Response: Yes. The short-form merger provisions under state law ordinarily relate to a merger between an issuer and the holder of a specified, large percentage of the issuer's outstanding securities. * * * Because a short-form merger may not require a vote of the issuer's unaffiliated security holders, a solicitation subject to Regulation 14A or a distribution subject to Regulation 14C would not be involved. Nevertheless, subparagraph (a)(4)(i)(A) of the Rule provides that the transactions covered by the Rule include a "purchase of any equity security by the issuer of such security or by an affiliate of such issuer," and the term "purchase," as defined in Rule 13e-3(a)(3), includes any acquisition pursuant to a merger. Thus, a short-form merger of an issuer into its affiliate, involving a class of securities of the issuer which is subject to Section 12 or Section 15(d) of the Exchange Act, is a Rule 13e-3 transaction and, absent an available exception, is subject to the provisions of Rule 13e-3. * * *

IV. *The Rule 13e-3 Exceptions*

Although an issuer or affiliate may engage in a transaction or series of transactions which constitutes a Rule 13e-3 transaction, the filing, disclosure and dissemination requirements and the antifraud provisions of the Rule will not be applicable if the transaction or series of transactions is within the scope of one of the paragraph (g) exceptions. * * *

Question 7: Does a statement, in connection with an any or all tender offer, that the bidder "may determine to engage" in a described follow-up transaction satisfy the Rule 13e-3(g)(1)(ii)(A) disclosure requirement?

Response: No. The availability of this exception is conditioned upon the disclosure of a binding agreement or a firm intent to engage in a specifically described second-step transaction. * * *

20. *Question*: Item 8(b) of the Schedule [now Item 1014(b) of Reg. MA, referred to in Item 8 of Schedule 13E-3] requires a discussion of the material factors upon which the belief as to fairness is based and, to the extent practicable, of the weight assigned to each such factor. The Item provides that this discussion should include an analysis of the extent,

if any, to which such belief is based on certain specified factors which will normally be important in determining the fairness of a Rule 13e-3 transaction. Must all of these factors be discussed in every case?

Response: The factors need be discussed only to the extent that they are material in the context of the transaction. Ordinarily, possible alternative courses of action should be discussed, and the absence of an intention to liquidate is not determinative of whether the discussion should address liquidation values. However, when a factor which would otherwise be important in determining the terms of the transaction is not considered or is given little weight because of particular circumstances, this may be a significant aspect of the decision-making process which should be discussed in order to make the Item 8 disclosure understandable and complete. For example, if liquidation value was disregarded because the issuer or affiliate believed that the company's assets would be very difficult to sell, or if historical market prices were believed not to be indicative of the value of the securities because of recent adverse developments, the bases for such beliefs should be discussed. In addition, the discussion of these factors must be that of the issuer or affiliate engaging in the transaction. Thus, a reference to or extract from an opinion of an investment banker, appraiser or similar advisor which fully analyses the factors does not satisfy the requirements of Item 8(b) unless the issuer or affiliate expressly adopts the advisor's discussion of the factors.

21. *Question*: Instruction 2 to Item 8(b) [now Item 1014(b) of Reg. MA, referred to in Item 8 of Schedule 13E-3] provides that, in discussing in reasonable detail the material factors upon which the belief as to fairness is based, "[c]onclusory statements, such as 'The Rule 13e-3 transaction is fair to unaffiliated security holders in relation to net book value, going concern value and future prospects of the issuer' will not be considered sufficient...." Is an itemization of the factors considered by the issuer or affiliate in approving the transaction adequate in response to Item 8(b)?

Response: No. The requirement of a reasonably detailed discussion of the material factors underlying the issuer's or affiliate's belief as to the fairness of the transaction is designed to assist security holders in making their investment decision by providing them with information, from the most knowledgeable source, regarding the terms and effect of the transaction in relation to the business and prospects of the issuer. The Division is concerned that in many instances the Item 8(b) disclosure being made to security holders is vague and non-specific and is therefore of limited utility to security holders. While the Division recognizes that the material factors upon which the fairness determination is based cannot always be addressed with mathematical precision, it believes that at least certain minimal elements should be included in the issuer's or affiliate's discussion. The discussion of factors relating to fairness should normally include the specific factors identified in Item 8(b), which are of two types.

The first type relates to whether the consideration offered to unaffiliated security holders constitutes fair value in relation to certain factors specified in subparagraphs (i) through (viii) of Instruction 1 to the Item. Each of these factors relates to a possible source of valuation of securities of the class which is the subject of the transaction. Each such factor which is material to the transaction should be discussed and, in particular, if any of the sources of value indicate a value higher than the value of the consideration offered to unaffiliated security holders, the discussion should specifically address such difference and should include a statement of the bases for the belief as to fairness in light of the difference.

The other type of factor identified in Instruction 1 relates to the existence of procedures designed to enhance the protection of unaffiliated security holders in the effectuation of the transaction. In discussing the issuer's or affiliate's belief as to the fairness of the transaction in the context of these factors, it is not sufficient simply to acknowledge the lack of one or more of the specified procedural safeguards. If any of these safeguards are not provided, the discussion should include a statement of the basis for the belief as to fairness despite the absence of these safeguards.

22. *Question*: Item 8(c) of Schedule 13E-3 [now Item 1014(e) of Reg. MA, referred to in Item 8 of Schedule 13E-3] requires disclosure of whether the transaction is structured so as to require the approval of at least a majority of unaffiliated security holders (as defined in paragraph (a)(5) of Rule 13e-3). Does this requirement relate to approval by a majority of the outstanding shares held by unaffiliated security holders or by a majority of the shares held by unaffiliated security holders and voted on the transaction?

Response: In the division's view, the information that must be disclosed in response to Item 8(c) of the Schedule is whether the transaction requires approval by the holders of at least a majority of the shares held by non-affiliates and actually voted on the transaction.
* * *

D. SEC's Current Issues Outline: 13e-3 Filing Obligation, Who Are "Affilliates?"

SEC Division of Corporation Finance, Current Issues and Rulemaking Projects

(November 14, 2000)

Schedule 13E-3 Filing Obligations of Issuers or Affiliates Engaged in a Going-Private Transaction. Generally, Exchange Act Rule 13e-3 requires that each issuer and affiliate engaged, directly or indirectly, in a going-private transaction file a Schedule 13E-3 with the Commission and furnish the required disclosures (e.g., the statement of "reasonable belief" as to the fairness or unfairness of the proposed transaction) directly to the holders of the class of equity securities that is the subject of the transaction. A joint filing may be permissible in this situation, provided each filing person individually makes the required disclosures and signs the Schedule 13E-3.

Two separate but related issues may be raised with respect to the determination of "filing-person" status in situations where a third party proposes a transaction with an issuer that has at least one of the requisite "going-private" effects: first, what entities or persons are "affiliates" of the issuer within the scope of Rule 13e-3(a)(1) and, second, when should those affiliates be deemed to be engaged, either directly or indirectly, in the going-private transaction. While resolution of both issues necessarily turns on all relevant facts and circumstances of a particular transaction, you should note the following:

[*The Senior Management Rule*] First, the staff consistently has taken the position that members of senior management of the issuer that is going private are affiliates of that issuer. Depending on the particular facts and circumstances of the transaction, such management also might be deemed to be engaged in the transaction. As a result, such management-affiliates may incur a Schedule 13E-3 filing obligation separate from that of the issuer. For example, the staff has taken the position that members of senior management of an issuer that will be going private are required to file a Schedule 13E-3 where the transaction will be effected through merger of the issuer into the purchaser or that purchaser's acquisition subsidiary, even though:

such management's involvement in the issuer's negotiations with the purchaser is limited to the terms of each manager's future employment with and/or equity participation in the surviving company; and

the issuer's board of directors appointed a special committee of outside directors to negotiate all other terms of the transaction except management's role in the surviving entity.

An important aspect of the staff's analysis was the fact that the issuer's management ultimately would hold a material amount of the surviving company's outstanding equity securities, occupy seats on the board of this company in addition to senior management positions, and otherwise be in a position to "control" the surviving company within the meaning of Exchange Act Rule 12b-2 (*i.e.*, "possession, direct or indirect, of the power to direct or cause the direction of the management and policies of a person, whether through the ownership of voting securities, by contract, or otherwise.").

Second, questions have arisen regarding the nature and scope of the Schedule 13E-3 filing obligation of an acquiring person, or "purchaser," in a merger or other going-private transaction. In the situation described above, where management of the issuer-seller that will be going private is essentially "on both sides" of the transaction, the purchaser also may be deemed to be an affiliate of the issuer engaged in the transaction and, as a consequence, required to file on Schedule 13E-3. *See* Exchange Act Release No. 16075 (August 2, 1979) (noting that "affiliates of the seller often become affiliates of the purchaser through means other than equity ownership, and thereby are in control of the seller's business both before and after the transaction. In such cases the sale, in substance and effect, is being made to an affiliate of the issuer * * *"). Accordingly, the issuer-seller, its senior management and the purchaser may be deemed Schedule 13E-3 filing persons in connection with the going-private transaction. Where the purchaser has created a merger subsidiary or other acquisition vehicle to effect the transaction, moreover, the staff will "look through" the acquisition vehicle and treat as a separate, affiliated purchaser the intermediate or ultimate parent of that acquisition vehicle. Accordingly, *both* the acquisition vehicle and the entity or person who formed it to acquire the issuer would have separate filing obligations (although, as noted, a joint filing may be permitted by the staff).

E. Excerpt from the Schedule 13E-3 Disclosures of *LNR* in Its Freezeout Merger/MBO

Documentary Appendix GG of *M&A Statutes, Rules, and Documents, supra* Section 1.1 contains the excerpts from the Schedule 13E-3 going private statement and related proxy statement filed for the 2005 freezeout merger/MBO, going private transaction for LNR, a Delaware corporation. As indicated in the discussion of the Delaware litigation regarding this case in Section 14.5.B, the court refused to dismiss the plaintiff's entire fairness claim.

F. Private Right of Action under Rule 13e-3 and Disclosure Standard

Howing Co. v. Nationwide Corp.

United States Court of Appeals, Sixth Circuit, 1987 826 F.2d 1470

MERRITT, Circuit Judge:

* * * The basic questions presented in this case are: (1) whether the plaintiffs have a private right of action under § 13e-3 to police non-compliance with Rule 13e-3; (2) and if so, whether the disclosure requirements of Rule 13e-3 have been met; and (3) if those requirements have not been met, whether defendant's conduct in violating Rule 13e-3 also gives rise to liability under the antifraud provisions of Rules 10b-5 and 14a-9. * * *

Private Right of Action Under § 13(e)

In the present case, we must decide a question of first impression in the federal courts of appeals: Does § 13(e) of the Securities and Exchange Act of 1934 allow a private right of action for damages? The District Court assumed that a private right of action exists, and we agree. Based upon our review of the statute, the legislative history, and the Supreme Court's decisions respecting private rights of action, we conclude that such a right of action does exist under § 13(e). * * *

The most serious problem in defendants' proxy statement concerns Item 8(b) compliance. Our review of the proxy statement indicates that defendants have made precisely the kind of conclusory statements prohibited by the Rule. In describing the fairness of the transaction as required by Item 8(b) [now Item 1014(b) of Reg. MA, referred to in Item 8 of Schedule 13E-3], defendants have done nothing more than provide a laundry list of factors considered by their investment banker.

This kind of non-specific disclosure runs counter not only to the SEC's position taken in the Commission release [dealing with Rule 13e-3] but also to the Instruction to Item 8(b) of Schedule 13E-3. The Instruction states that the issuer shall "[d]iscuss in reasonable detail the material factors upon which the belief stated in Item 8(a) is based and, to the extent practicable, *the weight assigned to each factor*." (emphasis added) Thus, the proxy statement is incomplete in that we are not provided with any indication of the weights given the various factors as required by Rule 13e-3, incorporating Schedule 13E-3. Moreover, we therefore have no indication as to whether any of the "sources of value indicate a value higher than the value of the consideration offered to unaffiliated security holders." * * *

Somewhere in the proxy materials the Nationwide shareholders should have received a reasonably detailed analysis of the various financial valuation methods discussed by the Rule and the weights attached thereto. Even if certain valuation methods were not particularly relevant, this should itself have been noted and explained. Without this disclosure, Nationwide shareholders did not possess the information necessary to make an informed decision concerning the going private transaction. * * *

D. *Rule 13e-3 Liability*

Subsection (b)(2) of Rule 13e-3 states that "it shall be unlawful for an issuer * * * to engage, directly or indirectly, in a Rule 13e-3 transaction unless [the] issuer * * * complies with the filing, disclosure, and dissemination requirements of the Rule." As discussed above, defendants did not comply with the disclosure obligation imposed by the Rule—

a failure declared unlawful by subsection (b)(2) of the Rule. Accordingly, since plaintiffs have a private right of action under § 13(e) to police such unlawful behavior, the District Court erred in its disposition of plaintiffs' Rule 13e-3 claims.

The Antifraud Claims

In addition to liability under subsection (b)(2) of Rule 13e-3, plaintiffs also contend that the defendants breached the antifraud provisions of Rules 10b-5, 13e-3(b)(1), and 14a-9. In essence, plaintiffs contend that a failure to disclose information required by Rule 13e-3 *ipso facto* constitutes an "omission" actionable under the antifraud provisions. They argue that Rules 10b-5 and 14a-9 incorporate Rule 13e-3 by reference in the going private context. * * *

The essence of plaintiff's claim is that a failure to provide items of disclosure required by Rule 13e-3(e) always constitutes a material omission under the antifraud rules. This is tantamount to incorporating the disclosure provisions of the securities laws into the antifraud provisions. No longer would omissions be actionable only where a half-truth resulted. Instead, any failure to comply with SEC disclosure obligations would be actionable by private litigants under the antifraud provisions.

Although the antifraud rules are the "catch-all" provisions of the securities laws, the Supreme Court has emphasized in the Rule 10b-5 context that they apply only where some fraud has been committed. Congress did not enact sections 10(b), 13(e), or 14(a) to give private litigants the same enforcement powers granted to the [SEC]. Allowing private suits based on any non-disclosure, without regard to the "half-truth" limitation, would contravene the congressional intent behind these statutes. Therefore, we hold that omission of disclosure required by Rule 13e-3(e) will constitute a violation of the antifraud provisions of sections 10(b), 13(e), and 14(a) only where the information is necessary to prevent half-truth. The violations of Rule 13e-3, Item 8, itemized above, do not constitute "fraud" under sections 10(b) and 14(a) but should be considered as violations only of the specific rule in question. * * *

G. Materiality under 13e-3

Howing Co. v. Nationwide Corp.

United States Court of Appeals, Sixth Circuit, 1991 927 F.2d 263

MERRITT, Chief Judge:

In this securities action by minority public shareholders arising from a freezeout merger of a subsidiary, Nationwide Corporation, with its parent, Nationwide Mutual, which at the time of the merger owned approximately 85% of the shares of the subsidiary, we previously reversed the District Court's dismissal of plaintiffs' claims under SEC Rule 13e-3, governing going-private transactions or freezeout mergers; and we then remanded the case to the District Court for further proceedings. * * *

In our earlier opinion, we found that the defendant corporations in their going-private offer to the minority public shareholders had violated Item 8 required under Rule 13e-3 by making no effort to state, discuss or explain in reasonable detail the net book value, the going concern value or the liquidation value of the company whose minority interests were purchased. On remand, the District Court concluded that such a discussion would not have provided a shareholder with information of "material" value under the legal standard of "materiality" in securities transactions set out in *TSC Indus. v. Northway, Inc.*, [Section 4.5.A]. The District Court therefore granted summary judgment for the defendant corporations which were responsible for the proxy statement we had previously found defective under Item 8 of Rule 13e-3.

The District Court based its grant of summary judgment on the ground that it is so clear and beyond dispute that the information on these values would not be of significance to a shareholder that no reasonable trier of fact—in this case a jury—could reach a contrary conclusion. We do not agree that the insignificance of the information is so clear, and we therefore remand the case for trial. * * *

Although we agree with the District Court that the general *TSC* standard of materiality is applicable to transactions governed by Rule 13e-3, the clear and specific language of the instructions to Item 8 [now Item 1014 of Reg. MA, referred to in Item 8 of Schedule 13E-3] creates in effect a presumption that a discussion of book, going concern and liquidation value in the proxy statement would be material to a reasonable shareholder. The presumed fact—that the investor would likely find disclosure of such information significant—follows from Item 8's insistence that the information be stated. * * *

H. Loss of State Remedy in a Rule 13e-3 Transaction—*Nationwide's* Response to *Virginia Bankshares*

Howing Co. v. Nationwide Corp.

United States Court of Appeals, Sixth Circuit, 1992 972 F.2d 700

Bailey Brown, Senior Circuit Judge:

This securities action brought by minority public shareholders of Nationwide Corporation arises from a [Rule 13e-3] freezeout merger of Nationwide Corporation with a parent corporation, Nationwide Mutual Insurance Company, which, with another parent, Nationwide Mutual Fire Insurance Company, immediately prior to the merger owned approximately 85% of the shares of the subsidiary. * * * [In view of the Supreme Court's decision in *Virginia Bankshares* [Section 13.17.C], the Defendants argued that the action by the minority shareholders should be dismissed.]

Unlike the Court in *Mills* [Section 13.17.A], the *Virginia Bankshares* Court had before it the claims of minority shareholders whose votes were not necessary for the authorization of the transaction. In the *Virginia Bankshares* decision, the majority rejected the first of the minority shareholders' two theories of causation. The first theory * * * was that the directors' desire to avoid minority shareholders' ill will by use of a misleading proxy solicitation should provide the causal nexus between the proxy statement and the merger. * * * The Court rejected this theory because it would give rise to speculative claims and procedural intractability. * * *

The minority shareholders in *Virginia Bankshares* derived their second theory of causation from Virginia's law of postmerger ratification. They noted that minority approval, though unneeded to authorize the transaction, would preclude a minority suit attacking the merger based on the alleged conflict of interest on the part of a director of the merged corporation. They argued that causation should be recognized when a misleading proxy statement induces minority shareholders to forfeit such a state-law remedy.

The Court in *Virginia Bankshares*, although not rejecting this theory, declined to decide its merits. The Court found that "there is no indication in the law or facts before us that the proxy solicitation resulted in any such loss [of the state law remedy]," because a favorable minority vote *induced by a materially misleading proxy solicitation* would not, under Virginia law, render the transaction invulnerable to such later attack by the minority. * * *

Defendants acknowledge that *Virginia Bankshares* arose under § 14(a), while this case arises under § 13(e). They contend, however, that the *Virginia Bankshares* analysis of causation applies. * * *

The Plaintiffs contend that the *Virginia Bankshares* analytical framework does not apply to § 13(e) claims. They contend that, because Rule 13e-3 imposes special disclosure obligations that are absent under Rule 14a-9, the dangers of speculative, hazy factual issues that concerned the Supreme Court in *Virginia Bankshares* do not arise under 13(e). * * *

Proceeding from the proposition that the *Virginia Bankshares* analysis of causation applies to this action under § 13(e), and noting the factual similarities of the two cases, the Nationwide Defendants contend that the Plaintiffs cannot demonstrate causation. They contend that, under *Virginia Bankshares*, minority shareholders can never establish causation when a majority shareholder holds sufficient raw voting power to authorize the transaction. The Plaintiffs, in response, distinguish their case from *Virginia Bankshares*. They correctly note that the state-law remedy of appraisal was unavailable to the plaintiffs in *Virginia Bankshares*. Such a remedy was, however, available to the minority shareholders of Nationwide Corporation, who are the class Plaintiffs here.

We must first determine whether the Plaintiffs' loss-of-state-law-remedy theory of causation can support a § 13(e) claim. * * *

* * * The Plaintiffs submit that their loss-of-state-law-remedy theory avoids the dangers of speculation[.] * * *

The Plaintiffs' loss-of-state-law-remedy theory relies on a presumption that is no more speculative than the presumption made by the Court in *Mills*, and less so than the one rejected by the Court in *Virginia Bankshares*. The presumption concerns likely action by shareholders, and the causal link arises from the enforceable terms of the corporate relationship.

Finally, there is another reason we favor recognition of the Plaintiffs' theory of causation. We previously have indicated our belief that Congress intended that an implied private right of action arise under § 13(e). Having found such congressional intent, we would certainly be hesitant to conclude that Congress also intended that causation could not be demonstrated in any case where the minority shareholders lack sufficient votes to block the transaction. * * *

Rule 13e-3 and § 13(e) embrace Congress' philosophy of full and fair disclosure of all material information in freezeout transactions. Absent such disclosure, the value of a state-law appraisal remedy declines precipitously. The goal of § 13(e) and Rule 13e-3 is to provide shareholders with all of the information they need to make informed decisions with respect to their investments. Faced with a vote on a proposed merger, and a ten-day window in which they had to exercise or forsake the appraisal remedy, the minority shareholder-Plaintiffs had their greatest need for such disclosure. The Nationwide Defendants' failure to provide such disclosure forced the Plaintiffs to make these pressing, important decisions in an atmosphere of ignorance and confusion.

We hold that, based upon the loss of their appraisal remedy, the Plaintiffs have established causation supportive of their § 13(e) claim. * * *

§ 14.7 Applicability to Freezeout Mergers of Section 14(c) of the 34 Act and the Following Provisions Thereunder: Regulation 14C, Rules 14c-1 through 14c-7, and Schedule 14C

Read and Study Section 14(c), Regulation 14C, and Schedule 14C.

Downe Communications, Inc., No Action Letter
(November 15, 1976)

This is in response to your letter of October 6, 1976 concerning the applicability of Section 14(c) of the Securities Exchange Act of 1934 and Regulation 14C thereunder to the proposed merger of Downe Communications, Inc. ("Downe") and its 66% owned subsidiary Bartell Media Corporation ("Bartell").

As explained in your letter, Downe intends to merge Bartell into itself pursuant to Section 251 of the Delaware General Corporation Law, dealing with the merger of domestic corporations. The merger agreement, approved by the respective board of directors of Downe and Bartell provides for payment by Downe of $1.25 per share for each outstanding share of Bartell common stock not owned by Downe or Bartell. Approval of the merger by Bartell was effected by the execution of a written consent by the board of directors of Downe pursuant to Section 228 of the Delaware General Corporation Law which authorizes the taking of corporate action by consent without a meeting by the holders of not less than a majority of shares entitled to vote.

You are of the view that since Downe by virtue of its 66% ownership interest in Bartell could unilaterally effect the merger without the consent of any other Bartell shareholder Regulation 14C does not apply. In this connection you indicate that Bartell shareholders have been provided with a statement describing the terms of the merger and informing them of their appraisal rights.

Based on the information presented, this Division is of the view that an information statement complying with Regulation 14C is required to be furnished to security holders of Bartell in connection with the above described transactions.

§ 14.8 Impact of Fraudulent Conveyance Law on an LBO

A. Introduction

In structuring an LBO, consideration must be given to the fraudulent conveyance provisions of the Bankruptcy Code and of state law. If the transaction is a fraudulent conveyance and the target/debtor goes bankrupt, the trustee in bankruptcy may be able to avoid the transfer or obligation, thereby possibly recovering proceeds paid out to shareholders and nullifying a recent creditor's security interest.

B. Section 548 of the Bankruptcy Code

Section 548. Fraudulent transfers and obligations.

(a) The trustee may avoid [legally undue by requiring a return of property] any transfer of an interest of the debtor in property [may, for example, avoid a dividend paid by the debtor], or any obligation incurred by the debtor [*i.e.*, may avoid an obligation the debtor incurs to a controlling shareholder or lender], that was made or incurred on or within one year before the date of the filing of the petition, if the debtor voluntarily or involuntarily—

(1) made such transfer or incurred such obligation with actual intent to hinder, delay, or defraud any entity to which the debtor was or became on or after the date that such transfer was made or such obligation was incurred, indebted; or

(2) (A) received less than a reasonably equivalent value in exchange for such transfer or obligation [*i.e.*, the debtor was not adequately compensated for the transfer of property or the incurrence of the debt]; and

(B) (i) was insolvent on the date that such transfer was made or such obligation was incurred, or became insolvent as a result of such transfer or obligation;

(ii) was engaged in business or a transaction, or was about to engage in business or a transaction, for which any property remaining with the debtor was an unreasonably small capital; or

(iii) intended to incur, or believed that the debtor would incur, debts that would be beyond the debtor's ability to pay as such debts matured. * * *

(c) Except to the extent that a transfer or obligation voidable under this section is voidable under [*inter alia*] section 544[b][state fraudulent conveyance law] * * * , a transferee or obligee of such a transfer or obligation that takes for value and in good faith [*i.e.*, someone who gave value for the transfer or obligation] has a lien on or may retain any interest transferred or may enforce any obligation incurred, as the case may be, to the extent that such transferee or obligee gave value to the debtor in exchange for such transfer or obligation.

C. Further Elaboration

Section 548(a) of the Bankruptcy Code gives the trustee the power to avoid (1) any transfer of an interest of the debtor in property, or (2) any obligation incurred by the debtor, if such transfer or obligation was made or incurred on or within one year before the date of the filing of the petition, if the debtor voluntarily or involuntarily engaged in actual fraud as specified in Section 548(a)(1) or constructive fraud as specified in Section 548(a)(2).

Actual fraud under Section 548(a)(1) occurs if the debtor voluntarily or involuntarily made the transfer or incurred the obligation with "actual intent to hinder, delay, or defraud any entity to which the debtor was or became, on or after the date that such transfer was made or such obligation was incurred, indebted. * * *"

Thus, for example, if in an LBO a target/debtor, in actually defrauding the unsecured creditors, transferred a security interest in its property to a secured creditor, the trustee could avoid the transfer.

Constructive fraud under Section 548(a)(2) occurs if the following two conditions are satisfied. First, under Section 548(a)(2)(A), the debtor received "less than reasonably equivalent value in exchange for such transfer or obligation." Thus, for example, the debtor makes a cash dividend payment to a controlling shareholder or distributes its own debt instrument to a controlling shareholder as a dividend. Since both transactions are unilateral transfers by the debtor, it has not received any value in exchange for the transfer or obligation. Second, under Section 548(a)(2)(B), the debtor must fall within one of the following three paragraphs, which bear on the debtor's ability to pay its debts:

(i) *Insolvency.* The debtor was "insolvent on the date that such transfer was made or such obligation was incurred, or became insolvent as a result of such transfer or obligation * * *." [*See* § 548(a)(2)(B)(i)]; or

(ii) *Unreasonably Small Capital.* The debtor was "engaged in business or a transaction, or was about to engage in business or a transaction, for which any property remaining with the debtor was an unreasonably small capital * * *." [*See* § 548(a)(2)(B)(ii)]; or

(iii) *Beyond Ability to Repay.* The debtor "intended to incur, or believed that the debtor would incur, debts that would be beyond the debtor's ability to pay as such debts matured" [*see* § 548(a)(2)(B)(iii)].

Thus, for example, a debtor corporation that pays a dividend has not made a fraudulent transfer if the debtor (1) is not insolvent at the time to the dividend and does not become insolvent as a result of the dividend, (2) does not have an unreasonably small capital, and (3) has not incurred debts beyond its ability to pay.

For an LBO to fall within the constructive fraud provision of Section 548(a)(2), the trustee must first establish that the target/debtor made the transfer or incurred the obligation for "less than a reasonably equivalent value." In most LBOs, the target/debtor pays out all of the consideration to the shareholders as a dividend or other distribution, for example, in a merger transaction, and consequently, the target/debtor may be deemed not to have received any consideration for making the transfer or incurring the obligation. Thus the first condition may be satisfied in most LBOs. If the trustee is successful in establishing that the target received less than reasonably equivalent value, to avoid the transfer or obligation, the trustee must also establish that the target/debtor was insolvent, or had an unreasonably small capital, or incurred debts beyond its ability to pay. For an illustration of the provisions of a merger agreement relating to the solvency of the buyer in an LBO, *see* Sections 5.2(j) of the TXU merger agreement, Documentary Appendix Z of *M&A Statutes, Rules, and Documents*, *supra* Section 1.1.

The focus here is on constructive fraud under Section 548(a)(2) and on the conditions for applicability of this provision:

(1) Determining whether the target/debtor received a reasonably equivalent value; and

(2) Determining whether the target/debtor

  (i) was insolvent,

  (ii) had an unreasonably small capital, or

  (iii) had incurred debts beyond its ability to repay.

In addition to the "avoiding" power under Section 548(a) of the Bankruptcy Code, Section 544(b) of this Code provides that "[t]he trustee may avoid any transfer of an interest of the debtor in property or any obligation incurred by the debtor that is voidable under *applicable law* by a creditor holding an unsecured claim * * *." The *applicable law* referred to is the relevant state fraudulent conveyance law, which in virtually all cases has both an actual and a constructive fraud provision structured similarly to those in Section 548(a)(1) and (2) of the Bankruptcy Code. The state fraudulent conveyance law, which will generally follow the Uniform Fraudulent Conveyance Act (UFCA), may, however, permit the avoidance of transfers made or obligations incurred within more than a year of the bankruptcy, which is the test under Section 548(a) of the Bankruptcy Code. Thus, it may be more advantageous for the trustee to proceed under the state fraudulent conveyance law and Section 544(b) of the Bankruptcy Code.

D. The Lender Prevails: No Fraudulent Transfer

Mellon Bank N.A. v. Metro Communicators, Inc.

United States Circuit Court, Third Circuit, 1991 945 F.2d 635

ROSENN, Circuit Judge:

* * * Mellon Bank, N.A. (Mellon or Bank) financed the acquisition; Mellon lent the acquiror [TCI] 1.85 million dollars to purchase all of the capital stock of the target corporation, Metro. Metro guaranteed and secured the acquisition loan with substantially all of its assets. Simultaneously with the leveraged buyout, Mellon extended a 2.3 million dollar credit line to Metro. At a later date, Mellon extended another 2.25 million dollars to Metro in the form of letters of credit. These loans were also collateralized by the security interest in substantially all of Metro's assets. Within a year of the leveraged buyout, Metro filed a bankruptcy petition under chapter 11. * * *

Fraudulent Transfer Under Section 548(a)(2). The bankruptcy court held that Metro's guaranty and the security interest collateralizing the guaranty of the 1.85 million dollar loan to TCI which was used to buy out Metro's shareholders constituted a fraudulent conveyance under 11 U.S.C. § 548(a)(2). * * *

Reasonably Equivalent Value. Section 548(a)(2)(A) requires the trustee to show that the debtor received "less than a reasonably equivalent value." Because Metro did not receive the proceeds of the acquisition loan, it did not receive any direct benefits from extending the guaranty and security interest collaterizing that guaranty. However, in evaluating whether reasonably equivalent value has been given the debtor under section 548, indirect benefits may also be evaluated. If the consideration Metro received from the transaction, even though indirect, approximates the value it gave TCI, this can satisfy the terms of the statute. * * *

The bankruptcy court rejected Mellon's argument that one of the indirect benefits that Metro received as a result of the LBO was the ability to borrow working capital from Mellon. The court reasoned that the 2.3 million dollar credit line extended contemporaneously with the 1.85 million dollar loan to TCI amounted to a *liability* because "all that Debtor really received was the opportunity to incur an additional $2.3 million of debt." The court concluded that because of accruing interest, Metro received "substantially less than a reasonably equivalent value in exchange." This analysis is flawed. The ability to borrow money has considerable value in the commercial world. To quantify that value, however, is difficult. Quantification depends upon the business opportunities the additional credit makes available to the borrowing corporation and on other imponderables in the operation or expansion of its business.

The bankruptcy court also did not account for the value created by the LBO itself. The Banks cite what appears to be legitimate and reasonable expectation that the affiliation of these two corporations, TCS and Metro, would produce a strong synergy. * * *

Thus, the indirect benefits to Metro of this guaranty were the ability to obtain substantial credit due to its new association with the TCS corporate group and the synergy expected to result from the combination of these corporations. The value, however, of the synergy obtained in the corporations' affiliation and the value of obtaining the credit are difficult to quantify in dollars without the aid of expert witnesses. Regrettably, no such testimony was forthcoming in this case. * * *

Insolvency or Undercapitalization. Under section 548, not only must the Committee prove that the debtor did not receive reasonably equivalent value, the Committee must also prove that the debtor was "insolvent on the date that such transfer was made or such obligation was incurred, or became insolvent as a result of such transfer." 11 U.S.C. § 548(a)(2)(B)(i). The bankruptcy court swiftly concluded that Metro was rendered insolvent by the LBO, stating that clear logic showed that "the very transactions themselves caused a *serious* case of insolvency."

The bankruptcy code defines insolvency as a "financial condition such that the sum of such entity's debts is greater than all of such entity's property, at a fair valuation." 11 U.S.C. § 101(31)(A). This test is frequently described as the "balance sheet test." The debtor's assets and liabilities are tallied at fair valuation to determine whether the corporation's debts exceed its assets. Under section 548, insolvency is to be measured at the time the debtor transferred value or incurred an obligation. In present case, Metro's solvency must be measured on April 6, 1984, the date on which Metro guaranteed the acquisition loan.

The bankruptcy court reasoned that the LBO rendered Metro insolvent because it assumed that the 1.85 million paid to the former shareholders of Metro reflected the fair market value of Metro and that Metro's pledge of its stock and assets in equal amount necessarily rendered it insolvent. * * *

When we examine the balance sheet of June 30, 1984, prepared on an accrual basis, after the ingestion of 2.3 million dollars working capital and the expansion of the company's broadcasting rights, we find accounts receivable of $1,828,016 and accounts payable of $762,745. The corporation's assets have now shot up to an aggregate $28,370,697 consisting primarily of broadcasting rights, and its liabilities amounted to $27,684,167, comprised principally of obligations under its broadcast rights and bank loans of $3,500,000. The net worth of the company shows improvement—now $343,265—despite the liability of the bank loans and demonstrates that the Mellon loans did not render Metro insolvent, even without considering the value of the guarantees of TCS and MCM, but improved its financial condition.

We conclude that the Committee failed to satisfy its burden of proving that Metro was insolvent on the date of the transfer or became insolvent as a result of the transfer. * * *

Note

In a subsequent case before the Third Circuit, *Moody v. Security Pacific Business Credit, Inc.*, 971 F.2d 1056 (3rd Cir. 1992), the court found that although the target of an LBO did not receive reasonably equivalent value, the target was not insolvent and did not have an unreasonably small capital. Consequently, there was no fraudulent conveyance under the Pennsylvania UFCA.

E. The Lender Loses: Fraudulent Transfer and Equitable Subordination

In Re the O'Day Corporation v. Meritor Savings Bank

United States Bankruptcy Court, D. Mass, 1991 126 B.R. 370

The structure of the acquisition [of the O'Day Corporation] involved the formation of LTF Acquisition Corp. The acquisition price was to be $13,915,000 * * *. * * * The amount of equity invested was to be $2,450,000. * * *

[The parties] contemplated borrowing the balance of the acquisition price from Meritor, which amount was to be secured by a security interest in all the real and personal property owned by [O'Day]. After the loan was granted, the loan proceeds plus a portion of the equity were to be wire transferred to [O'Day's shareholder] Bangor Punta. LTF Acquisition Corp. and O'Day were to merge at that time. LTF Acquisition Corp. was to be the surviving entity and was to change its name to The O'Day Corporation. * * *

The closing of the acquisition occurred on schedule on June 30, 1987. * * * [T]he Meritor loan facilities generated $9,571,411.10. [The new stockholders] contributed $2,450,000. From those sums, $12,066,000 was paid to Bangor Punta. The O'Day Corporation received $235,000 from which it paid $233,656.04 in fees * * *. In the end, O'Day was left with $1,343.96 in cash, and the balance of the money, approximately $120,000, went to Meritor. * * *

[**Issues**] The Trustee seeks to set aside Meritor's security interest in the collateral under sections 4, 5 and 7 of the UFCA. The Court has ruled that the version of the UFCA enacted in Massachusetts applies. * * *

The Trustee argues that O'Day did not receive "fair consideration" in exchange for Meritor's security interest in the collateral and that O'Day was insolvent or was rendered insolvent as a result of the transfer pursuant to section 4 of the UFCA. Section 4 provides as follows:

> Every conveyance made and every obligation incurred by a person who is or will be thereby rendered insolvent is fraudulent as to creditors without regard to his actual intent if the conveyance is made or the obligation is incurred without a fair consideration.

The Trustee claims that O'Day did not receive "fair consideration" and was left with "unreasonably small capital" as a result of the transfer pursuant to section 5 of the UFCA. Section 5 provides as follows:

> Every conveyance made without fair consideration when the person making it is engaged or is about to engage in a business or transaction, for which the property remaining in his hands after the conveyance is an unreasonably small capital, is fraudulent as to creditors and as to other persons who become creditors during the continuance of such business or transaction, without regard to his actual intent.

Section 3 of the UFCA defines "fair consideration." It states in pertinent part: Fair consideration is given for property or obligation—

> (a) When in exchange for such property or obligation, as a fair equivalent therefore, and in good faith, property is conveyed or an antecedent debt is satisfied * * *.

Section 2 of the UFCA defines "insolvency." It states as follows:

> A person is insolvent within the meaning of this chapter when the present fair salable value of his assets is less than the amount that will be required to pay his probable liability on his existing debts as they become absolute and matured. * * *

Lastly, the Trustee seeks to equitably subordinate Meritor's claims under section 510(c) of the Bankruptcy Code which provides as follows:

> (c) Notwithstanding subsections (a) and (b) of this section, after notice and a hearing, the court may—
>
> (1) under principles of equitable subordination, subordinate for purposes of distribution all or part of an allowed claim to all or part of another allowed claim or all or part of an allowed interest to all or part of another allowed interest; or

(2) order that any lien securing such a subordinated claim be transferred to the estate. 11 U.S.C. § 510.

FAIR CONSIDERATION. The threshold issue in examining the LBO under the UFCA is whether O'Day received fair consideration. If it did, the Court's inquiry under sections 4 and 5 of the UFCA necessarily must end because both sections require a showing that a conveyance was made (or an obligation incurred) without fair consideration. Fair consideration is given when in good faith, as a fair equivalent, and in exchange, property is conveyed or an antecedent debt is satisfied. Fair equivalence only requires that the value of the consideration be reasonably equivalent rather than exactly equivalent in value to the property transferred or obligation assumed. * * *

The Trustee, on the one hand, maintains, as he obviously must, that O'Day did not receive fair consideration. In his words, O'Day gave literally millions of dollars of liens to Meritor and encumbered virtually all of its existing assets in exchange for $1,344.00 in loan proceeds. Meritor, on the other hand, states that O'Day received fair consideration in the form of 1) the cancellation of the Intercompany Notes in the aggregate amount of $14,274,145; 2) the establishment of a $2.5 million revolving line of credit; and 3) the term and DIAL loans. Meritor argues that just because the Debtor utilized the proceeds to pay prior shareholders and that the Bank was aware of the payment does not mean that O'Day did not receive fair consideration in exchange for the security interests granted. In short, the Bank concludes that collapsing the transaction is unwarranted in this case. * * *

The Court is not persuaded that the loans advanced by Meritor constituted fair consideration. When the transaction is viewed in its totality, it is clear that the proceeds from the term loan and the DIAL loan were merely passed through O'Day to the selling shareholder. * * *

* * * In sum, the Court cannot find that the term loan, the revolving loan and the Intercompany Notes provided fair consideration to the Debtor.

Insolvency. * * * The Trustee's insolvency argument is predicated upon a balance sheet approach. * * *

The Court finds that the Trustee has sustained his burden of proof on the issue of insolvency. * * * The burden shifted to Meritor to come forward with another value. The Court finds that there was insufficient evidence to rebut the Trustee's case. * * *

EQUITABLE SUBORDINATION. The fraudulent conveyance action before the Court raises an issue pertaining to subordination: does a determination that Meritor's liens are avoidable as fraudulent conveyances leave Meritor with a general unsecured claim. The Trustee, on the one hand, contends that a creditor or creditors who successfully invoke the provisions of sections 4, 5 or 7 of the UFCA or section 548 of the Bankruptcy Code are entitled to be satisfied, in full, prior to any recovery by the fraudulent transferee. The Trustee further asserts that it would be anomalous for the Court to permit the avoidance of liens under the UFCA or section 548 and then allow the available recovery to injured O'Day creditors to be reduced by permitting Meritor to participate in that recovery as an unsecured creditor.

On the other hand, Meritor insists that there is simply no authority for the Trustee's position. In fact, Meritor contends that, should the Court sustain the Trustee's fraudulent conveyance action, it would remain as an unsecured creditor. Consequently, the Bank takes the position that, as a creditor of the estate with a proof of claim on file, it is entitled to its *pro rata* distribution of the estate's assets unless an objection to Meritor's proof of claim is filed and sustained by the Court or, alternatively, its claim is equitably subordinated under section 510 of the Bankruptcy Code. The Court disagrees. The language of the UFCA and the Bankruptcy Code supports the position taken by the Trustee. * * *

Assuming arguendo that Meritor's position is correct, equitable subordination is an equitable remedy available to the Trustee. * * *

[T]he Court is persuaded that Meritor's post-LBO conduct was tantamount to overreaching, although the Court believes that Meritor did not act to intentionally hinder, delay or defraud creditors, at the very outset of its relationship with O'Day. Thus, the Court finds that, even if authority exists to permit Meritor to share in the Debtor's estate as a general unsecured creditor, the Trustee has demonstrated the existence of sufficient grounds to subordinate the Bank's claim pursuant to section 510 of the Bankruptcy Code. * * *

F. Potential Liability of Public Shareholders in an LBO

Munford Inc. v. Valuation Research Corporation

United States Court of Appeals, Eleventh Circuit, 1996 98 F.3d 604

As a matter of first impression in this Circuit, we hold that 11 U.S.C. § 546(e) does not bar the trustee in bankruptcy from avoiding payments the debtor corporation made to its shareholders in a leveraged buy-out.

[**Facts**] In August 1987, Dillard Munford, the founder and chief executive officer of Munford, Inc., suggested to Munford, Inc.'s board of directors (the board) that it sell Munford, Inc. * * * Based on Dillard Munford's suggestion, the board retained Shearson Lehman Brothers (Shearson) to evaluate Munford, Inc.'s financial viability and its fair market value. Following this evaluation, Shearson would make recommendations regarding how to best maximize shareholder value in the event the board decided to sell Munford, Inc.

In September 1987, Shearson presented a written report to the board identifying several selling options. * * *

[T]he board received an offer from the Panfida Group to purchase its Majik and World Bazaar stores for $18.50 per share. On May 23 the board met with its lawyers and Shearson's representatives to consider the Panfida Group's offer. * * * After discovering potential environmental liability at some of the Majik stores, the Panfida Group decided to reduce its purchase price from $18.50 a share to $17 a share. The board approved the Panfida Group's new offering price and the proposed merger agreement. The proposed merger agreement required that the Panfida Group have a reasonable amount of working capital, and would have the ability to pay its debts as they came due. After receiving this assurance, Munford, Inc.'s lawyers prepared a detailed proxy statement for Munford, Inc.'s 3,100 shareholders outlining the merger agreement. On October 18, 1988, the shareholders approved the merger plan. As provided in the merger agreement, each share of common stock was converted into the right to receive the merger price of $17 per share and extinguished the shareholders' ownership interest in Munford, Inc. The Panfida Group retired the 291,177 shares it purchased prior to the LBO merger without payment. The sale of Munford, Inc. to the Panfida Group closed on November 29, 1988. Thirteen months after the LBO transaction, on January 2, 1990, the post-Munford Corporation filed a Chapter 11 case in bankruptcy court.

[**Issue**] In this case, the district court entered summary judgment in favor of the shareholders on Munford, Inc.'s fraudulent conveyance claim finding that the LBO payments Munford, Inc. made to the shareholders constituted settlement payments within the meaning of section 741(8). *See* 11 U.S.C. § 741(8). Consequently, the District Court held that 11 U.S.C. § 546(e) did not authorize a bankruptcy trustee or a debtor in possession acting as trustee to avoid such transfers under state law because the shareholders received their settlement payments from Citizens & Southern Trust Company, a financial institution. On appeal, Munford, Inc. contends that the District Court erred in concluding that the LBO payments the shareholders received for their shares constituted settlement payments for purposes of section 546(e). * * *

[**Analysis**] Here, the transfers/payments were made by Munford to shareholders. None of the entities listed in section 546(e)—*i.e.*, a commodity broker, forward contract merchant, stockbroker, financial institution, or a securities clearing agency—made or received a transfer/payment. Thus, section 546(e) is not applicable.

True, a section 546(e) financial institution was presumptively involved in this transaction. But the bank here was nothing more than an intermediary or conduit. Funds were deposited with the bank and when the bank received the shares from the selling shareholders, it sent funds to them in exchange. The bank never acquired a beneficial interest in either the funds or the shares.

Importantly, a trustee may only avoid a transfer to a "transferee." *See* 11 U.S.C. § 550. Since the bank never acquired a beneficial interest in the funds, it was not a "transferee" in the LBO transaction. Rather, the shareholders were the only "transferees" of the funds here. And, of course, section 546(e) offers no protection from the trustees avoiding powers to shareholders; rather, section 546(e) protects only commodity brokers, forward contract merchants, stockbrokers, financial institutions, and securities clearing agencies. Accordingly, regardless of whether the payments qualify as settlement payments, section 546(e) is not applicable since the LBO transaction did not involve a transfer to one of the listed protected entities. We conclude that the District Court erred with respect to this issue and reverse.

Note

The court in *In Re Kaiser Steel Corporation*, 952 F.2d 1230 (10th Cir. 1991) held for the shareholders in a similar situation. The court reasoned:

> [T]hose shareholders who tendered their shares one day after the LBO and received the LBO consideration are treated just the same under the Code as shareholders who sold their shares in the market one day prior to the LBO and received a settlement payment reflecting the market value of the LBO consideration. Neither type of investor will be forced to disgorge the payments several years later.

§ 14.9 Potential Liability for Making an Illegal Corporate Distribution

A. The Virginia View

In Re C-T of Virginia, Incorporated v. Barrett

United States Court of Appeals, Fourth Circuit, 1992 958 F.2d 606

Wilkinson, Circuit Judge:

This case presents the question of whether the leveraged acquisition of a corporation, structured in the form of a cash-out merger and consummated at arm's length, is subject to restrictions on distributions to shareholders under Virginia law. The case involves an action brought by an official committee of unsecured creditors of a corporation now in bankruptcy against the former directors of that corporation. The creditors, suing on behalf of the corporation, claimed that the leveraged acquisition created an illegal distribution to shareholders under the Virginia Stock Corporation Act, Va. Code Ann. § 13.1–601 *et seq.* We agree with the district court that the merger did not create a distribution under Virginia law and therefore affirm its judgment.

[**Facts**]* * * C-T of Virginia, Inc., formerly Craddock-Terry Shoe Corp., is a Virginia corporation engaged in the manufacture, wholesale, and mail-order sale of shoes. Prior to the purchase that is the subject of this action, C-T was a publicly owned corporation whose stock was traded on the over-the-counter market. * * *

C-T received [an] unsolicited offer on November 11, 1985, from HH Holdings, Inc. * * * Holdings agreed to [a] merger at $20 per share, and an Agreement in Principle was signed on December 11, 1985.

The parties formalized the transaction in an Agreement and Plan of Merger executed on January 24, 1986. The merger agreement structured the purchase in the form of a reverse triangular merger. For purposes of the merger, Holdings formed HH Acquisition, Inc., a wholly owned subsidiary. The merger agreement provided that on April 30, 1986, Acquisition would merge into C-T, leaving C-T as the surviving corporation wholly owned by Holdings. The funds necessary to purchase all outstanding shares of C-T, about $30 million, would be deposited with the exchange agent, Sovran Bank, before or at the closing of the transaction. At the moment that the merger was effected, the outstanding shares of C-T common stock would be automatically canceled, and the former shareholders would receive the right to submit their canceled stock certificates to Sovran for payment of $20 per canceled share. * * *

The financing for the merger was arranged solely by Holdings. Holdings provided about $4 million of its own money. It obtained the balance, approximately $26 million, in the form of bank loans secured by C-T's assets. The pre-merger directors did not solicit proposed financing, negotiate the terms of the financing or of the security, or participate in or authorize the encumbering of C-T's assets. * * *

C-T's board of directors approved the merger agreement and unanimously voted to recommend that the shareholders approve the merger, which they did on April 17, 1986. The transaction was consummated as planned on April 30. The surviving corporation struggled along for about eighteen months, and it filed for bankruptcy under Chapter 11 on October 21, 1987.

[**Issue**] In October 1989, the Official Committee of Unsecured Creditors of C-T filed this action in federal court against the pre-merger directors and officers of the corporation. The complaint alleged that the directors and officers breached their fiduciary duties owed to the corporation and that the directors had approved a distribution in violation of Va.Code Ann. § 13.1–653 and § 13.1–692. The district court granted the defendants' motion to dismiss both claim[s]. * * *

* * * The Virginia statute defines "distribution" as follows:

> "*Distribution*" means a direct or indirect transfer of money or other property, except its own shares, or incurrence of indebtedness by a corporation to or for the benefit of its shareholders in respect of any of its shares. A distribution may be in the form of a declaration or payment of a dividend; a purchase, redemption, or other acquisition of shares; a distribution of indebtedness of the corporation; or otherwise.

Va.Code Ann. § 13.1–603. Not all distributions are unlawful. Rather, a distribution is prohibited only if, after it is made, the corporation fails either of two insolvency tests:

> No distribution may be made if, after giving it effect:
>
> 1. The corporation would not be able to pay its debts as they become due in the usual course of business; or
>
> 2. The corporation's total assets would be less than the sum of its total liabilities plus (unless the articles of incorporation permit otherwise) the amount that would be needed, if the corporation were to be dissolved at the time of the distribution, to satisfy the preferential rights upon dissolution of shareholders whose preferential rights are superior to those receiving the distribution.

Id. § 13.1–653(C).

Directors face potential personal liability when the corporation makes an unlawful distribution:

> Unless he complies with the applicable standards of conduct described in § 13.1–690, a director who votes for or assents to a distribution made in violation of this chapter or the articles of incorporation is personally liable to the corporation and its creditors for the amount of the distribution that exceeds what could have been distributed without violating this chapter or the articles of incorporation.

Id. § 13.1–692(A). There is, however, no provision in the Virginia Stock Corporation Act by which creditors can recover a distribution from the shareholders directly. Rather, a creditor's only remedy is against the directors, who then may seek contribution from shareholders who received the distribution. *Id.* § 13.1–692(B)(2). * * *

We now address the central question in this case: whether the merger involved a distribution to shareholders within the meaning of § 13.1–603. For the reasons set forth below, we conclude that the transaction does not fall within the statutory definition of distribution and, therefore, that the directors cannot be subjected to potential liability under § 13.1–692. * * *

Appellant argues that the plain meaning of the statute contradicts the district court's conclusion that the merger did not create a distribution under Virginia law. It claims that the purchase of the pre-merger shareholders' shares in C-T entailed a distribution because the payment of the purchase price of $20 per share was a "transfer of money * * * by a corporation to * * * its shareholders." Since this purchase was funded primarily through loans secured by the assets of C-T, the argument runs, the value of the corporation—and hence the financial position of its creditors—was diminished. According to appellant, it is irrelevant whether the funds that are transferred to shareholders derive from the corporation's capital surplus, retained earnings, or new loans secured by corporate assets, and it is likewise immaterial that the payment resulted from a cash-out merger; appellant claims that the legislature intended the statute to have "the broadest range of inclusion" and thereby "pick up all forms of transfer of the assets of a corporation to its shareholders."

We do not share appellant's view of the statute. The Virginia Stock Corporation Act provides a precise definition of the word "distribution:" "[A] direct or indirect transfer of money or other property, except its own shares, or incurrence of indebtedness by a corporation to or for the benefit of its shareholders in respect of any of its shares." Va.Code Ann. § 13.1–603. Payment of the merger consideration to C-T's former shareholders simply does not fit within the plain language of this definition. The key language, for our purposes here, is the requirement that the transfer of money or property be "by a corporation to * * * *its* shareholders." When post-merger C-T transferred $20 per canceled share to C-T's pre-merger shareholders, they were no longer the corporation's—"its"—shareholders, for their ownership interest had been lawfully canceled as of the effective time of the merger.

Similarly, we must reject appellant's argument that the encumbering of C-T's assets to raise sufficient funds to pay for the merger was a distribution because it represented the "incurrence of indebtedness by a corporation * * * for the benefit of its shareholders." * * *

The distribution statute is aimed by its terms at actions taken by a corporation to enrich unjustly its own shareholders at the expense of creditors and to the detriment of the continuing viability of the company. It does not cover third-party payments to acquire the stock of a corporation or the encumbering of assets after a change in corporate ownership, and it is not intended to obstruct an arm's-length acquisition of an enterprise by new owners who have their own plans for commercial success. * * *

B. The Georgia View

In Re Munford, Inc. v. Valuation Research Corporation

United States Court of Appeals, Eleventh Circuit, 1996 97 F.3d 456

HATCHETT, Chief Judge:

In this corporate leveraged-buy-out merger case, we affirm the District Court's ruling that Georgia's stock distribution and repurchase statutes apply.

[The facts are set out in the Munford case in Section 14.8.F.]

In Count III of its complaint, Munford, Inc. asserted that the directors violated legal restrictions under Georgia's distribution and share repurchase statutes in approving the LBO merger. Specifically, Munford, Inc. asserts that the LBO transaction constituted a distribution of corporate assets that rendered Munford, Inc. insolvent. The directors moved for summary judgment contending that the Georgia distribution and repurchase statutes did not apply to LBO mergers. On August 10, 1994, the District Court, adopting the bankruptcy court's report and recommendation in part, denied the directors' motion for summary judgment on Munford, Inc.'s stock repurchase and distribution claim, ruling that Georgia's stock distributions and repurchase restrictions applied to LBO transactions. The District Court also found that a genuine issue of material fact existed as to whether the LBO merger rendered Munford, Inc. insolvent in violation of Georgia law. * * *

[**Issue**] The sole issue on appeal is whether the District Court erred in ruling that Georgia's stock distribution and repurchase statutes apply to a leverage acquisition of a corporation. * * *

[**Analysis**] Georgia's capital surplus distribution statute provides, in pertinent part:

> (a) The board of directors of a corporation may from time to time distribute to shareholders out of capital surplus of the corporation a portion of its assets in cash or property subject to the following [provision]: (1) No such distribution shall be made at a time when the corporation is insolvent or when such distribution would render the corporation insolvent[.]

O.C.G.A. § 14–2–91 (1988). Similarly, Georgia's stock repurchasing statute prohibits directors of a corporation from repurchasing the corporation's shares when such purchase would render the corporation insolvent. O.C.G.A. § 14–2–92(e) (1982). Under both statutes, directors who vote for or assent to a corporate distribution or stock repurchase in violation of these statutes are jointly and severally liable for the amount distributed or paid to the extent the payments violated the restrictions. O.C.G.A. §§ 14–2–154(a)(1), (2) (1982). * * *

[T]he bankruptcy court concluded that a reasonable jury could conclude that the merger rendered Munford, Inc. insolvent in violation of Georgia's distribution and stock repurchase statutes.

In reaching its conclusion, the bankruptcy court rejected a Fourth Circuit case that refused to apply Virginia's corporate distribution statute to recapture payments made to shareholders pursuant to an LBO merger. *See C-T of Virginia, Inc. v. Barrett,* [Section 14.9.A]. * * *

The bankruptcy court, in this case, rejected [the] line of reasoning in [*C-T of Virginia, Inc.*], reasoning that the legislature enacted the distribution and share repurchase statutes of the Georgia Code to protect creditors "by prohibiting transfers at a time when a corporation is insolvent or would be rendered insolvent." Such intent, the bankruptcy court noted, "furthers the longstanding principle that creditors are to be paid before shareholders." We agree with the District Court and the reasoning of the bankruptcy court and decline to join the Fourth Circuit in holding that "[a] corporate acquisition, structured as a merger, is simply a different animal from a distribution." *C-T of Virginia, Inc.*, 958 F.2d at 611.

We note that the LBO transaction in this case did not merge two separate operating companies into one combined entity. Instead, the LBO transaction represented a 'paper merger' of Munford, Inc. and AMC, a shell corporation with very little assets of its own. To hold that Georgia's distribution and repurchase statutes did not apply to LBO mergers such as this, while nothing in these statutes precludes such a result, would frustrate the restrictions imposed upon directors who authorize a corporation to distribute its assets or to repurchase shares from stockholders when such transactions would render the corporation insolvent. We therefore affirm the District Court's ruling that Georgia's restrictions on distribution and stock repurchase apply to LBO.

In the alternative, the directors argue that their approval of the LBO merger should not subject them to liability under the distribution and repurchase statutes because they approved the merger in good faith and with the advice of legal counsel. Because we are not aware of any Georgia courts that recognize good faith or reasonable reliance on legal counsel's advice as an affirmative defense to liability under Georgia's distribution and repurchase statutes, we reject this argument.

For the reasons stated above, we affirm the district court's denial of the directors' motion for summary judgment on Munford, Inc.'s stock distribution and repurchase claim.

C. Treatment of Revaluation Surplus under Delaware Law, *See Also* the Materials in Section 24.4.B

Klang v. Smith's Food & Drug Centers, Inc.

Delaware Supreme Court, 1997 702 A.2d 150

VEASEY, Chief Justice:

* * * Plaintiff in this purported class action alleges that a corporation's repurchase of shares violated the statutory prohibition against the impairment of capital. * * *

[**Facts**] On January 29, 1996, [Smith's Food & Drug Centers, Inc. ("SFD") a Delaware corporation,] entered into an agreement with The Yucaipa Companies ("Yucaipa"), a California partnership also active in the supermarket industry. Under the agreement, * * * Yucaipa [would acquire] slightly over 3 million newly-issued shares of SFD common stock [, and] SFD was to undertake a recapitalization, in the course of which SFD would assume a sizable amount of new debt, retire old debt, and offer to repurchase up to fifty percent of its outstanding shares (other than those issued to Yucaipa) for $36 per share. [Also,] SFD was to repurchase 3 million shares of preferred stock from Jeffrey Smith [a controlling shareholder] and his family.

SFD hired the investment firm of Houlihan Lokey Howard & Zukin ("Houlihan") to examine the transactions and render a solvency opinion. Houlihan eventually issued a report to the SFD Board replete with assurances that the transactions would not endanger SFD's solvency, and would not impair SFD's capital in violation of 8 Del.C. Section 160.

On May 17, 1996, in reliance on the Houlihan opinion, SFD's Board determined that there existed sufficient surplus to consummate the transactions, and enacted a resolution proclaiming as much. On May 23, 1996, SFD's stockholders voted to approve the transactions, which closed on that day. The self-tender offer was over-subscribed, so SFD repurchased fully fifty percent of its shares at the offering price of $36 per share. * * *

[**Analysis**] A corporation may not repurchase its shares if, in so doing, it would cause an impairment of capital, unless expressly authorized by Section 160. A repurchase impairs capital if the funds used in the repurchase exceed the amount of the corporation's "surplus," defined by 8 Del.C Section 154 to mean the excess of net assets over the par value of the corporation's issued stock.

Plaintiff asked the Court of Chancery to rescind the transactions in question as violative of Section 160. * * *

In an April 25, 1996 proxy statement, the SFD Board released a pro forma balance sheet showing that the merger and self-tender offer would result in a deficit to surplus on SFD's books of more than $100 million. * * * Plaintiff asks us to adopt an interpretation of 8 Del.C. Section 160 whereby balance-sheet net worth is controlling for purposes of determining compliance with the statute. Defendants do not dispute that SFD's books showed a negative net worth in the wake of its transactions with Yucaipa, but argue that corporations should have the presumptive right to revalue assets and liabilities to comply with Section 160.

Plaintiff advances an erroneous interpretation of Section 160. We understand that the books of a corporation do not necessarily reflect the current values of its assets and liabilities. Among other factors, unrealized appreciation or depreciation can render book numbers inaccurate. It is unrealistic to hold that a corporation is bound by its balance sheets for purposes of determining compliance with Section 160. Accordingly, we adhere to the principles of *Morris v. Standard Gas & Electric Co.* [Del.Ch., 63 A.2d 577 (1949)] allowing corporations to revalue properly its assets and liabilities to show a surplus and thus conform to the statute.

It is helpful to recall the purpose behind Section 160. The General Assembly enacted the statute to prevent boards from draining corporations of assets to the detriment of creditors and the long-term health of the corporation. That a corporation has not yet realized or reflected on its balance sheet the appreciation of assets is irrelevant to this concern. * * * Allowing corporations to revalue assets and liabilities to reflect current realities complies with the statute and serves well the policies behind this statute.

Plaintiff contends that SFD's repurchase of shares violated Section 160 even without regard to the corporation's balance sheets. Plaintiff claims that the SFD Board was not entitled to rely on the solvency opinion of Houlihan, which showed that the transactions would not impair SFD's capital given a revaluation of corporate assets. * * *

The record contains, in the form of the Houlihan opinion, substantial evidence that the transactions complied with Section 160. Plaintiff has provided no reason to distrust Houlihan's analysis. In cases alleging impairment of capital under Section 160, the trial court may defer to the board's measurement of surplus unless a plaintiff can show that the directors "failed to fulfill their duty to evaluate the assets on the basis of acceptable data and by standards which they are entitled to believe reasonably reflect present values." [*Morris*, 63 A.2d at 582] In the absence of bad faith or fraud on the part of the board, courts will not "substitute [our] concepts of wisdom for that of the directors." [*Id.* at 583] * * *

Note

The decision above is consistent with *Randall v. Bailey*, Section 24.4.B.3.a, which addresses spin-offs.

§ 14.10 Potential Breach of Implied Covenants in Bond Indenture of Pre-LBO Bondholders

Metropolitan Life Insurance Company v. RJR Nabisco, Inc.

United States District Court, S.D.N.Y., 1989 716 F. Supp. 1504

WALKER District Judge:

The corporate parties to this action are among the country's most sophisticated financial institutions, as familiar with the Wall Street investment community and the securities market as American consumers are with the Oreo cookies and Winston cigarettes made by defendant RJR Nabisco, Inc. (sometimes "the company" or "RJR Nabisco"). The present action traces its origins to October 20, 1988, when F. Ross Johnson, then the Chief Executive Officer of RJR Nabisco, proposed a $17 billion leveraged buy-out (LBO) of the company's shareholders, at $75 per share. Within a few days, a bidding war developed among the investment group led by Johnson and the investment firm of Kohlberg Kravis Roberts & Co. (KKR), and others. On December 1, 1988, a special committee of RJR Nabisco directors, established by the company specifically to consider the competing proposals, recommended that the company accept the KKR proposal, a $24 billion LBO that called for the purchase of the company's outstanding stock at roughly $109 per share. * * *

Plaintiffs [bondholders of RJR Nabisco] now allege, in short, that RJR Nabisco's actions have drastically impaired the value of bonds previously issued to plaintiffs by, in effect, misappropriating the value of those bonds to help finance the LBO and to distribute an enormous windfall to the company's shareholders. As a result, plaintiffs argue, they have unfairly suffered a multimillion dollar loss in the value of their bonds. * * *

Although the numbers involved in this case are large, and the financing necessary to complete the LBO unprecedented, the legal principles nonetheless remain discrete and familiar. Yet while the instant motions thus primarily require the Court to evaluate and apply traditional rules of equity and contract interpretation, plaintiffs do raise issues of first impression in the context of an LBO. At the heart of the present motions lies plaintiffs' claim that RJR Nabisco violated a restrictive covenant, not an explicit covenant found within the four corners of the relevant bond indentures, but rather an *implied* covenant of good faith and fair dealing, not to incur the debt necessary to facilitate the LBO and thereby betray what plaintiffs claim was the fundamental basis of their bargain with the company. The company, plaintiffs assert, consistently reassured its bondholders that it had a "mandate" from its Board of Directors to maintain RJR Nabisco's preferred credit rating. Plaintiffs ask this Court first to imply a covenant of good faith and fair dealing that would prevent the recent transaction, then to hold that this covenant has been breached, and finally to require RJR Nabisco to redeem their bonds.

RJR Nabisco defends the LBO by pointing to express provisions in the bond indentures that, *inter alia*, permit mergers and the assumption of additional debt. These provisions, as well as others that could have been included but were not, were known to the market and to plaintiffs, sophisticated investors who freely bought the bonds and were equally free to sell them at any time. Any attempt by this Court to create contractual terms *post hoc*, defendants contend, not only finds no basis in the controlling law and undisputed facts of this case, but also would constitute an impermissible invasion into the free and open operation of the marketplace.

For the reasons set forth below, this Court agrees with defendants. There being no express covenant between the parties that would restrict the incurrence of new debt, and no perceived direction to that end from covenants that are express, this Court will not imply a covenant to prevent the recent LBO and thereby create an indenture term that, while bargained for in other contexts, was not bargained for here and was not even within the mutual contemplation of the parties.

The indentures at issue clearly address the eventuality of a merger. They impose certain related restrictions not at issue in this suit, but no restriction that would prevent the recent RJR Nabisco merger transaction. The indentures also explicitly set forth provisions for the adoption of new covenants, if such a course is deemed appropriate. While it may be true that no explicit provision either permits or prohibits an LBO, such contractual silence itself cannot create ambiguity to avoid the dictates of the parole evidence rule, particularly where the indentures impose no debt limitations. * * *

Note

For a discussion of debt provisions that call for an acceleration of the payment of principal in the event of an LBO or similar event, *see* Section 23.7.

§ 14.11 Impact of Federal Reserve Margin Regulations on Acquisition Financing

A. Introduction

Committee on Developments in Business Financing the Impact of the Federal Reserve Margin Regulations on Acquisition Financing

35 Business Lawyer 517, 516–523 (1980)

INTRODUCTION

In recent years, corporate lawyers have become increasingly aware of the applicability of the securities credit provisions of the Securities Exchange Act of 1934 (the Exchange Act) to acquisition financing. This, in large part, has resulted from the bar's experience in the explosive new corporate acquisition movement. Because much of this new acquisition activity has been financed with bank loans and privately-placed debt, lawyers representing investment bankers, institutional lenders and corporate borrowers have frequently found themselves facing problems under the securities credit provisions.

The securities credit provisions consist of section 7 of the Exchange Act and the implementing Federal Reserve margin regulations. [Section 7 provides in part:

> For the purpose of preventing the excessive use of credit for the purchase or carrying of securities, the Board of Governors of the Federal Reserve System

shall * * * prescribe rules and regulations with respect to the amount of credit that may be initially extended and subsequently maintained on any [non-exempt] security.]

Congress included section 7 in the Exchange Act primarily as a reaction to the belief that heavily leveraged stock market speculation had contributed to the onset of the Great Depression. Although the legislative history is not free from ambiguity, it is generally believed that Congress' main purpose in enacting section 7 was to give the Federal Reserve Board an effective method of reducing the aggregate amount of the nation's credit resources which can be directed by speculation into the stock market. The reduction of securities-market volatility and protection of stock market investors are regarded as secondary purposes of the legislation.

The Federal Reserve Board has implemented section 7 by promulgating a series of technical and complex regulations designed to regulate the typical securities credit transaction in which an investor obtains a loan from a broker [Reg. T], a bank [Reg. U] or other lender [Reg. U] to finance a purchase of securities. The focus of the regulations is decidedly on the extension of credit at the retail level. Regulations T [and] U * * * cover the lending and credit arranging activities of broker-dealers, banks and other lenders, respectively. Regulation X prohibits borrowers from obtaining credit in the United States or abroad on terms that violate any of the lender regulations.

Although it can be argued that application of the margin regulations to acquisition financing is inconsistent with the objectives of section 7 of the Exchange Act and the retail-level focus of the regulations themselves, the Federal Reserve Board and the Securities Exchange Commission (the SEC) both take the position that acquisition financing is subject to the requirements of the regulations.

B. The Federal Reserve Board's 1998 Margin Rules Governing Acquisition Transactions

Federal Reserve System, Board of Governors, Securities Credit Transactions; Borrowing by Brokers and Dealers

63 FR 2806, (January 16, 1998)

SUMMARY: The Board is adopting final amendments to Regulations G [non-bank lenders], T [broker dealers] and U [banks]. * * * The final amendments include the extension of Regulation U to cover lenders formerly subject to Regulation G and the elimination of Regulation G. [Thus, there is one rule governing broker dealers, Reg. T, and one rule covering banks and other covered lenders, Reg. U.] The amendments reduce regulatory distinctions between broker-dealers, banks, and other lenders. * * * Conforming changes are also made to Regulation X [anti-avoidance provision]. * * *

Except as otherwise noted, substantive provisions of Regulation G have been incorporated into Regulation U.

Entities that were known as "lenders" under Regulation G will be known as "nonbank lenders" under Regulation U and the term "lender" will be used in Regulation U to refer to banks and former Regulation G lenders collectively. * * *

The Board has generally viewed section 7 of the § 34 Act as prohibiting broker-dealers from extending purpose credit [*i.e.*, credit for the purpose of buying, carrying, or trading in securities] that is either unsecured or secured by collateral other than securities. * * *

Prior to the adoption of today's amendments, the following United States traded stocks were subject to the Board's 50 percent margin requirement: (1) Stocks traded on a national securities exchange * * *. [Thus, for example, an investor can buy IBM stock with no more than 50% credit, that is, with a margin loan from a broker of no more than 50% of the purchase price of the stock.] * * *

Lenders other than broker-dealers and banks are responsible for applying Federal Reserve margin requirements only after they have extended margin stock secured credit in an amount that surpasses one of two dollar thresholds: $200,000 in credit extended in one calendar quarter or $500,000 in credit. * * *

12 CFR PART 220—CREDIT BY BROKERS AND DEALERS (REGULATION T)

§ 220.1—Authority, purpose, and scope. (a) *Authority and purpose.* [The] principal purpose [of Regulation T] is to regulate extensions of credit by brokers and dealers. * * *

§ 220.2—Definitions. * * * *Creditor* means any broker or dealer. * * *

Margin security means: (1) Any security registered [*i.e.*, exchange traded stock like IBM] or having unlisted trading privileges on a national securities exchange [and certain other tradable securities]. * * *

Purpose credit means credit for the purpose of: (1) Buying, carrying, or trading in securities. * * * [For example, a margin loan to buy IBM stock]

§ 220.3—General provisions. * * * (g) *Arranging for loans by others.* A creditor [*i.e.*, broker dealer] may arrange for the extension or maintenance of credit to or for any customer by any person, provided the creditor does not willfully arrange credit that violates parts 221 [Reg. U, applicable to banks and nonbank lenders other than broker dealers] or 224 [Reg. X, the antiavoidance provision] of this chapter. * * *

§ 220.6—Good faith account. * * * (e) *Nonpurpose credit.* (1) A creditor may: * * *

(iii) Extend and maintain secured or unsecured nonpurpose credit, subject to the requirements of paragraph (e)(2) of this section.

(2) Every extension of credit [with regard to securities] shall be deemed to be purpose credit unless, prior to extending the credit, the creditor accepts in good faith from the customer a written statement that it is not purpose credit. * * *

§ 220.12—Supplement: Margin requirements. The required margin for each security position held in a margin account shall be as follows:

(a) Margin equity security, [in general]: 50 percent of the current market value of the security or the percentage set by the regulatory authority where the trade occurs, whichever is greater. * * *

12 CFR PART 221—CREDIT BY BANKS AND PERSONS OTHER THAN BROKERS OR DEALERS FOR THE PURPOSE OF PURCHASING OR CARRYING MARGIN STOCK (REGULATION U)

§ 221.1—Authority, purpose, and scope. (b) *Purpose and scope.* (1) This part imposes credit restrictions upon persons other than brokers or dealers (hereinafter lenders) that extend credit for the purpose of buying or carrying margin stock if the credit is secured directly or indirectly by margin stock. Lenders include "banks" and other persons who are required to register with the Board under § 221.3(b) [*i.e.*, lenders meeting the $200K or $500K test]. Lenders may not extend more than the maximum loan value of the collateral securing such credit, as set by the Board in § 221.7 (the Supplement). * * *

§ 221.2—Definitions. * * *

Indirectly secured. (1) Includes any arrangement with the customer under which: (i) The customer's right or ability to sell, pledge, or otherwise dispose of margin stock owned by the customer is in any way restricted while the credit remains outstanding; or (ii) The exercise of such right is or may be cause for accelerating the maturity of the credit.

(2) Does not include such an arrangement if: (i) After applying the proceeds of the credit, not more than 25 percent of the value (as determined by any reasonable method) of the assets subject to the arrangement is represented by margin stock; * * *

Lender means: (1) Any bank; or (2) Any person subject to the registration requirements of this part. * * * *Margin stock* means: (1) Any equity security registered or having unlisted trading privileges on a national securities exchange; * * *

Maximum loan value is [50% of] the * * * current market value [of margin stock]. * * *

Nonbank lender means any person subject to the registration requirements of this part.

Purpose credit is any credit for the purpose, whether immediate, incidental, or ultimate, of buying or carrying margin stock.

§ 221.3—**General requirements.** (a) *Extending, maintaining, and arranging credit*- (1) *Extending credit.* No lender, * * *, shall extend any purpose credit, secured directly or indirectly by margin stock, in an amount that exceeds the maximum loan value of the collateral securing the credit. * * *

(3) *Arranging credit.* No lender may arrange for the extension or maintenance of any purpose credit, except upon the same terms and conditions under which the lender itself may extend or maintain purpose credit under this part.

(b) *Registration of nonbank lenders; termination of registration; annual report*—(1) *Registration.* Every person other than a [broker dealer] or a bank who, in the ordinary course of business, extends or maintains credit secured, directly or indirectly, by any margin stock shall register * * * within 30 days after the end of any calendar quarter during which: (i) The amount of credit extended equals $200,000 or more; or (ii) The amount of credit outstanding at any time during that calendar quarter equals $500,000 or more. * * *

§ 221.7—**Supplement: Maximum loan value of margin stock and other collateral.**(a) *Maximum loan value of margin stock.* The maximum loan value of any margin stock is fifty per cent of its current market value.

(b) *Maximum loan value of nonmargin stock and all other collateral.* The maximum loan value of nonmargin stock and all other collateral * * * is their good faith loan value. * * *

Interpretations

§ 221.102—**Application to committed credit where funds are disbursed thereafter.**

The Board has concluded that the date a commitment to extend credit becomes binding should be regarded as the date when the credit is extended, since: (a) On that date the parties should be aware of law and facts surrounding the transaction; and (b) Generally, the date of contract is controlling for purposes of margin regulations and Federal securities law, regardless of the delivery of cash or securities. * * *

§ 221.110—**Questions arising under this part.**

(a) This part governs "any purpose credit" extended by a lender "secured directly or indirectly by margin stock" and defines "purpose credit" as "any credit for the purpose, whether immediate, incidental, or ultimate, of buying or carrying margin stock," with certain exceptions, and provides that the maximum loan value of such margin stock shall be a fixed percentage "of its current market value." * * *

(2) *Loan to acquire controlling shares.* (i) The second question is whether this part governs a margin stock-secured loan made for the business purpose of purchasing a controlling interest in a corporation, or whether such a loan would be exempt on the ground that this part is directed solely toward purchases of stock for speculative or investment purposes. The Board answered that a margin stock-secured loan for the purpose of purchasing or carrying margin stock is subject to this part, regardless of the reason for which the purchase is made. * * *

§ 221.124—Purchase of debt securities to finance corporate takeovers [The Junk Bond Interpretation].

(a) Petitions have been filed with the Board raising questions as to whether the margin requirements in this part apply to two types of corporate acquisitions in which debt securities are issued to finance the acquisition of margin stock of a target company.

(b) In the first situation, the acquiring company, Company A, controls a shell corporation that would make a tender offer for the stock of Company B, which is margin stock (as defined in § 221.2) [*i.e.*, B is a public company]. The shell corporation has virtually no operations, has no significant business function other than to acquire and hold the stock of Company B, and has substantially no assets other than the margin stock to be acquired. To finance the tender offer, the shell corporation would issue debt securities which, by their terms, would be unsecured. If the tender offer is successful, the shell corporation would seek to merge with Company B. However, the tender offer seeks to acquire fewer shares of Company B than is necessary under state law to effect a short form merger with Company B, which could be consummated without the approval of shareholders or the board of directors of Company B [*see* Chapter 2].

(c) The purchase of the debt securities issued by the shell corporation to finance the acquisition clearly involves purpose credit (as defined in § 221.2). In addition, such debt securities would be purchased only by sophisticated investors in very large minimum denominations, so that the purchasers may be lenders for purposes of this part. *See* § 221.3(b) [the $200K and $500K tests]. Since the debt securities contain no direct security agreement involving the margin stock, applicability of the lending restrictions of this part turns on whether the arrangement constitutes an extension of credit that is secured indirectly by margin stock.

(d) As the Board has recognized, indirect security can encompass a wide variety of arrangements between lenders and borrowers with respect to margin stock collateral that serve to protect the lenders' interest in assuring that a credit is repaid where the lenders do not have a conventional direct security interest in the collateral. *See* § 221.124. However, credit is not "indirectly secured" by margin stock if the lender in good faith has not relied on the margin stock as collateral extending or maintaining credit. *See* § 221.2.

(e) The Board is of the view that, in the situation described in paragraph (b) of this section, the debt securities would be presumed to be indirectly secured by the margin stock to be acquired by the shell acquisition vehicle. The staff has previously expressed the view that nominally unsecured credit extended to an investment company, a substantial portion of whose assets consist of margin stock, is indirectly secured by the margin stock. *See* Federal Reserve Regulatory Service 5–917.12. This opinion notes that the investment company has substantially no assets other than margin stock to support indebtedness and thus credit could not be extended to such a company in good faith without reliance on the margin stock as collateral.

(f) The Board believes that this rationale applies to the debt securities issued by the shell corporation described in paragraph (b) of this section. At the time the debt securities are issued, the shell corporation has substantially no assets to support the credit other than the margin stock that it has acquired or intends to acquire and has no significant business function other than to hold the stock of the target company in order to facilitate the acquisition. Moreover, it is possible that the shell may hold the margin stock for a significant and indefinite period of time, if defensive measures by the target prevent consummation of the acquisition. Because of the difficulty in predicting the outcome of a contested takeover at the time that credit is committed to the shell corporation, the Board believes that the purchasers of the debt securities could not, in good faith, lend without reliance on the margin stock as collateral. The presumption that the debt securities are indirectly secured by margin stock would not apply if there is specific evidence that lenders could in good faith rely on assets other than margin stock as collateral, such as a guaranty of the debt securities by the shell corporation's parent company or another company that has substantial non-margin stock assets or cash flow. This presumption would also not apply if there is a merger agreement between the acquiring and target companies entered into at the time the commitment is made to purchase the debt securities or in any event before loan funds are advanced. In addition, the presumption would not apply if the obligation of the purchasers of the debt securities to advance funds to the shell corporation is contingent on the shell's acquisition of the minimum number of shares necessary under applicable state law to effect a merger between the acquiring and target companies without the approval of either the shareholders or directors of the target company. In these two situations where the merger will take place promptly, the Board believes the lenders could reasonably be presumed to be relying on the assets of the target for repayment.

(g) In addition, the Board is of the view that the debt securities described in paragraph (b) of this section are indirectly secured by margin stock because there is a practical restriction on the ability of the shell corporation to dispose of the margin stock of the target company. Indirectly secured is defined in § 221.2 to include any arrangement under which the customer's right or ability to sell, pledge, or otherwise dispose of margin stock owned by the customer is in any way restricted while the credit remains outstanding. The purchasers of the debt securities issued by a shell corporation to finance a takeover attempt clearly understand that the shell corporation intends to acquire the margin stock of the target company in order to effect the acquisition of that company. This understanding represents a practical restriction on the ability of the shell corporation to dispose of the target's margin stock and to acquire other assets with the proceeds of the credit.

(h) In the second situation, Company C, an operating company with substantial assets or cash flow, seeks to acquire Company D, which is significantly larger than Company C. Company C establishes a shell corporation that together with Company C makes a tender offer for the shares of Company D, which is margin stock. To finance the tender offer, the shell corporation would obtain a bank loan that complies with the margin lending restrictions of this part and Company C would issue debt securities that would not be directly secured by any margin stock. The Board is of the opinion that these debt securities should not be presumed to be indirectly secured by the margin stock of Company D, since, as an operating business, Company C has substantial assets or cash flow without regard to the margin stock of Company D. Any presumption would not be appropriate because the purchasers of the debt securities may be relying on assets other than margin stock of Company D for repayment of the credit. * * *

12 CFR PART 224—BORROWERS OF SECURITIES CREDIT (REGULATION X)

§ 224.3—Margin regulations to be applied by nonexempted borrowers. (a) *Credit transactions outside the United States.* No borrower shall obtain purpose credit from outside the United States unless it conforms to the following margin regulations: (1) Regulation T if the credit is obtained from a foreign branch of a broker-dealer; (2) Regulation U, as it applies to banks, if the credit is obtained from a foreign branch of a bank * * *; and (3) Regulation U, as it applies to nonbank lenders, if the credit is obtained from any other lender outside the United States * * *.

(b) *Credit transactions within the United States.* Any borrower who willfully causes credit to be extended in contravention of Regulations T and U, and who, therefore, is not exempted by § 224.1(b)(1), must conform the credit to the margin regulation that applies to the lender.

C. Impact of Regulation T (Regulation of Broker/Dealers) on Tender Offer Financing by Private Sale of Debt Securities

Letter from Federal Reserve Board to Sullivan & Cromwell

(November 29, 1979)

Dear Mr. Kirby:

This is in response to your letter of February 14, 1979 asking for an interpretation by the Board of Governors under the arranging provision of Regulation T (12 C.F.R. 220). Your question arises in the situation where an investment banker is asked to arrange a private placement of debt securities for a corporate client, with the proceeds to be used to finance the acquisition of a publicly-held company. One of the terms of the private placement is that it will not be consummated until the stock of the company to be acquired has ceased to be publicly-held.

Under the terms of section [§ 220.3(g), arranging loans for others] of Regulation T, a broker-dealer may not arrange for credit on different terms from those on which he may himself extend credit, with certain enumerated exceptions. In this particular instance the broker-dealer could not finance the acquisition himself unless it were secured by a margin security, and then only at the current permissible loan value of the collateral, which is 50 percent. [*See* § 220.112] One of the exceptions from the prohibition of this section is an arrangement by the broker-dealer.

> (2) For any person to extend or maintain credit for the purpose of purchasing or carrying a security * * * in a transaction which is exempt from the registration requirements of the Securities Act of 1933 by virtue of section 4(2) of that Act * * *. Provided, that: * * * (ii) the credit will not be used to purchase or carry a security that is publicly-held. [*See* § 221.102]

At the time the broker-dealer completes his "arranging" activities in the transaction which you described, the security is still publicly-held.

The Board has addressed previously the issue as to the date when credit is extended and concluded that

> * * * the date a commitment to extend credit becomes binding should be regarded as the date when the credit is extended, since (1) on that date the parties could be aware of law and facts surrounding the transaction and (2) generally, the date of contract is controlling for purposes of margin regulations and Federal securities law, regardless of the delivery of cash or securities. [*See*§ 221.102]

To argue that there is no firm commitment until the stock is eliminated, the Board feels is to ignore the realities of the situation since, without the promise of financing, the acquisition would not have been made in the proposed form. The certainty of financing set forth in the loan agreement is the catalyst enabling a company to attempt to purchase another company's stock. The buying of the stock and the use of credit to complete the transaction, by themselves, add to the volume of total credit in the securities market and the elimination of the securities purchased at a later date does not alter that fact.

Accordingly, it is the opinion of the Board that under the circumstances described, the credit is both extended and arranged when the stock is still a public stock. Therefore, the activities of the broker would not be in accordance with the terms of the regulation as presently in effect. * * *

D. Impact of Margin Regulations on Tender Offer Financing by Public Sale of Debt Securities (Former Reg G) and Bank Financing (Reg U)

Revlon, Inc. v. Pantry Pride, Inc.

United States District Court, Delaware, 1985 621 F. Supp. 804

FARNAN, District Judge:

Plaintiff, Revlon, Inc. (Revlon), filed a complaint * * * seeking preliminary injunctive relief against defendants Pantry Pride, Inc. (Pantry Pride) * * * from commencing a tender offer by Pantry Pride for any and all of Revlon' shares. * * *

Revlon also seeks injunctive relief against Chemical Bank, barring them from issuing a loan to Pantry Pride, on the ground that such a loan would violate Section 7 of the Securities Exchange Act of 1934 (Exchange Act), and the regulations thereunder.

Revlon, in its Second Amended and Supplemental Complaint has alleged seven causes of action. * * *

The fifth alleges that the proposed financing for the tender offer violates the margin requirements set forth in Section 7 of the Exchange Act and Regulations G, U and X thereunder. The sixth alleges that Chemical has violated the disclosure requirements of Sections 14(d) and 14(e) of the Exchange Act and the rules and regulations thereunder. * * *

[**Facts**] On August 19, 1985, Pantry Pride publicly announced its intention to make a tender offer for any and all of Revlon's shares at $47.50 per share. Pantry Pride, through its wholly-owned shell subsidiary, Nicole, commenced a cash tender offer on August 26, 1985, pursuant to an Offer to Purchase bearing the date August 23, 1985. The Offer to Purchase generally provides that if the tender offer succeeds, and if 90% of the outstanding common and preferred stock are tendered, then Pantry Pride will effectuate a short-form merger of Revlon and Nicole or an affiliate. If less than 90% are tendered, it will effectuate a statutory merger through a vote of the Board of Directors and shareholders. The Offer notes that Pantry Pride may have to replace a majority of the Board of Directors in order to consummate a statutory merger. The Offer to Purchase further advises that Pantry Pride intends to sell substantially all of Revlon's assets, except the Beauty Group, in order to reduce the size of the merged corporation, and to service the debt it will incur in financing the tender offer.

[**Issue**] Revlon contends that the Offer to Purchase violates Sections 14(d) and (e) of the Exchange Act because it fails to disclose: * * *

> (c) that the financing procured by Pantry Pride for the tender offer violates margin regulations; * * *

[Analysis] On July 12, 1985, Pantry Pride commenced a public offering (the July Offering) of $700 million in notes, debentures and exchangeable preferred stock (the July Prospectus) which advised that the proceeds of the offering would be used primarily "to finance acquisitions of new assets and business." However, it further advised that "[n]o specific determination has been made to acquire any particular company, assets, properties or business." * * *

On August 8, 1985, the Pantry Pride Group asked Chemical for a $500 million loan. * * *

Also on August 8, 1985, the Pantry Pride Group contacted Drexel for the first time to inquire as to its interest in participating in raising funds to finance a Revlon stock acquisition.

On August 14, 1985, Pantry Pride, Nicole and Chemical signed a commitment letter specifying the terms and conditions of the $500 million loan to Nicole. The terms give Chemical a "perfected first priority security interest" in all of Revlon's shares acquired by Nicole, and set forth default provisions restricting the sale, pledge or transfer of Revlon stock without Chemical's consent. On August 19, 1985, Pantry Pride announced its intention to acquire Revlon by an all-cash tender offer. * * *

Revlon alleges that the proposed financing for the Pantry Pride Group's tender offer violates the margin regulations promulgated under Section 7 of the Exchange Act. Revlon asserts that it has a private right of action for injunctive relief enforcing these margin regulations against the defendants.

Revlon also contends that Pantry Pride's failure to disclose margin violations of itself and others violates § 14(e) of the Williams Act. Although the nature of the alleged violations differ, Revlon contends violations of Regulations G, U and X, which will be discussed hereafter.

[Standing] It is settled in this circuit that there is no private right of action under Section 7 of the Exchange Act or the regulations thereunder. Although Revlon cannot maintain a private action on the margin regulations directly, it does have standing to allege failure to disclose margin violations. Thus, the court must determine whether these regulations were in fact violated.

[Reg. G now Reg. U] Regulation G, promulgated by the Federal Reserve Board under Section 7 of the Exchange Act, provides in pertinent part:

> No lender * * * shall extend any purpose credit, secured directly or indirectly by margin stock in an amount that exceeds the maximum loan value of the collateral securing the credit * * *.

[Now § 221.3(a)] The maximum loan value of any margin stock is set at 50% of its current market value. Therefore, in order for the September Securities Offering to violate Regulation G, (1) the purchasers of the securities must be "lenders" within the Board's definition, (2) the purpose of the offering must be to buy Revlon stock, (3) the debt must be secured directly or indirectly by Revlon stock, and (4) the amount of the debt must exceed 50% of the market value of the Revlon stock. The disputed issues between the parties are, first, whether the purchasers of the September securities are "lenders", and second, whether the securities are directly or indirectly secured by Revlon stock.

Regulation G defines "lender" to include every person who, in the ordinary course of business, extends credit secured directly or indirectly by margin stock in the amount of $200,000 or more in any calendar quarter. [§ 221.3(b)] However, the Federal Reserve Board staff has explicitly exempted purchasers of public offerings of debt securities from the definition of "lender" under Regulation G. Such public debt offerings have been construed not to involve the kind of extension of credit intended to be regulated by Section 7 of the Exchange Act, regardless of the purpose of that debt.

Revlon does not dispute the Board's interpretation. Rather it asserts that the public offering exception does not apply to the September Securities Offering, because Pantry Pride has imposed a minimum purchase requirement of $2.5 million on the offering. It asserts that this high minimum purchase requirement will assure that the $200,000 quarterly minimum will be met, thus all buyers would be within the definition of "lender" in the absence of the public offering exception. It asserts that the staff opinions contemplate "true" public offerings, and not the "nominal" public offering at issue here.

The Court believes, as a matter of public policy, there is much to commend Revlon's position. It is apparent that the Pantry Pride Group has taken advantage of a possible oversight on the part of the Board in formulating the public offering exception to the margin regulations. However, it is not the role of this Court to engage in the rulemaking activities delegated by Congress to the Federal Reserve Board. The Board and its staff bear primary responsibility for interpreting the Exchange Act, and this Court will accord substantial weight to the staff's opinions. Therefore, the Court finds that the Pantry Pride Group's September Securities Offering does not violate Regulation G, because it is a public debt offering exempt from the margin regulations. * * *

[**Reg.** X] Regulation X provides:

> Any borrower who willfully causes credit to be extended in contravention of Regulation G, T, or U * * * must conform the credit to the margin regulation that applies to the lender. 12 CFR § 224.3(b).

In order to find that the Pantry Pride Group violated Regulation X, the Court must find that credit was extended in violation of Regulations G or U. Since the Court has found no violations of those Regulations, the Pantry Pride Group cannot be found to have violated Regulation X.

Chemical-Margin Issues.Revlon has alleged that the Chemical loan in the amount of $500 million will violate Regulation U and that Chemical has "arranged" the Pantry Pride Group's financing, in further violation of Regulation U.

Regulation U provides, in pertinent part:

> No bank shall extend any purpose credit, secured directly or indirectly by margin stock, in an amount that exceeds the maximum loan value of the collateral securing the credit * * * 12 CFR § 221.3a (1985).

It is undisputed that Chemical Bank's loan to Pantry Pride will be directly secured by any Revlon stock that the Pantry Pride Group purchases. Revlon concedes that the Chemical loan, standing alone, is adequately margined.[1] However, Revlon asserts that the loan value of the Revlon stock Pantry Pride seeks to acquire must be shared with the $900 million of debt Pantry Pride anticipates from the September Securities Offering, since the September Offering is also indirectly secured by the Revlon stock. Thus, when these two debts are combined, the Chemical loan violates the margin requirements of Regulation U.

---

1. Chemical Bank is committed to loan the principle sum of $500 million to Nicole. The acquisition plan calls for the purchase of $1.85 billion worth of Revlon stock. Thus, the maximum loan value of this stock under the margin regulations is 50% of $1.85 billion, or $925 million.

For this claim to succeed, the Court must find that the September Offering is indirectly secured by Revlon stock. However, the September Offering, as a public offering, is exempt from the margin regulations and, thus, it cannot be directly or indirectly secured by Revlon stock within the requirements of Regulation U. * * *

Arranging Credit. Section 221.3(a)(3) of Regulation U provides:

> No bank may arrange for the extension or maintenance of any purpose credit, except upon the same terms and conditions under which the bank itself may extend or maintain purpose credit under this part. 12 CFR § 221.3(a)(3).

Revlon asserts that Chemical Bank has "arranged" the September Securities Offering in violation of Regulation U. However, since public offerings are exempt from the margin regulations, the September Offering cannot constitute an "extension of credit" within Regulation U. * * *

E. Application of the Junk Bond Rule

Caesars World, Inc. v. Sosnoff

United States District Court, Central District of California, 1987 Lexis 14293

William J. Rea, United States District Judge:

On the matter of Plaintiff's Motion for Preliminary Injunction now before this Court, the Court having considered the papers filed in support thereof and in opposition thereto and having heard oral argument,

IT IS HEREBY ORDERED that the Motion is GRANTED. The Court makes the following findings:

Plaintiff has established a probability of successfully demonstrating that,

(1) Caesars World, Inc. as an issuer of stock has standing to bring an implied cause of action under Section 7 of the Securities and Exchange Act and Federal Reserve Board Regulation U promulgated thereunder;

(2) In an action under Section 7, Caesars may assert the interests of its shareholders;

(3) If Defendants' Tender Offer with its current financing plan is not enjoined, the minority shareholders that would remain as owners of Caesars' common stock following the consummation of Defendants' Tender Offer would risk suffering the very harm that Section 7 was enacted to prevent. Defendants' acquisition of a large bloc of Caesars' stock on excessive margin credit would place minority shareholders at risk of a rapid deflation in the value of their stock. * * *

(4) Defendants' plan to finance their Tender Offer through MTS Holding Company's issuance of "$120 Increasing Dividend Cumulative Exchangeable Preferred Stock Exchangeable for Senior Subordinated Increasing Rate Notes." These are debt instruments due to the underlying and ultimate intentions of the issuer and the purchasers to create a creditor-debtor relationship;

(5) The Federal Reserve Board's Interpretative Ruling of January 1986 indicates [now 221.124, Section 14.11.B] that debt instruments issued by a shell corporation to finance acquisition of stock are secured by the stock so acquired. Applying this ruling to the present case, the debt securities issued by MTS Holding to finance its purchase of Caesars stock will be secured by the Caesars stock that MTS Holding acquires;

(6) Federal Reserve Board Regulation U provides that a purchaser may borrow no more than fifty percent of the funds used to purchase stock if that stock is to be pledged as security to the lender(s). Defendants' financing plan violates Regulation U because MTS Holding will issue debt securities to raise $475 million of the approximately $1 billion purchase price of Caesars stock, and Defendants plan to borrow just under $500 million in secured loans to raise most of the remainder of the purchase. Accordingly, nearly all of Defendants' purchase will be financed with borrowings secured by Caesars stock in violation of Regulation U; * * *

(7) Plaintiff and its shareholders would be irreparably harmed if defendants' Tender Offer is not preliminarily enjoined.

In light of these findings, IT IS HEREBY ORDERED that:

1. Defendants * * * are enjoined during the pendency of this action from purchasing any shares of the common stock of Caesars World, Inc. pursuant to their Tender Offer as originally constituted and as amended and supplemented.

2. Nothing herein shall prevent Defendants from commencing a new tender offer for Caesars shares in full compliance with all requirements of law, including the federal securities laws. * * *

F. Summary Problems on Margin Regulation

1. Acquiring Corporation (AC) is considering a leveraged acquisition of the stock of Publicly-Held Target Corporation (PHTC) for $100 million. AC is a small start-up firm that plans to engage in LBOs. Investment Banker (IB) is working with AC on the transaction. It is proposed that AC will make a tender offer for 70% of PHTC's stock at $10 a share for a total of $70 million and then do a second-step freezeout reverse subsidiary merger for the 30% balance of PHTC's stock also at $10 per share for a total of $30 million.

IB has proposed that the acquisition be financed pursuant to one of the following financing structures:

First Financing Plan

1. AC will provide $10 million, which will be used in the first step tender offer. These funds will come from equity contributions AC receives from its shareholders.

2. First Bank of Coral Gables will provide a $90 million loan for the balance of the purchase price.

Second Financing Plan

1. AC will provide $10 million as specified above.

2. IB will assist AC in doing a public issuance of junk bonds to raise the $90 million balance of the purchase price. What if the bonds are issued in a private offering?

Third Financing Plan

1. AC will provide $10 million as specified above.

2. IB will make AC a bridge loan of $90 million to cover the $90 million purchase price. The bridge loan will be replaced shortly after the acquisition with a public issuance of junk bonds.

Fourth Financing Plan

1. AC will provide $10 million as specified above.

2. First Bank of Coral Gables will provide a loan for $40 million, which will be used in the first-step tender offer.

3. IB will assist AC in doing a public offering of junk bonds to finance the $20 million balance of the funds needed for the first-step tender offer.

4. IB will assist AC in doing a private offering of junk debt in the amount of $30 million to be used in the second-step freezeout merger.

5. What would be the result under each of the above financing plans if instead of a tender offer followed by a freezeout merger the transaction were structured as a sale by PHTC of its assets to AC for $100 million or a transaction in which PHTC were acquired in a reverse subsidiary merger for $100 million?

§ 14.12 Potential Liability of PE's Investment Funds for Pension Liability of Bankrupt Portfolio Company

A. Introduction

Under the Employee Retirement Income Security Act of 1974 (ERISA), certain "basic pension benefits" are guaranteed by the Pension Benefit Guaranty Corporation (PBGC). Thus, if an employer goes into bankruptcy and a defined benefit pension plan is underfunded, the PBGC may pay the current retirees and current employees upon their retirement a minimum pension benefit.

In such case, ERISA grants to the PBGC the power to seek the amount of the underfunding from certain parties, such as controlling shareholders in certain cases. This is a potential problem for a PE firm and its related investment funds when one of the companies owned by the funds (*i.e.*, a portfolio company) goes into bankruptcy. While the details behind this issue are beyond the scope of this book, the short excerpt in the next section from the *Sun Capital* case illustrates the issue, and the issue is discussed in greater detail in Thompson, *Mergers, Acquisitions and Tender Offers*, *supra* Section 1.10, at Section 14:12.

B. Potential Liability in *Sun Capital*

Sun Capital Partners III, LP v. New England Teamsters & Trucking Indus. Pension Fund

First Circuit Court of Appeals, 2013 724 F.3d 129

LYNCH, Chief Judge. This case presents important issues of first impression as to withdrawal liability for the pro rata share of unfunded vested benefits to a multiemployer pension fund of a bankrupt company, here, Scott Brass, Inc. (SBI). *See* Employee Retirement Income Security Act of 1974 (ERISA), 29 U.S.C. § 1001 et seq., as amended by the Multiemployer Pension Plan Amendment Act of 1980 [2] (MPPAA), 29 U.S.C. § 1381 et seq. [The applicable statute imposes on certain parties' liability for accrued but unpaid pensions.]

This litigation considers the imposition of liability as to three groups: [1] two private equity funds [organized by Sun Capital, a PE firm], which assert that they are mere passive investors that had indirectly controlled and tried to turn around SBI, a struggling portfolio company [i.e., one of the companies owned by Sun Capital and its funds]; [2] the New England Teamsters and Trucking Industry Pension Fund (TPF), to which the bankrupt company had withdrawal pension obligations and which seeks to impose those obligations on the equity funds; and [3] ultimately, if the TPF becomes insolvent, the federal Pension Benefit Guaranty Corporation (PBGC), which insures multiemployer pension plans such as the one involved here.

If the TPF becomes insolvent, then the benefits to the SBI workers are reduced to a PBGC guaranteed level. According to the PBGC's brief, at present, that level is about $12,870 for employees with 30 years of service.

The plaintiffs are the two private equity funds, which sought a declaratory judgment against the TPF. The TPF, which brought into the suit other entities related to the equity funds, has counterclaimed and sought payment of the withdrawal liability at issue. * * *

We conclude that at least one of the private equity funds which operated SBI, through layers of fund-related entities, was not merely a "passive" investor, but sufficiently operated, managed, and was advantaged by its relationship with its portfolio company, the now bankrupt SBI. We also conclude that further factual development is necessary as to the other equity fund. We decide that the district court erred in ending the potential claims against the equity funds by entering summary judgment for them under the "trades or businesses" aspect of the two-part "control group" test under 29 U.S.C. § 1301(b)(1). *See* Sun Capital Partners III, LP v. New Eng. Teamsters & Trucking Indus. Pension Fund, 903 F. Supp. 2d 107, 116–18, 124 (D. Mass. 2012).

As a result, we remand for further factual development and for further proceedings under the second part of the "control group" test, that of "common control," in 29 U.S.C. § 1301(b)(1). The district court was, however, correct to enter summary judgment in favor of the private equity funds on the TPF's claim of liability on the ground that the funds had engaged in a transaction to evade or avoid withdrawal liability. *See* 29 U.S.C. § 1392(c); Sun Capital, 903 F. Supp. 2d at 123–24.

§ 14.13 Potential Antitrust Liability for PE Firms Engaging in "Club Deals"

Dahl v. Bain Capital Partners, LLC

Federal District Court Mass, 2013 937 F. Supp. 2d 119

[This case involves an antitrust action against certain PE firms that engaged in "club deals." These are deals in which two or more PE firms would combine in making an acquisition. Although a full discussion of this issue is beyond the scope of this book, the following description by the court of the plaintiffs' claims, which it did not dismiss, provides a perspective on the principal issues:]

The Alleged Overarching Conspiracy. Plaintiffs contend that the evidence supports a finding of an overarching conspiracy on the part of the Defendants to allocate the market for large LBOs. They contend that the evidence establishes a motive on the part of the Defendants to conspire, an opportunity to do so, and actions in furtherance of the overarching conspiracy, including the establishment of rules of conduct. They further assert that the economic evidence supports a finding of an overarching conspiracy.

Plaintiffs assert that the alleged overarching conspiracy was in effect by 2003. At that time, the private equity industry had entered an era of "mega-fund" investment, making the buyout of "mega-cap" targets—large multi-billion dollar companies—possible for a limited number of private equity firms who could garner sufficient funds to compete for the transactions.

Plaintiffs assert that the late 1980s marked the last time the market conditions in the industry were as fertile. During that time, the then-largest private equity firm, Defendant KKR, conducted a $31 billion LBO of RJR Nabisco. Leading up to the RJR Nabisco transaction, a bidding war between potential purchasers erupted, causing the price to rise substantially.

The transactions at issue were all "mega-cap" transactions and the Defendants, who are some of the largest private equity firms in the world, constituted a portion of the limited pool of potential participants in those transactions. Plaintiffs contend that Defendants understood that the large amounts of capital and access to cheap debt could create an RJR Nabisco-like bidding war for other large LBOs, where billions of dollars of capital could be deployed to muscle out competition. Plaintiffs contend that Defendants understood that, by working together, they could suppress competition and avoid another price escalation.

§ 14.14 Summary Problem on LBOs

RJR Corporation (RJR), a publicly-held Delaware corporation, has both common and non-convertible preferred stock outstanding. RJR also has publicly-held investment-grade debentures, which are rated AAA by Standard & Poor's (S&P). The debentures are RJR's only significant liability. RJR's summary balance sheet is as follows:

RJR SUMMARY BALANCE SHEET

Assets		Liabilities	
Assets:	$5 Billion	**Debentures:**	$1 Billion
		Equity	
		Preferred Stock Redemption Value:	$1 Billion
		Common Stock Paid in Capital and Retained Earnings:	$3 Billion
TOTAL ASSETS	$5 Billion	**TOTAL LIABILITIES and EQUITY:**	$5 Billion

The tax basis of RJR's assets is equal to the $5 billion book value of the assets. The current trading value of the debentures is $1 billion, because the interest rate currently paid on the debentures is equal to the current interest rate on AAA debentures. The current trading value of the preferred stock is also $1 billion, because the dividend rate on the preferred is equal to the dividend yield on preferred stock with similar risk. The current trading value of the common stock is $15 billion. Thus, RJR's implicit debt to equity ratio is one to sixteen, that is, $1 billion of debt to $16 billion of common and preferred.

KRK, a private equity firm, has decided that RJR is a good candidate for a leveraged buyout (LBO). On the basis of a discounted cash flow analysis [*see* Chapter 7], KRK has determined that in addition to RJR's balance sheet assets, which have a fair market value equal to the $5 billion book value, RJR also has goodwill of $25 billion. Thus, on a fair market value basis, RJR's summary balance sheet would look as follows:

RJR SUMMARY FAIR MARKET VALUE BALANCE SHEET

Assets		Liabilities and Equity	
Hard Assets:	$ 5 Billion	Debentures:	$ 1 Billion
Goodwill:	$25 Billion		
		Preferred Stock Redemption Value:	$ 1 Billion
		Common Stock Fair Market Value:	$28 Billion
TOTAL ASSETS	$30 Billion	TOTAL LIABILITIES and EQUITY:	$30 Billion

KRK has approached Ross Thompson, the Chairman and CEO of RJR, about the possibility of doing a leveraged management buyout of RJR. KRK has proposed that Ross and other senior management of RJR (Management Team), who in the aggregate own 1% of the stock of RJR, join KRK in making a bid for RJR's common stock at a price of $23 billion, which is $8 billion more than the current trading value of the common and $5 billion less than KRK's estimate of the actual value of that stock. The proposed transaction is as follows:

(1) KRK and the Management Team would form Holding Company (HC), a Delaware corporation. Management Team would contribute to HC its 1% holding of RJR stock, which for this purpose would be valued at $230 million (*i.e.*, 1% of $23 billion), and would receive 10% of the stock of HC. KRK would put in cash of $2.07 billion (*i.e.*, 9% of $23 billion) for 90% of the stock of HC.

(2) HC would form a subsidiary (Sub), and the $2.07 billion of cash received by HC from KRK would be contributed to Sub. HC would continue to own the RJR stock contributed to it by Management Team.

(3) With the assistance of KRK, Sub would raise in a private offering through the issuance of non-investment grade bonds (*i.e.*, junk bonds) $20.7 billion in cash to be used in the acquisition of the common stock of RJR. After this issuance Sub will have cash of $22.77 billion. (*i.e.*, 99% of the $23 billion offer price), and HC would own 1% of the stock of RJR.

(4) HC, Sub, and RJR would enter into a merger agreement providing for the merger of Sub into RJR in a reverse subsidiary merger, with the public shareholders of RJR receiving the $22.77 billion in cash for their shares, and with HC ending up with 100% of the stock of RJR. Pursuant to the merger, RJR would assume the $20.7 billion of junk debt issued by Sub. Thus, RJR's post-LBO summary balance sheet would look as follows:

RJR POST-LBO SUMMARY BALANCE SHEET

Assets		Liabilities	
Hard Assets:	$ 5 Billion	**Debentures:**	$ 1 Billion
Goodwill:	$20 Billion	**New Junk Bonds:**	$20.7 Billion
		Equity	
		Preferred Stock:	$ 1 Billion
		Common Stock Fair Market Value:	$2.3 Billion
TOTAL ASSETS	$25 Billion	TOTAL LIABILITIES and EQUITY:	$25 Billion

(1) Describe briefly the economics behind the above deal. What is driving this deal? What is the post-LBO debt-to-equity ratio?

(2) What are the tax consequences to the various parties to the transaction? *See* Chapter 5.

(3) What is the accounting treatment for KRK, HC and RJR? Assume that KRK is a publicly-held corporation. *See* Chapter 6.

(4) What steps should RJR's board take in considering this offer from KRK and Management Team? Should the board seek other offers? What standard governs the action of the board? Do the directors have any potential personal liability from this transaction? *See* Chapter 3.

(5) What are the implications for this transaction under the Federal securities laws?

(6) What result if RJR goes into bankruptcy within one year of the transaction? *See* Section 14.8.

(7) What is likely to happen to the value of RJR's old debentures and of its preferred stock as a result of this transaction? What remedies do the debenture holders and preferred holders have? *See* Section 14.10.

(8) Does this transaction comply with the federal margin rules? *See* Section 14.11. What if Sub made a public offering of the junk bonds?

References

ALI, *Principles of Corporate Governance: Analysis and Recommendation*, *supra* Section 1.10, at Section 5.15.

Blackwood, *Applying Fraudulent Conveyance Law to Leveraged Buyouts*, 42 Duke L.J. 340 (1992).

Easterbrook and Fischel, *The Economic Structure of Corporate Law* 134–139 (1991).

Kling and Nugent Simon, *Negotiated Acquisitions*, *supra* Section 1.10, at Chapter 20, (LBOs) and Section 5.07. (margin rules).

Lorne, *Negotiated and Contested Transactions*, *supra* Section 1.10, at Chapter 6.

Thompson, *Mergers, Acquisitions and Tender Offers*, *supra* Section 1.10, at Chapter 14.

Chapter 15

Drafting Stock Purchase Agreements, Asset Acquisition Agreements, and Merger Agreements

§ 15.1 Scope

This chapter focuses on the drafting of three types of acquisition agreements: stock purchase agreements, asset acquisition agreements, and merger agreements. These are the principal types of agreements for effectuating an acquisition. An acquisition can also be effectuated pursuant to variants of these forms of agreements or by use of a joint venture agreement (*see* Chapter 27). To facilitate an understanding of the issues, the Sections of this chapter refer to the following acquisition agreements, which are set out in *M&A Statutes, Rules, and Documents, supra* Section 1.1:

- The 1989 Time-Warner Merger Agreement, Documentary Appendix A, a reverse subsidiary stock merger;
- The 2005 J.P. Morgan-Bank One Merger Agreement, Documentary Appendix D, a direct stock merger;
- The 2005 Global Toys-Toys "R" Us Merger Agreement, Documentary Appendix F, a reverse subsidiary cash merger;
- Sample Stock Purchase Agreement, Documentary Appendix U; and
- Sample Asset Acquisition Agreement, Documentary Appendix V.

Section 15.2 sets out an introductory problem dealing with the three forms of acquisition agreements. Section 15.3 addresses some of the basic legal issues faced in structuring the various forms of acquisition agreements. This section refers to other sections in many of the chapters found in this book. Section 15.4 discusses common provisions found in acquisition agreements, including representations and warranties, covenants, closing conditions, and indemnification. Subsequent sections explore these concepts in greater detail.

Section 15.5 examines the section of an acquisition agreement designating the parties to the transaction, Section 15.6 addresses the "whereas" clauses, and Section 15.7 discusses the three ways of dealing with defined terms. Section 15.8 deals with the provision of an acquisition agreement describing the basic purchase and sale or merger transaction, and Section 15.9 addresses representations and warranties. Section 15.10 discusses the covenants made by the parties regarding actions to be taken between the signing of the agreement and the closing of the transaction. Section 15.11 addresses the conditions to closing. Section 15.12 considers termination provisions. This section includes the *IBP* decision, which deals with a public acquiror's right to terminate the transaction and a public target's right to seek specific performance. There, the public acquiror wanted to walk from the transaction because of its assertion that (1) the public target breached a representation and warranty, and (2) a material adverse effect (MAE) had occurred. Section 15.13 explores the provisions dealing with the survival or non-survival of the representations and warranties and the related concept of indemnification. This section contains the *ABRY* case, which addresses the exclusivity under Delaware law of indemnification as a remedy for breach of representations contained in the agreement, and the *AES* case, which deals with the applicability of Rule 10b-5 in the face of a purchaser's contractual agreement to rely only on representations in the agreement.

Section 15.14 addresses various types of deal protection devices, such as no talks, termination fees, and reverse termination fees. As will be seen there, other sections of the book also address these issues. Section 15.15 discusses provisions governing general matters, and Section 15.16 examines legal opinions. Section 15.17 addresses employment agreements and non-competition agreements. Section 15.18 deals with registration rights, which may be provided for when the consideration paid by the acquiring corporation is restricted stock.

The materials in this chapter are discussed in greater detail in Thompson, *Mergers, Acquisitions and Tender Offers, supra* Section 1.10, Chapter 2. For other discussions of various aspects of drafting acquisition agreements, *see e.g. ABA Model Stock Purchase Agreement, supra* Section 1.10; *ABA Model Asset Purchase Agreement, supra* Section 1.10; ABA, *Model Merger Agreement for the Acquisition of a Public Company* (2011), *supra* Section 1.10; Freund, *Anatomy of a Merger, supra* Section 1.10, at Chapters 5 to 12; Ginsburg and Levin, *Mergers and Acquisitions, supra* Section 1.10, at *Sample Acquisition Agreements with Tax and Legal Analysis*; and Kling and Nugent, *Negotiated Acquisitions, supra* Section 1.10, at Chapters 10 to 15.

§ 15.2 Introductory Problem on Drafting Acquisition Agreements

Acquiring Corporation (AC) is a publicly-held corporation, the stock of which is traded on the New York Stock Exchange. Target Corporation (TC) is held by five shareholders, each of whom owns 20% of the stock. One of the shareholders of TC, Shareholder A, wants very much to continue to be active in the business, but the other shareholders would like to cash out.

The board of directors of AC and the five shareholders of TC have tentatively agreed to a transaction, the form of which is addressed below, in which AC will acquire substantially all of the assets and assume substantially all of the liabilities of TC in exchange for $70 million in AC common stock, which will amount to 30% of AC's outstanding stock after the transaction. TC has $25 million of liabilities on its balance sheet. AC has agreed that A will become an employee of AC after the transaction and will receive an annual salary of $500,000 plus bonus.

A. Scene One

The parties have tentatively agreed to structure the transaction as a tax-free reorganization under Section 368(a)(2)(E), the reverse subsidiary merger reorganization. [*See* Chapter 5.] AC will issue its stock in a private offering under Regulation D. [*See* Chapter 4.] Although the TC shareholders are willing to take the AC stock in a Reg. D offering, they want to be able to sell the stock without restrictions.

The investment banker who put together the deal has sent to each of the parties the original merger agreement pursuant to which Time, Inc. was to acquire Warner Communications, Inc., in a reverse subsidiary merger reorganization. [*See* Documentary Appendix A of *M&A Statutes, Rules, and Documents, supra* Section 1.1.] The investment banker has asked the lawyers for the parties to be prepared to discuss the modifications of this Time-Warner merger agreement that would be necessary to reflect the terms of this deal. Also, the parties want to be advised on the tax, corporate, accounting, Hart-Scott-Rodino, and securities consequences of this type of transaction.

B. Scene Two

In the event the parties cannot come to terms on the merger agreement in Scene One, the investment banker has also sent to the parties the Sample Stock Purchase Agreement. [*See* Documentary Appendix U] The investment banker has tentatively advised the parties that if the transaction cannot be structured as a tax-free merger then it could be structured as a purchase by AC of the stock of TC for $70 million in cash. The investment banker has asked the lawyers for the parties to be prepared to discuss the modifications to the Sample Stock Purchase Agreement that would be necessary to reflect this type of stock purchase. Also, the parties want to be advised of the tax, corporate, accounting, Hart-Scott-Rodino, and securities consequences of this type of transaction.

In the course of conducting its due diligence, AC discovers that TC has a potential outstanding tax liability of approximately $25 million. This is a contingent liability, which is not required to be reflected on TC's balance sheet under generally accepted accounting procedures (GAAP). Also, TC's plant, where it manufactures widgets, may have some exposure under the environmental laws. How should the parties deal with these issues?

C. Scene Three

The investment banker realizes that this deal could possibly be restructured as a purchase by AC of TC's assets and an assumption of certain of TC's liabilities in exchange for $70 million in cash. He has, therefore, sent to each of the parties the Sample Asset Acquisition Agreement, Documentary Appendix V. The investment banker has asked the lawyers for the parties to be prepared to discuss the modifications to the Sample Asset Acquisition Agreement that would be necessary to reflect this type of asset purchase. Also, the parties want to be advised of the tax, corporate, accounting, Hart-Scott-Rodino and securities consequences of this type of transaction. In the asset acquisition, AC does not want to assume any unstated liabilities. How should the parties deal with TC's $25 million contingent tax liability and its potential environmental exposure? Is it beneficial to AC to do an asset acquisition?

D. Scene Four

The parties have signed a stock purchase agreement similar to the Sample Stock Purchase Agreement, Documentary Appendix U, which contains in Section 2.1(b) a representation by the selling shareholders to the effect that there are no undisclosed liabilities. During the conduct of its due diligence, AC discovers the potential $25 million tax liability and the potential exposure to environmental liability.

(1) Can AC refuse to consummate the transaction, that is, can AC "walk", and, if so, pursuant to what provision?

(2) Can AC refuse to close and sue for damages?

(3) Can AC close and then sue for damages? Should AC disclose to TC that it has discovered this problem?

(4) What if AC does not discover the contingent tax liability and environmental exposure during its due diligence and such liabilities arise after the closing? What rights does AC have under the agreement?

(5) Any suggestions for AC on the structuring of the purchase price to address the risk of discovery of undisclosed liabilities after the closing?

§ 15.3 Overview of Legal Considerations Applicable to the Structuring of Acquisition Agreements

A. Introduction and Purchase Price Considerations

Stock Purchase Agreements (SPAs) are entered into between the acquiring corporation (or a subsidiary), on the one hand, and the selling shareholders of the target corporation, on the other. An SPA may be used in the acquisition of all of the stock of a closely-held target where all of the shareholders are willing to sell. Also, it may be used in the acquisition of a subsidiary corporation. If the target is publicly-held, however, it will be practically impossible to arrange for all of the shareholders to enter into an SPA. Consequently, stock acquisitions of publicly-held corporations are effectuated pursuant to tender offers, which are addressed in Chapters 17 through 20. An SPA may, however, be used in the acquisition of a portion of the stock of a publicly-held corporation from a single or small group of shareholders, just as it can be used in the acquisition of a portion of the stock of a closely-held corporation. Certain corporate and securities issues arising in stock acquisitions are discussed in Chapter 11.

Asset Acquisition Agreements (AAAs) are entered into between the acquiring corporation (or a subsidiary), on the one hand, and the target corporation, on the other. An AAA may cover all or a portion of the target's assets and may provide for the assumption of all, some, or none of the target's liabilities. Often times the target will be liquidated after a sale of its assets. Although AAAs are generally used in the acquisition of the assets of a closely-held corporation, or of a division of a publicly-held or closely-held corporation, they may also be used in the acquisition of the assets of a publicly-held corporation. Certain corporate and securities issues arising in asset acquisitions are explored in Chapter 12.

Merger Agreements (MAs) are entered into between the acquiring corporation (or in the case of a triangular merger, both the acquiring corporation and its subsidiary), on the one hand, and the target corporation, on the other. MAs can be used in the acquisition of a closely-held corporation, a subsidiary, or a publicly-held corporation. Mergers, however, are much more common in the acquisition of a publicly-held corporation and are typically accomplished with an acquisition subsidiary in a triangular merger, which is most often structured as a reverse subsidiary merger. Certain corporate and securities issues arising in mergers are examined in Chapter 13.

SPAs, AAAs, and MAs have similar terms and conditions. For example, the acquisition agreement for a particular target corporation will contain similar provisions without respect to whether the transaction is structured as a stock acquisition, an asset acquisition, or a merger. There will, however, be different provisions in each of the agreements. For example, the stockholders of the target will be parties to the SPA but may not necessarily be parties to an AAA and an MA. On the other hand, the target must be a party to both an AAA and an MA. Also, all of the assets and liabilities of the target as of the closing date are acquired in a stock acquisition or merger, but only specified assets and liabilities are acquired in an asset acquisition. There are, however, potential issues with successor liability in asset acquisitions. [*See* Chapter 12]

The consideration paid in each form of transaction can be cash, common stock, preferred stock, debt instruments, other property, or any combination thereof. The consideration can be paid immediately or on a deferred basis, such as with (1) a payment contingent on the future performance of the target (*i.e.*, an earnout), (2) a hold back escrow that is paid out if certain conditions are satisfied, and (3) a deferred payment note. Also, a deferred payment may be used to secure the seller's indemnification undertaking with respect to the accuracy of its representations and warranties. There are, in essence, no limits on the structure of the purchase price. And, the purchase price may be subject to post-closing adjustment to take account of, for example, differences in the net worth or net current assets of the target, between that shown on its financials available at the signing and the actual amounts at closing, as determined by a post-closing audit. This method is utilized in Section 1.5 of the Sample Asset Acquisition Agreement, Documentary Appendix V.

In structuring acquisitions of publicly-held targets for stock of the acquiring corporation, the parties may not be willing to accept a fixed exchange ratio (*e.g.*, two shares of the acquiring corporation for each share of the target), because of the potential movements in the price of the stock of the acquiror prior to the closing.

For example, assume that at the time the deal is structured the target's shares are selling for $30 per share and the acquiror's shares are selling for $25 per share. Assume further that the exchange ratio is set at two acquiror shares for each target share, indicating the payment of $50 per share for the target stock, a $20 premium. The acquiror is concerned that if its price rises significantly by the time of the closing (say to $30 per share) the target's shareholders will receive a windfall (*i.e.*, $60 per share rather than $50 per share). On the other hand, the target's shareholders are concerned that if the acquiror's stock drops significantly by the time of the closing (say to $20 per share), then they will suffer an unfair loss (*i.e.*, $40 per share rather that $50 per share).

The parties could solve this dilemma by putting both a ceiling and a floor on the exchange ratio. To illustrate, they could provide that (1) if the acquiror's shares at the closing are trading above $27.50 per share, then the target shareholders will receive in the acquisition shares of the acquiror with a value of $55 (*i.e.*, a ceiling), and (2) if the acquiror's shares at the closing are trading below $22.50 per share, then the target's shareholders will receive in the acquisition shares of the acquiror with a value of $45 (a floor). If the ceiling is triggered the target's shareholders receive less than two shares of the acquiror for each of their target shares, and if the floor is triggered they receive more than two target shares for each target share. The combination of a ceiling and a floor is referred to as a collar.

As demonstrated in Chapter 5, each form of transaction can be structured as either a taxable acquisition or as a tax-free reorganization. To qualify as a reorganization, all or a substantial part of the consideration must be stock of the acquiring corporation.

Each form of acquisition has its own advantages and disadvantages, and the lawyer's role is to help the parties settle on the best form for the particular situation. The structure may be sensitive to tax considerations as illustrated in Chapter 5; however, the accounting treatment, that is, the required "acquisition" method, is not dependent upon whether the transaction is effectuated as a stock acquisition, an asset acquisition or a merger. [*See* Chapter 6] Also, as illustrated in Chapter 4, if the acquiring corporation issues securities to the target's shareholders, then without regard to the form of the transaction, the securities will either have to be registered as required by Section 5 of the Securities Act of 1933 or the transaction must be exempt from registration, generally under the private offering exemption under Section 4(a)(2) of the 33 Act.

The following sections discuss some of the advantages and disadvantages of each form of acquisition; they do not discuss such factors as pension law and ERISA, which are briefly introduced in Chapter 33. These factors can have an impact on the structuring of acquisition agreements, and experts in these and other regulatory areas must be consulted where appropriate.

B. Stock Purchase Agreements

For the reasons discussed in Chapter 5, in a taxable acquisition of a stand-alone target, the stock acquisition will avoid the corporate level tax under the federal income tax that would apply in an asset acquisition followed by a liquidation. Depending on the particular state law, there also may not be any state sales or income tax liability at the target level in a stock acquisition.

If the consideration paid is solely voting stock of the acquiring corporation the stock acquisition may qualify as a tax-free reorganization under Section 368(a)(1)(B).

Stock acquisitions generally are the simplest form of acquisition because the only items required to be transferred are the stock certificates held by the target's shareholders. Each selling shareholder signs the SPA, and there is no need to have a directors' or shareholders' meeting because no corporate action is required. Since there is no corporate action, there are no appraisal rights, unless the transaction is treated as a *de facto* merger, which would generally not be the case. [*See* Chapter 2]

There is generally no assignment required for outstanding contracts such as leases, supply contracts and debt instruments, unless the contract has a "change of control" provision. Such a provision terminates the contract upon a change of control, unless consent to the transaction is received. Consequently, it is imperative that the target's major contracts be reviewed to determine whether they contain change of control provisions.

Although the target's liabilities are not assumed by the acquiring corporation in a stock acquisition, if a consent is required pursuant to a change of control provision, the acquiring corporation may be required to guarantee the target's liability as a condition to receipt of such consent.

Because of its simplicity, a stock acquisition can generally be effectuated within a short period of time. However, if pre-merger notification forms must be filed under Hart-Scott-Rodino [*see* Chapter 9], the transactions cannot be completed until 30 days after the date of the filing of the forms, unless the parties receive early termination. If a second request is issued, the transaction will be further delayed.

As indicated in Section 11.3.B, the anti-fraud provisions of the federal securities laws apply to the sale by the selling shareholders of the stock of the target.

C. Asset Acquisition Agreements

As discussed in Chapter 5, a taxable asset acquisition of a stand-alone subchapter C corporation followed by a liquidation will generate a double tax under the federal income tax, and, therefore, this may be a strong reason for avoiding this form of transaction. State law may also impose a state income tax on the target's sale of assets; however, an exemption may apply for the state sales tax. If the consideration paid is voting stock of the acquiring corporation, the transaction may qualify as in tax-free reorganization under Section 368(a)(1)(C). [*See* Chapter 5]

One of the principal advantages of an asset acquisition is that the acquiror can acquire only those assets and assume only those liabilities specified in the AAA. Thus, the acquiring firm may be able to avoid assuming certain specific liabilities and also contingent and unknown liabilities, unless the transaction is treated as a *de facto* merger [*see* Chapter 2] or "successor liability" attaches [*see* Chapter 12]. To insure that the assets of the acquiring corporation are not exposed to the target's assumed liabilities, the acquisition may be made by a subsidiary of the acquiring corporation.

Balanced against the flexibility in acquiring specific assets and assuming specific liabilities is the complexity in effectuating an asset acquisition. Transfer documents must be prepared for each of the assets being transferred, although a global bill of sale may be used for certain assets. The bulk sales laws may have to be compiled with. [*See* Chapter 12] Also, assignments must be received for certain contracts, and the acquiror might have to pay something to obtain consent to the contract assignment.

If the transaction involves a sale of all or substantially all of the target's assets, the target's shareholders will have to vote to approve the transaction [*see* Chapter 2], and the target's shareholders may or may not have appraisal rights, depending on state law. [*See* Chapter 2]

The 30-day waiting period that applies if an HSR pre-merger notification filing must be made may be of little concern, because the transaction may take more than 30 days to complete in any event.

D. Merger Agreements

As discussed in Chapter 5, mergers can either be taxable or tax-free. Generally, the most efficient form of taxable merger is the reverse subsidiary merger in which a newly formed subsidiary of the acquiring corporation merges into the target with the target's shareholders receiving the merger consideration and with all of the post-merger stock of the target owned by the acquiring corporation. For example, this form of transaction was used in the Time-Warner Merger Agreement, Documentary Appendix A, a stock reverse subsidiary merger, and the Global Toys-Toys "R" Us Merger Agreement, Documentary Appendix F, a cash reverse subsidiary merger. The reverse subsidiary merger can be structured as a tax-free reorganization under Section 368(1)(a)(2)(E), provided, among other things, at least 80% of the consideration paid is voting stock of the acquiring corporation. [*See* Chapter 5] If cash is used, this type of transaction is treated as a stock acquisition and gives rise to only one level of federal income tax: A tax on the target's shareholders. Generally there is no state income or sales tax on the target corporation in a merger transaction, but the treatment depends on state law.

The boards of both the target and the acquiring corporation and in the case of a triangular merger, the board of the subsidiary must approve the MA, and the shareholders of the target, and in certain cases the shareholders of the acquiring corporation [*see* Chapter 2], must approve the transaction. Depending on the circumstances, the target's and acquiror's shareholders may or may not have dissenters' rights.

In the merger, the assets and liabilities of the target corporation are transferred to the acquiring corporation (or its subsidiary) by operation of law upon the filing of the merger certificate with the secretary of state. [*See* Chapter 2] In a reverse subsidiary merger, the target's assets and liabilities simply stay with the target. The target's contracts may, however, have "change of control" provisions that terminate the contract unless consent to the transaction is received.

An important reason for structuring the transaction as a triangular merger is to insulate the acquiring corporation's assets from the target's liabilities.

§ 15.4 Outline of Common Provisions of Acquisition Agreements

Most acquisition agreements, whether SPAs, AAAs, or MAs, have certain basic provisions. *See* Freund, *Anatomy of a Merger, supra* Section 1.10, at 147–148. Although the order of the various articles or sections in an acquisition agreement may differ, virtually every acquisition agreement will have a provision addressing the following items: 1. The Parties to the Transactions, 2. Whereas Clauses, 3. Defined Terms, 4. Description of the basic purchase and sale or merger transaction, 5. Representations and Warranties, 6. Covenants, 7. Conditions to Closing, 8. Termination, 9. Indemnification, generally in acquisitions of closely-held corporations, and 10. Miscellaneous Matters.

The discussion here deals with acquisition agreements for deals structured as deferred closings. These are transactions in which the acquisition agreement is signed and the closing occurs at a later date, which is the case with most acquisitions. Thus, there is a delay between the signing and the closing. If the execution of the acquisition agreement and closing occur simultaneously, certain provisions of the acquisition agreement may be omitted, such as the conditions to closing, pre-closing covenants, and rights to terminate the agreement.

§ 15.5 The Parties to the Transaction

The agreement will first set out the parties to the transaction. For example, the first paragraph of the merger agreement in the Time-Warner transaction, Documentary Appendix A, reads as follows:

> AGREEMENT AND PLAN OF MERGER dated as of March 3, 1989 * * * among Time, Incorporated [the acquiring corporation], a Delaware corporation (Time), TW SUB, INC., a Delaware corporation and a wholly owned subsidiary of Time (Sub), and Warner Communications, Inc. [the target], a Delaware corporation (WCI).

This transaction was a reverse subsidiary merger and, therefore, there were three parties to the transaction: the acquiring corporation, Time; the acquiring subsidiary, Sub; and the target corporation, WCI.

If an acquiring corporation were buying the stock of a closely-held target corporation pursuant to a SPA, the opening paragraph might read similarly to the opening paragraph of the Sample Stock Purchase Agreement in Documentary Appendix U, as follows:

> STOCK PURCHASE AGREEMENT, dated as of March 31, 1989 between Acquiring Corporation, Inc., a Delaware corporation (the Acquiring Corporation), and the individuals named in Exhibit 1 attached hereto (the Selling Shareholders), being all of the shareholders of Target Corporation, Inc., a Delaware Corporation (the Target Corporation).

In some SPAs the target corporation may also be a party to the transaction. [*See Model Stock Purchase Agreement, supra* Section 1.10, at 1 to 3]

If an acquiring corporation were buying the assets of a target pursuant to an AAA, the opening paragraph might read similarly to the opening paragraph of the Sample Asset Acquisition Agreement, Documentary Appendix V, which reads as follows:

> ASSET ACQUISITION AGREEMENT, dated as of March 3, 1989 between Acquiring Corporation, Inc., a Delaware Corporation (the Acquiring Corporation) and Selling Corporation, Inc., a Delaware corporation, (the Selling Corporation).

If the target is a closely-held corporation, the shareholders of the target may also be parties to the transaction. The target shareholders may become parties at the request of the acquiring corporation primarily for two reasons. The first is so that the acquiror knows the shareholders have approved the sale of all or substantially all of the assets of the target and that this will not be a condition of the closing. Secondly, if the target is liquidating following the sale, the proceeds will be distributed to the shareholders, and the buyer may wish to have the shareholders join in the indemnification undertaking of the target.

§ 15.6 The Whereas Clauses

Many acquisition agreements will contain several whereas clauses or recitals that set out the basic terms of the transactions. These clauses will follow the opening paragraph as illustrated in the Time-Warner merger agreement in Documentary Appendix A. *See also* Documentary Appendices D–F. Although not required, whereas clauses, which generally are "declarative statements of fact," can help the reader understand the basic aspects of the transaction. [*See Model Stock Purchase Agreement, supra*, Section 1.10, at 3] Depending upon the law of the governing jurisdiction, the whereas clauses may be "conclusively presumed to be true as between the parties * * *." *Id.*

§ 15.7 Defined Terms

An acquisition agreement will typically contain many defined terms. Such terms can either be defined in a section at the beginning or end of the acquisition agreement or defined at the point the term first appears in the text of the agreement. This latter device is followed in the Time-Warner merger agreement in Documentary Appendix A.

§ 15.8 Description of the Basic Purchase and Sale or Merger Transaction

The acquisition agreement will contain an article or articles setting out the basic terms of the transactions indicating what the acquiring corporation is acquiring and what the selling shareholders or target are selling. For example, Article I of the Time-Warner Merger Agreement, Documentary Appendix A, sets out the basic terms of the merger, and Article II specifies the exchange of shares that occurs at the closing upon the effective date of the merger. [*See also* Articles I and II of Documentary Appendix D and Articles II and III of Documentary Appendix F]

If Time were acquiring the stock of a closely-held target corporation in a stock acquisition, there would be an article specifying the consideration to be paid by Time to the selling shareholders upon delivery by them of the shares of the target corporation at the closing. [*See e.g., Model Stock Purchase Agreement, supra* Section 1.10, at 32 to 46] Such an article might look something like Article I of the Sample Stock Purchase Agreement, Documentary Appendix U.

If Time were purchasing the assets of the target corporation, there would be an article specifying (1) the assets to be sold to Time and those to be retained by the target, (2) the liabilities to be assumed by Time and those to be retained by the target, (3) the purchase price to be paid by Time, and (4) the documents to be exchanged at the closing. Such an article might look something like Article I of the Asset Acquisition Agreement, Documentary Appendix V.

§ 15.9 The Representations and Warranties: The Snapshot

A. In General

Generally each party to the transaction will be required to make certain representations and warranties. These are statements concerning the state of the business of the party at the time of the execution of the acquisition agreement. In other words, the representations and warranties present a "static" snapshot of the current state of the party's business. [*See* Freund, *Anatomy of a Merger, supra* Section 1.10., at 153–155]

The representations of the purchaser and seller will generally be the same without regard to whether the transaction is effectuated as a merger, a stock acquisition or an asset acquisition. However, a merger or asset acquisition will generally include only representations of the acquiring corporation and the target, whereas a stock acquisition will also include representations and warranties of the selling shareholders. In the acquisition of the assets of a closely-held target corporation, the shareholders of the target may also be parties to the transaction and, therefore, may be required to make certain representations and warranties.

Many of the representations and warranties will refer to a disclosure schedule to the acquisition agreement, such as follows:

> 2.8 *Real Property*. Schedule 2.8 attached hereto contains an accurate and complete list of all real property owned in whole or in part by the Target Corporation.

The disclosure schedules will elaborate on the information provided in the representation and warranties, and will be of great help in the due diligence process.

Section 3.1 of the Time-Warner merger agreement, Documentary Appendix A, contains the representations and warranties of Warner, the target corporation, and Section 3.2 contains similar representations and warranties of Time, the acquiror. This transaction involved an acquisition by Time of Warner in exchange for stock of Time. Therefore, the Warner shareholders were making an investment in Time, just as Time was making an investment in Warner. Consequently, both the target and the acquiror made a full set of representations and warranties. This would also be the case if the transaction were structured as an asset acquisition or as a stock acquisition in which the consideration paid by the acquiror was its securities. On the other hand, if Time were paying cash in the merger, Warner shareholders would not be making an investment in Time, and they would need only representations and warranties dealing with such items as (1) the organization and standing of the acquiror similar to the representation in Section 5.01 of the Global Toys-Toys "R" Us Merger Agreement, Documentary Appendix F, which is a cash acquisition, (2) the authority of the acquiror to enter into and consummate the transaction, similar to Section 5.02 of Documentary Appendix F, and (3) the availability of the financing for the merger similar to Section 5.05 of Documentary Appendix F. This is also true if the transaction were structured as an asset acquisition or a stock acquisition in which the acquiror paid cash. [*See e.g., Model Stock Purchase Agreement, supra*, Section 1.10, at 139 to 142.]

B. Materiality Qualification

Many of the representations and warranties may contain a materiality qualification, such as that contained in Section 3.1(f) of the Time-Warner Merger Agreement, Documentary Appendix A.

A materiality qualification may be used in a situation in which a party is not aware of all the possible facts, or where the party does not wish to be held responsible for the breach of an immaterial representation which is not really important to the other party. For example, in the acquisition of a publicly-held target by merger, the target's board may not be in a position at the time of the signing of the merger agreement, to represent that the merger does not violate "any" contract, whereas it should be in a position to represent that the merger does not violate "any material" contract.

In addition to the materiality qualifications in the representations and warranties, the conditions to closing will generally have a materiality qualification, but as indicated in the discussion of the conditions to closing [*see* Section 15.11], it is important to avoid double materiality, that is qualifying an already materially qualified representation and warranty with a second materiality closing condition.

C. Knowledge Qualification

Many representations and warranties will be qualified by the "knowledge" of the person making the representation. The Sellers will attempt to use knowledge qualifications to limit many of their representations and warranties. The inclusion of a knowledge qualification in the representation concerning threatened litigation has become accepted practice. [*See* § 3.1(g) of the Time-Warner Merger Agreement, Documentary Appendix A] Otherwise, there is no standard practice for determining which representations, if any, should contain such a qualification. Ultimately, the issue involves the allocation of risk between the buyer and the seller. Who bears the risk of the unknown? [*See Model Stock Purchase Agreement, supra* Section 1.10, at 20.]

§ 15.10 Covenants: The Undertakings

A. In General

Whereas the representations and warranties section of an acquisition agreement presents a snapshot picture of the business of the party making the representation, the covenant section of the agreement sets out the promises, agreements and undertakings of the parties for the period from the signing of the agreement to the closing of the acquisition. There also may be post-closing covenants, *i.e.*, undertakings of a party to do certain things following the completion of the closing. As explained by Freund, covenants relate to a "period of time (the movie rather than the snapshot)," and they are a way of saying:

> Here is what we commit ourselves to do and here is what we promise not to do, during the period between the date the agreement is signed and the closing.

> They relate to the future, whereas the usual representation relates to the present or the past. (Freund, *Anatomy of a Merger, supra* Section 1.10, at 155)

The covenants are generally both "affirmative," here is what we commit to do, and "negative," here is what we will not do. For example, in Article IV of the Time-Warner Merger Agreement, Documentary Appendix A, both Time and Warner agree "[d]uring the period from the date of this agreement and continuing until the Effective Time" [*i.e.* the date the merger becomes effective] to "carry on their respective business in the usual, regular, and ordinary course * * *." (§ 3.1(a), *i.e.*, an affirmative covenant), and not to "issue, deliver or sell any shares of its capital stock * * *." (§ 3.1(c), *i.e.*, a negative covenant).

In Section 4.1(e) of the Time-Warner Merger Agreement, both Time and Warner agree not to shop their companies, *i.e.* they enter "no shops." No shops, related fiduciary-out provisions, and termination fees are examined further in Section 3.19.F.

Article V of the Time-Warner Merger Agreement, which sets out "Additional Agreements" also sets out covenants of the various parties. The covenants in Article V generally relate to specific actions that each party is required to take during the period between the signing and closing. Whereas the Covenants article (Article IV) deals with obligations that are of a continuing nature during the period between signing and closing, the Additional Agreements article (Article V) generally addresses specific one shot obligations during this period, such as the obligation on both Time and Warner to "promptly prepare and file" the S-4. [*See* § 5.1]

B. The Efforts Clause

Some covenants will contain an "efforts clause." Depending on the formulation this clause could require the party giving the covenant to make one of the following efforts to accomplish a particular result: "best efforts," "all reasonable efforts," or "commercially reasonable efforts." For example, Section 5.1 of the Time-Warner Merger Agreement requires that that Time use its "best efforts to have the [SEC S-4 registration statement] declared effective[.]" For a more detailed discussion of "efforts" clauses, *see* Thompson, *Mergers, Acquisitions and Tender Offers, supra* Section 1.10, at Section 2:11.2.

§ 15.11 Conditions to Closing

A. Introduction

The conditions article sets out the conditions precedent to each party's obligation to close the transaction. As explained by Freund:

> The conditions article is a way of saying: Here is what you are entitled to get from me (or from others) at or prior to the closing. If you don't get it, you can walk away from the deal without recourse on my part. (Freund, *Anatomy of a Merger, supra* Section 1.10, at 157)

The effect of this statement can be illustrated by a quick review of Article VI of the Time-Warner Merger Agreement, Documentary Appendix A, which sets out the conditions precedent. Pursuant to Section 6.1(a) neither Time nor Warner has to close if shareholder approval of either Time or Warner is not received. In such case, the parties could walk away without any damages, as long as neither party had breached its covenant in Section 5.5 to call a shareholders' meeting and to recommend the merger to the shareholders. The Model Stock Purchase Agreement elaborates on this point as follows:

> If the Sellers fail to satisfy any of these closing conditions, the Buyer will have the right to terminate the acquisition, but unless there has also been a separate breach by the Sellers of a representation or covenant, the Sellers will not be liable to the Buyer for their failure to satisfy the condition. (*Model Stock Purchase Agreement, supra,* Section 1.10, at 156–157)

B. Accuracy of Representations and Warranties

Virtually every acquisition agreement has conditions precedent relating to the truthfulness of the representations and warranties. For example, in Section 6.2(a), of the Time-Warner Merger Agreement, Documentary Appendix A, a condition to Time's obligation to close is that Warner's representations and warranties be true and correct "in all material respects" when made on the signing of the agreement, and except when referring to a later date, as of the closing date. Two aspects of this condition deserve further elaboration: the materiality qualification and the reaffirmation of the representations and warranties as of the closing date.

With regard to the materiality qualification, the *Model Stock Purchase Agreement* explains:

> A materiality qualification is needed [in the closing conditions], because most of the Seller's representations do not contain any such qualification * * *. The materiality qualification * * * prevents the Buyer from using a trivial breach of the Sellers representations as an excuse for terminating the acquisition * * *. (*Model Stock Purchase Agreement, supra,* Section 1.10, at 159)

The *Model Stock Purchase Agreement* also gives the following explanation of the need to avoid "double materiality:"

> A few of Sellers' qualifications * * * already contain express materiality qualifications. It is appropriate to require that these representations be accurate [as of the closing] in all respects (rather than merely in all material respects) in order to avoid double materiality problems. *Id.*

The concept of, in essence, reaffirming the representations and warranties as of the closing is referred to as a "bring down," that is, bringing the representations and warranties down from the signing to the closing. It is important to recognize that the "bring-down" of the representations and warranties as a condition of closing effectively makes every one of the representations and warranties a separate condition of closing. The *Model Stock Purchase Agreement,* supra Section 1.10, contains an elaborate discussion of various bring down clauses. *Id.* at 162–166. Section 15.12.B sets out *IPB,* a good illustration of a case in which, *inter alia,* the buyer wanted to walk from the transaction because of an alleged breach by the seller of a representation and warranty.

C. No Material Adverse Change (MAC) or Effect (MAE) Conditions

Acquisition agreements generally will contain either a direct or indirect no "material adverse change" (MAC) or no "material adverse effect" (MAE) condition to closing. MACs and MAEs have the same purpose: (1) to alert the counter party to material events the other party has experienced since, for example, the signing of the agreement, and (2) to provide the counter party with certain rights, for example, the right to walk from the transaction as a result of the occurrence of the MAC or MAE.

Section 5.1(c) of the Sample Stock Purchase Agreement, Documentary Appendix U is an illustration of a direct MAC provision to closing, and Section 7.02(a)(i) of the Global Toys-Toys "R" Us Merger Agreement, Documentary Appendix F, is an MAE condition to closing, with MAE defined in the definitions in Section 1.01.

It may appear that there is no MAC or MAE condition to closing in Article VI of the Time-Warner Merger Agreement. However, the agreement contains an indirect MAE condition through the "bring down" of the representations and warranties. Section 3.1(m) of the Time-Warner merger agreement, relating to *Absence of Certain Changes of Events*, provides in relevant part:

> Except as disclosed in the [Warner] SEC documents * * * since the date of the [Warner] 1988 financials * * * there has not been * * * (iii) any transaction, commitment, dispute or other event or condition (financial or otherwise) of any character (whether or not in the ordinary course of business) individually or in the aggregate having or which, insofar as reasonably can be foreseen, in the future is reasonably likely to have, a material adverse effect on [Warner] and its Subsidiaries taken as a whole.

The similarity between the above MAE condition and a MAC condition is seen by comparing the above provision with the following MAC condition in the *Model Asset Purchase Agreement*, Section 1.10:

> Since the date of the Balance Sheet, there has not been any material adverse change in the business, operations, prospects, assets, results of operations or condition (financial or otherwise) of Seller, and no circumstance exists that may result in such a material adverse change.

In the context of the representations and warranties these provisions are designed to ensure that since the date of the last audited financials, (1) there has been no "MAE" on the company making the representation, or (2) no "MAC" has occurred at the company making the representation. Thus, in the context of the representations and warranties, these clauses cover the gap between the date of the last financials and the date of the agreement. Such clauses also act as a closing condition through the "bring down" of the representations and warranties. For example, Section 6.2(a) of the Time-Warner Merger Agreement discussed above extends the no material adverse effect clause in the representations and warranties from the date of signing to the date of closing.

Thus, while there may be no direct MAC or MAE clause in the conditions to closing, there usually will be an indirect clause through the "bring down." The *Model Asset Purchase Agreement, supra* Section 1.10 at 181, elaborates on the direct and indirect approaches:

> Some acquisition agreements contain a separate closing condition giving the buyer a walk right if there has been a material adverse change in the seller's business since the date of the agreement. The Model Agreement does not include a separate condition of this type because Buyer receives comparable protection by virtue of the Seller's no-material-adverse-change representation in [the representations and warranties] (which operates as a closing condition pursuant to the [bring down].

The Model Asset Purchase Agreement goes on to explain that the direct MAC may offer more protection because it focuses specifically on the period between the signing and closing, whereas the indirect approach focuses on the period between the date of the last audited financials and the date of the closing, and there could be a material adverse change between the signing and closing but not between the date of the last financials and the closing.

Section 15.12.B sets out *IPB*, a good illustration of a case in which, *inter alia*, the buyer wanted to walk from the transaction because the target had experienced an alleged MAE.

D. Performance of Covenants

Pursuant to Section 6.2(b) of the Time-Warner Merger Agreement, a condition of Time's obligation to close is that Warner shall have performed in "all material respects" all of its obligations set out in the Merger Agreement, that is, Warner shall have satisfied its covenants in Article IV and its Additional Agreements in Article V.

E. Legal Opinions

In public deals, such as the Time-Warner transaction, the parties may not have as a condition to closing the receipt of an opinion of counsel. However, such an opinion is generally required, particularly from the seller's attorney, in acquisitions of closely-held corporations, whether by merger, stock acquisition, or asset acquisitions. Also, the closing conditions for acquisitions of closely-held firms generally are broader than the closing conditions for the acquisition of publicly-held firms. This can be illustrated by comparing the closing conditions in Article V of the Sample Stock Purchase Agreement, Documentary Appendix U with the closing conditions in Article VI of the Time-Warner Merger Agreement. Section 15.16, below addresses the delivery of legal opinions in acquisition transactions.

§ 15.12 Termination and Allegations of Breach of Representations and Warranties and MAC Clauses

A. In General

Article VII of the Time-Warner Merger Agreement, Documentary Appendix A, contains standard provisions relating to the termination of the agreement. First, under, Section 7.1(a) the Merger Agreement may be terminated by mutual consent of the parties. Second, under Section 7.1(b), either party may terminate if the other party has materially breached any representation, warranty, covenant or agreement, subject to the obligation to negotiate in good faith for a reasonable period of time pursuant to Section 7.1(c). Third, each party may terminate if the merger does not occur before a specific date, a drop-dead date. Section 7.2 provides that except in certain specific circumstances, including willful breach, there is no liability for a breach leading to the termination of the contract. Termination payments (*i.e.*, "break-up fees") that are part of deal protection devices are addressed in Section 5.14.

B. Buyer's Alleged Right to Terminate Because of (1) Breach of Representation and Warranty, and (2) MAE; Seller Seeks Specific Performance—*IBP*

In Re IBP, Inc. Shareholders Litigation

Delaware Court of Chancery, 2001 Del. Ch. LEXIS 81

STRINE, Vice Chancellor:

This post-trial opinion addresses a demand for specific performance of a "Merger Agreement" by IBP, Inc., the nation's number one beef and number two pork distributor.

By this action, IBP seeks to compel the "Merger" between itself and Tyson Foods, Inc., the nation's leading chicken distributor, in a transaction in which IBP stockholders will receive their choice of $30 a share in cash or Tyson stock, or a combination of the two.

The IBP-Tyson Merger Agreement resulted from a vigorous auction process that pitted Tyson against the nation's number one pork producer, Smithfield Foods. To say that Tyson was eager to win the auction is to slight its ardent desire to possess IBP. During the bidding process, Tyson was anxious to ensure that it would acquire IBP, and to make sure Smithfield did not. By succeeding, Tyson hoped to create the world's preeminent meat products company[.]

During the auction process, Tyson was given a great deal of information that suggested that IBP was heading into a trough in the beef business. Even more, Tyson was alerted to serious problems at an IBP subsidiary, DFG, which had been victimized by accounting fraud to the tune of over $30 million in charges to earnings and which was the active subject of an asset impairment study. Not only that, Tyson knew that IBP was projected to fall seriously short of the fiscal year 2000 earnings predicted in projections prepared by IBP's Chief Financial Officer in August, 2000.

By the end of the auction process, Tyson had come to have great doubts about IBP's ability to project its future earnings, the credibility of IBP's management, and thought that the important business unit in which DFG was located—Foodbrands—was broken.

Yet, Tyson's ardor for IBP was such that Tyson raised its bid by a total of $4.00 a share after learning of these problems. Tyson also signed the Merger Agreement, which permitted IBP to recognize unlimited additional liabilities on account of the accounting improprieties at DFG. It did so without demanding any representation that IBP meet its projections for future earnings, or any escrow tied to those projections.

After the Merger Agreement was signed on January 1, 2001, Tyson trumpeted the value of the merger to its stockholders and the financial community, and indicated that it was fully aware of the risks that attended the cyclical nature of IBP's business. In early January, Tyson's stockholders ratified the merger agreement and authorized its management to take whatever action was needed to effectuate it.

During the winter and spring of 2001, Tyson's own business performance was dismal. Meanwhile, IBP was struggling through a poor first quarter. Both companies' problems were due in large measure to a severe winter, which adversely affected livestock supplies and vitality. As these struggles deepened, Tyson's desire to buy IBP weakened.

This cooling of affections first resulted in a slow-down by Tyson in the process of consummating a transaction, a slow-down that was attributed to IBP's on-going efforts to resolve issues that had been raised about its financial statements by the Securities and Exchange Commission ("SEC"). The most important of these issues was how to report the problems at DFG, which Tyson had been aware of at the time it signed the Merger Agreement. Indeed, all the key issues that the SEC raised with IBP were known by Tyson at the time it signed the Merger Agreement. The SEC first raised these issues in a faxed letter on December 29, 2000 to IBP's outside counsel. Neither IBP management nor Tyson learned of the letter until the second week of January, 2001. After learning of the letter, Tyson management put the Merger Agreement to a successful board and stockholder vote.

But the most important reason that Tyson slowed down the Merger process was different: it was having buyer's regret. Tyson wished it had paid less especially in view of its own compromised 2001 performance and IBP's slow 2001 results.

By March, Tyson's founder and controlling stockholder, Don Tyson, no longer wanted to go through with the Merger Agreement. He made the decision to abandon the Merger. His son, John Tyson, Tyson's Chief Executive Officer, and the other Tyson managers followed his instructions. Don Tyson abandoned the Merger because of IBP's and Tyson's poor results in 2001, and not because of DFG or the SEC issues IBP was dealing with. Indeed, Don Tyson told IBP management that he would blow DFG up if he were them.

After the business decision was made to terminate, Tyson's legal team swung into action. They fired off a letter terminating the Agreement at the same time as they filed suit accusing IBP of fraudulently inducing the Merger that Tyson had once so desperately desired.

This expedited litigation ensued, which involved massive amounts of discovery and two weeks of trial.

In this opinion, I address IBP's claim that Tyson had no legal basis to avoid its obligation to consummate the Merger Agreement, as well as Tyson's contrary arguments. * * *

At bottom * * * I conclude as follows:

- The Merger Agreement and related contracts were valid and enforceable contracts that were not induced by any material misrepresentation or omission;
- The Merger Agreement specifically allocated certain risks to Tyson, including the risk of any losses or financial effects from the accounting improprieties at DFG, and these risks cannot serve as a basis for Tyson to terminate the Agreement;
- None of the non-DFG related issues that the SEC raised constitute a contractually permissible basis for Tyson to walk away from the Merger;
- IBP has not suffered a Material Adverse Effect within the meaning of the Agreement that excused Tyson's failure to close the Merger; and
- Specific performance is the decisively preferable remedy for Tyson's breach, as it is the only method by which to adequately redress the harm threatened to IBP and its stockholders. * * *

Do The DFG Charges To Earnings Evidence A Breach Of Warranty? *The Merger Agreement Does Not Unambiguously Assign The DFG-Related Risks.* The first question I address is whether the DFG-related problems of IBP were a risk that was contractually accepted by Tyson, through the inclusion of Schedule 5.11 [a schedule to the "No Undisclosed Material Liability" representation setting forth information on the DFG problem]. The parties have starkly different views of whether the reference to DFG in Schedule 5.11 operates to qualify all of the representations and warranties in the Agreement. Tyson contends that Schedule 5.11 has no effect on any representation and warranty other than that contained in § 5.11 of the Agreement. There are no Schedules 5.07–5.09 attached to the Agreement that operate to qualify §§ 5.07–5.09 explicitly. And §§ 5.07, 5.08, and 5.09 are, by their own terms, unqualified by reference to Schedule 5.11, and generally stand for the proposition that IBP warranted that the Warranted Financial Statements were accurate in all material respects and comported with GAAP. Tyson thus claims that these "flat" representations were plainly breached when IBP restated the Warranted Financial Statements to record the additional losses at DFG. * * *

According to IBP, Schedule 5.11 specifically permits IBP to recognize further liabilities on account of the accounting improprieties at DFG. Thus, according to IBP, the Annexes protect IBP by ensuring that its specific contractual right to do so does not result in a technical breach of a more general representation and warranty that permits Tyson to walk. IBP supports this contention by pointing to the Model Stock Purchase Agreement produced by the American Bar Association's Committee on Negotiated Acquisitions. The Committee Commentary states:

> The Sellers may also request that the 'bring down' clause be modified to clarify that the Buyer will not have a 'walk right' if any of the Sellers' representations is rendered inaccurate as a result of an occurrence specifically contemplated by the acquisition agreement. The requested modification entails inserting the words 'except as contemplated or permitted by this Agreement' (or some similar qualification).[1]

Tyson's response to this line of argument is * * * quite literalistic and technical, rather than commonsensical. * * *

I conclude that Tyson's reading of the language of the contract is not the only reasonable one. Indeed, if forced to choose, I would find that IBP's reading of the Agreement is the one that is most reasonable in view of the overall language and structure of the Agreement, and commercial setting within which the parties were operating. The Tyson interpretation in essence reads the DFG disclosure in Schedule 5.11 out of the Agreement because it gives IBP no reasonable room to address additional charges to earnings on account of past accounting improprieties. Put differently, Tyson argues that it came out of a hotly contested auction with an option, rather than an obligation, to purchase IBP, having silently pocketed an almost sure walk-away right. By contrast, the IBP reading continues to give wide scope to §§ 5.07–5.09, but merely qualifies their application when necessary to give effect to a more specific provision of the contract.

The Parol Evidence Demonstrates That IBP's Reading Of The Agreement Is In Large Measure The Correct One. * * * Schedule 5.11 was created specifically to address the DFG issues that had been discussed by representatives of Tyson and IBP. * * *

From at latest January 16, 2001 onward, Tyson knew that IBP would almost certainly have to restate the Warranted Financials to record additional charges to earnings because of the DFG accounting problems. At no time did it express the view that such a restatement would, in itself, give rise to a right on Tyson's part to walk away. To the contrary, Tyson simply urged IBP to get the issue worked out with the SEC promptly. * * *

The reason for this later course of dealing is obvious: none of the Tyson negotiators harbored the belief that the particular filing in which IBP recognized the charges had any relationship to whether the Agreement was breached. * * * Therefore, it is reasonable to infer that Tyson's negotiators believed that these charges had been carved out entirely by Schedule 5.11.

Was Tyson's Termination Justified Because IBP Has Suffered A Material Adverse Effect? Tyson argues that it was also permitted to terminate because IBP had breached § 5.10 of the Agreement, which is a representation and warranty that IBP had not suffered a material adverse effect since the "Balance Sheet Date" of December 25, 1999, except as set forth in the Warranted Financials or Schedule 5.10 of the Agreement. Under the contract, a material adverse effect (or "MAE") is defined as "any event, occurrence or development of a state of circumstances or facts which has had or reasonably could be expected to have a Material Adverse Effect" * * * "on the condition (financial or otherwise), business, assets, liabilities or results of operations of [IBP] and [its] Subsidiaries taken as whole. . . ."[2]

---

1. Model Stock Purchase Agreement, 1995 A.B.A. Sec. Bus. L. Sec. 7, at 163.

2. Agreement Sec 5.10(a) (specific warranty dealing generally with MAE); Sec 5.01 (defining MAE for entire agreement).

Tyson asserts that the decline in IBP's performance in the last quarter of 2000 and the first quarter of 2001 evidences the existence of a Material Adverse Effect. It also contends that the DFG Impairment Charge constitutes a Material Adverse Effect. And taken together, Tyson claims that it is virtually indisputable that the combination of these factors amounts to a Material Adverse Effect.

In addressing these arguments, it is useful to be mindful that Tyson's publicly expressed reasons for terminating the Merger did not include an assertion that IBP had suffered a Material Adverse Effect. * * *

The simplicity of § 5.10's words is deceptive, because the application of those words is dauntingly complex. On its face, § 5.10 is a capacious clause that puts IBP at risk for a variety of uncontrollable factors that might materially affect its overall business or results of operation as a whole. Although many merger contracts contain specific exclusions from MAE clauses that cover declines in the overall economy or the relevant industry sector, or adverse weather or market conditions, § 5.10 is unqualified by such express exclusions.

IBP argues, however, that statements in the Warranted Financials that emphasize the risks IBP faces from swings in livestock supply act as an implicit carve-out, because a Material Adverse Effect under that section cannot include an Effect that is set forth in the Warranted Financials. I agree with Tyson, however, that these disclaimers were far too general to preclude industry-wide or general factors from constituting a Material Adverse Effect. Had IBP wished such an exclusion from the broad language of § 5.10, IBP should have bargained for it. At the same time, the notion that § 5.10 gave Tyson a right to walk away simply because of a downturn in cattle supply is equally untenable. Instead, Tyson would have to show that the event had the required materiality of effect. * * *

Taken together, the provisions [of the Merger Agreement] can be read to require the court to examine whether a MAE has occurred against the December 25, 1999 condition of IBP as adjusted by the specific disclosures of the Warranted Financials and the Agreement itself. This approach makes commercial sense because it establishes a baseline that roughly reflects the status of IBP as Tyson indisputably knew it at the time of signing the Merger Agreement. * * *

In large measure, the resolution of the parties' arguments turns on a difficult policy question. In what direction does the burden of this sort of uncertainty fall: on an acquiror or on the seller? * * * Practical reasons lead me to conclude that a New York court would incline toward the view that a buyer ought to have to make a strong showing to invoke a Material Adverse Effect exception to its obligation to close. Merger contracts are heavily negotiated and cover a large number of specific risks explicitly. As a result, even where a Material Adverse Effect condition is as broadly written as the one in the Merger Agreement, that provision is best read as a backstop protecting the acquiror from the occurrence of unknown events that substantially threaten the overall earnings potential of the target in a durationally-significant manner.[3] A short-term hiccup in earnings should not suffice; rather the Material Adverse Effect should be material when viewed from the longer-term perspective of a reasonable acquiror. * * *

When examined from this seller-friendly perspective, the question of whether IBP has suffered a Material Adverse Effect remains a close one. IBP had a very sub-par first quarter. * * *

3. A contrary rule will encourage the negotiation of extremely detailed "MAC" clauses with numerous carve-outs or qualifiers. An approach that reads broad clauses as addressing fundamental events that would materially affect the value of a target to a reasonable acquiror eliminates the need for drafting of that sort.

I am confessedly torn about the correct outcome. * * *

In the end, however, Tyson has not persuaded me that IBP has suffered a Material Adverse Effect. * * *

Therefore, I conclude that Tyson has not demonstrated a breach of § 5.10. I admit to reaching this conclusion with less than the optimal amount of confidence. The record evidence is not of the type that permits certainty. * * *

IBP Is Entitled To An Award Of Specific Performance. Having determined that the Merger Agreement is a valid and enforceable contract that Tyson had no right to terminate, I now turn to the question of whether the Merger Agreement should be enforced by an order of specific performance. * * *

A compulsory order will require a merger of two public companies with thousands of employees working at facilities that are important to the communities in which they operate. * * * I therefore approach this remedial issue quite cautiously and mindful of the interests of those who will be affected by my decision.

I start with a fundamental question: is this is a truly unique opportunity that cannot be adequately monetized? If the tables were turned and Tyson was seeking to enforce the contract, a great deal of precedent would indicate that the contract should be specifically enforced. In the more typical situation, an acquiror argues that it cannot be made whole unless it can specifically enforce the acquisition agreement, because the target company is unique and will yield value of an unquantifiable nature, once combined with the acquiring company.[4] In this case, the sell-side of the transaction is able to make the same argument, because the Merger Agreement provides the IBP stockholders with a choice of cash or Tyson stock, or a combination of both. Through this choice, the IBP stockholders were offered a chance to share in the upside of what was touted by Tyson as a unique, synergistic combination. This court has not found, and Tyson has not advanced, any compelling reason why sellers in mergers and acquisitions transactions should have less of a right to demand specific performance than buyers, and none has independently come to my mind.

In addition, the determination of a cash damages award will be very difficult in this case. And the amount of any award could be staggeringly large. No doubt the parties would haggle over huge valuation questions, if which (Tyson no doubt would argue) must take into account the possibility of a further auction for IBP or other business developments. A damages award can, of course, be shaped; it simply will lack any pretense to precision. An award of specific performance will, I anticipate, entirely eliminate the need for a speculative determination of damages.

Finally, there is no doubt that a remedy of specific performance is practicable. Tyson itself admits that the combination still makes strategic sense. At trial, John Tyson was asked by his own counsel to testify about whether it was fair that Tyson should enter any later auction for IBP hampered by its payment of the Rawhide Termination Fee. This testimony indicates that Tyson Foods is still interested in purchasing IBP, but wants to get

4. [Original footnote 202] The United States Court of Appeals for the Third Circuit has issued a thoughtful opinion to this effect, in a case dealing with a merger agreement between two public companies. *Allegheny* [171 F.3d 153 (1999)]. *See also C&S/Solvran, [cited in Allegheny]* (specifically enforcing merger agreement between two publicly traded banks). This court has embraced this reasoning on many occasions. *See, e.g., True North, 705 A.2d 244 (Del. 1997).* Indeed, this premise is a foundation of this State's jurisprudence in the takeover area, as exemplified by *Revlon*.

its original purchase price back and then buy IBP off the day-old goods table. I consider John Tyson's testimony an admission of the feasibility of specific performance. * * *

Probably the concern that weighs heaviest on my mind is whether specific performance is the right remedy in view of the harsh words that have been said in the course of this litigation. Can these management teams work together? The answer is that I do not know. * * *

What persuades me that specific performance is a workable remedy is that Tyson will have the power to decide all the key management questions itself. * * *

The impact on other constituencies of this ruling also seems tolerable. Tyson's own investment banker thinks the transaction makes sense for Tyson, and is still fairly priced at $30 per share. One would think the Tyson constituencies would be better served on the whole by a specific performance remedy, rather than a large damages award that did nothing but cost Tyson a large amount of money.

In view of these factors, I am persuaded that an award of specific performance is appropriate, regardless of what level of showing was required by IBP. That is, there is clear and convincing evidence to support this award. Such an award is decisively preferable to a vague and imprecise damages remedy that cannot adequately remedy the injury to IBP's stockholders.

Conclusion. For all the foregoing reasons, IBP's claim for specific performance is granted. Tyson's claims for relief are dismissed. * * *

C. Dealing with the Effect of (1) a Disclosure under One Representation or Warranty, on (2) a Second Representation and Warranty—The First Issue in *IBP*

In addressing the first issue in *IBP* (*i.e.*, whether the disclosure of the DFG problem in the schedule to Section 5.11 qualified the flat representations in 5.07–5.09), it has become common practice to include in the representations and warranties section of a merger agreement a provision like the following italicized clause in Section 3.1 of the Sirus-XM merger agreement, which is Appendix 2C to Thompson, *Mergers, Acquisitions and Tender Offers, supra* Section 1.10:

> Except (x) with respect to any subsection of this Section 3.1, as set forth in the correspondingly identified subsection of the disclosure schedule delivered by XM to Sirius concurrently herewith (the "XM Disclosure Schedule") (*it being understood by the parties that the information disclosed in one subsection of the XM Disclosure Schedule shall be deemed to be included in each other subsection of the XM Disclosure Schedule in which the relevance of such information thereto would be readily apparent on the face thereof*) [emphasis added] or (y) as disclosed in the XM SEC Documents (as defined below) filed with the SEC prior to the date hereof, XM represents and warrants to Sirius as follows: * * *

For a discussion of this point, *see* Thompson, Mergers, Acquisitions and Tender Offers, supra Section 1.10, at Section 2:10.2[B].

D. The Meaning of MAC and MAE—The Second Issue in *IBP*

In addressing the second issue in *IBP* (*i.e.*, the meaning of the no MAE clause), the court said:

> On its face, § 5.10 is a capacious clause that puts IBP at risk for a variety of uncontrollable factors that might materially affect its overall business or results of operation as a whole. Although many merger contracts contain specific exclusions from MAE clauses that cover declines in the overall economy or the relevant industry sector, or adverse weather or market conditions, § 5.10 is unqualified by such express exclusions.

Partly in response to this observation, in many transactions the parties will include in the merger agreement certain limits on what constitutes a MAC or MAE. For example, Section 3.1(a)(iv) of the Sirus-XM merger agreement, which is Appendix 2C to Thompson, *Mergers, Acquisitions and Tender Offers*, *supra* Section 1.10 provides:

> the term "material adverse effect" means, with respect to any entity, a material adverse effect on the financial condition, properties, assets, liabilities, businesses or results of operations of such entity and its Subsidiaries taken as a whole; provided that, * * * the following shall not be deemed "material" or to have a "material adverse effect": any change or event caused by or resulting from (A) changes in prevailing economic or market conditions in the United States or any other jurisdiction in which such entity has substantial business operations (except to the extent those changes have a materially disproportionate effect on such entity and its Subsidiaries relative to the other party and its Subsidiaries), (B) changes or events, after the date hereof, affecting the industries in which they operate generally (except to the extent those changes or events have a materially disproportionate effect on such entity and its Subsidiaries relative to the other party and its Subsidiaries), * * *.

For a discussion of this point, *see* Thompson, Mergers, Acquisitions and Tender Offers, supra Section 1.10, at Section 2:10.4.

§ 15.13 Survival of Representations and Warranties and Indemnification

A. Introduction

As indicated above, representations and warranties are statements of fact as of the date of the execution of the acquisition agreement, and the truthfulness of the representations and warranties as of both the date of execution and, when appropriate, the date of the closing is generally a condition to the closing. If prior to closing a party discovers that a representation or warranty is materially inaccurate, the party can refuse to close and possibly sue for damages. If, however, the party does not discover the inaccurate representation and warranty until after the closing, then the question becomes whether the breaching party can be sued for damages for breach of the representation and warranty.

The resolution of this issue depends at first instance on whether the representations and warranties survive the closing date, and this will in many cases be addressed in the acquisition agreement. In an acquisition of a publicly-held firm, such as the Time-Warner merger, the representations and warranties and other agreements typically do not survive the closing because as a practical matter it would be difficult to hold the public shareholders of the target liable for breach. [*See* Freund, *Anatomy of a Merger*, *supra* Section 1.10, at 161] Along this line, Section 8.1 of the Time-Warner Merger Agreement, Documentary Appendix A, provides that, except as otherwise provided, none of the representations, warranties or other agreements in the Merger Agreement survived the closing.

On the other hand, in acquisitions of closely-held corporations, it is common for the acquisition agreement to provide that the representations, warranties and other agreements survive the closing, because in many instances it would not be difficult for the acquiring corporation to seek damages from the target's shareholders. Along this line Section 6.1 of the Sample Stock Purchase Agreement, Documentary Appendix U, provides that the representations, warranties, covenants and other agreements survive the closing. This means that after the closing, the selling shareholders or the acquiring corporation, as the case may be, may be sued for damages for breach of a representation, warranty or other agreement.

Section 6.2 of the Sample Stock Acquisition Agreement also has an indemnification provision which in the words of Freund, "says, in effect: 'Here is what we will pay you if it turns out we have breached one of our representations.'" *Id.* at 159. Although as long as the representations and warranties survive, a non-breaching party would likely be able to recover damages from a breaching party without an indemnification provision, Freund points out that the following purposes that may be served by an indemnification provision:

> (i) eliminat[ing] any ambiguity as to whether the representations are intended to survive the closing; (ii) mak[ing] it clear that all misrepresentations are indemnifiable, thereby rebutting in advance any argument by the seller that a particular breach was unintentional or not sufficiently significant to require the purchaser being made whole; (iii) provid[ing] that the expenses (such as attorneys' fees) incurred by the buyer in connection with the misrepresented item fall into the protected area; (iv) fram[ing] particular remedies, and perhaps liquidat[ing] or provid[ing] a formula for damages; (v) set[ting] forth specific terms and procedures for indemnification to avoid future argument (*e.g.*, who is responsible for defending a third party lawsuit); (vi) includ[ing] breaches of covenants and other agreements as indemnifiable claims; and (vii) pick[ing] up matters that do not constitute misrepresentations but as to which the buyer has nevertheless insisted on protection (*e.g.*, seller's income taxes attributable to the period through the closing date, or a disclosed lawsuit that the parties agree will be the seller's responsibility). *Id* at 160.

One of the principal issues that must be faced in structuring an indemnification provision is determining whether there will be a limitation on the indemnification by, for example, any of the following: a basket, a threshold (otherwise known as a "tipping basket", or a ceiling. [*See* Kling and Nugent Simon, *Negotiated Acquisitions, supra. See* 1.10, at 15–29 to 15–21] If a basket is used, the breaching party is only liable for damages above a specific amount. For example, Section 6.2 of the Sample Stock Purchase Agreement, Documentary Appendix U, has a $25,000 basket, which means that the indemnifying party will have no liability until the damages exceed $25,000 and in that case will only be liable for damages in excess of $25,000.

If this provision were structured as a threshold, it would provide that if the damages exceeded $25,000, then the indemnifying party would be liable for all damages from the first dollar of damages, thus the name "tipping basket." Of course, this means that if the damages were exactly $25,000 there would be no claim; but if they were $25,001, the claim would be for $25,001. This "cliff" aspect is why most lawyers prefer the basket approach.

Section 6.2 does not contain a ceiling on the potential liability. Arguably the liability of the selling shareholders should be limited to the amount of the consideration received. On the other hand, if the acquiring corporation ends up with environmental or other liabilities in excess of the purchase price, arguably its damages should not be limited to the amount of the purchase price. The *ABRY* case set out below illustrates an indemnification provision with a ceiling and how a purchaser may be able to lift the ceiling.

To ensure payment pursuant to an indemnification provision, the acquiring corporation may hold back a portion of the purchase price, put a portion of the purchase price in an escrow account, or structure a portion of the purchase price in the form of a deferred payment note. Specific set-off provisions may be set forth in the indemnification provision granting the acquiring corporation the right to set-off the required indemnifiable amount against any sums owed by the acquiring corporation pursuant to any hold back, escrow, or deferred payment note.

As indicated in the comment to Section 6.2, that provision is a short-form indemnification. Many indemnification provisions cover other items, such as those mentioned in the comment.

B. Is an Exclusive Indemnification Provision with a Ceiling the Only Remedy in the Event of Fraud?—*ABRY*

ABRY Partners V, L.P. v. F&W Acquisition LLC.

Delaware Court of Chancery, 2006 Del. Ch. LEXIS 28

STRINE, Vice Chancellor:

This case involves a request by the buy-side of a corporate acquisition contract—the Stock Purchase Agreement—to rescind that contract. The plaintiffs—a group of entities affiliated with a sophisticated private equity firm named ABRY Partners (hereinafter, largely referred to collectively as the "Buyer")—bought a portfolio company from an entity owned by another sophisticated private equity firm, Providence Equity Partners (hereinafter, largely referred to collectively as the "Seller"). The portfolio company that was purchased by the Buyer, F&W Publications (hereinafter, largely referred to as the "Company"), was in the business of publishing magazines and selling books. * * *

[Basic] Facts * * * *After Closing The Sale, The Buyer Discovers That The Company's Financial Statements Were Inaccurate.* Once the Buyer assumed ownership of the Company, it began to uncover a host of serious financial and operational problems. So serious were these problems that the Buyer came to the conclusion that it had been defrauded by the Seller and the Company in connection with the Stock Purchase Agreement.

Specifically, the Buyer alleges that it has become apparent that the Seller and Company management, working in concert, schemed together to manipulate the Company's financial statements in order to fraudulently induce the Buyer into purchasing the Company at an excessive price. Thus, the Buyer claims that the Company's December 2004, March 2005, and June 2005 financial statements contained material misrepresentations and did not accurately portray the Company's financial condition. * * *

Aside from problems with financial statements, the Buyer also argues that the Company misrepresented the implementation status of a book order fulfillment system, which was named VISTA. * * * The Buyer alleges that the problems with VISTA were so serious that they constituted a material adverse effect ("MAE") under the Stock Purchase Agreement. Yet, the Company did not give the Buyer any pre-closing notice of these problems, and the Seller certified, as required by § 8.2(h)(i) of the Stock Purchase Agreement, that no MAE occurred before closing.

The Buyer contends that the various misrepresentations and non-disclosures resulted in it purchasing the Company for a grossly overstated value. Specifically, the Buyer alleges that the true value of the Company was more like $400 million than $500 million and that it would never have closed had it known that the Company was propping up its performance with unethical business and accounting practices.

When it learned of these improprieties, the Buyer asked the Seller to rescind the transaction and to take back ownership of the Company. The Seller refused and this suit ensued.

The Claims In The Complaint. The Complaint contains three major counts. Count I asserts a fraudulent inducement claim and seeks rescission of the Stock Purchase Agreement and related relief. The basis for the fraudulent inducement is the course of financial manipulation and non-disclosure I just detailed. Counts II (also a claim for fraudulent inducement) and III (a claim for negligent misrepresentation) rely on the same conduct and set forth alternative claims for damages in the event that rescission is not awarded. * * *

The Terms Of The Stock Purchase Agreement Bearing On The Seller's Liability. * * * The first specific provision of the Stock Purchase Agreement requiring recitation is § 7.8 [a clause asserting that the purchaser has not relied on representations or warranties outside of the merger agreement, *i.e.*, a non-reliance clause], which states:

> Acquiror acknowledges and agrees that neither the Company nor the Selling Stockholder has made any representation or warranty, expressed or implied, as to the Company or any Company Subsidiary or as to the accuracy or completeness of any information regarding the Company or any Company Subsidiary furnished or made available to Acquiror and its representatives, except as expressly set forth in this Agreement ... and neither the Company nor the Selling Stockholder shall have or be subject to any liability to Acquiror or any other Person resulting from the distribution to Acquiror, or Acquiror's use of or reliance on, any such information or any information, documents or material made available to Acquiror in any "data rooms," "virtual data rooms," management presentations or in any other form in expectation of, or in connection with, the transactions contemplated hereby.

This is a critical provision. It operates to define what information the Buyer relied upon in deciding to execute the Agreement. By its plain terms, the Buyer promised that neither the Company nor the Seller had made any representation or warranty as to the accuracy of any information about the Company except as set forth in the Agreement itself. The Buyer further promised that neither the Seller nor the Company would have any liability to the Buyer or any other person for any extra-contractual information made available to the Buyer in connection with the contemplated sale of the Company. Because of this provision, the Buyer was careful to amend its complaint and to premise its claims solely upon alleged misrepresentations of facts that are represented and warranted in the Stock Purchase Agreement itself. * * *

Article III, in § 3.23, also reinforces the promise of the Buyer that it was not relying on extra-contractual representations by stating:

> EXCEPT AS EXPRESSLY SET FORTH IN THIS ARTICLE III, THE COMPANY MAKES NO REPRESENTATION OR WARRANTY, EXPRESSED OR IMPLIED, AT LAW OR IN EQUITY IN RESPECT OF THE COMPANY OR THE COMPANY SUBSIDIARIES, OR ANY OF THEIR RESPECTIVE ASSETS, LIABILITIES OR OPERATIONS, INCLUDING WITH RESPECT TO MERCHANTABILITY OR FITNESS FOR ANY PARTICULAR PURPOSE, AND ANY SUCH OTHER REPRESENTATIONS OR WARRANTIES ARE HEREBY EXPRESSLY DISCLAIMED. ACQUIROR HEREBY ACKNOWLEDGES AND AGREES THAT, EXCEPT TO THE EXTENT SPECIFICALLY SET FORTH IN THIS ARTICLE III, THE ACQUIROR IS ACQUIRING THE COMPANY ON

AN "AS IS, WHERE IS" BASIS. THE DISCLOSURE OF ANY MATTER OR ITEM IN ANY SCHEDULE HERETO SHALL NOT BE DEEMED TO CONSTITUTE AN ACKNOWLEDGEMENT THAT ANY SUCH MATTER IS REQUIRED TO BE DISCLOSED. * * *

For the obvious reason that it would own the Company after closing, the Buyer naturally wanted the Seller to back up the Company's representations and warranties. The Buyer accomplished that objective to a precisely negotiated extent. For starters, as a closing condition, the Seller was required by § 8.2(h)(i) of the Stock Purchase Agreement to provide an Officer's Certificate stating that the closing conditions relating to the accuracy of not only the Seller's, but the Company's, representations and warranties were satisfied, that the Company and Seller had complied with the covenants applicable to them, and also that the Company had not suffered events that had had or would reasonably be expected to constitute an MAE. * * *

The Seller also put its wallet behind the Company's representations and warranties to a defined extent. This was accomplished through a promise by the Seller to indemnify the Buyer if the Company's representations and warranties were incorrect or in other similar, broadly-defined circumstances. Section 9.1 of the Agreement sets forth this obligation. It states in pertinent part at subsection (a) that:

> The Selling Stockholder agrees that, after the Closing Date, the Acquiror and the Company and ... each controlling shareholder of the Acquiror or the Company ... shall be indemnified and held harmless by the Selling Stockholder from and against, any and all claims, demands, suits, actions, causes of actions, losses, costs, damages, liabilities and out-of-pocket expenses incurred or paid, including reasonable attorneys' fees, costs of investigation or settlement, other professionals' and experts' fees, and court or arbitration costs but specifically excluding consequential damages, lost profits, indirect damages, punitive damages and exemplary damages ... to the extent such Damages ... have arisen out of or ... have resulted from, in connection with, or by virtue of the facts or circumstances (i) which constitute an *inaccuracy, misrepresentation, breach of,* default in, or failure to perform any of the *representations, warranties or covenants* given or made by the *Company* or the *Selling Stockholder* in this Agreement ...

Section 9.1(c), however, goes on to limit the aggregate liability of the Seller for conduct covered by § 9.1(a) to the amount of the escrowed Indemnity Fund, which was established to be $20 million in § 2.4(b). This limitation is part of a very textured subsection that also permits the Buyer to seek damages for breaches of representations and warranties, without reference to materiality qualifications placed on them in the bring-down clause—that is, the clause of the Agreement that brings the representations and warranties down from the time of signing to the time of closing in the form of closing conditions. In other words, through the Indemnity Claim process, the Buyer clawed back the materiality qualifiers the Company and Seller extracted on the representations and warranties for purposes of closing.

The Stock Purchase Agreement also addresses the exclusivity of the Indemnity Claim provisions of the Agreement. To that end, § 9.9(a) (the "Exclusive Remedy Provision") provides:

> Except as may be required to enforce post-closing covenants hereunder ... after the Closing Date the indemnification rights in this Article IX are and shall be the sole and exclusive remedies of the Acquiror, the Acquiror Indemnified Persons, the Selling Stockholder, and the Company with respect to this Agreement

> and the Sale contemplated hereby; provided that this sentence shall not be deemed a waiver by any party of its right to seek specific performance or injunctive relief in the case of another party's failure to comply with the covenants made by such other party.

In addition, § 9.9(b) clearly states that "the provisions of Article IX were specifically bargained for and reflected in the amounts payable to the Selling Stockholder in connection with the Sale pursuant to Article II." The provisions of Article IX include the Exclusive Remedy Provision, the Indemnity Claim provision, and the Indemnity Fund provision.

Further, the Agreement requires that Indemnity Claims be arbitrated in Massachusetts if they cannot be resolved consensually. Despite the selection of Massachusetts as an arbitration forum, the Agreement, in § 9.5 and § 11.9, also makes clear that Delaware law governs any claim submitted to arbitration. * * *

Legal Analysis. * * * *The Crux Of The Matter: Does The Stock Purchase Agreement Itself Bar Even An Otherwise Well-Pled Claim Of Rescission?* * * * For the purposes of addressing the remaining substantive arguments in [the defendant's motion to dismiss], I * * * will accept two of the Buyer's primary contentions as true for the sake of argument: (1) that the complaint sets forth facts supporting an inference that the Company made misrepresentations in its financial statements, the accuracy of which was represented and warranted in the Stock Purchase Agreement by the Company and in the Officer's Certificate by the Seller; and (2) that the problems with VISTA, particularly insofar as it led Amazon.com to terminate distribution of the Company's trade books, could have constituted a material adverse effect under § 8.2(c) of the Stock Purchase Agreement, thereby triggering a contractual duty to disclose the underlying facts to the Buyer on the Company's part, and on the Seller's part in the context of the Officer's Certificate. Relatedly, I assume that the complaint sufficiently alleges that the Seller knew that the Company's financial statements were not materially accurate. The Seller's key contention, however, rests on the notion that even if these assumptions are correct, the Buyer is not entitled to press this lawsuit and obtain rescission.

The Seller's primary argument is that the Stock Purchase Agreement precludes the Buyer from obtaining the relief it seeks in this court. That argument is premised on several elements of the Agreement, which I have described in detail. In summary, though, the argument proceeds as follows. The Stock Purchase Agreement is a carefully negotiated document that allocates economic risk. It was entered into by sophisticated players in the private equity markets. In that Agreement, the parties carefully set forth which representations and warranties were made by the Company and which were made by the Seller. The Buyer also explicitly promised that the only information it relied upon in entering into the Agreement was that represented and warranted in the Agreement itself, thus contractually pledging that it had not relied on extra-contractual representations. In addition, the Buyer agreed to the Exclusive Remedy Provision stating that the only remedy that it had against the Seller for contractual misrepresentations was limited to a claim in arbitration for damages, *i.e.*, an Indemnity Claim. And, in that event, the Seller's liability is capped at the extent of the Indemnity Fund for $20 million. Furthermore, the Agreement explicitly indicated that the Exclusive Remedy Provision and limitation on liability contained in the contract were bargained for and reflected in the sale price.

Instead of seeking the relief permitted to it by the Agreement—an Indemnity Claim—the Buyer is bringing a claim for rescission in court. Not only that, the Buyer is seeking to hold the Seller responsible for representations and warranties made by the Company, when the Seller only agreed to back Company representations to the extent of the Indemnity Fund.

The Seller believes that the Buyer's attempt to avoid the terms of the Stock Purchase Agreement is improper and mandates dismissal. Having signed a contract explicitly disclaiming access to the very remedy it now seeks, the Buyer has contractually forsaken its current preferred remedy and must be held to its bargain. The Seller contends that a deal between sophisticated parties with the free right to walk away is a deal, and the law of this State should honor it.

For its part, the Buyer makes two major counter-arguments. First, the Buyer argues that the Exclusive Remedy Provision of the Stock Purchase Agreement does not limit its remedial options in the manner that the Seller suggests. Second, the Buyer contends that even if the Stock Purchase Agreement does limit the Seller's liability for misrepresentation to an Indemnity Claim by the Buyer, public policy overrides that aspect of the Agreement. According to the Buyer, a provision limiting in any manner the liability of a contracting party for misrepresentation is void. The public policy interest in deterring fraudulent conduct is, says the Buyer, so powerful that it prevents even sophisticated private equity firms from shaping acquisition agreements in which parties trade off price for limitations on liability. Given this background, I will now address the Seller's arguments underlying the motion to dismiss.

Do The Terms Of The Stock Purchase Agreement Purport To Limit The Liability Of The Seller For Intentional, Fraudulent Misrepresentations? The Buyer argues that this court need not reach its argument that public policy precludes the Agreement from barring its fraud-based rescission claim. According to the Buyer, the Agreement cannot be reasonably read to subject fraud claims, rather than merely breach of contract claims, to the Exclusive Remedy Provision. I find that argument unpersuasive and inconsistent with the plain language of the Stock Purchase Agreement. * * *

Is The Buyer Permitted To Seek Rescission In This Court Despite The Exclusive Remedy Terms Of The Stock Purchase Agreement? Having determined that the Stock Purchase Agreement's plain terms would, if given legal effect, preclude the Buyer from seeking rescission, I must now consider the Buyer's argument that public policy intervenes to trump contractual freedom and to prevent that preclusion. * * *

When addressing contracts that were the product of give-and-take between commercial parties who had the ability to walk away freely, this court's jurisprudence has taken a different approach. We have honored clauses in which contracted parties have disclaimed reliance [*i.e.*, non-reliance clauses] on extra-contractual representations, which prohibits the promising party from reneging on its promise by premising a fraudulent inducement claim on statements of fact it had previously said were neither made to it nor had an effect on it. * * *

The teaching of this court * * * is that a party cannot promise, in a clear integration clause of a negotiated agreement, that it will not rely on promises and representations outside of the agreement and then shirk its own bargain in favor of a "but we did rely on those other representations" fraudulent inducement claim. The policy basis for this line of cases is, in my view, quite strong. * * *

[T]his court has therefore honored contracts that define those representations of fact that formed the reality upon which the parties premised their decision to bargain. * * *

Nonetheless, this court consistently has respected the law's traditional abhorrence of fraud in implementing this reasoning. Because of that policy concern, we have not given effect to so-called merger or integration clauses that do not clearly state that the parties disclaim reliance upon extra-contractual statements. Instead, we have held * * * that murky integration clauses, or standard integration clauses without explicit anti-reliance representations, will not relieve a party of its oral and extra-contractual fraudulent representations. The integration clause must contain "language that ... can be said to add up to a clear anti-reliance clause by which the plaintiff has contractually promised that it did not rely upon statements outside the contract's four corners in deciding to sign the contract." This approach achieves a sensible balance between fairness and equity—parties can protect themselves against unfounded fraud claims through explicit anti-reliance language. If parties fail to include unambiguous anti-reliance language, they will not be able to escape responsibility for their own fraudulent representations made outside of the agreement's four corners.

This case, however, raises a related, but more difficult, question: to what extent may a contract exculpate a contracting party from a rescission or damages claim based on a false representation of fact made within the contract itself. May parties premise a contract on defined representations but promise in advance to accept a less-than-adequate remedy if one of them has been induced by lies about one of those material facts?

As the Buyer notes, there is a strong tradition in American law that holds that contracts may not insulate a party from damages or rescission resulting from the party's fraudulent conduct. In that vein, the Restatement of Contracts states: "[a] term exempting a party from tort liability for harm caused intentionally or recklessly is unenforceable on grounds of public policy." [Restatement (Second) of Contracts § 195 (1981)] Specifically, "[a] provision in a bargain that fraud in its formation shall not be asserted is illegal." [Restatement (Second) of Contracts § 195 (1981)] The Restatement's position finds resonance in a deep body of case law as well as in leading treatises. * * *

On the other hand, there is also a strong American tradition of freedom of contract, and that tradition is especially strong in our State, which prides itself on having commercial laws that are efficient. The Seller stresses this strain in our law to buttress its argument that contracts between sophisticated parties with equal bargaining strength should be honored without intrusion by the policy concerns of unelected judges. * * *

As the Buyer notes, prior Delaware decisions have used language that is generally condemnatory of contractual limitations on a party's exposure to a fraud claim for making a false statement. To wit, our courts have said that "[a] perpetrator of fraud cannot close the lips of his innocent victim by getting him blindly to agree in advance not to complain against it" and "fraud vitiates every contract, and no man may invoke the law to enforce his fraudulent acts." Those decisions primarily involve the protection of a relatively unsophisticated party or a party lacking bargaining clout who signs a contract with a boilerplate merger clause.

But, as our recent case law indicates, Delaware is also sensitive to the need for commerce to proceed in a rational and certain way. We also respect the ability of sophisticated businesses, such as the Buyer and Seller, to make their own judgments about the risk they should bear and the due diligence they undertake, recognizing that such parties are able to price factors such as limits on liability. * * *

In considering how to allocate the risk of misrepresentations consistent with public policy, I also consider our General Assembly's approach to exculpation in the case of business entities. In the corporate context, the General Assembly has permitted corporate charters to exculpate directors for liability for gross negligence. [*See* Chapter 3] In the alternative entity context, where it is more likely that sophisticated parties have carefully negotiated the governing agreement, the General Assembly has authorized even broader exculpation, to the extent of eliminating fiduciary duties altogether.[5] Given these statements

5. 6 *Del. C.* § 17–1101(d) ("To the extent that, at law or in equity, a partner or other person has duties (including fiduciary duties) * * * to a limited partnership * * * the partner's * * * duties and

of policy by our General Assembly, it is appropriate for the judiciary in fashioning common law to give as much leeway to sophisticated business parties crafting acquisition agreements as is afforded to those who write the governing instruments of limited partnerships and limited liability companies. We should be reluctant to be more restrictive of freedom of contract than those elected by our citizens to write the statutory law.

With that in mind, I resolve this case in the following manner. To the extent that the Stock Purchase Agreement purports to limit the Seller's exposure for its own conscious participation in the communication of lies to the Buyer, it is invalid under the public policy of this State. That is, I find that the public policy of this State will not permit the Seller to insulate itself from the possibility that the sale would be rescinded if the Buyer can show either: 1) that the Seller knew that the Company's contractual representations and warranties were false; or 2) that the Seller itself lied to the Buyer about a contractual representation and warranty. This will require the Buyer to prove that the Seller acted with an illicit state of mind, in the sense that the Seller knew that the representation was false and either communicated it to the Buyer directly itself or knew that the Company had. * * *

By contrast, the Buyer may not obtain rescission or greater monetary damages upon any lesser showing. If the Company's managers intentionally misrepresented facts to the Buyer without knowledge of falsity by the Seller, then the Buyer cannot obtain rescission or damages, but must proceed with an Indemnity Claim subject to the Indemnity Fund's liability cap. Likewise, the Buyer may not escape the contractual limitations on liability by attempting to show that the Seller acted in a reckless, grossly negligent, or negligent manner. The Buyer knowingly accepted the risk that the Seller would act with inadequate deliberation. It is an experienced private equity firm that could have walked away without buying. It has no moral justification for escaping its own voluntarily-accepted limits on its remedies against the Seller absent proof that the Seller itself acted in a consciously improper manner.

In sum, I conclude that the Seller's motion to dismiss the complaint in its entirety must be denied. But the Buyer may only obtain its desired relief—rescission or in the alternative, full compensatory damages—if it meets the burden of proof described. * * *

Note

The parties in *ABRY* settled the matter.

C. Can a Purchaser Bring a Rule 10b-5 Action When It Has Agreed Not to Rely on Representations Outside of the Agreement?—*AES*

AES Corp. v. The DOW Chemical Company

United States Court of Appeals, Third Circuit, 2003 U.S. App. LEXIS 7041
cert denied 2003 U.S. LEXIS 8916

Stapleton, Circuit Judge:

Introduction. The AES Corporation ("AES") operates power facilities. AES alleges that Dow Chemical Company ("Dow") and its subsidiary, Destec Energy, Inc. ("Destec"),

liabilities may be expanded or restricted or eliminated by provisions in a partnership agreement."); 6 *Del. C.* § 18–1101(c) ("To the extent that, at law or in equity, a member or manager or other person has duties (including fiduciary duties) ... to a limited liability company ... the member's or manager's ... duties and liabilities may be expanded or restricted or eliminated by provisions in a limited liability company agreement.").

violated Sections 10(b) and 20(a) of the Securities Exchange Act of 1934 (the "Exchange Act") in connection with a transaction in which AES [acquired] the stock of one of Destec's subsidiaries, Destec Engineering, Inc. ("DEI"). * * * According to AES, Dow and Destec conspired to sell DEI at an artificially inflated price by making misrepresentations material to an evaluation of DEI. * * *

Section 4.6 of the Merger Agreement * * * provided as follows:

Except for the representations and warranties contained in this Article IV, neither Dow nor any other person makes any other express or implied representation or warranty on behalf of Dow.

The Merger Agreement provided that "[t]his Agreement and the Confidentiality Agreement, and certain other agreements executed by the parties hereto as of the date of this Agreement, constitute the entire agreement, and supersede all prior agreements and understandings (written and oral), among the parties with respect to the subject matter hereof."

According to AES, shortly after purchasing DEI * * * it realized that [i]nstead of providing the predicted $31 million in profit, the project ultimately occasioned a $70 million loss. AES contends that Dow knew specific facts about the [DEI] that contradicted the representations it had made [in the transaction documents] prior to and during due diligence. * * *

The District Court's opinion * * * "concludes that the 'no representation/non-reliance' clauses in the agreements between Dow and AES are enforceable." * * * In [the Confidentiality Agreement] AES "acknowledge[d]" that no "express or implied representations or warranty as to the accuracy or completeness of the Information" had been made and agreed (1) that Destec and Dow would not have "any liability relating to the Information" and (2) that AES would be entitled to rely solely on the representations and warranties it would be able to secure in "any definitive agreement." In order to avoid further repetition of this acknowledgment and agreement, we will refer to them hereafter as the "non-reliance" clause.

Analysis. *The Federal Law* * * * To state a valid claim under Rule 10b-5, a plaintiff must show that (1) the defendant made a misstatement or an omission of a material fact (2) with scienter (3) in connection with the purchase or the sale of a security (4) upon which the plaintiff reasonably relied and (5) that the plaintiff's reliance was the proximate cause of his or her injury.

The "reasonable reliance" element of a Rule 10b-5 claim requires a showing of a causal nexus between the misrepresentation and the plaintiff's injury, as well as a demonstration that the plaintiff exercised the diligence that a reasonable person under all of the circumstances would have exercised to protect his own interests. * * *

The District Court held that as a result of AES's contractual commitment not to rely on any representations other than those incorporated in the final agreements, its alleged reliance was unreasonable as a matter of law. AES insists that this holding is incorrect in light of Section 29(a) of the Exchange Act Section 29(a) provides: "Any condition, stipulation, or provision binding any person to waive compliance with any provision of this title or of any rule or regulation thereunder, or of any rule of an exchange required thereby shall be void." That is, by its terms, Section 29(a) "prohibits waiver of the substantive obligations imposed by the Exchange Act." * * *

The Applicable Law * * * Reasonable reliance is an element of a federal law claim and what constitutes such reliance is a matter of federal law. Federal law calls for the determination of reasonableness to be made on a case-by-case basis based on all of the surrounding circumstances. * * *

The Role of the Non-Reliance Clause. This brings us back to Section 29(a) of the Exchange Act which forecloses anticipatory waivers of compliance with the duties imposed by Rule 10b-5. We believe the conclusion inescapable that enforcement of the non-reliance clauses to bar AES's fraud claims as a matter of law would be inconsistent with Section 29(a).

As we have noted, reliance is an essential element of a Rule 10b-5 claim. It necessarily follows that, if a party commits itself never to claim that it relied on representations of the other party to its contract, it purports anticipatorily to waive any future claim based on the fraudulent misrepresentations of that party. The same is true if the commitment is more limited, *e.g.*, a promise not to claim reliance on any representation not set forth in the agreement. The scope of the anticipatory waiver is more limited, but it is nevertheless an anticipatory waiver of potential future claims under Rule 10b-5.

We, thus, find ourselves in agreement with the conclusion of the Court of Appeals for the First Circuit in *Rogen v. Ilikon*, 361 F.2d 260 (1st Cir. 1966). * * *

In reaching this conclusion, we have not been unmindful of the decision of the Court of Appeals for the Second Circuit in *Harsco Corp. v. Segui*, 91 F.3d 337 (2d Cir. 1996). The court there affirmed the dismissal of a Rule 10b-5 security fraud claim based on a stipulation in the stock purchase agreement that the sellers were "not [to] be deemed to have made ... any representation or warranty other than as expressly made by" the sellers in the agreement. *Id.* at 342. The *Harsco* court rejected the purchaser's argument that the District Court's dismissal had violated Section 29(a). Although acknowledging that "the underlying concern of § 29(a) is 'whether the agreement weakens the ability to recover under the Exchange Act'" and that the agreement before it could accurately be described as doing precisely that, the Court nevertheless found the "no other representation" clause enforceable. * * *

We find *Harsco*'s reasoning unpersuasive. Section 29(a) is not intended to protect substantive rights created by contract. It is designed to protect rights created by the Exchange Act, and it expressly forecloses contracting parties from "defin[ing] the boundaries of the[ir] transaction" in a way that relieves a party of the duties imposed by that Act. We do not dispute that there may be economic efficiency in allowing private parties the freedom to fashion their own bargains. But Congress has made a decision to limit that freedom when it comes to anticipatory waivers of Exchange Act claims. Accordingly, we conclude that we must side with the First Circuit Court of Appeals in *Rogen* rather than with the *Harsco* court. * * *

The Issue for Decision on Remand. This leaves for resolution the issue of whether, viewing all of the relevant circumstances and applying the reasonable reliance standard * * *, a reasonable trier of fact could only conclude that AES failed to exercise ordinary care in protecting its own interest. * * *

D. Must Acquiror Prove Reliance in an Action for Post Merger Damages for Breach by Seller of Representations and Warranties?

Giuffrida v. American Family Brands, Inc.

United States District Court, 1998 WL 196402 (E.D.Pa.)

O'Neill:

[**Facts**] These breach of contract actions concern the sale of substantially all of the assets of a family-owned business that distributed and manufactured various meat, poultry and other food products * * *. The buyer, American Family Brands, Inc. (AFB), purchased substantially all of the assets of Freda Corporation and its wholly-owned subsidiaries (collectively "Freda") for $19,434,129 pursuant to a lengthy and detailed Purchase Agreement executed on March 18, 1996. The sellers are five members of the Giuffrida family who ran the business from 1956 until 1996. AFB contends that the sellers breached various provisions of the Purchase Agreement. * * *

Included in the "Representations and Warranties of the Sellers" section of the Purchase Agreement is the following representation and warranty related to the change in the financial condition of sellers from the date of the last audited financial statements to the date of the closing:

> Except as set forth in Schedule 5(a) hereto, since August 26, 1995, there have been no material adverse changes in the condition (financial or otherwise), assets, liabilities, earnings, or properties, of any of the Sellers[.]

The Agreement also contains a section titled "Survival of Representations, Warranties, Etc." which reads:

> All of the representations, warranties, covenants and agreements made by the parties to this Agreement shall survive the execution and delivery of this Agreement and the consummation of the transactions contemplated hereunder for a period of two (2) years after the Closing Date[.]

Under the miscellaneous section of the Agreement there is also a non-waiver subsection which provides:

> No waiver of the provisions hereof shall be effective unless in writing and signed by the party to be charged with such waiver.

[**Issue**] AFB contends that there was a material adverse change in the sellers' financial condition resulting in a breach of the express representation and warranty in Section 5(e) of the Agreement that survived closing. Sellers, however, contend that AFB closed with knowledge of the change in the financial condition of sellers, and that therefore AFB did not rely on the truth of the warranty and waived any claim pursuant to Section 5(e).

Prior to executing the Purchase Agreement, the parties signed a "Letter of Intent" under which AFB had the right to cancel the purchase without any liability if it was dissatisfied with the results of its due diligence. As part of its due diligence AFB received Freda's interim financial statements for the "stub period"—the period between the last audited financial statements, August 25, 1995, and the date of the closing, March 18, 1996. Laurence Needleman, AFB's Chief Financial Officer, prepared an analysis of those interim financial statements which showed a significant reduction in earnings. The downturn was so severe that Needleman concluded that "[r]esults of operations for Freda Corp. through Jan., 1996 indicate that the company has been severely mismanaged during the last three months." *See* Needleman Memo, March 4, 1996.

Sellers contend that because AFB knew about the changes in the financial condition of Freda during the stub period, as evidenced by this memorandum, it is precluded from relying on the no material adverse change representation and warranty. AFB argues that under Pennsylvania law and the plain language of the Purchase Agreement reliance on the representation and warranty is not a requirement of its breach of warranty claim and therefore it did not waive its claim by closing.

[**Analysis**] The Pennsylvania Supreme Court has not decided whether reliance is a required element in a contractual breach of representation and warranty claim, and the decisions in other jurisdictions are divided. As a federal judge applying Pennsylvania law without guidance from the Pennsylvania Supreme Court, I must attempt to predict what that Court would hold if presented with this question.

In *Land v. Roper Corp.*, 531 F.2d 445 (10th Cir. 1976), the court held that under Kansas law reliance on an express warranty by the buyer of a business is essential to maintenance of its breach of express warranty claim. The Court found the Uniform Commercial Code's reliance requirement for breach of warranty claims could be applied by analogy to the sale of a business. It also supported its holding by reference to Kansas tort law, and the reliance requirement in tortious misrepresentation claims. The Court of Appeals for the Seventh Circuit, relying exclusively on Minnesota precedent, reached the same decision with regard to Minnesota law. *Hendricks v. Callahan*, 972 F.2d 190, 192–94 (7th Cir. 1992).

Reliance as an element of a breach express warranty claim, however, has been rejected in *Shambaugh v. Lindsay*, 445 N.E.2d 124, 126–27 (Ind.App. 3 Dist. 1983) and *Weschler v. Long Island Rehabilitation Center of Nassua, Inc.*, 1996 WL 590679, *21–22 (Mass. Super. Ct. 1996) (applying Indiana and Massachusetts law respectively). In *Shambaugh* the court examined the conflicting case law and concluded that:

> The problems of reliance, and a right to rely, on the representations do not appear when the action is grounded in warranty. The warranty is as much a part of the contract as any other part, and the right to damages on the breach depends on nothing more than the breach of warranty.

This holding was grounded in the view that a warranty "is an assurance by one party to a contract of the existence of a fact upon which the other party may rely. It is intended precisely to relieve the promisee of any duty to ascertain the fact for himself." The *Wechsler* court held that reliance was not a requirement for breach of express warranty claims using similar reasoning: "[a]n express warranty serves in substance as an agreement on the part of the warrantor to indemnify the other party if the fact or condition guaranteed to be true turns out not to be so."

In between these two lines of cases is New York law. Under New York law, reliance is generally not a requirement of a breach of an express warranty claim. The rationale supporting this view is similar to that of *Shambaugh* and *Weschler*:

> This view of "reliance"—*i.e.*, as requiring no more than reliance on the express warranty as being part of the bargain between the parties—reflects the prevailing perception that an action for breach of express warranty is one that is no longer grounded in tort, but essentially in contract. The express warranty is as much a part of the contract as any other term. Once the express warranty is shown to have been relied on as part of the contract, the right to be indemnified in damages for its breach does not depend on proof that the buyer thereafter believed that the assurances of fact made in the warranty would be fulfilled. The right to indemnification depends only on establishing that the warranty was breached.

CBS, Inc. v. Ziff-Davis Publishing Co., 75 N.Y.2d 496, 503–04, 554 N.Y.S.2d 449, 553 N.E.2d 997 (N.Y. 1990). New York law, however, also provides a defense to a breach of express warranty claim where the "buyer closes on a contract with full knowledge and acceptance of facts disclosed by the seller which would constitute a breach of warranty under the terms of the contract ... unless the buyer expressly preserves his rights under the warranties." *Galli v. Metz*, 973 F.2d 145, 151 (2d Cir. 1992).

In *Pegasus Management Co., Inc. v. Lyssa, Inc.*, 1998 WL 59394 (D.Mass. February 6, 1998) the Court was faced with predicting which line of authority the Connecticut Supreme Court would follow. While the Court rejected the *Roper/Hendricks* line of cases, it found it unnecessary to choose between the New York cases and the *Shambaugh/Weschler* line of cases because of the following language of the purchase agreement:

> Every ... warranty ... set forth in this Agreement and ... the rights and remedies ... for any one or more breaches of this Agreement by the Sellers shall ... not be deemed waived by the Closing and shall be effective regardless of any ... prior knowledge by or on the part of the Purchaser[.]

The *Pegasus* court held that, faced with the language of the agreement, the Connecticut Supreme Court would not require reliance with respect to plaintiff's breach of warranty claim.

I follow a similar approach in predicting that the Pennsylvania Supreme Court would not require AFB to prove reliance to maintain its breach of warranty claims. First, I conclude that the Pennsylvania Supreme Court would not adopt the *Roper/Hendricks* line of cases because that approach is inconsistent with the commercial realities of these complex purchase agreements negotiated over several months by sophisticated parties. The representations and warranties in these transactions define and apportion the risks that the parties negotiated. The amount of risk assumed by the sellers is part of the bargain and protects the investment that buyers make in sellers' business. If the sellers were not willing to take on the risk reflected in the representations and warranties, the buyers may have reduced their offer or not gone forward with the transaction at all. I find that the *Roper/Hendricks* approach is inconsistent with this commercial reality because it permits sellers to escape liability for negotiated representations and warranties by arguing to a fact-finder that buyers did not rely on the representations and warranties. Thus, in essence, the *Roper/Hendricks* approach allows contracting parties to avoid the plain meaning and effect of the contract to which they agreed.

The approach also injects a degree of unneeded uncertainty into these already complex transactions by making the enforceability of the representations and warranties subject to a fact-finder's determination. * * *

Finally, the *Roper/Hendricks* approach discourages complete due diligence because the more complete buyers' due diligence the more likely a fact-finder will find that they did not rely on the accuracy of the representations and warranties. The law, however, should encourage complete due diligence to ensure that buyers are aware of what they are purchasing and the associated benefits and risks of that purchase. For these reasons, I predict that the Pennsylvania Supreme Court would not adopt the *Roper/Hendricks* approach.

Like the court in *Pegasus*, however, I find it unnecessarily to predict which of the two remaining lines of cases the Pennsylvania Supreme Court would adopt because the language of the instant Purchase Agreement would compel the same conclusion whichever authority applies. Under the more pro-seller New York approach, sellers may avoid liability by showing that the buyer was aware of the inaccuracies in the warranties prior to closing and that the buyer did not expressly preserve a breach of warranty claim. Here, the Purchase Agreement included a non-waiver provision, and a provision providing that all representations and warranties shall survive closing plus two years. I conclude that these provisions unambiguously preserved buyer's breach of warranty claim against a defense of non-reliance such as asserted by the sellers. * * *

§ 15.14 Legality of (1) Various Deal Protection Measures: No Talks, Break-Up Fees, and Fiduciary Outs; and (2) Reverse Termination Fees

The law governing various types of deal protection devices is examined in Chapter 3, and particularly in Section 3.20, which is entitled: *Elaboration on Issues with "No Solicitations," "Lock-Ups," "Break-Up Fees" and Other Deal Protection Measures in Revlon and Other Transactions.* As explained there, merger agreements for public company acquisitions will generally have a non-solicitation provision, which will be subject to certain fiduciary outs, and a termination fee. The non-solicitation provision is generally found in the covenants section, sometimes referred to as "Additional Agreements," and the termination fee is generally found in the termination section of the agreement. *See e.g.*, Section 6.5 (No Solicitation) and Section 8.1 and 8.2 (Termination) of the MCI-Verizon merger agreement, which are in MCI-Deal Protection Devices, Documentary Appendix K.

A reverse termination fee is a fee paid by the acquiror to the target if the acquiror walks form the deal, for example, as a result of the absence of antitrust clearance. These fees are examined in Section 9.11.

§ 15.15 General Provisions

Article VIII of the Time-Warner Merger Agreement, Documentary Appendix A, contains standard general provisions found in all forms of acquisition agreements, including sections dealing with such items as notices, interpretation, counterparts, third party beneficiaries, publicity, and governing law. Also, the general provisions would normally include a section dealing with amendments, as specified in Section 7.3 of the Time-Warner Merger Agreement.

§ 15.16 Legal Opinions

Legal opinions are required as a condition to the closing of most acquisition agreements relating to the acquisition of a closely-held corporation [*see* § 5.1(a) of the Sample Stock Purchase Agreement, Documentary Appendix U] and may be required in the acquisition of a publicly-held corporation. However, it is becoming common in public acquisitions, particularly in "mergers of equals," or near equals as in the Time-Warner transactions, not to require legal opinions as a condition of closing. *See also* Article VII of the Global Toys-Toys "R" Us Merger Agreement, Documentary Appendix F. However, if the transaction is structured as a tax-free reorganization [*see* Chapter 5] a tax opinion to such effect will normally be required. *See e.g.*, Section 6.1(d) of the Time-Warner Merger Agreement, Documentary Appendix A.

In an acquisition of a closely-held corporation, the acquiring corporation is particularly interested in receiving the legal opinion of counsel to the selling shareholders in a stock acquisition or counsel to the target in an asset acquisition or a merger.

In rendering a legal opinion, the attorney must exercise the utmost care and must conduct the due diligence needed to render the opinion. At the point when the parties are first negotiating the opinions to be delivered, the attorneys should consult Section of Business Law, ABA, *Third Party Legal Opinion Report: Including the Legal Opinion Accord* (1991) [hereinafter the "*Legal Opinion Accord*"]; Section of Business Law, ABA, *The*

Collected TriBar Legal Opinion Reports 1979–1993 (1995); and Herbert S. Wander, Laurie G. Goldstein and Nancy A. Rose, *Issues in Legal Opinions*, 18 The Lawyers Brief 591 (1988) (containing opinions in various acquisition contexts).

The *Legal Opinion Accord* contains Guidelines for Negotiation and Preparation of Third-Party Legal Opinions. The *Accord*, which is not binding on attorneys, suggests, *inter alia*, that legal opinions (1) be negotiated early in the preparation of the acquisition agreement, (2) be limited to questions of law and questions requiring legal judgment, and (3) be reasonable and necessary.

Legal opinions required by acquisition agreements will generally be set forth as an exhibit to the agreement as is provided in Section 5.1(a) of the Sample Stock Purchase Agreement, Documentary Appendix U, and the provisions of the legal opinion will be heavily negotiated.

In general, the legal opinion of the counsel to the selling shareholders in a stock acquisition or to the closely-held target in an asset acquisition or merger will have the following provisions, which are tied into various representations and warranties and closing conditions.

First, the opinion generally will provide that the target is duly organized, validly existing, and is in good standing, thus confirming a representation commonly found in acquisition agreements. [*See* § 3.1(a) of the Time-Warner Merger Agreement, Documentary Appendix A]

Second, the opinion typically will specify the capitalization of the target, thus confirming a representation dealing with capitalization and also state that the selling shareholders own the stock free and clear, thus confirming a representation dealing with ownership of the target's stock. [*See* § 3.1(b) of the Time-Warner Merger Agreement, Documentary Appendix A]

Third, the opinion will generally deal with the authority of the seller to enter into the agreement and the binding effect of the agreement on the seller, thereby confirming a common representation. [*See* § 2.1 of the Sample Stock Purchase Agreement, Documentary Appendix U] The opinion regarding the binding effect of the agreement is the remedies part of the opinion, indicating the extent to which the acquiror's rights under the agreement will be respected by a court.

Fourth, the opinion typically will state that the completion of the transaction will not cause a default under any material contract or give rise to the right to terminate any material contract as a result of a change of control or similar provision. This provision confirms one of the common closing conditions as illustrated in Section 6.2(e) of the Time-Warner Merger Agreement, Documentary Appendix A.

Fifth, the opinion typically will provide that all governmental approvals for the transaction have been obtained, thus confirming a general condition of closing. [*See* § 6.1(c) of the Time-Warner Merger Agreement, Documentary Appendix A]

Sixth, the opinion typically will address the status of any litigation involving the target, thus addressing one of the common closing conditions. [*See* § 5.1(d) of the Sample Stock Purchase Agreement, Documentary Appendix U]

Finally, the opinion will generally state that the attorney has no reason to believe that any representation or warranty is untrue, thus confirming one of the typical closing conditions. [*See* § 6.2(a) of the Time-Warner Merger Agreement, Documentary Appendix A]

§ 15.17 Employment Contracts and Non-Competition Agreements

The acquisition agreement may contain as a closing condition the receipt by the acquiring corporation of executed employment agreements from certain key employees who will continue their employment after the acquisition. Such an agreement is typically an exhibit to the acquisition agreement. These agreements are specifically tailored to the situation, and, therefore, are not included here.

Also, the receipt by the acquiring corporation of non-competition agreements from the selling shareholders may be a condition of closing. Such agreements are also typically exhibits to the acquisition agreement.

§ 15.18 Registration Rights

If the consideration paid in the acquisition is non-registered stock or debt instruments, which are subject to resale restrictions under Regulation D or otherwise [*see* Chapter 4], the target's shareholders may negotiate for the right to have such stock registered.

There are two basic forms of registration rights: piggy-back and demand. Piggy-back rights permit the shareholder to include his or her shares in any registered offering that the acquiring corporation subsequently completes. Demand rights permit the shareholder to require the acquiring corporation to prepare a registration statement covering the shareholder's shares.

References

The references for this chapter are in the Scope.

Chapter 16

Proxy Contests

§ 16.1 Scope

This chapter focuses on both the state corporate law and federal securities law aspects of proxy contests and related issues. A proxy contests is similar to a political election; the contending parties make arguments in support of their positions and ask for the votes of the electorate, which in a proxy contest is the shareholders. The contest is generally over the annual election of directors, but can also be focused on a strategic or other issue, such as whether the company should engage in a merger as in the *HP* case discussed in Section 16.11.B.

The corporate law sections of this chapter build on Chapter 3, (director's duties) and the securities law sections build on Chapter 4 (securities regulation) and Chapter 13 (acquisitions of publicly-held corporations). Section 16.2 presents an introductory problem, and Section 16.3 provides background information on this topic. Section 16.4 provides a summary of the rules under Section 14(a) of the Securities Exchange Act of 1934 (the 34 Act) regarding proxy contests. Section 16.5 addresses the question of what constitutes a "solicitation" within Rule 14a-1(*l*) under the 34 Act. It will be seen that the concept of a solicitation is very broad and may arise inadvertently, thus making the soliciting party subject to the proxy rules. Section 16.6 addresses the provisions of the proxy rules that provide for (1) safe-harbors from the solicitation concept; (2) exemptions for certain solicitations; and (3) solicitations that can be made outside of a proxy statement. Section 16.7 introduces the rules regarding the Internet availability of proxy materials and Internet based proxy contests.

Section 16.8 deals with allegations of a failure to properly disclose all material information as required by Rule 14a-9 under the 34 Act. Rule 14a-9 was also addressed in Chapter 4, securities regulation, and Chapter 13, acquisitions of public companies. Finally, on the securities front, Section 16.9 briefly mentions the SEC's vacated proxy access rule.

Section 16.10 examines the 2006 amendments to the Model Business Corporation Act (MBCA) that make it easier to provide for majority voting for directors. Section 16.11 addresses state law standards governing directors' control of the proxy system. Section 16.12 deals with a fiduciary duty issue arising in an acquiror's contemporaneous tender offer and proxy contest to replace the target's board. Section 16.13, which addresses shareholder bylaw proposals to limit the board's ability to issue poison pills, refers to *Fleming*, Section 3.18.E.11, which addressed a pill redemption bylaw under Oklahoma law. Other pill cases are also set out in Chapter 3, directors' duties. Section 16.14 briefly addresses state law rules governing the production of shareholder lists, and Section 16.15 deals with the state law rules governing reimbursement of proxy expenses.

Various sections of this chapter refer to Documentary Appendix HH, *Documents Relating to the Air Products 2010 Proxy Contest to Elect Directors to the Board of Airgas*. The *Airgas* case is discussed in Section 3.18.E.10. The materials in this chapter are discussed in greater detail in Thompson, *Mergers, Acquisitions and Tender Offers*, *supra* Section 1.10, Chapters 5 and 8.

§ 16.2 Introductory Problem on Proxy Contests

RJR Nabisco, Inc. is a publicly-held Delaware corporation that is engaged in the tobacco business and the food business. Raider, Inc. would like to acquire RJR's food business but not its tobacco business. Raider, which owns 4% of RJR stock has proposed to RJR's board that it spin-off the tobacco business to the RJR shareholders [*see* Chapter 24] and that RJR then be acquired by Raider in a tax-free merger in which the RJR shareholders would end up with 55% of the stock of Raider. RJR's board has rejected Raider's proposal, and Raider is now searching for ways to pressure RJR's board into these transactions.

(1) Can Raider contact several of RJR's institutional shareholders and urge them to pressure RJR's board to complete the proposed transactions?

(2) Can Raider take-out a full-page ad in the *Wall Street Journal* urging RJR's shareholders to pressure the RJR board to accept the transaction?

(3) What steps is Raider required to take under Delaware and federal law if it decides to seek to replace the RJR directors at the next annual meeting? Can Raider expect to be reimbursed for its expenses?

(4) What standard applies to the actions taken by the RJR directors in opposing Raider's efforts to replace them? What if the RJR directors delay the annual meeting to give the shareholders more time to understand the nature of Raider's proposal? Can the directors expect to be reimbursed for the expenses incurred in opposing Raider?

(5) What if the controlling shareholder of Raider is alleged to have ties to a notorious member of the mob, who is presently serving time for securities fraud? Raider has not disclosed this in any of its communications to the RJR shareholders.

§ 16.3 Introduction

A. Overview of the Uses of a Proxy Contest

Mark A. Stach, An Overview of Legal and Tactical Considerations in Proxy Contests: The Primary Means of Effecting Fundamental Corporate Change in the 1990s

13 Geo. Mason U. L. Rev. 745, 746–749 (1991)

The Classic Proxy Fight. In the classic proxy fight, the insurgents seek to replace the incumbent board of directors with their own slate of candidates. In the past, the insurgents were likely to charge that the incumbent board had generally mismanaged the company. In more recent battles for control of the board, however, the insurgent has typically sought to elect directors to support a specific proposal. The insurgents, for example, may seek to terminate or to redeem a shareholders rights plan or simply to support a takeover plan.

The implementation by many companies of a staggered or classified board reduces the insurgents' chances of winning a classic proxy fight for control of the board. Companies which have provisions for classified boards elect only a minority of the board's members at each annual meeting. This precludes the insurgents from electing a majority of the board at one meeting and immediately implementing their takeover agenda. Such provisions may force insurgents to wage at least two successful proxy fights in order to elect enough directors to gain control of the target corporation's board. The election of insurgent candidates to even a minority of seats on a staggered board, however, may cause the incumbent directors to change policy in order to fulfill some or all to the insurgents' demands. * * *

Shareholders' Proposals [*See* **Rule 14a-8**] In the face of classified boards, many insurgents have chosen to offer proposals for economic reform or alterations in corporate governance rather than trying to elect a new board. An economic reform proposal generally calls for a "bust up" or "spin-off" designed to require the board of directors to sell all or part of the company. Corporate governance proposals often call for the redemption of rights plans. An insurgent proposal of this nature is sometimes accompanied by a challenge to the incumbent board. The effective use of such proposals by insurgents is illustrative of how a classified board structure does not act as a complete bar to obtaining the results for which the proxy contest was initiated.

When an insurgent's proposal is not accompanied by an attempt to gain control of the board, the proposal is precatory rather than mandatory. A precatory resolution is not binding on the incumbent directors and only seeks to encourage them to undertake certain actions. Even if a precatory proposal is passed, it need not be initiated by the incumbent board. It would be difficult, however, for the incumbents to ignore the wishes of the majority of shareholders who voted for a precatory resolution. * * *

B. The Simultaneous Tender Offer and Proxy Contest

Irwin H. Warren and Kevin G. Abrams, Evolving Standards of Judicial Review of Procedural Defenses in Proxy Contests

47 Bus. Law. 647, 650–651 (1992)

The simultaneous or staged commencement of a tender offer with a proxy contest or a consent solicitation has emerged in several prominent control contests as a means of pressuring the target directors to reject reliance solely on the corporation's shareholder rights plan and a "just say no" posture. A bidder can combine a tender offer with a stockholder solicitation to accomplish a number of significant objectives. Assuming the shareholder rights plan does not include a "continuing director" provision, an initial objective may be to install directors who will rescind the plan or redeem the target company's shareholder rights. The newly-installed directors also could exempt the insurgent's proposed business combination from the application of the pertinent state anti-takeover statute, to the extent that statute may provide. Even in the face of a staggered board, insurgents have recognized that electing one-third of the directors at the annual meeting could impose enormous pressures on the holdover directors. In addition, securing stockholder approval of a proposed transaction through a proxy contest may satisfy a supermajority or fair price requirement in the corporation's charter or bylaws, or otherwise nullify other target defenses. * * *

C. Does the Party Have a Winning Case?

Any party that is considering the possibility of a proxy contest must answer a fundamental question: Can I win? This will depend on many factors, including (1) the amount of the corporation's stock that is controlled by the insurgent and parties friendly to it; (2) the amount of stock controlled by the management and the parties friendly to it; (3) the percentage of the stock held by shareholders who are not aligned with either the insurgent or management; (4) the percentage of the stock held by institutions and other sophisticated shareholders; (5) the timing of the shareholders' meeting; (6) the percentage of the shares that are likely to be voted; and (7) the strength of the insurgent's case.

Obviously, a professional proxy solicitor can be of help in addressing these and other issues that can bear on the question of whether the insurgent can win. And, of course, in any proxy contest, the management of the company will be looking at similar factors and consulting the company's proxy solicitor.

In many cases the argument may come down to the merits of (1) a short-term premium transaction advanced by the insurgent, as compared to (2) possible future greater returns from the continued pursuit of management's long-term strategy.

D. Proxy Contest for the Five-Year Period, 2009 to 2013

Georgeson, a leading proxy solicitor, publishes an *Annual Corporate Governance Review.* The *2013 Annual Review* presents the following statistics on the number of proxy contests in each of the years during the five-year period from 2009 through 2013:

Number of Proxy Contests, 2009–2013

Year	Number of Contests
2009	57
2010	35
2011	20
2012	34
2013	37

Source: Figure 21, Georgeson, 2013 Annual Corporate Governance Review

An analysis of the statistics in the *2013 Annual Review* for the 37 proxy contests occurring in 2013 shows that management won 9 of the contests and the dissident won 8. The full data on the Winners is shown in the following table.

Results of the 37 Proxy Contests in 2013

Winner	Number
Management	9
Settled	9
Dissident	8
Withdrawn	4
Split	2
Pending	5
Total	37

Source: Figure 22, Georgeson, 2013 Annual Corporate Governance Review

The above data show that in 17 of the contests, the dissident either won (8) or settled (9), which would seem to be pretty good results for the dissidents.

§ 16.4 Summary of the SEC Rules Regarding Proxy Contests and Consent Solicitations

A. Introduction

The principles in Rules 14a-1 *et seq.* under the 34 Act, which are discussed in Chapter 13 in connection with proxy solicitations in the context of an M&A transaction, also generally apply to proxy contests. Rule 14a-1(f) defines the term "proxy" broadly to include "every proxy, consent or authorization within the meaning of section 14(a) of the [1934] Act." Thus, the federal proxy rules apply to solicitations of both proxies and consents.

B. What Is a "Consent"?

Section 228 of the Delaware General Corporate Law permits stockholders to take by written consents any action they could have taken at an annual or special stockholders' meeting, and the required vote is the same as would apply on the issue at a shareholders' meeting. Under Section 213(a) of the Delaware General Corporate Law, the board of directors may "exercise its business judgment in fixing a record date for shareholder action by written consent." *Empire of Carolina, Inc. v. The Deltona Corporation*, 514 A.2d 1091, 1097 (Del. 1986). However, the board cannot arbitrarily delay the consummation of shareholder action by consent. *See Datapoint Corp. v. Plaza Securities Co.*, 494 A.2d 1031 (Del. 1985).

C. Rules Relating to Access to Shareholder Lists and Reporting of Results

The SEC's 1992 revision of the proxy rules contained the following provisions relating to shareholder lists and reporting of election results. The exempt solicitation provision, Rule 14a-2(b), is discussed *infra.*

Access to Shareholder Lists [*See* Rule 14a-7] The Commission is adopting revisions to Rule 14a-7, which sets forth the obligations of registrants to either:

> (1) provide a requesting shareholder with a list of holders of securities of a class from which proxies have been solicited or are to be solicited on management's behalf in connection with a shareholder meeting or action by consent or authorization; or
>
> (2) mail the requesting shareholder's soliciting materials to shareholders or subgroups of shareholders of that class. * * *

Enhanced Disclosure Regarding Voting Results and Vote Tabulation Policies Voting Results The Commission proposed to amend Items 4(c) of Forms 10-K and 10-Q to require a brief description of each matter voted upon by shareholders during the period of the report, including contested and uncontested elections, as well as a statement of the number of votes cast for, against, or withheld with regard to each matter or nominee. * * * [T]he Commission has adopted the amendments as proposed. * * *

D. The "Filing-and-Distribution-Before-Solicitation" Rule

1. In General

Rule 14a-3(a) sets out the following "filing-and-distribution-before-solicitation" rule that applies to every "proxy, consent, or authorization" sought with respect to a 34 Act company:

> (a) No solicitation subject to this regulation shall be made unless each person solicited is concurrently furnished or has previously been furnished with a publicly-filed preliminary or definitive written proxy statement containing the information specified in Schedule 14A or with a preliminary or definitive written

proxy statement included in a registration statement filed under the Securities Act of 1933 on Form S-4 * * * and containing the information specified in such Form.

Rule 14a-6(a) requires that as a general matter "preliminary copies of the proxy statement and form of proxy [must] be filed with the Commission at least 10 calendar days prior to the date definitive copies of such material are first sent or given to security holders[.]"

The court in *Capital Real Estate Investors*[1] described as follows the "substance" of Rules 14a-3 and 14a-6:

> Rules 14a-3 and 14a-6 * * * provide in substance that no solicitation subject to Regulation 14A shall be made unless a preliminary or definitive proxy statement is filed with the Commission and each person solicited is provided with a copy concurrently with or in advance of the solicitation.[2]

2. Preliminary and Definitive Proxy Statements in the Airgas Proxy Contest

Section I of Documentary Appendix HH, *Documents Relating to the Air Products 2010 Proxy Contest to Elect Directors to the Board of Airgas*, is a press release by Airgas announcing the filing of its preliminary proxy statement. Section II of Appendix HH is an excerpt from Air Products definitive proxy statement regarding the matter.

E. What Constitutes a "Solicitation?"

The term "solicitation" in Section 14a-3(a) is broadly defined as follows in Rule 14a-1(*l*):

> (*l*) *Solicitation.* (1) The terms "solicit" and "solicitation" include:
>
> (i) Any request for a proxy whether or not accompanied by or included in a form of proxy;
>
> (ii) Any request to execute or not to execute, or to revoke, a proxy; or
>
> (iii) The furnishing of a form of proxy or other communication to security holders under circumstances reasonably calculated to result in the procurement, withholding or revocation of a proxy.

The breath of the term is illustrated in the *ConAgra* case in Section 16.5.

§ 16.5 Elaboration on What Constitutes a "Solicitation" under Rule 14a-1(*l*)

ConAgra, Inc. v. Tyson Foods, Inc.

United States District Court, Nebraska, 1989 708 F. Supp. 257

[Plaintiff, *ConAgra*, and Defendant, *Tyson Foods*, were both trying to acquire Holly Farms, the target corporation.]

1. Capital Real Estate Investors Tax Exempt Fund Ltd. Pshp. v. Schwartzberg, 917 F. Supp. 1050 (S.D. N.Y. 1996).

2. *Id.* at 1059.

* * * The Court shall now address the defendants' counterclaim in which Tyson alleges that plaintiffs violated sections 14(a) and 14(e) of the Securities Act of 1934 when they issued a January 24, 1989, press release concerning this litigation. In its section 14(a) claim Tyson alleges that ConAgra's news release constitutes a proxy solicitation in violation of the securities laws in that ConAgra has not furnished the persons solicited, *i.e.*, Holly shareholders, with a written proxy statement containing legally prescribed information and that ConAgra's alleged intentional violation of the federal securities law and regulations causes harm to shareholders by depriving them of information necessary for informed investment decisions in choosing between the Tyson and ConAgra proposals. Tyson relies on section 14(a) and Rule 14a-3 for support of its claim and seeks appropriate preliminary injunctive relief.

ConAgra responds to this argument by arguing that its January 24, 1989, press release was not in fact a solicitation of a proxy, therefore, since a solicitation is a requisite element of a section 14(a) violation, no violation can be demonstrated in the instant action. ConAgra contends that a communication to the general public contemporaneously with a significant corporate event, prior to the scheduling of any shareholder meeting, does not constitute a proxy solicitation. In support ConAgra cites *Brown v. Chicago Rock Island Company*, 328 F.2d 122 (7th Cir. 1964) where the court concluded that an advertisement published in a number of newspapers did not constitute a proxy solicitation but that the purpose of the advertisement was to inform and motivate the public. Under the prevailing circumstances, the court concluded that there was "nothing in the record to substantiate the conclusion that it was a 'communication reasonably calculated to result in the procurement' of proxies." *Id.* at 125. ConAgra also cites *Smallwood v. Pearl Brewing Company*, 489 F.2d 579, 600–601 (5th Cir. 1974) in support of its argument that its press release did not constitute a proxy solicitation. Relying upon these precedents ConAgra contends that its press release did not constitute a solicitation of proxies for the following reasons: a) its purpose was to inform the public about a significant corporate development; b) that at the time of issuance no shareholders meeting has been scheduled by either ConAgra or Holly to vote on the Merger; and c) that proxies were not mentioned in the press release. * * *

Rule 14a-3 states:

> (a) No solicitation subject to the regulation shall be made unless each person solicited is concurrently furnished or has previously been furnished with a written proxy statement containing the information specified in Schedule 14A or with a written proxy statement included in a registration statement filed under the Securities Act of 1933 on Form S-4 or F-4 * * * and containing the information specified in such Form.

Under Rule 14a-1(*l*), solicitation includes "(i) any request for a proxy whether or not accompanied by or included in a form of proxy; (ii) any request to execute or not to execute, or to revoke, a proxy; or (iii) the furnishing of a form of proxy or other communication to security holders under circumstances reasonably calculated to result in procurement, withholding or revocation of a proxy." Solicitation materials can take the form of press releases. In *Long Island Lighting Company v. Barbash*, 779 F.2d 793 (2nd Cir. 1985) the Second Circuit stated that the proxy rules applied "not only to direct requests to furnish, revoke or withhold proxies, but also to communications which may indirectly accomplish such a result or constitute a step in a chain of communications designed ultimately to accomplish such a step." *Id.* at 796. Furthermore, the court stated that the "question in every case is whether the challenged communication, seen in the totality of the circumstances, is 'reasonably calculated' to influence the shareholders' votes." * * *

Based on the circumstances of this action the Court finds that Tyson has established a reasonable probability of success on the merits that the plaintiffs, through the use of their press release, violated the proxy solicitation rules embodied in section 14(a), and Rule 14a-3. * * *

Questions

Is the result in *ConAgra* changed by the adoption of either (1) the exempt solicitation rule in Rule 14a-2(b)(1), or (2) the shareholder announcement exception to the solicitation definition in Rule 14a-1(*l*)(2)(iv)? Both of these provisions are discussed in Section 16.6.

§ 16.6 Solicitation Safe-Harbors; Exempt Solicitations; and Solicitations Outside of the Proxy Statement

A. Introduction

Notwithstanding the broad definition of the term "solicitation" in Rule 14a-1(*l*), there are several provisions that govern the following (1) safe-harbors from the solicitation concept; (2) solicitations that are exempt from some or all of the proxy rules; and (3) solicitations that can be made outside of the proxy statement. This section briefly addresses these exceptions by generally moving from the exceptions that are more ministerial to those that are more substantive.

B. Safe-Harbors from the "Solicitation" Concept

Pursuant to Rule 14a-1(2), the following activities are safe-harbors from the "solicitation" concept and are, therefore, not subject to the proxy rules:

> (i) [**Furnishing a Proxy**] The furnishing of a form of proxy to a security holder upon the unsolicited request of such security holder;
>
> (ii) [**Providing Shareholder List**] The performance by the registrant of acts required by Rule 14a-7 (relating to providing a shareholder list);
>
> (iii) [**Ministerial Acts**] The performance by any person of ministerial acts on behalf of a person soliciting a proxy; or
>
> (iv) [**Announcing How Shareholder Will Vote**] A communication by a security holder who does not otherwise engage in a proxy solicitation (other than a solicitation exempt under Rule 14a-2) stating how the security holder intends to vote and the reasons therefor, provided that the communication:
>
>> (A) [**Public Announcement**] Is made by means of speeches in public forums, press releases, published or broadcast opinions, statements, or advertisements appearing in a broadcast media, or newspaper, magazine or other bona fide publication disseminated on a regular basis,
>>
>> (B) [**Fiduciary Duty**] Is directed to persons to whom the security holder owes a fiduciary duty in connection with the voting of securities of a registrant held by the security holder, or
>>
>> (C) [**Requested**] Is made in response to unsolicited requests for additional information with respect to a prior communication by the security holder made pursuant to this paragraph (l)(2)(iv).

The Rule 14a-1(2)(iv) **Announcing How Shareholder Will Vote** safe-harbor from the "solicitation" concept was at issue in *Capital Real Estate Investors*.[3] There the court explained that the efforts of the defendant, Schwartzberg, to defeat proposed mergers was "part of a broader plan which include[d] supplanting [certain] * * * managing general partners[.]"[4] In rejecting Schwartzberg's claim that the Rule 14a-1(2)(iv) safe-harbor applied, the court reasoned:

> To construe "otherwise engage in a proxy solicitation" as Schwartzberg suggests would allow one in Schwartzberg's position to "spread the misinformation adequately before beginning to solicit." The Commission certainly intended no such result. The far more rational reading of the rule is that one loses any possibility of coming within the 14a-1(l)(2)(iv) safe harbor if the circumstances indicate that the press release or other communication at issue is a step in a campaign likely to end in the solicitation of proxies and, *a fortiori*, whereas here the issuer of the communication already has taken concrete steps to prepare for such a solicitation.[5]

C. Full Exemption for Certain Special Situations

Rule 14a-2(a) provides that the proxy rules, including the anti-fraud rule in Rule 14a-9, do not apply to the following: solicitations (1) by a person with "respect to securities carried in his name," (2) by a person with respect to securities of which he is the beneficial owner, (3) involved in an offer registered under the 33 Act, (4) with respect to bankruptcy reorganizations, and (5) by newspaper advertisement informing investors how they can get the proxy materials. These exemptions are not discussed further here.

D. Exemption (Except for Rule 14a-9) for Certain Transactions

Except for Rule 14a-9, the antifraud rule, the proxy rules generally to not apply to solicitations in connection with (1) providing proxy advice by financial advisors, (2) roll-up transactions, (3) distributions by brokers and dealers of research reports, (4) electronic shareholder forums, and (5) the formation of, and solicitations by, a nominating shareholder group. [*See* Rule 14a-2(b)(3)-(8)]

E. Exemption (Except for Rule 14a-9) for General Solicitations by Certain Third Parties

Rule 14a-2(b)(1) provides an exemption for a solicitation [*i.e.*, an Exempt Solicitation] by any person, whether or not a shareholder, who does not for himself or on behalf of another: (1) "seek, directly or indirectly, the power to act as proxy for a security holder, and (2) furnish or otherwise request * * * a form of revocation, abstention, consent or authorization." The following categories of persons cannot rely on this exemption:

(a) the registrant or an affiliate or associate of the registrant;

(b) any officer or director of the registrant, or person serving in a similar capacity, engaging in a solicitation financed by the registrant;

(c) any officer, director, affiliate or associate of an ineligible person other than the registrant, or any person serving in a similar capacity;

---

3. Capital Real Estate Investors Tax Exempt Fund Ltd. Pshp. v. Schwartzberg, 917 F. Supp. 1050 (S.D. N.Y. 1996).

4. *Id.* at 1061.

5. *Id.*

(d) any nominee for whose election as a director proxies are solicited;

(e) any person soliciting in opposition to a merger, recapitalization, reorganization, sale of assets or other extraordinary transaction recommended or approved by the board of directors of the registrant who is proposing or intends to propose an alternative transaction to which such person or one of its affiliates is a party; and

(f) any person required to report beneficial ownership of the registrant's equity securities on Schedule 13D, unless the person has filed a Schedule 13D and has not disclosed an intent, or reserved the right, to engage in a control transaction, or a contested solicitation for the election of directors.

Pursuant to Rule 14a-6(g), a special filing requirement applies to any person who "(i) Engages in a solicitation pursuant to Rule 14a-2(b)(1), and (ii) at the commencement of that solicitation owns beneficially securities of the class which is the subject of the solicitation with a market value of over $5 million[.]" Such a soliciting shareholder must, "furnish * * * to the Commission, not later than three days after the date the written solicitation is first sent or given to any security holder, * * * a statement containing the information specified in the Notice of Exempt Solicitation (Rule 14a-103)[.]"

This exempt solicitation rule was at issue in *MONY Group, Inc. v. Highfields Capital.*[6] In this case, a person opposing a merger sent with its opposition statement to the shareholders a duplicate of the management's proxy card and urged that the card be used to vote against the merger. In finding that the Rule 14a-2(b) exempt solicitation rule was not available, the court reasoned:

> [The Rule 14a-2(b)(1)] exemption is not available for solicitations by persons who "furnish" shareholders with a "form of revocation." We conclude that, in the circumstances of this case—including the circumstance that the transaction is a proposed merger under Delaware law—the duplicate of MONY management's proxy card that Appellees seek to provide, when it is included in a mailing that opposes the proposed merger, is a "form of revocation." * * *
>
> Moreover, revocation is the only utility of the duplicate proxy in this case because: (i) undecided MONY shareholders presumably retain blank copies of their (original) management proxy cards, and (ii) other than the (presumably few) MONY shareholders who have lost or discarded the multiple proxy cards sent to them by MONY and cannot, otherwise obtain new copies, the only MONY shareholders in need of proxy card duplicates are those who have already sent in their proxy cards and want to revoke their votes. In the absence of any indication by the SEC that the term "revocation" in Rule 14a-2(b)(1) has an unconventional legal meaning, Appellees' proxy duplicate serves as a "form of revocation" for MONY shareholders who have already voted for the merger. Such a duplicate is precluded by the plain text of the Rule 14a-2(b)(1) exemption.[7]

F. General Broadcast or Publication of Soliciting Material

In the 1992 liberalizations of the proxy rules, the SEC amended Rule 14a-3(f) to provide as follows:

---

6. MONY Group, Inc. v. Highfields Capital Mgmt., L.P., 2004 U.S. App. LEXIS 7190 (2nd Cir. 2004).

7. *Id.* at 1–3.

> [T]the proxy statement delivery requirement set forth [Rule 14a-3(a)] does not apply to a soliciting communication made solely by means of a speech in a public forum, or an opinion, statement or advertisement broadcast through radio or television media, or appearing in a newspaper, magazine or other publication disseminated on a regular basis. The provisions of the amendment include two proposed conditions: (1) no form of proxy, consent or authorization is provided to shareholders in conjunction with the communication; and (2) a definitive proxy statement is on file with the Commission pursuant to Rule 14a-6(b). * * *

G. The Ten Investor Exemption (Except for Rule 14a-9)

Except for Rule 14a-9, the proxy rules generally to not apply to "any solicitation made otherwise than on behalf of the registrant where the total number of persons solicited is not more than ten." [*See* Rule 14a-2(b)(2)] Thus, for example, a shareholder could, without being subject to the general proxy rules, contact no more than ten other shareholders and urge them to vote in a certain way. This exemption is not discussed further here.

H. Rule 14a-12 Written and Oral Communications before Filing a Proxy Statement

1. In General

Rule 14a-12, which as indicated in Chapter 13, has a significant impact on M&A transactions, also has an impact on the conduct of proxy contests. The following are relevant excerpts from the 1999 release that adopted the current Rule 14a-12, which should be carefully read.

Final M&A Release, Regulation of Takeovers and Security Holders Communications under the Proxy Rules, Securities Act Release No. 33-7760

(October 22, 1999)

[**Rule 14a-12**] We are revising Rule 14a-12, substantially as proposed, to permit both written and oral communications before the filing of a proxy statement so long as all written communications related to the solicitation are filed on the date of first use. * * * [Written communications by soliciting parties before a proxy statement is furnished to security holders must be filed on the date of first use and must provide information regarding the participants and their interests or include a legend advising security holders where they can obtain this information. *See* revised Rule 14a-12(a)(1). Once a proxy statement is furnished to security holders, any additional soliciting materials used must be filed on the date of first use but need not include participant information or a legend advising where to obtain that information. *See* revised Rule 14a-6(b)] * * *

This exemption is not limited to business combination transactions, but is available regardless of the subject matter of the solicitation. Oral communications do not need to be reduced to writing and filed. * * * [N]o form of proxy [may be] furnished until a proxy statement is delivered, [there is an] obligation to disclose participant information, and [there is a] requirement to file all written communications with a prominent legend advising security holders to read the proxy statement.

As a result of these changes to Rule 14a-12, management can communicate more freely with security holders about significant corporate events, including a proposed merger or acquisition, or other significant corporate governance matters that may require a security holder vote. Likewise, security holders are able to communicate more freely with one another. The revised rule does not, however, expand a company's or security holder's ability to secure promises to vote a certain way before a proxy statement is provided. * * *

Together with the antifraud provisions of Rule 14a-9, these requirements should maintain the integrity of the solicitation process and adequacy of information disseminated to security holders. In addition to these safeguards, security holders will receive a complete proxy statement before they can vote. * * *

2. A Rule 14a-12 News Release by Air Products Prior to the Furnishing of Its Proxy Statement in the Airgas Proxy Contest

Section II of Documentary Appendix HH, *Documents Relating to the Air Products 2010 Proxy Contest to Elect Directors to the Board of Airgas*, is a press release issued by Air Products, under the authority of Rule 14a-12, before Air Products furnished to the shareholders its definitive proxy statement.

I. Fight Letters and Press Releases after the Filing of the Proxy Statement

1. In General

In a proxy contest it is common for the parties to send to the shareholders or to publicly announce information that supports the party's position. As indicated above, under Rule 14a-12, information can be provided before the filing of the proxy statement. Letters sent to the shareholders after the filing of the proxy statement are sometimes referred to as "fight letters." The filing requirements with regard to "fight letters" and other similar communications is addressed in Rule 14a-6(b), which provides: "[T]he proxy statement, form of proxy and all other soliciting material, in the form in which such material is furnished to security holders, shall be filed with * * * the Commission not later than the date such material is first sent or given to any security holders."

2. A "Fight" Press Release by Air Products in the Airgas Proxy Contest

Section IV of Documentary Appendix HH, *Documents Relating to the Air Products 2010 Proxy Contest to Elect Directors to the Board of Airgas*, is a "fight" press release issued by Air Products after its distribution of its definitive proxy statement.

§ 16.7 Internet Availability of Proxy Materials and Internet-Based Proxy Contests

Rule 14a-16 deals with the Internet Availability of Proxy Materials, and the SEC has described these requirements as follows:

> Under the Internet Availability of Proxy Materials rules, companies and other soliciting parties are required to make their proxy materials available on

an Internet site (other than the SEC's EDGAR web site). A company or other party that is soliciting proxies has two options for providing the proxy materials to its shareholders — the "notice only" option or the "full set delivery" option. * * *

Under the "notice only" option, a company or other soliciting party must post its proxy materials on an Internet Web site and send a Notice of Internet Availability of Proxy Materials to its shareholders to inform them of the electronic availability of the proxy materials at least 40 days before the shareholder meeting to which the proxy materials relate. The soliciting party must provide paper or electronic copies of the proxy materials to a requesting shareholder and allow shareholders to make an election to receive paper or electronic copies of proxy materials for future shareholder meetings. * * *

The "full set delivery" option is similar to the traditional proxy delivery process. It allows a company or other soliciting party to deliver a full set of proxy materials to shareholders along with the Notice of Internet Availability of Proxy Materials.[8]

The notice and access rules apply, with certain conditions, to dissidents as well as to the company [*see* Rule 14a-16(l)]; however, these rules are not available for business combination transactions [*see* Rule 14a-16(m)].

An article entitled *New Internet Technology Permits New Proxy Contest Techniques*[9] provides helpful insights into the conduct of Internet based proxy contests. The article includes a discussion of the first such successful contest, in which the dissidents, led by Travis Street Partners LLC, were successful in electing three members to the board of ICO, a NASDAQ company. This article states:

[D]issidents have created special purpose websites shortly before or simultaneously with the launch of a proxy contest. A website serves not only to collect in one location all of the dissidents' communications regarding the proxy contest but also to intensify and increase the ability of the recipients to absorb the outsiders' message[.] * * * A typical website may comprise [for example] : a FAQs page, which answers investor questions and concerns about the dissidents' platform; a "press releases" page, which collects all press releases disseminated by the dissidents; an "SEC filings" page, which provides a convenient link into the target's SEC EDGAR database of all SEC filings relating to the target; and a "proxy materials" page, which provides ready access to the insurgent's most recently filed preliminary or definitive proxy statement.

Under SEC [Rules 14a-12 and 14a-6(b)], a full copy of the website content is required to be filed with the SEC.[10]

8. SEC, *Internet Availability of Proxy Materials, A Small Entity Compliance Guide* (as amended 3/23/2010).

9. Eugene F. Cowell III, *New Internet Technology Permits New Proxy Contest Techniques*, Insights (October 2001) available at http://cdn.akingump.com/images/content/9/8/v4/980/400.pdf.

10. Id.

§ 16.8 Allegations of a Failure to Properly Disclose under Rule 14a-9

GAF Corp. v. Heyman

United States Court of Appeals, Second Circuit, 1983 724 F.2d 727

George C. Pratt, Circuit Judge:

This is an expedited appeal from a judgment of the United States District Court for the Southern District of New York (Lloyd F. MacMahon, *Judge*), entered after a bitter proxy contest in which shareholders of plaintiff GAF Corporation voted decisively to replace the corporation's incumbent board of directors with an insurgent slate headed by defendant Samuel J. Heyman. The district court ruled that the insurgents violated § 14(a) of the Securities Exchange Act of 1934, and Rule 14a-9(a) thereunder, by failing to disclose in their proxy materials any information concerning an action for breach of trust, brought by Heyman's sister against him and his mother a year before the 1983 campaign began, which GAF alleged cast doubt on Heyman's fitness to serve as a director. Although this family dispute among the Heyman's did not involve GAF, the district court enjoined the entire insurgent slate from assuming the directorships to which they had been elected, set a new record date, and ordered a resolicitation of proxies and a new election. For the reasons below, we hold that non-disclosure of the Heyman family lawsuit was not a material omission in the context of this proxy contest. Accordingly, we reverse. * * *

[**Parties' Positions**] Heyman contends that the Committee had no obligation to disclose in a GAF proxy fight either the contested, unproven, and unpursued allegations of a complaint filed in an unrelated intra-family dispute or the circumstances surrounding a family loan transaction not even mentioned in that complaint. In any event, Heyman argues, GAF's dissemination of the "breach of trust" allegations in its March 13 press release cured these omissions, since the "total mix" of information available to GAF shareholders would not have been significantly altered by fuller disclosure. On the other hand, GAF argues that the fact that a candidate for a position as a corporate fiduciary is a defendant in a pending lawsuit, charging him with improper self-dealing and other fiduciary misconduct, is necessarily important to stockholders called upon to decide who should be entrusted with the stewardship of their collective investment.

[**Analysis**] In considering these competing arguments, we are guided not only by the principles outlined above, but also by SEC Regulation S-K. Regulation S-K, together with more general provisions such as Rule 14a-9, "states the requirements applicable to the content of * * * proxy and information statements under § 14 of the Exchange Act". The regulation provides the following instructions regarding involvement in legal proceedings that must be disclosed:

> (f) *Involvement in certain legal proceedings.* Describe any of the following events that occurred during the past five years and that are material to an evaluation of the ability or integrity of any director, person nominated to become a director or executive officer of the registrant:
>
> (1) A petition under the Federal bankruptcy laws or any state insolvency law was filed by or against * * * the business or property of such person * * * ;
>
> (2) Such person was convicted in a criminal proceeding or is a named subject of a pending criminal proceeding (excluding traffic violations and other minor offenses); * * *

(5) Such person was found by a court of competent jurisdiction in a civil action or by the Commission to have violated any Federal or State securities law, and the judgment in such civil action or finding by the Commission has not been subsequently reversed, suspended, or vacated.

Nothing in this detailed regulation, which has been relegated to a footnote in GAF's brief, required Heyman to make any disclosure about the unproven allegations in the Connecticut action, much less the disputed loan transaction. * * * [*See also* Rule 14a-9(b) and the note to the rule.]

In our view, the regulation's emphasis on orders, judgments, decrees, and findings in civil proceedings, in stark contrast to its express coverage of all pending criminal proceedings, strongly suggests that regardless of how serious they may appear on their face, unadjudicated allegations in a pending civil action against a director-nominee should not automatically be deemed material. * * *

* * * [A]ll of the relevant factual indicia militate against a finding of materiality. First, the Connecticut action was "pending" only in a technical sense. The action was stayed on consent only nine days after it was commenced, before Heyman even filed a responsive pleading. * * *

All available evidence suggests that the action was nothing more than the outgrowth of an intra-family feud between Abigail and her new husband on one side and her mother and brother on the other. * * * Furthermore, [Abigail] subsequently swore that she supported her brother's slate in the proxy contest.

Thus, viewed in context, the three specific allegations in Abigail's complaint seized upon by GAF raise no serious question about Heyman's fitness to serve as a corporate director. * * *

This was a proxy contest fought on the issues of GAF's financial performance and future corporate policy. Presented with a clear choice, the shareholders voted decisively in favor of the insurgent slate. Given this resounding mandate, it is inconceivable that fuller disclosure of the dormant Connecticut action would have had "a significant propensity to affect the voting process." *TSC*.

The judgment of the district court is therefore reversed. The mandate shall issue forthwith.

§ 16.9 SEC's Vacated Proxy Access Rule

In 2010, the SEC issued final proxy access rules that, *inter alia*, required 34 Act companies to include in their proxy statements certain nominations for directors made by the certain shareholders. However, the Court of Appeals for the District of Columbia vacated this rule on the grounds that the SEC failed to address the economic effects of the rule.[11] Although the Dodd-Frank Act presumably authorizes the SEC to issue the rule, as of May 2014, the SEC has not done so. In any event, the rule would not have been available to shareholders that had a change of control purpose. Rule 14a-8, which is not examined here, governs the current rules on shareholder proposals.

11. *See* Business Roundtable v. SEC, 647 F.3d 1144 (D.C. Cir. 2011).

§ 16.10 State Law: The Majority Vote for Directors Issue

A. Background and 2006 Amendments to the MBCA

The default rule for directors elections under both Delaware law and the MBCA is plurality voting, which means that the directors with the largest number of votes are elected, even though the number of votes is less than a majority of votes cast. [*See* MBCA Section 7.28(a) and DGCL 216(3)] Section 216(3) provides: "Directors shall be elected by a plurality of the votes of the shares present in person or represented by proxy at the meeting and entitled to vote on the election of directors[.]" Thus, even if recalcitrant shareholders withhold their votes for a nominee of the current board and thereby cause the director to receive less than a majority of votes cast, that nominee would still be elected as long as he or she received the requisite plurality of votes. Under both Delaware law and the MBCA the default rule can be changed by an amendment to the charter, which requires the votes of both the directors and shareholders. However, as a result of a June 2006 amendment to the MBCA, the default rule can now be changed unilaterally by either the directors or the shareholders by an amendment to the by-laws.

B. Shareholder Proposals for Majority Voting for Directors and ISS Position

There have been many shareholder proposals for companies to amend their charters to provide for majority voting for directors. Institutional Shareholder Services (ISS), which describes itself as "the world's leading provider of proxy voting and corporate governance services," has taken the following position on these proposals:

> **New Policy Position:** ISS will generally recommend FOR reasonably crafted shareholders proposals calling for directors to be elected with an affirmative majority of votes cast and/or the elimination of the plurality standard for electing directors (including binding resolutions requesting that the board amend the company's bylaws), provided the proposal includes a carve-out for a plurality voting standard when there are more director nominees than board seats (*e.g.* contested elections).
>
> ISS will consider recommending AGAINST a shareholder proposal if the company has adopted formal corporate governance principles that present a meaningful alternative to the majority voting standard and provide an adequate response to both new nominees as well as incumbent nominees who fail to receive a majority of votes cast.

§ 16.11 State Law Standards Governing Directors' Control of the Proxy and Voting System

A. Directors' Manipulation of Number of Board Members

See Blasius Industries v. Atlas Corp., Section 3.14.G.

B. Allegation of Vote Buying in the Hewlett-Packard Proxy Contest over Compaq Acquisition

Walter B. Hewlett v. Hewlett-Packard Company

Delaware Court of Chancery, 2002 Del. Ch. LEXIS 35

CHANDLER, Chancellor:

This lawsuit challenges the shareholder vote in connection with the proposed merger of defendant Hewlett-Packard Company ("HP") and Compaq Computer Corporation ("Compaq"). HP is a publicly traded Delaware corporation. * * * Plaintiff Walter B. Hewlett ("Hewlett") has been a director of HP for approximately 15 years. He is the son of the late William R. Hewlett, one of HP's founders. * * * [Hewlett and certain related parties (Hewlett Parties) solicited proxies in opposition to the proposed merger.]

After a hotly contested proxy battle between Hewlett and HP, HP's shareholders approved the issuance of shares in connection with the merger at a special meeting on March 19, 2002, by a very slim margin. On March 28, the Hewlett Parties filed this action pursuant to 8 *Del. C.* § 225(b) challenging the validity of that vote. The Hewlett Parties attack the vote on two grounds: first, they assert that HP management knowingly misrepresented material facts about the integration of the two companies throughout the proxy campaign; second, they contend that HP management improperly coerced and enticed Deutsche Bank into voting 17 million HP shares in favor of the transaction. Accordingly, the Hewlett Parties seek an order declaring Deutsche Bank's final voting proxy cards to be invalid, invalidating all proxies voted in favor of the merger, declaring that the proposal to issue additional HP shares in connection with the merger was defeated, or declaring that a new vote must be held on the proposed merger. [Only the vote buying claim is addressed here.] * * *

The Vote-Buying Claim The Hewlett Parties' vote-buying claim centers on the March 19, 2002 telephone conference at which members of Deutsche Bank's PWG entertained competing presentations on the merits of the proposed merger from Walter Hewlett and HP management. The plaintiffs contend that during the telephone conference, Deutsche Bank was coerced by threats, either implied or explicit, from HP management that Deutsche Bank's future business relationship with HP would suffer if the shares of HP held by Deutsche Bank were voted against the merger. Accordingly, they ask this Court to set aside the resulting vote of a portion of the HP shares held by Deutsche Bank in favor of the merger.

[T]he Hewlett Parties bear the following burden with respect to the vote-buying claim:

> At trial, the plaintiffs will have the significant burden of presenting sufficient evidence for me to find that Deutsche Bank was coerced by HP management during their March 19, 2002 telephone conference into voting 17 million shares in favor of the proposed merger and that the switch of those votes was not made by Deutsche Bank for independent business reasons.

Therefore, the plaintiffs must prove that HP management used the business relationship between HP and Deutsche Bank as a weapon to coerce Deutsche Bank into voting for the merger. That is, they must establish that it was HP management's improper influence that caused Deutsche Bank to switch some of the proxies it had voted against the merger on March 15 to favor the merger on March 19.

The vote-buying claim turns entirely on circumstantial evidence. The Hewlett Parties point to circumstances surrounding the arranging of the March 19 telephone conference and to one statement by Fiorina [the CEO of HP] at the end of HP's presentation during that call to support their claim of illegal vote-buying. Having considered all of the testimony and exhibits offered at trial, I conclude that plaintiffs have failed to meet their burden of proving the existence of such a vote-buying arrangement. * * *

The final circumstance offered by the plaintiffs to prove that the [Deutsche Bank] vote was the result of improper influence from HP management is Fiorina's closing remarks during the conference call. Fiorina ended her presentation by stating:

> Gentlemen, we appreciate your time. I need to go try and get ready for a shareowner meeting. We very, very much appreciate your willingness to listen to us this morning. This is obviously of great importance to us as a company. *It is of great importance to our ongoing relationship.* We very much would like to have your support here. We think this is a crucially important decision for this company.

This is the only statement from HP management that plaintiffs point to as evidence that Deutsche Bank was coerced during the March 19, 2002, telephone conference. That statement does not, in my opinion, demonstrate that Fiorina was attempting to coerce Deutsche Bank. Fiorina testified that the statement was the typical way she ended similar calls after making HP's standard presentation to investors. * * *

Conclusion * * * I conclude that plaintiffs have failed to prove that HP management improperly enticed or coerced Deutsche Bank into voting in favor of the merger.

§ 16.12 Fiduciary Duties of Acquiror's Nominee Directors in Combination Tender Offer Proxy Contest—*AMP*

AMP Incorporated v. Allied Signal, Inc.

United States District Court, Eastern District of Pennsylvania, 1998 U.S. Dist. LEXIS 15617

[Allied Signal made a tender offer for AMP, a Pennsylvania corporation, and launched a "consent solicitation among AMP shareholders to amend AMP by-laws in order to expand the board so that a majority of directors would be elected who would cause AMP to accept Allied Signal's takeover bid." Set out below is the court's discussion of the fiduciary duties of Allied Signal's nominees. The portion of the opinion dealing with AMP's nonredeemable poison pill is set out in Section 3.23.D] * * *

64. * * * Allied Signal's consent solicitation fails to state completely and, therefore, accurately that the directors of a registered corporation owe a fiduciary duty solely to the corporation. While it states that nominees, if elected, will have conflicts of interests and recites the general standard of care applicable to the discharge of a director's duty, the duty itself is not stated. * * *

66. The failure of Allied Signal to clearly state that the unequivocable fiduciary duty of a director is solely to the corporation, is material to AMP's motion that the consent solicitation should be enjoined. While Allied Signal has asserted on behalf of the nominees that they can discharge their duties to AMP, the nominees, themselves, have not. * * *

68. * * * The foreseeable practical consequence of electing Allied Signal's nominees as proposed in its consent solicitation, is to embroil some court continually in determining whether, in voting on matters of corporate governance, let alone corporate independence, the interested Allied Signal nominees have breached their fiduciary duties, as a group or

individually. Therefore, the burden upon Allied Signal by reason of this injunction is far outweighed by the public interest in avoiding unnecessary costs of litigation. * * *

72. If elected, interested directors stand in a fiduciary relation to the target corporation, owing undivided loyalty thereto, and must perform their duties in good faith, in a manner reasonably believed to be in the best interests of the corporation. Thus, if Allied Signal's nominees were elected to the AMP board, their fiduciary duty would have to be to AMP, not to shareholders, and not to Allied Signal.

73. Allied Signal is a Delaware corporation subject to Delaware corporate law. Under Delaware law, officers and directors of Allied Signal owe a fiduciary duty to Allied Signal and its shareholders to act in their best interest. If Allied Signal's directors and officers are elected to AMP's board of directors, they will have an inherent conflict that will necessarily put them at risk of violating Pennsylvania's fiduciary duty standard. Allied Signal has not suggested how their interested nominees may discharge their duty of exclusive loyalty to AMP. * * *

75. The reality not clearly spelled out in Allied Signal's consent solicitation is that, because of the nominees' fiduciary duties to Allied Signal, they may be disqualified as AMP directors by self-restraint or by judicial restraint, from voting on or implementing acquisition related transactions. * * *

79. Contrary to Allied Signal's suggestion in its proposed consent solicitation, Section 1728(a) [of the Pennsylvania Corporation Law], which permits shareholders to approve contracts or transactions between corporations that have some common directors or officers if the shareholders are aware of all material facts, would not operate to excuse conflicts of interest that are breaches of fiduciary duty. Under Section 2538, interested directors are prohibited from voting on merger transactions. Any pre-merger actions by interested directors would not qualify as transactions between corporations. * * *

81. * * * [T]he consent solicitation shall be enjoined until the duty of directors is stated as being solely to the corporation and each nominee undertakes to be bound personally by that duty, if elected. * * *

§ 16.13 Poison Pill Redemption Bylaw—*Fleming,* Section 3.18.E.11

§ 16.14 State Law Rules Concerning Production of Shareholder Lists

Under Section 220(b) of the Delaware General Business Corporation Law, a shareholder for a "proper purpose" may get a list of the corporation's shareholders.

§ 16.15 State Law: Reimbursement of Proxy Expenses

Rosenfeld v. Fairchild Engine and Airplane Corp.

Court of Appeal of New York, 1955 128 N.E.2d 291

FROESSEL, Judge:

[Issue] In a stockholder's derivative action brought by plaintiff, an attorney, who owns 25 out of the company's over 2,300,000 shares, he seeks to compel the return of $261,522, paid out of the corporate treasury to reimburse both sides in a proxy contest for their expenses. * * *

Of the amount in controversy $106,000 were spent out of corporate funds by the old board of directors while still in office in defense of their position in said contest; $28,000 were paid to the old board by the new board after the change of management following the proxy contest, to compensate the former directors for such of the remaining expenses of their unsuccessful defense as the new board found was fair and reasonable; payment of $127,000, representing reimbursement of expenses to members of the prevailing group, was expressly ratified by a 16 to 1 majority vote of the stockholders. * * *

[**Analysis**]* * * It should be noted that plaintiff does not argue that the aforementioned sums were fraudulently extracted from the corporation; indeed, his counsel conceded that "the charges were fair and reasonable", but denied "they were legal charges which may be reimbursed for". * * * [The court rejected this position, reasoning:]

The rule * * * which we adopt is simply this: In a contest over policy, as compared to a purely personal power contest, corporate directors have the right to make reasonable and proper expenditures, subject to the scrutiny of the courts when duly challenged, from the corporate treasury for the purpose of persuading the stockholders of the correctness of their position and soliciting their support for policies which the directors believe, in all good faith, are in the best interests of the corporation. The stockholders, moreover, have the right to reimburse successful contestants for the reasonable and bona fide expenses incurred by them in any such policy contest, subject to like court scrutiny. * * *

References

Fleischer and Sussman, *Takeover Defense, supra* Section 1.10.

Lorne, *Negotiated and Contested Transactions, supra* Section 1.10.

Thompson, *Mergers, Acquisitions and Tender Offers, supra* Section 1.10, Chapters 5 and 8.

Chapter 17

Introduction to the Williams Act

§ 17.1 Scope

This chapter introduces federal securities regulations under the Williams Act amendments to the Securities Exchange Act of 1934, principally Sections 13(d) and (e) and Sections 14(d) and (e). These sections regulate the purchase of stock of a publicly-held target corporation in open market transactions (*e.g.*, purchases on an exchange) and in tender offers (*e.g.*, public offers by an acquiror to purchase the stock of a target's shareholders). Some of the practical aspects of these transactions are explored in Chapter 1. Tender offers can be either hostile (*i.e.*, made without the support of the target's directors) or consensual (*e.g.*, made pursuant to an agreement that calls for a tender offer to be followed by a merger). As indicated in Section 1.8, most tender offers are consensual. Section 17.2 provides an introductory problem, and Section 17.3 sets out a general introduction to the Williams Act. Section 17.4 presents a brief look at the legislative purposes behind this Act. Finally, Section 17.5 looks at certain aspects of the report of the SEC's Advisory Committee on Tender Offers.

This chapter provides an introduction to topics addressed more completely in subsequent chapters. Chapter 18 examines the regulation of open market purchases under Section 13(d); Chapter 19 focuses on the definition of the term "tender offer" in Section 14(d); Chapter 20 addresses third-party tender offers under Sections 14(d) and (e); and Chapter 21 deals with issuer tender offers under Section 13(e). Going private transactions under Rule 13e-3 are examined in Chapter 14, which deals with freezeout mergers and LBOs. Chapters 22 and 23 deal with related issues, with Chapter 22 looking at state regulation of tender offers and Chapter 23 addressing defensive tactics, which are generally regulated by state corporate law and not the federal securities laws. The materials in this chapter are discussed in greater detail in Thompson, *Mergers, Acquisitions and Tender Offers*, *supra* Section 1.10, Chapter 8.

§ 17.2 Introductory Problem

J.P. Morgan Chase & Co. (J.P. Morgan) and The Goldman Sachs Group, Inc. (Goldman Sachs), both publicly-held Delaware corporations, have announced that they have entered into a merger agreement and that the agreement will be submitted to their shareholders for approval. Citigroup Inc. would like to acquire J.P. Morgan but not Goldman Sachs. To discourage the J.P. Morgan shareholders from voting to approve the merger, Citigroup plans to immediately acquire from 8% to 12% of J.P. Morgan's shares in open market purchases. Assume that under the notification threshold rules under Hart-Scott-Rodino, no pre-merger notification under the antitrust laws is required for these acquisitions. *See* Chapter 9. Does Citigroup have to give prior notice of these purchases? Suppose, instead, Citigroup makes a cash tender offer for any and all of J.P. Morgan's shares. Does Citigroup have to pre-clear the tender offer with the SEC? Suppose instead of a cash tender offer,

Citigroup makes an exchange tender offer pursuant to which it offers its debt instruments in exchange for J.P. Morgan stock. Does this exchange offer have to be pre-cleared with the SEC?

§ 17.3 Introduction to the Williams Act

Read and study Securities Exchange Act of 1934, § 13(d), (e), (f) and (g) and § 14(d), (e) and (f).

Excerpt from SEC Report on Tender Offer Law

(1980)

The primary objective in the enactment of the Williams Act was to provide for full disclosure in connection with cash tender offers and other techniques for accumulating large blocks of equity securities of publicly held companies. The principal provisions enacted to require such disclosure were Sections 13(d) and 14(d). As enacted in 1968, Section 13(d)(1) applied to any person who, after acquiring, directly or indirectly, the beneficial ownership of any equity security of a class of equity securities specified therein was, directly or indirectly, the beneficial owner of more than 10 percent of the class. Section 13(d)(1) required such persons to file a statement setting forth material information within 10 days of any such acquisition. As enacted in 1968, Section 14(d)(1) made it unlawful for any person to make a tender offer for any class of equity securities specified therein if after consummation of the offer, the person would be the beneficial owner of more than 10 percent of the class, unless that person met certain filing and disclosure obligations contained in the statute. Section 14(d) also contained regulatory provisions relating to shareholders' withdrawal rights and pro rata acceptance rights, as well as the obligation of a bidder to treat all tendering shareholders equally with respect to any increase in the offered consideration. And, Section 14(e) provided a general antifraud provision with regard to conduct "in connection with any tender offer * * *."

The Williams Act also dealt with the question of issuer repurchases of their own securities. Section 13(e) of the Securities Exchange Act authorized the Commission to adopt "such rules and regulations with respect to purchases by an issuer * * * of its own securities as [the Commission] may deem necessary or appropriate in the public interest or for the protection of investors, to define such acts and practices as are fraudulent, deceptive, or manipulative and to prescribe means reasonably designed to prevent such acts and practices." Like Sections 13(d) and 14(d), but unlike Section 14(e), Section 13(e) was, generally speaking, limited in its application to securities of issuers registered pursuant to Section 12 of the Securities Exchange Act.

Section 13(d) and Section 13(g) [*See* **Chapter 18**] Section 13(d) was intended to bring to the public's attention every accumulation of securities which carries the potential to affect the control of a corporation and through that, control the market's valuation of the issuer's securities. But an exemption was provided for acquisitions totaling less than two percent within a twelve-month period. The post-acquisition notification disclosure system under Section 13(d) would make "the relevant facts known so that shareholders would have a fair opportunity to make [investment] decisions." This information "if known to investors, might substantially change the assumptions on which the market price [of the securities of the subject company] is based." Thus, the objective of Section 13(d) was to provide to shareholders and the marketplace relevant information and a fair opportunity to evaluate the securities of a company in response to acquisitions with the potential to affect or change control of the company. To implement this objective the Commission has adopted Schedule 13D, and appropriate rules and regulations.

In 1970, the reporting threshold in Section 13(d) was reduced from 10 percent to 5 percent beneficial ownership. This amendment was adopted in response to a practice which had developed where persons contemplating stock acquisitions terminated their purchases at 8 or 9 percent as a means of avoiding the disclosure requirements of Section 13(d). It was believed that an investment of between 5 and 10 percent in the securities of a company could be a controlling interest in some large widely-held corporations and that such an investment could have a significant impact on the public market for the company's securities. Acquisitions of more than 5 percent may lead to important changes in the management or business of the company, and therefore shareholders should be fully informed of such acquisitions in order to have a fair opportunity to evaluate the company.

Present operation A review of the present operation of Section 13(d) indicates that the existing notification system often does not provide shareholders with relevant information in a timely manner and a fair opportunity to evaluate the company when an acquisition of a potentially controlling interest in the company has been effected. This is the result of an increasingly prevalent practice of acquiring additional securities of the class during the 10-day period after the acquisition which results in the beneficial ownership of more than 5 percent and before the disclosure statement is required to be, and normally is, filed with the Commission. * * *

Acquisitions on the open market or in a series of negotiated purchases of substantial amounts of securities in the 10-day filing period without public disclosure deprive security holders of a fair opportunity to adjust their evaluation of the securities of a company with respect to potential change in control of that company.

To correct these current problems, the Commission proposes that Section 13(d) * * * be amended. The filing requirements of Section 13(d) would be altered to: (1) require all persons who acquire, in the aggregate, more than 5 percent of a class to make a prompt public announcement (not later than 1 business day) of their identity and the amount of securities beneficially owned by them; (2) reduce the filing period from 10 days to 5 business days, or 1 calendar week; and (3) prohibit any person who becomes obligated to file a statement, or to amend a statement previously filed, from making any further acquisitions before the necessary filing is made and until a short time thereafter. It is the Commission's view that these revisions of Section 13(d) will materially advance the disclosure function of that Section. * * * [These proposals have not been adopted.]

Section 14(d) [***See*** **Chapter 20**] Section 14(d) of the Act was adopted to provide adequate disclosure in connection with cash takeover bids. Prior to the enactment of the Williams Act, no information was required to be filed or disclosed in connection with a cash tender offer, and as a result, investors were required to make investment decisions without access to the information which would enable them to decide upon the best course of action in response to the tender offer. The cash tender became increasingly significant as a corporate takeover technique, supplanting the proxy contest as the favored means of takeover, because it was found to be cheaper, and more effective, while providing the bidder with the further advantage of surprise. It was believed, however, that the cash tender offer was similar to a proxy contest and that there was no reason to continue this gap in the federal securities laws which left the cash tender offer exempt from disclosure provisions. Moreover, Section 14(d) was designed to provide tendering security holders with certain fundamental protections, such as withdrawal rights and pro rata acceptance of deposited securities. These provisions were adopted to combat the abuses prevalent before the Williams Act was adopted when a bidder was capable of pressuring shareholders into tendering hastily, due to the combined effect of a premium price, a time limit, a specified number of shares to be bought and a first-come-first-served purchase policy.

Similar to the amendment to Section 13(d), Section 14(d) was amended in 1970 to reduce the reporting threshold to 5 percent. At that time, the statute was further amended to cover exchange tender offers in addition to cash tender offers. * * *

The term "tender offer" is not defined in the Williams Act. Since the passage of the Williams Act, the Commission has been continually involved in the development of the meaning of the term but has not adopted a definition. This position has been premised upon the dynamic nature of these transactions and the need for the Williams Act to be interpreted flexibly in a manner consistent with its purposes to protect investors. Consequently, in 1976 and again in February, 1979, the Commission specifically declined to define the term. However, as is discussed below, the Commission has recently proposed for comment a rule containing such a definition. [*See* Section 19.4]

Present Operation. While there has been substantial compliance with the provisions of the Williams Act when people seek shares through a formal public announcement and filings with the Commission, many persons have not complied with the Williams Act when they have made tender offers for shares in other ways. Indeed, many persons have deliberately structured unconventional offers which they aver are not tender offers, and, as a result, have tried to evade the provisions and spirit of the Williams Act. These approaches have included purported privately negotiated transactions, wide-scale solicitation of members of one family and various forms of massive and rapid open market purchase programs. [*See* Chapter 19] In the judgment of the Commission, these transactions are tender offers and, however packaged, were intended to be subject to Section 14(d) and are required to be effected in accordance with its provisions. Recognizing the persistent occurrence of these "unconventional" tender offers, the Commission has proposed for comment a definition which would include within its coverage at least certain of these diverse forms of transactions. [*See* Section 19.4]

The scope of the proposed definition reflects the Commission's long-standing position that the term "tender offer" embraces not only tender offers formally announced by communications to shareholders but also offers accomplished by other means. This position is supported by the case law and legal commentators. * * *

Purchases by an Issuer of its Own Securities. **[*See* Chapter 21 and Chapter 14]** The Committee has raised several questions concerning the regulation of purchases by an issuer of its own securities. First, the Committee has inquired whether "going private" transactions [*see* Chapter 14] and tender offers by issuers [*see* Chapter 21] should be exempt from the disclosure requirements of Section 14(d). The Commission believes that, in view of existing legislation relating to issuer repurchases, including new rulemaking thereunder, and certain policy considerations more fully described below, it is not necessary to regulate these transactions under Section 14(d) of the Securities Exchange Act of 1934. * * *

Section 14(d) excepts issuer tender offers from the substantive and disclosure requirements of that provision. Rather, Congress determined to address separately all issuer repurchases, including repurchases by means of a tender offer, in a separate provision—Section 13(e) of the Act. Section 13(e)(1) makes it unlawful for an issuer with a class of equity securities registered pursuant to Section 12 of the Act * * * , to purchase any of its equity securities in contravention of rules adopted by the Commission "to define acts and practices which are fraudulent, deceptive or manipulative" and "to prescribe means reasonably designed to prevent such acts and practices." The Williams Act also added Section 13(e)(2) to the Act which provides that purchases by a person in a control relationship with an issuer shall be deemed to be purchases by the issuer.

Pursuant to its rulemaking authority under Section 13 and other sections of the Act, the Commission recently adopted Rule 13e-4, to regulate issuer tender offers. [*See* Chapter 21] This rule contains disclosure and substantive requirements applicable to issuer tender offers, which, to the extent appropriate, are patterned on the regulatory scheme established by Section 14(d) of the Act and existing rules thereunder. The Commission believes that these disclosure and substantive requirements are adequate, at the present time, to protect the shareholders of public companies in the context of issuer tender offers. In the Commission's view, it is unnecessary to impose substantially similar obligations on issuers under Section 14(d) of the Act. In addition, the Commission believes that, in view of the distinct concerns raised by issuer, as opposed to third party tender offers, it continues to be appropriate, as a policy matter, to regulate issuer tender offers under a separate section of the Act. * * *

The Commission has also recently adopted Rule 13(e)(3) to govern the conduct of so-called "going private transactions." [*See* Chapter 14] This Rule contains a general antifraud provision and disclosure requirements both of which apply to all going private transactions defined as "Rule 13(e)(3) transactions" whether accomplished by means of a tender offer or by means of some other transaction. * * * The disclosure obligations mandated by Rule 13(e)(3) are designed to provide security holders and other interested persons with sufficient information upon which to decide whether to participate in the transaction, to elect a right of appraisal where available, or to exercise available federal or state law remedies to challenge the transaction. The Commission expects to monitor closely developments in the practice under this new Rule and is mindful of the unusual potential for fraud and overreaching inherent in going private transactions. * * *

The Committee has also asked whether the antifraud provisions of Section 14(e) and the rulemaking authority under Section 13(e) are effective regulatory tools for the Commission. Section 13(e) of the Act expressly grants the Commission authority to adopt rules which define, and prescribe means reasonably designed to prevent fraudulent, deceptive or manipulative activity in connection with purchases by an issuer of its own equity securities. Section 14(e) of the Act gives the Commission similar authority in connection with any tender offer. As mentioned above, pursuant to these and other sections of the Act, the Commission has adopted Rules 13(e)(3) and 13(e)(4). * * * The Commission believes that Section 13(e) and 14(e) of the Act provide adequate statutory authority for the adoption of these rules. * * *

§ 17.4 The Legislative History of the Williams Act As Seen through Court Decisions

A. The Purpose of the Williams Act Generally

Electronic Specialty Co. v. International Controls Corp.

United States Court of Appeals, Second Circuit, 1969 409 F.2d 937

Friendly, Circuit Judge:

This the first case in which we or, so far as we are aware, any court of appeals has had to consider the amendment adding to § 14 of the Securities Exchange Act new subsections (d), (e) and (f) dealing with tender offers. * * *

The likeness of tender offers to proxy contests is not limited to the issue of standing. They are alike in the fundamental feature that they generally are contests. This means that the participants on both sides act, not "in the peace of a quiet chamber," but under the stresses of the market place. They act quickly, sometimes impulsively, often in angry response to what they consider, whether rightly or wrongly, to be low blows by the other side. Probably there will no more be a perfect tender offer than a perfect trial. Congress intended to assure basic honesty and fair dealing, not to impose an unrealistic requirement of laboratory conditions that might make the new statute a potent tool for incumbent management to protect its own interests against the desires and welfare of the stockholders. These considerations bear on the kind of judgment to be applied in testing conduct-of both sides-and also on the issue of materiality. * * *

B. The Purpose of § 13(d)

GAF Corp. v. Milstein

United States Court of Appeals, Second Circuit, 1971 453 F.2d 709

The 1960's on Wall Street may best be remembered for the pyrotechnics of corporate takeovers and the phenomenon of conglomeration. Although individuals seeking control through a proxy contest were required to comply with scction 14(a) of the Securities Exchange Act and the proxy rules promulgated by the SEC, and those making stock tender offers were required to comply with the applicable provisions of the Securities Act, before the enactment of the Williams Act there were no provisions regulating cash tender offers or other techniques of securing corporate control. According to the committee reports:

> "The [Williams Act] would correct the current gap in our securities laws by amending the Securities Exchange Act of 1934 to provide for full disclosure in connection with cash tender offers and other techniques for accumulating large blocks of equity securities of publicly held companies."

Specifically, we were told, "the purpose of section 13(d) is to require disclosure of information by persons who have acquired a substantial interest, or increased their interest in the equity securities of a company by a substantial amount, within a relatively short period of time." Otherwise, investors cannot assess the potential for changes in corporate control and adequately evaluate the company's worth.

That the purpose of section 13(d) is to alert the marketplace to every large, rapid aggregation or accumulation of securities, regardless of technique employed, which might represent a potential shift in corporate control is amply reflected in the enacted provisions. * * *

C. The Purpose of § 14(d)

Hanson Trust PLC v. SCM Corp.

United States Court of Appeals, Second Circuit, 1985 774 F.2d 47

Congress adopted § 14(d) in 1968 "in response to the growing use of cash tender offers as a means of achieving corporate takeovers * * * which * * * removed a substantial number of corporate control contests from the reach of existing disclosure requirements of the federal securities laws." * * *

Prior to the Williams Act a tender offeror had no obligation to disclose any information to shareholders when making a bid. The Report of the Senate Committee on Banking and Currency aptly described the situation: "by using a cash tender offer the person seeking control can operate in almost complete secrecy. At present, the law does not even require that he disclose his identity, the source of his funds, who his associates are, or what he intends to do if he gains control of the corporation." The average shareholder, pressured by the fact that the tender offer would be available for only a short time and restricted to a limited number of shares, was forced "with severely limited information, [to] decide what course of action he should take." "Without knowledge of who the bidder is and what he plans to do, the shareholder cannot reach an informed decision. He is forced to take a chance. For no matter what he does, he does it without adequate information to enable him to decide rationally what is the best possible course of action."

The purpose of the Williams Act was, accordingly, to protect the shareholders from that dilemma by insuring "that public shareholders who are confronted by a cash tender offer for their stock will not be required to respond without adequate information."

Congress took "extreme care," * * * however, when protecting shareholders, to avoid "tipping the balance of regulation either in favor of management or in favor of the person making the takeover bid." * * *

Congress * * * settled upon a statute requiring a tender offer solicitor seeking beneficial ownership of more than 5% of the outstanding shares of any class of any equity security registered on a national securities exchange first to file with the SEC a statement containing certain information specified in § 13(d)(1) of the Act, as amplified by SEC rules and regulations. Congress' failure to define "tender offer" was deliberate. Aware of "the almost infinite variety in the terms of most tender offers" and concerned that a rigid definition would be evaded, Congress left to the court and the SEC the flexibility to define the term. * * *

D. The Purpose of § 14(e)

Schreiber v. Burlington Northern, Inc.

United States Supreme Court, 1985 105 S.Ct. 2458

It is clear that Congress relied primarily on disclosure to implement the purpose of the Williams Act. * * *

Section 14(e) adds a "broad antifraud prohibition," modeled on the antifraud provisions of § 10(b) of the Act and Rule 10b-5. It supplements the more precise disclosure provisions found elsewhere in the Williams Act, while requiring disclosure more explicitly addressed to the tender offer context than that required by § 10(b).

While legislative history specifically concerning § 14(e) is sparse, the House and Senate Reports discuss the role of § 14(e). Describing § 14(e) as regulating "fraudulent transactions," and stating the thrust of the section:

> "This provision would affirm the fact that persons engaged in making or opposing tender offers or otherwise seeking to influence the decision of investors or the outcome of the tender offer are under an obligation to make full disclosure of material information to those with whom they deal."

Nowhere in the legislative history is there the slightest suggestion that § 14(e) serves any purpose other than disclosure, or that the term "manipulative" should be read as an invitation to the courts to oversee the substantive fairness of tender offers; the quality of any offer is a matter for the marketplace. * * *

Note

The substantive issue in *Schreiber* is addressed in Chapter 20.

§ 17.5 SEC's Advisory Committee on Tender Offers

SEC, Advisory Committee on Tender Offers Report of Recommendations (Summary Recommendations)

(July 8, 1983) [*See also* Sections 20.11 and 23.9]

Economics of Takeovers and their Regulation

1. The purpose of the regulatory scheme should be neither to promote nor to deter takeovers; such transactions and related activities are a valid method of capital allocation, so long as they are conducted in accordance with the laws deemed necessary to protect the interests of shareholders and the integrity and efficiency of the capital markets.

2. There is no material distortion in the credit markets resulting from control acquisition transactions, and no regulatory initiative should be undertaken to limit the availability of credit in such transactions, or to allocate credit among such trans-actions.

Objectives of Federal Regulation of Takeovers

3. Takeover regulation should not favor either the acquiror or the target company, but should aim to achieve a reasonable balance while at the same time protecting the interests of shareholders and the integrity and efficiency of the markets.

4. Regulation of takeovers should recognize that such transactions take place in a national securities market.

5. Cash and securities tender offers should be placed on an equal regulatory footing so that bidders, the market and shareholders, and not regulation, decide between the two.

6. Regulation of takeovers should not unduly restrict innovations in takeover techniques. These techniques should be able to evolve in relationship to changes in the market and the economy.

7. Even though regulation may restrict innovations in takeover techniques, it is desirable to have sufficient regulation to insure the integrity of the markets and to protect shareholders and market participants against fraud, non-disclosure of material information and the creation of situations in which a significant number of reasonably diligent small shareholders may be at a disadvantage to market professionals.

8. The evolution of the market and innovation in takeover techniques may from time to time produce abuses. The regulatory framework should be flexible enough to allow the Commission to deal with such abuses as soon as they appear.

9. a. *State Takeover Law.* State regulation of takeovers should be confined to local companies.

b. *State Corporation Law.* Except to the extent necessary to eliminate abuses or interference with the intended functioning of federal takeover regulation, federal takeover regulation should not preempt or override state corporation law. Essentially the business judgment rule should continue to govern most such activity.

c. *State Regulation of Public Interest Business.* Federal takeover regulation should not preempt substantive state regulation of banks, utilities, insurance companies and similar businesses, where the change of control provisions of such state regulation are justified in relation to the overall objectives of the industry being regulated, do not conflict with procedural provisions of federal takeover regulation and relate to a significant portion of the issuer's business.

d. *Federal Regulation.* Federal takeover regulation should not override the regulation of particular industries such as banks, broadcast licensees, railroads, ship operators, nuclear licensees, etc.

e. *Relationships with Other Federal Laws.* Federal takeover regulation should not be used to achieve antitrust, labor, tax, use of credit and similar objectives. Those objectives should be achieved by separate legislation or regulation.

References

Brown *et al.*, *Takeovers: A Strategic Guide*, *supra* Section 1.10.

Hazen, *Securities Regulation*, *supra* Section 1.10.

Lipton and Steinberger, *Takeovers and Freezeouts*, *supra* Section 1.10.

Loss & Seligman, *Securities Regulation*, *supra* Section 1.10.

Thompson, *Mergers, Acquisitions and Tender Offers*, *supra* Section 1.10, Chapter 8.

Chapter 18

Regulation of Open Market Purchases

§ 18.1 Scope

This chapter deals with Section 13(d) of the Securities Exchange Act of 1934 which requires a person or group that acquires more than 5% of the stock of a publicly-held target to file a Schedule 13D within 10 days of exceeding the 5% threshold. Section 18.2 provides an introductory problem. Section 18.3 presents an excerpt from an SEC release addressing issues under Section 13(d). Section 18.4 considers the standards for determining injunctive relief under Section 13(d) as set forth by the Supreme Court in *Rondeau v. Mosinee Paper Corp.* Section 18.5 addresses standing and remedy issues under Section 13(d), and Section 18.6 looks at the requirements for amending a Schedule 13D. Finally, Section 18.7 examines the group concept under Section 13(d). The materials in this chapter are discussed in greater detail in Thompson, *Mergers, Acquisitions and Tender Offers, supra* Section 1.10, Chapter 8.

§ 18.2 Introductory Problems on Section 13(d)

1. Citigroup, Inc. is planning to make a tender offer for J.P. Morgan Chase & Co. (J.P. Morgan), a publicly-held corporation, and prior to announcing the tender offer, Citigroup buys on the open market 8% of J.P. Morgan's shares. Assume that under the notification threshold rules under Hart-Scott-Rodino, it can do so without making another antitrust pre-merger notification filing. *See* Chapter 9. Given that Citigroup has definite plans to make a tender offer, can it purchase the shares on the open market before announcing the tender offer? If so, what SEC filings are required, when must they be made, and what must they disclose?

2. Citigroup has decided to purchase only 4% of J.P. Morgan's shares on the open market. What SEC filing is required, if any? The president of Citigroup (Citi Pres) has discussed his plans for the tender offer for J.P. Morgan with the president of Bear, Inc. (Bear Pres), and Citi Pres has suggested to Bear Pres that it would be good if Bear were to purchase some shares of J.P. Morgan on the open market. Bear then buys 4.5% of J.P. Morgan's shares. What SEC filings are Citigroup and Bear required to make, if any? What is the HSR impact on these purchases? Assume that neither Citigroup nor Bear made any SEC filings. What rights, if any, does J.P. Morgan have and what remedies can it practically expect? What rights do J.P. Morgan's shareholders have and what remedies can they expect?

§ 18.3 Background

Read Securities Exchange Act Section 13(d), Rules 13d-1 to -7 and Schedule 13D.

A. Introduction

The statutory requirements of Section 13(d) are amplified by the rules, which are briefly introduced here. Rule 13d-1(a) sets out the general filing requirement:

> Any person who, after acquiring directly or indirectly the beneficial ownership of any equity security [of a 34 Act reporting company] * * * is directly or indirectly the beneficial owner of more than five percent of the class shall, within 10 days after the acquisition, file with the Commission, a statement containing the information required by Schedule 13D.

Rules 13d-1(b)-(h) set out the rules for an alternative, less burdensome, filing requirement under Schedule 13G.. This schedule applies to certain institutional investors who satisfy the more than five percent ownership requirement, but whose ownership is not for the "purpose or effect of changing or influencing the control of the issuer." Schedule 13G is discussed further in Chapter 25, which deals with activist shareholders.

Rule 13d-2, deals with amendments to a Schedule 13D, and Rule 13d-2(a) requires that an amendment be filed if any "material change occurs in the facts set forth in the Schedule 13D."

Rule 13d-3 deals with the determination of beneficial ownership. Rulc 13d-3(a) sets out the following general rule:

> a beneficial owner of a security includes any person who, directly or indirectly, through any contract, arrangement, understanding, relationship, or otherwise has or shares:
>
> (1) *Voting power* which includes the power to vote, or to direct the voting of, such security; and/or,
>
> (2) *Investment power* which includes the power to dispose, or to direct the disposition of, such security.

This beneficial ownership concept and the *CSX* case are explored in greater detail in Chapter 25.

Rule 13d-5 sets out a group concept which applies broadly and even in the context where the members of the group have not acquired securities:

> (b)(1) When two or more persons agree to act together for the purpose of acquiring, holding, voting or disposing of equity securities of an issuer, the group formed thereby shall be deemed to have acquired beneficial ownership, for purposes of sections 13(d) and 13(g) of the Act, as of the date of such agreement, of all equity securities of that issuer beneficially owned by any such persons.

B. The 1977 SEC Release

Excerpt from Sec. Exch. Act. Rel. No. 13291

(Feb. 24, 1977)

Rule 13d-3(d)(1) provides that with respect to certain options relating to outstanding securities both the holder of the option and the person who presently owns the underlying securities would be deemed to be beneficial owners. * * *

Rule 13d-2, which required the prompt filing of an amendment to Schedule 13D to reflect any material change, has been re-adopted without change.

For the purposes of Section 13(d), new Rule 13d-3(a) provides that a beneficial owner of a security includes any person who directly or indirectly has or shares voting power and/or investment power of such security. * * * An analysis of all relevant facts and circumstances in a particular situation is essential in order to identify each person possessing the requisite voting power or investment power. * * *

In addition to being a beneficial owner by possession of voting power or investment power, a person is also deemed to be a beneficial owner of a security pursuant to new Rule 13d-3(d)(1) if such person has the right to acquire beneficial ownership of such security at any time within sixty days through the exercise of an option, warrant or right, conversion of a convertible security, or pursuant to the power to revoke a trust or similar arrangement.

New Rule 13d-3(d)(2) excludes from the definition of beneficial owner any person whose only interest in the securities is record ownership. * * *

New Rule 13d-6(b) deems the group formed by two or more persons who agree to act together for the purpose of acquiring, holding or disposing of securities to have "acquired," for the purpose of Section 13(d)(1), beneficial ownership, as of the date of their agreement, of all securities beneficially owned by any member of such group. A group has the option of either filing a joint acquisition statement or each member of the group may file an individual acquisition statement reporting both his ownership and the group's collective ownership.

New Rule [13d-3(d)(4)]: exempts an acquisition by an underwriter of securities as part of a good faith firm commitment underwriting where it is anticipated that such person will, as part of a distribution registered under the Securities Act, be immediately reselling such securities since such a transaction is not the type of acquisition that Section 13(d)(1) was intended to cover. * * *

The Commission has amended Schedule 13D, its current, long form acquisition statement, in order to make the disclosure therein more meaningful to investors and, to the extent feasible, less burdensome to beneficial owners. The amendments will require disclosure of the citizenship of the beneficial owner, the general nature of any non-purchase acquisitions; certain pledges of securities by the beneficial owner; and interests of other persons in the securities being reported on. * * *

[**Illustrations**] The following illustrations are intended to supplement the explanation and analysis set forth elsewhere in the release, and to demonstrate the manner in which the rules would be interpreted. It should be assumed in each of the following illustrations that the rules adopted in this release are in effect and that the securities of the subject company ("Z Corporation") are registered pursuant to Section 12 of the Exchange Act. * * *

Example 1. Rule 13d-3(a), indirect ownership; Rule 13d-3(d)(i), option to acquire. X, an individual, beneficially owns sixty-eight percent of Y Corporation. Y Corporation purchases four percent of a class of securities of Z Corporation and also an option, exercisable within thirty days of the date of purchase, to purchase an additional two percent of the outstanding shares of the same class of Z Corporation.

Question. Does X have a filing obligation and, if so, how may it be satisfied?

Interpretative Response. Yes, X has an obligation to file under Rule 13d-1 since under Rule 13d-3 he is the indirect beneficial owner of the Z shares held by Y Corporation due to his power to direct their voting or disposition. It should be noted that the operation of Rule 13d-3(d)(1)(i) puts X above the five percent threshold inasmuch as the shares subject to the option will be aggregated with those purchased. X's reporting obligation may be satisfied with a filing by X disclosing his indirect ownership and the intermediaries involved; alternatively, since Y Corporation also would be subject to a separate filing requirement with respect to the same securities, X may file jointly with Y disclosing the control position and other information required with respect to X pursuant to Instruction C to Schedule 13D.

Example 2. Rule 13d-3, indirect ownership by corporation; Rule 13d-5, use of short form; Instruction C, Schedule 13D.

Y Corporation, a wholly-owned subsidiary of X Corporation acquires six percent of a class of securities of Z Corporation. X is a widely-held company with no single shareholder owning in excess of one percent of X's shares and its directors beneficially own only directors' qualifying shares.

Question. Who has the obligation to report beneficial ownership of the Z shares, and how may this obligation be satisfied?

Interpretative Response. Both X and Y would be viewed as beneficial owners of the Z shares due to their power to direct the voting or disposition. X's obligation to report such ownership may be satisfied with a filing by either X or Y. If Y Corporation files on behalf of X and Y, the control position and the other information required with respect to X must be disclosed pursuant to Instruction C to Schedule 13D. If X Corporation files on behalf of X and Y, it must disclose that it is indirectly the beneficial owner of the Z shares as a result of its control over Y Corporation, which actually holds the shares. However, if all the conditions of Rule 13d-5 are satisfied, including paragraph (a)(2)(vi), X may satisfy its filing obligation by filing that form. * * *

C. Goldman Sach's 13D Relating to the Acquisition of Kinder Morgan, Inc.

For an illustration of a Schedule 13D *see* the Schedule 13D filed by Goldman Sachs and related entities relating to the acquisition of Kinder Morgan, Inc. by Goldman and certain other parties, including private equity firms, Documentary Appendix L of *M&A Statutes, Rules, and Documents*, *supra* Section 1.1.

§ 18.4 Availability of Injunctive Relief

Rondeau v. Mosinee Paper Corp.

United States Supreme Court, 1975 422 U.S. 49, 95 S.Ct. 2069

Mr. Chief Justice Burger:

We granted certiorari in this case to determine whether a showing of irreparable harm is necessary for a private litigant to obtain injunctive relief in a suit under § 13(d) of the Securities Exchange Act of 1934. The Court of Appeals held that it was not. We reverse.

[**Facts**] * * * In April 1971 petitioner Francis A. Rondeau, a Mosinee businessman, began making large purchases of respondent's [Mosinee Paper Corp.] common stock in the over-the-counter market. Some of the purchases were in his own name; others were in the name of businesses and a foundation known to be controlled by him. By May 17, 1971, petitioner had acquired 40,413 shares of respondent's stock, which constituted more than 5% of those outstanding. He was therefore required to comply with the disclosure provisions of the Williams Act, by filing a Schedule 13D with respondent and the Securities and Exchange Commission within 10 days. * * *

Petitioner did not file a Schedule 13D but continued to purchase substantial blocks of respondent's stock. By July 30, 1971, he had acquired more than 60,000 shares. On that date the chairman of respondent's board of directors informed him by letter that his activity had "given rise to numerous rumors" and "seems to have created some problems under the Federal Securities Laws * * *." Upon receiving the letter petitioner immediately stopped placing orders for respondent's stock and consulted his attorney. On August 25, 1971, he filed a Schedule 13D. * * *

On August 27 respondent sent a letter to its shareholders informing them of the disclosures in petitioner's Schedule 13D. The letter stated that by his "tardy filing" petitioner had "withheld the information to which you (the shareholders) were entitled for more than two months, in violation of federal law." * * *

[**Issue**] [R]espondent initiated this suit in the United States District Court * * * alleged that [petitioner and certain other parties] were engaged in a scheme to defraud respondent and its shareholders in violation of the securities laws. It alleged further that shareholders who had "sold shares without the information which defendants were required to disclose lacked information material to their decision whether to sell or hold," and that respondent "was unable to communicate such information to its stockholders, and to take such actions as their interest required." Respondent prayed for an injunction prohibiting petitioner and his codefendants from voting or pledging their stock and from acquiring additional shares, requiring them to divest themselves of stock which they already owned, and for damages. * * *

[Petitioner] readily conceded that he had violated the Williams Act, but contended that the violation was due to a lack of familiarity with the securities laws and that neither respondent nor its shareholders had been harmed. The District Court agreed. * * * Thus, although petitioner had committed a technical violation of the Williams Act, the District Court held that respondent was entitled to no relief and entered summary judgment against it.

The Court of Appeals reversed, with one judge dissenting. * * * [T]he majority was of the view that respondent "need not show irreparable harm as a prerequisite to obtaining permanent injunctive relief in view of the fact that as issuer of the securities it is in the best position to assure that the filing requirements of the Williams Act are being timely and fully complied with and to obtain speedy and forceful remedial action when necessary." The Court of Appeals remanded the case to the District Court with instructions that it enjoin petitioner and his codefendants from further violations of the Williams Act and from voting the shares purchased between the due date of the Schedule 13D and the date of its filing for a period of five years. It considered "such an injunctive decree appropriate to neutralize (petitioner's) violation of the Act and to deny him the benefit of his wrongdoing."

We granted certiorari to resolve an apparent conflict among the Courts of Appeals and because of the importance of the question presented to private actions under the federal securities laws. We disagree with the Court of Appeals' conclusion that the traditional standards for extraordinary equitable relief do not apply in these circumstances, and reverse.

[**Analysis**] As in the District Court and the Court of Appeals, it is conceded here that petitioner's delay in filing the Schedule 13D constituted a violation of the Williams Act. The narrow issue before us is whether this record supports the grant of injunctive relief, a remedy whose basis "in the federal courts has always been irreparable harm and inadequacy of legal remedies."

The Court of Appeals' conclusion that respondent suffered "harm" sufficient to require sterilization of petitioner's stock need not long detain us. The purpose of the Williams Act is to insure that public shareholders who are confronted by a cash tender offer for their stock will not be required to respond without adequate information regarding the qualifications and intentions of the offering party. * * *

The short of the matter is that none of the evils to which the Williams Act was directed has occurred or is threatened in this case. Petitioner has not attempted to obtain control of respondent, either by a cash tender offer or any other device. Moreover, he has now filed a proper Schedule 13D, and there has been no suggestion that he will fail to comply with the Act's requirement of reporting any material changes in the information contained therein. *See* Rule 13d-2. On this record there is no likelihood that respondent's shareholders will be disadvantaged should petitioner make a tender offer, or that respondent will be unable to adequately place its case before them should a contest for control develop. Thus, the usual basis for injunctive relief, "that there exists some cognizable danger of recurrent violation," is not present here.

Nor are we impressed by respondent's argument that an injunction is necessary to protect the interests of its shareholders who either sold their stock to petitioner at predisclosure prices or would not have invested had they known that a takeover bid was imminent. * * * In any event, those persons who allegedly sold at an unfairly depressed price have an adequate remedy by way of an action for damages, thus negating the basis for equitable relief. * * *

Respondent urges * * * that the "public interest" must be taken into account in considering its claim for relief and relies upon the Court of Appeals' conclusion that it is entitled to an injunction because it "is in the best position" to insure that the Williams Act is complied with by purchasers of its stock. This argument misconceives, we think, the nature of the litigation. Although neither the availability of a private suit under the Williams Act nor respondent's standing to bring it has been questioned here, this cause of action is not expressly authorized by the statute or its legislative history. Rather, respondent is asserting a so-called implied private right of action established by cases such as *J. I. Case Co. v. Borak*, *See* Section 13.16. Of course, we have not hesitated to recognize the power of federal courts to fashion private remedies for securities laws violations when to do so is consistent with the legislative scheme and necessary for the protection of investors as a supplement to enforcement by the Securities and Exchange Commission. However, it by no means follows that the plaintiff in such an action is relieved of the burden of establishing the traditional prerequisites of relief. Indeed, our cases hold that quite the contrary is true. * * *

Reversed and remanded with directions.

§ 18.5 Standing and Remedies under § 13(d)

A. Target's Standing to Force Corrective Disclosure

Florida Commercial Banks v. Culverhouse

United States Court of Appeals, Eleventh Circuit, 1985 772 F.2d 1513

Johnson, Circuit Judge:

This appeal challenges the district court's dismissal of claims brought under Sections 13(d), 14(d), and 14(e) of the Securities and Exchange Act of 1934 ("Exchange Act"). Appellant asserts that those provisions provide a target corporation (or "issuer corporation") with a private cause of action to obtain corrective disclosures from a tender offeror who has filed with the Securities and Exchange Commission ("SEC"), and disseminated to shareholders, false and misleading tender offer materials. The district court dismissed the claims on the grounds that appellant did not have standing under those provisions to maintain this cause of action. We reverse.

[**Facts and Issue**] Appellant Florida Commercial Banks, Inc. ("the Bank"), a Florida corporation, brought this action against Hugh F. Culverhouse, Sr. ("Culverhouse") and an unknown entity styled as the John Doe Group ("the Group"). In October 1981, Culverhouse's ownership of the Bank's common stock reached 5% of the shares outstanding; later that month Culverhouse filed with the SEC the required Schedule 13D, pursuant to Section 13(d) of the Exchange Act. Over the next three years, Culverhouse continued to acquire stock in the Bank and filed 12 amendments to the Schedule 13D. In August 1984, Culverhouse made a tender offer in which he sought to acquire enough shares to gain a controlling interest in the Bank, a total of approximately 54.8% of the Bank's outstanding common stock. At about that time, Culverhouse also filed with the SEC a Schedule 14D-1 Tender Offer Statement, pursuant to Section 14(d)(1) of the Exchange Act.

The Bank's amended complaint alleged that Culverhouse and the Group were engaged in a conspiracy that either would permit Culverhouse to acquire control of the Bank for later resale to the Group, or would permit the Group to sell the Bank's stock to, or merge the Bank with, another unnamed financial institution. The complaint alleged that the Schedule 13D and its amendments failed to disclose Culverhouse's intention systematically to purchase the Bank's stock for other than "investment purposes," and his simultaneous negotiations with others for the sale of the Bank's stock. The complaint further alleged that Culverhouse made 23 material misrepresentations and omissions in the tender offer materials that he filed with the SEC and disseminated to shareholders. The complaint charged Culverhouse with violations of Sections 10(b), 13(d), 14(d), and 14(e) of the Exchange Act. The Bank sought injunctive relief that would require Culverhouse to make corrective disclosures to cure the false statements and omissions in his tender offer materials, and would enjoin Culverhouse from proceeding further with the tender offer until such disclosures were made.

Culverhouse moved to dismiss for failure to state a claim, arguing that the Bank lacked standing under this Court's holding in *Liberty National Insurance Holding Co. v. Charter Co.*, 734 F.2d 545 (11th Cir. 1984). The district court dismissed the federal claims with prejudice on the standing issue, citing only *Liberty National*. * * *

[**Analysis**] In *Liberty National*, one company (Charter) accumulated approximately seven percent of the common stock of the target company (Liberty) and filed a Schedule 13D statement with several amendments. Liberty filed a complaint, alleging that Charter sought to accumulate enough shares of Liberty stock to enable Charter either to sell the shares at a control premium, or to coerce Liberty's management to give Charter business concessions to the economic detriment of the Liberty shareholders. Liberty alleged that Charter's actions violated Sections 13(d), 14(d), and 14(e) of the Exchange Act, as well as other securities laws. Liberty sought injunctive relief requiring Charter to divest itself of its holdings of Liberty stock and to refrain from voting its shares or otherwise exercising its rights in those shares pending such divestiture.

This Court held that Liberty did not have an implied right of action under Section 13(d) to expel an unwanted shareholder from the company. This Court also held that Sections 14(d) and 14(e) did not create implied rights of action on behalf of a target corporation for the type of injunctive relief sought. Although Sections 14(d) and 14(e) would apply only if Charter made a tender offer, this Court did not reach the question of whether Charter actually made a tender offer.

The main focus of *Liberty National* concerned the question of whether providing an issuer corporation with a private right of action under the Williams Act would have a greater tendency to effectuate the purposes of the Williams Act by protecting the shareholders or, instead, would have a greater tendency to give the management an unfair advantage over tender offerors in takeover battles, ultimately to the detriment of the shareholders. The remedy that was requested in that case divestiture was clearly relevant to the issue of whether providing Liberty with the private right of action would tend to effectuate or thwart the purpose of the Williams Act to benefit the investor. * * *

Appellants in the instant case do not seek to force the tender offeror to divest itself of its holdings in the Bank but, rather, seek to obtain corrective disclosures. In *Piper* [Section 20.8.A] the Supreme Court addressed the question of whether Section 14(e) of the Exchange Act permitted the Court to read into the statute a damages remedy for unsuccessful tender offerors. By focusing on whether that particular remedy was necessary to achieve the Congressional purpose of protecting the shareholders, the Court indicated that courts should consider the particular remedy sought in determining whether a statute implies a private right of action. Since the remedy that the plaintiffs sought in *Liberty National* was significantly different from the remedy sought in the instant case, this Court must independently determine whether the Bank should have a private right of action to obtain corrective disclosures from Culverhouse.

The Supreme Court has never directly decided the question of whether an issuer can obtain injunctive relief under the Williams Act. * * * Although the Court's denial of injunctive relief on the merits [in *Rondeau v. Mosinee Paper Corp.*, Section 18.4] could be interpreted to mean that an issuer has standing to obtain such relief, the *Rondeau* Court explicitly stated that the question of the issuer's standing to obtain injunctive relief was not before it. Nevertheless, the Court indicated that it might recognize issuer standing to seek certain remedies, saying: "Of course, we have not hesitated to recognize the power of federal courts to fashion private remedies for securities laws violations when to do so is consistent with the legislative scheme and necessary for investors as a supplement to enforcement by the Securities and Exchange Commission."

The Supreme Court has set forth four factors a court should consider in determining whether a statute creates an implied private right of action: (1) whether the plaintiff is a member of the class for whose especial benefit the statute was enacted; (2) whether there is any indication of legislative intent, explicit or implicit, either to create such a remedy or to deny one; (3) whether it is consistent with the underlying purposes of the legislative scheme to imply such a remedy for the plaintiff; and (4) whether the cause of action is one traditionally relegated to state law, so that it would be inappropriate to infer a cause of action based on federal law. *Cort v. Ash*, 422 U.S. 66, (1975). The Court has since held that these factors are not entitled to equal weight, and that the central inquiry must focus on the question of legislative intent. * * *

This Court will examine (1) whether the legislature has specifically indicated the intent to create or preserve such a private right of action, and (2) whether the purposes of the Williams Act would be furthered or thwarted by the creation of such a private right of action. * * *

Only four years before the passage of the Williams Act in 1968, the Supreme Court held that Section 14(a) of the Exchange Act permitted a shareholder to sue for damages on behalf of the corporation to redress injuries from false and misleading proxy solicitation materials distributed in violation of that provision. *J.I. Case Co. v. Borak*, [Section 13.16] It could be argued that, given the Williams Act's origin in Section 14(a), Congress had ample reason to assume that the federal judiciary would imply certain private rights of action to enforce the newly enacted mandates. * * *

[B]y the time the second amended version of [the Williams] Act was adopted in 1977, courts had consistently and routinely interpreted the Act to provide for private rights of action on behalf of target corporations. Because Congress in 1977 had ample notice of the existence of these judicially created private rights of action under the Williams Act, that Congress's failure to eliminate these rights of action legislatively is evidence that Congress intended the Williams Act to create private rights of action on behalf of target corporations.

The purpose of the Williams Act was to insure that shareholders who are confronted with a cash tender offer would not be required to respond without adequate information regarding the qualifications and intentions of the offering party. * * *

In deciding whether to provide the target corporation with a private cause of action under the Williams Act to seek a particular remedy, a court should balance the likelihood that the shareholders will benefit by obtaining necessary information, against (1) the likelihood that shareholders will be harmed by the potential misuse of the cause of action by management seeking to thwart takeover attempts, and (2) the likelihood that shareholders will be harmed by other aspects of the particular remedy sought. In the instant case, where the particular remedy sought is corrective disclosures, there is no chance that shareholders will be harmed by the remedy. This Court needs only to balance the likelihood that the shareholders will benefit from the availability of this cause of action to the target corporation, against the likelihood that the shareholders will be harmed by the misuse of that cause of action by management.

Applying this test, we hold that under the Williams Act an issuer has a private right of action to seek the remedy of corrective disclosures.[1] * * *

By providing issuers with this cause of action to enforce the Williams Act, this Court does not intend to allow the directors of corporations, who clearly have an economic interest in protecting their own positions, to use corporate resources simply to harass and burden aggressive outsiders. * * *

B. Cooling-Off Period

Kirsch Co. v. Bliss and Laughlin Industries, Inc.

United States District Court, W.D. Michigan, 1980 495 F.Supp. 488

Enslen, District Judge:

* * * Kirsch [the target] alleges that BLI [the acquiror] and its officers violated the federal securities laws by misrepresenting, on the Schedule 13D, its actual purpose in purchasing Kirsch's stock, by stating that the shares were purchased "for the purpose of investment." * * *

I am inclined to believe that the information in BLI's Schedule 13D would not fairly apprise investors of BLI's intent with regard to potential changes in Kirsch's corporate

1. Every other circuit which has addressed this question has held that an issuer has standing under the Williams Act to seek corrective disclosures from a tender offeror who has filed false and misleading disclosure statements. * * *

control. Although I realize that there is evidence to the contrary, I have little doubt that Kirsch's shareholders and the investing public were not adequately informed about possible courses of action BLI had considered and its policies or purpose behind the purchasing of Kirsch's stock. * * *

Plaintiff has alleged that irreparable harm will occur to the investing shareholders of Kirsch and to potential shareholders. While the Court recognizes that "the * * * injunctive process [is] designed to deter rather than punish", *Rondeau*, [*see* Section 18.4] and that disclosure requirements established by Congress are not intended to provide a weapon for management to prevent large accumulations of stock, *Piper*, [*see* Section 20.8.A] the Court cannot overlook the *raison d'etre* of § 13(d) which is: "Full and fair disclosure for the benefit of the investors".

The Court is convinced, based upon the evidence, that irreparable injury would occur to present shareholders of Kirsch and the investing public if BLI were allowed to continue its purchases of Kirsch stock without correcting and amending its Schedule 13D.

The Court hereby Orders a suspension period of 30 days, whereby BLI is enjoined from acquiring further shares of Kirsch stock. * * *

The court is not convinced, from the record, that irreparable injury will result to existing shareholders of Kirsch, or potential investors of Kirsch, if BLI votes its stock presently owned.

The Court, therefore, declines to rule that BLI may not vote its present Kirsch stock, absent any showing by Kirsch that such voting would cause irreparable injury.

[T]he court [has] recognized that disenfranchisement may be an appropriate remedy, where shares were rapidly acquired immediately prior to a control contest during a period of time in which the purchaser was in violation of 13(d). In the instant case, such a disenfranchisement of a stock would be more like punishment than deterrence and not within the spirit of judicial equitable principles. * * *

C. Disgorgement of Profits

SEC v. First City Financial Corp.

United States Court of Appeals, D.C. Circuit, 1989 890 F.2d 1215

[The portion of this decision dealing with the requirement for a group to file a 13D is set out in Section 18.7.D]

The district court directed disgorgement of profits, and appellants' challenge to this aspect of the order presents an issue of first impression—whether federal courts have the authority to employ that remedy with respect to section 13(d) violations and whether it is appropriate in this sort of case. Appellants also claim that the amount ordered disgorged is excessive. We reject both arguments and affirm the district court's order on these issues as well.

Appellants, by claiming that Congress did not explicitly authorize a monetary remedy for section13(d) violations, misapprehend the source of the court's authority. Disgorgement is an equitable remedy designed to deprive a wrongdoer of his unjust enrichment and to deter others from violating the securities laws. * * * "Unless otherwise provided by statute, all the inherent equitable powers of the District Court are available for the proper and complete exercise of that jurisdiction." * * * We see no indication in the language or the legislative history of the 1934 Act that even implies a restriction on the equitable remedies of the district courts. Disgorgement, then, is available simply because the relevant provisions of the Securities Exchange Act of 1934, sections 21(d) and (e), vest jurisdiction in the federal courts.

Indeed, appellants concede that disgorgement is rather routinely ordered for insider trading violations despite a similar lack of specific authorizations for that remedy under the securities law. But they seek to distinguish section 13(d) violations as a "technical" transgression of reporting rules that really do not cause injury. In contrast, they argue, insider trading under modern theory is tantamount to theft; an actual injury is inflicted on the individual or institution entitled to confidentiality. Section 13(d), however, is the pivot of the entire Williams Act regulation of tender offers. To be sure, some may doubt the usefulness of that statute generally or the section 13(d) requirement specifically, but it is hardly up to the judiciary to second-guess the wisdom of Congress' approach to regulating takeovers. Suffice it for us to note that section 13(d) is a crucial requirement in the congressional scheme, and a violator, it is legislatively assumed, improperly benefits by purchasing stocks at an artificially low price because of a breach of the duty Congress imposed to disclose his investment position. The disclosure of that position—a holding in excess of 5 percent of another company's stock—suggests to the rest of the market a likely takeover and therefore may increase the price of the stock. Appellants circumvented that scheme, and the theory of the statute, by which we are bound, is that the circumventions caused injury to other market participants who sold stock without knowledge of First City's holdings. We therefore see no relevant distinction between disgorgement of inside trading profits and disgorgement of post-section 13(d) violation profits. * * *

D. Standing of Acquiror's Shareholders

In Re Dow Chemical Securities Bhopal Litigation

U.S. District Court Southern District New York, 2000 U.S. Dist. LEXIS 18698

Chen, District Judge:

These consolidated securities fraud class actions arise from the proposed acquisition by defendant Dow Chemical Corporation ("Dow") of Union Carbide Corporation ("Union Carbide"). In connection with the transaction, Dow sent to Union Carbide and filed with the Securities Exchange Commission (the "SEC") a disclosure statement required by § 13(d) of the Securities Exchange Act of 1934 (the "1934 Act"). Plaintiffs—shareholders of Dow—contend that the disclosure statement was false and misleading, and they seek damages from Dow and certain of its officers and directors.

Defendants move to dismiss the complaints on a number of grounds, including plaintiffs' lack of standing under § 13(d). Defendants argue that § 13(d) was enacted to protect the shareholders of target corporations and not the shareholders of acquiring companies. Because the statute's language and its legislative history demonstrate that shareholders of an acquiring company lack standing to sue such a company under § 13(d), defendants' motion to dismiss is granted and the complaints are dismissed.

Factual Background. In 1984, a disastrous leak of poisonous gas occurred at a pesticide plant owned by a former subsidiary of Union Carbide in Bhopal, India. * * *

Pursuant to Dow's planned merger with Union Carbide, Dow filed a Schedule 13D on August 13, 1999. According to plaintiffs, the disclosure statement failed to disclose (i) pertinent facts regarding the Bhopal accident, (ii) the existence of ongoing prosecutions and investigations against Union Carbide, (iii) relevant decisions rendered by the Indian courts, (iv) the ongoing investigation into claims against Union Carbide, and (v), most significantly, the "material adverse effects of such ongoing prosecutions * * * on Dow, on the value of the [Union Carbide merger], and on Dow's own Indian assets and prospects for future business in India."

In this consolidated class action, plaintiffs assert [that] * * * defendants have violated and continue to violate § 13(d) by having filed a false and misleading Schedule 13D * * *.

Discussion. The threshold issue in this case—which both sides acknowledge is a matter of first impression—is whether shareholders of defendant Dow, the acquiring company, have standing to bring this cause of action against [Dow] for their alleged violations of § 13(d).

The issue of whether § 13(d) provides plaintiffs with a private cause of action "is, of course, one of statutory construction." * * *

Section 13(d) and Schedule 13D. Statutory Language.* * * [T]he intended recipients of the disclosure statement are not the shareholders of the acquiring company, as plaintiffs are here, but the shareholders of the target company, here Union Carbide. In fact, the statute does not require the Schedule 13D to be sent to shareholders of the acquiring company at all.

Legislative History.* * * In *Piper v. Chris-Craft Indus., Inc.* [Section 20.8.A], plaintiff, an unsuccessful contender for control of a target company, sued defendant, the successful contender, for violations of securities laws, including allegedly making false statements in its Schedule 13D. The primary issue before the Court was whether "tender offerors * * *, whose activities are regulated by the Williams Act, have a cause of action * * * against other regulated parties under the statute * * *." After an exhaustive analysis of the Williams Act, the Court concluded that Congress intended to benefit the target company's shareholders, and, thus, tender offerors, who were not the intended beneficiaries, lacked standing to sue for violations of the Act. * * *

[D]espite plaintiff's insistence that the statute contemplates protection for all shareholders, including those of the takeover company, the legislative history of the Williams Act, like the language of the statute itself, refutes that argument. * * *

E. Standing of Tender Offeror

E.ON AG v. Acciona

U.S. District Court, Southern District of New York,
2006 CCH Fed. Securities Law Report, ¶ 94,129

Opinion of COTE, District Judge.

This litigation raises the issue of whether a putative tender offeror has standing under Section 13(d) of the Securities Exchange Act of 1934 ("Section 13(d)" and "Exchange Act"), to bring an action for injunctive relief. The litigation arises in the context of a battle between European companies for control of Spain's largest electrical utility, Endesa, S.A. ("Endesa"). Finding that a tender offeror does have standing, and that the other grounds pressed by defendants to dismiss this action must be rejected, the defendants' motion to dismiss is denied. * * * .

Plaintiffs * * * (collectively "E.ON") are German power and gas companies that have announced their intention to make a tender offer for Endesa. Defendants Acciona, S.A. * * * (collectively "Acciona") are Spanish and international corporations engaged in the development and management of infrastructures, services, and renewable energies, which have recently acquired over 20% of the equity of Endesa. Endesa's shares are traded in the United States as American Depository Shares ("ADSs") [*see* Chapter 26]. Pursuant to Section 13(d), therefore, Acciona is required to file with the Securities and Exchange Commission ("SEC") and serve on Endesa documents describing its purchases and intentions. Plaintiffs' First Amended Complaint asserts two claims for injunctive relief under Section 13(d), alleging that Acciona's Section 13(d) filings contain material misstatements and omissions.

E.ON requests a preliminary injunction [*inter alia*] *1) compelling Acciona to file corrective disclosures under Section 13(d).*

Acciona's Schedule 13D. *On October 5, 2006, ten days after its purchase of 10% of Endesa's securities, Acciona filed a Schedule 13D. The Schedule 13D reported that Acciona acquired ADSs * * * through a "market transaction" financed through Santander. * * **

Acciona filed its Schedule 13D on October 5, 2006, a date on which it executed the fifth of fourteen total return swaps with Santander, yet did not disclose the existence of these agreements, their purpose, or their details. * * *

Discussion. Acciona has moved to dismiss this action and E.ON has moved for a preliminary injunction. Before addressing these two motions, the issue of subject matter jurisdiction must be resolved.

Subject Matter Jurisdiction. * * * Although the plaintiffs, defendants, and target company are all foreign entities, approximately 2% of Endesa shares are traded on the New York Stock Exchange, and 15.3% of the company's securities are held by U.S. investors. Although not essential to a finding of jurisdiction, Acciona's initial investment was through a purchase of ADSs. * * * [As a consequence, the court has subject matter jurisdiction.]

Motion to Dismiss. Acciona * * * contends that E.ON does not have standing under Section 13(d) as either a shareholder or tender offeror. * * * The motion fails.

Standing. Acciona claims that E.ON lacks standing either as a shareholder of or tender offeror for Endesa securities to bring a claim under Section 13(d) against Acciona for disclosure violations. * * *

Section 13(d) does not explicitly provide a private right of action, but the Court of Appeals for the Second Circuit has long found an implied private right of action for both issuers and shareholders to bring claims for injunctive relief under this provision. * * *

Section 13(d) also permits a tender offeror to bring a claim for injunctive relief. * * * This conclusion is not surprising. The analysis that implies the existence of a right of action for shareholders and issuers under Section 13(d) similarly supports the finding of an identical right for tender offerors. * * *

The central concern in deciding whether a private right of action has been created by Congress is the determination of congressional intent. * * *

As described in detail by both the Supreme Court and the Second Circuit, "the sole purpose of the Williams Act was the protection of investors who are confronted with a tender offer." *Piper*, 430 U.S. at 35. *See also GAF Corp.*, 453 F.2d at 717 & n.16. Shareholders, however, rarely have the knowledge of the violation or the resources to engage in the complex and expensive litigation associated with enforcement of Williams Act disclosure. In finding that Congress impliedly intended that issuers bring injunctive actions to enforce Section 13(d)'s disclosure requirements, the Second Circuit noted that the "Williams Act was entitled 'An Act Providing for full disclosure of corporate equity ownership of securities under the Securities Exchange Act of 1934.'" *Id.* at 720. It reasoned that the Act was intended to "alert investors to potential changes in corporate control" and that the issuer "can promptly and effectively police Schedule 13D filings." *Id.* at 720–21.

Similarly, a tender offeror has not only the resources, but also the self-interest which the *GAF Co.* court identified as "vital to maintaining an injunctive action," *id.* at 719, when it found standing for an issuer under Section 13(d). * * *

This takeover battle is an excellent illustration of an instance in which a tender offeror is uniquely motivated to identify deficiencies in Schedule 13D filings. It appears that the Spanish government, and perhaps Endesa as well, will resist to the extent permitted by law, any takeover bid by a foreign company. In this case, the issuer may have little incentive to act to enforce Section 13(d)'s requirements and compel Acciona to make all necessary disclosures as it maneuvers to block the E.ON bid. Endesa shareholders must rely on [E.ON], the tender offeror, to enforce compliance with Section 13(d) by litigating the adequacy of Acciona's filings. * * *

§ 18.6 Amendments

A. Failure to Promptly Amend

In Matter of Merry Land & Investment Co., Inc.

42 S.E.C. Docket 796 Release No. 34–26410 1988

The Commission deems it appropriate and in the public interest that proceedings be, and they hereby are, instituted pursuant to Section 15(c)(4) of the Securities Exchange Act of 1934 ("the Exchange Act") to determine whether Respondent Merry Land & Investment Company, Inc. ("MLIC") failed to comply with Section 13(d) of the Exchange Act and Rule 13d-2 thereunder. * * *

Section 13(d)(2) provides for the prompt amendment of a Schedule 13D in the event of "any material change" in the information stated in a previously filed Schedule 13D. Whether an amendment is prompt is to be determined "based on all of the facts and circumstances surrounding both prior disclosures by the filing person and the material changes which trigger the obligation to amend."

Schedule 13D sets forth categories of disclosure specifically required by Sections 13(d)(1) and 13(d)(2). Item 4 of Schedule 13D requires disclosure of the purpose of the acquisition of the securities, including any plans or proposals by the acquiring person to influence or control the subject company. By September 21, 1987, MLIC's Schedule 13D, as last amended in August 1985, became materially inaccurate. * * *

At the September 21, 1987 meeting between Knox [chairman of the MLIC's board] and Osteen [chairman of BFC's board], which was subsequently confirmed in the November 12, 1987 letter from Knox to BFC's Board of Directors, Knox expressed his dissatisfaction with BFC's management, pressed for an exchange of financial information regarding BFC, and suggested the possibility of pursuing a merger between BFC and Great Southern. In his September 21, 1987 meeting with Osteen, Knox also expressed a desire to obtain detailed proprietary information from BFC for a "side-by-side comparison of similar statistics [which] might help point out areas of potential improvement in both companies [BFC and Great Southern]." Osteen was not receptive to Knox's suggestion regarding sharing financial information. Osteen finally agreed to furnish the requested information only after Knox indicated that MLIC was prepared, if necessary, to commence a proxy contest to get the requested information. * * *

Contrary to the stated purposes publicly disclosed in its Schedule 13D, Knox's statements at the September 21, 1987 meeting with Osteen reflect that, at least by that date, MLIC had formed an intent to initiate or support hostile activities against BFC's management.

The Commission concludes that the events of September 21, 1987 were of such a nature as to have "significantly altered the total mix of information made available" regarding MLIC's intent not to initiate or support activities against the wishes of BFC's management, and thus, "would have been considered to be important by a reasonable shareholder." * * * MLIC was, therefore, required to amend promptly its Schedule 13D, to reflect the material change from its prior Schedule 13D Item 4 statements evidenced by events which had occurred by September 21, 1987. * * *

B. Prompt Amendment

Feldman v. Simkins Industries, Inc.

United States Court of Appeals, Ninth Circuit, 1982 679 F.2d 1299

* * * Section 13(d)(1) requires persons who acquire certain classes and amounts of securities to file disclosure statements. If any material changes occur in the facts set forth in the statements, § 13(d)(2) requires that an amended statement be filed. * * *

Simkins filed a schedule 13(d)(2) amendment the first day after its sales were completed (the fourth trading day after beginning its sales). The district court was justified in concluding that Simkins' filing was "prompt" as a matter of law. * * *

§ 18.7 The Group Concept

A. Formation of a Group to Buy: Is Formation of a Group an Acquisition?

Read Rule 13d-5(b)(1).

GAF Corporation v. Milstein

United States Court of Appeals, Second Circuit, 1971 453 F.2d 709

KAUFMAN, Circuit Judge:

[**Facts and Issue**]* * * GAF Corporation filed its complaint in the United States District Court for the Southern District of New York alleging that Morris Milstein, his two sons, Seymour and Paul, and his daughter, Gloria Milstein Flanzer, violated section 13(d) of the Securities Exchange Act first by failing to file the required statements and then by filing false ones. * * * Judge Pollack aptly framed the issues involved:

> The ultimate issue presented by the defendants' motion to dismiss the first count is whether, organizing a group of stockholders owning more than 10% [now 5%] of a class of equity securities with a view to seeking control is, without more, a reportable event under Section 13(d) of the Exchange Act. * * *

Judge Pollack granted the Milsteins' motion to dismiss, and GAF has appealed. We disagree with Judge Pollack's determination that GAF failed to state a claim under section 13(d) and Rule 13d-1 promulgated thereunder, and thus reverse his order in this respect. * * *

The four Milsteins received 324,166 shares of GAF convertible preferred stock, approximately 10.25% of the preferred shares outstanding, when The Ruberoid Company, in which they had substantial holdings, was merged into GAF in May, 1967. They have not acquired any additional preferred shares since the merger. * * *

[**Analysis**] Section 13(d)(3), which is crucial to GAF's claim, * * * provides that "[w]hen two or more persons act as a partnership, limited partnership, syndicate, or other group for the purpose of acquiring, holding, or disposing of securities of an issuer, such syndicate or group shall be deemed a 'person' for the purposes of [Section 13(d)]." On the assumption that the facts alleged in the complaint are true, we cannot conclude other than that the four Milsteins constituted a "group" and thus, as a "person," were subject to the provisions of section 13(d). Furthermore, the individuals collectively or as a "group" held more than 10% of the outstanding preferred shares—a registered class of securities. Since the section requires a "person" to file only if he acquires more than 2% of the class of stock in a 12-month period after July 29, 1968, the principal question presented to us is whether the complaint alleges as a matter of law that the Milstein *group* "acquired" the 324,166 shares of preferred stock owned by its members after that date. We conclude that it does and thus that it states a claim under section 13(d).

The statute refers to "acquiring directly or indirectly the beneficial ownership of securities." Thus, at the outset, we are not confronted with the relatively simple concept of legal title, but rather with the amorphous and occasionally obfuscated concepts of indirect and beneficial ownership which pervade the securities acts.

The Act nowhere explicitly defines the concept of "acquisition" as used in section 13(d). * * *

The legislative history, as well as the purpose behind section 13(d), bear out our interpretation. Any residual doubt over its soundness is obviated by the following clear statement appearing in both the House and Senate reports accompanying the Williams Act:

> "[Section 13(d)(3)] would prevent a group of persons who seek to pool their voting or other interests in the securities of any issuer from evading the provisions of the statute because no one individual owns more than 10 percent of the securities. *The group would be deemed to have become the beneficial owner, directly or indirectly, of more than 10 percent of a class of securities at the time they agreed to act in concert. Consequently, the group would be required to file the information called for in section 13(d)(1) within 10 days after they agree to act together, whether or not any member of the group had acquired any securities at that time.*"

The Senate and House reports and the Act as finally enacted, contrary to appellees' contention, are entirely consistent in our view. This conclusion is buttressed by a consideration of the purpose of the Act. * * *

The alleged conspiracy on the part of the Milsteins is one clearly intended to be encompassed within the reach of section 13(d). We have before us four shareholders who together own 10.25% of an outstanding class of securities and allegedly agreed to pool their holdings to effect a takeover of GAF. This certainly posed as great a threat to the stability of the corporate structure as the individual shareholder who buys 10.25% of the equity security in one transaction. A shift in the *loci* of corporate power and influence is hardly dependent on an actual transfer of legal title to shares, and the statute and history are clear on this.

In light of the statutory purpose as we view it, we find ourselves in disagreement with the interpretation of *Bath Industries, supra*, that the group owning more than 10%, despite its agreement to seize control, in addition, must agree to acquire more shares before the filing requirement of section 13(d) is triggered. The history and language of section 13(d) make it clear that the statute was primarily concerned with disclosure of potential changes in control resulting from new aggregations of stockholdings and was not intended to be restricted to only individual stockholders who made future purchases and whose actions were, therefore, more apparent. It hardly can be questioned that a group holding sufficient shares can effect a takeover without purchasing a single additional share of stock. * * *

Note

Goldman Sachs filed the Schedule 13D that is Documentary Appendix L of *M&A Statutes, Rules, and Documents*, *supra* Section 1.1, because of concern that it may be part of a group. *See* Item 5 of the Schedule 13D.

B. Formation of a Group to Sell: What Constitutes Concerted Action?

Wellman v. Dickinson

United States Court of Appeals, Second Circuit, 1982 682 F.2d 355,
cert. denied, 460 U.S. 1069 1983

LEONARD P. MOORE, Circuit Judge:

This appeal arises from seven separate actions brought against defendant-appellant, Fairleigh S. Dickinson, Jr., and eleven other defendants, for alleged violations of the federal securities laws * * * . All seven actions stem from the acquisition by Sun Company, Inc. of approximately 34% of the outstanding stock of Becton, a New Jersey corporation engaged in the manufacture of health care products and medical testing and research equipment. * * *

[**Facts and Issue**] One of the principal personalities was Fairleigh S. Dickinson, Jr., the son of a founder of Becton and a major stockholder of the company. He individually held 802,138 shares of Becton stock (4.2% of the outstanding shares). In addition, Dickinson held 140,794 shares (.64%) as a co-trustee and at least 198,922 shares (1%) as a member of the Dickinson family.

Dickinson personally managed Becton for over twenty-five years. In 1974, Dickinson relinquished his management responsibilities and became Chairman of the Board. In late 1976, however, differences between the new management and Dickinson emerged. On April 20, 1977, after a bitter internal power struggle over the course of several months, the new management team prevailed, and the board of directors voted to remove Dickinson as its chairman.

The day following his removal as chairman, Dickinson met with representatives of Salomon Brothers ("Salomon"), a New York limited partnership engaged in the investment banking and brokerage business, to obtain advice on how to regain control of Becton. * * * These men discussed several possible strategies. Dickinson ultimately agreed to a plan to vote with outside directors as a means of bringing pressure on Becton's management and selling a block of the company's shares, including his own, to a corporation interested in taking over Becton. * * *

Beginning in the spring of 1977, Salomon and Eberstadt worked earnestly to interest a major corporation in acquiring a minority interest or in effecting a complete takeover of Becton. * * *

The labors of the two brokerage houses eventually bore fruit when Sun Company, Inc. ("Sun"), a Pennsylvania corporation whose principal business involves oil and gas, entered the picture. On November 28, 1977, Kenneth Lipper of Salomon approached Horace Kephart, a senior vice president of Sun in charge of the company's corporate development and diversification program, and suggested that Sun might want to consider Becton as a possible acquisition. Lipper informed Kephart that 15% of Becton's stock was available and that this initial block included 1,200,000 shares owned by Dickinson, 300–400,000 shares owned by Dunning, 400,000 shares owned by Lufkin, and 500,000 shares owned by the Chemical Fund, one of the Eberstadt-managed mutual funds. Lipper also advised Kephart that Sun would be able to acquire quickly an additional 10%–20% of Becton stock. Kephart was aware of the rift between Dickinson and Becton's management and learned of Becton's public announcement in June of its desire to remain independent. * * *

To complete the first step in effecting the acquisition, on January 14, 1978, Lipper and Zeller went to Dickinson * * * and formally presented Sun's proposal to him. Lipper's brother, Jerome Lipper, was also present. Dickinson was told that the matter must be kept confidential and that Sun was the purchaser. After the price options were outlined, Dickinson indicated that he was ready to accept the $45 price but only on the condition that the proposal would be presented to Dunning as well.

With the favorable response from Dickinson, Dunning, Lufkin, and the Funds, the time was ripe for Sun to commence the second stage of its plan for acquiring 34% of the outstanding stock of Becton [which involved open market purchases of approximately 20% of the stock of Becton.] The central question on appeal is whether the district court erred in finding that Dickinson joined a group holding beneficial ownership of approximately 13% of the outstanding shares of Becton, and in finding that the members of this group agreed to dispose of the Becton stock under their control but failed to disclose this fact pursuant to Section 13(d). A group, under Section 13(d)(3), is defined as an aggregation of persons or entities who "act * * * for the purpose of acquiring, holding or disposing of securities * * * ." The statute contains no requirement, however, that the members be committed to acquisition, holding, or disposition on any specific set of terms. Instead, the touchstone of a group within the meaning of Section 13(d) is that the members combined in furtherance of a common objective. * * *

[**Analysis**] The evidence in this case supports the district court's determination that as part of an effort to effectuate a shift in the corporate control of Becton, Dickinson and others holding beneficial ownership of approximately 13% of the company's outstanding stock, reached an understanding to act in concert in disposing of their shares, but failed to disclose this fact as required by Section 13(d). * * *

The final issue which we consider is the claim raised by class plaintiffs that Dickinson should be required to disgorge the over-the-market premium he received from the sale of his stock to Sun. * * *

Although Dickinson violated Section 13(d), there is no evidence that Dickinson had breached any statutory or common law obligation he owed Becton's stockholders. * * *

With respect to class plaintiffs' claim that Dickinson should be required to disgorge the over-the-market premium he received from the Sun purchases because of his failure to file a Section 13(d) statement, we find that plaintiffs have not demonstrated that their alleged injury was directly caused by the Section 13(d) violation or that there was any injury in fact. To recover damages for violation of the Securities Exchange Act, "the loss complained of must proceed directly and proximately from the violation claimed and not be attributable to some supervening cause." Although Dickinson profited from the sale of his Becton shares, his profit was not derived from his failure to file a Section 13(d) statement. * * * Since class plaintiffs have not demonstrated that their alleged injury was directly caused by the Section 13(d) violation, the district court properly denied their claims for damages against Dickinson.

Affirmed.

C. Management Groups

Warner Communications, Inc. v. Murdoch

United States District Court, Delaware, 1984 581 F.Supp. 1482

* * * News International alleges that, in undertaking the W-CC Transaction, Warner and its directors have formed a § 13(d)(3) "group" with Chris-Craft, BHC, and Chris-Craft's directors for the purpose of holding a "veto block" of Warner's stock to prevent a hostile takeover of Warner. News International claims that Warner and its directors have violated § 13(d) of the Exchange Act by failing to disclose the existence of this group in a 13D Statement.

News International's claim raises the threshold question of whether "management groups" are subject to the disclosure provisions of § 13(d). There is some authority to support the general proposition that management-shareholders, like any other shareholders, are subject to § 13(d)'s disclosure provisions.

This Court, however, possesses serious doubts whether § 13(d)'s disclosure obligations should be broadly construed to apply to management groups *per se*. Corporate officers and directors are required to disclose their beneficial ownership of company stock in public documents regularly filed with the SEC. It is common knowledge that officers and directors generally possess a mutual interest in maintaining their corporate positions. This fact, in and of itself, serves as notice to investors of the existence of a "management group." Management's interest in maintaining corporate control should not be turned on its head and used as a basis for a § 13(d)(3) claim any time a management group that collectively owns 5% or more of a company's stock undertakes some action, which is itself disclosed, that serves to perpetuate management's control. Management is not obligated under the federal securities laws to publicly admit to engaging in an entrenchment scheme. * * * Section 13(d) should not be permitted to be used as a vehicle to circumvent this principle.

If a management group, however, engages in a voting or pooling arrangement with third parties, the arrangement should be subject to the disclosure provisions of § 13(d). * * * Such an arrangement might significantly alter the control structure of a company and effectively enlarge the contours of the management group beyond the scope that investors would ordinarily presume. News International has alleged the existence of such an arrangement between Warner's directors, Chris-Craft, BHC, and Chris-Craft's directors. The circumstances surrounding the W-CC Transaction provide a sufficient inference of the existence of a § 13(d) group to sustain News International's claim against the present motions to dismiss. * * *

D. Beneficial Ownership through Parking

See Rule 13d-3.

SEC v. First City Financial Corp.

United States Court of Appeals, D.C. Cir., 1989 890 F.2d 1215

Silberman, Circuit Judge:

* * * The SEC charged appellants, First City Financial Corporation, Ltd. ("First City") and Marc Belzberg, with deliberately evading section 13(d) and its accompanying regulations in their attempted hostile takeover of Ashland Oil Company ("Ashland") by filing the required disclosure statement after the 10 day period. * * * We think that the district court's

findings were not clearly erroneous and that the injunction and disgorgement orders were lawful and appropriate remedies for appellants' violations. We therefore affirm.

The SEC's case is based on its contention that on March 4, 1986 Marc Belzberg, a vice-president of First City, telephoned Alan ("Ace") Greenberg, the Chief Executive Officer of Bear Stearns, a large Wall Street brokerage firm, and asked Greenberg to buy substantial shares of Ashland for First City's account. Appellants claim that Greenberg "misunderstood" Belzberg: the latter intended only to recommend that Bear Stearns buy Ashland for its own account. * * *

Under Commission Rule 13d-3(a), whenever a person possesses investment or voting power through any agreement or understanding, he enjoys beneficial ownership. Rule 13d-3 is crafted broadly enough to sweep within its purview informal, oral arrangements that confer upon a person voting or investment power. * * *

The case before the district court turned on the question whether the put and call agreement between First City and Bear Stearns was entered into on March 4, as the SEC claims, or not until March 17 as First City argues. * * *

The government's affirmative case against First City, in sum, was quite strong, and not, as appellants claim, predicated on unwarranted inferences and weak circumstantial evidence. * * *

After carefully examining appellants' lengthy briefs and the record in this case, then, we conclude the district court's finding, that appellants deliberately violated section 13(d), [by parking stock of Ashland with Bear Stearns] should be affirmed. * * *

References

Brown *et al.*, *Takeovers: A Strategic Guide*, *supra* Section 1.10.

Hazen, *Securities Regulation*, *supra* Section 1.10.

Lipton and Steinberger, *Takeovers and Freezeouts*, *supra* Section 1.10.

Loss & Seligman, *Securities Regulation*, *supra* Section 1.10.

Thompson, *Mergers, Acquisitions and Tender Offers*, *supra* Section 1.10, Chapter 8.

Chapter 19

Definition of Tender Offer

§ 19.1 Scope

This chapter focuses on the definition of the term "tender offer." Although the term is not defined in the Williams Act, Section 14(d), governing third-party tender offers, and Rule 13e-4, governing issuer tender offers, do not apply unless there is in fact a "tender offer." Section 19.2 presents an introductory problem; Section 19.3 surveys the development of the term "tender offer" in the case law; Section 19.4 examines a previously proposed SEC definition of "tender offer"; and Section 19.5 addresses an SEC previously proposed rule dealing with market sweeps, that is, the purchase by a bidder of the target's stock after termination of a tender offer. The materials in this chapter are discussed in greater detail in Thompson, *Mergers, Acquisitions and Tender Offers*, *supra* Section 1.10, Chapter 8.

§ 19.2 Introductory Problem on the Definition of Tender Offer

J.P. Morgan Chase & Co. (J.P. Morgan) and The Goldman Sachs Group, Inc. (Goldman Sachs), both publicly-held corporations, have entered into a merger agreement. Citigroup, Inc., would like to acquire J.P. Morgan but not Goldman Sachs and is contemplating making a tender offer for J.P. Morgan. Prior to formally announcing a tender offer, however, Citigroup would like to acquire a significant position in J.P. Morgan's stock.

(1) Can Citigroup purchase 10% of J.P. Morgan's shares on the open market without triggering the tender offer rules? Assume that the acquisition could be made without violating the Hart-Scott-Rodino pre-merger notification rules. *See* Chapter 9.

(2) Can Citigroup purchase 10% of J.P. Morgan's shares in privately negotiated transactions with 12 institutional shareholders of J.P. Morgan? What if Citigroup had approached 40 institutions, but only purchased from 12?

(3) What would be the answers to Questions 1 and 2, if prior to making the purchases, Citigroup made a public announcement that it was thinking of making a tender offer and that in any event it would be purchasing a substantial stock interest in J.P. Morgan?

(4) Suppose that Citigroup announces a tender offer for J.P. Morgan, but because of defensive actions taken by J.P. Morgan, Citigroup subsequently terminates the tender offer. After announcing the termination, Citigroup acquires 25% of J.P. Morgan's shares in a combination of open market purchases and privately negotiated purchases. Is this permissible?

§ 19.3 Definition of Tender Offer: The Case Law

A. Definition in Context of an Organized Solicitation

Wellman v. Dickinson

United States District Court, S.D.N.Y., 1979 475 F.Supp. 783

Robert L. CARTER, District Judge:

This litigation stems from the acquisition by Sun Company, Inc. ("Sun"), a Pennsylvania corporation whose principal business is oil and gas, of roughly 34% of the stock of Becton, Dickinson & Company ("BD"), a New Jersey corporation which manufactures health care products and medical testing and research equipment. * * *

[**Facts**] Fairleigh S. Dickinson, Jr. was the son of one of the founders of BD. He held the reins of the company from 1948 until 1973. When he became BD chief in 1948, BD was a private family enterprise with gross sales of 10 million dollars annually. When he released the reins of the company in 1973, it was a public company with gross sales of $300 million annually. Dickinson loosened his hold on the helm but did not entirely let go. In 1974, he stepped upstairs to become Chairman of the Board, while Wesley Howe became Chief Executive and Marvin Asnes became Chief Operating Officer. Differences between the management team and the chairman became evident in late 1976 when Dickinson threatened to fire Asnes. * * *

Howe and Asnes * * * canvassed the board, found enough votes to get rid of Dickinson, and on April 18 sent out notices for an April 20 meeting. * * * Howe prevailed. Dickinson was deposed as chairman and nudged out the back door with the title of Honorary Chairman.

Obviously this must have been a terrible personal blow. Dickinson was now stripped of all power within what he must still have regarded as a family enterprise. On April 21, Dickinson had a meeting at Salomon to secure advice on how to proceed. * * * He * * * [decided] to sell his stock to a company interested in a takeover of BD and engaged Salomon for the latter purpose. * * *

In early December, Kephart [a Senior Vice President of Sun] attended a meeting of Sun's senior executives and mentioned BD as a possible acquisition opportunity. * * *

On January 9, there was a meeting of [Sun's] lawyers at Salomon. The lawyers indicated that the law regarding tender offers was still murky and that the concept of a tender offer had not been precisely defined. The lawyers wanted to structure a "privately negotiated" transaction. Fogelson [of Wachtell, Lipton] and Charles Nathan of Cleary, Gottlieb felt this required that those solicited be limited in number. One felt that up to 60 solicitees was safe; the other argued for an upper limit of 40, but within those limits the lawyers felt there would be no problem. * * *

The [Sun] study team concluded that the optimum percentage level for Sun to reach was over 33%. * * *

On January 13, the [Sun] executive committee approved the "private transaction" proposal and authorized a $350 million expenditure for a 34% acquisition. * * *

On January 11, Fogelson, Nathan and Blum carefully considered the approach to be made to solicitees. When they learned that the strategy envisioned approaches to a number of individuals and institutions, they initially wanted Rosenthal to make all the solicitations. When he said that was impossible because there were too many solicitees, the lawyers decided on preparing two scripts: one for those soliciting individuals and a second one for those soliciting institutions. The instructions stressed confidentiality and it was agreed that a lawyer would be at the side of each solicitor to monitor the latter's side of the conversation. * * *

Rosenthal's two tiered price offer with a most favored nation clause was agreed upon. At his suggestion, solicitees were to be offered a top price of $45 per share with no recourse or $40 per share with the right to receive the highest price subsequently paid to any other solicitee. * * *

Blum advised Rosenthal that the price should be negotiated, not fixed, and that if another price were suggested by solicitees, it should not be rejected but referred back to Sun. He told Rosenthal that there should be no specified time to respond, but Rosenthal said time deadlines would be set within the time frame normally allowable in block trading. Rosenthal was told that the principal was not to be disclosed and that solicitees should be told to keep the matter confidential, lest a 13(d) group develop as a result of leaks.

[Kephart] * * * authorized the making of an offer to Dickinson and Dunning prior to January 16. * * * After the price options were outlined, Dickinson indicated that he was ready to accept but only if the proposal was presented to Dunning as well. Dickinson chose the $45 price. * * *

At noon on January 16, there was a meeting at Salomon of those persons who were to solicit the institutions. * * * Each solicitor was given a script * * * . Nathan explained the purpose the script served, and the solicitors were told to specify that only shares held by discretionary accounts were desired. The institutions were then called to determine whether someone would be available after 4:00 P.M. to receive a proposal.

Nilsen of Chemical Fund was called at 3:45, and was offered the proposal before the offer was made to any other institution. Nilsen accepted the $45 price for the two Eberstadt funds, * * * and for Eberstadt's discretionary accounts.

At 4:00 P.M. all the persons assigned to do the solicitation met in the trading room of Salomon. Each solicitor had a script from which to read, and a lawyer was teamed up with each caller. Shortly after 4:00 P.M. the telephoning began. Some 30 institutions were contacted. [Several] institutions accepted the offer and sold their BD shares at $45 per share. * * *

[Several institutions] rejected the offer for various reasons. * * *

The callers followed the script. There were slight variations, but each solicitee was told that a non-disclosed purchaser, sometimes identified as in the top fifty of Fortune Magazine's 500, was looking for 20% of BD stock; that no transaction would be final unless 20% of the shares were acquired; that the $45 option was a top final price and the $40 option could be accepted with protection in the event shares were later bought at a higher figure; and that the desired 20% goal was within reach or that the order was filling up fast and a hurried response was essential. Each solicitee was asked to respond within one hour or less, although some were given until the next day. Sun was identified to a few institutions, but to most the purchaser's specific identity was not revealed.

The institutions solicited had to consult with their in-house officials hurriedly. By 4:45 Kephart advised Burtis that verbal commitments for 3.1 million shares had been obtained. At 5:35 P.M. the total had reached 20%, and Kephart was given authorization to seal the bargain with these institutions that had committed their shares. Those institutions were called again, and Kephart was put on the phone. He identified himself, and after confirming that the solicitees were interested in selling at $45 a share, he accepted on behalf of Sun's subsidiary L.H.I.W. [an acronym for *Let's Hope It Works*]. The project had gone so well that Kephart was concerned that the total might far exceed 34%, and he called Sharbaugh and asked whether he was to pro rate the shares if the 34% figure was exceeded. Sharbaugh replied that there would be no problem unless the figure was over 50%. Before retiring for the night on January 16, Sun officials knew that they had obtained their objective in that there were verbal commitments for at least 30% of BD's outstanding shares. Indeed, there was some concern that they might have overreached their goal by a wide margin.

On January 17 and 18, couriers were dispatched all over the country with Sun's checks to pay for the stock, to obtain signatures or collect prepared purchase agreements, to take physical possession of the stock certificates and to have the solicitees sign powers of attorney to allow Sun to vote their proxies.

Success had been achieved, but the lawyers were now concerned that the legal risks of the transaction were not entirely past. * * * Sun wanted to have physical possession of the stock certificates it had purchased before its identity was generally revealed. Blum feared that verbal commitments were not binding. The lawyers debated whether it was wiser to adopt a wait and see approach and react to the unfolding events or to seek to halt trading in BD stock on the NYSE. Fogelson and Nathan wanted trading halted.

The latter course was approved, but Sun executives forbade disclosure of Sun's identity to NYSE officials. [The NYSE officials first refused to halt trading without such disclosure, but later capitulated.]

Sun's Williams Act filing did not take place until January 19 when its 13(d) was filed. Jerome Lipper, after discussion with his partner and Fogelson, advised Dickinson and Turner to file 13(d) statements. The statements were prepared and filed on January 19, the same day Sun's statements were filed. Dunning made a 13(d) filing on January 24. * * *

[**Standing Issue**]* * * Defendants contend that BD lacks standing because it is not an intended beneficiary of the Williams Act and that the individual and class plaintiffs lack standing because they are not parties who were confronted with a decision as to whether or not to sell their shares. * * * I hold that both the class and individual plaintiffs have standing to bring an action for Section 14(d) and 14(e) violations. * * *

[**Private of Public Offering Issue**] The next threshold inquiry concerns whether this was a privately negotiated transaction or series of such transactions or a public offering. There can be no disagreement that a purely private transaction is not subject to the pre-filing strictures under Section 14. * * *

While no differentiation between private and public has been spelled out in the Williams Act or the debates leading to its enactment, we have not been cast totally adrift. Some guidelines developed in defining a private offering exemption under Section 4[(2)] of the Securities Act of 1933, should be of aid in determining whether this transaction may properly be classified as one privately negotiated or publicly offered. * * *

In the *Ralston Purina* case, the Court held that the proper way to interpret the private offering exemption provided under Section 4(2) of the Securities Act of 1933, was in the light of the statutory purpose. "Since exempt transactions are those as to which 'there is no practical need for * * * [the bill's] application,' the applicability of §4(2) should turn on whether the particular class of persons affected need the protection of the Act. An offering to those who are shown to be able to fend for themselves is a transaction 'not involving any public offering.'" *S.E.C. v. Ralston Purina Co.*, *supra*, 346 U.S. at 125. The Court held that the statute applied to a public offering whether "few or many," and while it concluded the Commission could rightfully use a "numerical test in deciding when to investigate particular exemption claims," the Court did not favor embellishing the statute with the addition of a quantitative test as a means for defining a private offering. Finally, the Court stated that those claiming the private offering exemption properly have the burden of persuasion.

It must be conceded, of course, that *Ralston Purina* was concerned with the meaning of a private offering exemption under the 1933 Act, and we are faced with an entirely different statutory provision in the case at hand. Yet logic does make its demands. If statutory purpose gives proper definitional aid in distinguishing a public from a private offering under the 1933 Act, it would seem to follow that the purposes of the Williams Act would help define the contours of privately negotiated transactions exempted from the reach of Section 14. * * *

Here, there were face to face transactions with four persons Dickinson, Dunning, Turner and Lufkin. A total of 39 individuals and institutions were solicited with holdings involving a variety of discretionary accounts. There was no common characteristic binding the solicitees together except that they were uniformly shareholders with substantial BD holdings. Among those approached were highly knowledgeable individuals like Lufkin as well as unsophisticated investors like Smith, Willock and Drake. There were insurance companies, mutual funds, banks, a state entity, partnerships and corporations. The solicitation was nationwide. Some institutions held shares in their own account; others held shares in discretionary and non-discretionary accounts. While the Sun solicitors had been instructed by their lawyers to limit their offer to discretionary accounts, some institutions sold shares in non-discretionary accounts when faced with the demand to respond quickly to the offer lest the opportunity be lost, while others overlooked some of their shares held in discretionary accounts. * * *

Since these were undoubtedly not "privately negotiated" transactions in which there was a mutual desire to avoid premature disclosure, the "access to information standard" derived from *Ralston Purina* and its cognate cases becomes even more relevant. The cases indicate that the supposed sophistication of the solicitees will not suffice to render the transaction private if they are given no information on which to exercise their skills. The procedure employed in this case required a hurried response on the basis of little information other than the price offered. The solicitors had no authorization to engage in negotiations with those they called. Their job was to obtain quick, oral commitments. * * *

Based on the decided case law distinguishing "public" from "private" transactions, defendants have failed to carry their burden of showing that Sun's acquisition was "privately negotiated." * * *

[**Tender Offer Issue**] This is not the end but merely the beginning of the inquiry. The conclusion that this was a public solicitation does not necessarily mean that the pre-acquisition filing requirements of the Williams Act apply. We now proceed to consider that issue.

The Senate subcommittee introduced its report on the proposed Williams Act with a brief description of a typical tender offer:

> The offer normally consists of a bid by an individual or group to buy shares of a company—usually at a price above the market price. Those accepting the offer are said to tender their stock for purchase. The person making the offer obligates himself to purchase all or a specified portion of the tendered shares if certain specified conditions are met.

A second characteristic common to many tenders but not an essential element of Congress' definition is universal publicity of the offer. * * *

All of these elements bid, premium price, obligation to purchase all or a specified portion of the tendered shares if certain specified conditions are met (in this instance, if 20% of the outstanding shares are acquired) are present here. * * *

What is probably more important than the fact that this transaction has all the characteristics of a tender offer that were identified by Congress in the debates on consideration of the Williams Act is that Sun's acquisition is infected with the basic evil which Congress sought to cure by enacting the law. This purchase was designed in intent, purpose and effect to effectuate a transfer of at least a 20% controlling interest in BD to Sun in a swift, masked maneuver. * * *

The argument that the solicitees were sophisticated investors and therefore did not need Section 14 disclosure is no more convincing in this connection than it was in relation to the issue of whether this was merely a private transaction. * * *

Even if this transaction were not seen as a *conventional* tender offer, it would not necessarily fall outside the ambit of Section 14(d). As discussed above, the concept of a tender offer has never been precisely defined either in the Williams Act itself or by the Commission. Congress left to the Commission the task of providing through its experience concrete meaning to the term. The Commission has not yet created an exact definition, but in this case and in others, it suggests some seven elements as being characteristic of a tender offer: (1) active and widespread solicitation of public shareholders for the shares of an issuer; (2) solicitation made for a substantial percentage of the issuer's stock; (3) offer to purchase made at a premium over the prevailing market price; (4) terms of the offer are firm rather than negotiable; (5) offer contingent on the tender of a fixed number of shares, often subject to a fixed maximum number to be purchased; (6) offer open only a limited period of time; (7) offeree subjected to pressure to sell his stock. These characteristics were recently accepted as appropriately describing the nature of a tender offer. *See Hoover v. Fuqua Industries, Inc.*, C. 79-1062A (N.D.Ohio June 11, 1979). In that case, the Commission also had listed an 8th characteristic not included here whether the public announcements of a purchasing program concerning the target company precede or accompany rapid accumulation of large amounts of the target company's securities. The reason this last characteristic was left out undoubtedly was because publicity was not a feature of this transaction.

At any rate, it seems to me that the list of characteristics stressed by the Commission are the qualities that set a tender offer apart from open market purchases, privately negotiated transactions or other kinds of public solicitations. With the exception of publicity, all the characteristics of a tender offer, as that term is understood, are present in this transaction. The absence of one particular factor, however, is not necessarily fatal to the Commission's argument because depending upon the circumstances involved in the particular case, one or more of the above features may be more compelling and determinative than the others. * * *

Measured by the size of the holdings solicited (34%), the geographic dimensions of the effort (from New York to California and from Massachusetts to North Carolina) and by the number of solicitees approached (30 institutions and 9 individuals, not including 3 institutions that were approached earlier * * *), there was widespread solicitation of BD's shareholders.

The second characteristic, substantial percentage, does not move us very far. * * *

The third element, premium over market, is regarded as one of the typical indicia of a conventional tender offer and was certainly present here.

The fourth element, the firm terms of the offer and the absence of opportunity for negotiation, is stressed by the Commission. Defendants argue that the solicitees were not told that negotiations were barred, but the price was so attractive that none sought to negotiate. No negotiation took place and indeed if any had occurred, the whole project would have been derailed. * * *

The fifth, sixth, and seventh elements were also present. The offer was contingent on Sun's achieving a stated percentage of BD shares. * * * Time constraints were placed on each solicitee, * * * most felt that they had to reply within the time constraints imposed. The solicitors tried to exert a maximum amount of pressure on the solicitees they contacted. * * *

The one element missing is publicity. Lack of publicity, however, should be no deterrent to classifying this transaction as a tender offer * * * . Accordingly, in acquiring 34% of BD stock in the transaction at issue here, Sun made a tender offer for BD stock without a pre-acquisition filing in violation of Section 14(d) of the Williams Act. * * *

B. Open Market Purchases

SEC v. Carter Hawley Hale Stores, Inc.

United States Court of Appeals, Ninth Circuit, 1985 760 F.2d 945

Skopil, Circuit Judge:

The issue in this case arises out of an attempt by The Limited ("Limited"), an Ohio corporation, to take over Carter Hawley Hale Stores, Inc. ("CHH"), a publicly-held Los Angeles corporation. The SEC commenced the present action for injunctive relief to restrain CHH from repurchasing its own stock in an attempt to defeat the Limited takeover attempt without complying with the tender offer regulations. The district court concluded CHH's repurchase program was not a tender offer. The SEC appeals from the district court's denial of its motion for a preliminary injunction. We affirm.

[Facts] On April 4, 1984 Limited commenced a cash tender offer for 20.3 million shares of CHH common stock, representing approximately 55% of the total shares outstanding, at $30 per share. Prior to the announced offer, CHH stock was trading at approximately $23.78 per share (pre-tender offer price). Limited disclosed that if its offer succeeded, it would exchange the remaining CHH shares for a fixed amount of Limited shares in a second-step merger. * * *

While CHH initially took no public position on the offer, it filed an action to enjoin Limited's attempted takeover. CHH's motion for an injunction was denied. From April 4, 1984 until April 16, 1984 CHH's incumbent management discussed a response to Limited's offer. During that time 14 million shares, about 40% of CHH's common stock, were traded. The price of CHH stock increased to approximately $29.25 per share. CHH shares became concentrated in the hands of risk arbitrageurs.

On April 16, 1984 CHH responded to Limited's offer. CHH issued a press release announcing its opposition to the offer because it was "inadequate and not in the best interests of CHH or its shareholders." CHH also publicly announced an agreement with General Cinema Corporation ("General Cinema"). CHH sold one million shares of convertible preferred stock to General Cinema for $300 million. The preferred shares possessed a vote equivalent to 22% of voting shares outstanding. General Cinema's shares were to be voted pursuant to CHH's Board of Directors recommendations. General Cinema was also granted an option to purchase Walden Book Company, Inc., a profitable CHH subsidiary, for approximately $285 million. Finally, CHH announced a plan to repurchase up to 15 million shares of its own common stock for an amount not to exceed $500 million. If all 15 million shares were purchased, General Cinema's shares would represent 33% of CHH's outstanding voting shares.

CHH's public announcement stated the actions taken were "to defeat the attempt by Limited to gain voting control of the company and to afford shareholders who wished to sell shares at this time an opportunity to do so." CHH's actions were revealed by press release, a letter from CHH's Chairman to shareholders, and by documents filed with the Securities and Exchange Commission ("SEC") a Schedule 14D-9 and Rule 13e-1 transaction statement. These disclosures were reported by wire services, national financial newspapers, and newspapers of general circulation. Limited sought a temporary restraining order against CHH's repurchase of its shares. The application was denied. Limited withdrew its motion for a preliminary injunction.

CHH began to repurchase its shares on April 16, 1984. In a one-hour period CHH purchased approximately 244,000 shares at an average price of $25.25 per share. On April 17, 1984 CHH purchased approximately 6.5 million shares in a two-hour trading period at an average price of $25.88 per share. By April 22, 1984 CHH had purchased a total of 15 million shares. It then announced an increase in the number of shares authorized for purchase to 18.5 million.

On April 24, 1984, the same day Limited was permitted to close its offer and start purchasing, CHH terminated its repurchase program having purchased approximately 17.5 million shares, over 50% of the common shares outstanding. On April 25, 1984 Limited revised its offer increasing the offering price to $35.00 per share and eliminating the second-step merger. The market price for CHH then reached a high of $32.00 per share. On May 21, 1984 Limited withdrew its offer. The market price of CHH promptly fell to $20.62 per share, a price below the pre-tender offer price.

[**Issue**] On May 2, 1984, two and one-half weeks after the repurchase program was announced and one week after its apparent completion, the SEC filed this action for injunctive relief. The SEC alleged that CHH's repurchase program constituted a tender offer conducted in violation of section 13(e) of the Exchange Act, and Rule 13e-4. [Rule 13e-4, which is similar to the third-party tender offer rules under Section 14(d), applies to issuer tender offers. *See* Chapter 21] On May 5, 1984 a temporary restraining order was granted. CHH was temporarily enjoined from further stock repurchases. The district court denied SEC's motion for a preliminary injunction, finding the SEC failed to carry its burden of establishing "the reasonable likelihood of future violations * * * [or] * * * a 'fair chance of success on the merits' * * *." The court found CHH's repurchase program was not a tender offer because the eight-factor test proposed by the SEC and adopted in *Wellman v. Dickinson*,[**Section 19.3.A**] had not been satisfied. The court also refused to adopt, at the urging of the SEC, the alternative test of what constitutes a tender offer as enunciated in *S-G Securities, Inc. v. Fuqua Investment Co.* On May 9, 1984 the SEC filed an emergency application for an injunction pending appeal to this court. That application was denied.

[**Analysis**] The SEC urges two principal arguments on appeal: (1) the district court erred in concluding that CHH's repurchase program was not a tender offer under the eight-factor *Wellman* test, and (2) the district court erred in declining to apply the definition of a tender offer enunciated in *S-G Securities*. Resolution of these issues on appeal presents the difficult task of determining whether CHH's repurchase of shares during a third-party tender offer itself constituted a tender offer. * * *

Issuer repurchases and tender offers are governed in relevant part by section 13(e) of the Williams Act and Rules 13e-1 and 13e-4 promulgated thereunder.

The SEC argues that the district court erred in concluding that issuer repurchases, which had the intent and effect of defeating a third-party tender offer, are authorized by the tender offer rules and regulations. The legislative history of these provisions is unclear. * * *

There is also little guidance in the SEC Rules promulgated in response to the legislative grant of authority. Rule 13e-1 prohibits an issuer from repurchasing its own stock during a third-party tender offer unless it discloses certain minimal information. The language of Rule 13e-1 is prohibitory rather than permissive. It nonetheless evidences a recognition that not all issuer repurchases during a third-party tender offer are tender offers. In contrast, Rule 13e-4 recognizes that issuers, like third parties, may engage in repurchase activity amounting to a tender offer and subject to the same procedural and substantive safeguards as a third-party tender offer. The regulations do not specify when a repurchase by an issuer amounts to a tender offer governed by Rule 13e-4 rather than 13e-1. * * *

Like the district court, we resolve the question of whether CHH's repurchase program was a tender offer by considering the eight-factor test established in *Wellman.* * * *

Under the *Wellman* test, the existence of a tender offer is determined by examining the following [eight] factors * * * . [*See* Section 19.3.A]

The district court concluded CHH's repurchase program was not a tender offer under *Wellman* because only "two of the eight indicia" were present. The SEC claims the district court erred in applying *Wellman* because it gave insufficient weight to the pressure exerted on shareholders; it ignored the existence of a competitive tender offer; and it failed to consider that CHH's offer at the market price was in essence a premium because the price had already risen above pre-tender offer levels.

A. Active and Widespread Solicitation. The evidence was uncontroverted that there was "no direct solicitation of shareholders." No active and widespread solicitation occurred. Nor did the publicity surrounding CHH's repurchase program result in a solicitation. The only public announcements by CHH were those mandated by SEC or Exchange rules.

B. Solicitation for a Substantial Percentage of Issuer's Shares. * * * In this case CHH did not engage in a solicitation under the first *Wellman* factor but did accumulate a large percentage of stock as defined under the eighth *Wellman* factor. An evaluation of the second *Wellman* factor does not alter the probability of finding a tender offer.

C. Premium Over Prevailing Market Price. The SEC contends the open market purchases made by CHH at market prices were in fact made at a premium not over market price but over the pre-tender offer price. At the time of CHH's repurchases, the market price for CHH's shares (ranging from $24.00 to $26.00 per share) had risen above the pre-tender offer price (approximately $22.00 per share). Given ordinary market dynamics, the price of a target company's stock will rise following an announced tender offer. Under the SEC's definition of a premium as a price greater than the pre-tender offer price, a premium will always exist when a target company makes open market purchases in response to a tender offer even though the increase in market price is attributable to the action of the third-party offeror and not the target company. The SEC definition not only eliminates consideration of this *Wellman* factor in the context of issuer repurchases during a tender offer, but also underestimates congressional concern for preserving the free and open market. The district court did not err in concluding a premium is determined not by reference to pre-tender offer price, but rather by reference to market price. This is the definition previously urged by the SEC, Exchange Act Release No. 16385 * * * and is the definition we now apply.

D. Terms of Offer Not Firm. There is no dispute that CHH engaged in a number of transactions or purchases at many different market prices.

E. Offer Not Contingent on Tender of Fixed Minimum Number of Shares. Similarly, while CHH indicated it would purchase up to 15 million shares, CHH's purchases were not contingent on the tender of a fixed minimum number of shares.

F. Not Open For Only a Limited Time. CHH's offer to repurchase was not open for only a limited period of time but rather was open "during the pendency of the tender offer of The Limited." * * * The time within which the repurchases were made was a product of ordinary market forces, not the terms of CHH's repurchase program.

G0–H. Shareholder Pressure and Public Announcements Accompanying a Large Accumulation of Stock. With regard to the seventh *Wellman* factor, following a public announcement, CHH repurchased over the period of seven trading days more than 50% of its outstanding shares. The eighth *Wellman* factor was met.

The district court found that while many shareholders may have felt pressured or compelled to sell their shares, CHH itself did not exert on shareholders the kind of pressure the Williams Act proscribes.

While there certainly was shareholder pressure in this case, it was largely the pressure of the marketplace and not the type of untoward pressure the tender offer regulations were designed to prohibit.

CHH's purchases were made in the open market, at market and not premium prices, without fixed terms and were not contingent upon the tender of a fixed minimum number of shares. CHH's repurchase program had none of the traditional indicia of a tender offer. * * *

The SEC finally urges that even if the CHH repurchase program did not constitute a tender offer under the *Wellman* test, the district court erred in refusing to apply the test in *S-G Securities*. Under the more liberal *S-G Securities* test, a tender offer is present if there are

> (1) A publicly announced intention by the purchaser to acquire a block of the stock of the target company for purposes of acquiring control thereof, and
>
> (2) a subsequent rapid acquisition by the purchaser of large blocks of stock through open market and privately negotiated purchases.

There are a number of sound reasons for rejecting the *S-G Securities* test. The test is vague and difficult to apply. It offers little guidance to the issuer as to when his conduct will come within the ambit of Rule 13e-4 as opposed to Rule 13e-1. A determination of the existence of a tender offer under *S-G Securities* is largely subjective and made in hindsight based on an *ex post facto* evaluation of the response in the marketplace to the repurchase program. The SEC's contention that these concerns are irrelevant when the issuer's repurchases are made with the intent to defeat a third-party offer is without merit. * * *

We decline to abandon the *Wellman* test in favor of the vague standard enunciated in *S-G Securities*. The district court did not err in declining to apply the *S-G Securities* test or in finding CHH's repurchases were not a tender offer under *Wellman*.

C. Open Market Purchase after Termination of Tender Offer

Hanson Trust PLC v. SCM Corp.

United States Court of Appeals, Second Circuit, 1985 774 F.2d 47

Mansfield, Circuit Judge:

Hanson Trust PLC, HSCM Industries, Inc., and Hanson Holdings Netherlands B.V. (hereinafter sometimes referred to collectively as "Hanson") appeal from an order of the Southern District of New York, * * * granting SCM Corporation's motion for a preliminary injunction restraining them, their officers, agents, employees and any persons acting in concert with them, from acquiring any shares of SCM and from exercising any voting rights with respect to 3.1 million SCM shares acquired by them on September 11, 1985.

The injunction was granted on the ground that Hanson's September 11 acquisition of the SCM stock through five private and one open market purchases amounted to a "tender offer" for more than 5% of SCM's outstanding shares, which violated § 14(d)(1) and (6) of the Williams Act, and rules promulgated by the Securities and Exchange Commission (SEC) thereunder. We reverse.

[**Facts**] The setting is the familiar one of a fast-moving bidding contest for control of a large public corporation: first, a cash tender offer of $60 per share by Hanson, an outsider, addressed to SCM stockholders; next, a counterproposal by an "insider" group consisting of certain SCM managers and their "White Knight," Merrill Lynch Capital Markets (Merrill), for a "leveraged buyout" at a higher price ($70 per share); then an increase by Hanson of its cash offer to $72 per share, followed by a revised SCM-Merrill leveraged buyout offer of $74 per share with a "crown jewel" irrevocable lock-up option to Merrill designed to discourage Hanson from seeking control by providing that if any other party (in this case Hanson) should acquire more than one-third of SCM's outstanding shares (66% being needed under N.Y. Bus.L.§ 903(a)(2) to effectuate a merger) Merrill would have the right to buy SCM's two most profitable businesses (consumer foods and pigments) at prices characterized by some as "bargain basement." The final act in this scenario was the decision of Hanson, having been deterred by the SCM-Merrill option (colloquially described in the market as a "poison pill"), to terminate its cash tender offer and then to make private purchases, amounting to 25% of SCM's outstanding shares, leading SCM to seek and obtain the preliminary injunction from which this appeal is taken. * * *

Hanson, faced with what it considered to be a "poison pill," concluded that even if it increased its cash tender offer to $74 per share it would end up with control of a substantially depleted and damaged company. Accordingly, it announced on the Dow Jones Broad Tape at 12:38 P.M. on September 11 that it was terminating its cash tender offer. A few minutes later, Hanson issued a press release, carried on the Broad Tape, to the effect that "all SCM shares tendered will be promptly returned to the tendering shareholders."

At some time in the late forenoon or early afternoon of September 11 Hanson decided to make cash purchases of a substantial percentage of SCM stock in the open market or through privately negotiated transactions. * * * If Hanson could acquire slightly less than one-third of SCM's outstanding shares it would be able to block the $74 per share SCM-Merrill offer of a leveraged buyout. This might induce the latter to work out an agreement with Hanson, something Hanson had unsuccessfully sought on several occasions since its first cash tender offer.

Within a period of two hours on the afternoon of September 11 Hanson made five privately-negotiated cash purchases of SCM stock and one open-market purchase, acquiring 3.1 million shares or 25% of SCM's outstanding stock. * * *

Following the NYSE ticker and Broad Tape reports of the first two large anonymous transactions in SCM stock, some professional investors surmised that the buyer might be Hanson. Rothschild [Hanson's investment banker] then received telephone calls from (1) Mr. Mulhearn of Jamie & Co. offering to sell between 200,000 and 350,000 shares at $73.50 per share, (2) David Gottesman, an arbitrageur at Oppenheimer & Co. offering 89,000 shares at $73.50, and (3) Boyd Jeffries of Jeffries & Co., offering approximately 700,000 to 800,000 shares at $74.00. Pirie [of Rothschild] purchased the three blocks for Hanson at $73.50 per share. The last of Hanson's cash purchases was completed by 4:35 P.M. on September 11, 1985.

[**Issue**] In the early evening of September 11 SCM successfully applied to Judge Kram in the present lawsuit for a restraining order barring Hanson from acquiring more SCM stock for 24 hours. On September 12 and 13 the TRO was extended by consent pending the district court's decision on SCM's application for a preliminary injunction. * * *

The district court, characterizing Hanson's stock purchases as "a deliberate attempt to do an 'end run' around the requirements of the Williams Act," made no finding on the question of whether Hanson had decided to make the purchases of SCM before or after it dropped its tender offer but concluded that even if the decision had been made after it terminated its offer preliminary injunctive relief should issue. From this decision Hanson appeals. * * *

[**Analysis**] Although § 14(d)(1) clearly applies to "classic" tender offers, * * * courts soon recognized that in the case of privately negotiated transactions or solicitations for private purchases of stock many of the conditions leading to the enactment of § 14(d) for the most part do not exist. * * * [T]he solicitee in the private transaction is less likely to be pressured, confused, or ill-informed regarding the businesses and decisions at stake than solicitees who are the subjects of a public tender offer.

These differences between public and private securities transactions have led most courts to rule that private transactions or open market purchases do not qualify as a "tender offer" requiring the purchaser to meet the pre-filing strictures of § 14(d). The borderline between public solicitations and privately negotiated stock purchases is not bright and it is frequently difficult to determine whether transactions falling close to the line or in a type of "no man's land" are "tender offers" or private deals. This has led some to advocate a broader interpretation of the term "tender offer" than that followed by us in *Kennecott* and to adopt the eight-factor "test" of what is a tender offer, which was recommended by the SEC and applied by the district court in *Wellman v. Dickinson*, [Section 19.3.A] and by the Ninth Circuit in *SEC v. Carter Hawley Hale Stores, Inc.*, [Section 19.3.B] * * * Although many of the above-listed factors are relevant for purposes of determining whether a given solicitation amounts to a tender offer, the elevation of such a list to a mandatory "litmus test" appears to be both unwise and unnecessary. As even the advocates of the proposed test recognize, in any given case a solicitation may constitute a tender offer even though some of the eight factors are absent or, when many factors are present, the solicitation may nevertheless not amount to a tender offer because the missing factors outweigh those present.

We prefer to be guided by the principle followed by the Supreme Court in deciding what transactions fall within the private offering exemption provided by § 4(2) of the Securities Act of 1933, and by ourselves in *Kennecott Copper* in determining whether the Williams Act applies to private transactions. That principle is simply to look to the statutory purpose. In *S.E.C. v. Ralston Purina Co.*, 346 U.S. 119,(1953), the Court stated, "the applicability of § 4(2) should turn on whether the particular class of persons affected need the protection of the Act. An offering to those who are shown to be able to fend for themselves is a transaction "not involving any public offering." Similarly, since the purpose of § 14(d) is to protect the ill-informed solicitee, the question of whether a solicitation constitutes a "tender offer" within the meaning of § 14(d) turns on whether, viewing the transaction in the light of the totality of circumstances, there appears to be a likelihood that unless the pre-acquisition filing strictures of that statute are followed there will be a substantial risk that solicitees will lack information needed to make a carefully considered appraisal of the proposal put before them.

Applying this standard, we are persuaded on the undisputed facts that Hanson's September 11 negotiation of five private purchases and one open market purchase of SCM shares, totaling 25% of SCM's outstanding stock, did not under the circumstances constitute a "tender offer" within the meaning of the Williams Act. Putting aside for the moment the events preceding the purchases, there can be little doubt that the privately negotiated purchases would not, standing alone, qualify as a tender offer * * * .

Last, Hanson's prior disclosures of essential facts about itself and SCM in the pre-acquisition papers it filed on August 26, 1985, with the SEC pursuant to § 14(d)(1), are wholly inconsistent with the district court's characterization of Hanson's later private purchases as "a deliberate attempt to do an 'end run' around the requirements of the Williams Act." On the contrary, the record shows that Hanson had already filed with the SEC and made public substantially the same information as SCM contends that Hanson should have filed before making the cash purchases. * * *

In the present case we conclude that since the district court erred in ruling as a matter of law that SCM had demonstrated a likelihood of success on the merits, based on the theory that Hanson's post-tender offer private purchases of SCM constituted a *de facto* tender offer, it was an abuse of discretion to issue a preliminary injunction. * * *

D. When Is a Tender Offer Abandoned?

See Field v. Trump, Section 20.4.K.2.

§ 19.4 SEC's Proposed (and Withdrawn) Definition of Tender Offer

Securities Exchange Release No. 34-16385

The term "tender offer" is not defined in the Williams Act. Since the passage of the Williams Act, the Commission has been continually involved in the development of the meaning of the term but has not adopted a definition. * * *

In developing the proposed definition, the Commission considered the provisions and purposes of the Williams Act, its legislative history, applicable case law, enforcement actions, administrative proceedings and positions, legal commentary and past and present tender offer practice. The proposed definition does distinguish between tender offers and transactions involving open market or privately negotiated purchases. However, not all so-called open market or privately negotiated purchases are automatically exempted from the definition simply because they occur on or off the market, and certain of these programs would be defined as tender offers. * * *

The proposal is divided into two tiers which would operate independently of each other. That is, an offer is a tender offer if it meets the test in either of the two tiers.

Under the first tier, proposed Rule 14d-1(b)(1)(i), the term "tender offer" consists of four elements: (1) one or more offers to purchase or solicitations of offers to sell securities of a single class; (2) during any 45-day period; (3) directed to more than 10 persons; and (4) seeking the acquisition of more than 5% of the class of securities.

In order to be a tender offer within the meaning of proposed Rule 14d-1(b)(1)(i), all four elements must be present. * * *

The second tier of the definition of tender offer is set forth in proposed Rule 14d-1(b)(1)(ii). Unlike the first tier, the second tier does not contain a specific percentage test, time period or number of solicitees.

Under the second tier, one or more offers to purchase, or solicitations of offers to sell, securities of a single class would be a tender offer if three conditions are present. First, the offers to purchase or the solicitation of offers to sell must be disseminated in a widespread manner. * * *

Second, the price offered must represent a premium in excess of the greater of 5% of or $2 above the current market price of the securities being sought. The third condition of the second tier is that the offers do not provide for a meaningful opportunity to negotiate the price and terms. Thus, truly negotiated purchases of securities would not be regulated as a tender offer under the second tier. * * *

§ 19.5 SEC's Proposed Rules on Market Sweeps

Excerpts from Securities Exchange Release No. 24976

(Oct 1. 1987)

Executive Summary.The Commission is proposing rules that expressly would include within the scope of its tender offer regulations acquisitions of substantial amounts of securities and related activity undertaken during and for a limited period following the scheduled expiration of a tender offer for that class of securities. * * *

[C]ommencement of a tender offer often results in a concentration of blocks of stock among market professionals and others. Issuers, bidders and others have acquired control or substantial amounts of securities by purchasing stock from such block holders without complying with the Williams Act and rules applicable to tender offers. * * * In the absence of Commission rulemaking, the courts that have addressed the issue have been unwilling to apply the procedural and substantive protections of the Williams Act and rules to such acquisition programs.[1] * * *

Accordingly, the Commission is proposing Rules 13e-2 and 14d-11 to subject these acquisitions and related market activity during or shortly after a tender offer for the same class of securities to the statutory provisions and regulations applicable to all tender offers.

Proposed Rules 13e-2 and 14d-11(a) would require, with certain exceptions compliance with the Williams Act and rules applicable to tender offers from dissemination and publication of a tender offer until the expiration of 10 business days following its scheduled expiration (including any extensions), by any person that seeks to increase its beneficial ownership of the class of securities subject to the tender offer by 10 percent or more of the class or who solicits offers to sell those securities that would increase any person's beneficial ownership by 10 percent of the class or more. Proposed Rule 14d-11(b) would further require, with certain exceptions, that a bidder's acquisition activities with respect to 10 percent or more of the class be conducted in compliance with the Williams Act and rules thereunder from commencement of a tender offer by public announcement until dissemination and publication of the offer or the expiration of 30 business days following withdrawal of the announcement. * * *

Note

Proposed Rule 13e-2 has been adopted as Rule 13e-4(f)(6), but proposed Rule 14d-11 has not.

---

1. . *See Hanson Trust PLC v. SCM Corp.*, [**Section 19.3.C**] and *SEC v. Carter Hawley Hale Stores, Inc.*, [**Section 19.3.B**].

References

Brown *et al.*, *Takeovers: A Strategic Guide*, *supra* Section 1.10.

Hazen, *Securities Regulation*, *supra* Section 1.10.

Lipton and Steinberger, *Takeovers and Freezeouts*, *supra* Section 1.10.

Loss & Seligman, *Securities Regulation*, *supra* Section 1.10.

Thompson, *Mergers, Acquisitions and Tender Offers*, *supra* Section 1.10, Chapter 8.

Chapter 20

Third-Party Tender Offers: The SEC's Rules under Sections 14(d) and (e)

§ 20.1 Scope

This chapter contains the SEC explanations of the rules under Sections 14(d) and (e) and certain related provisions governing third-party tender offers. This chapter also contains major cases interpreting these provisions. The explanations come from excerpts from the SEC releases that promulgated the rules, including the 1999 amendments relating to Regulation of Takeovers and Security Holder Communication. Be sure to read and study the applicable statutory provision and rule, which are set out in *M&A Statutes, Rules, and Documents, supra* Section 1.1, after reading the explanations in the book.

Section 20.2 presents an introductory problem on third-party tender offers. The discussion of the rules is divided as follows: (1) an introduction to the rules (Section 20.3), (2) basic rules governing the bidder (Section 20.4), (3) basic rules governing the target (Section 20.5), (4) rules governing unlawful tender offer practices (Section 20.6), (5) rules relating to the target's shareholders (Section 20.7), (6) legal actions under Section 14(e) (Section 20.8), and (7) legal actions under Section 14(d) (Section 20.9). Section 20.10 addresses the use of a negotiated tender offer followed by a second step merger. Finally, Section 20.11 considers recommendations of the SEC's Advisory Committee on Tender Offers.

Appendices M, N, and O of *M&A Statutes, Rules, and Documents, supra* Section 1.1 contain documents relating to Oracle's tender offer for PeopleSoft and are referred to throughout this chapter. The materials in this chapter are discussed in greater detail in Thompson, *Mergers, Acquisitions and Tender Offers, supra* Section 1.10, Chapter 2.

§ 20.2 Introductory Problem on Third-Party Tender Offers

Time, Entertainment, Inc. (Time) and Warner Entertainment Inc. (Warner), both publicly-held Delaware corporations have entered into a merger agreement pursuant to which Time will acquire Warner in a reverse subsidiary merger in exchange for Time stock. Paramount Entertainment, Inc. (Paramount), would like to acquire Time but not Warner, and Paramount is considering making a tender offer for Time's shares.

(1) Paramount would like to publicly announce that it plans to make a cash tender offer for Time at $175 per share today even though it has not yet prepared all of the tender offer papers. Can Paramount make such a public announcement?

(2) What steps is Paramount required to take and permitted to take in communicating the tender offer to the Time shareholders?

(3) How long must the tender offer stay open?

(4) After Paramount commences its tender offer for Time, another corporation makes a competing tender for Time. What effect does the competing offer have on the period during which Paramount's tender offer is required to stay open? May a shareholder who has previously tendered to Paramount retrieve her shares and tender them to the other party?

(5) Paramount's tender offer is for 75% of Time's outstanding common shares. What result if 90% of the Time shares are tendered to Paramount, and it is prepared to purchase only 75%?

(6) Paramount plans to follow its tender offer with a second-step freezeout merger of Time in which the Time shareholders would receive a new class of convertible preferred stock that would have, in the opinion of Investment Bankers, Inc., a value per share of Time equal to the $175 price paid in the tender offer. Can Paramount include in its tender offer documents a description of the preferred?

(7) Prior to closing the tender offer at $175 per share, Paramount is approached by Insurance Company, Inc., (IC) with an offer by IC to sell to Paramount all of IC's Time shares (*i.e.*, 4% of Time's outstanding shares) for $170 per share in cash. Can Paramount make this purchase? What if Paramount terminates its tender offer, purchases the shares from IC, and then makes a second tender offer?

(8) The President of Time (Prez) owns 8% of the Time shares, and Prez has indicated to Paramount that he might be inclined to support a tender offer by Paramount provided that a deal can be structured to give Prez tax-free treatment. Paramount has not yet launched its tender offer. Is there a way to give Prez tax-free treatment and to have Paramount complete its cash tender offer with the second-step freezeout merger. What are the risks under the tender offer rules with such a structure? Also, what if Paramount is interested in retaining Prez as the President of Time after the transaction at a substantial salary increase? What steps should Paramount take in structuring Prez's compensation arrangement?

(9) Paramount launches its tender offer at $175 per share. What are the obligations, if any, of the Time board with respect to the tender offer?

§ 20.3 Introduction to the Rules

Excerpt from Securities Exchange Act Release No. 34-16384

(November 1979)

The rules regulating the person making the tender offer (the "bidder") may be divided into four categories: filing requirements; dissemination provisions; disclosure requirements; and substantive provisions. Before discussing these categories, it should be noted that the operation of these rules is triggered by the date of commencement of the tender offer. * * *

The filing of Schedule 14D-1 [now Schedule TO] with the Commission is governed by Rule 14d-3. In addition, a bidder is required to make hand delivery of the initial filing and any amendments to the company whose securities are being sought (the "subject company"), and under certain conditions to give telephonic notice of certain information and to mail copies to national securities exchanges and to the NASD. A competing bidder is also required to hand deliver the initial filing to any previous bidder whose tender offer for the same class of securities has not yet expired.

Rule 14d-4 establishes three alternative methods of disseminating a cash tender offer to security holders: long-form publication; summary publication; and the use of shareholder lists and security position listings ("stockholder lists"). The dissemination process includes both the initial and subsequent soliciting materials published or sent or given to security holders during the tender offer. While tender offers may be disseminated by methods other than those specified in Rule 14d-4, summary publication and the use of stockholder lists and security position listings pursuant to Rule 14d-5 must comply with Rules 14d-4(a)(2) and (a)(3), respectively. The dissemination of an exchange tender offer is governed by the provisions of the Securities Act if the transaction is subject to the registration requirements of that Act.

Rule 14d-5 allows a bidder to disseminate its tender offer materials in a manner substantially similar to that permitted under present Rule 14a-7, which relates to proxy contests. The tender offer materials would be disseminated to security holders pursuant to the stockholder lists. The subject company would determine whether to retain the stockholder lists, in which case the subject company would distribute the bidder's tender offer materials, or furnish the stockholder lists to the bidder, in which case the bidder would distribute them.

While the dissemination provisions of Rule 14d-4 apply only to tender offers in which the consideration consists solely of cash and/or securities exempt from registration under Section 3 of the Securities Act and are not mandatory, the disclosure requirements of Rule 14d-6 apply to any tender offer subject to Section 14(d). The specific disclosure requirements generally depend on whether the tender offer is published or sent or given to security holders by means of summary publication pursuant to Rule 14d-4(a)(2) or the use of stockholder lists and security position listings pursuant to Rule 14d-5. The summary advertisement which is required to be published in connection with either of these means of dissemination must contain the disclosure called for by Rule 14d-6(e)(2). Tender offers which are disseminated other than by such means, such as cash tender offers which are published by means of long-form publication, registered exchange offers or unconventional tender offers, are subject to the disclosure requirements prescribed by Rule 14d-6(e)(1).

With respect to a tender offer in which the consideration consists solely of cash and/or securities exempt from registration under Section 3 of the Securities Act, Rules 14d-4, 14d-5 and 14d-6 are designed to operate in concert. This interrelationship may be demonstrated by the following brief description of the chronological operation of a cash tender offer by the use of stockholder lists: (1) the bidder requests the use of the stockholder lists pursuant to Rule 14d-5(a); (2) on or prior to the date of the request the bidder makes adequate publication of either a summary advertisement or long-form publication commencing the tender offer under Rule 14d-2; (3) the subject company makes its election either to disseminate the tender offer materials or to furnish the stockholder lists; (4) if the subject company conducts the dissemination, Rule 14d-5(b) governs the subject company's conduct and Rule 14d-5(f)(3) applies to the bidder; (5) if the subject company furnishes the stockholder lists to the bidder, Rule 14d-5(c) applies to the subject company and Rule 14d-5(f)(4) prescribes the method by which the bidder disseminates its tender offer materials; (6) under either option, the bidder's tender offer materials must include the disclosure required by Rule 14d-6(e)(1); and (7) a similar sequence will be followed with respect to material changes in the bidder's tender offer materials.

Substantive provisions concerning tender offer subject to Section 14(d) of the Exchange Act are set forth in Rules 14e-1, 14d-7, and 14d-8. Rule 14e-1 regulates the minimum length of a tender offer. Any tender offer (other than certain issuer tender offers) is required to remain open for a minimum of twenty business days from the date of commencement and for ten business days from the date of any notice of increase in the offered consideration or the dealer's soliciting fee. These time periods are designed to operate concurrently. Thus, if a tender offer commences on business day 1 and the bidder increases the consideration on business day 8, the ten business day period will expire during the minimum twenty business day period. * * *

Rule 14e-1(c) requires payment for or the return of the deposited securities to security holders promptly after the termination or withdrawal of the tender offer.

The subject company is regulated by three rules. If a bidder has determined to use the subject company's stockholder list, the subject company must comply with Rule 14d-5. Rule 14e-2 requires the subject company to disclose to security holders its position with respect to the tender offer and the reasons therefore within ten business days of the date the tender offer is first published or sent or given to security holders. This communication is, under Rule 14d-9(f), a solicitation/recommendation requiring compliance with Rule 14d-9. [*See* Section 20.5] Thus, the statement furnished under Rule 14e-2 or any other solicitation or recommendation to security holders with respect to the tender offer would under Rule 14d-9 require the filing of Schedule 14D-9 with the Commission and transmittal thereof to certain designated persons as soon as practicable on the date the solicitation/recommendation is first published or sent or given to security holders. The disclosure in the solicitation-recommendation disseminated to security holders by the subject company would be required to contain certain information, based on the provisions of Schedule 14D-9. Material changes to that Schedule would be filed, delivered and disseminated in a similar manner. * * *

§ 20.4 Basic Rules Governing the Bidder

A. Rule 14-d Scope of and Definitions Applicable to Regulations 14D and 14E

Excerpt from Securities Exchange Act Release No. 34-16384 Rule 14d-1
(November 1979)

Rule 14d-1: Scope of and Definitions Applicable to Regulations 14D and 14E. * * * Section 14(d)(1) of the Exchange Act imposes certain requirements upon a bidder who makes a tender offer for a class of equity securities described in that section if upon consummation of such tender offer the bidder would be the beneficial owner of more than five percent of such class. Rule 14d-1(a) limits the application of Regulation 14D to tender offers which are subject to Section 14(d)(1). Thus, tender offers by persons for securities of which they are the issuer are not subject to Regulation 14D. [*See* Chapter 21 for a discussion of issuer tender offers.]

Rule 14d-1(b) establishes a definitional framework in order to clarify terms frequently used in Regulations 14D * * * and to provide guidance concerning the operation of certain terms. Terms defined in the Exchange Act and in Rule 12b-2 promulgated thereunder have the same meaning in the Regulations unless the context otherwise requires. In addition, eight specific terms are defined. * * *

The term "beneficial owner" has * * * been revised by bifurcating the meaning of the term depending on the context in which it is employed. For purposes of filing a Schedule [TO] or a Schedule 14D-9 as well as stating the number of shares beneficially owned in response to Item 6 of Schedule [TO], the term "beneficial owner" has the same meaning as that set forth in Rule 13d-3. Thus, both voting power and investment power with respect to a specified security, or the right to acquire either of those powers, are relevant. However, for other purposes, which relate principally to dissemination of the tender offer, only investment power is operative. * * *

B. Rules 14d-2 and 14e-8: SEC'S Final M&A Release Adopts New Rules Regarding Commencement and Exchange Offers

1. Final M&A Release Rules Regarding "Commencement," Communications, and Filing Requirements

Final M&A Release, Regulation of Takeovers and Security Holder Communication, Commencement, Communications, and Filing Requirements, Securities Act Release No. 33-7760

(October 22, 1999)

Currently, the tender offer rules restrict a third-party bidder's communications regarding a proposed tender offer. The restrictions on communications stem from the concept of "commencement," the five business day rule for cash tender offers,[1] and the requirement that a registration statement be filed promptly for registered exchange offers. A target's communications regarding a tender offer are similarly restricted. To harmonize the treatment of communications regarding business combination transactions under the three regulatory schemes, and to promote the dissemination of information to all security holders on a more timely basis, we are modifying the definition of "commencement" and eliminating the five business day rule and the requirement to promptly file a registration statement after announcing a registered exchange offer. [Revised Rule 14d-2(c)]

In place of these rules, we are adopting a filing requirement for all written communications that relate to a tender offer beginning with and including the first public announcement of the transaction.[2] As with communications subject to the Securities Act and the proxy rules, written communications must be filed on the date that the communication is made.[3] In addition, written communications must contain a legend advising security holders to read the full tender offer or recommendation statement when it becomes available.

Under the revised rules, "commencement" is when the bidder first publishes, sends or gives security holders the means to tender securities in the offer.[4] We believe that security holders need the information required by the tender offer rules when they are either asked or able to tender their securities in an offer.[5]

---

1. Currently, an offer is deemed to "commence" on public announcement of the following limited information: the identity of the bidder, the identity of the subject company, the amount and class of securities sought and the price or range of prices offered, unless a tender offer statement is filed within five business days of the announcement and disseminated to security holders or the bidder makes a subsequent public announcement withdrawing the offer. *See* Rule 14d-2(b) and (c). We refer to this as the "five business day rule."

2. The public announcement also triggers the Rule 14e-5 restrictions on purchasing outside the tender offer.

3. Revised Rule 14d-2(b)(2). These communications will be filed under cover of Schedule TO or 14D-9, as appropriate. * * *

4. Generally, this will occur if the bidder provides security holders with a transmittal form to use to tender securities or if the bidder publishes an advertisement advising security holders how to tender in the offer or to contact the bidder for more information on how to tender securities in the offer. * * *

5. Although we are changing how a tender offer is commenced for purposes of the tender offer rules, we are not defining the term "tender offer" or changing our position on what activities may be deemed to constitute a tender offer. The tender offer rules still may apply to activities that function as unconventional tender offers. We maintain our position that the term "tender offer" should be interpreted flexibly in accordance with the intended purposes of Sections 14(d) and 14(e). A determination of whether a particular transaction or series of transactions constitutes a tender offer

To minimize the potential for dissemination of false offers into the marketplace in the absence of the five business day rule, we are adopting new Rule 14e-8. As proposed, this rule prohibits bidders from announcing an offer: without an intent to commence the offer within a reasonable time and complete the offer; with the intent to manipulate the price of the bidder or the target's securities; or without a reasonable belief that the person will have the means to purchase the securities sought. We believe that a specific rule prohibiting such conduct is appropriate. This antifraud rule is intended as a means to prevent fraudulent and misleading communications regarding proposed offers under the new communications scheme, in addition to the existing antifraud provisions. * * *

[W]e believe that the availability of more information on a timely basis will better assist security holders in making well informed individual investment decisions when confronted with news of a pending or proposed business combination. Accordingly, we are adopting the changes to the tender offer communications provisions substantially as proposed.

In reaching this conclusion, we note that communications regarding issuer tender offers are not similarly restrained.[6] * * *

We believe that courts would hold that any state law that conflicted with the new rule by attempting to establish a different commencement date or otherwise frustrating operation of the rule would be preempted. * * *

We encourage bidders to commence their offers as soon as they are able to do so, since security holders and other market participants will benefit from the complete information in the mandated tender offer materials. * * *

Targets need not file a formal recommendation statement until after the offer is formally commenced and a recommendation is made. The target remains obligated, however, to take a position with respect to the offer no later than 10 business days after the offer commences under Rule 14d-2(a). [*See* Section 20.4] If the target makes a recommendation after commencement, but before the tenth business day, then it must file a recommendation/solicitation statement on Schedule 14D-9 on or before the time the recommendation is first made.

These rules apply to issuer and third-party tender offers alike. In addition, the new rules make no distinction based on the form of consideration offered to security holders (*e.g.*, cash or stock). * * *

2. SEC's Final M&A Release Rules Regarding Exchange Offers

Final M&A Release, Regulations of Takeovers and Security Holder Communication, Exchange Offers May Commence on Filing, Securities Act Release No. 33-7760

(October 22, 1999)

[**Early Commencement**] We are adopting the early commencement provision substantially as proposed, but extended to cover issuer exchange offers. [*See* Rule 14d-2

will, of course, depend on the particular facts and circumstances and is not limited to "conventional" tender offers. *See* Release No. 34-15548 (Feb. 5, 1979) [*See* Chapter 19].

6. Issuer tender offers are subject to Rule 13e-4, which does not contain a comparable provision to the five business day rule or a requirement to file a registration statement promptly after announcing limited information about a registered exchange offer. [*See* Chapter 21]

and Rule 14d-4(b)] Currently, registered exchange offers may not commence until the related registration statement becomes effective. As we noted in the Proposing Release, this results in cash and stock tender offers being treated differently. Cash tender offers have a distinct timing advantage over stock tender offers because cash offers can commence as soon as a tender offer statement is filed and disseminated. This change should minimize this regulatory disparity by permitting stock tender offers to commence as early as the date the related registration statement is first filed. * * *

We recognized in the Proposing Release that early commencement alone may not be sufficient to level the playing field between cash and stock tender offers because bidders would not be able to purchase shares tendered in the offer until after the related registration statement is effective. Accordingly, cash offers could close earlier than stock tender offers due to possible staff review and comment on the registration statement. * * *

We are * * * committed to expediting staff review of exchange offers so that they may compete more effectively with cash tender offers.

[T]here is no reason to exclude issuer exchange offers from early commencement, and therefore, we have decided to treat third-party and issuer exchange offers alike under the new rule. * * *

Under the new rules,[7] to commence an exchange offer early (before effectiveness of a registration statement), a bidder must file a registration statement relating to the securities offered and include in the preliminary prospectus all information, including pricing information, necessary for investors to make an informed investment decision. Information may not be omitted under Rule 430 or Rule 430A under the Securities Act. Bidders also must disseminate the prospectus and related letter of transmittal to all security holders and file a tender offer statement with us before the exchange offer can commence.[8] Early commencement is at the option of the bidder. Exchange offers can commence as early as the filing of a registration statement, or on a later date selected by the bidder up to the date of effectiveness.[9] If a bidder does not commence its exchange offer before effectiveness of the related registration statement, then the exchange offer would need to commence on or shortly after effectiveness, as is the case today.

As proposed, we are adopting new Rule 162 to permit the tender of securities into an exchange offer before a registration statement is effective. New Rule 162(a) exempts the tender of securities from Section 5(a) of the Securities Act.[10] Security holders may withdraw tendered securities until they are purchased, and bidders may not purchase the tendered securities until the registration statement is declared effective, as is currently the case. * * *

---

7. New Rule 162 and revised Rules 13e-4(e)(2) and 14d-4(b).

8. Because tender offer statements generally incorporate by reference a substantial amount of the required information from the related registration statement, the actual filing of a tender offer statement would serve primarily as notice to us and the markets that the exchange offer commenced. Of course, any prospectus furnished to security holders before the registration statement is effective must include the red herring legend required by Item 501(b)(10) of Regulation S-K.

9. Regulation M [17 CFR 242.100 through 242.105] prohibits purchases of the bidder's securities during an exchange offer's restricted period, beginning when the bidder commences its offer. The restrictions under Rule 10b-13 (new Rule 14e-5) start when the bidder makes its first public announcement.

10. This exemption is necessary to prevent the tendering of securities into an offer from being viewed as a "sale" without an effective registration statement. We are using our exemptive authority under Section 28 of the Securities Act to adopt this new rule.

[T]he new rule provides bidders with greater flexibility in choosing the form of consideration to offer in a business combination transaction and should serve to facilitate the growth of our capital markets.

[**Dissemination of a Supplement and Extension of the Offer**] Under the early commencement provision adopted, bidders are required to disseminate a prospectus to all security holders. [*See* Rule 14d-4(b)] If a bidder wants to commence its exchange offer early, it must disseminate a preliminary prospectus to all security holders as discussed above. The new rules also provide that bidders sending a preliminary prospectus must disseminate a supplement to security holders if there are any material changes, whether as a result of staff review, or due to any other material changes in the information previously disclosed. Exchange offers must remain open for a specified minimum period of time after a supplement is sent to security holders containing the new information, depending on the significance of the change. This is to permit security holders to react to the information by tendering securities or by withdrawing securities already tendered.

Since the tender offer rules do not currently establish specific minimum time periods necessary for the disclosure and dissemination of material changes, other than those relating to changes in price or the amount of securities sought,[11] we are establishing well-defined periods necessary for the dissemination of a prospectus supplement that contains material changes under early commencement. The mandated periods we adopt today are consistent with our current rules and interpretive positions in this area. Therefore, we are revising Rule 14d-4[(d)(2)] [*see* Section 20.4.D] to specify the minimum time periods necessary for the dissemination of changes to preliminary prospectuses that are used to commence an exchange offer early. As a result, exchange offers that commence early must remain open for at least:

- five business days for a prospectus supplement containing a material change other than price or share levels;
- ten business days for a prospectus supplement containing a change in price, the number of shares sought, the dealer's soliciting fee, or other similarly significant change;
- ten business days for a prospectus supplement included as part of a post-effective amendment; and
- 20 business days for a revised prospectus when the initial prospectus was materially deficient; for example, failing to comply with the going-private rules or filing a "shell" document solely to trigger commencement and staff review. * * *

We agree that the informational purpose of the prospectus may best be served by requiring bidders to deliver to security holders prospectus supplements containing material changes rather than redeliver a final prospectus repeating substantial amounts of information that was previously delivered.[12] The use of prospectus supplements should adequately inform security holders of the information they need to make an informed investment decision.

Accordingly, we are using our exemptive authority to exempt exchange offers that commence early from the final prospectus delivery requirement.[13] In doing so, we are not

11. Rule 14e-1(b). A tender offer must remain open for ten business days after a notice of an increase or decrease in the percentage of the class of securities being sought, the consideration offered, or the dealer's soliciting fee.

12. Any supplements sent to security holders should present the informational changes in a clear, concise and understandable manner. *See* Rule 421 of Regulation C. * * *

13. *See* new Rule 162(b), which provides an exemption from Section 5(b)(2) of the Securities Act [15 U.S.C. 77e(b)(2)]. This rule does not provide an exemption for exchange offers that commence

changing the final prospectus delivery requirement in Exchange Act Rule 15c2-8(d).[14] * * * Although we are eliminating the requirement to deliver a final prospectus, bidders would still need to file a final prospectus.

3. Discussion of Regulatory Treatment of Cash and Stock Tender Offers in the SEC's Current Issues Outline

SEC Division of Corporation Finance, Current Issues and Rulemaking Projects

(November 14, 2000)

Balance the Regulatory Treatment of Cash and Stock Tender Offers. Registered stock tender offers (exchange offers) [were previously] subject to regulatory delays not imposed on cash tender offers. A cash tender offer may commence as soon as a tender offer schedule is filed and the information disseminated to security holders, while an exchange offer [previously could] not commence before a registration statement is filed and becomes effective. The delay associated with exchange offers may cause some bidders to favor cash over stock as consideration in a business combination transaction. In addition, the different regulatory treatment can give a bidder offering cash a timing advantage over a competing bidder offering stock. The amendments adopted balance the regulatory treatment of cash and stock tender offers to the extent practicable.

Under the new rules third-party or issuer exchange offers may commence as early as the filing of a registration statement, or on a later date selected by the bidder, before effectiveness of the registration statement. As a result, a bidder offering securities will not need to wait until effectiveness to commence an exchange offer. Early commencement is not mandatory, but rather at the election of the bidder. A bidder may file a registration statement, wait for staff comments, if any, and then decide to commence its offer. Any securities tendered in the offer could not be purchased until after the registration statement becomes effective, the minimum 20 business day tender offer period has expired, and all material changes are disseminated to security holders with adequate time remaining in the offer to review and act upon the information. A bidder need not deliver a final prospectus to security holders. Security holders may withdraw tendered securities at any time before they are purchased by the bidder.

C. Rule 14d-3: Filing and Transmission of Tender Offer Statement

Excerpt from Securities Exchange Act Release No. 34-16384 Rule 14d-3

(November 1979)

Rule 14d-3(a) requires the bidder to file a Schedule [TO] with the Commission as soon as practicable on the commencement date. This rule also requires the bidder to hand

---

on the date of effectiveness or later, for which a final prospectus must be delivered to security holders. * * *

14. 17 CFR 240.15c2-8(d). This rule requires all brokers or dealers that participate in a distribution of securities registered under the Securities Act to take reasonable steps to comply promptly with the written request of any person for a copy of the final prospectus. The broker or dealer must comply with this request until the expiration of the applicable 40-day or 90-day period under Section 4(3) of the Act. *See* Rule 174.

deliver a copy of the Schedule to the subject company and to any previous bidder which has filed a Schedule [TO] with respect to a tender offer for the same class of securities which has not yet terminated. * * * [E]ach national securities exchange where the class of the subject company's securities being sought in the tender offer is registered and listed for trading and, if the class of securities being sought in the tender offer is quoted in NASDAQ, the NASD, will receive telephonic notice of certain information and a copy of the schedule through the mail. * * *

Rule 14d-3(b) requires material changes in the information set forth in the bidder's Schedule [TO] to be filed as an amendment. In addition, such amendments must be hand delivered to the subject company and sent to any exchange and/or the NASD as required by Rule 14d-3(a). * * *

Rule 14d-3(b) requires additional tender offer material and amendments to the Schedule [TO] disclosing a material change to be filed and sent promptly but not later than the date such material or such change is first published or sent or given to security holders. Rule 14d-3(c) creates a limited exception to this requirement by providing that additional tender offer material or an amendment to Schedule [TO] which only discloses the number of shares deposited to a certain date and/or announces the extension of the tender offer may be filed and sent promptly after the date such material is first published or sent or given to security holders.

D. Rule 14d-4: Dissemination of Certain Tender Offers

Excerpt from Securities Exchange Act Release No. 34-16384 Rule 14d-4

(November 1979)

[T]he disclosure process envisioned by the Williams Act is not limited to the items of information which must be disclosed. It also includes the dissemination of material information to shareholders so that security holders have the opportunity to receive, consider and evaluate the disclosure required by Rule 14d-6. * * *

Rule 14d-4 provides * * * the prompt and widespread dissemination of * * * tender offers by establishing standards whereby information disseminated in compliance with its provisions would be deemed "published or sent or given to security holders" for purposes of Section 14(d)(1) of the Exchange Act. This is accomplished by providing three alternative definitions of what constitutes dissemination: long-form publication; summary publication and use of stockholder lists and security position listings. [Rule 14d-4(a)] A bidder is able to use more than one method so long as there is full compliance with each method used. Moreover, Rule 14d-4 is not mandatory and a tender offer in which the consideration consists of cash and/or securities exempt from registration under Section 3 of the Securities Act may be disseminated by other methods. * * *

Long-form publication * * * requires adequate publication of the tender offer in a newspaper or newspapers.

Summary publication under Rule 14d-4(a)(2) requires the adequate publication of a summary advertisement of the tender offer in a newspaper or newspapers. Additionally, this method requires a bidder to mail or otherwise furnish with reasonable promptness its tender offer materials to any security holder upon request. * * *

Rule 14d-4(a)(3) relates to the use of stockholder lists and security position listings. * * * Rule 14d-4(a)(3) has been revised in several respects. * * * [E]ither long-form or summary publication may be used with stockholder lists and security position listings.

[S]uch publication is required on or prior to the date of the request to the subject company, rather than on the date of mailing and transmittal of tender offer materials. * * *

Pursuant to Rule 14d-4[(d)], material changes in the information published or sent or given to security holders must be disseminated in a manner reasonably designed to inform security holders. * * * [The provisions of Rule 14d-4 relating to exchange offers are discussed in Section 20.4.B.2]

E. Rule 14d-5: Dissemination of Certain Tender Offers by the Use of Stockholder Lists and Security Position Listings

1. In General

Excerpt from Securities Exchange Act Release No. 14-16384 Rule 14d-5

(November 1979)

[For a discussion of the amendments made to Rule 14d-5 in the Final M&A Release regarding exchange offers *see* Section 20.4.B.2]

Rule 14d-5 gives bidders a Federal right to have their tender offer materials disseminated by means of the stockholder lists of the subject company and security position listings of clearing agencies. As described more fully below, the subject company is able to elect whether to retain the stockholder lists, in which case the subject company will mail and transmit the bidder's tender offer materials, or to furnish the stockholder lists to the bidder, in which case the bidder will mail and transmit the tender offer materials. The option feature of Rule 14d-5 is patterned after Rule 14a-7. * * * [T]he rights created by Rule 14d-5 are intended to be in addition to any rights the bidder may have to stockholder lists under state law. * * *

In order to assure the timely receipt of tender offer materials by security holders pursuant to the rule, the rule specifies the time periods for compliance as well as the principal obligations of both the bidder and the subject company. * * *

2. SEC's Final M&A Release Amendments to Rule 14d-5, Dissemination of Tender Offers by Stockholder Lists

Final M&A Release, Regulation of Takeovers and Security Holder Communication, Tender Offer and Proxy Rules Relating to the Delivery of a Security Holder List and Security Position Listing Harmonized, Securities Act Release No. 33-7760

(October 22, 1999)

We are adopting as proposed revisions to Rule 14d-5 to conform the tender offer dissemination requirements with the proxy dissemination requirements in Rule 14a-7. The revised rule expands the scope of information included in a security holder list under the tender offer rules so that it is consistent with the security holder list requirements in the proxy rules. Under the revised rule, a target company that elects to provide a bidder with a security holder list instead of mailing the bidder's materials to security holders must disclose the most recent list of names, addresses and security positions of non-objecting beneficial owners (as well as record holders) it has in its possession, or subsequently obtains. The security holder list must be in the format requested by the bidder if it can be provided without undue burden or expense. The purpose of the amendment to the rule is to give bidders the same ability as target companies to communicate directly with non-objecting beneficial owners of securities. * * *

F. Rule 14d-6: Disclosure Requirements with Respect to Tender Offers (Review Schedule TO)

1. In General

Excerpt from Securities Exchange Act Release No. 34-16384 Rule 14d-6
(November 1979)

Rule 14d-6 establishes disclosure requirements for any tender offer which is subject to Section 14(d)(1) of the Exchange Act. * * * The disclosure requirements continue to depend on the method by which the tender offer is disseminated to security holders but the distinction between the requirements which are applicable to tender offer materials disseminated on the date of commencement and to additional tender offer materials disseminated after the date of commencement has been clarified.

Rule 14d-6(a) provides the disclosure requirements which are applicable to tender offer materials published or sent or given to security holders on the date of commencement. When a bidder uses a method under Rule 14d-4 to disseminate a tender offer on the date of commencement, either sub-paragraphs (a)(1), (a)(2) or (a)(3) of Rule 14d-6 will determine what information specified in paragraph (e) will be required to be disclosed. * * *

Rules 14d-6(a) and (b) specify the information required in additional tender offer materials that are published or sent or given to security holders subsequent to the date of commencement. * * *

Rule 14d-6(c) establishes an express obligation to disclose promptly material changes in the information published or sent or given to security holders. This obligation comports with current practice and avoids any possible ambiguity, thus ensuring full disclosure of material information during the course of the tender offer.

Rule 14d-6(d) specifies the items of information to be included pursuant to Rules 14d-6(a) and (b). Rule 14d-6(d)(1) is applicable to tender offers which are published or sent or given to security holders other than by means of a summary advertisement. * * *

Rule 14d-6(d)(2) specifies the limited disclosure to be made in a summary advertisement published, sent or given on the date of commencement pursuant to Rule 14d-6(a)(2) or (3). * * *

2. SEC's Final M&A Release Amendments to Disclosure Requirements in Rule 14d-6

Final M&A Release, Regulation of Takeovers and Security Holder Communications, Dissemination Requirements Securities Act Release No. 33-7760
(October 22, 1999)

* * * [L]ong form publication is rarely used by bidders due to the cost associated with publishing extensive information about the offer in a newspaper. We proposed to eliminate long form publication.

[C]ommenters noted that, in the future, long form publication may become a viable means of disseminating an offer using the Internet or another electronic delivery system. At this time, we do not believe that technology has developed to the point where bidders can rely solely on electronic media to disseminate information about a tender offer to security holders. In particular, posting the information on a web site alone would not be adequate dissemination. Nevertheless, in response to commenters' requests that we retain long form publication as a means of commencement, we have decided not to eliminate it.

We solicited comment on whether the rules should continue to permit an offer to be commenced and disseminated by summary advertisement alone. [Rule 14d-6(a)(2)] Currently, bidders that rely on the summary advertisement method to disseminate an offer tend also to mail their offering documents to security holders using a security holder list under Rule 14d-5. We asked whether bidders should always be required to use security holder lists when disseminating an offer. * * * [W]e are not changing this aspect of the summary advertisement rule.[15] However, in keeping with the expansion of permissible communications, we are eliminating, as proposed, the current restriction on the information that may be included in a summary advertisement.[16]

Currently, bidders must hand deliver a copy of their tender offer statement and any additional tender offer materials to the target company as well as any other bidder that has made an offer for the same class of securities. * * * [W]e are adopting a requirement that the bidder deliver to the target and any other bidder the first written communication relating to the transaction that is filed, or required to be filed, with the Commission. This material must be delivered on the date of the communication.[Rule 14-2(b)(2)] * * *

G. Rule 14e-1: Unlawful Tender Practices

1. Initial 20-Day Period

Excerpt from Securities Exchange Act Release No. 34-16384

(November 1979)

Rule 14e-1: Unlawful Tender Offer Practices. With one exception Rule 14e-1(a) requires any tender offer to remain open for a minimum of twenty business days from the date it is first published or sent or given to security holders. * * *

There are several purposes to be served by Rule 14e-1(a). Tender offers which do not stay open for a reasonable length of time increase the likelihood of hasty, ill-considered decision making on the basis of inadequate or incomplete information as well as the possibility for fraudulent, deceptive or manipulative acts or practices by a bidder and others. * * *

For similar reasons, the Commission is adopting Rule 14e-1(b) which requires that any tender offer must remain open for at least ten business days after the date of the notice of an increase in either the offered consideration or the dealer's soliciting fee. The Commission believes that this provision will facilitate communication during tender offers and provide a realistic time frame for security holders to evaluate certain increases before making an investment decision. * * *

Rule 14e-1(c) has been revised to require a person making a tender offer to pay the consideration offered or to return the securities deposited by or on behalf of security holders promptly after the termination or withdrawal of the tender offer. * * *

---

15. Similarly, we are retaining the current requirement that bidders using stockholder lists also publish summary advertisements.

16. We are amending Rule 14d-6(a)(2) to delete the language limiting the information that can appear in a summary advertisement. We are retaining the prohibition against including a transmittal form with the summary advertisement. A summary advertisement may (and must, if it is designed to commence the offer) include the means to tender, *e.g.*, a telephone number to call to obtain the complete tender offer materials, including the transmittal form.

Finally, Rule 14e-1(d) has been revised to require notice of an extension of the tender offer to be issued through a press release or other public announcement no later than the earlier of: (i) 9:00 a.m. Eastern time, on the next business day after the scheduled expiration date of the offer; or (ii) if the class of securities which is the subject of the tender offer is registered on one or more national securities exchanges, the first opening of any one of such exchanges on the next business day after the scheduled expiration date of the offer. The notice is required to include a statement of the approximate number of securities deposited up to the date of such notice. * * *

2. Extensions of the Period

Excerpt from Securities Exchange Act Release No. 34-23421

(Aug. 13, 1986)

The ten business day time period will only be triggered as a result of changes in the offer effected by the bidder. Thus, if the target company increases the number of shares outstanding and the bidder does nothing, the ten business day time period will not be triggered despite the fact that the percentage of securities sought by the bidder has decreased. Only if the bidder's own actions cause a decrease or increase in the consideration offered or percentage of securities sought will the ten business day time period be triggered. * * *

H. Rule 14d-7: Additional Withdrawal Rights

Excerpt from Securities Exchange Act Release No. 34-23421

(August 13, 1986)

[T]he Commission is adopting, as proposed, the alternative requiring withdrawal rights to extend throughout the offer. * * * [Rule 14d-7]

The Commission * * * believes that given the significant extension of withdrawal rights there is no need to continue to require the additional withdrawal rights upon commencement of a competing bid. * * *

As a result of these amendments, security holders will have only one date to be concerned with the expiration date. Proration and withdrawal rights will exist throughout the offer. A bidder will be the master of its own bid; timing will not be altered by actions of a competing bidder. This should reduce the potential for gamesmanship in commencing competing bids. * * *

I. Rule 14d-8: Pro Rata Requirement

Excerpt from Securities Exchange Act Release No. 34-9336

(December 15, 1982)

Pursuant to revised Rule 14d-8, a bidder in an oversubscribed partial tender offer is required to accept securities on a pro rata basis according to the number of securities deposited by each depositor during the period such offer remains open. * * *

The Commission believes that, as stated in the Proposing Release, extension of proration rights throughout the term of the offer is essential to assure security holders the time necessary to consider the merits of an offer and to obtain sufficient information upon which to base their investment decisions and to minimize the potential security holder confusion and misunderstanding generated by changing proration periods and multiple proration pools.

J. SEC's Final M&A Release: Replacement of Rule 10b-13 with Rule 14e-5

Final M&A Release, Regulation of Takeovers and Security Holder Communication, New Rule 14e-5: Revision and Redesignation of Former Rule 10b-13, the Rule Prohibiting Purchases Outside an Offer, Securities Act Release No. 33-7760

(October 22, 1999)

Rule 10b-13 prohibits a person who is making a cash tender offer or exchange offer from purchasing or arranging to purchase, directly or indirectly, the security that is the subject of the offer (or any security that is immediately convertible into or exchangeable for the subject security), otherwise than as part of the offer. We proposed to clarify the rule's text, codify several interpretations and exemptions, and redesignate it as new Rule 14e-5. We are adopting the amendments substantially as proposed. * * * Rule 14e-5 has ten exceptions. * * *

The amendments to Rule 14e-5 being adopted today do not alter the rule's basic terms. Instead, they modify the rule's text to more clearly set forth the covered activities. Rule 14e-5 will continue to protect investors by preventing an offeror from extending greater or different consideration to some security holders outside the offer, while other security holders are limited to the offer's terms. * * * Rule 14e-5 prohibits a covered person from purchasing or arranging to purchase any subject securities or any related securities except as part of the tender offer. Rule 14e-5 does not explicitly include the term "exchange offer" as former Rule 10b-13 did because in Regulation 14E the term "tender offer" includes offers to exchange securities for cash and/or securities.

We are changing the language describing the time period of the rule's restrictions. As adopted, the restrictions of Rule 14e-5 start upon "public announcement," which is defined in the rule as any oral or written communication by the offeror, or any person authorized to act on the offeror's behalf, that is reasonably designed to, or has the effect of, informing the public or security holders in general about the tender offer.[17] Although the language regarding the commencement of the rule's restrictions is different from the language in Rule 10b-13, the scope is the same; the restrictions apply from the time holders of the subject securities, or the public more generally, are notified of the tender offer. * * *

As adopted, Rule 14e-5 does not apply to purchases or arrangements to purchase outside of a tender offer during a subsequent offering period [Section 20.4.L] if the consideration is the same in form and amount. * * *

Rule 10b-13 applied to the person who made the offer, which had been interpreted to cover the offeror, the offeror's affiliates, and the offer's dealer-manager. Under Rule 14e-5, the Rule 10b-13 term "person" is replaced by "covered person" to codify this interpretation. * * *

Covered person, as adopted, means: the offeror and its affiliates; the offeror's dealer-manager and its affiliates; any advisor to the offeror, dealer-manager or their affiliates, if such advisor's compensation is dependent on the completion of the offer; and any person acting, directly or indirectly, in concert with any of the other covered persons in connection with any purchase or arrangement to purchase any subject securities or any related securities. * * *

---

17. *See* new Rule 165(f)(3) and revised Rules 13e-4(c) and 14d-2(b).

[**Excepted Transactions**] * * * [Among other exceptions,] Rule 14e-5 will permit, as proposed, a covered person to convert, exchange, or exercise related securities [*e.g.*, options], if the covered person owned the related securities before public announcement. * * *

We proposed to add an exception for unsolicited purchases by a dealer-manager that are made on an agency basis. * * *

K. Rule 14d-10: All Holders Best Price Rule [*see also* Rules 13e-4(f), 14d-7 and 14e-1]

1. Introduction to the Original Release

Excerpt from Securities Exchange Act Release No. 34-23421

(August 13, 1986)

SUMMARY: [As indicated in Section 20.4.K.4, the best price rule was amended in 2006.] The Securities and Exchange Commission ("Commission") today announced the adoption of amendments to its issuer and third-party tender offer rules. The amendments provide that a bidder's or issuer's tender offer must be open to all holders of the class of securities subject to the tender offer and that any security holder must be paid the highest consideration paid to any other security holder during the tender offer. In addition, the Commission is amending existing rules concerning minimum offering periods and withdrawal rights. With respect to minimum offering periods, a tender offer would be required to remain open for ten business days upon the announcement of an increase or decrease in (i) the percentage of securities being sought or (ii) the consideration offered by the offeror. With respect to withdrawal rights, the amendments provide that withdrawal rights extend throughout the offering period and that the extension of withdrawal rights upon commencement of a competing bid is eliminated. [As the Court stated in *Polaroid v. Disney*, [Section 20.9.B], the all holders rule (and best price rule) were "responsive to the situation which gave rise to the litigation in *Unocal Corp., v. Mesa Petroleum Co.*, [Section 3.14.D], in which the Delaware Supreme Court upheld the power of a corporation to effect a self tender for its shares which excluded shares of a minority shareholder who was attempting to take over the corporation.]* * *

[**All Holders**] New Rule 14d-10 and amended Rule 13e-4(f) make explicit the Commission's position that the Williams Act requires that third-party as well as issuer tender offers be open to all holders of the class of securities sought. The all-holders requirement does not prohibit tender offers for fewer than all outstanding securities of a class, but provides that all security holders must be able to accept the tender offer if they so choose. * * *

[**Best Price**] In Release No. 33-6619, the Commission proposed to revise the best-price provision in proposed Rules 13e-4(f)(8)(ii) and 14d-10(a)(2) to provide that "[t]he consideration paid to any security holder pursuant to the tender offer is the highest consideration paid to any other security holder." * * * Under this proposal, both issuer and third-party bidders could reduce the consideration offered to security holders during the tender offer. The highest price paid to any tendering security holder, however, would need to be paid to any other tendering security holder. Commentators generally endorsed the best-price provision, as revised, and, accordingly, the Commission is adopting it substantially as proposed.

[**Alternative Consideration**] As proposed in Release No. 33-6619, where more than one type of consideration is offered, the types of consideration offered need not be substantially equivalent in value. Security holders, however, must be afforded the right to elect among all types of consideration offered. * * *

[**Exemptions**] Paragraph (f) of rule 14d-10 and redesignated paragraph (h)(9) of Rule 13e-4 permit the Commission to grant relief from the all-holders requirement and best-price provision on a case-by-case basis. * * *

[**Odd Lot Purchases**] Rule 13e-4(h) codifies those few special and recurring circumstances where relief from the all-holders requirement for issuer repurchases through tender offers is warranted. The Commission has adopted an amendment to paragraph (h)(5) of Rule 13e-4, providing that issuers are permitted to make odd-lot offers without complying with the general all-holders provision of Rule 13e-4(f)(8)(i). [*See* Section 21.5]

2. Termination of Tender Offer, Purchase of Shares and Start of New Tender Offer

Field v. Trump

United States Court of Appeals, Second Circuit, 1988 850 F.2d 938, cert. denied 109 S.Ct. 1112

WINTER, Circuit Judge:

[**Facts and Issue**] The legal issues in this appeal concern the meaning of the so-called "best-price rule" of Section 14(d)(7) of the Securities Exchange Act of 1934. * * *

[T]his dispute arises from a leveraged buy-out in which defendants Julius and Eddie Trump, through corporations they owned and controlled, commenced a tender offer at a price of $22.50 per share for shares of defendant Pay'n Save Corporation, a Washington state corporation. Shortly after the market closed on the fourth business day after the announcement of the tender offer, the Trumps "withdrew" the offer in order to arrange a purchase of a bloc of shares from certain dissident directors. Later that night, after acquiring an option to purchase the dissidents' shares, the Trumps announced a "new" tender offer at $23.50 per share. When the price of the option and a side payment for "fees and expenses" is taken into account, the dissidents received $25.00 per share, a $1.50 premium over the price paid to the tendering shareholders.

Bertram Field subsequently brought this class action [alleging] that the agreement between the Trumps and the dissident directors violated Section 14(d)(7), commonly known as the "best-price" provision of the Williams Act, and SEC Rule 10b-13 [now Rule 14e-5]. * * *

The district court held that plaintiff did not state a claim under Section 14(d)(7) because the Trumps had announced an effective withdrawal of their tender offer before they struck their deal with the dissident directors, and that plaintiff was not a proper party to invoke Rule 10b-13. * * * We reverse the dismissal of the Section 14(d)(7) claim and the pendent state claims but otherwise affirm. * * *

[**Analysis**] Plaintiff's principal claim arises under Section 14(d)(7) of the Williams Act, the so-called "best-price" provision. * * * The purpose of this provision is to prevent a tender offeror from discriminating in price among tendering shareholders. The position taken by the SEC thus is that:

> (i) a tender offer must be extended to all holders of the class of securities which is the subject of the offer (the "all-holders requirement"); and (ii) all such holders must be paid the highest consideration offered under the tender offer (the "best-price rule"). To codify the "all-holders requirement" and "best-price rule," the SEC has adopted Rule 14d-10. * * *

To the same end, the SEC has promulgated a rule prohibiting side transactions involving purchases of securities subject to a tender offer. [*See* Rule 14e-5] The essence of plaintiff's claim is that the $4,200,000 paid to the Stroums during the brief "withdrawal" of the offer was in law and fact a payment of a $1.50 per share premium intended to induce the Stroums to accept the tender offer. The failure to pay this premium to the other tendering shareholders, plaintiff argues, violated the "best-price rule."

No party disputes the proposition that payment of a premium to one shareholder and not others during a tender offer is illegal. The issue rather is whether the purported withdrawal effectively ended the offer so that the $4,200,000 payment was not during or part of a tender offer. In dismissing the Section 14(d)(7) claim, the district court relied upon SEC rules governing the commencement of a tender offer, specifically Rule 14d-2(b)[.] * * *

[G]iving effect to every purported withdrawal that allows a discriminatory premium to be paid to large shareholders would completely undermine the "best-price rule." For example, plaintiff has alleged that the purported withdrawal of the original tender offer was intended solely to allow the Trumps to pay a premium of $1.50 per share to the Stroums that was not offered to shareholders who tendered pursuant to the "new" tender offer announced immediately thereafter. The "best-price rule" of Section 14(d)(7) and Rule 14d-10 is completely unenforceable if offerors may announce periodic "withdrawals" during which purchases at a premium are made and thereafter followed by "new" tender offers. Unless successive tender offers interrupted by withdrawals can in appropriate circumstances be viewed as a single tender offer for purposes of the Williams Act, the "best-price rule" is meaningless.

Whether the purchase of the Stroum shares was a private purchase or part of a continuing tender offer is not determined simply by the Trumps' use of the labels "withdrawal" and "new" offer. Indeed, we have explicitly recognized that purchases after a purported withdrawal of a tender offer may constitute a continuation of the offer in light of the surrounding circumstances. *Hanson Trust*, [Section 19.3.C] Finally, Section 14(d)(7) itself explicitly treats a material change in the terms of a tender offer in the form of an increased price as a continuation of the original offer rather than as a new tender offer. Clearly, therefore, purchases of shares by an offeror after a purported withdrawal of a tender offer may constitute a continuation of the original tender offer. * * *

For purposes of the "best-price rule," therefore, an announcement of a withdrawal is effective when the offeror genuinely intends to abandon the goal of the original offer. * * * In determining the most appropriate analysis for evaluating the conduct of an offeror surrounding a purported withdrawal, we draw upon a suggestion of Professor Loss. He has noted that the determination of whether formally separate offerings of securities should be "integrated," and thus considered a single offering, for the purposes of the various registration exemptions, is closely analogous to the question of whether single or multiple tender offers have been made. * * *

In establishing criteria to govern the integration of formally separate offerings, the SEC has identified the following factors, *inter alia*, as relevant: "(1) are the offerings part of a single financing; (2) do the offerings involve issuance of the same class of security; (3) are the offerings made at or about the same time ... ?" Analogous factors may thus point to "integration" in the context of formally separate tender offers: (1) are the offers part of a single plan of acquisition; (2) do the offers involve the purchase of the same class of security; and (3) are the offers made at or about the same time? These factors are useful in determining the ultimate fact of whether an offeror has abandoned the goal of an initial tender offer in announcing a withdrawal of that offer. As previously noted, where the goal has not been abandoned, a purported withdrawal followed by a "new" offer must be treated as a single continuing offer for purposes of the "best-price rule."

Accepting as true the facts alleged in plaintiff's complaint, all of the listed factors weigh in favor of treating the Trumps' acquisition of Pay'n Save shares as a single tender offer. If the allegations are proven, the alleged $1.50 premium to the Stroums would violate Section 14(d)(7).

The parties and the district court have correctly assumed that Section 14(d)(7) impliedly affords a private right of action to shareholders. In *Pryor v. United States Steel Corp.*, 794 F.2d 52, 57–58 (2d Cir.), *cert. denied*, we held that the best-price provision's statutory neighbor, Section 14(d)(6) of the § 34 Act, which requires pro rata acceptance of tendered shares in oversubscribed offers, could be privately enforced. Section 14(d)(7) certainly provides at least as strong a basis for the implication of a private remedy as does Section 14(d)(6). * * * Accordingly, we hold that Section 14(d)(7) affords private plaintiffs an implied right of action, and we therefore reverse the dismissal of the Section 14(d)(7) claim.

3. Side Arrangements between Bidder and Controlling Shareholders under the Original Best Price Rule

a. Contemporaneous Section 351 and Option Purchases

Epstein v. MCA, Inc.

United States Court of Appeals, Ninth Circuit, 1995 50 F.3d 644

[**Essential Facts**] In 1990, Matsushita Electrical Co. Ltd. ("Matsushita") acquired MCA, Inc. ("MCA") for $6.1 billion. The acquisition was accomplished through a tender offer of $71 per share of MCA common stock.

Lew Wasserman, MCA's chairman and chief executive officer at the time, owned 4,953,927 shares of MCA common stock worth $351,728,817 at the tender price of $71 per share. His cost basis was 3 cents per share. Rather than tender his shares at the tender offer price, Wasserman entered into a separate agreement with Matsushita, known as the "Capital Contribution and Loan Agreement," pursuant to which Wasserman exchanged his shares for preferred stock in a wholly-owned Matsushita subsidiary called "MEA Holdings." Matsushita agreed to fund MEA Holdings by contributing 106% of the tender price multiplied by the number of MCA shares Wasserman exchanged. The MEA Holdings preferred stock Wasserman received pays a dividend of 8.75% annually, is secured by letters of credit, and is redeemable upon the death of either Wasserman or his wife, but in no event earlier than five years from the date of the exchange. Wasserman was 77 at the time. It is not disputed that the transaction was designed to be a tax-free exchange of Wasserman's MCA stock under Internal Revenue Code § 351(a).[18] * * *

[**Issues**] These consolidated appeals arise out of actions brought in the United States District Court for the Central District of California by former MCA shareholders who tendered their shares for the $71 tender price. They claim that Matsushita violated SEC

18. Upon the death of Wasserman or his wife, the basis of all their community property, including the Matsushita preferred stock, would "step up" to its fair market value. *See* Internal Revenue Code §§ 1014, 2032. [As a result of an amendment to the Code, the preferred stock used in this transaction would likely have been nonqualified preferred stock and, therefore, would not have qualified for tax-free treatment under Section 351.]

Rule 14d-10, by treating Wasserman * * * differently from other shareholders in the tender offer. Rule 14d-10, known as the "all-holder, best-price" rule, requires bidders to treat all shareholders on equal terms.

The district court denied plaintiffs' motion for summary judgment on their claim that Matsushita's agreement to pay Wasserman consideration that was different from the $71 per share tender offer violated Rule 14d-10, and later granted Matsushita's motion for summary judgment on this claim. We reverse. * * *

[**Private Right of Action**] [W]e hold that in enacting section 14(d)(7) of the Williams Act, Congress intended to provide a damage remedy as a means of enforcing its command that every security holder who tenders his shares be paid any "increased consideration" offered to others.

[**Analysis**] Captioned the "Equal treatment of securities holders," Rule 14d-10 prohibits a bidder from making a tender offer that is not open to all shareholders or that is made to shareholders at varying prices. The gist of plaintiffs' claims is that Matsushita violated the antidiscrimination requirements of the Rule by paying Wasserman and Sheinberg premiums pursuant to the tender offer. * * *

Performance of the Capital Contribution and Loan Agreement was conditioned on the tender offer in several respects. First, neither Matsushita nor Wasserman was obligated to perform the Agreement if any of the conditions of the tender offer were not satisfied. If, for example, Matsushita did not acquire 50% of MCA's common stock as a result of the tender offer, the Wasserman deal would be off. Second, the timing of performance was tied to the tender offer. The Wasserman exchange was scheduled to take place "immediately following the time at which shares of MCA Common Stock are accepted for payment pursuant to and in accordance with the terms of the offer * * *." Third, the amount of cash Matsushita was required to contribute in order to fund MEA Holdings was dependent upon the tender price, with Matsushita agreeing to contribute to MEA Holdings 106% of the "highest price paid * * * for any shares of MCA Common Stock pursuant to the [tender] offer." Finally, the redemption value of Wasserman's preferred stock was set as the tender price. Thus if Matsushita increased the tender price at the last minute in response to a competitive bid for MCA, Matsushita would have been required to increase both its funding of MEA Holdings and the amount paid upon the redemption of the Wasserman preferred stock.

Moments after signing the Capital Contribution and Loan agreement, Matsushita and MCA announced the $71 per share tender offer. Shareholders were given from the time of the announcement until 12:01 a.m. on December 29, 1990 to tender their shares. The owners of 91% of MCA's common stock did so, and at 12:05 a.m., Matsushita accepted all tendered shares for payment. At 1:25 a.m., Matsushita exchanged Wasserman's shares for MEA Holdings preferred stock pursuant to the Capital Contribution and Loan Agreement. MCA was merged into Matsushita as a wholly owned subsidiary on January 3, 1991.

Whether the Wasserman transaction violated Rule 14d-10 depends upon whether Wasserman received greater consideration than other MCA shareholders "during such tender offer," Rule 14d-10(a)(2), or whether he received a type of consideration not offered to other MCA shareholders "in a tender offer." Rule 14d-10(c).

Matsushita argues that the Wasserman transaction falls outside the Rule's ambit because it closed after the tender offer period expired. The tender offer period, Matsushita contends, ended when it accepted the tendered MCA shares for payment—at 12:05 a.m. on December 29, 1990, one hour and 20 minutes before Wasserman's shares were exchanged. In

Matsushita's view, liability under Rule 14d-10 boils down to a pure question of timing: the Rule is simply a "mechanical provision" concerned with "payments to shareholders of a target corporation only during a specifically-defined tender offer period." Outside that period, Matsushita insists, "Rule 14d-10 is without effect" because the Rule "is engaged (or not engaged) depending upon when payment is made."

Although Matsushita argues that Rule 14d-10 is designed to operate only during a "specifically-defined tender offer period," neither the phrase "tender offer period" nor a specific time frame is to be found in the Rule's text. To be sure, section (a)(2) of the Rule prohibits paying one security holder more than another "during such tender offer." But the term "tender offer," as used in the federal securities laws, has never been interpreted to denote a rigid period of time. On the contrary, in order to prevent bidders from circumventing the Williams Act's requirements, Congress, the SEC, and the courts have steadfastly refused to give the term a fixed definition. Instead, we have held that "[t]o serve the purposes of the Williams Act, there is a need for flexibility in fashioning a definition of a tender offer." *SEC v. Carter Hawley Hale Stores, Inc.*, [Section 19.3.B]

Even if the language of Rule 14d-10(a)(2) were to provide a measure of support for Matsushita's timing argument, Matsushita would still be unable to account for the language of Rule 14d-10(c), which prohibits a bidder from "offer[ing] * * * more than one type of consideration in a tender offer" if shareholders are not permitted to choose between the different types of consideration offered. * * *

Matsushita implicitly acknowledges that Rule 14d-10 does not contain a rigid time frame of its own when it urges us to read Rule 14d-10 as incorporating, *sub silentio*, the time frame set out in Rule 10b-13 [now Rule 14e-5], which prohibits side purchases "from the time [a] tender offer or exchange offer is publicly announced or otherwise made known * * *[to security holders] until the expiration of the period * * * during which securities tendered pursuant to such tender offer or exchange offer may by the terms of such offer be accepted or rejected." Matsushita justifies fusing elements of two separate regulations by asserting that "for purposes of the Williams Act and the SEC Rules promulgated thereunder," Rule 10b-13 defines the time period of a tender offer.

Matsushita offers no authority for incorporating Rule 10b-13's time frame into Rule 14d-10. In promulgating the all-holders, best-price Rule in 1986, the SEC gave no hint that its new regulation would be governed by Rule 10b-13's time clock. Nor does the Williams Act fully incorporate Rule 10b-13's timing provisions. Rule 10b-13 prohibits bidders from making side deals during a fixed period of time; it does not purport to serve as a general definition of when a tender offer begins and ends. In fact, in Rule 14d-2, the SEC rejected the notion that Rule 10b-13 timing determines when tender offers start for purposes of section 14(d)(7) and the rules promulgated thereunder.

We therefore reject Matsushita's timing argument. Indeed, if adopted, it would drain Rule 14d-10 of all its force. Under Matsushita's reading, even the most blatantly discriminatory tender offer—in which large shareholders were paid twice as much as small shareholders—would fall outside Rule 14d-10's prohibition, so long as the bidder waited a few seconds after it accepted all of the tendered shares before paying the favored shareholders. Rule 14d-10's equality requirements, which "expressly preclude bidders from discriminating among holders of the class of securities that is the subject of the offer, either by exclusion from the offer or by payment of different consideration," SEC Release No. 34-23421, (July 11, 1986), cannot be so easily circumvented.

An inquiry more in keeping with the language and purposes of Rule 14d-10 focuses not on when Wasserman was paid, but on whether the Wasserman transaction was an integral part of Matsushita's tender offer. If it was, Matsushita violated Rule 14d-10 because it paid him, pursuant to the tender offer, different, and perhaps more valuable consideration than it offered to other shareholders.

Matsushita contends that the Wasserman transaction cannot be deemed a part of the tender offer because it was merely a private exchange of stock, structured to take place after the tender offer finished. But Matsushita's assumption that the Wasserman transaction was private, rather than a part of the tender offer, begs the question. In *Field v. Trump*, [Section 20.4.K.2] the Second Circuit held that "[w]hether [an] acquisition of shares in a corporation is part of the tender offer for purposes of the Act cannot be determined by rubber-stamping the label used by the acquiror." To hold otherwise, the court stated, would render "virtually all of the provisions of the Williams Act, including its filing and disclosure requirements," subject to evasion "simply by an offeror's announcement that offers to purchase * * * stock were private purchases." * * *

Because the terms of the Wasserman Capital Contribution and Loan Agreement were in several material respects conditioned on the terms of the public tender offer, we can only conclude that the Wasserman transaction was an integral part of the offer and subject to Rule 14d-10's requirements. * * * The deal Matsushita made with Wasserman thus differed from the tender offer in only one material respect—the type (and possibly the value) of consideration provided. Rule 14d-10(c)(1) forbids just such a transaction.

To be sure, the fact that a private purchase of stock and a public tender offer are both part of a single plan of acquisition does not, by itself, render the purchase a part of a tender offer for purposes of Rule 14d-10. Rule 14d-10 does not prohibit transactions entered into or effected before, or after, a tender offer—provided that all material terms of the transaction stand independent of the tender offer. Thus a bidder who purchases shares from a particular shareholder before a tender offer begins does not violate Rule 14d-10. *See, e.g., Kahn v. Virginia Retirement Systems*, 13 F.3d 110 (4th Cir.1993) (bidder's unconditional private purchase of target's shares two days before tender offer was formally announced did not violate section 14(d)(7) and Rule 14d-10), *cert. denied*, 114 S.Ct. 1834.

If, in advance of the tender offer, Wasserman had become unconditionally obligated to exchange his MCA shares, the transaction would not have violated Rule 14d-10, even if Matsushita believed that acquiring Wasserman's shares was a first step in acquiring MCA. In such a case, both Wasserman and Matsushita would have assumed the burdens of their agreement despite the risk that an anticipated tender offer would fail, or command a different price. * * *

Matsushita argues, in the alternative, that the summary judgment should be affirmed because plaintiffs cannot prove that they suffered injury from the Wasserman deal. This argument, however, confuses the question of whether Matsushita complied with Rule 14d-10 with the question whether plaintiffs may recover damages. By paying Wasserman consideration that it failed to offer to other shareholders, Matsushita violated Rule 14d-10(c)(1). It remains to be determined on remand whether the preferred stock Wasserman received had a value greater than $326,959,182, the value of his 4,953,927 shares at the cash tender price of $66 per share.

Accordingly, we reverse the summary judgment in favor of Matsushita on plaintiffs' claim that the Wasserman transaction violated Rule 14d-10, reverse the district court's order denying plaintiffs' motion for partial summary judgment that the Wasserman transaction did violate Rule 14d-10, and remand for further proceedings on the question whether the consideration Wasserman received in exchange for his MCA stock had a greater value than what plaintiffs' received and, if so, how much greater. * * *

b. Contemporaneous Distributorship Agreement

Lerro v. Quaker Oats Company

United States Court of Appeals, Seventh Circuit, 1996 84 F.3d 239

EASTERBROOK, Circuit Judge:

[**Essential Facts**] The Quaker Oats Company acquired Snapple Beverage Corporation for $1.7 billion in 1994. A merger agreement was signed on November 1, 1994, and a tender offer was announced to the public on November 4. Quaker Oats offered $14 in cash for each share of Snapple stock; the merger agreement contemplated the same payment per share. Investors who thought $14 too low could refuse to tender, vote against the merger, and demand appraisal under § 262 of the Delaware Corporation Law. Nonetheless, the success of the transaction was assured by the support of Thomas H. Lee, who controlled at least 35 percent of Snapple's shares (this is plaintiffs' figure; the tender offer documents say that he controlled 47 percent). Lee not only promised to tender his shares but also gave Quaker Oats an option to purchase them even if the tender offer failed. When the offer closed, 96.5 percent of Snapple's stock had been tendered. Quaker Oats immediately effected a short-form merger under Delaware law between Snapple and LOOP Acquisition Corporation, which had been created for this purpose. * * *

One part of the offering document intrigued investors Joseph Lerro and John Duty: At the insistence of Parent [Quaker Oats] and to induce Parent to enter into the Merger Agreement, a number of agreements relating to employment, noncompetition, consulting and other matters were entered into and are described in the Schedule 14D-9. Additionally, the Company [Snapple] and Stokley-Van Camp, Inc., a subsidiary of Parent entered into a new Distribution Agreement (the "Distributor Agreement") with Select Beverages, Inc. ("Select") for the distribution of their respective products. A majority of the common stock of Select is held by affiliates of THL [Thomas H. Lee Company] and 20 percent of such common stock is held by the Company. The Distributor Agreement grants to Select the exclusive right to distribute in certain areas of Indiana, Illinois (including Chicago) and Wisconsin, certain sizes of Snapple and Gatorade in certain channels. The Agreement commences upon consummation of the Offer and is perpetual, and is subject to termination if Select fails to satisfy certain tests for increasing distribution penetration. * * *

[**Issue**] Lerro and Duty filed separate actions under § 14(d) of the Securities Exchange Act of 1934, as added by the Williams Act of 1968, contending that the Distributor Agreement provided Lee with extra compensation for his shares, in violation of § 14(d)(7) and the SEC's Rule 14d-10(a)(2). Section 14(d)(7) provides that when a bidder "varies the terms of a tender offer ... before the expiration thereof by increasing the consideration offered to holders of such securities," it must apply the increase to all shares acquired under the offer. The Distributor Agreement, which was in place from the start, is hard to characterize as an "increase" in compensation. Rule 14d-10(a)(2), adopted in 1986, is broader. It forbids any tender offer that does not satisfy this condition: The consideration paid to any security holder pursuant to the tender offer is the highest consideration paid to any other security holder during such tender offer. According to Lerro and Duty, profits anticipated under the Distributor Agreement are consideration Lee received in his role as a security holder, which per Rule 14d-10(a)(2) must be paid to everyone else who tendered into the offer. * * *

[**Analysis**] [T]he point of Rules 10b-13 [now Rule 14e-5], 14d-10, and their cousins is to demark clearly the periods during which the special Williams Act rules apply. Once the offer begins, professional investors and amateurs receive the same price. That is the objective of § 14(d)(7) and Rule 14d-10. * * *

Against this conclusion, which rests on both the language and the function of the rules, plaintiffs set *Field v. Trump*, [Section 20.4.K.2] and *Epstein v. MCA*, [Section 20.4.K.3.a]. *Field* applies a step-transaction approach to include within a tender offer a transaction that occurred between two offers. * * *

Epstein, * * * simply does not address the proper treatment of a transaction completed before a tender offer begins. * * *

Of course, all of this assumes that the transaction between Stokley-Van Camp and THL (and therefore between Quaker Oats and Lee) really did precede the commencement of the tender offer. Plaintiffs' complaint alleges, and we therefore assume, that the Distributor Agreement was integral to the transaction, in the sense that Quaker Oats would not have launched the bid unless it knew that Lee was satisfied with the terms. The Distributor Agreement was signed on November 1, but its effect depended on the merger and obviously was bound up with the tender offer too. * * *

Because transactions before or after a tender offer are outside the scope of Rule 14d-10, we must decide whether the transactions at issue preceded the tender offer. Rule 14d-2(a) addresses this directly: A tender offer shall commence for the purposes of section 14(d) of the Act and the rules promulgated thereunder at 12:01 A.M. on the date when the first of the following events occurs: (1) The long form publication of the tender offer is first published by the bidder pursuant to Rule 14d-4 (a)(1); (2) The summary advertisement of the tender offer is first published by the bidder pursuant to Rule 14d-4 (a)(2); (3) The summary advertisement or the long form publication of the tender offer is first published by the bidder pursuant to Rule 14d-4(a)(3); (4) Definitive copies of a tender offer, in which the consideration offered by the bidder consists of securities registered pursuant to the Securities Act of 1933, are first published or sent or given by the bidder to security holders; or (5) The tender offer is first published or sent or given to security holders by the bidder by any means not otherwise referred to in paragraphs (a)(1) through (4) of this rule. The Merger Agreement and Distributor Agreement were signed on November 1, 1994. News of an impending bid first reached the public, via the Dow Jones News Wire, on November 2, and the tender offer was formally announced on November 4, commencing it on that date.

Not so, plaintiffs insist. They believe that the offer commenced even before November 1 under Rule 14d-2(a)(5), because it was "given" to Lee and other Snapple insiders before then. How could they negotiate the agreements and promise to tender their shares, plaintiffs ask, if an offer had not been extended? Plaintiffs read "security holders" in Rule 14d-2(a)(5) to mean any security holder, rather than investors in general; on plaintiffs' understanding, a tender offer "commences" as soon as a potential bidder opens negotiation with a potential target's management. Yet no case or administrative interpretation supports that understanding. * * *

Treating private negotiations as the "commencement" of a tender offer would have effects far beyond requiring Quaker Oats to pay a little more than $14 per share to Snapple's public investors. * * *

Plaintiffs remind us that neither the Williams Act nor the SEC's regulations defines "tender offer." That term has been frustratingly difficult to encapsulate. * * * True enough, but our case is about "when" rather than "what." Quaker Oats made a traditional tender offer. The commencement date for such an offer is rigorously defined. This offer commenced at 12:01 A.M. on November 4, 1994. * * *

4. SEC's 2006 Amendments to the Best Price Rule

SEC Release No. 34-54685, Amendments to the Tender Offer Best-Price Rules

(November 1, 2006)

FINAL RULE. SUMMARY: We are adopting amendments to the language of the third-party and issuer tender offer best-price rules to clarify that the provisions apply only with respect to the consideration offered and paid for securities tendered in a tender offer. We also are amending the third-party and issuer tender offer best-price rules to provide that any consideration that is offered and paid according to employment compensation, severance or other employee benefit arrangements entered into with security holders of the subject company that meet certain requirements will not be prohibited by the rules. Finally, we are amending the third-party and issuer tender offer best-price rules to provide a safe harbor provision so that arrangements that are approved by certain independent directors of either the subject company's or the bidder's board of directors, as applicable, will not be prohibited by the rules. These amendments are intended to make it clear that the best-price rule was not intended to capture employment compensation, severance or other employee benefit arrangements. We are also making a technical amendment to correct a cross-reference in the rules that govern the ability to delegate authority for purposes of granting exemptions under the best-price rule. * * *

BACKGROUND. Introduction and summary. On December 16, 2005, we proposed changes to the issuer and third-party tender offer best-price rules[19] to make it clear that the best-price rule generally was not intended to apply to compensatory arrangements. We believed that these amendments were necessary to alleviate the uncertainty that the various interpretations of the best-price rule by courts have produced. We also intended that the amendments would reduce a regulatory disincentive to structuring an acquisition of securities as a tender offer, as compared to a statutory merger, to which the best-price rule does not apply. * * *

The amendments to the best-price rule will change the language of the rule to clarify that the provisions of the rule apply only with respect to the consideration offered and paid for securities tendered in a tender offer. The amendments are premised on our view that the best-price rule was never intended to apply to consideration paid pursuant to arrangements, including employment compensation, severance or other employee benefit arrangements, entered into with security holders of the subject company, so long as the consideration paid pursuant to such arrangements was not to acquire their securities. Accordingly, the amendments provide that consideration offered and paid according to employment compensation, severance or other employee benefit arrangements entered into with security holders of the subject company of a tender offer, where the arrangements meet certain requirements, are not prohibited by the best-price rule. The amendments also provide for a non-exclusive safe harbor, which states that arrangements, and any consideration offered and paid according to such arrangements, that are approved by either a compensation committee of the subject company's board of directors or a committee performing similar functions, regardless of whether the subject company is a party to the arrangement, are not prohibited by the best-price rules. Alternatively, if the bidder is a party to the arrangement, the arrangement may be approved by either a compensation

19. For purposes of this release, unless otherwise indicated, our references to the "tender offer best-price rule" or the "best-price rule" are intended to refer to both Exchange Act Rule 13e-4(f)(8)(ii) [the issuer rule, *see* Chapter 21] and Exchange Act Rule 14d-10(a)(2) [the third-party rule].

committee or a committee performing similar functions of the bidder's board of directors. In order to satisfy the safe harbor, we have provided certain alternatives for bidders or subject companies, as applicable, that do not have a compensation committee or that are foreign private issuers. * * *

History of the best-price rule and the reasons for today's amendments. Section 14(d)(7) of the Exchange Act requires equal treatment of security holders. Based on the objectives of the Williams Act and the protections afforded by Section 14(d)(7), the Commission adopted Rules 13e-4(f)(8) [the issuer best price rule, *see* Chapter 21] and 14d-10 [the third-party best price rule] in 1986. These rules codified the positions that both an issuer tender offer and a third-party tender offer must be open to all holders of the class of securities subject to the tender offer (commonly referred to as the "all-holders rule") and that all security holders must be paid the highest consideration paid to any security holder (commonly referred to as the "best-price rule"). The rules provided that no one may "make a tender offer unless: (1) [t]he tender offer is open to all security holders of the class of securities subject to the tender offer; and (2) [t]he consideration paid to any security holder pursuant to the tender offer is the highest consideration paid to any other security holder during such tender offer."

Since the adoption of these rules, the best-price rule has been the basis for litigation brought in connection with tender offers in which it is claimed that the rule was violated as a result of the bidder entering into new agreements or arrangements, or adopting the subject company's pre-existing agreements or arrangements, with security holders of the subject company. [*citing*, *inter alia*, *Epstein*, Section. 20.4.K.3.a. and *Lerro*, Section. 20.4.K.3.b.]. When ruling on these best-price rule claims, courts generally have employed either an "integral-part test" or a "bright-line test" to determine whether the arrangement violates the best-price rule.

The integral-part test states that the best-price rule applies to all integral elements of a tender offer, including employment compensation, severance and other employee benefit arrangements or commercial arrangements that are deemed to be part of the tender offer, regardless of whether the arrangements are executed and performed outside of the time that the tender offer formally commences and expires. Courts following the integral-part test have ruled that agreements or arrangements made with security holders that constituted an "integral part" of the tender offer violate the best-price rule. The bright-line test, on the other hand, states that the best-price rule applies only to arrangements executed and performed between the time a tender offer formally commences and expires. Jurisdictions following the bright-line test have held that agreements or arrangements with security holders of the subject company do not violate the best-price rule if they are not executed and performed "during the tender offer." These differing interpretations of the best-price rule have made using a tender offer acquisition structure unattractive because of the potential liability of bidders for claims alleging that compensation payments violate the best-price rule. This potential liability is heightened by the possibility that claimants can choose to bring a claim in a jurisdiction that recognizes an interpretation of the best-price rule that suits the claimant's case. These differing interpretations do not best serve the interests of security holders and have resulted in a regulatory disincentive to structuring an acquisition of securities as a tender offer, as compared to a statutory merger, to which the best-price rule does not apply. We believe that the interests of security holders are better served when all acquisition structures are viable options. We intend for the amendments we are adopting today to alleviate this regulatory disincentive. * * *

Overview of the proposed amendments. As we discussed in the Proposing Release, we do not believe that the best-price rule should be subject to a strict temporal test because such a test lends itself to abuse. However, we also do not believe that all payments that are conditioned on or otherwise somehow related to a tender offer, including payments under compensatory or commercial arrangements that are made to persons who happen to be security holders, whether made before, during or after the tender offer period, should be subject to the best-price rule. Accordingly, we proposed amendments to the best-price rule that did not follow the approach of either the integral-part or the bright-line test. Instead, we proposed to change the language of the best-price rule so that only consideration paid to security holders for securities tendered into a tender offer will be evaluated when determining the highest consideration paid to any other security holder for securities tendered into the tender offer.

Our proposed amendments to the third-party tender offer best-price rule also acknowledged that critical personnel decisions often are required to be made concurrently with decisions regarding whether to pursue a transaction with the subject company in a tender offer. We believed, and continue to believe, that these decisions generally are made independently from the consideration paid for securities tendered in the tender offer. We therefore proposed a specific exemption from the third-party tender offer best-price rule for consideration offered and paid according to employment compensation, severance or other employee benefit arrangements entered into with employees and directors of the subject company of a tender offer where the amounts payable under the arrangements meet certain requirements. We also proposed a safe harbor to the exemption from the third-party tender offer best-price rule for consideration offered and paid according to certain employment compensation, severance or other employee benefit arrangements that were approved by either the compensation committee or a committee performing similar functions as the compensation committee of the board of directors of either the subject company or bidder, depending on which entity was a party to the arrangement.

AMENDMENTS TO THE BEST-PRICE RULE. Amendments to the basic standard in Exchange Act Rules 13e-4(f)(8)(ii) and 14d-10(a)(2). Discussion. We proposed amendments to the issuer and third-party best-price rule to address the uncertainty that the various court interpretations have produced while ensuring that the intent of the best-price rule—equal treatment of security holders—is satisfied. The amendments revise the best-price rule to state that no one may make a tender offer unless "[t]he consideration paid to any security holder for securities tendered in the tender offer is the highest consideration paid to any other security holder for securities tendered in the tender offer." [*See* Rules 14d-10(a)(2) and 13e-4(f)(8)(ii)] The clause "for securities tendered in the tender offer" would replace the clauses "pursuant to the tender offer" and "during such tender offer," as the rule previously read, to clarify the intent of the best-price rule. Today, we adopt these changes as proposed. * * *

Exemption for consideration offered and paid pursuant to compensatory arrangements. Discussion. We are adopting an amendment to the issuer and third-party best-price rules so that consideration offered and paid pursuant to employment compensation, severance or other employee benefit arrangements that are entered into with security holders of the subject company and that meet certain substantive requirements are not prohibited by the best-price rules. [*See* Rules 14d-10(d)(1) and (2) and 13e-4(f)(12)(i) and (ii).] We believe that amounts paid pursuant to arrangements meeting the requirements of this provision should not be considered when calculating the price paid for tendered securities.

We have revised the proposed exemption for compensatory arrangements that meet specified substantive requirements to address a number of the comments received. We have expanded the persons who may enter into an employment compensation, severance or other employee benefit arrangement to include all security holders of the subject company, as opposed to only employees and directors of the subject company. We are also extending this exemption to issuer tender offers. Finally, we have modified the requirements of the exemption so that the amounts to be paid pursuant to an arrangement will have to be "paid or granted as compensation for past services performed, future services to be performed, or future services to be refrained from performing, by the security holder (and matters incidental thereto)" and may "not [be] calculated based on the number of securities tendered or to be tendered in the tender offer by the security holder." * * *

Arrangements approved by independent directors. Discussion. We proposed a safe harbor from the third-party tender offer best-price rule for consideration offered and paid according to employment compensation, severance or other employee benefit arrangements entered into with employees and directors of the subject company that are approved by certain committees of the subject company's or bidder's board of directors. As we stated in the Proposing Release, we believe that the fiduciary duty requirements of board members, coupled with significant advances in the independence requirements for compensation committee members and recent advances in corporate governance, provide safeguards to allow employment compensation, severance or other employee benefit arrangements that are approved by independent compensation committee members and groups of independent board members to be exempt from the best-price rule. As proposed, this provision would have operated as a safe harbor within the broader proposed exemption that included the two requirements discussed above. As we noted in the Proposing Release, we believed that providing such a safe harbor would provide increased certainty to bidders and subject companies in connection with the application of the best-price rule. We also believed that the proposed safe harbor struck the proper balance between the need for certainty in planning and structuring proposed acquisitions and the statutory purposes of the best-price rule. Most of the commenters agreed that providing the safe harbor was a good idea, although some commenters suggested certain changes to the provisions of the safe harbor to address issues on which we requested comment or that commenters identified.

We are adopting the safe harbor provision with certain modifications. First, we added the safe harbor to both the issuer and third-party tender offer best-price rules. [*See* Rules 14d-10(d)(2) and 13e-4(f)(12)(ii).] Next, we amended the language of the safe harbor so that arrangements can be approved by either a compensation committee or a committee performing similar functions of the subject company's board of directors, regardless of whether the subject company is a party to the arrangement. Alternatively, if the bidder is a party to the arrangement, the arrangement may be approved by either a compensation committee or a committee performing similar functions of the board of directors of the bidder. In the case of issuer tender offers, arrangements must be approved by either a compensation committee of the issuer's board of directors or a committee performing similar functions, regardless of whether the issuer is a party to the arrangement. Alternatively, if an affiliate is a party to the arrangement, the arrangement may be approved by either a compensation committee or a committee performing similar functions of the board of directors of the affiliate. We are also amending the safe harbor to allow a special committee of the approving entity formed to consider and approve the arrangement to approve the arrangement and meet the requirements of the safe harbor if the approving entity does not have a compensation committee or a committee of the board of directors that performs functions similar to a compensation committee or if all the members of either of those committees are not independent. All of the members of the committee used to approve an arrangement must be independent, as defined. We have made certain accommodations to these requirements for foreign private issuers, as discussed below.

Most of the commenters believed that providing the safe harbor would create certainty in an otherwise uncertain environment caused by the legal precedent that has evolved in this area. * * *

The safe harbor we are adopting today has been revised from the proposal to address the following concerns, as discussed in further detail below:

- The approval of the directors of the subject company will satisfy the safe harbor requirements, regardless of whether the subject company is a party to the arrangement;
- A special committee of the board of directors of the subject company or the bidder, as applicable, comprised solely of independent members and formed to consider and approve the arrangement may approve the arrangement and satisfy the safe harbor requirements if the subject company's or bidder's board of directors, as applicable, does not have a compensation committee or a committee of the board of directors that performs functions similar to a compensation committee or if none of the members of such committees is independent;
- Foreign private issuers may have the arrangement approved by any members of the board of directors or any committee of the board of directors authorized to approve the arrangement under the laws or regulations of their home country, and the members of the board or committee need not be independent in accordance with the U.S. listing standards but must be independent in accordance with the laws, regulations, codes or standards of their home country;
- The approving directors do not need to determine that the arrangements meet the additional requirements of the compensation arrangement exemption;
- A new instruction provides that a determination by the board of directors that the board members approving an arrangement are independent in accordance with the provisions of the safe harbor will satisfy the independence requirements of the safe harbor; and
- We have expanded the safe harbor to apply to issuer, in addition to third-party, tender offers.

L. SEC's Final M&A Release: Adoption of Rule 14d-11, Subsequent Offering Period

Final M&A Release, Regulation of Takeovers and Security Holder Communication, Bidders May Include a Subsequent Offering Period Without Withdrawal Rights Securities Act Release No. 33-7760

(October 22, 1999)

We are adopting the subsequent offering period rule with several modifications described below. [Rule 14d-11] Under the new rules third-party bidders may provide, at their election, a subsequent offering period during which security holders can tender securities into the offer without withdrawal rights. The purpose of the subsequent offering period is two-fold. First, the period will assist bidders in reaching the statutory state law minimum necessary to engage in a short-form, back-end merger with the target. Second, the period will provide security holders who remain after the offer one last opportunity to tender into an offer that is otherwise complete in order to avoid the delay and illiquid market that can result after a tender offer and before a back-end merger.

The subsequent offering period may be disclosed in the bidder's initial offering materials, or in a subsequent amendment to the tender offer materials that is disseminated to security holders. * * *

In short, we are adopting new Rule 14d-11, which permits bidders to include a subsequent offering period in a third-party tender offer during which no withdrawal rights are available,[20] so long as: the offer is for all outstanding securities of the class sought; the initial offering period (with withdrawal rights) remains open for at least 20 business days; all conditions to the offer are deemed satisfied or waived by the bidder on or before the close of the initial offering period; the bidder accepts and promptly pays for all securities tendered during the initial offering period on the closing of the initial offering period; the bidder announces the approximate number and percentage of outstanding securities that were deposited by the close of the initial offering period no later than 9:00 a.m. Eastern time on the next business day after the scheduled expiration date of the initial offering period; and the bidder immediately accepts and promptly pays for all shares as they are tendered in the subsequent offering period.

The rule, as proposed and adopted, permits bidders to use a subsequent offering period in both cash and stock tender offers. Similarly, the rule permits bidders to offer either cash or stock in any planned back-end merger. There is no specific requirement that a minimum number of shares be tendered in the initial offering period. Of course, the same consideration must be paid in both the initial and subsequent offering periods.

The new rule includes a requirement that bidders announce the results of the initial offering period (including the number and percentage of securities tendered) before 9:00 a.m. on the next business day following the close of the initial offering period. * * *

M. Final M&A Release Adopts Schedule TO As Replacement for Schedule 14D-1 and Amends Bidder Financial Information Requirements

1. Introduction to Regulation M&A and Schedule TO

Final M&A Release, Regulation of Takeovers and Security Holders Communications, Disclosure Requirements for Tender Offers and Mergers, Regulation M-A and Schedule TO
Securities Act Release No. 33-7760
(October 22, 1999)

[**New Regulation M-A and Schedule TO**] Currently, there are different disclosure schedules for issuer tender offers [Chapter 21], third-party tender offers [Chapter 20] and going-private transactions [Chapter 14].[21] Since a given transaction may involve more than one of these regulatory schemes, a company may be required to file a separate disclosure document to satisfy each applicable disclosure regime. In addition, the disclosure requirements appearing in the rules and schedules can often lead to duplicative, and

20. We also are amending Rule 14d-7 to provide an exemption so the withdrawal rights required by Section 14(d)(5) of the Exchange Act, which apply 60 days after the start of a tender offer, are not available during a subsequent offering period.

21. Schedules 13E-4, 14D-1 and 13E-3, respectively.

sometimes inconsistent, requirements. In light of the increased pressure to announce a business combination transaction soon after it is entered into and the attendant requirement to file mandated disclosure documents quickly, we proposed to integrate, simplify and update the disclosure requirements currently in the rules and schedules. Our basic approach was to combine all the disclosure requirements in one central location in a subpart of Regulation S-K, called Regulation M-A. The specific disclosure requirements in schedules were keyed to items under Regulation M-A in a manner consistent with the integrated disclosure system previously adopted for proxy and registration statements. * * *

We are adopting Regulation M-A substantially as proposed. This series of disclosure items incorporates all the current disclosure requirements for issuer and third-party tender offers, tender offer recommendation statements and going-private transactions. The new regulation includes some disclosure items for cash merger proxy statements as well. * * *

We are combining current Schedules 13E-4 and 14D-1 (the schedules now used for issuer and third-party tender offers, respectively), into new Schedule TO, as proposed.[22] In addition, we are changing the rules to allow one filing to satisfy both the tender offer and going-private [Chapter 14] disclosure requirements.[23] As a result, the information required by Schedules 14D-1[third party tender offers], 13E-4 [issuer tender offers] and 13E-3 [going private transactions] can be disclosed in one combined filing.[24] We believe that these revisions will reduce the need to file two or more schedules for what is essentially the same transaction.[25]

We have included an instruction in new Schedule TO, as proposed, listing the specific line items that must be complied with for different types of transactions.[26] In addition, we have revised the current instruction requiring information that is incorporated by reference to be filed as an exhibit. * * *

At this time we are not extending the one filing satisfies all approach to encompass transactions involving the Securities Act and proxy rules as well as the tender offer and going-private rules. In the future, we may consider integrating the requirements further, to permit the satisfaction of the disclosure required under all four regulatory schemes with one filing.

We also are revising the rules that require filing persons to include a fair and adequate summary of the information required by the schedules in the disclosure document sent to security holders. Instead of specifying some items and excluding others, as the current

22. The format and instructions for Schedules 13E-3 and 14D-9 are revised so that they are consistent with new Schedule TO. These schedules refer to Regulation M-A for all substantive disclosure requirements. * * *

23. New Schedule TO has boxes on the cover page to check to indicate whether the filing is an issuer tender offer, third-party tender offer, and/or going-private transaction. We are implementing conforming changes to the EDGAR filing tag system so that the type of transaction and filing persons are identified when viewing a document on EDGAR.

24. For example, an affiliate engaged in a tender offer having a going-private effect can now file a Schedule TO that also serves as a Schedule 13E-3. All filing persons and applicable schedules must be identified on the cover page. Separate cover pages are not required. Of course, a Schedule 13E-3 must be filed independently when the underlying transaction is not a tender offer.

25. Schedule TO also may be combined with an amendment to a previously filed Schedule 13D. *See* General Instruction G to Schedule TO. The ability to file a joint 13D amendment and tender offer statement is the same as currently permitted. *See* General Instruction E to Schedule 14D-1.

26. General Instruction J to new Schedule TO.

rules do, the revised rules simply require that the document given to security holders summarize all items in the schedule (except for exhibits).[27]

As noted in the Proposing Release, this change is not intended to increase the amount of information that is given to security holders. Instead, it is intended to simplify the requirements. We expect filers to exercise their judgment in determining the specific information that must be included in the disclosure document sent to security holders to provide a fair and adequate summary. We are not, however, changing the current requirement that certain disclosure required in a going-private transaction be set forth in full in the disclosure document delivered to security holders.[28] * * *

Under the revised rules, it is sufficient to include a general statement in the schedule that all information in the disclosure document filed as an exhibit is incorporated by reference in answer to all or some of the items in the schedule. * * *

2. Plain English Disclosure in Tender Offers

Final M&A Release, Regulation of Takeovers and Security Holder Communication, Plain English Disclosure Requirements in Tender Offers Securities Act Release No. 33-7760

(October 22, 1999)

[**"Plain English" Summary Term Sheet**] We proposed to require a plain English summary term sheet in all cash tender offers and all cash mergers, as well as going-private transactions. [Review the discussion in Section 13.12.E.2. *See* Item 1001 of Reg. MA and Item 1 of Schedule TO] * * *

[I]n most cases, we believe bidders should address the following questions in the summary term sheet accompanying their cash tender offers: Who is offering to buy my securities? What are the classes and amounts of securities sought in the offer? How much is the bidder offering to pay and what is the form of payment? Does the bidder have the financial resources to make payment? Is the bidder's financial condition relevant to my decision on whether to tender in the offer? How long do I have to decide whether to tender in the offer? Can the offer be extended, and under what circumstances? How will I be notified if the offer is extended? What are the most significant conditions to the offer? How do I tender my shares? Until what time can I withdraw previously tendered shares? How do I withdraw previously tendered shares? If the transaction is negotiated, what does my board of directors think of the offer? Is this the first step in a going-private transaction? Will the tender offer be followed by a merger if all the company's shares are not tendered in the offer? If I decide not to tender, how will the offer affect my shares? What is the market value (if traded) or the net asset or liquidation value (if not traded) of my shares as of a recent date? Who can I talk to if I have questions about the tender offer? * * *

In the context of a going-private transaction, we believe that the receipt of opinions, appraisals, or other similar reports[29] regarding the fairness of a transaction would be of material interest to security holders. In addition, the identity of the filing persons, including the affiliates engaged in the transaction, a description of their affiliation or relationship with the issuer, and their role in the transaction may be important disclosure. * * *

---

27. Revised Rules 14d-6(d), 14d-9(d), 13e-3(e) and 13e-4(d).
28. Items 7, 8 and 9 of current and revised Schedule 13E-3.
29. *See* current and revised Item 9 to Schedule 13E-3.

3. SEC's Final M&A Release Clarifies Bidder Information Required in a Cash Tender Offer and Certain Stock Tender Offers

Final M&A Release, Regulation of Takeovers and Security Holder Communication, Bidder Financial Information Clarified for Cash Tender Offers, Securities Act Release No. 33-7760

(October 22, 1999)

[When a Bidder's Financial Statements Are Not Required; Source of Funds] We are clarifying when financial statement information of the bidder must be disclosed in a cash tender offer.[30] Currently, this information is required in a cash tender offer when the information is material to a security holder's decision whether to tender, sell or hold. * * *

We noted in the Proposing Release that generally there are several factors that should be considered in determining whether financial statements of the bidder are material. * * *

In order to provide more guidance to bidders, we are adopting a new instruction to Schedule TO specifying when the financial statements of a bidder are not material and do not have to be provided. * * *

As adopted, Item 10 to new Schedule TO includes an instruction stating that a bidder's financial statement information is not material when: only cash consideration is offered; the offer is not subject to any financing condition; and *either*: the bidder is a public reporting company that files reports electronically on EDGAR; *or* the offer is for all outstanding securities of the target.[31] * * *

Regardless of the level of financial information that security holders receive, a bidder's ability to pay for the securities is a material disclosure item. We believe the disclosure that security holders currently receive in this area can be improved by clarifying the "Source of Funds" item requirement for tender offers and going-private transactions. As proposed, we are revising this item to require disclosure of information regarding the specific sources of financing, any conditions to the financing, and the filing person's ability to finance the transaction through alternative means if the primary source of financing should fall through.[32]

[Content of Bidder's Financial Statements in Cash Tender Offers; Financial Statements in Going-Private Transactions] In the Proposing Release we noted the disparity in the financial statements required in third-party tender offers, issuer tender offers, and going-private transactions. We are reducing the financial statement information required in third-party tender offers as proposed. This change harmonizes the requirements with those for issuer tender offers and going-private transactions. * * *

We are reducing the required information, [relating to book value etc.] to only the most recent balance sheet date.[33] * * *

We believe that summary financial information must include a reconciliation to the same extent full financial statements must include a reconciliation to U.S. GAAP. * * *

---

30. If a bidder offers securities instead of or in addition to cash, then financial statements are material. The registration statement form for the securities offered will specify the financial statements required. * * *

31. Instruction 2 to Item 10 of new Schedule TO.

32. Item 1007 of Regulation M-A.

33. Item 1010(a)(4), (b)(1) and (3) of Regulation M-A. As proposed, this change also applies to merger proxy statements.

[Pro Forma Financial Information Required in Two-Tier Transactions] We believe security holders need pro forma financial information for a bidder and target on a combined basis when deciding whether or not to tender in the first tier of a two-tier transaction.[34] Security holders need pro forma financial information to make an informed investment decision because if security holders do not tender in an offer they may receive securities of the bidder in exchange for the securities they hold in the target at a later date in a back-end securities transaction. Bidders frequently disclose information regarding expected synergies and other financial information to effectively sell their transaction to the market. We believe that pro forma information may be necessary to balance the disclosure disseminated to security holders and the markets. In addition, disclosure of pro forma financial information is generally consistent with our free communications scheme.[35] * * *

[W]e are adopting a requirement that bidders disclose pro forma financial information prepared in accordance with Article 11 of Regulation S-X, in addition to historical financial statements, when they intend to engage in a back-end securities transaction following a cash tender offer.[36] We limit this requirement, however, in two important respects.

First, the requirement is limited to "negotiated" transactions (*i.e.*, management of the target is cooperating with the bidder). Generally, in negotiated transactions, bidders have access to internal financial information of the target necessary to prepare pro forma financial information. In transactions where the bidder does not have access to the internal information necessary to prepare reliable pro forma financial information in compliance with Article 11 of Regulation S-X (*i.e.*, non-negotiated transactions), we are not requiring pro forma financial information. However, we encourage bidders to provide pro forma or other similar financial information that they consider useful and meaningful to security holders, regardless of whether the transaction is negotiated or not. Second, if an acquisition of a target is not significant to the bidder, we do not believe that pro forma financial information for the transaction would be helpful to security holders. Therefore, we are only requiring bidders to disclose pro forma financial information in a first-step tender offer when the acquisition is significant above the 20% level.[37]

[Financial Information Requirements in Certain Stock Tender Offers] [Review the discussion in Section 13.10.E.4]

34. A "two-tier transaction" is a business combination structured as a cash tender offer followed by a back-end securities transaction, typically a merger, where remaining security holders of the target receive the bidder's securities as consideration.

35. A requirement to disclose pro forma financial information in the first tier of a two-tier transaction extends the Division of Corporation's interpretive position that disclosure of certain material information known to the bidder regarding a planned back-end securities transaction would not result in "gun-jumping" under the Securities Act.

36. The pro forma financial information requirement applies whether the first step is a partial offer or an offer for all outstanding securities. In both cases, a bidder could intend to engage in a back-end securities transaction with the target.

37. Determination of the significance of an acquisition to the acquiror is made in accordance with Rule 3-05 of Regulation S-X. *See* Release No. 33-7355 (October 10, 1996).

N. SEC Interpretative Release Relating to the Bidder

Excerpt from Securities Exchange Commission Interpretative Release No. 34-16623

(March 5, 1980)

* * * *Question*: Assuming that a public announcement has been made which would require the bidder to file tender offer materials, need the bidder do anything more than file and deliver its tender offer materials in accordance with Rule 14d-3?

Response: Yes. The bidder must also make adequate dissemination of its offer to security holders. * * * In the Division's view, adequate publication, sending or giving is always required in order to assure that the information required by Rule 14d-6 is disseminated to security holders who are confronted with an investment decision to tender, sell or hold the securities being sought by the bidder. Rules 14d-4 and 14d-5 set forth procedures which, if followed, will be deemed to constitute adequate publication. Recognizing, however, that some flexibility should be afforded, Rules 14d-4 and 14d-5 are not mandatory; and each bidder is left free to select those means of dissemination which, under the particular circumstances, will reasonably assure that the information referred to in Rule 14d-6 will be disseminated adequately to security holders. In this regard when dissemination is not made pursuant to Rules 14d-4 and 14d-5, Rule 14d-6(a)(4) specifically indicates that the materials which are published or sent or given to security holders on the date of commencement must include specified information. * * *

Question: Once an offer has commenced, must the offer remain open continuously for 20 business days or may the offer be conditioned in such a way that it will not actually commence until a later date?

Response: Once commencement occurs (*i.e.* the offer is published or sent or given to security holders), the offer must remain open continuously from the date of commencement for at least the minimum twenty business day period referred to in Rule 14e-1, unless the tender offer is withdrawn by the bidder. The time periods set forth in the Williams Act and in the rules thereunder, including the time periods relating to proration and withdrawal rights, are generally computed from the date of commencement. These rights would be rendered ineffective if the offer were not concurrently open.

Question: Can a bidder's acceptance for payment of the securities tendered in response to a tender offer be conditioned upon the obtaining of a state or federal regulatory approval?

Response: Yes. Nothing in the rules prohibits offers under the terms of which the acceptance for payment is conditioned upon fulfillment of a condition requiring regulatory approval. * * * The nature and extent of any such condition must be fully described in the bidder's tender offer materials. * * *

Question: Must the bidder be prepared to receive shares for deposit immediately from and after the date of commencement or may the bidder indicate that no shares will be accepted for deposit until a state or federal regulatory approval has been obtained or some other condition has been fulfilled?

Response: The bidder must be willing at all times during its offer to accept shares for deposit. In order to have an offer, security holders must be in a position to accept the offer or tender for acceptance throughout the period of the offer. * * *

Question: When does the 20th business day end for purposes of computing the minimum tender offer period under Rule 14e-1?

Response: Pursuant to Rule 14d-1(b)(7) [now Rule 14d-1(g)3], the 20th business day ends at twelve midnight eastern time on the 20th business day and the offer must remain open continuously until at least that time. Accordingly, bidders may not indicate that shares must be deposited prior to the close of business on the 20th business day, since at that time the minimum period has not run. Bidders who wish to avoid the inconvenience of providing facilities for the deposit of shares after normal business hours may extend their offers into the day following the 20th business day. * * *

O. Who Is the Bidder?

SEC Division of Corporation Finance, Current Issues and Rulemaking Projects: Discussion of the Determination of the Bidder

(November 14, 2000)

Identifying the Bidder in a Tender Offer. Rule 14d-1(c)(1) of Regulation 14D defines "bidder" in a tender offer as "any person who makes a tender offer or on whose behalf a tender offer is made." The term bidder, for Regulation 14D purposes, does not include an issuer that makes a tender offer for its own securities. Each bidder in a tender offer subject to Regulation 14D must file a Schedule TO and disseminate the information required by that schedule.

The determination of who is the bidder does not necessarily stop at the entity used to make the offer and purchase the securities. Rule 14d-1(c)(1) also requires persons "on whose behalf" the tender offer is being made to be included as bidders. For instance, where a parent company forms an acquisition entity for the purpose of making the tender offer, both the acquisition entity and the parent company are bidders even though the acquisition entity will purchase all securities tendered. The staff views the acquisition entity as the nominal bidder and the parent company as the real bidder. They both should be named bidders in the Schedule TO. Each offer must have at least one real bidder, and there can be co-bidders as well.

The fact that the parent company or other persons control the purchaser through share ownership does not mean that the entity is automatically viewed as a bidder. Instead, we look at the parent's or control person's role in the tender offer. Bidder status is a question that is determined by the particular facts and circumstances of each transaction. A similar analysis of bidder status is made in a tender offer subject only to Regulation 14E. When we analyze who is the bidder, some relevant factors include:

(1) Did the person play a significant role in initiating, structuring, and negotiating the tender offer?

(2) Is the person acting together with the named bidder?

(3) To what extent did or does the person control the terms of the offer?

(4) Is the person providing financing for the tender offer, or playing a primary role in obtaining financing?

(5) Does the person control the named bidder, directly or indirectly?

(6) Did the person form the nominal bidder, or cause it to be formed?, and

(7) Would the person beneficially own the securities purchased by the named bidder in the tender offer or the assets of the target company?

One or two of these factors may control the determination, depending on the circumstances.

These factors are not exclusive.

We also consider whether adding the person as a named bidder means shareholders will receive material information that is not otherwise required under the control person instruction, Instruction C to Schedule TO. * * *

P. Oracle's Tender Offer for PeopleSoft

Documentary Appendix M of *M&A Statutes, Rules, and Documents, supra* Section 1.1 contains excerpts from Oracle's tender offer statement in which it offered to acquire PeopleSoft shares for $16 per share, and Documentary Appendix N contains Oracle's summary advertisement announcing the tender offer. The tender offer statement was mailed to the PeopleSoft shareholders, and the summary advertisement was published in newspapers. Review these documents in connection with your study of the above materials.

§ 20.5 Basic Rules Governing the Target

A. Rule 14e-2: Position of Subject Company with Respect to a Tender Offer

Excerpt from Securities Exchange Act Release No. 34-16384

(November 1979)

The Commission requested specific comment in the February release with regard to whether a rule should be adopted under the Williams Act which would require subject company management to disclose to security holders that: (1) the subject company recommends acceptance or rejection of a tender offer; (2) the subject company is expressing no opinion and is remaining neutral toward the tender offer; or (3) the subject company is unable to take a position with respect to the tender offer. It was also noted that if the subject company's position changed during the tender offer, timely disclosure of such change would be required. * * *

Rule 14e-2 implements this specific inquiry by requiring the subject company to publish or send or give to security holders a statement disclosing its position with respect to the tender offer within ten business days of the commencement of a tender offer by a person other than the issuer. The statement of position would take one of three forms: (1) the subject company recommends acceptance or rejection of a tender offer; (2) the subject company expresses no opinion and will remain neutral toward the tender offer; or (3) the subject company is unable to take a position with respect to the tender offer. In addition, the subject company is required to include the reason(s) for its position with respect to the tender offer, including the inability to take a position. If a subject company changes its position or other material changes occur in the disclosure required by the rule, the subject company is required to promptly publish or send or give to security holders a statement disclosing such material change.

As noted previously, a statement of position pursuant to Rule 14e-2 with respect to a tender offer which is subject to Section 14(d)(1) of the Act is deemed by Rule 14d-9(g) to constitute a solicitation or recommendation within the meaning of Rule 14d-9 and Section 14(d)(4) of the Act. In such case, a subject company is required to comply with the requirements of Rule 14d-9. Thus, among other things, a subject company is required to file a Schedule 14D-9 with the Commission and include the information required by certain items thereof in the information disseminated to security holders. Item 4 of the

Schedule is among the items of information which is required to be communicated to security holders and is intended to serve as the vehicle by which the subject company will satisfy its disclosure obligation under Rule 14e-2 with respect to tender offers subject to Section 14(d)(1).

Rule 14e-2 is predicated primarily on Section 14(e) which grants to the Commission authority to define and prescribe means reasonably designed to prevent fraudulent, deceptive or manipulative acts and practices in connection with any tender offer. * * *

B. Rule 14d-9: Solicitation/Recommendation Statements with Respect to Certain Tender Offers

Excerpt from Securities Exchange Act Release No. 34-16384

(November 1979)

Rule 14d-9 is applicable to any solicitation or recommendation with respect to a tender offer by a person described in Rule 14d-9(d). Rule 14d-9(a) requires the filing of Schedule 14D-9 with the Commission and transmittal of copies to certain persons as soon as practicable on the date the solicitation or recommendation is first published or sent or given to security holders. * * *

Under Rule 14d-9[c], material changes in the information contained in the Schedule 14D-9 are required to be filed with the Commission and transmitted to the same persons who received the initial filing under Rules 14d-9(b)(2) and (b)(3). [*See* Section 20.5.D] Such amendments must be filed and transmitted promptly but not later than the date the material change is first published or sent or given to security holders. * * *

Rule 14d-9[d] establishes minimum informational requirements for any solicitation or recommendation that is communicated to security holders. * * *

Rule 14d-9[e] specifies the persons who are required to comply with Rule 14d-9. Paragraph [e](1) identifies the persons whose solicitations/recommendations are subject to the rule and paragraph [e](2) exempts specific persons from the rule. * * *

A specific exemption is provided for the subject company's initial limited communication regarding a tender offer—the "stop-look-and-listen" letter under Rule 14d-9[f]. This provision has been reviewed to accommodate new Rule 14e-2, described below. A subject company which is sending a "stop-look-and-listen" letter is required to state that on or before a specified date (no later than 10 business days from the date of commencement) it will advise security holders of its position with respect to the tender offer. Thus, in order to avail itself of the exemption the subject company is required to make a subsequent communication which is deemed by Rule 14d-9(e) to constitute a solicitation/recommendation subject to Rule 14d-9.

C. Schedule 14D-9: Solicitation/Recommendation Statement

Excerpt from Securities Exchange Act Release No. 34-16384

(November 1979)

Schedule 14D-9 is intended to provide more meaningful information to security holders in the context of a tender offer. The Commission believes that the disclosure elicited by the Schedule will assist security holders in making their investment decision and in evaluating the merits of a solicitation/recommendation. * * * [The items in Schedule 14D-9 refer to disclosures required by Regulation M-A and include such information as past contacts and negotiations, the solicitation or recommendation, and the purpose of the transaction.]

D. Duty to Amend Schedule 14D-9

In the Matter of George C. Kern, Jr. (Allied Stores Corp.)

SEC Admin. Proceeding File No. 3-6869 (Nov. 14, 1988)
CCH Fed. SEC Law Rptr. ¶ 84, 342

[**Essential Facts and Issue**] These public proceedings were instituted by an order of the Commission dated June 29, 1987 ("Order") pursuant to Section 15(c)(4) of the Securities Exchange Act of 1934 ("Exchange Act") to determine whether, as alleged by the Division of Enforcement ("Division"), Allied Stores Corporation ("Allied") failed to comply with Section 14(d)(4) of the Exchange Act and Rule 14d-9 thereunder, whether George C. Kern, Jr., ("Kern") was a cause of Allied's failures to comply with Section 14(d)(4) of the Exchange Act and Rule 14d-9 thereunder, and whether the respondents should be ordered to comply or take steps to effect compliance with the requirements of Section 14(d)(4) of the Exchange Act and Rule 14d-9 thereunder.

In substance the Division alleged that Allied failed to comply, and Kern caused Allied to fail to comply, with Section 14(d)(4) of the Exchange Act and Rule 14d-9 thereunder by failing to promptly amend a Schedule 14D-9 filed with the Commission on September 24, 1988. The alleged lack of compliance involved failure of Allied to disclose that in response to a tender offer [by Campeau] (1) negotiations were under way with another party relating to or which would result in a sale of a material amount of Allied's assets and a material change in Allied's capitalization or result in an extraordinary transaction such as a merger or reorganization, (2) Allied and a third party reached an agreement in principle to a merger with the third party, and (3) Allied's Board of Directors adopted a resolution directing Allied's management to execute a merger agreement with a third party. * * *

Kern is a partner in Sullivan & Cromwell, a large well-known New York City law firm, and head of the firm's merger and acquisitions group. During the relevant period covered by the Division's allegations Sullivan & Cromwell, primarily through Kern, acted as Allied's principal outside counsel on the matters involved in these proceedings. Kern was also a member of Allied's Board of Directors during this time. * * *

[**Analysis**] *The Shopping Centers.* Allied was required by Rule 14d-9(b) under the Exchange Act to amend its Schedule 14D-9 to disclose promptly any material changes in the information set forth in its Schedule 14D-9. Allied's disclosure * * * that Allied's Board had "resolved that it was desirable and in the best interests of the Company and its stockholders to continue to explore and investigate" certain types of transactions including acquisition by another company of one or more of Allied's business segments did not encompass what must be deemed negotiations for the shopping centers that took place on September 25. Those negotiations, which culminated in an understanding between DeBartolo [the white knight] and Macioce [CEO of Allied] that $405 million dollars would be the price tag for the shopping centers and that a firm offer by DeBartolo might be forthcoming, constituted a "material change" in Allied's Schedule 14D-9 information. Consequently, Kern's decision not to amend Schedule 14D-9 to disclose promptly that material change caused Allied to violate Rule 14d-9(b), and Kern should have known that he was contributing to Allied's failure to comply with Section 14 of the Exchange Act.

Kern attempts to defend the failure to file a Schedule 14D-9 amendment disclosing the contemplated sale of Allied's six shopping centers by arguing that there was no agreement on price and terms on September 25 and that nothing occurred in the discussions that constituted a material change in Allied's initial disclosure. * * *

Kern agrees that *Basic*'s [Section 13.8.B] principles which were made applicable to the question of materiality in the context of Section 10(b) of the Exchange Act are equally applicable to a determination of materiality under Section 14(d) of the Exchange Act. He contends, however, that in exercising his judgment and reaching his conclusion that an amendment to Allied's Schedule 14D-9 was unnecessary he used the [probability/magnitude] guidelines set forth in *Basic*. * * *

The shopping center negotiations represented a material change in the Schedule 14D-9 information and required disclosure. * * *

The Merger Negotiations. Allied's plans for sale of the shopping centers and recapitalization were disrupted on September 29, 1986 by Campeau's revising its tender offer to $66 per share for 80% of Allied's stock. Although the possibility of recapitalization was not then entirely abandoned, it became clear to Allied's senior management and Kern at that time that the sale of the shopping centers and recapitalization would not suffice to counter Campeau's offer. One alternative considered was the possibility of a "white knight" merger with DeBartolo and a meeting with DeBartolo was arranged for the next day.

DeBartolo, Paul Bilzerian ("Bilzerian"), who was associated with EJDC in its efforts to acquire Allied, and other representatives of EJDC met on September 30 at Macioce's office with Macioce, Kern, and other representatives of Allied. In the course of that meeting the Campeau offer was discussed and analyzed and consideration was given to the mechanics and timing of a competing offer by EJDC. Before the conclusion of the meeting DeBartolo and Bilzerian indicated to Macioce that they were going to make an all-cash offer for Allied stock at a price of $66 to $67 per share. * * *

Continuing to exercise the legal discretion vested in him by Macioce, Kern, without consultation with any officer or other director of Allied, decided that no amendment to Allied's Schedule 14D-9 disclosing the merger negotiations with DeBartolo and Bilzerian during the period September 29 through October 3, 1986 would be filed. It appears from the record that Kern's decision not to file such amendment was erroneous and that as a result Allied failed to comply with Section 14(d)(4) of the Exchange Act and Rule 14d-9 thereunder. * * *

Without attempting to pinpoint the precise moment when Allied's merger negotiations reached the stage where its disclosure in the Schedule 14D-9 of September 24 no longer sufficed to cover the material change in Allied's situation with respect to EJDC's proposed merger, it is clear that by the close of October 2, 1986 a material change in the information previously disclosed had occurred and that the new developments would have been of significant interest to Allied shareholders. That new information should have been made known to them by way of an amendment to Allied's Schedule 14D-9. Bearing in mind the Supreme Court's approval in its recent *Basic Inc. v. Levinson* decision of the concept expressed in *S.E.C. v. Texas Gulf Sulphur Co.*, that materiality "will depend at any given time upon a balancing of both the indicated probability that the event will occur and the anticipated magnitude of the event in light of the totality of the company activity," there is little in the record to justify Kern's position that an amendment to disclose Allied's merger negotiations was not required. * * *

The Agreement in Principle and Board Resolution. Allied and EJDC reached an agreement in principle in the merger negotiations on October 3, 1986, with EJDC agreeing to offer $67 per share in cash for Allied stock and accepting a break-up fee of $1 per share plus expenses if the deal were not consummated. The only unresolved contingency was whether

EJDC could raise the financing needed to carry out the tender offer. As of the morning of October 3 Kern assumed, on the basis of DeBartolo's assurances, that the necessary funds would become available. * * *

Kern insists that Allied was under no obligation to file an amendment disclosing the "agreement in principle" or the merger resolution because he did not believe an "agreement in principle" was ever reached, and that by October 6 the Board Resolution of October 3 became a "non-event" when Allied learned that no financing was available. Those contentions are not persuasive. * * *

Note

Although the Administrative Law Judge found a violation, the full SEC vacated the decision on the grounds that it did not have the power to issue general prospective compliance orders under Section 15(c)(4). The SEC currently has such 'cease and desist' powers under Section 21C of the 34 Act, which was enacted in 1990 by the Remedies Act.

E. The 14D-9 Statement by PeopleSoft in Response to Oracle's Tender Offer

Documentary Appendix O of *M&A Statutes, Rules, and Documents, supra* Section 1.1 contains PeopleSoft's Schedule 14D-9 relating to Oracle's tender offer for PeopleSoft. Review this document in connection with your study of the above materials.

F. SEC'S Final M&A Release Amendments to Rule 13e-1, Purchases by Issuers during a Third Party Tender Offer

Final M&A Release, Regulation of Takeovers and Security Holder Communication, Target is Required to Report Purchases of Its Own Securities after a Third-Party Tender Offer Is Commenced Securities Act Release No. 33-7760

(October 22, 1999)

Rule 13e-1 prohibits an issuer whose securities are the subject of a third-party tender offer from repurchasing any of its equity securities until information about the intended acquisition is filed and disseminated to security holders. We proposed to clarify the timing of the disclosure called for by the rule so that the required information is disclosed only *after* a third-party tender offer is made, when it is most relevant. * * *

[W]e are adopting the rule substantially as proposed, but as a filing requirement only. The information would not be required to be sent to security holders. This will eliminate the cost to issuers of mailing the information, but the information will be publicly available to the marketplace.

§ 20.6 Unlawful Tender Offer Practices: Rule 14e-3: Transactions in Securities on the Basis of Material Nonpublic Information in the Context of Tender Offers

A. SEC Explanation of the Rule

Excerpt from Securities Exchange Act Release No. 34-17120

(Oct. 14, 1980)

SUPPLEMENTARY INFORMATION: The Securities and Exchange Commission today announced the adoption of Rule 14e-3 under Regulation 14E pursuant to Sections 14(e) and 23(a) of the Securities Exchange Act of 1934 (the "Exchange Act"). The rule pertains to trading by persons in securities which may be the subject of a tender offer as well as tipping of material, nonpublic information relating to a contemplated tender offer. It should be noted that the rule applies only in the context of tender offers. * * *

Rule 14e-3(a) establishes a "disclose or abstain from trading" rule under the Williams Act. A person who is in possession of material information that relates to a tender offer by another person which information he knows or has reason to know is nonpublic and which he also knows or has reason to know was acquired directly or indirectly from a person who has taken a substantial step or steps to commence or has commenced a tender offer (hereinafter also referred to as the "offering person"), the issuer whose securities are subject to the tender offer or any officer, director, partner or employee or any other person acting on behalf of the offering person or the issuer would be subject to the restrictions of the new rule. Any person subject to the rule would be prohibited from purchasing or selling or causing the purchase or sale of the securities to be sought or being sought in the tender offer unless, within a reasonable period of time prior to the purchase or sale, the information and its source are publicly disclosed.

Rule 14e-3(b) provides that certain transactions by multi-service financial institutions under certain circumstances which would otherwise be proscribed will not violate Rule 14e-3(a). This exception is available for purchases or sales by multi-service institutions where the institution can show that the individuals making the investment decision did not know the information and that the institution has established policies and procedures, reasonable under the circumstances, to ensure that individual decision maker(s) would not violate Rule 14e-3(a).

Rule 14e-3(c) provides that certain transactions which would otherwise be proscribed will not violate Rule 14e-3(a). These exceptions include: (1) the execution by a broker or another agent on behalf of the offering person; and (2) sales by any person to the offering person.

Rule 14e-3(d) is designed to prevent leaks of material, nonpublic information relating to a tender offer. Rule 14e-3(d) provides that, as a means reasonably designed to prevent fraudulent, deceptive or manipulative acts or practices within the meaning of Section 14(e), it shall be unlawful for certain specified persons to communicate such information to persons under circumstances in which it is reasonably foreseeable that such communication is likely to result in a violation of Rule 14e-3. An exception to the rule provides that a communication made in good faith to certain other persons involved in the planning, financing, preparation or execution of the tender offer, to the issuer and certain affiliated persons or to any person pursuant to applicable statute will not violate Rule 14e-3(d).

Rule 14e-3(a) does not proscribe purchases or sales of securities to be sought or sought in a tender offer by the person who has taken a substantial step or steps to commence or has commenced the tender offer. The offering person will be subject to liability, however, under Rule 14e-3(d) if he tips, *i.e.*, communicates material, nonpublic information relating to a tender offer to someone under circumstances in which it is reasonably foreseeable that he may violate Rule 14e-3. Persons other than the offering person will also be subject to liability for tipping under Rule 14e-3(d). * * *

B. The Supreme Court's View on the Validity of Rule 14e-3

United States v. O'Hagan

Supreme Court of the United States 1997, LEXIS 4033

[The portion of this opinion addressing the misappropriation theory under Rule 10b-5 is set out in Section 4.4.D. Review the facts of the case there.]

We consider next the ground on which the Court of Appeals reversed O'Hagan's convictions for fraudulent trading in connection with a tender offer, in violation of Section 14(e) of the Exchange Act and SEC Rule 14e-3(a). A sole question is before us as to these convictions: Did the Commission, as the Court of Appeals held, exceed its rulemaking authority under Section 14(e) when it adopted Rule 14e-3(a) without requiring a showing that the trading at issue entailed a breach of fiduciary duty? We hold that the Commission, in this regard and to the extent relevant to this case, did not exceed its authority. * * *

Relying on Section 14(e)'s rulemaking authorization, the Commission, in 1980, promulgated Rule 14e-3(a). * * *

As characterized by the Commission, Rule 14e-3(a) is a "disclose or abstain from trading" requirement. The Second Circuit concisely described the rule's thrust:

"One violates Rule 14e-3(a) if he trades on the basis of material nonpublic information concerning a pending tender offer that he knows or has reason to know has been acquired 'directly or indirectly' from an insider of the offeror or issuer, or someone working on their behalf. Rule 14e-3(a) is a disclosure provision. It creates a duty in those traders who fall within its ambit to abstain or disclose, without regard to whether the trader owes a pre-existing fiduciary duty to respect the confidentiality of the information."

In the Eighth Circuit's view, because Rule 14e-3(a) applies whether or not the trading in question breaches a fiduciary duty, the regulation exceeds the SEC's Section 14(e) rule-making authority. *Contra*, *Maio*, 51 F.3d, at 634–635(CA7); *Peters*, 978 F.2d, at 1165–1167 (C.A.10); *Chestman*, 947 F.2d, at 556–563(CA2) (all holding Rule 14e-3(a) a proper exercise of SEC's statutory authority). * * *

We need not resolve in this case whether the Commission's authority under Section 14(e) to "define ... such acts and practices as are fraudulent" is broader than the Commission's fraud-defining authority under Section 10(b), for we agree with the United States that Rule 14e-3(a), as applied to cases of this genre, qualifies under Section 14(e) as a "means reasonably designed to prevent" fraudulent trading on material, nonpublic information in the tender offer context.[38] * * * We hold, accordingly, that under Section

38. * * * We leave for another day, when the issue requires decision, the legitimacy of Rule 14e-3(a) as applied to "warehousing," which the Government describes as "the practice by which bidders leak advance information of a tender offer to allies and encourage them to purchase the target company's stock before the bid is announced." As we observed in *Chiarella*, one of the Commission's purposes in proposing Rule 14e-3(a) was "to bar warehousing under its authority to regulate tender offers." The

14(e), the Commission may prohibit acts, not themselves fraudulent under the common law or Section 10(b), if the prohibition is "reasonably designed to prevent ... acts and practices [that] are fraudulent."

Because Congress has authorized the Commission, in Section 14(e), to prescribe legislative rules, we owe the Commission's judgment "more than mere deference or weight." Therefore, in determining whether Rule 14e-3(a)'s "disclose or abstain from trading" requirement is reasonably designed to prevent fraudulent acts, we must accord the Commission's assessment "controlling weight unless [it is] arbitrary, capricious, or manifestly contrary to the statute." In this case, we conclude, the Commission's assessment is none of these. * * *

The United States emphasizes that Rule 14e-3(a) reaches trading in which "a breach of duty is likely but difficult to prove." "Particularly in the context of a tender offer," as the Tenth Circuit recognized, "there is a fairly wide circle of people with confidential information," notably, the attorneys, investment bankers, and accountants involved in structuring the transaction. The availability of that information may lead to abuse, for "even a hint of an upcoming tender offer may send the price of the target company's stock soaring." Individuals entrusted with nonpublic information, particularly if they have no long-term loyalty to the issuer, may find the temptation to trade on that information hard to resist in view of "the very large short-term profits potentially available [to them]."

"[I]t may be possible to prove circumstantially that a person [traded on the basis of material, nonpublic information], but almost impossible to prove that the trader obtained such information in breach of a fiduciary duty owed either by the trader or by the ultimate insider source of the information." The example of a "tippee" who trades on information received from an insider illustrates the problem. Under Rule 10b-5, "a tippee assumes a fiduciary duty to the shareholders of a corporation not to trade on material nonpublic information only when the insider has breached his fiduciary duty to the shareholders by disclosing the information to the tippee and the tippee knows or should know that there has been a breach." To show that a tippee who traded on nonpublic information about a tender offer had breached a fiduciary duty would require proof not only that the insider source breached a fiduciary duty, but that the tippee knew or should have known of that breach. "Yet, in most cases, the only parties to the [information transfer] will be the insider and the alleged tippee."

In sum, it is a fair assumption that trading on the basis of material, nonpublic information will often involve a breach of a duty of confidentiality to the bidder or target company or their representatives. The SEC, cognizant of the proof problem that could enable sophisticated traders to escape responsibility, placed in Rule 14e-3(a) a "disclose or abstain from trading" command that does not require specific proof of a breach of fiduciary duty. That prescription, we are satisfied, applied to this case, is a "means reasonably designed to prevent" fraudulent trading on material, nonpublic information in the tender offer context. * * *

C. Impact of Rule 14(e)(3) in the Pershing/Valeant Bid for Allergan, *see* Section 25.8.G.

Government acknowledges that trading authorized by a principal breaches no fiduciary duty. The instant case, however, does not involve trading authorized by a principal; therefore, we need not here decide whether the Commission's proscription of warehousing falls within its Section 14(e) authority to define or prevent fraud.

§ 20.7 Rules Relating to Target's Shareholders: Prohibition against Short Tendering and Hedged Tendering under Rule 14e-4

Securities Exchange Act Release No. 34-26609

(March 8, 1989) (Proposing to Redesignate Rule 10b-4 as Rule 14e-4)

SUPPLEMENTARY INFORMATION: The Securities and Exchange Commission is publishing for comment amendments to clarify current Rule 10b-4 ("Rule") under the Securities Exchange Act of 1934 ("Exchange Act") and to redesignate the rule as Rule 14e-4 [which is now the current rule]. The Commission is also soliciting comment on the possible deregulation of hedged tendering. The Commission's review of the Rule is prompted by the decision of the Second Circuit in *Merrill Lynch, Pierce, Fenner & Smith, Inc. v. Bobker.*[39]

Rule 10b-4 was adopted by the Commission in 1968 for the purpose of prohibiting "short tendering," *i.e.*, tendering more shares than a person owns in order to avoid or reduce the risk of *pro rata* acceptance in tender offers for less than all the outstanding securities of a class or series. The Rule was amended in 1984 to prohibit the practice of "hedged tendering" in connection with partial offers, *i.e.*, tendering and then selling a portion of the tendered shares in the market.

[**Background**] In making a tender offer for securities of a subject company, the bidder can tender for all the outstanding securities of the subject company or for a lesser amount. When a tender offer is made for less than all the outstanding equity securities of a class ("partial offer") and when a greater number of securities are tendered than is sought in the offer, the tendered securities must be accepted on a *pro rata* basis from all tendering security holders.

Partial offers involve a risk to security holders of the subject company that not all of the securities tendered will be accepted. This risk is referred to as "proration risk." Before the adoption of Rule 10b-4, security holders occasionally tendered more securities than they owned in order to diminish proration risk. * * *

The Commission adopted Rule 10b-4 in 1968 for the specific purpose of prohibiting short tendering. The rule currently provides that it is a "manipulative or deceptive device or contrivance" within the meaning of section 10(b) of the Exchange Act for any person, in response to an offer or invitation for tenders of any security, to tender securities that he does not own. * * *

Following the adoption of Rule 10b-4, it became apparent that requiring a shareholder to tender from a long position did not prevent market professionals from tendering shares they owned and then selling a portion of their shares before the proration deadline to a purchaser who would then also be able to tender the shares. This practice, known as hedged tendering, permitted tendering persons who hedged their tenders to shift proration risk to others who did not hedge. The avoidance of proration risk was similar to that achieved by short tendering. The Advisory Committee on Tender Offers recommended that the Commission prohibit hedged tendering.

In 1984, the Commission adopted amendments to Rule 10b-4 that were designed to prohibit hedged tendering without unduly affecting tendering practices or the structure of the trading markets during tender offers. The amendments required a tendering person

39. 808 F.2d 930 (2d Cir. 1986) (herein cited as Bobker).

to have a net long position to the extent of the tender not only at the time of tendering, but also at the end of the proration period. * * *

Jack Bobker, a customer of Merrill Lynch, Pierce, Fenner & Smith Inc. ("Merrill Lynch"), owned and tendered 4,000 shares of Phillips Petroleum Company ("Phillips") common stock in response to a tender offer by Phillips for approximately 50 percent of its outstanding common stock. Before the proration date of the Phillips offer, Bobker sold 2,000 shares of Phillips common stock short, making arrangements through Merrill Lynch to borrow the necessary shares. Shortly thereafter, Merrill Lynch's compliance department cancelled the short sale, apparently on the basis that Bobker would have been in violation of Rule 10b-4 if he had not covered his short position by the proration date. Bobker commenced an arbitration proceeding claiming that his tender and his short sale were "independent transactions" and seeking $23,000 in profits that he allegedly would have earned if Merrill Lynch had not cancelled his short sale. The arbitrators awarded Bobker $11,500 and Merrill Lynch appealed. The District Court adopted the analysis of Rule 10b-4 set forth in the Commission's brief as *amicus curiae* and vacated the arbitration award, finding that the arbitrators had acted in "manifest disregard of the law" with respect to the application of Rule 10b-4 to Bobker's activities. Bobker appealed.

The Second Circuit reversed and held that the arbitrators did not act in "manifest disregard of the law" in the manner in which they disposed of the arbitration proceeding. In reaching that conclusion, the court's opinion emphasized that the arbitrators' "careful and conscientious analysis" of the application of Rule 10b-4 to the facts of the case resulted in "serious doubts * * * about the rationality and interpretation of the 'net long' proviso and how it serves the Rule's avowed purpose of preventing a stockholder such as Bobker from increasing his *pro rata* share of stock tendered and accepted over the *pro rata* share of that tendered by other stockholders."

The court viewed Bobker as having tendered 4000 shares that he owned and continued to own, and then having separately sold 2000 "additional" shares borrowed from non-tendering shareholders.

The Commission believes that Bobker's short sale, assuming it was not covered by the end of the proration period, would have caused Bobker to violate the provisions of Rule 10b-4, which are intended to ensure that all tendering shareholders are subject to equal proration risk. The purpose of the Rule is not to limit the size of the proration pool (although it has that effect), but rather to promote equality of opportunity and of proration risk for all tendering security holders. * * *

[**Proposals**] In light of the Second Circuit's decision in *Bobker*, the Commission believes that it may be appropriate to clarify the Rule's rationale and substantive provisions. Accordingly, the Commission is requesting comment on a proposed redraft of the Rule to clarify its provisions, particularly the net long proviso. The amendments to the Rule are not intended to effect any substantive change in the operation of the Rule. [The amendments have been adopted in new Rule 14e-4] * * *

The Commission also is requesting comment on whether it would be desirable to deregulate hedged tendering, while continuing to restrict short tendering. The principal argument in favor of permitting hedged tendering, put forth by several commentators on the 1984 Rule Amendments, is that the practice of hedged tendering ultimately benefits those shareholders who choose not to tender but rather to sell into the market to avoid proration and other risks. [Hedged tendering is also prohibited by Rule 14e-4] * * *

§ 20.8 Actions under Section 14(e)

A. Acquiror's Standing under Section 14(e)

Piper v. Chris-Craft Industries, Inc.

United States Supreme Court, 1977 430 U.S. 1

Mr. Chief Justice BURGER:

We granted certiorari in these cases to consider, among other issues, whether an unsuccessful tender offeror in a contest for control of a corporation has an implied cause of action for damages under § 14(e) of the Securities Exchange Act of 1934, or under Securities and Exchange Commission (SEC) Rule 10b-6, 17 CFR § 240.10b-6 (1976), based on alleged antifraud violations by the successful competitor, its investment adviser, and individuals constituting the management of the target corporation. * * *

The legislative history * * * shows that the sole purpose of the Williams Act was the protection of investors who are confronted with a tender offer. As we stated in *Rondeau v. Mosinee Paper Corp.*,[Section 18.4]: "The purpose of the Williams Act is to insure that public shareholders who are confronted by a cash tender offer for their stock will not be required to respond without adequate information * * *." We find no hint in the legislative history, on which respondent so heavily relies, that Congress contemplated a private cause of action for damages by one of several contending offerors against a successful bidder or by a losing contender against the target corporation. * * *

Our conclusion as to the legislative history is confirmed by the analysis in *Cort v. Ash*, 422 U.S. 66, (1975). There, the Court identified four factors as "relevant" in determining whether a private remedy is implicit in a statute not expressly providing one. The first is whether the plaintiff is "'one of the class for whose *especial* benefit the statute was enacted * * *.'" As previously indicated, examination of the statute and its genesis shows that Chris-Craft is not an intended beneficiary of the Williams Act, and surely is not one "for whose *especial* benefit the statute was enacted." *Ibid.* To the contrary, Chris-Craft is a member of the class whose activities Congress intended to regulate for the protection and benefit of an entirely distinct class, shareholder-offerees. As a party whose previously unregulated conduct was purposefully brought under federal control by the statute, Chris-Craft can scarcely lay claim to the status of "beneficiary" whom Congress considered in need of protection. * * *

[A]s Judge Friendly observed in *Electronic Specialty Co., v. International Controls Corp.*, [Section 17.4.A], in corporate control contests the stage of preliminary injunctive relief, rather than post-contest lawsuits, "is the time when relief can best be given." * * *

We therefore conclude that Chris-Craft, as a defeated tender offeror, has no implied cause of action for damages under § 14(e). * * *

B. Requirement of Manipulation under Section 14(e)

Schreiber v. Burlington Northern, Inc.

United States Supreme Court, 1985 105 S.Ct. 2458

Chief Justice BURGER:

We granted certiorari to resolve a conflict in the Circuits over whether misrepresentation or nondisclosure is a necessary element of a violation of § 14(e) of the Securities Exchange Act of 1934.

[**Facts and Issue**] On December 21, 1982, Burlington Northern, Inc., made a hostile tender offer for El Paso Gas Co. Through a wholly owned subsidiary, Burlington proposed to purchase 25.1 million El Paso shares at $24 per share. Burlington reserved the right to terminate the offer if any of several specified events occurred. El Paso management initially opposed the takeover, but its shareholders responded favorably, fully subscribing the offer by the December 30, 1982, deadline.

Burlington did not accept those tendered shares; instead, after negotiations with El Paso management, Burlington announced on January 10, 1983, the terms of a new and friendly takeover agreement. Pursuant to the new agreement, Burlington undertook, *inter alia*, to (1) rescind the December tender offer, (2) purchase 4,166,667 shares from El Paso at $24 per share, (3) substitute a new tender offer for only 21 million shares at $24 per share, (4) provide procedural protections against a squeeze-out merger of the remaining El Paso shareholders, and (5) recognize "golden parachute" contracts between El Paso and four of its senior officers. By February 8, more than 40 million shares were tendered in response to Burlington's January offer, and the takeover was completed.

The rescission of the first tender offer caused a diminished payment to those shareholders who had tendered during the first offer. The January offer was greatly oversubscribed and consequently those shareholders who retendered were subject to substantial proration. Petitioner Barbara Schreiber filed suit on behalf of herself and similarly situated shareholders, alleging that Burlington, El Paso, and members of El Paso's board of directors violated § 14(e)'s prohibition of "fraudulent, deceptive, or manipulative acts or practices * * * in connection with any tender offer." She claimed that Burlington's withdrawal of the December tender offer coupled with the substitution of the January tender offer was a "manipulative" distortion of the market for El Paso stock. Schreiber also alleged that Burlington violated § 14(e) by failing * * * to disclose the "golden parachutes" offered to four of El Paso's managers. She claims that this January nondisclosure was a deceptive act forbidden by § 14(e).

The District Court dismissed the suit for failure to state a claim. The District Court reasoned that the alleged manipulation did not involve a misrepresentation, and so did not violate § 14(e). The District Court relied on the fact that in cases involving alleged violations of § 10(b) of the Securities Exchange Act, this Court has required misrepresentation for there to be a "manipulative" violation of the section.

The Court of Appeals for the Third Circuit affirmed. * * *

[**Analysis**] We are asked in this case to interpret § 14(e) of the Securities Exchange Act. The starting point is the language of the statute. * * *

Petitioner relies on a construction of the phrase, "fraudulent, deceptive, or manipulative acts or practices." Petitioner reads the phrase "fraudulent, deceptive, or manipulative acts or practices" to include acts which, although fully disclosed, "artificially" affect the price of the takeover target's stock. Petitioner's interpretation relies on the belief that § 14(e) is directed at purposes broader than providing full and true information to investors.

Petitioner's reading of the term "manipulative" conflicts with the normal meaning of the term. We have held in the context of an alleged violation of § 10(b) of the Securities Exchange Act:

> "Use of the word 'manipulative' is especially significant. It is and was virtually a term of art when used in connection with the securities markets. It connotes intentional or willful conduct *designed to deceive or defraud* investors by controlling or artificially affecting the price of securities." *Ernst & Ernst v. Hochfelder*, [Section 4.4.A] (emphasis added). * * *

Section 14(e) adds a "broad antifraud prohibition," modeled on the antifraud provisions of § 10(b) of the Act and Rule 10b-5. It supplements the more precise disclosure provisions found elsewhere in the Williams Act, while requiring disclosure more explicitly addressed to the tender offer context than that required by § 10(b). * * *

We hold that the term "manipulative" as used in § 14(e) requires misrepresentation or nondisclosure. It connotes "conduct designed to deceive or defraud investors by controlling or artificially affecting the price of securities." *Ernst & Ernst v. Hochfelder*, [Section 4.4.A] Without misrepresentation or nondisclosure, § 14(e) has not been violated.

Applying that definition to this case, we hold that the actions of respondents were not manipulative. * * *

The judgment of the Court of Appeals is *Affirmed.*

C. Target's Standing under Section 14(e) to Force Disclosure

Polaroid Corp. v. Disney

United States Court of Appeals, Third Circuit, 1988 862 F.2d 987

* * * Polaroid contends that Shamrock's September 9, 1988, Offer did not disclose all material information concerning the important issue of whether the Offer complied with Federal Reserve Board margin regulations. * * * A target company such as Polaroid has standing to sue, under section 14(e)'s implied right of action, to enjoin misrepresentations made by a tender offeror in connection with the offer. Our cases have not had occasion to explain why target companies may sue under section 14(e). Judge Friendly for the Second Circuit explained that allowing the target corporation to sue would "best accomplish the purposes of the legislature" because "the superior resources of the corporation * * * can be vital in this context[,] where remedial action must be speedy and forceful." *Electronic Specialty Co. v. International Controls Corp.* [Section 17.4.A] * * *

D. Section 14(e) Applicability to an Unregulated Tender Offer and Scienter Standard

Clearfield Bank and Trust Company v. Omega Financial Corporation

United States District Court, Pennsylvania, 1999 CCH Fed Sec Law Rep ¶ 90,655

D. Brooks Smith, District Judge:

* * * Plaintiff, [Clearfield Bank & Trust Company, which was held by a number of local shareholders], charges that defendant [Omega] has violated [the] federal securities law * * * in its aggressive efforts to buy shares of plaintiff's common stock directly from some of plaintiff's shareholders. * * *

[**Essential Facts**] [Anonick, a representative of Omega, met with 20 to 30 of Clearfield's shareholders and reviewed with them] some of the terms of Omega's May 10 letter of interest, emphasizing the $65 per share price and the promise that Clearfield would retain its name.

The shareholders attending the * * * meeting were invited to sign the Omega Agreement before leaving, or to take copies with them. Some shareholders signed the agreements and turned them in that day; others have since mailed signed agreements to Omega. As of the date of the evidentiary hearing, shareholders holding 20.42% of Clearfield common stock had executed the Omega Agreement. * * *

[**Issue**] The complaint alleges that Omega's May 10 letter of interest constitutes a tender offer which included misstatements and omissions of material fact in violation of Section 14(e) of the Securities and Exchange Act of 1934. * * *

[**Analysis**] Omega argues first that, even if this Court concludes that its written offer to shareholders constitutes a tender offer, the Act was not intended to reach "privately negotiated intrastate agreements," such as the one at issue here.* * *

Omega's attempt to establish a public/private dichotomy in shareholder trading upon which applicability of the Williams Act hinges is unsupported by either case law or the plain language of the statute. * * *

Although it may be the exception to apply the Williams Act to private transactions of stock in small companies which have a limited number of shareholders, "the case law clearly gives courts the discretion to apply the Act if its protections are needed." * * * Here, neither the fact that the agreement was privately negotiated nor the fact that it dealt with unregistered stock removes the transaction from the reach of Section 14(e).

The parties agree that if the Omega Agreement does not constitute a "tender offer," the protections of the Williams Act do not apply. * * *

[I]n this case it is appropriate to supplement the *Wellman* [Section 19.3.A] factors, which preponderate in favor of finding a tender offer, with an examination of the alleged misstatements and omissions at issue. * * *

I conclude that the two-page Omega Agreement contained omissions which a reasonable Clearfield shareholder would consider important in deciding how to vote and whether to exercise dissenters' rights in connection with the proposed merger. Those omissions were, therefore, material. * * *

Another question that remains is whether scienter is required in a proceeding for injunctive relief under Section 14(e) of the Act. * * * The Third Circuit has yet to address whether a plaintiff seeking a permanent injunction under Section 14(e) must prove scienter. * * *

This language [of Section 14(e)] was "modeled on the antifraud provisions of Section 10(b) of the Act and Rule 10b-5[.]" * * * It is well-settled that scienter is a necessary element of a claim under Section 10(b) and Rule 10b-5. *Ernst & Ernst* [Section 4.4.A]. For that reason, I conclude that scienter is also a necessary element of an action under Section 14(e) and will follow the principles governing scienter applied in a claim under Section 10(b) and Rule 10b-5. * * *

I can only conclude that the complete explanation of dissenter's rights omitted from the August 2 agreement was, if not intentional, at least reckless. * * *

* * * Omega has violated section 14(e) of the Williams Act. To remedy this violation, I am ordering the postponement of the scheduled shareholder meeting, the rescission of all Agreements executed by Clearfield shareholders and their return by Omega, and the distribution to Clearfield's shareholders of this Summary and Conclusion section of my opinion.

§ 20.9 Legal Actions under Section 14(d)

A. Target Shareholder's Right of Action under the Best Price Provision of Rule 14(d)(7)

See Field v. Trump, Section 20.4.K.2.

B. Target's Standing to Enforce All Holders Rule

Polaroid Corp. v. Disney

United States Court of Appeals, Third Circuit, 1988 862 F.2d 987

BECKER, Circuit Judge.

This is an appeal by Polaroid Corporation ("Polaroid") from an order of the district court denying Polaroid's motion for a preliminary injunction against a tender offer for Polaroid stock which, if successful, would vest control of Polaroid in interests controlled by appellees Roy and Patricia Disney. The appeal presents the first impression question of the standing of a target company to assert a violation of the Security and Exchange Commission's All Holders Rule, [Rule 14(d)-10(a)] * * *

Polaroid argues that Shamrock's tender offer violates the Rule because it is not open to all holders of Polaroid common stock; the Polaroid ESOP is a holder (of 9.7 million shares) of Polaroid common stock and Shamrock has not offered to purchase the ESOP shares. Shamrock's argument in response is that its tender offer is "premised on the invalidity of the ESOP shares." * * *

[T]his Court has held that target corporations have standing to raise a claim under section 14(e) that the tender offer contains fraudulent misrepresentations or omissions. The best argument for allowing target corporations standing to sue under the All Holders Rule may thus be that there is no reason to distinguish All Holders Rule standing from misrepresentation standing. There is, however, a reason to draw this distinction. The bar against misrepresentation is meant to protect all shareholders. Shareholder litigation under the aegis of the corporation makes greater sense in this context, where the class of persons whose rights the corporation is vindicating constitutes all of its shareholders. The All Holders Rule, by contrast, protects what are likely to be only a minority of shareholders. Moreover, it may be more difficult to detect fraud than to detect violations of the All Holders Rule, and the possibility of irreparable harm may be greater in the case of fraud because of the greater difficulty in computing monetary loss. The need for target corporation standing in the fraud context may thus be greater than in the context of the All Holders Rule. * * *

We therefore hold that, although the All Holders Rule creates a private right of action enabling injured shareholders to sue a tender offeror whose offer violates the Rule, a target corporation has no standing to sue under the Rule. * * *

§ 20.10 Negotiated Tender Offer and Second Step Merger under Section 251(h) of the DGCL or pursuant to a "Top-Up Option"

Tender offers may be structured as the first step in a negotiated transaction, in which case the merger agreement will specify the terms of both the tender offer and the second step merger. As a result of the 2006 amendments to the best price rule discussed in Section 20.4.K, these transactions are common, because they permit the acquiror to gain a controlling position in the target in a shorter period of time than with a single-step merger transaction, which requires a shareholder vote. [*See* Chapter 13]

As a result of the 2013 adoption of Section 251(h) of the Delaware General Corporation Law, which is discussed in Section 2.16.C, if a third party acquirer acquires pursuant to a negotiated tender offer/merger agreement more than 50% of the stock of a target, the acquirer can immediately effectuate a second-step merger without having a vote of the target's shareholders. This type of transaction is illustrated in Documentary Appendix II, *Documents Relating to the Tender Offer by Mallinckrodt Plc for the Stock of Cadence pursuant to a Merger Agreement with a Section 251(h) Second Step Merger Provision*, which is contained in *M&A Statutes, Rules, and Documents, supra* Section 1.1.

If Section 251(h) is not available the parties may consider having the merger qualify as a short-form merger, which is addressed in Section 2.16. For an illustration of this type of transaction *see* the *Cox Communications Going Private Tender Offer/Merger Offer Document*, which is Documentary Appendix Q of *M&A Statutes, Rules, and Documents, supra* Section 1.1.

To ensure that the acquiror can get the required number of shares to effectuate a short form merger (generally 90%), the merger agreement may also contain a "top-up option." Such an option comes into effect where an acquiror does not hold 90% of the shares of the target after the completion of the tender offer and, therefore, cannot effectuate a short-form merger. The top-up option gives such an acquiror the right to purchase shares directly from the target so that the 90% short-form merger condition is satisfied. An illustration of a "top-up option is contained in Documentary Appendix JJ, *Combination Tender Offer/Merger Agreement with a Top-Up Option—Wild Oats*, which is contained in *M&A Statutes, Rules, and Documents, supra* Section 1.1.

The operation of a "top-up option" can be illustrated as follows. Assume that a target has 100,000 shares outstanding, and the acquiror receives 87,000 of the target's shares in the tender offer. In such case, a top-up option would give the acquiror the right to purchase sufficient shares to take it to 90%. In this case, the acquiror would have to purchase an additional 30,000 shares directly from the target. Such a purchase would give the acquiror 117,000 shares of the target's 130,000 shares outstanding, which is exactly 90% of the post-purchase outstanding shares of the target. Of course, the target would have to have sufficient authorized but unissued shares to issue pursuant to the option.

It should be noted that with a "top-up option" the number of shares the target needs to issue is not simply the difference between (1) 90%, and (2) the percentage held by the acquiror after the tender offer. This is because the shares issued to the acquiror pursuant to the option increase the number of outstanding shares, that is, the newly issued shares increase both the numerator and the denominator used in determining if the 90% condition is satisfied.

§ 20.11 SEC's Advisory Committee on Tender Offers

SEC, Advisory Committee on Tender Offers Report of Recommendations

(Summary Recommendations) (July 8, 1983)

[*See also* Sections 17.5 and 23.9]

* * *

Regulation of Acquirors of Corporate Control * * *

13. No person may acquire directly or indirectly beneficial ownership of more than 5% of an outstanding class of equity securities unless such person has filed a Schedule 13D and that schedule has been on file with the Commission for at least 48 hours. Such person may rely on the latest Exchange Act report filed by the target company that reports the number of shares outstanding. The acquiror would have to report subsequent purchases promptly as provided by current law.

14. No person may acquire voting securities of an issuer, if, immediately following such acquisition, such person would own more than 20% of the voting power of the outstanding voting securities of that issuer unless such purchase were made (i) from the issuer, or (ii) pursuant to a tender offer. The Commission should retain broad exemptive power with respect to this provision.

15. The Committee encourages the Commission to study means to strengthen the concept and definition of "group" or concerted activity.

16. The minimum offering period for a tender offer for less than all the outstanding shares of a class of voting securities should be approximately two weeks longer than that prescribed for other tender offers.

17. The minimum offering period for an initial bid should be 30 calendar days; for subsequent bids the minimum offering period should be 20 calendar days, provided that the subsequent bid shall not terminate before the 30th calendar day of the initial bid. In each case, the minimum offering period will be subject to increase, if the bid is a partial offer. The period during which tendering shareholders will have proration and withdrawal rights should be the same length as the minimum offering period.

18. The minimum offering period and prorationing period should not terminate for five calendar days from the announcement of an increase in price or number of shares sought.

19. Where the bidder discloses projections or asset valuations to target company shareholders, it must include disclosure of the principal supporting assumptions provided to the bidder by the target. * * *

24. Except to the extent there already exists such a requirement in a particular context, the price paid by an acquiror unaffiliated with the target company should not be required to be "fair" nor should federal law provide for state law-type appraisal rights.

25. All shareholders whose shares are purchased in a tender offer should be entitled to the highest per share price paid in the offer.[*See* Rule 14d-10]

26. Current prohibitions of the purchase by a bidder of target company shares other than under the offer should be continued. [*See* Rule 14e-5] * * *

31. Approval by shareholders of a bidder with respect to an acquisition should continue to be an internal matter between shareholders and management, subject only to applicable state law.

32. The takeover process should not be permitted to become so complex that it is understood only by investment professionals.

References

Brown *et al.*, *Takeovers: A Strategic Guide*, *supra* Section 1.10.

Hazen, *Securities Regulation*, *supra* Section 1.10.

Lipton and Steinberger, *Takeovers and Freezeouts*, *supra* Section 1.10.

Loss & Seligman, *Securities Regulation*, *supra* Section 1.10.

Thompson, *Mergers, Acquisitions and Tender Offers*, *supra* Section 1.10, Chapter 8.

Chapter 21

SEC's Rules on Tender Offers by Issuers

§ 21.1 Scope

This chapter addresses tender offers by issuers for their own securities; thus, in these transactions a publicly-held corporation offers to purchase its stock from its public shareholders. In Securities Exchange Act of 1934 Release No. 16112 (August 16, 1979), the SEC promulgated Rule 13e-4 and Schedule 13E-4 (now Schedule TO) relating to these transactions. Section 21.2 presents an introductory problem on issuer tender offers, and Section 21.3 focuses on the meaning of the term "tender offer" in the context of these transactions. Section 21.4 contains excerpts from the SEC's explanation of the rule and the schedule. Section 21.5 deals with the exemption that applies to odd lot purchases, and Section 21.6 addresses the safe-harbor for issuer repurchases contained in Rule 10b-18. Rule 13e-4 has also been amended by Securities Exchange Release No. 34-23421, which sets forth the all holders best price rule for tender offers. [*See* Chapter 20] The materials in this chapter are discussed in greater detail in Thompson, *Mergers, Acquisitions and Tender Offers*, *supra* Section 1.10, Chapter 8.

§ 21.2 Introductory Problem on Issuer Tender Offers

J.P. Morgan Chase & Co. (J.P. Morgan) and The Goldman Sachs Group, Inc. (Goldman Sachs), both publicly-held Delaware corporations, have entered into a merger agreement. Citigroup, Inc. has made a tender offer for 60% of the stock of J.P. Morgan, at $100 in cash per share, conditioned on the termination of the J.P. Morgan-Goldman Sachs merger agreement. Citigroup proposes to effectuate a second-step freezeout merger at $100 in Citigroup stock. After consulting with its investment banker, J.P. Morgan's board has determined that the $100 price per share in the cash tender offer and the $100 price per share in the second-step are inadequate. In an attempt to discourage Citigroup from proceeding with its tender offer, J.P. Morgan's board is planning to repurchase 20% of its stock at the market price in open market purchases.

(1) Pursuant to Rule 13e-1, J.P. Morgan is prepared to announce the repurchase program and then immediately begin purchasing its stock on the market. Can it follow this course?

(2) What if J.P. Morgan decides to place bids for its stock at a price that is $2 above the current market price?

(3) At what point will J.P. Morgan's repurchase program become a tender offer? If the repurchase program is a tender offer, what are the required terms of such offer?

§ 21.3 What Is an Issuer Tender Offer?

See Carter Hawley Hale v. Limited (Section 19.3.B).

§ 21.4 SEC's Explanation of Rule 13e-4 and Schedule 13E-4, Now Schedule TO

[Rule 13e-4 Was Revised and Schedule 13E-4 Was Converted to Schedule TO by the SEC's Final M&A Release. *See* Section 20.4.M] Securities Exchange Act Release No. 34–16112

(1979)

(*See also* **Section 20.4.H., I., and K.** Relating to Withdrawal, Pro Rata Rules, and All Holders, Best Price)

Introduction.[T]he requirements of [Rule 13e-4 ("Rule") relating to issuer tender offers] are patterned substantially on the regulatory scheme established by Section 14(d) of the Act and existing rules thereunder which are applicable in the context of third party tender offers. * * * The information required to be disclosed in Schedule 13E-4 is substantially the same type of information which is required by Schedule 14D-1. * * *

Statutory Background. The Commission has adopted Rule 13e-4 under seven sections of the Act, including Sections 13(e) and 14(e). Sections 13(e) and 14(e) expressly grant the Commission authority to adopt rules which define, and prescribe means reasonably designed to prevent fraudulent, deceptive or manipulative activity in connection with purchases by an issuer of its own securities, and in connection with any tender offer, respectively. * * *

* * * The Commission has determined that regulation of issuer tender offers under Rule 13e-4 is appropriate to ensure that issuer tender offers are conducted in a manner free of the deceptive, manipulative and fraudulent acts and practices set forth in paragraph (b) of the Rule. By providing a regulatory framework governing issuer tender offers, Rule 13e-4 responds to a major Congressional concern underlying the Williams Act to ensure that tender offers are conducted on appropriate terms and conditions in light of the special market and investment decision problems which attend such offers.

Coverage of the Rule. * * *

[P]aragraph (g)(4) of the Rule excludes any tender offer already subject to Section 14(d).

As proposed and adopted, the Rule applies to issuers required to file periodic reports under Section 15(d) of the Act. * * *

Rule 13e-4[a].Paragraph (a) of the Rule defines certain terms used throughout the Rule and Schedule. * * *

Rule 13e-4[b].* * * Issuers and affiliates subject to the Rule are required to comply with * * * the requirements set forth in paragraphs (c), (d), (e) and (f) of the Rule.

Filing Requirements. Paragraph (c) of Rule 13e-4 imposes three filing obligations on the issuer or affiliate subject to the Rule. First, the person subject to the Rule must file with the Commission ten copies of Schedule 13E-4 prior to or as soon as practicable on the date of commencement of the issuer tender offer. Second, such person must report any material change in the information set forth in the Schedule by filing with the Commission ten copies of an amendment to the Schedule. Finally, the issuer or affiliate making the tender offer must report the results of the tender offer by filing with the Commission ten copies of a final amendment to the Schedule no later than ten business days after termination of the tender offer.

Disclosure and Dissemination Requirements. Rule 13e-4(d) sets forth specifically those terms of the tender offer which the issuer or affiliate is required to disclose to security holders in its offering materials. The offering materials must be disseminated to security holders pursuant to the requirements contained in paragraph (e) of the Rule. The issuer or affiliate will be deemed to have published, sent or given the tender offer to security holders upon compliance with the provisions relating to long-form publication, use of shareholder and other lists or summary publication. If any material change occurs in the information published, sent or given to security holders, the offeror is required by Rule 13e-4(e)(2) to disseminate promptly disclosure of such change in a manner reasonably calculated to inform security holders.

Manner of Making the Tender Offer. Rule 13e-4 (f)(1) requires that an issuer tender offer remain open for at least [twenty] business days from the date of commencement of the offer. * * *

The periods during which tendering security holders must be afforded the right to withdraw their securities under the Rule are set forth in paragraph (f)(2). [Under this rule security holders can withdraw at anytime during the period the issuer's tender offer remains open.] * * *

The requirements of the Rule relating to pro rata acceptance of tendered securities have been adopted substantially as proposed. Paragraph (f)(3) of the Rule requires that where a greater number of securities is tendered than the issuer will accept * * * the issuer or affiliate making the tender offer shall accept all such securities on a pro rata basis. * * *

Paragraph (f)(4) of the Rule requires that, if the issuer or affiliate subject to the Rule increases the consideration offered after the tender offer is commenced, the issuer or affiliate must pay the increased consideration to all security holders whose tendered securities are accepted for payment. * * *

As proposed, the Rule would have prohibited, for the ten business days after termination of the offer, any purchases by the issuer of the securities which are the subject of the tender offer. This provision is essentially an anti-manipulation restriction. A tender offer tends to peg the market price of the security which is the subject of the tender offer at or near the offering price, and the purpose of the prohibition on post-offer purchasing activity is to prevent the issuer from supporting the market at that artificial price after termination of the tender offer. * * *

As adopted, the Rule also prohibits, for the ten business days subsequent to the termination of the tender offer, purchases of securities of the same class and series as, or any "right to purchase," the securities which are the subject of the tender offer. [*See* Rule 13e-4(f)(6)]

[The all holders, best price rule is set out in Rule 13e-4(f)(8). The background on the adoption of this rule is set out in Section 20.4.K]

Disclosure Requirements—Schedule 13E-4 [**Now Schedule TO** *see* Section 20.4.M] * * *

§21.5 Amendment Relating to Odd Lot Offers

Excerpt from Securities Exchange Act Release No. 19988

(July 21, 1983)

[**Background**, Rule 13e-4(h)(5)] One type of issuer tender offer is an offer to purchase the shares of security holders who own a specified number of shares that is less than one hundred ("Odd-lot Offer"). Generally, the purpose of an Odd-lot Offer is to reduce the disproportionately high costs to the issuer of servicing large numbers of small shareholder accounts and to enable those shareholders to dispose of their securities without incurring the brokerage fees that normally attend odd-lot transactions. In light of their limited purpose and the fact that they are not characterized by large premiums or significant market impact. Odd-lot Offers present minimal potential for fraud and manipulation.

As noted in the Proposing Release, the Commission currently grants exemptions from the Rule to permit issuers to make Odd-lot Offers without complying with the filing and dissemination requirements of the Rule. * * *

§21.6 Rule 10b-18 Safe Harbor from Liability for Manipulation in Issuer Purchase Transaction

See Section 13.15.

References

Brown *et al.*, *Takeovers: A Strategic Guide*, *supra* Section 1.10.

Hazen, *Securities Regulation*, *supra* Section 1.10.

Lipton and Steinberger, *Takeovers and Freezeouts*, *supra* Section 1.10.

Loss & Seligman, *Securities Regulation*, *supra* Section 1.10.

Thompson, *Mergers, Acquisitions and Tender Offers*, *supra* Section 1.10, Chapter 8.

Chapter 22

State Regulation of Tender Offers

§ 22.1 Scope

This chapter focuses on state laws regulating tender offers and takeovers. These provisions are sometimes referred to as "Baby Williams Acts." Section 22.2 presents an introductory problem on state regulation of such offers. A state's takeover laws generally apply only to a target corporation incorporated in that state, and in some cases, only if the target also has significant business in the state or has a significant number of shareholders resident in the state. These statutes are generally classified as first, second, and third generation statutes. The first generation statutes, which regulated tender offers directly, are examined in Section 22.3. These statutes have been found to be unconstitutional and also preempted by the Williams Act.

Section 22.4 considers the second generation control share statutes, which have been found to be constitutional and not preempted. These statutes regulate the voting of control shares. Section 22.5 examines the third generation business combination statutes that also have been found to be constitutional and not preempted. Section 22.6 looks briefly at Pennsylvania's comprehensive approach to takeover regulation. Section 22.7 looks generally at other constituency statutes. Finally, Section 22.8 presents a policy perspective on state takeover law.

Just as it is essential for the corporate lawyer in a merger or acquisition transaction to master the intricacies of the voting and dissenting provisions of the applicable state corporate law [*see* Chapter 2], it is also essential for such a lawyer to master the intricacies of any applicable Baby Williams Act. The materials in this chapter are discussed in greater detail in Thompson, *Mergers, Acquisitions and Tender Offers*, *supra* Section 1.10, Section 8.6.

§ 22.2 Introductory Problems on State Takeover Statutes

1. J.P. Morgan Chase & Co. (J.P. Morgan) and The Goldman Sachs Group, Inc. (Goldman Sachs) both publicly-held Delaware corporations, have entered into a merger agreement and are about to submit the agreement to their shareholders for vote. Citigroup, Inc., makes a hostile tender offer for any and all J.P. Morgan shares at a price of $50 per share, which is a substantial premium over the pre-tender offer market price of J.P. Morgan's shares. Citigroup intends to follow the tender offer with a freezeout merger. Are there any restrictions in Delaware corporate law on Citigroup's ability to effectuate the freezeout merger?

2. The facts are the same as in Question 1, except that J.P. Morgan, as a defensive reaction and with the consent of the Goldman Sachs directors, makes a tender offer for any and all Goldman Sachs shares, to be followed by a freezeout merger. Are there any restrictions in Delaware corporate law on J.P. Morgan's ability to vote the Goldman Sachs shares it acquires in the tender offer? Are there any such restrictions on J.P. Morgan's ability to effectuate the freezeout merger?

§ 22.3 The First Generation Statutes: The Supreme Court's View of the Illinois Statute

Edgar v. Mite Corp.

United States Supreme Court, 1982 102 S.Ct. 2629

Justice WHITE delivered an opinion, Parts I, II, and V-B of which are the opinion of the Court.

The issue in this case is whether the Illinois Business Take-Over Act * * * is unconstitutional under the Supremacy and Commerce Clauses of the Federal Constitution.

[**Essential Facts and Issues**] Appellee MITE Corp. and its wholly owned subsidiary, MITE Holdings, Inc., are corporations organized under the laws of Delaware with their principal executive offices in Connecticut. Appellant James Edgar is the Secretary of State of Illinois and is charged with the administration and enforcement of the Illinois Act. Under the Illinois Act any takeover offer for the shares of a target company must be registered with the Secretary of State. A target company is defined as a corporation or other issuer of securities of which shareholders located in Illinois own 10% of the class of equity securities subject to the offer, or for which any two of the following three conditions are met: the corporation has its principal executive office in Illinois, is organized under the laws of Illinois, or has at least 10% of its stated capital and paid-in surplus represented within the State. An offer becomes registered 20 days after a registration statement is filed with the Secretary unless the Secretary calls a hearing. The Secretary may call a hearing at any time during the 20-day waiting period to adjudicate the substantive fairness of the offer if he believes it is necessary to protect the shareholders of the target company, and a hearing must be held if requested by a majority of a target company's outside directors or by Illinois shareholders who own 10% of the class of securities subject to the offer. If the Secretary does hold a hearing, he is directed by the statute to deny registration to a tender offer if he finds that it "fails to provide full and fair disclosure to the offerees of all material information concerning the take-over offer, or that the take-over offer is inequitable or would work or tend to work a fraud or deceit upon the offerees * * *."

On January 19, 1979, MITE initiated a cash tender offer for all outstanding shares of Chicago Rivet & Machine Co., a publicly held Illinois corporation, by filing a Schedule 14D-1 with the Securities and Exchange Commission in order to comply with the Williams Act. The Schedule 14D-1 indicated that MITE was willing to pay $28 per share for any and all outstanding shares of Chicago Rivet, a premium of approximately $4 over the then-prevailing market price. MITE did not comply with the Illinois Act, however, and commenced this litigation on the same day by filing an action in the United States District Court for the Northern District of Illinois. The complaint asked for a declaratory judgment that the Illinois Act was pre-empted by the Williams Act and violated the Commerce Clause. * * *

The United States Court of Appeals for the Seventh Circuit * * * agreed with the District Court that several provisions of the Illinois Act are pre-empted by the Williams Act and that the Illinois Act unduly burdens interstate commerce in violation of the Commerce Clause. * * *

[**Supremacy Clause Analysis**] We first address the holding that the Illinois Takeover Act is unconstitutional under the Supremacy Clause. We note at the outset that in passing the Williams Act, which is an amendment to the Securities Exchange Act of 1934, Congress did not also amend § 28(a) of the 1934 Act. In pertinent part, § 28(a) provides as follows:

> "Nothing in this title shall affect the jurisdiction of the securities commission (or any agency or officer performing like functions) of any State over any security or any person insofar as it does not conflict with the provisions of this title or the rules and regulations thereunder."

Thus Congress did not explicitly prohibit States from regulating takeovers; it left the determination whether the Illinois statute conflicts with the Williams Act to the courts. * * *

The Illinois Act requires a tender offeror to notify the Secretary of State and the target company of its intent to make a tender offer and the material terms of the offer 20 business days before the offer becomes effective. During that time, the offeror may not communicate its offer to the shareholders. Meanwhile, the target company is free to disseminate information to its shareholders concerning the impending offer. The contrast with the Williams Act is apparent. Under that Act, there is no pre-commencement notification requirement; the critical date is the date a tender offer is "first published or sent or given to security holders." * * *

For similar reasons, we agree with the Court of Appeals that the hearing provisions of the Illinois Act frustrate the congressional purpose by introducing extended delay into the tender offer process. The Illinois Act allows the Secretary of State to call a hearing with respect to any tender offer subject to the Act, and the offer may not proceed until the hearing is completed. * * *

The Court of Appeals also concluded that the Illinois Act is pre-empted by the Williams Act insofar as it allows the Secretary of State of Illinois to pass on the substantive fairness of a tender offer. * * * The Court of Appeals understood the Williams Act and its legislative history to indicate that Congress intended for investors to be free to make their own decisions. We agree. * * *

[**Commerce Clause Analysis**] The Commerce Clause provides that "Congress shall have Power * * * [t]o regulate Commerce * * * among the several States." U.S. Const., Art. I, § 8, cl. 3. "[A]t least since *Cooley v. Board of Wardens*, 53 U.S. (12 How.) 299, 13 L.Ed. 996 (1852), it has been clear that 'the Commerce Clause * * * even without implementing legislation by Congress is a limitation upon the power of the States.'" Not every exercise of state power with some impact on interstate commerce is invalid. A state statute must be upheld if it "regulates evenhandedly to effectuate a legitimate local public interest, and its effects on interstate commerce are only incidental * * * unless the burden imposed on such commerce is clearly excessive in relation to the putative local benefits." The Commerce Clause, however, permits only *incidental* regulation of interstate commerce by the States; direct regulation is prohibited. The Illinois Act violates these principles for two reasons. First, it directly regulates and prevents, unless its terms are satisfied, interstate tender offers which in turn would generate interstate transactions. Second, the burden the Act imposes on interstate commerce is excessive in light of the local interests the Act purports to further. * * *

We conclude with the Court of Appeals that the Illinois Act imposes a substantial burden on interstate commerce which outweighs its putative local benefits. It is accordingly invalid under the Commerce Clause.

The judgment of the Court of Appeals is *Affirmed*. * * *

[Concurring and dissenting opinions deleted]

§ 22.4 The Second Generation Statutes: The Supreme Court's View of the Indiana Control Share Statute

CTS Corp. v. Dynamics Corp. of America

United States Supreme Court, 1987 107 S.Ct. 1637

Justice POWELL:

These cases present the questions whether the Control Share Acquisitions Chapter of the Indiana Business Corporation Law, is pre-empted by the Williams Act, or violates the Commerce Clause of the Federal Constitution * * *.

[**Essential Facts and Issues**] On March 4, 1986, the Governor of Indiana signed a revised Indiana Business Corporation Law. That law included the Control Share Acquisitions Chapter (Indiana Act or Act). Beginning on August 1, 1987, the Act will apply to any corporation incorporated in Indiana, unless the corporation amends its articles of incorporation or bylaws to opt out of the Act. Before that date, any Indiana corporation can opt into the Act by resolution of its board of directors. The Act applies only to "issuing public corporations." The term "corporation" includes only businesses incorporated in Indiana. An "issuing public corporation" is defined as:

a corporation that has:

(1) one hundred (100) or more shareholders;

(2) its principal place of business, its principal office, or substantial assets within Indiana; and

(3) either:

(A) more than ten percent (10%) of its shareholders resident in Indiana;

(B) more than ten percent (10%) of its shares owned by Indiana residents; or

(C) ten thousand (10,000) shareholders resident in Indiana.

The Act focuses on the acquisition of "control shares" in an issuing public corporation. Under the Act, an entity acquires "control shares" whenever it acquires shares that, but for the operation of the Act, would bring its voting power in the corporation to or above any of three thresholds: 20%, 33%, or 50%. An entity that acquires control shares does not necessarily acquire voting rights. Rather, it gains those rights only "to the extent granted by resolution approved by the shareholders of the issuing public corporation." Section 9 requires a majority vote of all disinterested shareholders holding each class of stock for passage of such a resolution. The practical effect of this requirement is to condition acquisition of control of a corporation on approval of a majority of the pre-existing disinterested shareholders.

The shareholders decide whether to confer rights on the control shares at the next regularly scheduled meeting of the shareholders, or at a specially scheduled meeting. The acquiror can require management of the corporation to hold such a special meeting within 50 days if it files an "acquiring person statement," requests the meeting, and agrees to pay the expenses of the meeting. If the shareholders do not vote to restore voting rights to the shares, the corporation may redeem the control shares from the acquiror at fair market value, but it is not required to do so. Similarly, if the acquiror does not file an acquiring person statement with the corporation, the corporation may, if its bylaws or articles of incorporation so provide, redeem the shares at any time after 60 days after the acquiror's last acquisition.

On March 10, 1986, appellee Dynamics Corporation of America (Dynamics) owned 9.6% of the common stock of appellant CTS Corporation, an Indiana corporation. On that day, six days after the Act went into effect, Dynamics announced a tender offer for another million shares in CTS; purchase of those shares would have brought Dynamics' ownership interest in CTS to 27.5%. Also on March 10, Dynamics filed suit in the United States District Court for the Northern District of Illinois, alleging that CTS had violated the federal securities laws in a number of respects no longer relevant to these proceedings. On March 27, the board of directors of CTS, an Indiana corporation, elected to be governed by the provisions of the Act, *see* § 23-1-17-3.

Four days later, on March 31, Dynamics moved for leave to amend its complaint to allege that the Act is pre-empted by the Williams Act and violates the Commerce Clause.* * *

[**Preemption Analysis**] The first question in these cases is whether the Williams Act pre-empts the Indiana Act. As we have stated frequently, absent an explicit indication by Congress of an intent to pre-empt state law, a state statute is pre-empted only:

> "where compliance with both federal and state regulations is a physical impossibility * * *, or where the state 'law stands as an obstacle to the accomplishment and execution of the full purposes and objectives of Congress.' * * *"

Because it is entirely possible for entities to comply with both the Williams Act and the Indiana Act, the state statute can be pre-empted only if it frustrates the purposes of the federal law. * * *

The Indiana Act differs in major respects from the Illinois statute that the Court considered in *Edgar v. MITE Corp.*, [Section 22.3] * * *

* * * [T]he overriding concern of the *MITE* plurality was that the Illinois statute considered in that case operated to favor management against offerors, to the detriment of shareholders. By contrast, the statute now before the Court protects the independent shareholder against the contending parties. Thus, the Act furthers a basic purpose of the Williams Act. * * *

The Indiana Act operates on the assumption, implicit in the Williams Act, that independent shareholders faced with tender offers often are at a disadvantage. By allowing such shareholders to vote as a group, the Act protects them from the coercive aspects of some tender offers. * * * The desire of the Indiana Legislature to protect shareholders of Indiana corporations from this type of coercive offer does not conflict with the Williams Act. Rather, it furthers the federal policy of investor protection. * * *

Unlike the *MITE* statute, the Indiana Act does not give either management or the offeror an advantage in communicating with the shareholders about the impending offer. * * *

The Court of Appeals based its finding of pre-emption on its view that the practical effect of the Indiana Act is to delay consummation of tender offers until 50 days after the commencement of the offer. * * *

Even assuming that the Indiana Act imposes some additional delay, nothing in *MITE* suggested that *any* delay imposed by state regulation, however short, would create a conflict with the Williams Act.

Finally, we note that the Williams Act would preempt a variety of state corporate laws of hitherto unquestioned validity if it were construed to preempt any state statute that may limit or delay the free exercise of power after a successful tender offer. State corporate laws commonly permit corporations to stagger the terms of their directors. By staggering the terms of directors, and thus having annual elections for only one class of directors each year, corporations may delay the time when a successful offeror gains control of the board of directors. Similarly, state corporation laws commonly provide for cumulative voting. By enabling minority shareholders to assure themselves of representation in each class of directors, cumulative voting provisions can delay further the ability of offerors to gain untrammeled authority over the affairs of the target corporation.

In our view, the possibility that the Indiana Act will delay some tender offers is insufficient to require a conclusion that the Williams Act pre-empts the Act. * * *

[**Commerce Clause Analysis**] As an alternative basis for its decision, the Court of Appeals held that the Act violates the Commerce Clause of the Federal Constitution. * * *

[I]ts decision rested on its view of the Act's potential to hinder tender offers. We think the Court of Appeals failed to appreciate the significance for Commerce Clause analysis of the fact that state regulation of corporate governance is regulation of entities whose very existence and attributes are a product of state law. * * * Every State in this country has enacted laws regulating corporate governance. By prohibiting certain transactions, and regulating others, such laws necessarily affect certain aspects of interstate commerce. This necessarily is true with respect to corporations with shareholders in States other than the State of incorporation. * * *

These regulatory laws may affect directly a variety of corporate transactions. Mergers are a typical example. In view of the substantial effect that a merger may have on the shareholders' interests in a corporation, many States require supermajority votes to approve mergers. By requiring a greater vote for mergers than is required for other transactions, these laws make it more difficult for corporations to merge. State laws also may provide for "dissenters' rights" under which minority shareholders who disagree with corporate decisions to take particular actions are entitled to sell their shares to the corporation at fair market value. By requiring the corporation to purchase the shares of dissenting shareholders, these laws may inhibit a corporation from engaging in the specified transactions.

It thus is an accepted part of the business landscape in this country for States to create corporations, to prescribe their powers, and to define the rights that are acquired by purchasing their shares. * * *

[**Conclusion**] On its face, the Indiana Control Share Acquisitions Chapter evenhandedly determines the voting rights of shares of Indiana corporations. The Act does not conflict with the provisions or purposes of the Williams Act. To the limited extent that the Act affects interstate commerce, this is justified by the State's interests in defining the attributes of shares in its corporations and in protecting shareholders. Congress has never questioned the need for state regulation of these matters. Nor do we think such regulation offends the Constitution. * * *

[Concurring and dissenting opinions deleted]

§ 22.5 The Third Generation Statutes

A. The Seventh Circuit's View of the Wisconsin Business Combination Statute

Amanda Acquisition Corp. v. Universal Foods Corp.

United States Court of Appeals, Seventh Circuit, 1989 877 F.2d 496

Easterbrook, Circuit Judge:

[**Background and Issue**] States have enacted three generations of takeover statutes in the last 20 years. Illinois enacted a first-generation statute, which forbade acquisitions of any firm with substantial assets in Illinois unless a public official approved. We concluded that such a statute injures investors, is preempted by the Williams Act, and is unconstitutional under the dormant Commerce Clause. *MITE Corp. v. Dixon*, 633 F.2d 486 (7th Cir.1980). The Supreme Court affirmed the judgment under the Commerce Clause, *Edgar v. MITE Corp.*, [Section 22.3] * * *

Indiana enacted a second-generation statute, applicable only to firms incorporated there and eliminating governmental veto power. Indiana's law provides that the acquiring firm's shares lose their voting power unless the target's directors approve the acquisition or the shareholders not affiliated with either bidder or management authorize restoration of votes. We concluded that this statute, too, is inimical to investors' interests, preempted by the Williams Act, and unconstitutional under the Commerce Clause. *Dynamics Corp. of America v. CTS Corp.*, 794 F.2d 250 (7th Cir.1986). This time the Supreme Court did not agree. It thought the Indiana statute consistent with both Williams Act and Commerce Clause. *CTS Corp. v. Dynamics Corp. of America*, [Section 22.4] * * *

Wisconsin has a third-generation takeover statute. Enacted after *CTS*, it postpones the kinds of transactions that often follow tender offers (and often are the reason for making the offers in the first place). Unless the target's board agrees to the transaction in advance, the bidder must wait three years after buying the shares to merge with the target or acquire more than 5% of its assets. We must decide whether this is consistent with the Williams Act and Commerce Clause.

[**Essential Facts**] Amanda Acquisition Corporation is a shell with a single purpose: to acquire Universal Foods Corporation, a diversified firm incorporated in Wisconsin and traded on the New York Stock Exchange. Universal is covered by Wisconsin's anti-takeover law. Amanda is a subsidiary of High Voltage Engineering Corp., a small electronics firm in Massachusetts. * * *

In mid-November 1988 Universal's stock was trading for about $25 per share. On December 1, Amanda commenced a tender offer at $30.50, to be effective if at least 75% of the stock should be tendered. This all-cash, all-shares offer has been increased by stages to $38.00. Amanda's financing is contingent on a prompt merger with Universal if the offer succeeds, so the offer is conditional on a judicial declaration that the law is invalid. (It is also conditional on Universal's redemption of poison pill stock. For reasons that we discuss below, it is unnecessary to discuss the subject in detail.)

No firm incorporated in Wisconsin and having its headquarters, substantial operations, or 10% of its shares or shareholders there may "engage in a business combination with an interested stockholder * * * for 3 years after the interested stockholder's stock acquisition date unless the board of directors of the [Wisconsin] corporation has approved, before the interested stockholder's stock acquisition date, that business combination or the purchase of stock", Wis.Stat. § 180.726(2). An "interested stockholder" is one owning 10% of the voting stock, directly or through associates (anyone acting in concert with it), § 180.726(1)(j). A "business combination" is a merger with the bidder or any of its affiliates, sale of more than 5% of the assets to bidder or affiliate, liquidation of the target, or a transaction by which the target guarantees the bidder's or affiliates debts or passes tax benefits to the bidder or affiliate, § 1 80.726(1)(e). The law, in other words, provides for almost hermetic separation of bidder and target for three years after the bidder obtains 10% of the stock—unless the target's board consented before then. No matter how popular the offer, the ban applies: obtaining 85% (even 100%) of the stock held by non-management shareholders won't allow the bidder to engage in a business combination, as it would under Delaware law. *See BNS, Inc. v. Koppers Co.*, 683 F.Supp. 458 (D.Del. 1988); * * *.

Wisconsin firms cannot opt out of the law, as may corporations subject to almost all other state takeover statutes. In Wisconsin it is management's approval in advance, or wait three years. Even when the time is up, the bidder needs the approval of a majority of the remaining investors, without any provision disqualifying shares still held by the managers who resisted the transaction, § 180.726(3)(b). The district court found that this statute "effectively eliminates hostile leveraged buyouts". As a practical matter, Wisconsin prohibits any offer contingent on a merger between bidder and target, a condition attached to about 90% of contemporary tender offers.

Amanda filed this suit seeking a declaration that this law is preempted by the Williams Act and inconsistent with the Commerce Clause. * * * The district court declined to issue a preliminary injunction. It concluded that the statute is constitutional and not preempted * * *.

[**Analysis**] If our views of the wisdom of state law mattered, Wisconsin's takeover statute would not survive. Like our colleagues who decided *MITE* and *CTS*, we believe that antitakeover legislation injures shareholders. * * * Studies of laws similar to Wisconsin's produce the same conclusion: share prices of firms incorporated in the state drop when the legislation is enacted. * * *

Skepticism about the wisdom of a state's law does not lead to the conclusion that the law is beyond the state's power, however. * * * Unless a federal statute or the Constitution bars the way, Wisconsin's choice must be respected.

Amanda relies on the Williams Act of 1968 * * *. * * * Amanda believes that Congress created an entitlement for investors to receive the benefit of tender offers, and that because Wisconsin's law makes tender offers unattractive to many potential bidders, it is preempted.

[**Preemption**] Preemption has not won easy acceptance among the Justices for several reasons. First there is § 28(a) of the '34 Act, which provides that "[n]othing in this chapter shall affect the jurisdiction of the securities commission * * * of any State over any security or any person insofar as it does not conflict with the provisions of this chapter or the rules and regulations thereunder."* * * States have regulated corporate affairs, including mergers and sales of assets, since before the beginning of the nation. * * *

Any bidder complying with federal law is free to acquire shares of Wisconsin firms on schedule. Delay in completing a second-stage merger may make the target less attractive, and thus depress the price offered or even lead to an absence of bids; it does not, however, alter any of the procedures governed by federal regulation. * * *

Only if the Williams Act gives investors a right to be the beneficiary of offers could Wisconsin's law run afoul of the federal rule. No such entitlement can be mined out of the Williams Act, however. * * *

[**Commerce Clause**] The Commerce Clause, Art. I, § 8 cl. 3 of the Constitution, grants Congress the power "[t]o regulate Commerce * * * among the several States." * * *

Illinois's law, held invalid in *MITE*, regulated sales of stock elsewhere. Illinois tried to tell a Texas owner of stock in a Delaware corporation that he could not sell to a buyer in California. By contrast, Wisconsin's law, like the Indiana statute sustained by *CTS*, regulates the internal affairs of firms incorporated there. Investors may buy or sell stock as they please. * * *

Buyers of stock in Wisconsin firms may exercise full rights as investors, taking immediate control. No interstate transaction is regulated or forbidden. True, Wisconsin's law makes a potential buyer less willing to buy (or depresses the bid), but this is equally true of Indiana's rule. Many other rules of corporate law-supermajority voting requirements, staggered and classified boards, and so on-have similar or greater effects on some persons' willingness to purchase stock. *CTS.* States could ban mergers outright, with even more powerful consequences. Wisconsin did not allow mergers among firms chartered there until 1947. We doubt that it was violating the Commerce Clause all those years. * * *

The three district judges who have considered and sustained Delaware's law delaying mergers did so in large measure because they believed that the law left hostile offers "a meaningful opportunity for success". *BNS, Inc. v. Koppers Co.*, 683 F.Supp. at 469. *See also RP Acquisition Corp.*, 686 F.Supp. at 482–84, 488; *City Capital Associates*, 696 F.Supp. at 1555. Delaware allows a merger to occur forthwith if the bidder obtains 85% of the shares other than those held by management and employee stock plans. If the bid is attractive to the bulk of the unaffiliated investors, it succeeds. Wisconsin offers no such opportunity, which Amanda believes is fatal.

Even in Wisconsin, though, options remain. Defenses impenetrable to the naked eye may have cracks. Poison pills are less fatal in practice than in name (some have been swallowed willingly), and corporate law contains self-defense mechanisms. * * * Poison pills are dilution devices, and so pre-emptive rights ought to be handy countermeasures.[1] So too there are countermeasures to statutes deferring mergers. The cheapest is to lower the bid to reflect the costs of delay. * * *

At the end of the day, however, it does not matter whether these countermeasures are "enough". The Commerce Clause does not demand that states leave bidders a "meaningful opportunity for success". * * * The Constitution has room for many economic policies. "[A] law can be both economic folly and constitutional." *CTS*, 481 U.S. at 96–97, 107 S.Ct. at 1653–54 (Scalia, J., concurring). Wisconsin's law may well be folly; we are confident that it is constitutional.

B. Delaware

1. § 203 of Delaware General Business Corporation Law

See § 203 of Delaware General Business Corporation Law, Business Combinations with Interested Shareholders

Note

Section 203 has been found not to be preempted by the Williams Act and not to be in violation of the Commerce Clause. [*See e.g., BNS, Inc., v. Koppers Co.*, 683 F. Supp. 458, (D. Del. 1988), discussed in *Amanda* Section 22.5.A]

1. Imagine a series of Antidote rights, issued by would-be bidding firms, that detach if anyone exercises flip-over rights to purchase the bidder's stock at a discount. Antidote rights would entitle the bidder's investors, other than those who exercise flip-over rights, to purchase the bidder's stock at the same discount available to investors exercising flip-over rights. Antidotes for flip-in rights also could be issued. In general, whenever one firm can issue rights allowing the purchase of cheap stock, another firm can issue the equivalent series of contingent pre-emptive rights that offsets the dilution.

2. Interpretation of § 203—*Home Shopping*

Home Shopping Network, Inc. Shareholders Litigation

Delaware Chancery Court, 1993 CCH Fed.Sec. Law Rep. ¶ 97,619

CHANDLER, Vice Chancellor:

[**Essential Facts and Issue**] This is the decision on motions to preliminarily enjoin the consummation or closing of a partial tender offer by defendant Liberty Media Corporation ("Liberty"). In an offer that expires at midnight on May 20, 1993, Liberty seeks to purchase up to 15 million outstanding public shares of defendant Home Shopping Network Inc.'s ("HSN") common stock at $7 net per share. If Liberty's offer is fully subscribed, Liberty's equity interest in HSN will increase from 23 percent to 40 percent, while its voting power will grow from 65 percent to 70 percent. * * *

The plaintiffs (the "§ 203 plaintiffs") allege that Liberty's pending tender offer violates the Delaware Business Combinations Act, 8 *Del.C.* § 203. * * *

[**Analysis**] The statute begins:

> (a) Notwithstanding any other provisions of this chapter, a corporation shall not engage in any business combination with any interested stockholder for a period of 3 years following the date that such stockholder became an interested stockholder * * *

8 *Del.C.* § 203(a). The statute later provides a detailed definition of the term "business combination" in subsection (c)(3). Subsection 203(a) also contains numerous exceptions to the three-year moratorium on business combinations.

Plaintiffs argue that the tender offer is a business combination, as defined in § 203(c)(3)(iv). They note that the tender offer, if completed, will increase Liberty's proportionate share of HSN's stock from 23 percent to 40 percent, approximately. * * * [A]ccording to the language and intent of the statute, I believe Liberty's partial tender offer, in which its equity interest may be increased from 23 percent to 40 percent, is not a transaction covered by § 203's definition of a "business combination." * * *

Of greatest importance in statutory interpretation is the plain language of the statute itself. * * * In this regard, § 203(c)(3) specifically defines a "business combination." To paraphrase, the definition of business combination basically includes: 1) mergers and consolidations with interested stockholders; 2) any sale, lease, exchange, pledge, disposition, or similar transaction to or with an interested stockholder if the transaction involves corporate assets valued at over 10 percent of the market value of the corporation's stocks or aggregate assets; 3) issuance of stock or other securities or other transactions that increase an interested stockholder's proportionate ownership of any class or series of stock; 4) any other transaction that confers a financial benefit on an interested stockholder by or through the corporation; and 5) receipt of financial benefits by an interested stockholder in loans or other financial benefits provided by the corporation. 8 *Del.C.* § 203(c)(3).

Plaintiffs do not argue that Liberty's partial tender offer is a "business combination" as defined in categories 1, 2, 3, or 5. * * * Plaintiffs assert, however, that the fourth category of a "business combination", as stated in subsection 203(c)(3)(iv), applies to Liberty's partial tender offer because it has the effect of increasing the interested shareholder's (Liberty's) ownership of stock. This subsection states:

> (3) "business combination," when used in reference to any corporation and any interested stockholder of such corporation, means: * * *

> (iv) any transaction *involving the corporation* or any direct or indirect majority-owned subsidiary of the corporation which has the effect, directly or indirectly, of increasing the proportionate share of the stock of any class or series, or securities convertible into the stock of any class or series, of the corporation or of any such subsidiary which is owned by the interested stockholder, except as a result of immaterial changes due to fractional share adjustments or as a result of any purchase or redemption of any shares of stock not caused, directly or indirectly, by the interested shareholder;

8 *Del.C.* § 203(c)(3)(iv) (emphasis added).

The question before me, then, is whether the clause "involving the corporation" necessarily applies to a partial tender offer by an interested shareholder. Plaintiffs assert that it does; defendants disagree. The statute itself does not further clarify the phrase. * * *

It is clear that a tender offer is directed not at the target corporation, but at its shareholders. * * * Therefore, the target corporation is not automatically "involved" in any tender offer for its shares. Unlike each of the other transactions defined as a "business combination" under the statute * * * the corporation in the situation presented here is involved only through its shareholders. * * *

Plaintiffs have not demonstrated that HSN is "involved" in the current partial tender offer. * * * Therefore, I conclude that Liberty's partial tender offer is not a "business combination" within the meaning of § 203(c)(3)(iv). * * *

3. The Meaning of "Interested Shareholder" under Section 203—*Chesapeake*

Chesapeake Corporation v. Shore

Delaware Court of Chancery, 2000 Del. Ch. LEXIS 20

[The excerpt below deals with the issue of whether the acquiror, Chesapeake, became an interested party under Section 203 by reason of its purchase of 14.9% of the stock of Shorewood, the Delaware target, from Ariel.]

* * * An obvious target in the Chesapeake/Shorewood struggle was Ariel Capital Management, Inc., an investment advisory firm that was Shorewood's single largest stockholder. Ariel owned over 20% of Shorewood's shares. * * *

[T]he Chesapeake representatives raised the issue of purchasing enough of Ariel's shares to obtain 14.9% of Shorewood's stock with upside protection. * * * The record is clear that Chesapeake was careful to limit itself to the 14.9% level because of 8 Del. C. Section 203. Its intention was to stop short of any agreement that would make Chesapeake "an interested stockholder" under that statute. * * *

On November 26, 1999, an agreement was reached (the "Ariel Agreement") for Ariel to sell shares equal to 14.9% of Shorewood's outstanding shares (the "Purchased Shares") at $ 17.25 apiece. In the event of a future Majority Transaction, Ariel would receive additional consideration. * * *

The Ariel Agreement left Ariel still holding a substantial block of Shorewood shares (the "Non-Purchased Shares"). * * *

Is Chesapeake An "Interested Stockholder" Under 8 Del. C. Section 203? The defendants contend that Chesapeake is barred by 8 Del. C. Section 203 from entering into any business combination with Shorewood for three years from the date of its agreement to purchase Shorewood shares from Ariel. * * *

The defendants * * * contend that the Agreement [with Ariel] provides Chesapeake with rights as to the remaining Shorewood shares held by Ariel clients (heretofore defined as the "Non-Purchased Shares")—rights that under Section 203 are sufficient to make Chesapeake an owner of the Non-Purchased Shares as well and therefore the owner of over 20% of Shorewood's shares. More specifically, the defendants contend for two independent reasons that, as a result of the Agreement, Chesapeake became an "interested stockholder" under Section 203.

First, the defendants claim that Section 1(d)(ii) of the Agreement requires Ariel to cause its clients to execute consents in favor of Chesapeake with respect to all of the Shorewood shares beneficially owned by them, not just the Purchased Shares. Second, the defendants contend that Section 2 of the Agreement creates an economic incentive for Ariel to vote the Non-Purchased Shares with Chesapeake in circumstances where that would not be so absent the Agreement and that this incentive system also renders Chesapeake an owner of the Non-Purchased Shares under Section 203. Before addressing these arguments, I will set forth the basic provisions of 8 Del. C. Section 203 and how they relate to the defendants' claims.

Under Section 203, an "interested stockholder" is prohibited in most circumstances from entering into any "business combination" with the corporation for a period of three years following the time that the stockholder became an "interested" one. [Section 203(a)] An "interested stockholder" is one who acquires "ownership" of 15% or more of the corporation's outstanding voting stock. [Section 203(c)(5)(i)]

The statute defines "ownership" expansively, with the term "owner" including any "person that individually or with or through any of its affiliates or associates: (i) beneficially owns such stock, directly or indirectly; or (ii) has (A) the right to acquire such stock * * * or (B) the right to vote such stock pursuant to any agreement, arrangement or understanding." [203(c)(9)(i),(ii)] Thus if the defendants' first argument is correct and the contract between Chesapeake and Ariel vested voting control of over 20% of Shorewood's shares in Chesapeake, then Chesapeake would be an "interested stockholder."

The defendants' second argument relies on another part of Section 203's definition of an owner. That part provides that a person who has an "agreement, arrangement or understanding * * * for the purpose of acquiring, holding, voting * * * or disposing of such stock with any other person that beneficially owns, or whose affiliates beneficially own, directly or indirectly, such stock" is also deemed an owner of that stock. [203(c)(9)(iii)] By incentivizing Ariel to vote the Non-Purchased Shares with Chesapeake, the Ariel Agreement, the defendants claim, constitutes an "agreement * * * or understanding" between Chesapeake and Ariel for the purpose of * * * voting" those Shares. * * *

To the extent that the terms of the Agreement can be considered ambiguous, the extrinsic evidence of the parties' intent is abundant and consistent and undercuts the defendants' argument. Representatives of Chesapeake and Ariel involved in the drafting of the Agreement both intended that the Agreement apply only to the Purchased Shares. Therefore, nothing in Section 1(d) of the Agreement suffices to make Chesapeake an owner of the Non-Purchased Shares under Section 203.

The defendants' second argument is subtle. That argument turns on the provision of the Agreement requiring Chesapeake to pay additional consideration for the Purchased Shares if Chesapeake, a Chesapeake affiliate, or any third party not affiliated with Ariel or Chesapeake acquires ownership of a majority of Shorewood's outstanding shares pursuant to any type of transaction within one year of the closing date in the Agreement. * * *

The defendants argue that this incentive structure is sufficient to make Chesapeake a person that has "any agreement, arrangement or understanding for the purpose of * * * voting [the Non-Purchased Shares]." As such, Section 203(c)(9)(iii), they contend, renders Chesapeake an "owner" of the Non-Purchased Shares and therefore an interested stockholder. * * *

Because Section 203 has the practical effect of disenfranchising parties found to be "interested" under its terms, this court should be hesitant to strain the statute's language to cover situations that do not threaten the interests the statute was designed to protect. Seeing no such threat here, I decline to extend Section 203's reach.

To the extent I am incorrect, Chesapeake would still not be deemed an "interested stockholder" under Section 203. Rather, by the Agreement's terms, the Purchased Shares would be reduced to the number sufficient to satisfy Section 203. * * *

4. Waiver of Controlled Corporation's Section 203 Rights by Controlling Shareholder's Interested Directors—*Digex*

In Re Digex, Inc. Shareholders Litigation

Court of Chancery of Delaware, 2000 Del. Ch. LEXIS 171

CHANDLER, Chancellor:

This is my decision on plaintiffs' motion to preliminarily enjoin the proposed merger between defendants WorldCom, Inc. ("WorldCom") [the acquiring corporation] and Intermedia Communications, Inc. ("Intermedia") [the target], the controlling shareholder of Digex, Inc. ("Digex") [the potential target]. Plaintiffs, minority shareholders of Digex, seek either of two alternative forms of relief: (1) an order enjoining the defendants from consummating the Agreement and Plan of Merger dated September 1, 2000, (the "merger") [this issue is addressed in Section 3.17.C], or (2) an order enjoining the Digex board's waiver of 8 *Del. C.* § 203. * * *

Section 203 Claim. In their [§ 203] claim; the plaintiffs argue that the interested Digex directors breached their fiduciary duties by causing Digex to improperly waive § 203 of the DGCL. Specifically, the plaintiffs assert that because the waiver was accomplished by the vote of the four Intermedia-affiliated Digex directors, and against the vote and advice of the three independent Digex directors, the vote must be judged under the entire fairness standard. Plaintiffs contend that the defendants have failed to meet this standard. * * *

[O]nce an entity becomes an "interested stockholder," § 203, subject to certain exemptions, prohibits business combinations between a Delaware corporation and that shareholder for a period of three years. There is no dispute between the parties that WorldCom will become an interested shareholder in Digex as a result of the merger [with Intermedia a controlling shareholder of Digex] and that WorldCom intends to enter into transactions with Digex [*i.e.*, a freeze-out merger] where the prohibitions of § 203 would apply absent an exemption. As a result, although WorldCom believes that it would come within the statutory exemption provided by § 203(a)(2) for interested stockholders holding 85% or more of the "voting stock" of the corporation, WorldCom also sought the additional certainty that would come with a § 203(a)(1) waiver agreed to by the Digex board of directors [*i.e.*, the Digex board's approval for the transaction which would result in WorldCom becoming an interested shareholder, that is the merger with Intermedia]. WorldCom was not content to rely merely on the 85% shareholder exemption because it recognized that the application of the § 203(a)(2) exemption in situations involving "super-voting rights" has not been definitively ruled upon by the Delaware courts. There is also no dispute that the Digex board voted to waive the protections afforded by § 203. Instead, the plaintiffs contend that the vote to waive § 203 amounted to a breach of fiduciary duty. * * *

Was the § 203 Waiver Entirely Fair to the Digex Shareholders? On its face, § 203 does not bar interested directors from participating in a vote to approve a transaction in which an entity becomes an interested stockholder. Nevertheless, directors must at all times abide by their fiduciary duties owed to the shareholders of the corporation. When the directors of a Delaware corporation appear on both sides of a transaction, the presumption in favor of the business judgment rule is rebutted and the directors are required to demonstrate their "utmost good faith and the most scrupulous inherent fairness of the bargain."

Where a director holds dual directorships in the parent-subsidiary context, there is no dilution of this obligation to demonstrate the entire fairness of specific board actions. * * *

Here, the § 203 waiver decision must be analyzed under the rubric of entire fairness as all four votes to waive the protections were made by directors who not only sat on both the boards of Intermedia and Digex, but also possessed substantial direct, personal financial interests in the proposed transaction. The waiver by the Digex board therefore demands careful scrutiny, as the defendants bear the burden of establishing entire fairness. * * *

§ 22.6 Pennsylvania's Second and Third Generation Statutes and Beyond[2]

A. Introduction

In 1990 Pennsylvania enacted a comprehensive anti-takeover statute, which the Third Circuit in *Armstrong World Industries, Inc. v. Adams*, 961 F.2d 405 (3rd Cir 1992), described as follows: "Considered one of the nation's toughest anti-takeover statutes, the Act enhances the ability of management of Pennsylvania corporations to fend off hostile takeover attempts." The *Armstrong* court affirmed the district court's dismissal of a constitutional challenge to the statute which contained provisions relating to:

1. Fiduciary Duties,
2. Control Transactions,
3. Business Combinations,
4. Control Share Acquisitions,
5. Disgorgement of Certain Control Share Profits,
6. Severance Compensation, and
7. Labor Contract Continuation

The fiduciary duty provisions are discussed in Section 3.23. This section briefly outlines the other provisions.

B. Applicability of PA BCL to "Registered Corporations"

Pennsylvania's Takeover Statute applies to "registered corporations," which are defined in Section 2502 of the Pennsylvania Business Corporation Law (Pa BCL) as a PA corporation

2. I thank Taimoor Choudhry, a 2014 graduate of Penn State Law and my former research assistant, for his very helpful assistance in preparing the materials dealing with Pennsylvania law.

that is registered under the 34 Act, that is, a publicly held Pennsylvania corporation. There are certain provisions pursuant to which a registered corporation may "opt-out" of being a registered corporation.

C. Control Share Provisions of the PA Takeover Statute

Sections 2541–2548 of the PA BCL deal with "Control Transactions," which are transactions where a person or group acquires at least 20% of the voting power of a registered corporation. Pursuant to Section 2546 of the PA BCL, if a control transaction occurs, then:

> any holder of voting shares of the registered corporation may * * * make written demand on the controlling person or group for payment of * * * an amount equal to the fair value of each voting share as of the date on which the control transaction occurs, taking into account all relevant factors, including an increment representing a proportion of any value payable for acquisition of control of the corporation.

D. The Business Combination Provision of the PA Takeover Statute

The business combination provisions are similar to Delaware's Section 203, which prohibits for a period of three years certain business combinations between an interested shareholder and the target corporation, when such combinations were not previously approved by the target's board. [*See* §§ 2551–2558] Section 2555 provides, *inter alia*, that for a period of five years, a registered corporation shall not engage in a business combination with any interested shareholder [*i.e.*, a 20% shareholder] of the corporation other than:

> (1) A business combination approved by the board of directors of the corporation prior to the interested shareholder's share acquisition date [*i.e.*, date that the person first became an interested shareholder], or where the purchase of shares made by the interested shareholder on the interested shareholder's share acquisition date had been approved by the board of directors of the corporation prior to the interested shareholder's share acquisition date.

E. The Control Share Acquisition Provision of the PA Takeover Statute

The *Armstrong* case describes as follows the control-share acquisition provision of the PA Takeover Statute:

> The control-share acquisitions provision restricts the voting rights of any person who acquires shares in connection with a "control-share acquisition." [*See* § 2564] A control-share acquisition occurs whenever a person acquires voting power for the first time over 20%, 33%, or 50% of the voting shares of a corporation. [*See* § 2562] Persons who initiate control-share acquisitions are denied voting rights in "control shares," except where such rights are granted by a majority of disinterested shares and a majority of all voting shares. [*See* § 2564] * * *

F. The Disgorgement Provision of the PA Takeover Statute

The *Armstrong* case describes as follows the disgorgement provision of the PA Takeover Statute:

> The disgorgement provision enables corporations to recover short-swing profits realized by any "controlling person" from the sale of shares in connection with a control-share acquisition. [*See* § 2575] A controlling person is any person or group that (1) acquires, offers to acquire, or announces its intention to acquire voting power over at least 20% of the shares entitled to vote in an election of directors, or (2) announces that "it may seek to acquire control of a corporation through any means." All profits realized within eighteen months after obtaining controlling-person status from the sale of shares acquired two years prior to, or eighteen months subsequent to, attaining such status may be recovered by the corporation through an enforcement action. [*See* § 2575] * * *

G. The Severance Pay Provision of the PA Takeover Statute

A Senate Democratic Wrap-up for the 1989–1990 Legislative Session explains: "The law also provides protection to employees once a takeover is consummated under the control shares provision by requiring severance pay to terminated workers." [*See* § 2582]

H. The Labor Continuation Provision of the PA Takeover Statute

The Senate Democratic Wrap-up also explains: "Labor contracts cannot be terminated unless the bargaining unit and the new management agree." [*See* § 2587]

I. PA's "Other Constituencies" Statute

As pointed out in *Simmons*, Section 3.23.C, in the exercise of its general powers, a board of directors of a Pennsylvania corporation may consider constituencies other than shareholders. These provisions are commonly referred to as "other constituency" provisions. Specifically, Section 1715 of the PA BCL provides that "in considering the best interests of the corporation, [the directors may] consider to the extent they deem appropriate:"

> (1) The effects of any action upon any or all groups affected by such action, including shareholders, employees, suppliers, customers and creditors of the corporation, and upon communities in which offices or other establishments of the corporation are located.
>
> (2) The short-term and long-term interests of the corporation, including benefits that may accrue to the corporation from its long-term plans and the possibility that these interests may be best served by the continued independence of the corporation.
>
> (3) The resources, intent and conduct (past, stated and potential) of any person seeking to acquire control of the corporation.
>
> (4) All other pertinent factors.

§ 22.7 Illustration of Private Ordering: The Goldman Sachs "Other Constituency" Charter Provision

Although Goldman Sachs is a Delaware corporation, and Delaware does not have an "other constituency" statute, Goldman has an "other constituency" provision in its charter. [*See* Documentary Appendix W of *M&A Statutes, Rules, and Documents, supra* Section

1.1] This illustrates that unless specifically prohibited by the applicable corporate law, the shareholders of a corporation can adopt a provision in the charter that is different from the statutory default rule.

§ 22.8 Policy Perspectives: Three Views of the Economic Effect of State Takeover Legislation

A. Detrimental to Shareholders' Welfare

The effect on shareholder wealth from the adoption of state takeover statutes is addressed in Jonathan M. Karpoff and Paul H. Malatesta, *The Wealth Effects of Second-Generation Takeover Legislation*, 25 J. OF FIN. ECO. 291, (1989). This article examines in particular the wealth effects of the adoption of second-generation statutes. The article reaches the following conclusion:

> We find that, on average, the initial press announcement of a state takeover law is associated with a small but statistically significant decrease in the stock prices of firms incorporated in the state and of large firms headquartered in the state. This result is consistent with the hypothesis that state takeover laws tend to deter hostile takeover bids and entrench incumbent managers at the expense of stockholders. *Id.* at 321.

B. Delaware Statute Beneficial to Shareholders' Welfare

One recent study has found that Section 203 of the Delaware Corporate law, which is discussed in Section 22.5, is beneficial to shareholders. *See* John S. Hahera, Jr., and William Pugh, *State Takeover Legislation: The Case of Delaware*, 7 J. OF LAW, ECONOMICS AND ORGANIZATIONS, 410 (1991). The study reaches the following conclusions:

> We find that * * * there is little evidence that the Delaware law harms shareholders. In fact, for some methodologies, we observe that companies incorporated in Delaware tended to have positive excess returns on days associated with progress of the legislation. *Id.* at 411.

C. Pennsylvania's Statute Detrimental to Shareholders' Welfare

A study of Pennsylvania's takeover statute, which is discussed in Section 22.6, found an adverse effect on shareholders. *See* Samuel H. Szewczyk and George P. Tsetsekos, *State Intervention in the Market for Corporate Control*, 31 J. OF FIN. ECONOMICS 3, (1992). The conclusions are summarized as follows:

> Over the period in which the bill was making its way through the legislature, we observe a significantly negative abnormal return of 9.09% for 56 such firms. The total loss in shareholders' wealth is conservatively estimated at $4 billion. *Id.* at 4.

References

Brown *et al.*, *Takeovers: A Strategic Guide*, *supra* Section 1.10.

Hazen, *Securities Regulation*, *supra* Section 1.10.

Lipton and Steinberger, *Takeovers and Freezeouts*, *supra* Section 1.10.

Loss & Seligman, *Securities Regulation*, *supra* Section 1.10.

Thompson, *Mergers, Acquisitions and Tender Offers*, *supra* Section 1.10, Section 8.6.

Chapter 23

Target's Defensive Actions

§ 23.1 Scope

This chapter builds on Section 3.14, *The "Big Six" Foundational Delaware Fiduciary Duty Cases Dealing with Mergers and Acquisitions*, and Section 3.18, *Elaboration on the Enhanced Business Judgment Rule for Defensive Tactics and Introduction to Poison Pills*. As indicated in Section 23.3, it is important to review Sections 3.14 and 3.18 before proceeding with this chapter.

Section 23.2 sets out an introductory problem on defensive tactics. Section 23.4 focuses on various charter and bylaw provisions designed to shield a target from takeover; these are known generally as "shark repellent" provisions. Section 23.5 explores various contractual arrangements between a target and its senior employees providing for special payments in the event of a change in control; these are known as "golden parachute" payments. Section 23.6 deals with situations in which a target corporation buys its stock from a raider at a premium over the market. These are known as "greenmail" payments. Section 23.7 discusses poison debt, that is, debt that becomes due and payable in the event of a takeover. Section 23.8 refers to the ALI's proposed rules on defensive tactics, and Section 23.9 sets out the recommendations of the SEC's Tender Offer Advisory Committee. The final two sections look at two significant policy issues with defensive tactics. Section 23.10 presents two different views on the efficacy of defensive tactics: the board passivity approach developed by Easterbrook and Fischel, and the board action approach developed by Lipton. Section 23.11 looks at a policy debate on how courts should respond to a poison pill in combination with a staggered board. Finally, Section 23.12 addresses my proposal for a Change of Control Board or Change of Control Special Committee, which I believe would eliminate the need for judicial scrutiny of virtually every significant acquisition of a publicly held firm.

The materials in this chapter are discussed in greater detail in Thompson, *Mergers, Acquisitions and Tender Offers*, *supra* Section 1.10, Chapter 5.

§ 23.2 Introductory Problem on Defensive Tactics

(1) The boards of Time Entertainment, Inc. (Time) and Warner Entertainment, Inc. (Warner), both publicly-held Delaware corporations, are considering a combination transaction. Neither Time nor Warner has a poison pill or any shark repellent provisions. However, both are concerned that once the possible combination transaction becomes public knowledge, a third party or parties may attempt to acquire either Time or Warner. Can Time and Warner now adopt a poison pill or shark repellent provision in order to protect themselves from a hostile offer?

(a) What if the transaction is structured so that Time will acquire Warner in exchange for 40% of Time's stock? 60% of Time's stock?

(b) What if the transaction is structured so that Time will acquire all of the stock of Warner in exchange for cash?

(2) Under what circumstances and conditions, if any, can Time and Warner include in the merger agreement a provision prohibiting each firm from talking (a "no talk" provision) with any potential third party acquiror?

(3) The facts are the same as in question 1, and the transaction is structured so that Time will acquire Warner in exchange for 40% of Time's stock. Is the board of Time or of Warner required to auction the company?

(a) What if the transaction is structured so that Time will issue 60% of its stock in exchange for the Warner stock?

(b) What if Time will acquire the Warner stock for cash?

(4) Assume that both Time and Warner have adopted a standard flip-in and flip-over poison pill plan, with a 20% trigger on the flip-in. The boards of Time and Warner have agreed to a reverse subsidiary merger in which a newly formed subsidiary of Time (Time-Sub) will merge into Warner, with Warner becoming a subsidiary of Time and the shareholders of Warner receiving common stock of Time equal to 60% of Time's outstanding common stock after the transaction. Also, Time and Warner enter into a share exchange agreement pursuant to which in exchange for stock of each other Time can acquire 10% of Warner's stock and Warner can acquire 12% of Time's stock. The share exchange is triggered if, *inter alia*, a third party makes a tender offer for either Time or Warner. What standard governs the actions of Time's and Warner's boards in structuring this transaction?

(5) After the merger is announced, but before the vote by the Time and Warner shareholders on the transaction, Paramount Entertainment, Inc. (Paramount), makes an any and all tender offer for Time at a price of $175 per share. The tender offer is contingent on the redemption by Time of its pill, the termination of the merger agreement, and the termination of the share exchange agreement. Before the tender offer, Time's shares were selling at $135 per share. Paramount also announces that it has purchased on the open market 7% of Time's shares. Over 50% of Time's shareholders immediately tender to Paramount, and it is obvious that Time's shareholders will not vote to approve the merger. Paramount has announced that, if necessary, it will run a proxy contest to replace Time's board and then terminate the merger and redeem the pill.

(a) Time's board would like to reduce the trigger on the Pill to 10%. Can it and what standard governs the actions of the board in this regard?

(b) Time's board, with the consent of Warner's board, is considering restructuring the merger as a cash tender offer by Time for the stock of Warner at $70 per share in cash, to be followed up by a cash out merger at $70 per share. For various reasons, Paramount is not willing to make a tender offer for the combined Time-Warner, and, therefore, has also conditioned its tender offer on the termination of Time's tender offer. What standard governs Time's board in deciding whether to redeem its pill and terminate its tender offer for Warner?

(c) Warner decides to back out of the transaction with Time. Is Time required to redeem its pill or can it "Just say no"? What standard applies to Time's board? What if Time's board adopts a restructuring plan that purportedly offers the Time shareholders more than $175 per share?

(d) Time's board is concerned that many of its executives may resign. To what extent can Time provide these executives with substantial severance payments in the event Time is taken over?

(e) Paramount has suggested that it would be willing to sell to Time its 7% block of shares in Time for $200. What rules govern the decision of Time's board to make such a purchase? What would be the collateral effects of such a transaction?

§ 23.3 Review of the Principal Fiduciary Duty and Poison Pill Cases Applicable to Takeover Defenses

Before proceeding with this chapter it is important to review Section 3.14, *The "Big Six" Foundational Delaware Fiduciary Duty Cases Dealing with Mergers and Acquisitions*, and Section 3.18, *Elaboration on the Enhanced Business Judgment Rule for Defensive Tactics and Introduction to Poison Pills*. In particular, review *Unocal, Unitrin, Revlon, Blasius, Time Warner, QVC, Moran, Air Gas*, and all of the materials dealing with the poison pill, which is the principal defensive measure.

§ 23.4 Shark Repellent Provisions: Charter and Bylaw Provisions Designed to Prevent Takeovers and Protect Pills

A. Introduction to Shark Repellents

Shark repellents encompass a variety of anti-takeover provisions designed to make potential target corporations less attractive to potential acquiring corporations. These provisions generally involve amendments to the target's charter or to the target's bylaws, and they may be employed in addition to a poison pill, which is now the principal defensive measure. The following materials illustrate some of the issues that can arise with shark repellents.

B. SEC's Proxy Requirements Regarding the Disclosure of Shark Repellents in Proxy and Information Statements

SEC Exchange Act Release No. 15,230

(October 13, 1978)

Typically, a corporation proposing to adopt amendments [including defensive measures] to its charter or bylaws is required by state corporation law to submit the proposal to a shareholder vote. In such cases, corporations subject to, *inter alia*, Section 12 of the Securities Exchange Act of 1934 are required to furnish either proxy materials or information statements to shareholders, pursuant to Regulation 14A or Regulation 14C, respectively. Over the years, the Division has reviewed many proxy and information statements containing anti-takeover measures and has gained a great deal of experience in identifying issues, formulating comments and dealing with registrants and their counsel.

Since at least 1969, the Division has taken the position that when management sponsors anti-takeover proposals and other devices [*e.g.*, a classified or staggered board] to insulate management from removal, the issuer's proxy material or information statements should disclose in a prominent place that the over-all effect of the proposal is to render more difficult the accomplishment of mergers or the assumption of control by a principal stockholder, and thus to make difficult the removal of management. * * *

C. Issues Involving the Annual and Special Shareholders' Meetings

1. Introduction

Section 211 of the Delaware General Corporation Law sets out certain rules governing stockholder meetings. Section 211(b) requires that an annual meeting of shareholders be held for the election of directors unless directors are elected by written consent pursuant to that provision. Section 211(c) authorizes the Court of Chancery to order that an annual meeting be held in certain circumstances. Section 211(d) provides that "[s]pecial meetings of the stockholders may be called by the board of directors or by such person or persons as may be authorized by the certificate of incorporation or by the bylaws." *Read* Section 211.

Section 211 can be particularly important in an effort by a target to delay an attempt by a hostile acquiror to replace the target's board in a proxy contest held at an annual or special meeting of the target's shareholders. For example, a target's board may amend the bylaws to eliminate the right of the shareholders to call a special meeting. The materials below address attempts by the target's board to delay the shareholders' meeting. Section 23.4.E addresses issues involving the use of the consent provision.

2. Delaying the Shareholders' Annual Meeting of a Nevada Corporation

Hilton Hotels Corporation v. ITT Corporation

United States District Court, November, 1997 962 F.Supp. 1309

Pro, District Judge.

Before the Court for consideration is the Motion of Plaintiffs Hilton Hotels Corporation and HLT Corporation ("Hilton") [a hostile acquiror] for a Preliminary Injunction requiring Defendant ITT Corporation [the target] to conduct its annual meeting in May 1997. * * *

First, neither Nevada law nor ITT's bylaws require that the 1997 annual meeting be conducted in May. * * *

Hilton alternatively argues that even if consistent with Nevada law and ITT's bylaws, failure to conduct an annual meeting in May 1997 would constitute a breach of the fiduciary duty owed by ITT's incumbent Board of Directors to its shareholders.

Courts have consistently prevented actions by an incumbent board of directors which were primarily designed to impair or impede the shareholder franchise. * * *

The circumstances presented here are far different from those in * * * *Blasius* [Section 3.14.G], but are not unlike those confronted in *Stahl v. Apple Bancorp Inc.* Here, as in *Stahl*, a majority shareholder claims the incumbent Board of Directors has delayed its annual meeting to frustrate a proxy contest and public tender offer. Moreover, in *Stahl*, the incumbent board had set and then rescinded the record date for the annual meeting, although no specific date for the annual meeting had been scheduled. The *Stahl* court concluded that, "the action of deferring this company's annual meeting where no meeting date has yet been set and no proxies even solicited does not impair or impede the effective exercise of the franchise to any extent." The Court's reasoning in *Stahl* is fully applicable to the instant case. * * *

IT IS THEREFORE ORDERED that Hilton's Motion for Preliminary Injunction is denied.

D. Conducting a Proxy Contest to Replace the Target's Board and Redeem the Target's Pill

Review the materials in Chapter 16, Proxy Contests.

E. Shareholder Action by Consent to Replace a Target's Board and Redeem Its Pill

1. Introduction

Pursuant to Section 228 of the Delaware General Corporation Law, unless the charter provides otherwise, the shareholders may by written consent setting forth the action to be taken, take any action required or permitted to be taken at an annual or special meeting of stockholders, provided the consents are "signed by the holders of outstanding stock having not less than the minimum number of votes that would be necessary to authorize or take such action at a meeting at which all shares entitled to vote thereon were present and voted ..." Read Section 228. Balotti and Finkelstein, Delaware Corporate Law, *supra* Section 1.7, at 7–49, says that "shareholders may adopt certificate or bylaw amendments, elect or remove directors, and approve mergers and other transactions by written consent."

Hostile acquirors may use a consent solicitation to replace the target's board and redeem the target's pill. A consent solicitation can have a timing advantage over a proxy contest, because a proxy contest is conducted in connection with an annual or special stockholders' meeting. If no restrictions are otherwise present, a consent solicitation can commence at any time and, pursuant to Section 228(c), must be completed within 60 days of the earliest dated consent. The Federal proxy rules apply to a consent solicitation for a public company. *See* Chapter 16.

An acquiror that purchases more than 50% of a Delaware target's shares in a tender offer can effectuate a second step merger through the consent procedure as long as there is no prohibition against the use of consents in the target's charter. As discussed in Sections 2.16.C and 20.10, as a result of the enactment in 2013 of Section 251(h) of the Delaware General Corporate Law, a third party that acquires more than 50% of the stock of a target in a tender offer may immediately acquire the balance of the target's outstanding shares without a shareholder vote or consents.

The materials below address attempts by the target's board to restrict the use of the consent provision.

2. Adoption of Consent Solicitation Bylaw Delaying Effectiveness of Action by Consent

Allen v. Prime Computer, Inc.

Delaware Supreme Court, 1988 540 A.2d 417

Moore, Justice.

This expedited interlocutory appeal arises from the adoption by Computervision Corporation of consent solicitation bylaws which delayed for at least twenty days the effectiveness of certain stockholder action taken by written consent. Thus, we confront the validity of a bylaw purporting to provide ministerial review of such stockholder action under *Datapoint Corp. v. Plaza Securities Co.*, Del.Supr., 496 A.2d 1031 (1985). Computervision and its directors (collectively, Computervision) appeal a decision of the Court of Chancery preliminarily enjoining Computervision from enforcing its consent solicitation bylaws. * * *

On December 28, 1987 appellee, Prime Computer, Inc. (Prime), launched a tender offer for any or all of the outstanding shares of Computervision. In its Offer to Purchase, Prime expressed its intention to solicit stockholder consents to enable it to circumvent a Computervision defensive mechanism.

In the face of this hostile offer Computervision adopted the so-called Consent Solicitation Bylaws, the stated purpose of which was to give shareholders adequate time to become informed about the issues presented in a consent solicitation. * * * Basically, with an exception not pertinent here, Section 12 of the bylaws delayed for an absolute minimum period of twenty days, beginning with the commencement of a solicitation, the effectiveness of any action taken by written consent pursuant to § 228. Section 13 of the bylaws established a procedure for inspecting, counting and challenging the validity of the consents. It provided that within three days of receipt of the first valid consent the Computervision board was to appoint a nationally recognized independent inspector of elections to review the consents. The inspector was required to issue a preliminary report no sooner than twenty days from the commencement of the solicitation. The report could then be challenged, if notice of the challenge was delivered within 48 hours. Thus, the effect of Sections 12 and 13 was to prevent the consummation of shareholder action by consent for at least twenty days, and probably longer.

The Chancellor found that despite the reasonableness of the bylaws, both Sections 12 and 13 were void under *Datapoint*. On appeal Computervision argues that *Datapoint* is inapposite because these bylaws are less restrictive than those in *Datapoint*, and in any event, the bylaws are the type of reasonable regulation of consent solicitations which *Datapoint* contemplates. * * *

In evaluating the reasonableness of a bylaw, which purports to establish ministerial review of the validity of consents, several factors are relevant. First, a court must determine the purpose sought to be served. A bylaw whose real purpose is delay of shareholder action is *per se* unreasonable. Second, the court should consider the impact of the bylaw upon the effective exercise of the power conferred under § 228. Finally, the bylaw should contain only the minimal requisites for a reliable and prompt ministerial review to ensure the orderly function of corporate democracy. Such ministerial review must not be unduly elaborate, should contain reasonable time periods only necessary to the circumstances, and should be one which, when administered in good faith, is reasonable and balanced. The Computervision bylaws clearly fail to meet these standards.

Section 12 of the bylaws, with its absolute minimum twenty day delay provision, the reasonableness of which is not explained, did more than "defer consummation of shareholder action until a ministerial review of the validity of the consents" had occurred. In the absence of a provision in the certificate of incorporation, limiting the exercise of stockholder rights under § 228, such a bylaw is void.

Section 13 of the bylaws, while purporting to establish ministerial review, contains the same minimum, but fatal, twenty day delay provision as Section 12. It too is void, even though the form of ministerial review, were it not coupled with the twenty day period, would probably be reasonable under *Datapoint*. * * *

We are satisfied, based upon the defendant's interference with a fundamental stockholder franchise, that the preliminary injunction was properly issued.

The judgment of the Court of Chancery is AFFIRMED.

F. Use of Classified Board to Prevent Removal of Target's Directors and Redemption of Its Pill

1. Introduction

As a mechanism to slow down a potential acquiror that wants to conduct a tender offer and proxy contest or consent solicitation, a target may adopt a classified board, pursuant to which one third of the directors stand for election each year. In such case, an acquiror would have to successfully go through two annual meetings to install a majority of the target's directors. Of course, there is the possibility that if the acquiror succeeds in the first election, the other directors may voluntarily step down. Section 141(d) of the Delaware General Corporation Law permits the establishment of a classified board by certificate of incorporation or by an initial bylaw, or by a bylaw adopted by a vote of stockholders. Section 141(k) provides that "any director or the entire board may be removed, with or without cause, by the holders of a majority of the shares then entitled to vote at an election of directors." One of the exceptions to this rule provides that "[u]nless the certificate of incorporation otherwise provides, in the case of a corporation whose board is classified, * * * shareholders may effect such removal only for cause." *See* Section 141(k)(1). The materials below elaborate on these provisions.

2. Interpretation of the Removal for Cause Provision in the Context of a Classified Board

Roven v. Cotter

Delaware Court of Chancery, 1988 547 A.2d 603

Moore, Justice.

Alfred Roven, a director of Citadel Holding Corporation, has sued to enjoin certain corporate actions ultimately intended to remove him without cause from Citadel's presently classified board of directors. The novel issue before me is whether 8 Del.C. § 141 * * * permit[s] shareholders to amend a certificate of incorporation, thereby eliminating a bylaw establishing a classified board of directors, so that the stockholders can then remove a director without cause. The defendants seek both summary and declaratory judgments on this question. I find that the proposed corporate actions are consistent with Delaware law. Accordingly, judgment will be granted on the legal issues in defendants' favor. * * *

[I]n 1974 the issue of removal was settled when the General Assembly amended § 141 to permit removal with or without cause. *See* § 141(k). This included the specific recognition that even a classified board could be removed without cause if the certificate of incorporation so provided. 8 Del.C. § 141(k)(i) (1974). Thus, it is clear that the shareholders retain the right to remove directors without cause, even if the board is classified. This leaves to shareholders the ultimate decision of how they will balance concerns for continuity and director security against those of flexibility and accountability.

Roven concedes that the shareholders may remove a director without cause, where a board is unclassified, or if classified, where the charter so permits. However, his argument focuses on the time of adoption of the certificate provision permitting removal without cause. Roven contends that once elected to a "full term" of three years on a classified board, absent an existing contrary charter provision, he has a vested right under § 141(d) to serve the entire term, regardless of any later amendments to the charter or bylaws. * * *

Roven's interpretation of § 141(d) becomes impossible. If a director is potentially subject to removal without cause, even on a classified board, then § 141(d) could not possibly entitle a director to serve a "full term" contrary to basic principles of corporate democracy, and the expressed will of the majority. That is of particular significance here, since it is the shareholders who will make the final decisions respecting Citadel's corporate structure. * * *

3. Use of Spin-Off to Establish a Classified Board for a Target Subsidiary

Hilton Hotels Corporation v. ITT Corporation

United States District Court Nevada, 1997 WL 651211

Pro, District Judge:

[**Facts and Issue**] On January 27, 1997, Hilton announced a $55.00 per share tender offer for the stock of ITT [a Nevada corporation], and announced plans for a proxy contest at ITT's 1997 annual meeting. * * *

On July 15, 1997, ITT announced a Comprehensive Plan which, among other things, proposed to split, ITT into three new entities, the largest of which would become ITT Destinations. ITT Destinations would be comprised of the current ITT's hotel and gaming business which account for approximately 93% of ITT's current assets. A second entity, ITT Educational Services, would consist of the current ITT's technical schools, and ITT's European Yellow Pages Division would remain with the current ITT as ITT World Directories.

Most significantly, under the Comprehensive Plan, the board of directors of the new ITT Destinations would be comprised of the members of ITT's current board with one important distinction. The new board would be a "classified" or "staggered" board divided into three classes with each class of directors serving for a term of three years, and with one class to be elected each year. Moreover, a shareholder vote of 80% would be required to remove directors without cause, and 80% shareholder vote would also be required to repeal the classified board provision or the 80% requirement to remove directors without cause. * * *

Finally, and critical to this Court's analysis, ITT seeks to implement the Comprehensive Plan prior to ITT's 1997 annual meeting and without obtaining shareholder approval. * * *

[**Analysis**] * * * Coupling an unsolicited tender offer with a proxy contest to replace the incumbent board is a favored strategy of would-be acquirors. "[R]eplacing the incumbent directors of the target corporation is viewed as an efficient way to eliminate the target company's ability to utilize these anti-takeover defenses." * * *

[N]othing in the Nevada statutes, or elsewhere in the law of Nevada, authorizes the incumbent board of a corporation to entrench itself by effectively removing the right of the corporation's shareholders to vote on who may serve on the board of the corporation in which they own a share. * * *

Where, as here, there is no Nevada statutory or case law on point for an issue of corporate law, this Court finds persuasive authority in Delaware case law. * * *

As this case involves both a tender offer and a proxy contest by Hilton, the proper legal standard is a *Unocal/Blasius* analysis. * * *

Unocal requires the Court to consider the following two questions: 1) Does ITT have reasonable grounds for believing a danger to corporate policy and effectiveness exists? 2) Is the response reasonable in relation to the threat? * * *

Nine of ITT's eleven directors are outside directors. Under *Unocal*, such a majority materially enhances evidence that a hostile offer presents a threat warranting a defensive response. * * *

The ITT board has * * * failed to meet its burden of showing "good faith and reasonable investigation" of a threat to corporate policy or effectiveness which would meet the burden placed on the board under the first prong of the *Unocal* test. Since Hilton's tender offer was announced, the ITT board has not met with Hilton to discuss the offer. * * *

The sole "threat" ITT points to is that Hilton's offer of $70 a share is inadequate, primarily because this price does not contain a control premium. However, at the August 14, 1997, ITT board meeting, Goldman Sachs told the ITT board that the market valued ITT's plan at $62 to $64 dollars a share. * * *

The only attempt ITT has made to satisfy the first prong of the *Unocal* analysis is to argue that Hilton's price is inadequate. However, while inadequacy of an offer is a legally cognizable threat, *Paramount Communications. Inc. v. Time, Inc.*, [Section 3.19.F], ITT has shown no real harm to corporate policy or effectiveness. * * *

Assuming Hilton's offer constitutes a cognizable threat under *Unocal*, ITT's response cannot be preclusive or coercive, and it must be within the range of reasonableness. * * * The installation of a classified board for ITT Destinations, a company which will encompass 93% of the current ITT's assets and 87% of its revenues, is clearly preclusive and coercive under *Unitrin*. The classified board provision for ITT Destinations will preclude current ITT shareholders from exercising a right they currently possess—to determine the membership of the board of ITT. At the very minimum, ITT shareholders will have no choice but to accept the Comprehensive Plan and a majority of ITT's incumbent board members for another year. Therefore, the Comprehensive Plan is preclusive.

ITT's response to Hilton's tender offer touches upon issues of control, and this Court must determine whether the response purposefully disenfranchises ITT's shareholders. If so, * * * it is not a reasonable response unless a "compelling justification" exists. [*Blasius*] * * *

ITT's position is particularly anomalous given the fact that when ITT previously split the company in 1995, it sought shareholder approval. While shareholder approval may not be absolutely required to split ITT now anymore than it was in 1995, the fact that the ITT board decided to subject the 1995 split of the company to a shareholder vote is strong evidence that the primary purpose of its attempts to implement the Comprehensive Plan prior to the 1997 annual meeting is to entrench the incumbent ITT board. * * *

[T]he Court concludes that Hilton has prevailed on the merits of its claim for permanent injunctive relief. * * *

Question

Assume that after full disclosure, the shareholders of a corporation vote to amend the corporation's charter to provide for a classified board and to require an 80% majority vote to amend the provision. An acquiror now wants to replace the board in order to redeem its pill. How must the acquiror proceed?

G. Adoption of Tenure Voting Mechanism

Williams v. Geier

Delaware Supreme Court, 1994 671 A.2d 1368

Veasey, Chief Justice, for the majority:

In this appeal, we consider whether defendant below-appellee, Cincinnati Milacron ("Milacron"), may validly implement a recapitalization plan (the "Recapitalization") resulting from an amendment to Milacron's certificate of incorporation (the "Amendment"). The Amendment was recommended by resolution of the Milacron Board of Directors (the "Board") and approved by the requisite stockholder vote. Plaintiff below-appellant, Josephine L. Williams ("Williams"), an individual minority stockholder, brought suit in the Court of Chancery against Milacron and certain members of the Board, challenging the validity of the Amendment and Recapitalization.

The essence of the Recapitalization is to provide for a form of "tenure voting" whereby holders of common stock on the record date would receive ten votes per share. Upon sale or other transfer, however, each share would revert to one-vote-per-share status until that share is held by its owner for three years. The Recapitalization applied to every stockholder, whether a stockholder was a minority stockholder or part of the majority bloc. Williams argues that the Recapitalization disproportionately and invalidly favors stockholders who are part of the majority bloc and disfavors the minority stockholders. Williams further contends that the sole purpose of the Recapitalization was to entrench Milacron management in office and allow the majority bloc to sell a portion of its holdings while retaining control of the company.

The Court of Chancery granted summary judgment in favor of defendants, holding that Milacron's adoption of the Amendment and Recapitalization was valid. Specifically, the court held that *Unocal* applied, and found that the Board had reasonable grounds to believe that a corporate threat existed and that the Recapitalization was a reasonable response to that threat, there being no improper action or motive. * * *

Williams begins her attack on the grant of summary judgment by questioning the trial court's choice of the "more lenient standard of *Unocal*" [Section 3.14.D] to review the Board's actions, rather than the "heightened standard of scrutiny" used in *Blasius Industries v. Atlas Corp.*, [Section 3.14.G]. We hold that neither standard is implicated here because there was no unilateral board action. Here, there was stockholder approval of the Amendment. Accordingly, the Board action was not unilateral.* * *

The record does not rebut the business judgment rule presumption that the Board acted independently, with due care, in good faith and in the honest belief that its actions were in the stockholders' best interests.* * *

Williams contends that the action of the Board in recommending the Amendment and Recapitalization to the stockholders constituted either a breach of fiduciary duty or an impermissible effort at entrenchment, both of which are claimed to rebut the business judgment presumption and implicate entire fairness review. We disagree. * * *

Based on the undisputed evidence in this record, we conclude that the Board's action in recommending the Amendment and Recapitalization to the stockholders for approval, pursuant to 8 *Del.C.* Section 242(b)(1), is protected by the business judgment rule. We now turn to the issue of the validity of the stockholder vote. * * *

Stockholder approval of an organic, statutory change must comply with the statutory procedure and must be based on full and fair disclosure. The burden rests on the party relying on stockholder approval to establish that the approval resulted from a fully informed electorate and that all material facts relevant to the transaction were fully disclosed. * * *

In *Stroud II* this Court held that the stockholder vote, being both fully informed and devoid of any fraud, waste, manipulative or other inequitable conduct, effectively implemented the board recommendations adopting amendments to the certificate of incorporation and approving a bylaw change, both of which allegedly benefited the incumbent controlling majority. The presence of a controlling majority stockholder did not undermine the validity of the stockholder vote.

In the instant case, like *Stroud II*, the Board recommended the advisability of the Amendment to the stockholders who voted in favor of the Amendment. On its face, therefore, the corporate action was authorized and regular. Stockholders (even a controlling stockholder bloc) may properly vote in their own economic interest, and majority stockholders are not to be disenfranchised because they may reap a benefit from corporate action which is regular on its face. * * *

There is no requirement under the Delaware General Corporation Law that a majority of the outstanding minority shares must vote in favor of a transaction which benefits the majority. * * *

Accordingly, the judgment of the Court of Chancery granting summary judgment to defendants is AFFIRMED.

Hartnett, Justice, and Horsey, Justice (Retired), dissenting:

We respectfully dissent. * * *

It is clear from the record that the Recapitalization Plan will increase the relative voting power of the long-term holders of the common stock—who are likely to be Geier Family members. This fact mandates a factual inquiry into the purpose of the Board in adopting and recommending the Recapitalization Plan. If the change in shareholder voting power was an unintended byproduct of a defensive strategy, the heightened scrutiny standard in *Unocal* should be applied. If, however, the facts show that the Board's primary purpose was to dilute the franchise of the non-Geier Family shares, then, under *Blasius*, Defendants "[bear] the heavy burden of demonstrating a compelling justification for such action."

If the facts show that the purpose of the Recapitalization Plan was simply to favor the Geier Family at the expense of the other stockholders, then a breach of the duty of loyalty likely occurred. * * *

H. The SEC's Shark Repellent Study

Shark Repellents: The Role and Impact of Antitakeover Charter Amendments

Study of the Office of the Chief Economist of the SEC (September 7, 1984)

* * * In this study, we take a large sample of firms proposing antitakeover amendments and consider the impact of these amendments on share prices. We include 131 New York or American stock exchange firms and 40 firms traded over the counter. All of these firms introduced successful fair price amendments, most of which included supermajority provisions.

We find evidence which supports the hypothesis that antitakeover amendments reduce shareholder wealth. From forty trading days before through the mailing date of the proxy detailing the amendments we find that shareholder wealth decreases an average of approximately three percent. * * * [T]he aggregate loss to shareholders of these 127 NYSE, ASE, and OTC firms resulting from passage of antitakeover amendments is estimated to be about $1.35 billion. * * *

§ 23.5 Golden Parachute Payments

A. The Delaware Approach to Golden Parachutes Effectuated Through a Funding Trust

Tate & Lyle PLC v. Staley Continental, Inc.

Del. Ch., 1988 CCH Fed. Sec. L. Rep. ¶ 93,764

Hartnett, Vice Chancellor.

Plaintiffs seek a preliminary injunction enjoining the use by defendants of certain anti-takeover defenses. On April 8, 1988, plaintiffs commenced a cash tender offer for all the shares of defendant Staley Continental, Inc. ("Staley"). The tender offer materials state that the tender offer is conditioned upon this Court enjoining: (1) the operation of a trust created by Staley which would fund several employee compensation plans enacted over the last three years. * * *

I find the plaintiffs have borne their burden of showing that the funding of the Trust must be preliminarily enjoined to prevent its vesting, because it appears reasonably probable that the trust was improperly created. I also find that it is reasonably probable that irreparable harm will occur if the funding of the Trust is not preliminarily enjoined because once funded the Trust may be immune from further judicial scrutiny. * * *

Under Delaware law, anti-takeover measures, like all business decisions of the directors, are judged by the business judgment rule. Nevertheless, plaintiffs argue that the directors breached their fiduciary duty to the stockholders of Staley by adopting the Funding Trust and, in support of this argument, they rely upon *Unocal*, [Section 3.14.D]. * * *

In the present case, the Board adopted the Funding Trust while there was no then presently pending challenge to the corporate management, although there was a reasonable perception that an environment existed which would likely result in a takeover threat in the near future. The compensation plans funded by the Funding Trust were also adopted before any immediate takeover threat.

A stricter standard for determining the propriety of the directors' actions applies when the directors act in their own self-interest. In such a case a Board must show the entire fairness of the transaction. *Weinberger v. UOP, Inc.*, [Section 3.14.B].

A board decision which benefits its members may, nevertheless, be protected by the business judgment rule if a majority of disinterested directors or an independent committee approves the transaction. * * *

The purpose of the Funding Trust, however, is to fund compensation plans which benefit both the management and non-management directors upon a change of control, thus placing all the compensation plans beyond the ability of a court to examine them. All the directors who approved the creation of the Trust had a direct personal interest in one or another of the compensation plans to be funded by the Funding Trust. The interests of the Staley stockholders, (who include the plaintiffs), were not protected by any independent committee or group of directors. The plaintiffs therefore have shown a reasonable probability that the creation of the Funding Trust was not protected by the business judgment rule and the defendants have not shown the reasonable probability that it is intrinsically fair. * * *

B. Federal Income Tax Treatment of Golden Parachute

See Internal Revenue Code §§ 280G and 4999.

1. The Legislative History

General Explanation of the Deficit Reduction Act of 1984

199–200 (1984)

REASONS FOR CHANGE

In recent years, there has been a large volume of activity involving acquisitions and attempted acquisitions of corporations by other taxpayers. In many instances, the "target" corporation has resisted being taken over. In other cases, acquisitions have gone forward on a "friendly" basis. In both situations, however, arrangements were often made to provide substantial payments to top executives and other key personnel of the target corporation in connection with any acquisition that might occur.

In many "hostile" takeover situations, the Congress believed that such arrangements, commonly called "golden parachutes," were designed in part to dissuade an interested buyer, by increasing the cost of the acquisition, from attempting to proceed with the acquisition. * * *

In other situations, the Congress was concerned that the existence of such arrangements tended to encourage the executives and other key personnel involved to favor a proposed takeover that might not be in the best interests of the shareholders or others. * * *

EXPLANATION OF PROVISIONS

General rules

Under the Act, no deduction is allowed for "excess parachute payments." [*See* § 280G(a)] * * * [A] nondeductible 20-percent excise tax is imposed on the recipient of any excess parachute payment. [*See* § 4999]

* * *

2. The Regulations

Preamble to Proposed Regulations under § 280G

PS-217–84 (July 5, 1989)

OVERVIEW OF STATUTORY PROVISIONS

In applying the golden parachute provisions, the first step is to identify payments that constitute "parachute payments." Section 280G(b)(2)(A) defines a "parachute payment" as any payment that meets all of the following four conditions: (a) the payment is in the nature of compensation; (b) the payment is to, or for the benefit of, a disqualified individual; (c) the payment is contingent on a change in the ownership of a corporation, the effective control of a corporation, or the ownership of a substantial portion of the assets of a corporation ("change in ownership or control"); and (d) the payment has (together with other payments described above in (a), (b), and (c) with respect to the same individual) an aggregate present value of at least 3 times the individual's base amount.

For this purpose, an individual's base amount is, in general, the individual's average annualized includible compensation for the most recent 5 taxable years ending before the change in ownership or control. * * *

Once payments are identified as "parachute payments", the next step is to determine any "excess" portion of the payments. Section 280G(b)(1) defines the term "excess parachute payment" as an amount equal to the excess of any parachute payment over the portion of the disqualified individual's base amount that is allocated to such payment. * * *

Generally, excess parachute payments may be reduced by certain amounts of reasonable compensation. Section 280G(b)(4)(B) provides [generally] that * * * the amount of an excess parachute payment is reduced by any portion of the payment that the taxpayer establishes by clear and convincing evidence is reasonable compensation for personal services actually rendered by the disqualified individual before the date of change in ownership or control. * * *

[**Exempt Payments**] Section 280G specifically exempts several types of payments from the definition of the term "parachute payment." * * *

Section 280G(b)(5) provides an exemption for payments with respect to certain corporations. Pursuant to that section, the term "parachute payment" does not include any payment made to a disqualified individual with respect to a corporation if, immediately before the change in ownership or control, no stock in the corporation was readily tradable on an established securities market (or otherwise) and certain shareholder approval requirements are met with respect to the payment. * * *

[**Disqualified Individuals**] To be a parachute payment, a payment must be made to (or for the benefit of) a "disqualified individual." Section 280G(c) defines the term "disqualified individual" to include any individual who (a) is an employee or independent contractor who performs personal services for a corporation, and (b) is an officer, shareholder, or highly-compensated individual. * * *

[**Contingent on Change**] To be a parachute payment, a payment must be contingent on a change in ownership or control. * * *

Questions

Individual *A* is the president of Potential Target (*PT*), a publicly traded corporation. *A* is concerned that Acquiring Corporation (*AC*) is planning to attempt a hostile takeover of *PT* and that this takeover may cause *PT*'s 30 or so key employees to seek other employment. *A* would like to give these employees and also himself the maximum allowable golden parachute payments in the event of a takeover of *PT*. What advice do you give to *A*?

C. The SEC's "Say on Golden Parachute" Provision

See Section 13.12.B.3

§ 23.6 Greenmail

A. The Delaware Approach

Polk v. Good

Delaware Supreme Court, 1988 507 A.2d 531

MOORE, Justice:

Appellants, shareholders of Texaco, Inc., appeal a decision of the Court of Chancery approving the settlement and dismissal of these consolidated stockholders' class and derivative actions against Texaco, its board of directors, and several investors known collectively as the Bass Brothers group (the Bass group or Bass). The settlement disposed of claims challenging Texaco's repurchase at a premium of the Bass group's Texaco stock. * * *

A Delaware corporation has the power to deal in its own stock, 8 Del.C. § 160(a), and may acquire a dissident's shares provided the transaction is free from fraud or unfairness. Unless the primary or sole purpose was to perpetuate the directors in office, such an acquisition will be sustained if, after reasonable investigation, a board has a justifiable belief that there was a reasonable threat to the corporate enterprise. *Unocal*, [Section 3.14.D]. When properly accomplished, such matters are protected by the business judgment rule. *Unocal.* * * *

Here, the presence of the 10 outside directors on the Texaco board, coupled with the advice rendered by the investment banker and legal counsel, constitute a *prima facie* showing of good faith and reasonable investigation. With 10 of the 13 directors being independent, the plaintiffs thus bore a heavy burden of overcoming the presumptions thus attaching to the board's decisions. * * *

The events occurring from the outset of the Bass group's acquisition of Texaco stock, up to the repurchase, created reasonable grounds for a justifiable belief by the directors that there was a threat to Texaco. The payment of a premium of approximately 3% over market seems reasonable in relation to the immediate disruptive effect and the potential long-term threat which the Bass group posed. Clearly, that was a benefit to the company and most of its stockholders. * * *

B. SEC Study of Greenmail

The Impact of Targeted Share Repurchases (Greenmail) on Stock Prices: Study of the Chief Economist of the SEC

(September 11, 1984)

The term "Greenmail" is commonly used to describe [repurchases of blocks of common stock from a substantial shareholder at a premium], reflecting the widespread perception that this practice, or the process leading to it, is counter to the best interests of target shareholders. * * *

We conclude that the overall impact of targeted share repurchases on the wealth of non-participating target shareholders is negative. The stock price evidence indicates that the magnitude of the losses to non-participating target shareholders is at least equal to the wealth loss implied by the cash premium paid for the block repurchase.

C. The Federal Income Tax Treatment of Greenmail

House Report to the Revenue Act of 1987

1086–1087 (1987)

Reasons for Change

* * * The committee believes that taxpayers should be discouraged from realizing short-term profits by acquiring stock in a public tender offer and later being redeemed by the corporation in an effort by the corporation to avert the hostile takeover.

Explanation of Provisions

[U]nder the bill a person who receives "greenmail" is subject to a non-deductible 50-percent excise tax on any gain realized on such receipt. [*See* § 5881(a)] Greenmail is defined as any amount paid by a corporation in redemption of its stock if such stock has been held by the shareholder for less than two years and the shareholder (or any related person or person acting in concert with the shareholder) made or threatened a public tender offer for stock in the corporation during that period.

Question

Within the past two weeks, Acquiring Corporation (*AC*) purchased 7% of the stock of Publicly-Held Target Corporation (*TC*). *AC* has now suggested that *AC* acquire *TC* in a merger. *TC*'s board is considering having *TC* purchase the stock of *TC* held by *AC* at a price equal to 110% of the market value of such stock. What standard of review applies to *TC*'s board in making this decision. What are the tax consequences of such a purchase?

§ 23.7 Poison Debt

A. Introduction

Richard A. Steinwurtzel and Janice L. Gardner, Super Poison Puts as a Protection against Event Risk

3 Insights 3 (October, 1989)

The use of covenants in public debt instruments to protect bondholders is by no means a recent phenomenon. Historically, covenants took into account the existing capital structure of the issuer and, among other things, limited dividends to shareholders, set minimum net worth requirements and imposed net tangible asset tests for mergers and other business combination. [T]here has been increased use in recent years of so-called "poison put" provisions. These provisions serve as protection against a variety of corporate acts, referred to generally as "event-risks," that potentially or actually endanger the cash flows previously designated to support corporate debt. They have been dubbed "poison" because they may "make a company indigestible for a hostile bidder."

The first generation of poison put provisions gave bondholders the right to demand that the issuer repurchase the debt securities at the initial offering price upon the occurrence of certain events, generally limited to unfriendly takeovers. The principal shortcoming of these provisions, however, was that most hostile takeover attempts became "friendly" in the end and therefore did not trigger the poison put. Moreover, the poison put provisions were not triggered by recapitalizations that often were undertaken by issuers in response to hostile bids or other unfriendly action. Because substantial new debt is frequently incurred in recapitalizations, such transactions subject the bondholders to the same economic consequences that the poison put provisions were designed to prevent.

In response to institutional investors' demands for new safeguards, issuers began to utilize indentures with an enhanced bondholder protection which has become known as a "super poison put" or, less colloquially, an "event risk" provision. The terms of event risk provisions vary from issuer to issuer. They differ from their predecessors in that the trigger events include recapitalizations and leveraged buy-outs, other major dividend distributions that substantially affect the underlying value of the company, purchases of a controlling interest, and stock repurchase programs. In addition, the event risk provision often is contingent upon a trigger event resulting in a downgrading of the credit rating of the debt securities.

The purpose of these provisions is to "shift to the issuer the 'event risk' of the investment." These provisions, however, have proved beneficial to issuers from a financing standpoint as well. In addition to improving the general receptivity of investors to offerings of debt securities, event risk provisions arguably have resulted in low borrowing costs and better credit ratings. * * *

B. Challenges to Poison Debt

In an October 2014 bench ruling,[1] Vice Chancellor Laster of the Delaware Chancery Court refused to dismiss fiduciary duty claims brought by shareholders of Healthways against the board of Healthways for causing Healthways to enter a lending agreement that contained a dead hand, poison put. This put permitted the lenders, which included Sun Trust Bank, to "declare an event of default and accelerate the debt in the event that a majority of the Healthways board during a period of 24 months is comprised of 'non-continuing' directors, including directors initially nominated as a result of an actual or threatened proxy contest."[2] The court also refused to dismiss an aiding and abetting claim against Sun Trust. In rendering his decision, the Vice Chancellor referred to the following two cases, which also dealt with poison puts: *Kallick v. SandRidge Energy, Inc.*, 68 A.3d 242 (Del. Ch. 2013); and *San Antonio Fire & Police Pension Fund v. Amylin Pharmaceuticals, Inc.*, 983 A.2d 304 (Del. Ch. 2009).

§ 23.8 ALI's Proposed Rules Governing Defensive Tactics

See Section 3.25.

§ 23.9 SEC's Advisory Committee on Tender Offers

SEC, Advisory Committee on Tender Offers Report of Recommendations

(Summary Recommendations) (July 8, 1983) [*See also* Sections 17.4 and 20.10]

Regulation of Opposition to Acquisitions of Control

33. The Committee supports a system of state corporation laws and the business judgment rule. No reform should undermine that system. Broadly speaking, the Committee believes that the business judgment rule should be the principal governor of decisions that may alter the likelihood of a takeover.

34. State laws and regulations, regardless of their form, that restrict the ability of a company to make a tender offer should not be permitted because they constitute an undue burden on interstate commerce. * * *

35. Congress and the Commission should adopt appropriate legislation and/or regulations to prohibit the use of charter and by-law provisions that erect high barriers to change of control and thus operate against the interests of shareholders and the national marketplace.

36. To the extent not prohibited or otherwise restricted, companies should be permitted to adopt provisions requiring supermajority approval for change of control transactions only where the ability to achieve such a level of support is demonstrable.

---

1. *Pontiac General Employees Retirement System v. Healthways, Inc.*, C.A. No. 9789-VCL (Del. Ch. Oct. 14, 2014) (transcript ruling).

2. Harvard Law School Forum on Corporate Governance and Financial Regulation, *Pontiac General Employees Retirement System v. Healthways, Inc.*, available at http://blogs.law.harvard.edu/corpgov/2014/11/17/pontiac-general-employees-retirement-system-v-healthways-inc/#printable.

a. Any company seeking approval of a charter or by-law provision that requires, or could under certain circumstances require, the affirmative vote of more than the minimum specified by state law should be required to obtain that same level of approval in passing the provision initially. Ratification should be required every three years. * * *

37. The Commission should designate certain change of control related policies of corporations as "advisory vote matters" for review at each annual stockholders' meeting for the election of directors and for disclosure in the proxy statement.

a. *Matters Covered.* Advisory vote matters should include:

i. *Supermajority provisions.* To the extent not prohibited or otherwise restricted, charter provisions requiring more than the statutorily imposed minimum vote requirement to accomplish a merger, including provisions requiring supermajority approval under special conditions (*e.g.*, "fair value" and "majority of the disinterested shareholders" provisions); * * *

iv. *Change of control compensation.* Arrangements that provide change of control related compensation to company managers or employees.

b. *Proxy Statement Disclosure.* Companies should be required to disclose all advisory vote matters in a "Change of Control" section of the proxy statement.

c. *Vote.* Shareholders should be requested to vote on an advisory basis as to whether they are or continue to be in favor of the company's policy with respect to the advisory vote matters disclosed in the proxy statement. The board would not be bound by the results of the advisory vote but could, in its own judgment, decide whether company policy should be changed on the advisory vote matters. The outcome of an advisory vote would have no legal effect on an existing agreement.

38. a. *Change of Control Compensation During a Tender Offer.*

The board of directors shall not adopt contracts or other arrangements with change of control compensation once a tender offer for the company has commenced.

b. *Change of Control Compensation Prior to a Tender Offer.*

i. *Disclosure.* The issuer should disclose the terms and parties to contracts or other arrangements that provide for change of control compensation in the Change of Control section of the annual proxy statement.

ii. *Advisory Vote.* At each annual meeting, shareholders should be requested to vote, on an advisory basis, as to whether the company should continue to provide change of control compensation to its management and employees. * * *

39. a. In general, target company self-tenders should not be prohibited during the course of a tender offer by another bidder for the target company.

b. Once a third party tender offer has commenced, the target company should not be permitted to initiate a self-tender with a proration date earlier than that of any tender offer commenced prior to the self-tender.

40. There should be no general restrictions on the counter tender offer as a defense. The employment of the counter tender offer should be prohibited, however, where a bidder has made a cash tender offer for 100% of a target company.

41. Contracts for the sale of stock or assets to preferred acquirors should continue to be tested against the business judgment rule. During a tender offer, however, the issuance of stock representing more than 15% of the fully diluted shares that would be outstanding after issuance should be subject to shareholder approval.

42. The sale of significant assets, even when undertaken during the course of a tender offer, should continue to be tested against the business judgment rule.

§ 23.10 Two Opposing Views on Defensive Tactics

A. The Easterbrook/Fischel Managerial Passivity Model

Easterbrook and Fischel, The Proper Role of a Target's Management in Responding to a Tender Offer

94 Harv L. Rev.: 1161, 1161–1162, 1164, 1201–1204 (1981)

We argue in this Article that current legal rules allowing the target's management to engage in defensive tactics in response to a tender offer decrease shareholders' welfare. The detriment to shareholders is fairly clear where defensive tactics result in a defeat of a takeover, causing shareholders to lose the tender premium. Even where resistance leads to a higher price paid for the firm's shares, however, shareholders as a whole do not necessarily benefit. The value of any stock can be understood as the sum of two components: the price that will prevail in the market if there is no successful offer (multiplied by the likelihood that there will be none) and the price that will be paid in a future tender offer (multiplied by the likelihood that some offer will succeed). A shareholder's welfare is maximized by a legal rule that enables the sum of these two components to reach its highest value. Any approach that looks only at the way in which managers can augment the tender offeror's bid, given that a tender offer has already been made, but disregards the effect of a defensive strategy on the number of offers that will be made in the future and the way in which the number of offers affects the efficiency with which corporations are managed, ignores much that is relevant to shareholders' welfare. * * *

Although we have concluded that shareholders would want management to be passive in the face of a tender offer, we have not attempted to define precisely what we mean by passivity. Doubtless, managers must carry out the corporation's ordinary business. Perhaps, too, management should be able to issue a press release urging shareholders to accept or reject the offer. The offeror also will convey its views to the shareholders, who can act on these messages in light of the self-interest of both the management and the offeror. But almost any other defensive actions expend the target's resources and produce no gain to investors. Thus, management should not propose antitakeover charter or bylaw amendments, file suits against the offeror, acquire a competitor of the offeror in order to create an antitrust obstacle to the tender offer, buy or sell shares in order to make the offer more costly, give away to some potential "white knight" valuable corporate information that might call forth a competing bid, or initiate any other defensive tactic to defeat a tender offer. * * *

B. The Lipton Managerial Action Model in "Takeover Bids and the Target's Boardroom"

Lipton, Takeover Bids in the Target's Boardroom

35 The Business Lawyer 101, 109–110 (1979)

There is no logical distinction between a requirement that directors accept any takeover bid that represents a substantial premium over market and a requirement that the directors determine annually whether it would be possible to sell or liquidate the company at a substantial premium over market and that, if possible, the directors do so. The fact that a raider has taken the initiative is no basis for distinction. If the directors have an obligation to sell whenever a substantial premium is available, it should make no difference who initiates the activity. Indeed, if that is the rule, the directors should not await a raider's initiative, but are required to take the initiative themselves. Nor is the greater certainty created by a takeover bid as compared to the directors' assessment of what might be realized on sale or liquidation a basis for distinction. * * *

What, then, would be wrong with a requirement for annual assessment by the directors as to whether the company should be sold or liquidated? First, it shortens the directors' perspective to the present and forces them to ignore the long term. * * * Second, a requirement for an annual life or death assessment would have a fundamental impact on the way in which corporations operate. * * * Third, there is no reason to believe that the experience with mandated annual life or death assessments would be any different than the experience with rejection of unsolicited tender offers. In sum, there is no empirical evidence or logic to support a requirement that sale or liquidation of the company be treated any differently from any other major business decision. * * *

C. A 25th Year Reprise on Lipton's Original Position in "Takeover Bids and the Target's Boardroom"

The August 2005 issue of The Business Lawyer, 60 Bus. Law. 1369 (2005), contains several articles written for: *Symposium on Takeover Bids in the Boardroom: 25 Years Later*. In the lead article in the Symposium, Martin Lipton defended his initial position in *Takeover Bids* and indicated that the battle with the passivity theorists had been won:

> I am reminded of the primary impetus for *Takeover Bids*—a concern that the business judgment rule and the board's fundamental gatekeeping role were severely threatened by calls for director passivity in the context of hostile takeover attempts. At its core, *Takeover Bids* argued that a corporation's board of directors should be permitted, and indeed has a duty, to manage actively the business of the company, and that its discretion in doing so should not depend on the nature of the particular issue that is being decided (so long as the board satisfies its fiduciary duties). Those theories—a rejection of board passivity, an endorsement of the board as gatekeeper and an active role by the board in the context of hostile takeover bids—became part of the public discourse after the publication of *Takeover Bids* and were ultimately affirmed, either tacitly or explicitly, by both common law and legislative guidance [*i.e.*, in the form of state anti-takeover laws, *see* Chapter 22]. In short, that battle was won.[3]

However, he went on to indicate that future battles are on the horizon:

> But there is little rest for the battle-weary. Self-described "reformers" of the post-Enron era are now mounting a more trenchant, multi-level and multi-jurisdictional attack on the ability of the board and management to manage effectively the corporation. * * * At the level of state common law, new theories of director liability [*e.g.*, the good faith claim in *Disney*, Section 3.10.D] also threaten to restrict further a board's effective exercise of its business judgment. If successful,

3. Martin Lipton, Twenty-Five Years After Takeover Bids In The Target's Boardroom: Old Battles, New Attacks And The Continuing War, 60 Bus. Law. 1369, 70 (2005).

> these attacks may result in making boards a mere conduit for shareholder referenda, thus rekindling the very theories of director passivity that prompted *Takeover Bids.*[4]

In an article in the Symposium, Professor Allen, a former Chancellor of the Delaware Chancery Court, and Vice Chancellor (now Chancellor) Strine of that court, agreed with Lipton's observation that the battle had been won:

> On [the] front of the economic policy battlefield that involves the contest over the appropriate takeover policy of substantive corporate law, Lipton can take pride in the extent to which his arguments in *Takeover Bids in the Target's Boardroom* have been adopted. Even more dramatically, his audacious originality produced the innovation of the poison pill and its intellectual defense. However one feels about the social utility of the device, almost certainly the pill represents the most important private law innovation in the field of corporate law of the last fifty years. Nearly as consequential was Lipton's important role in the movement toward increasing the professionalism and power of independent directors. Lipton seized upon the emergence of independent board majorities as additional intellectual ballast for his argument that boards should be trusted to decide whether and to what buyer corporations should be sold or merged. To his continuing delight, many scholars * * * bemoan the rejection of their perspective by Delaware and other states and find themselves constantly reworking their policy proposals in order to come upon one that can shake the grip of the director-centered approach to takeovers that is at the heart of Lipton's Institutionalist View.[5]

§23.11 Policy Perspectives on the Use of a Classified Board in Connection with a Poison Pill

A. The Bebchuk/Coates/Subramanian Approach

Bebchuk, Coates & Subramanian, The Powerful Antitakeover Force of Staggered Boards: Theory, Evidence, and Policy

54 Stan. L. Rev. 887, 950,51 (2002)

Effective staggered boards ["a staggered board that is appropriately designed to prevent circumvention"] are [in combination with a poison pill] the most powerful antitakeover device in the current arsenal of takeover defense weapons. An ESB prevents a hostile bidder, no matter when it emerges, from gaining control of the target unless it can wait at least fourteen months and win two elections that are far apart in time. Because of these impediments, the ballot box route becomes illusory against an ESB target.

We find strong empirical support for this view of ESBs. ESBs substantially increase the likelihood that a target receiving a hostile bid will remain independent. We find that the increased odds of remaining independent are quite costly for target shareholders, without providing sufficient countervailing benefits in terms of higher acquisition premiums. We estimate that an ESB reduces the expected return of target shareholders in the nine months after a hostile bid is launched on the order of 8%–10%. * * *

---

4. Id.

5. Allen and Strine, When the Existing Economic Order Deserves a Champion: The Enduring Relevance of Martin Lipton's Vision of the Corporate Law, 60 Bus. Law. 1383, 1391–92 (2005).

C. Vice Chancellor Strine's View on the Staggered Board

Strine, The Professorial Bear Hug: The ESB Proposal as a Conscious Effort to Make the Delaware Courts Confront the Basic "Just Say No" Question

55 Stan. L. Rev. 863 (2002)

[T]his brief Response will highlight the basic policy choice that authors [Bebchuck/ Coates/ Subramanian] ask the Delaware courts to enshrine in the common law of corporations. The question the authors ask us to decide affirmatively is fundamental: Can control of the corporation be sold over the objections of a disinterested board that believes in good faith that the sale is inadvisable? That is, at bottom, the authors want to force the hand of the Delaware courts to decide, once and for all, that impartial and well-intentioned directors do not have the fiduciary authority to "just say no" for an indefinite—even perpetual—period to a noncoercive tender offer made to their company's shareholders.

Although staggered boards are critical to their proposal, the authors prescribe a judicial cure for a quite different toxin: the poison pill. Thus, the authors have continued a long-standing debate, but in a particularly valuable way, by forcing the contestants to grapple with empirical facts about the real-world effects of the combined defense of a poison pill and an "Effective Staggered Board" (ESB). * * *

The authors' proposal puts pressure on the Delaware courts to determine a fundamental, normative issue that is legislative in character. Our judiciary should not apologize for having taken a careful and case-by-case approach to takeover litigation posing such a choice. Faced with an important public policy issue, lacking firm policy guidance from the legislative branch of our government, and being uncertain about the effects new innovations in the market for corporate control would have, the Delaware courts responded to the M&A boom of the last twenty years by evolving the common law of corporations in an incremental manner that was provisional enough to allow for adjustments and changes in initial direction.

This approach has much to commend, because it reduced the scope of harmful impact from potential judicial errors while leaving ample room for adaptive solutions by market participants. * * *

In other jurisdictions, the legislative branch of government has [adopted] * * * one of the two predominant models of the corporation, at least insofar as those models apply to the Just Say No question. In England, for example, the London City Takeover Code largely adopts the property model of the corporation, and gives stockholders the ultimate say about whether a tender offer should be accepted. [*See* Chapter 26] In several American states, legislation adopts the entity model of the corporation, by giving directors explicit authority to deny stockholders the opportunity to accept a tender offer. [*See* Chapter 22] By contrast, the Delaware General Assembly has taken a more ambivalent approach, which has permitted talented advocates and scholars to argue both sides of the issue persuasively. * * *

E. The Bebchuk/Coates/Subramanian Rejoinder

Bebchuk, Coates, & Subramanian, The Powerful Antitakeover Force of Staggered Boards: Further Findings and a Reply to Symposium Participants

55 Stan. L. Rev. 885 (2002)

Earlier this year in the Stanford Law Review, we presented a theoretical, empirical, and policy analysis of staggered boards. We argued that "effective" staggered boards (ESBs) provide a powerful antitakeover defense, more powerful than is commonly recognized. * * *

This issue of the Stanford Law Review includes five commentaries that present responses and reactions to our article. * * *

To address the problems we face today, it would be helpful to place limits on the ability of boards to block hostile bids indefinitely. We have demonstrated in our original paper that the post-just say no effective staggered board has severely reduced the pressure that the market for corporate control can exert on disloyal boards. Surprisingly, Gordon, Bainbridge, and Stout wish to provide directors with expanded and what we believe amounts to practically unlimited powers to block even offers that shareholders find attractive. The evidence that our work has put forward, reinforced by the striking corporate governance failures of the past year, clearly indicates that this would be a step in the wrong direction.

An important element of an improved corporate governance system would involve reviving the hostile takeover—not in its full and uncontrolled form (with T. Boone Pickens playing the monster to academia's Dr. Frankenstein), but as a responsible yet viable mechanism for achieving value-creating changes in corporate control.

§23.12 My Proposals for a (1) Change of Control Board, or (2) Change of Control Special Committee

In Thompson, *The Missing Link in Sarbanes-Oxley: Enactment of the "Change of Control Board" Concept, or Extension of the Audit Committee Provisions to Mergers and Acquisitions*, 63 The Business Lawyer 1 (Nov. 2007), I argue that Sarbanes-Oxley should be amended to provide that in all types of M&A transactions an independent and knowledgeable three-person Change of Control Board should be appointed by the SEC's Office of M&A for (1) all publicly held corporations that become targets of an acquisition, and (2) publicly held acquirors that are contemplating major acquisitions. The Change of Control Board would have complete control over the acquisition process, including defensive tactics such as the issuance of a poison pill. As is the case for audit committees under Sarbanes-Oxley, the corporation would be required to pay all the expenses, including expenses for retention of an investment banker, for the Change of Control Board. Because of the pre-determined independence and knowledge of the members of the Change of Control Board, this board would receive protection under a federally mandated business judgment rule, thus eliminating much of the litigation in the M&A process. This federal preemption approach would eliminate the multiple and confusing standards of review that apply under Delaware law in M&A transactions (*see* Chapters 3 and 23) and also would preempt all state takeover laws, including the laws of states such as Pennsylvania (*see* Chapter 22) that, in essence, make their state corporations takeover proof. Thus, this approach would enhance the efficiency of the M&A marketplace and eliminate debates such as the one above concerning the combination of a classified board with a poison pill. The public shareholders of a corporation could vote to have the corporation elect-out of the provision.

I made an alternative proposal in Thompson, *Change of Control Special Committee: Breathing Life into CNX*, 36 Delaware Journal of Corporate Law 1053 (2011). There, I argue that to reduce the economically inefficient litigation surrounding M&A transactions, the Delaware General Corporation Law ("DGCL") should be amended to permit the shareholders of a corporation to adopt a provision requiring that if the corporation becomes a target of a bona fide acquisition proposal, the board of the corporation must petition the Delaware Court of Chancery for the appointment of an independent, disinterested, and knowledgeable special committee of the board (a "Change of Control Special Committee"). This Committee would have complete power over the acquisition transaction. At the discretion of the Delaware Court of Chancery, a member of the current board could be appointed to the Change of Control Special Committee.

All decisions of the Change of Control Special Committee, including any decision to employ, maintain, or terminate a poison pill, would be subject to the deferential business judgment rule standard of review. As a consequence, litigation involving the actions taken by the Committee would be rare, if not essentially eliminated, because it could be expected that the decisions made by the Committee would be in the interest of the target's shareholders. As a practical matter, the role of the Court of Chancery in such transactions would be moved from the back-end to the front-end, because the Chancery Court's determination of the independence, disinterestedness, and competence of the board members would be made on an *ex ante* as opposed to an *ex post* basis.

This type of amendment to the DGCL is consistent with the concept of this statute as an "enabling" law, permitting shareholders to adopt provisions that the shareholders determine are in their interests. Also, adoption of this proposal would breathe life into Vice Chancellor Laster's suggestion in *CNX* that the business judgment standard of review apply to freezeout (and other) mergers if a "unified standard" (*i.e.* an independent committee and a majority of minority vote) is satisfied.

What do you think about these approaches?

References

ALI, *Corporate Governance Project*, *supra* Section 1.10, at Section 6.02.

Balotti and Finkelstein, Delaware Corporate Law, supra Section 1.10.

Easterbrook and Fischel, *The Economic Structure of Corporate Law* 192–211 (1991).

Fleischer and Sussman, *Takeover Defense*, *supra* Section 1.10.

Lipton and Steinberger, *Takeovers & Freezeouts*, *supra* Section 1.10.

Thompson, *Mergers, Acquisitions and Tender Offers*, *supra* Section 1.10, Chapter 5.

Chapter 24

Spin-Offs

§ 24.1 Scope

This chapter addresses some of the legal issues that may arise in a spin-off transaction. In a spin-off, a parent corporation distributes the stock of a subsidiary corporation to the shareholders of the parent as a dividend. Thus, before the transaction, the shareholders of the parent hold the stock of the parent, which in turn holds the stock of the subsidiary. After the transaction, the shareholders of the parent own stock in the parent and stock in the subsidiary. The subsidiary can either be previously existing or newly formed for the purpose of the spin-off. The principal business reason for a spin-off is the rationalization of the business structure to maximize corporate efficiency and shareholder value. If properly structured, the spin-off transaction can be effectuated on a tax-free basis to the parent, to the subsidiary, and to the parent's shareholders. Thus, substantial tax benefits arise in a spin-off. A spin-off may be followed by the acquisition of or by either the parent or the spun off sub, and properly structured, both the spin-off and the subsequent acquisition may be tax-free.

Section 24.2 presents an introductory problem on spin-offs, and Section 24.3 addresses the federal income tax aspects of spin-offs. Section 24.4 looks at some of the corporate issues in spin-offs, including the corporate consents required, the surplus or retained earnings needed to effectuate the spin-off, and the question of whether a shareholder vote is required. Section 24.5 considers the federal securities issues, including the question whether the subsidiary stock distributed in the spin-off is required to be registered under the Securities Act of 1933. Section 24.6 addresses whether a spin-off may be a fraudulent conveyance. Section 24.7 refers to the Form S-4 and proxy statement for the AT&T-Comcast Spin-off and Merger, which is Documentary Appendix R of *M&A Statutes, Rules, and Documents*, *supra* Section 1.1. The materials in this chapter are discussed in greater detail in Thompson, *Mergers, Acquisitions and Tender Offers*, *supra* Section 1.10, Chapter 15.

§ 24.2 Introductory Problem on Spin-Offs

J.P. Morgan Chase & Co. (J.P. Morgan), a publicly-held Delaware corporation engaged in the financial services business, has decided to focus exclusively on the commercial and retail banking business. Therefore, it has decided to dispose of its investment banking and other businesses in a spin-off transaction that will be tax-free under Section 355 of the Internal Revenue Code (Code). Prior to the spin-off, J.P. Morgan will transfer all of its businesses to be spun off to a new subsidiary named JP Investment Bank, Inc. and will distribute the stock of JP Investment Bank to the J.P. Morgan shareholders. Once The Goldman Sachs Group, Inc. (Goldman Sachs), a publicly held Delaware corporation engaged in the investment banking business, learned of the proposed spin-off it approached J.P. Morgan about the possibility of Goldman Sachs acquiring the spun off JP Investment

Bank immediately after the spin-off in a tax-free reverse subsidiary merger under Section 368(a)(2)(E) of the Code. [*See* Chapter 5] Even though Goldman Sachs would be the acquiring company, the shareholders of JP Investment Bank would receive 55% of the stock of Goldman Sachs in the reverse subsidiary merger. Goldman has proposed that prior to the spin-off the shareholders of J.P. Morgan would vote on the acquisition by Goldman so that the acquisition would take place simultaneously with the spin-off. Thus, Goldman has proposed a transaction that is similar to the structure of the acquisition by Comcast of the AT&T Broadband properties from the former AT&T.

(1) Can the spin-off of JP Investment Bank be effectuated on a tax-free basis under the federal income tax law to J.P. Morgan, JP Investment Bank and the J.P. Morgan shareholders?

(2) J.P. Morgan's preferred shareholders have objected to the spin-off. What obligations do the J.P. Morgan directors have to these preferred shareholders in structuring the spin-off?

(3) Under Delaware law, do the J.P. Morgan shareholders have a right to vote on the spin-off assuming there is to be no merger with Goldman Sachs? What if J.P. Morgan were incorporated in a state that has adopted the Model Business Corporation Act?

(4) The common equity section of J.P. Morgan's balance sheet is as follows:

Par Value ($1 per 10 million shares)	$10,000,000
Paid in Capital ($9 per 10 million shares)	$90,000,000
Retained Earnings	$25,000,000
Total Equity	$125,000,000

The aggregate trading value of the J.P. Morgan shares is $500 million. Assume that the acquisition by Goldman Sachs will not take place. After the spin-off, the expected aggregate trading value of the JP Investment Bank shares is $125 million and the expected aggregate trading value of the J.P. Morgan shares is $375 million. Can J.P. Morgan effectuate the spin-off without violating the restrictions on dividends in Delaware Law? What if J.P. Morgan were incorporated in a state that had adopted the MBCA? Prior to the spin-off is J.P. Morgan required to register the JP Investment Bank shares under the Securities Act of 1933? Since the JP Investment Bank shares will be publicly traded, is J.P. Morgan required to register those shares under the Securities Exchange Act of 1934?

(5) Assume that the acquisition by Goldman Sachs does not take place and that J.P. Morgan distributes the stock of JP Investment Bank to the J.P. Morgan shareholders in a spin-off. Within six months J.P. Morgan goes into bankruptcy. Do the directors or shareholders of J.P. Morgan have any personal liability under the fraudulent conveyance laws?

(6) Suppose that as part of the transfer of property to JP Investment Bank, $50 million of liabilities of J.P. Morgan were assumed by JP Investment Bank. Within six months of the spin-off, JP Investment Bank goes into bankruptcy. Has JP Investment Bank made a fraudulent conveyance in assuming the $50 million of liabilities?

§ 24.3 Federal Income Tax Impact on Spin-Offs

A. Introduction

Tax-free spin-offs can involve the distribution by a parent corporation of (1) the stock of a previously existing subsidiary, or (2) the stock of a newly formed subsidiary. Section 355 alone deals with the spin-off of a previously existing sub, but both Sections 368(a)(1)(D) (the (D) reorganization) and 355 deal with the spin-off of a newly formed sub. Thus, if the assets to be spun off are not in a single sub, such assets can be contributed to a new sub that will be spun off.

In a (D) reorganization under Section 368(a)(1)(D), a corporation (the "distributing corporation") transfers all or part of its assets to another corporation (the "controlled corporation"), and immediately after the transfer, the distributing corporation or its shareholders, or a combination thereof, are in control (*i.e.*, own at least 80% of the stock) of the controlled corporation. The distribution by the distributing corporation to its shareholders of stock of the controlled corporation must qualify under Section 354, 355 or 356. The (D) can be either nondivisive or divisive, but only the divisive (D), which qualifies under Section 355, is discussed here. Under Section 361, the distributing corporation in a divisive (D) is not taxed on the contribution of its assets to the controlled corporation or on the distribution of the stock of the controlled corporation to the shareholders in the spin-off segment of the transaction. Also, the controlled corporation can generally assume liabilities of the distributing corporation in connection with such contributions of property without adverse tax treatment to either party. *See* § 357(c). And, under Section 355(a) the shareholders of the distributing corporation have tax-free treatment on the receipt of the stock of the controlled corporation. In a distribution of the stock of a previously existing controlled corporation, Section 355(c) provides that the distributing corporation has no gain, and Section 355(a) provides for tax-free treatment to the shareholders of the distributee on receipt of the stock of the controlled corporation.

B. Types of (D) Reorganizations and Spin-Offs: Split-Ups and Split-Offs

Section 355 distributions, whether in connection with a divisive (D) reorganization or in distributions of stock of a previously existing sub, fall into three broad categories: spin-offs, split-offs and split-ups. In a spin-off, a distributing corporation distributes to its shareholders the stock of the controlled corporation in a pro rata distribution. Thus, the shareholders continue their same pro rata interest but in two corporations rather than one. In a split-off, stock of the distributing corporation is redeemed in exchange for stock of the controlled corporation. Thus, the distribution is not pro rata. In a split-up, the distributing corporation contributes its assets to two or more controlled corporations and then liquidates, distributing the stock to its shareholders.

C. Conditions for Tax-Free Treatment under Section 355

For a transaction to be tax-free under Section 355(a), the following basic requirements must be satisfied:

- The distributing corporation must distribute to its shareholders or security holders "solely" stock or securities (*i.e.*, debt instruments of the controlled corporation [*see* §§ 355(a)(1)(A) and 355(a)(2)]; the distribution need not be pro rata. If cash or other property (i.e., boot) is distributed, the Section 356 boot gain rule will apply [*see* §§ 356(a) and (b)] (only distributions of stock are addressed here);
- The transaction must not be a "device" for the distribution of earnings and profits (*i.e.*, the corporation's after-tax earnings) [*see* § 355(a)(1)(B)];
- As illustrated in the *Gregory* case, the transaction must have a business purpose;
- A separate active trade or business that has been conducted for at least five years must continue to be conducted after the distribution by each of the distributing

and controlled corporations [*see* §§ 355(a)(1)(C) and 355(b)] (Thus, a five-year business must be both spun off and retained); and

- The distributing corporation must distribute all of the stock or securities of the controlled corporation or an amount of stock of the controlled corporation amounting to control (*i.e.*, at least 80%), provided that in the latter case it is established that the retention of stock or securities of the controlled corporation is not for tax avoidance purposes [*see* § 355(a)(1)(D)].

For transactions that fall within Section 355, the shareholders or security holders of the distributing corporation receive nonrecognition treatment on receipt of the stock of the controlled corporation. [*See* § 355(a)] Thus, Section 355 is analogous to Section 354, which gives nonrecognition treatment for reorganizations other than the divisive (D).

At the corporate level, the distributing corporation generally has nonrecognition treatment under § 355(c) or § 361(c) (in the case of a (D) reorganization) on the distribution of stock of the controlled corporation. However, the distributing corporation has gain recognition in the case of certain (1) distributions to a 50% or greater shareholder of the distributing corporation who recently acquired his stock in the corporation by purchase (§ 355(d)), and (2) distributions followed by certain acquisitions of the distributing corporation or the controlled corporation (§ 355(e)). Section 355(e) is examined below. A (D) reorganization spin-off is diagramed on the next page.

Because of the large tax stakes to both the distributing parent and its shareholders in a spin-off, the distributing parent will, in many cases, condition the transaction on receipt of a private letter ruling from the IRS to the effect that the transaction qualifies under Section 355. This was the case in the AT&T spin-off addressed in Documentary Appendix R of *M&A Statutes, Rules, and Documents, supra* Section 1.1.

D. Section 355(e) and the Reverse Morris Trust Transaction

Under the *Morris Trust* case, it is possible to structure a tax-free spin-off followed by a tax-free acquisition of either the distributing corporation or the controlled corporation in an acquisitive reorganization. Thus, *Morris Trust* provides a way for a corporation to dispose of a business on a tax-free basis with such corporation's shareholders receiving stock of an acquiring corporation tax-free. However, Section 355(e) limits the ability to structure a spin-off followed by an acquisition of either the distributed or controlled corporation. Under this section the distributing corporation recognizes gain on the distribution of appreciated stock of the controlled corporation if pursuant to a plan in existence at the time of the spin-off there is a change in control (measured at 50%) of either the distributing corporation or the controlled corporation. Thus, for example, if pursuant to a plan, a controlled corporation were spun off in a transaction otherwise qualifying under Section 355 and immediately thereafter the controlled corporation were acquired by an acquiror in an acquisitive reorganization in exchange for 20% of the acquiror's stock, the distribution would be taxable to the distributing corporation to the extent of the appreciation in the stock of the controlled corporation. The shareholders of the distributing corporation would, however, have tax-free treatment under Section 355(a). Thus, there is only taxable gain at the distributing level, but this tax is most certainly a deal killer. Fortunately, the control test in Section 355(e) focuses on the economics of the transaction and even if the distributing corporation or the controlled corporation are acquired in a post spin-off reorganization, Section 355(e) does not apply as long as the shareholders of the

Divisive Spin-off under §§ 368(a)(1)(D) and 355

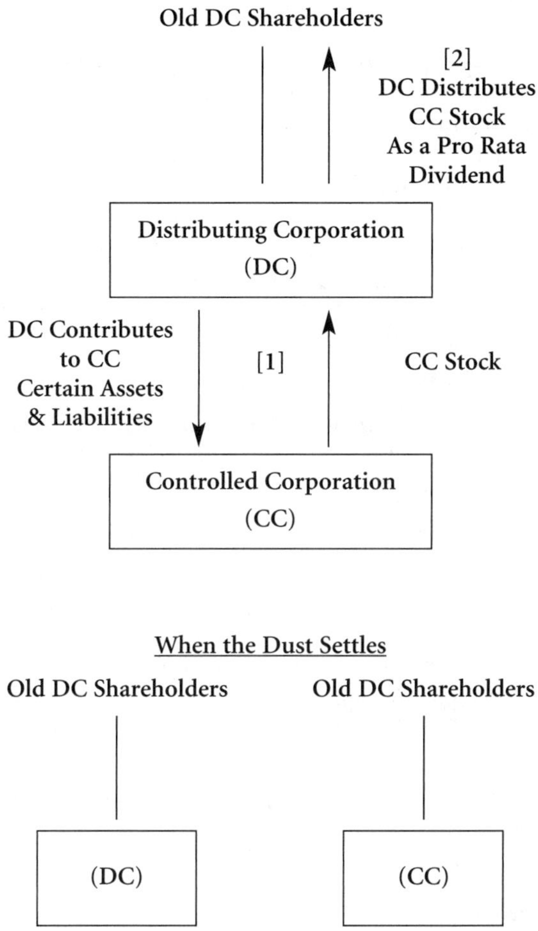

acquired corporation own more than 50% of the acquiring corporation. This was the type of structure used in the acquisition by Comcast of the ATT Broadband properties, which is discussed in Section 24.7.

E. Cash Rich Split-Offs

In December 2014, it was announced that Berkshire Hathaway, which is controlled by Warren Buffett, would acquire Duracell, the battery maker, from Procter & Gamble in a cash-rich split-off. In this transaction, Berkshire would exchange (1) shares it owns in P&G, for (2) all of the stock of Duracell held by P&G. Thus, P&G is essentially redeeming its stock from Berkshire in exchange for stock P&G holds in its subsidiary, Duracell. The redemption is a "split-off" because in exchange for P&G stock held by Berkshire, P&G is splitting off to Berkshire its stock in Duracell.

Prior to the transaction, P&G will transfer to Duracell significant cash, thus making the transaction a cash rich split-off. If structured correctly (*e.g.*, the cash can be no more than two thirds of Duracell's assets), this type of transaction can come within Section 355 and all parties will receive tax-free treatment.

After the transaction, Berkshire will own all of the stock of Duracell and can cause Duracell to distribute its cash to Berkshire on a tax-free basis under the consolidated return rules. Thus, Berkshire will (1) have received some cash for its P&G stock while avoiding tax on the disposition, and (2) also own Duracell. On the other hand, P&G will have disposed of Duracell without paying tax on its significant gains in such stock. Obviously, this type of transaction is a tax efficient transaction for both P&G and Duracell.

§ 24.4 Corporate Issues in Spin-Offs

A. Directors' Duties in Spin-Offs: Duty to Preferred Stockholders

See HB Korenvaes Investments L.P. v. Marriott Corporation, Section 3.5 and *Puma v. Marriott*, Section 3.7.

B. The Restriction on Dividends

1. Introduction

A spin-off is a dividend payment by the parent corporation, and, therefore, the transaction must satisfy the dividend provisions of the applicable state corporate law. Directors are personally liable for paying illegal dividends and the limitation on liability statutes, such as Section 102(b)(7) of the Delaware Corporate Law, do not free directors of liability for paying illegal dividends.

The following sections consider the dividend provisions of Delaware law, New York law, and the Model Business Corporation Act.

2. Dividend Provisions of Delaware Law

See §§ 154, 170, 172, 173, and 174 of the General Corporation Law of Delaware.

3. Payment of Dividends out of Revaluation Surplus

a. The New York Approach

Randall v. Bailey

Supreme Court of New York, 1940 23 N.Y.S.2d 173

WALTER, Justice:

A trustee of Bush Terminal Company, *** here sues former directors of that company to recover on its behalf the amount of dividends declared and paid between November 22, 1928, and May 2, 1932, aggregating $3,639,058.06. At the times of the declarations and payments, the company's books concededly showed a surplus which ranged from not less than $4,378,554.83 on December 31, 1927, down to not less than $2,199,486.77 on April 30, 1932. The plaintiff claims, however, that in fact there was no surplus, that the capital was actually impaired to an amount greater than the amount of the dividends, and that the directors consequently are personally liable to the corporation for the amount thereof under Section 58 of the Stock Corporation Law. [*Cf.* § 174 of Delaware Law] Defendants claim that there was no impairment of capital and that the surplus was actually greater than the amount which plaintiff concedes as the amount shown by the books.

The claims of the plaintiff, although branching out to a multitude of items, are basically reducible to four:

1. It was improper to "write-up" the land values above cost and thereby take unrealized appreciation into account. * * *

Until 1915 the company's land was carried upon its books at cost. In 1915 the land was written up to 80% of the amount at which it was then assessed for taxation, and in 1918 it was written up to the exact amount at which it was then so assessed. Those two write-ups totaled $7,211,791.72, and the result was that during the period here in question the land was carried on the books at $8,737,949.02, whereas its actual cost was $1,526,157.30. Plaintiff claims that the entire $7,211,791.72 should be eliminated because it represents merely unrealized appreciation, and dividends cannot be declared or paid on the basis of mere unrealized appreciation in fixed assets irrespective of how sound the estimate thereof may be. That obviously and concededly is another way of saying that for dividend purposes fixed assets must be computed at cost, not value, and plaintiff here plants himself upon that position, even to the point of contending that evidence of value is immaterial and not admissible. If that contention [is] sound, the company indisputably had a deficit at all the times here involved in an amount exceeding the dividends here in question. * * *

* * * The question I have to decide is whether or not an existing statute has been violated. The problem is one of statutory construction.

The words of the statute, as it existed during the period here involved, are: "No stock corporation shall declare or pay any dividend which shall impair its capital or capital stock, nor while its capital or capital stock is impaired, nor shall any such corporation declare or pay any dividend or make any distribution of assets to any of its stockholders, whether upon a reduction of the number of its shares or of its capital or capital stock, unless the value of its assets remaining after the payment of such dividend, or after such distribution of assets, as the case may be, shall be at least equal to the aggregate amount of its debts and liabilities including capital or capital stock as the case may be." Stock Corporation Law, § 58. [*Cf.* §§ 170 and 154 of Delaware Law] * * *

In summary, I think that it cannot be said that there is a single case in this State which actually decides that unrealized appreciation cannot be taken into consideration, or, stated in different words, that cost and not value must be used in determining whether or not there exists a surplus out of which dividends can be paid. * * *

* * * I am of the opinion that the same reasons which show that unrealized appreciation must be considered are equally cogent in showing that unrealized depreciation likewise must be considered. In other words, the test being whether or not the value of the assets exceeds the debts and the liability to stockholders, all assets must be taken at their actual value.

b. The Delaware Approach to Revaluation Surplus

See Klang v. Smith Food & Drug Centers, Inc., Section 14.9.C.

4. Dividend Provisions of the Model Business Corporation Act

See §§ 6.40 (distributions to shareholders) and 8.33(directors liability for paying unlawful dividends).

Official Comment to § 6.40 of the Revised Model Business Corporation Act

Section 1.40 defines "distribution" to include virtually all transfers of money, indebtedness of the corporation or other property to a shareholder in respect of the corporation's shares. * * *

Section 6.40 imposes a single, uniform test on all distributions. * * *

[**Equity Solvency Test**] As noted above, older statutes prohibited payment of dividends if the corporation was, or as a result of the payment would be, insolvent in the equity sense. This test is retained, appearing in section 6.40(c)(1).

For an on-going business enterprise the equity insolvency test requires that decisions be based on a cash flow analysis that is itself based on a business forecast and budget for a sufficient period of time to permit a conclusion that known obligations of the corporation can reasonably be expected to be satisfied over the period of time that they will mature. * * *

[**Balance Sheet Test**] Section 6.40(c)(2) requires that, after giving effect to any distribution, the corporation's assets equal or exceed its liabilities plus (with some exceptions) the dissolution preferences of senior equity securities. Section 6.40(d) authorizes asset and liability determinations to be made for this purpose on the basis of either (1) financial statements prepared on the basis of accounting practices and principles that are reasonable in the circumstances or (2) a fair valuation or other method that is reasonable in the circumstances. The determination of a corporation's assets and liabilities and the choice of the permissible basis on which to do so are left to the judgment of its board of directors. * * *

[**Voting Rights in Spin-offs**] The shareholders of the parent will not have the right to vote in the spin-off, unless the spin-off amounts to a disposition of substantially all of the corporation's assets. For example, under Section 271 of the Delaware Law * * * a shareholder vote is required for sale or other disposition of all or substantially all of a corporation's assets.

C. Use of Spin-Off with Spin Company Having a Classified Board As a Defensive Tactic

See Hilton Hotels Corporation v. ITT Corporation, Section 23.8.F.3.

§ 24.5 Federal Securities Issues Relating to Spin-Offs

Spin-Offs, SEC Division Of Corporation Finance, Staff Legal Bulletin No. 4

(September 16, 1997)

3. What Are the Basic Concerns about Spin-Offs?

A subsidiary must register a spin-off of shares under the Securities Act if the spin-off is a "sale" of the securities by the parent. Also, when a company that reports under the Exchange Act spins-off shares of a company that does not report under the Exchange Act, the spin-off raises concerns because it may:

- result in an active trading market for the spun off shares without adequate public information about their issuer; and
- violate the anti-fraud provisions of the Securities Act and the Exchange Act.

4. Does the Subsidiary Have to Register the Spin-Off under the Securities Act?

The Subsidiary does not have to register the spin-off if five conditions are met.

It is the Division's view that the subsidiary does not have to register a spin-off under the Securities Act when:

- the parent shareholders do not provide consideration for the spun-off shares;
- the spin-off is *pro rata* to the parent shareholders;
- the parent provides adequate information about the spin-off and the subsidiary to its shareholders and to the trading markets;
- the parent has a valid business purpose for the spin-off; and
- if the parent spins-off "restricted securities," it has held those securities for at least two years.

An Explanation of the Conditions

1. The parent shareholders do not provide consideration for the spun-off shares.

If the parent shareholders provide consideration for the spun-off shares, the parent would be transferring the spun-off securities for value. This transfer of securities for value is a "sale" under the Securities Act. So, when shareholders provide consideration, the subsidiary must register the spin-off unless an exemption is available.

2. The spin-off must be *pro rata.*

When the spin-off is pro rata, the parent shareholders have the same proportionate interest in the parent and the subsidiary both before and after the spin-off. If a spin-off is not *pro rata*, the shareholders' relative interests change and some shareholders give up value for the spun-off shares. Ordinarily, Securities Act registration would be required if a spin-off is not *pro rata.*

3. The parent must provide adequate information to its shareholders and the trading markets.

Whether the parent provides adequate information about the spin-off and the subsidiary to its shareholders and the trading markets depends on whether the subsidiary is an Exchange Act reporting company or a non-reporting company before and after the spin-off. In this discussion, we assume the parent is a reporting company.

> Non-reporting subsidiary
>
> If the subsidiary is a non-reporting company, the parent provides adequate information if, by the date it spins-off the securities:
>
> • it gives its shareholders an information statement that describes the spin-off and the subsidiary and that substantially complies with Regulation 14A or Regulation 14C under the Exchange Act; and
>
> • the subsidiary registers the spun-off securities under the Exchange Act.
>
> Reporting Subsidiary
>
> If the subsidiary is a reporting company, the parent may provide less information about thc spin-off to its shareholders. * * *

4. Valid Business Purpose for Spin-Off

When there is a valid business purpose for a spin-off, it is less likely that the parent indirectly will receive value for the spun-off shares through the creation of a market in those securities.

The Division has recognized the following as examples of valid business purposes for a spin-off:

- allowing management of each business to focus solely on that business;
- providing employees of each business stock-based incentives linked solely to his or her employer;
- enhancing access to financing by allowing the financial community to focus separately on each business; or
- enabling the companies to do business with each other's competitors.

In our view, there is not a valid business purpose for a spin-off when the purpose is:

- creating a market in the spun-off securities without providing adequate information to the shareholders or to the trading markets;
- the creation of a public market in the shares of a company that has minimal operations or assets; or
- the creation of a public market in the shares of a company that is a development stage company that has no specific business plan or whose business plan is to engage in a merger or acquisition with an unidentified company.

Other than the business purposes discussed above, the facts of a particular situation will determine whether the business purpose is valid. Accordingly, the parent must determine whether there is a valid business purpose for the spin-off.

5. If the parent spins-off "restricted securities," the parent must have held those securities for at least two years.

*** This two-year holding period position does not apply where the parent formed the subsidiary being spun-off, rather than acquiring the business from a third-party.

5. Does Securities Act Rule 145 Require the Subsidiary to Register a Spin-Off?

Securities Act Rule 145 requires specified transactions to be registered under the Securities Act when investors decide whether to accept a new or different security in exchange for their existing security. For example, when shareholders vote on a plan or an agreement for the transfer of assets in consideration for the issuance of securities, Rule 145(a)(3) may deem that vote to be a "sale" under the Securities Act.

Parent companies often ask their shareholders to vote on proposed spin-offs. Further, spin-offs may include the transfer of assets to the subsidiary. Based on Rule 145(a)(3), the Division generally has refused to say that the subsidiary does not have to register a spin-off where the parent's shareholders vote on an asset transfer from the parent to the subsidiary. However, we have reconsidered this position where the parent wholly owns the subsidiary. In this situation, we will no longer require Securities Act registration of a spin-off solely as a result of a shareholder vote on the asset transfer. The reason for the change in our view is that, when the other conditions described in response to Question 4, immediately above, are met, the vote on the asset transfer does not change the overall nature of the transaction. ***

6. Are Spun-Off Securities "Restricted Securities" under Rule 144?

It is the Division's view that securities received by shareholders in a spin-off that meets the conditions described in response to Question 4, above, generally are not "restricted securities."

In rare situations, however, a large shareholder of the parent so controls the parent that the shareholder essentially decides whether to do the spin-off. In these infrequent situations, we view the spin-off as a privately negotiated transaction between the parent and that shareholder, with that shareholder getting restricted securities. The other shareholders get securities that are not restricted.

7. Can the Subsidiary Consider Itself to Meet the Exchange Act Reporting Requirements of Rule 144 on the Date of the Spin-Off, Rather than Wait 90 Days?

Affiliates of a spun-off company may want to sell securities that they received in the spin-off. Absent registration under the Securities Act, affiliates must sell these securities under Rule 144 or another appropriate exemption.

These affiliates can only rely on Rule 144 if the subsidiary has been a reporting company for at least 90 days. [Rule 144(c)] We believe that the subsidiary satisfies this reporting requirement on the date the parent spins-off the securities (that is, before 90 days have passed) if:

- the spin-off meets the conditions described in response to Question 4, above;
- the parent is current in its Exchange Act reporting;
- the subsidiary will have substantially the same assets, business, and operations as a segment or subsidiary about which the parent has reported extensive segment data and other financial and narrative disclosure in its Exchange Act periodic reports for at least 12 months before the date it spins-off the securities. * * *

8. Does Exchange Act Section 16 Apply to Spin-Offs?

Exchange Act Section 16 applies to the officers, directors, and principal security holders of most companies with a class of equity securities registered under the Exchange Act. Section 16 requires these people to file ownership reports and subjects them to potential "short-swing" profit liability for their purchases and sales of the company's equity securities. Exchange Act Rule 16a-9(a) exempts the receipt of securities in a spin-off from Section 16 if all holders of a class of securities participate in the spin-off on a *pro rata* basis. * * *

§ 24.6 Is the Spin-Off a Fraudulent Conveyance?

VFB LLC v. Campbell Soup Co.

United States District Court for the District of Delaware, 2005
U.S. Dist. LEXIS 19999, aff'd 2007 U.S. App. LEXIS 7407 (3d Cir.)

Jordan, District Judge:

INTRODUCTION. VFB L.L.C. ("VFB") brought this action against Campbell Soup Company, [and related entities] (collectively "Campbell"), alleging that Campbell engineered a fraudulent transfer from VFB's predecessor in interest, Vlasic Foods International Inc. ("VFI"), to Campbell of more than $600 million in cash and assumed liabilities. * * *

FINDINGS OF FACT. *Parties.* 1. Plaintiff VFB is the successor-in-interest to VFI which was a wholly-owned subsidiary that Campbell spun-off to its shareholders (the "Spin" or "Spin-off") on March 30, 1998. Campbell transferred to VFI a group of businesses (the "VFI Businesses") which had been grouped together within Campbell prior to the Spin and were known as the "Specialty Foods" division. As part of the Spin-off, Campbell also transferred a $500 million debt obligation to VFI. On the date of the Spin-off, Campbell transferred its shares of VFI stock to its shareholders, so that Campbell's shareholders then owned shares of Campbell and, separately, shares of VFI. [The transfer to VFI and the subsequent spin-off qualified under Sections 368(a)(1)(D) and 355]

2. For reasons discussed in detail herein, VFI did not succeed as an independent company, and, on January 29, 2001, it filed a petition for reorganization under Chapter 11 of the Bankruptcy Code. VFB was created pursuant to VFI's Chapter 11 plan to permit creditors an opportunity to pursue the claims now at issue. (*Id.*) * * *

10. Campbell decided that, by leveraging [*i.e.*, causing VFI to assume Campbell debt] the Spin-off, it could "receive value similar to a sale" while "controlling the process." * * *

The Spin-off.

54. * * * [T]he Spin-off promised, and ultimately delivered an enormous tax benefit to Campbell. Specifically, the payment it received from VFI was tax free. * * *

55. The means Campbell employed to take cash was provided by the Banks. Campbell had arranged with the Banks to establish a $750 million line of credit for VFI (the "Credit Facility"). Campbell decided that it would take $500 million in cash from the Credit Facility and that VFI would take on the burden of that debt as part of the VFI capital structure. The $500 million thus became payment to Campbell in exchange for the transferred business assets.

56. The Spin-off occurred on March 30, 1998. During the Spin-off, Campbell transferred all of the businesses within the "Specialty Foods" division, *i.e.,* the VFI Businesses, along with the business specific debt, to VFI. (*Id.*) In addition, as noted, Campbell transferred the $500 million Credit Facility debt to VFI. (*Id.*)

57. By the close of trading on the day of the Spin-off, VFI's stock price stood at $25.31 per share on the New York Stock Exchange. At that time, VFI had approximately 45 million shares outstanding, yielding an equity market capitalization of approximately $1.1 billion. (*Id.*) That figure represented the value the market placed on all of the businesses transferred to VFI at the time of the Spin-off, taking account of the attendant debt. * * *

Bankruptcy. 88. In FY2000, VFI hired Lazard, an investment banking firm, to explore "strategic alternatives." Lazard and VFI concluded that VFI was "not viable" due to its "excess leverage" and that the only feasible alternative was to sell the businesses that comprised VFI at that time.

CONCLUSIONS OF LAW * * * *Fraudulent Transfer.*

2. VFB alleges that VFI fraudulently transferred $500 million to Campbell by assuming the $500 million debt obligation during the Spin-off. VFB argues that the transfer was illegal because it was constructively fraudulent and, alternatively, that it was made with actual intent to "hinder, delay or defraud" VFI's creditors. (*Id.*) The two sections of the New Jersey Uniform Fraudulent Transfer Act ("N.J. UFTA") that VFB relies upon for these allegations are Section 25:2–25[1] and Section 25:2–27.[2] (*Id.*) * * *

---

1. Section 25:2–25 states: A transfer made or obligation incurred by a debtor is fraudulent as to a creditor, whether the creditor's claim arose before or after the transfer was made or the obligation was incurred, if the debtor made the transfer or incurred the obligation: a. With actual intent to hinder, delay, or defraud any creditor of the debtor; or b. Without receiving a reasonably equivalent value in exchange for the transfer or obligation, and the debtor: (1) Was engaged or was about to engage in a business or a transaction for which the remaining assets of the debtor were unreasonably small in relation to the business or transaction; or (2) Intended to incur, or believed or reasonably should have believed that the debtor would incur, debts beyond the debtor's ability to pay as they become due.

2. Section 25:2–27 states in pertinent part: A transfer made or obligation incurred by a debtor is fraudulent as to a creditor whose claim arose before the transfer was made or the obligation was incurred if the debtor made the transfer or incurred the obligation without receiving a reasonably equivalent value in exchange for the transfer or obligation and the debtor was insolvent at that time or the debtor became insolvent as a result of the transfer or obligation.

Constructive Fraudulent Transfer.

8. Under both Section 25:2–25 and 25:2–27, a finding of constructive fraudulent transfer requires that a debtor make a transfer or incur an obligation and not receive "reasonably equivalent value." Section 25:2–25 also requires that, at the time of the transfer, the debtor "was engaged or was about to engage in a business or a transaction for which the remaining assets of the debtor were unreasonably small in relation to the business or transaction; or * * * [the debtor] intended to incur, or believed or reasonably should have believed that the debtor would incur, debts beyond the debtor's ability to pay as they become due," *i.e.*, it was inadequately capitalized. N.J. STAT. § 25:2–25. Section 25:2–27 requires that the "debtor was insolvent at [the time of the transfer] or the debtor became insolvent as a result of the transfer or obligation." N.J. STAT. § 25:2–27. Bad faith is not an element of a constructive fraudulent transfer claim under either section.

9. As discussed below, VFB has failed to prove by a preponderance of the evidence that VFI did not receive "reasonably equivalent value" during the Spin-off, or that VFI was inadequately capitalized or insolvent at the time of the Spin-off. Therefore, VFB's constructive fraudulent transfer claim fails.

Reasonably Equivalent Value.

10. New Jersey's version of the UFTA does not describe how to determine if an asset received by a debtor is reasonably equivalent in value to an obligation incurred by the debtor. The Bankruptcy Code also lacks a definition of "reasonably equivalent value." Consequently, I must look to case law for guidance on this subject. *Id.* * * *

12. Some cases have held that if the fair market value of the consideration received by the debtor is less than 70% of the fair market value of the consideration given by the debtor, then there is a lack of reasonable equivalence. * * * Later cases, however, used a different approach, known as the "*Bundles*" standard, after the Seventh Circuit decision in *In re Bundles*, 856 F.2d 815, 823–24 (7th Cir. 1988). *See In re Grissom*, 955 F.2d 1440 (11th Cir. 1992); *Barrett v. Commonwealth Fed. Sav. & Loan Ass'n*, 939 F.2d 20, 23 (3d Cir. 1991); *In re Morris Communications NC*, 914 F.2d 458, 466 (4th Cir. 1990). The *Bundles* standard arose in the context of determining if the proceeds from a sale of assets at foreclosure represented reasonably equivalent value. *Bundles*, 856 F.2d at 823–24. In that case, the Seventh Circuit, held that:

> In determining reasonably equivalent value, the court must focus on what the debtor received in return for what he surrendered. Consequently, it is appropriate to consider, as a starting point, the fair market value. However, the fact that the sale was the result of a foreclosure rather than an arm's length transaction between a willing buyer and a willing seller is also of considerable importance. Therefore, the bankruptcy court must focus ultimately on the fair market value as affected by the fact of foreclosure. * * * The bankruptcy court therefore must consider such factors as whether there was a fair appraisal of the property, whether the property was advertised widely, and whether competitive bidding was encouraged.

14. In non-foreclosure situations, courts have * * * continued to use the totality of the circumstances to determine if reasonably equivalent value has been received. * * *

15. Information from the most disinterested source imaginable, the securities market, helps to establish the fair market value of the VFI Businesses. This is not a case involving a distress sale, in which an asset's value may be skewed downward. In fact, neither party argues that the transfer of assets at issue here was distressed in any way.

Instead, the determination of reasonably equivalent value here is a straightforward comparison of the amount of consideration paid to Campbell and the fair market value of the assets transferred to VFI on the date of the Spin-off. I have already found that the value of the consideration paid to Campbell was $500 million. Consequently, all that is left to be determined is the fair market value of the VFI Businesses at the time of the Spin.

16. To determine the fair market value of businesses, courts have looked to market data about similar assets as the most trusted source of information. * * *

17. Comparable sales from the time in question are one type of market data that can be used to determine the value of a company. * * *

18. Another method used to determine the fair market value of a company is discounted cash flow ("DCF") analysis. [*See* Chapter 7] * * *

19. The price of a company's publicly traded common stock at the time of the transaction is presumably an ideal data point for the determination of fair market value. * * *

20. The stock of VFI was traded on the New York Stock Exchange at the time of the Spin-off. Because of the open and public nature of the trading, the only real concern in determining the fair market value of the company is whether the investing public had the information necessary to properly evaluate the VFI Businesses. Consequently, I have used the trading price of VFI's stock as the primary factor in determining if the fair market value of the VFI Businesses was greater than $500 million. In addition, I have considered the opinions expressed by market participants both during and after the Spin-off, as well as the market price of comparable companies at the time of the Spin-off, and I have considered the opinions of the parties' experts.

21. As previously noted, the value that the market placed on the VFI Businesses at the time of the Spin-off, as inferred from VFI's public stock price, was $1.6 billion. Considering the information that VFB asserts the market did not have at the time of the Spin-off, and the market's reaction when it indisputably acquired such information, as reflected in the price of VFI common stock during and after the Spin-off, I conclude that the value of the businesses transferred in the Spin-off was greatly in excess of the purchase price of $500 million. * * *

Inadequate Capitalization.

57. A debtor is inadequately capitalized if its assets were unreasonably small in relation to its business or the business that it was about to engage in, or the debtor reasonably believed that it would be unable to pay its debts as they came due. N.J. STAT. § 25:2–25. The test for unreasonably small capital and ability to pay debts as they come due is reasonable foreseeability. * * *

60. VFB has not proven by a preponderance of the evidence that VFI was inadequately capitalized at the time of the Spin-off.

Insolvency.

61. "A debtor is insolvent if the sum of the debtor's debts is greater than all of the debtor's assets, at a fair valuation." N.J. STAT. § 25:2–23(a). As discussed above, the value of VFI's assets at the time of the Spin was greater than $646 million, the sum that VFB asserts was the total amount of VFI's debts. Therefore, VFI was not insolvent at the time of the Spin-off.

Actual Intent to Defraud.

62. "A transfer made or obligation incurred by a debtor is fraudulent as to a creditor * * * if the debtor made the transfer or incurred the obligation * * * with actual intent to

hinder, delay, or defraud any creditor of the debtor * * *." N.J. STAT. § 25:2–25. Actual intent to defraud, by its nature, is rarely susceptible to direct proof, and, thus, circumstantial evidence must suffice. Each piece of circumstantial evidence is often referred to as a "badge of fraud." *Id.* * * *

65. I have already concluded that the $500 million obligation VFI incurred was reasonably equivalent to the businesses it received and that VFI was solvent at the time of the Spin-off. In addition, the conduct of VFI and Campbell does not suggest an intent to hinder, delay, or defraud any creditor. * * *

§ 24.7 Proxy Statement in the AT&T-Comcast Spin-Off and Merger

Many of the principles discussed in this chapter are illustrated in the Form S-4 and proxy statement for the AT&T-Comcast Spin-off and Merger, which is Documentary Appendix R of *M&A Statutes, Rules, and Documents, supra* Section 1.1. In this transaction AT&T effectuated a spin-off of its broadband cable properties and this company was immediately acquired by Comcast in what is known as a "reverse *Morris Trust*" tax-free transaction.

References

For a discussion of tax aspects of spin-offs, *see* Ginsburg and Levin, *Mergers and Acquisitions, supra* Section 1.10, at Chapter 10, Bittker and Eustice, *Corporate Tax, supra* Section 1.10, at Chapter 3, and Thompson, *Corporate Tax Through The Lens of M&A, supra* Section 1.10, at Chapter 9.

For a discussion of dividend payments under Delaware law, *see Folk on Delaware Corporate Law, supra* Section 1.10, at §§ 154 and 170.

For a discussion of the federal securities laws issues in spin-offs, *see* Hazen, *Securities Regulation, supra* Section 1.10.

See also Thompson, *Mergers, Acquisitions and Tender Offers, supra* Section 1.10, Chapter 15.

Chapter 25

Introduction to Shareholder Activism and Merger Arbitrage

§ 25.1 Scope

The principal focus of this chapter is on issues arising with shareholder activism, principally by activist hedge funds. The chapter also presents a brief introduction to merger arbitrage, a market strategy employed by various investment firms, including hedge funds and mutual funds.

Section 25.2 introduces three 2014 activist campaigns by the following leading hedge funds: Pershing Square, Icahn Capital, and Third Point. To help set the stage, Section 25.3 addresses the question: What is a hedge fund? And, Section 25.4 addresses the question: What is the basic mode of operation of activist hedge funds and the reactions of the targets? Section 25.5 discusses the "one-day pop," that is, the immediate increase in the price of the target's stock upon the announcement of the activist's position in the target's shares. Section 25.6 looks at the structure of hedge funds and their investments.

Section 25.7 discusses the Delaware Chancery Court's decision regarding Sotheby's two-trigger pill, which was deployed against the Third Point hedge fund. Section 25.8 examines several aspects involved in the joint bid in 2014 by Pershing Square, a hedge fund, and Valeant, a publicly held corporation, for Allergan, a publicly held corporation. This was the first transaction in which a hedge fund joined with a strategic buyer in making a joint bid for a publicly held firm. Finally, Section 25.9 provides a brief introduction to merger arbitrage. These and additional issues are explored in greater detail in Chapter 28 of Thompson, *Mergers, Acquisitions and Tender Offers*, *supra* Section 1.10.

§ 25.2 Three 2014 Activist Campaigns: (1) Pershing Square/Valeant–Allergan; (2) Icahn Capital–Family Dollar Stores; and (3) Third Point–Sotheby's

To illustrate many of the issues discussed in this chapter, references are made to the following three 2014 classic examples of activist hedge fund campaigns:

(1) Pershing Square's establishment (together with Valeant, a large publicly held pharmaceutical firm) of a 9.7% position in Allergan, another large publicly held pharmaceutical firm, with a view to facilitating the acquisition of Allergan by Valeant;

(2) Icahn Capital's establishment in June 2014 of a 9.4% interest in Family Dollar Stores, a publicly held firm, with a view to enhancing shareholder value by changing Family Dollar's business strategy; and

(3) Third Point's establishment of a 9.4% position in Sotheby's, a publicly held firm, with a view to changing its business strategy.

Pershing Square is run by William "Bill" Ackman; Icahn Capital is run by Carl Icahn; and Third Point LLC is run by Daniel Loeb. A May 2014 Conference Board article entitled *The Activism of Carl Icahn and Bill Ackman*[1] describes them as "prominent figures in the activist world."[2] The same is true of Dan Loeb.

The Third Point campaign against Sotheby's was also the subject of a 2014 court decision in Delaware, *Third Point v. Ruprecht*,[3] which is discussed later as an illustration of how Delaware law deals with a target's adoption and use of a poison pill. Although the court decision went against Third Point, it continued to wage a "short-slate" proxy contest against Sotheby's, and the contest was settled with Sotheby's agreeing to add three Third Point designees to its board, one of whom was Dan Loeb. Although as of the time of the writing of this chapter in early July 2014, the Third Point campaign had come to an end, at least temporarily, the results of the Allergan and Family Dollar Store campaigns have not yet been determined.

§ 25.3 What Is a Hedge Fund?

Hedge funds are privately held investment funds that are run by a management company that acts as the investment advisor to the fund. The investors in the hedge fund are generally accredited investors, which, as defined in Reg. D, generally include wealthy individuals and sophisticated institutions. The SEC describes a hedge fund as follows:

> Like mutual funds, hedge funds pool investors' money and invest the money in an effort to make a positive return. Hedge funds typically have more flexible investment strategies than mutual funds. Many hedge funds seek to profit in all kinds of markets by using leverage (in other words, borrowing to increase investment exposure as well as risk), short-selling and other speculative investment practices that are not often used by mutual funds.
>
> Unlike mutual funds, hedge funds are not subject to some of the regulations that are designed to protect investors. Depending on the amount of assets in the hedge funds advised by a manager, some hedge fund managers may not be required to register or to file public reports with the SEC. [Such non-SEC registered hedge funds generally will have to register under the applicable state law.] Hedge funds, however, are subject to the same prohibitions against fraud as are other market participants, and their managers owe a fiduciary duty to the funds that they manage.
>
> Hedge fund investors do not receive all of the federal and state law protections that commonly apply to most mutual funds. For example, hedge funds are not required to provide the same level of disclosure as you would receive from mutual funds. Without the disclosure that the securities laws require for most mutual funds, it can be more difficult to fully evaluate the terms of an investment in a hedge fund. It may also be difficult to verify representations you receive from a hedge fund.[4]

---

1. Richard Lee and Jason D. Schloetzer, *The Activism of Carl Icahn and Bill Ackman*, Director Noes, The Conference Board (May 2014) [hereinafter *Activism of Icahn and Ackman*].
2. *Id.* at 1–2.
3. Third Point LLC v. Ruprecht, 2014 Del. Ch. LEXIS 64 (May 2, 2014).
4. SEC, Hedge Funds, available at https://www.sec.gov/answers/hedge.htm (last visited July 2, 2014).

§ 25.4 What Is the Basic Mode of Operation of Activist Hedge Funds and What Are the Usual Reactions of the Targets?

Although activist hedge funds can follow any number of strategies, the basic mode of operation by these funds is as follows:

> First, identify a publicly held firm whose stock is undervalued because of an ineffective business strategy;
>
> Second, with capital provided by investment funds organized and controlled by the hedge fund, secretly acquire a significant amount of a target's stock at the undervalued prices, thus becoming a large block holder of the target's shares;
>
> Third, after the running of the 10-day window period under Section 13(d) (see Chapter 18), publicly announce that stock position, with the expectation that there will be an immediate increase in the stock price of the target, that is a "one-day pop"; and
>
> Fourth, by the use of, for example, (1) a proxy contest, and (2) the presentation of a white paper on the need for change, advocate for a change in the target's corporate strategy, which could include the sale of the target.

As one would expect, the target will generally react to the public announcement by the activist by (1) adopting a poison pill if it has not already done so, and (2) employing other defensive measures, such as modifications in the manner in which special shareholder meetings may be called.

The above mode of operation by the hedge fund and the reaction by the target is precisely what happened in the three campaigns discussed in this chapter: (1) Pershing Square/Valeant-Allergan, (2) Icahn Capital-Family Dollar Stores, and (3) Third Point-Sotheby's.

Two hot issues with this structure are (1) whether the 10-day window under Section 13(d) should be closed, and (2) to what extent should derivative positions count as beneficial interest for purposes of Section13(d). Both of these issues are discussed in Chapter 28 of Thompson, *Mergers, Acquisitions and Tender Offers, supra* Section 1.10.

§ 25.5 The "One-Day Pop" in Pershing Square-Allergan

As an illustration of the economic impact on the activist hedge fund from recent "one-day pops," this section focuses on the pop in the Pershing Square/Valeant-Allergan campaign. The following table shows that the one-day pop resulted in an economic gain to Pershing Square and Valeant of approximately $1 billion, the overwhelming majority of which was allocated to the participating Pershing Square funds:

Calculations of Pershing Square/Valeant's "One-Day POP"

Opening Price Day after Disclosure	$163.65
Average Price Per Share	$129.28
Increase in Price as Result of Disclosure	$34.37
Total Number of Shares	28,878,538
Single Day Aggregate Profit	$992,555,351.06
Profit as a Percent of Total Cumulative Purchase Price	26.59%

§ 25.6 How Are Activist Hedge Funds and Their Investments Structured?

A. Introduction

This section focuses on the ownership structure of Icahn's investment in Family Dollar. As will be seen, the ownership structure is quite complex. Keep in mind, however, that the hedge fund itself provides financial advice to various investor funds that the hedge fund, or an affiliate, (1) has organized, and (2) manages. The investment funds are the principal sources of capital for the purchase of the target's shares.

B. The Structure of the Icahn Acquisition of the Stock of Family Dollar Stores

Documentary Appendix KK provides a diagram of the ownership structure of Icahn's investment in Family Dollar. The bottom line is that the following three investor funds made the investment in the stock of Family Dollar Stores: High River Limited Partnership, [1]; Icahn Master Fund Limited, [2]; and Icahn Partners LP, [3].

§ 25.7 Fiduciary Duties and the Two Trigger Pill; 10% for 13D Filers; 20% for 13G Filers — *Third Point*

A. Background

In *Third Point v. Ruprecht*,[5] Vice Chancellor Parsons of the Delaware Chancery Court was faced with a challenge to a poison pill adopted by Sotheby's, a publicly held Delaware corporation. The pill was adopted in response to the acquisition by activist hedge funds and others of stock of Sotheby's, and the pill, which had a one-year life unless approved by shareholders, had (1) a 10% trigger for 13D filers, and (2) a 20% trigger for 13G filers, who because of their passive ownership have a reduced disclosure obligation.

Sotheby's has an unstaggered board consisting of twelve directors, and the only management representative on the board is Ruprecht, the Chairman, CEO, and President. Ten of the other eleven directors are "independent" within the meaning of the NYSE rules, and the directors as a group own approximately 0.87% of Sotheby's outstanding shares. The composition of the board turns over more frequently than the average for a publicly traded firm.

The primary plaintiff, Third Point, an activist hedge fund, sought a preliminary injunction against the dual trigger feature of the pill, asserting:

> [Sotheby's] board violated their fiduciary duties by adopting the rights plan and refusing to provide it with a waiver from the rights plan's terms, so that the Board could obtain an impermissible advantage in an ongoing proxy contest with [Third Point]. [R]egardless of the board's intent in adopting and refusing to waive certain features of the rights plan, [Third Point] does not pose a legally

5. Third Point LLC v. Ruprecht, 2014 Del. Ch. LEXIS 64 (May 2, 2014).

> cognizable threat to [Southeby's] and ... in any event, the rights plan is not a proportionate response to any threat the board might have perceived.[6]

The following discussion focuses principally on the activities of the activist hedge funds, the structure of the pill, and a brief overview of the court's reasoning in denying Third Point's motion for a preliminary injunction. Also, discussed are (1) the basic documents used in the proxy contest, and (2) the post-decision settlement that put three representatives of Third Point on Sotheby's board.

B. Description of the Acquisition of Stock of Sotheby's by Activist Hedge Funds and Others

The court described as follows the purchases of Sotheby's stock by various hedge funds and investment banking firms:

> On May 15, 2013, in a Form 13F filed with the SEC, Third Point disclosed that it had acquired 500,000 shares of Sotheby's stock. [Third Point is an investment manager for a series of investment funds that, collectively, manage approximately $14.5 billion in assets, and Daniel Loeb is Third Point's CEO.] On June 11, 2013 ... Trian Fund Management, L.P. ("Trian"), an activist hedge fund with ties to Nelson Peltz, ... acquired 250,000 shares in the Company. [Sotheby's was advised] ... that "[Trian's] usual MO is to buy 4.9% and then call us and make a lot of noise." ... Morgan Stanley [an investment banking firm] recently had announced a "passive" 5.1% stake in Sotheby's, but [Sotheby's was concerned] that such a stake might be a front for one or more funds, including Third Point and those associated with Peltz or Bill Ackman, another well-known activist investor, wishing to obtain as large an interest as possible in the Company "before announcing their intentions, probably through a 13D filing."
>
> On July 30, 2013, another activist fund, Marcato Capital Management LLC ("Marcato"), filed a Schedule 13D disclosing its acquisition of 6.61% of Sotheby's common stock. Marcato's filing stated that it may enter into discussions with the Board, the Company's management, or other stockholders about "various strategic alternatives," including "M&A." Marcato also reserved the right to acquire additional shares in the Company and to pursue "[a]n extraordinary corporate transaction, such as a merger, reorganization or liquidation, involving the issuer or any of its subsidiaries." ...
>
> On August 1, 2013, [Sotheby's was informed] that Third Point owned over 500,000 shares in the Company and [had asked] for a meeting with Ruprecht "as part of [Third Point's] efforts to better understand the company and strategic plans."[7]

C. Sotheby's View That the Hedge Funds Had a Short-Term View

The court pointed out that Ruprecht was concerned that activists "were likely to want to have the Company pursue a strategy emblematic of the 'classic tension [of] short term

6. *Id.* at 3–3.
7. *Id.* at 9–13.

vs long term thinking and strategies' [and that the activists] likely plan [on] 'stripping capital from the company and increasing ... annual P&L costs' "[8]

D. Advice from Sotheby's Lawyers, Wachtell Lipton, and Investment Banker, Goldman Sachs

The court explains that the board received a joint presentation by Wachtell and Goldman dealing with (1) the stockholder activism market generally, and (2) activism issues that are specific to Sotheby's. With regard to general shareholder activism, Wachtell and Goldman reported:

> [S]tockholder activism levels were "high," at least in part because of activists' prior successes in waging proxy contests. The presentation also contained a slide titled "Activist Investor Tactics Typically Follow a Familiar Pattern." According to the presentation, this pattern usually consists of activists building a stake in an entity, individually or by teaming up with other institutional or activist stockholders to form a "wolf pack," applying pressure on the entity, including threatening to agitate against a board's preferred strategic alternatives, and finally taking action against the board by threatening "withhold the vote" campaigns, demanding board seats, launching a short-slate proxy contest, or making aggressive use of derivatives.[9]

Turning to the activism issues currently facing Sotheby's, the court explained that Wachtell and Goldman presented an overview of each of the hedge funds that had invested in Sotheby's: Trian, Marcato, and Third Point. The court summarized as follows the overview:

> For Third Point, the overview noted Loeb's penchant for authoring "poison-pen" letters and the fund's focus on "event-driven situations such as mergers, acquisitions, tender offers, recapitalizations, spin-offs, exchange offers and liquidations." On a slide comparing the "agendas" Trian, Marcato, and Third Point had pursued in previous activist campaigns, Goldman and Wachtell reported that Third Point had, among other things, bid for a company in which it had invested. The Board's financial and legal advisors also discussed with them Third Point's previous successes in negotiating a transaction with entities it had invested in that arguably allowed it to obtain a benefit that was not available to the entity's other stockholders. An example was the repurchase by Yahoo! of 40 million of its shares from Third Point.[10]

E. Discussions about Returning Capital and the "Hedgies" Keep Buying

Representatives of Sotheby's met with Third Point and Marcato, and the hedge funds urged Sotheby's management to return to shareholders a significant part of the cash-on-hand. The funds continued to acquire stock of Sotheby's with Trian filing a Form 13F stating that it had acquired approximately 3% of Sotheby's outstanding common stock. Also, Third Point quintupled its stake in Sotheby's to a position of 3.6% of the outstanding

8. *Id.* at 13–14.
9. *Id.* at 15–16.
10. *Id.* at 16.

stock, and shortly thereafter filed its initial Schedule 13D, disclosing it had acquired a 5.7% position in Sotheby's. The 13D stated:

> [It] intended to "engage in a dialogue with members of the Board or management," and also might pursue discussions with other stockholders or "knowledgeable industry or market observers (including art market participants)." [T]hese discussions "may relate to potential changes of strategy and leadership at" Sotheby's.... [It] reserved the right to purchase additional Sotheby's shares and to pursue "[a]n extraordinary corporate transaction, such as a merger, reorganization or liquidation, involving the issuer or any of its subsidiaries."[11]

Shortly after the filing of Third Point's 13D, Marcato received clearance from the FTC under the HSR pre-notification law to acquire over 50% of Sotheby's outstanding shares, if it so chose to do so. And shortly thereafter, Sotheby's Finance Committee was informed that "Trian, Marcato, and Third Point had accumulated approximately 15% of the Company's outstanding shares, and that Third Point held derivative positions that, if exercised, would increase that figure to over 20%."[12]

At a Finance Committee meeting Goldman recommended a $200-$250 million share repurchase, explaining:

> One of the "potential consequences of inaction" was that "vocal shareholders" would "[p]ropose a short slate of 2 to 3 alternative directors," and ... the "key risks" of engaging in a share buyback [is] adding "additional leverage to a highly cyclical business," and creating the "[p]otential for Marcato/Third Point to 'claim victory,'" and the "[p]otential loss of operational flexibility in the U.S."[13]

F. Third Point's Form 13D and Letter to Sotheby's

Third Point filed an amended Form 13D showing that it had increased its stake in Sotheby's to approximately 9.4%, and attached to the 13D was a letter in which Loeb of Third Point raised several concerns about Sotheby's, including:

> "[T]he Company's chronically weak operating margins and deteriorating competitive position relative to Christie's," "Management's lack of alignment with shareholders," Ruprecht's "generous package of cash, pay, perquisites, and other compensation," "a sleepy board and overpaid executive team," and "lack of expense discipline."[14]

The court gave the following description of Loeb's "prescriptions for repairing Sotheby's" and his objective for sending the letter:

> [Loeb] asserted that the Company [should bring] in "the right technicians," such as Loeb himself, several new directors recruited by Loeb, and "a designee from another large shareholder." According to the letter, "[o]nce installed, these new directors would determine what other steps are necessary to ensure that the Company benefits from the rigor and direction that comes with having an 'owners perspective' in the boardroom." In addition, Loeb emphasized the need to replace Ruprecht as CEO. In that regard, his letter stated that Third Point already had

---

11. *Id.* at 20.
12. *Id* at 22.
13. *Id.* at 26–27.
14. *Id.* at 28.

> identified potential CEO candidates, both internal and external to the Company, and had already commenced informal discussions with the external candidates.
>
> Loeb apparently made several of the accusations in his letter without actual knowledge of their veracity. In addition, the record supports an inference that Loeb included the letter with the Schedule 13D as part of an "all out assault" meant to destabilize the Company. In contemporaneous emails, Loeb described his letter as both part of a "holy jihad" intended to "make sure all the Sotheby's infidels are made aware that there is only one true God," and part of a "Special Operation on Sotheby's," which was intended to "shock and awe" the Company and "undermine the credibility" of Ruprecht. Loeb acknowledged that the letter may have caused some "collateral damage" to the Board, but believed that was "an acceptable risk" to have taken.[15]

G. Sotheby's Adopts a Poison Pill

After carefully considering Loeb's letter and other factors, and on the advice of Wachtell and Goldman, the board of Sotheby's adopted a poison pill, and the court described the terms of the pill as follows:

> By its own terms, the Rights Plan expires in one year unless it is approved by a stockholder vote. Nothing in the Rights Plan, however, appears to prohibit the Board from re-adopting it in whole or in part after it expires. In addition, the Rights Plan contains a "qualifying offer" exception, in which the Rights Plan will not apply to an "any-and-all" shares offer for the Company that cashes out all Sotheby's stockholders and gives them at least 100 days to consider the offer.
>
> Of greater relevance to the current litigation, however, is the Rights Plan's two-tiered structure. Under the Rights Plan's definition of "Acquiring Person," those who report their ownership in the Company pursuant to Schedule 13G may acquire up to a 20% interest in Sotheby's. A person is eligible to file a Schedule 13G only if, among other things, they have "not acquired the securities with any purpose, or with the effect of, changing or influencing the control of the issuer, or in connection with or as a participant in any transaction having that purpose or effect" and they own less than 20% of the issuer's securities. All other stockholders, including those who report their ownership pursuant to Schedule 13D, such as Third Point and Marcato, are limited to a 10% stake in the Company before triggering the Rights Plan or "poison pill."[16]

Third Point and Sotheby's continued to interact, including having discussions about putting Loeb on the board. Also, Sotheby's continued its capital allocation review.

H. Third Point's Request for a Waiver of the 10% Trigger and Sotheby's Response

In March 2014, Third Point "sent a letter to Sotheby's requesting that the Company grant it a waiver from the Rights Plan's 10% trigger, and allow it to purchase up to a 20%

---

15. *Id.* at 28–30.
16. *Id.* at 32–33.

stake in the Company."[17] The court describes, in part, as follows Sotheby's reaction to this request:

> With its advisors, the Board considered the basis for the Rights Plan in the context of Third Point's letter and discussed at length whether Third Point and other activist investors continued to pose a threat to corporate policy and effectiveness and a risk of creeping control. The Board reviewed the interactions over the past eight months between Sotheby's, on the one hand, and Third Point and Mr. Loeb, on the other, including the risk that Third Point could obtain "negative control" or effectively a controlling influence without paying a premium with respect to certain matters if it achieved a 20% stake.... The Board considered [Wachtell's] Mr. Brownstein's advice and ultimately concluded that nothing had changed that would warrant a change in the Rights Plan, including the exemption requested by Third Point.[18]

I. Brief Summary of the Court's Reasoning in Denying Third Point's Motion for a Preliminary Injunction Re Its Request for a Waiver of the 10% Trigger and Sotheby's Response

The court started by pointing out the three elements that must be satisfied in order for the court to issue a preliminary injunction: "(1) a reasonable probability of success on the merits; (2) that absent injunctive relief, they will suffer irreparable harm; and (3) that the balance of the parties' harms weighs in favor of injunctive relief."[19] Only the reasonable probability of success element is discussed here.

Although the court found that *Unocal* applies to the resolution of this dispute, the court, citing *Liquid Audio*, said: "It is possible, but unlikely, that *Blasius* nevertheless may be implicated within the *Unocal* framework in this case."[20]

Turning to the application of the first prong of *Unocal* (that is, was there a legally cognizable threat to Sotheby's) to the adoption of the pill, the court concluded:

> [O]n the record before me, there is sufficient support for the Board's assertion that its good faith investigation led it to determine that Third Point posed a legally cognizable threat, and I consider that threat objectively reasonable. Thus, Plaintiffs have not demonstrated a reasonable probability of success with respect to the first prong of the *Unocal* analysis for the October 2013 adoption of the Rights Plan.[21]

Turning to the second prong of *Unocal* (that is, was the defensive measure reasonable in relation to the threat posed), the court first concluded that the plaintiffs "have not shown a reasonable likelihood that they will be able to demonstrate that the Rights Plan is either coercive or preclusive."[22] Further, the court said that having found that the pill was not Draconian, that is coercive or preclusive, it would have to determine if the adoption of the pill was within the range of reasonableness. On this point the court reasoned:

17. *Id.* at 41.
18. *Id.* at 42–43.
19. *Id.* at 48.
20. *Id.* at 50.
21. *Id.* at 59.
22. *Id.* at 64–65.

> The gravamen of Plaintiffs' argument that the Rights Plan is disproportionate pertains mostly to its two-tier structure which permits "passive" investors to buy 20% of the Company shares while "activist" stockholders cannot purchase more than 10%. As an initial matter, I note that while the Rights Plan is "discriminatory" in that sense, it also arguably is a "closer fit" to addressing the Company's needs to prevent an activist or activists from gaining control than a "garden variety" rights plan that would restrict the ownership levels for every stockholder, even those with no interest in obtaining control or asserting influence. In any event, the importance of the "discriminatory" nature of the challenged Rights Plan appears to be overstated in the circumstances of this case. Because I already have determined that the Board is likely to be able to show that the Rights Plan's 10% trigger for activist stockholders is reasonable and proportionate, the reason the discriminatory nature of the Rights Plan would be most likely to be found unreasonable or disproportionate is that it allows Schedule 13G filers, who may be more inclined to vote with the Company's management, to acquire up to 20% of the Company's shares, and not because a 10% cap on activist stockholders is, itself, unreasonable or disproportionate.
>
> In this case, Third Point is the Company's largest stockholder meaning that there are no Schedule 13G filers who own more than 10% of Sotheby's stock. Thus, while the question of whether Schedule 13G filers should be permitted under a rights plan to buy a larger interest in a company than activist stockholders is important in a general sense, I am not persuaded it can or should serve as a basis to enjoin the Sotheby's annual meeting when, as a practical matter, it is a complete non-issue in terms of the current composition of Sotheby's stockholders.
>
> Based on the record before me, Plaintiffs have not shown that there is a reasonable probability that the Board will be unable to establish that the adoption of the Rights Plan in response to a legitimate control threat was a reasonable and proportionate response. As such, Plaintiffs have not demonstrated a likelihood of success on the merits of their claim that the Board breached its fiduciary duties in adopting the Rights Plan in October 2013.[23]

Turning to Third Point's claim that the Sotheby's directors violated their fiduciary duty in failing to grant Third Point's request for a waiver of the 10% trigger, the court reasoned as follows with regard to the threat prong of the *Unocal* standard:

> I am skeptical that there is a reasonable probability that the Board could establish that when it rejected the request for a waiver, it had an objectively reasonable belief that Third Point continued to pose a "creeping control" risk to the Company, either individually or as part of a "wolf pack."
>
> Nevertheless, ... I am persuaded that Sotheby's has made a sufficient showing as to at least one objectively reasonable and legally cognizable threat: negative control. Plaintiffs are correct that the Delaware case law relating to the concept of negative control addresses situations in which a person or entity obtains an explicit veto right through contract or through a level of share ownership or board representation at a level that does not amount to majority control, but nevertheless is sufficient to block certain actions that may require, for example,

23. *Id.* at 70–72.

a supermajority vote. The evidence currently available indicates that Sotheby's may have had legitimate real-world concerns that enabling individuals or entities, such as Loeb and Third Point, to obtain 20% as opposed to 10% ownership interests in the Company could effectively allow those persons to exercise disproportionate control and influence over major corporate decisions, even if they do not have an explicit veto power.

The notion of effective, rather than explicit, negative control obviously raises some significant concerns, chief among them being where does one draw the line to ensure that "effective negative control" does not become a license for corporations to deploy defensive measures unreasonably. In this case, however, on the preliminary record developed to date there appears to be an objectively reasonable basis to believe that Third Point could exercise effective negative control over the Company. If Third Point was given the waiver it requested and achieved 20% ownership it would, by far, be Sotheby's largest single stockholder. That fact, combined with the aggressive and domineering manner in which the evidence suggests Loeb has conducted himself in relation to Sotheby's, provides an adequate basis for legitimate concern that Third Point would be able to exercise influence sufficient to control certain important corporate actions, such as executive recruitment, despite a lack of actual control or an explicit veto power. Therefore, I find that Plaintiffs have not satisfied their burden of showing that there is a reasonable probability that the Board will not be able to demonstrate that it identified an objectively reasonable and legally cognizable threat to Sotheby's corporate policy and effectiveness.[24]

In finding that the Sotheby's board had satisfied the "reasonable in relation to the threat posed" element of the Unocal standard, the court reasoned as follows:

For the reasons already discussed *supra*, the Rights Plan does not implicate issues of preclusion or coercion. Consequently, the relevant inquiry is whether the Board's refusal to grant Third Point a waiver from the 10% trigger falls within the range of reasonableness. The Board's refusal to grant Third Point a waiver was a response to the threat that it posed to the Company of obtaining, at least, negative control and threatening corporate policy and effectiveness. The refusal to waive the Rights Plan's 10% trigger level is consistent with the Board's stated purposes, and the operation of the Rights Plan at the 10% level would help the Board achieve that end. While it is of course conceivable that there is some level of ownership between 10% and 20% that the Board could have allowed Third Point to increase its stake in the Company to without allowing it to obtain negative control, the 10% cap must be reasonable, not perfect. Based on the record before me, I find that Plaintiffs have not shown that there is a reasonable probability that the Board will be unable to demonstrate that its refusal to waive the 10% trigger in the Rights Plan was within the "range of reasonable" responses to the negative control threat posed by Third Point. Therefore, Plaintiffs have not established a likelihood of success on the merits of their claim that the Board breached its fiduciary duties by refusing to allow Third Point in March 2014 to acquire up to 20% of the Company's stock.[25]

---

24. *Id.* at 74–76.
25. *Id.* at 78–80.

§ 25.8 The Pershing Square-Valeant Co-Bid for Allergan—The Potential Game Changer

A. Introduction

This section introduces the Pershing Square-Valeant co-bid for Allergan. It must be emphasized that this section was written in early July 2014 before the final resolution of this transaction. It appears that this type of co-bid arrangement could be employed by other hedge funds and strategic buyers.

B. What Happened to the Allergan Stock Price on the Announcement of the Pershing Square/Valeant Position?

As discussed previously, the "one-day pop" in the Allergan shares as a result of the announcement of the Pershing Square/Valeant position gave rise to about a $1 billion increase in the value of Allergan stock held by PS Fund 1 LLC.

C. The Agreement between Pershing Square and Valeant

Item 6 of the Schedule 13D filed on April 11, 2014 by Pershing Square with regard to the purchase of stock of Allergan provides the following background on the agreement between Pershing Square and Valeant:

> On February 25, 2014, Pershing Square and Valeant entered into a Letter Agreement (the "[Co-Bidder Agreement]") relating to [PS Fund 1 LLC's] investment in Common Stock. Pursuant to the [Co-Bidder Agreement], the parties thereto agreed, among other things, that:
>
> - Valeant and Pershing Square will become members in a newly formed jointly owned entity (which thereafter became known as PS Fund 1) and that entity will be the exclusive entity through which Pershing Square and funds advised by Pershing Square will acquire Issuer equity;
> - Valeant will contribute $75.9 million [the threshold above which Hart-Scott-Rodino pre-merger notification would have been required] to the entity; Funds advised by Pershing Square will contribute in its discretion additional amounts to the entity and the entity will purchase equity in the Issuer [Allergan];
> - Valeant will not, while Valeant, Pershing Square and/or the entity may be deemed a group, acquire beneficial ownership of Issuer equity, except in a business combination transaction with the Issuer or as a result of transactions by Pershing Square, the entity or any of their respective affiliates;
> - The entity will dissolve following the earliest to occur of several events, including the consummation of a business combination transaction with the Issuer or at such time that Valeant informs Pershing Square or the Issuer that it is no longer interested in pursuing a business combination transaction with the Issuer;
> - Income, gain and loss on $75.9 million in value of shares of Common Stock purchased by the entity will be allocated to Valeant and the remaining net profit realized by the entity will be allocated to funds advised by Pershing Square, except that Valeant will have a right to 15% of the net profits otherwise allocable to funds advised by Pershing Square if, before dissolution and at a time when a Valeant

business combination proposal for the Issuer is outstanding, a proposal for a third party business combination with the Issuer is outstanding or made;

- Valeant will consult with Pershing Square before making any material decisions relating to a business combination with the Issuer;
- Pershing Square will direct the management of the entity (including the manner and timing of purchases and sales of Issuer equity) and will generally decide how the entity votes any securities it owns, except that until the Termination Time (as defined in the [Co-Bidder Agreement]) the entity will vote all of its shares of Common Stock in favor of a proposal by Valeant to acquire the Issuer and other proposals supported by Valeant and against proposals reasonably likely to impair the ability of Valeant to consummate a business combination with the Issuer, and, subject to limited exceptions, will not sell or otherwise reduce its economic ownership in Issuer equity;
- At the election of Valeant, immediately prior to consummation of a Valeant business combination with the Issuer, Pershing Square will purchase, for $400 million, shares of Valeant common stock at a per share price reflecting a 15% discount to the then current market price;
- If Valeant and the Issuer consummate a business combination transaction that permits stockholders of the Issuer to elect to receive Valeant common stock, Pershing Square will cause the entity to elect to receive Valeant common stock for all shares of Common Stock over which it controls that election; and
- If Valeant and the Issuer consummate a business combination transaction, Pershing Square will, on the date of consummation, hold Valeant common stock with a then current value of at least $1.5 billion and, for a period of one year after that consummation, it will not sell shares of Valeant common stock unless after giving effect to the sale it continues to own at least $1.5 billion in value of Valeant common stock (and during that one year period it will not hedge its investment in that minimum number of shares).

D. Allergan Common Stock Purchased by PS Fund 1 LLC

Although it is not clear from the Schedule 13D, the trading data in Exhibit 99-2 of the Schedule 13D indicates that PS Fund 1 LLC purchased a total of $75.9 million shares of common stock of Allergan on February 25 and 26, 2014. Pursuant to Section 1(a) of the [Co-Bidder Agreement], these shares are "[Valeant] Allocated Shares" and the "gain or loss will be allocated to [Valeant]." Thus, the full $75.9 million contributed by Valeant went directly to the purchase of Allergan common stock in that amount. Although this amount was allocated to the account of Valeant, it did not exceed the HSR threshold and, therefore, at this point clearly no HSR filing was required. *See* Chapter 9.

Also, clearly no Schedule 13D had to be filed because the $75.9 million constituted only 2 tenths of 1% of the Allergan shares.

E. PS Fund 1 LLC's Options and Forward Purchase Contracts on Allergan Common Stock

Item 6 of the Schedule 13D filed on April 11, 2014 by Pershing Square with regard to the purchase of stock of Allergan also provides the following information regarding the options and forward contracts on Allergan stock owned by PS Fund 1 LLC:

> As of April 21, 2014, PS Fund 1 holds options to purchase 24,831,107 shares of Common Stock pursuant to various American-style call options with strike prices ranging from $1.20 to $1.33 and exercisable through dates ranging from March 4, 2015 to April 20, 2015. PS Fund 1 has also entered into certain forward purchase contracts with an expiration of April 22, 2015, covering 3,450,000 notional shares of the Issuer's Common Stock. The forward purchase contracts may be settled by physical settlement or cash settlement. The consideration for the forward purchase contracts will be paid at settlement based on a forward price of $140.37 and 3,450,000 notional shares of the Issuer's Common Stock. None of the options or forward purchase contracts gives the Reporting Persons direct or indirect voting, investment or dispositive control over any securities of the Issuer or requires the counterparty thereto to acquire, hold, vote or dispose of any securities of the Issuer. The counterparty to the options and the forward purchase contracts is an international investment bank.

Thus, while all of the $79.6 million contributed to PS Fund 1 LLC by Valeant went to the purchase of common stock of Allergan, all of the money contributed to this fund by Pershing Square advised funds went to the purchase of American style options and forward purchase contracts.

It is interesting to note that of the $3.2 billion dollar purchase price for the Allergan equity, $3.1 billion went to the purchase of options and forward purchase contracts.

The options gave rise to a beneficial ownership for purposes of Section 13(d) but they were not considered as effectuating an acquisition for purposes of HSR. This discontinuity in the treatment of options under Section 13(d) and HSR is explored in Chapter 28 of Thompson, *Mergers, Acquisitions and Tender Offers, supra* Section 1.10.

F. Filing of HSR and Exercise of the Options

After filing the Schedule 13D, pursuant to the co-bidder agreement, Pershing Square immediately filed a HSR notification. Shortly thereafter, Pershing was given early termination of the HSR waiting period. This permitted Pershing to exercise the options and buy the Allergan stock. This is one of the big advantages to Valeant from the use of this structure: it permits the early acquisition of the Allergan shares.

If Valeant had done the transaction alone, once it filed the HSR notification, it would probably not have received early termination because of potential antitrust concerns with the acquisition. In such case it could not exercise the options and buy the Allergan stock. The same was not true with Pershing. This issue is discussed in greater detail in Chapter 28 of Thompson, *Mergers, Acquisitions and Tender Offers, supra* Section 1.10.

G. Did Pershing Square Engage in Insider Trading or Violate Rule 14e-3?

1. Introduction

Some have raised the possibility that by entering into the co-bidder arrangement with Valeant, Pershing Square may have engaged in insider trading in violation of Rule 10b-5 or Rule 14e-3. In the case of Rule 10b-5, Pershing did not receive inside information from Allergan, and therefore, it seems clear that it did not violate Rule 10b-5. It is less clear with respect to Rule 14e-3, which is discussed in Section 20.6. Although Valeant did not initially make a tender offer for Allergan, after a period of time, Valeant made a tender offer and this presented a more problematic issue under Rule 14e-3, which was addressed by the California District Court in *Allergan v. Valeant*, which is set out next.

2. California District Court's Decision on Rule 14e-3

Allergan, Inc. v. Valeant Pharms. Int'l, Inc.

U. S. District Court, Central District of California, 2014 U.S. Dist. LEXIS 156227, Nov. 4, 2014

David O. Carter,

Background

This case arises from a live battle for corporate control that has spilled over into the courts. In February 2014, Canadian-based pharmaceutical company Valeant and hedge fund management company Pershing Square teamed up to help Valeant pursue a combination with Irvine-based pharmaceutical company Allergan. Between February and April, Pershing Square acquired 9.7% of Allergan's shares. In June 2014, Valeant publicly announced a tender offer for Allergan shares after Allergan's board of directors had rebuffed an unsolicited merger proposal. Valeant and Pershing Square then went directly to Allergan's shareholders to urge them to call a special shareholder meeting to replace Allergan's current directors with directors friendlier to Valeant. At the much-publicized urging of Pershing Square and some other shareholders, and after settling litigation in Delaware, Allergan agreed to hold a special shareholders meeting on December 18, 2014.

In this case, Plaintiffs Allergan, Inc. and Karah H. Parschauer allege that Defendants violated federal securities laws and regulations in connection with Valeant's tender offer for Allergan and in connection with Valeant's and Pershing Square's proxy solicitations. * * * [After discussing in detail the arrangement described above between Pershing Square and Valeant, the court proceeded as follows:]

Plaintiffs allege that Defendants' conduct constituted insider trading in violation of Section 14(e) of the Exchange Act and Rule 14e-3. Plaintiffs also allege that Defendants violated Section 14(a) and Rule 14a-9, *inter alia*, by not adequately disclosing the above facts to Allergan shareholders. * * *

Discussion

Likelihood of Success on the Merits/Serious Questions Going to the Merits.

[In seeking an injunction,] Plaintiffs argue that they are likely to succeed or at least raise serious questions going to the merits of their Section 14(e) and Rule 14e-3 claim as well as their Section 14(a) and Rule 14a-9 claim. The Court addresses each in turn.

Section 14(e) and Rule 14e-3 Claim

Plaintiffs' core allegations are based on Section 14(e) of the Williams Act, 15 U.S.C. § 78n(e) and Rule 14e-3, 17 C.F.R. § 240.14e-3. In *Brody v. Transitional Hospitals Corp.*, the Ninth Circuit assumed without deciding that a private right of action exists under Rule 14e-3. 280 F.3d 997, 1002-03 (2002). The Court held that only contemporaneous traders who could have purchased from or sold to the alleged inside trader can bring suit under Rule 14e-3. *Id.* at 1005. Here, Ms. Parschauer sold shares on February 26 and March 11, 2014, during the time period that PS Fund 1 purchased shares. Thus, Ms. Parschauer has standing to bring suit under Rule 14e-3. Allergan, however, was not a contemporaneous trader and therefore cannot bring suit under Rule 14e-3. The Court thus restricts its Rule 14e-3 analysis to Ms. Parschauer's claim.

Section 14(e) prohibits "fraudulent, deceptive, or manipulative acts or practices, in connection with any tender offer." Under Rule 14e-3(a), once an "offering person" "has taken a substantial step or steps to commence ... a tender offer," "any other person who is in possession of material information relating to such tender offer" that he knows or has reason to know is nonpublic and that he received directly or indirectly from the offering person must either abstain from trading or disclose the information to the public before trading. 17 C.F.R. § 240.14e-3(a). Relatedly, Rule 14e-3(d) makes it unlawful for an "offering person" to communicate "material, nonpublic information relating to a tender offer to any other person under circumstances in which it is reasonably foreseeable that such communication is likely to result in a violation of this section." 17 C.F.R. 240.14e-3(d).

Here, there is no dispute that Pershing Square possessed nonpublic information and did not disclose that information to the public before causing PS Fund 1 to purchase Allergan shares between February 25 and April 21, 2014. The parties dispute only whether any substantial steps toward a tender offer were taken by then, *i.e.*, whether the nonpublic information in Pershing Square's possession was related to a tender offer at that point. Even if substantial steps were taken, the parties dispute whether it was unlawful for PS Fund 1 to buy Allergan shares because it is unclear whether PS Fund 1 and other Pershing Square Defendants were "offering person[s]." The Court addresses each area of disagreement in turn.

a. Whether Substantial Steps Were Taken to Commence a Tender Offer

In order for Rule 14e-3's "disclose or abstain" requirement to be triggered, there must have been "a substantial step or steps to commence ... a tender offer" before PS Fund 1 began purchasing Allergan equity. To determine whether a "substantial step or steps" toward a tender offer were taken, a court looks mainly to the offering person's objective conduct. The SEC chose an objective standard in order to avoid "the difficulty of identifying when a person has actually determined to make a tender offer." Tender Offers, 45 Fed Reg. 60,410, 60,413 n.33 (Sept. 12, 1980) ("SEC Adopting Release"). In adopting the "substantial step or steps" standard, the SEC stated:

> [S]ubstantial step or steps to commence a tender offer include, but are not limited to, voting on a resolution by the offering person's board of directors relating to the tender offer; the formulation of a plan or proposal to make a tender offer by the offering person or the person(s) acting on behalf of the offering person; or activities which substantially facilitate the tender offer such as: arranging financing for a tender offer; preparing or directing or authorizing the preparation of tender offer materials; or authorizing negotiations, negotiating or entering into agreements with any person to act as a dealer manager, soliciting dealer, forwarding agent or depository in connection with the tender offer.

Id.

Courts have interpreted this list as only a list of examples and have found that other actions are sufficient to constitute substantial steps. *E.g., SEC v. Ginsburg*, 362 F.3d 1292, 1303 (11th Cir. 2004) (finding that a meeting between executives, followed by due diligence, a confidentiality agreement, and an awareness that "the deal had to go down fast" constituted substantial steps); *SEC v. Mayhew*, 121 F.3d 44, 53 (2d Cir. 1997) (finding that bidder and target companies' representatives signing a confidentiality agreement and holding a series of confidential discussions regarding a possible merger, and retaining McKinsey to do financial analysis and come up with strategy for the combination constituted substantial steps). The courts in *Ginsburg* and *Mayhew* both found that substantial steps toward a tender offer had taken place even though the offeror had not yet settled on a tender offer as the form of the merger. *See Ginsburg*, 362 F.3d at 1303.

Here, the Court must determine whether a substantial step was taken toward a tender offer before PS Fund 1's purchases of Allergan stock between February 25 and April 21, 2014. * * *

Defendants stating in a contract that they had not taken any steps toward a tender offer does not necessarily make it so. Evidence that Defendants took more definite steps toward a tender offer in May does not necessarily mean that a "substantial step" did not happen in February. Defendants have not adequately explained why the February 25 Relationship Agreement used the term "Co-Bidder Entity" and required Pershing Square and Valeant to identify themselves as "co-bidders" in the event that Valeant launched a tender offer if there was no plan for a tender offer at that time, or at least a strong possibility at that time that their actions would lead toward and facilitate a tender offer. With further discovery and upon presentation of the evidence to the jury, a jury could find for Defendants on the substantial steps issue. However, based on this record, the Court concludes that Plaintiffs have at least raised serious questions as to whether substantial steps to commence a tender offer were taken before PS Fund 1 began purchasing Allergan shares.

b. Whether Rule 14e-3 Contains a "Co-Offering Person" Exception

Even if Pershing Square purchased Allergan shares based on confidential information about a forthcoming tender offer, Defendants argue that their conduct was not illegal. There are two potential theories under which Pershing Square would be permitted to trade on confidential information that it received from Valeant: (1) if Pershing Square is Valeant's "broker" or "agent" within the meaning of Rule 14e-3(c)(1) or fits into the exception under Rule 14e-3(b), or (2) if Pershing Square and Valeant are collectively an "offering person" and it is possible for two persons to work together as one "offering person" within the meaning of Rule 14e-3. Since Defendants do not argue that Pershing Square fits into Rule 14e-3(b) or (c), the Court addresses the second theory, the "co-offering person" theory. Plaintiffs argue based on the text and legislative and regulatory history of Rule 14e-3, an "offering person" cannot be more than one person. However, the Court concludes from its review of the relevant statutory and regulatory text that the term "offering person" can include multiple persons. * * *

c. Who is a Co-Offering Person

The Court's conclusion that Rule 14e-3 allows multiple persons to act as one "offering person" does not end the analysis. If a co-offering person exception is not to swallow the general rule that an offering person cannot tip off another person and other persons cannot then trade on that confidential tip, there must be certain characteristics that distinguish a co-offering person from "any other person" for Rule 14e-3 purposes. The parties have not cited nor has the Court been able to find any legal authority directly addressing how to distinguish between a co-offering person and "any other person" for Rule 14e-3 purposes. Neither Congress nor the SEC has provided guidance directly on point.

Defendants urge the Court to equate "offering person" with "bidder" and "offeror" as the SEC already defines them for disclosure purposes, that is, as "any person who makes a tender offer or on whose behalf a tender offer is made." SEC Regulation M-A; 17 C.F.R. § 229.1000(d); Rule 14d-1(g)(2); 17 C.F.R. 240.14d-1(g)(2). When the SEC analyzes "bidder" status for Regulation 14D purposes, the staff consider factors such as:

- Did the person play a significant role in initiating, structuring, and negotiating the tender offer?

- Is the person acting together with the named bidder?
- To what extent did or does the person control the terms of the offer?
- Is the person providing financing for the tender offer, or playing a primary role in obtaining financing?
- Does the person control the named bidder, directly or indirectly?
- Did the person form the nominal bidder, or cause it to be formed?, and
- Would the person beneficially own the securities purchased by the named bidder in the tender offer or the assets of the target company?

One or two of these factors may control the determination, depending on the circumstances. These factors are not exclusive. * * *

Plaintiffs argue that "offering person" cannot be defined identically as "bidder" or "offeror" because effecting the purpose of the Williams Act—to ensure that investors have access to the material information they need to decide how they will respond to a tender offer—requires defining "bidder" broadly to ensure broad disclosures under Sections 13(d) and 14(d) while defining "offering person" narrowly to restrict the number of persons allowed to trade on insider information about tender offers. The Court finds Plaintiffs' argument persuasive because, in promulgating Rule 14e-3, the SEC was concerned about the practice of "warehousing" (the practice of the tender offeror intentionally leaking information to institutional investors to allow those other entities to make early trades before other investors heard about the tender offer) because such a practice is unfair to investors who are trading at an informational disadvantage. SEC Adopting Release at 60,412; Proposed Rule 14e-2 at 9976-77; *see also Chiarella v. United States*, 445 U.S. 222, 234, 100 S. Ct. 1108, 63 L. Ed. 2d 348 (1980) (noting that the SEC promulgated Rule 14e-3 to prevent warehousing).

Although Plaintiffs did not explicitly frame it as such, the Court also finds compelling their proposed test for distinguishing an "offering person" from a "bidder" or "offeror." Plaintiffs argue that an offering person should be more than a financier, and should actually make an offer to purchase shares and should have some degree of control over the terms of the tender offer and over the surviving entity. These factors are included among the factors used by the SEC to determine whether someone is a "bidder" or "offeror" for disclosure purposes. Thus, in essence, Plaintiffs would use the same test as that proposed by Defendants. The only difference is that, similar to how the SEC considers whether adding a person as a named bidder for Regulation 14D purposes would result in more material information being disclosed to shareholders, in determining whether someone is an "offering person," Plaintiffs would add the consideration of whether labeling the person an "offering person" would be consistent with Rule 14e-3's purpose of limiting the universe of persons permitted to trade on inside information only to the person making the tender offer. This may involve emphasizing control factors, such as control over the terms of the offer, control over the surviving entity, and control over and identity with the named bidder.

In adopting this test, the Court is aware that the SEC may one day issue a clarifying interpretation or even promulgate an amended rule that imposes a different test. However, in the absence of action by the SEC and Congress, the Court must do its best to interpret existing laws and regulations and to apply them to the cases before the Court in a manner faithful to their text and purpose. With these considerations in mind, the Court must determine if Pershing Square was a co-offering person within the meaning of Rule 14e-3.

d. Whether Pershing Square Was a Co-Offering Person

In crafting the February 25 Relationship Agreement, Defendants appear to have been trying to fit their relationship into what they hoped would be recognized as a co-offering person or "co-bidder" exception to Rule 14e-3. Neither the SEC nor the Congress has provided clear guidance in this area. Based on the existing legal authorities and the factual record currently before the Court, the Court concludes that, in this case, Plaintiffs have raised serious questions as to whether Pershing Square is a co-offering person.

In reaching this conclusion, the Court considers the following factors. First, the Court recognizes that Pershing Square did play an active role from the beginning in helping Valeant craft its acquisition strategy. It is likely that the tender offer could not have been launched without Pershing Square's assistance in strategizing the bid, financing it by acquiring a toehold through PS Fund 1, agreeing to accept Valeant shares if the Allergan-Valeant transaction included an offer for cash and shares to Allergan's shareholders, and agreeing to buy $400 million of Valeant shares at Valeant's request. The Court also recognizes that, technically, PS Fund 1 was a creature of both Valeant and Pershing Square at the time that it crossed the 5% threshold and triggered Schedule 13D disclosure obligations because, pursuant to the February 25 Relationship Agreement, Valeant was added as a member of the LLC and made a small $75.9 million contribution shortly before that point. (Prior to that point, PS Fund 1's only members and funders were Pershing Square entities.) Additionally, Pershing Square was listed as an "offeror" on the Schedule TO at the SEC's request, Defs.' App'x Ex. 37 at 1, and thus may be jointly and severally liable if Valeant fails to pay the consideration offered to Allergan's shareholders. *See* Rule 14e-1(c); 17 C.F.R. § 240.14e-1(c).

However, although Pershing Square was active as a strategist and financier to Valeant and even listed itself as an "offeror," the Court is doubtful that Congress and the SEC meant for these factors to be sufficient to exempt an entity like Pershing Square from the "disclose or abstain" rule of Rule 14e-3. While the February 25 Relationship Agreement required Pershing Square to give its consent before a tender offer could be formally launched, Pershing Square had no control over the price to be offered to Allergan's shareholders, whether the tender offer would involve cash and/or an exchange of stock, or even whether to call off the tender offer at some point. Pershing Square is helping to finance the tender offer; however, there is no evidence that it will actually acquire any Allergan stock through the tender offer. In fact, Defendants' Form S-4 Registration Statement states the opposite:

> Q: WHO IS OFFERING TO ACQUIRE MY SHARES OF ALLERGAN COMMON STOCK?
>
> A: This offer is being made by Valeant through [AGMS], a wholly owned subsidiary of Valeant....
>
> Q: WHAT DOES IT MEAN THAT PERSHING SQUARE AND PS FUND 1, A PERSHING SQUARE AFFILIATE, ARE CO-BIDDERS?
>
> A:.... [N]one of Pershing Square, PS Fund 1 or any of Pershing Square's affiliates is offering to acquire any shares of Allergan common stock in the offer....

In addition, there is no evidence that Pershing Square has any interest or involvement with AGMS, Inc., the wholly-owned subsidiary of Valeant listed as the "Purchaser" on the Schedule TO. There is also no requirement that Pershing Square be involved in the surviving entity beyond the requirement that Pershing Square hold an equity interest in the surviving entity for at least one year. *See supra* note 8; Feb. 25 Relationship Agreement

§ 2(c). Given that Defendants took care to explain in their tender offer materials that Pershing Square and PS Fund 1 were "co-bidder[s]" only "for SEC purposes," it appears that even Defendants do not really see Pershing Square and PS Fund 1 as the persons actually making an offer to pay Allergan shareholders consideration in exchange for their shares.

Based on these considerations, the Court finds that Plaintiffs have, at minimum, raised serious questions regarding whether Pershing Square is an "offering person" or "co-offering person" exempt from Rule 14e-3's "disclose or abstain" rule.

e. Conclusion

In conclusion, the Court finds that Plaintiffs have raised serious questions going to the merits of their Rule 14e-3 claim.

Section 14(a) and Rule 14a-9 Claim

The Court next turns to Plaintiffs' Section 14(a) and Section 14a-9 claim. As a current shareholder, Ms. Parschauer has standing to bring a Section 14(a) and Rule 14a-9 claim. * * *

Section 14(a) of the Securities Exchange Act of 1934, 15 U.S.C. § 78n(a), and Rule 14a-9, 17 C.F.R. 240.14a-9, prohibit the use of false or misleading statements or omissions in soliciting proxies. Section 14(a) and Rule 14a-9 are violated when (1) the proxy solicitation contains either a false or misleading statement of fact or omits a material fact; (2) the misstatement or omission was made with the requisite level of culpability and (3) the solicitation was an essential link in accomplishing the proposed transaction. *Desaigoudar v. Meyercord*, 223 F.3d 1020, 1022 (9th Cir. 2000). Defendants do not dispute factors (2) and (3), so the Court addresses only the first factor.

Plaintiffs allege that Defendants' September 24, 2014 proxy solicitation and Form S-4 Registration Statement fail to fully disclose that Valeant and Pershing Square had begun planning a tender offer to Allergan's shareholders in early February 2014 before PS Fund 1 began purchasing Allergan shares. Plaintiffs also allege that Defendants failed to disclose specifics about Pershing Square's involvement in Valeant's acquisition plans and that Defendants' conduct could make each Defendant liable under Rule 14e-3. Defendants argue that they have satisfied their disclosure obligations by disclosing that Allergan filed this lawsuit. The Court agrees with Plaintiffs.

Although Defendants have disclosed many details about their early discussions in February 2014, they failed to disclose several key facts. First, they did not disclose that the February 25 Relationship Agreement includes a provision whereby Valeant, Pershing Square, and the Co-Bidder Entity agreed to be listed as "co-bidders" if the acquisition proceeded by way of tender offer. Second, they failed to disclose that they were cognizant of potential liability under Rule 14e-3 when structuring the Relationship Agreement. Finally, although Defendants did disclose that Plaintiffs had filed this lawsuit, they did not disclose that the lawsuit involved their potential liability under Rule 14e-3. * * *

A reasonable shareholder would consider facts regarding Defendants' potential Rule 14e-3 liability important in deciding whether to vote for proposals advocated by Defendants, which are part of Defendants' plan for Valeant to acquire Allergan. *See SEC v. Fehn*, 97 F.3d 1276, 1291 (9th Cir. 1996) (requiring disclosure of contingent liability). Even if it was true that a shareholder would have to be "living under a rock" not to know about Plaintiffs' insider trading claims from the news or from Allergan's own disclosures, *see* Defs.' App'x Ex. 14 (Pyott Dep.) 184:12, that does not change Defendants' obligation to make their own required disclosures. *E.g., Kohn v. Am. Metal Climax, Inc.*, 458 F.2d 255, 265 (3d Cir. 1972).

Accordingly, the Court finds that Plaintiffs have raised serious questions going to the merits of their Section 14(a) and Rule 14a-9 claims. * * *

Disposition

For the reasons discussed above, the Court GRANTS IN PART Plaintiffs' Motion for Preliminary Injunction. The Court hereby ORDERS as follows:

(1) Defendants must make corrective disclosures to their September 24, 2014 proxy solicitation statement in compliance with Section 14(a) of the Securities Exchange Act and Rule 14a-9 promulgated thereunder, including disclosure of the facts underlying Defendants' exposure to liability under Section 14(e) of the Securities Exchange Act and Rule 14e-3 promulgated thereunder. Specifically, Defendants must disclose that:

a. Pershing Square and Valeant's February 25 Relationship Agreement included an agreement that Pershing Square and Valeant agreed to be called "co-bidders" if the Allergan-Valeant transaction occurred by way of tender offer.

b. Allergan and Karah M. Parschauer's federal lawsuit against Pershing Square, Valeant, and PS Fund 1 alleged that they violated Rule 14e-3 by causing PS Fund 1 to acquire Allergan shares between February and April 2014 without publicly disclosing information about Valeant's plans for a tender offer.

c. The Court found that Plaintiff Parschauer raised serious questions as to whether Defendants' conduct between February and April 2014 violated Rule 14e-3.

(2) Defendants and all of their officers, agents, representatives, employees, assigns, and/or anyone acting on their behalf or in concert with them are preliminarily enjoined from voting any proxies solicited by Defendants on the basis of their September 24, 2014 proxy solicitation and are enjoined from soliciting any further proxies until corrective disclosures are made.

(3) Defendants shall file their proposed corrective disclosures for the Court's review on or before November 7, 2014.

(4) Plaintiffs shall file their objections, if any, to Defendants' proposed corrective disclosures on or before November 11, 2014. Plaintiffs' objections shall be no more than 10 pages. If any objections are filed, Plaintiffs shall also file their own proposal for corrective disclosures.

IT IS SO ORDERED.

H. Actavis Spoils the Pershing/Valeant Offer

The Pershing/Valeant offer for Allergan was ultimately unsuccessful, as in November 2014, Allergan agreed to be acquired by Actavis, Plc, at a significant premium over the Valeant offer. However, as explained by Reuters, the transaction was a big success for Pershing Square:

> Hedge fund mogul William Ackman told investors they could see a $6 billion payday when he closes the chapter on Allergan Inc., his firm's biggest bet of 2014. * * *
>
> One week after Allergan agreed to sell itself to rival Actavis Plc., Ackman wrote in his quarterly investment letter that his Pershing Square Capital Management, the Botox-maker's biggest investor, still owns 26.6 million shares.

> Currently Pershing Square's stake is worth $5.64 billion and the stock was trading at a $15.70 discount to the transaction value, which translates into about a 19 percent annualized return assuming the deal closes next April.[26]

§ 25.9 Brief Introduction to Merger Arbitrage

A. What Is Merger Arbitrage?

Merger arbitrage may be engaged in by hedge funds and also by mutual funds, such as The Merger Fund. Merger arbitrage involves investing in targets of takeovers with a view to making a profit on the spread between (1) the post-announcement trading price of the target's shares, and (2) the price that is paid for those shares at closing. The amount of the spread is dependent upon (1) the risk that the transaction may not close, and (2) the time value of money between the date of the announcement of the merger and the date of the expected closing.

The strategy is sometimes referred to as "risk arbitrage," because of the risk that the transaction may not close because of, for example, an antitrust challenge to the transaction or the failure of some other condition to closing (*see* Chapter 15). In most transactions, the acquiror is offering a premium over the pre-announcement trading price of the target's stock, and if the transaction does not close, the trading price of the target may return to that pre-merger trading price or even a lower price, thus generating substantial losses for the fund.

In a merger where cash is the consideration, the fund will buy only the stock of the target, and if the transaction closes, the fund will have a profit equal to the spread between (1) the purchase price of the target's shares, and (2) the cash received at closing, less the transaction cost.

If an acquiror is issuing its stock in a merger, the fund will (1) buy the target's stock, and (2) sell short the acquiror's stock in the same ratio as the exchange ratio specified in the merger agreement. By selling short the acquiror's stock, the fund is "hedging" its position in the target's stock.

For example, assume that the exchange ratio is two shares of the acquiror's stock for each one share of the target's stock. For every one share of the target's stock the fund buys, it will sell short two shares of the acquiror's stock. At the closing, the fund will (1) receive for each of its target shares, two of the acquiror's shares, and (2) immediately close out the short sale with the two acquiror shares. The fund will then have a profit equal to the spread between (1) the purchase price of the target shares, and (2) the closing price of the acquiror's shares, less the transaction cost.

B. Potential Impact on the Market's Reaction to the Target's Stock

As pointed out in Chapter 1, in many cases, upon the announcement of a merger transaction, the stock of the acquirer will fall. This could be an indication that the market thinks the acquirer is overpaying or has otherwise made a bad deal. This is probably the case where the consideration is cash. However, if the consideration is stock of the acquirer,

---

26. Svea Herbst-Bayliss, *Ackman's Pershing Square Sees Big Payoff from Allergan Deal*, Reuters (Nov. 26, 2014), Available at http://www.reuters.com/article/2014/11/26/us-hedgefunds-pershingsquare-idUSKCN0JA1CG20141126.

some (and maybe all) of any drop in the price of the acquirer's stock could be attributable to the short sales of such stock by merger arbitrageurs.

References

Thompson, *Mergers, Acquisitions and Tender Offers, supra* Section 1.10, Chapters 28 and the references cited therein.

Chapter 26

International Acquisitions

§ 26.1 Scope

This chapter addresses some of the basic issues arising in cross-border acquisitions involving U.S. firms. Thus, the focus is on (1) inbound acquisitions in which a foreign acquiring corporation acquires the stock or assets of a U.S. target, and (2) outbound acquisitions in which a U.S. acquiring firm acquires the stock or assets of a foreign target. Although such cross-border acquisitions present numerous legal issues, the focus here is on corporate, securities, tax, antitrust, and investment restrictions relating to acquisitions involving a U.S. target firm and a target firm organized in the European Union (EU). Rather than focusing on the specific laws of any one EU country, this chapter examines various directives the EU has issued on corporate law, takeovers, and income tax matters. The member states of the EU are required to adopt internal laws that comply with these directives; thus, these directives give the reader a sense of how a particular member state may approach the particular issue. In the antitrust area, the EU applies its rules (and not the antitrust rules of a member state) to certain mergers and acquisitions, and this chapter examines these EU rules under its Merger Control Regulation (MCR).

There are two cross-border M&A case studies at the end of this chapter. The first case study illustrates some of the issues under South African law in an acquisition by a U.S. acquiror of a publicly-traded South African target. The South African laws regulating mergers and acquisitions, which are very sophisticated, follow the UK in many respects. I have selected South Africa for this study because I had the privilege of having the following experiences in dealing with its M&A laws: (1) serving in 1999–2000, on behalf of the U.S. Treasury, as the Tax Policy Advisor to the South African Ministry of Finance in Pretoria, (2) consulting with the South African competition authorities on their regulations, and (3) serving as a member of a group from the ABA's Section of Business Law that advised South Africa on the recently adopted revisions of its company law.

The second case study briefly introduces some of the issues under Chinese law when a U.S. acquirer acquires the stock or assets of a Chinese target. The Chinese laws regulating mergers and acquisitions are unique and developing. These laws are significant in view of the growing level of cross-border M&A activity between the U.S. and China.

In any inbound acquisition, the foreign acquiring corporation must comply with the U.S. laws discussed in other chapters of this book, and in addition, the foreign acquiring corporation may be subject to other U.S. laws governing, for example, tax and investment restrictions on certain foreign acquisitions. In any outbound transaction, the U.S. firm must comply with the laws of the country or countries governing the target and in addition may be subject to special regulation under U.S. laws, such as the tax and securities laws.

The employment laws in many foreign countries place serious restrictions on the ability of an employer to terminate employees, and such laws may prevent an acquiror from significantly decreasing a target's staff after an acquisition. Also, many countries, including less developed countries, have strict environmental laws. Obviously, the due diligence process [*see* Chapter 10] is particularly important in any cross-border acquisition. It is obviously important for the U.S. lawyer advising on a cross-border acquisition to have a fundamental understanding of the legal rules governing the foreign parties to the transaction. Further, in any acquisition with international dimensions, including acquisitions by a U.S. acquiror of a U.S. target where foreign operations are involved, it may be necessary to consult counsel in each of the countries where the firms operate. For example, as will be seen below in the examination of South African Competition law, the acquisition by a U.S. Acquiror of a U.S. Target may be subject to reporting and review under the South African Competition Act if both firms have business operations in South Africa.

This chapter is divided into five parts. Part I, *Introduction*, consists of Section 26.2, which presents an introductory problem, and Section 26.3, which presents an introduction to cross-border acquisitions.

Part II, *U.S. Issues in Cross-Border M&A*, looks at the U.S corporate, securities, tax, antitrust, and CFIUS (*i.e.*, investment restrictions) considerations in inbound, outbound, and in some case, foreign-to-foreign (*e.g.*, foreign acquiror and target) transactions. Sections 26.4 through 26.8, focus on inbound acquisitions. Section 26.4 covers corporate issues of such transactions, and Section 26.5 deals with issues under the federal securities laws. Section 26.6 briefly introduces the federal income tax issues arising in (1) acquisitions by foreign corporations of U.S. targets in tax-free reorganizations under Section 368 of the Internal Revenue Code, and (2) taxable acquisitions by foreign acquiring corporations of U.S. targets, including the impact of the interest stripping provisions of the Code. These provisions are designed to reduce the tax benefits a foreign acquiring corporation can receive from acquiring a U.S. target in an LBO.

Section 26.7 addresses the regulation of acquisitions of U.S. targets under both the substantive antitrust laws and the Hart-Scott-Rodino pre-merger notification rules. Finally, with regard to inbound acquisitions, Section 26.8 considers the Exon-Florio law, pursuant to which acquisitions of U.S. firms by certain foreign firms may be prohibited on national security grounds.

Sections 26.9 through 26.13 address U.S considerations in outbound and foreign-to-foreign transactions, with Section 26.9 focusing on corporate issues, Section 26.10 dealing with securities laws issues, Section 26.11 considering federal income tax issues, Section 26.12 looking at substantive antitrust and HSR pre-merger notification issues of foreign-to-foreign transactions, and Section 26.13 introducing the impact on M&A of the U.S. Foreign Corrupt Practices Act (FCPA).

Part III, *Regulation of Mergers and Acquisitions in the European Union*, contains Sections 26.14 through 26.21, and Section 26.14 provides an introduction to these sections, which includes a basic discussion of the structure of the EU.

Part IV, *Case Study No 1: Acquisition By U.S. Acquiror of South African Public Target*, with an emphasis of Walmart's acquisition of South Africa's Massmart, contains Sections 26.22 through 26.30, and this part is introduced in Section 26.22.

Part V, *Case Study No 2: Acquisition By U.S. Acquiror of a China Target*, contains Sections 26.31 through 26.41, and this part is introduced in Section 26.31.

Much of the material in this chapter is discussed in greater detail in the following chapters of Thompson, *Mergers, Acquisitions and Tender Offers*, *supra* Section 1.10: Chapters 19 (inbound M&A), 20 (outbound M&A), 21 (taxable cross border M&A), and 22 (tax-free cross border M&A).

Part I
Introduction

§ 26.2 Introductory Problem on Cross-Border Acquisitions

Time Entertainment, Inc., a publicly-traded Delaware corporation, is planning to acquire Warner Entertainment, PLC, a publicly traded United Kingdom corporation. The stock of Warner is principally traded on the London Stock Exchange and to a lesser extent is traded on exchanges in Germany, France, and through American Depositary Receipts (ADRs), in the U.S. Time and Warner have significant operations in the U.S., U.K., Germany and France. Time has proposed a friendly merger in which the shareholders of Warner would receive two shares of Time in exchange for each share of Warner. At the completion of the acquisition, Time will control all of the stock of Warner, and Warner shareholders will own 40% of the stock of Time. Warner is engaged in the movie production and distribution business and has 40% of the market in the U.K., 30% of the market in France, 20% of the market in Germany and 10% of the U.S. market. Time is also engaged in the movie production and distribution business and has 5% of the market in the U.S., the U.K., Germany and France.

1. How can a merger or acquisition of assets transaction be structured under the U.K. company law?

2. Assume that Time proceeds with an exchange offer for the stock of Warner to be followed by some type of freezeout transaction. What result under U.K. law? What if the tender offer is for cash?

3. What is the impact under the Securities Act of 1933 upon the issuance by Time of its shares in either a negotiated acquisition or an exchange offer? What is the impact of the Williams Act if Time makes either an exchange offer or a cash tender offer for Warner?

4. What is the treatment of the negotiated transaction under the U.K. tax law assuming that U.K. law is consistent with the EU's directive on tax treatment of mergers and acquisitions? What if the consideration paid is cash?

5. Assume that the jurisdictional threshold under the EC Merger Control Regulation is satisfied. In general, what is the impact of the acquisition under the MCR? What additional information is needed to complete the analysis? In general, what if the jurisdictional threshold in the MCR is not satisfied?

6. Warner decides that it does not want to complete the merger, and Time is now considering a hostile tender offer for the Warner shares. How must Time proceed and what defensive measures can Warner employ?

7. Because of certain legal barriers to completing the proposed acquisition by Time of Warner, the parties have restructured the transaction as a merger of a newly formed U.S. subsidiary of Warner into Time with the Time shareholders receiving voting common shares of Warner amounting to 60% of Warner's post-merger outstanding stock.

(a) What are the corporate and federal securities issues arising in this transaction?

(b) Will this merger be a tax-free reorganization under Section 368(a)(2)(E)?

8. In general, what result if Warner acquires Time in an LBO, with Warner borrowing 90% of the acquisition price in London and loaning that amount to a U.S. holding company that makes the acquisition of Time? Time's earnings are used by the holding company to

repay the debt to Warner. The U.S. and the U.K. have a tax treaty that exempts interest from withholding. What is the likely federal income tax treatment of the interest payments? What are the antitrust and Hart-Scott-Rodino considerations in this transaction?

§ 26.3 Introduction to Cross-Border Acquisitions

UNCTAD Global Investment Trends Monitor

28 January 2014

Developing economy M&A sales bounced back to the pre-crisis level, mainly driven by sales to developing economy TNCs

Expectations of a rebound in cross-border M&A activity in 2013 did not materialize as TNCs maintained a cautious approach. The value of cross-border M&A sales increased only modestly by 5% to reach US$337 billion, in 2013. This increase was mainly driven by deals in East and Southeast Asia, particularly in China, Singapore and Thailand. Latin America's increase in sales was due to the US$18 billion mega deal in Mexico, mentioned above.

Cross-border sales in developed countries decreased by about 10% on both sides of the Atlantic. However there are signs that confidence is returning in Europe. Germany, for example, more than doubled its sales with some major deals including Vodafone's acquisition of Kabel Deutschland for US$7.7 billion. Increases in FDI flows to Japan in 2013 were mainly owing to a number of mega deals, including United States-based Micron Technology Inc's merger with Elpida Memory Inc for US$2.5 billion.

Developing economy M&A sales' value in 2013 increased by 64% to US$88 billion, bouncing back to their pre-crisis levels. Almost 68% of the acquisitions were from other developing countries (up from about 50% in 2006). An example of this trend is the acquisition of Chinese Ping An Insurance Co. by a group of Thai investors for US$9.4 billion.

The value of announced greenfield projects continued to decline in 2013, although only minimally, by 1.7% from the previous year (figure 6). A 17% decrease of project values in developed economies was counterbalanced by a few developing countries (such as Nicaragua, Mexico, Iraq, Jordan, Myanmar and Vietnam) that saw announced greenfield activity increase.

Part II
U.S. Issues in Cross-Border M&A

§ 26.4 U.S. Corporate Issues in Inbound Acquisitions

In a negotiated acquisition, the foreign acquiring corporation will generally form a U.S. subsidiary (U.S. Sub-1) which may itself have a U.S. subsidiary (U.S.-Sub-2), and either U.S. Sub-1 or U.S. Sub-2 will enter into the transaction (*i.e.*, merger or acquisition of assets) with the U.S. target. The corporate rules discussed in preceding chapters, including Chapters 2, 3, and 13, apply to U.S. Sub-1 or U.S. Sub-2.

As an example of this structure, in the November 3, 1996 proposed acquisition by British Telecommunications PLC (BT), a UK corporation, of MCI Communications Corporation (MCI), a Delaware corporation, BT formed a U.S. subsidiary which was to merge into MCI pursuant to Delaware corporate law. *See* Documentary Appendix S of *M&A Statutes, Rules, and Documents*, *supra* Section 1.1.

§ 26.5 Federal Securities Issues in Inbound Acquisitions

A. Negotiated Acquisitions

If the acquisition is for cash, the Securities Act of 1933 (the 33 Act) is not applicable to the foreign acquiror. If the foreign acquiror issues its securities and the target is closely-held, the transaction may qualify for the private offering exemption under Section 4(2) of the 33 Act or under one of the Regulation D safe harbors. [*See* Chapters 4.14]. If, on the other hand, the target is publicly-held, the foreign acquiring corporation must register its stock under the 33 Act [*see* Chapter 4] and the proxy rules under the 34 Act apply to the transaction. [*See* Chapter 13] Rather than issuing its shares directly to the target's shareholders, the foreign acquiring corporation may issue American Depositary Receipts (ADRs), representing an interest in its shares. The ADRs would have to be registered under the 33 Act.

B. Tender Offers

In a tender offer by a foreign acquiring corporation for the stock of a U.S. target, the acquiror is subject to the Williams Act to the same extent as a domestic acquiring corporation. [*See* Chapters 17 to 20]

§ 26.6 Federal Income Tax Issues in Inbound Acquisitions

A. Acquisition by Foreign Acquiring Corporation of U.S. Target in a Tax-Free Reorganization

The rules regarding tax-free reorganizations discussed in Chapter 5 also generally apply to acquisitions by foreign acquirors of U.S. targets. Also, as a result of a 2006 amendment to the regulations, a merger of a domestic target corporation into a foreign acquiring corporation can now qualify as a reorganization under Section 368(a)(1)(A). The prototypical structure of an acquisition by a foreign acquiror of a U.S. target in a tax-free reorganization will involve the formation by the foreign acquiring corporation of a domestic subsidiary and that subsidiary will engage in a triangular merger with the domestic target, pursuant to which the target's shareholders receive stock of the foreign acquiring corporation. The transaction may qualify as a tax-free reorganization under Section 368(a)(2)(D) (forward subsidiary mergers) or Section 368(a)(2)(E) (reverse subsidiary merger), provided all other conditions for reorganization treatment are satisfied. [*See* Reg. § 1.367(a)-3] This type of reorganization must, however, also pass muster under Section 367, a provision designed to prevent tax avoidance through the use of foreign corporations. *See generally* Thompson, *International Tax Planning and Policy*, Section 1.10. If, however, as long as (1) the U.S. shareholders of the target do not end up with more than 50% of the stock of the foreign parent acquiror, (2) the U.S. shareholders of the target receive only stock in the foreign parent acquiror, and (3) no U.S. shareholder ends up with more than 5% of the stock of the foreign parent acquiror, then each such U.S. shareholder has tax-free treatment.

B. Acquisition by Foreign Acquiror of U.S. Target in a Taxable Acquisition

In a taxable acquisition of a U.S. target by a foreign acquiring corporation, the rules discussed in Chapter 5 apply. In addition, after completion of the acquisition, the foreign acquiring corporation will be subject to a 30% withholding tax on the receipt of dividend, interest and royalty payments from the U.S. subsidiary. [*See* Code §§ 882 and 1442] The withholding tax may be reduced or eliminated by the tax treaty, if any, between the country in which the foreign acquiring corporation is incorporated and the U.S. The U.S. has restrictions on the ability to organize a foreign acquiring corporation in a country with a favorable tax treaty. These are referred to as the anti-treaty shopping rules.

The foreign acquiring corporation must also be concerned about the U.S. interest stripping rules. [*See* § 163(j)] These rules apply where a foreign acquiror receives interest payments from a U.S. target that it has acquired and now holds as a subsidiary. If the target has a heavy debt load and the interest payments are exempt from U.S. withholding tax because of a tax treaty, then the interest stripping rules may deny the U.S. target a deduction for certain interest paid to the foreign acquiror. *See generally* Thompson, *International Tax Planning and Policy*, Section 1.10.

§ 26.7 Antitrust and HSR Issues in Inbound Acquisitions

A. Substantive Antitrust

The acquisition by a foreign acquiring corporation of the stock or assets of a U.S. target corporation is subject to scrutiny under Section 7 of the Clayton Act. [*See* Chapter 8]

B. Hart-Scott-Rodino

The acquisition by a foreign acquiring corporation of the stock or assets of a U.S. target is subject to pre-merger filing under Hart-Scott-Rodino assuming the reporting thresholds are satisfied. [*See* Chapter 9]

C. Possible Impact of the EU's Merger Control Regulation or Antitrust Regulation in Foreign State if a U.S. Target Has Foreign Operations

The European Union's Merger Control Regulation may apply if the U.S. target has operations in the EU. [*See* Section 26.20] Also, the antitrust laws of the foreign states in which the U.S. firm operates may apply. [*See e.g.* Section 26.22, for the South African approach to antitrust regulation]

§ 26.8 U.S. Investment Restrictions in Inbound Acquisitions—CFIUS

A. Introduction to CFIUS from the Treasury's Website

The Committee on Foreign Investment in the U.S. (CFIUS) is an inter-agency committee [chaired by the Department of Treasury] authorized to review transactions that could result in control of a U.S. business by a foreign person ("covered transactions") in order to determine the effect of such transactions on the national security of the United States. CFIUS operates pursuant to section 721 of the Defense Production Act of 1950, as amended by the Foreign Investment and National Security Act of 2007 (FINSA) (section 721) and as implemented by Executive Order 11858, as amended, and regulations at 31 C.F.R. Part 800.

The CFIUS process has been the subject of significant reforms over the past several years. These include [1] numerous improvements in internal CFIUS procedures, [2] enactment of FINSA in July 2007, amendment of Executive Order 11858 in January 2008, revision of the CFIUS regulations [which are set out in *M&A Statutes, Rules, and Documents*, *supra* Section 1.1] in November 2008, and [3] publication of guidance on CFIUS's national security considerations in December 2008.

B. The Foreign and National Security Act of 2007 Amendments to Exon-Florio (CFIUS)

Senate Report to the Foreign Investment and National Security Act of 2007

110 S. Rpt. 80 (June 13, 2007) (Signed by the President July 26, 2007)

Section 721 of the Defense Production Act, also known as the Exon-Florio Amendment ("Exon-Florio"), established a statutory framework for the United States Government to analyze foreign acquisitions, mergers, and takeovers (hereafter "transactions") of privately-owned entities within the United States to determine whether such transactions affect the national security of the United States. The Foreign Investment and National Security Act of 2007 (hereafter "the Act") amends Section 721 for the purpose of strengthening the process by which such transactions are reviewed and, when warranted, investigated for national security concerns. In addition, the Act provides for a system of Congressional notification so that Congress is able to conduct proper oversight of the national security implications of foreign direct investment in the United States to ensure that it is beneficial and has no adverse impact on U.S. national security. * * *

Major Provisions of the Bill

The Foreign Investment and National Security Act of 2007

1. Establishes the membership of the Committee on Foreign Investment in the United States (CFIUS) in statute.

2. Strengthens the role of the Director of National Intelligence (hereafter "DNI") by making the DNI an ex-officio member of CFIUS and requiring that the Director undertake a thorough analysis of the transaction with respect to any national security implications, engage the intelligence community, and report the DNI's findings to the committee within 20 days of the commencement of the CFIUS review. Requires the DNI to update CFIUS with any additional relevant intelligence information that becomes available during the course of a review and/or investigation.

3. Mandates the designation of a lead agency or agencies for each covered transaction, in addition to the Treasury Department, charged with negotiating any mitigation agreement or other conditions to ensure that national security is protected, and for follow up compliance with the terms of the agreement after the transaction has been approved by CFIUS.

4. Provides for the 30-day review of covered transactions by CFIUS to determine its effects on national security, and for sign-off at the assistant secretary-level (or above) that there is no threat to national security by the proposed transaction.

5. Provides for the 45-day investigation of covered transactions that threaten to impair national security, including transactions involving foreign government-owned companies and control of critical infrastructure, and for sign off at the Deputy Secretary level that there is no threat to the national security by the proposed transaction.

6. Provides for certain exceptions for the requirement that a state-owned entity automatically go to the investigation stage if the Secretary or Deputy Secretary of the Treasury, and the equivalent level official in the Lead Agency, determine after review of the transaction that national security will not be impaired by the transaction.

7. Requires assessment of a country's compliance with U.S. and multilateral counter-terrorism, non-proliferation and export control regimes for acquisitions by state-owned companies in the investigation stage.

8. Provides authority to the President to suspend or prohibit a covered transaction if there is credible evidence that such transaction threatens to impair U.S. national security.

9. Provides authority to CFIUS, or the lead agencies acting on behalf of CFIUS, to negotiate, impose and enforce conditions necessary to mitigate any threat to national security related to a covered transaction.

10. Adds to the list of factors that CFIUS should consider in the conduct of its reviews and investigation to include among other things consideration of the potential impact of a transaction on critical infrastructure, energy assets, or critical technologies.

11. Provides for written notice, to the Congress at the conclusion of the CFIUS process for both reviews and investigations, providing details about the transaction, including written assurance that the transaction does not threaten to impair national security or that any initial concerns have been mitigated through binding agreements between the parties and CFIUS (or the lead agency or agencies designated by the Chairman of CFIUS.).

12. Provides for detailed annual reports to Congress on the activities of CFIUS, including information concerning the transactions that have been reviewed or investigated during the previous 12 months. * * *

Note

As noted previously, the CFIUS regulations are set out in *M&A Statutes, Rules, and Documents, supra* Section 1.1.

C. Treasury's "Process Overview" of CFIUS

Prior to filing a voluntary notice, parties may consult with CFIUS or submit a draft notice * * * to ensure that the review will proceed as efficiently as possible. The CFIUS process generally begins formally when parties to a proposed or pending transaction jointly file a voluntary notice with CFIUS containing information required by § 800.402 of the regulations. Upon receiving the notice, the Staff Chairperson will promptly determine whether the notice is complete and satisfies the requirements stated in the regulations. If the notice is complete, the Staff Chairperson will circulate the notice to all CFIUS members. A review period of up to 30 days begins on the next business day.

During the review period, CFIUS members examine the transaction in order to identify and address, as appropriate, any national security concerns that arise as a result of the transaction. During the review period, CFIUS members, through the Department of the Treasury as Committee Chair, may request additional information from the parties. Parties must respond to such follow-up requests within three business days of the request or within a longer time frame if the parties so request in writing and the Staff Chairperson grants that request in writing.

CFIUS concludes action on the preponderant majority of transactions during or at the end of the initial 30-day review period. In certain circumstances defined in section 721 and at § 800.503 of the regulations, CFIUS may initiate a subsequent investigation, which must be completed within 45 days. In certain circumstances described at section 6(c) of Executive Order 11858, as amended, and § 800.506 of the regulations, CFIUS may also refer a transaction to the President for decision. In such case, section 721 requires the President to announce a decision with respect to a transaction within 15 days of CFIUS's completion of the investigation.

Parties to a transaction may request withdrawal of their notice at any time during the review or investigation stages. Such a request must be approved by CFIUS and may include conditions on the parties, such as requirements that they keep CFIUS informed of the status of the transaction or that they re-file the transaction at a later time. CFIUS tracks withdrawn transactions. * * *

If CFIUS finds that the covered transaction does not present any national security risks or that other provisions of law provide adequate and appropriate authority to address the risks, then CFIUS will advise the parties in writing that CFIUS has concluded all action under section 721 with respect to such transaction.

If CFIUS finds that a covered transaction presents national security risks and that other provisions of law do not provide adequate authority to address the risks, then CFIUS may enter into an agreement with, or impose conditions on, parties to mitigate such risks or may refer the case to the President for action.

Where CFIUS has completed all action with respect to a covered transaction or the President has announced a decision not to exercise his authority under section 721 with respect to the covered transaction, then the parties receive a "safe harbor" with respect to that transaction, as described in § 800.601 of the regulations and section 7(f) of Executive Order 11858, as amended.

Parties to a transaction that choose to file notice of the transaction with CFIUS must do so in accordance with the procedures stated in the regulations at § 800.401. Such notice must include the information required in the regulations at § 800.402.

D. 2012 Annual Report to Congress Filed December 2013 and the Ralls Decision[1]

The Treasury is required to submit an annual report to Congress on the operations of CFIUS, and the report for 2012 was filed in December 2013.[2] This report contains the following summary data on 2012 covered transactions:

> The classified version of this report contains a table listing all 114 notices of transactions that were filed with CFIUS in 2012 and that CFIUS determined to

1. This section is adapted from Thompson, *Mergers, Acquisitions and Tender Offers*, *supra* Section 1.10, at Section 19:7.5.

2. U.S. Treasury, Committee on Foreign Investment in the U.S. Annual Report to Congress, 2–3 (Dec. 2013) (public version).

be covered transactions under section 721. That table sets forth information on the acquirer and the U.S. business acquired, including the nature of their business activities or products, and details on any withdrawal. That table is not included here because section 721 prohibits its public disclosure, but aggregate information regarding those 114 notices is provided below:

- CFIUS conducted a "review" with respect to the 114 notices of covered transactions filed with CFIUS.

- CFIUS also conducted a subsequent "investigation" with respect to 45 of those 114 notices.

- Twenty-two of the notices were withdrawn. In 10 of these cases, the parties filed new notices in 2012; in two cases, the parties filed new notices in 2013.

- The President took action to prohibit one transaction in 2012. The President issued an order prohibiting the acquisition and ownership of four wind farm project companies by Ralls Corporation, its owners, its subsidiaries, and its affiliates. The order directs Ralls Corporation to divest its interest in the wind farm project companies that it acquired in 2012, and to take other actions related to the divestment. Ralls Corporation is owned by Chinese nationals, and is affiliated with a Chinese construction equipment company that manufactures wind turbines. The wind farm sites are all within or in the vicinity of restricted air space at Naval Weapons Systems Training Facility Boardman in Oregon.[3]

In an October 2013 decision of the D.C. District Court in Ralls matter,[4] the court concluded that (1) Ralls had not alleged a protected interest under the due process clause of the Fifth Amendment to the U.S. Constitution, and (2) "[e]ven if the Court were to find that the President's Order deprived Ralls of some protected interest ... [Ralls'] due process claim fails because Ralls received sufficient process."[5]

E. The 2013 Smithfield Decision[6]

Shuanghui International Holdings Limited, now named WH Group Limited, is the majority shareholder of China's largest meat processing enterprise and China's largest publicly traded meat products company. Shuanghui and Smithfield, a large, publicly held U.S. meat producing company, entered into a merger agreement pursuant to which Shuanghui would acquire Smithfield. On September 6, 2013, Shuanghui and Smithfield announced that the companies had received CFIUS clearance for the transaction.[7] The approval came notwithstanding concerns expressed by some people in Congress that transaction could lower food safety standards.

---

3. *Id.* at 2.

4. Ralls Corp. v. Comm. on Foreign Inv. in the United States, 2013 U.S. Dist. LEXIS 145949 (D.C. D.C. Oct. 10 2013).

5. *Id.* at 33.

6. This section is adapted from Thompson, *Mergers, Acquisitions and Tender Offers, supra* Section 1.10, at Section 19:7.6.

7. Press Release, Shuanghui International and Smithfield Foods Receive CFIUS Clearance, Smithfield Shareholder Vote Scheduled for September 24, 2013 (Sept. 6, 2013).

§ 26.9 U.S. Corporate Law Issues in Outbound Acquisitions

The principal corporate law question regarding an outbound acquisition concerns the approval of the transaction by the U.S. acquiror's directors. Also, if stock of the U.S. acquiror is going to be issued, there must be an adequate number of authorized but unissued shares. As is the case with inbound acquisitions, the U.S. acquiror may set up a subsidiary in the country where the acquisition is to be made and have the sub make the acquisition.

§ 26.10 Federal Securities Laws Issues in Outbound and Foreign-to-Foreign Acquisitions

A. Impact of Securities Act of 1933 on Outbound Acquisitions by U.S. Acquiror of Foreign Target in Exchange for Securities of U.S. Acquiror

1. The 1990 Adopting Release

Regulation S, Offshore Offers and Sales

Securities Act Release No 6863 (April 24, 1990)

Executive Summary. On June 10, 1988, the Commission published for comment Regulation S, which was intended to clarify the extraterritorial application of the registration requirements of the Securities Act of 1933 (the Securities Act). * * *

[T]he final Regulation consists of a general statement of applicability of the registration provisions (the General Statement) and two safe harbors. The General Statement provides that Section 5 of the Securities Act does not apply to offers or sales of securities that occur outside the United States. [*See* Rule 901] In order for a transaction to fall within the provisions of the General Statement, both the sale and the offer relating to that sale must be made outside the United States.* * *

As with the Proposals, Regulation S as adopted includes two safe harbors. One safe harbor applies to offers and sales by issuers, securities professionals involved in the distribution process pursuant to contract, their respective affiliates, and persons acting on behalf of any of the foregoing (the issuer safe harbor), [*See* Rule 903], and the other applies to resales by persons other than the issuer, securities professionals involved in the distribution process pursuant to contract, their respective affiliates (except certain officers and directors), and persons acting on behalf of any of the foregoing (the resale safe harbor). [*See* Rule 904] An offer, sale or resale of securities that satisfies all conditions of the applicable safe harbor is deemed to be outside the United States within the meaning of the General Statement and thus not subject to the registration requirements of Section 5.

Two general conditions apply to the safe harbors. First, any offer or sale of securities must be made in an "offshore transaction," which requires that no offers be made to persons in the United States and that either: (i) the buyer is (or the seller reasonably believes that the buyer is) offshore at the time of the origination of the buy order, or (ii) for purposes of the issuer safe harbor, the sale is made in, on or through a physical trading floor of an established foreign securities exchange, or (iii) for purposes of the resale safe harbor, the sale is made in, on or through the facilities of a designated offshore securities market, and the transaction is not pre-arranged with a buyer in the United States. [*See* Rule 903(a)] Second, in no event could "directed selling efforts" be made in the United States in connection with an offer or sale of securities made under a safe harbor. [*See* Rule 903(b)] "Directed selling efforts" are activities undertaken for the purpose of, or that could reasonably be expected to result in, conditioning of the market in the United States for the securities being offered.* * *

The issuer safe harbor distinguishes three categories of securities offerings, based upon factors such as the nationality and reporting status of the issuer and the degree of U.S. market interest in the issuer's securities. The first category of offerings has been expanded from the Proposals and includes: securities offered in "overseas directed offerings" * * *. [*See* Rule 903(c)(1)] The term "overseas directed offerings" * * * includes an offering of a foreign issuer's securities directed to any one foreign country, whether or not the issuer's home country, if such offering is conducted in accordance with local laws, offering practices and documentation. * * * The second category has been revised to include offerings of securities of U.S. reporting issuers and offerings of debt securities, asset-backed securities and specified preferred stock of foreign issuers with a substantial U.S. market interest. [*See* Rule 903(c)(2)] The third, residual category has been adopted substantially as reproposed. [*See* Rule 903(c)(3)]

The issuer safe harbor requires implementation of procedural safeguards, which differ for each of the three categories, to ensure that the securities offered come to rest offshore. * * *

The resale safe harbor has been expanded from the Proposals to allow reliance thereon by certain officers and directors of the issuer or distributors. [*See* Rule 904] In such a transaction, no remuneration other than customary broker's commissions may be paid. * * *

Question

Time-Warner, a publicly-held Delaware corporation, is planning an exchange offer for the stock of Publicly-Held French Target Corporation (PHFTC). Time-Warner will issue its voting common stock to the shareholders of PHFTC, all of whom are residents of France. Is Time-Warner required to register this stock under Section 5 of the 33 Act?

B. Impact of Williams Act on Tender Offers for Stock of Foreign Corporation Traded in U.S. Market: 1999 Final SEC Rules on Cross-Border M&A

Securities Act Release No. 33-7759, Cross-Border Tender and Exchange Offers, Business Combinations and Rights Offerings

(October 22, 1999)

Executive Summary. U.S. security holders are often excluded from tender and exchange offers, business combinations and rights offerings involving foreign private issuers. It is very common for bidders to exclude U.S. security holders from these transactions to avoid the application of the U.S. securities laws, particularly when U.S. security holders own a small amount of the securities of the foreign private issuer. When bidders exclude U.S. security holders from tender or exchange offers, they deny U.S. security holders the opportunity to receive a premium for their securities and to participate in an investment opportunity. * * *

Today, the Commission is adopting exemptive rules that are intended to encourage issuers and bidders to extend tender and exchange offers, rights offerings and business combinations to the U.S. security holders of foreign private issuers. The purpose of the exemptions adopted today is to allow U.S. holders to participate on an equal basis with foreign security holders. * * *

The U.S. anti-fraud and anti-manipulation rules and civil liability provisions will, however, continue to apply to these transactions. * * *

The Tier I Exemption. Under the Tier I exemption adopted today, eligible issuer and third-party tender offers will not be subject to Rules 13e-3, 13e-4, Regulation 14D or Rules 14e-1 and 14e-2. [*See* Rule 13e-4(h)(8) (issuer tender offers) and Rule 14d-1(c) (third party tender offers)] These provisions contain disclosure, filing, dissemination, minimum offering period, withdrawal rights and proration requirements that are intended to provide security holders with equal treatment and adequate time and information to make a decision whether to tender into the offer. The Tier I exemption provides that tender offers for the securities of foreign private issuers are exempt from these U.S. tender offer requirements, so long as: U.S. security holders hold 10 percent or less of the class of securities sought in the tender offer; In the case of an offer that otherwise would be subject to Rule 13e-4 or Regulation 14D under the Exchange Act, bidders submit, rather than file, an English language translation of the offering materials to the Commission under cover of Form CB and, in the case of a foreign offeror, file a consent to service on Form F-X; U.S. security holders participate in the offer on terms at least as favorable as those offered to any other holders; and Bidders provide U.S. security holders with the tender offer circular or other offering documents, in English, on a comparable basis to that provided to other security holders.

The exemption is available to U.S. and foreign bidders. * * *

The Tier II Exemption. Commenters generally supported the proposed scope and conditions of the Tier II exemption, under which offerors would be entitled to limited relief from the U.S. tender offer rules to minimize conflicts with foreign regulatory schemes. This relief will be available for both issuer and third party tender offers when the subject company is a foreign private issuer and U.S. ownership is no greater than 40 percent. [*See* Rule 13e-4(i) (issuer tender offers) and Rule 14d-1(d) (third party tender offers)] The offeror must comply with the remaining tender offer provisions, including the procedural, disclosure, and filing requirements of the Williams Act. Because the offeror would file a Schedule TO, a Form CB or F-X is not required. * * *

We are adopting the Tier II provisions relating to the All-Holders/Best Price provisions, notice of extensions, prompt payment, and the interpretation regarding a waiver or reduction of minimum conditions as proposed. * * *

Exemption from the Securities Act for Exchange Offers [and] Business Combinations. The rules adopted today also provide exemptions from Securities Act registration requirements for securities issued to U.S. security holders of a foreign private issuer in exchange offers, business combinations, and rights offerings. These exemptions are being adopted as Rule 801 for rights offerings and Rule 802 for business combinations and exchange offers. Rule 800 provides common definitions for both rules. The exemptions are available only if the subject company (or the issuer in an issuer tender offer or rights offering) is a foreign private issuer and U.S. security holders hold no more than 10 percent of the subject securities.

The exemptions are not available for any transaction or series of transactions that technically complies with the exemptions but is part of a plan or scheme to evade the registration provisions of the Securities Act. * * *

The terms and conditions of the offer must be at least as favorable for U.S. security holders as foreign holders. Rules 801 and 802 provide exceptions to the equal treatment requirement similar to the Tier I exemption with respect to state blue-sky requirements.

The new exemptions restrict the transferability of the securities acquired in an exempt transaction. To the extent that the subject securities are "restricted securities" under Rule 144 in the hands of a U.S. investor prior to the Rule 801 or 802 transaction, securities acquired by that investor in the Rule 801 or 802 transaction will be "restricted securities." Conversely, if the securities that are the subject of the transaction made pursuant to Rule 801 or 802 are unrestricted, then securities acquired in the transaction will be unrestricted. In the latter case, the securities would be freely tradable by non-affiliate security holders, so long as they are not participating in the offer under circumstances in which they could be deemed statutory underwriters. * * *

As adopted, Rule 802 does not contain any limitations based on the domicile or reporting status of the offeror. * * *

Finally, neither Rule 801 nor 802 impose a dollar limitation on the value of securities that may be sold to U.S. investors in an exempt transaction. * * *

Rules 801 and 802 do not mandate that specific information be sent to U.S. security holders. Instead, when any document, notice or other information is provided to offerees, copies (translated into English) must be provided to U.S. security holders in a similar manner. The documents must include a legend regarding the foreign nature of the transaction and the issuer's disclosure practices. The legend also must state that investors may have difficulty in enforcing rights against the issuer and its officers and directors. * * *

We are adopting, as proposed, the requirement that an offeror submit a notification to the Commission on new Form CB. A foreign company also must file a Form F-X at the same time it submits the Form CB to appoint an agent for service of process in the United States. The new form will include as an attachment a copy of any document, notice or other information disseminated to U.S. offerees.

We are adopting, as proposed, a new rule under Section 304(d) of the Trust Indenture Act that would exempt any debt security issued pursuant to Rule 802 under the Securities Act from having to comply with the provisions of the Trust Indenture Act. * * *

C. Impact of Securities Fraud Provision or Cross-Border Tender Offer

1. Rule 10b-5 and Section 14(e)

The potential reach of the antifraud provisions of the Federal securities laws is illustrated in *Consolidated Gold Fields v. Minorco, S.A.*[8] There Minorco (AC), a Luxembourg company, made a tender offer for Consolidated Gold Fields (TC), a U.K. company. AC was controlled by a South African interest and AC owned 29.9% of TC. TC owned substantial U.S. properties. Approximately 2.5% of TC's shareholders were U.S. persons, some of whom held American Depositary Receipts (ADRs) of TC. AC excluded the U.S. shareholders of TC from the tender offer, but the tender offer documents indicated that AC would accept shares from U.S. persons if the shares were mailed from outside the U.S.

TC alleged that AC violated the antifraud provisions of the Federal securities laws, Rule 10b-5 and Section 14(e) of the 34 Act, by making false and misleading statements about

8. Consolidated Gold Fields PLC v. Minorco, SA, 871 F.2d 252 (2d Cir. 1989).

the extent to which AC was controlled by the South African interests. TC argued that it was important that TC's shareholders be aware of such interests because ownership of AC by persons in pre-Democratic South Africa could make it difficult for TC, which after the acquisition would be a subsidiary of AC, to continue its business in certain countries.

Reversing the district court's holding that the antifraud provisions did not apply because the tender offer had only "indirect effects on a relatively small number of Americans," the Second Circuit reasoned:

> The anti-fraud laws of the United States may be given extraterritorial reach whenever a predominantly foreign transaction has substantial effects within the United States....
>
> In applying the so-called "effects" test ... the District Court determined that the number of Americans holding stock in the allegedly defrauded British company was "insignificant" and that Minorco [AC] had taken "whatever steps it could to assure that the tender offer documents would not reach Gold Fields [TC] ADR holders." Because Minorco had sent the offering documents to British nominees of American shareholders, the District Court concluded that the transaction between Minorco and Gold Fields had only indirect effects on a relatively small number of Americans. However, the District Court's analysis cannot be reconciled with this Court's prior holding in [*Bersch v. Drexel Firestone, Inc.*, 519 F.2d 974 (2d Cir 1975)]. In that case, purchasers of common stock of I.O.S., Ltd., a Bahamian corporation, brought a class action for damages, alleging that fraudulent financial statements were included in prospectuses that were used in offerings of 3.95 million shares of I.O.S. stock. The prospectus stated that the shares were not being offered in the United States. Nevertheless, at least 22 United States residents purchased 41,936 shares. Although the record did not indicate how the Americans came to purchase the shares, Judge Friendly assumed that the allegedly misleading documents must have been sent into the United States, and he asserted subject matter jurisdiction on the basis of that assumption.
>
> In this case, the District Court should have asserted jurisdiction once it noted that Minorco knew that the British nominees were required by law to forward the tender offer documents to Gold Fields' shareholders and ADR depository banks in the United States. This "effect" (the transmittal of the documents by the nominees) was clearly a direct and foreseeable result of the conduct outside the territory of the United States.[9]

The court also distinguished the treatment of fraud claims from the treatment of claims that an SEC filing was required:

> In rejecting subject matter jurisdiction, the District Court relied on *Plessey Co. PLC v. General Electric Co. PLC*, 628 F. Supp. 477 (D. Del. 1986), and *IIT v. Vencap, Ltd.*, 519 F.2d 1001 (2d Cir. 1975). Both are inapposite. In *Plessey*, the target company sought to compel the bidder to make certain filings with the Securities and Exchange Commission (SEC) under the Williams Act. No allegations of fraud were made. As we observed in *Bersch*, however, the antifraud provisions of American securities laws have broader extraterritorial reach than American filing requirements.[10]

9. *Id.* at 261–262.
10. *Id.* at 262.

Under the current exemption rules, this tender offer would be exempt from certain tender offer rules under the Tier I exemption under Rule 14d-1(c), discussed previously. As noted, this exemption does not, however, extend to the antifraud provisions of the securities laws. Thus, *Consolidated Gold Fields* is good law even after adoption of the Tier I and Tier II exemptions.

However, the limit of cases like *Consolidated Gold Fields* is illustrated by the Second Circuit's 2008 decision in *Morrison v. National Australia Bank Ltd.*[11] There a publicly held Australian bank (NAB) with its shares traded on several exchanges including the New York Stock Exchange through ADRs, allegedly made false statements relating to the income of its Florida mortgaging servicing subsidiary, which produced around 5% of NAB's income. Both foreign and U.S. shareholders of NAB brought a Rule 10b-5 action in the Southern District of New York, and the district court dismissed the action of the foreign shareholders for lack of subject matter jurisdiction and the action of the U.S. shareholders for failure to state a claim, that is, a failure to claim damages. Only the foreign shareholders appealed. The Second Circuit explained that this is the "first so-called 'foreign-cubed' securities class action to reach [the court]."[12] In a "foreign-cubed" action "a set of (1) foreign plaintiffs is suing (2) a foreign issuer in an American court for violations of American securities laws based on securities transactions in (3) foreign countries."[13] In affirming the dismissal of the action, the court reasoned, *inter alia*, that the "actions taken and the actions not taken by NAB in Australia were ... significantly more central to the fraud and more directly responsible for the harm to investors than the manipulation of the numbers in Florida."[14]

The Supreme Court affirmed the dismissal by the Second Circuit in *Morrison v. National Australia Bank*[15] but on different grounds. After examining the reach of Rule 10b-5, the Supreme Court reasoned that since Rule 10b-5 is promulgated under Section 10(b) of the 34 Act, if Section 10(b) "is not extraterritorial, neither is Rule 10b-5."[16] The court went on to hold:

> Section 10(b) reaches the use of a manipulative or deceptive device or contrivance only in connection with the purchase or sale of a security listed on an American stock exchange, and the purchase or sale of any other security in the United States. This case involves no securities listed on a domestic exchange, and all aspects of the purchases complained of by those petitioners who still have live claims occurred outside the United States. Petitioners have therefore failed to state a claim.[17]

§ 26.11 Federal Income Tax Issues in Outbound Acquisitions

There are a variety of federal income tax issues arising in an outbound acquisition. *See generally*, Thompson, *U.S. International Tax Planning and Policy*, Section 1.10. In general, there is no reason to structure such transactions as tax-free reorganizations because the foreign shareholders and foreign target are generally not subject to U.S. taxation.

---

11. Morrison v. National Australia Bank Ltd., 547 F.3d 167 (2d Cir. 2008).
12. *Id.* at 172.
13. *Id.*
14. *Id.* at 176.
15. Morrison v. National Australia Bank Ltd., 130 S. Ct. 2869 (2010).
16. *Id.* at 2881.
17. *Id.* at 2888.

At the end of an outbound acquisition, the U.S. acquiror will generally end up controlling the stock of the foreign target corporation. If the U.S. acquiror owns more than 50% of the stock of the foreign target, the target becomes a "controlled foreign corporation" (CFC). [*See* Code § 957] Although the income of foreign corporations generally is not subject to U.S. taxation until distributed to a U.S. shareholder, in certain cases, the U.S. shareholders of a CFC are subject to immediate taxation on the earnings of the CFC. Immediate taxation applies if the CFC has certain tax haven income, referred to in the Code as subpart F income. [*See* Code § 951 *et seq.*] In general, if the foreign target is engaged in active business it will not have subpart F income.

§ 26.12 Antitrust and HSR Issues in Outbound and Foreign-to-Foreign Acquisitions

A. Impact of Section 7 of the Clayton Act

DOJ and FTC Antitrust Enforcement Guidelines for International Operations

§§ 1,3.1, 3.14, 3.2 April 15, 1995

INTRODUCTION. * * *

The 1995 Antitrust Enforcement Guidelines for International Operations (hereinafter "Guidelines") are intended to provide antitrust guidance to businesses engaged in international operations on questions that relate specifically to the Agencies' international enforcement policy. * * *

THRESHOLD INTERNATIONAL ENFORCEMENT ISSUES. **Jurisdiction.** * * * The reach of the U.S. antitrust laws is not limited * * * to conduct and transactions that occur within the boundaries of the United States. Anticompetitive conduct that affects U.S. domestic or foreign commerce may violate the U.S. antitrust laws regardless of where such conduct occurs or the nationality of the parties involved. * * *

Jurisdiction Under Section 7 of the Clayton Act. Section 7 of the Clayton Act applies to mergers and acquisitions between firms that are engaged in commerce or in any activity affecting commerce. The Agencies would apply the same principles regarding their foreign commerce jurisdiction to Clayton Section 7 cases as they would apply in Sherman Act cases.

ILLUSTRATIVE EXAMPLE H. *Situation:* Two foreign firms, one in Europe and the other in Canada, account together for a substantial percentage of U.S. sales of a particular product through direct imports. Both firms have sales offices and are subject to personal jurisdiction in the United States, although neither has productive assets in the United States. They enter into an agreement to merge.

Discussion: The express language of Section 7 of the Clayton Act reaches the stock and asset acquisition of persons engaged in trade and commerce "with foreign nations." Thus, in assessing jurisdiction for this merger outside the United States the Agencies could establish U.S. subject matter jurisdiction based on its effect on U.S. imports. * * *

B. Impact of Hart-Scott-Rodino on Acquisitions of Foreign Assets and Stock

1. Introduction

FTC Notice of Proposed Rulemaking Relating to Pre-Merger Notification of Foreign Transactions

February 1, 2001

Sections 802.50 and 802.51 Acquisitions of Foreign Assets and Voting Securities [These proposed amendments have been adopted and are in *M&A Statutes, Rules, and Documents, supra* Section 1.1] * * * The PNO receives numerous calls each year requesting advice on the applicability of sections 802.50 and 802.51 of the rules. As global merger activity has increased, the exemptions for foreign assets and foreign voting securities have become more relevant to determinations of a party's HSR reporting requirements. In response to input from the private sector, the Commission proposes revising these rules for greater ease of comprehension. * * *

The first major proposed change to these sections consists of raising both the $15 million and $25 million thresholds that trigger reporting obligations for foreign transactions to $50 million. This change is intended to preserve the principle underlying these sections, that acquisitions of foreign assets or voting securities should not be subject to the reporting requirements unless the assets or voting securities being acquired have a direct impact on U.S. commerce. That direct impact would be measured by the $50 million threshold amount established in the new legislation. For asset transactions, the impact would be reflected by the amount of sales in or into the U.S. For voting securities transactions, the impact would be reflected either by the amount of sales in or into the U.S. or by the total value of assets, measured by fair market value, held by the issuer in the U.S. * * *

The Commission also proposes to exempt an acquisition between foreign persons that do not meet the $110 million aggregate sales and assets test only where such acquisition is not valued at over $200 million. The 1978 Statement of Basis and Purpose explains that the $110 million threshold was adopted to approximate the size-of-person criteria of Section 7A(a)(2), as it seemed appropriate and consistent with congressional intent not to exempt a transaction involving two foreign persons with a U.S. presence similar in size to the general criteria of the act for all persons. 43 FR 33498 (July 31, 1978). Since the new legislation removes the size-of-person test for acquisitions valued at over $200 million, the Commission believes it is appropriate and consistent with congressional intent to require filings from foreign persons, regardless of the size of their U.S. presence, where the transaction is valued at over $200 million and the $50 million threshold of these exemption rules is satisfied.

The remaining substantive proposed change is the extension of reportability to acquisitions of foreign assets by foreign persons. The 1978 Statement of Basis and Purpose justified the blanket exclusion of these transactions * * * on the grounds that asset transactions were less likely to affect the U.S. economy than voting securities transactions. Experience at both agencies has shown that foreign assets acquisitions can and do have a direct impact on the U.S. economy. This is more likely to be true where the assets generate over $50 million in sales in or into the U.S. Thus, it appears to be appropriate to require that their acquisition be reported where minimum contacts are present. * * *

2. HSR Rules Relating to Filing in Multiple Jurisdictions

Pre-Merger Notification; Reporting and Waiting Period Requirements and Rules of Practice

February 1, 2001

Transactions Subject to Foreign Antitrust Reporting Requirements The [HSR Report Form, excerpts from which are in *M&A Statutes, Rules, and Documents*, *supra* Section 1.1] is further amended to add a space for reporting persons to indicate if the filing is subject to foreign antitrust reporting requirements and requests the voluntary submission of the name(s) of any foreign antitrust or competition authority that, based upon the knowledge or belief of the filing person at the time of the filing, has been or will be notified of the proposed transaction and the date or anticipated date of such notification. * * *

[E]arly notice of multiple jurisdiction filings will * * * enable the agencies, where appropriate, to seek consent of the parties to enable more extensive cooperation between or among antitrust authorities in conducting their investigations. Because numerous foreign jurisdictions may be involved, some of which may not have been identified at the time the parties to a transaction are otherwise prepared to file their notification, the question has been modified from the 1994 proposal to provide that the response to this item should be made "to the knowledge or belief of the filing person at the time of the filing of this notification."

§ 26.13 Impact of Foreign Corrupt Practices Act (FCPA) on Outbound M&A

Introduction to the Foreign Corrupt Practices Act (FCPA)

In any acquisition of a company with foreign operations, consideration must be given to the impact of the U.S. Foreign Corrupt Practices Act (FCPA), which was enacted in 1977. The Act, reflected principally in Sections 30A and 13(b) of the Securities Exchange Act, contains both anti-bribery and accounting provisions. A DOJ Resource Guide to the FCPA contains the following summary of the Act:

> The anti-bribery provisions [Section 30A] prohibit U.S. persons and businesses (domestic concerns), U.S. and foreign public companies listed on stock exchanges in the United States or which are required to file periodic reports with the Securities and Exchange Commission (issuers), and certain foreign persons and businesses acting while in the territory of the United States (territorial jurisdiction) from making corrupt payments to foreign officials to obtain or retain business. The accounting provisions [principally Section 13(b)] require issuers to make and keep accurate books and records and to devise and maintain an adequate system of internal accounting controls. The accounting provisions also prohibit individuals and businesses from knowingly falsifying books and records or knowingly circumventing or failing to implement a system of internal controls.
>
> The Department of Justice (DOJ) and the Securities and Exchange Commission (SEC) share FCPA enforcement authority[.][18]

---

18. U.S. Department of Justice and Securities Exchange Commission, FCPA, A Resource Guide to the U.S. Foreign Corrupt Practices Act 2 (Nov. 14, 2012).

In any acquisition of a target that has foreign operations, the acquiror will have to give consideration to the target's potential liability under the FCPA.

Part III
Regulation of Mergers and Acquisitions in the European Union

§ 26.14 Scope of Regulation of Mergers and Acquisitions in the European Union

Before examining the manner in which the European Union (EU) regulates mergers and acquisitions, it is first important to have a general understanding of the structure of the EU and its principal institutions, and Section 26.15 provides that introduction. As will be seen there, the principal organ of the EU involved in merger regulation is the European Commission (EC). Section 26.16 looks at the EU directive dealing with domestic mergers. As previously indicated directives set out rules that the member states of the EU are required to adopt. Section 26.17 considers the EU directive addressing cross-border mergers. Section 26.18 looks at the EU's Takeover Directive, the analogue of the Williams Act legislation in the U.S., which provides for the regulation of tender offers and related transactions under the federal securities laws. [*See* Chapters 17–20] This section also examines the regulation of takeovers under the UK's City Code on Takeovers and Mergers, which is the basic model of takeover regulation followed in the EU's Takeover Directive and by many other countries in the world. In considering the UK's Takeover Code, the section discusses the 2011 amendments to the Code, which were adopted as a result of Kraft's takeover of Cadbury.

Section 26.19 presents the EU's directive on taxation of mergers and acquisitions. Section 26.20 looks at the EU's enforcement of the antitrust aspects of mergers and acquisitions under its Merger Control Regulation (MCR), related documents, and the *GE-Honeywell* decision of the reviewing court, the Court of First Instance. Thus, while the directives instruct the member states on laws they are to adopt, the MCR provides for preemptive regulation by the EU of the antitrust aspects of M&A transactions subject to the jurisdiction of the MCR. Member state antitrust regulation may apply to transactions not covered by the MCR. Finally, Section 26.21 examines the EU Treaty and directive prohibitions against investment restrictions.

An examination of the directives will give the reader a general understanding of how a member state is likely to regulate the particular aspect of M&A, but of course, every transaction will require a careful examination of the laws of the particular country involved. Also, member states may not adopt the directive in a timely manner or in a manner that complies fully with the requirements. For example, as of May 20, 2006, the deadline for implementing the Takeover Directive discussed in Section 26.18, only France, the U.K., Denmark, Luxembourg, and Hungary had adopted the provision.

With this introduction, we begin our examination of the EU's regulation of the corporate, securities, tax, and antitrust aspects of M&A with a brief look at the structure of the EU and its institutions.

§ 26.15 Introduction to the Structure of the European Union (EU) and Its European Commission (EC)

The EU at a Glance

EU Website, August 26, 2005

The European Union(EU) is a family of democratic European countries, committed to working together for peace and prosperity. * * * Its Member States have set up common institutions to which they delegate some of their sovereignty so that decisions on specific matters of joint interest can be made democratically at the European level. This pooling of sovereignty is also called "European integration". * * *

There are five EU institutions, each playing a specific role: European Parliament (elected by the peoples of the Member States); Council of the European Union (representing the governments of the Member States); European Commission (driving force and executive body); Court of Justice (ensuring compliance with the law); Court of Auditors (controlling sound and lawful management of the EU budget).

The European Parliament * * * has three main roles: (1) Passing European laws—jointly with the Council in many policy areas; * * * (2) [E]xercise[ing] democratic supervision over the other EU institutions, and in particular the Commission; and * * * (3) [Exercising] the power of the purse. * * *

The Council * * * represents the member states, and its meetings are attended by one minister from each of the EU's national governments. * * *

The Council has six key responsibilities [including]: To pass European laws—jointly with the European Parliament in many policy areas. * * *

As a rule, the Council only acts on a proposal from the Commission, and the Commission normally has responsibility for ensuring that EU legislation, once adopted, is correctly applied. * * *

The European Commission (EC) is independent of national governments. Its job is to represent and uphold the interests of the EU as a whole. It drafts proposals for new European laws, which it presents to the European Parliament and the Council.

It is also the EU's executive arm—in other words, it is responsible for implementing the decisions of Parliament and the Council. That means managing the day-to-day business of the European Union [*e.g.*, the Competition Commission is the EU's antitrust enforcer]: implementing its policies, running its programmes and spending its funds. * * *

Informally, the appointed Members of the Commission are known as 'commissioners' [*e.g.*, the Competition Commissioner]. * * *

The European Commission has four main roles: to propose legislation to Parliament and the Council; to manage and implement EU policies and the budget; to enforce European law (jointly with the Court of Justice); and to represent the European Union on the international stage, for example by negotiating agreements between the EU and other countries. * * *

The Commission also has to manage the policies adopted by Parliament and the Council, such as * * * competition policy, where the Commission has the power to authorise or prohibit mergers between companies. [*See* the discussion below] * * *

The Commission's staff is organised in departments, known as 'Directorates-General' (DGs) and 'services' (such as the Legal Service). Each DG is responsible for a particular policy area and is headed by a Director-General [*e.g.*, the Director-General of the Competition Commission] who is answerable to one of the commissioners. * * *

It is the DGs that actually devise and draft legislative proposals [*e.g.*, the DG for Internal Affairs drafted the EU's Takeover Directive, Section 26.18, and the DG Competition drafted the EU's Merger Control Regulation, Section 26.20], but these proposals become official only when 'adopted' by the Commission at its weekly meeting. * * *

To help the Court of Justice cope with the large number of cases brought before it, and to offer citizens better legal protection, a 'Court of First Instance' (CFI) was created in 1989. This Court (which is attached to the Court of Justice) is responsible for giving rulings on certain kinds of cases, particularly actions brought by private individuals, companies and some organisations, and cases relating to competition law. * * *

§ 26.16 The EC's Directive Regarding Corporate Law Aspects of Mergers

A. Introduction

The European Commission (EC) has promulgated a directive, set out in the next section, requiring member states to adopt in their internal company law provisions permitting mergers of domestic companies. The directive deals with such issues as the shareholder vote required for a merger. Not all member states have provisions that are similar to those in the directive. The U.K. recently added merger provisions to its company law. The U.K. also retained its long-existing "scheme of arrangement" provision, which has a similar effect.

B. The Directive

78/855/EEC: Third Council Directive of 9 October 1978 Based on Article 54(3)(G) of the Treaty, Concerning Mergers of Public Limited Liability Companies

CHAPTER I. Regulation of merger by the acquisition of one or more companies by another and of merger by the formation of a new company.

Article 2. The member states shall, as regards companies governed by their national laws, make provision for rules governing merger by the acquisition of one or more companies by another and merger by the formation of a new company.

Article 3. 1. For the purposes of this directive, "merger by acquisition" shall mean the operation whereby one or more companies are wound up without going into liquidation and transfer to another all their assets and liabilities in exchange for the issue to the shareholders of the company or companies being acquired of shares in the acquiring company and a cash payment, if any, not exceeding 10% of the nominal value of the shares so issued or, where they have no nominal value, of their accounting par value. * * *

CHAPTER II. Merger by acquisition.

Article 5. 1. The administrative or management bodies of the merging companies shall draw up draft terms of merger in writing.

2. Draft terms of merger shall specify at least:

(a) The type, name and registered office of each of the merging companies.

(b) The share exchange ratio and the amount of any cash payment. * * *

Article 6. Draft terms of merger must be published in the manner prescribed by the laws of each member state in accordance with Article 3 of directive 68/151/EEC, for each of the merging companies, at least one month before the date fixed for the general meeting which is to decide thereon.

Article 7. 1. A merger shall require at least the approval of the general meeting of each of the merging companies. The laws of the member states shall provide that this decision shall require a majority of not less than two thirds of the votes attaching either to the shares or to the subscribed capital represented.

The laws of a member state may, however, provide that a simple majority of the votes specified in the first subparagraph shall be sufficient when at least half of the subscribed capital is represented. * * *

Article 9. The administration or management bodies of each of the merging companies shall draw up a detailed written report explaining the draft terms of merger and setting out the legal and economic grounds for them, in particular the share exchange ratio.

The report shall also describe any special valuation difficulties which have arisen.

Article 10. 1. One or more experts, acting on behalf of each of the merging companies but independent of them, appointed or approved by a judicial or administrative authority, shall examine the draft terms of merger and draw up a written report to shareholders. However, the laws of a member state may provide for the appointment of one or more independent experts for all the merging companies, if such appointment is made by a judicial or administrative authority at the joint request of those companies. Such experts may, depending on the laws of each member state, be natural or legal persons or companies or firms.

2. In the report mentioned in Paragraph 1 the experts must in any case state whether in their opinion the share exchange ratio is fair and reasonable. Their statement must at least: (a) Indicate the method or methods used to arrive at the share exchange ratio proposed; and (b) State whether such method or methods are adequate in the case in question, indicate the values arrived at using each such method and give an opinion on the relative importance attributed to such methods in arriving at the value decided on. The report shall also describe any special valuation difficulties which have arisen. * * *

Article 12. Protection of the rights of the employees of each of the merging companies shall be regulated in accordance with directive 77/187/EEC(2).

Article 13. 1. The laws of the member states must provide for an adequate system of protection of the interests of creditors of the merging companies whose claims antedate the publication of the draft terms of merger and have not fallen due at the time of such publication. * * *

Article 19. 1. A merger shall have the following consequences *ipso jure* and simultaneously:

(a) The transfer, both as between the company being acquired and the acquiring company and as regards third parties, to the acquiring company of all the assets and liabilities of the company being acquired;

(b) The shareholders of the company being acquired become shareholders of the acquiring company. * * *

CHAPTER IV. Acquisition of one company by another which holds 90% or more of its shares.

Article 27. In cases of merger where one or more companies are acquired by another company which holds 90% or more, but not all, of the shares and other securities of each of those companies the holding of which confers the right to vote at general meetings, the Member States need not require approval of the merger by the general meeting of the acquiring company, provided that the following conditions at least are fulfilled:

(a) The publication provided for in Article 6 must be effected, as regards the acquiring company, at least one month before the date fixed for the general meeting of the company or companies being acquired which is to decide on the draft terms of merger;

(b) At least one month before the date specified in (a), all shareholders of the acquiring company must be entitled to inspect the documents specified in Article 11(1)(a), (b) and (c) at the company's registered office. * * *

Questions

Does the directive encompass triangular mergers, which are common in the U.S.? [*See* Chapter 2] Does the directive encompass a merger in which 100% of the consideration paid is cash, which is common in the U.S.?

§ 26.17 The EC's 2005 Directive on Corporate Law Aspects of Cross-Border Mergers

Directive 2005/56/EC of the European Parliament and of the Council of 26 October 2005 on Cross-Border Mergers of Limited Liability Companies

(Text with EEA Relevance) October 26, 2005

Whereas: (1) There is a need for cooperation and consolidation between limited liability companies [corporations and other limited liability entities] from different Member States. However, as regards cross-border mergers of limited liability companies, they encounter many legislative and administrative difficulties in the Community. It is therefore necessary, with a view to the completion and functioning of the single market, to lay down Community provisions to facilitate the carrying-out of cross-border mergers between various types of limited liability company governed by the laws of different Member States.

(2) This Directive facilitates the cross-border merger of limited liability companies as defined herein. The laws of the Member States are to allow the cross-border merger of a national limited liability company with a limited liability company from another Member State if the national law of the relevant Member States permits mergers between such types of company. * * *

Article 1 Scope. This Directive shall apply to mergers of limited liability companies formed in accordance with the law of a Member State and having their registered office, central administration or principal place of business within the Community, provided at least two of them are governed by the laws of different Member States (hereinafter referred to as cross-border mergers).

Article 2 Definitions. For the purposes of this Directive: * * * 2. "Merger" means an operation whereby: (a) one or more companies, on being dissolved without going into liquidation, transfer all their assets and liabilities to another existing company, the acquiring company, in exchange for the issue to their members of securities or shares representing the capital of that other company and, if applicable, a cash payment not exceeding 10% of the nominal value, or, in the absence of a nominal value, of the accounting par value of those securities or shares. * * *

Article 5 Common draft terms of cross-border mergers. The management or administrative organ of each of the merging companies shall draw up the common draft terms of cross-border merger. The common draft terms of cross-border merger shall include at least the following particulars: (a) the form, name and registered office of the merging companies and those proposed for the company resulting from the cross-border merger; (b) the ratio applicable to the exchange of securities or shares representing the company capital and the amount of any cash payment; * * * (d) the likely repercussions of the cross-border merger on employment; * * * (h) any special advantages granted to the experts who examine the draft terms of the cross-border merger or to members of the administrative, management, supervisory or controlling organs of the merging companies; (i) the statutes of the company resulting from the cross-border merger; * * * (k) information on the evaluation of the assets and liabilities which are transferred to the company resulting from the cross-border merger; * * *

Article 6 Publication. 1. The common draft terms of the cross-border merger shall be published in the manner prescribed by the laws of each Member State in accordance with Article 3 of Directive 68/151/EEC for each of the merging companies at least one month before the date of the general meeting which is to decide thereon. * * *

Article 7 Report of the management or administrative organ. The management or administrative organ of each of the merging companies shall draw up a report intended for the members explaining and justifying the legal and economic aspects of the cross-border merger and explaining the implications of the cross-border merger for members, creditors and employees. * * *

Article 8 Independent expert report. 1. An independent expert report intended for members and made available not less than one month before the date of the general meeting referred to in Article 9 shall be drawn up for each merging company. * * *

3. The expert report shall include at least the particulars provided for by Article 10(2) of Council Directive 78/855/EEC of 9 October 1978 concerning mergers of public limited liability companies [Section 26.16.B]. * * *

Article 9 Approval by the general meeting. 1. After taking note of the reports referred to in Articles 7 and 8, the general meeting of each of the merging companies shall decide on the approval of the common draft terms of cross-border merger. * * *

Article 11 Scrutiny of the legality of the cross-border merger. 1. Each Member State shall designate the court, notary or other authority competent to scrutinise the legality of the cross-border merger as regards that part of the procedure which concerns the completion of the cross-border merger and, where appropriate, the formation of a new company resulting from the cross-border merger where the company created by the cross-border merger is subject to its national law. * * *

Article 14 Consequences of the cross-border merger. 1. A cross-border merger carried out as laid down in points (a) * * * of Article 2(2) shall, from the date referred to in Article 12, have the following consequences: (a) all the assets and liabilities of the company being acquired shall be transferred to the acquiring company; (b) the members of the company being acquired shall become members of the acquiring company; and (c) the company being acquired shall cease to exist. * * *

Article 16 Employee participation. 1. Without prejudice to paragraph 2, the company resulting from the cross-border merger shall be subject to the rules in force concerning employee participation, if any, in the Member State where it has its registered office. [However, certain employers are subject to EU rules on employee participation.] * * *

Transposition. Member States shall bring into force the laws, regulations and administrative provisions necessary to comply with this Directive by 15 December 2007.

§ 26.18 The EC's 2004 Takeover Directive and the U.K.'s Takeover Code

A. Introduction

European Parliament and Council Directive on Takeover Bids

2004/25/EC of 21 April 2004

ACT SUMMARY

The EU wishes to offer European businesses greater legal certainty with regard to takeover bids * * * while protecting the interests of shareholders (and particularly minority shareholders), employees and any other interested parties. It is using a directive to introduce transparent rules that will apply throughout the EU to cross-border takeover bids, in the interests of all concerned. This means, for example, strengthening the rules on informing shareholders about bids (period for acceptance, consideration, financing of the bid, etc.) The EU is also promoting corporate restructuring to help boost the competitiveness of the European market. * * *

B. The Directive

European Parliament and Council Directive on Takeover Bids

2004/25/EC of 21 April 2004

Article 1 Scope. 1. This Directive lays down measures coordinating the laws, regulations, administrative provisions, codes of practice or other arrangements of the Member States, including arrangements established by organisations officially authorised to regulate the markets (hereinafter "rules"), relating to takeover bids for the securities of a company governed by the law of a Member State, where all or some of those securities are admitted to trading on a regulated market within the meaning of Council Directive 93/22/EEC in one or more Member States (hereinafter "regulated market"). * * *

Article 2 Definitions. 1. For the purposes of this Directive: (a) "takeover bid" or "bid" means a public offer (other than by the offeree company itself) made to the holders of the securities of a company to acquire all or some of the said securities, whether mandatory or voluntary, which follows or has as its objective the acquisition of control of the offeree company in accordance with national law; (b) "offeree company" means a company whose securities are the subject of a bid; (c) "offeror" means any natural or legal person governed by public or private law making a bid; (d) "persons acting in concert" means natural or legal persons who co-operate with the offeror or the offeree company on the basis of an agreement, either express or tacit, either oral or written, aimed respectively at obtaining control of the offeree company or frustrating the successful outcome of a bid; (e) "securities" means transferable securities carrying voting rights in a company; (f) "parties to the bid" means the offeror, the members of the offeror's board if the offeror is a company, the offeree company, holders of securities of the offeree company and the members of the board of the offeree company, and persons acting in concert with such parties; (g) "multiple voting securities" means securities included in a distinct and separate class and carrying more than one vote. * * *

Article 3. General principles. 1. For the purpose of implementing this Directive, Member States shall ensure that the following principles are complied with:

(a) all holders of securities of an offeree company of the same class are to be afforded equivalent treatment; moreover, if a person acquires control of a company, the other holders of securities are to be protected;

(b) holders of securities of an offeree company are to have sufficient time and information to enable them to reach a properly informed decision on the bid; where it advises the holders of securities, the board of the offeree company is to give its views on the effects of implementation of the bid on employment, conditions of employment and the locations of the company's places of business;

(c) the board of an offeree company is to act in the interests of the company as a whole and must not deny the holders of securities the opportunity to decide on the merits of the bid;

(d) false markets must not be created in the securities of the offeree company, of the offeror company or of any other company concerned by the bid in such a way that the rise or fall in the prices of the securities becomes artificial and the normal functioning of the markets is distorted;

(e) an offeror must announce a bid only after ensuring that it can fulfill in full any cash consideration, if such is offered, and after taking all reasonable measures to secure the implementation of any other type of consideration;

(f) an offeree company must not be hindered in the conduct of its affairs for longer than is reasonable by a bid for its securities.

2. With a view to ensuring compliance with the principles set out in paragraph 1, Member States: (a) shall see to it that the minimum requirements set out in this Directive are observed; (b) may lay down additional conditions and more stringent provisions than those required by this directive.

Article 4 Supervisory authority and applicable law. 1. Member States shall designate the authority or authorities competent for supervising a bid for the purposes of the rules made or introduced pursuant to this Directive. * * *

2. (a) The authority competent for supervising the bid shall be that of the Member State in which the offeree company has its registered office if the securities of that company are admitted to trading on a regulated market in that Member State. * * *

Article 5 Protection of minority shareholders; mandatory bid; equitable price. 1. [Mandatory Bid] Where a natural or legal person who, as a result of his own acquisition or the acquisition by persons acting in concert with him, holds securities of a company referred to in Article 1(1) which, added to any existing holdings and the holdings of persons acting in concert with him, directly or indirectly give him a specified percentage of voting rights in that company, conferring on him the control of that company, Member States shall ensure that this person is required to make a bid as a means of protecting the minority shareholders of that company. This bid shall be addressed at the earliest opportunity to all holders of securities for all their holdings at the equitable price defined in paragraph 4.

2. Where control has been obtained following a voluntary bid made in accordance with this Directive to all holders of securities for all their holdings, the obligation to launch a bid laid down in paragraph 1 shall no longer apply.

3. The percentage of voting rights which confers control for the purposes of paragraph 1 and the method of its calculation shall be determined by the rules of the Member State in which the company has its registered office.

4. [All Holders, Best Price] The highest price paid for the same securities by the offeror, or by persons acting in concert with him, over a period, to be determined by Member States, of not less than six and not more than twelve months prior to the bid referred to in paragraph 1 shall be regarded as the equitable price. If, after the bid has been made public and before the offer closes for acceptance, the offeror or any person acting in concert with him purchases securities at above the offer price, the offeror shall increase his offer to not less than the highest price paid for the securities so acquired. * * *

5. The offeror may offer as consideration securities, cash or a combination of both. However, where the consideration offered by the offeror does not consist of liquid securities admitted to trading on a regulated market, such consideration has to include a cash alternative. In any event, the offeror shall offer a cash consideration at least as an alternative where he or persons acting in concert with him, over a period beginning at the same time as the period decided by the Member State in accordance with paragraph 4 and ending when the offer closes for acceptance, he has purchased in cash securities carrying 5% or more of the voting rights of the offeree company. Member States may provide that a cash consideration shall be offered, at least as an alternative, in all cases. * * *

Article 6 Information on the bid. 1. Member States shall ensure that the decision to make a bid is made public without delay and that the supervisory authority is informed of the bid. * * *

2. Member States shall ensure that the offeror is required to draw up and make public in good time an offer document containing the information necessary to enable the holders of securities of the offeree company to reach a properly informed decision on the bid. * * *

3. The offer document referred to in paragraph 2 shall state at least: (a) the terms of the bid; (b) the identity of the offeror * * *; (c) the securities * * * for which the bid is made; (d) the consideration offered for each security * * *and, in the case of mandatory bids, the method employed in determining it, with particulars of the way in which that consideration is to be paid; (d) the compensation offered for the rights which might be removed as a result of the breakthrough rule laid down in Article 11(4), with particulars of the way in which that compensation is to be paid and the method employed in determining it; (e) the maximum and minimum percentages or quantities of securities which the offeror undertakes to acquire; (f) details of any existing holdings of the offeror, and of persons acting in concert with him, in the offeree company; (g) all the conditions to which the bid is subject; (h) the offeror's intentions with regard to the future business of the offeree company * * *; (i) the period for acceptance of the bid; (j) where the consideration offered by the offeror includes securities of any kind, information about those securities; (k) information on the financing for the bid; (l) the identity of persons acting in concert with the offeror or with the offeree company * * *; (m) indication of the national law which will govern contracts concluded between the offeror and holders of securities of the offeree company as a result of the bid and the competent courts. * * *

Article 7 Period for acceptance. 1. Member States shall provide that the period for acceptance of the bid [generally] may not be less than two weeks or more than ten weeks from the date of publication of the offer document. * * *

Article 8 Disclosure. 1. Member States shall ensure that a bid must be made public in such a way as to ensure market transparency and integrity for the securities of the offeree company, of the offeror or of any other company affected by the bid, in particular in order to prevent the publication or dissemination of false or misleading information. * * *

Article 9 Obligations of the board of the offeree company. 1. Member States shall ensure that rules laid down in paragraphs 2 to 5 below are complied with.

2. [Prohibition on Defensive Actions] During the period referred to in the second subparagraph, the board of the offeree company must obtain the prior authorization of the general meeting of shareholders given for this purpose before taking any action other than seeking alternative bids which may result in the frustration of the bid and in particular before issuing any shares which may result in a lasting impediment to the offeror in obtaining control over the offeree company. * * *

5. [Rule 14D-9 Statement by Target's Board] The board of the offeree company shall draw up and make public a document setting out its opinion on the bid, together with the reasons on which it is based, including its views on the effects on all the interests of the company, including employment, and on the offeror's strategic plans for the offeree company and their likely effects on employment and the locations of the company's places of business as set out in the offer document in accordance with Article 6(3)(h). The board of the offeree company shall at the same time communicate that opinion to the representatives of its employees or, where there are no such representatives, the employees themselves. * * *

Article 10 Information on companies referred to in Article 1(1). 1. Member States shall ensure that companies referred to in Article 1(1) publish detailed information on the following: (a) the structure of their capital, including securities which are not admitted to trading on a regulated market in a Member State, where appropriate with an indication of the different classes of shares and, for each class of shares, the rights and obligations attaching to it and the percentage of total share capital that it represents; * * * (f) any restrictions on voting rights, such as limitations of the right to vote for holders of a given percentage or number of votes, deadlines for exercising the right to vote, or systems whereby, with the company's co-operation, the financial rights attached to securities are separated from the holding of securities; * * *

Article 11 Breakthrough. 1. Without prejudice to other rights and obligations laid down in Community law for companies referred to in Article 1(1), Member States shall ensure that the provisions referred to in paragraphs 2 to 6 apply when a bid has been made public.

2. Any restrictions on the transfer of securities provided for in the articles of association of the offeree company shall not apply vis-à-vis the offeror during the period for acceptance of the bid laid down in Article 7(1).

Any restrictions on the transfer of securities provided for in contractual agreements between the offeree company and holders of its securities, or contractual agreements between holders of securities of the offeree company entered into after the adoption of this Directive, shall not apply vis-à-vis the offeror during the period for acceptance of the bid laid down in Article 7(1).

3. Restrictions on voting rights provided for in the articles of association of the offeree company shall not have effect at the general meeting which decides on any defensive measures in accordance with Article 9.

Restrictions on voting rights provided for in contractual agreements between the offeree company and holders of its securities, or contractual agreements between holders of securities of the offeree company entered into after the adoption of this Directive, shall not have effect at the general meeting which decides on any defensive measures in accordance with Article 9. Multiple voting securities shall carry one vote only at the general meeting which decides on any defensive measures in accordance with Article 9.

4. Where, following a bid, the offeror holds 75% of the capital carrying voting rights, any restrictions on the transfer of securities and on voting rights referred to in paragraphs 2 and 3 and any extraordinary rights of shareholders concerning the appointment or removal of board members provided for in the articles of association of the offeree company shall not apply and multiple voting securities shall carry one vote only at the first general meeting following closure of the bid, called by the offeror in order to amend the articles of association or to remove or appoint board members.

To that end, the offeror shall have the right to convene a general meeting at short notice, provided that the meeting does not take place within two weeks of notification.

4a. Where rights are being removed on the basis of paragraphs 2, 3, 4 and/or Article 11A, equitable compensation must be provided for any loss incurred by the holders of these rights. The terms for determining such compensation and the modalities of its payment will be set by Member States.

5. Paragraphs 3 and 4 shall not apply to securities where the restrictions on voting rights are compensated for by specific pecuniary advantages.

6. This Article shall not apply where Member States hold securities in the offeree company which confer special rights on the Member State which are compatible with the Treaty and to special rights provided for in national law which are compatible with the Treaty and to cooperative enterprises.

Article 11A Optional arrangements. 1. Member States may reserve the right not to require companies referred to in Art. 1(1) which have their registered offices on their territory to apply Articles 9(2) and (3) [prohibition against defensive actions] and/or 11 [breakthrough].

2. When Member States make use of the option referred to under paragraph 1, they must nevertheless give companies which have their registered offices on their territory an option, which is reversible, to apply Articles 9(2) and (3) and/or 11, without prejudice to Article 11(6).

The decision of the company must be taken by the general meeting of shareholders, based on the applicable law where the company has its registered office in accordance with the rules applicable to amendments of the Articles of association. The decision must be notified to the supervisory authority of the Member State where the company has its registered office and to all supervisory authorities of Member States where its securities are admitted to trading on a regulated market or where such admission has been requested. * * *

Article 12 Other rules applicable to the conduct of bids. Member States shall also lay down rules which govern the conduct of bids at least as regards the following: (a) lapse of the bid; (b) revision of bids; (c) competing bids; (d) disclosure of the results of bids; (e) irrevocability of the bid and conditions permitted.

Article 13 Information for and consultation of employees' representatives. The provisions of this Directive are without prejudice to the rules relating to information and to consultation of representatives of and, if Member States so provide, codetermination with the employees of the offeror and the offeree company governed by the relevant national provisions, and in particular those adopted pursuant to Directives 94/45/EC, 98/59/EC, 2001/86/EC and 2002/14/EC.

Article 14 Squeeze-out right. 1. Member States shall ensure that, following a bid made to all the holders of securities of the offeree company for all their securities, the provisions in paragraphs 2 to 5 apply.

2. Member States shall ensure that an offeror is able to require all the holders of the remaining securities to sell him those securities at a fair price. Member States shall introduce this right in one of the following situations: (a) where the offeror holds securities representing not less than 90% of the capital carrying voting rights and 90% of the voting rights of the offeree company, or (b) where he has acquired or has firmly contracted to acquire, following acceptance of the bid, securities representing not less than 90% of the offeree company's capital carrying voting rights and 90% of the voting rights comprised in the bid. * * *

4. The offeror must exercise the squeeze-out right within a period of three months after the end of the period for acceptance of the bid referred to in Article 7.

5. Member States shall ensure that a fair price is guaranteed. That price shall take the same form as the consideration offered in the bid or consist of cash. Member States may provide that cash shall be offered at least as an alternative.

Following a voluntary bid, in both cases referred to in points (a) and (b) of paragraph 2, the consideration offered in the bid shall be presumed to be fair where the offeror has acquired, through acceptance of the bid, securities representing not less than 90% of the capital carrying voting rights comprised in the bid.

Following a mandatory bid, the consideration offered in the bid shall be presumed to be fair.

Article 15 Sell-out right. 1. Member States shall ensure that, following a bid made to all the holders of securities of the offeree company for all their securities, the provisions in paragraphs 2 and 3 apply.

2. Member States shall ensure that a holder of remaining securities is able to require the offeror to buy his securities from him at a fair price under the same circumstances as provided for in Article 14(2). * * *

Note

The E.C.'s Takeover Directive is based in principal part on the U.K.'s City Code on Takeovers and Mergers, which is set out in the next section.

C. The U.K.'s City Code on Takeovers and Mergers

1. Introduction to the Takeover Panel

Information from the Panel's Website

June 30, 2006

The panel on takeovers and mergers. The Panel on Takeovers and Mergers (the "Panel") is an independent body, established in 1968, whose main functions are to issue and administer the City Code on Takeovers and Mergers (the "Code") and to supervise and regulate takeovers and other matters to which the Code applies in accordance with the Rules set out in the Code. It has been designated as the supervisory authority to carry out certain regulatory functions in relation to takeovers pursuant to the Directive on Takeover Bids (2004/25/EC) (the "Directive") [Section 26.18.B]. * * *

Membership of the panel. The Panel draws its members from major financial and business institutions, giving it an unrivalled expertise in takeovers and securities markets. The Panel comprises up to 34 members. The Chairman, Deputy Chairmen and up to twenty independent members are appointed by the Panel on the recommendation of its Nomination Committee. * * * [The Panel has two committees: the Code Committee and the Hearings Committee.] The Code Committee carries out the rule-making functions of the Panel and is solely responsible for keeping the Code * * * under review and for proposing, consulting on, making and issuing amendments to * * * the Code. The principal function of the Hearings Committee is to review rulings of the Executive. The decisions of the Hearing Committee can be appealed to the Takeover Appeal Board, an independent body. Prior to adoption of the EC's Takeover Directive, decisions of the Takeover Panel were generally not subject to court review. As a result of the requirements of the Directive [Section 26.18.B], decisions of the Panel are now subject to court review in certain circumstances. * * *

Functions of the panel. The Panel regulates takeover bids and other merger transactions (however effected) for companies which have their registered offices in the United Kingdom, the Channel Islands or the Isle of Man if any of their securities are admitted to trading on a regulated market in the United Kingdom or on any stock exchange in the Channel Islands or the Isle of Man. Its remit also extends to unlisted companies and certain private companies which are resident in the United Kingdom. * * *

In all cases, the Panel's function is to ensure that shareholders are treated fairly and are not denied an opportunity to decide on the merits of a takeover and that shareholders of the same class are afforded equivalent treatment by an offeror. The Code is not concerned with the financial or commercial advantages of a takeover. * * *

The Code. The Code has been developed since 1968 to reflect the collective opinion of those professionally involved in the field of takeovers as to appropriate business standards and as to how fairness to shareholders and an orderly framework for takeovers can be achieved. Following the implementation of the Takeovers Directive (2004/25/EC) (the "Directive") [Section 26.18.B] by means of the Takeovers Directive (Interim Implementation) Regulations 2006, the rules set out in the Code which are derived from the Directive have a statutory basis and comply with the relevant requirements of the Directive.

General principles and rules. The Code is based upon a number of General Principles, which are essentially statements of standards of commercial behaviour. These General Principles are the same as the general principles set out in Article 3 of the Directive. They apply to takeovers and other matters to which the Code applies. * * *

In addition to the General Principles, the Code contains a series of rules. Although most of the rules are expressed in less general terms than the General Principles, they are not framed in technical language, and like the General Principles, are to be interpreted to achieve their underlying purpose. Therefore, their spirit must be observed as well as their letter. * * *

The panel executive. The day-to-day work of takeover supervision and regulation is carried out by the Executive. In carrying out these functions, the Executive operates independently of the Panel. * * *

2. The City Code

[It must be emphasized that the Code is over 300 pages in length, and consequently, the discussion here only addresses some of the more important provisions, particularly relating to the structure of the transaction. As a result of the acquisition by Kraft, a U.S. company of Cadbury, a U.K. company, the Code was amended in 2011. The discussion below of specific provisions of the Code identifies those provisions that were adopted in 2011.][19]

Excerpts from The City Code on Takeovers and Mergers

General Principles. The Code has General Principles that are essentially the same as the General Principles in the Takeover Directive, Section 26.18.B.

Definitions and Rules 1 and 2: The definitions give a very broad meaning to the term "acting in concert," and for purposes of the rules, any prohibition on a person extends to those acting in concert. The term "control" is defined to mean a holding of 30% or more of the voting rights of a company. The term "offer period" means, in essence, the period between the announcement of an offer and the first closing date.

Rules 1 and 2 deal respectively with "The Approach" and "Secrecy Before Announcement; The Timing and Contents of Announcements." Under Rule 1(a), the "offer must be put forward in the first instance to the board of the offeree company [the target]." Under Rule 2.2, an announcement is required, *inter alia,*"(a) when a firm intention to make an offer ... is notified to the board of the offeree company from a serious source..., [and] (b) immediately upon acquisition of shares which gives rise to an obligation to make an offer under Rule 9 [relating to mandatory offers]." Under Rule 2.5, an announcement of a "firm intention to make an offer should be made only when the offeror has every reason to believe it can and will ... implement the offer."

Rules 2.5, 2.6 and 2.8, The Put Up or Shut Up (PUSU) Requirement. The 2011 amendments altered the put-up or shut-up (PUSU) rules, which require a potential offeror to either commit to the offer or not make an offer for six months. The purpose of the rules is to curtail "virtual bids," which are "possible" bids announced by a potential offeror. Virtual bids could keep the target's board occupied for an unwarranted period. While there are many twists and turns with these rules, the discussion here outlines the basic principles.

Rules 2.5 and 2.6 implement the "put-up" requirement. Rule 2.5 requires that the Panel be consulted regarding any possible offers that the potential offeror proposes to make public.

Under Rule 2.6, if a possible offer is publicly announced, whether by the potential offeror or the target, then within 28 days, the "put-up" period, following the date of the announcement, the potential offeror must either:

(i) announce a firm intention to make an offer ... ; or

(ii) announce that it does not intend to make an offer, in which case the announcement will be treated as a statement to which Rule 2.8 applies, unless the Panel has consented to an extension of the deadline....

Under Rule 2.6(c), the Panel will normally consent to an extension of the 28-day period "at the request of the board of the offeree company."

Pursuant to Rule 2.8, the "shut-up" requirement, a potential offeror that does not make an offer within the 28-day period, or the period as extended by the Panel, is prohibited for a period of six months from the date of the statement, from:

---

19. The materials dealing with these 2011 changes are discussed in greater detail in Thompson, *Mergers, Acquisitions and Tender Offers, supra* Section 1.10, Chapter 20. For a more complete discussion of the 2011 amendments, see Richard May, *Changes to the UK Takeover Code: A Hostile Regime for Hostile Bids?*, 15 The M&A Lawyer 8 (2011).

(a) announc[ing] an offer or possible offer for the offeree company (including a partial offer which would result in the offeror and persons acting in concert with it being interested in shares carrying 30% or more of the voting rights of the offeree company);

(b) acquir[ing] any interest in shares of the offeree company if any such person would thereby become obliged under Rule 9 [the mandatory offer provision, see discussion *infra*] to make an offer....

Since the trigger on the 28-day period is an announcement of a possible offer by either the potential offeror or the offeree, the new PUSU rules "may encourage target companies to announce the identity of potential bidders in order to make them subject to the [PUSU] requirement."[20]

Pfizer, a U.S. company, became subject to the put-up or shut-up rule in 2014 as a result of the rejection of its offer by AstraZeneca, a U.K. company. After the running of the 28 day period, Pfizer announced that it was abandoning its offer.

Rule 3. Independent Advice. [*Cf. Van Gorkom*, Section 3.10.A] **3.1 Board of the Offeree Company.** The board of the offeree company must obtain competent independent advice on any offer and the substance of such advice must be made known to its shareholders. * * *

3.2 Board of an Offeror Company. The board of an offeror must obtain competent independent advice on any offer when the offer being made is a reverse takeover or when the directors are faced with a conflict of interest. The substance of such advice must be made known to its shareholders. * * * Reverse takeovers: A transaction will be a reverse takeover if an offeror might as a result need to increase its existing issued voting equity share capital by more than 100%. * * *

3.3 Disqualified Advisors. The Panel will not regard as an appropriate person to give independent advice a person who is in the same group as the financial or other professional adviser * * * to an offeror or who has a significant interest in or financial connection with either an offeror or the offeree company of such a kind as to create a conflict of interest.

4.1 Prohibited Dealings by Persons Other than the Offeror. (a) No dealings of any kind in securities of the offeree company, by any person, not being the offeror, who is privy to confidential price-sensitive information concerning an offer or contemplated offer may take place between the time when there is reason to suppose that an approach or an offer is contemplated and the announcement of the approach or offer or of the termination of the discussions. * * *

Rule 5. Timing Restrictions on Acquisitions. 5.1 Restrictions. [*Cf.* Section 13(d), Chapter 18] Except as permitted by Rule 5.2: (a) when a person (which for the purpose of Rule 5 includes any persons acting in concert with him) holds shares or rights over shares which in the aggregate carry less than 30% of the voting rights of a company, he may not acquire any shares carrying voting rights in that company or any rights over such shares which, when aggregated with the shares or rights over shares which he already holds, would carry 30% or more of the voting rights; * * *

20. Richard May, *Changes to the UK Takeover Code: A Hostile Regime for Hostile Bids?*, 15 The M&A Lawyer 8, 9. (2011).

5.2 Exceptions to Restrictions. The restrictions in Rule 5.1 do not apply to an acquisition of shares carrying voting rights in a company, by a person: (a) at any time from a single shareholder if it is the only such acquisition within any period of 7 days * * *; (b) immediately before the person announces a firm intention to make an offer [which is recommended by the board of the offeree company]; * * *

Rule 6. Purchase Resulting in an Obligation to Offer a Minimum Level of Consideration. 6.1 Purchases Before A Rule 2.5 Announcement (Announcement Of A Firm Intention To Make An Offer) [*Cf.* Treatment of market sweeps, Chapter 19] Except with the consent of the Panel * * *, when an offeror * * * purchased shares in the offeree company: (a) within the three month period prior to the commencement of the offer period; or (b) during the period, if any, between the commencement of the offer period and an announcement made by the purchaser in accordance with Rule 2.5; or (c) prior to the three month period referred to in (a) [in certain cases], the offer to the shareholders of the same class shall not be on less favorable terms.

6.2 Purchases After A Rule 2.5 Announcement. [*Cf.* Rule 14e-5, Chapter 20] (a) If, after an announcement made in accordance with Rule 2.5 [firm intention to make an offer] and before the offer closes for acceptance, an offeror * * * purchases shares at above the offer price * * *, it shall increase its offer to not less than the highest price paid for the shares so acquired. * * *

Rules 7 and 8. These rules deal respectively with "Consequences of Certain Dealings and Disclosure of Dealings During the Offer Period and Indemnity." Under Rule 8.3, all shareholders holding 1% or more of the securities of the offeror or offeree must publicly disclose dealings in such shares. This rule is much more onerous than the rules of Section 13(d). *See* Chapter 18.

Section F. The Mandatory Offer and Its Terms

Rule 9. 9.1 When A Mandatory Offer Is Required And Who Is Primarily Responsible For Making It. Except with the consent of the Panel, when: (a) any person acquires, whether by a series of transactions over a period of time or not, shares which (taken together with shares held or acquired by persons acting in concert with him) carry 30% or more of the voting rights of a company; or (b) any person, together with persons acting in concert with him, is interested in shares which in the aggregate carry not less than 30% of the voting rights of a company but does not hold shares carrying more than 50% of such voting rights and such person, or any person acting in concert with him, acquires an interest in any other shares which increases the percentage of shares carrying voting rights in which he is interested, such person shall extend offers, on the basis set out in Rules 9.3, 9.4 and 9.5 [the mandatory offer rules], to the holders of any class of equity share capital whether voting or non-voting and also to the holders of any other class of transferable securities carrying voting rights. * * *

9.3 Conditions And Consents. Except with the consent of the Panel (a) offers made under this Rule must be conditional only upon the offeror having received acceptances in respect of shares which, together with shares acquired or agreed to be acquired before or during the offer, will result in the offeror and any person acting in concert with it holding shares carrying more than 50% of the voting rights; * * *

9.5 Consideration To Be Offered. (a) Offers made under this Rule must, in respect of each class of share capital involved, be in cash or be accompanied by a cash alternative at not less than the highest price paid by the offeror or any person acting in concert with it for shares of that class during the offer period and within 12 months prior to its commencement. * * *

Section G. The Voluntary Offer and Its Terms

Rule 10. The Acceptance Condition. It must be a condition of any offer for voting equity share capital which, if accepted in full, would result in the offeror holding shares carrying over 50% of the voting rights of the offeree company that the offer will not become or be declared unconditional as to acceptances unless the offeror has acquired or agreed to acquire (either pursuant to the offer or otherwise) shares carrying over 50% of the voting rights.

Rule 11. Nature Of Consideration To Be Offered. 11.1 When A Cash Offer Is Required. Except with the consent of the Panel in cases falling under (a) or (b), a cash offer is required where:

(a) the shares of any class under offer in the offeree company in which interests are acquired for cash by an offeror and any person acting in concert with it during the offer period and within 12 months prior to its commencement carry 10% or more of the voting rights currently exercisable at a class meeting of that class, in which case the offer for that class shall be in cash or accompanied by a cash alternative at not less than the highest price paid by the offeror or any person acting in concert with it for any interest in shares of that class acquired during the offer period and within 12 months prior to its commencement; or

(b) subject to paragraph (a) above, any interest in shares of any class under offer in the offeree company is acquired for cash by an offeror or any person acting in concert with it during the offer period, in which case the offer for that class shall be in cash or accompanied by a cash alternative at not less than the highest price paid by the offeror or any person acting in concert with it for any interest in shares of that class acquired during the offer period; or

(c) in the view of the Panel there are circumstances which render such a course necessary in order to give effect to General Principle 1.

Rule 12. The [U.K.] Competition Commission And The European Commission. 12.1 Requirement For Appropriate Term In Offer. (a) Where an offer comes within the statutory provisions for possible reference to the [U.K.] Competition Commission, it must be a term of the offer that it will lapse if there is a reference [by the Fair Trade Commission of the case to the Competition Commission] before the first closing date or the date when the offer becomes or is declared unconditional as to acceptances, whichever is the later.

(b) Where an offer would give rise to a concentration with a Community dimension within the scope of Council Regulation 139/2004/EC, it must be a term of the offer that it will lapse if either:—(i) the European Commission initiates proceedings under Article 6(1)(c) [initiates a Phase II investigation]; or (ii) following a referral by the European Commission under Article 9.1 to a competent authority in the United Kingdom, there is a subsequent reference to the Competition Commission, in either case before the first closing date or the date when the offer becomes or is declared unconditional as to acceptances, whichever is the later. * * *

Rules 13 Through 15. Rule 13 prohibits conditions to an offer that "depend solely on the subjective judgments of the directors of the offeror * * *." Rule 14 sets out rules regarding multiple classes of stock, and Rule 15 addresses the treatment of convertible securities.

Rule 16. Special Deals With Favorable Conditions. Except with the consent of the Panel, an offeror * * * may not make any arrangements with shareholders and may not deal or enter into arrangements to deal in shares of the offeree company, * * * if there are favorable conditions attached which are not being extended to all shareholders.

Rules 17 Through 20. Rule 17.1 requires the offeror to announce on the day after the closing of the offer the number of shares that have been tendered. Rule 18 addresses the treatment of proxies with regard to tendered shares. Rule 19.1 requires each public document to "satisfy the highest standards of care and accuracy * * * ."

Rule 21. Restrictions On Frustrating Action. [*Cf.* Defensive Actions, Chapter 23] **21.1 When Shareholders' Consent Is Required.** During the course of an offer, or even before the date of the offer if the board of the offeree company has reason to believe that a bona fide offer might be imminent, the board must not, without the approval of the shareholders in general meeting: (a) take any action which may result in any offer or bona fide possible offer being frustrated or in shareholders being denied the opportunity to decide on its merits; or (b) (i) issue any authorised but unissued shares or transfer or sell, or agree to transfer or sell, any shares out of treasury; (ii) issue or grant options in respect of any unissued shares; (iii) create or issue, or permit the creation or issue of, any securities carrying rights of conversion into or subscription for shares; (iv) sell, dispose of or acquire, or agree to sell, dispose of or acquire, assets of a material amount; or (v) enter into contracts otherwise than in the ordinary course of business. The Panel must be consulted in advance if there is any doubt as to whether any proposed action may fall within this Rule. * * *

Rule 21.2 Inducement Fees. Prior to the 2011 amendments, Rule 21.2 permitted "*de minimis*" break fees of no more than 1% of the transaction value, and parties generally included such a break fee, as well as other deal protection measures, in friendly deals. Except as noted below, the amended Rule 21.2 eliminated this *de minimis* rule and restricted other deal protection devices. Rule 21.2 now reads as follows:

> RULE 21.2 INDUCEMENT FEES AND OTHER OFFER-RELATED ARRANGEMENTS
>
> (a) Except with the consent of the Panel, neither the offeree company nor any person acting in concert with it may enter into any offer-related arrangement with either the offeror or any person acting in concert with it during an offer period or when an offer is reasonably in contemplation.
>
> (b) An offer-related arrangement means any agreement, arrangement or commitment in connection with an offer, including any inducement fee arrangement or other arrangement having a similar or comparable financial or economic effect, but excluding:
>
> > (i) a commitment to maintain the confidentiality of information provided that it does not include any other [prohibited] provisions ... ;
> >
> > (ii) a commitment not to solicit employees, customers or suppliers;
> >
> > (iii) a commitment to provide information or assistance for the purposes of obtaining any official authorisation or regulatory clearance;
> >
> > (iv) irrevocable commitments and letters of intent;
> >
> > (v) any agreement, arrangement or commitment which imposes obligations only on an offeror [*e.g.*, reverse termination fees, see chapters 2 and 13] ... ; and
> >
> > (vi) any agreement relating to any existing employee incentive arrangement.

Rule 21.2(c) requires that the parties consult with the Panel "[i]f there is any doubt as to whether any proposed agreement, arrangement or commitment is subject to [the] Rule...."

Note 1 to Rule 21.2 relaxes this prohibition against inducement fees where there is a hostile bid and a *de mininmis* fee is paid to a White Knight (*i.e.*, a third party offeror that is making a topping bid). Also, Note 2 to Rule 21.2 relaxes the prohibition against inducement fees paid, for example, to the winning bidder of an auction originated by the offeree.

Rules 22 through 24. Rule 22 sets out rules regarding the responsibilities of the offeree company regarding registration procedures, and Rules 23 and 24 deal with documents and other information required to be provided by the boards of the offeree and offeror.

Rule 24.1. Rule 24.1 generally requires that the offer be commenced within 28 days of an announcement by an offeror that it will be making an offer. This provision reads as follows:

> (a) The offeror must, normally within 28 days of the announcement of a firm intention to make an offer, send an offer document to shareholders of the offeree company and persons with information rights[.]

Rule 25. Offeree Board Circulars. [*Cf.* Rule 14d-9, Chapter 20] **25.1 View Of The Board.** Rule 25.1(a) was amended in 2011 and now reads as follows:

> (a) The board of the offeree company must, normally within 14 days of the publication of the offer document, send a circular to the offeree company's shareholders and persons with information rights ... and must, at the same time, make it readily available to its employee representatives or, where there are no employee representatives, to the employees themselves.

Rules 26 And 27. Rule 26 deals with documents required to be on display, and Rule 27 addresses the treatment of material changes.

Section K. Profit Forecasts

Rule 28.1 Standards Of Care. There are obvious hazards attached to the forecasting of profits; this should in no way detract from the necessity of maintaining the highest standards of accuracy and fair presentation in all communications to shareholders in an offer. * * *

Section L. Asset Valuations

Rule 29.1 Valuations To Be Reported On If Given In Connection With An Offer. When a valuation of assets is given in connection with an offer, it should be supported by the opinion of a named independent valuer. * * *

Section M. Timing And Revision

Rule 30.1 provides that the "offer document should normally be posted within 28 days of the announcement * * * of the offer." Rule 30.2 provides that the board of the offeree "should advise its shareholders of its views on the offer as soon as practicable after publication of the offer document and normally within 14 days." This is the analogue to the Schedule 14D-9. [*See* Chapter 20]

Rule 31. Timing Of The Offer. [*Cf.* Rule 14e-1, Chapter 20] **31.1 First Closing Date.** An offer must initially be open for at least 21 days following the date on which the offer document is posted. * * *

Rule 32. Revision. [*Cf.* Rule 14e-1, Chapter 20] **32.1 Offer Open For 14 Days After Revision.** If revised, an offer must be kept open for at least 14 days following the date on which the revised offer document is posted. * * *

Rule 33. Rule 33 addresses the treatment of alternative offers.

Rule 34. Right Of Withdrawal [*Cf.* Rule 14d-7, Chapter 20] An acceptor must be entitled to withdraw his acceptance from the date which is 21 days after the first closing date of the initial offer, if the offer has not by such date become or been declared unconditional as to acceptances. This entitlement to withdraw must be exercisable until the earlier of (a) the time that the offer becomes or is declared unconditional as to acceptances and (b) the final time for lodgment of acceptances which can be taken into account in accordance with Rule 31.6. * * *

Rules 35 To 38. Rule 35 deals with restrictions following offers, Rule 36 addresses partial offers, Rule 37 focuses on redemptions by the offeree, and Rule 38 addresses dealings by certain connected persons.

D. U.K. Compulsory Acquisition of Minority Shares and Minority Put After a Tender Offer[21]

Section 979 of the Companies Act of 2006, which is titled "Squeeze-out," applies where an acquirer makes an offer for "any and all" of a target's shares. In such case, if the acquirer acquires not less than 90% "in value of the shares to which the offer relates [then the acquirer] may give notice to the holder of any shares to which the offer relates which the [acquirer] has not acquired or unconditionally contracted to acquire that [it] desires to acquire those shares." The 90% rule applies to the shares the acquirer tenders for and does not include shares held by the acquirer at the beginning of the tender. Thus, this test is different from the short form merger test under U.S. law discussed in Chapter 4. Under Section 981, the notice must be given within three months of the closing of the offer, and, once the acquirer has given the notice, it is "entitled and bound to acquire the shares to which the notice relates on the terms of the offer."

The most common form of acquisition of a public target in the U.K. is a tender offer for 90% of the target's stock followed by a compulsory acquisition. For example, this was the model followed by NASDAQ in its tender offer for the London Stock Exchange (LSE).[22]

Under Section 983, which is titled "Sell-out," if an acquirer who has acquired the requisite 90% or more does not give a compulsory acquisition notice under Section 979, the minority shareholders have the right to put their shares to the acquirer, and under Section 985(2), the acquirer is "entitled and bound to acquire those shares on the terms of the offer. . . ."

E. U.K. Company Act Disclosure Requirements Regarding a Target's Shares

In addition to the rules under the City Code requiring disclosure of interests in the target's shares, the U.K.'s Financial Conduct Authority (FCA), a successor to the Financial Services Authority, and the U.K. equivalent of the SEC, also has disclosure rules. In the Disclosure and Transparency Rules (DTR) section of the FCA's Handbook, the FCA has promulgated Voter Holder and Issuer Notification Rules. These rules, which were previously

---

21. Sections D through G are adapted from Thompson, *Mergers, Acquisitions and Tender Offers, supra* Section 1.10, at Section 20:6.2–20:6.5.

22. *See* Appendix 20-A, NASDAQ Stock Market Offer for LSE pursuant to City Code, of Thompson, *Mergers, Acquisitions and Tender Offers, supra* Section 1.10.

in the Companies Act of 1985, are the U.K.'s analogue to the U.S. early warning system in Section 13(d) of the 34 Act, discussed in Chapter 8. Rule 5.1.2 of these Notification Rules requires the following disclosure of the acquisition or disposal of an interest in a U.K. public company:

> [A] person must notify the issuer of the percentage of its voting rights he holds as shareholder or through his direct or indirect holding of [certain] financial instruments ... if the percentage of those voting rights:
>
> > (1) reaches, exceeds or falls below 3%, 4%, 5%, 6%, 7%, 8%, 9%, 10% and each 1% threshold thereafter up to 100% ... as a result of an acquisition or disposal of shares or [certain] financial instruments....

Also, the U.K. Companies Act of 2006 imposes certain disclosure requirements regarding the acquisition of shares of a company. Under Section 793, a "public company may by notice ... to any person whom the company knows or has reasonable cause to believe ... to be interested in the company's shares...." require such person to "confirm that fact or ... to state whether or not it is the case...." Thus, a target could use the Section 793 device to force a disclosure by a suspected hostile acquirer who owns the target's stock. Elaborate procedures govern the operation of Section 793.

F. Schemes of Arrangement and Mergers of Public Companies in the U.K.

1. Introduction

For a substantial period of time, the U.K.'s Companies Act has contained provisions dealing with "Arrangements and Reconstructions" referred to as schemes of arrangement, and the Companies Act of 2006 retains the scheme of arrangement provisions (Sections 895 to 901) and also adopts provisions dealing with Mergers and Divisions of Public Companies (Sections 902 to 941). The Mergers and Divisions provisions are apparently designed to satisfy the E.U.'s Directive on Mergers, discussed previously.

2. Schemes of Arrangement—GE's Acquisition of Amersham

A scheme of arrangement can be used where, for example, an acquirer and a target agree that the acquirer will acquire all of the target's shares in exchange for shares of the acquirer. This was the type of scheme of arrangement pursuant to which GE, a Delaware corporation, in 2004 acquired Amersham, a U.K. company, in exchange for the stock of GE.[23] This type of scheme is referred to here as a "share acquisition scheme." One benefit of a share acquisition scheme is that all the shareholders in the target company must exchange their shares for shares of the acquirer, which is the case with mergers in the U.S.

Schemes of arrangement are now governed by Sections 895 to 901 of the U.K. Companies Act of 2006. A scheme requires, *inter alia*, (1) a court order for a shareholders' meeting on the transaction (§ 896), (2) the vote of a majority of the outstanding shares (§ 899), (3) the vote of at least 75% of the value of the shares (§ 899), and (4) a final court approval

23. *See* Appendix 20-B, GE's Acquisition of the U.K.'s Amersham in a Scheme of Arrangement, of Thompson, *Mergers, Acquisitions and Tender Offers*, *supra* Section 1.10.

of the transaction (§ 899). For a discussion of these aspects in the GE-Amersham deal *see* §§ II.F and G, Appendix 20-B, GE's Acquisition of the U.K.'s Amersham in a Scheme of Arrangement.

Appendix 7 of the City Code addresses Schemes of Arrangement, and paragraph 1 provides: "The provisions of the Code apply to an offer effected by means of a scheme of arrangement in the same way as they apply to an offer effected by means of a contractual offer, except as set out in this Appendix 7."[24]

In several no action letters the SEC has expressed the view that a U.K scheme of arrangement qualifies for the Section 3(a)(10) "fairness hearing" exemption to the registration requirements of the Securities Act of 33. GE relied on this exemption in its acquisition of Amersham. Apparently the U.S. shareholders of Amersham held more than 10% of Amersham's shares, and for that reason, the issuance of the shares did not qualify for the exemption from registration available under Rule 802, which is discussed previously.

In the event the GE-Amersham transaction could not be completed by a scheme of arrangement, GE had the right to convert the transaction into a tender offer under the City Code, with a 90% tender condition, which would have permitted GE to acquire the non-tendered shares in a compulsory acquisition.

3. Mergers

The merger provisions of the Companies Act of 2006 operate similarly to the scheme of arrangement provisions, except that they contemplate, *inter alia*, the transfer by the target of its assets and liabilities to the acquirer in what is referred to in Section 904 as a "merger by absorption." Under Section 907, a 75% shareholder vote is required for both the acquirer and the target, but court approval is not required. Unlike mergers in the U.S., the provisions do not provide for triangular mergers.

G. Impact of the U.K.'s Prospectus Requirements

The U.K.'s FCA has regulations dealing with the preparation and issuance of prospectuses relating to public offerings of securities. Section 1.2.2 of these rules makes it clear that they do not generally apply to takeovers and mergers:

> In accordance with section 85(5)(b) of the Act, section 85(1) of the Act does not apply to offers of the following types of transferable securities: ...
>
> (2) transferable securities offered in connection with a takeover by means of an exchange offer, if a document is available containing information which is regarded by the SA as being equivalent to that of the prospectus, taking into account the requirements of Community legislation;
>
> (3) transferable securities offered, allotted or to be allotted in connection with a merger, if a document is available containing information which is regarded

24. For an illustration of how the City Code applied in the GE-Amersham deal *see e.g.*, §§ I.C.4, relating to dealings; II.K, relating to conditions; III.A relating to the responsibility of directors; and III.B relating to interests in the shares of Amersham and GE, Appendix 20-B, GE's Acquisition of the U.K.'s Amersham in a Scheme of Arrangement, of Thompson, *Mergers, Acquisitions and Tender Offers*, *supra* Section 1.10.

> by the FCA as being equivalent to that of the prospectus, taking into account the requirements of Community legislation....

Also, they do not apply in a scheme of arrangement, which is subject to court supervision. Although not technically applicable in these M&A transactions, the prospectus rules can provide guidance on the preparation of offering documents in these transactions.

§ 26.19 The EC's 2005 Directive on Income Tax Aspects of Mergers, Asset Acquisitions, Share Exchanges, and Divisions

A. The Directive

Council Directive 90/434/EEC of 23 July 1990 on the common system of taxation applicable to mergers, divisions, partial divisions, transfers of assets and exchanges of shares concerning companies of different Member States and to the transfer of the registered office, of an SE or SCE, between Member States

As amended Council Directive 2005/19/EC of 17 February 2005

Excerpt from Council Directive 90/434 of 23 July 1990

Having regard to the Treaty establishing the European Economic Community, and in particular Article 100 thereof, * * *

Whereas mergers, divisions, transfers of assets and exchanges of shares concerning companies of different Member States may be necessary in order to create within the Community conditions analogous to those of an internal market and in order thus to ensure the establishment and effective functioning of the common market; whereas such operations ought not to be hampered by restrictions, disadvantages or distortions arising in particular from the tax provisions of the Member States; whereas to that end it is necessary to introduce with respect to such operations tax rules which are neutral from the point of view of competition, in order to allow enterprises to adapt to the requirements of the common market, to increase their productivity and to improve their competitive strength at the international level; * * *

Whereas the common tax system ought to avoid the imposition of tax in connection with mergers, divisions, transfers of assets or exchanges of shares, while at the same time safeguarding the financial interests of the State of the transferring or acquired company; * * *

Excerpt from Council Directive 2005/19/EC of 17 February 2005

Whereas:

(2) The objective of Directive 90/434/EEC is that taxation of the income, profits and capital gains from business reorganisations should be deferred and Member States taxing rights safeguarded. * * *

(5) On 8 October 2001 the Council adopted Regulation (EC) No 2157/2001 on the Statute for a European Company (SE). * * * One of the most important features of [this Directive is that] the SE * * * will be able to transfer [its] registered office between Member States without being dissolved and going into liquidation. * * *

(18) Directive 90/434/EEC should therefore be amended accordingly,

Title I General provisions

Article 1. Each Member State shall apply this Directive to the following: (a) mergers, divisions, partial divisions, transfers of assets and exchanges of shares in which companies from two or more Member States are involved, (b) transfers of the registered office from one Member State to another Member State of European companies (Societas Europaea or SE), as established in Council Regulation (EC) No 2157/2001 of 8 October 2001, on the statute for a European Company (SE) * * *.

Article 2. [*Cf.* Code § 368, Chapter 5] For the purposes of this Directive:

(a) 'merger' shall mean an operation whereby:

- one or more companies, on being dissolved without going into liquidation, transfer all their assets and liabilities to another existing company in exchange for the issue to their shareholders of securities representing the capital of that other company, and, if applicable, a cash payment not exceeding 10% of the nominal value, of the accounting par value of those securities,
- two or more companies, on being dissolved without going into liquidation, transfer all their assets and liabilities to a company that they form, in exchange for the issue to their shareholders of securities representing the capital of that new company, and, if applicable, a cash payment not exceeding 10% of the nominal value, or in the absence of a nominal value, of the accounting par value of those securities,
- a company, on being dissolved without going into liquidation, transfers all its assets and liabilities to the company holding all securities representing its capital; * * *

(b) "division" shall mean an operation whereby a company, on being dissolved without going into liquidation, transfers all its assets and liabilities to two or more existing or new companies, in exchange for the pro rata issue to its shareholders of securities representing the capital of the companies receiving the assets and liabilities, and, if applicable, a cash payment not exceeding 10% of the nominal value or, in the absence of a nominal value, of the accounting par value of those securities; * * *

(c) "transfer of assets" shall mean an operation whereby a company transfers without being dissolved all or one or more branches of its activity to another company in exchange for the transfer of securities representing the capital of the company receiving the transfer;

(d) "exchange of shares" shall mean an operation whereby a company acquires a holding in the capital of another company such that it obtains a majority of the voting rights in that company, or, holding such a majority, acquires a further holding, in exchange for the issue to the shareholders of the latter company, in exchange for their securities, of securities representing the capital of the former company, and, if applicable, a cash payment not exceeding 10% of the nominal value, in the absence of a nominal value, of the accounting par value of the securities issued in exchange; * * *

(e) "transferring company" shall mean the company transferring its assets and liabilities or transferring all or one or more branches of its activity;

(f) "receiving company" shall mean the company receiving the assets and liabilities or all or one or more branches of the activity of the transferring company;

(g) "acquired company" shall mean the company in which a holding is acquired by another company by means of an exchange of securities; * * *

(j) "transfer of the registered office" shall mean an operation whereby an SE or an SCE, without winding up or creating a new legal person, transfers its registered office from one Member State to another Member State;

Title II Rules applicable to mergers, divisions, partial divisions, and exchanges of shares

Article 4. [*Cf.* Code §§ 361 and 362, Chapter 5] 1. A merger, division or partial division shall not give rise to any taxation of capital gains calculated by reference to the difference between the real values of the assets and liabilities transferred and their values for tax purposes [the target thus gets tax free treatment as in § 361].

For the purpose of this Article the following definitions shall apply:

(a) "value for tax purposes": the value on the basis of which any gain or loss would have been computed for the purposes of tax upon the income, profits or capital gains of the transferring company if such assets or liabilities had been sold at the time of the merger, division or partial division but independently of it;

(b) "transferred assets and liabilities": those assets and liabilities of the transferring company which, in consequence of the merger, division or partial division, are effectively connected with a permanent establishment of the receiving company in the Member State of the transferring company and play a part in generating the profits or losses taken into account for tax purposes. * * *

3. Paragraphs 1 * * * shall apply only if the receiving company computes any new depreciation and any gains or losses in respect of the assets and liabilities transferred according to the rules that would have applied to the transferring company or companies if the merger, division or partial division had not taken place [the acquiror must take a carryover basis as in § 362]. * * *

Article 6. [*Cf.* Code § 382, Chapter 5] To the extent that, if the operations referred to in Article 1, paragraph A, were effected between companies from the Member State of the transferring company, the Member State would apply provisions allowing the receiving company to take over the losses of the transferring company which had not yet been exhausted for tax purposes, it shall extend those provisions to cover the take-over of such losses by the receiving company's permanent establishments situated within its territory.

Article 8. [*Cf.* Code §§ 354, 355 356, and 358, Chapters 5 and 25] 1. On a merger, division or exchange of shares, the allotment of securities representing the capital of the receiving or acquiring company to a shareholder of the transferring or acquired company in exchange for securities representing the capital of the latter company shall not, of itself, give rise to any taxation of the income, profits or capital gains of that shareholder [this is the analogue to § 354, which gives the target's shareholders tax-free treatment]. * * *

4. Paragraphs 1 and 3 shall apply only if the shareholder does not attribute to the securities received a value for tax purposes higher than the value the securities exchanged had immediately before the merger, division or exchange of shares [a target shareholder must take a substituted basis for the securities received, compare § 358]. * * *

7. In this Article the expression "value for tax purposes" means the value on the basis of which any gain or loss would be computed for the purposes of tax upon the income, profits or capital gains of a shareholder of the company. * * *

9. Paragraphs 1, 2 and 3 shall not prevent a Member State from taking into account when taxing shareholders any cash payment that may be made on the merger, division, partial division or exchange of shares [thus, boot can be taxed as under § 356].

Title III Rules applicable to transfers of assets

Article 9. [*Cf.* Code § 368,Chapter 5] The provisions of Articles 4 [mergers, divisions, partial divisions, and share exchanges] * * * and 6 [carryover of losses] shall apply to transfers of assets. * * *

B. Discussion of Impact of the Directive

David R. Tillinghast and Karina Haum, A Primer on the Impact of the EC Directive on Mergers and Divisions on U.S. Companies with Interests in Europe

Tax Notes International 575, 577–579 (May 1991)

In July 1990, the Council of the European Communities (EC) published a Directive mandating a common system of taxation for cross-border mergers, divisions, asset transfers, and exchanges of shares by companies resident in member countries. EC countries are directed to implement the Directive by conforming their national laws before January 1, 1992. Some of the transactions contemplated by the Directive are not now provided for under the company laws of some EC countries. * * *

In general, the objective of the Directive is to assure that cross-border corporate realignments resulting from increased economic integration within the EC are not impeded by taxes on "paper" gains realized by participating companies and their shareholders. In effect, it constructs a set of community-wide nonrecognition rules. While these are comparable in general scope and purpose to the "tax-free reorganization" rules applicable to U.S. companies under the Internal Revenue Code, there are substantial differences. As American multinationals plan their own responses to developments in the EC—whether these be internal restructuring of their existing European operations or new investments or alliances—they will need not only to be familiar with the EC tax rules, but also to understand how these dovetail with the U.S. nonrecognition rules that may apply to the same transactions. * * *

§ 26.20 Antitrust Regulation of Mergers and Acquisitions by the European Commission (EC)

A. The Statutory Provisions

General antitrust regulation in the European Community (EC) is provided for under Articles 81, 82 and 83 of the EU Treaty. (These provisions were formerly Articles 85, 86 and 87) Article 81, which reads as follows, is similar to Section 1 of the Sherman Act.

Article 81

1. The following shall be prohibited as incompatible with the common market: all agreements between undertakings, decisions by associations of undertakings and concerted practices which may affect trade between Member States and which have as their object or effect the prevention, restriction or distortion of competition within the common market, and in particular those which:

(a) directly or indirectly fix purchase or selling prices for any other trading conditions;

(b) limit or control production, markets, technical development, or investment;

(c) share markets or sources of supply;

(d) apply dissimilar conditions to equivalent transactions with other trading parties, thereby placing them at a competitive disadvantage;

(e) make the conclusion of contracts subject to acceptance by the other parties of supplementary obligations which, by their nature or according to commercial usage, have no connection with the subject of such contracts. * * *

Article 82, which is similar to Section 2 of the Sherman Act, reads as follows:

Article 82

Any abuse by one or more undertakings of a dominant position within the common market or in a substantial part of it shall be prohibited as incompatible with the common market in so far as it may affect trade between Member States. Such abuse may, in particular, consist in:

(a) directly or indirectly imposing unfair purchase or selling prices or other unfair trading conditions;

(b) limiting production, markets or technical development to the prejudice of consumers;

(c) applying dissimilar conditions to equivalent transactions with other trading parties, thereby placing them at a competitive disadvantage;

(d) making the conclusion of contracts subject to acceptance by the other parties of supplementary obligations which, by their nature or according to commercial usage, have no connection with the subject of such contracts.

Article 83 authorizes the promulgation of regulations or directives giving "effect to the principles set out in Articles 81 and 82." Pursuant to this regulatory authority the Council of the European Communities adopted on December 21, 1989 the Merger Control Regulation (No 4064/89), which was significantly amended in 2004.

B. General Description of Operation of Articles 81 and 82

European Competition Policy: A Brief Overview—Antitrust and Cartels

EU Website, August 26, 2005

"Antitrust" covers two prohibition rules set out in the EC Treaty: * * *

Agreements which restrict competition are prohibited (Article 81 of the Treaty). This is for example the case of price-fixing agreements and cartels between competitors;

Firms in a dominant position may not abuse that position (Article 82 of the EC Treaty). This is for example the case for predatory pricing aiming at eliminating competitors from the market.

The Commission is empowered by the Treaty to apply these prohibition rules and enjoys a number of investigative powers (inspection in business and non business premises, written requests for information * * *) to that end. It may impose substantive fines for their violations. Since 1 May 2004, all National competition authorities are also empowered to apply fully the provisions of the Treaty in order to ensure that competition is not distorted or restricted. National courts may also apply directly these prohibitions so as to protect the individual rights conferred to citizens by the Treaty.

C. The EU's Microsoft Abuse of Dominance Case

New Release Announcing Competition Commission's Decision
(24 March 2004)

The European Commission has concluded, after a five-year investigation, that Microsoft Corporation broke European Union competition law by leveraging its near monopoly in the market for PC operating systems (OS) onto the markets for work group server operating systems and for media players. Because the illegal behaviour is still ongoing, the Commission has ordered Microsoft to disclose to competitors, within 120 days, the interfaces required for their products to be able to 'talk' with the ubiquitous Windows OS. Microsoft is also required, within 90 days, to offer a version of its Windows OS without Windows Media Player to PC manufacturers (or when selling directly to end users). In addition, Microsoft is fined A497 million for abusing its market power in the EU.

"Dominant companies have a special responsibility to ensure that the way they do business doesn't prevent competition on the merits and does not harm consumers and innovation—said European Competition Commissioner Mario Monti. "Today's decision restores the conditions for fair competition in the markets concerned and establish clear principles for the future conduct of a company with such a strong dominant position," he added.

After an exhaustive and extensive investigation of more than five years and three statements of objections, the Commission has today taken a decision finding that US software company Microsoft Corporation has violated the EU Treaty's competition rules by abusing its near monopoly [Microsoft's operating systems equip more than 95% of the worlds personal computers] (Article 82) in the PC operating system.

Microsoft abused its market power by deliberately restricting interoperability between Windows PCs and non-Microsoft work group servers, and by tying its Windows Media Player (WMP), a product where it faced competition, with its ubiquitous Windows operating system.

This illegal conduct has enabled Microsoft to acquire a dominant position in the market for work group server operating systems, which are at the heart of corporate IT networks, and risks eliminating competition altogether in that market. In addition, Microsoft's conduct has significantly weakened competition on the media player market.

The ongoing abuses act as a brake on innovation and harm the competitive process and consumers, who ultimately end up with less choice and facing higher prices.

For these very serious abuses, which have been ongoing for five and a half years, the Commission has imposed a fine of 497.2 million. * * *

Note

As of June 2006, this decision is still on appeal to the EU's Court of First Instance.

D. The European Commission's (EC) Merger Control Regulation (MCR)

1. The Preamble to the EC's 2004 Merger Control Regulation

European Council Regulation (EC) No 139/2004 of 20 January 2004 on the Control of Concentrations between Undertakings

(The EC Merger Regulation)

Whereas:

(1) Council Regulation (EEC) No 4064/89 of 21 December 1989 [the original MCR, which was adopted under the authority of Article 83 (formerly 87)] on the control of concentrations between undertakings has been substantially amended. Since further amendments are to be made, it should be recast in the interest of clarity.

(2) For the achievement of the aims of the Treaty, Article 3(1)(g) gives the Community the objective of instituting a system ensuring that competition in the internal market is not distorted. Article 4(1) of the treaty provides that the activities of the Member States and the Community are to be conducted in accordance with the principle of an open market economy with free competition. These principles are essential for the further development of the internal market.

(3) The completion of the internal market and of economic and monetary union, the enlargement of the European Union and the lowering of international barriers to trade and investment will continue to result in major corporate reorganisations, particularly in the form of concentrations.

(4) Such reorganisations are to be welcomed to the extent that they are in line with the requirements of dynamic competition and capable of increasing the competitiveness of European industry, improving the conditions of growth and raising the standard of living in the Community.

(5) However, it should be ensured that the process of reorganisation does not result in lasting damage to competition; Community law must therefore include provisions governing those concentrations which may significantly impede effective competition in the common market or in a substantial part of it. * * *

(7) Articles 81 and 82, while applicable, according to the case-law of the Court of Justice, to certain concentrations, are not sufficient to control all operations which may prove to be incompatible with the system of undistorted competition envisaged in the Treaty. This Regulation should therefore be based not only on Article 83 but, principally, on Article 308 of the Treaty, under which the Community may give itself the additional powers of action necessary for the attainment of its objectives. * * *

(8) The provisions to be adopted in this Regulation should apply to significant structural changes, the impact of which on the market goes beyond the national borders of any one Member State. Such concentrations should, as a general rule, be reviewed exclusively at Community level, in application of a 'one-stop shop' system and in compliance with the principle of subsidiarity. Concentrations not covered by this Regulation come, in principle, within the jurisdiction of the Member States.

(9) The scope of application of this Regulation should be defined according to the geographical area of activity of the undertakings concerned and be limited by quantitative thresholds in order to cover those concentrations which have a Community dimension. * * *

(10) A concentration with a Community dimension should be deemed to exist where the aggregate turnover of the undertakings concerned exceeds given thresholds; that is the case irrespective of whether or not the undertakings effecting the concentration have their seat or their principal fields of activity in the Community, provided they have substantial operations there.

(11) The rules governing the referral of concentrations from the Commission to Member States and from Member States to the Commission should operate as an effective corrective mechanism in the light of the principle of subsidiarity; these rules protect the competition interests of the Member States in an adequate manner and take due account of legal certainty and the 'one-stop shop' principle. * * *

(17) The Commission should be given exclusive competence to apply this Regulation, subject to review by the Court of Justice.

(18) The Member States should not be permitted to apply their national legislation on competition to concentrations with a Community dimension, unless this Regulation makes provision therefore. * * *

(24) In order to ensure a system of undistorted competition in the common market, in furtherance of a policy conducted in accordance with the principle of an open market economy with free competition, this Regulation must permit effective control of all concentrations from the point of view of their effect on competition in the Community. Accordingly, Regulation (EEC) No 4064/89 established the principle that a concentration with a Community dimension which creates or strengthens a dominant position as a result of which effective competition in the common market or in a substantial part of it would be significantly impeded should be declared incompatible with the common market.

(25) In view of the consequences that concentrations in oligopolistic market structures may have, it is all the more necessary to maintain effective competition in such markets. Many oligopolistic markets exhibit a healthy degree of competition. However, under certain circumstances, concentrations involving the elimination of important competitive constraints that the merging parties had exerted upon each other, as well as a reduction of competitive pressure on the remaining competitors, may, even in the absence of a likelihood of coordination between the members of the oligopoly, result in a significant impediment to effective competition. The Community courts have, however, not to date expressly interpreted Regulation (EEC) No 4064/89 as requiring concentrations giving rise to such non-coordinated effects to be declared incompatible with the common market. Therefore, in the interests of legal certainty, it should be made clear that this Regulation permits effective control of all such concentrations by providing that any concentration which would significantly impede effective competition, in the common market or in a substantial part of it, should be declared incompatible with the common market. The notion of 'significant impediment to effective competition' in Article 2(2) and (3) should be interpreted as extending, beyond the concept of dominance, only to the anti-competitive effects of a concentration resulting from the non-coordinated behaviour of undertakings which would not have a dominant position on the market concerned.

(26) A significant impediment to effective competition generally results from the creation or strengthening of a dominant position. With a view to preserving the guidance that may be drawn from past judgments of the European courts and Commission decisions pursuant to Regulation (EEC) No 4064/89, while at the same time maintaining consistency with the standards of competitive harm which have been applied by the Commission and the Community courts regarding the compatibility of a concentration with the common market, this Regulation should accordingly establish the principle that a concentration

with a Community dimension which would significantly impede effective competition, in the common market or in a substantial part thereof, in particular as a result of the creation or strengthening of a dominant position, is to be declared incompatible with the common market.

(27) In addition, the criteria of Article 81(1) and (3) of the Treaty should be applied to joint ventures performing, on a lasting basis, all the functions of autonomous economic entities, to the extent that their creation has as its consequence an appreciable restriction of competition between undertakings that remain independent. * * *

(29) In order to determine the impact of a concentration on competition in the common market, it is appropriate to take account of any substantiated and likely efficiencies put forward by the undertakings concerned. It is possible that the efficiencies brought about by the concentration counteract the effects on competition, and in particular the potential harm to consumers, that it might otherwise have and that, as a consequence, the concentration would not significantly impede effective competition, in the common market or in a substantial part of it, in particular as a result of the creation or strengthening of a dominant position. The Commission should publish guidance on the conditions under which it may take efficiencies into account in the assessment of a concentration. * * *

(32) Concentrations which, by reason of the limited market share of the undertakings concerned, are not liable to impede effective competition may be presumed to be compatible with the common market. Without prejudice to Articles 81 and 82 of the Treaty, an indication to this effect exists, in particular, where the market share of the undertakings concerned does not exceed 25 % either in the common market or in a substantial part of it. * * *

(34) To ensure effective control, undertakings should be obliged to give prior notification of concentrations with a Community dimension following the conclusion of the agreement, the announcement of the public bid or the acquisition of a controlling interest. Notification should also be possible where the undertakings concerned satisfy the Commission of their intention to enter into an agreement for a proposed concentration and demonstrate to the Commission that their plan for that proposed concentration is sufficiently concrete, for example on the basis of an agreement in principle, a memorandum of understanding, or a letter of intent signed by all undertakings concerned. * * *

(35) A period within which the Commission must initiate proceedings in respect of a notified concentration and a period within which it must take a final decision on the compatibility or incompatibility with the common market of that concentration should be laid down. * * *

HAS ADOPTED THIS REGULATION:

2. The EC's 2004 Merger Control Regulation

Article 1 **Scope.** 1. [T]his Regulation shall apply to all concentrations with a Community dimension as defined in this Article.

2. A concentration has a Community dimension where: (a) the combined aggregate worldwide turnover of all the undertakings concerned is more than EUR 5 000 million; and (b) the aggregate Community-wide turnover of each of at least two of the undertakings concerned is more than EUR 250 million, unless each of the undertakings concerned achieves more than two-thirds of its aggregate Community-wide turnover within one and the same Member State.

3. A concentration that does not meet the thresholds laid down in paragraph 2 has a Community dimension where:

(a) the combined aggregate worldwide turnover of all the undertakings concerned is more than EUR 2 500 million;

(b) in each of at least three Member States, the combined aggregate turnover of all the undertakings concerned is more than EUR 100 million;

(c) in each of at least three Member States included for the purpose of point (b), the aggregate turnover of each of at least two of the undertakings concerned is more than EUR 25 million; and

(d) the aggregate Community-wide turnover of each of at least two of the undertakings concerned is more than EUR 100 million, unless each of the undertakings concerned achieves more than two-thirds of its aggregate Community-wide turnover within one and the same Member State. * * *

Article 2 **Appraisal of concentrations [The substantive rule for examining mergers].** 1. Concentrations within the scope of this Regulation shall be appraised in accordance with the objectives of this Regulation and the following provisions with a view to establishing whether or not they are compatible with the common market. In making this appraisal, the Commission shall take into account:

(a) the need to maintain and develop effective competition within the common market in view of, among other things, the structure of all the markets concerned and the actual or potential competition from undertakings located either within or without the Community;

(b) the market position of the undertakings concerned and their economic and financial power, the alternatives available to suppliers and users, their access to supplies or markets, any legal or other barriers to entry, supply and demand trends for the relevant goods and services, the interests of the intermediate and ultimate consumers, and the development of technical and economic progress provided that it is to consumers' advantage and does not form an obstacle to competition.

2. A concentration which would not significantly impede effective competition in the common market or in a substantial part of it, in particular as a result of the creation or strengthening of a dominant position, shall be declared compatible with the common market.

3. A concentration which would significantly impede effective competition, in the common market or in a substantial part of it, in particular as a result of the creation or strengthening of a dominant position, shall be declared incompatible with the common market. * * *

5. In making this appraisal, the Commission shall take into account in particular:— whether two or more parent companies retain, to a significant extent, activities in the same market as the joint venture or in a market which is downstream or upstream from that of the joint venture or in a neighboring market closely related to this market,— whether the coordination which is the direct consequence of the creation of the joint venture affords the undertakings concerned the possibility of eliminating competition in respect of a substantial part of the products or services in question.

Article 3 **Definition of concentration.** 1. A concentration shall be deemed to arise where a change of control on a lasting basis results from:

(a) the merger of two or more previously independent undertakings or parts of undertakings, or

(b) the acquisition, by one or more persons already controlling at least one undertaking, or by one or more undertakings, whether by purchase of securities or assets, by contract or by any other means, of direct or indirect control of the whole or parts of one or more other undertakings.

2. Control shall be constituted by rights, contracts or any other means which, either separately or in combination and having regard to the considerations of fact or law involved, confer the possibility of exercising decisive influence on an undertaking. * * *

Article 4 **Prior notification of concentrations and pre-notification referral at the request of the notifying parties.** 1. Concentrations with a Community dimension defined in this Regulation shall be notified to the Commission prior to their implementation and following the conclusion of the agreement, the announcement of the public bid, or the acquisition of a controlling interest. Notification may also be made where the undertakings concerned demonstrate to the Commission a good faith intention to conclude an agreement or, in the case of a public bid, where they have publicly announced an intention to make such a bid, provided that the intended agreement or bid would result in a concentration with a Community dimension. * * *

Article 5 **Calculation of turnover.** 1. Aggregate turnover within the meaning of this Regulation shall comprise the amounts derived by the undertakings concerned in the preceding financial year from the sale of products and the provision of services falling within the undertakings' ordinary activities after deduction of sales rebates and of value added tax and other taxes directly related to turnover. * * *

Article 6 **Examination of the notification and initiation of proceedings.** 1. The Commission shall examine the notification as soon as it is received.

(a) Where it concludes that the concentration notified does not fall within the scope of this Regulation, it shall record that finding by means of a decision.

(b) Where it finds that the concentration notified, although falling within the scope of this Regulation, does not raise serious doubts as to its compatibility with the common market, it shall decide not to oppose it and shall declare that it is compatible with the common market. * * *

(c) Without prejudice to paragraph 2, where the Commission finds that the concentration notified falls within the scope of this Regulation and raises serious doubts as to its compatibility with the common market, it shall decide to initiate proceedings. Without prejudice to Article 9, such proceedings shall be closed by means of a decision as provided for in Article 8(1) to (4), unless the undertakings concerned have demonstrated to the satisfaction of the Commission that they have abandoned the concentration.

2. Where the Commission finds that, following modification by the undertakings concerned, a notified concentration no longer raises serious doubts within the meaning of paragraph 1(c), it shall declare the concentration compatible with the common market pursuant to paragraph 1(b). The Commission may attach to its decision under paragraph 1(b) conditions and obligations intended to ensure that the undertakings concerned comply with the commitments they have entered into vis-à-vis the Commission with a view to rendering the concentration compatible with the common market. * * *

Article 7 **Suspension of concentrations.** 1. A concentration with a Community dimension as defined in Article 1, or which is to be examined by the Commission pursuant to Article 4(5), shall not be implemented either before its notification or until it has been declared compatible with the common market pursuant to a decision under Articles 6(1)(b), 8(1) or 8(2), or on the basis of a presumption according to Article 10(6).

2. Paragraph 1 shall not prevent the implementation of a public bid or of a series of transactions in securities including those convertible into other securities admitted to trading on a market such as a stock exchange, by which control within the meaning of Article 3 is acquired from various sellers, provided that:

(a) the concentration is notified to the Commission pursuant to Article 4 without delay; and

(b) the acquirer does not exercise the voting rights attached to the securities in question or does so only to maintain the full value of its investments based on a derogation granted by the Commission under paragraph 3. * * *

Article 8 **Powers of decision of the Commission.** 1. Where the Commission finds that a notified concentration fulfils the criterion laid down in Article 2(2) and, in the cases referred to in Article 2(4), the criteria laid down in Article 81(3) of the Treaty, it shall issue a decision declaring the concentration compatible with the common market. A decision declaring a concentration compatible shall be deemed to cover restrictions directly related and necessary to the implementation of the concentration.

2. Where the Commission finds that, following modification by the undertakings concerned, a notified concentration fulfils the criterion laid down in Article 2(2) and, in the cases referred to in Article 2(4), the criteria laid down in Article 81(3) of the Treaty, it shall issue a decision declaring the concentration compatible with the common market. The Commission may attach to its decision conditions and obligations intended to ensure that the undertakings concerned comply with the commitments they have entered into vis-à-vis the Commission with a view to rendering the concentration compatible with the common market. * * *

3. Where the Commission finds that a concentration fulfils the criterion defined in Article 2(3) or, in the cases referred to in Article 2(4), does not fulfill the criteria laid down in Article 81(3) of the Treaty, it shall issue a decision declaring that the concentration is incompatible with the common market. * * *

Article 10 **Time limits for initiating proceedings and for decisions.** 1. Without prejudice to Article 6(4), the decisions referred to in Article 6(1) [to not oppose or to initiate proceedings] shall be taken within 25 working days at most. [This is what is known as a Phase I decision]* * * That period shall be increased to 35 working days where * * * the undertakings concerned offer commitments pursuant to Article 6(2) with a view to rendering the concentration compatible with the common market.

2. Decisions pursuant to Article 8(1) or (2) [decisions after initiation of proceedings, that is, during Phase II, not to oppose] concerning notified concentrations shall be taken as soon as it appears that the serious doubts referred to in Article 6(1)(c) have been removed, particularly as a result of modifications made by the undertakings concerned, and at the latest by the time limit laid down in paragraph 3.

3. [D]ecisions pursuant to Article 8(1) to (3) concerning notified concentrations [Phase II decisions] shall be taken within not more than 90 working days of the date on which the proceedings are initiated. That period shall be increased to 105 working days where the undertakings concerned offer commitments pursuant to Article 8(2), second subparagraph, with a view to rendering the concentration compatible with the common market, unless these commitments have been offered less than 55 working days after the initiation of proceedings. The periods set by the first subparagraph shall likewise be extended if the notifying parties make a request to that effect not later than 15 working days after the initiation of proceedings pursuant to Article 6(1)(c). * * *

Article 18 **Hearing of the parties and of third persons.** 1. Before taking any decision provided for in Article 6(3), Article 7(3), Article 8(2) to (6), and Articles 14 and 15, the Commission shall give the persons, undertakings and associations of undertakings concerned the opportunity, at every stage of the procedure up to the consultation of the Advisory Committee, of making known their views on the objections against them. * * *

Article 20 **Publication of decisions.** 1. The Commission shall publish the decisions which it takes pursuant to Article 8(1) to (6), Articles 14 and 15 with the exception of provisional decisions taken in accordance with Article 18(2) together with the opinion of the Advisory Committee in the *Official Journal of the European Union.* * * *

Questions

When and under what circumstances is prior notification of a merger or acquisition required under the EC's Merger Control Regulation? [*See* Articles 1 and 4] Under what circumstances can a notification be filed prior to the completion of an acquisition agreement? [*See* Article 4] How long after receipt of the notification does the Commission have to decide whether to initiate a proceeding? [*See* Articles 6(1) and 10(1)] What standards does the Commission apply in assessing the competitive effects of an acquisition? [*See* Article 2] Is there an efficiency defense? [*See* Article 2] How long after initiation of a proceeding under Article 6(1)(c), that is, a Phase II investigation, does the Commission have to decide whether the acquisition is incompatible with the common market? [*See* Articles 2(2), 2(3), 8 and 10)]

E. Pre-Merger Notification in the EC

Commission Regulation (EC) No 802/2004 of 7 April 2004 Implementing Council Regulation (EC) No 139/2004 on the Control of Concentrations between Undertakings

Annex I

Form CO Relating to the Notification of a Concentration pursuant to Regulation (EC) No 139/2004

Section 1. Introduction. 1.1. * * * This Form specifies the information that must be provided by notifying parties when submitting a notification to the European Commission of a proposed merger, acquisition or other concentration. * * *

1.6. **Definitions and instructions for purposes of this Form** * * * **Affected markets:** Section 6 of this Form requires the notifying parties to define the relevant product markets, and further to identify which of those relevant markets are likely to be affected by the notified operation. This definition of affected market is used as the basis for requiring information for a number of other questions contained in this Form. The definitions thus submitted by the notifying parties are referred to in this Form as the affected market(s). This term can refer to a relevant market made up either of products or of services.

Description of the concentration. Provide an executive summary of the concentration, specifying the parties to the concentration, the nature of the concentration (for example, merger, acquisition, or joint venture), the areas of activity of the notifying parties, the markets on which the concentration will have an impact (including the main affected markets (1)), and the strategic and economic rationale for the concentration. * * *

Section 6. Market definitions. The relevant product and geographic markets determine the scope within which the market power of the new entity resulting from the concentration must be assessed.[25] The notifying party or parties must provide the data requested having regard to the following definitions:

Relevant product markets: A relevant product market comprises all those products and/or services which are regarded as interchangeable or substitutable by the consumer, by reason of the products' characteristics, their prices and their intended use. A relevant product market may in some cases be composed of a number of individual products and/or services which present largely identical physical or technical characteristics and are interchangeable. Factors relevant to the assessment of the relevant product market include the analysis of why the products or services in these markets are included and why others are excluded by using the above definition, and having regard to, for example, substitutability, conditions of competition, prices, cross-price elasticity of demand or other factors relevant for the definition of the product markets (for example, supply-side substitutability in appropriate cases).

Relevant geographic markets: The relevant geographic market comprises the area in which the undertakings concerned are involved in the supply and demand of relevant products or services, in which the conditions of competition are sufficiently homogeneous and which can be distinguished from neighbouring geographic areas because, in particular, conditions of competition are appreciably different in those areas.

Affected markets: For purposes of information required in this Form, affected markets consist of relevant product markets where, in * * * the Community, * * * [or] in any Member State:

(a) two or more of the parties to the concentration are engaged in business activities in the same product market and where the concentration will lead to a combined market share of 15 % or more. These are horizontal relationships;

(b) one or more of the parties to the concentration are engaged in business activities in a product market, which is upstream or downstream of a product market in which any other party to the concentration is engaged, and any of their individual or combined market shares at either level is 25 % or more, regardless of whether there is or is not any existing supplier/customer relationship between the parties to the concentration. These are vertical relationships.

On the basis of the above definitions and market share thresholds, provide the following information: * * * Identify each affected market * * * at: the * * * Community * * * level; [and] the individual Member States * * * level.

Section 7. Information on affected markets. For each affected relevant product market, for each of the last three financial years * * * (b) for the Community as a whole; [and] (d) individually for each Member State * * * where the parties to the concentration do business; * * *; provide the following:

7.1. an estimate of the total size of the market in terms of sales value (in euros) and volume (units). * * *;

25. *See* Commission Notice on the definition of the relevant market for the purposes of Community competition law. Factors relevant to the assessment of the relevant geographic market include inter alia the nature and characteristics of the products or services concerned, the existence of entry barriers, consumer preferences, appreciable differences in the undertakings' market shares between neighboring geographic areas or substantial price differences.

7.2. the sales in value and volume, as well as an estimate of the market shares, of each of the parties to the concentration;

7.3. an estimate of the market share in value (and where appropriate, volume) of all competitors (including importers) having at least 5% of the geographic market under consideration. On this basis, provide an estimate of the HHI index pre- and post-merger, and the difference between the two (the delta). Indicate the proportion of market shares used as a basis to calculate the HHI. Identify the sources used to calculate these market shares and provide documents where available to confirm the calculation; * * *

7.9. the nature and extent of vertical integration of each of the parties to the concentration compared with their largest competitors.

Section 8. General conditions in affected markets. [Structure of Supply in the affected markets] 8.1. Identify the five largest independent suppliers to the parties to the concentration and their individual shares of purchases from each of these suppliers (of raw materials or goods used for purposes of producing the relevant products). * * *

Structure of demand in affected markets. 8.6. Identify the five largest independent customers of the parties in each affected market and their individual share of total sales for such products accounted for by each of those customers. * * *

Market entry. 8.8. Over the last five years, has there been any significant entry into any affected markets? If so, identify such entrants. * * * If any of the parties to the concentration entered an affected market in the past five years, provide an analysis of the barriers to entry encountered.

8.9. In the opinion of the notifying parties, are there undertakings * * * that are likely to enter the market? * * *

8.10. Describe the various factors influencing entry into affected markets, examining entry from both a geographical and product viewpoint. * * *

Section 9. Overall market context and efficiencies. * * * 9.3. Should you wish the Commission specifically to consider from the outset whether efficiency gains generated by the concentration are likely to enhance the ability and incentive of the new entity to act pro-competitively for the benefit of consumers, please provide a description of, and supporting documents relating to, each efficiency (including cost savings, new product introductions, and service or product improvements) that the parties anticipate will result from the proposed concentration relating to any relevant product. * * *

F. European Commission's Guidelines on Market Definition

Commission Notice on the Definition of the Relevant Market for the Purposes of Community Competition Law

(1997)

Introduction. The purpose of this notice is to provide guidance as to how the Commission applies the concept of relevant product and geographic market in its ongoing enforcement of Community competition law, in particular the application of Regulations 17/62 and 4064/89 [the prior MCR]. * * *

Market definition is a tool to identify and define the boundaries of competition between firms. It allows to establish the framework within which competition policy is applied by the Commission. The main purpose of market definition is to identify in a systematic way the competitive constraints that the undertakings involved face. The objective of defining a market in both its product and geographic dimension is to identify those actual competitors of the undertakings involved that are capable of constraining their behaviour and of preventing them from behaving independently of an effective competitive pressure. It is from this perspective, that the market definition makes it possible, *inter alia*, to calculate market shares that would convey meaningful information regarding market power. * * *

Definition of Relevant Market. Definition of relevant product and relevant geographic market. * * *

Relevant product markets are defined as follows:

"A relevant product market comprises all those products and/or services which are regarded as interchangeable or substitutable by the consumer, by reason of the products' characteristics, their prices and their intended use."

Relevant geographic markets are defined as follows:

"The relevant geographic market comprises the area in which the undertakings concerned are involved in the supply and demand of products or services, in which the conditions of competition are sufficiently homogeneous and which can be distinguished from neighbouring areas because the conditions of competition are appreciably different in those areas".

The relevant market within which to assess a given competition issue is therefore established by the combination of the product and geographic markets. * * *

Basic principles for market definition. Competitive constraints: Firms are subject to three main sources of competitive constraints: demand substitutability, supply substitutability and potential competition. From an economic point of view, for the definition of the relevant market, demand substitution constitutes the most immediate and effective disciplinary force on the suppliers of a given product, in particular in relation to their pricing decisions. A firm or a group of firms cannot have a significant impact on the prevailing conditions of sale, such as prices, if its customers are in a position to switch easily to available substitute products or to suppliers located elsewhere. Basically, the exercise of market definition consists in identifying the effective alternative sources of supply for the customers of the undertakings involved, both in terms of products/services and geographic location of suppliers.

The competitive constraints arising from supply side substitutability * * * and from potential competition are in general less immediate and in any case require an analysis of additional factors. As a result such constraints are taken into account at the assessment stage of competition analysis. * * *

Demand substitution: The assessment of demand substitution entails a determination of the range of products which are viewed as substitutes by the consumer. One way of making this determination can be viewed, as a thought experiment, postulating a hypothetical small, non-transitory change in relative prices and evaluating the likely reactions of customers to that increase. * * *

Conceptually, this approach implies that starting from the type of products that the undertakings involved sell and the area in which they sell them, additional products and areas will be included into or excluded from the market definition depending on whether competition from these other products and areas affect or restrain sufficiently the pricing of the parties' products in the short term.

The question to be answered is whether the parties' customers would switch to readily available substitutes or to suppliers located elsewhere in response to an hypothetical small (in the range 5%–10%), permanent relative price increase in the products and areas being considered. If substitution would be enough to make the price increase unprofitable because of the resulting loss of sales, additional substitutes and areas are included in the relevant market. This would be done until the set of products and geographic areas is such that small, permanent increases in relative prices would be profitable. * * *

Supply substitution: Supply-side substitutability may also be taken into account when defining markets in those situations in which its effects are equivalent to those of demand substitution in terms of effectiveness and immediacy. This requires that suppliers be able to switch production to the relevant products and market them in the short term without incurring significant additional costs or risks in response to small and permanent changes in relative prices. When these conditions are met, the additional production that is put on the market will have a disciplinary effect on the competitive behaviour of the companies involved. Such an impact in terms of effectiveness and immediacy is equivalent to the demand substitution effect. * * *

Potential competition: The third source of competitive constraint, potential competition, is not taken into account when defining markets, since the conditions under which potential competition will actually represent an effective competitive constraint depend on the analysis of specific factors and circumstances related to the conditions of entry. * * *

Evidence Relied Upon to Define Relevant Markets. * * * The type of evidence the Commission considers relevant to assess whether two products are demand substitutes can be categorized as follows: Evidence of substitution in the recent past * * * [and] quantitative tests that have specifically been designed for the purpose of delineating markets. These tests consist of various econometric and statistical approaches: estimates of elasticities and cross-price elasticities[26] for the demand of a product, tests based on similarity of price movements over time, the analysis of causality between price series and similarity of price levels and/or their convergence. * * *

G. European Commission's 2004 Horizontal Merger Guidelines

European Commission Guidelines on the Assessment of Horizontal Mergers under the Council Regulation on the Control of Concentrations between Undertakings

Introduction. 1. Article 2 of Council Regulation (EC) No 139/2004 of 20 January 2004 on the control of concentrations between undertakings (hereinafter: the 'Merger Regulation') provides that the Commission has to appraise concentrations within the scope of the Merger Regulation with a view to establishing whether or not they are compatible with the common market. For that purpose, the Commission must assess, pursuant to Article 2(2) and (3), whether or not a concentration would significantly impede effective competition, in particular as a result of the creation or strengthening of a dominant position, in the common market or a substantial part of it. * * *

5. The purpose of this notice is to provide guidance as to how the Commission assesses concentrations when the undertakings concerned are actual or potential competitors on the same relevant market. In this notice such mergers will be denoted 'horizontal mergers'. While the notice presents the analytical approach used by the Commission in its appraisal of horizontal mergers it cannot provide details of all possible applications of this approach.

---

26. Own price elasticity of demand for product X is a measure of the responsiveness of demand for X to percentage change in its own price. Cross-price elasticity between products X and Y is the responsiveness of demand for product X to percentage change in the price of product Y.

The Commission applies the approach described in the notice to the particular facts and circumstances of each case. * * *

Overview. * * * 11. This notice is structured around the following elements:

(a) The approach of the Commission to market shares and concentration thresholds.

(b) The likelihood that a merger would have anticompetitive effects in the relevant market. * * *

(c) The likelihood that buyer power would act as a countervailing factor. * * *

(d) The likelihood that entry would maintain effective competition in the relevant markets.

(e) The likelihood that efficiencies would act as a factor counteracting the harmful effects on competition which might otherwise result from the merger.

(f) The conditions for a failing firm defense. * * *

Market Share and Concentration Levels. 14. Market shares and concentration levels provide useful first indications of the market structure and of the competitive importance of both the merging parties and their competitors.

15. Normally, the Commission uses current market shares in its competitive analysis. However, current market shares may be adjusted to reflect reasonably certain future changes, for instance in the light of exit, entry or expansion. Post-merger market shares are calculated on the assumption that the post-merger combined market share of the merging parties is the sum of their pre-merger market shares. * * *

16. The overall concentration level in a market may also provide useful information about the competitive situation. In order to measure concentration levels, the Commission often applies the Herfindahl-Hirschman Index (HHI). [*See* Section 8.23.A for computation of the HHI] * * *

Market share levels: 17. According to well-established case law, very large market shares—50% or more—may in themselves be evidence of the existence of a dominant market position. However, smaller competitors may act as a sufficient constraining influence if, for example, they have the ability and incentive to increase their supplies. A merger involving a firm whose market share will remain below 50% after the merger may also raise competition concerns in view of other factors such as the strength and number of competitors, the presence of capacity constraints or the extent to which the products of the merging parties are close substitutes. The Commission has thus in several cases considered mergers resulting in firms holding market shares between 40% and 50%, and in some cases below 40%, to lead to the creation or the strengthening of a dominant position.

18. Concentrations which, by reason of the limited market share of the undertakings concerned, are not liable to impede effective competition may be presumed to be compatible with the common market. Without prejudice to Articles 81 and 82 of the Treaty, an indication to this effect exists, in particular, where the market share of the undertakings concerned does not exceed 25% either in the common market or in a substantial part of it.

HHI levels. 19. The Commission is unlikely to identify horizontal competition concerns in a market with a post-merger HHI below 1 000. Such markets normally do not require extensive analysis.

20. The Commission is also unlikely to identify horizontal competition concerns in a merger with a post-merger HHI between 1 000 and 2 000 and a delta below 250, or a merger with a post-merger HHI above 2 000 and a delta below 150, except where special circumstances such as, for instance, one or more of the following factors are present:

(a) a merger involves a potential entrant or a recent entrant with a small market share;

(b) one or more merging parties are important innovators in ways not reflected in market shares;

(c) there are significant cross-shareholdings among the market participants;

(d) one of the merging firms is a maverick firm with a high likelihood of disrupting coordinated conduct;

(e) indications of past or ongoing coordination, or facilitating practices, are present;

(f) one of the merging parties has a pre-merger market share of 50 % of more.

21. Each of these HHI levels, in combination with the relevant deltas, may be used as an initial indicator of the absence of competition concerns. However, they do not give rise to a presumption of either the existence or the absence of such concerns.

Possible Anti-Competitive Effects Of Horizontal Mergers. 22. There are two main ways in which horizontal mergers may significantly impede effective competition, in particular by creating or strengthening a dominant position:

(a) by eliminating important competitive constraints on one or more firms, which consequently would have increased market power, without resorting to coordinated behaviour (non-coordinated effects);

(b) by changing the nature of competition in such a way that firms that previously were not coordinating their behaviour, are now significantly more likely to coordinate and raise prices or otherwise harm effective competition. A merger may also make coordination easier, more stable or more effective for firms which were coordinating prior to the merger (coordinated effects).

23. The Commission assesses whether the changes brought about by the merger would result in any of these effects. Both instances mentioned above may be relevant when assessing a particular transaction.

Non-coordinated effects. 24. A merger may significantly impede effective competition in a market by removing important competitive constraints on one or more sellers, who consequently have increased market power. The most direct effect of the merger will be the loss of competition between the merging firms. For example, if prior to the merger one of the merging firms had raised its price, it would have lost some sales to the other merging firm. The merger removes this particular constraint. Non-merging firms in the same market can also benefit from the reduction of competitive pressure that results from the merger, since the merging firms' price increase may switch some demand to the rival firms, which, in turn, may find it profitable to increase their prices. The reduction in these competitive constraints could lead to significant price increases in the relevant market.

25. Generally, a merger giving rise to such non-coordinated effects would significantly impede effective competition by creating or strengthening the dominant position of a single firm, one which, typically, would have an appreciably larger market share than the next competitor post-merger. Furthermore, mergers in oligopolistic markets involving the elimination of important competitive constraints that the merging parties previously exerted upon each other together with a reduction of competitive pressure on the remaining competitors may, even where there is little likelihood of coordination between the members of the oligopoly, also result in a significant impediment to competition. The Merger Regulation clarifies that all mergers giving rise to such non-coordinated effects shall also be declared incompatible with the common market. * * *

Coordinated effects. 39. In some markets the structure may be such that firms would consider it possible, economically rational, and hence preferable, to adopt on a sustainable basis a course of action on the market aimed at selling at increased prices. A merger in a concentrated market may significantly impede effective competition, through the creation or the strengthening of a collective dominant position, because it increases the likelihood that firms are able to coordinate their behaviour in this way and raise prices, even without entering into an agreement or resorting to a concerted practice within the meaning of Article 81 of the Treaty. A merger may also make coordination easier, more stable or more effective for firms, that were already coordinating before the merger, either by making the coordination more robust or by permitting firms to coordinate on even higher prices. * * *

Reaching terms of coordination 44. Coordination is more likely to emerge if competitors can easily arrive at a common perception as to how the coordination should work. * * *

Monitoring deviations. 49. Coordinating firms are often tempted to increase their share of the market by deviating from the terms of coordination, for instance by lowering prices, offering secret discounts, increasing product quality or capacity or trying to win new customers. Only the credible threat of timely and sufficient retaliation keeps firms from deviating. Markets therefore need to be sufficiently transparent to allow the coordinating firms to monitor to a sufficient degree whether other firms are deviating, and thus know when to retaliate. * * *

Deterrent mechanisms. 52. Coordination is not sustainable unless the consequences of deviation are sufficiently severe to convince coordinating firms that it is in their best interest to adhere to the terms of coordination. It is thus the threat of future retaliation that keeps the coordination sustainable. * * *

Merger with a potential competitor. 58. Concentrations where an undertaking already active on a relevant market merges with a potential competitor in this market can have similar anti-competitive effects to mergers between two undertakings already active on the same relevant market and, thus, significantly impede effective competition, in particular through the creation or the strengthening of a dominant position. * * *

Mergers creating or strengthening buyer power in upstream markets. 61. The Commission may also analyse to what extent a merged entity will increase its buyer power in upstream markets. * * *

Countervailing Buyer Power. 64. The competitive pressure on a supplier is not only exercised by competitors but can also come from its customers. Even firms with very high market shares may not be in a position, post-merger, to significantly impede effective competition, in particular by acting to an appreciable extent independently of their customers, if the latter possess countervailing buyer power. * * *

Entry. 68. When entering a market is sufficiently easy, a merger is unlikely to pose any significant anti-competitive risk. Therefore, entry analysis constitutes an important element of the overall competitive assessment. For entry to be considered a sufficient competitive constraint on the merging parties, it must be shown to be likely, timely and sufficient to deter or defeat any potential anti-competitive effects of the merger. * * *

Efficiencies. 76. * * * It is possible that efficiencies brought about by a merger counteract the effects on competition and in particular the potential harm to consumers that it might otherwise have. In order to assess whether a merger would significantly impede effective competition, in particular through the creation or the strengthening of a dominant position, within the meaning of Article 2(2) and (3) of the Merger Regulation, the Commission performs an overall competitive appraisal of the merger. In making this appraisal, the Commission takes into account the factors mentioned in Article 2(1), including the development of technical and economic progress provided that it is to the consumers' advantage and does not form an obstacle to competition.

77. The Commission considers any substantiated efficiency claim in the overall assessment of the merger. It may decide that, as a consequence of the efficiencies that the merger brings about, there are no grounds for declaring the merger incompatible with the common market pursuant to Article 2(3) of the Merger Regulation. This will be the case when the Commission is in a position to conclude on the basis of sufficient evidence that the efficiencies generated by the merger are likely to enhance the ability and incentive of the merged entity to act pro-competitively for the benefit of consumers, thereby counteracting the adverse effects on competition which the merger might otherwise have.

78. For the Commission to take account of efficiency claims in its assessment of the merger and be in a position to reach the conclusion that as a consequence of efficiencies, there are no grounds for declaring the merger to be incompatible with the common market, the efficiencies have to benefit consumers, be merger-specific and be verifiable. These conditions are cumulative. * * *

Failing Firm. 89. The Commission may decide that an otherwise problematic merger is nevertheless compatible with the common market if one of the merging parties is a failing firm. * * *

H. EU-U.S. Best Practices in Merger Enforcement

United States and European Union Antitrust Agencies Issue "Best Practices" for Coordinating Merger Reviews

Department of Justice Press Release
(October 30, 2002)

WASHINGTON, D.C. Charles A. James, Assistant Attorney General for the Antitrust Division, Federal Trade Commission Chairman Timothy Muris and European Union Competition Commissioner Mario Monti today released a set of "best practices" for coordinating future merger reviews. * * *

The objectives of the best practices are to enhance cooperation between the U.S. antitrust agencies and the European Commission in merger review, minimize the risk of divergent outcomes and reduce burdens on parties participating in merger investigations. * * *

"The 'best practices' we released today institutionalize important forms of cooperation between the U.S. and EU antitrust authorities on merger reviews and publicly confirm our commitment to cooperate closely with our friends across the Atlantic," said Mr. James. * * *

The best practices recommend that investigative staffs establish schedules for conferring with each other and encourage senior antitrust officials in the United States and the European Union to engage in discussions at key moments of one another's investigations. They also offer merging parties a meeting at an early point in each review to discuss timing issues. In addition, the best practices encourage joint interviews of parties and third-parties, where appropriate, and provide for increased coordination with respect to remedies. * * *

I. European Commission's Decision in the Boeing Acquisition of McDonnell Douglas

See also FTC action in this case in Chapter 8.

The Commission Clears the Merger between Boeing and McDonnell Douglas under Conditions and Obligations

Press Release

(July 30, 1997)

The European Commission has decided to declare the acquisition by The Boeing Company (Boeing) of the McDonnell Douglas Corporation (MDC) compatible with the common market subject to full compliance by Boeing with commitments submitted to the Commission. The Commission has found that the proposed merger leads to a significant strengthening of Boeing's already existing dominant position in the worldwide market for large commercial jet aircraft. The Commission considers that this strengthening arises from MDC's own competitive potential in large commercial jet aircraft, from the enhanced opportunity for Boeing to enter into long-term exclusive supply deals with airlines (already exemplified by those with American, Continental and Delta), and from the acquisition of MDC's defense and space activities, which latter confer advantages in the commercial aircraft sector through "spill-over" effects in the form of R&D benefits and technology transfer.

Boeing, in the course of intensive negotiations with the Commission, has offered commitments to resolve the competition problems identified by the Commission.

These include: the cessation of existing and future exclusive supply deals. * * *

These commitments are considered adequate to resolve the identified competition problems, and the Commission has therefore decided to declare the operation compatible with the common market subject to conditions and obligations. * * *

The market for large commercial jet aircraft is world-wide and the EU is an integral and important part of this world market, with a similar competitive structure. European airlines are forecast to account for almost a third of future demand over the next ten years, and Boeing and MDC's combined market share is about two thirds of the EU market.

In arriving at this decision the Commission has taken into account concerns expressed by the U.S. Government relating to important US defense interests. The Commission took the US Government's concerns into consideration to the extent consistent with EU law, and has limited the scope of its action to the civil side of the operation, including the effects of the merger on the commercial jet aircraft market resulting from the combination of Boeing's and MDC's large defense and space interests.

[T]he Commission has found that Boeing, a fully integrated civil and military aerospace company, already has a dominant position in the world-wide market for large commercial jet aircraft. Boeing's existing dominance stems from its very high market share (64% world-wide), the size of its fleet in service (60% world-wide), and the fact that it is the only manufacturer that offers a complete family of aircraft. This position cannot be challenged by potential new entrants, given the extremely high barriers to entry in this hugely capital intensive market. Boeing's dominance is further demonstrated by the recent conclusion of long-term exclusive supply deals with three of the world's leading carriers, American, Delta and Continental Airlines, who would have been unlikely to lock themselves into twenty year agreements with a supplier who did not already dominate, and seem likely to continue to dominate, the large jet aircraft market.

The most immediate reinforcement of Boeing's dominance in large commercial jet aircraft would arise through Boeing's increase in overall market share (in terms of current order backlog) from 64% to 70%. Moreover, Boeing could add to its already existing monopoly in the largest wide-body aircraft segment (the segment of the Boeing 747) a further monopoly in the smallest narrow-body segment.

The Commission recognises that Douglas Aircraft Company (DAC, the commercial aircraft division of MDC) has suffered a decline in its business performance in recent years (although the potential success of the MD95 has not yet been tested). This decline has been due to a level of investment which has been low relative to that of Boeing and Airbus, and seems likely to have been exacerbated by a fall in customer and investor confidence following MDC's abandonment of the MDXX program, and indeed the announcement of the proposed Boeing take-over. Nevertheless, Boeing itself has declared since that announcement that it would be able to benefit from DAC's remaining competitive potential. The acquisition of such an advantage constitutes a strengthening of a dominant position under EU law.

Another vital element in the strengthening of Boeing's dominance would result from the large increase of Boeing's customer base, from 60% to 84% of the current world-wide fleet in service. By ensuring preferential access to this customer base, Boeing would increase opportunities for future sales through significant leverage over existing MDC aircraft users (through customer support services for example). * * *

Although the Commission's investigation did not lead it to conclude that the proposed merger would create or strengthen dominance in the defense or space sectors, the Commission considers that Boeing's dominant position on the civil aircraft market would be significantly strengthened as a result of the addition of MDC's defense and space business. * * *

Boeing has proposed remedies. * * * In view of the impossibility of a divestment of DAC, Boeing commits itself to maintain DAC as a separate legal entity for a period of ten years and to supply to the Commission reports, publicly available and certified by an independent auditor, on DAC's results. * * *

J. Appeals of Commission Decisions to the Court of First Instance

1. Introduction to the Court of First Instance

The decisions of the European Commission on competition matters are appealable to the Court of First Instance, which is a division of the European Court of Justice. In certain limited cases, competition decisions of the Court of First Instance are appealable to the Court of Justice. Appeals from Commission decisions may be filed not only by the merging parties but also by competitors or customers of the merging parties. For example, in the BMG-Sony merger, the Commission approved the transaction, and certain competitors successfully appealed the decision in the Court of First Instance.

A brief excerpt from the Court of First Instance's decision in *GE-Honeywell* is set out below, and several of the Court's principal cases under the Section 2 of the 1989 MCR are discussed in Section 20:4.2[C] of Thompson, *Mergers, Acquisitions and Tender Offers*, *supra* Section 1.10. Paragraph 26 of the preamble to the 2004 MCR (Section 26.20.D.1), makes it clear that the court decisions rendered under this 1989 substantive standard have precedential value under the 2004 MCR.

2. The Substantive Standard under the 1989 MCR and Its Relationship to the Substantive Standard under the 2004 MCR

Article 2(3) of the 1989 MCR provides:

> A concentration which creates or strengthens a dominant position as a result of which effective competition would be significantly impeded in the common

market or in a substantial part of it shall be declared incompatible with the common market.

The "significantly impede effective competition" standard of Article 2 of the 2004 MCR is set out in Section 26.20.D.2. Paragraph 25 of the preamble to the 2004 MCR (Section 26.20.D.1) makes it clear that this standard can apply to "non-coordinated" behavior. This new standard was adopted to address what many thought was a "gap" in the coverage of the 1989 test as indicated in the *Airtours* case.

3. Single Firm Dominance—Court of First Instance's 2005 Decision in *GE-Honeywell*

General Electric Company v. Commission of the European Communities

Judgment of EU's Court of First Instance, Case T-210/01, December 14, 2005

Registrar: J. Plingers, Administrator,

Legal context * * *

4 On 22 October 2000, GE and Honeywell entered into an agreement under which GE would acquire Honeywell's entire share capital ('the merger'), Honeywell becoming a wholly-owned subsidiary of GE. * * *

11 On 3 July 2001, [the Commission declared] the merger incompatible with the common market * * * ('the contested decision'). * * *

14 According to the Commission, GE was itself already in a dominant position on the world market for jet engines for * * * large regional aircraft (hereinafter also referred to as 'large regional jet aircraft engines') * * *

16 In addition, the Commission concluded that GE's pre-merger dominance on the world market for large regional jet aircraft engines would be strengthened. * * *

Horizontal overlaps

474 The applicant submits, with regard to the reasons in the contested decision concerning horizontal overlaps between the merging parties' products for large regional jet aircraft engines * * * [the Commission] was wrong to conclude that dominant positions would be created with anti-competitive effects. * * *

b) Findings of the Court

Market definition * * *

538 [I]t is not established in the present case that the Commission made an error of fact in finding four-engine large regional aircraft powered by Honeywell engines to be in competition with two-engine large regional aircraft powered by GE engines. * * *

The applicant's pre-merger dominance

539 Having thus defined the market for large regional aircraft, the Commission found that the applicant was dominant on that market and that its dominance would be strengthened as a result of the merger. To support that finding, it states that, as regards the installed base of engines on aircraft in that category, the merger would allow GE to move from a market share of [40–50]% to [90–100]% for those aircraft overall and from [60–70]% to 100% for only those aircraft still in production (recital 84 of the contested decision). * * *

540 It is sufficient to observe, in relation to the existence of the applicant's pre-merger dominance in the present case, that, according to settled case-law, although the importance of the market shares may vary from one market to another, very large shares are in

themselves, and save in exceptional circumstances, evidence of the existence of a dominant position. * * *

The strengthening of a dominant position

543 The applicant submits that, in any event, the strengthening of a pre-existing dominant position resulting from the addition of a market share of [10–20]% for existing platforms currently in production, measured in terms of orders, is of little significance, relying in this regard on the fact that the Commission itself recognised, at recital 429 of the contested decision, that the increase was 'rather small'. * * * [T]he increase in market share of around [10–20]% of the market in terms of the order backlog for existing platforms in production must be regarded as significant, since it takes the merged entity's market share to 100%. * * *

563 It must therefore be held, in the context of these proceedings, that the pillar of the contested decision concerning the strengthening of the applicant's dominance by virtue of the horizontal overlap on the market for large regional jet aircraft engines between the manufacturing activities of the two parties to the merger, as a result of which competition on that market would have been significantly impeded in the common market, is sufficiently established. * * *

§ 26.21 EU's Directive on Free Movement of Capital—Prohibitions against Investment Restrictions

A. Introduction

Article 56 of the Treaty Establishing the EU requires that the member states provide for the free movement of capital:

> ***Article 56.***1. Within the framework of the provisions set out in this chapter, all restrictions on the movement of capital between Member States and between Member States and third countries shall be prohibited.
>
> 2. Within the framework of the provisions set out in this chapter, all restrictions on payments [*i.e.*, capital contributions and repatriations] between Member States and between Member States and third countries shall be prohibited.

[A]s indicated in the press release set out below, in April 2006 the EC initiated proceedings against France for violating Article 56 in its adoption of certain investment restrictions (analogues to but much broader than Exon-Florio in the U.S.) designed to wall-off certain French industries from acquisition by non-French firms.

B. EC's 2006 Proceedings against French Investment Restrictions

Free movement of capital: Commission scrutinises French law establishing authorisation procedure for foreign investments in certain sectors

Press Release, IP/06/438
(Brussels, 4 April 2006)

The European Commission has decided to send a formal request to France to submit its observations on the provisions of Decree 2005-1739 of 30 December 2005, which creates an authorisation procedure for foreign investments in certain sectors of activities that could affect public policy, public security or national defence. After informal dialogue on this

text, the Commission has expressed its concern that some of these provisions could act as a disincentive to investment from other Member States, in contradiction with EU Treaty rules on the free movement of capital (Article 56) and the right of establishment (Article 43). The Commission's request takes the form of a letter of formal notice, the first stage of infringement procedures under Article 226 of the EC Treaty. France is asked to send its reply within two months. Depending on the analysis of this reply and the continued dialogue that has taken place on this Decree, the Commission will decide whether or not to issue a formal request to the French Government to amend the legislation in the form of a 'reasoned opinion'.

Although objectives of public policy, public security and national defence may require measures that restrict the fundamental freedoms established by the EC Treaty, the Commission is concerned that the authorisation procedure detailed in the French decree lacks the required proportionality with regard to these objectives.

The Commission considers that the authorisation of investment operations provided for in the Decree might not be suitable for reaching the intended objectives, if the damages that the procedure is supposed to prevent may occur without any investment operation. France is also asked to justify that the procedure would not go beyond what is necessary to the extent that foreign investment operations might not necessarily induce the risks that motivate the requirement for authorisation.

In addition, France is asked to clarify why companies established in the EU but under the control of third-country investors could be submitted to the more stringent procedure applicable to third-country companies, whereas that a company legally and genuinely established in a Member State should normally be treated as a national of that Member State. * * *

Finally, the Commission considers that the inclusion of casinos within the scope of the decree is unsatisfactory given that casinos should be covered by the appropriate transposition of the Money Laundering Directive (2005/60/CE). * * *

Part IV
Cross-Border M&A Case Study No. 1, South African M&A Transactions and Walmart's Acquisition of Massmart[27]

§ 26.22 Scope of Part

A. Introduction to Cross-Border M&A Case Study No. 1: Acquisition by U.S. Acquiror of South African Public Target

This part focuses on various transactions in which a U.S. acquiror corporation (U.S. Acquiror) acquires the stock or assets of a South African target corporation (SA Target),

---

27. I would like to thank Joshua Bam, a 2013 graduate of Penn State Law and a Fellow with the Center for the Study of Mergers and Acquisitions, for his assistance with the preparation of this Part IV.

From 1999 to 2000, I had the great privilege of serving on behalf of the U.S. Treasury Department as the Tax Policy Advisor to the South African Ministry of Finance in Pretoria, South Africa. During that time, I also consulted with the South African Competition Commission on antitrust merger policy and taught a course on Comparative Merger and Acquisition Law at the University of Pretoria which is a publicly held corporation traded on the Johannesburg Stock Exchange (JSE). The part discusses principles of South African corporate, tax, antitrust, and securities laws[28] for a U.S. Acquiror's acquisition of SA Target in three prototypical transactions: (1) a tender offer, (2) a "scheme of arrangement," and (3) a sale of assets and liquidation. This part also discusses general accounting principles and the impact of South African exchange controls.

By necessity, the following transactions are kept simple and designed to illustrate fundamental principles. In the first transaction U.S. Acquiror or its wholly owned South African subsidiary (SA Sub) acquires the stock of SA Target in a tender offer followed by an anticipated second step compulsory acquisition. (Section 26.28) As in the UK, this is the most common form of acquisition transaction in South Africa. As will be seen below, the South African Takeover Regulation Panel prescribes the regulations that govern tender offers and monitors compliance with such regulations.

In the second transaction, U.S. Acquiror or SA Sub acquires all of the stock of SA Target in a transaction that qualifies as a "scheme of arrangement" under the Companies Act of 2008 as amended in 2011 (the SA Companies Act) (Section 26.29). The provisions of the Act governing schemes of arrangements are analogues to U.S. state corporate law merger provisions and are based in large part on similar provisions in UK law. However, unlike the apparent infrequent use of the UK scheme of arrangement provisions, in South Africa, "[t]akeover bids are frequently effected by using the scheme of arrangement procedure."[29] For example, as discussed below, Walmart used a scheme of arrangement in acquiring a controlling interest in South Africa's Massmart.

In the final transaction, U.S. Acquiror or SA Sub acquires all of the assets and certain liabilities of SA Target, which then liquidates, pursuant to provisions of the SA Companies Act of 1973 which are preserved by the Companies Act of 2008, as will be seen *infra*. (Section 26.30)

The consideration paid by U.S. Acquiror in each of the three transactions will either be cash or its stock. Under Part E of Chapter 2 of the SA Companies Act, stock issued to the public must be registered with the Companies and Intellectual Property Commission, which is known as CIPC. The registration requirement is similar to the registration requirement of U.S. law under the Securities Act of 1933 (33 Act). (*See* Chapters 4 and 13) Also, stock issued to a small number of investors may qualify for an exemption from registration that is similar to the private offering exemption that applies under the 33 Act. (*See* Chapter 4)

The income tax aspects of these transactions under the Income Tax Act (the SA Tax Act) is introduced in Section 26.26 and examined in the context of each transaction. The South African Companies Act and Regulations are introduced in Section 26.27 and also examined in the context of each transaction.

Since the antitrust (*i.e.*, competition), exchange control (*i.e.*, getting money into and out of South Africa), and accounting aspects of these transactions are the same for each transaction, this part first examines (1) the impact of the Competition Act of 1998 as amended (the SA Competition Act) on mergers (Section 26.23), (2) the applicability of the South African Exchange Control rules to investments into and remittances from South Africa (Section 26.24), and (3) the accounting treatment of mergers and acquisitions

Law School. Beginning in 2000, I served on an ABA sponsored panel of foreign advisors to the South African Department of Trade and Industry on a project to modernize South Africa's company law, which as discussed *supra* was revised in 2008.

28. South African laws can be accessed via the Acts Online website at http://www.acts.co.za/.

29. Cilliers et al., *South African Entrepreneurial Law*, 298 (2nd Ed. 1999).

under the rules for business combinations promulgated by the South African Institute of Chartered Accountants (SA Accounting Rules) (Section 26.25).

B. Introduction to Walmart's Acquisition of Massmart in Scheme of Arrangement

In order to explore the frequently used scheme of arrangement provisions in South Africa, this part discusses various aspects of Walmart's acquisition of 51% of Massmart in a scheme of arrangement under the SA Companies Act of 1973. Details of the transaction are discussed later in this part, but summarily, Walmart Stores Inc. (a U.S. company publicly traded on the NYSE) acquired a controlling interest in Massmart Holdings Limited (a South African company publicly traded on the JSE) by purchasing, through the use of a scheme of arrangement, 51% of each ordinary shareholder's stock and with Massmart continuing to be traded on the JSE. Walmart proposed the transaction in 2010 and received final approval for the transaction from South Africa's Competition Appeal Court in 2012.

A September 27, 2010 press release by Walmart announcing a preliminary agreement on the deal gives the following background on the transaction and the rationale for it:

> Walmart * * * announced today that it has made a preliminary, non-binding proposal which could, if successful, lead to Walmart making a cash offer to acquire Massmart Holdings Limited (JSE: MSM) for ZAR148 per share.
>
> This is an indicative, non-binding offer, and is subject to a number of conditions, including due diligence, and a period of reciprocal exclusivity granted by Massmart and Walmart. In accordance with the South African legal requirements, Massmart today filed a Cautionary Announcement indicating the terms of the Contemplated Offer.
>
> Massmart, headquartered in Johannesburg, is one of the largest distributors of consumer goods on the African continent and is the leading African retailer of general merchandise, home improvement equipment and supplies. Massmart is also the market-leading retailer of basic foods in the region. The company runs 290 stores in 13 countries in Africa, with the vast majority of its stores in South Africa, and manages eight wholesale and retail chains operating under a variety of different brand names.
>
> Doug McMillon, President and CEO of Walmart International, said, "Walmart's mission is to save people money so that they can live better lives. We believe this proposed acquisition is a great opportunity to deliver on that mission for all the people in the regions of the African continent where Massmart currently operates. We have the opportunity to leverage our experience from around the world to more effectively serve customers, create opportunities for our associates and add shareholder value. We are continuing to deploy our strategy to accelerate growth and improve returns in our international business and this region of the world fits with our focus on large, high growth markets. This potential combination with a market leader will enable us to add value to an already successful business through investments in people and technology. We respect and honor pre-existing union relationships and are committed to abiding by South African labor laws. We also look forward to serving communities and working with the leaders to support the continued development and momentum in the region."
>
> Andy Bond, Executive Vice President with responsibility for Walmart's operations in the region, including the United Kingdom and Africa, said, "South

Africa presents a compelling growth opportunity for Walmart and offers a platform for growth and expansion in other African countries. South Africa possesses attractive market dynamics, favorable demographic trends and a growing economy. We are fully aware and supportive of Massmart's Broad Based Black Economic Empowerment (BEE) program, and if the transaction is completed, we expect to continue and build on these efforts, working diligently with appropriate parties to grow skills and socio-economic development, and to be a corporate and retail role model. We also look forward to moving towards a deal with Massmart to offer their associates enhanced opportunities to grow and prosper."

§ 26.23 The South African Competition Act of 1998, as Amended

A. Introduction

Mergers and acquisitions involving South African firms are subject to antitrust scrutiny under the SA Competition Act. The Act establishes (1) a Competition Commission that is responsible for the day-to-day operations under the Act; (2) a Competition Tribunal that is required to adjudicate on certain matters, including large mergers; and (3) a Competition Appeal Court that hears appeals from the Competition Tribunal.

Chapter 3 of the Act deals with "Merger Control," and Section 11 of that chapter categorizes mergers as small, intermediate, and large, depending on whether certain thresholds are satisfied. For example, Section 11(5)(c) provides that "'a large merger' means a merger or proposed merger with a value at or above the higher threshold established [by the Minister of Trade and Industry]." Different procedures apply to these types of mergers, and this discussion focuses only on large mergers.

Subsection 11(1)(a) requires that the thresholds be set on the basis of combined annual turnover (*i.e.*, sales) and assets. Under the thresholds, which have remained the same since July 2009, a large merger is one in which the combined South African turnover/asset value of the acquiror and target is at least R6.6 billion (approximately $623 million) and the South African turnover/asset value of the target is at least R190 million (approximately $18 million).[30] Thus, if U.S. Acquiror has significant sales in South Africa and acquires a relatively small SA Target, the transaction may be subject to the Competition Act as a large merger. Also, even if both the acquiror and target are U.S. corporations, if they have significant operations in South Africa, the transaction may be subject to scrutiny by the South African Competition Commission.

Walmart's acquisition of Massmart was a large merger.

B. Definition of Merger

Section 12 of the Act defines the term "merger" broadly:

12. Merger defined

(1)(a) For purposes of this Act, a merger occurs when one or more firms directly or indirectly acquire or establish direct or indirect control [e.g. more than 50%

30. Determination of Merger Thresholds and Method of Calculation, Notice 216 of 2009, Department of Trade and Industry (March 6, 2009). Department of Trade and Industry, Merger Thresholds, available at http://www.compcom.co.za/merger-thresholds/ (last visited June 20, 2014).

stock ownership, see Section 12, Subsection 2] over the whole or part of the business of another firm.

(b) A merger contemplated in paragraph (a) may be achieved in any manner, including through-

(i) purchase or lease of the shares, an interest or assets of the other firm in question; or

(ii) amalgamation or other combination with the other firm in question. * * *

Since Walmart acquired 51% of the stock of Massmart, the transaction was a merger under this definition.

C. Prior Notification and Delayed Implementation

Section 13A of the Act requires that a party to an intermediate or large merger notify the Competition Commission and delay implementing the merger as follows:

13A. Notification and implementation of other mergers

(1) -A party to an intermediate or a large merger must notify the Competition Commission of that merger in the *prescribed* manner and form.

(2) -In the case of an intermediate or a large merger, the *primary acquiring firm* and the *primary target firm* must each provide a copy of the notice contemplated in subsection (1) to (a) any *registered trade union* that represents a substantial number of its employees; or (b) the employees concerned or representatives of the employees concerned, if there are no such *registered trade unions*.

(3) -The parties to an intermediate or large merger may not implement that merger until it has been approved, with or without conditions, by the Competition Commission * * *, the Competition Tribunal * * *, or the Competition Appeal Court * * *.

D. Competition Commission Procedures for Large Mergers

Under Section 14A, the Competition Commission is required to make a recommendation regarding a large merger to the Competition Tribunal and to the Minister of the Department of Trade and Industry as follows:

14A. Competition Commission large merger proceedings

(1) -After receiving notice of a large merger, the Competition Commission—

(a) must refer the notice to the Competition Tribunal and to the Minister; and

(b) within 40 business days after all parties to a large merger have fulfilled all their prescribed notification requirements, must forward to the Competition Tribunal and the Minister a written recommendation, with reasons, whether or not implementation of the merger should be-

(i) approved;

(ii) approved subject to any conditions; or

(ii) prohibited. * * *

Note that the Competition Commission does not make the final decision; it merely makes recommendations to the Competition Tribunal, which as discussed below is the decision maker.

E. Competition Tribunal Proceedings for Large Mergers

Under Section 16(2), the Competition Tribunal is required to make a decision on large mergers as follows:

16. Competition Tribunal merger proceedings * * *

(2) -Upon receiving a referral of a large merger and recommendation from the Competition Commission in terms of section 14A(1) * * * the Competition Tribunal must consider the merger in terms of section 12A and the recommendation or decision, as the case may be, of the Competition Commission, and must within the prescribed time—

a) approve the merger;

b) approve the merger subject to any conditions; or

c) prohibit implementation of the merger. * * *

F. Appeals to the Competition Court of Appeals

The Competition Appeal Court hears appeals from decisions of the Competition Tribunal as provided in Section 17:

17. Competition Appeal Court merger proceedings

(1) -Within 20 business days after notice of a decision by the Competition Tribunal in terms of section 16, an appeal from that decision may be made to the Competition Appeal Court, subject to its rules, by—

(a) any party to the merger; or

(b) a person who * * * is required to be given notice of the merger, provided the person had been a participant in the proceedings of the Competition Tribunal.

G. Standards for Appraising Mergers

Section 12A, which is analogues to Section 7 of the Clayton Act [see Chapter 8], sets out the standards that the Competition Commission and the Competition Tribunal are to apply in evaluating a merger:

12A. Consideration of Mergers

(1) -Whenever required to consider a merger, the Competition Commission or Competition Tribunal must initially determine whether or not the merger is likely to substantially prevent or lessen competition, by assessing the factors set out in subsection (2), and—

(a) [**A SLC Standard, *see* Chapter 8**] if it appears that the merger is likely to substantially prevent or lessen competition, the Commission or the Tribunal must then determine-

(i) [**Efficiencies Defense, *see* Chapter 8**] whether or not the merger is likely to result in any technological, efficiency or other pro-competitive, gain which will be greater than, and offset, the effects of any prevention or lessening of competition, that may result or is likely to result from the merger, and would not likely be obtained if the merger is prevented; and

(ii) [**Parties' Public Interest Defense**] whether the merger can or cannot be justified on substantial public interest grounds by assessing the factors set out in subsection (3); or

(b) [**Government's Public Interest Offense**] otherwise, determine whether the merger can or cannot be justified on substantial public interest grounds by assessing the factors set out in subsection (3).

(2) When determining whether or not a merger is likely to substantially prevent or lessen competition, the Competition Commission or the Competition Tribunal must assess the strength of competition in the relevant market, and the probability that the firms in the market after the merger will behave competitively or co-operatively, taking into account any factor that is relevant to competition in that market, including-

(a) the actual and potential level of import competition in the market;

(b) the ease of entry into the market, including tariff and regulatory barriers;

(c) the level and trends of concentration, and history of collusion, in the market;

(d) the degree of countervailing power in the market;

(e) the dynamic characteristics of the market, including growth, innovation, and product differentiation;

(f) the nature and extent of vertical integration in the market;

(g) [**Failing Firm Defense, *see* Chapter 7**] whether the business or part of the business of a party to the merger or proposed merger has failed or is likely to fail; and

(h) whether the merger will result in the removal of an effective competitor.

(3) [**Public Interest Standards**] -When determining whether a merger can or cannot be justified on public interest grounds, the Competition Commission or the Competition Tribunal must consider the effect that the merger will have on-

(a) a particular industrial sector or region;

(b) employment;

(c) the ability of small businesses, or firms controlled or owned by historically disadvantaged persons, to become competitive; and

(d) the ability of national industries to compete in international markets.

H. Antitrust Review of Walmart's Acquisition of Massmart

1. Introduction

Under the provisions of the Competition Act noted above, Walmart's acquisition of Massmart required antitrust approval before it could be completed because Walmart was acquiring control of Massmart in a transaction that was a merger under the Competition Act. The transaction also was a large merger.

2. Decisions of the Competition Commission and Competition Tribunal

The scheme initially received unconditional approval from the Competition Commission in early 2011. However, the Commission later recommended that the Competition Tribunal require the re-employment of 503 Massmart employees who had been dismissed after the merger was announced. After 6 days of hearings before the Competition Tribunal, conditional approval of the scheme was granted in May of 2009.[31] In its analysis, the Tribunal focuses less on the antitrust analysis of the transaction and more on the public interests at stake should the scheme be completed. In paragraph 28 of the Tribunal's Reasons for Decision, the Tribunal notes that "One of the unusual features of the Competition Act, 1998 (Act No. 89 of 1998, as amended) ("the Act") is that despite the fact that a merger may raise no competition concerns it may still be susceptible to prohibition, or approval subject to conditions, on public interest grounds."

With regard to this public interest prong of the test, the Tribunal reasoned:

> A survey of the merger decisions since the Act came into being shows that in no case has an adverse public interest condemned an otherwise unproblematic merger, nor has a problematic merger from a competition perspective been rescued on public interest grounds. This does not mean that no public interest grounds have been found to exist in a merger context. Rather these have been thought adequately addressed by the imposition of conditions on a particular transaction.
>
> The Tribunal has under certain circumstances been reluctant to venture too far in its public interest mandate. As an early decision showed, the Tribunal considered that it ought to show deference to other regulators when it tread upon territory outside its expertise. This however does not mean that the Tribunal has shied away from its responsibilities under the Act and in numerous cases conditions have been imposed to protect unjustified employment loss post merger.
>
> The Tribunal has also viewed its public interest mandate as linked to its competition analysis. Although this does not go as far as amounting to a balancing exercise as required with an efficiency analysis, it also does not mean that the competition and public interest considerations are analysed without regard to each other.[32]

The SA government argued, *inter alia*, that "even a 1 percent shift of [Massmart's] procurement to sources abroad could result in the loss of up to 4,000 jobs * * * ."[33]

The conditions imposed on the acquisition by the Tribunal aptly summarize the Tribunal's public interest concerns:

> 1.1 The merged entity must ensure that there are no retrenchments [lay-offs], based on the merged entity's operational requirements in South Africa, resulting from the merger, for a period of two (2) years from the effective date of the transaction * * * .
>
> 1.2 The merged entity must, when employment opportunities become available with the merged entity, give preference to the re-employment of the 503 employees that were retrenched during June 2010 * * * .
>
> 1.3 The merged entity must honour existing labour agreements and must continue to hounour * * * SACCAWU's current position, as the * * * representative union * * * .

31. Walmart Stores Inc. and Massmart Holdings Ltd, Order, 73/LM/Nov10, Competition Tribunal of South Africa.

32. *See* Walmart Stores Inc. and Massmart Holdings Limited, Reasons for Decisions, Case No. 73/LM/Nov10, paragraphs 34–36, Competition Tribunal of South Africa (31 May 2011).

33. Stinson, Paul, Walmart Unveils Local Procurement Fund, Mergers and Acquisitions, 100 ATRR 613.

1.4 The merged entity must establish a programme aimed exclusively at the development of local South African suppliers * * * in the fixed amount of R100 million to be contributed by the merged entity * * * . In addition the merged entity must establish a training programme to train local South African suppliers on how to do business with the merged entity and with Walmart. * * * [34]

In conclusion, "the merger raises no competition concerns," but it does "raise certain public interest concerns" that are "adequately remedied by the imposition of the conditions."

3. Decisions of the Competition Appeal Court

In July 2011 the Ministers of Economic Development, Trade and Industry and Agriculture, Forestry and Fisheries appealed the Competition Tribunal's approval of the scheme. The Ministers asserted that they had not enjoyed a fair hearing, based on the Tribunal's denial of certain discovery requests, and that the Tribunal failed to properly analyze the antitrust and public interest prongs of the standard, especially concerning the importation of foreign goods and the impact on local suppliers and job creation. In emphasizing that public interest concerns cannot be the sole impediment to antitrust approval, the Competition Appeal Court reasoned:

> The legitimate criticism about insufficient evidence notwithstanding, it is clear from the record as a whole that consumer benefits will flow from this merger. It does not appear to be disputed either that there is the potential for small and medium sized South African suppliers to gain benefit from the presence of Walmart and its unique access to global value supply chains. * * *
>
> In summary, the evidence, as made available to the Tribunal and which forms the record placed before this court, cannot justify the conclusion that the public interest considerations raised by the appellant would so trump the benefits which, it is common cause, will flow to consumers, to sustain a decision that the merger should be prohibited.[35]

Although the Court dismissed the Ministers' petition for reconsideration as a whole, it did impose an extra condition on the scheme requiring the merged entity to commission a study to "determine the most appropriate means together with the mechanism by which local South African suppliers may be empowered to respond to challenges posed by the merger and thus benefit thereby."

A second decision of South Africa's Competition Appeal Court in this case came in October 2011 when experts involved with the local supplier development fund disagreed about the fund's scope and purpose. Summarily, the court found that the original R100 million invested in the fund was "plainly too little," and required Walmart/Massmart to invest R200 million more. The Court also clarified the purpose of the fund: "... to minimize the risks to micro, small and medium-sized producers of South African products' triggered by the merger," and "incentivize the merged entity to purchase products from South African producers over and above the kinds of products that would in any event be so purchased."

---

34. Walmart Stores Inc. and Massmart Holdings Ltd, Order, 73/LM/Nov10, Competition Tribunal of South Africa.

35. The Ministers, et al., and The Tribunal and Commission, et al., and Walmart and Massmart, et al., Case No: 110CAC/Jul11, Competition Appeal Court of South Africa Held in Cape Town (March 9, 2012).

Walmart "received regulatory approval for the takeover of Massmart operations in Tanzania, Malawi, Swaziland, and Zambia; * * * a Namibian high court ruling [also] * * * found in favor of the American retailer."

§ 26.24 South African Exchange Controls

Although South Africa has exchange controls for South African citizens and companies, such controls generally do not apply to foreign companies investing in South Africa. Such companies can, in general, get investment funds in and out of South Africa without limitation. Section Q.6.2 of the South African Reserve Bank's Exchange Control Manual[36] explains:

> Non-residents may freely invest in the Republic, provided that suitable documentary evidence is viewed in order to ensure that such transactions are concluded at arms length, at fair market related prices and are financed in an approved manner. In this regard, such financing must be in the form of [1] the introduction of foreign currency, [or] [2] Rand from a Non-Resident account[.]

§ 26.25 South African Accounting Rules for Business Combinations

The South African Institute of Chartered Accountants, which is comparable to the Financial Accounting Standards Board (FASB) in the U.S., has promulgated a Statement of Generally Accepted Accounting Practice for Business Combinations, AC 140. The statement generally adopts International Financial Reporting Standard (IFRS) 3, which is promulgated by International Accounting Standards Committee (IASC). This statement aligns South African accounting for business combinations with the treatment in the U.S. and other countries that have adopted the principles in IFRS 3. Under this standard, all business combinations are accounted for under the acquisition method, which is similar to the purchase method, and no amortization deduction is allowed for goodwill and similar intangibles. [*See* Chapter 6] Rather, goodwill is tested for impairment yearly under AC 129, which is similar to International Accounting Standard 38, which was promulgated by the IASC. AC 140, mandating the Acquisition method for business combinations, and AC 129, requiring goodwill to be tested annually for impairment, are similar to the U.S. accounting rules promulgated under FASB Statements 141 and 142 respectfully. The U.S. accounting rules are discussed in greater detail in Chapter 6, which also notes that FASB and the IASB (International Accounting Standards Board) are currently engaged in a project to further harmonize the accounting treatment of business combinations.

§ 26.26 Introduction to Taxation in South Africa

South Africa imposes income taxes at the national level and not at the provincial level. South Africa also imposes a value added tax (VAT) at the national level on goods and services at a rate of 14%. The VAT, which is similar to a sales tax, is not generally applicable in mergers and acquisitions.

Under the SA Income Tax Act, individuals are subject to a maximum rate of 40% on ordinary taxable income and corporations are subject to a maximum rate of 28%.

---

36. Available at: https://www.resbank.co.za/RegulationAndSupervision/FinancialSurveillanceAndExchangeControl.

Individuals and companies are also subject to a 15% withholding tax on Dividends (DT) received. The DT replaced SA's former "Secondary Tax on Corporations" (STC), which was a tax imposed on corporations measured by the amount of the dividends paid. A FAQ dealing with the transition from STC to DT provides the rationale behind the change:

> To align the level of the taxation in South Africa with international norm where the recipient of the dividend, not the company paying it, is liable for the tax relating to the dividend, [and T]o make South Africa a more attractive international investment destination by eliminating the perception of a higher corporate tax rate (STC is an additional corporate tax) * * * .

Article 10 of the U.S.-South Africa Tax Convention (i.e., Tax Treaty) reduces or eliminates South Africa's dividend tax on dividends paid to U.S. individuals or companies if certain conditions are met. For example, paragraph 2 of Article 10 reduces the dividend tax to 5% on all dividends paid to companies that beneficially own at least 10% of the voting stock of the payor.

The maximum effective tax rate on capital gains for individuals is 13.3% and the maximum effective rate on corporations is 18.6%.

South Africa also levies a securities transfer tax (STT) on "every transfer of a security," listed or unlisted.[37] The current STT rate is .25% of the value of each transfer of securities.

In 2001 South Africa moved from a "source" basis income tax system to a "residence" basis system, subject to certain exceptions and credits. Thus, South Africa now taxes its residents on worldwide income. Thus, for example, if SA Target earns income in a foreign country, the income generally is subject to tax in South Africa, with a credit allowed for any foreign taxes paid on that income. This is similar to the residence system that applies in the U.S.

§ 26.27 Introduction to the South African Companies Act and Regulations

The Companies Act of 2008 mostly replaced the Companies Act of 1973, and the Companies Regulations of 2011 completely replaced the Securities Regulation Code, which dealt principally with tender offers. The 2008 Companies Act specifically addresses three "Fundamental Transactions:" (1) a Scheme of Arrangement, which was also addressed in the Companies Act of 1973; (2) a sale of all or the greater part a company's assets or undertaking, which was also addressed in the Companies Act of 1973; and (3) a merger or amalgamation, a concept borrowed from U.S. law.[38] Under the new act, there are also three general concepts which are applicable to all three fundamental transactions: (1) shareholder approval; (2) court approval in limited circumstances; and (3) the right to appraisal (*See generally* the Companies Act of 2008). As will be seen below, the SA Companies Regulations, which deals with tender offers and related transactions, are authorized by the Companies Act and, thus, can be enforced by the courts.

---

37. Securities Transfer Tax, South African Revenue Service, available at http://www.sars.gov.za/Tax-Types/STT/Pages/default.aspx (lasted visited July 24, 2014).

38. DLA Cliffe Dekker Hofmeyer, Key Aspects of the New Companies Act, available at http://www.cliffedekkerhofmeyr.com/en/legal/sectors/companies-act.html (last visited July 14, 2014).

The SA Companies Regulations are largely based on the UK City Code, which is discussed in Section 26.17. However, both the Regulations and the Act borrow concepts from U.S. law such as, *inter alia*, the business judgment rule and personal liability for directors.[39] The SA Companies Regulations are authorized under Section 120 of the SA Companies Act of 2008.[40] Section 196 of the SA Companies Act establishes a Takeover Regulation Panel, which replaces the Securities Regulation Panel, to administer the regulations: "The Takeover Regulation Panel is hereby established as a juristic person, to function as an organ of state within the public administration, but as an institution outside the public service." Regulation 201 gives the Panel the authority to "regulate affected transactions," "investigate complaints" and apply for court orders to wind up a company operating illegally or fraudulently.

Like the City Code, the SA Companies Regulations contain a set of general principles, such as the requirement to treatment of shareholders equally, as well as a series of specific rules. Unlike the City Code, the SA Companies Regulations generally apply even if the target is a private company, unless certain conditions are met. *See* Companies Act of 2008 Section 118(1)(c) and Regulation 91.

The SA Companies Regulations generally apply to "affected transactions," which are defined broadly in Section 117 of the Companies Act as follows:

(c) "**affected transaction**" means-

(i) a transaction or series of transactions amounting to the disposal of all or the greater part of the assets or undertaking of a regulated company [§ 112] * * * ,

(ii) an amalgamation or merger, * * * if it involves at least one regulated company [§ 113];

(iii) a scheme of arrangement between a regulated company and its shareholders [§ 114] * * * [such as the Walmart/Massmart transaction if it had been proposed under the 2008 Companies Act];

(iv) the acquisition of, or announced intention to acquire, a beneficial interest in any voting securities of a regulated company [§ 122] * * * ;

(v) the announced intention to acquire a beneficial interest in the remaining voting securities of a regulated company not already held by a person or persons acting in concert;

(vi) a mandatory offer [§ 123] * * * ; or

(vii)compulsory acquisition [§ 124][.]

The sections below discuss various provisions of the SA Companies Act and Regulations as they apply to each prototypical transaction.

§ 26.28 Tender Offer by U.S. Acquiror for Stock of SA Target

The discussion here focuses on a tender offer by U.S. Acquiror for all of the stock of SA Target, which is publicly traded on the JSE. Thus, under Sections 117 and 120 of the

39. *Id.*

40. This is similar to the UK's City Code, which is authorized by the Takeovers Directive (2004/25/EC). The City Code is implemented under part 28 of the UK Companies Act of 2006.

Companies Act, the transaction is subject to the SA Companies Act and the SA Companies Regulations.

A. Outline of the Transaction

U.S. Acquiror or its South African subsidiary (SA Sub) makes a tender offer for all of the shares of SA Target which is publicly traded on the JSE. Thus, the transaction is subject to the SA Companies Regulations. The consideration offered is either cash or stock of U.S. Acquiror or stock of its SA Sub. Assume in the alternative that the tender offer is friendly and hostile. Also assume in the alternative that two months before the tender offer U.S. Acquiror purchased for cash in the alternative 15% and 40% of SA Target's stock from a single shareholder. The next subsection briefly outlines the impact of the SA Companies Regulations and the disclosure of beneficial interest provision of the Companies Act on this transaction.

B. Impact of SA Companies Regulations and Disclosure Requirement of Beneficial Interest

1. Analogue to Section 13(d) of the 34 Act

Section 122 of the Companies Act of 2008, which is analogous to Section 13(d) of the 34 Act, requires the disclosure of beneficial interests "within three days after that person acquires a beneficial interest in * * * securities amounting to 5 percent, 10 percent, 15 percent, or any further whole multiple of 5 percent, of the issued securities of that class" and so on. Under Section 56 of the Companies Act an issuer of securities may ask a registered shareholder to "confirm or deny" whether they hold a beneficial interest and provide the particulars dating back three years from the date of notice.[41] Thus, U.S. Acquiror is prevented from secretly acquiring SA Target's shares.

2. Some of the Requirements Relating to an Offer

Regulation 99 requires that U.S. Acquiror approach SA Target's board before commencing a tender offer. Regulation 110 requires the board of SA Target to get "appropriate [independent] external advice" on the transaction. Regulation 108 governs the duties of SA Target's directors, including the required disclosure of conflicts of interest.

Under Regulation 102, the offer document must be "posted within 20 business days after the date of publication of a firm intention announcement." (*See* Regulation 101) Regulation 89 also deals with general notice requirements in "Fundamental Transactions," such as a merger.

If U.S. Acquiror acquires "control" (see Regulation 86 and § 123 of the Companies Act) of SA Target, U.S. Acquiror is required to make a mandatory offer to all SA Target shareholders. Control is defined in Regulation 81 as "the holding of a beneficial interest in a regulated company equal to or exceeding the specified [or proscribed] percentage of voting rights in that regulated company. Regulation 86(t) states that the "prescribed per-

---

41. In the U.K., a similar "confirm or deny" requirement is imposed on shareholders who own at least 1% of the issuing companies stock.

centage" means the percentage contemplated in Section 123(5) of the Companies Act [not more than 35%] and prescribed in regulation 86(1) [35%]. Consequently, for example, if U.S. Acquiror purchases 35% or more of SA Target's shares, then U.S. Acquiror would have to make a mandatory offer on the same terms to the other shareholders. The U.K's City Code has a similar provision.

Under a rule analogous to and an extension of the all holders, best price rule under the U.S. tender offer regulations discussed in Chapter 20, under the Section 111 of the SA Companies Regulation, any acquisition of securities in a 6 month period before an offer is announced must be acquired for consideration that is "identical * * * [or] similar to, the highest consideration paid" in the offer.

Under Regulation 106(4)(i), the offer document must contain a statement by the acquiror's directors taking responsibility for the information in the document. Regulation 111(4)(b) requires that in a cash offer there must be an independent confirmation that the acquiror has sufficient funds to complete the offer. Under Regulation 102(4), the offering must remain open for at least 30 days. Regulation 103(4) states that a general offer terminates at midnight on the 45th day from the date the offer was opened unless the Conditions in Regulation 103 are met. Regulation 102(9) requires the board of SA Target to mail its position on the offer to shareholders within 20 days from the date of commencement. This is the analogue to Rule 14D-9 under the 34 Act. Section 126 of the Companies Act of 2008 prohibits the board of SA Target from engaging in any defensive actions without the approval of its shareholders.

C. Compulsory Second Step Transactions

After the tender offer U.S. Acquiror will want to acquire the non-tendered shares of SA Target, and it can do so if the conditions of Section 124 of the Companies Act are complied with. This section, which only applies if U.S. Acquiror acquires 90% of SA Target's shares (excluding the shares held by the Acquiror prior to the offer), is similar to the U.K.'s Compulsory acquisition provision discussed in Section 26.18.D.

D. Put Right If No Compulsory Acquisition

Under Section 124(4) of the Companies Act, if U.S. Acquiror does not exercise the above compulsory acquisition device, the remaining public shareholders of SA Target will have a put right similar to the U.K.'s put right discussed in Section 26.18.D.

E. Tax Treatment of SA Target and the Selling Shareholders in a Tender Offer, Briefly[42]

1. Cash Tender Offer

Since SA Target is not disposing of its assets in the tender offer, it is not subject to tax. However, the individual and corporate shareholders of SA Target who sell their shares to

42. For a general discussion of South African Income Tax *see* Taxation in South Africa 2014, available in the "National Budget" section of the South African Treasury's website at http://www.treasury.gov.za (last visited June 20, 2014).

U.S. Acquiror will be subject to capital gains tax, depending on their holding periods, at the rates discussed above on the appreciation in their shares occurring after October 1, 2001.

2. Exchange Offer

Sections 43 and 44 of the South Africa Tax Act provide for tax-free treatment for certain stock-for-stock exchanges and other amalgamations. These provisions are similar to the stock-for-stock B reorganization, the A merger reorganization, and the stock-for-asset C reorganization under Section 368 of the Internal Revenue Code. [*See* Chapter 5] However, Sections 43 and 44 only apply when the acquiring corporation is a resident. Consequently, if stock of U.S. Acquiror is used in the exchange offer the transaction is taxable to the South African shareholders of SA Target. If, on the other hand, stock of SA Sub is the consideration, the transaction may qualify for tax-free roll over treatment.

3. Tax Treatment of U.S. Acquiror on Receipt of Dividends, Interest, and Royalties from SA Target

In structuring its investment in SA Target, U.S. Acquiror should be concerned with South Africa's treatment of repatriation payments made by SA Target to U.S. Acquiror in the form of (1) dividends on stock of SA Target held by U.S. Acquiror, (2) interest on debt of SA Target held by U.S. Acquiror, and (3) royalties paid by SA Target in respect of intellectual property rights provided to it by U.S. Acquiror.

Dividends paid by SA Target to U.S. Acquiror are generally subject to the South African 15% withholding DT. However, under Article 10(2) of the U.S.-South Africa Tax Treaty, since U.S. Acquiror owns more than 10% of the stock of SA Target, the rate is reduced to 5%. Under Article 11 of the U.S.-South Africa Tax Treaty, interest paid by SA Target to U.S. Acquiror is exempt from taxes in South Africa. Although royalties paid by SA Target to U.S. Acquiror are subject to a 12% withholding tax under the SA Tax Act, under Article 12 of the U.S.-South Africa Tax Treaty, royalties are exempt from tax.

4. Tax Treatment to U.S. Acquiror on the Sale of Its Stock in SA Target

Although South Africa now has a capital gains tax, the tax does not apply to nonresidents, such as U.S. Acquiror. Thus, U.S. Acquiror will not be subject to South Africa tax on gain realized on the sale of the stock of SA Target. This is the same rule that applies in the U.S.

§ 26.29 Acquisition by U.S. Acquiror of SA Target in a "Scheme of Arrangement" under the SA Companies Act and Walmart's Acquisition of Massmart

A. Outline of the Transaction

In this transaction, SA Target proposes to its shareholders that the shareholders agree to the acquisition by U.S. Acquiror or its SA Sub of all of the shares of SA Target in a "scheme of arrangement" under Sections 114 and 115 of the Companies Act of 2008. The South African courts have held that cash consideration can be paid in a scheme. The transaction may require court approval under the circumstances listed in Section 115(2)(c) of the Companies Act, which provides that notwithstanding the adoption of a shareholder resolution approving the transaction, a court hearing is required if the "resolution was opposed by at least 15%" of the voting shares and a shareholder who voted against the transaction requires the company to seek court approval.

The end result of a scheme of arrangement in which all of the target's stock is acquired is that SA Target will become a wholly-owned subsidiary of U.S. Acquiror or SA Sub, and the shareholders of SA Target will receive the consideration specified in the scheme. Thus, the effect of the transaction is the same as a reverse subsidiary merger under U.S. law, which is the most common technique for acquiring a publicly held corporation in the U.S. [*See* Chapters 1, 2, and 5] In a reverse subsidiary merger an acquiror forms a subsidiary and the subsidiary merges into the target, with the target's shareholders receiving the merger consideration and the acquiror owning all of the target's outstanding stock after the transaction. [*See* Chapter 2] The transaction is similar to a stock acquisition, but the merger makes the transaction compulsory for the target's shareholders.

Kevin Markman and Craig Atkinson contrast a scheme of arrangement under the 1973 Companies Act (the Old Act) against a scheme of arrangement under the 2008 Companies Act (the New Act):

> The three most important distinctions between Schemes under the Old Act and those under the New Act are that: (a) in terms of the New Act there now exists an appraisal right (*See* Section 164), where no such right existed under the Old Act; (b) in terms of the Old Act two court approvals/orders are always required (one to convene the scheme meeting and one to sanction the Scheme), whereas in terms of the New Act court approval is only required under the limited circumstances described * * * above [*i.e.*, 15% dissenters and request for hearing]; and (c) in terms of the New Act a report, which appears to be akin to a "fair and reasonable" report, must be provided by an independent expert to the board and distributed to shareholders. * * *
>
> The advantage of the Scheme under the Old Act is that it is tried and tested [and] has no appraisal right[.] * * * The disadvantage is that it requires two court applications. The advantage of the Scheme under the New Act is that it only requires court approval in limited circumstances. The disadvantages are that it is not tried and tested, has the appraisal right and has the fair and reasonable report requirement. * * * [T]he simpler scheme process introduced by the New Act may not necessarily be more advantageous to the target company than * * * under the Old Act.

B. Schemes of Arrangement under the SA Companies Act

Section 106 of the Companies Regulations requires that certain information be distributed to target shareholders in the form of a Circular addressing the proposed scheme of arrangement. The basic requirements for effectuating a scheme of arrangement are set out in Sections 114, 115, and 65:

> **114. Proposals for scheme of arrangement.** (1) [T]he board of a company may propose and * * * implement any arrangement between the company and holders of any class of its securities by way of * * * (a) a consolidation of securities of different classes, (b) a division of securities into different classes, * * * (d) exchanging any of its securities for other securities * * * .
>
> **115. Required approval for transactions contemplated in Part.** A [Scheme of Arrangement] must be approved (a) by a special resolution adopted by persons

entitled to exercise voting rights on such a matter, at a meeting called for that purpose and at which sufficient persons are present to exercise, in aggregate, at least 25% of all of the voting rights that are entitled to be exercised [quorum] on that matter, or any higher percentage as may be required by the company's Memorandum of Incorporation; and (b) by a special resolution, also adopted in the manner required by paragraph (a), by shareholders of the company's holding company if any * * * ; and (c) by the court [in the circumstances described in Sections 115 (3–9) * * *.] *See also* Section 65(11)(i) of the Companies Act of 2008.

65. Shareholder resolutions. (9) For a special resolution to be approved by shareholders, it must be supported by at least 75 percent of the voting rights exercised on the resolution.

To summarize: to approve a scheme, a quorum of no less than 25% of the voting shares must vote, and at least 75% of the voting shares must vote for the transaction.

As indicated previously, under Section 115, court approval is needed for the scheme of arrangement if, for example, "the resolution was opposed by at least 15% of the voting rights that were exercised on that resolution and * * * any person who voted against the resolution requires the company to seek court approval. *See* § 115(3). The above procedure is similar to a merger under state law in the U.S., but no court approval is required for a merger in the U.S.

Appraisal rights are established in Section 164 of the Companies Act. Section 112 applies to schemes of arrangement that concern a transfer of a target company's assets.

C. Applicability of the South African Companies Regulations

Sections 118 and 117 of the SA Companies Regulations make it clear that the Regulations apply to schemes of arrangement. *See also* Regulations 81 (o) and (p)(iii). Some of the provisions of the Regulations that would apply in a scheme of arrangement include the requirement of an independent opinion of an investment banker for the target as required by Regulation 110, a directors' responsibility statement as required by Regulation 106(3), and an independent confirmation that the acquiror has sufficient funds to complete a cash offer as required by Regulation 111(4)(b).

D. Income Tax Considerations of a Scheme of Arrangement, Briefly

1. Tax Treatment of Selling Shareholders and SA Target in the Scheme of Arrangement

Assuming the scheme of arrangement does not involve a transfer of the assets of SA Target but rather an acquisition of the shares of SA Target by U.S. Acquiror or its SA Sub, SA Target will not be subject to tax, and the individual and corporate shareholders of SA Target will be subject to the same tax rules that apply in the tender offer, as discussed above in Section 26.28.E.

2. Tax Treatment of U.S. Acquiror on Receipt of Dividends, Interest, and Royalties from SA Target

The treatment of U.S. Acquiror under the SA Tax Act on the receipt of repatriation payments from SA Target is the same here as when SA Target is acquired in a tender offer as discussed above. [*See* Section 26.28.E]

3. Tax Treatment to U.S. Acquiror on the Sale of Its Stock in SA Target

The treatment here is the same as discussed in connection with the tender offer above; no tax for non-residents selling SA Target stock in South Africa. [*See* Section 26.28.E]

E. Walmart's Acquisition of 51% of Massmart in a Scheme of Arrangement

1. Structure of the Scheme Under the Companies Act of 1973 with a Discussion of Provisions from the Companies Act of 2008

Walmart's acquisition of control of Massmart in a scheme of arrangement was proposed under Section 311 of the Companies Act of 1973, which is now governed by Sections 114 and 115 of the Companies Act of 2008. In the scheme of arrangement, Walmart acquired 51% of each ordinary shareholders' shares in return for cash, at about a 19% premium. Walmart's acquisition of only a 51%, instead of a 100%, shows the flexibility of a scheme of arrangement.

Walmart also secured letters of commitment in support of its offer from certain trusts holding Massmart stock as well as other institutional investors, not discussed further here. However, such support did not give rise to an obligation on Walmart to make a "mandatory offer."

2. The Joint Announcement of the Walmart-Massmart Transaction

The first step in the Walmart-Massmart transaction was the *Joint Announcement of a Firm Intention by Walmart to Make an Offer to Acquire 51% of South Africa's Masssmart. See* Appendix KK. As indicated in this Joint Announcement, Walmart would acquire "51% of Massmart ordinary shares, equivalent to 51 out of every 100 Massmart ordinary shares held ... by way of a scheme of arrangement [Scheme]." Section 3 of the Joint Announcement sets out the Conditions Precedent to the Scheme, which include:

> 4.1. the Scheme having been approved by a requisite 75% majority of Massmart ordinary shareholders at the Scheme meeting present in person or by proxy, the Scheme being sanctioned by the Court and the order of Court sanctioning the Scheme being registered with the Registrar of Companies;
>
> 4.2. the receipt of regulatory approvals, to the extent required by law, in relation to the Offer ... from all applicable regulators in South Africa and in any other country in which Massmart operates, including without limitation, the JSE, the Securities Regulation Panel ("SRP"), the competition authorities established under the (South African) Competition Act, 89 of 1998, and the Financial Surveillance Department of the South African Reserve Bank;
>
> 4.3. from the date of the firm intention letter referred to above until 17h00 (SA time) on the business day immediately preceding the finalisation date of the Scheme, no material adverse change having arisen in the business of Massmart....
>
> 4.4. where such consent is necessary, the consent for the proposed transaction contemplated in this announcement being obtained from the relevant counterparties to certain key contracts, as identified by Walmart during the due diligence review conducted by Walmart on the Massmart group. These consents relate primarily to "change of ownership" clauses in property leases, certain

banking facilities and certain commercial agreements, which clauses are usual for agreements of that nature;

4.5. the approval by the holders of Massmart ordinary and preference shares of all resolutions required to successfully implement the Offer..., including but not limited to the Whitewash Resolution (as defined in paragraph 5.4 below)...;

4.6. the SRP (a) accepting the Whitewash Resolution and waiving the requirements of Rule 8 of the Securities Regulation Code on Takeovers and Mergers ("SRP Code") relating to the obligation for Walmart to make a mandatory offer to acquire shares in Massmart held by Massmart's minority shareholders[.]

3. The Shareholder Circular for the Walmart-Massmart Transaction

The shareholder circular for the Walmart/Massmart transaction is Documentary Appendix L, *Shareholder Circular for Walmart's Acquisition of 51% of Shares of South Africa's Massmart.* This type of shareholder disclosure document (which is now required under Regulation 106 of the Companies Regulations of 2011) incorporated, *inter alia*: a notice of general and scheme meetings (now required by Section 62 of the Companies Act of 2008), an explanatory statement (now required by Regulation 106), a valuation statement (now required by Regulation 90), a statement of directors interests (now required by Regulation 106), and forms of proxy as required by the Old Companies Act and Takeover Code (now required by Section 58 of the Companies Act of 2008). The Massmart board retained Morgan Stanley as an "appropriate external advisor" to provide the board with a fairness opinion letter. Morgan Stanley ultimately offered a letter stating that the scheme was financially fair, in its opinion, to Massmart shareholders.

Section 3.1.2 of the Massmart Circular stated that the scheme must be approved by not less than 75% of the votes exercisable by scheme members presented and entitled to vote (*See* Sections 115 and 65 of the Companies Act of 2008, which generally provides the same rule). Section 4 of the Circular provided that if the requisite shareholder and court approval is received and if all conditions precedent are satisfied, then Massmart shareholders will be entitled to the cash consideration, and Walmart will be entitled to 51% of each ordinary shareholder's share holdings.

4. The Shareholder Vote and Court Approval of the Scheme

In January of 2011, 97% of Massmart shareholders approved[43] the Scheme of Arrangement, subject to the outstanding conditions precedent, which included, *inter alia*, regulatory approvals, no material adverse change (*see* Section 10.3 of the Circular), and the required court order sanctioning the transaction. The South Gauteng High Court sanctioned the scheme on February 1, 2011.

5. When Court Approval is Required Under the New Scheme Provision

As noted above, under the Companies Act of 2008, no court order is required to consummate a scheme of arrangement that all relevant South African regulatory bodies have approved unless, for instance, 15% of the voting shareholders dissent and at least one of the dissenting shareholders applies for court approval. Thus, if the Walmart/Massmart scheme had taken place under the new Companies Act and there had been no appeals

43. Walmart/Massmart, Results of The General Meeting and Scheme Meeting, paragraph 3, January 17, 2014.

from regulatory approval orders, such as the Competition Tribunal's Order, the scheme could have been implemented completely without court supervision.

6. Tax Treatment of the Parties

The tax treatment of the parties is the same as in Section 26.28.E. The Walmart/Massmart circular does not discuss tax implications to shareholders except to note that:

> The tax treatment of scheme participants is dependent on their individual circumstances and on the tax jurisdiction applicable to such scheme participants. It is recommended that scheme participants seek appropriate advice in this regard.

§ 26.30 Acquisition by U.S. Acquiror of Assets of SA Target followed by Liquidation of SA Target

A. Outline of the Transaction

U.S. Acquiror reaches agreement with the management of SA Target on a transaction in which U.S. Acquiror will form SA Sub for the purpose of acquiring the assets and certain specified liabilities of SA Target. SA Target will be liquidated pursuant to the transaction.

B. Impact of Section 390 of the Companies Act of 1973

This sale of assets followed by liquidation transaction is still governed by Section 390 of the SA Companies Act, which continues to apply under Schedule 5, Item 9 of the Companies Act of 2008 to any matters not specifically covered by the New Act. *See also* Regulation 41. Section 390 requires a 75% vote of shareholders and confers appraisal rights on dissenting shareholders. *See also* Sections 112 and 164(2)(b) of the Companies Act of 2008.

C. Applicability of the South African Companies Regulations

As indicated above, Schedule 5, Item 9 makes it clear that Section 390 continues to apply unless the Minister makes it inapplicable—as of June 2014, the Minister has not done so. Any conflicting provisions between Section 390 and the New Act will result in the application of the New Act. Further, any concept not specifically covered by Section 390 will be governed by either the Companies Regulations of 2011 or the Companies Act of 2008. *See also* Sections 112, 118, and 117 of the Companies Act of 2008 and Regulation 81 (o) and (p)(i).

D. Income Tax Considerations in an Asset Acquisition, Briefly

1. Tax Treatment of Selling Shareholders and SA Target in the Sale of Assets

In a sale of assets for cash or stock of U.S. Acquiror, SA Target will be subject to recoupment (recapture) with respect to depreciation it has taken on plant and equipment. Thus, the 28% rate will apply to this income. Also, SA Target will be subject to capital gains tax on the post October 1, 2001 appreciation in its assets. However, if stock of SA Sub is issued in the acquisition, SA Target may qualify for roll over relief on the disposition of its assets.

Shareholders will be subject to capital gains tax on the receipt of liquidating distributions unless an exemption applies for tax-free treatment. (*See* Section 26.28.E)

2. Tax Treatment of U.S. Acquiror on Receipt of Dividends, Interest, and Royalties from SA Sub

The treatment of U.S. Acquiror under the SA Tax Act and the U.S.-South Africa Tax Treaty on the receipt of repatriation payments from SA Sub is the same here as when a SA Target is acquired in a tender offer, as discussed in Section 26.28.E above.

3. Tax Treatment to U.S. Acquiror on the Sale of Its Stock in SA Sub

The treatment here is the same as discussed in connection with the tender offer: no tax for a non-resident on the sale of its stock in SA Sub in South Africa. Even if U.S. Acquiror decides to sell the assets of SA Target, U.S. Acquiror will not be subject to SA tax; however, SA Target would be subject to tax on such a sale.

Part V
Cross-Border M&A Case Study No. 2: China M&A Transactions and Coca-Cola's Blocked Acquisition of China's Huiyuan Juice Group[44]

§ 26.31 Scope of Part

Part V, *Case Study No. 2: Acquisition by U.S. Acquiror of a China Target*, contains Sections 26.31 through 26.41. This part provides a brief introduction to some of the issues that can arise in an acquisition by a U.S. firm of a Chinese firm. For the purpose of this discussion, the focus is on the laws of mainland China and not of Hong Kong, Macao, and Taiwan, which have separate legal systems. However, many companies with their principal business activities in China are incorporated in, for example, Hong Kong, which, as indicated below, is the case for WH Group Ltd., a Hong Kong listed company, which recently acquired Smithfield Foods. Other Hong Kong listed companies may be incorporated in, for example, the Cayman Islands, which is the case with Huiyuan Juice Group Ltd., which was the target of an acquisition by Coca-Cola that was blocked by China's antitrust authorities. Other principal China based businesses may be listed on the New York Stock Exchange or NASDAQ and incorporated in, for example, the Cayman Islands, which is the case with Alibaba, which completed an IPO on the NYSE in September 2014, raising $25 billion, the largest IPO ever.

Section 26.32 discusses the level of cross border M&A between the U.S. and China, and explains why from the U.S. perspective there has been more inbound (*i.e.*, acquisitions by China firms of U.S. firms) than outbound (*i.e.*, acquisitions by U.S. firms of China firms) M&A activity. Section 26.33 explains why China's entry into the World Trade Organization (WTO) has had the effect of opening some of its markets to foreign ownership. Section 26.34 provides a basic introduction to Chinese corporate law with a look at (1) selected provisions of the China Company Law; (2) the manner in which publicly traded shares of Chinese companies are traded; (3) the Chinese laws governing foreign-invested enterprises (FIEs); (4) China's concept of the Wholly Foreign Owned Enterprise (WFOE); and (5) the corporate and Variable Interest Entity (VIE) structure employed by Alibaba and many other China based companies.

---

44. I would like to thank Dao Fu, a former Penn State Law student and now an associate at Davis Polk in New York, for his helpful comments on this Part V on China M&A.

Section 26.35 briefly introduces Chinese restrictions on foreign investment through its Foreign Investment Catalogue. Section 26.36 discusses the general rules governing M&A transactions in which a China target is acquired by foreign investors. Section 26.37 introduces the China Takeover Code, which is applicable to tender offers for China targets; Section 26.38 looks at the potential acquisition of a China target through the merger provisions of the China company law and the *Provisions on the Merger and Division of Enterprises with Foreign Investment.* Section 26.39 discusses the acquisition of a closely-held China target through an asset acquisition or a stock acquisition.

Section 26.40 discusses Coca-Cola's tender offer for China's Huiyuan Juice Group, which was blocked under the China Anti-Monopoly Law (AML). Appendix MM contains the document pursuant to which the parties agreed to the transaction.

Finally, Section 26.41 looks at review under the AML of M&A transactions and presents the decision of MOFCOM that blocked Coca-Cola's acquisition.

For a discussion of China business law generally, *see* James M. Zimmerman, *China Law Deskbook* (4TH Ed 2014) [hereinafter *China Law Deskbook*]. For excellent introductions to China M&A law, *see* Baker & McKenzie, *China Guide to Mergers and Acquisitions* in Asia Pacific Guide to M&A (2013) and O'Melveny & Myers, *Mergers and Acquisitions in China* (January 2006).

§ 26.32 The Level of Cross-Border M&A Activity Between the U.S. and China

There has been a significant amount of cross-border M&A activity between the U.S. and China. The activity has gone both ways; however, there have been more inbound than outbound transactions.

Two notable inbound acquisitions are (1) the 2005 acquisition by Lenovo, a China controlled publicly-held Hong Kong company, of the personal computing division of IBM for $1.25 billion, and (2) the 2013 acquisition by China's publicly held Shuanghui International Holdings (now WH Group Ltd.) of Smithfield Foods Inc., for $4.7 billion, the largest acquisition of an American company by a Chinese firm. The transaction was approved by more than 96% of the Smithfield shareholders. One source explains that in 2013 "Chinese companies [were] on a North American buying spree, investing $14 billion in the U.S." Dexter Roberts, *Chinese Investment in U.S. Doubles to $14 Billion in 2013*, Bloomberg Businessweek (Jan. 8, 2014).

The outbound M&A has not been as active as the inbound, and one probable reason is that, as reported in the Wall Street Journal, "[g]rowing numbers of U.S. businesses ... feel unwelcome in China" as a result of a "crackdown on monopoly pricing and corruption" that U.S. and other non-Chinese firms believe unfairly targets them. *See* Andrew Browne and Laurie Burkitt, *U.S. Firms Feel Unwelcome in China, According to Survey*, Wall Street Journal (Sept. 2, 2014). In addition, a post on the China Law Blog gives the following reasons for a cautious approach by a U.S. firm acquiring a Chinese manufacturing firm:

> [T]here is a good chance the Chinese manufacturer is paying half of its employees completely under the table[.] * * * [T]here is also a good chance the Chinese manufacturer is underpaying its taxes[.] * * * [I]f the US manufacturer were to buy * * * a Chinese manufacturer, it would need to do so as a WFOE [*see* discussion

> below of Wholly Foreign Owned Entity] and it would then immediately be on [another level] with respect to China's various tax authorities. * * * [I]f you have no profits, the Chinese tax authorities will figure that is because your Chinese WFOE is intentionally under-pricing the product it is selling to your United States operations and it will then impute a profit to your Chinese WFOE."

Dan Harris, *Buying a Chinese Company? Why China Deals Don't Get Done*, (Jan 6, 2012), China Law Blog.

§ 26.33 China's Entry into the WTO

Notwithstanding the difficulties of doing business in China, one of the reasons for the M&A activity that is taking place in China is the entry of China into the World Trade Organization (WTO), which is described in the following WTO press release:

WTO Press Release, WTO successfully concludes negotiations on China's entry

17 September 2001

* * *

As a result of the negotiations, China has agreed to undertake a series of important commitments to open and liberalize its regime in order to better integrate in the world economy and offer a more predictable environment for trade and foreign investment in accordance with WTO rules.

Among some of the commitments undertaken by China are the following:

China will provide non-discriminatory treatment to all WTO Members. All foreign individuals and enterprises, including those not invested or registered in China, will be accorded treatment no less favourable than that accorded to enterprises in China with respect to the right to trade. * * *

§ 26.34 Introduction to Chinese Business Entities

A. China's Company Law

1. Introduction

Although China is a communist country, its laws governing business entities are similar to the business entities laws in a capitalist country. The Company Law of the Peoples Republic of China, which was first enacted in 1994 and last amended in 2014, provides for two types of companies: (1) a limited liability company, which can have no more than 50 shareholders, and (2) a company limited by shares, which may be a publicly traded company. Both of these entities provide for shareholders, a board of directors, and limited liability for the shareholders. The Company Law has provisions governing, *inter alia*, mergers and dissolutions. Although China's laws also provide for partnerships and joint ventures, the focus here is on limited liability companies and companies limited by shares.

2. Selected Provisions of China's Company Law (Revised 2014): Limited Liability Companies and Companies Limited by Shares

a. Chapter 1: General Provisions * * *

Article 2 For the purpose of this Law, a company shall refer to a limited liability company or a company limited by shares established within the territory of the People's Republic of China in accordance with this Law.

Article 3 [**Limited Liability**] A company is an enterprise legal person with independent legal person property, and is entitled to legal person property rights. The company shall bear liabilities for its debts with all its assets. The shareholders of a limited liability company shall bear liabilities for the company to the extent of their respective subscribed capital contribution. The shareholders of a company limited by shares shall bear liabilities for the company to the extent of their respective subscribed shares. * * *

Article 11 To establish a company, the company's articles of association shall be formulated in accordance with the law. * * *

Article 18 The staff members of a company shall organize a labor union in compliance with the Labor Union Law of the People's Republic of China[.] * * *

Article 19 An organization of the Communist Party of China ("CPC") shall be established in a company to carry out activities of the CPC[.] * * *

Article 21[**Duty of Loyalty**] The controlling shareholders, actual holders, directors, supervisors and senior management personnel of a company shall not make use of their affiliation to prejudice the interests of the company.* * *

b. Chapter 2: Establishment and Organizational Structure of a Limited Liability Company

Section 1: Establishment * * *

Article 24 The establishment of a limited liability company shall be subject to the capital contribution by not more than 50 shareholders.

Article 25 The articles of association of a limited liability company shall set forth the following matters:

(1) Name and domicile of the company;

(2) Business scope of the company;

(3) Registered capital of the company;

(4) Names of the shareholders;

(5) Form, amount, and schedule of capital contributions by the shareholders;

(6) Organizations of the company and the methods of formation, authorities, and rules of procedure thereof;

(7) Legal representative of the company; and

(8) Any other matter deemed as necessary to be specified by the shareholders' meeting. * * *

Article 42 The shareholders of a company shall exercise their voting rights at shareholders' meetings in proportion to their respective capital contributions, unless otherwise specified in the company's articles of association.

Article 43 [**Two-Thirds Vote**] * * * Any resolutions made at a shareholders' meeting on the amendment of the company's articles of association, increase or decrease of the registered capital and on the merger, division, dissolution, or conversion of the company, shall be adopted by the shareholders representing more than two thirds of the voting rights.

Article 44 A limited liability company shall have a board of directors that is to be composed of 3 to 13 members, unless otherwise specified in * * * this Law. * * *

Article 49 A limited liability company may have a manager whose employment or dismissal shall be subject to the decision of the board of directors. * * *

Article 50 A limited liability company with relatively few shareholders or of a relatively small size may have one executive director instead of a board of directors. * * *

Article 51 A limited liability company shall have a board of supervisors that is to be composed of at least three members. A limited liability company with relatively few shareholders or of a relatively small size may have one or two supervisors instead of a board of supervisors. * * *

Section 4: Special Provisions on Wholly State-Owned Companies * * *

c. Chapter 3: Equity Transfer of a Limited Liability Company

Article 71 [**Restrictions on Sales**] The shareholders of a limited liability company may transfer all or part of their equity among each other. The proposed transfer of equity by a shareholder to any non-shareholder party shall be subject to the consent of more than half of the other shareholders. * * *

d. Chapter 4: Establishment and Organizational Structure of a Company Limited by Shares

Section 1: Establishment * * *

Article 81 The articles of association of a company limited by shares shall set forth the following matters:

(1) Name and domicile of the company;

(2) Business scope of the company;

(3) Form of establishment of the company;

(4) Total shares, price per share, and registered capital of the company;

(5) Names of the promoters, number of shares they have subscribed for, and forms and schedule of their capital contributions;

(6) Composition, authorities and rules of procedure of the board of directors;

(7) Legal representative of the company;

(8) Composition, authorities and rules of procedure of the board of supervisors;

(9) Methods for profit distribution of the company;

(10) Causes for dissolution, and methods for liquidation, of the company;

(11) Methods of notification and public announcement by the company; and

(12) Any other matters deemed as necessary to be specified by the general meeting. * * *

Section 2: General Meeting

Article 98 The general meeting of a company limited by shares shall be composed of all the shareholders. * * *

Section 3: Board of Directors; Managers

Article 108 A company limited by shares shall have a board of directors that is to be composed of 5 to 19 members. * * *

Section 4: Board of Supervisors

Article 117 A company limited by shares shall have a board of supervisors that is to be composed of at least three members. * * *

Section 5: Special Provisions on the Organizational Structure of a Listed Company * * *

Article 121 [**Shareholder Vote on Significant Transactions**] Where the value of the purchase or sale of any substantial assets by a listed company or the provision of guarantee exceeds 30 percent of the total asset value of the listed company within a given year, a resolution shall be made by the general meeting, and shall be passed by the shareholders representing more than two thirds of the voting rights of all the shareholders present at the meeting.

Article 122 A listed company shall have independent directors. * * *

Article 124 [**Interested Party Transactions**] Any director of a listed company who is affiliated with any enterprise involved in the matters under any resolution made at a meeting of the board of directors shall be prohibited from exercising voting rights concerning that resolution, nor may that director vote on behalf of any other directors. * * *

e. Chapter 5: Issuance and Transfer of Shares Held of a Company Limited by Shares

Section 1: Issuance of Shares

Article 125 The capital of a company limited by shares shall be divided into shares, and each share shall have the same value. * * *

Article 126 Shares shall be issued in accordance with the principles of fairness and impartiality. Each share of the same class shall be entitled to the same rights. * * *

Section 2: Transfer of Shares

Article 137 The shares held by shareholders are transferrable under the law.

f. Chapter 13: Supplementary Provisions * * *

Article 217 [**Applicable to Foreign Invested Limited Liability and Companies Limited By Shares**] This Law shall be applicable to foreign-invested limited liability companies and companies limited by shares. The provisions otherwise prescribed by the laws on foreign investment shall prevail. * * *

B. Shares of a Publicly-Held China "Joint Stock Limited Company": "A," "B," "H," and "N" Shares

As indicated, a company limited by shares may be listed on an exchange, and the shares are categorized according to (1) the exchange on which they are listed, and (2) in the case of shares listed on either the Shanghai or Shenzhen Exchange, the two Chinese exchanges, the investors who are permitted to purchase the shares. At the end of 2012, there were 954 companies listed on the Shanghai Stock Exchange.

Two classes of shares are traded on Chinese exchanges: "A" shares and "B" shares. "A" shares can be traded by domestic Chinese investors and by Qualified Foreign Institutional Investors (QFIIs). The *Provisional Measures on Administration of Domestic Securities Investments of Qualified Foreign Institutional Investors* (November 5, 2005) defines QFII:

> Article 2. Qualified Foreign Institutional Investors (hereinafter referred to as "QFII") are defined in this Regulation as overseas fund management institutions, insurance companies, securities companies and other assets management institutions which have been approved by China Securities Regulatory Commission (hereinafter referred to as "CSRC") to invest in China's securities market and granted investment quota by State Administration of Foreign Exchange (hereinafter referred to as "SAFE").

"B" shares are shares that are designated in the renminbi (yuan), the Chinese currency, but quoted in foreign exchange and traded by foreigners. "H" shares are listed on the Hong Kong Stock Exchange, and "N" shares are listed on an exchange based in New York.

C. Foreign-Invested Enterprises [FIE]

China has laws regulating what it refers to as "foreign-invested enterprises" (FIEs), which are enterprises that are owned at least in part by foreigners and conduct business in China. *See generally China Law Deskbook, supra*, Section 26.31, at Chapter 4. As indicated above, Article 217 of the China Company Law provides that the law is applicable to "foreign-invested limited liability companies and [foreign-invested] companies limited by shares" and that the "provisions otherwise prescribed by the laws on foreign investment shall prevail." A foreign-invested limited liability company may be organized as a Wholly Foreign Owned Enterprise (WFOE), which is discussed in the next section.

An elaborate application process applies for an entity seeking to be designated as an FIE. *See China Law Deskbook, supra* Section 26.31, at Chapter 4. An FIE can only engage in certain businesses as specified in the Foreign Investment Catalogues, which is discussed subsequently. An FIE can be a newly formed entity or arise as a result of the acquisition by foreign persons of a Chinese business entity.

FIEs receive the benefit of a lower corporate tax rate. The standard corporate tax rate is 25%, but the rate applicable to many FIEs is 15%. *See Income Tax Law of the Peoples Republic of China for Enterprises with Foreign Investment and Foreign Enterprises.* Also, there is an exemption from the withholding tax on dividends paid by FIEs to foreign shareholders.

D. China Wholly Foreign Owned Enterprises (WFOE)

Pursuant to China's Wholly Foreign Owned Enterprise (WFOE) law, foreign persons can organize Chinese business entities, *e.g.*, limited liability companies or companies limited by shares that are wholly owned by foreign investors. The purpose of the law is set forth as follows:

> Article 1 In order to increase foreign economic cooperation and technology exchange and promote the development of China's national economy, the People's Republic of China permits foreign enterprises and other economic organizations or individuals (hereinafter, "Foreign Investors") to establish wholly foreign-

> owned enterprises (hereinafter, "WFOEs") in China and protects the lawful rights and interests of WFOEs.

See generally China Law Deskbook, *supra* Section 26.31, at Chapter 4.

The WFOE law makes it clear that the assets of a WFOE will not be nationalized and that the owners can repatriate profits. If a limited liability company or company limited by shares is acquired by a foreign acquirer, the company becomes a WFOE.

E. Introduction to Variable Interest Entities and the Corporate Structure of Alibaba

1. Introduction

Many Chinese companies, including publicly held companies, have what is known as Variable Interest Entities (VIEs). The basic principles of VIEs are discussed as follows in a report by O'Melveny & Myers:

> VIE structures are typically adopted as part of an offshore restructuring of a PRC domestic company in preparation for venture capital or private equity financing and eventual listing on an offshore stock exchange. But unlike a straight-forward offshore "red-chip" restructuring where the offshore holding company would acquire the domestic company's equity interest from its PRC resident founders, in a VIE structure the offshore holding company would form a new wholly owned subsidiary ("WFOE") in China which would control, and receive the economic benefits of, the domestic company ("VIE") through a series of contractual arrangements. The VIE, whose shareholders of record would be PRC individuals or companies (typically with the founders retaining majority ownership), would hold those licenses and assets that cannot be legally owned by or transferred to the WFOE under PRC foreign investment restrictions. As a result of the contractual arrangements, the offshore holding company would be able to consolidate the financials of the VIE into the group's overall financial statements under applicable accounting standards (the term "variable interest entity" being a U.S. GAAP accounting term describing an entity consolidated in this way).

David Roberts and Thomas Hall, *VIE Structures in China, What You Need to Know*, Topics in Chinese Law, an O'Melveny & Myers LLP Research Report (Oct. 2011).

The next section discusses the corporate and VIE structure employed by Alibaba in connection with its 2014 IPO.

2. Alibaba Corporate Structure Set Out in Form F-1A, Filed with the SEC on July 11, 2014

Our Corporate Structure

Alibaba Group Holding Limited is a Cayman Islands holding company established on June 28, 1999, and we conduct our business in China through our subsidiaries and variable interest entities. * * *

Contractual Arrangements among Our Wholly-foreign Owned Enterprises, Variable Interest Entities and the Variable Interest Entity Equity Holders

Due to PRC legal restrictions on foreign ownership and investment in, among other areas, value-added telecommunications services, which include the operations of Internet content providers, or ICPs, we, similar to all other entities with foreign-incorporated holding company structures operating in our industry in China, operate our Internet businesses and other businesses in which foreign investment is restricted or prohibited in the PRC through wholly-foreign owned enterprises, majority-owned entities and variable interest entities. The relevant variable interest entities, which are incorporated in the PRC and 100% owned by PRC citizens or by PRC entities owned by PRC citizens, where applicable, hold the ICP licenses and other regulated licenses and operate our Internet businesses and other businesses in which foreign investment is restricted or prohibited. * * * Each of these variable interest entities other than Zhejiang Taobao Network Co., Ltd. is 80%-owned by Jack Ma, our lead founder, executive chairman and one of our principal shareholders, and 20%-owned by Simon Xie, one of our founders and a member of our management. Zhejiang Taobao Network Co., Ltd. is 90%-owned by Jack Ma and 10%-owned by Simon Xie. We have entered into certain contractual arrangements, as described in more detail below, which collectively enable us to exercise effective control over the variable interest entities and realize substantially all of the economic risks and benefits arising from, the variable interest entities. As a result, we include the financial results of each of the variable interest entities in our consolidated financial statements in accordance with U.S. GAAP as if they were our wholly-owned subsidiaries.

Other than the ICP licenses and other licenses and approvals for businesses in which foreign ownership is restricted or prohibited held by our variable interest entities, we hold our material assets in, and conduct our material operations through, our wholly-foreign owned and majority-owned enterprises, which primarily provide technology and other services to our customers. We generate the significant majority of our revenue directly through our wholly-foreign owned enterprises, which directly capture the profits and associated cash flow from operations without having to rely on contractual arrangements to transfer such cash flow from the variable interest entities to the wholly-foreign owned enterprises.

The following diagram is a simplified illustration of the ownership structure and contractual arrangements that we typically have in place for our variable interest entities:

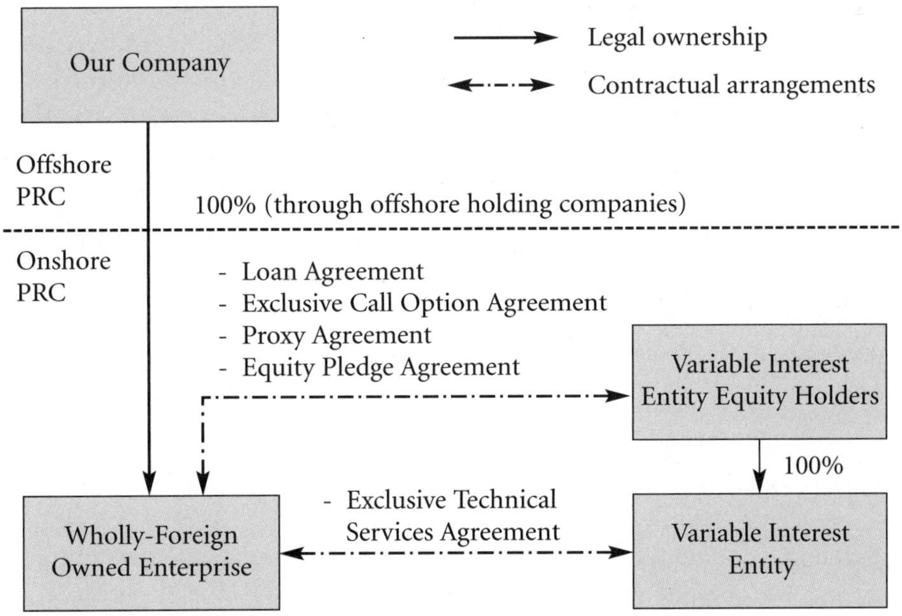

The following is a summary of the common contractual arrangements that provide us with effective control of our material variable interest entities and that enable us to receive substantially all of the economic benefits from their operations.

Contracts that give us effective control of the variable interest entities *[Loan Agreements, Exclusive Call Option Agreements, Proxy Agreements, and Equity Pledge Agreements].*

Contracts that enable us to receive substantially all of the economic benefits from the variable interest entities *[Exclusive Technical Services Agreements].*

§ 26.35 China Foreign Investment Catalogue

The *Provisions on Guiding Foreign Investment Direction* (2002) provide guidance on industries open to investment by foreign persons through FIEs and other business entities:

> Article 4. Foreign investment projects shall be classified into four categories: encouraged, permitted, restricted and prohibited projects. Foreign investment projects belonging to encouraged, restricted and prohibited categories are listed in Catalogue for the Guidance of Foreign Investment Industries. Those permitted foreign investment projects which do not belong to the above three categories are not to be listed in Catalogue for the Guidance of Foreign Investment Industries [amended 2011].

§ 26.36 Introduction to Provisions on M&A of a China Domestic Enterprise by Foreign Investors, the Foreign Investor M&A Rules

A. Introduction

China has adopted *Provisions on M&A of a Domestic Enterprise by Foreign Investors* (Foreign Investors M&A Rules), which govern all types of acquisitions of Chinese companies by foreign persons. As discussed below, Article 2 of these Foreign Investors M&A Rules deals with the following two types of transactions: (1) stock acquisitions, which are referred to as Equity Merger and Acquisition, and (2) asset acquisitions, which are referred to as Asset Merger and Acquisition.

The Foreign Investor M&A Rules apply in addition to other applicable laws and regulations, such as the China Takeover Code and the merger provisions of China Company Law. As a general matter, the M&A Rules require that the foreign investor comply with all aspects of Chinese law, including the Catalogue of Foreign Investment Industries, which is discussed *supra*, and the Anti-Monopoly Law, which is discussed *infra*. The M&A Rules are organized as follows:

Chapter 1 General Provisions

Chapter 2 Basic System

Chapter 3 Approval and Registration

Chapter 4 Foreign Investors Merge Domestic Companies Using Equity as the Means of Payment

Section 1 Conditions for Equity Merger

Section 2 Application Documents and Procedures

Section 3 Special Provisions on Special Purpose Companies

Chapter 5 Supplementary Provisions

Selected articles of the M&A Rules are set out in the next section.

B. The Provisions on M&A of Domestic Enterprise by Foreign Investors, the Foreign Investor M&A Rules

Excerpt from Provisions on M&A of a Domestic Enterprise by Foreign Investors

June 22, 2009

Chapter 1 General Provisions

Article 1 With a view to promoting and regulating foreign investors' investment in China, introducing advanced technologies and management experience from abroad, improving the utilization of foreign investment, rationalizing the allocation of resources, ensuring employment and safeguarding fair competition and our country's economic security, the Provisions are hereby formulated under the laws and administrative regulations governing foreign investment enterprises, the Company Law, and other relevant laws and administrative regulations.

Article 2 For the purposes of the Provisions, mergers and acquisitions of a domestic enterprise by foreign investors shall mean that [1] foreign investors, by agreement, purchase equity interest from shareholders of domestic enterprise with no foreign investment (hereinafter referred to as the "Domestic Company") or subscribe to the increase in the registered capital of the Domestic Company with the result that such Domestic Company changes into a foreign investment enterprise (hereinafter referred to as "**Equity Merger and Acquisition**"); or [2] the foreign investors establish a foreign investment enterprise and then, through such enterprise, purchase the assets of a domestic enterprise by agreement and operate such assets; or the foreign investors purchase the assets of a domestic enterprise by agreement and use such assets as investment to establish a foreign investment enterprise to operate such assets (hereinafter referred to as "**Asset Merger and Acquisition**").

Article 3 In mergers and acquisitions of domestic enterprises, foreign investors shall comply with the laws, administrative regulations and departmental rules and adhere to the principles of fairness, reasonableness, compensation for equal value, and honesty and good faith, and shall not create excessive concentration, eliminate or hinder competition, disturb the social economic order or harm the societal public interests, or lead to the loss of state-owned assets.

Article 4 In mergers and acquisitions of domestic enterprises, foreign investors shall comply with the requirements regarding the investors' qualifications and industrial, land and environmental protection policies as set forth in the laws, administrative regulations and departmental rules and the relevant requirements under industry policies. In the case of industries where no wholly foreign ownership is allowed under the Guidance Catalog of Foreign Investment Industries, any merger or acquisition of a domestic enterprise engaging in the industry shall not lead to the foreign investors' ownership of all equity interest in the acquired enterprise. In the case of industries which require the Chinese party to be controlling or relatively controlling, the Chinese party shall remain to be in the controlling or relatively controlling position in the acquired enterprise after any merger or acquisition of the domestic enterprise engaging in such industries. In the case of industries where operation by foreign investors is prohibited, no foreign investors may merge with or acquire any enterprise engaging in such industries. The business scope of the enterprise previously invested by the merged domestic enterprise shall meet the relevant requirements on foreign investment industrial policies; otherwise it shall be modified accordingly. * * *

Article 6 A foreign investor shall, when merging a domestic enterprise to establish a foreign-funded enterprise, be subject to the approval of the examination and approval authorities in accordance with the Provisions, and make registration of modification or establishment in the registration authority. If the enterprise to be merged is a domestic listed company, the foreign investor shall also go through relevant procedures with the securities regulatory authority under the State Council in accordance with Administration Rules on Foreign Investors' Strategic Investment in Listed Companies.

Article 7 All parties involved in the merger of domestic enterprises by foreign investors shall pay the taxes and accept the supervision of taxation authorities in accordance with China's relevant laws and regulations on taxation.

Article 8 All parties involved in the merger of domestic enterprises by foreign investors shall comply with China's relevant laws and regulations on foreign exchange control[.] * * *

Chapter 2 Basic System

Article 9 [**25% Test for FIE**] If the contribution made by a foreign investor to the registered capital of the foreign investment enterprise established after the merger or acquisition is more than 25%, such enterprise shall be treated as a foreign investment enterprise [**FIE**]. * * *

The foreign investment enterprise established after the merger of domestic listed companies by the foreign investor shall be treated in accordance with China's relevant laws and regulations.

Article 10 For the purposes of this Provisions, the approval authority [is MOFCOM]. * * *

Article 12 If foreign investors merge a domestic enterprise and obtain the actual control over the enterprise, and if such merger involves any critical industry, affects or may affect the security of national economy, or causes transference of actual control over the domestic enterprise who possesses a resound trademark or China's time—honored brand, the parties to the merger shall apply to [MOFCOM].

Article 13 [**Creditors' Rights**] Where a foreign investor carries out equity merger, the foreign investment enterprise established after the merger shall succeed to the claims and debts of the merged domestic company.

Where a foreign investor carries out asset merger, the domestic enterprise that sells assets shall assume its original claims and debts.

The foreign investor, the merged domestic enterprise, the creditors and other parties may reach an agreement additionally on the disposition of the claims and debts of the merged domestic enterprise, provided that the agreement shall not damage a third person's interests or public interests. The agreement on disposition of the claims and debts shall be submitted to the approval authority.

At least fifteen (15) days prior to the submission of application documents to the approval organ by the investors, the domestic enterprise that sells assets shall notify all creditors, and shall make a public announcement on the newspaper of provincial level or above published nationwide.

Article 14 [**Transaction Price**] The parties to a merger or acquisition shall determine the transaction price on the basis of the result of the evaluation of the equity interest to be transferred or of the assets to be sold conducted by the asset evaluation institution. The parties to a merger or acquisition may agree on an asset evaluation institution established within the territory of China in accordance with the law. Asset evaluation shall be conducted by adopting internationally recognized evaluation methods. * * *

Article 16 A foreign investor shall, when merging a domestic enterprise to establish a foreign investment enterprise, within three (3) months as of the day when the foreign investment enterprise is issued its business license, pay all the consideration to the shareholders who transfer the equities or to the domestic enterprise which sells the assets. * * *

[Articles 22 and 23 specifiy the documents that are required to be submitted for approval of the transaction by MOFCOM.]

§26.37 Acquisition of a Publicly Held China Target Pursuant to the China Takeover Code

A. Introduction

Most acquisitions of publicly held China targets are effectuated through a tender offer. Such transactions would be governed by the China Takeover Code, which, as seen from the excerpts below, is similar to the U.K. Takeover Code.

B. Excerpts from the China Takeover Code

[Selected Provisions of] Measures for the Administration on Acquisition of listed Companies, China Securities Regulatory Commission, May 17, 2006 as Amended 2012

Chapter 1: General Provisions * * *

Article 3 Acquisition of listed companies and change of relevant equity interests must be in conformity with the principles of openness, fairness, and impartiality. Information disclosure obligors in acquisition of listed companies and change of relevant equity interests shall fully disclose their rights and interests in the listed companies and information on the change of equity interest, strictly perform the obligations of making reports and public announcement as well as other statutory obligations pursuant to the law. They shall be obligated to keep the relevant information confidential before the information is disclosed.

Information reported or announced by the information disclosure obligor shall be truthful, accurate, and complete, and shall be free from any false records, misleading statements, or major omissions.* * *

Article 8 [**Fiduciary Duties, No Defensive Measures**] The directors, supervisors, and senior management personnel of the target company shall be obligated to be faithful and diligent to the company, and shall treat all the purchasers of the company on a fair basis. Decisions made and measures taken by the board of directors of the target company regarding the acquisition shall be conducive to maintaining the rights and interests of the company and its shareholders. Improper barriers shall not be established to the acquisition by abusing powers, no financial assistance in any form shall be provided to the purchasers by using the resources of the company, and the lawful rights and interests of the company and its shareholders shall not be harmed.

Article 9 A purchaser shall, when conducting acquisition of a listed company, engage a professional institution registered in China that has the qualification of conducting financial advisory services to be its financial advisor. * * *

Article 10 The CSRC shall supervise and administrate the acquisition of listed companies and change of relevant equity interests. * * *

Chapter 2: Equity Disclosure

Article 13 [Analogue to Section 13(d)] If the equity interests held by an investor and its persons acting in concert reach five percent of the issued shares of a listed company through securities transactions at securities exchanges, a report on the equity interest change shall be formulated within three days of the occurrence of the said fact[.] * * *

Chapter 3: Tender Offer

Article 23 An investor that voluntarily adopts the way of tender offer to acquire the shares of a listed company may send out to all the shareholders of the target company a tender offer for acquiring all their shares (hereinafter, "general tender offer"), and may also send out to all the shareholders of the target company a tender offer for acquiring part of their shares (hereinafter, "partial tender offer").

Article 24 [Mandatory Offer] Where, through securities transactions at securities exchange, the shares of a listed company held by a purchaser reaches 30 percent of the issued shares of the company, the purchaser shall, if continuing to increase the shareholding, adopt the way of tender offer and send out a general tender offer or a partial tender offer. * * *

Article 26 [Equal Treatment] Where a purchaser acquires a listed company by way of tender offer, the purchaser shall treat all the shareholders of the target company fairly. Shareholders that hold the same type of shares shall be treated equally. * * *

Article 35 Where a purchaser conducts tender offer pursuant to the provisions of these Measures, the offered price for the same type of stocks shall not be lower than the highest price paid by the purchaser for that type of stocks within six months before the brief announcement is made on the tender offer. * * *

Article 37 The period of acquisition agreed upon in the tender offer shall not be less than 30 days and shall not exceed 60 days, except for any occurrence of competing tender offers.

Within the acceptance period agreed upon in the tender offer, the purchaser shall not cancel its tender offer.

Article 38 If the way of tender offer is adopted, the purchaser shall not, after making a public announcement and before the expiry of the acquisition term, sell the stocks of the target company, nor shall it buy any stocks of the target company by any method that is not specified in the tender offer or by exceeding the conditions of the tender offer.

Article 39 All the acquisition conditions proposed in a tender offer shall apply to all the shareholders of a target company. * * *

Article 42 [Withdrawal Rights] * * * Within three trading days before the expiry of the period of the tender offer, the shareholders that have preliminarily accepted the tender offer may entrust a securities company to go through the formalities for withdrawing the preliminarily accepted tender offer, and the securities registration and settlement institution shall, upon application for withdrawal filed by the shareholders that have preliminarily accepted the tender offer, release the temporary custody of the shares of which the holders have preliminarily accepted the tender offer. * * *

Article 46 An investor shall not purchase the shares of a listed company outside the securities exchange, except by means of tender offer.

Article 51 [Management Buyouts] Where any director, supervisor, senior management personnel, staff member of a listed company, and any legal person or other organization that it controls or entrusts, intends to acquire that listed company or obtain the controlling right of that company by the means specified in Chapter 5 of these Measures (hereinafter, "management buyout"), that listed company shall have a well-established and well-performing organizational structure and effective internal control system, and the proportion of independent directors among the members of the board of directors shall reach or exceed one half. The company shall engage an asset evaluation institution with practice qualifications related to securities and futures to provide an asset evaluation report for the company. The present acquisition shall be subject to a resolution made by the non-affiliated directors from the board of directors, and the resolution shall be submitted to the general meeting of shareholders for deliberation upon consent of two thirds or more of the independent directors, and shall be subject to adoption by more than one half of the non-affiliated shareholders with voting rights that are present at the meeting of the general meeting of shareholders. Before independent directors express opinions, an independent financial advisor shall be engaged to present professional opinions concerning the present acquisition, and the opinions of the independent directors and independent financial advisor shall be jointly announced. * * *

§ 26.38 Acquisition of a China Target Through the Use of the Merger Provisions of China Company Law

A. Introduction

In effectuating the acquisition of a China target, consideration should be given to utilizing the merger provisions of China's Company Law. If these provisions are used, (1) the assets and liabilities of the target will pass to the acquiror by operation of law, thus eliminating the need for asset transfer documents, and (2) all shareholders will be forced to give up their shares for the merger consideration. There does not appear to be a prohibition against merging a China company controlled by Chinese persons into a China company controlled by foreigners, such as a WFOE. In addition to complying with the China Company Law relating to mergers, the parties must also comply with the MOFCOM's *Provisions on the Merger and Division of Enterprises with Foreign Investment* (FIE Merger Regulation). The merger provisions of the China's Company Law, which are not very detailed, are set out below followed by selected provisions of the FIE Merger Regulation.

B. Merger Provisions of China Company Law

Article 172 Merger of companies may either be merger by consolidation or merger by incorporation. Merger by consolidation shall mean that a company absorbs other companies while the absorbed companies shall be dissolved. Merger by incorporation shall mean that two or more companies merge into a newly incorporated company while all the merged parties shall be dissolved.

Article 173 In the case of a merger of companies, the parties thereto shall conclude a merger agreement and prepare the balance sheet and a list of property. The companies shall notify their creditors within ten days after the resolution on merger is made, and shall publish an announcement in newspapers within 30 days. The creditors may, within 30 days upon receipt of the written notice or, in the case of failure to receive the written notice, within 45 days of the public announcement, request the company to repay the debts or provide the corresponding guaranty.

Article 174 In the case of a merger of companies, the claims and debts of each of the companies to the merger shall be succeeded to by the company continuing to exist after the merger or the newly incorporated company. * * *

[Shareholder Vote on a Merger, *See* Article 43 of Chinese Corporate Law, *supra*, Two-Thirds Vote Required.]

C. Provisions on the Merger and Division of Enterprises with Foreign Investment, the FIE Merger Regulation

MOFCOM's Provisions on the Merger and Division of Enterprises with Foreign Investment

September 25, 1999

Article 1 These Provisions are formulated in accordance with the Company Law of the People's Republic of China and the laws and administrative regulations concerning enterprises with foreign investment for the purpose of regulating the acts relating to the merger and division of enterprises with foreign investment and protecting the legitimate rights and interests of the investors and creditors thereof.

Article 2 These Provisions shall apply to the merger or division of Chinese-foreign equity joint ventures, incorporated Chinese-foreign contractual joint ventures, foreign-capital enterprises and joint stock limited companies with foreign investment (hereinafter referred to as companies) that have been set up within the territory of the People's Republic of China in accordance with the laws of the land.

The merger of such a company with a Chinese-invested company shall be handled with reference to the relevant laws, administrative regulations and these Provisions.

Article 3 The term "merger" as used in these Provisions refers to the consolidation through the conclusion of agreements into one company of two or more companies in accordance with the relevant provisions of the Company Law.

The merger of companies may be achieved in two forms: merger by absorption or merger by new establishment.

Merger by absorption refers to a company that absorbs other companies as its own future components, the absorbing company continues to exist while the participating ones are dissolved.

Merger by new establishment refers to the merging of two or more companies into a new company, with all the participating companies dissolved after the establishment of the new company. * * *

Article 5 The merger or division of companies shall be carried out in strict observance of the laws and administrative regulations of China and these Provisions, and on the basis of the principle of free, equal and fair competition, and the public interests of society and the legitimate rights and interests of the creditors shall not be jeopardized. * * *

Article 10 The company that emerges from the merger between two or more liability limited companies shall be a liability limited company.

The company that emerges from the merger of two or more joint stock companies [*i.e.*, now a company limited by shares] shall be a joint stock company. The company emerging from the merger between a listed joint stock company and a limited liability company shall be a joint stock company. The company that emerges from the merger between an unlisted joint stock company and a limited liability company may either be a joint stock company or a limited liability company. * * *

Article 16 The merger or division involving listed joint stock companies shall conform to the pertinent laws and administrative regulations and the provisions on listed companies of the state securities regulatory authorities and be subjected to the necessary procedures for examination and approval.

Article 17 The merger between a foreign-invested company and a domestic Chinese-invested company must be in conformity with the provisions of the relevant laws and administrative regulation governing the utilization of foreign investment in China and with the requirements of the industrial policies, and must meet the following conditions:

1. The Chinese company to be merged with must either be a limited liability company or a joint stock company set up in accordance with the norms of the Company Law of the People's Republic of China;

2. The investors of the new company emerging from the merger shall satisfy the qualification requirements as contained in the relevant laws, administrative regulations and sector regulations for investors in the relevant industry the new company is engaged in;

3. The equity proportion of foreign investors in the new company shall be no less than 25% of the registered capital of the new company resulting from the merger; and

4. All the parties to the merger agreement shall see to it that the original employees of the companies to be merged are fully re-employed or reasonably re-assigned to jobs. * * *

§ 26.39 Asset or Stock Acquisition of a Closely-Held China Target

A. Asset Acquisition

A U.S. acquiror could acquire a closely-held China target through an asset acquisition. Although the China Company Law does not have a provision dealing with a sale of all or substantially all of a target's assets, it does have the following provision governing the dissolution and liquidation of a company:

Article 180 A company may be dissolved for any of the following reasons:

(1) The term of operation specified in the company's articles of association expires or any of the other causes of dissolution specified in the company's articles of association occurs;

(2) The shareholders' meeting or the general meeting makes a resolution to dissolve the company [A two-thirds vote is required, *see* Article 43];

(3) Dissolution is required by a merger or division of the company[.] * * *

B. Stock Acquisition and H.B. Fuller's Acquisition of China's Tonsan

An acquirer could acquire a closely-held China target through a stock acquisition. A stock acquisition was used in 2014 by H.B. Fuller, a publicly-held U.S. corporation, in its acquisition, through a Singaporean subsidiary, of Tonsan, a closely held Chinese company limited by shares. The stock purchase agreement for the transaction, which is Appendix NN, looks very much like a stock purchase agreement for an American target.

§ 26.40 Introduction to Coca-Cola's Blocked Tender Offer for China's Huiyuan Juice Group

A. The Press Release

In 2008, Coca-Cola and China Huiyuan Juice Group Ltd, a Hong Kong publicly held corporation, announced that Coke was going to acquire Huiyuan, which has its principal business activities in China. Appendix MM sets out the *Joint Announcement of the Deal*, and the September 3, 2008 press release on the deal explains:

> The Coca-Cola Company announced today its intention to make cash offers to purchase China Huiyuan Juice Group Limited, a Hong Kong listed company which owns the Huiyuan juice business throughout China.
>
> The Coca-Cola business in China has been operating since 1979[.] "Huiyuan is a long-established and successful juice brand in China and is highly complementary to the Coca-Cola China business[.]" * * *
>
> The making of the offers is subject to preconditions relating to Chinese regulatory approvals. * * *
>
> The Coca-Cola Company is offering HK$12.20 per share, and an equivalent price for outstanding convertible bonds and options.
>
> The Company has accepted irrevocable undertakings from three shareholders for acceptance of the offers, in aggregate representing approximately 66 percent of the Huiyuan shares.
>
> Assuming full acceptance of the offers, the deal is valued at approximately US $2.4 billion. The transaction is expected to be dilutive to the Company's earnings per share by $0.03 to $0.04 in the first full year following completion of the acquisition and accretive to earnings per share in year 3 after completion. * * *

B. The Joint Announcement under the Hong Kong Takeover Code

As indicated in Appendix MM, the transaction was to be effectuated through a tender offer by Coke for the shares of Huiyuan. The offer was to be made pursuant to the Takeover Code of Hong Kong. The Joint Announcement provides as follows with respect to the transaction:

> 1. INTRODUCTION
>
> The Coca-Cola Company, Atlantic Industries and Huiyuan jointly announce that ABN AMRO will, on behalf of Atlantic Industries, a wholly-owned subsidiary of The Coca-Cola Company, subject to the satisfaction of the Pre-Condition, make voluntary conditional cash offers: (a) to acquire all of the issued shares in the share capital of Huiyuan; (b) to acquire all the outstanding convertible bonds of Huiyuan; and (c) for the cancellation of all the outstanding options of Huiyuan. All references to the Offers in this Announcement are possible Offers which will be made if and only if the Pre-Condition is satisfied. * * *

3. PRE-CONDITION TO THE SHARE OFFER AND CONDITIONS OF THE OFFERS

The making of the Offers is subject to the satisfaction of the Pre-Condition, namely that any applicable waiting periods for a response from the relevant governmental or regulatory body have expired or been terminated and/or any consent or approval (including any antitrust approval) of any governmental or regulatory body in relation to the Share Offer or the completion thereof have been obtained in terms reasonably satisfactory to the Offeror pursuant to the provisions of any laws or regulations in the PRC, in each case where necessary for completion of the Share Offer.

Atlantic Industries will issue a Further Announcement after the Pre-Condition has been satisfied. * * *

9. COMPOSITE DOCUMENT

It is expected that a Composite Document [i.e., Offering Circular], comprising the offer document and the response document, which sets out the terms and details of the Offers, the advice of the Huiyuan IBC, the letter from the Huiyuan IFA, together with the acceptance and transfer forms in respect of the Offers, will be despatched to the Huiyuan Shareholders, the Huiyuan Bondholders and the Huiyuan Optionholders by the Latest Despatch Date.

C. Similarities of the Hong Kong Approach to Tender Offers to the Approaches in the U.K., the E.U., South Africa, and China

It should be noted that the Joint Announcement of the deal by Coke and Huiyuan in Appendix MM is similar in structure to the Joint Announcement of the deal by Walmart and Massmart in Appendix KK. If the Coke-Huiyuan deal had gone forward, an offering circular similar to the offering circular in Appendix LL for the Walmart-Massmart deal would have been used. The similarity in approaches to these issues in Hong Kong and South Africa is attributable to the similarities of each of their takeover codes to the takeover code in the U.K., which is the basis of the E.U.'s Takeover Directive. Also, a similar approach is taken under the China's Takeover Code, which is discussed *supra*.

§ 26.41 Antitrust Review of Mergers and Acquisitions in China

A. China's 2007 Anti-Monopoly Law (AML)

Anti-Monopoly Law of the People's Republic of China

Adopted at the 29th meeting of the Standing Committee of the 10th National People's Congress of the People's Republic of China on August 30, 2007.

Article 1 This Law is enacted for the purpose of preventing and restraining monopolistic conducts, protecting fair competition in the market, enhancing economic efficiency, safeguarding the interests of consumers and social public interest, promoting the healthy development of the socialist market economy.

Article 2 This Law shall be applicable to monopolistic conducts in economic activities within the People's Republic of China.

This Law shall apply to the conducts outside the territory of the People's Republic of China if they eliminate or have restrictive effect on competition on the domestic market of the PRC.

Article 3 For the purposes of this Law, "monopolistic conducts" are defined as the following:

(1) monopolistic agreements among business operators;

(2) abuse of dominant market positions by business operators; and

(3) concentration of business operators that eliminates or restricts competition or might be eliminating or restricting competition. * * *

Article 9 The State Council shall establish the Anti-monopoly Commission, which is in charge of organizing, coordinating, guiding anti-monopoly work[.] * * *

Article 10 The anti-monopoly authority designated by the State Council (hereinafter referred to as the Anti-monopoly Authority under the State Council) shall be in charge of anti-monopoly law enforcement in accordance with this Law. * * *

Article 20 **[Definition of Concentration]** A concentration refers to the following circumstances:

(1) the merger of business operators;

(2) acquiring control over other business operators by virtue of acquiring their equities or assets; or

(3) acquiring control over other business operators or possibility of exercising decisive influence on other business operators by virtue of contract or any other means.

Article 21 Where a concentration reaches the threshold of declaration stipulated by the State Council, a declaration must be lodged in advance with the Anti-monopoly Authority under the State Council, or otherwise the concentration shall not be implemented.

Article 22 Where a concentration is under any of the following circumstances, it may not be declared to the Anti-monopoly Authority under the State Council:

(1) one business operator who is a party to the concentration has the power to exercise more than half the voting rights of every other business operator, whether of the equity or the assets; or

(2) one business operator who is not a party to the concentration has the power to exercise more than half the voting rights of every business operator concerned, whether of the equity or the assets.

Article 23 A business operator shall, when lodging a concentration declaration with the Anti-monopoly Authority under the State Council, submit the following documents and materials:

(1) a declaration paper;

(2) explanations on the effect of the concentration on the relevant market competition;

(3) the agreement of concentration;

(4) the financial reports and accounting reports of the proceeding accounting year of the business operator; and

(5) other documents and materials as stipulated by the Anti-monopoly Authority under the State Council. * * *

Article 25 **[Initial 30-Day Review]** The Anti-monopoly Authority under the State Council shall conduct a preliminary review of the declared concentration of business operators, make a decision whether to conduct further review and notify the business operators in written form within 30 days upon receipt of the documents and materials submitted by the business operators pursuant to Article 23 of this Law. Before such a decision is made by the Anti-monopoly Authority under the State Council, the concentration may be not implemented.

Where the Anti-monopoly Authority under the State Council decides not to conduct further review or fails to make a decision at expiry of the stipulated period, the concentration may be implemented.

Article 26 **[Further 90-Day Review]** Where the Anti-monopoly Authority under the State Council decides to conduct further review, they shall, within 90 days from the date of decision, complete the review, make a decision on whether to prohibit the concentration, and notify the business operators concerned of the decision in written form. A decision of prohibition shall be attached with reasons therefor. Within the review period the concentration may not be implemented.

Under any of the following circumstances, the Anti-monopoly Authority under the State Council may notify the business operators in written form that the time limit as stipulated in the preceding paragraph may be extended to no more than 60 days:

(1) the business operators concerned agree to extend the time limit;

(2) the documents or materials submitted are inaccurate and need further verification;

(3) things have significantly changed after declaration.

If the Anti-monopoly Authority under the State Council fails to make a decision at expiry of the period, the concentration may be implemented.

Article 27 **[Factors to be Considered]** In the case of the examination on the concentration of business operators, it shall consider the relevant elements as follows:

(1) the market share of the business operators involved in the relevant market and the controlling power thereof over that market,

(2) the degree of market concentration in the relevant market,

(3) the influence of the concentration of business operators on the market access and technological progress,

(4) the influence of the concentration of business operators on the consumers and other business operators,

(5) the influence of the concentration of business operators on the national economic development, and

(6) other elements that may have an effect on the market competition and shall be taken into account as regarded by the Anti-monopoly Authority under the State Council.

Article 28 **[Enforcement Standard]** Where a concentration has or may have the effect of eliminating or restricting competition, the Anti-monopoly Authority under the State Council shall make a decision to prohibit the concentration. However, if the business operators concerned can prove that the concentration will bring more positive impact than negative impact on competition, or the concentration is pursuant to public interests, the Anti-monopoly Authority under the State Council may decide not to prohibit the concentration.

Article 29 [**Approval with Conditions**] Where the concentration is not prohibited, the Anti-monopoly Authority under the State Council may decide to attach restrictive conditions for reducing the negative impact of such concentration on competition.

Article 30 Where the Anti-monopoly Authority under the State Council decides to prohibit a concentration or attaches restrictive conditions on concentration, it shall publicize such decisions to the general public in a timely manner.

Article 31 [**National Security Concerns**] Where a foreign investor merges and acquires a domestic enterprise or participate in concentration by other means, if state security is involved, besides the examination on the concentration in accordance with this Law, the examination on national security shall also be conducted in accordance with the relevant State provisions. * * *

B. MOFCOM's Procedural Aspects of the Anti-Monopoly Law

MOFCOM, Guiding Opinions on the Antitrust Thresholds

June 2014

[B]usiness operators shall apply to the Ministry of Commerce ("MOFCOM") in advance for proposed transactions of concentration of business operators that reach the application thresholds, and shall not carry out such concentration transactions without application. * * *

Article 1 For the purpose of these Guiding Opinions, concentration of business operators shall refer to any of the following circumstances prescribed by Article 20 of the Anti-monopoly Law:

(1) Where business operators merge;

(2) Where one business operator gains the controlling power of another business operator by acquiring the latter's equities or assets; or

(3) Where one business operator gains the controlling power of another business operator or is able to exert decisive influence on another business operator through contracts or by other means.

Article 2 [Reporting Thresholds] For the purpose of these Guiding Opinions, application thresholds shall refer to any of the following thresholds prescribed by Article 3 of the Provisions:

(1) Where the combined worldwide turnover of all business operators participating in a concentration transaction in the preceding fiscal year exceeds RMB 10 billion, and the turnover within the Mainland of at least two of the participating business operators in the preceding fiscal year exceeds RMB 400 million each; or

(2) Where the combined turnover within the Mainland of all business operators participating in a concentration transaction in the preceding fiscal year exceeds RMB 2 billion, and the turnover within the Mainland of at least two of the participating business operators in the preceding fiscal year exceeds RMB 400 million each.

Article 13 A transaction of concentration of business operators by way of merger shall be reported by all the business operators participating in the merger. * * *

Article 14 An applicant shall apply to the MOFCOM for a transaction of concentration of business operators after the conclusion of concentration agreements but prior to the implementation of the concentration. Where a listed company is to be acquired by way of a public take-over offer, a written report on acquisition by take-over offer that has been announced may be deemed as a concentration agreement that has been signed. * * *

Article 20 The application documents and materials submitted by an applicant for a transaction of concentration of business operators shall include the following: * * *

(2) Descriptions of the impact of the concentration transaction on competition on relevant markets, covering the overview of the concentration transaction; the motive, purposes and economic rationality analysis of the concentration; definitions of the relevant markets; the shares held by each participating business operator in the relevant markets and the Controlling Power thereof over the relevant markets; main competitors and their market shares; the degree of market concentration; market entry; current situations of industry development; the impact of the concentration on the market competition structure, industry development, technological progress, national economic development, consumers and other business operators, etc[.] * * *

Article 26 Applications for simple cases shall be submitted by reference to the Guiding Opinions on the Application for Simple Cases of Concentration of Business Operators (for Trial Implementation). * * *

C. MOFCOM's Decision in Coke's Proposed Acquisition of Huiyuan

China's Ministry of Commerce (MOFCOM), Statement Blocking Coca-Cola's Acquisition of Huiyuan

March 18, 2009

On September 18, 2008, the Ministry of Commerce received the anti-monopoly notification materials for a concentration of business operators, Coca-Cola Co.'s acquisition of China Huiyuan Co. After additional materials were submitted to meet the requirements of Article 23 of the Antimonopoly Law, the Ministry of Commerce opened its review of this concentration on November 20 and, based on this preliminary review, on December 20 decided to conduct a further examination.

In accordance with the relevant provisions of the Antimonopoly Law, the Ministry of Commerce reviewed various aspects of this concentration including: market share and market control, the degree of market concentration, the impact on market access and technological progress, the impact on consumers and other business operators, and the impact of brands on market competition in the juice market. The review was in strict compliance with relevant laws and regulations. The views of parties concerned were fully aired during the review process.

Through its review, the Ministry of Commerce found that this concentration will have an adverse impact on competition. After the concentration is completed, Coca-Cola could use its market dominance in carbonated soft drinks to limit competition in the market for juice through tying, bundling or other exclusive transactions, resulting in consumers being forced to accept higher prices and reduced variety. At the same time, because brands can restrict entry to the market, it would be hard for the threat of potential competition to remove the restrictive effect on competition. In addition, the concentration will also reduce the room for small and medium-sized juice companies to survive, and will have an adverse effect on the structure of competition in China's juice market.

In order to reduce this concentration's adverse effects on competition, the Ministry of Commerce negotiated with Coca-Cola Co. about adding restrictive conditions, and asked it to submit a workable solution. Coca-Cola Co. expressed their views on the issues raised by the Ministry of Commerce, and submitted a preliminary resolution proposal and a revised proposal.

After an assessment, the Ministry of Commerce concluded that the revised proposal still could not effectively reduce this concentration's adverse impact on competition. Therefore, under Article 28 of the Antimonopoly Law, the Ministry of Commerce decided to forbid the concentration.

The goal of antimonopoly review is to protect fair market competition, and to safeguard the interests of consumers as well as the public interest. Since the Antimonopoly Law went into effect on August 1, 2008, the Ministry of Commerce has received 40 notifications of a concentration of business operators. In accordance with the law, 29 of these cases have been reviewed. Of the 24 cases that have been completed, 23 were approved unconditionally. For the one concentration that had the effect of eliminating or limiting competition, the Ministry of Commerce negotiated with the notifying party, who made commitments and proposed a plan to reduce the effects on competition. The Ministry of Commerce approved this concentration after adding restrictive conditions to reduce the adverse effect on competition.

References

Lorne, *Negotiated and Contested Transactions, supra* Section 1.10, at Chapter 8.

Thompson, *Mergers, Acquisitions and Tender Offers, supra* Section 1.10, at Chapters 19 and 20.

Chapter 27

Special M&A Situations: Regulated Industries, Bankruptcy, Joint Ventures

§ 27.1 Scope

This chapter provides a brief introduction to the following special M&A situations: (1) banking acquisitions (Section 27.2), (2) telecom acquisitions (Section 27.3), (3) public utility acquisitions (Section 27.4), (4) health care acquisitions (Section 27.5), (5) bankruptcy acquisitions (Section 27.6), and (6) joint ventures (Section 27.7). Each of these topics is covered by separate chapters in Thompson, *Mergers, Acquisitions and Tender Offers*, *supra* Section 1.10.

In addition to the rules introduced in this chapter, in each of these situations, the pre-merger notification rules (Chapter 9) are generally applicable, and the transactions are subject to substantive antitrust scrutiny under Section 7 of the Clayton Act (Chapter 8).

§ 27.2 Brief Introduction to Bank Acquisitions

A. In General

The issues with bank acquisitions are covered in greater detail in Chapter 17 of Thompson, *Mergers, Acquisitions and Tender Offers*, *supra* Section 1.10.

Since banks play a key role in the economy, the safety and soundness of banks is an important factor in economic growth. Therefore, bank regulation is extensive and complex, with many different acts and institutions involved. This section presents a very basic introduction to bank regulation, with an emphasis on regulation of acquisition activity.

Banks may be incorporated (chartered) under state or federal law. This note focuses only on national banks. The National Bank Act, which was enacted in 1863 and extensively amended since, sets out the basic regulation for national banks. The principal regulator for national banks is the Office of the Comptroller of the Currency (COC), which is a division of the U.S. Treasury Department. The charter for a national bank is issued by the COC (National Bank Act, 12 U.S.C. §§ 21–24). The terms of a national bank charter are similar to the terms of a certificate of incorporation under state law, and the National Bank Act sets out specific voting and dissenting rules for mergers involving national banks. *See* National Bank Act 12 U.S.C. § 215a. Also, under the Bank Merger Act amendments to the National Bank Act, bank mergers require the approval of the COC pursuant to specific standards. *See* National Bank Act § 1828(c), as amended by the Bank Merger Act.

National banks are required to have deposit insurance from the Federal Deposit Insurance Corporation (FDIC), and the FDIC applies certain factors set out in the National Bank

Act (12 U.S.C. § 1816) in deciding whether to grant a request for such insurance. Also, national banks are required to be members of the Federal Reserve System (12 U.S.C. § 222), which was established by the Federal Reserve Act (12 U.S.C. 241 *et. seq.*), enacted in 1913 and extensively amended since 1913. The System is run by the Board of Governors of the Federal Reserve [Bank] System (FRB), which has its headquarters in Washington, D.C. In addition to its bank regulatory role, the FRB is responsible for the conduct of monetary policy. This System membership by national banks subjects them to expanded regulation and gives them the ability to borrow from the FRB through what is known as the "discount window."

The Glass-Steagall Act of 1933 required banking to be separated from other business activity, including investment banking. As a result of the Bank Holding Company Act of 1956 (BHC Act), which relaxed to a degree the Glass-Steagall Act, a bank may be a subsidiary of a holding company that holds other non-bank subsidiaries that are engaged in businesses that are "closely related" to banking. Because of the "closely related" requirement, a bank holding company cannot own, for example, an industrial firm. Bank holding companies are incorporated under state general corporate law, such as the Delaware General Corporate Law, and they have at least one subsidiary that is a bank.

Most large and sophisticated banks are subsidiaries of publicly-held bank holding companies. For example, J.P. Morgan Chase Bank is a wholly-owned subsidiary of J.P. Morgan Chase & Co., a publicly-held Delaware corporation that is a bank holding company engaging in non-banking business activities through its other subsidiaries. Large bank holding companies, like J.P. Morgan Chase, are "financial holding companies," a concept adopted by the Gramm-Leach-Bliley Act (GLB Act), which was enacted in November 1999. As a financial holding company, J.P. Morgan Chase, Inc. through separate subsidiaries can engage in a broader range of non-banking activities (including insurance and investment banking without limitation) than is permitted for bank holding companies that are not also financial holding companies. Thus, the GLB Act further relaxed the Glass-Steagall Act. It must be remembered that all financial holding companies are bank holding companies, but not all bank holding companies are financial holding companies.

The Dodd-Frank Wall Street Reform and Consumer Protection Act of 2010 (Dodd-Frank Act) was enacted in response to the 2007–2008 financial crisis, and a part of the Act, known as the Volcker Rule, prevents banks, bank holding companies, and financial holding companies from engaging in certain proprietary trading, hedge fund, and private equity activities. Thus, the Volcker Rule cuts back on some of the liberalizations to the Glass-Steagall Act brought on by the Bank Holding Company Act and the GLB Act.

The FRB is the principal regulator of bank holding companies and financial holding companies. Thus, the FRB has regulatory authority over the acquisition of bank holding companies, including financial holding companies. Even though the FRB regulates bank holding companies, the COC is the principal regulator of any national bank that is a subsidiary of a bank holding company.

The Change in Bank Control Act of 1978 (CBCA) amended the National Bank Act to require prior approval of a change of control of an insured depository institution. *See* § 1817(j) of the National Bank Act, as amended by the CBCA. This provision applies generally to changes of control of banks that do not involve (1) bank mergers, or (2) acquisitions of bank holding companies. The approval standards under the Bank Merger Act, the BHC Act, and the CBCA are essentially the same. Thus, the standards discussed below for mergers under the BHC Act generally apply also under the Bank Merger Act and the CBCA.

B. Criteria Applied by the FRB in Deciding Whether to Approve an Acquisition of a Bank Holding Company or Financial Holding Company

Section 3 of the Bank Holding Company Act (12 U.S.C. § 1842(c)), as amended by the Dodd-Frank Act, sets out the factors the FRB is required to consider in determining whether to approve an application for an acquisition of a bank holding company:

(c) **Factors for consideration by Board**

(1) **Competitive factors**

The Board shall not approve—

(A) any acquisition or merger or consolidation under this section which would result in a monopoly, or which would be in furtherance of any combination or conspiracy to monopolize or to attempt to monopolize the business of banking in any part of the United States, or

(B) any other proposed acquisition or merger or consolidation under this section whose effect in any section of the country may be substantially to lessen competition, or to tend to create a monopoly, or which in any other manner would be in restraint or trade, unless it finds that the anticompetitive effects of the proposed transaction are clearly outweighed in the public interest by the probable effect of the transaction in meeting the convenience and needs of the community to be served.

(2) **Banking and community factors**

In every case, the Board shall take into consideration the financial and managerial resources and future prospects of the company or companies and the banks concerned, and the convenience and needs of the community to be served.

(3) **Supervisory factors**

The Board shall disapprove any application under this section by any company if—

(A) the company fails to provide the Board with adequate assurances that the company will make available to the Board such information on the operations or activities of the company, and any affiliate of the company, as the Board determines to be appropriate to determine and enforce compliance with this chapter; or

(B) in the case of an application involving a foreign bank, the foreign bank is not subject to comprehensive supervision or regulation on a consolidated basis by the appropriate authorities in the bank's home country.

(4) **Treatment of certain bank stock loans** * * *

(5) **Managerial resources**

Consideration of the managerial resources of a company or bank under paragraph (2) shall include consideration of the competence, experience, and integrity of the officers, directors, and principal shareholders of the company or bank.

(6) **Money laundering** * * *

(7) **Financial stability**

> In every case, the Board shall take into consideration the extent to which a proposed acquisition, merger, or consolidation would result in greater or more concentrated risks to the stability of the United States banking or financial system.

Paragraph (1)(A) is analogous to Section 2 of the Sherman Act (*see* Chapter 8) and will not normally be of issue. Paragraph (1)(B) is the analogue to Section 7 of the Clayton Act (*see* Chapter 8); however, the provision has a public interest exception that is not available under Section 7. The financial stability factor was added by the Dodd-Frank Act.

The above factors are also applicable to mergers of banks under the Bank Merger Act and to acquisitions of control of banks under the Change in Bank Control Act.

C. Basic Merger and Acquisition Principles Applicable to Acquisitions of Financial Holding Companies

In addition to the bank regulatory requirements discussed in this chapter, the basic principles governing mergers and acquisitions discussed in preceding chapters, such as directors' duties, tax, accounting, and antitrust are generally applicable to acquisitions of financial holding companies. This can be seen from a review of the merger agreement and Form S-4 Registration Statement and Joint Proxy Statements for the J.P. Morgan Chase, Inc. acquisition of Bank One, set out in Documentary Appendices D and E of *M&A Statutes, Rules, and Documents, supra* Section 1.1.

§ 27.3 Brief Introduction to Telecom Acquisitions

A. In General

The issues with telecom acquisitions are covered in greater detail in Chapter 18 of Thompson, *Mergers, Acquisitions and Tender Offers, supra* Section 1.10.

This section focuses on some of the issues arising in mergers and acquisitions in the telecommunications industry. This industry encompasses local phone companies, long distance phone companies, cellular companies, satellite operators, cable operators, and broadcasters, that is, radio and TV stations. The principal focus here is on the rules and regulations governing mergers and acquisitions under the Communications Act of 1934, which is administered by the Federal Communications Commission (FCC).

B. Provision of the Communications Act of 1934 Governing Mergers and Acquisitions of Telephone Companies [*i.e.*, Common Carriers] and of Holders of FCC Licenses

1. Introduction

The extension, acquisition or operation of a telephone line requires the approval of the FCC under Section 214(a) of the Communications Act of 1934, which is set out below. Also, telephone companies may be involved in several businesses, such as wireless operations, that require "licenses" from the FCC, and the transfer of any such license requires approval of the FCC under Section 310(d) of the Communications Act of 1934, which also is set out below.

2. Section 214(a) of the Communications Act of 1934, Extension of Lines

(a) No carrier [*i.e.*, telephone company] shall undertake the construction of a new line or of an extension of any line, or shall acquire or operate any line, or extension thereof, or shall engage in transmission over or by means of such additional or extended line, unless and until there shall first have been obtained from the Commission a certificate that the present or future public convenience and necessity require or will require the construction, or operation, or construction and operation, of such additional or extended line * * *.

3. Section 310(d) of the Communications Act of 1934

(d) No construction permit or station license, or any rights thereunder, shall be transferred, assigned, or disposed of in any manner, voluntarily or involuntarily, directly or indirectly, or by transfer of control of any corporation holding such permit or license, to any person except upon application to the Commission and upon finding by the Commission that the public interest, convenience, and necessity will be served thereby. * * *

4. Application of the Public Interest Standards in Sections 214(a) and 310(d)

In 1999 SBC (now AT&T), a Baby Bell, acquired Ameritech, a Baby Bell. In addition to their local telephone operations both companies were engaged, *inter alia*, in the cellular business. In the order approving the transaction, the FCC discussed the manner in which it applies the public interest standard in both Sections 214(a) and 310(d):

FCC, Memorandum Opinion and Order, In Re Applications of Ameritech Corp., Transferor, and SBC Communications Inc., Transferee

(October 8, 1999)

* * * **Public Interest Framework.** Pursuant to sections 214(a) and 310(d) of the Communications Act, the Commission must determine whether the Applicants have demonstrated that the public interest would be served by transferring Ameritech's numerous licenses and lines used in interstate or foreign communications to SBC. * * *

The public interest standard of sections 214(a) and 310(d) involves a balancing process that weighs the potential public interest harms of the proposed transaction against its potential public interest benefits. The Applicants bear the burden of proving, by a preponderance of the evidence, that the proposed transaction, on balance, serves the public interest. In applying this public interest test, the Commission considers four overriding questions: (1) whether the transaction would result in a violation of the Communications Act or any other applicable statutory provision; (2) whether the transaction would result in a violation of Commission rules; (3) whether the transaction would substantially frustrate or impair the Commission's implementation or enforcement of the Communications Act, or would interfere with the objectives of that and other statutes; and (4) whether the merger promises to yield affirmative public interest benefits. In summary, the Applicants must demonstrate that the transaction will not violate or interfere with the objectives of the Communications Act or Commission rules, and that the predominant effect of the transfer will be to advance the public interest.

The Commission's analysis of public interest benefits and harms includes, but is not limited to, an analysis of the potential competitive effects of the transaction, as informed by traditional antitrust principles. While an antitrust analysis, such as that undertaken by the DOJ in this case, focuses solely on whether the effect of a proposed merger "may be substantially to lessen competition," the Communications Act requires the Commission to make an independent public interest determination, which includes evaluating public interest benefits or harms of the merger's likely effect on future competition. In order to find that a merger is in the public interest, therefore, the Commission must "be convinced that it will enhance competition." * * *

C. Mergers in the Broadcast Industry

1. Introduction

An acquisition of a TV or radio station requires approval of the license transfer from the FCC under Section 310(d) of the Communications Act of 1934 [*see* Section 27.3.B.3], which applies a "public interest" standard. In addition, such transactions must not violate various FCC objective restrictions on ownership of such companies. The various ownership limitations are in a state of flux after several courts have found them to be arbitrary and capricious.

2. Summary of Regulation after the 1996 Telecommunications Act

Michael I. Meyerson, Ideas of the Market Place: A Guide to the 1996 Telecommunications Act

49 Federal Communications Law Journal 251, 277–78, 279–280 (1997)

The lowest-tech players in the telecommunications revolution, the broadcasters, received significant regulatory relief from the 1996 Act. In addition to the changes in the rules governing cable ownership of stations and networks, broadcasters also benefited from the deregulatory tradewinds. Ironically, though, most of the changes affecting broadcasters actually serve to limit intramedia competition. * * *

Many of the limits on multiple ownership of broadcast licenses have been eased or eliminated [by the Telecommunications Act of 1996]. On a national level, the limit on the number of AM or FM radio stations which can be controlled by one entity was eliminated. [Section 202(a)] The national limit on the number of television stations was also removed, [Section 202(c)(1)(A)] and now the only remaining national ceiling is that one entity cannot own television stations which, together, reach more than 35 percent of the nation's television households. [Section 202(b)]

The rules governing multiple-ownership within a particular local market have been relaxed, though not eliminated. For radio, a complicated matrix was created, with the number of permissible co-owned stations dependent both on the number of available commercial radio stations and whether the stations are concentrated in the same "service," either the AM or FM band. [Section 202(b)] * * *

Congress was not willing to make a final decision as to local ownership limits for television stations. Instead, the 1996 Act directs the FCC to "conduct a rulemaking proceeding to determine whether to retain, modify or eliminate" the current ban on owning more than one station in a market (the so-called "duopoly rule"). [Section 202(c)(2)] While not expressing any position on this issue directly, Congress did state in the Conference Report that if the duopoly rules were revised, VHF-VHF combinations should only be allowed in "compelling circumstances." [H.R. Conf. Rep. No. 104–458, at 163]

Congress also liberalized the rules as to television/radio co-ownership. Prior to the Act, the FCC permitted common ownership of a radio and a television station in the same market only if thirty broadcast owners were operating in that market, and the market was in any of the top twenty-five largest. The 1996 Act extends that policy to include any of the top fifty markets. [Section 202(d)]

The 1996 Act also provides a little more flexibility than in the past for broadcast television networks to combine. Previously, all television networks were barred from common-ownership. The "Big-4" networks (ABC, CBS, NBC, and Fox) are still barred from merging either with each other or the fledgling WB and UPN networks. Mergers are permitted, though, between either the WB and UPN networks, or between any existing network and some new network formed after the Act. [Section 202(e)]

D. Mergers in the Cable Industry[1]

1. Background

Mergers in the cable industry will likely require FCC approval because any substantial cable company will also have licenses under Section 301 of the Communications Act of 1934, and FCC approval of the license transfer will, therefore, be required under Section 310(d), discussed previously, which sets out a "public interest" standard. Also, the FCC has both horizontal and vertical ownership restrictions that could apply. As previously discussed, such transactions are subject to antitrust scrutiny, and a HSR pre-merger notification filing may be required. Finally, cable mergers may be subject to state or local regulation, a topic not considered here.

2. Horizontal and Vertical Ownership Restrictions for Cable Operators

As explained by the court in *Time Warner Entertainment Co., L.P. v. FCC*, a cable operator is subject to horizontal ownership restrictions on the number of cable subscribers it may reach and vertical restrictions regarding the number of channels through which it can provide its own content:

> Section 11(c) of the Cable Television Consumer Protection and Competition Act of 1992 ("1992 Cable Act"), amends [Section 613 of the Communications Act of 1934], to direct the Federal Communications Commission to set two types of limits on cable operators. The first type is horizontal, addressing operators' scale: "limits on the number of cable subscribers a person is authorized to reach through cable systems owned by such person, or in which such person has an attributable interest." Section 613(f)(a)(1)(A). The second type is vertical, addressing operators' integration with "programmers" (suppliers of programs to be carried over cable systems): "limits on the number of channels on a cable system that can be occupied by a video programmer in which a cable operator has an attributable interest." Section 613(f)(a)(1)(B).[2]

Pursuant to this authority, the FCC had adopted (1) a horizontal rule prohibiting a cable operator from reaching more than 30% of homes nationally, and (2) a vertical rule limiting a cable operator's own content to 40% of channel capacity, thereby reserving 60% for content provided by non-affiliated firms. *Time Warner Entertainment* challenged (1) the horizontal limit as in excess of the FCC's statutory authority and an unconstitutional infringement of their freedom of speech, and (2) the vertical limit as arbitrary and capricious.

---

1. This section is adapted from Thompson, *Mergers, Acquisitions and Tender Offers*, *supra* Section 1.10, at Section 18:2.5.

2. Time Warner Entm't Co., L.P. v. FCC, 240 F. 3d 1126 (D.C. Cir. 2001).

The court concluded that the 30% horizontal limit was in excess of the FCC's statutory authority. Additionally, the court held that the vertical limit was invalid because the FCC seemed to have "plucked the 40% limit out of thin air." The Court remanded both limits to the Commission for further consideration holding that the agency must reveal a "rational connection between the facts found and the choice made," and that the standards they set must meet First Amendment intermediate scrutiny.

In December 2007, six years after this decision, the FCC reissued the 30% horizontal limit and asked for comments on the vertical limit.[3] The FCC also gave the following justification for its retention of the 30% limit: "The 30 percent cable horizontal ownership limit set by the Commission will ensure that no single cable operator can create a barrier to a video programming network's entry into the market or cause a video programming network to exit the market simply by declining to carry the network."

3. Prohibition against Certain Telco-Cable Buyouts: Impact of the Telecommunications Act of 1996

Section 652 of the Communications Act of 1934, which was added by the Telecommunications Act of 1996, prohibits, subject to certain exceptions, local telephone companies from acquiring a more than 10% interest in a local cable company and vice versa.

4. The Proposed Comcast-Time Warner 2014 Merger

Time Warner Cable to Merge with Comcast Corporation to Create a World-Class Technology and Media Company

February 13, 2014

Comcast Corporation * * * and Time Warner Cable * * * today announced that their Boards of Directors have approved a definitive agreement for Time Warner Cable to merge with Comcast. The agreement is a friendly, stock-for-stock transaction in which Comcast will acquire 100 percent of Time Warner Cable's 284.9 million shares outstanding for shares of CMCSA amounting to approximately $45.2 billion in equity value. * * *

The new cable company * * * will generate multiple pro-consumer and pro-competitive benefits, including an accelerated deployment of existing and new innovative products and services for millions of customers. * * *

[In an attempt to address the FCC's public interest standard under Section 310(d), the Press Release explains:] Through this merger, more American consumers will benefit from technological innovations, including a superior video experience, higher broadband speeds, and the fastest in-home Wi-Fi. The transaction also will generate significant cost savings and other efficiencies. * * *

[In an attempt to address the FCC's and DOJ's antitrust concerns, the Press Release explains:] Through the merger, Comcast will acquire Time Warner Cable's approximately 11 million managed subscribers. In order to reduce competitive concerns [regarding overlapping cable subscribers], Comcast is prepared to divest systems serving approximately 3 million managed subscribers. As such, Comcast will, through the acquisition and management of Time Warner Cable systems, net approximately 8 million managed subscribers in this transaction. This will bring Comcast's managed subscriber total to approximately

3. FCC News Release, FCC Adopts Rules to Promote Video Programming Diversity by Ensuring New Video Programmers Can Enter and Compete in Video Market (Dec. 2007).

30 million. Following the transaction, Comcast's share of managed subscribers will remain below 30 percent of the total number of MVPD subscribers in the U.S. [*i.e.*, below the FCC's 30% horizontal limitation]. * * *

E. Satellite Mergers

1. The FCC Blocked Proposed 2002 Acquisition by Echostar of Direct TV

FCC Press Release Re: EchoStar-Direct TV

(October 10, 2002)

FCC Declines to Approve EchoStar-DirecTV Merger

Today, the Federal Communications Commission ("FCC") declined to approve the transfer of licenses from EchoStar Communications Corporation and Hughes Electronics Corporation, a subsidiary of General Motors Corporation, to a new entity. [EchoStar and Direct TV are the only satellite TV providers.] The FCC said that the companies have not demonstrated that approval of the transaction will serve the public interest, convenience, and necessity. * * *

2. The Proposed AT&T-Direct TV 2014 Merger

AT&T to Acquire DIRECTV

Press Release May 18, 2013

AT&T * * * and DIRECTV * * * today announced that they have entered into a definitive agreement under which AT&T will acquire DIRECTV in a stock-and-cash transaction for $95 per share based on AT&T's Friday closing price. The agreement has been approved unanimously by the Boards of Directors of both companies.

The transaction combines complementary strengths to create a unique new competitor with unprecedented capabilities in mobility, video and broadband services.

DIRECTV is the premier pay TV provider in the United States and Latin America, with a high-quality customer base, the best selection of programming, the best technology for delivering and viewing high-quality video on any device and the best customer satisfaction among major U.S. cable and satellite TV providers. AT&T has a best-in-class nationwide mobile network and a high-speed broadband network that will cover 70 million customer locations with the broadband expansion enabled by this transaction.

The combined company will be a content distribution leader across mobile, video and broadband platforms. * * *

The transaction enables the combined company to offer consumers bundles that include video, high-speed broadband and mobile services using all of its sales channels—AT&T's 2,300 retail stores and thousands of authorized dealers and agents of both companies nationwide.

* * *

DIRECTV has premier content, particularly live sports programming. It has the exclusive pay TV rights to NFL SUNDAY TICKET that provides every out-of-market game, every Sunday afternoon, on TV, laptops and mobile devices. * * * [In an attempt to address the FCC's public interest standard under Section 310(d), the Press Release explains:] With the benefits of the transaction, AT&T is able to commit [*inter alia*] to do the following, when the deal closes: [1] 15 Million Customer Locations Get More High Speed Broadband, [2] Stand-Alone Broadband, and [3] Nationwide Package Pricing on DIRECTV.

§ 27.4 Acquisitions of Public Utilities

The issues with acquisitions of public utilities are covered in greater detail in Chapter 18 of Thompson, *Mergers, Acquisitions and Tender Offers, supra* Section 1.10.

Mergers involving public utilities present substantial regulatory issues under federal and state law, and this section provides a brief introduction to mergers involving public utilities engaged in the production and distribution of electricity. Electric utility mergers and acquisitions may require the approval of the Federal Energy Regulatory Commission, FERC. Prior to 2006, the SEC administered the Public Utility Holding Company Act of 1935 (PUHCA of 1935), which, *inter alia*, required a registered holding company to be a "single integrated public-utility system." Under this provision, the SEC required as a condition of approving a merger of such holding companies that the "combined utility assets be physically interconnected." The PUHCA of 1935 has been replaced by the PUHCA of 2005, which eliminates this interconnection requirement and appoints FERC as the administrator of that act.

Section 203(a) of the Federal Power Act (16 U.S.C. § 824b(a)) sets out the following requirement for FERC approval of certain electric utility acquisitions:

> (a)(1) No public utility [Electric Utility Company] shall, without first having secured an order of the Commission [*i.e.*, FERC] authorizing it to do so—
>
> (A) sell, lease, or otherwise dispose of the whole of its facilities subject to the jurisdiction of the Commission, or any part thereof of a value in excess of $10,000,000;
>
> (B) merge or consolidate, directly or indirectly, such facilities or any part thereof with those of any other person, by any means whatsoever;
>
> (C) purchase, acquire, or take any security with a value in excess of $10,000,000 of any other public utility; or
>
> (D) purchase, lease, or otherwise acquire an existing generation facility—
>
> (i) that has a value in excess of $10,000,000; and
>
> (ii) that is used for interstate wholesale sales and over which the Commission has jurisdiction for ratemaking purposes.
>
> (2) No holding company in a holding company system that includes a transmitting utility [*i.e.*, "electric utility * * * which owns or operates electric power transmission facilities which are used for the sale of electric energy at wholesale," *see* 16 U.S.C. § 796(23)] or an electric utility [*i.e.*, "any person * * * which sells electric energy * * *, *see* 16 U.S.C. § 796(22)] shall purchase, acquire, or take any security with a value in excess of $10,000,000 of, or, by any means whatsoever, directly or indirectly, merge or consolidate with, a transmitting utility, an electric utility company, or a holding company in a holding company system that includes a transmitting utility, or an electric utility company, with a value in excess of $10,000,000 without first having secured an order of the Commission authorizing it to do so.
>
> (3) Upon receipt of an application for such approval the Commission shall give reasonable notice in writing to the Governor and State commission of each of the States in which the physical property affected, or any part thereof, is situated, and to such other persons as it may deem advisable.
>
> (4) [*The Public Interest Standard*] After notice and opportunity for hearing, the Commission shall approve the proposed disposition, consolidation, acquisition,

> or change in control, if it finds that the proposed transaction will be consistent with the public interest, and will not result in cross-subsidization [*e.g.*, using a utility's assets to benefit a non-utility sister company] of a non-utility associate company or the pledge or encumbrance of utility assets for the benefit of an associate company, unless the Commission determines that the cross-subsidization, pledge, or encumbrance will be consistent with the public interest.

The Nuclear Regulatory Commission must approve any acquisition of a utility that has a nuclear plant, and the approval of the applicable state Public Utility Commission (PUC) is often required in a utility merger. For an illustration of provisions of an acquisition agreement relating to the required regulatory approvals for an electric utility, *see* Sections 5.1(d), 6.5(d) and (e) of the TXU merger agreement, Documentary Appendix Z of *M&A Statutes, Rules, and Documents*, *supra* Section 1.1.

§ 27.5 Health Care Acquisitions

A. In General

The issues with health care acquisitions are covered in greater detail in Chapter 27 of Thompson, *Mergers, Acquisitions and Tender Offers*, *supra* Section 1.10.

This section presents a brief introduction to some of the issues deal lawyers face with M&A transactions in the health care industry. This topic is particularly important in view of the enactment in 2010 of health care reform: the Affordable Care Act (ACA), otherwise known as Obamacare. The health care industry plays a significant role in the economy and in merger and acquisition activity. The purpose of this section is to provide a basic introduction to the principal federal and state laws and regulations impacting mergers and acquisitions in the health care industry.

B. The "Five Ps" of the Health Care Industry

In approaching regulatory issues in the health care industry it is helpful to focus on the "Five Ps of the Health Care Industry: Patients, Providers, Pharma, Producers, and Payors."[4] The "Patients" and "Pharma" concepts are self-explanatory; the "Providers" concept encompasses, *inter alia*, hospitals, physicians, and clinical laboratories; the "Producer" concept includes the manufacturers of medical devices; and the "Payors" concept encompasses the health insurance companies and Medicare and Medicaid.

M&A activity among the "Five Ps" includes (1) acquisitions of physician practices; (2) acquisitions of both for-profit and not-for profit hospitals; (3) acquisitions of pharmaceutical firms; (4) acquisitions of medical device manufacturers; and (5) acquisitions of health care insurers and health plans.

There is significant fraud and abuse in the health care industry, and as discussed below, in any merger or acquisition in this industry, the acquiror will want to ensure that the target has complied with all health care laws. Antitrust is the principal Federal regulatory barrier to each of these acquisitions, and state insurance laws could be a barrier to an acquisition, particularly acquisitions involving a health care insurer. The following sections briefly discuss recent mergers involving hospitals, physicians, and a health insurer.

---

4. The term "Five Ps" is an expansion of the "Three Ps" concept (Patents, Providers, and Payors) I learned from Bob Harper in our Health Care M&A course at Penn State.

C. The Overarching Concern with Fraud and Abuse[5]

Physicians and hospitals (as well as other players in the health care industry) must pay particular attention to the laws and regulations governing fraud and abuse in the health care industry. The Executive Summary of Annual Report for 2009 by the DOJ and Department of Health and Human Services (HHS) on Fraud and Abuse provides the following summary:

> The Health Insurance Portability and Accountability Act of 1996 (HIPAA) established a national Health Care Fraud and Abuse Control Program (HCFAC or the Program) under the joint direction of the Attorney General and the Secretary of [HHS], acting through the Inspector General, designed to coordinate Federal, state and local law enforcement activities with respect to health care fraud and abuse....
>
> During Fiscal Year (FY) 2009, the Federal Government won or negotiated approximately $1.63 billion in judgments and settlements, and it attained additional administrative impositions in health care fraud cases and proceedings.[6]

The following is a list of the Federal fraud and abuse statutes that can apply generally and to any provider of services pursuant to a Federally funded health care plan, such as Medicare and Medicaid: (1) the Federal False Claims Act (FCA); (2) The Civil Monetary Penalty Statute (CMPS); (3) the Anti-kickback Statute (AKS); (4) the Health Care Fraud Statute (HCFS); (5) the physician anti-referral law (the Stark Law); and (6) the fraud policy of the Food and Drug Administration.

The following is an illustration of how "Health Care Legal Matters" were addressed in the representations and warranties section (*see* Chapter 15) of an acquisition agreement for a physician's practice. This representation and warranty was given by the Target, Southern Plains Medical Center, and its Shareholders concerning Southern Plains' compliance with Health Care Laws:

> **Section 3.19 Health Care Legal Matters.**
>
> **Section 3.19.1** Target has complied, and is in compliance, with all applicable Laws regulating the financing, reimbursement, payment, acquisition, construction, operation, maintenance or management of a health care practice, facility, provider or payor, including, without limitation: (i) 42 U.S.C. §§ 1320a-7 7a and 7b, which are commonly referred to as the "Federal Anti-Kickback Statute"; (ii) 42 U.S.C. § 1395nn, which is commonly referred to as the "Stark Law"; (iii) 31 U.S.C §§ 3729–3733, which is commonly referred to as the "Federal False Claims Act"; (iv) Titles XVIII and XIX of the Social Security Act, implementing regulations and program manuals; and (v) 42 U.S.C. §§ 1320d-1320d-8 and 42 C.F.R. §§ 160, 162 and 164, which is commonly referred to as "HIPAA" (the foregoing hereinafter collectively referred to as "Health Care Laws"). Target has maintained all records required to be maintained and made all required filings in connection with the Medicare and Medicaid programs established under Titles XVIII and XIX of the

5. This section is adapted from Thompson, *Mergers, Acquisitions and Tender Offers*, *supra* Section 1.10, at Section 27:3.3[B].

6. The Department of Health and Human Services and The Department of Justice, *Health Care Fraud and Abuse Control Program, Annual Report for Fiscal Year 2009*, 1 (May 2010).

Social Security Act, and such other similar federal, state or local reimbursement or governmental programs, managed care plans and any other private health care insurance programs and employee assistance programs, as well as any future similar programs, for which Target is eligible (the foregoing hereinafter referred to collectively as the "Payor Source Programs") as required by applicable Health Care Laws.

Section 3.19.2 Without limiting the foregoing, neither Target nor any Target Shareholder has engaged in any activities that are prohibited under any Health Care Laws or any other federal or state statutes related to illegal remuneration or false or fraudulent claims, the regulations promulgated pursuant to such statutes, or any related state or local statutes or regulations, including, without limitation, the following:

(a) knowingly and willfully making or causing to be made any false statement or representation of material fact in any application for any benefit or payment;

(b) knowingly and willfully making or causing to be made any false statement or representation of a material fact for use in determining rights to any benefit or payment;

(c) failing to disclose knowledge by a claimant of the occurrence of any event affecting the initial or continued right to any benefit or payment on its own behalf or on behalf of another, with intent to fraudulently secure such benefit or payment; or

(d) knowingly and willfully soliciting or receiving any remuneration (including any kickback, bribe or rebate), directly or indirectly, overtly or covertly, in cash or in kind or offering to pay or receive such remuneration in return for (A) referring an individual for the furnishing or arranging for the furnishing of any item or service for which payment may be made in whole or in part by any Payor Source Programs; or (B) purchasing, leasing, or ordering or arranging for or recommending the purchasing, leasing or ordering of any good, facility, service or item for which payment may be made in whole or in part by a Payor Source Program.[7]

D. PA's Challenge to the Geisinger Acquisition of Lewistown Hospital and Its Physician Practice[8]

In November 2013, the Commonwealth of Pennsylvania (Pa.) entered into an Amended Final Order (Order) with Geisinger Health System Foundation (GHSF) and Lewistown Health Care Foundation (LHF) concerning the planned acquisition by GHSF of LHF.[9] The Order states that Pa. "filed its Complaint on October 25, 2013 under Section 7 of the Clayton Act ... and under the common law of the Commonwealth of Pennsylvania alleging

7. This excerpt is from Section III.B of Appendix 27-A, Acquisition of Southern Plains Medical Center by First Physician Capital Group, of Thompson, *Mergers, Acquisitions and Tender Offers, supra* Section 1.10.

8. This section is adapted from Thompson, *Mergers, Acquisitions and Tender Offers, supra* Section 1.10, at Section 27:5.6[B][16].

9. Commonwealth of Pennsylvania v. Geisinger Health System Foundation, Amended Final Order, U.S. Dist. Ct. M.D. Pa., Civil Action No. v. 1:13 CV-02647-YK (Nov. 1, 2013).

that the proposed acquisition of [LHF] and its affiliates including, Lewistown Hospital [LH] and Family Health Associates of Lewistown Hospital [FHA] by [GHSF] will substantially lessen competition in one or more relevant health care services markets."

A press release[10] on the transaction issued by the Pa. Attorney General's Office gives the following background on Geisinger: "Geisinger is the non-profit parent of five hospitals, including Geisinger Medical Center in Danville, Montour County; Geisinger Clinic, a multi-specialty physician group practice with more than 1,000 primary and specialty care physicians; and Geisinger Health Plan."

The Complaint in this action asserts that the "combination is likely to substantially lessen or eliminate competition in [1] the provision of primary care physician services [the Primary Care Market] and [2] primary and secondary inpatient acute hospital services [the Hospital Market] in Mifflin and Juniata Counties [the Geographic Market]." The Complaint asserts that the combination will result in higher prices in both of these markets and that the higher prices will be "borne by health care purchasers, particularly Health Plans, employers and unions, and will likely result in an increase in prices that individual consumers pay for health insurance coverage."

The Complaint states that (1) GHSF operates principally in Northeast and Central Pa., and (2) LHF is a non-profit corporation based in Lewistown in Central Pa. and is the parent of the LH and of FHA, an organization of physicians. Although Geisinger does not own a hospital in Lewistown it has a "significant physician presence with primary and specialty care physicians" located in several offices in and near Lewistown."

With respect to market concentration, the Complaint asserts that pre-merger (1) for the Primary Care Market, LHF through FHA controls 39% and GHSF controls 42%, and (2) for the Hospital Market, LHF through LH was in first place with 63% and GHSF was in second place with 11%. The Complaint says that these high market shares will result in the elimination of significant competition between LHF and GHSF, thereby resulting in higher prices to consumers in both of these markets. The Complaint further asserts that there are significant barriers to entry and that GHSF and LHF have not set forth any substantial efficiencies.

The Order sets forth several terms pursuant to which Pa. will abandon its challenge to the transaction. These terms include, for example, the commitment of GHSF to (1) "continue to provide the community [LHF serves] with quality, affordable health care services in accordance with [its] mission and as part of a health care system of which GHSF, a non-profit, tax exempt, corporation, is the parent;" (2) "[m]aintain [LH] as an Acute Care Hospital" for at least eight years; (3) honor LH's contracts with various health plans; (4) not enter into any agreement with any Health Plan that includes a Most Favored Nation (MFN) clause[11] to the benefit of LH; (5) release from any "Restrictive Covenant," such as a non-compete, any physician currently employed by FHA who decides not to work for a GHSF controlled entity; and (6) "maintain an open medical staff and continue

---

10. Press Release, PA. Attorney General's Office, Attorney General Kathleen G. Kane reaches accord with Geisinger to ensure regional access to quality and affordable health care (Oct. 28, 2013), Available at http://www.attorneygeneral.gov/press.aspx?id=7281.

11. The Order explains that MFN "means any written or unwritten agreement between a Health Care Provider and a Health Plan that allows the Health Plan to receive the benefit of a better payment rate, term or condition that the Health Care Provider gives to another Health Plan."

all categories of appointment and staff privileges for all qualified physicians who have staff privileges at [LH]." The Order also sets out Complaint and Compliance procedures.

E. The Highmark-West Penn Affiliation[12]

In 2011, Highmark, a health insurance company, and its affiliated insurance companies entered into an affiliation agreement with West Penn Allegheny Health System (West Penn), a Pittsburgh based hospital network. The purpose of the affiliation is to create an integrated delivery network (IDN). The DOJ approved the transaction in April of 2012, and in April 2013 the Pennsylvania Insurance Commission approved the transaction, which was described as follows in the Pittsburgh Post-Gazette:

> West Penn Allegheny Health System [WPAHS] is under new ownership, the Pittsburgh region has a newly named hospital network, and the nation may soon have a "vibrant" new model for treating patients, now that the state Department of Insurance has conditionally approved Highmark's acquisition of the financially ailing WPAHS.
>
> The approval, issued Monday morning after nearly 18 months of vetting, puts [WPAHS] under Highmark's control and lays the foundation for Highmark's plans to establish an integrated health care delivery system—now being called the Allegheny Health Network—to compete with, and be an alternative to, the regionally dominant UPMC [University of Pittsburgh Medical Center].[13]

The DOJ's Statement said that the agency had concluded that (1) "the affiliation agreement likely will not reduce competition in the markets for hospital, physician or health insurance services," and (2) the "proposed affiliation holds the promise of bringing increased competition to western Pennsylvania's health care markets by providing WPAHS with a significant infusion of capital and increases the incentives of market participants to compete vigorously."

The Pa. Insurance Department's Approval and Determination Order[14] states that Section 1402 of the Insurance Holding Companies Act requires the Department to approve Highmark's application for a change in control unless the Department finds any of the following:

> (i) After the Change of Control, the Highmark Insurance Companies would not be able to satisfy the requirements for the issuance of a license to write the line or lines of insurance for which they are presently licensed;
>
> (ii) The effect of the Change of Control would be to substantially lessen competition in insurance in this Commonwealth or tend to create a monopoly therein;

12. This section is adapted from Thompson, *Mergers, Acquisitions and Tender Offers*, *supra* Section 1.10, at Section 27:5.7.

13. Bill Toland and Steve Twedt, Pennsylvania approves Highmark-West Penn Allegheny Health System merger, Pittsburg Post-Gazette (April 30, 2013), Available at http://www.post-gazette.com/business/businessnews/2013/04/29/Pennsylvania-approves-Highmark-West-Penn-Allegheny-Health-System-merger/stories/201304290231.

14. In re: Application of UPE for Approval of Request by UPE to Acquire Control of Highmark [and related health insurance companies], Approving and Determination Order, PA Insurance Department, ID-RC-13-06 (April 29, 2013), Available at http://www.post-gazette.com/attachment/2013/10/17/Full-state-Insurance-Department-approval-order.pdf.

(iii) The financial condition of the Applicant is such as might jeopardize the financial stability of one or more of the Highmark Insurance Companies or prejudice the interests of any policyholders;

(iv) The Change of Control, including but not limited to any material change in the business or corporate structure or management of the Applicant or the Highmark Insurance Companies as described in the Application, is unfair and unreasonable to policyholders of the Highmark Insurance Companies and not in the public interest:

(v) The competence, experience and integrity of those Persons who would control the operations of any of the Highmark Insurance Companies are such that it would not be in the interest of the policy holders of the Highmark Insurance Companies and the public to permit the Change of Control;

(vi) The Change of Control is likely to be hazardous or prejudicial to the insurance buying public; and

(vii) The Change of Control is not in compliance with laws of the Commonwealth.

In approving the transaction, the Order explains that (1) the "burden is on the Department to show a violation of the standards," and (2) the "standards are in the negative and the Department is required to approve a transaction unless it finds that any of the standards are met."

§ 27.6 Acquisitions of Bankrupt Companies

A. In General

The issues with acquisitions of bankrupt companies are covered in greater detail in Chapter 16 of Thompson, *Mergers, Acquisitions and Tender Offers, supra* Section 1.10.

Mergers and acquisitions may arise in connection with the sale of all or substantially all of the assets of a company that is in bankruptcy pursuant to Section 363(b) of the Bankruptcy Code, which provides:

§ 363. **Use, sale, or lease of property** * * *

(b) (1) The trustee [and a debtor in possession], after notice and a hearing, may use, sell, or lease, other than in the ordinary course of business, property of the estate.

(2) If [premerger] notification is required under [the HSR Act, *see* Chapter 9, then, *inter alia*, a 15 day waiting period applies]. * * *

(f) The trustee [and a debtor in possession] may sell property under subsection (b) or (c) of this section free and clear of any interest in such property of an entity other than the estate, only if—

(1) applicable nonbankruptcy law permits sale of such property free and clear of such interest;

(2) such entity consents;

(3) such interest is a lien and the price at which such property is to be sold is greater than the aggregate value of all liens on such property;

(4) such interest is in bona fide dispute; or

(5) such entity could be compelled, in a legal or equitable proceeding, to accept a money satisfaction of such interest. * * *

B. Third Circuit's Decision in *Trans World Airlines* on Successor Liability

In Re Trans World Airlines, Inc.

United States Court of Appeals, Third Circuit, (2003) U.S. App. LEXIS 4530

FUENTES, Circuit Judge:

The issues in this bankruptcy appeal involve the doctrine of successor liability and arise out of the Bankruptcy Court's order approving the sale of the assets of Trans World Airlines ("TWA") to American Airlines ("American"). The primary question is whether the District Court erred in affirming the Bankruptcy Court's order, which had the effect of extinguishing the liability of American, as successor to TWA, for (1) employment discrimination claims against TWA and (2) for the Travel Voucher Program awarded to TWA's flight attendants in settlement of a sex discrimination class action. Because section 363(f) of the Bankruptcy Code permits a sale of property "free and clear" of an "interest in such property[,]" and because the claims against TWA here were connected to or arise from the assets sold, we affirm the Bankruptcy Court's order approving the sale "free and clear" of successor liability. * * *

§ 27.7 Introduction to Joint Ventures

The issues with joint ventures are covered in greater detail in Chapter 24 of Thompson, *Mergers, Acquisitions and Tender Offers, supra* Section 1.10.

This section briefly introduces joint ventures and other strategic alliances (JVs). JVs are generally formed as either partnerships or limited liability companies (LLCs). These transactions, which are becoming quite common, involve the partial coming together of the parties for a specific purpose and may be an alternative to a full merger or acquisition. The rights and obligations of the members of the JV are determined by the JV agreement (i.e., the partnership or LLC agreement). In the absence of a contractual provision, the default rules are governed by the applicable partnership or LLC law.

For Federal income tax purposes, JVs that are formed as partnerships or LLCs are treated as partnerships for federal income tax purposes. As a consequence, (1) contributions to the joint venture are generally tax free; (2) the partners or LLC members include in their individual returns their pro rata shares of the profits or losses of the JV; and (3) distributions, including liquidating distributions from the JV are generally tax-free.

The formation of a JV may be subject to the Hart-Scott-Rodino pre-merger notification rules, and in considering the substantive antitrust issues with JVs, consideration has to be given to the Joint Venture Guidelines adopted by the FTC and the DOJ in 2000.

Chapter 28

Ethical Issues Facing Attorneys in M&A: A Problem Approach

§ 28.1 Scope

This chapter explores ethical issues facing attorneys in M&A and related transactions.[1] The answers to many of the issues are uncertain, and many of the issues are not peculiar to mergers and acquisitions and could arise in other business contexts. In addition to ethical dilemmas, some of the issues raise potential violations of common law fraud principles, fiduciary duty principles, or Rule 10b-5. [*See* Chapter 4] However, the focus of this chapter is on ethical issues faced by the attorneys in these transactions.

The principal sources referred to in this chapter are (1) the American Bar Association's *Model Rules of Professional Conduct* (Model Rules);[2] (2) the American Law Institute's *Restatement of the Law Governing Lawyers* (ALI Restatement);[3] (3) the SEC's new "up-the-ladder" reporting rules[4] and proposed "noisy withdrawal" rules,[5] issued under Section 307 of the Sarbanes-Oxley Act of 2002 (SOX),[6] which requires the SEC to prescribe minimum standards of professional conduct for attorneys appearing and practicing before the SEC; and (4) the SOX rules on whistle blowing. These items are set out in *M&A Statutes, Rules, and Documents, supra* Section 1.1.

The hypothetical is set out in Section 28.2, and each of the ethical issues is identified at the point it is raised in the hypothetical. The authorities dealing with each of the ethical issues are listed by issue in *M&A Statutes, Rules, and Documents, supra* Section 1.1. The materials in this chapter are covered in greater detail in Chapter 26 of Thompson, *Mergers, Acquisitions and Tender Offers, supra* Section 1.10.

---

1. The hypothetical problem set out below is based on, and a modification of, the hypothetical problem in Barry S. Alberts and Samuel C. Thompson, Jr., *Ethics Issues Faced by Lawyers and Investment Bankers in Mergers and Acquisitions: A Problem Approach and Report of Panel Discussion*, 54 U. Miami L. Rev. 697 (2000). The problem was the basis of the discussion of ethical issues at the UCLA Law Second Annual Institute on Corporate, Securities and Related Aspects of Mergers and Acquisitions (Oct. 2005).
2. American Bar Association, *Model Rules of Professional Conduct* (5th Ed 2003) [hereinafter ABA Model Rules]. *See also* American Bar Association, *Annotated Model Rules of Professional Conduct*(5th Ed 2003) [hereinafter ABA Model Rules Annotated].
3. American Law Institute, *Restatement of The Law Governing Lawyers* (1998) [hereinafter ALI, Law Governing Lawyers].
4. 17 CFR Part 205, promulgated in SEC Release Nos 33-8185 and 34-47276, RIN 3235-AI72, Effective August 5, 2003.
5. Promulgated in SEC Release Nos 33-8186 and 34-47282, RIN 3235-AI72, (2003).
6. 15 U.S.C. 7245.

§ 28.2 Hypothetical Problem: The Public Acquisition Scene

A. Introduction

Set forth below is a summary of the events surrounding a hypothetical in which a public company, Consumers Choice, Inc. was approached by ALO.com, Inc., a public company, about the possibility of combining in a merger of equals. Before that transaction was consummated, Macro Ware Inc., a large publicly held computer software company, made a hostile tender offer for ALO. Thus, the facts present a merger of equals between publicly held companies and a hostile tender offer.

B. The Cast of Characters

Consumers Choice is a leading manufacturer and merchandiser of a wide range of consumer goods. Through its domestic and international operations, Consumers Choice caters to mass retailers and wholesalers, home centers and office superstores, doing business through more than 20 subsidiaries, affiliates and divisions. Consumers Choice has annual revenues of approximately $10 billion. Its stock trades on the New York Stock Exchange.

ALO.com, Inc., a NASDAQ traded company, is a leading marketer of consumer products over the Internet, and it sees the possibility of substantial synergies and new business opportunities arising from a combination with Consumers Choice. It has been following Consumers Choice for a significant period and thinks that the time is right to combine the two firms.

Macro Ware is a leading software company that is traded on the New York Stock Exchange. The CEO of Macro Ware, Bill King, has for a significant time been following the developments of ALO and has been thinking of making an offer for ALO. He is not interested at all in Consumers Choice, and thinks that the announced merger between ALO and Consumers Choice does not make sense.

C. ALO's Approach to Consumers Choice

Recently the CEO of ALO, Steve Vision, contacted the CEO of Consumers Choice, Jenny Sharpeye, about a "merger-of-equals" between ALO and Consumers Choice. The market capitalization of the two companies is similar, and Steve has proposed that the shareholders of each firm end up with 50% of the combined entity, with Steve and Jenny serving as Co-CEOs in all respects. The board of the combined entity would consist of an equal number of members appointed by each company. Thus, the proposed deal is a true merger-of-equals.

Jenny's immediate reaction is that the deal makes very good sense and should be pursued but with the shareholders of Consumers Choice receiving 55% of the stock of the combined firm. This would give the shareholders of Consumer Choice a slight premium to compensate for the faster growth in earnings at Consumers Choice. Jenny also thinks the timing is right for doing this type of deal now, assuming Steve is willing to go with the premium, Jenny wants to move as quickly as possible.

Jenny called Stu Stone, the senior partner of Consumers Choice's principal outside law firm, Stone & Cold, which has represented Consumers Choice on several recent acquisitions, and asked for the assistance of Stone & Cold on the potential deal with ALO. It turns out that Steve Vision, ALO's CEO, had already contacted Keith Cold, another senior partner at Stone & Cold and asked Stone & Cold to represent ALO on the transaction.

Thus, Steve Vision and Jenny Sharpeye have attempted to retain members of the same law firm for the transaction. Stu Stone and Keith Cold think that they probably cannot represent both parties even with consent and firewalls; however, they are being urged by their partners to at least explore the possibility. The partners are arguing that Wachtell Lipton represented both parties in a public transaction and Stone & Cold should be able to do so also as long as there are appropriate consents. An article in the New York Times addressing dual representation by both law firms and investment bankers explains:

> "Wachtell Lipton Rosen & Katz gave legal advice to both the Banc One Corporation and the First Chicago NBD Corporation in a $30 billion merger; Merrill Lynch & Company advised Italy's Credito Italiano and Unicredito in a $10 billion combination, and ... Goldman advised the Norwest Corporation and Wells Fargo & Company on their $34 billion merger."[7]

Steve and Jenny are mainly interested in doing the deal fast, and they are each willing to give their consent to the dual representation if that will help expedite the deal. So, they need to know quickly whether this dual representation by the lawyers is doable. **First Issue.** The first issue is whether Stone & Cold can undertake this dual representation, and if so under what conditions. In answering this question, Stone & Cold will have to consider such issues as: what if the parties are unable to agree on the exchange ratio, and what if a third party makes a competing offer for one of the merging firms?

Both Steve and Jenny read the article in the Wall Street Journal about the $35 million dollar success fee that Time Warner Inc. agreed to pay the law firm of Cravath, Swaine & Moore upon completion of its merger with America Online Inc.[8] If the deal had not been completed Cravath would have been paid a much smaller fee. As an inducement to expediting the deal, Steve and Jenny are each proposing to pay Stone & Cold a success fee if the deal closes and a fraction of the standard hourly rates if the deal does not close. They both think it is appropriate to have this type of incentive for lawyers, who can sometimes be deal breakers. **Second Issue.** The second issue is whether and under what conditions Stone & Cold can agree to this success fee arrangement.

After due consideration, they proceed with the dual representation. In the course of tough negotiations over the exchange ratio, with Jenny insisting on 55% for the Consumer Choice shareholders, Steve suggests to Jenny that Jenny should get a new employment contract with a significant increase in salary and other benefits that will even put Jenny substantially ahead of Steve in compensation. Steve is not much concerned with salary, because he owns 30% of ALO's stock. Shortly after this proposal, Jenny and the board settle on a 50–50 split in the shareholdings. **Third Issue.** The issue here is whether the lawyers for Consumers Choice can merely accept this deal on salary even though there are grounds to believe that Jenny may have settled on the 50–50 split because she is being given the higher salary. What are the lawyer's responsibilities in this situation under both the Model Rules and the SEC "up-the-ladder" rules? What impact would adoption of the SEC "noisy withdrawal" rules have in this situation?

7. Laura M. Holson, It Takes 2 to Merge but One Firm to Give Advice, The New York Times, Section D, page 1, June 13, 1998.

8. Cravath, Swaine to Receive Huge Fee if Merger Occurs, Wall Street Journal Interactive Edition, Jan. 21, 2000.

D. Macro Ware's Unsolicited Offer for ALO

As indicated, Bill King, the CEO of Macro Ware, has for a long period been interested in ALO, and he thinks the time is right to make a bid for ALO prior to the completion of its deal with Consumers Choice. Bill has retained the law firm of Blue & Blood to represent Macro Ware on the transaction.

In consultation with Blue & Blood, it is decided that Bill King will approach Steve Vision, ALO's CEO, with an offer that is 40% higher than the trading price of ALO's shares on the date of the offer. ALO's shares are currently trading at $100 per share and thus the offer would be at $140 per share. It is also decided that Bill will not approach Steve until the FTC has issued its expected second request for information relating to the antitrust aspects of the Consumers Choice deal. It is expected that the second request, which will delay the potential FTC clearance of the transaction, will be issued within ten days. The thought is that it will be best to make the offer to Steve at the point when the antitrust clearance of the Consumers Choice transaction is in doubt. It is decided that if Steve does not react favorably to Bill's offer, then Macro Ware would make a tender offer for ALO.

When Bill King presented the offer to Steve Vision, Steve immediately said: "No way. I did not build this company to turn it over to you." Steve immediately called the lawyers for ALO, Stone & Cold and told them to make sure Bill King's offer does not succeed. He said: "I don't care what it takes, erect every barrier to a take over by Macro Ware." Further, he reminded Stone & Cold that its success fee was tied to the Consumers Choice deal and not to any deal with Macro Ware. The board of ALO went along with Steve's judgment on this matter.

With Stone & Cold's advice, ALO launched an extensive defense to Macro Ware's offer, and Macro Ware was required to launch a hostile tender offer at $150 per share (a premium of $10 over the price initially offered), with a proxy contest to remove ALO's poison pill.

Fourth Issue. The fourth issue concerns the appropriateness of the defensive tactics recommended by Stone & Cold in response to Steve's direction. As with the Third Issue, what are the lawyer's responsibilities in this situation under both the Model Rules and the SEC "up-the-ladder" rules? What impact would adoption of the SEC "noisy withdrawal" rules have in this situation?

E. Proposed Sale of Steve Vision's Controlling Shares to Macro Ware

1. The Facts

While the proxy contest was still proceeding it began to look like Macro Ware might prevail, Steve, with the assistance of Stone & Cold, decided to approach Bill King, CEO of Macro Ware, about the possibility of immediately selling to Macro Ware Steve's 30% controlling block of shares at a price of $175 per share (a premium of $25 over the tender offer price). Steve has assured Bill that the ALO board would exempt such a sale from its poison pill. Also, Steve has argued that this would allow Macro Ware to get an immediate controlling interest in ALO and that Macro Ware could at a later time freeze out the public shareholders at a much lower price than the $140 which Macro Ware initially offered.

Fifth. The fifth issue is whether Stone & Cold can represent Steve on the sale of his shares to Macro Ware. In considering this question, read the *Dow* and two *Airgas* cases set out next.

2. Three Recent Cases Dealing with a Lawyer's Conflicts in Representing Clients — *Dow/Wachtell,* Delaware Chancery Court; *Airgas/Cravath,* Delaware Chancery Court; and *Airgas/Cravath,* Pa. Fed District Court

a. *Dow/Wachtell,* Delaware Chancery Court

Rohm & Haas Co. v. Dow Chem. Co.

Delaware Court of Chancery, 2009 Del. Ch. LEXIS 249 (Feb. 11, 2009)

William B. Chandler III, Chancellor

Opinion

Before me is defendants' motion to disqualify Wachtell, Lipton, Rosen & Katz ("Wachtell") from conducting discovery against The Dow Chemical Company and examining Dow witnesses. * * * For the reasons set forth briefly below, the motion to disqualify is denied.

Dow argues that Wachtell should be disqualified because the firm's representation of Rohm and Haas Company in this matter presents a conflict of interest as a result of Wachtell's representation of Dow. Dow alleges that Wachtell is in violation of the Delaware Rules of Professional Conduct because Dow is both a current client of Wachtell and a client whom Wachtell has previously represented in matters substantially related to the instant proceedings. Dow alleges that it is prejudiced in this action because Wachtell was privy to sensitive information in its capacity as Dow's counsel.

Dow argues that it is a current client of Wachtell because the firm never took steps to inform Dow that it was no longer a client following Wachtell's representation of Dow in 2007 and 2008 in connection with the termination of two Dow executives and potential defensive measures in response to rumors of a takeover bid. Dow further argues that Wachtell represented Dow in matters substantially related to this proceeding and in the course of that representation obtained confidential information that will materially advance Rohm and Haas's position in the instant litigation.

Plaintiff Rohm and Haas counters that there is not a concurrent conflict of interest because Dow is no longer a Wachtell client. According to Rohm and Haas, it should have been clear to Dow that Dow was no longer a Wachtell client when the firm appeared opposite Dow in its representation of Rohm and Haas in the negotiations of the initial confidentiality agreement and the merger agreement in mid-2008. Rohm and Haas further argues that the nature and scope of the prior representation and the current litigation are distinct and that Wachtell received no confidences from Dow that could be used to advantage Rohm and Haas in this proceeding.

While the Court's evaluation of these issues is guided by the Delaware Rules of Professional Conduct, the moving party is not entitled to disqualification merely by showing a violation of the ethical rules. [A] mere showing that a law firm violated the Rules of Professional Conduct is not sufficient to warrant disqualification. Instead, I must determine whether allowing Wachtell to continue its representation of Rohm and Haas will affect the fair and efficient administration of justice. * * *

After careful consideration of the parties' arguments, I am not convinced that allowing Wachtell to continue representing Rohm and Haas in this matter will prejudice the fairness of the proceedings or affect the fair and efficient administration of justice. First, I am not convinced by the argument that Dow reasonably believes it is a current client of Wachtell or that Dow relied on such a belief. Dow knew that Wachtell was representing Rohm and Hass during the negotiations of the merger agreement and did not object. Rather, Dow obtained its own separate counsel to represent Dow in the merger negotiations. Wachtell sent its final bill to Dow in June 2008, and there is no convincing evidence that Wachtell continued to perform services for Dow that would justify a reasonable belief by Dow that it is a current Wachtell client. I am also not convinced by Dow's argument that there was an implicit promise by Wachtell that they would represent Rohm and Haas in the negotiations but would discontinue the representation if litigation arose. * * *

Second, I am not convinced that Wachtell possesses confidential information that it obtained during its representation of Dow that will materially enhance the position of Rohm and Haas in this litigation. Wachtell represented Dow in 2007 and early 2008 regarding matters related to a possible takeover attempt and the termination of two Dow executives. * * *

Dow has failed to convince me that the information Wachtell had access to regarding Dow's strategies and asset values in 2006 and 2007 will substantially advance the interest of Rohm and Haas in this litigation. Additionally, Wachtell has assured the Court that its attorneys who obtained confidential Dow information have not and will not share Dow's client confidences with the Wachtell attorneys working on this matter. While Dow is correct that the ethical rules impute knowledge of one attorney to other attorneys in the firm, the issue before the Court is not whether there was a violation of the ethical rules. To justify disqualification, the Court must find that allowing the representation to continue would threaten the fair and efficient administration of justice, a threat that is greatly reduced by a credible representation to the Court that the firm will ensure that the attorneys working on this matter do not have access to Dow's client confidences. Dow has failed to point to information or confidences obtained by Wachtell in its 2006-2007 work for Dow that will have a material influence on the proceedings before me today.

For the foregoing reasons, the motion to disqualify is denied.

b. *Airgas/Cravath*, Delaware Chancery Court

Air Prods. & Chems., Inc. v. Airgas, Inc.

Delaware Court of Chancery, 2010 Del. Ch. LEXIS 35 (March 5, 2010)

Top of Form

Opinion, William B. Chandler IIII, Chancellor.

TELECONFERENCE RULING OF THE COURT * * *

The Court: * * *

Now, the real meat of this lawsuit, as you know, is a dispute about the potential business combination of two Delaware firms, Air Products and Chemicals Inc. and Airgas Inc. [*See Airgas*, Section 3.18.E.10] * * *

Airgas filed a lawsuit in the Pennsylvania Court of Common Pleas * * * against Cravath, Swaine & Moore, the New York law firm representing Air Products in connection with the proposed business combination[.] * * * Cravath had Airgas' State Court action removed to the United States District Court for the Eastern District of Pennsylvania [which] stayed Airgas' lawsuit against Cravath until this Court ruled on Air Products' motion seeking a determination here that Cravath may properly represent Air Products in this lawsuit. * * *

Airgas * * * objects to Cravath's continuing role as an advisor to Air Products with respect to the proposed business combination with Airgas. * * *

First, I hold that Delaware law, in particular, the Delaware Lawyers Rules of Professional Conduct, and Delaware's common law rules regarding lawyer disqualifications applies to this dispute.* * *

Second, * * * I find and determine that no basis exists for me to disqualify Cravath, Swaine & Moore from representing Air Products in the litigation pending in this court.

Although the parties strenuously disagree regarding the propriety of Cravath's role in connection with its previous work for Airgas while it was simultaneously engaged as counsel for Air Products, and although the ethics experts diverge over whether Cravath has complied with the strict requirements of Rules 1.7 or 1.9 of the Professional Conduct rules, I need not formally decide that question in order to dispose of the motion and objections before me.

Before this Court may enter the Draconian order of disqualification, a moving party seeking that drastic relief must come forward with clear and convincing evidence establishing a violation of the Delaware Rules of Professional Conduct so extreme that it calls into question the fairness or the efficiency of the administration of justice. * * *

[I]n the *Dow Chemical* case [Section 28.2.E.2.a], I refused to disqualify counsel when there was no showing that counsel's participation as an advocate unfairly benefited its present client, in that instance Rohm & Haas, or unfairly prejudiced its former client, the Dow Chemical Company, even though the representation of the two clients may have overlapped.

Like Dow Chemical and the Rohm & Haas case, Airgas here has not demonstrated even simply persuasively, let alone clearly and convincingly, that it would be disadvantaged by the presence of its former counsel as advocate for its opponent, Air Products.

Nothing before me shows that Cravath had access to or learned internal and non-public confidential information, corporate strategies or defensive tactics during the course of its narrowly focused work for Airgas from 2001 until late October of 2009, or that such information, even if available to Cravath, would prejudice the fairness or the integrity of this proceeding.

The evidence presented to me indicates that Cravath's work for Airgas between 2001 and 2009 was limited in scope and nature, confined to advising Airgas regarding the completion of debt financings, and involved neither contact nor advice regarding corporate governance, litigation matters, charter or by-law issues, merger and acquisition advice, defensive tactics or corporate counseling. * * *

[E]ven if Cravath had access from its earlier representation to information that might be relevant in this proceeding, it has represented to this Court that it has no intention of using such information, and as is customary, Cravath has erected an ethical wall to seal off those members of the firm who worked on the Airgas debt financings from those members of the firm working on the Air Products proposed business combination with Airgas.

A similar ethical wall was erected in the Rohm & Haas matter as a means to further assure this Court that no prejudice or unfairness in the proceedings would result to Dow Chemical, the former client in that case. The same is true here. * * *

Accordingly, I grant Air Products' motion, declare that Cravath may continue to represent it in this litigation, and deny Airgas' objection to the Cravath lawyers who have been previously admitted *pro hac vice* in this matter. * * *

c. *Airgas/Cravath*, Pa. Federal District Court

Airgas, Inc. v. Cravath, Swaine & Moore LLP

U.S. District Court PA, 2010 U.S. Dist. LEXIS 78162 (E.D. Pa, Aug 3, 2010

Opinion, Memorandum, Eduardo C. Robreno, J.

Defendant Cravath, Swaine and Moore LLP ("Cravath") moves for judgment on the pleadings arguing that the pleadings fail to establish that Cravath's conduct caused Plaintiff to suffer any legally cognizable injury. Plaintiff Airgas, Inc. ("Airgas"), opposes the motion. For the following reasons, the motion will be denied. * * *

Airgas claims that Cravath violated Rule 1.7 of the Pennsylvania Rules of Professional Conduct by simultaneously representing Airgas in financing related matters and advising Air Products on a potential takeover of Airgas. [*See* Rule 1.7 in *M&A Statutes, Rules, and Documents*, *supra* Section 1.1]

As discussed herein, the Pennsylvania Supreme Court in *Maritrans* established that a cause of action may be maintained against an attorney for breach of his or her fiduciary duty to a client through concurrent representation that results in a conflict of interest. * * *

To support its claim for breach of fiduciary duty, Airgas claims that it has suffered four discrete injuries as a result of Cravath's alleged misconduct.

First, Airgas alleges that, "[a]s a proximate result of Cravath's wrongful conduct, Airgas has been required to retain new outside counsel to seek to enforce Cravath's ethical and fiduciary obligations, and has incurred legal fees and costs in doing so, which legal fees and costs should be reimbursed by Cravath." Second, Airgas contends that it was "proximately damaged to the extent it has been required to retain replacement outside counsel to develop an understanding of Airgas's financing needs and objectives in order to provide legal services concerning the Airgas credit facilities and financing requirements that would otherwise have been provided by Cravath." Third, Airgas alleges that it has been "proximately damaged in that it has been unable to obtain new financing because of Air Products' takeover offer, and Cravath, Air Products' counsel with respect to the takeover, knew that the timing of Air Products' offer letter could negatively affect Airgas's ability to seek new financing." Fourth, Airgas seeks disgorgement of $322,800 in fees paid to Cravath in October 2009, during the time period Airgas alleges that Cravath simultaneously was working for and against its client Airgas. * * *

ANALYSIS.

Breach of Fiduciary Duty

Elements of a Breach of Fiduciary Duty claim

To establish a breach of fiduciary duty under Pennsylvania law, Airgas must first prove that a fiduciary relationship existed between the parties. Then, Airgas must prove "'(1) that the defendant negligently or intentionally failed to act in good faith and solely for the benefit of plaintiff in all matters for which he or she was employed; (2) that the plaintiff suffered injury; and (3) that the agent's failure to act solely for the plaintiff's benefit … was a real factor in bring[ing] about plaintiff's injuries.'" * * *

Airgas has pleaded its claim in detail and alleged facts that Cravath disregarded its duty of undivided loyalty to its client Airgas by accepting, without prior disclosure, a representation of Air Products designed explicitly to help Air Products take over Airgas. Airgas alleges that at the same time (August—October 2009) that Airgas had engaged Cravath and assumed its undivided loyalty, Cravath was covertly advising Air Products on how to end Airgas's independent corporate existence. This pleading sufficiently sets forth a claim for breach of fiduciary duty. * * *

Injury and Causation

Airgas alleges that Cravath's representation of Air Products in the takeover bid and the related Delaware Action caused Airgas to suffer four specific harms: (1) attorneys' fees related to this litigation; (2) the cost of finding replacement counsel for Cravath; (3) Airgas's inability to obtain new financing because of Air Products' takeover offer; and (4) disgorgement of fees paid to Cravath. * * * [On each of these grounds, the court found that the Complaint states a cause of action and judgment on the pleadings is not appropriate.]

Punitive Damages

Cravath argues that because Airgas's complaint fails to state a claim for breach of fiduciary duty, its punitive damages claim must also fail. * * *

However, as the Court has already explained, Airgas has properly pleaded a claim for breach of fiduciary duty against Cravath, and therefore Airgas's claim for punitive damages cannot be dismissed at this stage of the litigation.

CONCLUSION

For the reasons discussed above, Cravath's motion for judgment on the pleadings is denied. * * *

Note

In June 2011, Airgas announced that it had settled its action against Cravath.[9] The terms of the settlement were not disclosed.

F. Tommy Whistle's Reaction to Steve Vision's Sale of Controlling Shares to Macro Ware

One of ALO's in house lawyers, Tommy Whistle, thinks that in making this offer to Macro Ware, Steve is violating his fiduciary duties to the ALO shareholders. Tommy has advised Steve that he should advise the ALO board to seek an opinion of counsel other than Stone & Cold on the propriety of the transaction prior to exempting this sale from the poison pill. Tommy argues that Stone & Cold has an inherent conflict in representing Steve on this sale. Steve responds: "Tommy, as usual, you do not know what you are talking about; this transaction has been cleared by one of the best law firms in the country; you are fired for your clear incompetence."

Sixth Issue. The sixth issue involves the appropriateness of the action taken by Steve in firing Tommy Whistle.

References

See the references in the footnotes.

Thompson, *Mergers, Acquisitions and Tender Offers, supra* Section 1.10, Chapters 26.

9. Sophia Pearson, *Airgas Settles Suit Against Cravath Swaine Over Air Products*, Bloomberg (June 17, 2011), available at http://www.bloomberg.com/news/2011-06-17/airgas-settles-suit-against-cravath-swaine-over-air-products-1-.html.

Index of Major Concepts

References are to book sections.